GENEALOGY COLLECTION

# HISTORY

OF THE

# CITY OF OMAHA

NEBRASKA

BY
JAMES W. SAVAGE
AND
JOHN T. BELL

AND

# SOUTH OMAHA

BY
CONSUL W. BUTTERFIELD

NEW YORK AND CHICAGO
MUNSELL & COMPANY
1894.

COPYRIGHTED 1894
MUNSELL & COMPANY
NEW YORK AND CHICAGO

Printed by Rees Printing Company
Omaha

## PREFACE.

Tacitus, appreciating the great value of history to mankind, wrote, nearly twenty centuries ago, that its chief object was "to rescue virtuous actions from oblivion to which the want of records would consign them." Even in this practical, speculative age, there seems to be a tendency all over our country to preserve the record of the past. This growing regard for American history is an evidence of increasing national intelligence, pride and dignity.

Fortunately for the citizens of Omaha, with all their love of home, pride of material prosperity, and ambition for a still greater future, that is so intimately blended therewith, Judge James W. Savage, long a resident, prominent in life and deeply mourned in death, had for years preserved many facts and incidents of historical association with the city, intending to publish them when opportunity offered.

Professional and business responsibilities caused this important work to be deferred from time to time, until, in December, 1888, the opportunity to secure an early consummation of his plans was presented. Judge Savage at this time associated with him, in the work of detailed preparation, John T. Bell, Esq., and they jointly arranged with the publishers, and issued to the public the following:

"To the Citizens of Omaha:

Having been requested to prepare the proposed work, we have pledged to the publishers, and do now pledge to our fellow-citizens our best endeavors to render it a comprehensive, discriminating, truthful and readable history.

Yours truly,

Jas. W. Savage,

John T. Bell."

These gentlemen, with their accustomed zeal, at once entered upon the task of writing the book, and prior to his last illness, Judge Savage had the early chapters completed, and, with his associate, had outlined the work now presented to

COPYRIGHTED 1894
MUNSELL & COMPANY
NEW YORK AND CHICAGO

Printed by Rees Printing Company
Omaha

## PREFACE.

Tacitus, appreciating the great value of history to mankind, wrote, nearly twenty centuries ago, that its chief object was "to rescue virtuous actions from oblivion to which the want of records would consign them." Even in this practical, speculative age, there seems to be a tendency all over our country to preserve the record of the past. This growing regard for American history is an evidence of increasing national intelligence, pride and dignity.

Fortunately for the citizens of Omaha, with all their love of home, pride of material prosperity, and ambition for a still greater future, that is so intimately blended therewith, Judge James W. Savage, long a resident, prominent in life and deeply mourned in death, had for years preserved many facts and incidents of historical association with the city, intending to publish them when opportunity offered.

Professional and business responsibilities caused this important work to be deferred from time to time, until, in December, 1888, the opportunity to secure an early consummation of his plans was presented. Judge Savage at this time associated with him, in the work of detailed preparation, John T. Bell, Esq., and they jointly arranged with the publishers, and issued to the public the following:

"To the Citizens of Omaha:

Having been requested to prepare the proposed work, we have pledged to the publishers, and do now pledge to our fellow-citizens our best endeavors to render it a comprehensive, discriminating, truthful and readable history.

Yours truly,

*Jas. W. Savage*

*John T. Bell.*"

These gentlemen, with their accustomed zeal, at once entered upon the task of writing the book, and prior to his last illness, Judge Savage had the early chapters completed, and, with his associate, had outlined the work now presented to the public. Mr. Bell thereupon devoted himself to the compiling of the remaining portions of the book, and to the performance of their joint responsibility.

In addition to those contributors who have written certain chapters, or of certain subjects, and whose names appear in connection therewith, the publishers acknowledge their obligations to the late Byron Reed, Dr. George L. Miller, Hon. A. J. Poppleton, Hon. Edward Rosewater, Judge George W. Doane, Judge E. Wakeley, Hon. John C. Cowin, Hon. James M. Woolworth, Hon. B. E. B. Kennedy, Lyman Richardson, Judge A. N. Ferguson, James G. Megeath, Jesse H. Lacy, Judge George B. Lake, Hon. Charles H. Brown, Gen. W. W. Lowe, J. J. Brown, Thomas Gibson, Hon. Charles A. Baldwin, M. R. Risdon, Dr. S. D. Mercer, Hon. Geo. I. Gilbert, E. L. Stone, William P. Snowden, E. L. Eaton, Major Geo. Armstrong, Miss Jessie Allan, Herman Kountze, H. W. Yates, William Wallace, Frank Murphy, Charles W. Hamilton, Gen. Experience Estabrook, Mr. and Mrs. C. F. Catlin, Henry W. Kuhns, D. D., and many others,—all of whom have, by their counsel and contributions of valuable facts, enhanced the value of the work, thus adding to the completeness of this history.

We are also indebted to the hearty co-operation of the press of Omaha, especial acknowledgment being due the *Bee*, *World-Herald* and *Excelsior*.

In addition, it is proper to mention that Samuel Rees and Julius C. Jennings have contributed to the following pages, and have had charge of the completion of portions of the work.

C. W. Butterfield, of South Omaha, author of its history, desires to have his grateful acknowledgments extended, for kindly assistance, to Thomas Hoctor, John F. Ritchhart, J. B. Erion, W. G. Sloane, Samuel P. Brigham, C. H. Rich, Denna Allbery, J. C. Sharp, and C. M. Hunt.

The time and expense given to this work, and the reputation of its authors, fully justify, it is believed, the undersigned in trusting to the public for a favorable recognition of its value.

THE PUBLISHERS.

OCTOBER 2D, 1893.

# CONTENTS

## HISTORY OF OMAHA

CHAPTER I — Early Explorations West of the Missouri River — Expeditions of Spanish Adventurers — The Search for Mythical Stores of Wealth — Supposed Location of the City of Quivira  1-7

CHAPTER II — Father Marquette's Maps — The Rivalry of France and Spain — Exploration in 1739 by the Mallet Brothers — Naming of the Platte — The French Purchase  8-14

CHAPTER III — The Title to the Province of Louisiana Acquired by the United States — Governor Claiborne's Proclamation — A Real Estate Deal Satisfactory to Both Grantor and Grantee  15-21

CHAPTER IV — The Lewis and Clark Expedition from St Louis to the Pacific Ocean — Personnel of the Expedition — Council with the Indians near Omaha — Death of Sergeant Floyd — Floyd's River Named in his Honor — Journal of Patrick Gass — The Missouri and American Fur Companies — Trading Expedition of Manual Lisa in 1811 — Brackenridge's Account of it — Hunt's Expedition up the Missouri — Bradbury's Visit to the Mouth of the Elkhorn  22-32

CHAPTER V — Journey from the Columbia to the Mouth of the Platte in 1812 — Major Long's Expedition — The Western Engineer, the First Steamboat that Ascended the Missouri Above the Site of Omaha — First White Family Locating at Bellevue — Establishment of a Baptist Mission in 1833, and a Presbyterian Mission in 1834 — General Fremont at Bellevue — The Oldest Settlement of White Civilians in Nebraska 1805 — Peter A Sarpy, Post Trader — J B Royce's Stockade and Trading Post on the Site of Omaha in 1825  33-37

CHAPTER VI — Our Indian Predecessors — Catlin's Visit to the Missouri Valley — The Famous Omaha Chief Blackbird — An Indian Tragedy — Burial of Blackbird on the Hill Named after Him — His Skull taken to Washington by Catlin — Om-pah-tou-ga, or Big Elk Succeeds to the Chieftaincy — Big Elk's Address  38-49

CHAPTER VII — Francis Burt Appointed Governor of Nebraska Territory — His Death at Bellevue — Thomas B Cuming Becomes Acting Governor of the Territory — Location of the Capitol at Omaha — Assembling of the First Legislature — Names of Members of the Legislature — Acting Governor Cuming's Message — The Platte Valley and Pacific Railroad — Capitol Removal Schemes — Civil and Criminal Codes Enacted — Mark W Izard Appointed Governor of Nebraska — His Arrival in the Territory, February 20, 1855 — Capitol Removal Agitation in the Session of 1857 — Passage of a Bill by the Legislature to Locate the Capitol at the Town of Douglas — Governor Izard Vetoes the Bill — Governor Izard's Departure — The City of Omaha Incorporated  50-63

viii                                   CONTENTS.

CHAPTER VIII.—Secretary Cuming Again Acting Governor—The Fourth Session of the Legislature—The Territorial Capitol Building About Completed—Legislators Adjourn to Florence—How the Difficulty Occurred—Arrival of Governor Richardson—He Repudiates the Florence Legislature—That Body Issues a Manifesto—Headline from the *Omaha Nebraskian*—An Article from the *Nebraska Pioneer*—A List of Nebraska's Governors ................................................................. 64–72

CHAPTER IX.—Douglas County—Mormon Settlers at "Winter Quarters," now Florence, in 1845—The First County Officials—Washington Square—The First Court House—The County Farm—Purchase of the Present Court House Site—The New Court House—Comparative Statement of Taxes Raised—List of County Officers and Legislators ... 73–82

CHAPTER X.—The Municipal Government of Omaha—First Officers Elected—Early Doings of the City Council—The Old Capitol Building—Omaha's Early Financial Straits—Committees Sent to Washington to Urge Certain Legislation—Failure of all Attempts to Recover Money Spent on the Territorial Capitol Building by the City of Omaha—A Resolution Regarding Small Pox—A Resolution Against the Opening of a Saloon in the Territorial Capitol Building—Other Scraps of Local Legislation—List of City Officers ................................................................. 83–97

CHAPTER XI.—The Claim Club—The Purpose of its Organization—Its Membership—John I. Redick's Experience with the Club—Some Facts Regarding Early Land Titles—George Francis Train's Omaha Real Estate ................................................. 98–103

CHAPTER XII.—The Pioneers—Laying Out the Townsite—Tracts of Land Included in the Same—Names of the Early Settlers—Biographical Sketches of Pioneers ........ 104–126

CHAPTER XIII.—Indian Graves at Bellevue—Logan Fontenelle—His Death and Burial at Bellevue—Departure of the Omaha from Bellevue—Biographical Sketch of Peter A. Sarpy—An Account of Stephen Decatur ................................................. 127–134

CHAPTER XIV.—Vigilance Committees—Pioneer Bands of Horse Thieves—Two Horse Thieves Publicly Whipped in Omaha—Mrs. Taylor Robbed by Bouve and Iler in 1861—Lynching of Bouve—Execution of Tator for the Murder of Neff in 1863—Execution of Baker for the Murder of Higgins in 1868—Execution of Neal for the Murder of Allen Jones and Wife, 1891—Lynching of George Smith, 1891 ..................... 135–139

CHAPTER XV.—Incidents and Experiences—Early Newspaper Items—Fee Paid Indians for Relinquishment of Claims to Lands—First Election in Nebraska—Facts and Figures as to Omaha, from the *Times* of June 7, 1857—First Things—First Grist Mill—First Saw Mill—First Child Born in Omaha—A. J. Hanscom's First Location—The City Marshal's Duty to Drive Indians Away from the Town—Major Armstrong Exposes the Character of Supplies Furnished the Indians—Dr. Vincent Insulted and Shot at—Slavery Prohibited—Location of Nave, McCord & Co. in Omaha—Why John R. Meredith was not Appointed Chief Justice of Nebraska—Why St. Mary's Avenue Runs at an Angle—E. L. Emery as a Stock Breeder—Pattee's Lottery—Many Suspicious Characters Arrested—The Great Flood of 1881—Old Time Buildings—Boring for Coal—First Asphalt Pavement ................................................................. 140–148

CONTENTS ix

CHAPTER XVI—Military History—"The Catfish War"—The Mormon Scare—The Pawnee War—Verses by General Estabrook—Military Movements in 1861—Governor Saunders' Order—List of Commissioned Officers of the First Nebraska Regiment—Second Nebraska Cavalry—Curtis Horse—First Battalion Nebraska Veteran Volunteers—Militia Organizations—Fort Omaha—Names of Commandants—The Manderson Bill—Location of Fort Crook—Department Headquarters—Commandant and Staff Officers 149-161

CHAPTER XVII—Notable Persons Visiting Omaha—Grand Duke Alexis—King Kalakaua's First Visit—President Grant's First Visit—Dom Pedro—President Grant's Second Visit—President Hayes—King Kalakaua's Second Visit—Marquis of Lorne—President Cleveland—Henry M Stanley—President Harrison 162-166

CHAPTER XVIII—The Press of Omaha—Newspapers Now Published—A List of the Dead and Buried 167-174

CHAPTER XIX—The Liquor Traffic—Prohibitory Act Passed by the First Territorial Legislature—The Act of 1881—The Act of 1889—The Contest of 1890—Prohibitionists Organize—A Circular—Joint Debates—Anti-Amendment Organizations—Miss Willard's Address—The Election—The Contest Following—Good Templars—W C T Union 175-187

CHAPTER XX—Governor Boyd's Election—The Contest Before the Legislature—Governor Thayer's Claim—The Case in the Courts—Governor Boyd Declared a Citizen by the United States Supreme Court—Takes his Seat 188-196

CHAPTER XXI—Navigation—The First Steamer on the Missouri—Celebration of the Event at Franklin, Mo—The First Steamer Above Franklin—A Story of Indian Warfare—Indians Tell of their Prowess—Sufferings of the Omahas—Boats on the Missouri River—A Steamer's Flag 197-200

CHAPTER XXII—Benevolent and Charitable Institutions—Nebraska State Institute for the Deaf and Dumb—The Woman's Christian Association—St Joseph's Hospital—Immanuel Hospital and Deaconess' Institute—The Crèche—The Bishop Clarkson Memorial Hospital—The Open Door—The County Poor Farm—Contest for Title thereto—A Great Sale of Lots—The Douglas County Hospital—Defective Construction—Fall of the North Wing—Legal Complications—Convent of Mercy Orphanage—Methodist Episcopal Hospital—Presbyterian Hospital—City Mission 201-212

CHAPTER XXIII—Financial Facts—Public and Private Improvements—Grading Down Hills and Filling Depressions—The City Hall—Laying the Corner Stone—Cost of Same—Omaha Business Houses—Loan Associations 213-220

CHAPTER XXIV—The Bench and Bar—Personal Mention of a Member of a Distinguished Profession—Organization of Territorial and State Courts 221-250

CHAPTER XXV—Hotels of Early and Modern Days—The Herndon House—Changes of Management—A Pleasant Occasion—How the Grand Central was Named—Destruction by Fire—Hotels of the Present Time 251-256

CONTENTS.

CHAPTER XXVI.—Libraries—Early Efforts in this Direction—The Great Public Library of To-day—Byron Reed's Bequest—Law Library in the New York Life Insurance Building—Omaha Law Library Association—Creighton College Libraries—Other Collections of Books..................................................................................257–266

CHAPTER XXVII.—Omaha's System of Waterworks—Early Safeguards against Fire—The Contest in the City Council—The City Waterworks Company's Works—Sale to the American Waterworks Company—Removal of the Pumping Station to Florence—The New Works—Description of the Method Now in Use...........................267–272

CHAPTER XXVIII.—Indians as Litigants—Arrest of a Band of Ponca Indians—Their Previous Sufferings—Omaha Citizens Become Interested in their Case—Petition for their Release—Indians Released—John Elk's Case—Heirs of Sophia Felix Claim Land in Omaha—An Unsuccessful Suit................................................273–276

CHAPTER XXIX.—County Fairs—Driving Park Association—Board of Trade—Real Estate Exchange—Manufacturers' and Consumers' Association—Real Estate Owners' Association.........................................................................277–281

CHAPTER XXX.—Bridges and Viaducts—The Union Pacific Bridge—Bridge of the Omaha & Council Bluffs Railway Bridge Company—Viaducts—Litigation Resulting from the Construction of the Tenth Street Viaduct—Proposition of the Nebraska Central Railroad Company..............................................................282–291

CHAPTER XXXI.—The Initial Point—The Legal Contest—Bridging the Missouri....292–298

CHAPTER XXXII.—The Union Depot—Legal Complications—Eastern Railroad Connections and Terminal Facilities....................................................299–302

CHAPTER XXXIII.—Theatres and Opera-Houses—The Academy of Music—Redick's Opera-House—A Project that Failed—Boyd's Opera-House—Opening and Congratulatory Resolutions—The Exposition Building—Formal Opening—Notable Entertainments There—The Eden Musee—Boyd's New Theatre—The Opening—The Coliseum.....303–307

CHAPTER XXXIV.—Educational—The First School in Omaha—Simpson University—Another Institution of Learning—Valuable Lots Offered the Catholic Church—The Offer Declined—Inauguration of the Public School System of Omaha—Howard Kennedy in Charge—Professor Beal's School—Names of Pupils—Transfer of the Capitol Grounds—The High School Building Erected—The First Graduating Class—The Metropolitan School District—Statistics—Propositions to Enlarge the High School Building Defeated—A Mandamus Case—Normal Department—Brownell Hall—First Graduates—Other Schools—Commerical Colleges—Presbyterian Theological Seminary—Dr. Miller's Offer—Professor Kellom....................................308–321

CHAPTER XXXV.—Church Organizations—Young Men's Christian Association—Personal Sketches of Bishops and Pioneer Clergymen.........................................322–344

CONTENTS. xi

CHAPTER XXXVI.—Catholicism in Omaha—First Church Services in Nebraska—St Mary's Church—St Philomena Cathedral—Other Churches—Creighton College  345-350

CHAPTER XXXVII.—Cemeteries—Prospect Hill Cemetery—Burial Ground in Shull's Addition—Holy Sephulchre, St Mary's and Cassidy's Cemeteries—Forest Lawn Cemetery—Mount Hope—Other Places of Final Repose  351-352

CHAPTER XXXVIII.—The Medical Profession—Early Practitioners in Omaha—The Nebraska Medical Society—The Omaha Medical Society—Action Regarding Baker's Body—Douglas County Medical Society—Omaha Medical Club—Omaha Academy of Medicine—Members of the Omaha Medical Society—Omaha Medical College of 1869—Nebraska School of Medicine, Preparatory—The Present Omaha Medical College—John A Creighton Medical College—The *Omaha Clinic*—Omaha Microscopic Society—Douglas County Medico-Legal Association—Homeopathy—Its First Representative here—Other Early Homeopathic Physicians—Their Successors—State Medical Society—Officers  353-365

CHAPTER XXXIX.—Dentistry in Omaha—The Pioneers in that Line—Improvements of Later Years  366-367

CHAPTER XL.—Police and Fire Departments—Organization of the Police Force—Its Growth—Conflict between the Commissioners and City Council—Statistics—Early Efforts for Protection Against Fire—Pioneer Hook and Ladder Company No 1—The First Fire Bell—The Fire King Engine—An Engine House Erected—Purchase of a Rotary Steam Engine—Electric Alarm System—Present Status of the Department—Names of Officers—The Durant Fire Company—Prominent Firemen—Lots for New Engine Houses Purchased—Omaha Veteran Fireman's Association  368-375

CHAPTER XLI.—Labor Disturbances—The Smelting Works Strike—Militia Called Out—Peace Restored—Labor Strike of 1882—Public Meetings—Laborers from Plattsmouth Take the Strikers Places—Driven from the Works—Militia and Regulars Called Out—Killing of Armstrong—Telegraphers' Strike—The Missouri Pacific Strike in Omaha—Difficulties Over the Eight Hour Law of 1891  376-379

CHAPTER XLII.—Grand Army Posts—A Private who Became Grand Commander—Woman's Relief Corps—Sons of Veterans—Nebraska Commandery of the Military Order of the Loyal Legion of the United States  380-382

CHAPTER XLIII.—Masonic History—First Lodge of Freemasons in Nebraska—The Second and Third Lodges—Early Members—Other Facts—Odd Fellows—Omaha Lodge No 2 Organized—A Remarkable Announcement—The First New Member—More Accessions—Present Membership—Grand Officers Furnished by this Lodge—Where the Lodge has Met—Knights of Pythias—First Lodge in Omaha—Early Members—History of Succeeding Lodges—Prominent Members  383-390

CHAPTER XLIV.—Transportation Lines—Early History of the Union Pacific—First Surveys—The Hoxie Contract—Durant's Probable Motive—Resignation of Chief Engineer Dey—The City Council Grants the Union Pacific Railroad Company Certain

## CONTENTS.

Rights and Privileges on the Levee — Breaking Ground for the Railroad — Resolutions of the Council — The Railroad Asks for Valuable Real Estate — Right of Way on Fourteenth Street Given — Right of Way over Other Streets Given — Locating the Bridge — Bonds Voted — More Real Estate Conveyed to the Railroad Company — Proposed Returns Therefor — Resolutions Regarding Transfers — Time for Building General Offices Extended — Purchase of the Herndon House — Executive Officers of the Company — The Omaha & Southwestern and the Omaha & Northwestern — The Burlington Route — The Kansas City Line — The Chicago, Rock Island & Pacific Railway — The Sioux City & Pacific Railroad — The Fremont, Elkhorn & Missouri Valley Railroad — The Missouri Pacific Railway — The Belt Line — The Chicago, St. Paul, Minneapolis & Omaha Railway — Other Railroad Schemes............................................391–411

CHAPTER XLV.— Street Railways — Early Legislation — The Omaha Horse Railway Company — The Cable Tramway Company — The Omaha Street Railway Company — The Omaha Motor Railway Company — The Benson Motor Company — The Omaha & Southwestern Street Railway Company — The Council Bluffs & Omaha Line — The Dundee Line — The Inter-State Bridge & Street Railway Company...........................412–415

CHAPTER XLVI.— Telegraph and Telephone — Line from Omaha to Sacramento — A "Big Lie" — Omaha's First Telegraph Line — "Mr. Peck Probably Drowned!"— Formation of the Western Union — Statistics — Other Lines — Telephone Companies — Electric Light Companies.......................................................................416–419

CHAPTER XLVII.— Grain Elevators — Their Development — Those now in Operation...420–421

CHAPTER XLVIII.— Banks and Banking — Early Banking Institutions — Brief History of Each of Omaha's Banks — Handsome and Costly Bank Buildings — Some Statistics...422–434

CHAPTER XLIX.— Omaha's Park System — The Struggle for Jefferson Square — Hanscom Park — The Present Park Law — The Park Commission — New Parks — Elmwood Park — Boulevards — Syndicate Park......................................................435–440

CHAPTER L.— The Post-Office — Early History — Business of Late Years — The New Post-Office — Plan of the Building — The Custom House — Early History — Official Terms Explained — Annual Collections of Duties — Internal Revenue District of Nebraska — Its History — Statement of Annual Collections — Express Companies — Sketch of Each Line Entering Omaha................................................................441–448

CHAPTER LI.— Art in Omaha — Early Organizations of Artists — Western Art Association — Art Exhibitions — The Lininger Art Gallery — Other Collections — Academy of Fine Arts — Some Artists..............................................................449–454

CHAPTER LII.— East Omaha — Origin — Graded Streets — Railroad Facilities — The Omaha Bridge and Terminal Railway — Origin of the Undertaking — Proposed Scope — The Bridge — Terminal Lines of Railroads — Terminal Grounds — The Largest Single Transfer of Real Estate in the History of Omaha — The Passenger Depot..................455–459

CONTENTS xiii

CHAPTER LIII — Commerce — Early Commercial Houses — Mercantile Firms of To-day — Dry Goods and Clothing — Hats and Caps — Millinery and Notions — Rubber Goods — Toys — Tents — Furniture and Carpets — Boots and Shoes — Department Stores — Jewelers — Book Stores — Paper Dealers — Wall Paper Dealers and Decorators — Art Goods — Crockery and Glassware — Billiard Merchandise — Guns and Sporting Goods — Plumbers' Supplies — Iron and Hardware — Printing Material — Stove Stores — Farm Machinery — Vehicles — Storage — Grocers — Wholesale Flour Dealers — Drugs — Commission Houses — Seed Houses — Saddlery Leather and Hides — Oil, Lead, Paints and Glass — Tobacco and Cigars — Wholesale Liquor Stores — Wholesale Dealers in Beer — Lumber — Coal — Ice — Livery Stables — Explosives — Laundries — Undertaking — Classified List and Estimate of Capital Employed 460-491

CHAPTER LIV — Manufacturing Interests — First Manufacturers — Carriage Factories — Iron Workers — Union Pacific Railroad Shops — Tinware Factories — Shot Works — Smelting Works — White Lead Works — Gas Works — Stone Cutting — Planing Mills — Box Factories — Furniture Factories — Linseed Oil Works — Printing — Clothing and Bag Factories — Merchant Tailors — Button Factories — Manufactories of Food Supplies — Brewing — Malt, Soda Water, Weiss Beer — Distilling — Manufacturing Pharmacists — Soap Factories — Cigar Factories — Asphalt Paving — Marble Works — Saddlery — Brick Manufacturers — Miscellaneous — The Manufacturers' and Consumers' Association of Nebraska 492-512

CHAPTER LV — Events of 1892 — The National Drill — National Infantry Drills — The General Conference of the M E Church — The National Convention of the Peoples' Party — The Mystic Shriners — The Omaha and Platte River Canal — The Hanging of Dixon — Political Notes — Some Statistics — Public Improvements 513-518

CHAPTER LVI — Some of Omaha s Representative Citizens — George W Ambrose — George B Ayres — Samuel DeWitt Beals — George Pickering Bemis — James E Boyd — Clinton Briggs — William James Broatch — Amelia Burroughs — Robert Harper Clarkson — Victor H Coffman, M D — Thomas B Cuming — Charles H Dewey — George W Doane — Robert Doherty — H D Estabrook — N B Falconer — Fenner Ferguson — Arthur Northcote Ferguson — Joseph Warren Gannett — W A L Gibbon — John Andrew Gillespie — George Paul Albrecht Grossmann — William Henry Hanchett — Pierce C Himebaugh — George A Hoagland — James Kerr Ish — Benjamin Eli Barnet Kennedy — Thomas Lord Kimball — Frederick Krug — Enos Lowe — Jesse Lowe — John W Lytle — William Wallace Marsh — Hon John A McShane — David Henry Mercer — Samuel David Mercer — George L Miller — George Morgan O Brien — Samuel A Orchard — William A Paxton — James Henry Peabody — Andrew J Poppleton — Arthur S Potter — Lyman Richardson — O D Richardson — Edward Rosewater — Alvin Saunders — James Stephenson — John Mellen Thurston — George Francis Train — Eleazer Wakeley — John L Webster — Solon L Wiley — Orlando Scott Wood — James M Woolworth 519-588

CHAPTER LVII — James Woodruff Savage — His Early Life and Subsequent Career — His Death in Omaha — Tributes of Respect to his Memory 589-691

## HISTORY OF SOUTH OMAHA.

CHAPTER I.— Origin and Opening of the Union Stock Yards ...................... 593-600

CHAPTER II.— Progress and Present Condition of the Union Stock Yards .......... 601-612

CHAPTER III.— The "Syndicate" and South Omaha Land Company ................ 613-620

CHAPTER IV.— Dressed Meat and Packing Concerns — The G. H. Hammond Company — The Omaha Packing Company — The Cudahy Packing Company — Swift & Company. 621-634

CHAPTER V.— Pioneers and Pioneer Times ........................................... 635-644

CHAPTER VI.— South Omaha as a Municipality ....................................... 645-656

CHAPTER VII.— Minor Industries and Public and Private Institutions .............. 657-663

CHAPTER VIII.— Social Life ........................................................... 664-665

CHAPTER IX.— Some of South Omaha's Enterprising Men .......................... 666-671

CHAPTER X.— South Omaha of To-day ............................................... 672

## BIOGRAPHIES

| | | | |
|---|---|---|---|
| Ambrose, George W | 519 | Krug, Frederick | 558 |
| Ayres, George B | 521 | Lowe, Enos | 558 |
| Beals, Samuel DeWitt | 522 | Lowe, Jesse | 560 |
| Bemis, George Pickering | 524 | Lytle, John W | 561 |
| Boyd, James E | 527 | Marsh, William Wallace | 562 |
| Briggs, Clinton | 529 | McShane, John A | 563 |
| Broatch William James | 530 | Mercer, David Henry | 563 |
| Burroughs, Amelia | 533 | Mercer, Samuel David | 564 |
| Clarkson Robert Harper | 533 | Miller, George L | 565 |
| Coffman, Victor H | 534 | O'Brien, George Morgan | 566 |
| Cuming, Thomas B | 537 | Orchard, Samuel A | 567 |
| Dewey, Charles H | 540 | Paxton, William A | 567 |
| Doane, George W | 541 | Peabody, James Henry | 569 |
| Doherty, Robert | 543 | Poppleton, Andrew J | 570 |
| Estabrook, Henry D | 544 | Potter, Arthur F | 572 |
| Falconer, N. B | 546 | Richardson, Lyman | 574 |
| Ferguson, Fenner | 546 | Richardson, O D | 574 |
| Ferguson Arthur Northcote | 547 | Rosewater, Edward | 575 |
| Gannett, Joseph Warren | 548 | Saunders, Alvin | 577 |
| Gibbon, W A L | 549 | Savage, James Woodruff | 589 |
| Gillespie John Andrew | 550 | Stephenson, James | 579 |
| Grossmann, George Paul Albrecht | 550 | Thurston, John Mellen | 580 |
| Hanchett, William Henry | 552 | Train, George Francis | 581 |
| Himebaugh, Pierce C | 553 | Wakeley, Eleazer | 582 |
| Hoagland, George A | 554 | Webster, John L | 584 |
| Ish, James Kerr | 555 | Wiley, Solon L | 585 |
| Kennedy, Benjamin Eli Barnet | 555 | Wood, Orlando Scott | 586 |
| Kimball, Thomas Lord | 556 | Woolworth, James M | 587 |

## PORTRAITS

| | | | |
|---|---|---|---|
| Ambrose George W | 248 | Krug, Frederick | 506 |
| Ayres, George B | 360 | Lowe, Enos | 106 |
| Beals, Samuel DeWitt | 308 | Lowe, Jesse | 78 |
| Bemis, George Pickering | 94 | Lytle, John W | 246 |
| Boyd, James E | 188 | Marsh, William Wallace | 412 |
| Briggs, Clinton | 224 | McShane, John A | 425 |
| Broatch, William James | 83 | Mercer, David Henry | 517 |
| Burroughs Amelia | 365 | Mercer, Samuel David | 353 |
| Clarkson, Robert Harper | 328 | Miller, George L | 108 |
| Coffman, Victor H | 354 | O'Brien, George Morgan | 228 |
| Cuming, Thomas B | 50 | Orchard, Samuel A | 466 |
| Dewey, Charles H | 104 | Paxton, William A | 115 |
| Doane, George W | 234 | Peabody, James Henry | 356 |
| Doherty, Robert | 318 | Potter Arthur F | 457 |
| Estabrook, Henry D | 250 | Richardson, Lyman | 116 |
| Falconer, N B | 463 | Richardson, O D | 52 |
| Ferguson, Arthur Northcote | 236 | Rosewater, Edward | 167 |
| Gannett, Joseph Warren | 401 | Saunders, Alvin | 111 |
| Gibbon, W A L | 465 | Savage, James Woodruff | 1 |
| Gillespie, John Andrew | 202 | Stephenson, James | 489 |
| Grossmann, George Paul Albrecht | 358 | Thurston, John Mellen | 391 |
| Hanchett, William Henry | 364 | Train, George Francis | Title page |
| Himebaugh, Pierce C | 339 | Wakeley, Eleazer | 232 |
| Hoagland, George A | 485 | Webster, John L | 242 |
| Ish, James Kerr | 479 | Wiley, Solon L | 267 |
| Kennedy, Benjamin Eli Barnet | 240 | Wood, Orlando Scott | 363 |
| Kimball Thomas Lord | 397 | Woolworth, James M | 221 |

## ILLUSTRATIONS.

| | |
|---|---|
| Farnam Street from Sixteenth Street East—1866 | 20 |
| Farnam Street from Sixteenth Street East—1889 | 20 |
| The Old Capitol Building | 70 |
| Douglas County Court House | 73 |
| The Territorial Capitol | 86 |
| Looking Northwest from Fifteenth and Farnam Streets—1876 | 91 |
| Residence of Hon. W. A. Paxton, 206 South Twenty-fifth Avenue, Built in 1887 | 114 |
| Looking Northeast from Court House Square—1886 | 141 |
| Looking Southeast from High School Ground—1886 | 141 |
| Omaha Public Library | 145 |
| Looking Northwest from Twelfth and Farnam Streets—1867 | 160 |
| Withnell Building, Headquarters Department of the Platte, Fifteenth and Harney Sts.—1876 | 160 |
| Looking North from South Eighth Street—1875 | 162 |
| Bee Building | 169 |
| Omaha & Grant Smelting and Refining Works | 192 |
| Omaha as seen from East Side of Missouri River—1889 | 192 |
| Glimpses of Omaha | 196 |
| View of the Levee before the Construction of the Union Pacific Bridge | 198 |
| Looking Northwest from South Ninth Street—1876 | 213 |
| The Late Byron Reed's Library | 265 |
| Power House and Settling Basins at Florence—American Waterworks Company | 271 |
| High School Building | 315 |
| Brownell Hall | 317 |
| Hanscom Park M. E. Church | 323 |
| Trinity M. E. Church | 324 |
| Congregational Church—First Protestant Church Built in Omaha | 325 |
| First Congregational Church | 326 |
| Trinity Cathedral | 328 |
| Kountze Memorial English Lutheran Church | 330 |
| Swedish Mission | 335 |
| First Universalist Church, Kountze Place | 336 |
| Young Men's Christian Association Building | 339 |
| St. Mary's Roman Catholic Church—First Catholic Church in Omaha | 346 |
| St. Mary's Convent, Twenty-fourth Street and St. Mary's Avenue—1868 | 346 |
| St. Philomena Cathedral | 347 |
| St. John's Collegiate Church | 349 |
| Creighton College | 350 |
| First Bank Building in Omaha | 425 |
| Looking North from Fourteenth and Farnam Streets—1873 | 441 |
| Looking Northwest from Fourteenth and Farnam Streets—1873 | 441 |
| The Lininger Art Gallery | 452 |
| The Smelting Works during the Flood of 1881 | 496 |
| Ruins of the Grand Central Hotel, Burned September, 1878 | 496 |
| City Hall | 518 |
| Exchange Building, Union Stock Yards, South Omaha | 592 |
| High School Building (South Omaha) | 659 |

## ILLUSTRATIONS.

| | |
|---|---|
| Farnam Street from Sixteenth Street East—1866 | 20 |
| Farnam Street from Sixteenth Street East—1889 | 20 |
| The Old Capitol Building | 70 |
| Douglas County Court House | 73 |
| The Territorial Capitol | 86 |
| Looking Northwest from Fifteenth and Farnam Streets—1876 | 91 |
| Residence of Hon. W. A. Paxton, 206 South Twenty-fifth Avenue, Built in 1887 | 114 |
| Looking Northeast from Court House Square—1886 | 141 |
| Looking Southeast from High School Ground—1886 | 141 |
| Omaha Public Library | 145 |
| Looking Northwest from Twelfth and Farnam Streets—1867 | 160 |
| Withnell Building, Headquarters Department of the Platte, Fifteenth and Harney Sts.—1876 | 160 |
| Looking North from South Eighth Street—1875 | 162 |
| Bee Building | 169 |
| Omaha & Grant Smelting and Refining Works | 192 |
| Omaha as seen from East Side of Missouri River—1889 | 192 |
| Glimpses of Omaha | 196 |
| View of the Levee before the Construction of the Union Pacific Bridge | 198 |
| Looking Northwest from South Ninth Street—1876 | 213 |
| The Late Byron Reed's Library | 265 |
| Power House and Settling Basins at Florence—American Waterworks Company | 271 |
| High School Building | 315 |
| Brownell Hall | 317 |
| Hanscom Park M. E. Church | 323 |
| Trinity M. E. Church | 324 |
| Congregational Church—First Protestant Church Built in Omaha | 325 |
| First Congregational Church | 326 |
| Trinity Cathedral | 328 |
| Kountze Memorial English Lutheran Church | 330 |
| Swedish Mission | 335 |
| First Universalist Church, Kountze Place | 336 |
| Young Men's Christian Association Building | 339 |
| St. Mary's Roman Catholic Church—First Catholic Church in Omaha | 346 |
| St. Mary's Convent, Twenty-fourth Street and St. Mary's Avenue—1868 | 346 |
| St. Philomena Cathedral | 347 |
| St. John's Collegiate Church | 349 |
| Creighton College | 350 |
| First Bank Building in Omaha | 425 |
| Looking North from Fourteenth and Farnam Streets—1873 | 441 |
| Looking Northwest from Fourteenth and Farnam Streets—1873 | 441 |
| The Lininger Art Gallery | 452 |
| The Smelting Works during the Flood of 1881 | 496 |
| Ruins of the Grand Central Hotel, Burned September, 1878 | 496 |
| City Hall | 518 |
| Exchange Building, Union Stock Yards, South Omaha | 592 |
| High School Building (South Omaha) | 659 |

# CHAPTER 1.

EARLY EXPLORATIONS WEST OF THE MISSOURI RIVER—EXPEDITIONS OF SPANISH ADVENTURERS—THE SEARCH FOR MYTHICAL STORES OF WEALTH—SUPPOSED LOCATION OF THE CITY OF QUIVIRA.

The State of Nebraska, though admitted to the Federal Union so lately as the year 1867 and containing, prior to its creation into a territory in 1854, no inhabitants of European ancestry except the handful whom the demands of trade or fondness for a nomadic life had drawn within its borders, still catches occasional glimpses of a past which antedates that of those which we are accustomed to regard as the early settlements, and does not lack even a tinge of romance to reward the investigation of the curious student. The mysterious habitations of the mound-builders still crown the conspicuous bluffs which border the Missouri, weapons and domestic implements of the stone age are still thrown up by the share or the spade from the fertile earth, bits of fragile pottery of strange fashions and devices still bestrew its prairies, and countless similar indications unite with aboriginal tradition to testify to the presence upon its soil in pre-historic ages, of populous communities.

The earliest record of its territory having been visited by Europeans dates back to the year 1540. This expedition, which certainly reached at least the southern boundary of Nebraska, has been the subject of much thought and study, and of more contradictory and diverse theories than any event of the kind in ancient or modern times. Into the vexed questions relating to the initial and terminal points of Coronado's great march through the wilderness, it is impossible, in a work of this character, to enter at any length. A brief synopsis of the principal features of that expedition, taken from the relations of participants in it, will be sufficient to enable those familiar with the topography of the region traversed to form their own conclusions as to the principal features of the journey.

The two decades following the conquest of Mexico by Cortez brought to the shores of the New World numerous cavaliers, grandees and adventurers of Spanish birth who burned to rival that dashing commander in the splendor of his enterprises and the renown of his career. Among these was one Francisco Vasquez de Coronado, a Spaniard of Salamanca, bold, well educated, ambitious, of pleasing address, adventurous, handsome and, like all Spanish commanders of his age, covetous and cruel. To him had been entrusted the command of the northern province of Mexico at a time when general interest had been aroused in reports, seemingly well founded, of rich and populous cities far to the northward, where dwelt a prosperous and happy people, with lofty dwellings and shops, rich in gold, silver, precious stones and all articles of luxury. No disciple of Cortez, recalling his romantic fame, could hesitate long in coming to a conclusion that it was his duty to despoil and rob the mansions of these peaceful, harmless and gentle barbarians. Coronado, therefore, early in the spring of 1540, led an expedition of some twelve or thirteen hundred men to the northward, on a journey which was destined to last for more than two years, and which has given rise to more discussion than any similar march known to history. It is certain, however, that somewhere in the territory now known as Arizona or New Mexico, he found the romantic seven cities of Cibola, of which he had been in search, and discovered also, to his sorrow and chagrin, that the marvellous tales of their grandeur and wealth were clever fictions which had but the very slightest basis of truth to support them. "There were farms in Mexico better than Cibola; the seven cities were seven hamlets, the houses were small, gold was not found, the minerals were of but little value, and in short, the puissant realms and populous cities which he had promised, the metals, the gems and the rich stuffs of which he had boasted in all his discourses, had faded like an insubstantial pageant into thin air."*

But as Coronado, mortified at so ignoble a close of an expedition which he had fondly hoped would rival the splendid achievements of Cortez, twenty years before, hesitated to retrace his steps with no greater renown than might accrue from the destruction of a few weak villages, and the slaughter of their unresisting inhabitants, his attention was called to a region far to the northeast by one whose motives are difficult to discern. A native of the region waited upon the General with much affectation of mystery and ill-will towards his own countrymen, and described with highly colored details, a land remote from the seven cities, which surpassed in its gorgeous magnificence the wildest day dreams of the avaricious Spaniard. He spoke of a region of unexampled fertility, of a river so wide as to seem like an arm of the sea, upon whose capacious bosom was carried the puissant navy of the realm—canoes of twenty oars, vessels with sails adorned with gold and sumptuous in all their appointments. The monarch of this romatic region, a long-bearded, gray-haired and powerful king named Tatarrax, prayed, by the aid of a string of beads, and worshipped a golden cross and the image of a woman, the queen of heaven. Throughout the whole of this land, which he named Quivira, the meanest and most common domestic articles were of wrought silver, while their bowls, plates and more pretentious utensils were of beaten gold. This story was cunningly framed to excite both the cupidity and the superstition of the Spaniards, and perhaps the best explanation of it is, that the narrator had resolved to sacrifice himself for the good of his people, and hoped to draw them so far into the wilderness before his treachery was discovered, that the Spaniards would not be able to return to the cities of Cibola. That the story had some foundation of truth, however, there can be no doubt, as we shall see further on. Coronado himself found the land described in such exaggerated terms, and visits to it in succeeding years were more than once repeated. The adventurous Coronado believed enough of the tale so skillfully told, to induce him to follow the track pointed out by his informant. So on the 5th day of May, 1541, he set out to discover the new and rich country so brought to his notice. The story of his march has been told by three of those who participated in it, Coronado himself, his lieutenant, Jaramillo, and a private soldier in his army, Castaneda, a patient, pious, honest and quaint old soul, to whose journal sedulously kept, we are indebted for most of the details of the march.

In order to fix, however, definitely the itinerary of this expedition, and the probable point at which it terminated, it is necessary for us to determine with accuracy the place of its commencement. This, we are informed, was a well fortified village called Cicuye, situated near a river of the same name, in a narrow valley, among mountains covered with pines. No one can visit and study the ruins of Pecos, on the Pecos River, only a mile or two from the line of the Atchison, Topeka & Santa Fe Railroad, without being convinced that that is the place referred to

*See the Discovery of Nebraska, Vol. 1, Trans. Neb. Hist. Soc.

by Castaneda as Cicuye. Its situation is absolutely impregnable to assaults by men carrying only barbarous weapons, traces of its four stories, of which Castaneda speaks, may still be discerned, it is in a narrow valley among mountains covered with pines and although fish are not found in any great numbers in the little stream which runs by it, the grooved stones which antiquaries suppose the Indians used as sinkers for their nets, may still be found among the stern and melancholy ruins to reward the search of the curious student of the past. It is true that a remark of Castaneda has somewhat perplexed those who have endeavored to fix the exact site of the initial point of Coronado's march. He says, "when the army left Cicuye we entered the mountains, which it was necessary to cross to reach the plains, and on the fourth day we reached a deep river which passes also near Cicuye, and is for this reason called the Cicuye River." That it should take four days to reach the Pecos River, which flows almost within sight of the village of Pecos, is the puzzle to those commentators who have never visited the spot. But as the crossing of the Santa Fe trail over the Pecos at San Miguel is twenty-two miles from the ruins, and the railroad bridge is several miles further, and as the words, "the fourth day," by no means necessarily implies that four days had been occupied in the march the passage rather strengthens than impairs the conclusion that Cicuye and Pecos are identical.

From Pecos, the little army, under Coronado, marched seven hundred miles northeastwardly, reaching a considerable river, which could have been no other than the Arkansas. Here the scarcity of provisions, and suspicions that reported magnificence of Quivira was a mere exaggeration to lure them away from the dwellers in New Mexico, induced the leader to order the main body back to the vicinity of the Pecos, while the General, with thirty of his bravest and best mounted men and six foot soldiers should take a northwestern course for the land of splendor and riches.

The little party so detached turned somewhat to the northwest and reached a point on the southern boundary of Nebraska, where they found the Kingdom of Quivira so long sought for. The reports of its wealth and magnificence, however, were for the most part unfounded. It occupied a fertile and well watered country and supported a numerous population, but of the precious metals or stones nothing was found. So after spending twenty-five days in the exploration of the new found land, Coronado set out upon his return home, which in due time he reached, chagrined and out of favor.

That this account of the celebrated march of Coronado is not universally accepted as true must be conceded. There are some arguments, however, in favor of its correctness which have never been successfully controverted. A strong one is the internal evidence of the reports themselves. The private soldier, Castaneda, seems to have been a somewhat credulous chronicler, but where he relates his own personal experiences he is modest and apparently worthy of credit. All the contemporaneous historians of the expedition agree with him. The itinerary agrees strikingly with what at this day we know a march northwestwardly from Pecos must have been. We have the word of Coronado that he reached the southern boundary of Nebraska and there entered upon the realm of Quivira. The explorers' accounts of the animals, fruits, people and natural features of their route agree in a most remarkable manner with the facts as we now know them. All these circumstances taken together would seem to render the doubts which have from time been thrown over the various narratives of this expedition, unreasonable.

Fifty-seven years after the journey of Coronado, in the year 1599, the Spaniard Onato made an effort to reach Quivira, but the accounts of his expedition are so ambiguous and indistinct that the point to which he penetrated cannot yet be very definitely ascertained. We gather from them, however, that he marched from Santa Fe over prairies and by rivers of varying magnitude, some seven or eight hundred miles, to a populous Indian city, extending for several leagues. Here the cowardice of his followers constrained him to relinquish his undertaking and return to Santa Fe. Of him and his expedition we can only say that he may have reached Nebraska. He declares in his narration that he traveled over two hundred leagues. This distance, of course, if taken in the right direction, would have brought him within the limits of Nebraska. But the obscurity and indefiniteness of his report forbid us to say more than that it was supposed at the time that he had advanced north of the fortieth parallel.

The passionate ardor of the Catholic clergy in the cause to which, with sublime enthusiasm, they had devoted alike their fortunes and lives, would have supplied us with more geographic material had the zealous fathers in their reports thought of, or cared for such mundane matters as dates, courses or descriptions. Several pious pilgrimages were set on foot to reach the heathen of this unknown region, but none of them has added much to our stock of information. One of these journeys is said to have ended seven hundred miles from Santa Fe, upon the banks of a large and rushing river, whose terrors proved too much for their Indian guides, so that they were forced to return without having Christianized any pagans. Another party had a happier fortune. They reached a nation north of Nebraska, in the region now known as Dakota, and converted the tribes so suddenly and effectually that the venerable priests could attribute the result only to the direct and miraculous interposition of Divine grace.

In the year 1662 took place, if we are to believe his own story, the expedition of the Count of Penalosa, from Santa Fe to Quivira. The narration shows him to have been a man of inordinate vanity, arrogant, high spirited and supercilious. It is usual to add to these characteristics that of an untruthfulness so great as to discredit the entire account. The story is professedly written by Nicholas de Freytas, one of his chaplains, and while there are not wanting evidences of its unreliability, there are many circumstances which show that the chronicler was well acquainted with the route which the expedition is said to have pursued.

In brief, the story is that on the 6th of March, in the year 1662, Penalosa marched from Santa Fe in absurd state, with a numerous and pompous retinue, and an army of considerable strength. For three months the Count led his force in a northeasterly direction, through pleasant and fertile prairies, "so agreeable," says the friar, "that not in all the Indies of Peru and New Spain, nor in Europe have any other such been seen so delightful and pleasant." Coming to a wide and rapid river, they encountered a war party of the Escauzaques nation, who dwelt along the fortieth parallel of latitude, and who represented themselves as bound for one of the great cities of Quivira, with whose inhabitants they were at war. With these warriors, who numbered about three thousand, Penalosa marched westwardly for a day along the right bank of the rushing river until it made a bend so that it came from the north. Following up its course, they marched northward for a day, and thereafter, pursuing the sinuosities of the stream, and guided by it, they proceeded on their course until they perceived to the northward, beyond the river, a high ridge whose sides were dotted with signal smokes, and understood that the natives were advised of their approach. Still proceeding westward, they at last halted at a spot where, on the opposite side, another beautiful river, flowing from the ridge, entered the stream they had previously followed. Here looking across the latter river, they could discern upon both banks of its attractive affluent a vast settlement or city, in the midst of a spacious prairie

This, the chronicler assures us, was the city, or one of the cities, of Quivira. It contained thousands of houses, circular in shape for the most part, some two, three, and even four stories in height, framed of a hard wood and skillfully thatched. It extended on both sides of this second river for more than two leagues, at which distance a third stream flowed into the second. Beyond this, the city again stretched out for many miles, just how far is uncertain, for the troops never reached its ultimate boundary. The plain upon which this huge village lay, was some eighteen or twenty miles in breadth. The city was very populous, the inhabitants being gentle submissive, curious and hospitable.

According to the story of De Freytas, the Escauzaques, their new found allies, crossed the river during the night under cover of the darkness, in spite of positive orders to the contrary, and falling upon the peaceful dwellers of the city, so ravaged, burned and murdered, that at sunrise when the General (who, with some difficulty, had also crossed the stream before dawn) encamped before the city, not a living soul was to be found within it. The timid and unwarlike natives who had survived the slaughter had all fled.

These are the principal features of the narration of Father Nicholas de Freytas. All the Count of Penalosa with his army could do after that, was to endeavor to extinguish the flames and make abortive efforts to repress the fury of the Escauzaques. The next day they marched through the town, admiring the vast number of dwellings, the innumerable paths which entered the city from the high lands below it, the fertility of the soil, which was black, strong and covered with rich grasses, and the beauty of the scene which, from the city to the ridge seemed to them like a paradise. But the Spaniard of those days, however sensible of natural beauty, deemed no expedition a successful one which did not yield some store of gold or precious stones. As the populous city furnished no signs of these, all zeal and interest in the undertaking at once vanished, and about the middle of June the Count set out on his return journey to New Mexico.

As has been suggested above, it is a matter of small importance whether this story is, in its details, true or not, if the descriptions of the routes, rivers, soils, natural objects, distances, directions and general features prove, so far as they can be verified at this day, correct, we shall hardly fail to be convinced that some one had taken the journey from Santa Fe northeastwardly, whether Penalosa did or not. And certainly if the route of the march as described, carefully followed, brings us to a spot where at some time in the past a populous city has stood, there is certainly some ground, however slight, for supposing that it was the magnificent city of the Spaniards' dreams.

Many of those interested in the early annals of Nebraska, believe that the site of this city was at the spot where now the city of Columbus stands, and not far from where the Loup River empties into the Platte. A few of the evidences, which are claimed to support this theory, are as follows:

*First.* Quivira lay northeasterly from Santa Fe. This was the line of Coronado's march, as we are informed both by his own report and those of his lieutenant, Jaramillo, and the soldier, Castaneda. Gomara, in his narrative of the expedition, declares that the march was towards the northeast. The missionary fathers previously mentioned, traveled in the same direction. Freytas constantly speaks of it as "the northeast land," and the Indian guides always persisted that the route to it, by way of Taos, was shorter and more direct than that usually followed.

*Second.* It was north of the southern boundary of Nebraska—the fortieth parallel of latitude. Coronado reported that he penetrated thus far to the north, and in this statement he was supported by the evidence of all who accompanied him. Penalosa, or whoever furnished that governor with the data for his narration, found, more than a century later, the Escauzaques, enemies of the Quiviras, dwelling along this parallel and ranging over the country northward. With them he marched north to attack the wondrous city.

*Third.* The distances asserted to have been traveled by the several explorers, while not always definitely given, or harmonious, all indicate that the region sought by them was at least as far from Santa Fe as Nebraska. The march of Coronado was of a sufficient length to have ended in this State. The march of Onato from Santa Fe in 1599, was, according to his account, upwards of two hundred leagues. The Spanish league being, as appears by the United States Ordinance Manual, 3.42 American miles, we may fairly suppose that he traveled between six hundred and seventy-five and eight hundred and fifty miles. Freytas, writing from Santa Fe, declares that "this northeast land, so populous and wealthy, begins one hundred and fifty leagues from here and stretches to where the city commences almost as far again." In other words, he makes the distance of the chief city of Quivira from Santa Fe between two hundred and fifty and three hundred leagues, that is, between eight hundred and fifty and a thousand miles.

By the "map of the territory of the United States west of the Mississippi River, prepared by the authority of the Honorable the Secretary of War, in the office of the Chief of Engineers" in the year 1879, the distance in an air line from Santa Fe to Columbus, Nebraska, is nearly six hundred miles. By rail, the distance from Santa Fe to the river Platte is nine hundred and eighty-six miles, and inasmuch as the Atchison and Santa Fe Railroad follows very closely the old and natural route so well known to travelers as the Santa Fe trail, it is probable that so easy and obvious a pathway would be the one pursued by the early adventurers. It would seem, then, that the distance to the city of Quivira, as reported, would, after making the most liberal allowances for guesses, imperfect measurements and exaggerations, require its location to be as far from New Mexico as Nebraska.

It has been objected to this hypothesis, that those early chroniclers described the land of Quivira as nearly surrounded by the sea. But when we reflect that the name given by the Pawnees to the Missouri was the "medicine," or "miraculous" water, and that this term translated to visitors might readily be understood as referring to the ocean, the circumstance is an argument in favor of, rather than against, the present theory. Freytas declares that the sea encircles and surrounds all that land to the east, northeast, north and northwest. This can only mean that the early explorers of the region were assured that the "wonderful water" so bounded it; and as from the entire eastern half of Nebraska the majestic current of the Missouri can be reached by a short journey towards either of the above mentioned points of the compass, there is some reason for believing that the region known as Quivira comprehended that portion of the State.

It is at least a curious diversion, with these considerations in mind, to follow the route which the chronicler declares was taken by Penalosa and his men, to see how far the features of the journey correspond with geographical and topographical facts. If the narrator's story is entitled to any credit whatever, the expedition struck the Platte River not far west of its junction with the Missouri. Thence, they marched for a day westward, to an abrupt bend in the river; thence northward for another day, and thence followed up the current of the river towards the west. These courses and distances are identical with those to be found by a party marching up the right bank of the Platte at the present day Proceeding up the river they found, on the opposite side, the city of which they were in search, situated on both sides of another beautiful stream, which, coming from the north, emptied into that which they had been following If our premises thus far are correct, this picturesque river was the Loup They forded the river, up which they had been marching, this fact showing that it could not have been the Missouri, which, unlike the Platte, is nowhere in this vicinity and for hundreds of miles at any season of the year, fordable

It is worthy of remark that the valley of the Loup, near its entrance into the Platte, is between fifteen and twenty miles wide, and evidences of ancient habitation along its banks for many miles exist in great abundance  Fragments of pottery, even at this day, are turned up by the plow of the farmer or the spade of the railway grader, mounds, evidently artificial, are to be found, the soil is fertile and so black as to excite the notice of the traveler now, as it did the Spaniards three centuries ago

Speculations such as these can hardly be considered as entirely fanciful  After deducting from the tales of these early explorers much that is marvelous and incomprehensible, and making all due allowance for their vain glory, pride, ambition, self-conceit and boastfulness, the conscientious student is still forced to admit that there exists in their narrations and reports a substratum of truth  From these we have a right at least, to consider it proved, that at the time of the Spanish conquests in America there was in the eastern half of the territory, which now forms the State of Nebraska, populous communities, having many traits in common with the Aztecs, living together in towns and cities, not unacquainted with the ruder arts of agriculture, dwelling in houses, and able to fashion the necessary weapons for the chase, and, by the art of the potter, the common utensils of domestic use

# CHAPTER II.

FATHER MARQUETTE'S MAP—THE RIVALRY OF FRANCE AND SPAIN—EXPLORATION IN 1739 BY THE MALLET BROTHERS—NAMING OF THE PLATTE— THE FRENCH PURCHASE.

IN the latter part of the sixteenth century we begin to emerge from the region of myth and marvel, and to gain a reasonably accurate knowledge of the denizens of the country which afterwards became the State of Nebraska. As early as the year 1673, Father Joseph Marquette, the pious French Jesuit and missionary, descended the Mississippi on an expedition to determine its situation and course. A map prepared by his own hand of his voyage, of undoubted authenticity, after lying concealed and forgotten for two centuries in the archives of St. Mary's College, in Montreal, was, a few years since, recovered from its hiding place. The Missouri river is depicted upon this map with remarkable accuracy, considering the fact that his information concerning it must have been derived from such wandering Indians as he chanced to meet along the banks of the Mississippi. His description of this passage of the mouth of the Missouri, which he calls the Pekatanoni, is as follows: "We descend, following the course of the river, towards the other called Pekatanoni, which empties into the Mississippi, coming from the northwest, of which I shall have something to say after what I have remarked of this river.

\* \* \* \* \* \* \* \*

"As we were discoursing, sailing gently down a still, clear water, we heard the noise of a rapid into which we were about to plunge. I have never seen anything more frightful! A mass of large trees, with roots and branches entire, real floating islands, came rushing from the mouth of the river Pekatanoni with such impetuosity that we could not venture across without serious risk. The agitation was so great that the water was all muddy and could not get clear.

"Pekatanoni is a considerable river, which, coming from very far in the northwest, empties into the Mississippi. Many Indian towns are situated on this stream, and I hope by its means to make the discovery of the Red, or California Sea.

"We judged, by the direction the Mississippi takes, that if it keeps on the same course it has its mouth in the Gulf of Mexico; it would be of great advantage to find that which leads to the South Sea towards California; and this, as I said, I hope to find by Pekatanoni, following the account which the Indians had given me; for from them I learn that ascending this river for five or six days, you come to a beautiful prairie twenty or thirty leagues in extent, which you must cross to the northwest. It terminates at another little river on which you can embark, it not being difficult to transport canoes over so beautiful a country as that prairie. This second river runs southwest for ten or fifteen leagues, after which it enters a small lake, which is the source of another deep river running to the west, where it empties into the sea. I have hardly any doubt that this is the Red Sea, and I do not despair of one day making the discovery, if God does me this favor and grants me health, in order to be able to publish the gospel to all the nations of this New World, who have so long been plunged in heathen darkness."

Upon the map above referred to, the general course of the Missouri is given to a point far above the site of the City of Omaha, the Platte River is laid down in almost its exact position, corresponding remarkably with its actual relative situation to the Missouri and other streams, and the mountains to the westward, among the Indian tribes which he enumerates as distributed throughout this region, we find such names as Panas, Mahas and Otontantes This map, it is probable, contains for the first time, written in a Christian tongue, the designation of the wild tribe for which the City of Omaha is named. The charitable wish of the good Father Marquette to visit this region and instruct its dusky natives in the doctrines of his faith, was, unfortunately for history, never gratified. The exposure and hardships of his travels were too much for his frail constitution, and he died on the shores of Lake Michigan before his devout dream of spiritual conquest could be realized.

The rivalry between France and Spain for the possession of the territory lying between the Rocky Mountains and the Mississippi was more effective in giving the world information concerning the prairies of the west than even the indefatigable labors of Catholic priests. Spain, secure in her possession of Mexico, looked with an eye of envy and desire over the beautiful plains traversed by countless herds of buffalo, antelope and deer, while France, from her strongholds at the mouth of the Mississippi, watched with cautious jealousy any movements of the successors of Cortez towards that coveted region. Suspicions, rivalries and antagonisms, were rife on both sides. If the French made a move in one quarter, the Spaniards endeavored to meet it by a counter stroke in another. If one nation established a trading post in the wilderness, the other sought to seduce its servants and to render the enterprise abortive. Spies and other emissaries everywhere abounded. With an ostentatious display of peace on both sides there was constant suspicion and constant watchfulness. Contemporary documents show that the richness and the beauty of the country, the fertility of the soil and the salubrity of the climate, made the possession of the region a matter of deep interest to both sides.

Thus, a letter from M de Bienville, then in command of Louisiana, to the French Minister of Marine, dated April 22 1734, has the following report: "A Frenchman, who for some years has lived among the Panimahas established on the Missouri, has, with these savages, visited the Ricaras, who inhabit about the headwaters of that stream. They had not before seen any Frenchmen. He found in the vicinity several silver mines which appeared to him very rich, among others one which he thinks virgin. Two travelers will go with him to verify his report."* The same officer had written in 1706: "Among the Canadians who have arrived, there are two who have for two years been roaming from village to village on the Missouri. They report that having been near to the mines of the Spaniards, they were arrested at a savage village sometimes visited by the Spaniards who came there for hides with which to make harness for their mules, that the Spaniards are at war with three or four large tribes, and march only with cuirass and helmet, proof against arrows, which causes the Indians to look upon them as devils. These men have assured Bienville that this country is the most beautiful of the world, with navigable streams communicating with nations who use horses. They have brought specimens of copper from these mines, and a metal with which they are unacquainted."

LaSalle wrote, in 1708: "The Missouri River empties into the Mississippi about five hundred leagues from the Gulf of Mexico. There are Canadian voyagers who have ascended it for three or four hundred leagues

---
*Exploration des affluents du Mississippi et decouverte des Montagnes Rocheuses Par Pierre Margry

to the northwest and west through the most beautiful country in the world, without being able to ascertain whence it has its source If His Majesty desires that this discovery should be made, the expense will not be great; not over forty thousand livres worth of merchandise, munitions and rations. This would be sufficient to cover all expenses, including the pay of one hundred men selected for the enterprise, and who would be able to accomplish it in canoes. The journey would not consume more than twelve or fifteen months from the time of setting out from the fort in Louisiana. It would be necessary to send along a young engineer to draw a chart of the river to give you a clear idea of it, and to designate the officers intended for the expedition."

The Sieur Mandeville, an ensign in the company of Vanlezard, in Louisiana, writes in 1709: "In ascending we reach the river Missouri where the great abundance of oxen and cows passes the imagination. These beasts grow upon their backs both hair and wool according to the season of the year. The river is beautiful and large. There is every reason to believe that here is a place for discoveries of great magnitude.

The following is extracted from a memorial by Sieur Hubert to the naval council in 1717: "I am assured by those who have ascended the Missouri that it is the veritable source of the Mississippi, which latter stream should indeed more properly be called the Missouri. The region explored by them in the vicinity of this river is, in beauty and healthfulness, far superior to any other portion of this colony; it is one of those happy climates which produce everything in great abundance and without difficulty. The air is quite salubrious, the seasons regular and temperate. The country is studded with trees of all varieties; the immense prairies covered with wild cattle, antelope, deer, and all other kinds of wild animals; and salt abounds, although the country is far from the sea, which is a sensible and certain proof of abundance, and of the neighborhood of mines."

Writing from Fort Louis, of Louisiana. on the 25th of April, 1722, Bienville says that he learns from the savages of the Missouri that the Spaniards are meditating an establishment on the Kansas River. and that he had ordered Sieur de Boisbriant to prevent this by sending a detachment of twenty soldiers to build a little fort and to remain in garrison on that river. The ruins of a stone edifice, still visible in northeastern Kansas, which have excited a good deal of local interest and curiosity, may possibly be the remains of the post established in pursuance of those instructions.

The foregoing extracts are sufficient to show the interest taken by the French government in their possessions near the Missouri and Platte Rivers, its belief in their value and the desire felt for a more thorough and systematic exploration of them. As early as the year 1700, complaints were made that unhappily those who had been sent upon tours of discovery had not been scientific men, competent to make the necessary observations and calculations, to prepare plans and itineraries, and to draw charts. "It is certain," said these fault-finders, "that the region west of the Mississippi, with the exception of three or four leagues from its banks, is absolutely unknown to us; and that to derive some benefit from the immense expense incurred during the last twenty years for this discovery, it is necessary to send *coureurs des bois* to the strait which separates California from the main land; and to detail people to accompany them who know enough to draw plans and make astronomical observations."

So far as our knowledge goes, the first formal exploration of this part of the country took place in the year 1739. A document recently unearthed by M. Margry gives many details of this expedition, not always accurate and sometimes uninteresting. The abridgment of the journal kept by the explorers, after slumbering for nearly a century and a half in the archives of the French government, cannot fail to be of use to the student of the early history of this region. The leaders of the party were two brothers, Canadians, named Peter and Paul Mallet, who, with six companions, successfully accomplished a task which, considering their numbers, the length of their journey, the barren regions traversed and the Spanish jealousy which their trip must have excited, may well be reckoned as among the most daring and successful of modern times. Their ostensible object was to visit Santa Fe, and endeavor to bring about a regular commerce with the people of New Mexico. That they were expected to keep their eyes open and make report of all matters which might prove advantageous to the French government, can hardly be doubted.

"To understand," they say in extracts from their journal prepared for the Governor and Intendant of Louisiana, "the course which these Canadians took to discover New Mexico it is well to know that it is one hundred leagues from the Illinois to the Missouri villages, on the river of that name, eighty leagues from there to the Cauzes, one hundred leagues from the Cauzes to the Otoctlatas, and sixty from there to the mouth of the river of the Panimahas in the Missouri country. This nation is established near the mouth of the Panimaha River, and it is at this that the discoverers made their point of departure on the 29th of May, 1739." There can be from the context, but little doubt that this river of the Panimahas was the stream now called the Loup.

"Those who had previously endeavored," they say, "to penetrate to New Mexico have expected to find that country at the head waters of the Missouri River. They have, therefore, ascended that stream as far as the Ricaras, who are more than one hundred and fifty leagues from the Pawnees." Following the advice of certain savages whom they met, these explorers determined upon an entirely different route, and upon leaving their savage allies, the Pawnees, they crossed the prairies, returning upon their steps in a course almost parallel with the course of the Missouri.

On the 2d of June they came upon a river to which they gave the name of the Platte, and observing that it did not deviate materially from the route which they had determined upon, they followed up its course to the right for a distance of twenty-eight leagues, where they ascertained that a fork was made by the river of the Padoncas, which there emptied into the Platte. That this river of the Padoncas was the stream now known as the south fork of the Platte, there can be no reasonable doubt. They continued to ascend the river which they had called the Platte, and on the 13th of June they turned to the left, probably finding that the further ascent of that river would take them too far to the northwest and crossing the stream and a tongue of land, they bivouacked on the 14th on the further bank of the river des Costes, which they supposed also emptied into the Platte.

On the 15th and 16th they continued across the country, and on the 17th came upon another stream which they called des Costes Blanches. Still pressing forward they traversed a level country, which barely sufficed to furnish wood for their camp fires. They note in their journal that these plains extend as far as the mountains bordering on Santa Fe. On the 18th they encamped on the bank of another stream which they crossed, and which they named the River Aimable. On the 19th they crossed still another watercourse, to which they gave the name of the River des Soucis. The following day they encountered a deep and rapid river, which they ascertained was the Cauces, seeing which they were encouraged to believe that they were upon the route which had been recommended to them at the time of their departure from the Pawnee nation. In attempting to make a crossing, however, they met with their first serious misfortune, losing in its turbulent current seven horses laden with valuable merchandise. Another stream which they crossed two days later, they named the River a la Fleche. On the following day the passage of still another river brought them out upon even more barren plains, where they were obliged to depend solely upon the *bois de vache*, or buffalo chips, for their necessary fuel. From that time to the 30th of June, they daily encountered streams of greater or less magnitude, until, on the last mentioned day, they discovered upon the banks of one of them traces of the Spaniards of whom they were in search. The water which they had then reached they conjectured to be a branch of the Arkansas, and at this point they estimated their distance from their starting place in the Pawnee country to be about one hundred and fifty-five leagues.

Up this stream they marched, keeping it on their left until the 5th of July, when they came upon an Indian village, of a tribe which they understood to be called Lalitanes.* To the inhabitants of this village they made a small present from their diminished stock of merchandise, and received in return a gift of antelope. Distrusting, however, the intentions of their new acquaintances and suspecting that they had evil designs, they were cautious enough to make their encampment some two or three miles away from their village. But the night passed without any hostile demonstrations, and on the next day they pursued their course.

But as they were leaving the river, which for several days they had been ascending, their apprehensions were again excited by a visitor, who proved to be a Ricara slave, held in bondage among the Lalitanes. He declared that the inhabitants of the village were determined to attack and destroy them. The adventurers put a bold face upon the matter and sent the slave back with a message, which apparently prevented the attack, as the Lalitanes made no hostile movement. The Ricara having returned to the Frenchmen, they inquired if he knew the road to the Spanish settlements. He replied that he was well acquainted with it, having been a slave among the Spaniards, by whom, as he alleged, he had been baptised into the Christian religion. This Indian the Frenchmen endeavored to engage as a guide for them to the City of Santa Fe, and in the hope of thereby procuring his liberty, he consented so to act. Setting forth therefore, again, with their new found ally, they found themselves when night fell some ten leagues away from the nation whose hostility they had shunned to encounter.

On the 10th of July they perceived for the first time a range of mountains which they called the Spanish Mountains. At this time their distance from them was about ten leagues; two days later they reached and encamped at the foot of one of them. On the following day, that is on the 13th of July, they encamped at a miserable little village containing three Lalitane cabins; ensuring the good will, or at least the tranquility of the inhabitants by a trifling present. On the next day they came upon another river to which they gave the name of Red River, but suspected it to be a branch of the Arkansas. Doubtless this was the stream now called the Gallinas, for we find that at twenty-one leagues from it they encountered the first Spanish post at a mission called Piquoris. This mission must have been at the deserted and dismantled rock now known as Pecos, whose striking situation and crumbling but massive walls show that before heavy artillery could have been brought to bear upon it, it was a place of no small strength and importance. We have seen before, when speaking of the expedition of Coronado, that it was in all

---

*Called also Laitanes, Litanes, Tetes Pelees, and Halitanes, by other travelers.

probability the spot from which that chivalrous commander launched forth on his vague and perilous journey. When they arrived within three or four miles of this settlement they were met by the governor and the priest of the station, who were attended by a vast crowd of natives. These received the wayworn travelers with great hospitality, and even, as they state in their journal, with the clamor of bells.

Prior to this time they had been enabled to avail themselves of the services of three wandering Indians whom they met, and to whom they entrusted a letter to the commandant at Taos. This officer seemed inclined to treat them in a friendly spirit, and sent them as a token of his good will on the next day, a supply of mutton and excellent bread, to which their appetites, sharpened by some six weeks' travel over the inhospitable and parched prairies, were ready to furnish that sauce, which the proverb establishes as the best. Leaving Pecos on the 15th, they arrived at noon at another mission, called Santa Cruz, where they dined, and passing another in the afternoon named Cagnada, they encamped at nightfall at the village of Santa Marie. At all these halting places they seem to have been cordially received by the cautious but hospitable Spaniard, perhaps from the paucity of their numbers, which prevented any inquietude as to their intentions, perhaps from a wish to elicit from them by kindness of treatment the real object of their long and dangerous journey. It is, of course, impossible that suspicious and jealous officers on the very frontier of Spanish occupation, surrounded by savage tribes, acquainted with the covetous disposition of their French neighbors, should have viewed such an incursion, even of six men, into their privacy with absolute indifference.

From the village of Santa Marie they reached Santa Fe in one day's march, having, since leaving the river of the Pawnees, on the 29th of May, fifty-four days previously, marched two hundred and sixty-five leagues over trackless and unfertile plains, at the hottest period of the year, without shade or shelter, crossing rapid and dangerous streams, exposed to attacks from hostile barbarians, and liable to be shot as spies at the end of their journey. It is certainly not too much to claim for these heroic men, whose exploits have been so long buried and forgotten, the credit of having participated in an enterprise which tested the highest qualities of manhood, and entitles them to rank with great leaders and explorers whose deeds have been the theme of commendatory pens since their performance, and will continue to be for all time. Their names, which follow, ought not to be longer unremembered. They are, Peter Mallet, Paul Mallet, Philip Robitaille, Louis Morin, Michael Beslot, Joseph Bellecourt, Manuel Gallien and John David, all of French extraction, and all, except David, who was a native of France, born in Canada.

They were received no less courteously by the Spanish authorities of Santa Fe than they had been by those of the villages along their route. It is evident, however, that during the nine months of their stay, a period rendered necessary by the infrequency and tardiness of communication with the viceroy at the City of Mexico, they were subjected to a strict surveillance, and were allowed to glean as little as might be concerning matters which would be useful to the French. The answer of the viceroy to their request to be allowed to institute a regular commerce across the plains between the French and Spanish settlements, was, when it did at last come, temporizing and indecisive. He thought, in fact, to detach them from their allegiance to the French monarch, and to induce them to engage in still further explorations in his own service. His offers were, however, declined, and seven of the original number—one of them, Louis Morin, having found Santa Fe a veritable Capua, and married in that city—started to the northwest and west through the most beautiful country in the world, without being able to ascertain whence it has its source If His Majesty desires that this discovery should be made, the expense will not be great; not over forty thousand livres worth of merchandise, munitions and rations. This would be sufficient to cover all expenses, including the pay of one hundred men selected for the enterprise, and who would be able to accomplish it in canoes. The journey would not consume more than twelve or fifteen months from the time of setting out from the fort in Louisiana. It would be necessary to send along a young engineer to draw a chart of the river to give you a clear idea of it, and to designate the officers intended for the expedition."

The Sieur Mandeville, an ensign in the company of Vanlezard, in Louisiana, writes in 1709: "In ascending we reach the river Missouri where the great abundance of oxen and cows passes the imagination. These beasts grow upon their backs both hair and wool according to the season of the year. The river is beautiful and large. There is every reason to believe that here is a place for discoveries of great magnitude.

The following is extracted from a memorial by Sieur Hubert to the naval council in 1717: "I am assured by those who have ascended the Missouri that it is the veritable source of the Mississippi, which latter stream should indeed more properly be called the Missouri. The region explored by them in the vicinity of this river is, in beauty and healthfulness, far superior to any other portion of this colony; it is one of those happy climates which produce everything in great abundance and without difficulty. The air is quite salubrious, the seasons regular and temperate. The country is studded with trees of all varieties; the immense prairies covered with wild cattle, antelope, deer, and all other kinds of wild animals; and salt abounds, although the country is far from the sea, which is a sensible and certain proof of abundance, and of the neighborhood of mines."

Writing from Fort Louis, of Louisiana, on the 25th of April, 1722, Bienville says that he learns from the savages of the Missouri that the Spaniards are meditating an establishment on the Kansas River, and that he had ordered Sieur de Boisbriant to prevent this by sending a detachment of twenty soldiers to build a little fort and to remain in garrison on that river. The ruins of a stone edifice, still visible in northeastern Kansas, which have excited a good deal of local interest and curiosity, may possibly be the remains of the post established in pursuance of those instructions.

The foregoing extracts are sufficient to show the interest taken by the French government in their possessions near the Missouri and Platte Rivers, its belief in their value and the desire felt for a more thorough and systematic exploration of them. As early as the year 1700, complaints were made that unhappily those who had been sent upon tours of discovery had not been scientific men, competent to make the necessary observations and calculations, to prepare plans and itineraries, and to draw charts. "It is certain," said these fault-finders, "that the region west of the Mississippi, with the exception of three or four leagues from its banks, is absolutely unknown to us; and that to derive some benefit from the immense expense incurred during the last twenty years for this discovery, it is necessary to send *coureurs des bois* to the strait which separates California from the main land; and to detail people to accompany them who know enough to draw plans and make astronomical observations."

So far as our knowledge goes, the first formal exploration of this part of the country took place in the year 1739. A document recently unearthed by M. Margry gives many details of this expedition, not always accurate and sometimes uninteresting. The abridgment of the journal kept by the explorers, after slumbering for nearly a century and a half in the archives of the French government, cannot fail to be of use to the student of the early history of this region. The leaders of the party were two brothers, Canadians, named Peter and Paul Mallet, who, with six companions, successfully accomplished a task which, considering their numbers, the length of their journey, the barren regions traversed and the Spanish jealousy which their trip must have excited, may well be reckoned as among the most daring and successful of modern times. Their ostensible object was to visit Santa Fe, and endeavor to bring about a regular commerce with the people of New Mexico. That they were expected to keep their eyes open and make report of all matters which might prove advantageous to the French government, can hardly be doubted.

"To understand," they say in extracts from their journal prepared for the Governor and Intendant of Louisiana, "the course which these Canadians took to discover New Mexico it is well to know that it is one hundred leagues from the Illinois to the Missouri villages, on the river of that name, eighty leagues from there to the Cauzes, one hundred leagues from the Cauzes to the Otoctlatas, and sixty from there to the mouth of the river of the Panimahas in the Missouri country. This nation is established near the mouth of the Panimaha River, and it is at this that the discoverers made their point of departure on the 29th of May, 1739." There can be no doubt from the context, but little doubt that this river of the Panimahas was the stream now called the Loup.

"Those who had previously endeavored," they say, "to penetrate to New Mexico have expected to find that country at the head waters of the Missouri River. They have, therefore, ascended that stream as far as the Ricaras, who are more than one hundred and fifty leagues from the Pawnees." Following the advice of certain savages whom they met, these explorers determined upon an entirely different route, and upon leaving their savage allies, the Pawnees, they crossed the prairies, returning upon their steps in a course almost parallel with the course of the Missouri.

On the 2d of June they came upon a river to which they gave the name of the Platte, and observing that it did not deviate materially from the route which they had determined upon, they followed up its course to the right for a distance of twenty-eight leagues, where they ascertained that a fork was made by the river of the Padoncas, which there emptied into the Platte. That this river of the Padoncas was the stream now known as the south fork of the Platte, there can be no reasonable doubt. They continued to ascend the river which they had called the Platte, and on the 13th of June they turned to the left, probably finding that the further ascent of that river would take them too far to the northwest and crossing the stream and a tongue of land, they bivouacked on the 14th on the further bank of the river des Costes, which they supposed also emptied into the Platte.

On the 15th and 16th they continued across the country, and on the 17th came upon another stream which they called des Costes Blanches. Still pressing forward they traversed a level country, which barely sufficed to furnish wood for their camp fires. They note in their journal that these plains extend as far as the mountains bordering on Santa Fe. On the 18th they encamped on the bank of another stream which they crossed, and which they named the River Aimable. On the 19th they crossed still another watercourse, to which they gave the name of the River des Soucis. The following day they encountered a deep and rapid river, which they ascertained was the Cauces, seeing which they were encouraged to believe that they were upon the route which again across the plains. Three of them retraced their steps and returned to their allies, the Pawnees of the Loup. The four others, however, determined to reach New Orleans by way of the Arkansas River, and succeeded finally in making their way to that city after continued labors, hardships, discouragements and perils, which makes it marvellous that they should have accomplished their object in tolerable health and without the loss of a single man. They reported that the village of Santa Fe was an unfortified city, built of frail material, guarded by few ill-equipped and ill-conditioned soldiers; that the vicinity was rich in mines of silver and other precious material, and that they thought that they had made a favorable impression by their gifts upon the savage nations of the region round about. Nothing further, however, was heard of hostile movements, and the two nations, hereditary enemies, continued separated by vast plains regarded as well nigh impassable; until after the lapse of more than two decades diplomacy effected what hostilities had been unable to bring about, and France, in 1762, ceded to Spain the territory then known as Louisiana. The Spaniard, however, who in those days was nothing if not glittering and showy, cared but little for the development of the immense agricultural resources of the magnificent territory so conveyed, and his rule was careless, neglectful and unpopular. In 1800 Bonaparte prevailed upon the Spanish government to reconvey to his nation the lands which during the thirty-eight years of Spanish occupancy it had found alike vexatious and unprofitable. Bonaparte, however, was but little more in this transaction than a conduit, to hold the title for the only nation which could at that time make any adequate use of the vast possession, and in the year 1803, in consideration of the sum of fifteen millions of dollars, the whole of Louisiana passed by solemn treaty into the hands of the United States.

# CHAPTER III.

### THE TITLE TO THE NORTHWESTERN TERRITORY ACQUIRED BY THE UNITED STATES—GOVERNOR CLAIBORNE'S PROCLAMATION—A REAL ESTATE DEAL SATISFACTORY TO BOTH GRANTOR AND GRANTEE.

On the 20th day of December, 1803, the flag of the United States first floated as a symbol of sovereignty over the city of New Orleans. It signified that not only the present State of Louisiana, but the entire French territory from the Mississippi River to the Pacific and south of the British Possessions had become the property of the young republic. From the land so acquired have grown rich and powerful States; and territories hardly less wealthy and populous are knocking at the doors of the Federal Union for admission. To be more specific, the cession of those portions of the States of Alabama and Mississippi south of the thirty-first parallel, the entire area of the States of Louisiana, Arkansas, Missouri, Iowa, Nebraska, the two Dakotas, Montana, Washington, all of Minnesota west of the Mississippi River, all of Kansas, except a small portion west of the one hundredth meridian and south of the Arkansas river, part of Colorado, the whole of Idaho and Indian territories, with a part of Wyoming.

The history of the transactions which led to the possession by the United States of this enormous addition to their domain shows the wisdom, foresight and prophetic skill of Jefferson and the statesmen who surrounded him in a most brilliant light. The rule of Spain had never been satisfactory to our government. The Spaniards were fond of stirring up hostile Indians to open warfare against our settlers. To the State of Kentucky, which depended on the mouth of the Mississippi as the natural outlet for its produce, the restrictions on her trade and the threats of closing that gateway altogether to vessels from the United States, were especially galling and exasperating. Still the borderers preferred to bear the ills they had than fly to others that they knew not of. They would rather endure the insults of Spain, studied and violent as they were, than to see possession transferred to France, whose ambition under the rule of Bonaparte and whose love of dominion might make their annoyances even harder to bear, and might lead to enunciation by a force of armed and determined men of the doctrine that navigable rivers are, by the great law of nature, free to all the dwellers upon their banks.

Such was the situation when, in the early part of 1801, shortly after Jefferson's accession to the Presidency, a despatch from Rufus King, the American Minister near the Court of St. James, gave information which was calculated to excite the deepest interest and concern. There was a report in circulation, he said, that a sale of Louisiana had been made to France. His view was that we should not interfere so long as the country remained in the hands of Spain, but that no alienation of it except to ourselves should be allowed. For more than a year the verification of Mr. King's rumor, though anxiously sought, could not be had. Napoleon's ministers uniformly and constantly denied that any such cession had been made. By degrees, however, all parties became assured these denials were untrue, and the anger and apprehension which the belief excited found expression in the well known letter from Jefferson to Mr. Livingston, at that time our Minister to France.

"There is," says he, "on the globe one single spot, the possessor of which is our natural and habitual enemy. It is New Orleans, through which the produce of three-eighths of our territory must pass to market; and from its fertility it will, ere long, yield more than half of our whole produce, and contain more than half of our inhabitants France, placing herself in that door, assumes to us the attitude of defiance. Spain might have retained it quietly for years. Her pacific dispositions, her feeble state, would induce her to increase our facilities there, so that her possession of the place would be hardly felt by us, and it would not, perhaps, be very long before some circumstance might arise which would make the cession of it to us the price of something of more worth to her. Not so can it ever be in the hands of France; the impetuosity of her temper, the energy and restlessness of her character, placed in a point of eternal friction with us; and our character, which, though quiet and loving peace and the pursuit of wealth, is high minded, despising wealth in competition with insult or injury, enterprising and energetic as any nation on earth—these circumstances render it impossible that France and the United States can continue long friends, when they meet in so irritating a position. They, as well as we, must be blind if they do not see this; and we must be very improvident if we do not begin to make arrangements on that hypothesis. The day that France takes possession of New Orleans fixes the sentence which is to restrain her forever within her low water mark. It seals the union of two nations, who, in conjunction, can maintain exclusive possession of the ocean. From that moment we must marry ourselves to the British fleet and nation. We must turn all our attention to a maritime force, for which our resources place us on very high ground; and having formed and connected together a power which may render reinforcement of her settlements here impossible to France. make the first cannon which shall be fired in Europe the signal for tearing up any settlement she may have made, and for holding the two continents of America in sequestration for the common purposes of the British and American nations."

Sentiments so bold and outspoken as the above were calculated to warn Napoleon that the retention of his power in the New World would be far more hazardous and expensive than his European schemes; but he temporized and hesitated long before he could bring himself to part with an empire which was destined at no distant day in the life of a nation, to add both power and wealth to its possessors. Kentucky fumed and threatened to open the gateway with her own militia. The Federalists taunted their opponents with the supineness, indifference and cowardice of the ruling powers. The whole country was indignant at the threatened occupation. Napoleon, however, was calm, quiet and obstinate in his refusal to treat.

But at last the fear of an alliance on the part of the United States with England, and the feeling, also, that even without such an alliance, New Orleans would be at the mercy of an English fleet in the event of a renewal of hostilities, led him to deliberate; and deliberation speedily convinced him of the advisability of getting rid of a possession which would, in war, be a source of anxiety and expense to him, and receiving in return funds sufficient to enable him to resume the offensive towards his ancient foes, should he so determine. It was not without a struggle that he came to this conclusion. "I know," said he, "the full value of Louisiana, and have been desirous of repairing the fault of the French negotiator who abandoned it in

1763 A few lines of a treaty have restored it to me, and I have scarcely recovered it when I must expect to lose it But if it escapes from me, it shall one day cost dearer to those who oblige me to strip myself of it, than to those to whom I wish to deliver it The English have successively taken from France, Canada, Cape Breton, Newfoundland, Nova Scotia, and the richest portions of Asia They shall not have the Mississippi, which they covet I have not a moment to lose in putting it out of their reach I think of ceding it to the United States. I can scarcely say that I cede it to them for it is not yet in our possession If, however, I leave the least time to our enemies, I shall only transmit an empty title to those republicans whose friendship I seek They only ask of me one town in Louisiana; but I already consider the colony as entirely lost, and it appears to me that in the hands of this growing power it will be more useful to the policy, and even to the commerce of France than if I should attempt to keep it "

Thus peaceably passed into the possession of the United States Government the richest and most valuable part of her domain The negotiations which followed were merely concerning price and terms of cession, and when one party is anxious to sell and the other to buy, these are usually matters which are arranged without much trouble The entire cost as summed up on final settlement, according to the original treaty stipulations, was 60,000,000 francs, or $15,000,000 in money and bonds, to which if added the interest on bonds to the time of redemption $8,529,353, and claims of citizens of the United States, due from France and assumed by the United States, $3,738,268 98, the total amount will be $27,267,621 98 The territory conveyed added to the public domain 1,183,752 square miles, or 760,961,280 acres The few acres which comprise the City of Omaha would now, if put up at auction, pay several times over the consideration for the entire purchase

The United States, safely at last established in the possession of a gateway which had acted as a constant menace to the citizens of Kentucky, and others living on the banks of the Ohio and tributary streams, lost no time in beginning to improve and make use of their new purchase On the 23d of October the following act was approved

AN ACT to enable the President of the United States to take possession of the territories ceded by France to the United States, by the treaty concluded at Paris on the thirtieth day of April last, and for the temporary government thereof

*Be it enacted by the Senate and House of Representatives of the United States of America in Congress assembled*

That the President of the United States be, and he is hereby, authorized to take possession of and occupy the territory ceded by France to the United States, by the treaty concluded at Paris on the thirtieth day of April last, between the two nations, and that he may, for that purpose, and in order to maintain in the said territories the authority of the United States, employ any part of the army and navy of the United States and of the force authorized by an act passed the third day of March last entitled, "An act directing a detachment from the militia of the United States and for erecting certain arsenals," which he may deem necessary, and so much of the sum appropriated by the said act as may be necessary, is hereby appropriated for the purpose of carrying this act into effect to be applied under the direction of the President of the United States

SEC 2 AND BE IT FURTHER ENACTED, That until the expiration of the present session of Congress, unless provision for the temporary government of the said territories be sooner made by Congress, all the military, civil and judicial powers exercised by the officers of the existing government of the same, shall be vested in such person and persons, and shall be exercised in such manner as the President of the United States shall direct for maintaining and protecting the inhabitants of Louisiana in the free enjoyment of their liberty, property and religion

On the 10th of November, 1803, an act was approved providing for bonds to the amount of $11,250,000, for the purpose of carrying into effect the first convention under the treaty, and making provision for paying the same This was carried into effect, the stock issued, delivered to the agent of France, and duly acknowleged. The financial agents were Messrs. Hope and Labouchere of Amsterdam, and the Barings of London. On the same day an act was approved making provision for payment of claims of citizens of the United States on the government of France, the payment of which had been assumed by the United States by virtue of the second convention of the 30th of April under the treaty.

President Jefferson at once proceeded to occupy and obtain actual possession of the province, which had been ordered to be delivered to France by writ of the King of Spain, dated Barcelona, October 15th, 1802, General Victor to receive it on the part of France, or any other officer duly authorized by the Republic of France. On the 30th of November, 1803, at New Orleans, Pierre Clement Laussat, colonial prefect, Commissioner on the part of France, received the colony and province of Louisiana from El Marques de Casa Calvo, Commissioner on the part of Spain, under an order of February 18, 1803. This was only twenty days prior to its transfer by France to the Commissioners on the part of the United States. The manner of taking and receiving possession by the United States was, as detailed in the following message from the President of the United States to Congress, transmitted on the 16th of January, 1804:

In execution of the act of the present session of Congress for taking possession of Louisiana, as ceded to us by France, and for the temporary government thereof, Governor Claiborne of the Mississippi Territory and General Wilkinson were appointed Commissioners to receive possession. They proceeded with such regular troops as had been assembled at Fort Adams from the nearest posts, and with some militia of the Mississippi Territory, to New Orleans. To be prepared for anything unexpected which might arise out of the transaction, a respectable body of militia was ordered to be in readiness in the States of Ohio, Kentucky and Tennessee, and a part of those of Tennessee was moved on to the Natchez. No occasion, however, arose for their services. Our Commissioners, on their arrival at New Orleans, found the province already delivered by the Commissioners of Spain to that of France, who delivered it over to them on the 20th day of December, as appears by their declaratory act accompanying this. Governor Claiborne, being duly invested with the powers heretofore exercised by the Governor and Intendant of Louisiana, assumed the government on the same day, and, for the maintenance of law and order, immediately issued the proclamation and address now communicated.

On this important acquisition, so favorable to the immediate interests of our western citizens, so auspicious to the peace and security of the nation in general; which adds to our country territories so extensive and fertile, and to our citizens new brethren to partake of the blessings of freedom and self-government, I offer to Congress and our country my sincere congratulations.

TH: JEFFERSON.

The report of the Commissioners, the record of the transfer and the proclamation and address follow in regular order:

CITY OF NEW ORLEANS, }
December 20, 1803. }

SIR: We have the satisfaction to announce to you that the Province of Louisiana was this day surrendered to the United States by the Commissioner of France: and to add that the flag of our country was raised in this city amidst the acclamations of the inhabitants. The enclosed is a copy of an instrument in writing, which was signed and exchanged by the Commissioners of the two governments, and is designed as a record of this interesting transaction.

Accept assurances of our respectful consideration.
WILLIAM C. C. CLAIBORNE.
JA. WILKINSON.

The HON. JAMES MADISON,
Secretary of State, City of Washington.

The undersigned, William C. C. Claiborne and James Wilkinson, Commissioners or agents of the United States, agreeable to the full powers they have received from Thomas Jefferson, President of the United States, under date of the 31st October, 1803, and twenty-eighth year of the independence of the United States of America (8 Brumaire, 12th year of the French Republic), countersigned by the Secretary of State, James Madison, and Citizen Peter Clement Laussat, Colonial Prefect and Commissioner of the French government for the delivery, in the name of the French Republic, of the country, territories and dependencies of Louisiana to the Commissioners or agents of the United States, conformably to the powers, commission, and special mandate which he has received in the name of the French people from Citizen Bonaparte, First Consul, under date of the 9th of June, 1803 (17 Prairial 11th year of the French Republic), countersigned by the Secretary of State, Hugues Maret, and by His Excellency the Minister of Marine and Colonies, Decres, do certify by these presents, that on this day, Tuesday, the 20th December, 1803, of the Christian era (28th Frimaire, 12th year of the Republic), being convened in the hall of the Hotel de Ville, of New Orleans, accompanied on both sides by the chiefs and officers of the army and navy, by the municipality and divers respectable citizens of their respective republics, the said William C. C. Claiborne and James Wilkinson delivered to the said citizen Laussat their aforesaid full powers, by which it evidently appears that full power and authority has been given them jointly and severally, to take possession of and to occupy the territories ceded by France to the United States by a treaty concluded at Paris on the 30th day of April, last past (10th Floreal), and for that purpose to repair to the said territory, and there to execute and perform all such acts and things touching the premises, as may be necessary for fulfilling their appointment, conformable to the said treaty and laws of the United States; and thereupon, the said Citizen Laussat declared that in virtue of, and in the terms of the powers, commission and special mandate, dated at St. Cloud, 6th June, 1803, of the Christian era (17 Prairial, 11th year of the French Republic), he put from that moment the said Commissioners of the United States in possession of the country, territories and dependencies of Louisiana, conformably to the 1st, 2d, 4th and 5th articles of the treaty, and the two conventions, concluded and signed the 30th April, 1803 (10th Floreal, 11th year of the French Republic), between the French Republic and the United States of America, by Citizen Francis Barbe Marbois, Minister of the Public Treasury, and Messieurs Robert R. Livingston and James Monroe, Ministers Plenipotentiary of the United States, all three furnished with full powers, of which treaty and two conventions, the ratifications, made by the First Consul of the French Republic on the one part, and by the President of the United States, by and with the advice and consent of the Senate, on the other part, have been exchanged and mutually received at the city of Washington, the 21st of October, 1803, (28 Vindemaire, 12th year of the French Republic), by Citizen Louis Andre Pichon, *charge des affaires* of the French Republic, near the United States, on the part of France, and by James Madison, Secretary of State of the United States, on the part of the United States, according to the *proces verbal* drawn up on the same day;

and the present delivery of the country is made to them, to the end that, in conformity with the object of the said treaty, the sovereignty and property of the colony or province of Louisiana may pass to the said United States, under the same clauses and conditions as it had been ceded by Spain to France, in virtue of the treaty concluded at St. Ildefonso, on the 1st of October, 1800, (9th Vindemaire, 9th year), between these two last powers, which has since received its execution by the actual re-entrance of the French Republic into possession of the said colony or province.

And the said Citizen Laussat, in consequence, at this present time, delivered to the said Commissioners of the United States, in this public sitting, the keys of the City of New Orleans, declaring that he discharges from their oaths of fidelity towards the French Republic, the citizens and inhabitants of Louisiana, who shall choose to remain under the dominion of the United States.

And that it may forever appear, the undersigned have signed the *proces verbal* of this important and solemn act in the French and English languages, and have sealed it with their seals, and have caused it to be countersigned by their Secretaries of Commission, the day, month and year above written.

    WM. C. C. CLAIBORNE. [L. S.]
    JAMES WILKINSON. [L. S.]
    LAUSSAT. [L. S.]

## PROCLAMATION

*By his Excellency William C. C. Claiborne, Governor of the Mississippi Territory, exercising the powers of Governor-General and Intendant of the Province of Louisiana:*

WHEREAS, By stipulations between the governments of France and Spain, the latter ceded to the former the colony and province of Louisiana, with the same extent which it had at the date of the above mentioned treaty in the hands of Spain, and that it had, when France possessed it, and such as it ought to be after the treaties subsequently entered into between Spain and other States; and,

WHEREAS, The government of France has ceded the same to the United States by a treaty duly ratified, and bearing date the 30th of April, in the present year, and the possession of said colony and province is now in the United States, according to the tenor of the last-mentioned treaty; and,

WHEREAS, The Congress of the United States, on the 31st day of October, in the present year, did enact that until the expiration of the session of Congress then sitting, (unless provisions for the temporary government of the said territories be sooner made by Congress), all the military, civil and judicial powers, exercised by the then existing government of the same, shall be vested in such person or persons, and shall be exercised in such manner, as the President of the United States shall direct, for the maintaining and protecting the inhabitants of Louisiana in the free enjoyment of their liberty, property and religion: and the President of the United States has, by his commission, bearing date the same 31st day of October, vested me with all the powers, and charged me with the several duties heretofore held and exercised by the Governor-General and Intendant of the Province :

I have, therefore, thought fit to issue this my proclamation, making known the premises, and to declare that the government heretofore exercised over the said province of Louisiana, as well under the authority of Spain, as of the French Republic, has ceased; and that of the United States of America is established over the same; that the inhabitants thereof will be incorporated in the Union of the United States, and admitted as soon as possible, according to the principles of the Federal Constitution, to the enjoyment of all the rights, advantages and immunities of citizens of the United States; that in the meantime they shall be maintained and protected in the free enjoyment of their liberty, property and the religion which they profess; that all laws and municipal regulations which were in existence at the cessation of the late government, remain in full force; and all civil officers charged with their execution, except those whose powers have been specially vested in me, and except also such officers as have been entrusted with the collection of the revenue, are continued in their functions during the pleasure of the governor for the time being, or until provision shall otherwise be made.

And I do hereby exhort and enjoin all the inhabitants and other persons within the said province, to be faithful and true in their allegiance to the United States, and obedient to the laws and authorities of the same, under full assurance that their just rights will be under the guardianship of the United States, and will be maintained from all force or violence from without or within.

In testimony whereof, I have hereunto set my hand.

Given at the City of New Orleans, the 20th day of December, 1803, and of the Independence of the United States of America the twenty-eighth.

WM. C. C. CLAIBORNE.

ADDRESS TO THE CITIZENS OF LOUISIANA.
*Fellow Citizens of Louisiana :*

On the great and interesting event now finally consummated—an event so advantageous to yourselves and so glorious to United America, I cannot forbear offering you my warmest congratulations. The wise policy of the Consul of France has, by the cession of Louisiana to the United States, secured to you a connection beyond the reach of change, and to your posterity the sure inheritance of Freedom. The American people receive you as brothers; and will hasten to extend to you a participation in those inestimable rights which have formed the basis of their own unexampled prosperity. Under the auspices of the American government you may confidently rely upon the security of your liberty, your property, and the religion of your choice. You may with equal certainty, rest assured that your commerce will be promoted and your agriculture cherished : in a word, that your true interests will be among the primary objects of our National Legislature. In return for these benefits the United States will be amply remunerated, if your growing attachment to the Constitution of our country, and your veneration for the principles on which it is founded be duly proportioned to the blessings which they will confer. Among your first duties, therefore, you should cultivate with assiduity among yourselves the advancement of political information; you should guide the rising generation in the paths of republican economy and virtue; you should encourage literature, for without the advantages of education your descendants will be unable to appreciate the intrinsic worth of the government transmitted to them.

As for myself, fellow citizens, accept a sincere assurance that, during my continuance in the situation in which the President of the United States has been pleased to place me, every exertion will be made on my part to foster your internal happiness and forward your general welfare, for it is only by such means that I can secure to myself the approbation of those great and just men who preside in the councils of the nation.

WM. C. C. CLAIBORNE.

New Orleans, December 20, 1803.

The proceedings which thus culminated in transferring to the United States so large and fertile a tract gave general, though not unmixed satisfaction to the country. The party known as federalists opposed it. Notwithstanding this, there has seldom been a transaction of bargain and sale in which

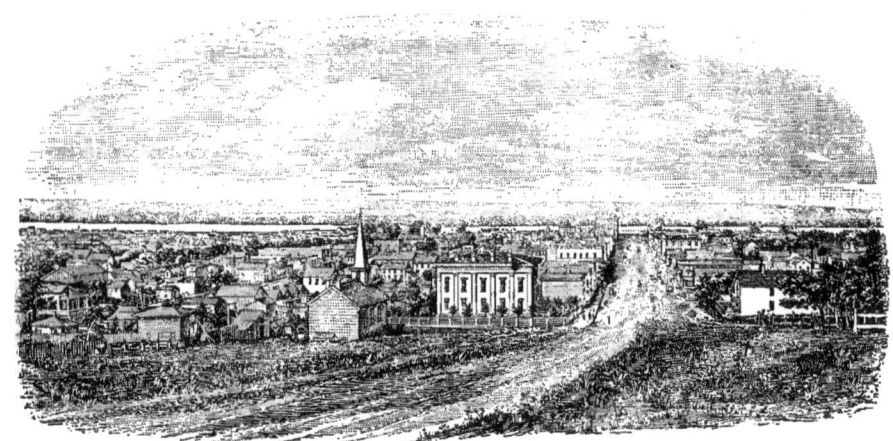

FARNAM STREET FROM SIXTEENTH STREET EAST—1866.

FARNAM STREET FROM SIXTEENTH STREET EAST—1889.

both parties were so well satisfied at its conclusion. Bonaparte presented Marbois, his factor, with the sum of nearly forty thousand dollars as his commission upon the negotiation, remarking that sixty millions of francs was no small price for a province of which he had never taken possession, and which he might not be able to retain twenty-four hours. Nor was his cause for self-gratulation due alone to the amount of the purchase money. He saw a blow at England in the transfer. "This accession of territory," said he, "strengthens forever the power of the United States, and I have just given to England a maritime rival that will sooner or later humble her pride." It is a singular fact, that the British government expressed its approval of the cession. Whether England's approval was sincere or assumed for the occasion matters little. It is a fact that the whole civilized world either openly rejoiced or sullenly acquiesced in it, except as has been already stated the irreconcilable remnant of the Federalist party who, from the first rumor of the purchase to the voting of the last dollar necessary to complete it, opposed the acquisition. The majority admitted that they could see no good in any measure set on foot or advocated by Jefferson, some honestly deplored any expansion of our territory, some disbelieved in the alleged value of the purchase, and some, Josiah Quincy, of Massachusetts, among the number, foresaw in the enlargement of the slave territory of the United States, the very disasters which, in fact, more than half a century thereafter, followed. The victorious followers of Jefferson, however, were jubilant. Trade revived in the West. Confidence in the future of the country was stronger than ever, and the general sentiment was expressed by a colored print of New Orleans, still occasionally to be seen, in which the American eagle with outstretched pinions hovered, with a scroll on which was written, "Under my wings every thing prospers."

# CHAPTER IV.

THE LEWIS AND CLARKE EXPEDITION—COUNCIL WITH THE INDIANS NEAR OMAHA—JOURNAL OF PATRICK GASS—THE MISSOURI AND AMERICAN FUR COMPANIES.

By an act of Congress passed March 26, 1804, the territory ceded by France was divided into two portions. Under the name of Orleans, a territory was formed of the part lying south of the Mississippi territory, and of an east and west line to commence on the Mississippi River at the thirty-third degree of north latitude, and extending west to the boundary of the cession. The remainder of the ceded lands, embracing, of course, what is now the State of Nebraska, was called the district of Louisiana, and became a part of the vast country known as the Indiana territory.

Statutes speedily followed establishing land offices, providing for ascertaining and adjusting the titles and claims to land within the territory, either under French or Spanish grants, directing the appointment of commissioners to decide summarily, according to justice and equity on all complete titles under such grants; to authorize General LaFayette to locate the eleven thousand five hundred and twenty acres already in recognition of his distinguished services, granted to him, in an unoccupied portion of the territory of Orleans. Provision was also made to prevent the unlawful location of pretended grants, and generally to encourage immigration into the valley of the Mississippi.

The time had come to put into execution what had long been a favorite scheme of Jefferson's, namely, the scientific and thorough examination and exploration of the country west of the Mississippi, and a report thereon by experienced and qualified men. Long before Jefferson became President, and sixteen years before the purchase of Louisiana had been consummated, he had, while American Minister in Paris, proposed such an expedition.

There was, in 1787, sojourning in Paris a young man of thirty-six, born in Connecticut, and by choice a citizen of the world, whose short but remarkable career was distinguished by zeal, activity, courage, honor and intelligence. His name was John Ledyard. He had been a student in Dartmouth College, a stroller among the Six Nations, a student of divinity, a sailor, a soldier, a corporal of marines under the renowned navigator, Captain Cook; at one time disappointed, ragged and penniless; at another, the honored and trusted associate of eminent professors and celebrated travelers. He had a manly form, a mild, but animated and expressive eye, perfect self-possession, a boldness not obtrusive, but showing a consciousness of his proper dignity, an independent spirit, and a glow of enthusiasm giving life to his conversation and his whole deportment. Ledyard had come to France to attempt a business arrangement in the fur trade on the northwest coast of America; but was ready for any adventure, from an exploration of Alaska to an expedition to the heart of Africa. Jefferson met him just as his effort to establish his fur trade had failed, and proposed to him a land journey through northern Europe and Kamtschatka to the Pacific, and thence across the

Rocky Mountains, and through the unknown regions of the northwestern territory, to what was then the United States. The consent of Russia having been obtained, the youthful explorer set out on his perilous trip, but before he had reached the confines of Kamtschatka, the Russian powers became suspicious, put an end to his journey, and compelled him to return. Had it not been for his sudden and untimely death in 1788, he would undoubtedly have been offered in 1804, some responsible position in the exploring expedition organized in that year.

Still later, in 1792, Mr. Jefferson proposed to the American Philosophical Society, that an expedition to be supported by private subscriptions should be organized to explore the northwest territory as far as the Pacific coast. Meriwether Lewis, a young captain in the First Regiment of United States Infantry, who had formerly been private secretary to Mr. Jefferson, and M. Michaux, a noted French botanist, were employed to make the trip, and started on the expedition. Hardly, however, had they commenced their journey, when the French savan was recalled by a message from his minister at Washington, and this attempt also, was rendered abortive.

But, on the 18th of January, 1803, prior to the actual completion of the Louisiana purchase, and when the negotiations began to show some probability of success, Mr. Jefferson, then President, in a confidential message to Congress, recommended that a certain act establishing trading houses among the Indians (which was then about to expire by limitation), be not only continued, but extended to the tribes dwelling on the Mississippi River. He also proposed that a party of explorers should be organized, and sent up to the sources of the Missouri, and thence to the Pacific. Congress approved the suggestion, and made the necessary appropriation. Captain Lewis was, at his own request, detailed to command the expedition, and First Lieutenant William Clarke, a brother of George Rogers Clarke, was subsequently detailed to accompany him. It was an expedition of discovery and inquiry. Its instructions, which were prepared by President Jefferson himself, were to notice and detail the geography and character of the country, to enter into negotiations with the Indians for commerce, and to describe their habits, characteristics and history.

The names of those who composed this celebrated party are worthy of being held in remembrance. They were Meriwether Lewis, captain, William Clarke, first lieutenant, John Ordway, Nathaniel Prior and Patrick Gass, sergeants; Charles Floyd, William Bratton, John Colter, John Collins, Pierre Crozatte, Robert Frazier, Joseph Fields, George Gibson, Silas Goodrich, Hugh Hall, Richard Worthington, Thomas P. Howard, Peter Wiser, John Baptiste Le Page, Frances Labinche, Hugh McNeal, John Potts, John Shields, George Shannon, John B. Thompson, William Werner, Alexander Willard, Richard Windsor, Joseph Whitehouse, John Newman, privates, George Drulyard and Toussaint Chabono, interpreters, Chabono's wife, a Snake squaw and her child, and York, a colored servant.

The party entered the Missouri in boats on the 4th day of May, 1804. In the summer of the following year they crossed the Rocky Mountains, and on the 15th of November, 1805, they landed at Cape Disappointment, having passed down the Lewis River (now known as Snake River) to its junction with the Columbia, and thence down the last mentioned river to its mouth.

Wintering at Fort Clatsop, on the left bank of the Columbia, they set their faces homeward in the spring, and reached St. Louis on the 23d of September, 1806, after a sojourn in the wilderness of two years and three months. It furnished more particular and reliable information of the region between the Mississippi River and the Pacific Ocean than had ever before been accessible.

Many editions of their report of the expedition were published, and also the diary or journal of Sergeant Patrick Gass. The success of the undertaking, in the face of peril and hardship, was considered by Congress deserving of special reward. By an act passed in March, of the year following their return, warrants for sixteen hundred acres of land each were given to Capt. Lewis and Lieut. Clarke; and warrants for three hundred and twenty acres to each of those mentioned above as composing the expedition, with the single exception of the negro York, who was not recognized in the distribution of rewards. These warrants were located on the west side of the Mississippi River, or were to be received at two dollars per acre for any such lands. Extra pay, double the regular amount, was voted to all for the entire time occupied in the expedition.

They passed up the Missouri River in the month of July, 1804. An account in full detail, and nearly their own language, of their voyage in the vicinity of the City of Omaha, will not be found devoid of interest:

"On the 11th of July they landed on a sand island opposite the River Nemaha, where they remained a day for the purpose of taking lunar observations and refreshing the party. They had now ascended the Missouri to the distance of about 480 miles. The Nemaha empties itself into the Missouri from the south, and is eighty yards wide at the confluence, which is in latitude 39 deg. 55 min. 56 sec. Captain Clarke ascended it in the pirogue about two miles, to the mouth of a small creek on the lower side. On going ashore, he found in the level plain several artificial mounds or graves, and on the adjoining hills others of a larger size. This appearance indicates sufficiently the former population of this country, these mounds being certainly intended as tombs, the Indians of the Missouri still preserving the custom of interring the dead on high ground.

From the top of the highest mound a delightful prospect presented itself. The level and extensive meadows watered by the Nemaha, and enlivened by the few trees and shrubs skirting the borders of the river and its tributary streams; the lowland of the Missouri covered with undulating grass, nearly five feet high, gradually rising into a second plain, where rich weeds and flowers are interspersed with copses of the Osage plum; farther back were seen small groves of trees, an abundance of grapes, the wild cherry of the Missouri, resembling our own but larger, and growing on a small bush; and the choke-cherry, which was observed for the first time.

"On the 14th, elk were seen for the first time. They passed the Nishnahbatona and the Little Nemaha Rivers, and found the former to be only three hundred yards from the Missouri, at the distance of twelve miles from its mouth. Farther on they reached an island to the north, near which the banks overflow; while on the south, hills project over the river in the form of high cliffs. At one point a part of the cliff, nearly three-fourths of a mile in length and two hundred feet in height, had fallen into the river. On the 20th they passed a creek called by the French l'Eau qui Pleure, or the Weeping Water."

They reached the great river Platte on the 21st, and it is thus described: "The highlands, which had accompanied us on the south for the last eight or ten miles, stopped at about three-quarters of a mile from the entrance of the Platte. Captains Lewis and Clarke ascended the river in a pirogue for about one mile, and found the current very rapid, rolling over sands, and divided into a number of channels, none of which are deeper than five or six feet. One of our Frenchmen, who spent two winters on it, says that it spreads much more at some distance from the mouth; that its depth is generally not more than five or six feet; that there are many small islands scattered through it and that, from its rapidity and quantity of its sand, it cannot be navigated by boats or pirogues, though the Indians pass it in small flat canoes made of hides, that the Saline or Salt River, which in some seasons is too brackish to be drank, falls into it from the south, about thirty miles up, and a little above it, Elkhorn River from the north running nearly parallel with the Missouri. The river is in fact, much more rapid than the Missouri, the bed of which it fills with moving sands, and drives the current on the northern shore, on which it is constantly encroaching. At its junction the Platte is about six hundred yards wide, and the same number of miles from the Mississippi. With much difficulty we worked round the sand bars near the mouth, and came to the above point, having made fifteen miles

"Our camp is by observation, in latitude 41 deg 3 11 sec. Immediately behind it is a plain about five miles wide, one half covered with wood and the other dry and elevated. The low grounds on the south, and near the junction of the two rivers are rich, but subject to be overflowed. Farther up the banks are higher, and opposite our camp the first hills approach the river, and are covered with timber, such as oak, walnut and elm. The intermediate country is watered by the Papillion, or Butterfly Creek of about eighteen yards wide, and three miles from the Platte, on the north are high open plains and prairies, and at nine miles from the Platte, the Moscheto Creek and two or three small willow islands. We stayed here several days, during which we dried provisions, made new oars, and prepared our dispatches and maps of the country we had passed, for the President of the United States, to whom we intend to send them by a pirogue from this place. The hunters have found game scarce in this neighborhood, they have seen deer, turkeys and grouse, we have also an abundance of ripe grapes, and one of our men caught a white catfish, the eyes of which were small and its tail resembling that of a dolphin

'On the 29th they passed the spot where the Ayauway Indians, a branch of the Ottoes, once lived and who had emigrated from this place to the River Des Moines. 'Our hunter brought to us in the evening,' continues the narrative, 'a Missouri Indian, whom he had found with two others, dressing an elk; they were perfectly friendly, gave him some of the meat, and one of them agreed to accompany him to the boat. He is one of the few remaining Missouris who live with the Ottoes, he belongs to a small party whose camp is four miles from the river; and he says that the body of the nation is now hunting buffalo in the plains. He appeared quite sprightly, and his language resembled the Osage, particularly in his calling a chief *inca*. We sent him back with one of our party the next morning, with an invitation to meet us above on the river, and then proceeded

"July 30. We went early in the morning three and a quarter miles, and encamped on the south, in order to wait for the Ottoes. The land here consists of a plain, above the high water level, the soil of which is fertile and covered with a grass from five to eight feet high, interspersed with copses of large plums, and a currant like those of the United States. * * * Back of this plain is a woody ridge about seventy feet above it, at the edge of which we formed our camp. This ridge separates the lower from the higher prairie, of a good quality, with grass ten or twelve inches in height, and extending back about a mile to another elevation of eighty or ninety feet, beyond which is one continued plain. Near our camp we enjoy from the bluffs a most beautiful view of the river and the adjoining country. At a distance, varying from four to ten miles, and of a height between seventy and three hundred feet, two parallel ranges of highland afford a passage to the Missouri, which enriches the low grounds between them. In its winding course it nourishes the willow islands, the scattered cottonwood, elm, sycamore, linn, and ash, and the groves are interspersed with hickory, walnut, coffeenut, and oak.

"July 31. The meridian altitude of this day made the latitude of our camp 41 deg., 18 min., 1¼ sec. One of our men brought in yesterday an animal, called by the Pawnees *chacartoosh*, and by the French, *blaireau*, or badger."

The narrative continues: "We waited with much anxiety the return of our messenger to the Ottoes. The men whom we despatched to our last encampment returned without having seen any appearance of its having been visited. Our horses, too, had strayed; but we were so fortunate as to recover them at the distance of twelve miles. Our apprehensions were at length relieved by the arrival of a party of about fourteen Ottoes and Missouri Indians, who came at sunset, on the 2d of August, accompanied by a Frenchman who resided among them, and interpreted for us. Captains Lewis and Clarke went out to meet them, and told them that we would hold a council in the morning. In the meantime we sent them some roasted meat, pork, flour and meal; in return for which they made us a present of watermelons. We learned that our man Liberte had set out from their camp a day before them; we were in hopes that he had fatigued his horse, or lost himself in the woods, and would soon return; but we never saw him again.

"The next morning the Indians, with their six chiefs, were all assembled under an awning formed with the mainsail, in presence of our party, paraded for the occasion. A speech was then made, announcing to them the change in the government, our promises of protection, and advice as to their future conduct. All the six chiefs replied to our speech, each in his turn, according to rank. They expressed their joy at the change in the government; their hopes that we would recommend them to their Great Father (the President), that they might obtain trade and necessaries; they wanted arms as well for hunting as for defence, and asked our mediation between them and the Mahas. with whom they are now at war. We promised to do so, and wished some of them to accompany us to that nation, which they declined, for fear of being killed by them. We then proceeded to distribute our presents. The grand chief of the nation not being of the party, we sent him a flag, a medal, and some ornaments for clothing. To the six chiefs who were present, we gave a medal of the second grade to one Ottoe chief and one Missouri chief; a medal of the third grade to two inferior chiefs of each nation: the customary mode of recognizing a chief being to place a medal round his neck, which is considered among his tribe as a proof of his consideration abroad. Each of these medals was accompanied by a present of paint, garters, and cloth ornaments of dress; and to this we added a canister of powder, a bottle of whisky, and a few presents to the whole, which appeared to make them perfectly satisfied. The air-gun, too, was fired, and astonished them greatly. The absent grand chief was an Ottoe, named Weahrushhah, which, in English, degenerates into Little Thief. The two principal chieftains present were Shongotongo, or Big Horse, and Wethen, or Hospitality; also Shosguscan, or White Horse, an Ottoe; the first an Ottoe, the second a Missouri. The incidents just related induced us to give to this place the name of the Council Bluffs; the situation of it is exceedingly favorable for a fort and trading factory, as the soil is well calculated for bricks, and there is an abundance of wood in the neighborhood, and the air being pure and healthy. It is also central to the chief resorts of the Indians: one day's journey to the Ottoes; one and a half to the Great Pawnees; two days from the Mahas; two and a quarter from the Pawnee Loups' village, convenient to the hunting grounds of the Sioux, and twenty-five days' journey to Santa Fe

"Omaha is in about 41 deg 16 min., 41 deg 18 min., is given as the place where the council was held"

There has, within the last few years, been some question and controversy as to the true location of this place, arising from the fact that a city in Iowa, opposite the site of Omaha, formerly called Kanesville, has now received the appellation of Council Bluffs, the same name as was given by Lewis and Clarke to the spot where their conference with the Indians was held The evidence, however, is overwhelming that it took place on the beautiful plateau now called Fort Calhoun, about sixteen miles north of Omaha The reasons for this belief are briefly as follows First The traditions of the neighborhood, never to be disregarded when the distance of time is so small, point to this bluff Second The latitude given corresponds as accurately as could be expected to that of the present Fort Calhoun, and at all events could not possibly apply to the old Kanesville Third We read that after the conference they set sail and reached Floyd's Bluffs under some bluffs—the first near the river since we left the Ayauway village This description could not apply to any portion of the river in the vicinity of the place which now claims the appellation Fourth In a journal of a voyage up the Missouri in 1811, by H. M Brackenridge, Esq, he speaks of passing the river Boyer, and afterwards, in the evening of sailing by some high, clean meadows called the Council Bluffs, from the circumstance of Lewis and Clarke having held a council with the Ottoe and Missouri Indians, when ascending this river Fifth In the journal of Patrick Gass, which will be hereafter more particularly referred to, he describes the spot as follows "At nine we came to some timber land at the foot of a high bluff and encamped there in order to wait for the Indians At the top of the bluff is a large, handsome prairie, and a large pond or small lake, about two miles from camp on the south side of the river." This pond or lake, much reduced doubtless, in size, as is common with all the lakes in the Missouri Valley, may still be discovered about a mile and a half or two miles northwest from the site of the old fort. In short, there can hardly be any question that the location of the council was on the beautiful spot which now forms the town of Fort Calhoun

"In the afternoon of August 18th, the party arrived with the Indians, consisting of the Little Thief and the Big Horse, whom we had seen on the 3d, together with the six other chiefs, and a French interpreter We met them under a shade, and after they had finished a repast with which we supplied them, we inquired into the origin of the war between them and the Mahas, which they related with great frankness It seems that two of the Missouris went to the Mahas to steal horses, but were detected and killed, the Ottoes and Missouris thought themselves bound to avenge their companions, and the whole nations were at last obliged to share in the dispute, they are also in fear of a war from the Pawnees, whose village they entered this summer while the inhabitants were hunting, and stole their corn This ingenious confession did not make us the less desirous of negotiating a peace for them, but no Indians have as yet been attracted by our fire The evening was closed by a dance, and the next day, the chiefs and warriors being assembled at 10 o'clock, we explained the speech we had already sent from the Council Bluffs, and renewed our advice They all replied in turn, and the presents were then distributed We exchanged the small medal we had formerly given to the Big Horse for one of the same size with that of Little Thief, we also gave a small medal to a third chief, and a kind of certificate or letter of acknowledgement to five of the warriors, expressive of our favor and their good intentions One of them, dissatisfied, returned us the certificate; but the chief, fearful of our being offended, begged that it might be restored to him; this we declined, and rebuked them severely for having in view mere traffic instead of peace with our neighbors. This displeased them at first, but they at length all petitioned that it should be given to the warrior, who then came forward and made an apology to us; we then delivered it to the chief to be given to the most worthy, and he bestowed it upon the same warrior, whose name was Great Blue Eyes. After a more substantial present of small articles and tobacco, the council was ended with a dram to the Indians. In the evening we exhibited different objects of curiosity, and particularly the air-gun, which gave them great surprise. Those people are almost naked, having no covering except a sort of breech-cloth round the middle, with a loose blanket.

"The next morning, August 20th, the Indians mounted their horses and left us, having received a canister of whisky at parting. We then set sail, and, after passing two islands on the north, came to, on that side, under some bluffs—the first near the river since we left the Ayauway village. Here we had the misfortune to lose one of our sergeants, Charles Floyd. He was yesterday seized with a bilious colic, and all our care and attention were ineffectual to relieve him. A little before his death he said to Captain Clarke: 'I am going to leave you.' His strength failed him as he added: 'I want you to write me a letter;' but he died with a composure which justified the high opinion we had formed of his firmness and good conduct. He was buried on the top of the bluff with the honors due to a brave soldier, and the place of his interment marked by a cedar post, on which name and the day of his death were inscribed. About a mile beyond this place, to which we gave his name, is a small river about thirty yards wide, on the north, which we called Floyd's River, where we encamped. We had a breeze from the southeast and made thirteen miles."

Patrick Gass, one of the persons employed in the expedition, as he modestly styles himself, also wrote an account, in journal form, of the voyage, which was published in 1809, before the report of Messrs. Lewis and Clarke appeared. It was received with considerable interest because the reading public had long looked with impatience for the official report, and was chafing at the delay of over three years, which had been allowed to lapse without any publication. The *Monthly Anthology and Boston Review* for June, 1809, says of it: "In the meantime this journal, written without lofty pretensions, will afford some amusement to those who are fond of perusing the relations of travelers in new and difficult situations." The *Quarterly Review* for the month of May, of the same year, remarks: "We ought not, however, to complain of Mr. Gass, whose journal of each day, taken on the spot, does him credit in his subordinate situation; and to whom alone, of all that were engaged in the expedition the public, as far as we can hear, are under any obligations."

This journal, evidently the work of an uncultivated man, is still not without interest, and is undoubtedly a correct diary of the expedition as it appeared to the writer. It consists, however, of little else than a dry log of the voyage, and the interest taken in it at the time of its appearance must be ascribed rather to the inherent importance of the subject than to any charm of style. So far as it relates to the region about Omaha it is no less brief and uninteresting than the remainder of the work.

On the 20th of July, 1804, he says that the voyagers embarked early, passing high yellow banks on the south side and a creek called the Water-which-cries, or the Weeping-stream, opposite a willow island, and encamped on a prairie on the south side Of the next day he says "At nine the wind fell and at one we came to the great river Platte, or shallow river, which comes in on the south side, and at the mouth is three-quarters of a mile broad The land is flat about the confluence. Up this river live three nations of Indians, the Otos, Panis, and Loos or Wolf Indians On the south side there is also a creek called Butterfly Creek"

It will be noticed that in the reports of all the early explorers of the Missouri, the west side of the stream from what is now Kansas City to the present site of Sioux City, in Iowa, is invariably spoken of as the south side This arises, doubtless, from the fact that upon entering the river at its confluence with the Mississippi the travelers found its course an easterly one, so that the right bank of the stream was the south bank This description, therefore, they continued to give it even after the course of the Missouri had changed to north and south

On Sunday, the 22d of July, they left the river Platte and proceeded early on their voyage, with fair weather, finding high prairie land on the south side, with some timber on the northern parts of the hills Nine miles from the mouth of the Platte River they landed on a willow bank, at what was probably the present site of Bellevue Here their hunters killed five deer and caught two beaver, and messengers were sent up the Platte to inform the Indians along its banks of the change in the government of the country, and of Lewis and Clarke's desire to treat with them After the lapse of five days, however, during which the main body remained at Bellevue busily engaged in hunting, making oars, dressing skins and airing stores, provisions and baggage, the messengers returned from the Indian village unsuccessful in their object, as they found it silent and deserted They set sail, therefore, at about noon on the last mentioned day, and after proceeding about twelve miles they encamped on a handsome prairie on the south side The changes in the course of the Missouri, which has ever since been swaying from bluff to bluff on both sides of the valley, render it impossible to ascertain the precise location of this handsome prairie It could not, however, have been far from where the packing houses of South Omaha are now situated 'On the next day, says the narrator, "we set out early, had a cloudy morning, passed some beautiful hills and prairies, and a creek called Round Knob Creek, on the north side, and high bluffs on the south Here two of our hunters came to us, accompanied by one of the Oto Indians"

There can be no doubt that among the 'beautiful hills and prairies" which Gass mentions was the graceful elevation from which, at a later period the territorial capitol and now the Omaha High School have looked down upon the thriving city, which was then only a convenient hunting ground None of the voyagers, however, except the hunters and those who conducted the lead horses along the banks of the river, seem to have set foot on its soil Two days later, while bewailing the loss of a gray horse which had died the previous night, they came to some timber land at the foot of a high bluff and encamped there to wait for the Indians This was the present site of Fort Calhoun The large, handsome prairie of which Gass speaks, is that on which Fort Atkinson was subsequently erected and which the charming village of Fort Calhoun now occupies 'This place," says Gass, "we named Council Bluffs, and by observation we found it to be in latitude 41 deg 47 min north" This latitude differs slightly from that given in the official report of the expedition, which was, as we have seen, 41 deg 18 min 1¼ sec That the spot is the same, however, as that mentioned by Lewis and Clarke there can be no possible doubt Gass even speaks of the singular little animal which excited so much curiosity in the camp: "Two of our hunters," he says, "went out and killed an animal called a prarow, about the size of a ground hog and nearly of the same color. It has a head similar to that of a dog, short legs and large claws on its fore feet; some of the claws are an inch and a half long."

Some two or three years after the visit of Lewis and Clarke, Manuel Lisa, an enterprising French trader, ascended the Missouri for furs and peltries almost to its source. The success of his venture led to the formation of an association under the name of the Missouri Fur Company, a corporation having its headquarters at St. Louis, and formed in the hope of carrying on the fur trade more extensively than it had theretofore been practiced, and in time of rivaling even the British associations in Canada. The company was composed of twelve persons, with a capital of about forty thousand dollars; and they engaged about two hundred and fifty men, Canadians and Americans; the first for the purpose of navigating the boats, for the Canadians were renowned boatmen, and the latter as hunters; it being their intention to hunt as well as trade. In the spring of 1808 they ascended the Missouri in barges, and left trading establishments in the Sioux country, and also among the Arickaras and Mandans. Owing to the jealousies and hostilities of the Blackfeet Indians, however, the expedition of 1808 proved abortive. Instead of three hundred packs of skins, upon which they might have calculated had they remained unmolested, they hardly procured thirty the first year, and the second none at all. The party was reduced to about sixty persons, by the detachments left at the different trading stations, by persons sent off with such furs as had been collected, and by skirmishes with the Indians, in which some twenty had fallen. Mr. Henry, who was in command, thought it best, in this state of affairs, to cross the Rocky Mountains and establish himself on the Columbia River, a movement which took him so much further from his base that he was not heard of at St. Louis for more than a year.

In this state of things it was resolved in the spring of 1811, by the company, to make one more effort, and, if possible, retrieve their losses. Humanity also demanded that, if possible, their distressed companions should be relieved and brought back to civilization. Manuel Lisa, already spoken of, a man of bold and daring character, energetic, enterprising, well acquainted with the Indian character and trade, of indefatigable industry, and with a powerful and vigorous frame, was selected to lead the enterprise. Mr. H. M. Brackenridge, a Maryland barrister, in a spirit of curiosity and fondness for adventure, decided to accompany the expedition, and to him we are indebted for another glimpse of the site of Omaha in its original, wild state. Mr. Lisa, with his party, including Mr. Brackenridge, set off from the village of St. Charles on Tuesday, the 2d of April, 1811, and ascending the Missouri with the usual monotonous adventures and provoking delays, passed the mouth of the Platte on the 10th of May. This river, he remarks, was at that time regarded by the jolly and rough boatmen of that day, as a point of as much importance as the equator among the navigators of the sea. All who had never passed its mouth before were required, amidst a good deal of jocose horse-play, to undergo the ceremony of being shaved with a rusty piece of hoop for a razor, and a bucket of slush for lather; unless they chose to compound for this unpleasant discipline by a treat for the men. Mr. Brackenridge declares that much merriment was indulged on the occasion, but leaves us in doubt whether he submitted to the operation or purchased immunity.

Above the Platte at that time, the river was called the Upper Missouri, and the change from the closely wooded country below the Platte to the open bare plains was then perceptible and great The habit of burning the prairies was not then so common south of the river as on the other side The face of the land however, he remarks, was so varied as to be pleasing and picturesque On Sunday the 12th of May, after passing the old Otoe village which was then not far from the southern boundary of Omaha, Mr Brackenridge went on shore, as he tells us, and wandered several miles through shrubby hills, seeing several elk and deer, without being able to approach them Towards evening he entered a charming prairie, and noted its rich black soil He speaks, too, of following a rivulet until it formed a lake in the river bottom, its banks for six or eight feet deep a rich black earth There can be no possible doubt that this afternoon's walk was, over a portion at least, of the ground which now forms Omaha and it was perhaps the first walk for recreation ever taken upon its site by a white man About this point the journalist concludes that the party has reached the highest point to which settlements will probably extend for many years In the evening of the 13th they passed the high, clean meadows called the Council Bluffs, of which he says " It is a beautiful scene The Council Bluffs are not abrupt elevations, but a rising ground, covered with grass as perfectly smooth as it the work of art They do not exceed in height thirty or forty feet above the plain below On ascending, the land stretches out as far as the eye can reach, a perfect level The short grass, with which the soil is covered, gives it the appearance of a sodded bank, which has a fine effect, the scene being shaded by a few slender trees or shrubs in the hollows " It would not be easy at this day to give a more vivid and correct picture of the natural beauties of this charming spot

Twenty-three days before the expedition of Lisa had started on their voyage, another party, employed by the American Fur Company and under the command of Wilson P Hunt, (gentleman then and long afterwards renowned in the history of the northwestern fur trade, had set sail from St Charles, and Lisa had been straining every nerve to meet him before he entered the lands of the Sioux nation The meeting finally took place not far from the villages of the Poncas In Mr Hunt's party were two scientific gentlemen enthusiasts on the subject of botany and mineralogy One of these, Mr Bradbury a few days before Mr Brackenridge reached the sight of Omaha, made an excursion with some Indians and hunters of the Hunt party to the mouth of the Elkhorn River He described this as a deep, navigable stream, containing nearly as much water as the Thames at London Bridge, soon swallowed up, however, in the shoals and quicksands of the Platte, into which it discharges Mr Bradbury reported that he had passed for one hundred and fifty miles through a delightful champaign country, of rich, open, smooth meadows, and the borders of the streams fringed with wood, that within eight or ten miles of the Missouri, the country is more broken and hilly, and with a still smaller proportion of wood Of course, from the above meagre account of this short trip it will be seen that it is by no means evident that Mr Bradbury passed over the ground where Omaha now stands, but it is probable that he either did so or came very near it It may not be uninteresting to state as a sequel to Mr. Brackenridge's story, that having ascended the Missouri as far as the Mandan and Arickara villages, and having fully satisfied his curiosity concerning the Indians, whose filthy habits were offensive to his civilized senses, he took charge of two of Mr Lisa's boats laden with peltries, descended the Missouri at the rate of about one hundred miles per day, passed the Blackbird hill, the site of Omaha and the mouth of the Platte on the same day, and after an absence of nearly five months, arrived at St Louis early in August, 1811, having made by their reckoning fourteen hundred and forty miles in a little more than fourteen days. He summed up the advantages of the region he had been exploring as follows: "This immense tract of country has now become the theatre of American enterprise. There prevails among the natives west of the mountains a spirit of wild adventure, which reminds us of the fictitious characters of Ariosto. The American hunters constitute a class different from any people known to the east of the mountains. The life which they lead is exceedingly fascinating; their scene ever changing—ever presenting something new. Confined by no regular pursuit, their labor is amusement. I have called the region watered by the Missouri and its tributaries *the paradise of hunters;* it is indeed to them a paradise. I have been acquainted with several who, on returning to the settlements, became in a very short time dissatisfied, and wandered away to these regions as delightful to them as are the regions of fancy to the poet.

"'Theirs the wild life, in frolic still to range,
From toil to rest, and joy in every change.'"

# CHAPTER V.

JOURNEY FROM THE COLUMBIA TO THE MOUTH OF THE PLATTE IN 1812—FIRST WHITE FAMILY LOCATING AT BELLEVUE—ESTABLISHMENT OF A BAPTIST MISSION IN 1833, AND PRESBYTERIAN MISSION IN 1834—GENERAL FREMONT AT BELLEVUE

A notable journey from the Columbia River to the mouth of the Platte was made during the years 1812 and 1813. On the 28th of June, in the first named year, Messrs Robert Stewart, Ramsey Crooks and Robert McClellan left the Pacific Coast with dispatches for their employers in New York After almost incredible adventures and hardships, in the course of which the Crow Indians stole every horse belonging to the party, leaving them on foot, two thousand miles from St Louis, in a desert which for fifteen hundred miles was utterly unknown to them, they at last succeeded in reaching St Louis on the 30th of May, 1813, having consumed more than eleven months in the journey They wintered on the Platte, six hundred miles from its mouth, and in the spring they followed its course undeviatingly to the Otoe villages near its mouth

Six years after this journey, another exploring expedition, pursuant to the orders of John C Calhoun was undertaken by Major Stephen H Long This expedition is famous, not only for the topographical results obtained, but as having been conveyed on the first steamboat which ever passed the spot now occupied by the City of Omaha This steamer, to which had been given the name of the Western Engineer, passed the plateau on which that city stands on the 15th or 16th of September, 1819 Major Long, the commander of this expedition, was a brave, enterprising and industrious officer, born in the town of Hopkinton,

in the State of New Hampshire, in the year 1784 Five years after his graduation from Dartmouth College, in that State, he was commissioned a lieutenant in the corps of engineers of the United States army, and in April, 1816, he was transferred to the topographical engineers with the rank of major During eight years thereafter he was assiduously and almost constantly engaged in a series of explorations of the western frontier, from the northern boundary of Texas to Lake Superior and the sources of the Mississippi, and traversed within that period more than twenty-six thousand miles of wilderness, procuring much information, till then unknown, concerning those portions of the national domain The account of the expedition now under consideration was published in 1823 For a long time afterwards he was engaged in explorations and improvements of western rivers, in superintending the construction of hospitals and steam vessels, in surveys of harbors and roads, and in other labors connected with the engineering department of the United States army His name is perpetuated by one of the loftiest peaks in Colorado

By this time the muddy current of the Missouri was so frequently vexed with the keels of the fur traders, going to and returning from their hunting and trading grounds, that the trip up that river had ceased to be a novelty, A trading post and fort was established at Bellevue, long the abode of Peter A. Sarpy His trading post at Bellevue was originally established by the American Fur Company, in 1810. Francis DeRoin was the person first appointed to the post of Indian trader. He was succeeded by Joseph Robidoux (who afterwards founded the city of St. Joseph, Mo.), who held the position for six years, when he was superseded by John Cabanne, who in turn gave place in the year 1824 to Colonel Sarpy. The last gave soul, vivacity and notoriety to that picturesque and beautiful spot for more than thirty years.

Up to the year 1823 the Indian agency was established at Council Bluffs, now known as Fort Calhoun, but in the last mentioned year that agency was removed to Bellevue, which then for a time assumed the name of Council Bluffs, the Iowa town now called by that appellation, being entitled Mormon Hollow and Kanesville. The agency at that date included within its limits the Omaha, Otoe, Pawnee and Pottawotamie tribes of Indians. In 1833 the first protestant missionary ventured to settle within the limits of this, then, wild and dangerous region. This honor belongs to the Baptists. One of their number, the Rev. Moses Merrill, in the year last named, created a mission house among the Otoes, at a point on the present farm of Mr. John F. Payne, where a stone chimney long remained, and perhaps still is visible, to mark the spot where a faithful apostle of God was willing to sacrifice his life upon the altar of duty. He did not long endure the hardships, privations and sufferings of life in a new country, among barbarous tribes. He died in 1835 and was, at the request of his widow, buried on the left bank of the Missouri, at a point which has long since yielded to the irreverent surges of the river, all traces of his grave having been swept away. His son, Rev. S. P. Merrill, born at Bellevue in July, 1834, is now a resident of Rochester, N. Y.

Just before his death, in the fall of 1834, Samuel Allis and Rev. John Dunbar, under the direction of the Presbyterian Board of Missions, arrived at the agency at Bellevue, in company with Major John Dougherty, Indian agent to the Otoes, Omahas and Pawnees. Major Dougherty paid to the Indians their annuities at this point, and Messrs. Allis and Dunbar opened a school among the Pawnees at a place known as Council Point, some distance up the Platte River. The hostility of the Sioux, however, caused the abandonment of this pious enterprise, and Mr. Allis returned to Bellevue, where he taught the children of the Pawnees at the agency.

In 1835 the American Board of Commissioners for Foreign Missions appointed an exploring mission, to ascertain by personal observation the condition of the country west of the Mississippi, the character of the Indian nations and tribes, and the facilities for introducing the gospel and civilization among them. The Rev. Samuel Parker undertook this difficult task, and starting from New York on the 14th of March, 1835, was joined at St. Louis by Dr. Marcus Whitman, who had been appointed by the Board as Mr. Parker's associate. They went by land, passing along the left bank of the Missouri, drew near to Council Bluffs, that is, Bellevue, on the 30th of April, and were amazed at the immense number of mounds which they were inclined to believe were not artificial.

An interesting account of this trip, which extended through Oregon, the Columbia River and the Pacific to the Sandwich Islands, was written and published by Mr. Parker in the year 1838. A few sentences follow: " We crossed the Maragine River, which, though very deep, was not so wide but that we constructed a bridge over it. Proceeding many miles through the rich bottom lands of the Missouri, we crossed this noble river over against Bellevue in a large canoe, and swam our horses and mules across; this, on account of the width of the river and the strength of the current, required much effort. I went to the agency

## ESTABLISHMENT OF MISSIONS

house, where I was happy to find Brethren Dunbar and Ellis, missionaries to the Pawnees, under the direction of the American Board of Commissioners for Foreign Missions There is a Baptist Mission here, composed of Rev Moses Merrill and wife, Miss Brown, and a Christian Indian woman, a descendant of Rev D Brainard's Indians They are appointed by the Baptist Board to labor among the Otoe Indians, about twenty-five miles from this place, on the River Platte These Indians are away from their intended residence about half the time on hunting excursions A little more than a half mile below the agency the American Fur Company have a fort, and in connection they have a farming establishment and large numbers of cattle and horses, and a horse-power mill for grinding corn

" We continued in this place three weeks, waiting the movements of the caravan, who made slow progress in preparing their packages for the mountains During our detention here I frequently walked over the hills bordering upon the west of the valley of of the Missouri, to enjoy the pure air of the rolling prairies and to view the magnificent prospects unfolded in the vale below From the summit of those prominences the valley of the Missouri may be traced until lost in its far winding course among the bluffs Three miles below is seen the Papillion, a considerable stream from the northwest, winding its way round to the east, and uniting with the Missouri, six miles above the confluence of the Platte, coming from the west These flow through a rich alluvial plain, opening to the south and southwest as far as the eye can reach Upon these meadows are seen feeding some few hundred of horses and mules, and a herd of cattle, and some fields of corn diversified the scenery The north is covered with woods, which are not less valuable than the rich vales. But few places can present a prospect more inviting, and when a civilized population shall add the fruits of their industry, but few can be more desirable ''

Mr Parker's stay in Bellevue was much longer than he had anticipated, from the fact that two weeks after their arrival a disease, which Dr Whitman called spasmodic cholera, broke out with a great degree of malignity. This disease was aggravated by the extreme warmth of the weather, by daily showers and by the intemperate habits of the men and their mode of living Three of the company died, and it was only through the assiduousness of Dr Whitman, and the use of powerful medicines and heroic treatment that the mortality was not much greater.

After the long delay caused by this epidemic the travelers with the trading party to which they were attached, recommenced their journey to the Pacific Coast on the 21st day of June, 1835 Mr Parker noted in his diary that their route was over a rich and extensive prairie, but so poorly watered that not a single stream was encountered during the whole day, and that they encamped before night on a high prairie where they could find but little wood and it was difficult to make a fire If these statements are literally true, and there would be, certainly, no possible motive for misrepresentation, the course of these travelers, who were bound for the Black Hills as their first objective point, would have been northwestwardly from Bellevue, a direction which would have taken them very near to, if not within the present boundary lines of the City of Omaha In no other direction could they have traveled more than an hour or two, without finding both wood and water in abundant profusion The fact also, that towards noon of the 24th, having been detained some forty-eight hours by a heavy, cold rain, with thunder, lightning and hail, they crossed the Papillion, would seem to point to the same conclusion

All the tourists who traveled over the

country about Omaha before its settlement, have noticed with a pleased surprise the salubrity of its climate and the fertility of its soil. Mr. Parker was similarly impressed with these characteristics. "No country," says he, "could be more inviting to the farmer, with only one exception, the want of woodland. The latitude is sufficiently high to be healthy; and as the climate grows warmer as we travel west, until we approach the snow-topped mountains, there is a degree of mildness not experienced east of the Allegheny Mountains. The time will come, and probably is not far distant, when this country will be covered with a dense population. The earth was created for the habitation of man, and for a theater on which God will manifest his moral government among his moral creatures, and therefore the earth, according to divine prediction, shall be given to the people of God. Although infidels may sneer and scoffers mock, yet God will accomplish his designs and fulfill every promise contained in his Word. Then this amazing extent of most fertile land will not continue to be the wandering ground of a few thousand Indians, with only a very few acres under cultivation; nor will millions of tons of grass grow up to rot upon the ground or to be burned up with the fire enkindled to sweep over the prairie, to disencumber it of its spontaneous burden. The herds of buffalo which once fattened upon these meadows are gone; and the deer which once cropped the grass have disappeared; and the antelope have fled away; and shall solitude reign here to the end of time? No, here shall be heard the din of business, and the church going bell shall sound far and wide. The question is, by whom shall this region of country be inhabited. It is plain that the Indians, under their present circumstances, will never multiply and fill this land. They must be brought under the influence of civilization and Christianity, or they will continue to melt away, until nothing will remain of them but the relics found in museums, and some historical records. Philanthropy and the mercy of God plead in their behalf."

It is curious to notice in the references of all western travelers of that day, how invariably, as they approach the region of Omaha, they devote a few sentences or pages to the natural beauties of the situation, the fertility of its soil, the charms of its climate, and the certainty of its being in some far distant future the home of a vast population. Generally, they express themselves as confidently, if not as beautifully as our own poet Bryant, who heard the murmurings of the bee upon the prairies:

"I listen long
To his domestic hum, and think I hear
The sound of that advancing multitude
Which soon shall fill these deserts. From the ground
Comes up the laugh of children, the soft voice
Of maidens, and the sweet and solemn hymn
Of Sabbath worshippers. The low of herds
Blends with the rustling of the heavy grain
Over the dark brown furrows. All at once
A fresher wind sweeps by, and breaks my dream,
And I am in the wilderness alone."

By 1837, the date of the publication of Mr. Parker's journal, the visitors to the territory now called Nebraska, and the voyages up the Missouri, had become so numerous and frequent that their tales of the border had ceased to excite especial interest.

The Rocky Mountain Fur Company and the Missouri Fur Company had for many years been familiar, through their boatmen and hunters and trappers, with the entire country west of the Missouri, and it is doubtless to these men, that we owe a number of French names still largely scattered over the State, despite the efforts of prosaic materialists to change and obliterate these euphonious appellations. The names of William H. Ashley, Dr. Pilcher, William O'Fallon and others were for years famous in this vicinity as distinguished travelers and traders.

Colonel Henry Dodge, an enterprising officer in the service of the United States, explored the Platte River to its source in 1835, and doubtless came near the town site of Omaha, but probably did not actually set foot upon the ground. General, then Lieutenant Fremont, in one of his expeditions, visited Bellevue, and made the acquaintance of Peter A. Sarpy, then the head of the trading house at that place, and speaks with enthusiasm of the beauty and scenery, and the hospitality of that distinguished frontiersman. At this point, the oldest settlement of white civilians in Nebraska, a trading post had been established as long ago as 1805. At its head was Manuel Lisa, a Spanish gentleman of considerable wealth, unbounded energy, and more taste than usually falls to the lot of the fur trader. Touched with the beauty of the surrounding landscape, and especially with the view from the commanding eminence on which now stands the buildings of the institution known as Bellevue College, he, as it is said, gave the place the name by which it has ever since that day been known. Lisa was a man of a bold and daring character, with a spirit of enterprise and audacity which caused him to be likened by his admirers to his countrymen, Cortez and Pizarro. We have already had some account of him in the description by Mr. Brackenridge of his travels. No one was better acquainted than he with the peculiarities of the Indian character, no one better fitted to secure their trade and overcome their prejudices. He had quick apprehension, a frame capable of sustaining every hardship, indomitable perseverance, and indefatigable industry. In addition to these qualities he displayed a kindness and hospitality which made him many friends, though for some reason, not now known, many of the members of the Missouri Fur Company lacked that confidence in him which his merits would seem to demand. It is doubtful how long Lisa remained in Bellevue. Certain it is that in 1811, six years after the establishment of his post, we find him in command of an expedition up the Missouri River from St. Louis, undertaken by the Missouri Fur Company for the purpose of retrieving the losses which that unfortunate association had, from one cause or another sustained. The fact, also, that in 1810 the American Fur Company established a trading post at Bellevue would seem to indicate that the former trading depot had been abandoned.

Up to this period there had been no actual settlement on the present site of the City of Omaha. But in 1825 the year after Colonel Sarpy had succeeded Cabanne in the management of the trading post at Bellevue, there was erected a stockade and trading post at a point on or near the present block formed by Dodge Street, Capitol Avenue, Ninth and Tenth Streets. Up to within a few years past the remains of this defensive work were plainly visible. It was the post of one J. B. Royce, or Roye (for even his name has vanished into oblivion), who for some three years maintained his trade with the Indians at this spot, when for some unknown cause he left. Hardly anything more than this bare fact is known of him. Father De Smet, who calls him T. B. Roye speaks of him as a noted trader in his day, and says that he was probably 'the first white man who built the first cabin on the beautiful plateau where now stands the flourishing City of Omaha.''

From this time until 1854, the site of the city was uninhabited and unvisited save by wandering Indians, emigrants to the far West, Mormons fleeing from persecution, and occasionally, curious and covetous claim-seekers from the State of Iowa.

# CHAPTER VI.

OUR INDIAN PREDECESSORS — CATLIN'S VISIT TO THE MISSOURI VALLEY—THE FAMOUS OMAHA CHIEF, BLACKBIRD—AN INDIAN TRAGEDY—BURIAL OF BLACKBIRD.

At the time of the first formal exploration of the region about Omaha, the principal tribes or nations of Indians inhabiting the territory, now Nebraska, in the region near Omaha, were four, namely, the Otoes, the Omahas, the Poncas and the Pawnees. The first three of these belonged to the great Dakota family, which embraces also the Sioux, the Osages, the Iowas, the Kansas, the Missouris, the Minatarees and Crows. This family once occupied the larger portion of the country bounded on the east by the great lakes, on the north by the British Possessions, on the west by the Rocky Mountains and on the south by the Platte River. According to their traditions they came eastward from the Pacific Ocean, meeting with little difficulty in their immigration, until they reached the vicinity of the headwaters of the Mississippi, where the Algonkins succeeded in checking the movement eastward of the main body. One of the tribes, however, the Winnebagos, or men from the fetid water, that is, the sea, succeeded in pushing through the barrier, and reached the shores of Lake Michigan.

Of the early history of the Pawnees but little is definitely known, although they were among the earliest tribes west of the Mississippi. It has heretofore been suggested that they may have been some offshoot of the Aztec nation, which separated from the main body as it passed to the southward. Be that as it may, they are noted on the map of Father Marquette, in 1773, as divided into various bands. They are undoubtedly the Panimahas of later explorers. In 1803 their principal villages were on the south side of the Platte. Three years later, Pike estimated the population of three of their villages at 6233, with nearly two thousand warriors, engaged in fierce combat with neighboring tribes. In the year 1820, three of the four bands into which they had been for a long time divided, resided on the banks of the Platte and its tributaries, with a reservation on Loup Fork, now Nance County. At that time their numbers were supposed to be about ten thousand souls, living in earth covered lodges, and much devoted to the cultivation of the soil, but engaging every season in a grand buffalo hunt. The Delawares in 1823 burned the great Pawnee village on the Republican, and these Pawnees, becoming much reduced in numbers by small-pox, soon after sold all their lands south of the Platte and removed to the reservation on Loup Fork. The means were provided and many exertions made to enable them to live here in prosperity; but their inveterate foes, the Sioux, harrassed them continually, repeatedly drove them from their reservation and despoiled their villages. This warfare and disease soon reduced them to half their former number. In 1861 they raised a company of scouts for service against the Sioux, and a much larger force under the volunteer organization, incurring in consequence the increased hostility of their enemies, who annoyed them so continually that in 1874, the chiefs in general council, yielded to the suggestions of United States agents, and consented to the removal of the tribe to a new reservation in the Indian Territory, lying between the forks of the Arkansas and the Cimarron, east of the 97th P M All who have sojourned long enough among the Pawnees to become familiar with their oral records, have noticed their tradition of a once great city on what was, from 1859 to 1876, their reservation on the Loup Loath to leave its site, when a Christian civilization drove them southward, they yearn in their new home for its familiar scenes, and a few remnants of the tribe yet linger unmolested, within its loved boundaries Their population at the present time is hardly over one thousand souls, showing a steady decrease from year to year The deaths, it is said, largely outnumber the births, and it seems only a question of time when the tribe will become extinct

The Poncas were a small tribe, said to have been related to the Omahas Their home was, when they were first known, in Dixon County, in the State of Nebraska, on the right bank of the Missouri River They are said to have lived originally on the Red River of the North, but being driven southwestwardly across the Missouri by the Sioux, they have seldom numbered in this State more than one thousand Selling their lands in Dixon County in 1858, they went on a reservation near the Yanktons, in Dakota, but being too near their old foes, and unable to raise any crops, they were, in 1865, removed to the mouth of the Niobrara for a permanent home, which, however, remained permanent only some twelve years, when they were, against their will transported to the Indian Territory, where their numbers are said to be still decreasing

Mr Catlin visited the tribe at their home on the Missouri, in 1832 "They are," he says, "contained in seventy-five or eighty lodges, made of buffalo skins, in the form of tents, the frames for which are poles of fifteen or twenty feet in length, with the but ends standing on the ground and the small ends meeting at the top, forming a cone which sheds off the rain and wind with perfect success. This small remnant of a tribe are not more than four or five hundred in number, and I should think at least two-thirds of these are women, this disparity in numbers having been produced by the continual losses which their men suffer who are penetrating the buffalo country for meat, for which they are now obliged to travel a great way (as the buffalo have recently left their country), exposing their lives to the more numerous enemies about them "

Of Shoo-de-ga-chas, or the Smoke Chief of the tribe in 1832, a very philosophical and dignified man, the artist says "The chief, who was wrapped in a buffalo robe, is a noble specimen of native dignity and philosophy I conversed much with him, and from his dignified manners, as well as the soundness of his reasoning, I became fully convinced that he deserved to be sachem of a more numerous and prosperous tribe He related with great coolness and frankness the poverty and distress of his nation, and, with the method of a philosopher, predicted the certain and rapid extinction of his tribe, which he had not the power to avert. Poor, noble chief, who was equal to and worthy a greater empire! He sat upon the deck of the steamer overlooking the little cluster of his wigwams mingled amongst the trees, and like Caius Marius weeping over the ruins of Carthage, shed tears as he was descanting on the poverty of his ill-fated little community, which he told me had once been powerful and happy, that the buffalo which the Great Spirit had given them for food, and which formerly spread all over their green prairies, had all been killed or driven out by the approach of white men who wanted their skins, that their country was now entirely destitute of game, and even of roots for their food, as it was one continued prairie, and that his young men, penetrating the countries of their enemies for buffalo, which they were obliged to do, were cut to pieces and destroyed in great numbers. That his people had foolishly become fond of *fire-water* (whiskey), and had given away everything in their country for it; that it had destroyed many of his warriors, and soon would destroy the rest; that his tribe was too small and his warriors too few to go to war with the tribes around them; that they were met and killed by the Sioux on the north, by the Pawnees on the west, and by the Osages and Kansas on the south; and still more alarmed from the constant advance of the pale faces—their enemies from the east, with whisky and small-pox, which already had destroyed four-fifths of his tribe, and soon would impoverish, and at last destroy the remainder of them."

A touching story is told by the same author of a superannuated chief left by his people to die on the prairie: "When we were about to start," he says, "on our way up the river from the village of the Poncas, we found that they were packing up all their goods and preparing to start for the prairies, further to the west, in pursuit of buffalo, to dry meat for their winter's supplies. They took down their wigwams of skins to carry with them, and all were flat to the ground and everything packing up ready for the start. My attention was directed by Major Sanford, the Indian agent, to one of the most miserable and helpless-looking objects I had ever seen in my life—a very aged and emaciated man of the tribe, who, he told me, was to be exposed.

"The tribe were going where hunger and dire necessity compelled them to go; and this pitiable object, who had once been a chief and a man of distinction in his tribe, who was now too old to travel—being reduced to mere skin and bones—was to be left to starve, or meet with such death as might fall to his lot, and his bones to be picked by the wolves. I lingered around this poor, old, forsaken patriarch for hours before we started, to indulge the tears of sympathy which were flowing for the sake of this poor, benighted and decrepit old man, whose worn-out limbs were no longer able to support him, their kind and faithful offices having long since been performed, and his body and his mind doomed to linger into the withering agony of decay and gradual solitary death. I wept, and it was a pleasure to weep, for the painful looks and the weary prospects of this old veteran, whose eyes were dimmed, whose venerable locks were whitened by a hundred years, whose limbs were almost naked and trembling as he sat beside a small fire which his friends had left him, with a few sticks of wood within his reach and a buffalo skin stretched upon some crotches over his head. Such was to be his only dwelling, and such the chances for his life, with only a few half-picked bones that were laid within his reach, and a dish of water, without weapon or means of any kind to replenish them, or strength to move his body from its fatal locality. In this sad plight I mournfully contemplated this miserable remnant of existence, who had unluckily outlived the fates and accidents of wars to die alone at death's leisure. His friends and his children had all left him, and were preparing in a little time to be on the march. He had told them to leave him; he was old, he said, and too feeble to march. 'My children,' said he, 'our nation is poor, and it is necessary that you should all go to the country where you can get meat; my eyes are dimmed and my strength is no more, my days are nearly all numbered, and I am a burden to my children; I cannot go, and I wish to die. Keep your heart stout and think not of me; I am no longer good for anything.' In this way they had finished the ceremony of exposing him, and taking their final leave of him. I advanced to the old man and was undoubtedly the last human being who held converse with him. I sat by the side of him, and though he could not distinctly see me, he shook me heartily by the hand and smiled, evidently aware that I was a white man, and that I sympathized with him in his inevitable misfortune I shook hands again with him and left him, steering my course towards the steamer, which was a mile or more from me, and ready to resume her voyage up the Missouri

" When passing by the site of the Ponca village a few months after this, on my return voyage in the fall of 1832, in my canoe, I went ashore with my men and found the poles and the buffalo skin, standing as they were left over the old man's head The fire-brands were lying nearly as I left them, and I found at a few yards distance the skull and others of his bones, which had been picked and cleaned by the wolves, which is probably all that any human being can ever know of his final and melancholy fate

" This cruel custom of exposing their aged people belongs, I think, to all the tribes who roam about the prairies, making severe marches, when such decrepit persons as are totally unable to go, unable to ride or to walk, when they have no means of carrying them It often becomes absolutely necessary in such cases that they should be left, and they uniformly insist upon it, saying, as this old man did, that they are old and of no further use, that they left their fathers in the same manner, that they wished to die, and that their children must not mourn for them"

The Commissioner of Indian Affairs, in his report for the year 1878, declares that the Poncas are good Indians, and in mental endowment, moral character, physical strength and cleanliness superior to any he had ever met

The Otoes and Missouris have long been confederated and are supposed by some to have been originally the same tribe The latter are a tribe of the Dakota family and first became known to the whites about the year 1673 They called themselves Nudarchas, the name Missouris, or people living by the muddy water, having been given them by the Illinois In 1804 they numbered only about three hundred persons, having been reduced from their former considerable numbers by the small-pox, which so reduced them that they again affiliated with the Otoes and have for a long time been treated and considered as the same tribe The Otoes were known to the French by the name of Otontantes, and at the time of the expedition of Lewis and Clarke, their possessions extended to the present City of Omaha on the north, though their villages were principally on the south side of the Platte River, where they lived in mud lodges At the time of the first settlement of Omaha they occupied a reservation south of the Platte, though their visits to their old hunting grounds about the city were not infrequent In the year 1882 the poor remains of these two ill-fated tribes, reduced by wars, hardships, small-pox and civilizing influences to four hundred and fifty-seven souls, were removed to the Indian Territory, where easy, good natured, lazy and shiftless, they depend on the government for their livelihood, doing just work enough to entitle them to a distribution of rations, and finding it exceedingly difficult to abandon their nomadic habits

There remains to be mentioned, of the four principal tribes inhabiting the eastern portion of Nebraska at the time of the advent of the whites, the nation of the Omahas, or as they were until a comparatively recent period, called the Mahas The signification of the name is said to be "the up-river people" Its proper pronunciation is O-maw-haw, with the accent on the second syllable, the prevailing tendency of the English speaking people to throw back the accent beyond the penult having at present, however, so far established its present pronunciation, with the stress on the first syllable, as to render any change impossible In fact the Indian accents were never strongly marked, and the native sound of the word can best be represented as given above, with no accent whatever on either of its three syllables.

The Mahas were one of the tribes mentioned by Father Marquette in his account of his voyage down the Mississippi, and their location was given on his map with considerable accuracy. Nearly one hundred years later they are said to have been visited by Jonathan Carver during his journey to the west. At that time they seem to have been roaming as far east as St. Peter's River.

His own account states that he arrived among the Nandowessie Indians on the 7th of December, 1766, and resided with them seven months. These Nandowessies are supposed to have been the Sioux or Dakota Indians. These Sioux are always reluctant to acknowledge this name, which was first given them by the French, and is now in general use. There are many theories as to its origin, perhaps the most acceptable of which is that it is a corruption of the word Nadonessioux, a general Chippewa designation for enemies; which was gradually applied by missionaries and traders through an imperfect comprehension of the language to the tribes thus designated. Carver declares that the band with which he resided constituted a part of the eight bands of the Nandowessies of the plains; "and are termed the Wawpuntowahs, the Tintons, the Afrahcootans, the Mawhaws, and the Schians. The other three bands whose names are the Schianese, the Chongonseeton, and the Waddapawjestin, dwell higher up to the west of the River St. Pierre, on plains that, according to their account, are unbounded; and probably terminate on the coast of the Pacific Ocean." His description of his first encounter with these Indians is as follows:

"As soon as I had reached the land two of the chiefs presented their hands to me, and led me amongst the astonished multitude, who had, most of them, never seen a white man before, to a tent. Into this we entered, and according to the custom that universally prevails among every Indian nation, began to smoke the pipe of peace. We had not sat long before the crowd became so great, both around and upon the tent, that we were in danger of being crushed by its fall. On this we returned to the plain, where, having gratified the curiosity of the common people, their wonder abated, and ever after they treated me with great respect.

"From the chiefs I met with the most friendly and hospitable reception; which induced me, as the season was so far advanced, to take up my residence among them during the winter. To render my stay as comfortable as possible, I first endeavored to learn their language. This I soon did, so as to make myself perfectly intelligible, having before acquired some slight knowledge of the language of those Indians that live on the back of the settlements; and in consequence, met with every accommodation their manner of living would afford. Nor did I want for such amusements as tended to make so long a period pass cheerfully away. I frequently hunted with them; and at other times beheld, with pleasure, their recreations and pastimes, which I shall describe hereafter.

"Sometimes I sat with the chiefs, and whilst we smoked the friendly pipe, entertained them, in return for the accounts they gave me of their wars and excursions, with a narrative of my own adventures, and a description of all the battles fought between the English and French in America, in many of which I had a personal share. They always paid great attention to my details, and asked many pertinent questions relative to the European methods of making war.

"I held these conversations with them in a great measure, to procure from them some information relative to the chief point I had constantly in view, that of gaining a knowledge of the situation and produce, both of their own country and those that lay to the westward of them. Nor was I disappointed in my designs; for I procured from them much useful intelligence. They likewise drew for me plans of all the countries with which they were acquainted; but as I entertained no great opinion of their geographical knowledge, I placed not much dependence on them, and therefore think it unnecessary to give them to the public. They draw with a piece of burnt coal, taken from the hearth, upon the inside bark of the birch tree; which is as smooth as paper, and answers the same purposes, notwithstanding it is of a yellow cast. Their sketches are made in a rude manner, but they seem to give us as just an idea of a country, although the plan is not so exact as more experienced draughtsmen could do.''

Carver left the habitations of these hospitable Indians at the latter end of April, 1767, not forgetting, after he had learned their language, to give them in it some idea of the glory and power of the great king that reigned over the English and other nations; descended from a very ancient race of sovereigns as old as the earth and waters; whose feet stood on two great islands larger than any they had ever seen, amidst the greatest waters in the world; whose head reached to the sun, and whose arms encircled the whole earth; the number of whose warriors were equal to the trees in the valleys, the stalks of rice in the marshes, or the blades of grass in the great plains; who had hundreds of canoes of his own, of such amazing bigness that all the waters in their country would not suffice for one of them to swim in; each of which have guns of such magnitude that a hundred young braves would, with difficulty, be able to carry one. And these were equally surprising in their operation against the king's great enemies when engaged in battle; the Indian language wanting words to express the terror they carried with them.

To this harangue the Indians, by the mouth of their principal chief responded, that they believed and were well satisfied of the truth of everything told them about the great English nation and its great king, and implored Carver, on his return, to acquaint their powerful father how earnestly the Nandowessies yearned to be counted among his good children.

It is painful to be obliged to record that poor Carver, after all his magniloquent speeches and romatic exaggerations of fact, did not receive from the British Government the consideration to which he thought himself entitled. Soliciting from the king a reimbursement of his expenses, he was not only refused this favor, but was ordered to deliver up all his charts, journals and manuscripts, as the property of the crown, Carver having been a captain of the provincial troops in America. Disappointed in his hopes of fame, abandoned by those whose duty it was to support him, it is said that he died at the early age of forty-eight, in want of the common necessaries of life.

The Omahas are said to be of the same linguistic family as the Poncas, Osages, Kansas, Otoes, Mandans, Winnebagos, and many other tribes. Some of these tribes, notwithstanding the long period which has elapsed since their separation, can still understand each others' speech.

Their period of greatest renown and prosperity was doubtless during the chieftancy of their distinguished chief Wah-shinguh-saba, or the Blackbird, who died in the year 1800, and of whose career such wild and romantic tales are narrated.

In the days of their prosperity, before the small-pox, that dread scourge of the red men, had reduced their numbers and conquered their haughty spirits, the Omahas conceived themselves to be superior to all other tribes or nations of men, and looked upon the birds of the air, the beasts of the field, and even the human race as created especially for their comfort and aggrandizement. Among this people Blackbird, the chief, ruled with a rigor never surpassed in eastern lands. And to this day his name is never mentioned among his people save with veneration. He soon learned the great advantage of being on good terms with the white traders, and was among the first of the dusky potentates along the Missouri to welcome them to a commerce with his tribe, a reasonable but not prohibitory tariff for the support of his royal dignity being always claimed and exacted with unfailing success and regularity.

No autocrat was ever so selfish; no prince ever more liberal with whatever did not belong to him. When the pirogues of the fur traders came in sight of his encampment, on the high bluffs of the right bank of the Missouri, on the spot now occupied by the Omaha reservation, he was always among the first to meet them, and his invariable habit was always to help himself from their store of merchandise, to whatever his royal fancy might indicate as desirable. For such articles he never deigned to give any compensation whatever, nor by those who knew his habits was it ever expected. The stores of blankets, beads, paint, ammunition and whisky were laid aside without a word, and when his appetite was satiated he sent for the rest of his tribe, who brought their peltries, and commenced their barter. The traders then found the advantages of his friendship, for they were allowed to fix their own prices upon both their own goods and those of the Indians, and soon, no doubt, indemnified themselves for any losses they might have sustained through him.

It is needless to say that such liberality in trade endeared him to the French and Spanish traders, and through them to the commanding officers of the province of Louisiana. There is still extant a curious certificate or diploma, given by the Baron Carondelet to this barbaric Chieftain, in the year 1790, which was, until a very recent date, preserved as a precious heirloom by the descendants of Blackbird, and which is now in the custody of the Nebraska Historical Society. The parchment is enriched with rude pen and ink drawings of the arms of Spain, trophies of war, and an Indian and white man shaking hands in token of amity. In records in magniloquent Spanish phrase the proofs of fidelity and friendship which the Blackbird had shown to the Spanish government, and recites the bestowal of a medal upon him as a token of the estimation in which he was held by the Catholic monarch of Spain. The original text of this interesting document is given in a note.[*]

The Blackbird was undoubtedly a warrior of unquestionable bravery and remarkable skill, so that his exploits in battle would alone have enabled him to rank among the first of the Indian sachems. Upon the Pawnees of the Republican River he had inflicted a signal and bitter vengeance for an insult offered by them to one of his Omaha braves. The Otoes, living south of Omaha's present site, had felt the bloody effects of his irresistible fury so often, that it seemed that if the warfare would end at last in the absolute extinction of one nation, if not both. This would probably have been the case, had not the white traders, who could not afford to lose such ready purveyors of bear, beaver, otter, buffalo and other valuable skins, offered themselves as arbitrators, and finally succeeded in patching up a peace between them. In the fierceness of his charges, the celerity of his movements, the irresistible fury of his onsets, the pride with which he exposed himself personally to the weapons of his enemies, he was a very Prince Rupert among the wandering tribes of the prairies. His forays extended even to the Kansas, and that tribe of horsemen had more than one occasion to mourn their devastated villages and their slaughtered braves. By his sudden incursions, his fulfilled prophesies, which seemed to indicate the possession of supernatural powers, by his miraculous escapes,

[*] El Baron de Carondelet Caballero de la Religion de San Juan, Mar. de Campo de les Reales Exercitos Gobernador General Vice-Patrono de las Provincias.

his astonishing personal prowess, and his daring and dazzling exploits, he was the pride and boast of his own tribe, and the terror and detestation of all surrounding ones

Irving gives an incident in the career of this barbaric warrior, which exhibits him in a different light, and gives a color of romance also to the more sombre tints of his military career He says that with all his savage and terrific qualities, he was not unsusceptible to the charm of female beauty, and not incapable of love "A war party of the Poncas had made a foray into the lands of the Omahas, and carried off a number of women and horses The Blackbird was roused to fury, and took the field with all his braves, swearing to eat up the Ponca nation—the Indian threat of exterminating war The Poncas, sorely pressed, took refuge behind a rude bulwark of earth, but the Blackbird kept up so galling a fire that he seemed likely to execute his menace In this extremity they sent forth a herald bearing the calumet, or pipe of peace, but he was shot down by order of the Blackbird Another herald was sent forth in similar guise, but he shared a like fate The Ponca chief then, as a last hope, arrayed his beautiful daughter in her finest ornaments, and sent her forth with the calumet to sue for peace The charms of the Indian maid touched the stern heart of the Blackbird, he accepted the pipe at her hand, smoked it, and from that time a peace took place between the Poncas and the Omahas

"This beautiful damsel, in all probability, was the favorite wife, whose fate makes so tragic an incident in the story of the Blackbird Her youth and beauty had gained an absolute sway over his rugged heart so that he distinguished her above all his other wives The habitual gratification of his vindictive impulses, however, had taken away from him all mastery over his passions and rendered him liable to the most furious transports of rage In one of these his beautiful wife had the misfortune to offend him, when, suddenly drawing his knife, he laid her dead at his feet with a single blow

"In an instant his frenzy was at an end He gazed for a time in mute bewilderment upon his victim, then drawing his buffalo robe over his head, he sat down beside the corpse, and remained brooding over his crime and his loss Three days elapsed, yet the chief continued silent and motionless, tasting no food and apparently sleepless It was apprehended that he intended to starve himself to death His people approached him in trembling awe, and entreated him once more to uncover his face and be comforted, but he remained unmoved At length one of his warriors brought in a small child, and laying it on the ground, placed the foot of the Blackbird upon its neck The heart of the gloomy savage was touched by this appeal, he threw aside his robe, made a harangue upon what he had done, and from that time forward seemed to have thrown the load of grief and remorse from his mind" The sorrowing monarch, his obsequious servants, their vain tenders of consolation and the sudden change at last from the stupor of despair to the habits of ordinary life, can hardly fail to remind the readers of this story of similar recorded incidents in the life of the great Israelitish king

One dark and fearful charge has been brought against the Omaha Sachem, which has blackened his reputation and left a stigma upon him which no lapse of years can efface It has been asserted that the great celebrity and absolute authority he acquired among his tribe were due to a long series of the most diabolical murders committed by him upon the ignorant and trusting children of the plains who believed in his prescience and trembled at his prowess One of the fur traders, so runs the story, who was accustomed to visit him at his village on the Missouri, seeking to ingratiate himself with so valuable a customer, made him acquainted with the deadly properties of arsenic, and undertook to keep him supplied with that noxious poison. From this time it was easy to induce the belief among his people that he was endowed with supernatural powers, and this rendered his despotism the more absolute and fearful. Whenever any one had offended him or thwarted his schemes or measures, he was wont to prophesy that at a certain time and with certain symptoms his recalcitrant subject would surely die. With his deadly drug it was never difficult to insure the fulfillment of his prediction. It has even been said that he administered the potent poison sometimes to friends, as well as to foes, that his prophecies might not all seem the effect of malice or ill-will.

The Omahas were entirely ignorant of the means by which this horrible result was produced, but they saw the effect, and knew from mournful experience that the displeasure of the chief was the forerunner; and their superstitious minds easily adopted the belief that he possessed a power which enabled him to will the destruction of his enemies. He thus acquired a despotic sway over the minds of his people which he exercised in the most tyrannical manner. So great was their fear of him that even when he became superannuated and so corpulent as to be unable to walk, they carried him about, watched over him when he slept, and awoke him, when necessary, by tickling his nose with a straw, for fear of disturbing him too abruptly. One chief, the Little Bow, whom he attempted ineffectually to poison, had the sagacity to discover the deception, and the independence to resist the influence of the imposter, but being unable to cope with so powerful an oppressor, he withdrew with a small band of warriors and remained separated from the nation until the decease of the Blackbird.

This, if true, is a sad record for the Chief of the Omaha nation; so discreditable that in the horror and detestation it excites we are apt to have lost sight of the incredible enormity of those who conferred upon him the power of perpetrating such barbarous homicides. If the guilt of the uncivilized and untaught denizen of the wilderness appeals to us with its iniquity, surely that of his civilized tempters and accomplices ought not to pass unnoticed and unreproved.

It is but just, however, to the memory of this haughty and invincible friend of the white man, to say that this story of his atrocities has not received universal acceptance. Mr. Catlin who, as we have seen, visited the Omahas while their great chief's memory was still fresh among them, says: "This story may be true and it may not. I cannot contradict it and I am sure the world will forgive me if I say I cannot believe it. It is said to have been told by the fur traders, and although I have not always the highest confidence in their justice to the Indian, yet I cannot, for the honor of my own species, believe them to be so depraved and so wicked, nor so weak as to reveal such iniquities of this chief, if they were true, which must directly implicate themselves as accessories to his most wilful and unprovoked murders.

"I have learned much of this noble chieftain," he continues, "and at a proper time shall recount the modes of his civil and millitary life; how he exposed his life and shed his blood in rescuing the victims to horrid torture, and abolished that savage custom in his tribe; how he led on and headed his brave warriors against the Sacs and Foxes, and saved the butchery of women and children; how he received the Indian agent and entertained him in his hospitable wigwam in his village, and how he conducted and acquitted himself on his embassy to the civilized world.

"So much I will take pains to say of a man whom I never saw, because other historians have taken equal pains just to mention his name, and a solitary (and doubtful) act of his life, as they have said of hundreds of others, for the purpose of consigning him to infamy

"How much more kind would it have been for the historian who never saw him, to have enumerated with this, other characteristic actions of his life for the verdict of the world, or to have allowed, in charity, his bones and his name to have slept in silence, instead of calling them up from the grave to thrust a dagger through them and throw them back again"

Towards the close of the eighteenth century that fearful scourge of Indian tribes, the small-pox, fell upon the tribes in Nebraska with fearful violence Neither the Poncas, the Otoes nor the Pawnees escaped its deadly visitation, and upon the Omahas it precipitated itself, as if with a full determination to leave no soul of the tribe remaining The loathsome pestilence swept like a conflagration over the prairies, and the poor doomed savages, dismayed at the progress of a malady against which their own prayers and the incantations of their medicine men were alike ineffective, at first sat in stoical silence as one after another of their sons, daughters and wives were taken away from them, and at last in despair, sought in suicide and human sacrifice either to appease the offended Deity or to secure for themselves and their friends an easier way to a happier region beyond the grave.

In the height of its ravages, Blackbird fell a victim to the pestilence He who was supposed to have power over the issues of life and death was found utterly powerless before the approach of the grim monster But in his last moments, surrounded by the grieving and despairing remnants of the proud tribe he had led to so many victories, he exhibited that fondness for the whites, which for years had made him a prominent object among the chieftains of his race There is, at a distance of less than a hundred miles north of Omaha, a conspicuous hill which rises high above the bluffs bordering the Missouri, of which it forms a part In the year 1811, when it was visited by Manuel Lisa, the river at its base began a strange winding course, several times returning upon its steps and at length coming within nine hundred yards of where the hills first approached, so that it was visible, and not far off for a course of thirty miles

Upon the summit of this hill the fierce and bloody warrior had often stood gazing upon the bends and mazes of the tortuous channel, and watching for the bateaux of his friends, the white traders When he became aware that death was approaching, he enjoined upon his weeping attendants that he he buried on the spot where he had gazed down the valley, so that he could see, after death, the Frenchmen passing up and down the river in their boats The Omaha village was then about sixty miles above his eminence, but in obedience to his dying command, his warriors took his body down the river to the pinnacle of this towering bluff, his favorite haunt He had owned, amongst many horses, a noble white steed that was led to the top of the grass-covered hill, and with great pomp and ceremony in the presence of the whole nation, and several of the fur traders, he was placed astride of his horse's back with his bow in his hand, and his shield and quiver slung, with his pipe and his medicine bag, with his supply of dried meat, and his tobacco pouch replenished to last him through his journey to the beautiful hunting grounds of the shades of his fathers, with his flint and steel and his tinder to light his pipe by the way The scalps that he had taken from his enemies could be trophies for nobody else, and were hung to the bridle of his horse. He was in full dress and fully equipped, and on his head waved, to the last moment, the beautiful head-dress of the war-eagle's plumes In this plight, and the last funeral honors having been performed by the medicine men, every warrior of his band painted the palm and fingers of his right hand with vermillion, which was stamped and perfectly impressed on the milk-white sides of his devoted horse.

This all done, turfs were brought and placed around the feet and legs of the horse, and gradually laid up to its sides, and at last over the back and head of the unsuspecting animal; and last of all over the head and over the eagle plumes of its valiant rider. On the top of the mound was planted a staff from which long waved the banner of the dead chief, and this conspicuous eminence is to this day known by the name of the Blackbird Hill. The mound, covered with green turf and spotted with wild flowers, with its cedar post in the center, was readily seen at the distance of fifteen miles by the voyageur, and formed for him for years a familiar and useful landmark. So late as 1811, the pious custom of placing near the grave articles of food and drink for the sustenance of the warrior during his long journey, was still kept up. Even to this day the crest of the grassy hill is pointed out to the passing traveler as the grave of a great chief.

It must be confessed, however, that Blackbird's sightless eyesockets were not permitted for more than a generation to scan the valley for his returning friends. When Mr. Catlin visited the romantic spot in 1832, for the purpose of making a sketch of the hill, he carried away more than his drawings. "Whilst visiting this mound," he says, " in company with Major Sanford, on our way up the river, I discovered in a hole made in the mound by a ground hog or other animal, the skull of a horse, and by a little pains also came at the skull of the chief, which I carried to the river side and secreted till my return in my canoe, when I took it in, and brought with me to this place, where I now have it, with others, which I have collected on my route.'' From the Catlin collection it found its way to the National Museum in Washington, where it is still to be seen, and where, if it possessed the power of vision, which its rightful owner expected, it might behold more wonderful objects and more rapacious traders than it could ever have observed in the now peaceful and pastoral valley of the Missouri.

Blackbird's curious and poetic fancy of being buried where he could see vessels and sailors may remind the classical student of Plutarch's description of the tomb of Themistocles. "Diodorus, the geographer, says in his work on Tombs, but by conjecture rather, than of certain knowledge, that near the port of Piraeus, where the land runs out like an elbow from the promontory of Alcinus, when you have doubled the cape and passed inward where the sea is always calm, there is a large piece of masonry, and upon this the tomb of Themistocles.'' Plato, the comedian, confirms this, he believes, in these verses:

"Thy tomb is fairly placed upon the strand,
Where merchants still shall greet it with the land;
Still in and out 'twill see them come and go,
And watch the galleys as they race below."

The successor of Blackbird was Om-pah-tou-ga, or the Big Elk, who held the chieftaincy, it is said, until the year 1846, when he died. He was an able and highly respectable man, exercising vast influence over his tribe. His power was used with moderation, and all white men who visited this country during his life were ready to bear witness to his uniform fair dealing, hospitality and friendship. Less brilliant than his distinguished predecessor, he was no less successful in accomplishing the ends at which he aimed, by the sagacity and common sense with which he laid his plans. It was the boast of the Big Elk, when Captain Long visited him in 1819, that neither his own hands, nor those of any of his tribe, had ever been stained with the blood of a white man. He was in his day a famous orator, and there has come down to our days a short specimen of his eloquence.

which has in it a not ineffective element of sad pathos. Black Buffalo, a chief of the Sioux, had died during a conference with the United States authorities, while arranging with the chiefs of various other tribes the preliminaries of a treaty. He was buried by a detachment of United States soldiers under the command of Colonel Miller, afterwards the hero of Lundy's Lane, with the honors of war. Big Elk was much impressed with the ceremonies, and made an address, in the course of which he said: "Would that I could have died today instead of the chief that lies before us. The loss to my people would have been but trifling. The honors of my burial would have repaid it twice over. Instead of being covered with a cloud of sorrow, my warriors would have felt the sunshine of joy in their hearts. To me it would have a glorious triumph. But now, when I die at my little Omaha village on the Missouri, instead of a noble grave and a grand procession, the rolling music and the thundering cannon, with a banner waving at my head, I shall be wrapped in a tattered robe and hoisted on a slender scaffold, soon to be by the whistling winds blown down again to the earth—my flesh to be devoured and my bones scattered on the plain by the wolves. Chief of the soldiers, my nation shall know the respect that you pay to the dead. When I return I will echo the sound of your guns."

# CHAPTER VII.

### The State Organized — Location of the Capitol at Omaha — Assembling of the First Legislature — Platte Valley & Pacific Railroad — Capitol Removal Schemes — Governor Izard's Departure.

The Hon. Francis Burt, a native of South Carolina, was the first governor appointed for the new territory of Nebraska after its organization by act of Congress, on the 30th of May, 1854. The Governor reached the western bank of the Missouri on the 6th of October of that year, in a delicate state of health, which had been rendered still more precarious by the hardships and exposures of the journey from his home. He was a man of delicate and refined mental organization; remarkable for kindness of heart and suavity of manner; of absolute and sterling integrity; of limited means, but incapable of seeking wealth by any indirection.

To this gentleman in infirm health, in need of entire repose, suffering from anxiety and trouble, every influential man in the territory at once resorted in the hope of inducing him to fix the capitol of the territory at some one or other of the numberless sites suggested for that location. It was, of course, of vital importance to every man who owned or possessed a large interest in any town site within the limits of that extensive territory. It is supposed that the prejudices of Gov. Burt were in favor of Bellevue as a location for the capitol, but doubtless he had made up his mind to give all portions of the eastern part of the territory an impartial and candid examination, and to place the capitol, honestly and fairly, where it would be most beneficial to the population of the entire commonwealth. But he never made any decision known. Harrassed beyond measure in the weak state of his health, and worn out by the vexatious trials incident to his new position, and the persistency with which the conflicting claims of rival town site speculators were forced upon him, the new Governor, in just ten days after his arrival in the territory, relinquished the struggle and sought in the grave that repose which it was evident he could never find in Nebraska.

He was, during his last illness, a guest of the Rev. William Hamilton, at that time the head of the Presbyterian mission at Bellevue. Mr. Hamilton has recorded it as his belief that the Governor had virtually decided to fix the capitol at Bellevue, and refers to some death-bed expressions, which seem to corroborate his views. However, that may be, no paper of any kind was left by him to indicate his intention, and the whole subject was left to his successor, Thomas B. Cuming, the secretary, who, upon the decease of Governor Burt, became the acting Governor of the territory.

Gov. Cuming was younger, stronger, and of sterner stuff than his predecessor, and took the importunities, of which he immediately became the victim, with much more coolness than Mr. Burt, though he was "plied, begged, pressed, entreated, assailed and even threatened" by almost every township in the territory. At last he was enabled to escape from further importunity, by designing Omaha as the place where the first session of the legislature should be held.

There were not wanting disappointed aspirants who charged the new Governor with selfish and even corrupt motives in this determination. But when we reflect that

## LOCATION OF THE CAPITOL AT OMAHA.

the last hours of Governor Burt were troubled by rival delegations, forcing their way to his bedside, to urge the respective claims of Omaha, Florence, Plattsmouth or Nebraska City for the seat of government, we can readily imagine that bribes would have readily been offered by the representatives of either of these places, and that wherever the capitol might have been fixed, the Governor could not have escaped like imputations, whether slanderous or not. On this subject Mr. C. H. Gere remarks: "By what pathways the acting Governor was led to pitch the imperial tent upon the plateau of Omaha, it is not our province to inquire. If the statesmen of Kanesville, later Council Bluffs, had a hand in the matter, the city soon had reason to mourn that the nest of the new commonwealth was lined with plumage from her own breast. From its very cradle her infant despoiled her of her commercial prestige, and now scoffs at her maternal ancestor every time she glances across the dreary bottom that separates the waxing from the waning metropolis."

Whatever the motive or reason, the action of Governor Cuming settled the question so far as the first assemblage of the Legislature was concerned, and gave to the ambitious little City of Omaha that prestige which enabled her, not without importunity, lavish expenditure of money, great parliamentary shrewdness and even at times a resort to the powerful logic of fisticuffs, to retain its position as the metropolis for nearly thirteen years.

It was hoped that the first Legislature called to meet at Omaha would be able to wrest from Omaha the sceptre thus put into her hands by the Governor. In November 1854, this officer caused an enumeration of the inhabitants of the new territory to be made, upon which he based the representation of the members of the Territorial Council and House of Representatives. Under this enumeration to the four counties north of the Platte River. Douglas (of which Sarpy was then a part), Washington, Burt and Dodge were apportioned seven Councilmen and fourteen Representatives, and to the four south of that stream, Cass, Pierce, now Otoe, Forney, now Nemaha, and Richardson, were given six Councilmen and twelve Representatives. It was loudly claimed on the part of the opponents of Omaha, that this basis of representation was forced and partial, and that the South Platte territory contained a larger population, and was entitled to a larger representation than the northern portion of the State.

Under these circumstances, various persons not holding the Governor's election certificates applied for admission to the first session of the Legislature. The organic act provided that the Governor should organize the territory, laying out counties and election districts, and set in motion the machinery of the territorial government. When the members of the first Legislature assembled, those holding certificates of election from the acting Governor favored, as was supposed, the permanent establishment of the capital at Omaha; while several of those who were contesting seats favored a change. When it became the business of the Legislature to pass upon these cases of contested seats, the legislators who favored Omaha as the permanent capital, under the leadership of Mr. Poppleton, took the ground that under the organic act the Governor's certificates of election were conclusive, and put it out of the power of the Legislature to seat any who were unable to exhibit such evidences of their election.

The careful training and education of the legislative friends of Omaha was shown in the fact that this somewhat startling proposition was assented to by the members of the first Legislature, though it is in direct opposition to one of the fundamental doctrines governing such bodies; that every legislature has the right to pass upon and decide the qualification and election of its own members.

Probably Mr. Poppleton, after his long years of honorable labor at the bar, would hardly at this day contend that his interpretation of the law was strictly accurate, but there can be no doubt but that this refusal to go behind the Governor's certificates of election had an important bearing upon the question of capital location, and contributed materially to the success of Omaha in the struggle of which the first session was the scene.

At that session were gathered together, either in or out of the Legislature, all who were disappointed in the selection of Omaha by Governor Cuming, and loud threats and declarations as to what the coming session would accomplish were indulged in on the streets. Warmth of argument and the irreconcilable differences not unfrequently led to pugilistic encounters, but on the whole the determination seemed to be to submit the question of capital location to the arbitrament of the Legislature.

The first session of the first Legislative Assembly for the new Territory of Nebraska, began at Omaha, on Tuesday, the 16th day of January, 1855. There were present as members of the House of Representatives from Douglas county, Messrs. Andrew J. Hanscom, Alfred D. Goyer, Andrew J. Poppleton, William Clancy, William N. Byers, Thomas Davis, Fleming Davidson and Robert B. Whitted. Three of these gentlemen, together with Mr. J. W. Paddock, who was elected Chief Clerk of the House, are still, after the lapse of thirty-five years, living in Omaha, with constitutions and mental faculties unimpaired, and in the enjoyment of well earned reputations and competence.

The Council organized on the same day. Joseph L. Sharp, of Richardson county, was elected President, and Messrs. Samuel E. Rogers, O. D. Richardson, A. D. Jones and T. G. Goodwill were announced as members elect from the county of Douglas.

Mr. Andrew J. Hanscom was elected Speaker of the House, and the first motion made in that body, being the first ever made in any legislative body in the State, was one by Mr. Poppleton for the temporary organization of the House.

In the afternoon of that day the two branches of the Legislature met together in the hall of the House and listened to the reading of the message of acting Governor Cuming. This first message from the young Governor, whose public utterances always gave promise of distinguished success in public life, too soon to be frustrated by his untimely decease, merits notice from its wise forethought, its enlarged conception of the future, and its prophecies then deemed extravagant by some, long since brilliantly realized.

After some graceful references to the recent death of Governor Burt, and the unexpected responsibilities thus devolved upon him, the acting Governor proceeded:

One of the principal subjects of general interest to which, next to the enactment of your laws, your attention will be directed this winter, is that of a Pacific Railroad. You have acquired, in respect to this, an acknowledged precedence; and the expression in your representative capacity, of the wishes of your constituents, throughout the vast extent of your Territory, may have a potent influence, together with the efforts of your friends, in promoting the construction of such a road up the valley of the Platte.

Many reasons lead to the conclusion that such a memorial from you will be of practical efficacy in contributing to the speedy consummation of such an enterprise—an enterprise of such absolute necessity as a means of intercommunication between the Atlantic and Pacific States and as the purveyor of a lucrative commerce with India, China and the Pacific islands. Among these are the facts that the valley of the Platte is on the nearest and most direct continuous line from the commercial metropolis of the east by railroad and the great lakes, through the most practical mountain passes to the metropolis of the West; that it is fitted by nature for an easy grade; and that it is central and convenient to the great majority of grain growing States, and of the northern portion of the Union, being situated in latitude 41 degrees north, while the majority of the people of the whole country are between the 38th and 46th degrees of north latitude. It seems to me

that it will be the desire of the friends of this great enterprise—one of the most prominent and important of all the measures of national development upon this continent now under the consideration of the people of the United States—to act immediately in the selection of routes, and to establish a permanent policy, the details of which may be practically prosecuted in the coming spring, and I sincerely hope and believe that your legislative memorial in Congress may have its legitimate weight in the decision of a question of such momentous interest

In view, however, of the uncertainty arising from the sectional conflict with which the subject is surrounded I would respectfully suggest that such a memorial should urgently, if not principally, ask for a preliminary provision from granting which, the general government will scarcely be deterred by considerations of policy or economy I refer to a proposition presented to Congress eight years ago for ' Telegraphic and Letter Mail Communication with the Pacific,' including the protection of emigrants and formation of settlements along the route through Nebraska, Utah, California and Oregon, the promotion of amicable relations with the Indians, and facilitating intercourse across the American continent between Europe and Asia, and the islands and American coasts of the Pacific

The plan is substantially, that instead of or in addition to garrisons at isolated points—parties of twenty dragoons shall be stationed at stockades twenty to thirty miles apart, on a route designated by the Executive of the United States as a "Post Road" between the Missouri River and the Pacific, that express mails shall be carried by said dragoons riding each way and meeting daily between the stockades, and affording complete supervision and protection of a line of electric telegraph constructed by private enterprise

By such an arrangement, in which every detail is subject to free public competition a line of telegraph may be opened within one year to the Rocky Mountains and a largely increased mail transported in half the time now required and with perfect security, between the Atlantic and Pacific States at the same time giving complete protection to the thousands who annually travel on the route, and conducing not only to the settlement of Nebraska, but of the vast regions between us and our fellow pioneers upon our western coasts

Such an emigrant highway would afford one of the best and speediest mail lines in the world, giving efficiency to troops already in service for purposes of protection encouraging emigration and making a continuous series of settlements and cultivated farms around the stockades, between which individual or corporate enterprise will the more speedily construct the long desired and expected " Pacific Railroad '

The location of Nebraska, remote from, but intermediate between the Atlantic and Pacific, indicates the necessity of facilitating intercourse between its inhabitants and their fellow citizens on the shores of both oceans It is the duty of governments to defend life and property, and protect and quicken communication between all portions of their domain, and this requirement is especially imperative upon the Federal and State governments of our widely extended Union in respect to territories where civilization is struggling for a foothold, and the farms and firesides of whose pioneers have a just claim upon the protection of a power, whose fleets are traversing every sea for the defense of its citizens

Aside, too, from the direct practical blessings of such a system faithfully carried out in all its details, and its immense effect on the correspondence and business of the world, the project acquires additional importance from the fact that it will contribute to bind together States far separate and of diverse interests, in the commercial fraternity and sympathy of an inseparable Union

We may reasonably expect that a memorial advocating the advantages of the Platte Valley, as a route for the Pacific Railroad, and urging especially and strenuously, the immediate adoption of a policy similar to the above would not be without its influence upon the deliberations of Congress

On the 24th day of January Mr Latham, of Cass County, gave notice in the House that on the morrow, or at an early day thereafter, he would present a bill "to locate the Capital of Nebraska "

Thus commenced a contest which lasted with great vehemence for more than twelve years, produced more ill-feeling, gave rise to more difficulties, and was more troublesome to manage, than any question ever decided in the State In the House at this time the parties for and against Omaha seemed nearly equally divided, but the location at Omaha was finally secured by a vote of fourteen to eleven Those voting in favor of Omaha were Messrs Arnold,

Byers, Clancy, Davidson, Davis, Goyer, Kempton, Latham, Poppleton, Purple, Richardson, Robertson, Thompson and Whitted. Those opposed were: Messrs. Bennett, Cowles, Decker, Doyle, Finney, Hail, Johnston, Maddox, Smith, Singleton and Wood.

In the Council the votes on nearly all the preliminary motions stood seven for Omaha to six opposed; and the final vote was as follows: Messrs. Clark, Folsom, Goodwill, Jones, Mitchell, Richardson and Rogers voted for Omaha, and Messrs. Bennett, Bradford, Brown, Cowles, Nuckolls and Sharp against it.

The bill thus passed by both branches of the Legislature was transmitted to the Governor for his signature; and notice being given by him on the 31st of January that the bill had received his signature, the vexed question was for the first session laid at rest, and the members were at liberty to proceed to other subjects of legislation.

One of the most important of these was a bill, pursuant to the recommendation of the acting Governor, chartering the Platte Valley & Pacific Railroad Company. The report of the Committee on Corporations, to which in the Council this bill was referred, contains some paragraphs which possess much interest. The Committee says:

"The valley of the Platte is well known in the West, it being the great highway through which nine-tenths of the overland emigration passes *en route* for the Pacific. Those coming by St. Louis travel by water up the Missouri to Independence, Weston, St. Joseph, Council Bluffs, and occasionally to Sargeant's Bluffs; and, uniting at these points with those who came by land from the east, pursue their way westward by converging lines that unite in the Platte Valley at various points within two hundred miles, a little north of a due west line from the cities of Omaha, Bellevue and Florence, in our infant territory.

"Although roads can be easily constructed over the rolling prairies of the west, yet it is only upon the valley of the Platte, after passing the great bend thirteen miles west of Omaha, Bellevue and Florence, that a straight level and solid road bed can be found which leads in the direct line of commerce east and west for near a thousand miles. This peculiar fitness would of itself be sufficient to attract all travel and railroad enterprise that might come within a hundred miles of the Platte; but there are other influences, outside of the valley, that tend to throw the migration through the center of Nebraska. The great channel of the St. Lawrence and the lakes, extended by railroads and common roads through Chicago, Iowa City, Fort Des Moines (the Capital of Iowa by a recent act of the General Assembly), and Council Bluffs, the frontier city of Iowa, and the great daily mail running in four-horse coaches, all tend to bring travel to the valley of the Platte. Several great lines of railroad south of these lakes, and all the leading roads which extend them through Iowa, converge towards Council Bluffs, directly east of the great line of the Platte valley. The greatest States, the largest cities, the most dense portion of our Union, are directly east and near this parallel of 41°, and it is, therefore, natural that these elements should flow through the center of Nebraska.

"But another great advantage of the Platte valley is the convenience it offers to branches westward. It leads to those great mountain passes, which are the gateways to Utah, California, Oregon and Washington. It is the best route, and the adopted road to all these States and Territories, and it is believed by your committee, some of whom have been through these routes, and for years intimate with those who traverse the mountains, that it is the Platte valley alone that affords to all those western divisions any natural and easy common way, which will commingle their travel with that of the Eastern States.

"There are still other attractions which

lead emigration through this channel Starting from this more westerly point on the Missouri there is less of land travel than any other route affords. There is a better connected line of good water, wood, stone, coal, soil and grass, than can be found on any other route, and it is far more inhabited, passing as we may, through the valley of the Great Salt Lake, Carson Valley, and the tributaries of the Sacramento. This route lies also in a zone of the earth's surface, where the greatest variety of useful articles can be produced, where men are capable of the greatest amount of endurance, and where the greatest amount of population and wealth are most likely to accumulate

"Although the Platte valley offers such pre-eminent advantages, and has for years been adopted as the natural emigrant route across this continent, yet it cannot be denied that other routes from east to west have their attractions, and that for years past commercial, financial and political efforts have been exhausted to direct and establish the trade and travel through other channels Millions have been expended annually in transports around Cape Horn and through Central America Extensive surveys have been made to find routes for railroads—far south and north—routes which a distinguished Senator has recently shown are far more convenient to Mexico and Canada, than to the United States Southern conventions have been held, and earnest efforts made to secure a route through by El Paso, and much has been said and done to direct public attention to a route leading southwest from St Louis But relying on the wisdom and prudence of our government, and the discerning scrutiny which characterizes those engaged in commerce and railroad enterprises, your committee confidently believe that the great emigrant route by the Platte valley will ultimately, not only retain its pre-eminence as the overland route, but absorb the business that now travels thousands of miles around a southern continent, instead of passing directly across our own country This, your committee believe, will be effected by the construction of a Pacific railroad The substitution of locomotives, or *land-steamers* that will run through or assist to develop and enrich our common country for *ocean steamers* that are now erected mainly at our expense, and sent off to enrich other parts of the world, is the only remedy that will secure our common interests Thirty years ago Colonel Leavenworth, who then commanded a post in sight of this locality, called the attention of our government to the importance, practicability and expediency of constructing a railroad by way of the Platte valley to the Pacific Subsequently the Rev J Parker, J. Plumber, Colonel Fremont, Mr Whitney, Captain Stansbury, and thousands of others at a still later period have urged the expediency of adopting a railroad to the emigrant route, thereby connecting all parts of our Republic

"But the importance of such a work is so manifest to all, and the consequent advantage which must result to the section of country through which such a road would pass, that a contest has arisen among States and cities to secure its location, and that contest has for years paralyzed all government effort, and retarded the progress and success of private enterprise. Engineers compute the distance from this navigable point of the Missouri to Sacramento City, a navigable point on the Sacramento River, at eighteen hundred miles At least one thousand miles of this would be in the valleys of the Platte and Humboldt, where it is generally conceded, at least by those conversant with the route in question, that the natural grade can hardly be improved Much of the remaining eight hundred miles would be on the valley of the Sweetwater, Bear River and other easy grades, leaving not over four hundred miles of what may be deemed heavy work Most of this would be in California and Utah, where the present inhabitants would be able and ready to execute their proper sections of the work. The State of Illinois has constructed railroads about equal in length to this Pacific road within the last two years; and the aid of the general government, and the application of State and private means, in the consummation of so great a work has not been felt by the community.

"Most of the Pacific road could be graded more easily than any of the roads of Illinois, and the worst sections do not present obstacles of serious moment to those engineers who have explored or ascertained the character of the country. Similar aid extended to Nebraska, Utah and California, would enable them to do on the Pacific line, what Illinois has done on various lines, and without regard to other projects, the old emigrant route by the Platte, through the center of Nebraska, would become the highway of nations.

"The completion of a line of railroad to Council Bluffs, on the opposite side of the Missouri, is a matter so self-evident that your committee have not deemed it necessary to advert to that section. Four companies are organized, four lines have been surveyed through Iowa to that point, and the Lyons road, Rock Island road, Air Line road and Burlington road are all contending for an early connection with that point in western Iowa. It is the desire of your committee, and doubtless of the entire population of our Territory, to secure their united efforts in carrying a great trunk line up the valley of the Platte, thereby securing to all of them a share of the Pacific road and to Nebraska a trunk that will expand into a thousand branches.

"With this view and in consideration of our remoteness from the wealth and influence of the Atlantic States, and our financial inability to carry forward, in the morning of our territorial existence, a great though practicable project, your committee have deemed it expedient to present a trunk line, with a liberal charter, in order to encourage capitalists to invest their means, and proceed with such a work at the earliest possible period. Your committee do this, not only to supply Nebraska with an early railroad connection but to protect her against powerful efforts which are being made to divert from her the travel which now comes through her great natural artery, and also to secure that great national highway that will revolutionize the commerce of the world. If, then, by the adoption of liberal measures and extending to capitalists the strongest inducements to invest their means, we succeed in accomplishing this great result, we will secure to Nebraska an advantage that she cannot hope otherwise to acquire.

"Some idea of the importance of an overland national channel of commerce can be found by inserting here some estimates of the business of this route. The Hon. Mr. McDougal, in a speech made in Congress on the second day of May last, stated that 443 merchant vessels had arrived in one year (1853) at San Francisco, carrying 423,230 tons, at $30 per ton, costing for its transportation $12,696,900.

| | |
|---|---|
| Cost for transportation, as above.... | $12,696,900 |
| Insurance on $100,000,000, the value of this merchandise at 4 per cent .... | 4,000,000 |
| Losses on merchandise not included as above ................................. | 7,000.000 |
| Interest on capital.................. | 5,000,000 |
| 110,000 passengers at an average of $250 each, with $2 per day for 40 days, the time of transit.......... | 36,300,000 |
| Transportation of mails and naval and military stores.................... | 3,739,000 |
| Freights crossing the Isthmus....... | 3,050,000 |
| Total for one year............. .... | $71,785,900 |

This is only a partial statement, because it only takes note of the merchandise which goes to San Francisco. Therefore, add merchandise transportation to other parts of California and Oregon, say ⅓ of $27,696,000, that which goes to San

| | |
|---|---|
| Francisco........................ | 9,232,000 |
| Isthmus freight on same............ | 1,000,000 |
| Transportation of many of these articles from western States to New York, estimated 200,000 tons at $6 per ton............................. | 12,000,000 |
| Travel of passengers and expense in New York $30 each.............. | 3,300 |
| Annual cost to the United States.. | $83,221,000 |

This is mainly the business of this country, that passes from the east to the west side of the Republic. There is the trade of our country and all Europe with India. Who can compute that? It is reasonable to suppose that good railroad facilities across this continent would secure more than half of the above items, amounting then to ......... 41,610,600
Add for increase which a railroad would naturally create—50 per cent 20,805,300
Add local business that would come to the line and equal the through.. 62,415,900

Total ............................. $124,831,800

"To this add whatever may be drawn from the commerce of the world, and the apparent business of the road would be greater than one single trunk road can do—not less than two hundred millions per annum. Like all the great east and west lines, it will immediately require doubling, and will produce a large profit on the cost.

"This gross income could only be secured after several years of business; but it is easy to see that the vast amount of trade and travel which does now follow the tedious route by ocean, would immediately pass through this new, safe and speedy channel of commerce. The millions of Europe would be brought into contact with the hundred millions of Asia, and their line of quick transit would be, to a great extent, across our continent. Their mails, their ministers, their most costly and interesting travel and trade would take this route and augment our business and multiply our resources.

"In view of the comparative cost to the wonderful changes that will result, your committee cannot believe the period remote when this work will be accomplished; and with liberal encouragement to capital, which your committee are disposed to grant, it is their belief that before fifteen years have transpired, the route to India will be opened and the way across this continent will be the common way of the world. Entertaining these views, your committee report the bill for the Platte Valley & Pacific Railroad, feeling assured that it will become not only a basis for branches within Nebraska, but for surrounding States and Territories."

It is doubtful if any prophetic vision of the future of a country was ever more accurately realized. Within a few months less than the fifteen years given for the completion of the road, the last spike was driven connecting the Union Pacific and the Central Pacific roads, and the "common way" of the world became what the author of this report had declared it should become.

The remaining proceedings of the first Nebraska Legislature are devoid of any special interest. They consisted of the enactment of civil and criminal codes, boundaries of counties, incorporation of cities, universities and private associations, establishment of ferries and the numberless acts which, necessary as they may be at the time of laying the foundations of a commonwealth, possess little general interest after the occasion which gave rise to them have passed.

The codes, however, enacted at that session, principally adopted from the several codes of the adjoining States, were found by experience to be incongruous and conflicting in many important respects and the doubts and difficulties arising in their application led to many errors and omissions in the administration of territorial affairs.

Governor Mark W. Izard, of Arkansas, had been appointed to succeed Governor Burt, and arrived in the Territory on the 20th of February, 1855, immediately entering upon the discharge of his duties and superseding acting Governor Cuming. At the second session of the Legislature, which was held on the 13th of December, 1855, Governor Izard recommended the adoption of a civil code which had, during the summer, been prepared by a board of commissioners. The criminal code of Iowa was adopted as the code of Nebraska, the necessary laws to provide for the local machinery of government were passed, and much useful work done. Prior to this time, James C. Mitchell had been appointed sole Commis sioner to locate the capitol building, and the envious and censorious asserted that this office accounted with exactness for his sudden change of front on the question of capital removal. He reported to the Governor on the 17th day of March, 1855, that he had that day selected the centre of Capitol Square, in Omaha, at present the site of the Omaha High School, as the locality for the edifice. By December, when the second session was held, Governor Izard was able to announce that the foundation of the capitol building was completed. For the present the danger of an early removal of the seat of government from Omaha seemed to be at an end.

The disastrous year of 1857 dawned upon Omaha with brightness, and the prospect for the future seemed unusually cheering. "Another year of unexampled prosperity, crowned with the blessings of health, peace, and an ample remuneration to the labors of our people in all the industrial pursuits of life has passed away," said the Governor, in his message of January in that year, and he added, "No citizen of Nebraska can look around him and contemplate the unexampled degree of prosperity which has crowned the efforts of our infancy without feelings of the profoundest gratitude and satisfaction. And when we reflect that but two short years have passed since Nebraska (almost unknown except by name) was a vast, uncultivated and unsettled region, with scarcely a mark to indicate that civilization had reached its borders, its present condition almost startles us with the conviction that the hand of magic, rather than enterprise, wrought the change. We can boast of a population of more than fifteen thousand intelligent, orderly and energetic citizens, who may challenge comparison with those of any State or Territory in the Union; of flourishing towns and prosperous cities, with their handsome church edifices, well regulated schools and busy streets; of our broad and beautiful prairies, thickly dotted with comfortable farm houses and well cultivated fields, yielding their rich treasures to the hand of peaceful industry. The appreciation of property has far exceeded the expectations of the most sanguine. Business lots upon streets where the wild grass still flourishes, are readily commanding from five hundred to three thousand dollars each; lands adjacent to our more prosperous towns, sell readily at from fifty to four hundred dollars per acre; credit is almost unknown in our business circles; no citizen oppressed for debt nor crippled in his energies by the hand of penury or want; but all encouraged by the success of the past look forward to the future with eager hopes and bright anticipations—stimulated to greater efforts and renewed exertion. * * * * * Our banks, the chartering of which by the last Legislative Assembly, was considered of doubtful expediency by many of our citizens, have so far worked well. By reference to their annual reports, made to the Auditor and published in conformity with law, it will be seen that they are in a healthy condition." Just nine months from the delivery of this message occurred in the City of New York the failure of the great Ohio Life and Trust Company, with its capital of millions and its ramifications extending over the whole country. From that grave disaster the City of New York soon recovered; two or three days of terror, apprehension and gloom passed away and business at that metropolis assumed its wonted appearance. But when the blow reached Omaha, the cardboard institutions of Nebraska went down like a claim shanty before a tornado. One or two of the Omaha banks, founded and managed on sound business principles, weathered the storm and still exist as monuments of the sagacity of their founders, but of most of the banking concerns in this vicinity, there remain only the exquisitely engraved and beautiful circulating bills, to remind the credulous of that day of then glowing anticipations and the unhappy reality

Early in the session of 1857 the agitation respecting capital removal was again started by Mr Jacob Safford, who was what is termed a "float" representative, representing the counties of Dodge, Cass and Otoe jointly His resolution, which was agreed to was " that a select committee of three be appointed by the President of the Council, to take into consideration the expediency of relocating the seat of government of Nebraska Territory, with instructions to report at their earliest convenience by bill or otherwise " The committee so appointed consisted of Mr Safford, Mr Kirkpatrick, of Cass, and Mr Clancy, of Washington This committee, appointed on Tuesday, the 6th, was ready to make its report on the morning of Thursday, the 8th Through Mr. Safford, their chairman, they declared "That they are unanimously of the opinion that the best interests of the Territory, present and future, demand that the capitol be removed from its present locality to some point in the interior In arriving at this conclusion your committee have been influenced by so many considerations that they deem it impossible to go into them at length without making their report too voluminous, but which will be well understood by those who have been conversant with the history of our Territory from the beginning Your committee will therefore merely state some of their reasons in as concise and general a form as possible

"When the first Governor arrived in this Territory he found but one place entitled to the name of village even, anywhere north of the Platte River The town of Bellevue, the first fine townsite north of the Platte, was the place where it is well known it was his intention to locate the capital His death, however, left the matter in other hands, and the capital was located at its present site

"Your committee are loth to say what influences are universally believed to have been brought to bear in inducing the present location It is, perhaps, sufficient for them to say that the people of the Territory are by no means satisfied with the location or with the means by which it was located, and still less by the means by which it has been kept there

"Again, the capital as located is not in the center of our population, or nearly so, as will be seen by the fact that there are only six representatives north, while there are twenty south of Omaha, and this disparity from the nature of the country will probably not be lessened when we become a State

"Again, it is important to the rapid growth of our population, that the capital be established at some point at a suitable distance from the Missouri River

"Again, it is manifest to your committee that the appropriations made by Congress for the erection of our Capitol building have been expended in a manner to enhance the interests of Omaha City, and to the detriment of the Territory, and to the injury of other points, to say the least, equally deserving That in fact immense speculations have been made in the whole affair, by the exercise of the public patronage and offices; and that the power thus acquired in conjunction with the public patronage and offices has been and is still operating to force everything into one channel, to the manifest injustice of other points. It would always seem that those having the control of the Capitol appropriations are determined not only to impress the public with the idea that this is to be the permanent capital, but to make it in fact so by the most lavish and unnecessary expenditure of public money

'It will be remembered that the appropriation by Congress for the purpose of erecting a capitol was fifty thousand dollars, this was deemed and is in fact amply sufficient for the purpose, if properly applied. But by reference to the Governor's message of Dec. 18, 1855, it will be seen that the Executive indulges in the most pleasing reflections on the magnificence and grandeur of the future capitol; challenging in fact the whole architecture of the Union and at the same time estimating the cost at $79,705.79, which will appear by reference to the Council journal of 1855, pages 6 and 7. At the last session of Congress the Territory failed to get an additional appropriation, and now, after the lapse of another year, we are told by the Executive that it will be necessary to ask of Congress an additional appropriation.

"Your committee forbear to give, at this time, any further reflections on this subject, under the belief that under another form the matter will undergo a full investigation. But this much they will say, that the object of all this seems manifest; and that they are impressed with the belief that Congress neither will or ought to appropriate one cent to complete the building if it is to cost that sum. But your committee are of the opinion that Congress ought and doubtless would appropriate $50,000, under the circumstances, to a new capitol, which will be amply sufficient to erect a capitol which will answer every purpose.

"Your committee would further state that there are other interests in the Territory that require the fostering hand of general government; among others, universities, colleges, and prisons for the confinement of convicts, &c., &c. But the course of policy heretofore pursued and still recommended absorbs everything in this enormous building and other interests around Omaha.

"For these reasons your committee have been induced to offer the accompanying bill as a part of their report, entitled 'An Act for the Relocation of the Seat of Government of the Territory of Nebraska.'"

This report was straightway adopted and the bill accompanying it read the first time. As the members of the Council apparently stood nine in favor of relocation to four against it, the opposition was feeble and the bill finally passed that body on the 10th of January, 1857. In the House of Representatives, to which the bill was immediately sent for concurrence, the opposition, led by Mr. Hanscom, was more active, and from the fact that on the 12th the Governor thought it necessary to assure the House, by a verbal message, that the disposition of the citizens of Omaha was peaceful, and that the body might proceed with legislation in safety, it is manifest that no little excitement was felt throughout the city relative to the pending question.

The opposition by the minority continued so vigorous that on the 13th Mr. Finney, of Nemaha, offered a resolution that the rules be suspended and that the Council bill for relocation be taken up and read a first and second time, and that the said bill be the order of the day from day to day, and no other business be transacted until the same shall be finally disposed of. This resolution was adopted by a vote of twenty-three to eleven. Things were beginning to look dark for the future of Omaha. Dilatory motions of all kinds were made, but the majority made short work with them. Among them was one that James C. Mitchell be prohibited from advising or counseling the Speaker or members of the House on what course they shall pursue in relation to their deliberations, and that unless he refrains from so doing he shall be prohibited from coming within the bar of the House. On the 15th the bill was finally passed, by a vote of twenty-three to twelve. This act provided that the seat of government should be located at the town of Douglas, in the county of Lancaster. It is not a little singular that ten years later, after Douglas was in his grave, and the war of the rebellion had largely changed the politics and thoughts of men, almost this identical spot should be chosen for the capital of the State of Nebraska, just admitted to the Federal

Union, its name, however, being changed to Lincoln,* in former days the friend, competitor and townsman of Douglas

It was found, however, that the bill had still another ordeal to undergo when it was transmitted to Governor Izard for his signature. On the 19th of January he sent a message to the Council in which the bill had originated, declining to give it his approval. His reasons were given at considerable length, owing to the fact that the measure had passed both Houses of the Legislature by so decided a majority. Stated briefly, however, they were

*First* That the removal of the seat of government was not made an issue before the people in any county in the territory at the time the legislature was elected, and he was therefore, constrained to believe that the movement had " been gotten up and passed hurriedly and inconsiderately through both branches of that body by a dominant majority, not only in the absence of any positive instructions from the people, but contrary to their wishes, and most certainly to the injury of their best interests "

*Second* That it was a universally conceded fact that the principal settlements in the territory would for many years be confined to a tract of country extending not more than thirty miles westward from the Missouri

*Third* That the location of Omaha was then central and readily accessible, not only from the territory, but from the country east

*Fourth* That " a costly and substantial building, sufficient to meet and accommodate the growing demands of the territory for many years, is now in course of erection at the present location, and will be completed during the present year, if not retarded by ill-advised and hasty legislation, without the cost of a single dollar to the people of the territory "

*The name "Lincoln" was suggested by Mr Poppleton The legislators of 1867 were on the point of giving to their new Capital the unmeaning and hackneyed designation of Central City

*Fifth* That the point selected, even " it it has an existence at all except upon paper is entirely removed from the center of population, and equally remote from the center of the territory It is not pretended that a single house, or even a sod shanty, has been erected on the site of the proposed capitol, or in the vicinity It appears to be a floating town, not only without a location, but without inhabitants Its existence, if it has any, seems to be confined at present to the brain of some desperate fortune-hunter and its identity reposes in an indefinable number of certificates of stock for $500.00 each neatly gotten up and handsomely executed with all the requisites of president, secretary, &c Where the precise location of this town is intended to be, I am unable to determine By some it is said to be somewhere on Salt Creek, and by others at a point further removed from the settlements, and in the vicinity of the southern boundary of the territory All agree, however, that there are two towns in Lancaster County by the name of Douglas, already made upon paper To which of these it is the intention of the Legislature to remove the seat of government I am left wholly to conjecture It might so happen, and from my knowledge of the speculative genius of a certain class of our citizens, I think it highly probable that should the bill under consideration become a law, each of these rival towns would set up a claim to the capital which it might require long and tedious litigation to settle, leaving the people of the territory in the meantime without a seat of government "

*Lastly* That under the organic act the seat of government having been once located, could thereafter be removed only by the concurrent action of the Governor and Legislative Assembly The latter, even by an unanimous vote, would have no such power And the act of Congress, appropriating money for the erection of a Capitol building, was passed in evident recognition of the fact that the Capital had been permanently located during the existence of the territory.

It soon became evident that it would be futile, if not impracticable, to pass the bill over the Governor's veto, and after several ineffective attempts to secure its passage, the bill was, on the 5th of February, on motion of Mr. Kirkpatrick, indefinitely postponed, allowing the citizens of Omaha to breathe more freely for another year.

Governor Izard did not remain in office to witness another attempt to destroy the prestige of Omaha. In October, 1857, he bade adieu to this cold northern clime, and betook himself to the balmier region of Arkansas, from which State he had been appointed. Coming to this city with but little experience in public life, he took home with him the reputation of an honest, painstaking and judicious officer. As usual, opinions concerning him varied. Those who were opposed to the City of Omaha on the Capital question insisted that he was vain, pompous, illiterate and inefficient. The citizens of Omaha esteemed him highly as a dignified, upright, firm and courteous gentleman of the old school. Mention has above been made of an oral message from the Governor, assuring the legislators that they need have no apprehension of violence in the discharge of their duties. Mr. Sorensen's story, which has been long current in Omaha, of this message, is as follows: "The South Platte party asked the Governor to call out three hundred militia to protect them from the Omaha crowd, which was composed of eight men. The next morning Governor Izard, whom they had called 'grandmother,' assembled both branches of the Legislature together, and made them a speech. It was short and pointed. He said: 'Gentlemen, it is entirely unnecessary to call out the militia. Go on and attend to the legislative business. Behave yourselves, and your grandmother will protect you.'"

That the Governor magnified his office, and delighted in marks of honor and respect, is not to be denied. Nor can it be questioned that he had never received the critical and liberal education which enabled him to comprehend the full signification of many long words. His enemies declared that he used to speak of "decimating" intelligence among the people, and that once, in response to a speech of welcome, he expressed his gratification with the climate, people and situation of Omaha, and declared it to be his most earnest desire and prayer, that when he died, he might be buried on some one of the beautiful "premonitories" in the neighborhood of that city.

It is certain that he was a stern and uncompromising democrat of the Jackson school, with a strong love for the Union, and the most bitter hatred for all whom he regarded as assailing its integrity. "I regard," he says in his first message, "the election of James Buchanan and John C. Breckenridge to the Presidency of the United States at this juncture, as not only having cemented the Union of the States, by reassuring the South that her constitutional rights are sacred from invasion, and as having settled forever the great question of Congressional interference in the domestic affairs of the States and Territories, by banishing the vexed question of slavery from the halls of the Capitol, and committing it for settlement to the hands of the people directly interested in its establishment or prohibition, but as having had a most salutary effect upon the business of the country." The denunciations and invectives of heated partisans on both sides of the then impending conflict vexed and harrassed his peaceful-natured soul, and he soon began to long for the more quiet retreat of his Arkansas plantation. As he advanced in years, the delights of office seemed less attractive to him. He built on the northeast corner of Twenty-Second and Burt Streets a brick edifice, modeled on the plan of the southern plantation mansion, so familiar in those days to the traveler, and, of course, utterly unsuited to the rigors of our winter climate. This house was standing until 1887. In October, as we have seen, dismayed at the thought of another winter like that of 1857, and not anxious to see the Legislature again in session, he disappeared from Omaha. For several years he was unheard of in the turmoil and excitement of arms and revolution. The Rebellion, and what he regarded as the certain loss of his beloved Union, seem to have stupefied him. Sometime during the war, it is said that a detachment of one of our Nebraska regiments passing his plantation, saw on the wide, southern gallery a gray withered and bent old man, whom they recognized as the former Governor of Nebraska.

The session of 1857 passed an act incorporating the City of Omaha. This became a law on the 2d of February of the last-mentioned year, and the settlement from that time became entitled to its added dignity. Up to about this time it had always been known as Omaha City. When it really became entitled to the designation of a city, it dropped the pretentious suffix

# CHAPTER VIII.

SECRETARY CUMING AGAIN ACTING-GOVERNOR—LEGISLATORS ADJOURN TO FLORENCE—HOW THE DIFFICULTY OCCURRED—LIST OF GOVERNORS OF NEBRASKA—OMAHA CITIZENS AS SENATORS AND CONGRESSMEN.

By the withdrawal of Governor Izard the Secretary of the Territory, Mr. Thomas B. Cuming, became again acting Governor of the Territory. The fourth session of the Legislature found him in that position and it soon became evident that the struggle for another capital was soon to be commenced. Governor Cuming, in his message, congratulated the Legislature that they met for the fourth time, "at the place first chosen for the Territorial Capital; and in the spacious and imposing edifice, nearly completed, under the appropriation by the General Government, and through the public spirit of the City of Omaha." The mutterings of the coming storm were first heard in a motion in the Council by Mr. Bowen, that a committee of two be appointed to report to the Council at their earliest convenience, the condition of the Territorial capitol buildings; what amount had been expended; by whom expended; the estimated cost to complete the same upon the present plan; when it would probably be completed; what party or parties were the owners of the ground upon which the same was situated; what party or parties were the contractors, and calling upon acting Governor Cuming for all facts within his knowledge and all papers in his office bearing upon the subject of inquiry. On the 2d of January Mr. Abbe, of Otoe county, gave notice of a bill to relocate the seat of Government of the Territory of Nebraska. This bill was read in the House the first time on the 6th of January, and the excitement in Omaha was so great that the majority of the Legislature either saw or feigned to see, imminent personal danger to themselves in the passage of such a bill. This apprehension led to a scheme on the part of the majority to adjourn the further sittings of the Legislature to Florence, some six miles away. It is now manifest that under the organic act of the Territory this was an unwise move on the part of the opponents of Omaha, for it is, to say the least, doubtful whether, under that act, even a two-thirds vote of the Legislature would have been sufficient to make the change without the assent of the Governor; and that the Governor, responsible to the general government, would not hazard his standing by giving his approval to such a law, might be reasonably inferred, even without any knowledge of his wishes or prejudices on the mere question of removal.

The vote to adjourn to Florence by the Council, its transmission to the House, the peculiarly unhandsome reception it met there, and the subsequent proceedings, were the subject of an investigation by both Houses, and the report of the joint committee is as follows:

Report of the Joint Committee of Investigation Appointed to Examine into the Causes and Consequences of the Difficulty in the Legislature of Nebraska, which occurred January 7th and 8th, 1858:

"*To the President of the Council and Speaker of the House of Representatives:*

"Your joint committee, to whom was referred the subject matter of the late disturbances in the Legislative Assembly of Nebraska, and the investigation of the causes of the precipitous exodus of a majority of the members thereof to Florence have had the same under consideration, and beg leave to report as follows

"Your committee deeply deplore the unfortunate circumstances which have rendered such a report necessary, but justice to the people of the Territory at large and to the minority of the members of the Legislative Assembly, demands that the responsibility in this matter be fixed where it properly belongs

' We hold that minority to be guiltless of wrong in the premises and submit the sworn statements of disinterested and reliable men as the basis for our opinion and invite for them a candid and careful consideration

"The charge of having deliberately and premeditately broken up the sitting of the Legislature, paralyzed its action and prevented the transaction of all legitimate legislation, is a grave and serious one, but solemnly and seriously we make it holding the majority to a just responsibility for what we are compelled to regard its unwarranted and revolutionary course

' We are unable to find any palliation or excuse for its action So far as we have been enabled to procure the facts in the progress of our investigation, the minority at no time asserted or attempted to exercise rights which did not clearly and unquestionably belong to them, and for which they had not the authority of precedent and undisputed parliamentary laws

"That the House was properly and regularly in committee of the whole when the difficulty occurred there can be no doubt, the Chairman having been nominated by a member of the majority and elected by the House

"That it could in that condition receive a message from the Council, is true, and that the House, sitting as such, could not receive a message from the Council while that body was not in session is equally true This was all as we understand it, that the minority claimed—the fact having been made known to the satisfaction of the Speaker that the Council was not in session, and that, consequently, under the rules of the House no message from it could be received But even had the facts been different, the conduct of the majority was unwarranted and unjustifiable, since no motion was made that the committee rise and report their proceedings to the House In derogation as we conceive, of all parliamentary law and all rules of order and decorum, Mr Decker attempted to take possession of the Speaker's chair by force, and his intended violence only prevented by the interference of Messrs Murphy and Paddock It does not appear to the committee that any demonstrations of violence or force were made or offered on the part of the minority, but that their efforts were confined to an attempt to prevent it, and to restore order and decorum, that the business of the House might be proceeded with

' We are forced to conclude that the action of the majority was unwarranted and revolutionary, without the sanction of law or precedent and without pretext or excuse With a full knowledge of the consequences of their acts they have not only violently broken up the law-making power of the Territory, and left the people without redress except at the ballot-box, but they have inaugurated anarchy destroyed the public peace, trampled upon and disregarded the public interests and fastened a stigma of disgrace upon a public reputation hitherto unblemished It is not for us to pass that public judgment upon their conduct which it merits, but to the wisdom of a people whom they have so shamefully outraged, we submit the facts, confident that justice will be meted out and responsibility lodged where it properly belongs

"The minority have remained at their posts from day to day, ready and anxious, as the facts disclose, to consummate the important legislation which the best interests of the Territory demand, but their action is paralyzed by the persistent and unjustifiable course of the majority Under these circumstances, all business has been frustrated, and the Territory robbed of that legislation which is so much needed and to which she was entitled at the hands of the majority by whom she has been so shamefully outraged and so dastardly betrayed

"In regard to the occurrence in the House which is made the pretext upon the part of the majority for abandoning their posts of duty the proof herewith submitted clearly shows it to have been precipitated by the design or folly of the Speaker Indeed, there is evidence of a premeditated design upon the part of the majority to obtain the possession of the chair by force, that they repaired to the House on the afternoon of the 7th with a determination to carry out such design and that the occurrence which then took place was the consequence This course on the part of the majority is the more extraordinary from the fact that the subject-matter under discussion at the time in the committee of the whole (the election of a printer), was comparatively of an unimportant character in no respect calculated to excite unusual feeling or arouse the passions This, together with the facts elicited by the testimony affords strong ground for the belief—which your committee would otherwise be reluctant to entertain—that the course pursued by the majority was in accordance with a predetermined plan to break up and disorganize the Legislature. We are further strengthened in this conclusion from the fact, that while it is not pretended that anything had occurred in the Council to disturb its deliberations, yet the majority of that body saw fit to adjourn to Florence, without any joint action by resolution with the other House.

"Your committee are reluctant to make these charges against a class of men with whom they have acted in a representative capacity on behalf of a common constituency, but we cannot shrink from the performance of a responsible duty, however unpleasant it may be, and relying upon the adequacy of the testimony upon which their conclusions are based, they beg leave to submit it for your consideration and as a part of this report.

Council
{
A. F. SALISBURY, Douglas County.
S. E. ROGERS, Douglas County.
CHAS. McDONALD, Pawnee County.
A. W. PUETT, Dakota County.
}

House
{
J. STERLING MORTON, Otoe County.
J. S. MINICK, Nemaha County.
A. F. CROMWELL, Richardson County.
J. VAN HORN, Cass County.
J. W. PADDOCK, Douglas County.
}

A portion of the testimony taken, which is entitled, "Testimony taken before the joint committee appointed by the Council and House of Representatives, in relation to the secession of certain members from the Fourth Legislative Assembly of Nebraska," is as follows:

JOHN C. TURK, sworn: My name is John C. Turk, aged twenty-six years; reside at Dakota City; am Receiver of Public Moneys in the Dakota Land District. I was present in the hall of the House of Representatives on Thursday, January 7th, 1858. I occupied a seat close to the Speaker's stand at the time the difficulty occurred; the House was in Committee of the Whole on the public printing; Dr. Thrall, of Douglas County, was in the chair; Mr. Clayes, of Douglas, had the floor; Mr. Decker, the Speaker, was promenading the floor with his cap on, conferring with the members with the view of taking the chair by force, as it was understood at that time; a message from the Council was announced; Mr. Poppleton got up and read from the rules of the House, having first inquired whether the Council was in session, and being answered that it was not, made the remark that no message could be received. Mr. Speaker Decker marched up to the stand took hold of the gavel in the hands of Dr Thrall; said he was Speaker of the House, and declared it adjourned, remarking soon after that he would bear the message from the Council or die right there; he asked Dr. Thrall to give up the chair; the doctor refused; Mr. Decker drew the gavel in a threatening manner in his right hand, and with his left took hold of the Speaker's chair, and endeavored to force Mr. Thrall forcibly out; at that stage of the proceedings Mr. Murphy caught hold of his right arm and the gavel, pulled him down on the floor of the House; about that time Mr. Paddock also caught hold of him; there was a great deal of confusion; a number of members rushed forward, and Mr. Hanscom rushed in, took Mr. Decker out of the hands of Murphy and Paddock, and rolled him under the table, after which Dr. Thrall, Chairman of the Committee succeeded in restoring order, and Mr. Clayes proceeded with his remarks. Mr. Speaker Decker, and others who were acting with him, endeavored to interrupt the business of the Committee by remarks, sneers and threats; Mr. Decker had his cap on at the time; treated the Chairman and Committee with contempt; promenading around the hall and whistling; and when ordered to take off his cap and desist by the Chairman, he refused; soon after Mr. Decker and his friends withdrew, and the business of the Committee was regularly gone through with; Mr. Morton was elected Speaker *pro tem.*, prior to which Mr. Morton requested the lobby to withdraw, stating that he had heard that the House was unable to do business on account of lobby influence; in obedience to which request every member of the lobby at once withdrew. Upon the election of Mr. Morton Speaker *pro tem.*, the Committee reported through their Chairman. Dr. Thrall. The House then adjourned. Up to the time of Mr. Speaker Decker's attempt to take the Chair, there had been no disturbance, and the Committee was proceeding regularly and in order. I saw no disposition or attempt on the part of any member of the lobby to interfere, and no attempt on the part of the minority in the House to do anything more than to restore order.

*Int.*—You have spoken of Mr. Hanscom. Was he within the bar at the time of this occurrence?

*Ans.*—I had not seen Mr. Hanscom until after the assault of Mr. Decker upon the Chairman of the Committee. Mr. Hanscom was an ex-member, and as such entitled to a seat within the bar.

*Int.*—With what apparent intention did Mr. Hanscom take hold of Mr. Decker?

*Ans* —I think Mr Hanscom's intention was to separate Mr Decker from Messrs Murphy and Paddock, which he did do

*Int* —Was there any interference or attempt at interference by any one not a member of the House and if so by whom ?

*Ans* —Judge Kinney, of Nebraska City standing upon a desk attempted to make a speech not being a member he was refused a hearing by the Chairman there being a great deal of confusion, I could not hear what he said

W R THRALL, sworn  I am a citizen of Omaha City aged twenty-eight years, am a practicing physician am a member of the House of Representatives from Douglas County was in the House on Thursday, January 7th 1858 pending the reading of the journal on that morning a discussion arose on a point of order which continued until 10 o'clock at which hour the House had by motion determined to go into Committee of the Whole on a special order—the joint resolution in relation to public printer, the House accordingly resolved itself into Committee of the Whole  Mr Strickland in the Chair, Mr Poppleton had the floor  Mr Strickland shortly after desiring to discuss the question, called Mr Armstrong to the Chair, Mr Armstrong declined  Mr Strickland then called upon Mr Morton of Otoe, who took the Chair, Mr Poppleton then raised the question whether the Chairman had the power to call upon another member to take the Chair  whereupon Mr Strickland standing in front of the Speaker's stand nominated Mr Morton who was elected by acclamation  Mr Strickland putting the question  Mr Poppleton continued his remarks which were of a humorous and good-natured character, he was occasionally interrupted by Mr Strickland, who approached him and made suggestions in a whisper, which I did not hear—but which appeared to be of a friendly character, as both were laughing at the time  After Mr Poppleton had been speaking a half hour or more  Mr Strickland and others left the hall, after which Mr Decker interrupted Mr Poppleton, and raised the point of order that there was not a quorum present and moved that the Committee rise  The Chairman ruled that a motion could not be entertained while a member occupied the floor  Mr Decker then advanced toward the Chair, and remarked that the Committee could not sit when there was not a quorum present  The Chairman decided Mr Decker out of order, and ruled that Mr Poppleton had the floor and should proceed  Mr Morton continued in the Chair until after one o'clock P M, when I was nominated and elected to take the Chair

Mr Poppleton yielded the floor to Mr Clayes at half past 1 or 2 o'clock  Mr Clayes continued speaking, and was on the floor when the Sergeant-at-Arms announced a message from the Council, Mr Decker rose from his seat and approached the Chair to receive the message, when Mr Poppleton inquired of the Clerk of the Council if the Council was in session, which question was answered in the negative  He protested against the message being received, as the rules provided that no message from one House to the other should be received, unless both Houses were in session  The Speaker continued to advance, mounted the rostrum, and declared in excited manner that "he would have that message or die right here," and as he spoke, snatched from my hand the gavel  Up to this time no demonstration of violence had been made from any quarter, except from the Speaker Mr Decker, as before stated  Upon his taking the gavel and making the declaration he did at the time, a scene of great confusion ensued, at this point Mr Decker grasped the arm of the Speaker's chair in which I was sitting, and commenced tipping the same, ordering me at the same time to leave  Mr Murphy then grasped the Speaker's right arm, and pulled him out of the stand on the floor of the House, I still retaining my seat  While Mr Decker and Mr Murphy were scuffling on the floor, Mr Paddock rushed in to the aid of Mr Murphy, all three holding on to the gavel  Mr Hanscom advanced behind Mr Decker, took hold of him, and rolled him under the table releasing him from the grasp of Murphy and Paddock  While this scene was occurring I was endeavoring, as Chairman of the Committee to maintain order using a copy of Swan's Revised Statutes for the purpose in the absence of the gavel  After Mr Decker got upon his feet he declared the committee dissolved, and the House adjourned, while Mr Clayes had the floor, having continued to speak during the entire melee  Mr Kinney, of Nebraska City, was called upon by Mr Decker and his friends to speak and, standing upon a desk he attempted to do so  but not being a member of the House was ordered by me to take his seat which he did  Mr Decker and his friends at that time and subsequent thereto, were walking about the floor with their hats on, endeavoring to create as much disturbance as possible  Order being finally restored Mr Morton requested the lobby to withdraw which they immediately did  After the lobby was thus cleared, Mr Clayes yielded the floor to Mr Morton, of Otoe, who moved that the committee rise and report progress, and ask leave to sit again, which was carried. The Speaker having left the House, Mr. Poppleton nominated Mr. Morton Speaker *pro tem.* and put the motion, which was carried, and thereupon Mr. Morton took the chair and received the report of the committee, which was adopted; and then, upon motion, the House adjourned. On the morning of the 8th the House assembled as usual, Mr. Decker in the chair. After prayer by the Chaplain, Mr. Donelan, of Cass, sprang to his feet and moved that the House adjourn to meet in Florence to-morrow, the 9th, at 10 o'clock A. M., which, being seconded by Mr. Cooper, I think the Speaker put it in a hurried manner and declared it carried ; whereupon he, with twenty-one other members, took their hats and left the hall. During the confusion of leaving Mr. Morton, of Otoe, nominated Mr. Poppleton Speaker *pro tem,* which, being seconded and carried, Mr. Poppleton took the chair; the remaining members continued in their seats, and have assembled and adjourned from day to day regularly since, up to the present time, doing little or no business except to appoint a committee to investigate the matter in reference to which I am now testifying.

DANIEL H. NELSON sworn : I reside in Omaha City ; age 29 years. I was present at the Douglas House on Thursday, January 7th, 1858. between the hours of 1 and 5 o'clock P. M. Mr. Strickland and other members of the House of Representatives, and other persons were there at the same time. Mr. Decker came in and stated to Mr. Strickland that he was going up to take his seat in the chair. Mr. Strickland said : "We do not want it this afternoon—let them talk against time ; to-morrow morning we can get the chair. Mr. Decker said, in substance, "I am going to have it this afternoon or die trying." Mr. Strickland made some remark to dissuade him from the attempt, and when Mr. Decker insisted, said, "There are twenty-three with you." Either Strickland or Decker remarked, " Let us go up stairs and talk the matter over." I then made up my mind, from what had been said, that there would be a fuss and went up to the capitol. When I got there Mr. Clayes was speaking. About ten minutes before Mr. Decker came I got within the bar. I was present during the time of the melee. I have read the testimony of Dr. Thrall and find it correct according to my observation. I was prompted by curiosity merely in going to the House ; did not intend to interfere and did not do so. Saw Dr. Rankin, Marshal of the Territory, endeavoring to assist the Chairman in preserving order; did not notice any attempt on the part of persons in the lobby to interfere. They seemed desirous merely, as I and others were, to get nearer to the scene to gratify their curiosity. I saw the whole of the performance, excepting the throwing down of Mr. Decker, and I fully corroborate the statements of Dr. Thrall.

Sterrett M. Curran, Chief Clerk of the House of Representatives, corroborated the statements already given, and added that during the session of the committee he met Mr. Welsh in the hall of the capitol and was told by him that there was a caucus in the unoccupied room set apart for the Governor's room. That he entered the room and there met a majority of the members of the House in consultation about getting the chair by some peaceable and legal method. That upon being asked his opinion he told them that in his opinion the only method of getting possession of the chair, was for some member friendly to them to get the floor, and move for the committee to rise, assuring them that they had the necessary votes to carry the motion. He also testified that he stated to them that one means was by getting a message from the Council, but that as the Council was not in session, if there were any objections raised it could not be received.

Messrs. Wm. Larimer Jr., Charles W. Cox, John Rickley, William F. Wilder, James Smith Jr., Robert A. Howard, J. McF. Hagood, Joel T. Griffen, Charles McDonald, George A. Graves and Jackson Barrett gave similar testimony and all concurred in the declaration, that during the session the most scrupulous order and decorum had been preserved ; and that up to the moment the majority of the Council adjourned to Florence, no disturbance had occurred in the Council Chamber, nor had its members been in any respect interfered with in the discharge of their duties. This testimony was designed to meet allegations of the other side, that owing to the actions of the disorderly lobby they were unable to transact their business with composure.

The seceding members of both Houses met pursuant to adjournment at Florence, and made application to acting Governor T. B. Cuming for the journals and papers belonging to their respective houses. The following is the text of the resolution:

*Be it Resolved by the Council and House of Representatives of the Territory of Nebraska,* That a joint committee, to be composed of one member of the Council and two members of the House of Representatives be appointed to wait upon His Excellency the Governor, and inform him that the journals, bills and papers belonging to the Legislature have been placed by persons without its sanction, beyond the control of their respective

## THE FLORENCE LEGISLATURE REPUDIATED.

bodies, and that amongst them are several bills of great importance to the welfare of the Territory, now nearly perfected, among which is an act providing the Criminal Code, a Homestead bill, a Revenue bill, a Fee bill, and various other bills which may become laws if legitimate legislation be not further interrupted by the illegal acts of irresponsible persons, who are in possession of such bills journals and other papers, and that therefore he be respectfully requested to issue an order and to enforce the same, for the immediate delivery of such papers to said committee for the Legislature

This resolution having been presented to Governor Cuming by the committee, Messrs Reeves, Hail and Taggart, was responded to as follows

EXECUTIVE OFFICE, NEBRASKA TERRITORY,
OMAHA, January 9th, 1858

*Messrs Reeves, Hail and Taggart*

GENTLEMEN I have received from you a communication purporting to be a "Resolution of the Council and House of Representatives of the Territory of Nebraska"

The General Assembly of the Territory is now in session according to law at Omaha City, the seat of government, where the executive office is required to be kept, and where the public documents and records must be preserved The communication furnished by you is not from that body but was sent from the town of Florence, to which place a portion of the members of each House have adjourned

My convictions, under the law and facts are clear—that no act of such recusant members can be legal Under such circumstances any communication from them as a legislative body will not require the official attention from this department Respectfully

T B CUMING,
Acting Governor of Nebraska

On the 11th day of January, 1858, Messrs Bowen, Campbell and Donelan were appointed a committee to wait upon Governor Richardson, who had arrived in Omaha, and present the following communication

*Be it Resolved by the Council and House of Representatives of the Territory of Nebraska, that,*

WHEREAS, It is understood that his Excellency, the Governor of the Territory, Hon William A Richardson has arrived at Omaha City, then be it

*Resolved,* That a joint committee consisting of one member of the Council and two of the House, be appointed to wait upon his Excellency, and inform him that the Council and House of Representatives of the Territory of Nebraska are now in session at Florence, having been forced to adjourn to that, the nearest place of safety, by the disorganizing and turbulent acts of a minority of their own body, aided by the violence of an unrestrained mob at Omaha, causing a well-grounded apprehension as to the personal safety of the majority, and requesting his Excellency to communicate with the Legislature at this place, at his earliest convenience

On the day following the presentation of this communication Governor Richardson sent to the committee the following reply, which, as will be seen, was a stern rebuke to the majority of the Legislature

GENTLEMEN I received from you on yesterday the following resolution [Here follows the resolution above quoted ]

I deem it my duty under existing circumstances, as an act of courtesy from me to you as members of the Legislative Assembly of Nebraska, to state frankly that looking at the question as a mere legal one, I cannot recognize that portion of the members of the Legislature now assembled at Florence as the Council and House of Representatives of this Territory

By reference to the Organic Act Section 13, it will be seen that the power to locate and establish the seat of government is conferred upon the ' Governor and Legislative Assembly " Under that authority Omaha City, Douglas County was determined upon as said seat of government by an act of the Territorial Legislature, approved January 30th, 1855 Omaha City must then continue to be the only legal place of holding the sessions of the Legislature, unless some other place is fixed upon by the joint action of the Governor and Legislative Assembly

I have been unable to find any enactment upon the statute books of the Territory making such change, and in its absence the Legislature can only transact its business legally at Omaha City, Douglas County But should it be insisted that this change is but temporary, and not designed as a removal of the seat of government even then, if I have been properly informed, the proceeding is not authorized by law I understand the following to be the facts

The House of Representatives, without reference to the action of the Council, or the approval of the Governor, upon a mere motion, adjourned to meet at Florence The Council, also, independent of the House and the Executive adjourned to meet at the same place If now I should recognize the meeting at Florence as the Legislative Assembly of the Territory, what is the doctrine which I endorse? Is it not that either branch of the Legislature, without the concurrent action of the other, has power to adjourn, to meet at any place it may select—a doctrine the establishment of which, might at some future day present the strange spectacle of a Council at one place, the House at another, and the Executive at still another place.

I cannot endorse a doctrine from the operation of which such consequences might result.

Without inquiring into or expressing an opinion upon transactions said to have taken place prior to my arrival in the Territory, I deem it sufficient for me to say that at the Capitol is the place of your right and your duty as legislators; and having entered upon the discharge of the functions of the Executive office, I am prepared to guarantee that no act of violence by any man, or set of men, will be perpetrated upon the rights or persons of members of the Legislature, while in the discharge of their duties as such. The fullest and most ample protection is warranted to freedom in discussion, and independence in action.

The public necessity requires that the Legislature should proceed to business and perform its appropriate duties. It would be exceedingly gratifying therefore to me, if you would return to the Capitol, accept the protection which it is my duty and pleasure to tender to the representatives of the people, and by just and needful legislation, relieve the citizens of the Territory from the apprehension of being left for another year without sufficient laws for that absolute protection which is guaranteed by the Constitution of the United States.

I need scarcely add, gentlemen, that no one regrets so sincerely as I do the necessity which compels me, upon the first assumption of the duties of my office, to differ with a majority of the members of the Legislative Assembly: nothing but a conviction so clear as to leave no doubt upon my mind would induce me to take upon myself so great a responsibility, but when the line of duty is so plainly marked, I should be faithless to the trust confided in me if I should for a moment falter or hesitate.

I have the honor to be, gentlemen,
Your obedient servant,
W. A. RICHARDSON.

Notwithstanding this rebuke, however, the seceding members continued their sessions at Florence, and even went through the form of passing an act by which the Territorial Capital was removed from Omaha, and a commission appointed to re-locate it. But no formal record exists of this action, for no money was available for the purpose of printing, or even for the pay of members thus absenting themselves. Mr. Poppleton had been elected Speaker of the House in place of Mr. Decker, drawing as such double the pay of a mere member, while Mr. Decker, the first Speaker, was obliged to content himself with the empty honor of presiding over an unrecognized body. Mr. Byron Reed is authority for the statement that Mr. Poppleton was oppressed, or feigned to be so, by the feeling that this extra compensation so coming to him, was not his by right. There stood at that time, and long afterwards, a two-story brick edifice on the south side of Douglas Street,

THE OLD CAPITOL BUILDING.

between Fourteenth and Fifteenth Streets, which was known as the Hamilton House, an inn of no mean pretensions, the favorite social resort of citizens. To the dining room of this hotel Mr. Poppleton invited all those who in the controversy of the session had shown themselves friendly to the interests of Omaha, and the festivities that ensued, enabled him without difficulty before morning, to relieve himself from any anxiety as to his having in his possession any money which rightfully belonged to another.

The contemporaneous views entertained of this singular escapade by its participants, and those directly interested in it, may perhaps be most satisfactorily shown by two documents which were printed during the controversy. The first is a manifesto, issued at Florence, the 9th of January, 1858, by the seceding members, and printed for general distribution as a circular

TO THE PEOPLE OF NEBRASKA—FELLOW CITIZENS The General Assembly of the Nebraska Territory is no longer able to discharge its legitimate functions at the Omaha seat of government Owing to the organized combination of a minority of its members aided by an Omaha mob and encouraged by the Omaha Executive they have been compelled to adjourn their present session to the nearest place of safety They accordingly assemble to-day at Florence, pursuant to adjournment

The sovereign power of legislation for this Territory is now exercised alone at this place The House of Representatives, J H Decker Speaker, retains twenty-four of its thirty-five members The Council, L L Bowen President, retains nine of the thirteen members, being two-thirds of their respective bodies

It has long been supposed that whenever the interests of Omaha became concerned, it became hazardous to attempt legislation at Omaha The course of the minority during the whole session has been characterized by tricks and chicanery, unworthy a manly system of legislation It culminated in violence on the 7th instant On that day the factionists allied with Omaha ruffians, dragged the Speaker of the House by force from his stand while attempting to discharge his duties and the Omaha mob armed and ready for any emergency applauded the foul act—affixing to Nebraska legislation an indelible stain, and covering the fair name of Omaha with ineffaceable INFAMY

Omaha can boast of having degraded the sovereignty of the people by thus exposing the person of her elected representative to the unresisted violence of an irresponsible rabble'

Omaha can boast of having arrested the wheels of legislation at the Capital!'

Omaha can boast of having driven the Legislature from the seat of government

Yet Omaha still retains the Capital, bought with such an infamous past of corruption violence and crime but the sceptre of legislation has departed from the ill-fated city, and the law givers from its riotous halls forever

The issue now made by Omaha with the squatter sovereigns of the whole Territory can have but ONE solution'

The interests and the rights of the whole of the masses will no longer be made subservient to the intrigues or machinations of one locality It is no longer a question as to the location of the city of their government merely It has now become a question as to the right of the people to rule' It can have but ONE answer—*the majority must prevail*

The Legislature is now free from faction and from violence Its acts will be free and untrammeled It will finish out its organization at this place zealously devoted to the legitimate legislation required by the wants of the public and the interests of the Territory, and if such honest efforts shall fail of consummation, they will leave the whole responsibility with the accidental Executive, who, albeit not elected by or responsible to the people, while clothed in a little brief authority, in the absence of the Governor, *may* dare to thwart their sovereign will'

For the full justification of our course we confidently appeal to our own *constituencies*, to whom alone we acknowledge responsibility

The members of the House who signed the foregoing manifesto, were the Speaker, James H Decker, Messrs J G Abbe, W B Beck, W G Crawford, J C Campbell, S A Chambers, P G Cooker, E A Donelan, James Davidson, Joseph Van Horn, Amos Gates, W B Hail, C T Holloway, Wingate King, T M Marquette, D B Robb, P M Rogers, J S Stewart, L Sheldon, S A Strickland, J M Taggart A J. Benedict, and Alonzo Perkins While the senators affixing their names were the President, Leavitt L Bowen, and Messrs. Mills S Reeves, James S Allen, Jacob Safford, A A Bradford, S M Kirkpatrick, William Clancy, R W Furnas and A. W. Puett

The Omaha side of the question may be gleaned from the headlines of an extra issued by the *Omaha Nebraskian* on the 8th of January, 1858 These are as follows

BORDER RUFFIANISM IN NEBRASKA!
KANSAS OUTDONE"
BOLD ATTEMPT AT REVOLUTION'''
SPEAKER DECKER HEADING THE REVOLUTION''''
REVOLUTIONISTS TO ORGANIZE ANOTHER GOVERNMENT AT FLORENCE UNDER THE PROTECTION OF BRIGHAM YOUNG'''''

The *Nebraska Pioneer*, a newspaper published at Cuming City, in Washington

County, gives the following account of the scene in the House, and of an occurrence which preceded it, as follows:

"Then commenced a scene which places border ruffianism far in the shade. One of the members from our county (Mr. Perkins) was rudely assaulted by two prominent citizens of Omaha, and it is with deep regret that we state that one of these *gentlemen* was a member of the Council. The war was now fairly open—Omaha against the Territory. All manner of means was used to stave off the bill, but the minority not being able to stave it off any longer at that time 'condescended' to allow it to be read the first time, which being done the House adjourned.

"Thursday morning the House convened as usual and went into committee of the whole on the election of a public printer, Mr. Strickland in the chair. Mr. Strickland wishing to make some remarks on the question, called Morton to the chair; the minority then boasted that they had the chair and would keep in committee of the whole the balance of the session unless the majority would agree to withdraw the capital bill. Mr. Poppleton getting the floor, commenced his famous speech against time; he spoke of all conceivable subjects except public printing, beginning as far back as Gulliver's famous history of the Lilliputian war. The lobbies were crowded and Mr. Poppleton was loudly applauded by the Omaha lobby members. Leaving to get something to eat, the editor of the *Pioneer* on his return found Dr. Thrall, of Omaha, in the chair and Mr. Clayes on the floor. Mr. Clayes asserted that it did not much matter what he said as he had to talk nine days.

"About this time a message was received and the Speaker went to the stand to receive it. Hanscom rushed to the Speaker and dragged him from the chair and after some scuffling threw him violently under a table."

Upon the whole the anti-Omaha men seem to have had the advantage in the newspaper warfare, but the citizens of Omaha could well afford to concede this advantage, having the acting Governor and the new Governor on their side. Nor can it well be doubted that under the guidance of sharp and active tacticians, the city managed throughout to have parliamentary law on her side, and that the move to Florence was a fatal one for her opponents.

But the struggle for the removal of the capital from Omaha was continued, year after year, until, in 1867, it culminated in the appointment, by the Legislature, of Governor David Butler, Secretary of State Thomas P. Kennard and Auditor John Gillespie as a Board of Commissioners to re-locate Nebraska's seat of government. The present site of the City of Lincoln was chosen, and from that date Omaha has been relieved of what had been for a dozen years a source of bitter strife and turmoil.

The following is Nebraska's list of Governors:

FRANCIS BURT, Democrat, appointed October 16, 1854.
MARK W. IZARD, Democrat, appointed February 20. 1855.
WILLIAM A. RICHARDSON, Democrat, appointed January 12, 1858.
SAMUEL W. BLACK, Democrat, appointed May 2, 1858.
ALVIN SAUNDERS. Republican, appointed May 15 1861.
DAVID BUTLER. Republican. elected, term began February 21. 1867; re-elected in 1868 and 1870; impeached and removed in 1871; and unexpired term filled by W. H. JAMES. Secretary of State.
ROBERT W. FURNAS, Republican, elected 1872.
SILAS GARBER, Republican, elected 1874 and re-elected 1876.
ALBINUS NANCE, Republican, elected 1878 and re-elected 1880.
JAMES W. DAWES, Republican, elected 1882 and re-elected 1884.
JOHN M. THAYER, Republican, elected 1886 and re-elected 1888.
JAMES E. BOYD, Democrat. elected 1890.

At Washington, Nebraska has been represented at various times by Omaha men. The first Delegate to Congress, Hon. Bird Chapman, was a resident of this city. The second, Judge Fenner Ferguson, was a resident of the county. The fifth, Hon. P. W. Hitchcock—also elected Senator in 1871—resided here; Hon. John M. Thayer, Mr. Hitchcock's predecessor in the United States Senate, was one of Omaha's pioneers. Hon. Alvin Saunders, elected Senator in 1877, was then and is yet a citizen of Omaha. Hon. Charles F. Manderson, now serving his second term in the United States Senate, resides here; Hon. John A. McShane, elected to the House of Representatives in 1886, has long been a resident of this city, as has also his successor, Hon. William J. Connell, whose term expired March 4, 1891.

Douglas County Court House.

# CHAPTER IX

DOUGLAS COUNTY—WASHINGTON SQUARE—THE NEW COURT HOUSE—COUNTY OFFICIALS, DISTRICT JUDGES AND LEGISLATORS

Douglas is one of the original counties, eight in number, created by Acting Governor Thomas B Cuming in 1854, and until February 7th, 1857, included the present County of Sarpy within its limits It contains about 321 square miles, with abundance of water, and a soil of unsurpassed fertility The early importance assumed by Omaha resulted in the land in the eastern part of the county being purchased by speculators as soon as the title could be secured from the general government, and for twenty years following but little improvement was made thereon, as farmers and stock-raisers could buy excellent land a few miles farther west, north or south for much less money The past ten years, however, have witnessed great changes in this respect, and now Douglas County will compare favorably with any other in the State, as regards the development of stock-raising, agriculture and fruit-growing resources

The first white settlers in the immediate vicinity of the present site of Omaha were the Mormons, who located six miles above, in 1845 and 1846, when driven out of Nauvoo, Illinois This settlement was first called "Winter Quarters," and the name afterwards changed to Florence It was from this point that the expedition was sent out in 1847, under the leadership of Brigham Young, to seek a location for the "New Zion," which resulted in the settlement of the Mormons in Utah, which country they first named "Deseret," and under that title soon after sought admission to the Union of States

When the county was organized, the following county officials were appointed Probate Judge, William Scott, Register of Deeds, Lyman Richardson, Treasurer, T G Goodwill, Sheriff, P. G. Peterson At an election held October 8th, 1856, Jesse Lowe, Thomas Davis and James H McArdle were elected Commissioners, Samuel Moffatt, Treasurer, Thomas O'Connor, Register, and Cameron Reeve, Sheriff Moffatt failed to qualify, and George W Forbes was elected Treasurer January 16th, 1857

The records were kept very carelessly in those days, hence the official doings of our county officers cannot be traced further back than the month of December, 1856, on the 27th day of which month it was decided to levy a tax of two mills on the dollar in order to provide funds for building a court house and jail, and at a special meeting was held March 13th, 1857, the following was spread upon the records

Articles of agreement made and entered into the 18th day of March, 1857, at the City of Omaha, in the Territory of Nebraska, by and between the City Council of Omaha of the first part, and the County Commissioners of the County of Douglas, and Territory of Nebraska, of the second part witnesseth That the said party of the first part, in consideration of the covenants and agreement hereinafter made by the party of the second part, doth hereby agree to, and with the party of the second part that they will and do from and after this date, lease and forever let and convey and relinquish to the said party of the second part, all right title to, and interest in, that parcel of ground known as the Washington Square and so marked and named on the plat of Omaha City, surveyed and platted by A D Jones, to the said party of the second part and their successors forever, for the uses and purposes of a court house and jail in the County of Douglas, Territory of Nebraska, and said County Commissioners are hereby authorized and empowered to give deeds for the said lots to any and all persons purchasing any part of said Washington Square, except 132 feet square of the southwest corner of said square, to be used for the purpose of building said court house and jail thereon but for no other purpose. without the consent of the City Council of Omaha. and when the said party of the second part shall cease to use said property as a court house and jail, then the said property so used for a court house and jail, viz: 132 feet square of the southwest corner of said Washington Square as above. together with all the buildings thereon, to revert to the party of the first part, and the title to rest in the party of the first part as though the agreement conveying the same to the said party of the second part had never been made. And the said party of the second part in consideration of the foregoing covenants and agreements on the part of the party of the first part, doth hereby agree to and with the said party of the first part that they will build a good and sufficient jail and court house for the County of Douglas, and will furnish to the party of the first part four rooms in said building which is to be constructed after the plan and specification drawn by E. C. Barker, one room suitable for a Council room and Mayor's Court Room, one for a City Recorder's office and two for watch houses, or for such other purposes as the Council may direct, said rooms to be completed by the 1st of January, 1858.

This paper was signed by T. G. Goodwill and William N. Byers on the part of the city, and by Jesse Lowe and Thomas Davis on behalf of the county.

The work of erecting the building was pushed rapidly for a time, the contract for the brick and iron work being let to Bovie & Armstrong for $25,000.00; for the carpenter, tinwork, painting and glazing to James E. Boyd & Brother (John M. Boyd) at $11,975.00; the plastering to Hunt & Manning at $1,975.00, and the stone work to John Green at $1,510.00. The building was two stories high, 40x70 feet, with a stone foundation of ten feet, which afforded a basement six feet high, the height of the building from the top of the water table to the top of the cornice being 35 feet.

In April, 1857, there was a public sale of lots in Washington Square (bounded by Farnam, Douglas, Fifteenth and Sixteenth), with the following result: George M. Mills bought the east 22 feet of lot 8 (northwest corner of Farnam and Fifteenth) for $1,140; H. H. Visscher purchased the 22 feet next adjoining on the west for $960 and the remaining third of lot 8 was sold to Dr. G. C. Monell and J. S. Izard for $890. The east 44 feet of lot 1 (southwest corner of Douglas and Fifteenth) was sold to W. R. Demerest for $1,905 (this ground, including a two-story brick building, sold in 1887 for $85,000) and the west 22 feet of lot 1 was purchased by J. S. Izard for $975, making the total amount received by the county from the two lots, $5,690, of which $1,896.65 was paid in cash and the balance in notes, one-half payable in three and the remainder in six months.

The following June the remainder of the property was offered at auction, when one Nicholls bought the east 22 feet of lot 7, (now occupied by the Merchant's Hotel) for $400; John H. Shahler paid $1,020 for the west 44 feet of said lot; the east 22 feet of lot 2, (fronting on Douglas and now covered with a portion of Falconer's store) and the west 22 feet of lot 3 were bought by W. A. Collins for $960; the middle 22 feet of lot 2 was sold to M. Rudowsky for $445; the west 22 feet of 2 and the east 44 feet of lot 3 were bought by T. Martin for $1,420, and lot 4 was sold to J. J. Brown and W. F. Sweesy for $1,425. It is on the west half of this lot that Mr. Brown has recently erected a magnificent stone business block at a cost of $150,000. The total amount realized from this sale was $5,670, of which $1,890.05 was paid in cash and notes were given payable in two and four months for the remainder. Thus these six lots were sold in 1857, and before the financial disaster of that year, at a period of great prosperity for Omaha, for $11,360. To-day the ground, stripped of buildings, would be a bargain at $600,000.

The money thus obtained was put into the

court house fund, the work on that building having dragged slowly for lack of means On the 4th of January, 1858, Commissioner Davis was empowered to present to the city the four rooms which had been finished in pursuance of the agreement of March 18th 1857 But a question arose as to the rights of the city in that respect, the outcome of which was that the city was adjudged to have no ownership in the building, as the deed to the county, made January 10th, 1859, signed by George Armstrong, Mayor, was a clear transfer without conditions of any kind In later years, however the city prisoners were confined in two of the basement rooms In July, 1861, John Davis was awarded the contract to complete the court house for $1,336, and in November of that year the Presbyterian Society was granted permission to hold services in the court room on Sundays, at a rental of $50 for the year A Mr Bruning, applying to the Commissioners for the privilege of giving a public ball Christmas night, it was accorded him on condition that he pay ten dollars "in advance," and at the same time the County Clerk was authorized to rent the court room for evening meetings at a rental of "not less than two dollars" for each meeting A few days later that official reported the receipt of $23 from the Presbyterian Society and $20 for the use of the court room two nights for balls, and was instructed to use $33 75 of the money to "pay the express charges on a package of books addressed to the register of deeds," evidently held by the express company for want of funds to pay the charges

The assessed valuation of Douglas County in 1855 was $311,116, personalty and realty, in 1862, as shown by a report made to the Commissioners in June of that year, it was as follows Lands and town lots, $850,-941 33 Personalty, $352,990, Total, $1,203,-931 33 On this return a levy of three and a half mills was made for Territorial purposes, eleven mills for county tax and a poll tax of one dollar. The valuation for taxation for 1890 was Lands, $3,213,000 Lots, $16,909,-581 Personalty, $4 900,839 Total, $25,023,-420 The balance on hand in the county treasury January 1st, 1890, was $131,925 43 The last report printed by the County Commissioners was dated July 26, 1890, and brings the financial business of the county up to January 1st of that year The levy was 18 mills on the dollar.

In illustration of the financial straits through which the people of Nebraska were passing in those early days, may be mentioned the fact that in building the court house, the Commissioners signed one note for $3,000 and another for $1,000, and in September, 1862, a special election was called to vote upon a proposition to levy a tax of a half mill to provide a sinking fund for the payment of these notes The note for the larger sum was then drawing thirty per cent interest, and the other twenty per cent At the election 138 votes were cast in favor of the proposition, and none against In November of that year the assets of the county were shown to be $17,474 04, liabilities, $49,343 74, excess of liabilities over assets $31,869 70.

The record of the Commissioners' proceedings for July 2d 1866, shows that action was taken on an account presented by Joel T Griffin "for killing seven wolves," by the drawing of a warrant on the Territorial treasury "to pay for the same," but the market price of wolves at that time is not stated

In March, 1869, a resolution was adopted by the County Commissioners reciting that "the public interests will in a few years imperatively demand the erection of a new court house, jail and other county buildings and, *whereas*, the present site of the court house is wholly insufficient in and for the purpose aforesaid, and, *whereas*, it is deemed expedient that immediate action be taken to secure to the county ample grounds for the purposes above indicated," it was resolved, "that the owners of property in Omaha be, and they are hereby invited to make propositions to convey to the county not less than two acres of ground for the purpose aforesaid, in some convenient and acceptable location, and that such proposition be received until the 1st day of May, 1869." Evidently there was a dearth, at that time, of property owners holding ground by the acre within the city limits, as there is no further reference made to the matter in the Commissioners' records.

In April, 1869, a resolution was offered providing for the enclosing and improving of forty acres of the county farm. Commissioners Gise and Eicke voted in favor of the resolution, but Chapman opposed it "for the reason that a case is now pending in the Circuit Court of the United States for the District of Nebraska against the county and in favor of William Arthur Esq., for the foreclosure of a certain mortgage upon the county farm, and it is inexpedient to expend any money in improving the said farm until said case is disposed of." The county farm of 160 acres, so valuable now, was purchased in 1859 by the Commissioners for either $6,000 or $7,000, which price also included a ten-acre timber tract south of Omaha, to which the title afterwards proved defective. As to whether the purchase price was the greater or less amount named depends upon how Douglas County warrants were rated at that time. The seller took, as cash payment of $1,000, warrants of the face value of double that sum, and so considered, he was getting $6,000 for the property, while the Commissioners called it a cash payment of $2,000, which brought the total up to $7,000, as notes to the amount of $5,000, secured by mortgage, were given for the balance of the purchase price. The Commissioners afterwards found that they could not legally bind the county in that manner, and of course refused to pay the notes when they became due, and suit was brought to recover possession of the property. In defense, the county, by its attorneys, John C. Cowin and James M. Woolworth, claimed that the failure of the title to the timber land rendered the sum actually received by the seller full value for the 160 acres, as land was then selling (a number of witnesses testifying it was worth only $10 an acre), and also pleaded the statute of limitation. The county won the case in the lower Court, but upon an appeal being to the Supreme Court of the United States, the verdict was set aside, and the county finally required to pay about $12,000 additional to acquire perfect title.

The project of improving the county farm was carried out, and in September, 1869, a contract was let with Reuben Barringer to erect a building thereon for $8,474, which was afterwards added to at various times, until a very comfortable and commodious structure was provided for the accommodation of the destitute of the county.

In 1878, the block bounded by Farnam, Harney, Seventeenth and Eighteenth, was purchased for a court house site at a cost of $35,913, and the following year the county jail was built on the south-west corner thereof, at an outlay of about $35,000. In November, 1880, an election was held to vote upon the proposition to issue bonds to the amount of $125,000 for the building of a court house, the total cost of which was to not exceed $150,000, which proposition carried by a vote of 3,550 for to 1,541 against. The plans of E. E. Meyers, of Detroit, Michigan, were accepted by the Commissioners, with the understanding that the cost of the building, including heating, would not exceed $139,000. There was some delay in getting to work, and the price of material increased somewhat meanwhile, and in November, 1881, another election was held to pass upon the proposition to authorize an expenditure of $198,000 instead of $150,000. To this the voters of the county assented, an additional $50,000 was voted, and the contract was awarded to John F. Coots, of Detroit, at $198,616. Certain changes were made in the plans, however, as the work progressed, and the total cost of the building was $204,787, exclusive of the cost of the retaining wall, which a change of grade on surrounding streets rendered necessary. D. L. Shane was employed by the county as superintendent, during the erection of the building, in which capacity he gave eminent satisfaction.

There were three bids for supplying the new court house with furniture, one by Ernest Feige, of East Saginaw, Michigan, of $13,875; one by Contractor Coots of $20,031 and the third was by Dewey & Stone, of Omaha, of $25,318. The former received the contract. The corner stone of the building was laid with great ceremony October 25th, 1882, and the structure formally received by the Commissioners, May 28th, 1885, at which time an invitation was extended the public to inspect the building. This invitation was generally accepted and the handsome structure was thronged during the entire day with visitors, all eloquent in their praises of the beauty of the building and its adaptability to the purposes for which it was erected. In the evening there were formal dedicatory exercises in the main court room, which was handsomely decorated. Music was furnished by the bands of the Hibernian Society, the Union Pacific and the Musical Union. Geo. W. Ambrose, Esq., presided, and addresses were made by John C. Cowin, Esq., Judge Eleazer Wakeley, Judge James Neville, Judge James W. Savage and County Commissioner Richard O'Keefe, the latter closing the exercises by presenting to Superintendent D. L. Shane a handsome gold-headed cane, in appreciation of the valuable services he had rendered the County Board and the taxpayers, generally, during the erection of the building.

The Douglas County records were kept in a very small space in the early days, as compared with that now required. Thomas O'Connor, the first elected Register of the county (his only predecessor, Lyman Richardson, having been appointed by Governor Cumings), says that for some time a case, with pigeon holes, about two feet square, was sufficient. This case was made by James E. Boyd & Bro., contractors for the wood work on the old court house, and whose carpenter shop was located on the south side of Harney street, directly west of the present site of Stephenson's livery establishment. Speaking of Register O'Connor, that official became involved in a difficulty in 1855 of a somewhat personal character. A fellow countryman, Pat. McDonough, employed by Governor Cumings, was directed by the latter to hurry up the transfer across the river of certain government supplies and came in contact, on the ferry boat, with one of the Wells brothers, then engaged in building the Douglas House, who was insisting that their material be given the preference by the overworked ferry manager. High words ensued and McDonough was thrown into the river by Wells, who was at once siezed by O'Connor and tossed overboard. Fortunately the men escaped drowning, but it was a close call for both.

In the spring of 1887 a tract of fifty acres, the east side of the county farm, was platted into building lots as Douglas addition. Real estate was selling rapidly at that time and the proposition to sell this property at public auction met with general favor. The sale took place in June, and having been well advertised was largely attended. Competition was very lively and prices obtained far beyond what had been hoped for, the result being that an aggregate of $330,480 was received for the fifty acres platted, this amount being increased considerably by interest on deferred payments.

## HISTORY OF THE CITY OF OMAHA.

Comparative statement of taxes raised:

| YEAR | *LEVY. | AMOUNT. |
|---|---|---|
| 1859 | 10 | $ 28,635 61 |
| 1860 | 18 2-10 | 31,437 38 |
| 1861 | 16¼ | 22,146 53 |
| 1862 | 13⅝ | 24,996 26 |
| 1863 | 12 | 21,016 40 |
| 1864 | 10 21-40 | 34,567 75 |
| 1865 | 11 43-60 | 45,383 06 |
| 1866 | 17¾ | 108,461 91 |
| 1867 | 13 11-24 | 93 974 21 |
| 1868 | 9 | 80,086 81 |
| 1869 | 12¼ | 114,408 63 |
| 1870 | 16½ | 223,438 07 |
| 1871 | 21 | 258 321 64 |
| 1872 | 20½ | 212,815 02 |
| 1873 | 21 | 207,492 20 |
| 1874 | 20¾ | 205 342 70 |
| 1875 | 21 39-40 | 217,661 04 |
| 1876 | 20 | 185,001 76 |
| 1877 | 20 | 158,816 80 |
| 1878 | 21½ | 169,597 90 |
| 1879 | 22 | 181,905 78 |
| 1880 | 19½ | 174 874 08 |
| 1881 | 21 | 197,498 03 |
| 1882 | 23 | 237,067 08 |
| 1883 | 23¼ | 287,176 33 |
| 1884 | 23⅝ | 309,512 11 |
| 1885 | 25⅜ | 325,478 67 |
| 1886 | 23¼ | 419,183 41 |
| 1887 | 22⅔ | 481,204 53 |
| 1888 | 20 | 555,566 00 |
| 1889 | 20 4-5 | 549,279 11 |
| 1890 | 18 | 487,903 16 |

*Levy in mills.

Under the heading "Benevolent Institutions" will be found a history of the erection of a county hospital on the west side of the county farm.

Following is a list of Douglas County officers, with date of election:

(Until 1887, the Board of Commissioners consisted of three members, elected, one each year, to serve three years. In 1887 the number was increased to five.)

COMMISSIONERS—Jesse Lowe. Thomas H. Davis and James H. McArdle, 1856; James H. McArdle and Sylvanus Dodge, 1857; Harrison Johnson and A. J. Critchfield. 1859; J. W. Parker, 1860; O. P. Hurford, 1861; James H. McArdle, 1862; Thomas H. Allison. 1863; St John Goodrich, 1864; James H. McArdle and Edward M. Chaplin, 1865; James G. Megeath, John M. Kelley. M. C. Wilbur and Haman Chapman, 1866; (Samuel E. Rogers and Charles W. Burt also served a few months during 1866, to fill vacancies caused by resignations of Megeath and Kelley); Jonas Gise, 1867; Henry Eicke. 1868; E. H. Sherwood. 1869; M. W. E. Purchase, 1870; James H. McArdle, 1871; Benjamin P. Knight and Thomas Wilkinson, 1872; Josiah B. Redfield, 1873; James H. McArdle, 1874; Benjamin P. Knight, 1875; Fred Drexel, 1876; F. W. Corliss, 1877; Benjamin P. Knight, 1878; Fred Drexel, 1879; F. W. Corliss, 1880; Benjamin P. Knight, 1881; Richard O'Keefe, 1882; F. W. Corliss 1883; George E. Timme, 1884; Richard O Keefe, 1885; W. J. Mount, 1886; William R. Turner. Peter Corrigan and Leavitt M. Anderson, 1887; Richard O'Keefe; 1888; Peter J. Corrigan and Richard S. Berlin, 1887; George Timme and Charles L. Van Camp. 1890. J. W. Paddock was selected, in 1891. to fill vacancy caused by the decease of Peter J. Corrigan; E. M. Stenberg, 1891.

PROBATE AND COUNTY JUDGES—William Scott, 1855; George Armstrong, 1859; Hiram M. Dickinson. 1862; Isaac S. Hascall, 1865; R. J. Stuck, 1867; J. R. Hyde. 1868; L. B. Gibson, 1869; Robbert Townsend 1871; William L. Peabody, 1873; C. H. Sedgewick. 1875; William O Bartholomew, 1877-9; (resigned, and Howard B. Smith appointed); A. M. Chadwick, 1881-3; (died, and J. H. McCulloch appointed); J H. McCulloch. 1885; George W. Shields. 1887-9; J. W. Eller, 1891.

COUNTY CLERKS—Thomas O'Connor, 1856; James E. Boyd and Charles P. Birkett. 1857; James W. Van Nostrand, 1859; Peter Hugus. 1861; Byron Reed, 1863; Frank Murphy, 1865; C. A. Downey, 1867; Thomas Swobe, 1869; William H. Ijams, 1871; Lewis S. Reed, 1873-5; John R. Manchester. 1877-9; John Baumer, 1881; Herbert T. Leavitt. 1883-5; (resigned October 24th, 1885, and Gustave Beneke appointed); Charles P. Needham, 1886; M D. Roche. 1887; Peter J. O'Malley. 1889; Fred J. Sackett, 1891.

COUNTY TREASURERS—T. G. Goodwill, 1855; Samuel Moffatt. 1856; George W. Forbes, 1857; A. C. Althaus, 1859; James K. Ish. 1861-3-5; William J. Hahn, 1867-9; Edward C. McShane, 1871; A. C. Althaus. 1873-5; William F. Hines, 1877-9; John Rush. 1881-3; Henry Bolln, 1885-7; Adam Snyder. 1889; H. B. Irey, 1891.

SHERIFFS—P. G. Peterson. 1855; Cameron Reeves, 1856; John C. Heilman, 1859; Thomas L. Sutton, 1861-3; Andrew Dellone, 1865; Aaron R. Hoel. 1867; Henry Grebe, 1869-71; Alfred Burley, 1873-5; George H. Guy, 1879-81; David N. Miller. 1883; William Coburn. 1885-7; John F. Boyd, 1889; George Bennett, 1891.

REGISTER OF DEEDS—Lyman Richardson, 1855; Thomas O'Connor, 1855-6-7. The office was then merged into that of County Clerk but was revived in 1887 when T. A. Megeath was elected and re-elected in 1889.

COUNTY AUDITOR—J T. Evans, October 1, 1889. Still in office.

SUPERINTENDENTS OF INSTRUCTION—A. A. Seagrave, 1869; Jeremiah Behm, 1871; S. D. Beals, 1873; John Rush, 1875; John J. Points, 1877-9-81; James B. Bruner, 1883-5-7; A. Mathews, 1889; George W. Hill, 1891.

## LIST OF DOUGLAS COUNTY OFFICERS.

SURVEYORS—Benjamin P. Knight, 1833; B. E. B, Kennedy, 1865; Benjamin P. Knight, 1867; Andrew Rosewater, 1869; George Smith, 1871-3-5-7-9-81-3-5; Charles H. Howes, 1887; J. E. House 1889; George Smith, 1891.

CORONERS—Emerson D. Seymour, 1860-2; E. Dallow, 1863; J. R. Conkling, 1865; C. H. Pinney, 1867; Jacob Gish, 1869; J. R. Conkling, 1871; Jacob Gish. 1873-5; Joseph Neville. 1877; John G. Jacobs 1879-81; W. H. Kent. 1883; John C. Drexell. 1885-7; C. P. Harrigan. 1889; M. O. Maul, 1891.

COUNTY PHYSICIANS—J. C. Denise. 1867-9-71; William McClelland, 1873; S. D. Mercer, 1875; Joseph Quinlan, 1877-9; J. R. Conkling. 1881; John D. Peabody, 1883; W. S. Gibbs, 1885; J. S. Deories, 1887; P. S. Keogh, 1888-9.

COUNTY ATTORNEYS—Before the admission of the Territory as a State, County Attorneys were also Prosecuting Attorneys. When Nebraska became a State. E. Estabrook was appointed Prosecuting Attorney by Judge Lake, to serve until the election in the fall of 1868, when John C. Cowin was elected and served from January, 1869, to January. 1873. He was succeeded by William J. Connell, who served until January, 1877, his successor being E. H. Buckingham, who died soon afterwards and Charles J. Greene was appointed to fill out the unexpired term. Arthur N. Ferguson was elected in the fall of 1878 and served until January, 1881 when he was succeeded by Nathan J. Burnham. Park Godwin succeeded Mr. Burnham in January, 1883; Lee Estelle filled the office from January, 1885, to January, 1887, and was succeeded by Edward W. Simeral, who served until January. 1889, the present incumbent, T. J. Mahoney, being his successor.

CONSTITUTIONAL CONVENTIONS—George B. Lake, Charles F. Manderson, James M. Woolworth, Eleazer Wakeley, Isaac S. Hascall. Experience Estabrook, James E. Boyd, John C. Myers, Silas A. Strickland, 1871; Clinton Briggs, John L. Webster, Charles F. Manderson. William A. Gwyer, Henry Grebe James E. Boyd, Charles H. Brown, 1875. Of the convention of 1871 Silas A. Strickland was President and John L. Webster presided over that of 1875.

SOLDIERS' RELIEF COMMITTEE—appointed under a recent act of the Legislature—M. D. Roche. Dr. R M. Stone and John P. Henderson. This committee has the charge of the disbursement of a sum, to not exceed three-tenths of a mill of the amount of the annual tax levy, in aid of dependent ex-soldiers and their families. The fund for 1890 amounted to about $7,500.

Members of the Legislature from Douglas County:

FIRST SESSION, CONVENED JANUARY 16, 1855.

REPRESENTATIVES—A. J. Hanscom, Alfred D. Gayer. A J. Poppleton, William Clancy. William N. Byers. Thomas Davis, Fleming Davidson and Robert B Whitted. A. J. Hanscom, Speaker; J. W. Paddock, Chief Clerk.

COUNCILMEN—Samuel E. Rogers, O. D. Richardson, A D. Jones and T. G. Goodwill. Joseph L. Sharp, President; George L. Miller, Chief Clerk.

SECOND SESSION, CONVENED DEC. 18, 1855.

REPRESENTATIVES—George L. Miller, William Larimer, Jr., Levi Harsh, William E. Moore, Alexander Davis, Leavitt L. Bowen, Alonzo F. Salisbury and William Clancy. P. C. Sullivan, Speaker; J. L. Gibbs, Chief Clerk.

COUNCILMEN—Samuel E. Rogers, O. D. Richardson. T. G. Goodwill and A. D. Jones.  B. R. Folsom President; E. G. McNeely, Chief Clerk.

THIRD SESSION, CONVENED JAN. 5, 1857.

REPRESENTATIVES—S. A. Strickland. Joseph Dyson. C. T. Halloway, John Finney, William E. Moore, H Johnson, J. Steinberger, M. Murphy, R. Kimball. Jonas Seely, A. J. Hanscom and George Armstrong. I. L. Gibbs, Speaker; J. H. Brown, Chief Clerk.

COUNCILMEN—A. F. Salisbury, Dr. George L. Miller, Samuel E. Rogers, L. L. Bowen. L. L. Bowen, President; O. F. Lake, Chief Clerk.

FOURTH SESSION, CONVENED DEC. 8, 1857.

REPRESENTATIVES—George Armstrong. J. Steinberger, George Clayes, J. S. Stewart, M. Murphy, A. J. Poppleton, W. R. Thrall and J. W. Paddock. J. H. Decker and A. J. Poppleton, Speakers; S. M. Curran, Chief Clerk.

COUNCILMEN—George L. Miller, S. E. Rogers, George Armstrong, William Clancy and A. F. Salisbury. George L. Miller, President; W. Safford, Chief Clerk.

FIFTH SESSION, CONVENED SEPT. 21, 1858.

REPRESENTATIVES—James H. Seymour, Clinton Briggs, ugustus Roeder. James Stewart, William A. Gwyer, R. W. Steele, John A. Steinberger and George Clayes. H. P. Bennett, Speaker; E. G. McNeely, Chief Clerk.

COUNCILMEN—George W. Doane, William E. Moore, George L. Miller and John R. Porter. L. L. Bowen, President; S. M. Curran, Chief Clerk.

SIXTH SESSION, CONVENED DEC. 5, 1859.

REPRESENTATIVES—A. J. Hanscom, David D. Belden, Harrison Johnson, George F. Kennedy,

George B. Lake and A. B. Malcomb. S. A. Strickland, Speaker: James W. Moore, Chief Clerk.

COUNCILMEN—George W. Doane, William A. Little. George L. Miller and John R. Porter. E. A. Donelan, President; S. M. Curran, Chief Clerk.

SEVENTH SESSION, CONVENED DEC. 2, 1860.

REPRESENTATIVES—John I. Redick, Samuel A. Lowe, Joel T. Griffin, Merrill H. Clark, Henry Grebe and Ezra Millard. Henry W. De Puy, Speaker; George L. Seybolt, Chief Clerk.

COUNCILMEN—David D. Belden, William A. Little and John M. Thayer. William H. Taylor, President: E. P. Brewster, Chief Clerk.

EIGHTH SESSION CONVENED, DEC. 2, 1861.

REPRESENTATIVES—James H. Seymour, Joel T. Griffin, A. D. Jones, Merrill H. Clarke, Oscar F. Davis and Aaron Cahn. A. D. Jones, Speaker; George L. Seybolt, Chief Clerk.

COUNCILMEN—David D. Belden, William A. Little and William F. Sapp. John Taffe. President; R. W. Furnas. Chief Clerk. (A direct tax of $19,312 was levied against Nebraska in 1861, which was remitted by the government in consideration of their being no session of the Legislature the following year, the expense of which the government would have had to pay. The amount was, by act of Congress, 1891, refunded to the State).

NINTH SESSION, CONVENED JAN. 7, 1864.

REPRESENTATIVES—John Ritchie, George B. Lake, Daniel Gantt, Joel S. Smith, B. E. B. Kennedy and Henry Grebe. George B. Lake, Speaker; Rienzi Streeter, Chief Clerk.

COUNCILMEN—William A. Little, John R. Porter, and John McCormick. E. A. Allen, President; J. W. Hollinshead, Chief Clerk.

TENTH SESSION, CONVENED JAN. 5, 1865.

REPRESENTATIVES—E. L. Emery. A. J. Critchfield, Charles M. Conoyer, Charles H. Brown and James W. Pickard. S. M. Kirkpatrick Speaker: John Taffe, Chief Clerk.

COUNCILMEN—John R. Porter and B. E. B. Kennedy. O. P. Mason, President; John S. Bowen, Chief Clerk.

ELEVENTH SESSION, CONVENED JAN. 4, 1866.

REPRESENTATIVES—George B. Lake, J. W. Paddock, Charles H. Brown, Frederick Drexel and James G. Megenth. James G. Megenth, Speaker; George May, Chief Clerk.

COUNCILMEN—B. E. B. Kennedy and John R. Porter. O. P. Mason. President; W. E. Harvey, Chief Clerk.

TWELFTH SESSION, CONVENED JULY 4, 1866.

REPRESENTATIVES—Phillip O'Hanlon, A. J. Critchfield, J. W. Paddock. V. Burkley and W. A. Denton. W. A. Pollock, Speaker; Joseph H. Brown, Chief Clerk.

SENATORS—James G. Megeath and M. C. Wilbur. Frank Welch, President; Casper E. Yost, Secretary.

THIRTEENTH SESSION, CONVENED JAN. 10, '67.

REPRESENTATIVES—George W. Frost, Dan S. Parmalee, Harvey Link. S. M. Curran and E. P. Child. W. F. Chapin, Speaker; John S. Bowen, Chief Clerk.

SENATORS—George W. Doane and William Baumer. E. H. Rogers, President: O. B. Hewett, Secretary.

FOURTEENTH SESSION, CONVENED FEB. 20, '67.

REPRESENTATIVES—Joel T. Griffin. Martin Dunham, Dan S. Parmalee and George W. Frost. W. F. Chapin, Speaker; H. W. Merrille, Chief Clerk.

SENATORS—Isaac S. Hascall. E. H. Rogers, President; O. B. Hewett, Secretary.

FIFTEENTH SESSION, CONVENED MAY 16, 1867.

REPRESENTATIVES—George W. Frost. Martin Dunham and Joel T. Griffin. W. F. Chapin, Speaker; John S. Bowen, Chief Clerk.

SENATORS—Isaac S. Hascall and J. N. H. Patrick. E. H. Rogers, President; L. L. Holbrook, Secretary.

Up to this date the sessions were held at Omaha; subsequent sessions at Lincoln, to which place the capital was removed in 1867. The session of July, 1866, was convened under the supposition that Nebraska would be admitted as a State by that date, a State Constitution having been previously adopted. It provided, however, for the exercise of the elective franchise by whites only. Congress required an amendment in that particular in order that it might conform to the amendment to the Constitution of the United States by which, suffrage was conferred upon the colored race. In consequence of this a delay of some months resulted and the session of January following was under the Territorial form of government.

## SESSIONS OF THE LEGISLATURE.

SIXTEENTH SESSION, CONVENED JAN. 7, 1869.

REPRESENTATIVES—S. C. Brewster, Joseph Fox, John B. Furay, Joel T. Griffin, Dan S. Parmalee and Edwin Loveland. William McLennan, Speaker; John S. Bowen, Chief Clerk.

SENATORS—E. B. Taylor and George W. Frost. E. B. Taylor, President; Samuel M. Chapman, Secretary.

SEVENTEENTH SESSION, CONVENED FEB. 17, '70.

REPRESENTATIVES—Joel T. Griffin. Edwin Loveland, Dan S. Parmalee, C. A. Leary, S. C. Brewster, Joseph Fox. William McLennan, Speaker; Charles H. Walker, Chief Clerk.

SENATORS—George W. Frost and E. B. Taylor. E. B. Taylor, President; Samuel M. Chapman, Secretary.

EIGHTEENTH SESSION, CONVENED JAN. 5, 1871.

REPRESENTATIVES—John Ahmanson, Thomas F. Hall John C. Myers, Edward Rosewater, William M. Ryan and Lewis S. Reed. George W. Collins, Speaker; Lew. E. Cropsey, Chief Clerk.

SENATORS—Isaac S. Hascall and Frederick Metz, E. E. Cunningham, President; Charles H. Walker, Secretary.

NINETEENTH SESSION, CONVENED JAN. 9, 1873.

REPRESENTATIVES—W. R. Bartlett, Charles F. Goodman, John L. Webster, Martin Dunham, Hugh L. Dodge and Erwin G. Dudley. M. H. Sessions, Speaker; J. W. Eller, Chief Clerk.

SENATORS—William A. Gwyer and O. Wilson. William A. Gwyer, President; Dan. H. Wheeler, Secretary.

TWENTIETH SESSION, CONVENED JAN. 7, 1875.

REPRESENTATIVES—B. H. Barrows, John M. Thurston, Jacob Wiedensall. John Baumer, Frank Murphy and Alexander H. Baker. Edward S. Towle, Speaker; George L. Brown, Chief Clerk.

SENATORS—Charles B. Rustin and Jacob S. Spaun. N. K. Griggs, President; Dan. H. Wheeler, Secretary.

The Twenty-first was a special session, convened December 5, 1876, to canvass the vote cast for Amasa Cobb, as a Presidential elector, in order to correct an alleged irregularity.

TWENTY-SECOND SESSION, CONVENED JAN. 2, 1877.

REPRESENTATIVES—Alexander H. Baker, James S. Gibson, William Neville, P. P. Shelby, George E. Pritchett. James Creighton, L. L. Wilcox and Thomas Blackmore. Albinus Nance, Speaker; B. D. Slaughter, Chief Clerk.

SENATORS—George W. Ambrose and Charles H. Brown. George F. Blanchard, President; Dan. H. Wheeler, Secretary.

October 27, 1868, a session of one day was held for the purpose of correcting an omission in the law with respect to election of Presidential electors.

TWENTY-THIRD SESSION, CONVENED JANUARY 7, 1879.

REPRESENTATIVES—George Plumbeck, Lewis M. Bennett, Ralph E. Gaylord, Patrick McArdle and Charles J. Karbach. C. P. Mathewson, Speaker; B. D. Slaughter, Chief Clerk.

SENATORS—Charles K. Contant and Charles H. Brown. William Marshall, President; Sherwood Burr, Secretary.

TWENTY-FOURTH SESSION, CONVENED JANUARY 4, 1881.

REPRESENTATIVES—Edmund M. Bartlett, P. O. Mullen, William A. Paxton. Henry Bolln, John A. McShane, William J. Broatch, Stephen K. Jackson and James H. Kyner. H. H. Shedd, Speaker; B. D. Slaughter, Chief Clerk.

SENATORS—George W. Doane, John D. Howe. J. B. Dinsmore, President; Sherwood Burr, Secretary.

The Twenty-fifth was a special session, convened May 10, 1882, in which there was no change in the membership from Douglas County.

TWENTY-SIXTH SESSION, CONVENED JAN. 2, '83.

REPRESENTATIVES—Fred. W. Gray, Frank Colpetzer, Alexander McGavock, Hugh G. Clark, John Christopherson, William Turtle and Henry Sussenbach. George M. Humphrey, Speaker; B. D. Slaughter, Chief Clerk.

SENATORS—Charles H. Brown and George Canfield. A. H. Conner, President; George L. Brown, Secretary.

TWENTY-SEVENTH SESSION, CONVENED JANUARY 6, 1885.

REPRESENTATIVES—James E. Riley, Thomas C. Bruner, William Turtle, William G. Whitmore, James H. Winspear, John Mulvihill, P. McArdle and A. C. Troup. Allen W. Field, Speaker; James F. Zediker, Chief Clerk

SENATORS—John A. McShane and Frederick Metz. Church Howe, President; Sherwood Burr. Secretary.

TWENTY-EIGHTH SESSION, CONVENED JANUARY 4, 1887.

REPRESENTATIVES—William G. Whitmore, Geo. Heimrod, John Mathieson, J. R. Young, Patrick Garvey, C. J. Smyth, David Knox and Philip Andres. N. V. Harlan, Speaker; Brad. D. Slaughter, Chief Clerk.

SENATORS—George W. Liniuger and Bruno Tzschuck. George D. Meikeljohn, President; Walter M. Seely, Secretary.

TWENTY-NINTH SESSION, CONVENED JAN. 1, '89.

REPRESENTATIVES—R. C. Cushing, R. S. Berlin, W. A. Gardner, J. H. Hungate, F. R. Morrissey (the last named was afterwards declared by the committee on elections to be not entitled to a seat, and a certificate was given to George M. O'Brien), William Neve, Adam Snyder, John McMillan and S. B. Fenno (unseated and place given to Christian Specht). John C Watson, Speaker; Brad. D. Slaughter, Chief Clerk.

SENATORS—J. T. Paulsen and William A. Paxton. Church Howe, President; Walter M. Seely, Secretary.

THIRTIETH SESSION, CONVENED JAN. 6, 1891.

REPRESENTATIVES—George Bertrand, W. S. Felker, Jesse B. Huse James C. Brennan, Joseph J. Breen, George J. Sternsdorf, Patrick Ford, Thomas Capek, W. A. Gardner. S. M. Elder, Speaker; Eric Johnson, Chief Clerk.

SENATORS—Warren Switzler, John C. Shea, George Christofferson. W. A. Poynter, President; C. H. Pirtle, Secretary.

# CHAPTER X.

MUNICIPAL—EARLY DOINGS OF THE CITY COUNCIL—THE OLD CAPITOL BUILDING—SCRAPS OF LOCAL LEGISLATION—LIST OF CITY OFFICIALS

The municipal government of Omaha dates from the spring of 1857, public business previous to that time having been conducted by the county officials. The original charter, passed by the Territorial Legislature, was approved February 2d of that year, a supplemental act, approved February 7th, and an election held on the first Monday in March, when the following officials were elected

Jesse Lowe, Mayor, H C Anderson, Recorder, Lyman Richardson, Assessor, J A Miller, City Marshal, A D Jones, T G Goodwill, G C. Bovey, H H Visscher, Thomas Davis, William U Wyman, William N Byers, C H Downs and Thomas O'Connor, Aldermen

Pursuant to a call of the Mayor, the Council convened March 5. 1857, and the rules of the Council of the Legislative Assembly were adopted for its guidance At this meeting work was at once entered upon with characteristic western vigor, notice being given of the introduction, at an early day, of bills for ordinances upon the following subjects "To prescribe the duties of the City Recorder, respecting official bonds and oaths, to protect the Marshal in the execution of his duties; to establish the boundaries of wards, to prevent hogs from running at large, to create the office of City Engineer, and define the duties thereof, to establish and build a city pound, to regulate the sale of intoxicating liquors, to regulate billiard and bowling alleys, and for the suppression of gambling and gambling rooms"

In order to insure enough business to keep itself occupied, this first Board of Aldermen adopted the following, which the Recorder was directed to have printed and posted in conspicuous places

"Notice is hereby given that the City Council of the City of Omaha has organized for the transaction of such business as may be brought before them for the welfare of said city, and at the first session thereof it was resolved that all petitions to their honorable body be addressed or presented to the City Recorder and by him presented to the Council for their consideration, and that the citizens of said city be and are hereby requested to make their wishes known by petition at as early a day as possible"

At the second meeting of the Board, evidence of modesty in a marked degree was given by the adoption of a motion recommending that hereafter the Recorder omit the use of the word "Alderman" in making up his minutes, and the wild character of the surroundings is shown by the notice given by Mr Jones that he proposed introducing a bill for an ordinance " to prevent the setting of fires," which referred, of course, to prairie fires A report is presented to the effect that "Hapburn & Chapman would furnish city printing at the following figures

| | | |
|---|---|---|
| "One-fourth sheet bills | 1st 100 | $4 00 |
| "Each subsequent . | 100 | 3 00 |
| "One-half sheet bills . | 1st 100 | 8 00 |
| "Blanks | per 100 | 4 00 |
| "Blank ordinances, 1000 ems, first time | | 75 |
| "Blank ordinances, each subsequent | | 40 |

"Printing proceedings of Council, gratis"

As T H Robertson was at this meeting elected city printer, there is a good reason to suppose that the scale of prices above given were not considered satisfactory. The standing committees of the Council were: Judiciary, Claims, Streets and Grades, Improvements and Printing. The first ordinance introduced was by A. D. Jones to established ward boundaries, and one to regulate the sale of liquors was No. 5, introduced by T. G. Goodwill.

Early in the history of the government the Recorder was directed to procure from Chicago, "or some other well regulated city," ten copies of its city ordinances for the use of the Council. Thus left with a wide discretion, the Recorder evidently concluded that Chicago was not a proper model for Omaha, as later on in the records appears mention of a bill from the Recorder of "the city of Iowa" for ten copies of city ordinances, hence we may conclude that it was to Iowa, and not to Illinois, that our first city law makers turned for forms and precedents, and that, after a calm and careful investigation, Recorder Anderson decided that, even in that early period, Chicago was not "a well regulated city."

It is interesting to follow the official record of this first Board of Aldermen, then planning ways and means for governing a hamlet, since grown into a mighty city. That they were an industrious body of men, is shown by the fact that they met in the daytime, and almost every day, for the first few months, afterwards changing to Tuesday night of each week. There was a strong desire to have erected a large hotel, and the Council was willing to aid in an enterprise of so much importance. March 13, 1857, a petition was presented by "George L. Miller and 129 others" in relation to appropriating a part of "the Park" (seven blocks bounded by Eighth, Ninth, Jackson and Davenport) towards such building, which was referred to the committee on public grounds. At this meeting the following resolutions were adopted:

*Resolved,* That a portion of the public grounds known as "the Park" be donated for the purposes of securing the erection of a hotel, worth not less than ———— thousand dollars, said hotel to be located between Fifth and Twentieth, and Howard and Webster Streets, said location, with the above restrictions, to be determined by the builder; and, be it further

*Resolved,* That a committee of three be appointed to receive proposals for the building of said hotel, and that they be authorized to close a contract with a responsible party who will undertake to build said hotel for the least quantity of said grounds.

The committee to whom this matter was referred recommended that a "plan and specifications of such house be made by a proper and experienced architect, to be reported to and acted upon by this Council, and after said plan and specifications shall have been agreed upon, the same shall be published in the papers of Omaha and Council Bluffs for two weeks, and give notice that all bids shall contain all the securities' names which may be offered, and the bids sealed and directed to the President of the City Council, which bids shall specify what number of lots on said Park they will ask as a donation by the city as a bonus towards the erection. Said proposals shall be handed in before the 1st day of April, and shall be opened and acted upon in open Council at the first regular session after that date."

This report was adopted and at the Council meeting, held April 7th, four bids were presented, and, on motion of Alderman Byers, "Dr. George L. Miller was declared the successful bidder for the hotel contract," and the City Attorney was directed to draw up a contract, to be signed by the Mayor and Dr. Miller. It was the intention then to have the proposed hotel built on some portion of the ground known as "The Park," and the City Engineer was directed to proceed at once in platting that tract into lots and blocks, to correspond with those adjacent. Later on Dr. Miller and his associates, Lyman Richardson and George Bridge, were given permission to erect the hotel on lots 7 and 8, block 124, and the brick building, four stories high, known as the Herndon House, was erected by those gentlemen, at a cost of $75,000. It is now, very much enlarged and improved, occupied by the Union Pacific Railway headquarters.

One of the first duties of the Council was to elect a City Attorney, and this important matter was attended to at the meeting held March 12th. John A. Horbach, John I. Redick, Charles Grant and Jonas Seeley were the candidates. On the first ballot Horbach received one vote, Redick and Seeley two each, and Grant three. On the second ballot Grant received four votes, Redick one, and Seeley three. Grant was declared elected. June 23d following he resigned and James M. Woolworth was elected in his place. At this meeting of March 12, a City Engineer was also elected, A. S. M. Morgan.

March 13th a committee, "to whom was referred the matter of releasing to Douglas County, Washington Square,'' reported the matter back to the Council, and the following was offered and laid over under the rules:

"*Resolved*, That a committee be appointed to make arrangements with the Commissioners of Douglas County to provide for the disposition of Washington Square, in Omaha City, for the purpose of having erected thereon such buildings as may be agreed upon, to be used as a court house and jail, a portion of which to be appropriated for the use of Omaha City, with instructions to report to this body at its earliest convenience."

March 18th a special session of the Council was held "to ratify the contract made by the committee appointed to confer and stipulate with the County Commissioners of Douglas County, for the appropriation of Washington Square, to be used in the erection of a court house and jail thereon.'' A contract, prepared by the City Solicitor and signed by Jesse Lowe and Thomas Davis on the part of the county, and T. G. Goodwill and William N. Byers on behalf of the Council, was presented and approved by the Council.

Washington Square was the block bounded by Farnam, Douglas, Fifteenth and Sixteenth, now the most valuable square in the city. The court house was built on lots 5 and 6, the present site of the Paxton Block, the title to which lots was conveyed by the city to the county. The desire of the city to occupy a portion of the court house free of expense was not complied with, however, the county claiming and exercising exclusive ownership in the building after it was finally completed.

March 14th, 1857, the Mayor was authorized "to enter, without unnecessary delay, in the name of the City of Omaha, in accordance with the provisions of an act of Congress of May 23d, 1844, the following subdivisions of the government land, to-wit: The northeast quarter and the north half of the northwest quarter of section twenty-two, and lot two in fractional section number twenty-three, township fifteen, north of range thirteen, east of the sixth principal meridian.'' The Mayor was further instructed to (after having made such entry) "proceed to deed to the proper owners thereof all lots and grounds situated within the above named tracts of land upon payment by such owner of his proportion of the cost of said entry and all other charges as are prescribed by the laws of this territory, in such cases made and provided.''

And thus was inaugurated a tedious and vexatious system of dealings in connection with real estate titles which circumstances combined to complicate and render exceedingly difficult to carry out successfully. The fact that the city was located upon land which still belonged to the government, and had not even been surveyed, caused much difficulty, bitter personal feuds, the perpetration of gross wrongs in isolated cases, and litigation as to titles which kept the courts occupied for many subsequent years. All this, however, resulted from the situation and not from the method adopted by the Council to perfect the city's title to the real estate within its boundaries.

The providing of funds to carry on the city government proved a very serious problem, and one which the Council had to confront early in its history. Money had been furnished to erect a capitol building on the ground now occupied by the High School, with the understanding that the sum thus advanced would be refunded by the general government. May 26th, 1857, Alderman

THE TERRITORIAL CAPITOL.

Bovey (who, with Major George Armstrong, erected the capitol building) offered the following, which was adopted:

"*Resolved*, That the Mayor of the City of Omaha be and is hereby instructed, to proceed immediately with the erection of the capitol building, expending thereon such money as there may be in the treasury, appointed for that purpose, which funds he may increase at such times as he may think best, by selling the lands set apart for that purpose, or by using the credit of the city."

Following this, appropriations were made at various times, until $110,000 had been expended on the building.

June 23d the Mayor was authorized " to procure plates and to have $30,000 of city scrip issued and to enter into a contract with the different banks for the circulation and redemption of said scrip on the best possible terms," and July 8, John H. Kellom (who had been elected to fill a vacancy caused by the failure of a man named Allen to qualify after having been elected), moved by a desire to uphold the city's credit, offered the following, which, however, was not adopted:

"WHEREAS, The City of Omaha is about to issue its bills of credit to the large amount of $30,000, for purposes of vital importance, and it is both just and expedient that security of a tangible nature, and which will inspire business men and the public generally with entire confidence, be provided to protect said issue:

*Resolved*, That deeds of trust be executed in the manner provided in Ordinance No. ——, conveying to ————————, as trustee, the public property of said city, not otherwise pledged or appropriated, to be held by him in trust as security for the redemption of the scrip issued.

The Mayor's authority as to the issuance of city scrip was extended at a special session held August 29th, when the following proposition was received, and the issuance of $50,000 authorized:

"We, the undersigned, do hereby agree to receive from the Mayor of the City of Omaha, of the scrip to be issued by the city, the amount set opposite our names, and to protect the same for nine months from the date of the scrip, for ten per cent interest for the nine months, to be promptly redeemed in currency, provided the amount issued shall not exceed $30,000, unless protected by a responsible party who shall stamp the same, and redeem it either in Omaha City or the City of Council Bluffs, but in no event shall the issue exceed $50,000. It is understood that this agreement shall not be binding on us until arrangements be entered into to protect the whole amount issued. (Signed,)

A. U. Wyman, W. E. F. & M. Ins. Co. ..... $5,000
Samuel Moffatt, Cashier Bank, Nebraska .. 5,000
Bank of Tekamah, F. M. Akin, Cashier .... 5,000
F. Gridley & Co .......................... 3,000
G. C. Monell ............................. 3,000
Banking House, S. E. Rogers & Co., B. B.
  Barkalow, Cashier...................... 3,000
William Young Brown .................... 3,000
John McCormick & Co.................... 2,000

This proposition was accepted by the Council, and the Mayor empowered to close the contract.

At a meeting held September 22d, an additional $10,000 worth of scrip was ordered printed, to be loaned to the Hotel Company, "upon their giving satisfactory security to the city that they will pay all expenses incurred in printing, procuring and issuing said scrip, to protect the circulation of said scrip, and redeem the same and deliver it up to the city authorities at the end of one year, provided the said company procure the concurrence of the bankers with whom the city has made contract, before the resolution shall take effect."

The bankers evidently made no objection, for the loan was made, and the Mayor instructed to take security on the property of the Hotel Company "for the sum of $10,000 heretofore agreed upon," thus making the total amount of city scrip issued $60,000. In the meantime the financial disaster of 1857, which affected the entire country, was bringing peculiar hardship to the new metropolis of Nebraska. November 10th of that year a resolution was adopted, reciting that the Farnam Street Hotel Company had displayed remarkable energy in the erection of their hotel "under the most depressing circumstances, owing to the unprecedented pressure in the money market, and conseqent stagnation in business and decline in the value of real estate," and asked that the time for the completion of said building be extended from January 1st, 1858, to June 1st of that year.

December 14th, a resolution was adopted favoring the issuing of city bonds to the amount of $50,000, and declaring against a proclamation previously issued by the Mayor for an election to be held December 24th, on a proposition to issue $60,000 in bonds to redeem city scrip to that amount; also directing the City Recorder to notify Messrs. Westwood, Hay & Whitney to print no more Omaha scrip, except by order of the Council. At a meeting held the following day, the Mayor was directed to issue his proclamation for an election to be held December 26th, to pass upon the question of issuing bonds to the amount of $57,500 to redeem city scrip, and the City Recorder was directed to have 2,000 affirmative ballots printed and 500 negative. When the ballots cast at said election were counted, it was found there were 598 in favor of and 43 against the bonds, a total of 641 votes cast at an election of so much importance, that it may be deemed a fair showing of the voting strength of Omaha at that time.

Notwithstanding the "unprecedented pressure in the money market, decline in the value of real estate," etc., the Omaha councilmen of those days retained their lofty aspirations, and their energy and zeal suffered no abatement. March 30, 1859, Dr. George L. Miller was elected "to proceed to Washington and use the best efforts to procure the passage of acts of Congress to reimburse the City of Omaha for money expended on the capitol building ; to locate the Surveyor General's office in the City of Omaha ; to locate the Pacific Railroad north of the Platte River and in the Platte valley; to make Omaha the military depot for the Utah war; to make an appropriation for the removal of snags from the Missouri River; to make the City of Omaha a port of entry; to make the postoffice at Omaha a distributing office, and to aid and assist in the enacting of such other acts as may be to the advantage of the City of Omaha."

Hopeful words these, and hopeful, enthusiastic and courageous hearts back of them! A task of generous proportions this, entrusted to one who has continued for more than thirty years since that date laboring to develop and promote the highest interests of the city which claimed his affection and loyalty in the days of his energetic young manhood, and which has since witnessed no abatement of his ardor. To the zeal, energy, confidence and ability of the chosen few who attended to the public affairs of Omaha in those early days of difficulty, hardships, poverty and privation, can be directly traced much of the prosperity which has attended her in these later years, and in none of their recorded acts are those qualities more clearly shown than in the instructions thus given their ambassador to Washington.

But there was very little in the treasury in those days. The Treasurer was directed to receive only gold and silver in the redemption of lots sold for non-payment of taxes; and a committee, appointed to inquire of that official why he had not complied with an order by the Council to pay the claim of one Shennehan to a small amount, received the reply that he had previously been directed " to reserve the first $500 received as a special fund to pay the expenses of the poor and the land office trials."

Certain repairs being demanded on the capitol building, a special committee was appointed to investigate the matter, which committee reported that " it would require $150 to make the necessary repairs; and, taking in consideration the large amount already expended by the city to preserve from total ruin the materials of which it was erected, and the indifference manifested by the general government to reimburse the city, together with the embarrassing state of the financial affairs of the country in general, and of this city in particular, it would be neither wisdom nor policy for the city to incur any further expense on the capitol building, until other demands were paid; and your committee recommend that no further action be taken at this time." The report was adopted.

But the desperate condition of the city finances is probably more clearly shown in certain proceedings had by the Council, August 10th, 1858, than elsewhere in the Clerk's records. An ordinance, of which, unfortunately, but a brief mention is made (hence its provisions cannot be given), had been previously referred to the judiciary committee; and, at this meeting of the Council, Mr. Thomas Davis, chairman, presented the following: " The committee on judiciary, to whom was referred the ordinance providing for the payment of city warrants, would respectfully report that they have had the same under consideration and would recommend that the bill do not pass, for the reason that your committee are fully of the opinion that the bill is a virtual repudiation of the debt of the city, known as the scrip debt, which has been ratified by a vote of over two-thirds of the citizens." Mr. M. W. Keith, of the same committee, took an entirely different view of the situation, and thus reported: " In the first place the city cannot proceed to make any improvements of streets and bridges, payment of its officers, relieving of the poor, or even burying the dead, in those cases of citizens who are so unfortunate as to die poor, unless we re-establish the credit of the city by paying its legitimate indebtedness in preference to any other class of claims. The undersigned is fully of the opinion, from information derived from citizens, that nine-tenths of the citizens are in favor of the bill now under consideration, and therefore he respectfully recommends that the report of the chairman be laid on the table and that the bill do now pass and become a permanent ordinance of the city." The Keith report was adopted.

November 30th, 1859, O. D. Richardson and John H. Sahler were appointed a committee to go to Washington and urge certain legislation in behalf of the city, and were voted $1,000 for their expenses, and later on they were authorized to expend money " upon contingency of success to an amount not to exceed $3,000." These gentlemen proceeded to Washington, where they spent some time, and upon their return presented the following report:

In pursuance of your appointment, we repaired to Washington and consulted with our delegates upon the best mode of effecting the passage of the bill to remunerate the City of Omaha for the outlay upon the capitol; the bill for an appropriation for the completion of the capitol; the bill for the bridging of the Loup Fork; the bill allowing the Mayor to pre-empt outside the 230 acres, and the bill appropriating lands for railroads in the Territory. etc. After agreeing upon the course to be pursued, we devoted our time and best energies to the business we had in charge.

The several bills were introduced and referred to the committees and, as a general thing, they met with a favorable reception, none denying the justness of our claims, but we were met with the fact that there was a short session, with scarcely time to pass the bills in their regular order, and even if there was, there was no money in the treasury. Aside from these obstacles there seemed to be a strong disinclination on the part of a majority in Congress, especially in the House, to do the business before them and which the public interests demanded. This was manifested by long speeches on things relevant and irrelevant and by constant calling for the yeas and nays at almost every opportunity. Notwithstanding all this we succeeded in getting two of our bills reported, the one appropriating $33 000 for a penitentiary and the one appropriating $30,000 for the completion of the capitol. These, under the rules of the House (in bills appropriating money), must be referred to the committee of the whole, and they were so referred, but were never reached in their order, and, though a strong effort was made to pass them by tacking them to another bill, that effort failed. In addition to the foregoing matters we were often at the general land office to put our lands in market, both those within the city limits and throughout the Territory. The Secretary of the Interior decided that all lands should be put in market by the 10th of July.

The subject of the division of our Territory came up after we arrived there. Several persons appeared there to represent those favorable to the measure. When the subject had been referred to a committee we appeared before the committee and stated our reasons against the proposed dismemberment and the absurdity and injustice of such dismemberment were so apparent that the committee reported adversely to the purpose of the bill.

We very much regret that we could not accomplish more for the benefit of the Territory and city than we did, but we believe the failure of the passage of our bills was not owing to any want of labor or effort on our part, but to causes over which we had no control, and which were manifest to all who were familiar with the transactions of the late Congress.

Later on Doctor Lowe presented the following additional statement:

TO THE CITY COUNCIL OF OMAHA:

*Gentlemen:* Under a commission of your predecessors, of December 21, 1858, I proceeded to Washington in the winter of 1858 and 1859, to urge upon the general land office prompt action in considering and canceling. the private preemptions illegally made within the corporate limits of the city and to do what else I could in matters of interest to Omaha, which were then pending in Congress. I reached Washington about the 20th of January, and, remained there until the 4th of March, 1859, devoting all my time to the objects of my mission, and succeeded in obtaining a hearing and favorable decision of much the larger and most important portion of the cases; but, not being able to get all of them taken up within that time, and being unable to remain longer, I employed M. Thompson, Esq., to attend to the remaining cases; and having no money to pay him I agreed to send him a deed for five of my own lots, within the limits of Council Bluffs, where the titles were complete, for $250. This I have done, as you will more satisfactorily learn from his own acknowledgment, herewith submitted, and I now respectfully ask to be reimbursed therefor. I disclaimed at the outset any compensation for my time and services, but I cannot afford to give also the money actually paid out for necessary personal expenses in going and returning, and for my board while there. Therefore I submit the following charges and ask their allowance in cash or its equivalent, viz: Paid to Thompson for city, $250; actual expenses going to and returning from Washington, $120; board forty-two days, at $1.50 per day $63—$433." The doctor was voted an equal number of lots in Omaha to reimburse him for the Council Bluffs lots, which he had deeded away, and in addition was given $183 in cash, on account of his expenses.

In November, 1864, the following was presented and adopted, as the report of a special committee, appointed in that behalf·

TO THE CITY COUNCIL:

Your committee, to whom was referred the proposition to employ P. W. Hitchcock, Esq, to procure from Congress an appropriation to reimburse the city the money expended by it in completion of the capitol building, respectfully report that they have had the matter under consideration and have had interviews with Mr. Hitchcock and others interested in the subject; that in consequence of his position they do not deem it advisable to enter into the engagement proposed, and we understand Mr. Hitchcock himself to be understood as desiring no compensation for himself, but only necessary means to receive the support of influential parties in aid of the measure. We believe Mr. Hitchcock will aid this matter to the utmost of his ability, out of regard to his position as delegate elect and interest in the affairs of our city, and so understood him to state; and we think his aid will be much more efficient in supporting some other person than it would be under the engagement proposed. Mr. J. M. Woolworth is to be in Washington this winter, on professional business, and he would undoubtedly enter into like engagements and at the same time have the aid of Mr. Hitchcock in the matter. It seems to your committee likely to meet with more success if entrusted in the first instance to the hands of some person whose official position did not seem to compromise his honor. No person can doubt the justice of the claim made upon the government, nor the advantage to the city of securing the appropriation.

Your committee, therefore, present the following resolutions:

WHEREAS, In order to complete the capitol of this Territory, the City of Omaha issued scrip to a large amount, which was expended for that purpose under the promise of Governor Izard, the agent of the United States, that they would reimburse the city the sum so expended, which, as yet, the government has failed to do, and by reason of large claims made against the city on account of these said scrip, our credit is greatly impaired.

*Resolved,* That J. M. Woolworth, Esq., be and hereby is appointed the agent of the City of Omaha in this behalf, and is empowered to use all proper means to obtain from the United States the funds to liquidate the sums so expended, and to that end this committee and the proper officers of the city make to him a power of attorney, authorizing him so to act in the premises, and that for his services he receive twenty-five per cent of the sum which he may obtain from the United States for said purpose, he to receive no other compensation for his services, whether he succeed or fail in the said business.

*Resolved,* That whatever sum is realized for the benefit of the City of Omaha from the general government in accordance with the foregoing resolution shall, when received, be applied to the settlement of the claims against the city arising from the completion of the capitol by the said City of Omaha, and for re-imbursing the city for its outlay upon said capitol, and such equitable manner as the City Council may determine.

These gentlemen having all failed to accomplish the object in view, September 27, 1865, a resolution was adopted giving to "Samuel Clinton, of Iowa, a power of attorney to solicit an appropriation by the United States government to refund the money expended upon the capitol building, by the City of Omaha," and for his services he was to receive twenty-five per cent of the money collected. And again, January 9th, 1867, O. P. Hurford was appointed the agent of the city to prosecute this claim for money expended on the capitol building, and was to receive as compensation the twenty-five per cent, which seemed to be the regular figures in fixing the remuneration to be received by the various parties designated by the city to make periodical assaults upon the National Congress. A year later a resolution was adopted by the Council revoking the authority previously given Samuel Clinton, James M. Woolworth, "and any and all persons" to whom such authority had been granted, and full power was conferred upon A. J. Poppleton to represent the city in the premises; and in June, 1869, all previous appointments were revoked, and David L. Collier was selected by the Council as the proper man to collect this money from the general government. All these efforts proved futile, however, the government at Washington adding to a long list of instances of its injustice to individuals and communities by ignoring entirely the claim the City of Omaha had upon it for the large sum expended in providing a capitol building for the Territory.

The amount appropriated by the general government for the erection of a Capitol building was $50,000; the City of Omaha expended $60,000 additional, and in his message to the Legislature in 1859, Governor Izard stated that a further sum of $30,000 would be required to complete the building in good shape, and recommended memorializing Congress to that effect, when, in his opinion, the amount required would be promptly voted by the National law makers. The building never was completed, but

Looking Northwest from Fifteenth and Farnam Streets, 1878.

served the purpose until the capitol was moved to Lincoln in 1867, and a few years later was torn down to give place to the High School building, as elsewhere referred to at length.

These old records are full of interesting facts. For instance, Omaha, in those early days, seemed to be threatened very frequently with outbreaks of hydrophobia in an epidemic form, and legislation of the most vigorous character was directed against the dogs of that period. Mr. Charles P. Birkett, after he came into the Board, was particularly active in this direction. Then there was much fear of small pox. In July, 1857, the following resolution was adopted:

WHEREAS, The small pox has commenced to prevail in the City of Omaha ; and,

WHEREAS, It is currently reported and believed that said disease prevails to a considerable extent among the Indians temporarily staying in and about said city, and among the Mormon emigrants passing through said city on their way to the west, and that the said disease has been introduced by said Indians and Mormons ; now, therefore, be it

"*Resolved,* That the City Marshal be instructed and required forthwith to cause said Indians to remove from and remain outside the corporate limits of said city, and also to cause such Mormon emigrants as may be camped within the said limits to remove without the same, unless it shall satisfactorily appear to the City Marshal and the City Physician that said camps are not infected with said disease; and that the City Marshal be instructed to immediately notify the officers and proprietors of the ferry boat, plying between Omaha and Council Bluffs, that said boat will not be allowed to carry over and land, within the corporate limits of said City of Omaha, any trains of emigrants coming from the east, until this order is annulled; and in enforcing the above orders the City Marshal is hereby vested with all the powers granted in the ordinances creating his said office, for the purpose of making arrests, quelling riots, and other like duties."

In the winter of 1857-8 the following was adopted:

WHEREAS, It has but recently come to the knowledge of the members of the Council that it is in contemplation by certain parties to open a saloon in one of the rooms in the basement story of the Territorial Capitol building ; and,

WHEREAS. We believe that the establishment of such an institution in the place named is an insult upon the dignity of the Territorial Legislature soon to convene in said building, and that it will be detrimental to the reputation of the City of Omaha, and injurious to its future prospects ; therefore, be it

*Resolved,* By the City Council of Omaha that we hereby instruct, empower and direct the present superintendent of said building to proceed forthwith to take measures to prevent the establishment and opening of said saloon in the place named, and for that purpose he will, if necessary call in the aid of the City Marshal, with such aides as the Marshal may deem necessary.

Upon this resolution, Aldermen Kellom, Byers, Downs, Davis, Creighton and Visscher voted in the affirmative, and Aldermen Wyman and O'Connor in the negative.

Various suggestions were made as to means to increase the city funds, including schemes to sell all of the city property, including Jefferson Square; and, in 1858, the City Solicitor (George I. Gilbert, Esq.,) presented a report on that subject, adverse to the proposition, in the course of which he cited instances in the cities of Detroit, Cincinnati and Allegheny, where sales of the city property had been made by the municipal authorities of those cities, and deeds given to purchasers, and in some instances the parties had erected buildings upon the property purchased; that legal measures were subsequently resorted to for the recovery of the property by others, on the part of the cities mentioned, and the courts vacated the deeds, and declared the buildings that had been erected on the property a public nuisance. Steps were afterwards taken to dispose of various lots owned by the city, but Jefferson Square was not included. At that time that block of ground was estimated to be worth $4,000, or $500 per lot. (The property is now valued at $400,000.) At one time it was proposed to use lots 3, 4, 5 and 6, in this block, for public school purposes, but the scheme was not carried into effect.

All sorts of enterprises calculated to benefit the city were encouraged in the most liberal manner. In 1859, three hundred lots were donated by resolution to "Messrs. Irving & Co., said lots supposed to be of the average value of $200 per lot, upon condition that said Irving & Co. will keep and maintain during the continuance of their contract with the United States, at or within two miles of the City of Omaha, a deposit (depot?) for the reception and delivery of goods to be transported by them for said government."

June 11, 1860, a committee was appointed to prepare a memorial to Howell Cobb, Secretary of the Treasury of the United States, in relation to repairing the damages done the capitol building by the late storm; and at the same meeting of the Council the Mayor was directed to issue a notice, to be recorded in the office of the Register of Deeds, warning all persons to not purchase from D. C. Sutphen lot 3, in fractional section 23, township 15, range 13, "the same being within the incorporated limits of the City of Omaha, and the title to the same having been illegally obtained by the said Sutphen." The tract referred to in this "warning" lies near the river bank, and consists of a trifle over 31 acres. Mr. Sutphen obtained his patent for the land, but it was afterwards annulled, and Mr. Durant filed on it on behalf of the Union Pacific Company; the land was ordered sold at public auction, and Mr. Sutphen bid it in at a dollar and a quarter an acre, Additional difficulty was experienced, however. Mr. Sutphen's money being tendered him by the land officers at Washington, Mr. Byron Reed became interested in the matter, and the result was that a second patent was granted Mr. Sutphen, with the understanding that he was to deed an undivided half of the property to Mr. Reed, which he did.

In July, 1860, a special meeting of the Council was held to take action with regard to a tract of 160 acres north of town, in which Mr. E. V. Smith, and the city were rival claimants. Mr. Smith had made a proposition to the Council to the effect that he should be permitted to purchase the 80 acres in section 15, and the city should take 80 acres in section 10, and after considerable discussion the proposition was accepted.

The pre-emption undertaken to be made by Mr. Heman Glass was the subject of a good deal of controversy. September 18th, 1860, Mr. Glass made a statement to the Council with regard to his case, and the following was adopted by the Board:

*Resolved*, That on condition that Heman Glass give a bond to the City of Omaha that he will pay to the city $1,000 in city scrip when his pre-emption is sustained, the City of Omaha hereby consents that the entry of the said Glass be perfected, and that the Mayor be and is hereby instructed to withdraw all opposition to the confirmation of the pre-emption title of Heman Glass to the south-west quarter of the south-west quarter of section 21, township 15, range 13.

This description comprises 80 acres of land, extending from Twentieth Street on the east to Twenty-Seventh Street on the west, and from Leavenworth on the north to Pacific Street on the south, which boundaries include Millard Place, McCandlish Place, Marsh's Addition, Redick's Second Addition, and Briggs' Place.

October 29th, 1860, the Council adopted a resolution to withdraw all opposition to the confirmation of the pre-emption of Paul Neilson to the east half of the south-west quarter of section 22, and the east half of the north-west quarter of section 27, township 15, range 13, in consideration of receiving $1,250 in scrip from said Neilson. This tract is a mile in length, north and south, and a quarter of a mile wide, extending from Center Street on the south to the alley south of Harney Street on the north, and from Sixteenth Street on the east to Twentieth on the west. It includes Hartman's Addition, Kountze & Ruth's Addition, and the triangular tract north of St. Mary's Avenue and east of Twentieth Street,

## REAL ESTATE AND OTHER LEGISLATION.

platted as Kountze's Reserve. With respect to this entry, on the 13th of March, 1862, this record appears in the proceedings of the City Council:

On leave, Messrs. Kountze and Ruth made a statement to the Council in relation to their note held by the city. Alderman Kennedy presented the following resolution, which was adopted: *Resolved*, That Messrs. Kountze and Ruth be released from all liability upon their note now held by the City of Omaha for the payment of $1,250 in city scrip or orders, dated October 30, 1860, and from all obligation to the said city in relation to the Paul Neilson entry, being the east half of the south-west quarter of section 22, and the east half of the north-west quarter of section 27, upon payment by said Kountze and Ruth to the City Treasurer the sum of $1,000 in city scrip or orders ; and, further, that they take up the note of Heman Glass to said city for $920, dated September 17, 1860, payable in city scrip or orders.

For many years this man Neilson lived in a small house on this tract, just north of St. Mary's Avenue. July 21, 1874, he hung himself in an out-building. He was then 66 years old, and lived with his married daughter and her husband, Christian Peterson. It was reported that he had been poisoned, and the body was taken up after burial and a *post mortem* examination had. Mr. and Mrs. Peterson, who discovered the dead body in the barn, at first reported that death had resulted from an attack of cholera-morbus, but the coronor's inquest disclosed the facts; when the body was dug up, it was found that a good suit of clothes in which it had been dressed for burial had been removed by someone, and an old suit substituted.

There was evidently "a watch dog of the treasury" in the earlier history of our city government, however it may have been in later years, as the records show an almost universal habit of cutting down on claims presented for payment. For instance, in 1860, the city printer, M. H. Clark, presented one bill for $110.00, which was referred to the Judiciary Committee, which committee reported, recommending that he be paid $70.00, but the Council thought this was too much, and voted the sum of $50.00 as a payment in full; M. W. Keith wanted $11.50 for the use of a room for election purposes, and was voted $3.50; Jerry McCheane asked for $3.00 for his services as clerk of election, and was given just fifty per cent. of his claim, and Timothy Kelly was treated in like manner when he demanded $5.00 to pay for his services as judge of election, and for the use of a room for election purposes.

In those early days there seemed to be no lack of poor in the city, as frequent references are made to that class in the Council proceedings. At one time the City Clerk was instructed to "issue city orders on the treasury, not exceeding $100 in the aggregate, as any person will volunteer to cash at par, the money to be appropriated for the relief of the poor of the city." At another time, in 1862, a committee was appointed to solicit donations from citizens for the support of the poor. Mr. Kellom seemed to be an active conservator of the public morals in those early days. Mr. Peter Hugus presented a petition in 1863, praying that steps be taken to prevent steamboats discharging their cargoes at the Omaha levee on Sunday, which petition was referred to a committee, of which Mr. Kellom and Mr. D. C. Sutphen were members. The former presented a report, recommending that the prayer of the petitioner be granted. An adverse report was presented by Mr. Sutphen, and the petition was re-referred to the same committee and evidently never saw the light of day again.

In December, 1864, an appropriation of $100 was made to pay for clearing away the brush on Ninth, Tenth and Eleventh streets, south of Jones, and as late as 1866 residents in that part of the city were allowed to work out their poll tax by cutting out brush from the public streets.

In 1865 there was an ordinance passed "Dedicating streets, alleys, levee, Jefferson Square, and the Park, to public uses." The same year Ebenezer Dallow was granted license "to open and keep a theatre in his building, on block 119, in said city, for the term of one month," for which privilege he was taxed $10. General W. T. Sherman, being expected to visit the city, the Council, at its meeting of October 7, 1865, adopted a resolution tendering him the hospitalities of Omaha. The schools were evidently very modest in their demands in those days, as we find the Board of Education, consisting of George B. Lake, B. E. B. Kennedy and Lorin Miller, petitioning the Council for a deed, February 21, 1866, to the west half of lot 5, in block 232, for school purposes. This lot is situated at the northeast corner of Pacific and Tenth.

Early in 1866 the Council passed a resolution declaring that the privilege heretofore granted E. B. Chandler to stack hay in certain streets of the city shall expire on the first day of May, 1866. March 22d, of that year, a police force was elected by the Council, consisting of Patrick Swift, John Morrissey, Thomas Welch and John Logan; and the "Captain of the City Police" was instructed to "place his men on their beats from 8 o'clock until sunrise." A few weeks later this army was increased by an addition of two, but as John Morrissey had been dismissed in the meantime, there was a net gain of but one.

During this same month an ordinance was passed requiring barbers to close their shops on Sunday, which action evidently created considerable dissatisfaction, as a few weeks later Alderman Ingalls gave notice that he would introduce a resolution to rescind the action previously taken; but, as no further record was made with regard to it, his purpose was evidently not carried out.

The following list comprises the principal city officers since the organization of the city government:

MAYORS—Jesse Lowe, 1857; A. J. Poppleton, 1858; George Armstrong, 1859; D. D. Belden, 1860; Clinton Briggs, 1861; George Armstrong, 1862; B. E. B. Kennedy, 1863; A. R. Gilmore, 1864; Lorin Miller, 1865; Charles H. Brown, 1867; George M. Roberts, 1868; Ezra Millard, 1869; Smith S. Caldwell, 1871; Joseph H. Millard, 1872; William M. Brewer, 1873; C. S. Chase, 1875; Reuben H. Wilbur, 1877; C. S. Chase, 1879; James E. Boyd, 1881; C. S. Chase, 1883; P. F. Murphy (to complete the unexpired term of C. S. Chase), 1885; James E. Boyd, 1886; W. J. Broatch, 1887; R. C. Cushing. 1889; George P. Bemis 1891. [In 1887, Judge Wakeley decided, in a *quo warranto* proceeding brought by C. S. Chase, that the latter had been illegally ousted as Mayor by the Council in 1884, and in a hearing before Judge Clarkson in June, 1890. the Court directed the jury to find for plaintiff in a case where Chase was seeking to recover the amount of the Mayor's salary paid to Murphy while acting as Mayor, to the amount of nearly $1,000.]

CITY CLERKS—H. C. Anderson, 1857; James W. VanNostrand, Joseph R. Stokes, R. C. Jordan, 1858; James W. Van Nostrand, 1859; George R. Smith, Byron Reed, 1860; Byron Reed, 1861-2-3-4-5-6; William L. May, 1867; C. L. Bristol, 1868-9-70-71; Joseph M. McCune, 1872-3-4; O. C. Ludlow, 1875-6-7; Zachary Taylor, 1878; James F. McCartney, 1880; J. J. L. C. Jewett, 1881-2-3-4-5; J. B. Southard, 1886-7-8; John Groves, 1889-90-91 (still in office).

CITY TREASURERS—John H. Kellom, 1858; Joseph H. Millard, 1859; R. H. Brown, 1860; Daniel Gantt, 1861 to 1864; Frank Murphy, 1864 to 1868; Henry Gray, 1868 to 1871; John Steen, 1871 to 1873; Edward A. Johnson, 1873 to 1875; C. Hartman, 1875 to 1879; Samuel G. Mallette, 1879 to 1882; Truman Buck, 1882 to 1887; John Rush, 1887 to 1891; Henry Bolln, 1891.

POLICE JUDGES—(Previous to 1868 the Mayor served as Police Judge also). John Sahler, 1868; John R. Porter, 1868 to 1873; Erwin G. Dudley, 1873; R. H. Wilbur, 1874; John R. Porter, 1875; Gustave Anderson, 1877; P. O. Hawes, 1879; Gustave Beneke, 1881 to 1885; E. M. Stenberg, 1885; Louis Berka, 1887; Lee Helsey, 1889; Louis Berka, 1891.

CITY ATTORNEYS—(This official was formerly called City Solicitor)—Charles Grant, James M. Woolworth, 1857; George I. Gilbert, 1858; no record to 1866, in which last named year George B. Lake filled the position; B. E. B. Kennedy, 1866-7; George W. Ambrose, 1868; J. P. Bartlett, 1869 to 1870; George E. Pritchett, 1873; John M. Thurston, 1874; Charles F. Manderson, 1877; John D. Howe, 1881; William J. Connell, 1883; John L. Webster, 1887; A. J. Poppleton. 1889; W. J. Connell, 1891.

## CITY OFFICERS — PAST AND PRESENT.

CITY ENGINEER—A. S. Morgan, 1857; Chauncy Wiltse, 1858; O. F. Davis, 1860 to 1866; George Smith, 1866; R. C. Barnard, A. J. Wilgocke, 1867; William Kipp, 1868 to 1871; J. E. House, 1871; Andrew Rosewater, 1871 to 1874; Edmund Dutton, 1874; Andrew Rosewater, 1875; Wilbur F. Hawes, 1876 to 1878; Henry Rohwer, 1878 to 1881; Andrew Rosewater, 1881 to 1887; George W. Tillson 1889; Andrew Rosewater, 1891.

CITY MARSHALS AND CHIEFS OF POLICE—J. A. Miller, J. H. Wheeler, 1857; J. H. Wheeler, 1858; Thomas L. Sutton, 1859 to 1861; T. J. Torrey, A. L. King, 1862; Thomas Riley, 1863 to 1864; Crockett Wilson, 1865; Thomas Riley, William P. Snowden, 1866; William P Snowden, 1867; W. W. Angel, H. L. Seward, 1868; William G. Hollins, 1869 to 1870; H. L. Seward, 1871; Richard Kimball, 1872; Gilbert Rustin, 1873 to 1874; William P. Snowden 1875 to 1876; John H. Butler, 1877 to 1878; C. J. Westerdahl, 1879; D. P. Angel, 1881 to 1883; Roger C. Guthrie, 1884; Thomas Cumings, 1885; Webb S. Seavey, 1887 (still in office).

GAS INSPECTOR—George W. Gratton, 1869 to 1872. The office was then vacant until the present incumbent, James Gilbert, was appointed in 1886.

FIRE WARDENS AND CHIEFS OF FIRE DEPARTMENT—Benjamin Steckles, 1862 to 1866; W. J. Kennedy, 1866; Andrew J. Simpson, 1866; Joseph F. Sheely, 1869; J. E. Markel, 1871; Charles Simpson, 1872; Stephen N. Mealio, 1874; John J. Galligan, 1874; Frank Kleffner, 1875; John J. Galligan, 1876 to 1882; John H. Butler, 1882 to 1886; John J. Galligan, 1886 (still in office).

HEALTH OFFICERS AND CITY PHYSICIANS—A. Chappel, 1857; J. P. Peck, 1858; George L. Miller, 1861; A. Roeder, 1862; G. C. Monell, 1864; J R. Conkling, 1865 to 1868, from which date the office was vacant for several years. R. C. Moore, 1876 to 1879; P. S. Leisenring, 1879 to 1887; J. B. Ralph, 1887 to 1889; Clark Gapen, 1889; A. B. Somers, 1891.

STREET COMMISSIONERS—Jeremiah Mahoney, 1858 to 1859; Jeremiah Mahoney, 1867; John Logan, 1868; William Knight, A. R. Hoel, 1869; B. B. Case, 1870; Jerry Dee, 1871; Robert G. Jenkinson, 1872 to 1874; Patrick Ford, 1881 to 1884; Michael C. Meaney, 1884 to 1889; Josiah Kent, 1889; J. H. Winspear, 1892.

BOARD OF PUBLIC WORKS—See chapter entitled "Public Improvements."

FIRE AND POLICE COMMISSIONERS—See chapter on Police.

BUILDING INSPECTORS—George C. Whitlock, 1887; James F. Filley, 1891.

COMPTROLLERS—Charles S. Goodrich, 1887; Theodore Olsen, 1891.

PLUMBING INSPECTORS—Robert D. Duncan, 1887; George Dennis, 1889.

CITY AUDITORS—Eben K. Long, 1885 to 1887, Mr. Long is the only person filling this office, the title being changed in 1887 to City Comptroller.

COUNCILMEN—(The city was first divided into three wards, with the Council composed of three members from each ward, to serve two years, after the first year, when half the Board was elected for only one year. Afterwards the city was re-districted into six wards, each having two members in the Board. At present there are nine wards, with a Council composed of eighteen members, half of whom are elected from the respective wards, and the others from the city at large). A. D. Jones, T. G. Goodwill, G. C. Bovey, H. H. Visscher, Thomas Davis, William N. Byers, William W. Wyman, Thomas O'Connor, C. H. Downs, John H. Kellom and James Creighton—the last two named being elected to fill vacancies caused by the resignation of A. D. Jones and death of T. G. Goodwill—1857; John E. Dailey, William W. Keith, Lorin Miller, B. T. C. Morgan, G. W. Wood, Jonas G. Seely, O. P. Ingalls, D. F. Richards, John Campbell, H. M. Judson, Albert S. Clarke, John Richards and O. D. Richardson—there were six vacancies caused by resignations during the year—1858; Thomas Davis, William A. Gwyer, Harrison Johnson, A. J. Hanscom, John McCormick, John Ritchie and Joseph Barker, Jr., 1859; G. C. Monell, John R. Meredith, J. G. Megeath, H. Z. Curtis, Edwin Loveland, Moses F. Shinn and Francis Smith, 1860; James K. Ish, Charles P. Birkett, J. J. Brown, John R. Porter, Asa Hunt and W. J. Kennedy, 1861; B. E. B. Kennedy, St. John Goodrich, D. C. Sutphen, Henry Gray, Joseph F. Sheely and William F. Sapp, 1862; Thomas O'Connor, St. John Goodrich, George B. Lake, Henry Grebe, John Campbell and John H. Kellom, 1863; Vincent Burkley, George M. Mills, Joseph E. Sheely, L. C. Huntington, John R. Porter, J. B. Allen and William E. Harvey, 1864; James B. Callahan, Jonas Gise, Charles H. Brown, O. P. Ingalls and George Smith, 1865; C. P. Birkett, A. J. Simpson, O. P. Ingalls and D. F. Richards, 1866; John H. Green, Charles Maguire, John R. Porter, Julius Rudowsky, Henry Bruning, James Creighton, William Jones and Edwin Patrick, 1867; George W. Doane, Robert C. Jordan, John R. Meredith, N. P. Isaacs, C. L. Gambell, J. C. Ambrose, David T. Mount and John Evans, 1868; Julius Rudowsky, Thomas Davis, George C. Merrill, George W. Homan, J. E. Kelley, David T. Mount, L. C. Richards, J. S. McCormick, George

O. Williams, James Creighton, Joseph W. Paddock, S. C. Rose and Jesse H. Lacey, 1869; E. A. Allen, Richard P. Kimball, John A. Horbach and George Smith, 1870; M. J. McKelligon, George W. Homan, James S. Gibson, Henry Luhens, John Campbell, John A. Horbach, Byron Reed, James Creighton, J. P. Bartlett and Thomas Martin, 1871; Thomas Swobe, A. J. Doyle, John M. Thurston, John D. Jones, L. L. Bristol and Henry J. Lucas. 1872; James Stephenson, James S. Gibson, W. J. Hamilton, D. C. Sutphen, A. A. Gibson and W. W. Marsh, 1873; O. C. Campbell. A. McGavock, Charles Bankes, Lewis Brown, H. J. Lucas M. H. Brown, Isaac W. Miner and Thomas Swobe, 1874; John P. Kelley, Charles J. Karbach, M. Cumings Charles C. Sperry, William N. Dwyer and Edwin Loveland, 1875; A. McGavock. Edward C. McShane, August Aust, Bernard Shannon Lewis S. Brown, C. V. Gallagher and E. V. Smith. 1876: Robert G. Jenkinson, James G. Megeath Charles Bankes, George H. Boggs, Fred W. Gray, William M. Dwyer and Robert K. Taft, 1877; Isaac S. Hascall, Owen Slaven, Dennis Cunningham, Bernard Shannon, George W. Lininger, Orrin G. Dodge and Joseph Redman, 1878; Charles Kaufman, George F. Labagh, Fritz Riepen, John D. Jones, Levi J. Kennard, Thomas H. Dailey and James Stephenson, 1879; Edward Roddis, Charles A. Thieman, Henry Hornberger, Thomas Blackmore, James E. Boyd and William Dailey, 1880; A. McGavock, M. A. McNamara, Martin Dunham, W. I. Baker. Richard O'Keefe, Fred Dellone, Homer Stull. J. O. Corby and Samuel H. Herman, 1881; C. C. Thrane, Fred Behm, D. L. McGuckin, Martin Dunham Edward Leeder and W. I. Baker, 1882; William Anderson, Isaac S. Hascall, Charles Kaufman, Charles D. Woodworth, P. F. Murphy and Josiah B. Redfield 1883; C. C. Thrane, Fred Behm, D. L. McGuckin, Martin Dunham Edward Leeder and W. I. Baker, 1884; Patrick Ford, W. F. Bechel, John B. Furay, Charles Kaufman, Isaac S. Hascall and P. F. Murphy, 1885; Charles F. Goodman, Michael Lee, Louis Shroeder, Charles S. Goodrich. Thomas H. Dailey and Francis E. Bailey, 1886; Adam Suyder, John F. Boyd, Charles Van Camp. Jacob M. Counsman, Jeff. W. Bedford, Leavitt Burnham, T. J. Lowry, Frank S. Kasper and Charles D. Cheney, 1887; William G. Shriver, Dan. H. Wheeler, Edward O'Connor. A. H. Sanders, Edwin P. Davis, Clarence L. Chaffee, F. E. Bailey, Isaac S. Hascall and Patrick Ford, 1888; William F. Bechel, F. L. Blumer, F. D. Cooper, James Donnelly, Sr., B. F. Madsen, John McLearie, Edward F. Morearty, Theodore Olsen and Henry Osthoff, 1889; Clarence L. Chaffee, Edwin P. Davis, Thos. J. Lowry, Charles E. Bruner, Thomas F. Tuttle, Richard Burdish, Peter Elsasser, Timothy Conway and Christian Specht, 1890; Peter M. Back, William S. Bechel, A. G. Edwards, Edward E. Howell, Halfdan Jacobsen, George F. Munro, John McLearie, Sol Prince and John Steel, 1891.

BOARD OF EDUCATION (since the establishment of the present school system)—Theodore Baumer. Charles M. Conoyer, Flemon Drake, Vincent Burkley, Charles W. Hamilton, A. Boehme, Howard Kennedy, Alvin Saunders, Thomas F. Hall. James Creighton, John T. Edgar, 1872; P. P. Shelby, Flemon Drake, James Morris, Howard Kennedy, David Harpster, Charles K. Coutant, 1873; Alvin Saunders, C. A. Baldwin. James Creighton, A. Boehme, Vincent Burkley, William Stephens, Jr., 1874; Eben K. Long, John Newell, I. R. Steel, M. G. McKoon, W. Mulhall. Charles K. Coutant 1875; W. H. S. Hughes, John Morrell. Charles Powell, William A. Gwyer. H. G. Clark. Howard Kennedy, Robert McConnell, Joseph W. Paddock, W. W. Marsh, 1876; W. J. Broatch, T. J Staley, George Wilkins, Daniel Sullivan, J. J. Points, Thomas H. Dailey, Robert Calderwood. 1877: George C. Bonner, Simeon Bloom, Peter O'Malley, 1878; Charles M. Conoyer, E. K. Long, R. E. Gaylord, Robert McConnell. W. W. Marsh, John Dwyer, 1879; John Bamford. John Morrell, Charles D. Woodworth, Howard Kennedy, M. G. McKoon, A. A. Gibson, 1880; George Thrall, F. J. McShane, A. N. Ferguson, William Anderson, Charles M. Conoyer, 1881; J. J. Points, E. K. Long, Charles M. Conoyer, 1882; A. N. Ferguson, F. J. McShane, William Anderson, 1883; W. E. Copeland, W. A. L. Gibbon, R. S. Hall, Henry Livesey, A. A. Parker, Christian Specht, 1884; Henry Livesey, William Coburn. H. G. Clark, 1885; R. S. Hall, J. J. Points, Charles Conoyer, W. E. Copeland, R. S. Hall, W. A. L. Gibbon, 1886; H. G. Clark, E. K. Long, Henry Livesey, William Coburn, T. W. Blackburn, H. E Davis. 1887; Frederick W. Gray, D. V. Sholes, Edward A. Parmalee, Robert McConnell, Aug. Pratt, William A. Kelley, W. E. Copeland, J. J. Saville. S. S. Auchmoedy, Morris Morrison, Henry T. Clarke. 1888; Charles Wehrer, Frederick R. McConnell, Frank Spoor, S. K. Spaulding. S. K. Felton, C. F. Goodman, Alfred Millard, Samuel Rees. 1889; W. S. Gibbs, Morris Morrison, H. B. Coryell, C. J. Smyth, Charles E. Babcock, 1890; W. N. Babcock. Charles S. Elgutter, R. W. Gibson, Clinton N. Powell, C. L. Jaynes. 1891.

The city has nine wards, and the Council is composed of eighteen members, one half of whom are elected from the city at large, at the regular city election, and the other

## SALARIES OF PRESENT CITY OFFICIALS.

half are elected by the respective wards on intervening years, for a term of two years, so that but one half the membership is made up of new members at any time. Following named are the present city officials.

MAYOR—George P Bemis
TREASURER—Henry Bolln
COMPTROLLER—Theodore Olsen
POLICE JUDGE—Louis Berka
COUNCILMEN AT LARGE (terms expire January 1, 1894)—Peter M Back, William F Bechel, A G Edwards, Edward E Howell, Halfdan Jacobson, George F Munro, John McLearie, Sol Prince, John Steel
WARD COUNCILMEN (terms expire January 1, 1893)—T J Lowry, Peter Elsasser, Richard Burdish, Thomas F Tuttle, Timothy J Conway, Christian Specht, Clarence L Chaffee, Charles E Bruner and Edwin P Davis
BOARD OF PUBLIC WORKS—P W Birkhauser, Chairman, A E Egbert, J B Furay
ENGINEER—Andrew Rosewater
BUILDING INSPECTOR—James F Tilly
BOILER INSPECTOR—Charles Soudenberg
CITY CLERK—John Groves
PLUMBING INSPECTOR—Robert L Duncan
GAS INSPECTOR—James Gilbert
STREET COMMISSIONER—J H Winspear
SIDEWALK INSPECTOR—John E Bonewitz

MEAT INSPECTORS—Frederick Hickstein, A. Halle
CITY PHYSICIAN—Dr A B Somers
CITY VETERINARIAN—Dr H L Ramacciotti

Omaha's officials are paid as follows

Mayor, $3,100, City Clerk, $2,000, Treasurer, $6,000, City Attorney, $3,000, Chief of Police, $2,000 Police Judge, $2,500, Comptroller, $2,500, City Physician, $2,000 City Clerk, $2,000, City Engineer, $3,000, Assistant City Engineer, $2 000, Chief of Fire Department, $2,000, Board of Public Works—Chairman, $2,500, other members, $1,000 Assistant City Attorney, $2,000, Building Inspector, $2,000, City Prosecutor, $1,500, Gas Inspector, $1,500, Boiler Inspector, $1,500, Plumbing Inspector, $1,800, Sidewalk Inspector, $1,200, Street Commissioner, $1 800 License Inspector, $1,200, Meat Inspectors (two), $1,200 each, Superintendent of City Schools, $3,600, Clerk of Board of Education, $1,800, Fire and Police Commissioners, $1,000, City Councilmen, $800, Chairman Park Commissioners, $600, the other four members $200 each, Policemen, $85, Captains and Sergeants not exceeding $100

In the early history of Omaha the Mayor had the legal jurisdiction of a Justice of the Peace, and tried the class of cases now disposed of by the Police Judge

# CHAPTER XI.

### THE CLAIM CLUB—THE PURPOSE OF ITS ORGANIZATION—SOME FACTS REGARDING EARLY LAND TITLES.

Claim clubs were a feature in the early settlement of Nebraska which the situation rendered necessary. The land had not been surveyed, hence titles could not be perfected and the protection of the rights of the settlers by a combination of interests was the only method possible. The Omaha Claim Club was organized precisely as clubs were organized in every town in the Territory, with the exception that it allowed its members to hold 320 acres of land, while the rule with others was to protect their members in claiming but 160 acres each. The good of the many was secured by these organizations, though in some instances injustice may have been done the few. The Omaha Club was composed of such men as John M. Thayer, A. D. Jones, A. J. Hanscom, A. J. Poppleton, Lyman Richardson, Governor Cuming, Dr. George L. Miller, Dr. Enos Lowe, Jesse Lowe, Joseph and George E. Barker, Joseph Barker, Sr., O. D. Richardson, Byron Reed, M. C. Gaylord, Robert B. Whitted, S. Lewis, John I. Redick and James M. Woolworth—indeed its membership comprised almost all of the male residents of the town in 1854 and 1855. In many instances valuable improvements were made upon claims taken by members of the club, and the transfer of the rights of claimants formed a considerable part of the commercial transactions of those early days, in the absence of anything more substantial. The difficulties which followed were attributable, chiefly, to the fact that a half section, instead of a quarter section, could be held by each claimant, and the further fact that nearly 4,000 acres were claimed by the original town site company. Later comers objected to so wide an expanse of territory being held by so few; claims were "jumped" and conflicts with the claim club resulted. Under its regulations the only course to be pursued was to notify each intruder that the land he claimed had previously been taken by a member of the club; that the latter's rights would be protected and that the newcomer must vacate to avoid trouble. In a very few instances personal resistance was made, and, of course, the club carried out the purposes for which it was organized.

Jacob S. Shull, locating in 1855 on a quarter section just south of town, a portion of which had previously been platted by Roswell G. Pierce as Pierce's Addition, received a visit from the club; but, being warned of the intended honor, did not wait to receive his unwelcome guests. His shanty was destroyed and for several days Mr. Shull was concealed under the counter of J. J. Brown & Brothers' store, corner of Douglas and Fourteenth, fearing personal violence. He finally decided to surrender his claim to the land and that ended the difficulty. The following spring he brought his family to Omaha, and died a few months later. Mrs. Shull then made claim to the land; the circumstances of the case were brought to the attention of the land department at Washington, an investigation followed and she was declared the legal owner of the property—now of great value.

The tract now known as Redick's Addition, Terrace Addition and Bartlett's Addition was claimed by Governor Cuming; and in order to hold it he had a small house built and hired a man named Callahan, at $45 per month, to occupy it. Callahan concluded that this was an excellent opportunity to get some land of his own, and made his filing at the land office. He was taken in charge by the club, asked to surrender his certificate, and, upon his refusal, was ducked in the Missouri River, and thereupon concluded that he did not care very much for that particular tract of land, and gave up the paper.

The claim club was first organized as "The Omaha Township Claim Association," July 22, 1854, with A. D. Jones as Judge; S. Lewis, Clerk; M. C. Gaylord, Recorder; and Robert B. Whitted as Sheriff. The duty of the judge was to preside at all the meetings; the clerk kept a record of the proceedings; the recorder kept a register of quit claim deeds, description of claims and decisions of arbitrators in disputed cases; and the sheriff executed the judgment of arbitrators and the orders of the club, and was empowered to call out the entire membership, if necessary, in the performance of his duties. Under the re-organization afterwards effected Dr. Lowe and A. J. Hanscom served at different periods as president of the club, and Jesse Lowe as captain. Moral suasion was first used in all cases where conflicts arose, but where that failed the club was prepared to adopt harsher methods to carry out its objects.

Judge John I. Redick had a little experience with the claim club in the winter of 1856, which he tells in this way: "Several of us who were boarding at the Tremont House, on Douglas Street, attended a temperance meeting one night, held in the Methodist Church, just around the corner on Thirteenth Street. It was proposed to organize to secure the adoption of the Maine Liquor Law, and I was asked to say something. I objected to the proposition, and said that such a law could not be carried out in Nebraska, and remarked, incidentally, that the United States laws allowed a man to enter but 160 acres of land, while the Omaha Claim Club said he could hold twice that amount and declared its readiness to defend him in claiming that amount. Next morning I went to my office, and was met with a scolding by my partner, James G. Chapman, who said I had got myself and the firm of Redick & Chapman in a nice muddle. He kept on with a regular tirade, but I finally got him to explain what he was talking about, and learned, to my astonishment, that I had been reported as using treasonable language against the claim club. I soon found the town was posted with notices for a meeting of the club, and concluded that I had stirred up a good deal of a rumpus, without intending to. The club was a powerful organization, I knew, for I was a member of it. I laid in a revolver that day, loaded it, and put it in my overcoat pocket. Then I told Chapman that he owed it to me to see that I had a chance to speak when the club met. The meeting was held in the Pioneer Block, and the first speech was made by A. J. Hanscom, the president, who spoke in a very reasonable, moderate way. He was followed by Mitchell, of Florence, who was very abusive of new people who were coming into the Territory to break down local institutions. Then a man from Bellevue talked, and he was followed by John M. Thayer in a ponderous sort of a way, and in a tone similar to that of Mitchell; and then Jim Chapman said that his partner ought to be given a chance to explain his views as to claim clubs and other domestic institutions. Thereupon I came to the front, and for ten minutes dwelt upon the advantages of the Territory of Nebraska, and predicted its glorious future. Then I praised the claim club, and said I had improved the first opportunity I had to join it upon coming to Omaha, a few months previously. I then said that I had had no intention to reflect upon the club, and that what I had said had not been correctly reported. I added that I knew that every man present was at least an ordinarily brave man, and with that I produced my revolver with one hand, and took out my watch with the other, and said: 'I denounce the man who has thus misrepresented me as a liar, a coward and a sneak, and will give him one minute in which to come out and face me.' As the time was ticked off, no one moved, and when I announced that the time had expired, there was a burst of applause, and I was convinced that I had nothing to fear.''

The tracts in North Omaha, afterwards entered by John A. Horbach and George Smith, were included in an addition platted by the Council Bluffs & Nebraska Ferry Company in 1855, and known at that period as Scrip Town. The survey was made by Colonel Lorin Miller, who received as pay for his services a block of eight lots and $2,000 in money. He selected his block of ground, No. 172½, but made no improvements thereon. Years afterwards, that portion of the Scrip Town plat having, in the meantime, passed into the ownership of Mr. Horbach, and the stakes defining lots and blocks being obliterated, he sued Mr. Horbach to gain possession of his property. The latter demanded that its exact location be defined by Colonel Miller, which proved a matter of considerable difficulty, but was finally accomplished to the satisfaction of the District Court and the Supreme Court. The litigation lasted for several years, and resulted in a single block being platted in that portion of the Horbach tract, then used for market garden purposes, designated by the number it bore in the original platting made more than a quarter of a century before, and for several years this block stood solitary and alone on the city maps. It is located about the intersection of Paul and Twenty-First Streets.

The first tract of land owned in this vicinity by the Kountze family—now such extensive real estate proprietors—consisted of three fifteen-acre lots, purchased by Augustus Kountze, located in what was called the Clancy Claim. Additional ground adjoining was secured, and the 160 acres, now platted as Kountze Addition, grew out of the original tract of forty-five acres.

The main town site was entered by Jesse Lowe, as Mayor, March 17, 1857, and certain odds and ends claimed by the Council Bluffs & Nebraska Ferry Company were bid in by John McCormick as Trustee, July 5, 1859. The opening of the land office in 1857 was awaited with great anxiety by the settlers, as, previous to that time, valid titles to their land could not be obtained, and the country was overrun with men known as claim jumpers, whose chief characteristic was a reckless disregard for the rights of other people, and who usually carried revolvers and indulged in a great deal of bluster about what they would do if interfered with. Killings on one side or the other were not infrequent, and the chance to purchase the land claimed was hailed as a period which would end an unsettled condition of society which all law-abiding citizens deplored.

The claim of 400 acres of land which Thomas Davis traded to Samuel S. Bayliss for the sawmill, elsewhere referred to, Mr. Bayliss traded to A. J. Hanscom; and a portion, 160 acres, was pre-empted by Mr. Hanscom when the land came into market in 1857. He sold part of his claim to Roswell G. Pierce, who laid it out as "Pierce's Addition.'' It was within the boundaries of the Shull tract, however, and Pierce was not able to perfect his title. The pre-emption laws allowed the entry of only 160 acres by each settler, but the hiring of others to pre-empt was a very common thing at that period; and in this way one purpose of the law—securing a general ownership of land—was frustrated.

The first paper put on record in the Douglas County deed records was a description of tracts of lands claimed by A. D. Jones, dated November 6, 1854, and recorded February 20, 1855, by Lyman Richardson, the first register of deeds for this county. It is as follows:

Commencing at the mouth of Purgatory Creek and running thence east to the Missouri River; thence down the said river to near the mouth of the slough ; thence west to the bluff ; thence up, under the bluff to the place of beginning, containing about 40 acres between the slough and the river, and bounded as follows: north by Peterson; east by the Missouri River; south by Reeves and west by Hanscom and Allen. The lines are all distinctly and well marked so they can be easily traced, and all the improvements are on the part of my claim, south of Omaha City, and also another part of my claim north of Omaha City, described as follows : north by H. D. Johnson ; west by W. Johnson ; south by W. Clancy ; and east by T. Jeffries, containing about 160 acres ; and is well staked, so the lines can be easily traced ; and a furrow on the north, west and south.

The second transfer recorded was one by which Enos Lowe conveyed the title to six lots to A. J. Hanscom, for a consideration of $600.00 ; in the third, Lyman Richardson deeds away an undivided one-twentieth part of a claim, " bounded on the north by A. J. Hanscom; on the east by Clancy and Jeffries; on the south by Hadley D. Johnson, and on the west by Murphy ; containing 273½ acres.'' The fourth transfer recorded recites, that in consideration of the building of a house, the town site company convey to A. J. Hanscom lots seven and eight, in block 105 ; and lots one and two, in block 138. The first lots are situated at the northwest corner of Douglas and Fourteenth, and the other two at the southwest corner of Farnam and Fourteenth, the ground now occupied by the Paxton Hotel. These two lots he sold in 1867 for $15,000. The building referred to, the erection of which was the consideration, was put up on one of the Paxton Hotel lots for a printing office—the first in Omaha.

George Francis Train became identified with Omaha at an early period, through his connection with the Union Pacific Railroad. In 1865 he purchased of the Kountze Brothers and Samuel E. Rogers a tract of 500 acres of land, of irregular form, the extreme northern boundary being a line 132 feet south of Pierce Street, the southern, the north line of Deer Park, the western, Twentieth Street, and the eastern, Second Street, as now platted. Eighty acres in the northeast corner of this tract he platted into lots and christened it " Credit Foncier Addition.'' Here he had erected ten houses, at a cost of $1,200 each, the buildings being framed and prepared for erection in Chicago, from which city even the bricks used for foundations and chimneys were brought. This addition he sold to the organization known as the " Credit Foncier of America,'' of which he was president, and George P. Bemis, secretary. James G. Chapman was local superintendent. These Chicago-built cottages were rented to some of the leading people of Omaha at a rental of $60 per month. Train paid from $100 to $200 per acre for the land, and sold the platted portion for $250 per acre. He paid only $38,000 cash, giving notes secured by mortgages for the remainder; and the court records of Douglas County, Nebraska, disclose much interesting information as to the result of this investment, suits being brought in 1872 by the Messrs. Kountze and Rogers to foreclose the mortgages held by them, which suits were finally successful. Train fought this litigation at long range, and under decidedly unfavorable circumstances, being confined in the Tombs Prison, New York City, a portion of the time, on the charge of publishing obscene literature in his newspaper, *The Train Ligue*. He had been making a lecture tour throughout the country, ostensibly as a candidate for the presidency of the United States, and his arrest occurred in November, immediately following the election of 1872. He had somewhat championed the cause of the Woodhull Sisters, and thereby incurred public ill will; and when he printed in his paper certain quotations from the Bible, in a spirit of bravado, he was arrested at once, and that edition of the *Ligue* confiscated by the authorities. He was confined in the Tombs for several months, and an effort was made to prove that he was insane. The charge of circulating obscene literature, it was found, could not be established, and Train was finally discharged. In the meantime the foreclosure proceedings were carried on in Omaha against Train personally, and his counsel undertook to have them set aside on the ground that a guardian should have been appointed to protect his interests, claiming that, as a matter of fact, he was then of unsound mind, at least temporarily, and citing this experience with the New York authorities in support of their position. The direct action against Train was held by the court to be legal, however, and in due time decisions in favor of the plaintiffs were rendered, and they recovered all of the land except the "Credit Foncier Addition." The notes drew twelve per cent. interest, and with the costs of foreclosures, added very considerably to the amount of the principal, so that there was nothing left for the defendant. In these suits, George W. Ambrose was counsel for Mr. Rogers; James M. Woolworth and George I. Gilbert appeared for the Kountzes, and John I. Redick, Arthur N. Ferguson and William J. Connell for Mr. Train. The tract thus recovered includes the ground since platted as Kountze's Addition, Supplement Addition, Kountze's Second Addition, Kountze's Supplemental Addition, Kountze's Fourth Addition, S. E. Rogers' Addition, Bowery Hill, Rogers' Plat of Okahoma, Improvement Association Addition, the Hascall Tract of ten acres on Thirteenth Street, and a large tract of unplatted ground, east of Thirteenth Street and west of Supplement Addition, and is now of immense value. The various mortgages, now included in the court files, are embellished with the internal revenue stamps then required by the government.

One of them, given to secure three notes, amounting to $24,999, bears two ten dollar stamps and one of five dollars, indicating that the general government was enriched to the extent of twenty-five dollars by that one mortgage.

May 2, 1876, a petition was filed in the District Court by George P. Bemis, in a suit against Mr. Train, as follows:

The plaintiff, George P. Bemis, represents to the Court that about the month of November, 1864, he entered into a verbal contract with one George Francis Train, in the capacity of his private secretary; that the said Train, at that time, was a man of large influence, and was indirectly connected with some of the largest enterprises in the United States, to-wit: the corporation known as the "Credit Mobilier of America," and the successful construction, in the shortest possible time, of the Union Pacific Railroad, procured the passage of an act in Nebraska, by its legislature, incorporating what is known as the "Credit Foncier of America," whose pretended object was to buy large tracts of land along the line of the Union Pacific Railroad; as well also being engaged in the construction of street railways in London, as well also being an aspirant for the highest office in the gift of the American people.

Plaintiff further says: That, by reason of his various business connections with these important enterprises and his unbridled ambition for political preference and glory, he deemed it important and necessary to employ some competent and true man to act as his confidante and private secretary, in all his business and political relations.

Plaintiff further says: That, to that end, about the date aforesaid, he, the said Train, employed this plaintiff by the year, agreeing to pay him for his services the sum of $5,000 per annum; and, in consideration of said promise and agreement in that behalf, the plaintiff entered into his service and employ about the 15th day of November, 1864, and continued in his employ, faithfully performing the services demanded or required by him, of every kind and nature, in many instances jeopardizing his own personal safety and life, while acting as his secretary, to carry out his wishes and desires; in many instances working nights as well as days, and has so continued in his employ up to and including November 15th, 1874; that all of said services were accepted by said defendant, and to his entire satisfaction; that he has paid said plaintiff, upon said contract, from time to time, in cash and otherwise, the first payment being made from the date first aforesaid to January 1, 1865, and at divers and sundry times since that, upon said contract, to December 10, 1875, amounting to $17,974.65, leaving a balance due this plaintiff of $47,660.68.

Plaintiff further says: That is all he has received upon said contract, and here submits to the Court an itemized statement of account between plaintiff and defendant, marked "A," and asks that it be made a part of the petition herein.

Plaintiff further says: That he has performed in every respect his part of said agreement, and that the said sum of $47,660.68 is the balance due and owing to him on said contract, and for that amount he prays judgment against said defendant, with costs.

Mr. Bemis clearly established his case and was awarded judgment for the full amount claimed. Mr. Train's interest in the Credit Foncier Addition was levied upon, and the property sold, and a portion of the judgment thus satisfied, Mr. Train's interest not being sufficient to pay the full amount. The City Directory for 1871 contains the following, under the heading Real Estate: "Train, George Francis—N. P. A. (Owner of 5,000 lots, a hotel and ten other buildings in Omaha, 1,000 lots in Council Bluffs and 7,000 lots and a hotel in Columbus). Represented by his private secretary and agent, George P. Bemis, Cozzens House." The N. P. A. stood for "Next President of America." Mr. Train's connection with the Cozzens' House enterprise is referred to elsewhere, in the chapter relating to hotels.

# CHAPTER XII.

### The Pioneers — Biographical Sketches — Personal Points Concerning the Early Settlers — "Sons of Omaha."

Much of the prosperity of a city depends upon its founders—their energy, liberality, public spirit, judgment, general information, knowledge of man, foresight, appreciation of the situation, or the lack of these qualities — all becoming important factors in the development or retarding the growth of a new settlement. In these respects, Omaha was peculiarly fortunate, its founders being men of far more than ordinary sagacity and enterprise. The first plat was made by the Council Bluffs & Nebraska Ferry Company, an organization perfected under the laws of Iowa for the purpose of establishing a ferry opposite Council Bluffs, across the Missouri River. This company was composed of Dr. Enos Lowe, Milton Tootle, James Jackson, Samuel S. Bayliss, Joseph H. D. Street, Bernhardt Henn, Jesse Williams, General Samuel R. Curtis, Tanner & Downs and Street & Redfield. Upon the admission of Nebraska as a Territory, May 23, 1854, the importance of securing a town site on the west bank of the river became apparent to these gentlemen, and Alfred D. Jones was employed to make a survey, in which work Captain C. H. Downs (both of these gentlemen are still residents of Omaha) assisted by carrying the chain and driving the stakes. The task was completed early in July of 1854, the town site consisting of 320 blocks, each 264 feet square, with streets 100 feet wide, and alleys of 20 feet. Mr. Jones says that if he had the work to do again he would make the lots 75 by 100 feet, twelve in a block. Capitol Avenue, running eastward from Capitol Square, and Twenty-First Street, running northward from the same point, were each made 120 feet wide. The event was celebrated on the 4th of July by the owners of the town site and their friends coming over from Council Bluffs and having a picnic on Capitol Hill, the present site of the High School building. The task of building upon this spot, so recently diverted from the possession of the Indians, homes and successful business enterprises for a populous community was at once entered upon with zeal and earnestness, a rapid increase of population marking the good judgment of the founders of the town.

The legislative enactment by which Omaha was incorporated, dated February 2, 1857, defines the following described tracts of lands as constituting the site: Sections 15 and 22; fractional sections 11, 14 and 23; the south half of fractional section 10; the south half of the north half of fractional section 10; the south-east quarter of section 9; the east half of section 16; the north-east quarter of section 21; the east half of the south-east quarter of section 21; the north-east quarter of the north-east quarter of section 28; the north half of the north half of section 27; the north half of the north half of fractional section 26 — all in township 15, north of range 13, east of the sixth principal meridian. The name, "The City of Omaha," was given in the charter, and the "middle of the main channel of the Missouri River" was defined as the east line of the city. The officers designated were: Mayor, nine Aldermen, Recorder, Treasurer, Assessor and Marshal. The Legislature of 1858 amended the charter, reducing the number of Aldermen to six.

## LIST OF NAMES OF THE PIONEERS.

To Captain William P. Wilcox and Charles M. Conoyer belong the distinction of having first, of those now resident in the city, seen the site upon which Omaha is now built. In 1849, the former as clerk and the latter, then a boy of eight years of age, were on the steamer El Paso, while that boat was engaged for several weeks in transporting, across the Missouri, emigrants to the newly discovered gold fields of California, at a point just below the plateau on which Omaha now stands. Mr. Conoyer's father was at that time an employe of the American Fur Company, and the father of Captain Wilcox was one of the few passengers aboard the first steamboat which ascended the Missouri River, as is noted elsewhere in these pages. Captain Wilcox became a resident of Omaha in 1864, and for many years, as a member of the firm of Stephens & Wilcox, was extensively engaged in business in this city. Mr. Conoyer located in Omaha in June, 1860, and has since made this his home. He is now Secretary of the Board of Education, and has served many years in that capacity. Mr. and Mrs. William P. Snowden, however, enjoy the honor of being the oldest continuous residents of this city, they having located here July 4, 1854, moving into the old Claim House, a log structure erected by the Town Site Company, on the 11th of July. They were employed by the company to board the hands then engaged in manufacturing brick for a building which the company erected for Territorial Capitol purposes. The enterprise proved a failure, however, as the brick makers were not familiar with the soil of Nebraska, and the result was that Council Bluffs brick entered into the erection of the first brick structure in Omaha.

In the fall of 1854, Mr. A. D. Jones built a home on a claim he had taken south-east of the town site. Previous to the organization of the Steam Ferry Company, Mr. William B. Brown, father of Mrs. Alfred Sorenson and Mrs. Alexander McKenzie, was engaged in transporting passengers across the river at this point by means of a flat-boat. He became interested with the Steam Ferry Company in their enterprise on this side of the river, and located here in 1854.

Among the pioneers who gave tone and character to the new settlement may be mentioned the following, all of whom located here in 1854, several bringing their families, and others a newly acquired wife:

Dr. George L. Miller,
A. J. Poppleton,
O. D. Richardson,
John Davis,
Lyman Richardson,
Thomas Swift,
John M. Thayer,
Samuel E. Rogers,
P. G. Peterson,
Maurice Dee,
Michael Dee,
John Riley,
Jesse Lowe,
Hadley D. Johnson,
Tim Sullivan,
James Ferry,
M. C. Gaylord,
O. B. Selden,
John Withnell,

Col. Lorin Miller,
George Armstrong,
Alexander Davis,
Thomas Davis,
Patrick Swift,
Gen. E. Estabrook,
Thomes O'Connor,
William Rogers,
Joseph W. Paddock,
Dennis Dee,
John Kenneally,
Dr. Enos Lowe,
A. J. Hanscom,
A. B. More,
Thomas Barry,
Joseph Mannien,
Timothy Kelley,
James G. Megeath,
A. D. Jones.

Among those who settled here the following year were:

H. H. Visscher,
David Richards,
John Logan,
John P. McPherson,
Moses Shinn,
Allen Root,
A. U. Wyman,
John Mulvihill,
Patrick Quinland,
Dennis Carroll,
G. C. Bovey,
Richard Kimball,

R. N. Withnell,
Edwin Patrick,
O. P. Ingalls,
Rev. Reuben Gaylord,
S. M. Marston,
W. W. Wyman,
W. N. Byers,
Jerry Mahoney,
Rev. Thomas B. Lemon,
Charles B. Smith,
Byron Reed,
Theodore H. Robertson.

The list of those who came here in 1856 and 1857 is considerably larger. Among these may be mentioned:

Charles W. Hamilton,
Herman Kountze,
John Breen,
Henry A. Kosters,
Thomas Murray,

Augustus Kountze,
O. F. Davis,
James E. Boyd,
Michael Roebling,
Harrison Johnson,

George Smith,
Aaron Cahn,
James Creighton,
Joseph Creighton,
Frank Creighton,
John A. Horbach,
Henry Pundt,
John Smiley and sisters,
George B. Lake,
Col. John Patrick and daughter, now Mrs. Joseph Barker,
S. R. Brown,
A. J. Simpson,
E. F. Cook,
Joseph F. Sheely,
John R. Porter,
Edwin Loveland,
George W. Homan,
Peter Hugus,
P. W. Hitchcock,
Joseph Millard,
John Campbell,
Joel T. Griffin,
Henry Grebe,
A. F. Salisbury,
Peter J. Karbach,
Charles Childs,
George Barker,
Charles Behm,
Robert C. Jordan,
Philip Von Windheim, (known as Peter Windheim),
Marsh Kennard,
William G. Florkee,
J. S. Gibson,
Harry Deuel,
Jacob Shull and family,
William A. Gwyer,
B. E. B. Kennedy,
Joseph P. Manning,
J. C. Carson,
Dr. G. C. Monell,
A. R. Orchard,
James M. Woolworth,
J. B. Plummer,
W. H. Demarest,
Charles B. King,
O. P. Hurford,
Judge J. R. Hyde,
Henry Gray,
Robert S. Knox,
J. Cameron Reeves,
Harrison J. Brown,
John M. Yerga,
M. Hellman,
John Creighton,
Edward Creighton,
Harry Creighton,
William Sexauer,
George M. Mills,
George H. Guy,
Vincent Burkley,
James M. Woolworth,
J. N. H. Patrick,
M. T. Patrick,
A. S. Patrick,
William F. Sweesy,
Charles Beindorf,
Frederick Schneider,
John R. Meredith,
Dr. J. P. Peck,
Augustus Roeder,
Edward P. Peck,
Eb. Dallow,
Ezra Millard,
William A. Little,
E. L. Eaton,
Frederick Drexel,
Jonas Seeley,
Charles J. Karbach,
W. J. Kennedy,
Joseph Barker,
John I. Redick,
S. S. Caldwell,
John F. Behm,
William Lehmer,
Frank Murphy,
Levy Kennard,
David L. Collier,
A. S. Paddock,
Joseph Frenzer,
Charles Powell,
Henry Yates,
W. H. S. Hughes,
George I. Gilbert,
John H. Kellom,
William F. Wilder,
Dr. N. C. Richardson,
Samuel A. Orchard,
Charles C. Woolworth,
The Durnall family,
William Ruth,
N. W. Keith,
Daniel Gantt,
Benjamin Stickles,
James G. Chapman,
Joseph Clark,
George W. Rust,
Thomas L. Sutton,
Henry L. James,
W. L. Pickard,
Henry C. Crowell,
David Whitney,
Frank Smith,
Moritz Roebling,
William Gray,
F. Bunn,
A. R. Gilmore,
George A. McCoy,
George Herzog,
John F. Taylor,
David H. Moffatt,
Rev. H. W. Kuhns,
Rev. William Leach,
The Latey family,
John Shoaf,
N. P. Isaacs,
Chris Hartman,
George W. Doane,
E. B. Chandler,
J. C. Wilcox,
Dr. William McClelland,
Luke McDermott,
Frederick Krug,
Jacob King,
Mrs. C. W. Koenig,
Patrick Clifford,
John McCreary,
Frederick Davis,
S. M. Curran,
Jacob Tex,
Porter Redman,
James T. Allan,
Daniel Sullivan,
James M. Winship,
The Barkalow family,
John M. Sheely,
E. V. Smith,
Charles P. Birkett,
Thomas O'Connor,
The Forbes family,
Charles M. Aumock,
Paul Harmon,
Michael Linahan,
A. N. Ferguson,
Patrick Connolly,
Patrick Dinan,
Frederick Kumpf,
Andrew J. Bruner,
John H. Sahler,
George Sylvester,
John McCormick,
George W. Crowell,
William B. Crowell,
John McBride,
Henry B. Meyers,
William Nile,
Thomas Martin,
F. L. Ruf,
Ralph Bowman,
Emerson S. Seymour,
Michael Cormody,
Samuel Moffatt,
Wiley Dixon,
Rev. Peter Cooper,
Rev. Isaac F. Collins,
Randal Shoaf,
Bernard Koster,
Frederick Court,
William A. Paxton,
Randall Brown,
George Medlock,
Martin Dunham,
Henry Livesey,
Charles Turner,
Andrew Wasserman,
Dr. James H. Seymour,
Jeremiah McCheane,
John M. Clarke,
H. M. Judson,
J. S. McCormick,
Julius Rudowsky,
Joseph Redman,
David Harpster,
Clinton Briggs,
Frank Dellone,
Frederick Dellone,
The McAusland family,
Rubin Wood,
Frank Kleffner,
Jerry Mahoney,
J. W. VanNostrand,
John Pety,
Samuel Megeath,
A. J. Harmon,
Jerry Linahan,
A. F. Frick,
Michael Connolly,
Patrick McDonough,
John J. Bruner,
Uriah Bruner,
Frank Coffman,
J. W. Tousley,
J. J. Brown.

Dr. Enos Lowe, President of the original Town Site Company, was one of the organizers of the Council Bluffs & Nebraska

## BIOGRAPHICAL SKETCHES OF EARLY SETTLERS.

Ferry Company. He was born at Guilford Courthouse, North Carolina, May 5, 1804, moving to Bloomington, Indiana, with his parents at an early age. He graduated with high honors at the Ohio Medical College, of Cincinnati, and practiced medicine for a number of years in Indiana. In 1837 he located at Burlington, Iowa, where he remained ten years, during which period he was a member of two constitutional conventions, of one of which he was President. In 1847, President Van Buren appointed him receiver of public moneys at the Land Office in Iowa City, and in 1853 he removed to Kanesville (Council Bluffs), Iowa, where he held the same position for two years. The platting of Omaha was done under the supervision of Dr. Lowe, as President of the Ferry Company and Town Site Company; and from that date until his death, February 12, 1880, he was actively identified with the best interests of Omaha, and during that period was a continuous resident here. In securing the location of the Union Pacific bridge at Omaha, Dr. Lowe rendered peculiarly efficient service, being a member of the committees sent by the City Council and the citizens to the headquarters of the railroad company at New York. This was a critical period in the history of this city on account of the many antagonisms with which Omaha had to contend in connection with the building of the Union Pacific Railroad. During the war, Dr. Lowe served for some time as surgeon, entering the service with the First Nebraska Infantry. He built the first brick residence of considerable size in Omaha, which building is yet standing at the southwest corner of Harney and Sixteenth Streets. He was a man of large means, broad and liberal views, of the highest personal character, and devoted to the advancement of the best interests of the city he had seen spring up from the prairie sod. He was President of the Omaha Gas Manufacturing Company; Vice President of the State Bank of Nebraska; a director and moving spirit in the Omaha and Southwestern Railway Company; and took an active part in the building of the Grand Central Hotel. He was prominent in the initial steps taken to secure the building of the Union Pacific Railroad, and was one of the incorporators of the Council Bluffs & St. Joseph Railroad. Dr. Lowe's only son, General W. W. Lowe, is the only survivor of the family. He was educated at West Point, served with distinction during the war, and, since his resignation from the army in 1869, has been a resident of this city, actively engaged in many important enterprises.

Alfred D. Jones, who surveyed the original town site of Omaha, and also of Des Moines and Council Bluffs, Iowa, was born in Philadelphia, Pennsylvania, January 30, 1814, and learned a trade as plasterer and bricklayer. He located in Omaha, in 1854; was a member of the first City Council; served as a member of the Territorial Council in 1855, and was Speaker of the Territorial House of Representatives in 1861; he was the first postmaster of Omaha, and was elected Judge of its first Claim Club; he was admitted to the Douglas County bar in an early day, but has never practiced; was a charter member of the first Odd Fellows Lodge instituted here, and in that Order has served as Grand Master and Sovereign Representative. Mr. Jones is also a Mason in high standing, and a member of the Knights of Pythias, of which latter order he has been Grand Chancellor and Supreme Representative. Since the day of his location here Mr. Jones has been a continuous resident in Omaha, a useful, honored citizen. For several years past his time has been fully occupied with looking after his property interests.

General Samuel R. Curtis, another member of the Council Bluffs & Nebraska Ferry Company, was a man with a national reputation. He was born in 1803, in Champlain, N. Y. He graduated at West Point in 1832, and served in the Indian Territory at Fort Gibson, about a year, when he resigned and was appointed Chief Engineer of the Muskingum River, Ohio, Improvement Company, where he served from 1836 to 1840. From 1840 to 1846, he practiced law at Worcester, Ohio, during which period he served as Adjutant General of Ohio. During the Mexican War he was Colonel of the Third Ohio Volunteers, and in 1847 came to Iowa as Chief Engineer of the Des Moines River Improvement Company. From 1849 to 1853 he was City Engineer of St. Louis. From 1853 to 1855, he was Chief Engineer of the projected railroad from Fort Wayne, Indiana, to Council Bluffs, Iowa. He was elected Mayor of Keokuk, Iowa, in the spring of 1856, and in the fall of that year, was elected to Congress, where he served three terms in succession. He was appointed Colonel of the Second Iowa Infantry, upon the breaking out of the war in the spring of 1861, and resigned his position as Congressman. In July of that year, he was appointed Brigadier-General, and in the spring of 1862, was appointed Major-General. In 1862 he commanded the army of the Southwest; in 1863 the Department of Missouri; in 1864 the Department of Kansas, and in 1865 the Department of the Northwest. He served as Indian Commissioner in 1866, and as Commissioner of the Union Pacific Railroad, also. He died at Council Bluffs, on the 22d of December, 1866. He became interested in the Council Bluffs & Nebraska Ferry Company in 1853; and, from the date of the acquirement of California, was an ardent advocate of the building of the Pacific Railroad, and contributed materially to the success of that great enterprise. He was Chairman of the Pacific Railroad Committee in the House of Representatives for three years, and passed through the House the first Union Pacific Bill. He was tendered the Presidency of the Union Pacific Railway Company upon its organization, but, it being a time of war, and having been educated at West Point, he declined this tempting offer, believing that at that period his services belonged to his country. His son, Major Henry Z. Curtis, was the proprietor of the first daily paper printed in Omaha, *The Telegraph.* Another son, Colonel Samuel S. Curtis, has been for many years a resident of this city. Both of these gentlemen were officers in the Union Army during the war, the former giving his life in support of the flag.

Dr. George L. Miller, the first practicing physician in Omaha, was born at Booneville, New York, July 1, 1831. He graduated, in 1852, from the New York College of Physicians and Surgeons, and practiced for two years at Syracuse, New York. He located in Omaha, October 19, 1854, and the following year was elected a member of the Territorial Council, in which body he served three terms, being the presiding officer of the last Council of which he was a member. From 1861 to 1864 he held the position of sutler at Fort Kearney, and, upon his return to Omaha in 1864, was nominated by the Democratic party as a candidate for Congress. The following year, in connection with Dan W. Carpenter, he established the *Omaha Herald,* as an evening paper, and continued his connection therewith as editor and joint proprietor until March 1, 1887; Mr. Lyman Richardson, who purchased Mr. Carpenter's interest soon after the establishment of the paper, being associated with Dr. Miller during all this period. As a strong and fearless editorial writer, Dr. Miller soon acquired a national reputation, and almost from the start *The Herald* was recognized as a paper of commanding influence. It was especially active in advocating every measure that tended to build up Nebraska and Omaha; and during the trying days of the early history of the Union Pacific Railroad, when the life of Omaha was at stake, no man rendered more valuable services in behalf of the city than did Dr. Miller, which fact is more fully appreciated

by the older residents of Omaha than by those who have located here in later years, and who cannot possibly appreciate the critical position our city occupied at that time, when it was only by the most persistent effort that the Union Pacific bridge was secured for this point, a powerful pressure being brought to bear to locate it six miles down the river, at a point known as Child's Mills. In the National Democratic nominations, Dr. Miller has always exercised a powerful influence, and could have secured political preferment on many different occasions, had he not chosen, instead, to retain his place with *The Herald*, which he deemed a place of much greater importance. Dr. Miller has large real estate interests in the city, the management of which occupy a considerable portion of his time. In 1888 he was appointed manager for Nebraska of the New York Life Insurance Company. He is President of the Board of Park Commissioners, and is taking an active interest in the development of the park and boulevard system of Omaha. He has recently built an elegant stone residence just outside the city limits on a large tract of ground, known as Seymour Park, of which he is the owner, and is now disposed to enjoy the comforts and advantages of a quiet life. The doctor's family consists of but himself and Mrs. Miller.

Andrew J. Hanscom was born in Detroit, Michigan, February 3, 1828. He served during the Mexican war as First Lieutenant of Company C, in the 1st Michigan Infantry. In the fall of 1849, he located in Council Bluffs, being then on his way to California, that being the year of the great gold excitement. During his residence in Council Bluffs, he built a mill, established himself in the mercantile business, and also practiced law. In 1854, he moved to Omaha and was elected a member of the House of Representatives of the first Legislature, of which body he was chosen Speaker. He also served in the sessions of 1857 and 1859. In the early days he was a member of the School Board and also of the City Council, and was active in building the first public school house of the city, which was erected on Jefferson Square. He has always been largely interested in real estate in this city, and for the past twenty years has devoted all of his time to those interests; though in the early years of his residence here, he was engaged in the practice of law. His second home here was the block bounded by Capitol Avenue, Davenport, Sixteenth and Seventeenth Streets, on which he built what was then considered one of the best houses in the city, planted the ground out in fruit, shade and ornamental trees, and transformed the square into a beauty spot, which was for many years one of the attractions of the city. Mr. and Mrs. Hanscom brought to their Nebraska home a family of three children, two daughters, Georgia and Virginia, and a son, Duane—after whom three important streets of this city were named. In the early history of Omaha, especially in the capital location fights, which were a feature of every session of the Territorial Legislature, Mr. Hanscom was particularly efficient. A man of strong character, and excellent judgment, he was specially adapted for leadership in critical emergencies. As President of the Omaha Claim Club, he was a powerful factor in securing to those who located here in an early day, and endured all of the hardships and privations incident to frontier life, that protection which the law of the land seemed to be inadequate to give; and, while he was always earnest and energetic in carrying out the duties of that position, he was ever disposed to recognize the just and proper claims of others.

James T. Allan located at Bellevue, Nebraska, in December, 1855, coming from Pontiac, Michigan, where he was born September 30, 1831. In April, 1856, he removed to Bellevue, bringing with him fruit trees, ornamental shrubs, and a bushel of apple seeds, for the future orchards of treeless and fruitless Nebraska. The failure of Bellevue to be designated the capital of the Territory induced his removal to Omaha in 1859. He took charge of the Herndon House, then recently completed by Dr. Miller and Lyman Richardson, in the spring of 1861, and conducted it for six years. Afterwards, he held positions in the Omaha postoffice, under Postmasters Wyman, Kellom, Griffin, Yost and Hall. He was superintendent of the first free delivery system of this city, inaugurated by Mr. Yost, and superintended the removal of the postoffice into the building it now occupies. He was a deputy for E. B. Chandler, Clerk of the District Court, when he had his office in the old Pioneer Block. In 1869, he embarked in the seed, plant and tree business, and in 1880 was made superintendent of tree planting by the Union Pacific Railway Company. For many years he was a member of the State Horticultural Society, serving as Secretary and President, holding the first mentioned position at the time of his death, November 20, 1885. Mr. Allan was the author of several works on horticulture, and was enthusiastic and tireless in his efforts to develop the fruit and timber interests of Nebraska. His widow and six daughters are still residents of Omaha.

Governor James E. Boyd, who was born September 9, 1834, in County Tyrone, Ireland, arrived in America June 10, 1844, and first settled in Belmont County, Ohio, moving from there to Zanesville, Ohio, in the fall of 1847, and locating in Omaha August 19, 1856. He left school at the age of thirteen, and, after working three years in a grocery store, began work at the carpenter's trade, and continued until 1858. August 22, 1858, he was married, in the Pacific House, Council Bluffs, to Miss Ann H. Henry, a sister of Dr. Henry. In December, 1858, Mr. Boyd moved to Wood River, Buffalo County, Nebraska, and engaged in farming and raising cattle. He began contracting for the Union Pacific Road in 1867, and had contracts for the grading of over three hundred miles of the road bed. In February, 1868, he moved back to Omaha and helped to build the Omaha Gas Works, of which he had the management for a year or two. He built the first packing house in Omaha, in 1872, and slaughtered 4,500 hogs that season—all that could be purchased in the country. This business he continued for fifteen years, in some seasons killing as many as 150,000 hogs. He built Boyd's Opera House in 1880-81, at that time by far the best building in the city. He was president of the Omaha & Northwestern Railroad Company at the time of its being built from Omaha to Blair, in 1869-71. He organized the Omaha Savings Bank, of which he was president for some time. He was elected Clerk of Douglas County in 1857; was a member, from Buffalo County, of the first State Legislature; represented Douglas County in the Constitutional Conventions of 1871 and 1875; served as President of the Omaha City Council in 1880; was Mayor in 1881 and 1882; declined re-nomination in 1883, but was again elected Mayor in 1885, and served two years. During his administration in 1881, the high license law went into effect,—the first city in the United States to enforce it—and its enforcement here met with great opposition on the part of the saloon interests, which was finally overcome with much difficulty. During his first administration, Mayor Boyd visited Detroit, Michigan, and made a careful investigation of its laws with respect to paving and other public improvements, and it was at his suggestion that the city charter was amended so as to provide that paved intersections of streets and alleys should be paid for by the city, and that the property holders should have five years in which to pay for the remainder. The present system of paving, curbing, guttering and sewerage, was adopted during Mr. Boyd's administration as Mayor. He erected, in

1891, another opera house, on a much more extensive scale, at the southeast corner of Harney and Seventeenth Streets November 7, 1890, he was elected Governor of Nebraska A question being raised as to Governor Boyd's citizenship, he was ousted out of office by the Supreme Court of the State shortly after being inaugurated, and did not again enter into the discharge of his duties until February 8, 1892, the United States Supreme Court having decided that he was and had been a citizen ever since 1867 A more extended account of this celebrated contest will be found elsewhere in this work Governor and Mrs Boyd have three children, Eleanora, Margaret, and James E, Jr The eldest, now Mrs Ellis L Bierbower, born May 6, 1860, was the first white child born in Buffalo County

Ex-Governor Alvin Saunders was appointed Governor of Nebraska by President Lincoln, in 1861, locating in Omaha in the spring of that year, and re-appointed in 1865 In 1868 he was a delegate to the National Convention which nominated General Grant, and in 1877 was elected to the United States Senate He was active in the efforts made to secure the location of the Union Pacific bridge at this point, being chairman of a committee appointed by the citizens for that purpose, and the city lots which were donated to the company in aid of the construction of said bridge and depot were deeded to Governor Saunders by the city and the various parties owning them, in trust, to be by him transferred to the Railroad Company, upon certain conditions He was one of the builders of the Omaha & Southwestern Railroad, and at one time vice president of the company, and was also president of the Board of Regents of the High School which had charge of the erection of the High School Building For several years he was president of the State Bank of this city, and was one of the original stockholders in the Omaha Smelting Works He was born in Fleming County, Kentucky, July 12, 1817, locating at Mount Pleasant, Iowa, at an early date He was a member of the Constitutional Convention in 1846, and in 1854 and 1858, served as a member of the Iowa State Senate. He was a member of the Iowa delegation to the Chicago Convention which nominated Mr Lincoln, in 1860. Governor Saunders has two children, Charles, now engaged in the practice of law, and a daughter, now Mrs Russell Harrison

Byron Reed located in this city November 10, 1855, and the following year established himself in the real estate business, which he has continuously followed since that date In 1860 he was elected city clerk, and served for seven years From 1861 to 1863 he was deputy county clerk, and in the fall of 1863 was elected county clerk, and served two years. In 1871 and 1872 he was a member of the City Council, serving as president during the latter year. Prospect Hill Cemetery, comprising fourteen acres of land, was given to the city for that purpose, by Mr Reed, in 1859 For many years he devoted much time and energy to the collection of coins, rare books, etc His collection of coins, valued at $50,000, is one of the most extensive in the country He was a corresponding member of the American Numismatic and Archæological Society, of New York He was one of the largest owners of real estate in Omaha and was one of its wealthiest citizens Some three years since he organized the Byron Reed Company, with a paid up capital of $200,000, and gave less attention to business, entrusting his affairs to a considerable extent to his son. Abraham L Reed, secretary and treasurer of the Byron Reed Company. Mr Reed died June 6, 1891, leaving a widow and two children, a son, Abraham L Reed, and a daughter, Mrs Frank B Johnson He quite generously remembered the city, which he had seen grow from a small hamlet to a prosperous metropolis, by bequeathing to it a lot for a library building and his very valuable collection of coins, rare books, etc. This bequest is more fully set forth in the chapter on the public library.

Edward Creighton, who rendered such valuable services to the West in pushing the construction of the telegraph line from the Missouri River to the Pacific, aided materially in bringing Omaha to the attention of the whole country in the earlier years of its existence. He was born August 31, 1820, in Belmont County, Ohio, and came to this city in 1856, and in 1858 engaged in building telegraph lines in Missouri and Arkansas. In 1860 he constructed the telegraph line from St. Louis to Omaha, and the following year entered upon the great undertaking which made him famous, and completed direct telegraphic communications between the two oceans. Mr. Creighton became a heavy stockholder in the Pacific and Western Union Telegraph Companies, purchasing when these organizations were in their infancy and the stock in little demand, and accumulated an immense fortune in consequence of the rapid rise in value of the interest so purchased. He made large and wise investments in Omaha real estate, and at the time of his death, Nov. 5, 1874, was reputed to be the wealthiest man in Omaha. For several years he had had large sums invested in the cattle business on the plains, being one of the pioneers in this line, and his profits from this source were very great. He was one of the incorporators of the First National Bank, and was its first president. He was also interested in the building of the Omaha and Northwestern Railroad. He was a man of broad and liberal ideas, and in his will bequeathed large sums of money for the benefit of various Catholic institutions of Omaha.

Closely identified with Mr. Creighton were his brother, John A. Creighton, and cousin, James Creighton, in his various enterprises. In 1883 these two gentlemen took a cattle train loaded with supplies to Montana, then in the midst of the great gold excitement, and the former located in Virginia City, where he remained for three years, engaged in mercantile pursuits. For two years he was connected with the building of a telegraph line from Salt Lake City to Helena, Montana, and in 1868 engaged in the wholesale grocery business with Frank C. Morgan, under the firm name of Creighton & Morgan. Upon the death of his brother he became administrator of the estate, charged with the disbursement of large sums of money. He was one of the incorporators of the Nail Works; a large stockholder in the Cable Street Railway, and in the South Omaha Land Syndicate. He was a delegate to the Chicago Convention in 1884, which nominated Grover Cleveland. He has been very generous in behalf of the interests of the Catholic Church. Mr. Creighton was born in Licking County, Ohio, October 15, 1831, and came to Omaha June 10, 1856. In 1859 he was clerking in the store of J. J. and R. A. Brown. His wife died in 1888, leaving no children.

Mr. James Creighton, born in Guernsey County, Ohio, March 1, 1822, located in this city May 26, 1856, and for several years was engaged in the freighting business between Omaha and the western gold mines. In 1861 he had the contract to deliver poles for the Pacific Telegraph line on the section between Fort Laramie and Fort Bridger. He had grading contracts on the Union Pacific during its construction. He was appointed a member of the City Council in 1857 to fill out the unexpired term of T. G. Goodwill, and was re-elected to several terms afterwards. He was a member of the House of Representatives in 1877, and appointed chairman of the Board of Public Works upon its organization in July, 1882. He was also a member of the first Board of Education under the present system.

Ezra Millard, who located in Omaha, in 1856, bore a prominent and useful part in the early history of this city. Upon coming here he became a member of the banking firm of Barrows, Millard & Co., the style of which was soon changed to Millard, Caldwell & Co. Upon the organization of the Omaha National Bank, in 1866, Mr. Millard was elected president, and held that office until 1884, when he severed his connection with that institution and organized the Commercial National Bank, of which he was elected president. This position he held at the time of his death, August 26, 1886. Mr. Millard served this city as mayor in 1870 and 1871, and was a member of the Territorial Council in 1860. In 1886 he assisted in organizing the Cable Railway system of Omaha, and was elected treasurer of the company. He was a man of great energy of character, of the strictest integrity, possessed unusual business ability, and was held in the highest esteem by all classes of citizens. Everything concerning the best interests of Omaha he made a matter of personal concern, and for thirty years this city had the benefit, at all times, and on all occasions, of his ripened judgment and foresight. His son, Alfred Millard, is cashier of the Commercial National Bank, and bears evidence of having inherited to a considerable degree the father's financial ability.

Herman Kountze, president of the First National Bank, has been identified with the interests of this city since the fall of 1856, when he engaged in the banking business with his brother Augustus, under the firm name of Kountze Bros. Upon the organization of the First National Bank of this city, in 1864, he was appointed cashier and afterwards vice president, and upon the death of Mr. Edward Creighton, in 1874, became president of the bank. In connection with his brothers, Augustus, Luther and Charles, he is interested in the Colorado National Bank, of Denver, and the New York Banking House of Kountze Bros., of which latter institution Augustus Kountze is president. Herman Kountze owns a great deal of valuable real estate in Omaha, including, until recently, a tract of 160 acres in the northern part of the city, which he platted a few years since as Kountze Addition, and which is now one of the choice residence localities of the city. Mr. Kountze was married to Miss Elizabeth Davis, of this city, May 10, 1864.

Joseph H. Millard located here in 1856, beginning business as a real estate dealer, in a small building near the corner of Farnam and Tenth, handling chiefly wild lands in various portions of the Territory. He became a member of the banking firm of Barrows, Millard & Co., upon its organization, and in the spring of 1864 established a banking business at Virginia City and Helena, Montana, which he continued for nearly three years. He became identified with the Omaha National Bank in January, 1867, which relationship he still maintains, having been its president since 1884. In 1872 and 1873 he served the city acceptably as mayor, and was for six years a Government Director of the Union Pacific Railroad. He was married at Davenport, Iowa, in 1861, to Miss Carrie G. Barrows, and has two children, Willard D. and Jessie H. He was born in 1836, in Hamilton, Canada.

Charles W. Hamilton, president of the United States National Bank, located in this city in May, 1856, and in the spring of 1862, was employed as book-keeper in the firm of Barrows, Millard & Co., bankers, becoming a member of the firm three years later, when the style was changed to Millard, Caldwell & Co. In 1868, the style was again changed and became Caldwell, Hamilton & Co., and so remained until 1883, when the United States National Bank was organized, with Mr. Hamilton as president. During all this time, the business has been conducted at the south-west corner of Farnam and Twelfth Streets. The present bank building is one of the most substantial structures in the city, built of Ohio blue stone, and is five stories in height. Mr. Hamilton was married in 1858 to Miss Fannie Murphy, of this city, a sister of Frank Murphy and Mrs. Thomas Cumings. Mr. and Mrs. Hamilton have six children, C. Will, Frank, Millard Caldwell, Stella, May and Frederick. The first son is assistant cashier of the United States National, and the second paying teller in the Merchants' National.

Jesse Lowe, the first mayor of Omaha, was a man of strong character. At the time of the passage of the Nebraska-Kansas Bill, he was a resident of Council Bluffs, and, crossing the Missouri in a skiff, on the 23rd of July, 1853, one year before the town was platted, he took up a claim just west of the land upon which the town site was located, in 1854, and this property he still had at the time of his death, April 3, 1868. He was an active member of the Omaha Claim Club, and prominent in everything relating to the best interests of the city in its early history. He was born in Raleigh, N. C., March 11, 1814, and educated in Bloomington College, Indiana. During the Mexican War, he was Commissary of the Missouri Regiment commanded by Colonel Sterling Price, afterwards prominent as a Major-General in the Confederate army. Mr. Lowe was employed in the office of his brother, Dr. Lowe, Receiver of the Land Office, during his residence in Council Bluffs. He dealt extensively in real estate in this city, and was recognized as one of Omaha's leading business men from the date of his arrival here. At the time of his death he owned valuable real estate in all portions of the city, in addition to his homestead of 320 acres west of town, all of which is now within the city limits and is of immense value.

William A. Paxton came to Omaha in January, 1857, in the employ of a contractor named Regan, who was engaged in building bridges on the old military road, and afterwards in the construction of the telegraph line between Omaha and Salt Lake. During the construction of the Union Pacific Railroad, Mr. Paxton was a contractor, and his profits earned in this business he invested in cattle in 1869, and for the next twelve years was extensively engaged in the cattle business on the plains, and accumulated a handsome fortune therefrom. In the meantime, he had contracts with the government for supplying beef to the Indian agencies. Mr. Paxton is one of the leading stockholders in the First National Bank; is vice president of the Union Stock Yards National Bank; is president of the Union Trust Company; vice president of the South Omaha Land Company; a member of the firm of the Paxton & Vierling Iron Works Company, and of the firm of Paxton & Gallagher, wholesale grocers. He has invested in buildings in this city three-fourths of a million dollars, and, for a dozen years past, has been recognized as one of Omaha's most enterprising and public-spirited citizens. His block at the northeast corner of Farnam and Sixteenth, six stories high, and 132 feet square, cost nearly half a million dollars. He was married February 21, 1858, to Mary J. Ware, and has one son, William A., Jr.

Samuel E. Rogers, who was born in Fleming County, Kentucky, in 1822, came to Omaha from Havana, Illinois, in August, 1854, locating here as a resident, with his family, October 28th, of that year, his first home being in a house which stood on the present site of the Dodge Street School building. His father, William R. Rogers, claimed a tract of 320 acres just south of town, in 1854, but died October 14th of that year, his property rights descending to his son Samuel, who moved upon the land in 1856, and for four years lived in a little house on the ground now covered by the residence of Thomas L. Kimball, on Sixth Street. At that time Mr. William Ruth, a brother of Mrs. Augustus Kountze, lived in a log house in the same vicinity, on the present site of Herman Kountze's home. Mr. Rogers served in the first four sessions of the Territorial Council. He was one of

Residence of Hon. W. A. Paxton, 206 South Twenty-fifth Avenue.—Erected in 1887.

the original stockholders in the State Bank, now Merchants' National, of which he became vice president in 1875, and has held that position ever since Twelve years ago he became interested in Florida lands, and owns nearly 700 acres in the vicinity of Sutherland, where he spends the winters In 1879, in company with Frank Murphy, General W. W. Lowe and James L Lovett, he secured valuable oil interests in Wyoming, these gentlemen now owning 3,200 acres of patented lands in the Shoshone Basin, Beaver and Rattlesnake Districts, and have developed three spouting wells, with a capacity of 1,200 barrels per day. These wells are now plugged, as the exportation of the oil will not pay expenses until railroad facilities are secured Mr Rogers is a graduate of Wabash College, Indiana, and received therefrom the degree of Bachelor of Arts, in 1852 He was married to Miss Martha Brown, in Michigantown, Indiana, in 1848 Their only child is G S Rogers, the third teller of the Merchants' National Bank. Mr Rogers, Sr, is one of the wealthiest men in the city

One of the first notaries appointed for Douglas County was Major J H Cryer, now living on his five hundred acre farm, five miles west of the city, a portion of which land he entered as a pre-emption claim in 1857. His mother, it is said, was the first woman ever naturalized in the United States, her papers as a citizen being taken out February 14, 1857, at the Douglas County Court House At that time Major Joseph W Paddock was clerk of the court During the war Major Cryer was an officer of a Pennsylvania regiment, and afterwards resided for many years in Philadelphia, where he is yet a large property holder

Major Joseph W. Paddock came to this city September 24, 1854 He was clerk of the first House of Representatives, and the first clerk of the first District Court held in this District, Judge Ferguson presiding He served as a member of the House of Representatives in 1858, 1865, 1866, and as a member of the City Council in 1869. Upon the organization of the first Nebraska Infantry, he was appointed captain of Company K, and served four months with the regiment, when he was detailed on staff duty, in November, 1861 He was appointed to the Adjutant General's Corps in 1862, and attached to the staff of General Steele After getting out of the army at the close of the war, he was secretary and manager of the Western Transportation Company, which was engaged in freight transportation from the end of the Union Pacific Railroad to the mountains For a number of years he was the Stock and General Claim Agent for the Union Pacific Railroad, and of late years his time has been devoted to his own interests. In January, 1891, he was appointed by President Harrison Government Director of the Union Pacific Railroad He was born in Matena, New York, April 27, 1825, and was married at Canton, New York, in 1858, to Miss Susie A Mack He has two children, Ben S, and a daughter, now Mrs W E Annin He is now living a few miles west of the city on a handsome place of 340 acres, a portion of which is his original claim, made before the land came into market, of 160 acres It was by the merest chance that Major Paddock lived to accomplish what he has during the past thirty-six years In January, 1855, while crossing the Missouri River on the ice, he stepped into an air-hole, and would undoubtedly have drowned but for the fact that he was holding under his right arm a buffalo robe rolled up in a long bundle, and this, catching on the ice, held him until assistance could be given him Major Paddock is now serving Douglas County in the capacity of commissioner, having been appointed to fill a vacancy

Jesse H Lacey and John McCormick established the first wholesale grocery house in Omaha, and, for that matter, the first established in the territory, beginning business in the spring of 1859 under the firm name of Lacey & McCormick, which was afterwards changed to John McCormick & Co., the company including Jesse H. Lacey, Josiah S. McCormick, Finley McCormick and Albert McCormick. Finley was accidentally drowned in Mill Creek, on the Iowa side of the river, in 1865, and Albert died in 1878. In the old Pike's Peak mining days, this firm did an immense business in furnishing supplies to the miners, and for many years their annual sales reached an enormous figure. John McCormick and Mr. Lacey married sisters, the Misses Miser. In 1875, John McCormick, with Messrs. Barringer and Davis, erected the first grain elevator built in this city, and was engaged in that business at the time of his death, in 1885. When he came to Nebraska in 1856, he established himself in the banking business, and took an active part in the financial affairs of the city. As trustee for the various claimants, he bid off at the public land sale July 5, 1859, a considerable portion of the town site. Mr. Lacey, who now occupies a responsible position in the First National Bank, came to Omaha in 1859. He served as a member of the City Council in 1869-70, and was Government Inspector of Indian Supplies for several years, receiving his appointment in 1870. Mr. J. S. McCormick has also served the city in the Council. He was married January 3, 1863, to Miss Hannah Mills, who died February 27, 1888.

Among the pioneer merchants of this city were J. J. and R. A. Brown, who were born in Stephentown, New York, and located here in 1856, in a frame building which they erected at the south-east corner of Fourteenth and Douglas, where they were engaged in the dry goods and grocery business, wholesale and retail, for many years. J. J. Brown served as a member of the City Council for one year, and R. A. acted as City Treasurer for one year. The former was married to Miss Missouri Kennedy, in Florence, New York, March 1, 1865. They have five children, Clara, Randall K., James J., Charles H., and Jeanie Dean. Mr. Brown was one of the incorporators of the Omaha National Bank, in which he has, since its establishment, been a director. He is vice president of the Omaha Loan & Trust Company, and also of the Omaha Fire Insurance Company. He was one of the incorporators of the Omaha Motor Line, and is a director of the Consolidated Line of Street Railway. He is one of the leading capitalists of the city, and has been active in advancing its material interests. R. A. Brown carried on for several years an extensive dry goods business on Douglas Street, near Fourteenth, but of late years has devoted his time to the management of his real estate interests. Associated with J. J. Brown for many years was a younger brother, Lewis, whose high ability as a business man and prominence warrant personal mention here, though he was not, strictly speaking, a pioneer. Lewis Brown located in Omaha, in 1868, entering at once into partnership with J. J. Brown in his mercantile business. Just previous to his death, which occurred about 1879, he served as a member of the City Council.

Lyman Richardson was the first Register of Douglas County, and also the first Assessor of the city. He located here with his father in January, 1855, studied law in the office of Judge Lake, and was admitted to the bar in 1858, but never practiced his profession. He enlisted in the First Nebraska Infantry in July, 1862, and was promoted to the position of captain in that regiment. He became a partner of Dr. George L. Miller in the management of *The Herald*, soon after its establishing, and remained as the business manager of the paper for nearly twenty years, during which period he was also half owner. He has been engaged for the past eight years in real estate transactions on his own account, and by the rapid rise of Omaha property has

accumulated a fortune. Mr. and Mrs. Richardson have but two children, Minnie, now Mrs. W. R. Morris, and Ralph. The success of *The Herald* was due in a large measure to the rare financial ability of Mr. Richardson, who gave to the management of the paper all of his time and attention. He was born in Michigan in 1834, and graduated at the State University at Ann Arbor, in 1854. His father, Origen D. Richardson, was Lieutenant Governor of Michigan from 1844 to 1848. During his twenty-three years in Omaha, he was one of the leading lawyers of the city. He took a prominent part in preparing the first code of laws for the Territory in 1855, and, in 1867, assisted by J. S. Sharp and Andrew J. Poppleton, prepared the revised statutes of Nebraska.

From the date of his arrival here, in the spring of 1859, until his death, June 26, 1884, Smith S. Caldwell was recognized as one of the leading business men of Omaha. He came from Marion, New York, where he was born in 1834, with a view of practicing law, having been admitted to the bar shortly before his departure from New York, but soon after locating in Omaha entered upon the banking business with Barrows, Millard & Co. The style was then changed to Millard, Caldwell & Co., and so continued for several years. When the Omaha National Bank was organized another change was made, and the firm of Caldwell & Hamilton, consisting of Mr. Caldwell and Charles W. Hamilton, was formed. Later on the firm became Caldwell, Hamilton & Co., and so continued until that banking house was merged into the United States National Bank, in 1883. Mr. Caldwell was one of the incorporators of the Omaha & Southwestern Railroad Company, of which he was president in 1869; was active in securing the erection of the Grand Central Hotel, and contributed very materially to the success of that important enterprise. In 1871 he was elected Mayor of Omaha, and served with credit to himself and satisfaction to the people. An addition in the northern part of the city was platted by Mr. Caldwell and Mr. Ezra Millard as Millard & Caldwell's Addition, now solidly built up. In April, 1863, Mr. Caldwell was married to Miss Henrietta M. Bush, of Tioga, Pennsylvania. His family, consisting of Mrs. Caldwell and two sons, Victor and Samuel, now live on a beautiful plat of two and a half acres of land, covered with a natural grove, which he purchased in 1864 from John I. Redick for residence purposes. It was then far out from the settled portion of the city, but is now considered "down town," and is of great value. It fronts on Twentieth Street, and joins on the north the homestead of Charles W. Hamilton, purchased of Mr. Redick at the same time and of like dimensions.

William F. Sweesy is a New Jersey man, who dates his residence in Omaha from May, 1856. During that year, in company with his brother-in-law, Aaron Root, he built the Tremont House, on Douglas just west of Thirteenth Street, and they also managed it until the spring of 1857, when a man named Hornberger became proprietor, Messrs. Sweesy & Root retaining ownership of the building, however, until the Caldwell Block was built, in 1865 and 1866. In 1866 he purchased from A. J. Poppleton and J. M. Woolworth a tract of land of twenty-two acres, just south and west of the present site of Creighton College, which he platted as Sweesy's Addition. The following year he was appointed Register of the United States Land Office here, which place he held for four years, O. F. Davis being his chief clerk a considerable portion of that period. In 1876 he was appointed United States Marshal for Wyoming Territory, and served three years. He has valuable real estate interests here, which now occupy his time and attention. In 1891 Mr. Sweesy erected and opened the Hotel Brunswick, on the corner of Sixteenth and Jackson streets. Mr. and Mrs. Sweesy have three children—Frank, Charles C. and Willard K.

John A. Horbach has been for thirty-four years a prominent resident of Omaha, locating here April 24, 1856. He came from Pittsburg, where he had been engaged in the railroad business for five years previously, and for three years was a clerk in the office of Colonel Gilmore, United States Receiver of the Land Department, and then engaged in the steamboat forwarding and commission business. He bore an active part in the building of the Omaha & Northwestern Railroad, of which company he was the vice president and manager, buying all of the material for the construction of the line between Omaha and Tekamah. He remained with the company until the consolidation of this line with others in 1880, and represented the old company in closing up its business during the next two years. Since 1874 he has been connected with various railroad enterprises, and in establishing a large cattle ranch business in south-western Kansas. He has extensive real estate interests here, and is classed among the wealthiest citizens of Omaha. He was married in Allegheny City, Pennsylvania, in December, 1854, to Miss Sallie Wallace. Mr. and Mrs. Horbach have two children, Mollie F. (now the wife of Major John G. Bourke) and Paul W.

Harry P. Deuel, as a member of the firm of Porter & Deuel, conducted a very large business in the old steamboat days, as agent for the St. Joseph Packet Line. Upon the completion of the Kansas City & St. Joseph Railroad, he was appointed the Omaha agent of that line, and was afterwards ticket agent for the Chicago, Burlington & Quincy and Burlington & Missouri Railroad Companies, until January, 1888, when he was appointed the City Ticket Agent for the Union Pacific Railroad Company. He was married January 6, 1858, at Tiskima, Illinois, to Miss F. J. Miller. They have had two children, Blanche, who died in November, 1881, and Charles.

John Evans, one of the best known men throughout the West in Odd Fellow circles, came to Nebraska in April, 1855, and has been a continuous resident here since. He was a member of the School Board, as treasurer, for many years previous to the establishment of the present school system. He represented Dodge County in the Territorial House of Representatives, at the second session, and was a member of the City Council of Omaha in 1864. He has served as Grand Secretary of the Grand Lodge I. O. O. F. and as Grand Representative for several years, and has also been the Grand Scribe of the Grand Encampment of that order. He rendered the city efficient service as secretary of the Committee of Fifteen which drafted the Metropolitan Charter of Omaha, in 1886, and as Chairman of the Committee of Twenty-one which was selected to draft certain amendments to the Charter in 1888. He was married in Philadelphia, to Miss Eliza P. Davis. He has five children— Charles, John B., Perla (Mrs. Samuel Houston), Mary and Edward D. Since 1864, Mr. Evans has been engaged in business in this city, first in the general grocery line, and for the last eight years dealing in seeds, garden implements, etc.

John and Richard N. Withnell have been for thirty-five years the leading brick manufacturers and contractors for the erection of brick buildings in the city. In the year 1855 they were sub-contractors under Bovey & Armstrong in the erection of the Territorial Capitol and the Douglas County Court House. They established a brick making business about that time, which they have gradually and steadily increased until their plant is by far the most extensive in the city. John Withnell located in Omaha September 15, 1854; his brother, Richard, arriving here in the spring of 1855, both coming from St. Joseph, Missouri. The former has been married twice, the first time in February, 1853, at St. Louis, and the second in January, 1887, at Omaha. He has eight children, Eliza A., Elizabeth C.,

Cora B., Charles H., Blanch C., John H., Alwilda, and Frank R. Richard Withnell was married at Omaha in 1858 to Miss Alwilda Boegle.

Meyer Hellman, born in 1834, in Germany, came to America in 1850, and located at Cincinnati. In 1856 he became a resident of this city, and entered into the clothing business with Aaron Cahn, under the style of M. Hellman & Co., which firm continued in business until 1887, when Mr. Hellman purchased Mr. Cahn's interest. M. Hellman & Co. always conducted a very extensive business, and for many years occupied a large, five-story building at the south-west corner of Farnam and Thirteenth Streets. Mr. Hellman died March 29, 1892, at his home in this city at St. Mary's Avenue and Twenty-fourth Street. In 1871, at Louisville, Kentucky, he was married to Miss Maria Rau. His widow and six children were left in comfortable circumstances.

William J. Kennedy, one of the best known men in Nebraska, was born in 1832, in Baltimore, Maryland; married, November 4, 1856, at St. Louis, Missouri, to Miss Mary M. Mundie, and located in Omaha, December 9, 1856, engaging in the watch and jewelry business. He was a member of the City Council in 1861, and closed up the business of the last "wildcat" bank of this city, known as the Omaha & Chicago Bank. In 1865, he became connected with the steamboat, storage and general commission business established by John A. Horbach. Afterwards he carried on a large agricultural implement business on his own account, until 1887. The Omaha Fire Department received in its formative period much valuable assistance from Mr. Kennedy, who was one of the originators of the volunteer system, of which he was a member for many years. Mr. Kennedy was strongly recommended by the leading business men of Omaha for appointment to the chairmanship of the Board of Public Works, at the expiration of Mr. Balcombe's term in 1890. He has but one child, Theodocia C.

Dr. Gilbert C. Monell, who located in Omaha in 1857, was born in Montgomery, New York, October 20, 1816, and at the age of nineteen graduated at Union College. In 1836 he was married to Miss Lucinda Carpenter. Graduating at New York as a physician, he was engaged in active practice for twenty years in the east, and for a considerable period after coming to Omaha. In 1859, he was associated with Thomas Gibson and W. N. Byers in establishing Denver's first newspaper, *The Rocky Mountain News*. He was instrumental in establishing in this city the Deaf and Dumb Asylum, which was conducted for two years as a private institution, and its final success was due in a great measure to the energy and business ability of Dr. Monell. He was likewise active in the erection of the Presbyterian Church building, on the corner of Dodge and Seventeenth Streets, and contributed freely of his means to that important enterprise. He bore an active part in the organization of the Union Pacific Railroad Company, and during his entire life here was recognized as a man of rare judgment, honorable and upright in his dealings, and of benevolent and sympathetic nature. He died September 30, 1881. Doctor and Mrs. Monell had two children, John J. Monell, still a resident of Omaha, and a daughter, the late Mrs. P. W. Hitchcock.

The residence in Nebraska of Captain W. W. Marsh, dates from February, 1856. For six years he was interested in the mail business between Dakota City, Nebraska, and Niobrara, Nebraska, and Sioux City, Iowa, and Fort Randall. In 1863 he bought an interest in the Council Bluffs & Nebraska Ferry Company, and managed its business for ten years; and for a large portion of this time he was superintendent of the Missouri River and Union Pacific Transfer Company, and had charge of the running of all their steamboats, until the completion of the railroad bridge in 1873. In July of that year he bought a controlling interest in the

Omaha Horse Railway Company, and since that date has devoted his energies and money to its development, and has lived to see the street railway system become one of the most complete in the country, as the result of the merging of the original horse railway with the cable and electric motor systems established during the past few years. Captain Marsh is now the treasurer of the consolidated lines incorporated as the Omaha Street Railway Company. He has served several terms in the City Council and on the Board of Education. In 1866, upon the organization of the Union National Bank, he was elected president of that institution, which place he still retains. He was married to Miss Florence M. Atwood, at Livermore Falls, Maine, in January, 1863. They have four sons, Charles, Frank, William and Allan. The former is assistant cashier of the Union National Bank, Frank is assistant treasurer of the Street Railway Company, William is teller of the Union National Bank, and Allan is a student at Phillips Academy, Andover, Massachusetts.

Henry Grebe is one of the best known residents of Omaha. He was born in Giessen, Hesse Darmstadt, Germany, May 28, 1828. Coming to this country in 1850, he located at Wheeling, Virginia, where he learned the trade of carriage and wagon making. In 1853 he moved to Davenport, Iowa, and four years later came to this county, locating six miles north of town, at Florence, moving into Omaha in 1861, and engaged in the wagon making business, which he has continued since. He was elected to the Territorial Legislature in 1860, and to the City Council in 1863. He served as a member of the Town Board of Florence in 1859, and as treasurer in 1860. In 1869 he was elected sheriff of Douglas County, and re-elected in 1871, serving four years. During this period he succeeded in breaking up the notorious gang of three-card monte men which infested this part of the country, under the leadership of William Jones, *alias* Canada Bill. In 1870 he took to Lincoln the first lot of prisoners confined in the new penitentiary. He served as a member of the State Convention, in 1875, which drafted our present Constitution. Mr. Grebe was married at Davenport, Iowa, April 24, 1856, to Miss Emily Kroeger, the daughter of a well-known Lutheran clergyman of that city. They have had seven children, three of whom are living, and residents of Omaha: Louis, Henry and Theodore. Mrs. Grebe died in this city August 11, 1890.

Charles J. Karbach, now a wealthy man, simply because he could not sell his Omaha real estate when it was cheap and did not have money enough to get away with his family and locate elsewhere, unless he could sell, located here in May, 1858, and engaged with Peter Frenzer in the wagon-making and blacksmithing business, at the southeast corner of Fifteenth and Dodge, where the Frenzer Block now stands. In 1859 he established a business of his own, on the present site of the Continental Block. In 1862 he bought a full lot, 66x132 feet, at the southwest corner of Douglas and Fifteenth for $2,100, and has owned it ever since. It is now worth about $200,000. In 1861 he bought the lot 66x132 feet at the corner of Howard and Fifteenth, now covered by the Karbach Block, for $1,090, but an offer of $100,000 for the ground to-day would not be a sufficient inducement for Mr. Karbach to part with it. He was elected to the City Council in 1867, and to the legislature in 1869. His residence property on Twentieth Street, near Leavenworth, is valued at $25,000.

Dr. James P. Peck took high rank among the physicians of Omaha. He learned the printing business in the offices of the *Ohio Observer*, and *Ohio Statesman*, devoting nine years to that calling. He was born October 11, 1821, in what is now Summit County, Ohio. In 1842 he commenced the study of medicine in the office of Dr. Wills, of Chillicothe, Ohio; but for want of means went back to the printing business, and for a time published a Democratic paper at Chillicothe, resuming his medical studies in the fall of 1848, graduating at the Cleveland Medical College in 1850, and locating in Akron, Ohio. He was married at Cleveland in June, of that year, to Miss Elizabeth H. Ames. In 1856 he removed to Omaha with his wife and two sons, the eldest, William Ames, dying in this city the following April. The other son, Edward P., is an active member of the Omaha Elevator Company. Dr. Peck built up a very large and profitable practice in this city. He died February 20, 1887.

Captain C. H. Downs is one of the oldest residents of this city—in fact, he resided on the ground now included in the town site before it was platted. He purchased an interest in the Council Bluffs & Nebraska Ferry Company, April 25, 1854, and on the following day took charge of the steam ferry boat, the General Marion, and shortly afterwards moved into a cabin the company had erected on the Nebraska shore, and lived therein during the summer of that year, superintending the men employed on the boat, and also assisting Mr. Jones in surveying the town site, which work, he claims, was commenced July 17, 1854, and completed in August. Captain Downs retained the management of the ferry, in a general way, until 1862. In 1869 he took an active part in the organization of the Smelting Works Company, and was its first president. He was also one of the leading spirits in the Omaha & Northwestern Railroad Company, and one of the directors of that company. On the 14th of February, 1860, Captain Downs and Miss Cornelia C. Smith were married at Ludlow, Vermont. They have two children, Anna and Carlotta, both born in Omaha. In 1857-8, Captain Downs served a term in the City Council. In the early history of Omaha he was a conspicuous figure, and took an active interest in everything calculated to advance the interests of the city.

Charles Turner has been a resident of Omaha since the 4th day of April, 1855, coming from Oconto, Wisconsin. He was for many years actively engaged in the lumber business in Wisconsin, where he had large and valuable interests. At an early date he purchased considerable real estate here, from which he has amassed a fortune. About the date of his removal to Omaha, he was married to Miss Charlotte Kennedy, a sister of B. E. B. Kennedy, Esq. Mr. and Mrs. Turner have one son, Curtis Turner, a civil engineer by profession, and a daughter, Miss Mary Turner.

Milton Rogers located in Council Bluffs, then called Kanesville, August 26, 1850. He was born in Horford, Maryland, June 22, 1822. In New Lisbon, Ohio, he learned the tinner's trade, and followed the business at Muncie, Indiana, and at Cincinnati, before coming West. Seeking a new location, he visited St. Louis, Weston, Lexington, Independence, Savannah and St. Joseph, Mo., and would have established himself at the latter point, but was unable to rent a building, the town being then filled with people on their way to the newly discovered gold mines in California, for which St. Joseph was the chief outfitting place. Establishing a tin and stove store in Council Bluffs, upon deciding to locate there, he started a branch business in Omaha in June, 1855, probably the first of that kind in Nebraska. In October, 1861, he moved to Omaha, and has made his home here ever since, continuing the same line of business. He was first located in a frame building, 20 by 40 feet in size, on a lot now covered by a portion of the old *Bee* building, on lower Farnam Street. This frame building was gradually added to, until it was 132 feet deep. He then rented one of the stores of the Pioneer Block, on Farnam Street, between Eleventh and Twelfth. In 1861 he put up a frame building, 22 by 60 feet, on a lot, 22 by 132 feet, he had bought at the south-east corner of Farnam and Fourteenth, and moved into it in March, 1862. In 1867-8 he joined with other property holders in that block in building the three-story brick structure which now covers that side of Farnam Street, and first occupied it in June, 1868. A few years later he bought of Dr. Ish the twenty-two feet joining him, and throwing the two stores into one has, since that date, carried on a very extensive business. His sons are now associated with him, the style of the firm being Milton Rogers & Sons. Mr. Rogers was married at Council Bluffs, November 27, 1856, to Miss Jennie S. Spoor, a sister of Captain N. D. Spoor. They have had five children, Thomas J., Warren M., Alice L. (now Mrs. Oscar Williams), Herbert M. and Will S. In the purchase of the tract of land now platted as South Omaha, Mr. Rogers bore an active part, being one of the original stockholders of the South Omaha Land Company. He was also one of the organizers of the South Omaha Stock Yards Company, and of the City Water Works Company.

Vincent Burkley dates his residence in Omaha from the 12th of May, 1856. He was born in Germany, April 5, 1818, and came to America in 1839, settling at Columbus, Ohio, where he was married, August 8, 1842. His first business enterprise in Omaha was the establishment of the Morning Star Clothing House, on Farnam street, the pioneer clothing house of the city. He served two terms in the City Council, was a member of the first Board of Education and was also a member of the first State Legislature. For three years, 1886 to 1889, he was Inspector of Customs for the Port of Omaha. He is now the head of the Burkley Printing Company, which includes also his sons Frank J. and Harry. For many years Mr. Burkley was connected with the business department of the *Omaha Herald*.

James G. Megeath located in Omaha in 1854, stopping here while on his way to Virginia from the gold mines of California, where he had been extensively engaged in merchandizing for several years, in Calaveras County. He entered upon the same line of business in Omaha, in company with his brother, Samuel A. Megeath, and Burr H. Richards, in 1856, and so continued for eleven years, though the style of firm was changed, in the meantime, from S. A. Megeath & Co. to Megeath, Richards & Co. and then to Megeath Brothers & Co. Their first store was a frame building, on the south side of Farnam, three doors east of Fourteenth, and their second in the building now occupied by John S. Caulfield's book store, on the north side of Farnam, just west of Thirteenth, which building they erected. The full lot, sixty-six feet front, was bought by Colonel Cochran from Samuel Bayliss, in 1854, for $31.25. It could not be purchased now for $100,000. Samuel A. Megeath died in March, 1868, and Mr. Richards returned to the South, and has been for many years engaged in business in Baltimore. In 1867 James G. Megeath formed a company under the style of Megeath & Co. and engaged in the receiving, forwarding and commission business, operating from the terminus of the Union Pacific Railroad, wherever that happened to be, and was so engaged until the completion of the line. This business assumed such proportions that during the last fourteen months it was conducted the firm paid to the Union Pacific Company $2,000,000 on freight bills, paying $40,000 in a single day, on one occasion. Mr. Megeath secured 380 acres of land in an early day, and has also been the owner of valuable city property since first locating here. His acre property included the ground now covered by Burr Oak Addition, the south two-fifths of Hanscom Park, Clark Place, Arbor Place, Windsor Place, Annavale, Dwight & Lyman's Addition, Lyman's Addition and other tracts of land not yet platted. The north line of his property was the present line of Park Street, and the present Twenty-seventh Street marks the east line. He joined with Andrew J. Hanscom, in 1872, in donating to the city the beautiful plat of ground known as Hanscom Park, comprising fifty-seven and a half acres, together with a street eighty feet wide all around it, the only condition exacted being that the city should expend $25,000 in developing the Park and keep that and the streets in repair. Mr. Megeath was born November 18, 1824, in Loupoum County, Virginia, and was married in 1851 to Miss Virginia Cooter, of that State. Their children are: George W., Joseph P., S. J., Samuel A. and Bettie T., the latter the wife of Lieutenant E. B. Robertson, of the Eighth United States Infantry. Mr. Megeath was Speaker of the House in the Territorial Legislature of 1866, and a member of the special session of the State Senate held in July, 1866, to ratify the New Constitution. He has also served in the City Council with distinction and to the advantage of the city.

George Armstrong was born in Baltimore, Maryland, August 1, 1819, and when eight years old moved with his father to Ohio, where, at an early age, he learned the trade of printer. In 1843, local division in the Democratic party caused him to found the *True Democrat*, of which he was editor and proprietor until 1845, when, the object of its existence having been attained, it was discontinued and its name changed to the *Ancient Metropolis*, a family paper independent in politics, of which Mr. Armstrong was editor and proprietor until 1854, when he sold it and journeyed to the west to select a place for a future home. After visiting various cities and towns, he decided that Omaha was the place for his little family to "grow up with the country," and in 1855 he moved to this place. In the following year, he formed a partnership with George C. Bovey, a practical builder. The firm of Bovey & Armstrong immediately began the manufacture of brick and built the territorial capitol, the Pioneer Block and other buildings. In 1856 and in 1857, Mr. Armstrong was elected representative from Douglas County and served during the third and fourth sessions of the territorial legislature. During these two years, he assisted in organizing a lodge of Odd Fellows and a Masonic lodge, in each of which he presided for several years; and, at the organization of the Masonic Grand Lodge, in 1857, he was elected Grand Secretary, and in 1861 was made Grand Master, to which office he was re-elected the year following. In 1859, he joined the volunteers called out by Governor Black against the Pawnee Indians, who were committing depredations upon the frontier settlements. The campaign was energetically conducted, and the Indians were trailed, overtaken and brought to terms. He was elected mayor of the young City of Omaha, in 1861, to fill the vacancy caused by the resignation of A. J. Poppleton. To this office he was re-elected in 1862. During a portion of his mayoralty he was Probate Judge of Douglas County. Resigning both these offices in 1862, he responded to the Nation's call for defenders and engaged in organizing the Second Nebraska Cavalry, the first battalion of which was mustered into the United States service in November, of that year, and George Armstrong was commissioned major. At the expiration of its nine months term of service, Major Armstrong was commissioned to raise an independent battalion of cavalry to serve during the war; and the following year the First Battalion of Veteran Cavalry was mustered in, and George Armstrong, Captain of Company A, was commissioned major commanding, and senior major after the consolidation of this battalion with the "Old Nebraska First," which was from that time known as the First Regiment of Nebraska Veteran Cavalry. Major Armstrong's military services were confined to Nebraska and Colorado, in expeditions against the

Indians, and to staff duty under Generals Craig, McKeon, Mitchel, Connor and Wheaton. After the war had closed, for meritorious services, Major Armstrong was commissioned Brevet Lieutenant Colonel, and later Brevet Colonel, by President Johnson. After the organization of the State government, Colonel Armstrong, in 1866, was appointed clerk of the District Court of Douglas County, and served in that capacity for nine years. In 1866, he was also appointed clerk of the Supreme Court of Nebraska, but, after a year's service, and when the court was removed to Lincoln, he resigned the office. In 1877, he was employed in the law department of the Union Pacific Railroad Company, in Omaha. From 1878 to 1883, he filled the office of chief deputy and cashier during the terms of United States Revenue Collectors Robb and Crounse. Mr. Armstrong erected a large warehouse at 1308, 1310, 1312 Izard street, in 1886, and engaged in the agricultural implement trade with his son, Ewing L., under the firm name of Armstrong & Co., and continued in that business till January, 1891, when he retired from the firm and active business, and now passes his time in leisure and the enjoyment of his ample fortune. Colonel Armstrong, in 1844, married Miss Julia A. Ewing, daughter of Alexander Ewing, of Chillicothe, Ohio. Mr. and Mrs. Armstrong came to Omaha with three children, viz: Ewing Latham, George Robert and Rose. The latter died in 1857. Another daughter, Ella Rebecca, now the wife of George S. Gould, of Bellwood, Nebraska, was born in Omaha.

Joseph and George E. Barker have been identified with the business interests of Omaha since the spring of 1856, coming here from Salem, Ohio, with their father, mother, and sister. The father, Joseph Barker, Sr., died in this city in 1873. One of the first investments in real estate which the Barkers made in Nebraska was in a large tract lying four miles west of town, a portion of which has been platted as Bellaire. Here they engaged in farming and stock raising on an extensive scale, and in the meantime carried on an extended real estate business in the city, purchasing many corner lots which they still own, and which are now of great value. The family removed to Ohio from England in 1851, and in 1868 George E. returned to Sheffield, England, to get a wife, Joseph, Jr., marrying Miss Eliza E. Patrick, of this city, in 1873. The Barker Brothers were among the incorporators of the Omaha Gas Company, and have always retained their interests therein. In 1886 they became identified with the private bank established on Sixteenth Street, by Messrs. Garlich & Johnson, and the style was then changed to the Bank of Commerce. When the National Bank of Commerce was organized in 1888, they were also active as incorporators and were, and have been ever since, heavy stockholders. Mr. George Barker is a director in the Nebraska Savings Bank, which institution he assisted in establishing.

Silas A. Strickland was born in Rochester, New York, and was of a good family, being a cousin of President Millard Fillmore on his mother's side. When he was but a year old his father died. At the age of seven he left his mother and her family and went to live with a brother-in-law, with whom he remained till he was twelve, and for three years after that he labored on a farm for an uncle for six dollars a month through the summer. During these years he attended the winter term of the district school. About the time he was fifteen years old his mother married a thriving farmer near Rochester and Silas returned home and entered Rochester Collegiate Institute, and later attended an academy in Cayuga County and another in Orleans County. Subsequently he taught school during the day and read law at night, finally entering the office of Fillmore, Hall & Haren, in Buffalo, and was admitted to the bar in 1850, but was too poor to enter upon the practice of his profession.

On the passage of the Kansas-Nebraska Bill by Congress he came to Nebraska, taking up his residence in the territory October 18, 1854. Mr. Strickland located at Bellevue and was soon appointed district attorney for the first judicial district. In 1856 he resigned that office and was elected to the territorial legislature. This was a stormy session and he was most active in organizing a majority of the house for the removal of the capital and the division of Douglas County, which latter resulted in the formation of the County of Sarpy. Mr. Strickland soon became a leader in the house and was elected a member of the legislature for the two succeeding terms. In 1859 he was made speaker of the lower house and the following year he was elected to the territorial council.

At the breaking out of the rebellion, in 1861, his patriotism prompted him to resign his seat in the legislature and assist in raising the First Nebraska Regiment.

Mustered in a private he was elected Second Lieutenant by his company and commissioned by acting Governor Paddock. Later he was promoted to the rank of adjutant. After the battles of Donaldson and Shiloh he resigned his commission and went to Cincinnati.

Within two months he again enlisted and was immediately commissioned by Governor Todd as Lieutenant Colonel of the Fiftieth Ohio Volunteers. He commanded the regiment at the battle of Perryville, losing 156 men in fifteen minutes. Later in the battle his brigade and division commanders were killed and Colonel Strickland was assigned to their command by General Rosecrans. In command of his brigade he crossed the Cumberland Mountains in a severe snow storm, the baggage and cannon being hauled by hand. He served through the entire Atlanta campaign. He was at Columbia, Tennessee, cut his way through the rebel lines at Spring Hill, and held the post of honor at Franklin, where he lost 503 men, twenty-three line and seven staff officers. For gallant service he was brevetted Brigadier General. At the close of the war he resumed the practice of law.

In 1867, when Nebraska was admitted into the Union, General Strickland was appointed United States District Attorney for Nebraska, which office he filled until 1871.

In 1868 he was chairman of the Nebraska delegation to the Chicago Convention which nominated General Grant and Schuyler Colfax for the chief offices of the Nation. After resigning the office of district attorney, in 1871, General Strickland was elected delegate to the convention called to frame a new State Constitution, of which body he was elected president. He was one of the founders of the order of the Grand Army of the Republic in Nebraska, a charter member of G. A. Custer Post of Omaha, and Past Department Commander.

General Silas A. Strickland, when at the zenith of his career, was one of the foremost lawyers in Nebraska. Possessing the inherent qualities of leadership he soon became powerful in the political arena and won for his name an abiding place in the annals of Nebraska politics. He died at his home in Omaha, in 1878. His widow and a daughter, Mrs. J. B. Haynes, still survive him.

In the chapter entitled " Bench and Bar " will be found additional sketches of the pioneer settlers of Omaha.

In the " Sons of Omaha," Omaha has a most unique society. The founder of the society is Dr. George L. Miller. He conceived " the plan to call together the representative young men of the best families of Omaha and form them into a society to perpetuate the memory and deeds of their fathers, the founders of Omaha." The members of this society are natives of Omaha, who have passed the age of twenty-one years. The objects of the society are: art, history and literature; and every thing that tends toward culture and refinement is in its scope. Already the society has a creditable collection of historical documents, and the munificent gift of four hundred volumes by the founder, Dr. George L. Miller, has created the nucleus for a fine library. In the not distant future this society contemplates erecting a handsome club house. To promote this purpose a scheme is already operative, and funds are collecting in the hands of the treasurer. The present membership is forty-five. The officers are: Mr. W. S. Poppleton, president; Mr. C. D. Sutphen, vice president; Mr. Augustus F. Kountze, secretary; Rev. Luther M. Kuhns, librarian; Mr. W. H. Koenig, treasurer.

On the 26th of April, 1890, the Nebraska Society of the Sons of the American Revolution was organized in Omaha. The purposes of the society are " to keep alive the patriotic spirit of the men who achieved American independence; to collect and secure for preservation the manuscript rolls, records, and other documents relating to the War of the Revolution, and to promote social intercourse and fellowship among its members, now and hereafter." Any person may be eligible for membership who is above the age of twenty-one years, and who is descended from an ancestor who assisted, while acting in any of the following capacities, in establishing American independence during the Revolutionary War: A military or naval officer; a soldier or a sailor; an official in the service of any one of the thirteen original states or colonies; an official in the United States or colonies; a recognized patriot who rendered material service to the cause of independence. The officers are: W. W. Copeland, Omaha, president; Dr. Aurelius Bowen, Nebraska City, first vice president; W. H. Alexander, Omaha, second vice president; P. L. Perine, Omaha, secretary; Paul W. Kuhns, Omaha, treasurer; Rev. L. M. Kuhns, Omaha, registrar.

# CHAPTER XIII.

INDIAN GRAVES AT BELLEVUE—TWO FAMOUS OMAHA CHIEFS—HOW LOGAN FONTENELLE WAS KILLED—SARPY AND DECATUR.

The following interesting sketch is furnished by A. N. Ferguson, Esq., who located at Bellevue, a mere lad, in 1854, when his father, the first Chief Justice of Nebraska, removed to the Territory:

The pioneer of 1854, in crossing the Missouri River to reach the trading post of Peter A. Sarpy, afterwards known as Bellevue, noticed on the summit of a high hill to the south and west of the Fur Company's buildings a number of Indian graves, surrounded by palisades of circular form. On a plateau, north-east of this hill, was another burial place, with the graves protected in like manner. It was the custom of some of the Indian tribes to bury their dead braves in a sitting posture, wrapped in buffalo robes or blankets, though the Sioux place the bodies of their dead, securely tied, upon high scaffolds, where they are left until decomposed by the action of the elements. In the case of the death of a noted chief of the Omahas, his favorite horse would be led to the grave and there sacrificed, so that its spirit might accompany the former owner to the other world. On the highest point of the hill referred to, known as Elk Hill, was the grave of Big Elk, one of the most noted of the Omaha chiefs, known to have been a resident of that vicinity as far back as 1811. His Indian name was Ongpatonga. He was a man of dignified and solemn mien, devoted to the advancement of his people, and prominent in the treaties of those years. Mr. Brackenridge, who visited the Omahas in 1811, says the village then had a population of three thousand souls. On the occasion of the death of Black Buffalo, a famous Sioux chief, Big Elk made a speech of great dramatic power.[*] He was a party to several treaties made by his tribe with the government previous to 1821. In 1854, the advancing line of whites began to surge against the barriers of the red man in Nebraska, and the palisades surrounding these Indian graves gradually disappeared, until, in 1856, the last vestige marking their location was swept away. Now this spot is a portion of a cultivated field, covered annually by fields of cultivated grain. The elevation is still known as Elk Hill, which name, I trust, it may bear forever.

Another distinguished Omaha chief, Logan Fontenelle, was buried at Bellevue. He was a firm friend of the whites in the first settlement of the country. The town of Fontenelle, in Washington County, was named in his honor, in 1854, as was also Logan Creek, a stream of considerable size which empties into the Elkhorn River just above Fontenelle. In order to get the exact facts in relation to the tragic death of this famous man I wrote to his brother Henry, now residing with the tribe at Blackbird, and received the following reply:

"Logan Fontenelle was born at Fort Atkinson, at or near the present site of Fort Calhoun, on May 6, 1825. Fort Atkinson, at that time, was a garrison. Father, Lucien Fontenelle, at that time was trading with the Indians. He afterwards went to Bellevue and built the trading post that P. A.

[*]This address is printed elsewhere in this work, in the chapter headed, "Our Indian Predecessors."—EDITOR.

Sarpy occupied. From that place Logan was sent, with a younger brother, to St. Louis to school. He was there but two years when father died, and Logan and brother were brought home. At sixteen years old, he was appointed United States interpreter for the Omahas, and held that position until 1853. When overtures were made by the United States to purchase their country, he was created principal chief, by acclamation, of the Omahas, and was such until he was killed by the Sioux, on the 15th of June, 1855, in a battle on the head of Beaver Creek, a tributary of the Loup Fork River.

"His influence over his tribe was absolute, and he was respected and honored. Years before he was chief, he used all his influence in trying to instill into them the great advantage of becoming civilized, educated, and to follow the peaceful pursuits of agriculture. But their one great vice of drunkenness—that must be rid of before any civilizing influence could be brought to bear on them—he determined to put his foot down upon. The first step was to appoint twenty trustworthy young men as police to protect the village and to arrest any fellow that was caught intoxicated, give him a good threshing with their whips and demolish his jugs of whisky. Many a hard tussle they had with some pugnacious fellows, but it had the desired effect, and the Omahas became a sober, virtuous and law-abiding people, and are so to-day.

"He generally went with them on their semi-annual buffalo hunts. About the 20th of May, 1855, the Omahas received their first installment of annuities in money for their lands. As soon as they could get ready, they started off on their buffalo hunt and traveled up the Elkhorn River until they found buffalo, when, in making their first surround of buffalo, they (not unexpectedly) found their enemies, the Sioux, awaiting to give them battle, when two of the Omahas were killed. The Sioux purposely kept with the buffalo, in order to give battle every time the Omahas made a surround after them. The Sioux were too numerous for the Omahas, when, after considering in council, the Omahas concluded to retreat towards home. After traveling four days, and thinking they were out of danger, Logan, in company with three Omahas, started ahead of the caravan and were off three or four miles, when they espied some elk, off in the distance, and Logan proposed chase. When they got among the elk, each one took after his game and scattered. That was the last seen of Logan alive. Soon after they got among the elk, the others espied the enemy and made a hasty retreat for camp. They no sooner reached camp than the Omahas were surrounded by the Sioux. A battle ensued, which commenced about 10 o'clock A. M. and lasted until about 3 P. M., when the Omahas saw a Sioux riding (they thought) Logan's mare, and holding a stick with a scalp dangling on the end. A Ponca Indian, who could speak every language, that was with the Omahas, was sent to the Sioux with a truce, to ask for a parley for the purpose of knowing if Logan was killed. He returned with the woeful announcement that their fears were verified. The whole village sent up a wail for the loss of their loved and honored chief. The Sioux then went off and the battle ended.

"The first impulse of Logan's nearest friends and relatives was to find his body, which they did, about five miles from the village, or battle ground. They found him, pierced with seven arrows in the breast, and gun wounds in other parts of the body, the side of his head broken by a tomahawk, and a small piece of scalp taken off. Two pools of blood were found near him. They tenderly took up the body and laid it on a blanket and washed it, and put it into another suit of clothes, and wrapped it in a 'sar-flesh' (a partly tanned hide, so called by the French voyageurs), as no such a thing as a coffin could be procured by them where they were. They put the body upon a litter, carried by a horse, which was presented to the dead body for the purpose, until they struck the emigrant trail, where they found a deserted wagon and harness, which they took possession of and put the body on. To this they harnessed a span of horses and hauled it into Bellevue, where he was buried by the side of his father. At his funeral a concourse of about 150 people, from Council Bluffs, and other places, came to pay their respects to the dead. At the grave Stephen Decatur gave to the assembly a fitting eulogy, touching upon the character, life and death of Logan. After all the people dispersed, his trusted friends, about twenty of the braves, gathered around his grave, when one of them, gifted in oratory, expressed the worth and goodness of their departed friend and benefactor, and regretting the loss of him they so much depended upon. When he finished they paid their last tribute of love in bedewing his grave with hearty and earnest tears, invoking his departed spirit to guard over them.

"When Logan separated from the others, in the chase after the elk, twenty Sioux made chase after him, but as he was mounted on a very fleet mare they could not near him. After chasing him about fifteen miles they gave up and stopped. At that moment Logan was seen to go down into a creek. They looked to see him come out on the opposite side, but, as they did not see him come out, they sent one of their men to go and see what had become of him. He approached the place in a stealthy manner and found Logan in the act of trying to get his horse out of the mire. He signalled the others to approach, and, as they did so, Logan ran up the bank on the other side and stood to fight, and, as the first one made a charge at him, Logan sent him rolling off of his pony. The next one met the same fate, but was not killed and is still living, to relate the deathly encounter. After Logan discharged the two shots they closed in on him with their arrows, guns and tomahawks, and killed him instantly. His memory is fresh in the minds of the Omahas to-day, and he is often spoken of, especially in their times of trials and privations. Had Logan lived till now, no doubt the Omahas would have been further advanced in civilization than they are, as his influence was so potent in reasoning with them, but as it is the Omahas are making rapid strides toward civilization, and I hope they may keep on until they are upon the same status with their white brethren, and be a people among people."

When the townsite of Omaha was platted, the Omaha Indians were located on the Papillion, just west of Bellevue. Under the treaty made just previous to this date, they were to remove to the Blackbird Hills, their present location. As a boy, I had for playmates the lads of the Omaha tribe, and spent many happy days in their village, and in hunting and fishing excursions. Major Hebburn was the agent for the Omahas at that time. When Colonel Manypenny, the Indian Commissioner, visited the tribe in 1852, to learn whether they would sell their lands, the principal chiefs were White Cow, Village Maker, Little Chief, Yellow Smoke, Fire Chief and Standing Hawk. Joseph La Flesche, a half-blood Ponca, was there as the guardian of Big Elk's grandson, who would have been chief of the tribe, had he lived. Logan Fontenelle was the interpreter, and spoke the English language readily. Peter A. Sarpy's trading post buildings were at the river landing. The Indians named were all called to Washington in the winter of 1853 and 1854 to close the treaty, at which time Logan Fontenelle was made head chief of the tribe. La Flesche, who had some hopes of filling that position, always claimed that it was Sarpy's influence that made Fontenelle the chief. Major Gatewood endeavored to get the Omahas to locate on the Blue River, with the Otoes, but they chose their present home.

In the spring of 1855, the Indians planted corn in their fields—near Sohlings Grove—and soon after received orders from Washington to prepare for immediate removal to their new reservation. This was done, the government assuring them of protection from the Sioux, but they had scarcely got settled before they were attacked by the Sioux. The killing of their chief, White Ant, on the hunt that summer, added to their distressed condition. They returned to their old village, at Bellevue, to spend the winter, poverty-stricken and discouraged. Rev. William Hamilton, missionary for the Presbyterian Board, rendered them much assistance in getting through the winter. Efforts to prevent the settlement of the Indians at Blackbird were at once resumed, and finally some of their friends brought the matter directly to the attention of President Pierce, who promptly decided that the Indians should be sustained in their choice of a home, and in the summer of 1856 a final removal to that point was effected. The day they started out a drizzling rain added to the gloom of the occasion, the Indians leaving their old home with great reluctance. For a long time we watched the procession slowly wending its way over the bluffs. My father then occupied, with his family, a large log house known as the agency building, in front of which still remained the upright posts and brush covering under which the Fourth of July had first been celebrated by the whites, in 1854. Suddenly the people of the agency were startled by a tremendous whoop and a band of about forty painted Omaha braves, including the leading men of the tribe, dashed up. A scene of leave-taking followed, marked by deep feeling on the part of both whites and Indians, and then, with a loud yell, the latter dashed away to rejoin their people. So passed away from this locality those who had, for so many years, occupied the country, who loved it for its old associations, to seek a new home, where the remnant of the tribe have since made much progress in civilization and usefulness.

From Hon. Bruno Tzschuck, ex-Secretary of State, the following points, with respect to Colonel Peter A. Sarpy, have been obtained. Mr. Tzschuck was in Sarpy's employ for several years, from the spring of 1853, having charge of the business conducted on the Iowa side of the river. Sarpy came to Nebraska in the service of the American Fur Company (the successor of the Astor Fur Company), in 1825, and was given the management of the trading post at Bellevue, which had been located there some years previously. In the course of time Colonel Sarpy also established a business on the Iowa shore opposite, at a place called Traders' Point, for the accommodation, more particularly, of the whites, as the store at Bellevue was for the Indian trade. In consequence of the encroachments of the river, Traders' Point was abandoned in the spring of 1853, and a new location made at St. Mary's, a small town four miles down the river. Here a very large business was conducted, the furnishing of outfits for miners and plainsmen being an important feature. A ferry boat, to be managed with oars, was built in St. Louis in 1853, for Sarpy's use, but he failed in getting it up the river and the ferrying that year was done by the Highland Mary, a small steamer which was hired for the season, to be succeeded in the spring of 1854 by the fine steam ferry boat, Nebraska No. 1. This boat he sold in 1856, to the Council Bluffs & Nebraska Ferry Company, and for many years it was used between Omaha and Council Bluffs. The furs handled by the American Fur Company, at St. Mary's and Traders' Point, were mainly brought down the Missouri in Mackinaw boats, and it was nothing unusual for thousands of bales, many of them of great value, to be stored in the company's warehouses, awaiting the arrival of a steamer to carry them down to St. Louis. Mr. Tzschuck describes Colonel Sarpy as possessing remarkable vigor and endurance. He was a keen business man, kind to his employes, and of courteous and polished manners. Like nearly all frontiersmen of that day he would indulge, at times, in the use of liquor to excess, and, on those occasions was wont to indulge in much loud talk, of a boasting character, but was never vicious or abusive. At these times he could not be induced to do any business, for fear of being overreached. His knowledge of the Indian character, gained by a lifetime spent in the West, was not surpassed by that of any of his associates throughout the Indian country. In the spring of 1854, the Omahas were driven in by a band of Sioux, while out on a hunt, and a large party took refuge in a willow grove two miles up the river from Bellevue. Decatur then had charge of the trading post at Bellevue, and sent word to Sarpy that he feared an attack by the Sioux. It was late at night, but Sarpy, accompanied by Mr. Tzschuck and one or two others, crossed the river in a row boat, landing at the hiding place of the Omahas, where they had a talk and then proceeded down to the post. Sarpy persisted in dropping behind the others, and in talking to them in a very loud voice, as they passed along the edge of the bluffs in which the besieging Indians were concealed. The party succeeded in reaching the post safely, and then Sarpy explained that they would have certainly been killed by the ambushed Sioux if his loud talk had not served to inform them that the persons passing were white men.

Colonel Sarpy removed to Plattsmouth about 1862, and there made his home during the few remaining years of his life. He owned, at one time, considerable St. Louis real estate. His brother, John A. Sarpy, resided at St. Louis and was a prominent member of the American Fur Company.

In 1853 Colonel Sarpy established flat boat ferries across the Elkhorn River, near where Elkhorn City was afterwards located, and on the Loup Fork near the present site of Columbus. He came to Omaha, on the occasion of the first meeting of the Legislature, as a contestant for a seat in that body; but the adoption of Mr. Poppleton's resolution to not go behind the certificates of election issued by acting Governor Cuming, shut him out. On that occasion he appeared in all the glory of a semi-civilized garb, and with an abundance of revolvers and bowie knives, which weapons were assumed more for effect than with a view of anticipated need. Sarpy had no children, and was never married to a white woman, though he had an Indian wife for whom he always cherished a high regard. He was of French parentage, was about five and a half feet in height, strongly built, remarkably active and famous far and near for his bravery and determination.

The following sketch of a man well-known in the early history of Omaha is furnished by Mr. John A. MacMurphy: Among the characters who figured in the early days in Nebraska, and served to give force and piquancy to its earlier days, was one calling himself Stephen Decatur, and as he claimed to be a nephew of the old original Commodore Decatur, the title of Commodore was tacked to his name too, and as "Commodore Decatur," he cut a pretty wide swath at times. He claimed to have come here from Jackson County, Missouri, and to have served in the Mexican war in Donovan's famous Missouri regiment, and I think this was true. About the first that was known of him here, he was one of Sarpy's employes at the old Trading Post there, and afterwards at Bellevue.

He could speak the Omaha Indian language fairly, as well as Ponca, Pottowatamie and Sioux. During the earlier California emigration he ran a ferry across the Loup Fork for Sarpy, and lived there. Later on he was found at Bellevue, part owner with Sarpy in the town site there, as well as at Tekamah and Decatur, Burt County, which last mentioned town was named after him. This was in 1856. About this time he married the widow of a Mr. Thompson, at Council Bluffs, a former editor of the *Bugle*. Mrs. Thompson was of a most excellent family in Michigan. The principal original owners of the town sites of Tekamah and Decatur were P. A. Sarpy, Benjamin R. Folsom and Stephen Decatur.

In the summer of 1857, Decatur moved up to the town of Decatur, taking his wife and her three children, a large number of cattle, some ponies, wagons, etc. He settled just west of the town, on "Decatur's Claim," as it was then known, and which he had selected in 1856, at the laying out of the town, on account of a large spring thereon, still known as Decatur Spring.

The Omahas were troublesome then, at times, and on account of his knowledge of their language, his connection with Sarpy, his ownership of the lots and the name of the town, he became at once the most prominent man in and about the new village. Disputes with Indians were left with him to settle, lots to be donated for various purposes were selected by him, he kept peace among the members of town company, and was in truth and verity the Commodore, or commandant of local affairs.

He bore himself with dignity, his decisions were just and moderate, he had a good deal of influence with the Indians, and may be said to have been sailing in high feather. Once in a while he took a little too much liquor, but who did not in those days? Old Sarpy took his "periodicals," and raised Cain, too, while Decatur generally got out of the way, and was quiet until the spell was over. He was a striking figure, rather short, very straight, square and strongly built, with a marked face, flashing eyes set deeply in the head and unusually long, overhanging eyebrows. He knew how to dress picturesquely, too, so as to set these advantages off.

The original proprietors had sold half the town site of Decatur to a New York City town site company, or "syndicate," as it would be called now, of which Roswell G. Pierce, then of some note in Wall Street, was the head, and a Dr. Thompson the local agent at Decatur. The town company having offered lots to any one free, who would build a house, a fellow took up the best of these, erected a small shanty, and then claimed his deed. It was refused, upon the ground that he had not built a house within the meaning of the term. Just then Decatur rode in from his place, and the dispute was left for him to decide. Straightening himself up, he rode around the structure once and then burst out: "Call that a house? Give a lot for that? It ain't a house, it's an abortion; pull it down!" and, jumping from his pony, he caught some loose planks and almost tore the thing to the ground himself.

During that summer, 1858, quite a tragedy occurred on the Omaha Reservation. Tecumseh Fontenelle—brother of Logan Fontenelle, the old chief whom the Sioux killed in 1855—was stabbed to death by his brother-in-law, a part-blood Indian, named Louis Neil, who had married Susan Fontenelle, a fine-looking, well-educated woman. They lived on the half-breed tract down on the Nemaha, in this State. Neil and his wife were up to the Omaha Reservation on a visit, by the wish of Tecumseh, or "Dick" Fontenelle, as he was always called. Dick and Neil had some trouble down at the Nemaha tract, about some ponies, but it had all been made up, presents exchanged, and Neil and his wife were living in one of Dick's tepees. One afternoon they both came down to Decatur, got some liquor and went tearing and whooping home about dark. Somehow, on the way home, the old quarrel broke out; and no sooner had they rolled off their horses at Dick's tent than he grabbed a butcher knife and attacked Neil, cutting him badly, and would probably have killed him, but Susan, his sister, who was cooking supper, turned a hot frying pan of grease over on Dick's back, making him let go his hold. Neil, in his turn, thoroughly enraged, drew a weapon and stabbed Dick so effectually that he died that night. Neil fled to the bushes, while the squaws were howling over Dick, and, wounded as he was, some friends threw Neil on a horse and brought him down to Decatur for protection. About midnight, when it was found Dick would die, a yelling band of Omahas, Dick's friends, came down to the town, surrounded the hotel where Neil was and demanded his life. The Indians outnumbered all the whites in town and the little band of pioneers were at a loss what to do. They did not want to see Neil murdered before their eyes (for it was known that Dick began the affair), and they were not strong enough to resist the Indians in an attack. Some one suggested Decatur, and a mounted man was sent after the "Old Commodore," the Indians agreeing to wait his return, and through the influence of Decatur and others, bloodshed was avoided and, on a solemn promise, made by the whites to Henry Fontenelle, Dick's brother, it was agreed that Neil should be taken to Omaha, and delivered over to the Agent, to be dealt with by white man's law, part of the escort to be composed of Omahas, to see that no escape could be planned. Neil was tried, but never hanged. He was sentenced to the Iowa Penitentiary for a term of years, came out and is alive now on his own land in the Indian Reservation, near Pender. It is said that he never drank liquor afterwards, and is now a substantial citizen.

In some way it got about that "Commodore Decatur" was not what he seemed—not a nephew of the Old Commodore, not even a Decatur. Some pooh-poohed the whole thing, and said the Commodore was all right, while others insisted there was something in it. One story was that one time Decatur and others of the set, were at Keith's saloon, in Omaha, drinking together one evening, when a young army officer and his friends walked in. Keith's saloon was on the northeast corner of Thirteenth and Harney, and was the swell place of the town then. The moment this young officer saw the Commodore he said: "You're the man they call Decatur, ain't you? You are my brother and your name is not Decatur. Why don't you acknowledge your family, and give your true name?" Decatur denied ever seeing the party, said his name was Stephen Decatur, and that he would fight any man who said it was not. "There is a scar on your hand," said the other, "that I made with a hatchet. If the scar is there, you are my brother, if not, you may be Decatur for all I know." Decatur refused to allow an examination, said he would not be dictated to, or forced, by any man, talked fight, and, in short, braved it out so boldly, that the new comer half acknowledged he was mistaken, and his friends took him away. Singular as it may seem this matter was hushed up at the time, and it was agreed that nothing should be said about the affair. The Commodore stood as well as ever with most of his friends. His family, of course, never heard any of these stories.

Decatur was not a good manager, and ran through his property in Nebraska, and suddenly left his home, telling his wife he was going away to make his fortune again, and would then return. Some years after, they got track of him as being connected with the Georgetown *Miner*, a newspaper at Georgetown, Colorado. It was a wild and rough country then, but he had wandered over the ridge, and there, in the heart of the mountains, had named another little town and mining camp Decatur. In the wildest spot he could find, he erected a cabin and for years lived there alone, except for those he entertained—for he was as hospitable as he was reckless — and he would come over to Georgetown now and then, bringing specimens, discourse learnedly on mines and minerals, leave some articles for the *Miner*, and then back to his cabin again. Some years since a party of noted gentlemen took a trip across the continent. One of these was Horace Greeley; Schuyler Colfax, Vice President of the United States, was another, and William Bross, editor of the Chicago *Tribune*, and once Lieutenant Governor of Illinois, was a third. At Denver, Bross said, "I want to stop here a bit; I believe I have a long-lost brother here, somewhere, shut up in the mountains, a kind of hermit. I have traced him once or twice and now I intend to find him and settle the fact whether he is the man or not." So off poked the good deacon to Georgetown to hunt his brother. Whether he had to go clear over to the cabin, at Decatur, or found his man at Georgetown, I do not know, but when he struck the fellow he thought was his brother, it was our old friend "Commodore Decatur." The deacon tried to convince him of the relationship, but Decatur would not have it that way, and Bross came away, partly in sorrow, partly in anger. From this time forth it came to be pretty well understood by many that our Commodore was really Stephen Decatur Bross, brother to Deacon Bross and the Bross family of Illinois, who left his family in Scranton, Pennsylvania, years before, changed his name, soldiered in Mexico, traded for Sarpy, became familiar with the Indian tribes, lived with them and learned their language, pioneered through the mines of Colorado, and did other curious things. He was well educated and could talk, or write, intelligently upon almost any subject.

From Georgetown he drifted down to Silver Cliff, in southern Colorado, and in 1876 was appointed Centennial Commissioner for Colorado at the Philadelphia Exposition, where a number of us old Nebraskans saw him, straight as an arrow, his gray whiskers shaved off, a long drooping mustache alone setting off his fine features, and he was cock of the walk there too. He had the most curious collection on the grounds, and was proud of it. He was followed by crowds wherever he went, seeming to possess a special fascination for women; they'd stick to him like a burr. He died in Colorado in 1889.

# CHAPTER XIV.

VIGILANCE COMMITTEES—THE COURT HOUSE TRAGEDY—EXECUTION OF TATOR AND BAKER—HANGING OF NEAL—LYNCHING OF SMITH.

There have been but three legal executions in Douglas County. In the early days the country was infested with a band of horse thieves, regularly organized, with stations for the concealing of stolen stock, extending across Iowa, Illinois and Indiana. In the bluffs, near DeSoto, a cave was found, in 1859, which had been occupied as headquarters by these gentry. Valuable papers were here discovered, including articles of organization, signed by the members of the band, which contained the names of several settlers who had previously been supposed to be men of good character. These settlers at once left the country, without waiting to be asked for explanations. Just north of Fontenelle resided, for several years, an Ohio man who had an abundance of horses, vehicles and harness at intervals, and who came and went in a mysterious sort of way. When the headquarters at DeSoto were broken up, the man disappeared for good, and it was then found that he was a member of the gang and that his farm was one of the stations for the collection of stolen property. This man was well connected in Ohio, and his wife was the daughter of a man of prominence and high character. He had been defended in an assault and battery case by an Omaha lawyer—still residing here—and one day drove up to his office with a horse and buggy, which he turned over to the attorney for services rendered, and also left an envelope well filled with papers, and securely sealed, which he asked to have kept for him for a short time. The envelope was put in the office safe and no further attention paid to it for the time. The horse was afterwards traded off, or sold, by the lawyer, who was waited upon some time after that transaction by a man who claimed that the horse and buggy had been hired at a St Joseph, Mo., livery stable by the man who had sold them to the attorney. The latter then, in the presence of witnesses, opened the sealed package and found it contained $5,000 in bills. A year and three months after leaving the parcel the owner suddenly re-appeared and claimed it, stating that he wanted to pay some debts with the money.

In 1856, two horse thieves were publicly whipped, in the presence of a large crowd, near the Douglas House, and in the spring of 1858 Harvey Braden and John Daley were hung by a vigilance committee for the crime of horse stealing. The execution took place on the hill northwest of Florence, near the Fort Calhoun road, the prisoners being taken from the jail in Omaha, placed in a wagon and driven rapidly to the scene of the tragedy. A convenient tree being found, no time was lost in adjusting a rope to the necks of the prisoners and they were at once suspended. A coroner's inquest disclosed the fact that there were many witnesses of the hanging, but those who took an active part therein were never arrested.

In February, 1861, Mrs George Taylor, who kept a famous hotel at the point where the military road crosses the Big Papillion, twelve miles west of Omaha, was robbed by two men, who entered her bed room in the night, tied her, hand and foot, and, presenting a revolver at her head, threatened instant death if she did not disclose the whereabouts of her money and other valuables. Mrs. Taylor happened to be the only occupant of the house that night, with the exception of a hired man, who was also bound and gagged, so that he was entirely helpless. Under the circumstances the robbery was effected without risk and with but little delay, a considerable amount of booty being obtained, after which the two men returned to Mrs. Taylor's room, and one of them insisted upon killing her to prevent a possible identification, in case they should be arrested. To this the younger and smaller of the two robbers made such earnest opposition that the other abandoned his purpose. A man driving in to Omaha from the west stopped at the house about 10 o'clock the following day, and found Mrs. Taylor and the hired man so securely bound as to be unable to help themselves. He at once relieved them, heard their story and spread the news of the outrage. Several persons were arrested on suspicion, among them James F. Bouve and John S. Iler, two strangers who seemed to have considerable money in their possession. Mrs. Taylor was brought to town by her husband and taken into a room where these men, with a large number of others, were ranged in line, and she was directed to identify the two who had robbed her. Stopping first in front of Bouve she cried out, in great excitement: "You are one of them. Oh, those eyes! those eyes!" Iler was next identified without hesitation and the two were confined in separate rooms, on the east side of the court house, then in the course of completion, on the corner where the Paxton building now stands. Here Iler broke down and confessed, telling where the booty was buried. The following day a mass meeting of citizens was held in front of the Pioneer Block, on Farnam street, and arrangements made to try the two prisoners by Lynch law, twelve men being selected as jurors. William A. Little and Robert A. Howard were assigned to protect the rights of the two men. A full investigation of the case was had and the prisoners found guilty, with a recommendation to leniency as to Iler. The verdict was reported to the waiting crowd outside, who ratified the action of the jury. At midnight that night Marshal Thomas Riley was overpowered at the jail by a body of masked men who hung Bouve to a beam in his cell. An inquest was held, by Coroner Emerson S. Seymour, over the remains, the following verdict being returned: "An inquest, holden at the county jail, in the City of Omaha and County of Douglas, on the 9th day of March, 1861, before me, coroner of said county, upon the body of James F. Bouve (supposed to be) hanging dead, by the jurors whose names are hereto subscribed, and said jurors, upon their oath, do say that he came to his death by hanging, by persons unknown to the jury." This was signed by Francis Smith, A. J. Hanscom, M. W. Keith, Benjamin Stickles and T. L. Shaw, jurors, and the coroner. Iler was soon afterwards released, on condition that he would leave the Territory immediately.

August 28th, 1863, Cyrus H. Tator was executed, by due process of law, for the murder of Isaac H. Neff, the hanging taking place north of town, near Sulphur Springs. Neff and Tator were encamped in that vicinity the June previous, having come in from Denver together with several empty wagons belonging to Neff, who disappeared, and Tator started on his return to Denver with one of the teams, which he claimed he had bought of Neff. The body of the latter was found, weighted down with heavy chains, in the Missouri River. Tator was arrested, brought back to Omaha and tried before Judge Kellogg, George B. Lake and Charles H. Brown appearing for the prosecution and A. J. Poppleton and William A. Little for the defense. The accused was a man of character and ability, thirty years old, who had been a probate judge and a member of the legislature in Kansas He protested his innocence to the last, and on the scaffold read a carefully prepared statement of his case The Supreme Court was appealed to, but to no effect beyond the affirming of the proceedings in the District Court. The execution was witnessed by several thousand people

February 14, 1868, Ottway G Baker was hanged, by order of the court, the scaffold being erected in a valley about half a mile west of the site of the High School building In November, 1866, he was employed as porter in the store of Will R King, and slept in the building with Woolsey D. Higgins, the bookkeeper After banking hours, on the 21st of that month, $1,500 in money was received and placed in the safe, of which Higgins carried the key While the latter was sound asleep, the night following, Baker quietly arose, procured an axe, and killed his bedfellow, took the safe keys and secured the money. This he placed in an empty oyster can and hid it under the plank sidewalk on the west side of Eleventh Street, near Harney He then set the store on fire, and shot himself through the arm in order to give color to his pretense that the building had been entered by burglars His conduct excited suspicion, however, and his arrest and conviction followed His trial was had before Judge George B Lake, District Attorney George W Doane being assisted in the prosecution by John I Redick Baker was defended by James W Savage, Ben Sheiks, George C Hopkins and Mr Parks The Supreme Court having affirmed the verdict of the jury, finding him guilty of murder in the first degree, Baker made a confession of the crime and told where the stolen property was concealed

On the morning of February 14, 1890, the bodies of Allen Jones and his wife. the former seventy-one years of age and the latter sixty, were found concealed in some rubbish about the stable on the Di Pinney farm, six miles west of Omaha, bearing marks of a brutal murder The old couple were the only tenants of the farm and had been left to care for several head of cattle, none of which could be found on the premises Investigation disclosed the fact that eight head of cattle and six horses had been driven from the farm into South Omaha and there sold by a stranger a day or two previously. A description of this man was given with such accuracy that E D Neal was arrested at Kansas City, February 20th, and brought to Omaha City Editor Edward O'Brien. of the Omaha Bee, achieved much distinction by his persistance in following up various clues which resulted in the capture of Neal Several other parties were arrested on suspicion, but these were all discharged after a full investigation of the circumstances in each case The trial of Neal was commenced before Judge J R Clarkson, May 14, 1890, Prosecuting Attorney J J Mahoney being assisted by J C Shea in the conduct of the case on behalf of the State, and Lee Estelle, since one of the judges of the District Court, and William F Gurley, appearing on behalf of the defendant May 22nd the jury returned a verdict of murder in the first degree against "Ed D Neal, alias C. E Neal, alias Livingstone, alias Katon," as the prisoner had been referred to in the proceedings by all of these names The case was appealed to the Supreme Court The Supreme Tribunal, however, refused to interfere with the verdict as rendered by the District Court, and the day of execution was set for the 9th day of October, 1891 He was executed within an enclosure which was erected for the purpose at the southwest side of the county jail, Sheriff John F Boyd officiating. Notwithstanding Neal had maintained his composure during the whole time from his arrest until the day of his execution, and had always claimed to be innocent, he made a full confession on the scaffold, acknowledging his guilt and admitting that he alone had committed the heinous crime. There were but few witnesses of the execution, except members of the jury, the relatives of the victims, the necessary officers and the reporters.

A day or so before Neal was hanged there had been committed upon a little girl, in the northern part of the city, a dastardly assault. It was reported that her assailant was a negro, and that she was so badly injured that she could not possibly live. A negro named George Smith was arrested, charged with the crime, and he was in jail at the time of Neal's execution. Smith had, a short time before, been arrested on a charge for a similar crime, committed in East Omaha, and had been discharged at the preliminary examination, at Council Bluffs, by reason of the unsettled condition of the boundary line between Nebraska and Iowa, the justice holding that the crime had been committed in Nebraska.

While Neal's execution had been as private as such affairs are usually, the city was filled with suppressed excitement. Not much was said, but apparently nearly every one felt that there would be an attempt made to lynch Smith during the night. The officers of the city and county, however, did not believe that there was any danger, and hence made no effort to remove him to a more secure place. With this indescribable feeling in the community, that one good act had been performed in the hanging of Neal, and that the work would be complete now if Smith was hanged, it was no wonder that, when one of the evening papers announced that the little girl had died, a crowd of determined fellow-workmen of the father of the child should have organized for the purpose of wreaking avenging justice on the negro, who was guilty of the crime. Soon after dark, as it appeared afterward, an organization was effected in the northern part of the city and the crowd marched to the jail, where a large number of people had gathered before their arrival. By 9 o'clock in the evening there must have been at least five thousand people on Harney Street side of the court house, and the leaders of the mob demanded entrance to the jail, which was refused. Sheriff Boyd, tired out by his unpleasant duties of the day, had gone to his home; but hearing of the trouble immediately repaired to the jail, and addressed the crowd, telling them that the law made it his duty to protect the prisoner, and that he should endeavor to do so. Before he had finished speaking, however, he was made a prisoner, disarmed, hurried into a hack and taken up to a point back of the High School, where he was kept until the affair was over. Governor James E. Boyd, Judge George W. Doane and others spoke to the excited multitude, urging them to disperse and to allow the law to take its course, but without effect. Every minute gave accessions to the crowd, not alone of men, but of women, also; and while many were there out of curiosity it was plain to be seen that very many were in sympathy with the mob, and by half-past 10 o'clock there must have been at least ten thousand persons present.

Several ineffectual attempts were made to disperse the crowd. The fire department was ordered out for the purpose of turning the hose on them, but no sooner did the hose carts arrive than shouts arose to cut the hose. As fast as the hose were unreeled there were many willing hands, with knives flashing in the weird light shed by the electric lamps, putting into effect the suggestion, and many lengths of valuable hose were irretrievably ruined. In the meantime the leaders of the mob were not idle. They had effected an entrance into the jail by way of one of the heavily barred windows, which had been broken in by means of a battering ram, improvised from an ordinary street car rail. On the approach of the mob the negro was placed in an almost impregnable steel cage, and the mob found it the work of at least two hours to break into this cage. After breaking into it and securing the negro there was quite a halt in the proceedings for the purpose of being sure of identification. Becoming satisfied that there was no mistake a rope was fastened around Smith's neck, and he was rushed across Harney Street and an effort made to throw the rope over one of the arms of a telegraph pole. Not being successful here, the poor wretch, more dead than alive, was dragged down across Seventeenth Street, a rope passed over one of the wires which sustains the trolly wires of the electric motor lines, and Smith was drawn up to the wire, where he was left hanging. It was about 1 o'clock on the morning of the 10th day of October, 1891, that Smith was hanged. The report of the death of the little girl was an error.

After Smith was in the hands of the mob the police made several attempts to rescue him, but were powerless and unable to do anything.

The better element of the community deplored the resort to violence, but very few felt otherwise than that Smith was justly dealt with.

District Attorney T. J. Mahoney filed complaints charging the most active leaders of the mob with murder, but, after doing his full duty in bringing them to trial, they were discharged.

## CHAPTER XV.

INCIDENTS AND EXPERIENCES—THE GREAT FLOOD—OLDEN TIME BUILDINGS—PATTEE'S LOTTERY, ETC., ETC.

The first issue of the Omaha *Arrow*, dated July 28, 1854, printed the following editorial:

"The Indians require ten dollars from each settler for the right to build and make improvement upon the lands for which they have not yet received payment nor relinquished their rights. We consider this a just demand and have, ourselves, fully complied. The amount should only be paid to Logan Fontenelle (the chief), H. D. Johnson or ourselves."

When Nebraska's first election was held, in the fall of 1854, there were but two voting places in Douglas County, which included the present Sarpy County, one being at Bellevue and the other designated in Governor Cuming's proclamation as "the brick building in Omaha," otherwise the State House, the first brick building erected in the Territory.

Under the heading, "The Future of Omaha," the *Times* of June 7, 1857, presents these facts and figures:

"The growth of Omaha astonishes—is a fact few can comprehend. Look at its chronology:

1853, June—Town claim made by the company and kept by them by paying tribute to the Indians, whose title had not been extinguished.

1854, June—No settlements but a single house, the old St. Nicholas, of round logs, sixteen feet square, built by the company as an improvement to hold the claim.

1855, June—Number of inhabitants 250 to 300. Best lots sold at $100.

1856, June—Number of inhabitants about eight hundred. Best lots sold at $600.

1856, October—Number of inhabitants 1,600. Best lots sold at $2,500.

1857, April—Number of inhabitants 2,000. Best lots sold at $3,500.

1857, June—Number of inhabitants 3,000. Best lots sold at $4,000.

"Judging the future by the past, we can safely calculate upon numbering five thousand people by the first of October, and property will, on Farnam, Douglas and Harney streets, run up to one hundred dollars a foot. The rapidity of growth in the past establishes public confidence in the future and tends to run prices up partly in anticipation. We were shamefully cheated out of our appropriation to finish the capitol, in Congress. The City Council has made the Mayor, Jesse Lowe, sole commissioner, in behalf of the city, to do this work of necessity to the honor and comfort of our Territory, and an ornament to our place, by an expenditure of $50,000. The work has begun.

"Jesse Lowe and Thomas Davis, county commissioners, are in charge of the erection of a court house, at an expense of $35,000. G. L. Miller & Co. are building the finest hotel west of St. Louis, to cost $60,000. Fifty houses have already been erected here this spring. As many more are in course of erection; three hundred will be erected this year."

The first resolution offered in the House of Representatives at the first session of the Territorial Legislature was presented by A. J. Poppleton, and the second motion made in the Council, at the same session, convened January 16, 1855, was made by Samuel E. Rogers. Omaha men were then, as now, always prominent in public affairs.

Looking Northeast from Court House Square—1886.

Looking Southeast from High School Grounds—1886.

INTERESTING SKETCHES OF EARLY INCIDENTS    141

The first marriage in Omaha was that of John Logan and Caroline M Mosier, the ceremony being performed by Rev Isaac F. Collins, Nov 11, 1855 Mr. Logan died in this city March 13, 1891.

W J. Kennedy established the first watch-repairing and jewelry store in Omaha, in 1856

Charles S Goodrich, late city comptroller, and Charles Sherman, editor of the Plattsmouth Journal, set the type on the first regular daily paper printed here, The Telegraph, the edition consisting of four hundred copies, half of which were distributed in Omaha, and the other half in Council Bluffs. Mr Goodrich came to Omaha in 1860, with his father, S J Goodrich

Mr Hellman came to Omaha from Cincinnati in 1856, driving a two-horse wagon

David T Mount, who came here in 1863, made the first light buggy harness and the first Shafto saddle made in this city The former was for Dr McClelland and the latter for Jesse Lowe

Peter Windheim, who died March 14, 1891, was induced to locate here in 1857, by the great quantity of ducks which he saw in this vicinity, he being at that time on his way up the Missouri River, on a steamer. Mr Windheim, with the Bruners, Henry A Kosters, Chas Behm and others of Omaha, were interested in platting West Point and Columbus

Daniel W Carpenter came to Bellevue in October, 1854, and assisted in the publication of the *Palladium*, J Sterling Morton and Thomas Morton being associated with him in that enterprise In 1864 he came to Omaha and formed a partnership with Dr George L Miller, for the publication of the *Herald*, first printed as an evening paper. It has been generally believed that the *Herald* succeeded the *Nebraskian*, but such is not the fact The paper was supplied with an entire new outfit, which Mr. Carpenter brought from Cincinnati.

James G Megeath's first visit to Omaha, in 1854 was for the purpose of voting He was at that time temporarily stopping at Council Bluffs, and in 1857 removed to this city with his family

Charles Childs established the first grist-mill in this vicinity In May, 1856, he erected a steam saw-mill, six miles south of the city, and put in one run of stone to grind corn, farmers coming from as far west as Grand Island and the Wood River settlements to patronize his establishment, though he ground only on one day in the week Afterwards he put in a flour mill and made the first flour manufactured in Nebraska

The first saw-mill in Omaha was put up by Samuel S Bayliss and Alex Davis, his brother-in-law, on Otoe Creek, just north of the present site of the Union Pacific depot, and traded to Thomas Davis for a claim on four hundred acres of land The explosion of the boiler of this mill, about 1856, created a great sensation Mr Davis afterwards built a large flour-mill in the same locality and for many years carried on a very extensive business His residence, which was in the same block, is still standing, at the corner of Jackson and Ninth Streets

There has been some difference of opinion as to who was the first white child born in Omaha On this point Mr. John Rush, city treasurer, says. "My father-in-law, James Ferry, came here with his family in the spring of 1854 He had no time to make proper preparations for his wife and children, so a 'dug-out' was scooped in the bank at what is now Twelfth and Jackson Streets, where the family and several men that Mr Ferry had working for him lived during the winter of 1854 and 1855 But even before this primitive excuse for a house had been made, he had constructed a hay hut near where the Union Pacific depot now stands, the tall grass of the bottoms affording material for one of the first and certainly one of the crudest habitations in Nebraska The first white child born in Omaha could, if she had lived, boast of having had this unique dwelling for her birth-place. It is contended that William Nebraska Reeves, son of the late Jesse Reeves, was the first white child born in Omaha, but this is a mistake. It is true that Mr. Reeves' son was born before Mr. Ferry's child, a month or so, but he was born outside of the city of Omaha as it was then platted, his birthplace being in what is known as Park Wilde." Mr. Ferry's child was born in October, 1854.

Mr. A. J. Hanscom first located on what is now known as Shinn's Addition, in 1854. Here he built a claim house and about the same time put up a frame house, at the southwest corner of Fifteenth and Farnam, which building was used as a printing office by the proprietors of the *Nebraskian*. When the land was surveyed he found that his claim was on the school section; and, fearing he would have difficulty in getting his title, accepted a proposition to trade, which was made him by Mr. Samuel Bayless, of Council Bluffs, and exchanged the 240 acres he had claimed for a tract of four hundred acres southwest of town, a part of which, now known as Hanscom Place, is one of the choicest residence portions of the city. The land he had first claimed was finally entered by Moses F. Shinn, who secured the passage of a special act of Congress in order to get possession of the land.

Elias L. Emery, who came here in 1862, lived for several years in the only building west of the Capitol Hill, a frame structure on the ground now occupied by Howard Kennedy's comfortable residence on West Dodge Street.

E. L. Eaton is the oldest photographer in the city. Locating here May 1, 1856, he opened a gallery in the old Pioneer Block the following year. In 1858 and 1859, he was engaged a considerable portion of the time in taking photographs, at Florence, of the Mormons and their outfits. During the war he spent four years in the camps of the Union soldiers, following his profession, in various portions of the country. For more than twenty years he has occupied his present location, on Farnam Street.

When Thomas Riley was city marshal in an early day, it was a part of his official duty to at intervals drive the Indians away from their camps in the suburbs of the town. At times the original owners of the soil refused to recognize his authority and on those occasions he would be compelled to call the citizens to his assistance.

When Mr. St. A. D. Balcombe purchased the Hanscom homestead, the block bounded by Capitol Avenue, Davenport, Sixteenth and Seventeenth Streets, in 1865, for seventeen thousand dollars, the old settlers told him he was throwing his money away, although the ground was covered with bearing fruit trees, shade trees and ornamental shrubbery, with a large house and barn, the contents of both buildings being included in the purchase price, the furniture being valued at two thousand dollars. The ground alone is now worth $400,000.

During the war J. C. McBride was given a lot at the southwest corner of Thirteenth and Jackson Streets, by the city, in consideration of his taking care of certain smallpox patients which the city officials were burdened with. This he afterwards sold and with the proceeds purchased a good farm in Sarpy County. The lot is now worth forty thousand dollars.

Thomas O'Connor was the second register of deeds, being first elected in the fall of 1855, and for two years thereafter was re-elected. He crossed the river November 28, 1854, in a canoe, and since that date has never been outside the city limits for a period of three days at a time. He had for fellow-passengers, on the occasion referred to, General John M. Thayer and an Irishman known as General Boyle, who had views of his own on the important topics of the day. These two became engaged in a violent discussion and Mr. O'Connor says that he was impelled to call out "For Heaven's sake keep still gentlemen, or we'll all go to the bottom of the river with this rickety old dug-out!" clutching, meanwhile, both sides of the craft in his endeavor to preserve the balance

Acting Governor Cuming came to Nebraska from Keokuk, Iowa, and most of the Irishmen who located in Omaha in 1854 and 1855 were induced to do so by that official Governor Cuming was a private, during the Mexican war, in the company of the Second Michigan Infantry which was commanded by A J Hanscom The latter and A. J Poppleton were schoolmates in Michigan in their boyhood days

Major George Armstrong won the life-long esteem, in 1855, of Colonel Sarpy and Commodore Decatur, by exposing the character of supplies then being furnished the Indians by an agent who made his headquarters on the Iowa side of the river, opposite Bellevue In coming to Nebraska, in the fall of 1854. Major Armstrong journeyed for some distance by stage with Colonel Manypenny, then Commissioner of Indian Affairs, in whose newspaper office in Ohio Major Armstrong had acquired a knowledge of the art of printing Samples of the supplies being shown him after his arrival here, Major Armstrong wrote some sharp articles on the subject for the *Nebraskian*, and also addressed a communication to the Indian Commissioner, the result being that the agent was promptly removed and the father of T H Robertson, editor of the *Nebraskian*, appointed in his stead Major Armstrong removed with his family to Omaha in the spring of 1855, driving all the way from Chillicothe, Ohio, in a carriage His firm, Bovey & Armstrong, built the Territorial Capitol, the Congregational Church, Pioneer Block and many other buildings of the ante-bellum days

Law and order were not as closely observed in the early history of Omaha as at present At the session of the Territorial Legislature of 1858 a resolution was adopted in the House, providing that the speaker and members of that body should "be exempt from arrest during the session"

Christmas day, 1860, a Dr Vincent, of Tabor, Iowa, then famous as a station of the "underground railroad" for assisting runaway slaves, called at the residence of Colonel Gilmore, the brick building owned by Aaron Cahn, on the south side of Dodge, just west of Fifteenth Street, recently torn down, and in the course of a conversation was asked by John A Parker, Jr, a hot-blooded young Virginian, where he lived, to which Vincent replied "Tabor, Iowa," whereupon Parker inquired if he "was one of those men who stole niggers?" Vincent responded "When a colored man comes there hungry we feed him, naked, we clothe him, foot-sore, we take him in a buggy and carry him on his way rejoicing" Thereupon Parker jumped up in a rage, drove the visitor from the house, striking him as he left the door and then fired at him twice with a revolver, but fortunately failed to hit him

A bill prohibiting slavery in Nebraska was passed by the Legislature of 1861, vetoed by Governor Black and passed over his veto by a vote of ten to three in the Council, and thirty-three to three in the House

In one of the early sessions of the Legislature a bill was introduced "prohibiting the settlement of free negroes and mulattoes in the Territory of Nebraska" It was referred to the House judiciary committee and, in the rush and hurry of business, was evidently lost

Referring to the appearance of Omaha in 1860, Mrs Silas A Strickland, who removed to the city from Bellevue with her husband in that year, says that Farnam was then the only well-defined street in the place From her residence, at the corner of Eighteenth and Capitol Avenue then the outskirts of town, she had an unobstructed view of the river landing, where she could see boats loading and unloading

E. F. Cook, who came here in September, 1856, and managed the Omaha Branch of Milton Rogers' store business, the main store being in Council Bluffs, found no town to speak of, but a community full of hope and enterprise, with a lively real estate market. The winter following, vegetables, eggs and apples were received and sold in a frozen condition. Prairie wolves could be seen skipping about over the town site. On the Council Bluffs side of the river, he saw the dead body of a man hanging to a tree, placarded: "Hung for his many crimes!"

When the firm of Nave, McCord & Co., wholesale grocers of St. Joseph, Mo., located a branch house in Omaha in 1861, then a village of but 3,000 inhabitants, it was considered a very important event. Henry W. Yates, now president of the Nebraska National Bank, came up to assist in taking care of the business, being ten days in making the trip, by Missouri River steamer. The firm had previously established a branch house at Council Bluffs, in charge of Will R. King, but upon locating here Mr. King was transferred to Omaha. In the fall of 1863 Mr. Yates became identified with the banking house of Kountze Brothers, which was merged into the First National Bank, and remained with it until the organization of the Nebraska National Bank, in 1882.

It is a fact not generally known that the interference of the wife of President Lincoln prevented the appointment of an Omaha attorney to the chief justiceship of Nebraska Territory. The members of the bar of Omaha, Republicans and Democrats, with a single exception, joined in presenting applications for the appointment of John R. Meredith, Esq., backed by the highest endorsements as to his character and professional standing; but Mrs. Lincoln had her candidate for the place, in the person of William Pitt Kellogg, who afterwards achieved celebrity, if not distinction, as Governor of Louisiana, and he secured the appointment, though Mr. Meredith was the President's choice. The position of associate justice was then tendered him and afterwards that of collector of internal revenue for Nebraska, but both offers were respectfully declined by Mr. Meredith.

The first city directory of Omaha was published in 1866, by Charles Collins, a newspaper man of this city who was active in the publication of the *Evening Times*. He afterwards became identified with the press of Sioux City and took a prominent part in opening up the Black Hills mining region to white settlers.

The fact that St. Mary's Avenue runs at an angle is due to the desire of Harrison Johnson to get to and from the village of Omaha by the most direct route from his homestead, a log house which occupied a sightly spot just west of Mr. Woolworth's present home. In time this private way became a county road and additions platted later on were conformed thereto. In recent years strong efforts were made to secure a change, so that the street might run directly east and west, but were not successful.

Elias L. Emery, who has been a continuous resident of Omaha since June 1, 1862, has borne a very active part in the improvement of cattle and swine in Nebraska. He was one of the first importers and breeders of shorthorns in the North Platte country, and in various sections of the State are now found entire herds of the direct decendants of Mr. Emery's importations. To this gentleman is also due the credit of establishing pedigrees for hogs, now a feature of swine breeding all over the civilized world. In February, 1871, in a letter to the *National Live Stock Journal*, of Chicago, now the *Breeders' Gazette*, he called attention to the importance of this subject. The Farmers' Institute of New York at once took the matter up and appointed a committee to consider the subject in all its bearings. The leading breeders and dealers all over the land became interested and the result was the establishment of a swine herd book, as

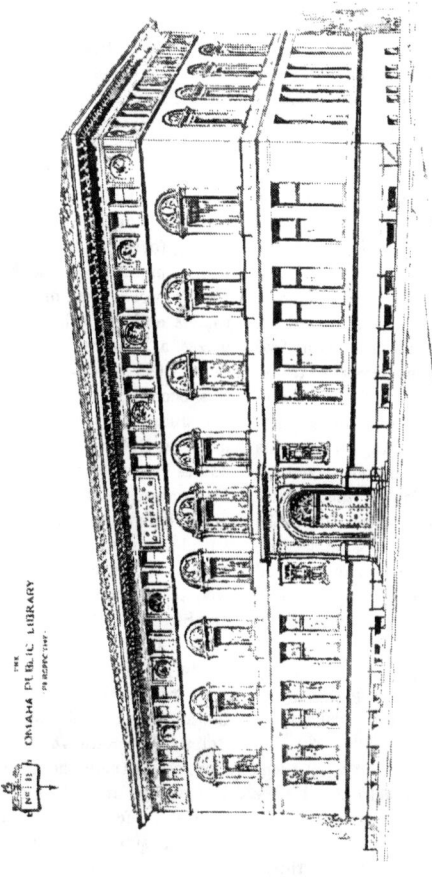

New Public Library.

accurately kept as are the records of horses and cattle For many years Mr Emery has been a contributor to the leading stock and horticultural journals of the country

In August, 1871, a lottery was established in Omaha by J M Pattee, and styled "The Omaha Library Legal Gift Enterprise Concern," Lyford & Co being the ostensible managers, the alleged object being to provide the city with a public library Just what was done in that regard will be found elsewhere printed in this work, in the chapter devoted to "Libraries" The first drawing took place at the Academy of Music, on Douglas Street, November 7, 1871, in the presence of a large audience The principal prize of $20,000 was announced as having been drawn by E H Dillingham, of Boston The enterprise was carried on in a very successful manner for about two years, during which time Pattee transacted a large business through the postoffice, his correspondence covering a large extent of country In May, 1873, his mail in the Omaha postoffice was seized by Postmaster Yost, by order of the department at Washington, and forwarded to the dead letter office The impression having been given out that the scheme had received the official endorsement of the City Council, the following resolution was adopted by that body, February 25, 1873

"*Resolved*, That in the opinion of this Council the lottery now advertised by J M Pattee, in this city, is a fraud, and the same is not and will not be endorsed by any member of this Council"

This was published in the city papers as an advertisement Previous to this Pattee had purchased the Redick Opera House building (afterwards known as the city hall), corner of Farnam and Sixteenth, for thirty thousand dollars, and here was employed a large number of young ladies in sending circulars out all over the country May 20, 1873, the fourth drawing occurred in this building, in the presence of a large audience Considerable formality was observed, Judge John R Porter being elected president of the assemblage, General S A Strickland, vice president and J M McCune, city clerk, secretary, Councilmen D C Sutphen, John M. Thurston, A. J. Doyle and Henry J Lucas, ex-City Marshals, Richard Kimball, J C Lea, ex-City Attorney, J P. Bartlett, Colonel Saunders, Colonel Burke and L P Hale were chosen as a committee to see that the proceedings were fair and regular, Judge Porter administering an oath binding them to a faithful performance of their duties in that regard A short address was made by General Strickland, who introduced Mr Pattee The latter made a brief speech, setting forth his honesty of purpose in the management of his gift enterprise Two wheels were used, one a large one for the tickets and the other a smaller one for the prizes, a blindfolded boy being stationed at each wheel to draw for the numbers On this occasion the grand prize was $75,000, one John B Duff, of Council Bluffs, being declared the winner thereof A month later James Donnelly, who had been employed by Pattee as a clerk, swore out a warrant in the police court, charging the lottery proprietor with having carried on a fraudulent business by the issuance of duplicate and triplicate tickets Pattee was then at Leavenworth, and Sheriff Grebe went after him and brought him to Omaha Being taken before Judge Porter, of the police court, an examination was waived by the prisoner and he was bound over in the sum of three hundred dollars to appear for trial in the District Court, and there the case terminated Mr. Pattee died at St Louis, where he was then residing, a few years since

In the summer of 1877, the great army of tramps was so largely represented in Omaha that heroic measures were resorted to to abate the nuisance A vigilance committee of two hundred men was quietly organized and each member sworn as a special officer, with power to make arrests. Captains were selected and the force divided into squads and assigned to the various wards. At a late hour at night this force started out on a general "round-up" and by daylight had arrested nearly four hundred men, some of whom were able to give a satisfactory account of themselves and were released. The others were locked up until their cases could be investigated, box cars on the railway tracks being utilized for the purpose after the city jail had been filled. Sensational disclosures were made, in which men of alleged respectability figured, and many dangerous characters were arrested. One of the incidents of the night was the finding of a pair of shoes under a window of the bishop's residence, on Ninth Street, and the discovery of the owner of the shoes inside the building in the act of burglary.

The spring of 1881 witnessed the highest recorded stage of water in the Missouri Valley. The flood reached Omaha April 6th, a heavy ice gorge at Yankton, Dakota, having given way, and soon the banks of the river were overflowed. The rip-rap, which had been put in by the government, and which protected the Union Pacific shops and smelting works, gave way, and the grounds and buildings were flooded so that all work was suspended. The coal and lumber yards in the vicinity were submerged and it was only by the most active exertions on the part of a large force of men that any of the material in the lumber yards was saved. The bottom lands lying between Omaha and Council Bluffs were covered by a rushing torrent, varying from two to ten feet in depth. Steamboats anchored in the neighborhood of the Transfer Hotel, and, from that point eastward, the Union Pacific built a bridge, half a mile long, of flat cars. Steamers wended their way over the Union Pacific grounds on the west side of the river and took on coal from the company's supply. For four days a steady gain of water was reported, the highest stage being reached at 6 o'clock P. M. of the 9th, when a depth of twenty-two feet above low water mark, two feet higher than ever before known, was reported, at which time the river extended from the bluffs just east of the Union Pacific headquarters to the Northwestern depot in Council Bluffs, a distance of five miles, the surface covered with broken ice, trees, timbers, fence rails, lumber, logs, fragments of houses and all the debris which a sudden flood of such awful magnitude would gather in its restless course. The loss of property here was considerable but there were, fortunately, but two lives sacrificed. Thaddeus Wren, Michael Cunningham and Nicholas Keenan were coming in a skiff from a barn belonging to the Union Pacific Company and attempted to cross a stream some fifty feet wide which poured into the river through a break in the rip-rap, when they were whirled out into the river. Mr. Wren clung to the boat and was rescued but the others jumped out and were drowned. Since that date immense sums of money have been expended by the government in protecting the river bank, and by the Union Pacific and Smelting Works people in raising the ground upon which their buildings are located, and they are now considered perfectly safe from damage by water. The increase in the value of the bottom lands on this side of the river has caused a general raising of the grade for a distance of two miles north of the Smelting Works, and the extension of the river protection system by the government adds to the security of that part of the city.

Doubtless the oldest house now standing in Omaha is one built by Timothy Kelly, a frame structure on Thirteenth Street, between Cass and Chicago, which he built in 1854, moving into it December 20th. Until recently a log house, weatherboarded and presenting the appearance of a frame building, stood on the south side of St. Mary's Avenue, just west of Mr. Woolworth's residence, which was built by Harrison Johnson in 1854. The property had been owned for many years by W. J. Connell and a two-story building had been erected by him on the south of the old structure Mrs Cuming's residence, at the southwest corner of Dodge and Eighteenth Streets, was built in 1855 A small brick building at the northeast corner of Harney and Fourteenth, used for many years as a blacksmith shop, was erected in 1855, by J. B. Allen The John M. Clarke house, northwest corner of Seventeenth and Capitol Avenue, was built in 1857, as was also the Cahn house a brick building on the south side of Dodge between Sixteenth and Seventeenth, recently torn down On the north side of Dodge, between Fifteenth and Sixteenth, is a brick residence which James Izard, son of the governor, built in 1856 In that year George Clayes built a frame building, which is still standing, on the west side of Eleventh, between Douglas and Dodge The small brick building just west of the First Presbyterian Church, on Dodge Street, was erected by John Withnell, in 1856 The Thomas Davis house, a brick building at the southeast corner of Howard and Ninth, was built in 1856 or 1857 The frame building, No. 1111 Davenport, was erected by Byron Reed, in 1857 The brick residence on Davenport, near Seventeenth, known as the Patrick property, was built by M. T Patrick, in 1857. The Goodwill house, on the same street, near Fifteenth, was built by T. G Goodwill, in 1856 In that year the brick structure standing at the southeast corner of Thirteenth and Capitol Avenue, owned by Frederick Dellone, was built in 1856

East of the Williams Block, on Dodge Street, is a brick dwelling, and on the northwest corner of Harney and Ninth is another, both of which were erected by Jesse Lowe, in 1856 The brick residence occupied by General W W Lowe, southwest corner of Harney and Sixteenth, was erected by his father, Dr Enos Lowe, about the year 1857

The frame house on the south side of Capitol Avenue, near Fifteenth, was moved to that lot, in 1860, from Florence, by Captain C H. Downs That same year a frame building, which now stands on the south side of Cass, near Thirteenth, was erected by William Florkee, on the lot now occupied by the American National Bank Building, and was known for several years as the Union Hotel The brick house yet standing at the northwest corner of Dodge and Eighteenth Streets was built at an early date by John McCormick, who died within its walls June 2, 1884 In the first city directory of Omaha, printed in 1866, this house is referred to as "next to the capitol itself, it is the first thing that attracts the eye of the stranger visiting or passing through the city" Near the northeast corner of Jackson and Eleventh Streets, facing south, is yet standing an old frame building which was occupied as a home for many years by the family of Rev Reuben Gaylord, two rooms of which Mr Gaylord bought in the summer of 1856 They were a mere shell, built of cottonwood lumber the year previously.

For many years it was generally believed that coal in paying quantities could be found in the vicinity of Omaha. In September, 1871, Thomas Wardell, an experienced miner, made a proposition to the Council to prospect for coal within the city limits for a reasonable bonus, and in October a resolution was offered calling for a special election to vote upon the proposition to issue bonds to the amount of $7,000 in aid of the project Another resolution was offered increasing the amount to $10,000, to be expended in boring for coal "within a reasonable distance of the city," which was adopted Later the amount was reduced to $4,000, and then a resolution was adopted to the effect that, if private individuals desire to bore for coal, in or about Omaha, at their own expense, they were at liberty to do so, and with that the subject was dropped In the spring of 1871 Professor Hayden, of the United States Geological Corps, was invited to address the Board of Trade upon the subject of coal formations of the West and to give his opinion as to the probability of finding coal near Omaha. He spoke at considerable length, describing the coal beds of the West, and gave it as his opinion that if coal were found at all near Omaha, in veins of sufficient thickness to be worked, it would be at such great depth as to be practically valueless. In 1887 half a dozen public-spirited citizens of Omaha contributed generously to a purse to be used in boring for coal in the vicinity of the Willow Springs Distillery. The best machinery obtainable for such purposes was procured and the work carried on for several months with great zeal but was finally abandoned. In the meantime, as the price of coal has been steadily reduced to Omaha consumers, and manufacturing interests correspondingly benefited, the incentive to experiments in this line has been, to a large degree, removed. A hole 1,400 feet deep was drilled last year on the Little Papillion, near Lawnfield, in a vain search for natural gas, at the expense of a number of Omaha capitalists.

The first asphaltum pavement laid in the city was on Douglas street, from Fourteenth to Sixteenth Street, in the fall of 1882. It was put down at a cost to the city of $2.98 a yard, by the Barber Asphalt Company, under the superintendency of John Grant. It was composed of a six inch concrete base, one-half inch of cushion top and two inches of asphaltum. There are three classes of this work now done in Omaha, that above described being called class "A," and is the most expensive. Class "B" has four inches of concrete base and two inches of asphalt top. Class "C" has a base of three inches of broken stone coated with coal tar, one and a half inches of broken stone, or slag, covered by a hot preparation of tar, and on this an inch and a half of asphalt paving material.

# CHAPTER XVI.

### Military History—Indian Difficulties—Fort Omaha.

The military history of Omaha dates back to 1855, when, pursuant to an act of the Territorial Legislature of the preceding session, two regiments of militia were "officered" (and they consisted entirely of officers) as follows

First Regiment—A J. Hanscom, colonel; William C James, lieutenant-colonel, Hascal C Purple, major, J D N Thompson and Thomas L Griffey, adjutants, John B. Roberts, quartermaster, Anselum Arnold, commissary, M B Clark, surgeon, George L Miller, assistant surgeon

Second Regiment—David M Johnson, colonel, Richard Brown, quartermaster, Gideon Bennet, commissary, William McLennan, adjutant, Isaiah H Crane, surgeon, William Hamilton, assistant surgeon

In July of that year a Mr Porter and his wife, and a young man named Demaree, while encamped at Sam Francis' Lake, near Fontenelle, were surprised by a straggling band of Sioux Indians, who came upon them suddenly A short parley was had, when one of the Indians snatched up Demaree's hat and was riding off with it when Demaree called out to him to bring the hat back, whereupon the Indians opened fire upon the whites, killing both the men, and rode hurriedly away. Great excitement followed this affair. The settlers at Fontenelle hastily made preparations to resist the attack, which it was supposed would be made, as the country then abounded with Indians of various tribes, all more or less hostile, and the Governor was appealed to for aid A few days later a company was sent up from Omaha, of which William E. Moore was captain,
John Y. Clopper first lieutenant and George Hepburn second lieutenant A company was also organized at Fontenelle, with William Kline as captain, Russell McNealy first lieutenant, and John W. Pattison (formerly editor of the Omaha Arrow), second lieutenant These "troops" encamped in the little settlement gave the people a sense of security As no attack was attempted, the militiamen had no chance to show their bravery, or want of it, but spent so much of their time in fishing along the banks of the Elkhorn that their campaign was christened "the catfish war," by the grateful and appreciative settlers.

At the time of the expedition against the Mormons, which was organized by the government in the fall of 1857, anxiety was felt throughout the West as to the outcome In April, 1858, the following contribution, signed "Fair Warning," was printed in the Omaha *Times*

"Circumstances of the most alarming character are being developed which should arouse attention to the movements of the Mormons in this locality and which already warrant and loudly demand of the United States Government that a military point (post?) be established not far distant from this city Not less than one hundred of these people are now housed in our midst It is well-known that near Florence, but six miles distant from us, the Saints have a village on the north bank of Mill Creek, where are their warehouses, hotel and other fixtures requisite for fitting up a small army without risk of detection. There, too, are their powder magazines.

"In our city just now a great stir is going on amongst them, but for what immediate purpose is not known. It is known, however, that every saintly dollar not absolutely required to keep together body and soul is given for the purchase of munitions of war. A large number of Mormons are leaving this vicinity this spring. They do not, as usual, go in hand or ox-cart trains, but small, straggling squads are seen moving westward toward South Pass. Horses and mules are used instead of oxen on account, as is supposed, of their better adaptation to quick motion movements. When met thus on their journey and asked their destination, the common reply is, "Washington Territory, Oregon or California." By this means they hope to pass Colonel Johnston and his army, or, perhaps, slip around him by some of the secret mountain passes.

"In the event of failure in both these moves, then the Mormon city (Genoa), some twenty miles west of the Loup Fork, will afford a very suitable retreat whence to sally forth and lay waste the towns and settlements west of this point—Columbus, Monroe, Buchanan, Fontenelle, Fremont, North Bend, Elkhorn, and many others, now without the least show of protection. Last fall this Mormon city contained not less than five hundred souls; at this time it no doubt numbers one thousand. It is well-known that the Mormons are in possession of the mails whilst they are being transported across the plains; instance the recent depredations under the walls of Fort Kearney, where, in an old smith shop by the wayside, the United States mail was held twelve days and all the government dispatches for the army stolen and sent slyly to Brigham Young.

"When our army in Utah shall enter the valley of Salt Lake the Mormons *en masse* will rise in hostile array, for they are sworn to resist. At that moment let the good people west of us look well to their safety. We hesitate not to say that those one thousand Mormons near Loup Fork, armed and equipped as they are, can and will sweep from existence every Gentile village and soul west of the Elkhorn. As to Omaha City, the nursling of a government hostile to Mormon rule, the rival of Mormon towns and the victim of sworn Mormon vengeance, how shall she share in this strife? In the space of one night the one hundred Saints now here could lay in ashes every house in our city, whilst the armed bands in our vicinity should pillage and revel in our blood. The Deseret *News* proclaims to the wide world from the great leader of the hosts of the annointed thus: 'Winter Quarters is Mine, saith the Lord. Nebraska will I lay waste: With fear and with sword shall my people blot out from the face of the earth all those who kill the Prophets and stone the Lord's annointed.'

"Aside from the teachers in the Mormon Church the laymen are fully pursuaded in their minds that they are the chosen of the Lord. One thousand Mormons, imbued with this spirit, will, on the field of battle, defeat ten thousand of the regular soldiery and lay waste a territory whilst the government is yet beginning to oppose.

"For verity of the statements herein contained as to the movements of this sect, let those who wish inquire of the merchants who sell ammunition here, at Florence and at Crescent City. Let them see if Council Bluffs merchants are not drained of these articles by the train which lately left that place. Then let the store houses of the Saints near Florence be searched, place scouts on the plains and there examine wagons and packs. That certainly should satisfy one and all, even the most sceptical."

This writer's fears proved to be unfounded, however, and from the date of the occupancy of Utah by the military forces of the government, in the winter of 1858 and 1859, there has been no occasion for any anxiety with regard to the attitude of the Mormons towards the national authorities.

In June, 1859, there was an outbreak of

the Pawnee Indians, then living near Fremont, but on the south side of the Platte River. They proceeded up the Elkhorn River, in a northwesterly direction, on their annual buffalo hunt, and as they journeyed committed many depredations upon the opposite side of the river, especially at West Point, from which place all the settlers fled in terror, leaving their homes to be ransacked by the Indians. A party of whites from Fontenelle went up to West Point, well armed and equipped, but found no Indians. Proceeding six miles farther up the river to the settlement of DeWitt, several Indians were enticed into a log cabin in which the whites had concealed themselves, with a view of capturing them. The attempt proved unsuccessful, however, though several of the Indians were shot in the melee.

A general uprising of the Indians being feared Governor Black organized a force of about two hundred men, which assembled on Maple Creek, near Fontenelle, early in July, to pursue and punish the Indians. In this there was much of "the pomp and glorious circumstance of war." The Governor himself was present, attended by a staff of half a dozen officers. General John M Thayer, who was in active command of the expedition, was similarly supplied with aides, and a squad of United States dragoons, under command of Lieutenant Beverly H. Robertson (who afterwards became a cavalry general in the Confederate army), contributed materially in giving a military appearance to the command. Colonel Samuel R Curtis (afterwards a major general in the Union army in the war of the rebellion) also accompanied the expedition. Omaha contributed John McCombie, Charles D. Woolworth, Robert H Howard, Witt Black, A S Paddock, Samuel A. Lowe and R. E Bowie as staff officers, the following named being appointed battalion officers. William A. West, colonel, Beverly H Robertson, lieutenant-colonel, Peter Reed, major, Samuel R. Curtis, inspector, Experience Estabrook, adjutant, W T Clarke, quartermaster; A U Wyman, commissary, Henry Page, wagonmaster, J P Peck and William McClelland, surgeons. The various companies composing the command were officered as follows —

Omaha Gun Squad (with a brass six-pounder) James H Ford, captain, E G McNeeley, first lieutenant, William Searight, sergeant

First Dragoons George F Kennedy, captain, J C Reeves, first lieutenant, C. A Henry, second lieutenant, John S Bowen, sergeant

Second Dragoons: R W Hazen, captain, William West, first lieutenant, H C Campbell, second lieutenant, Abram McNeil, sergeant

Fontenelle Mounted Rifles (so called because the members of the company rode in wagons and were armed with shot guns and old army muskets) William Kline, captain, James A. Bell, first lieutenant, William S Plack, second lieutenant, John H Francis, sergeant

About the 6th of July the expedition thus organized started in its pursuit of the Indians and overtook them some distance west of the forks of the Elkhorn River, encamped on the west side of a stream (since named Battle Creek) where it emptied into the Elkhorn. A lively chase for a distance of a couple of miles followed and the Indians were induced to call a halt and a parley ensued. The result was that half a dozen young Pawnees were surrendered by the tribe as the survivors of the party which had been perpetrating the outrages, and, with the agreement that the expenses of the expedition were to be paid out of certain moneys then due the tribe from the government, peace was declared. The following day all but one of the prisoners escaped, and after being confined in the jail at Omaha a few months that one was restored to liberty. Those who took part in this expedition were disappointed in their expectation of receiving pay from the government for their services, as were also the men who furnished horses, wagons and other supplies for the occasion.

In commemoration of this expedition, the following verses were composed by General Experience Estabrook, of this city:

Ye warriors from battle fields gory,
 Come listen a moment to me,
While I sing of the deeds of glory
 In the war with the bloody Pawnee.

Beneath our commander's broad pennant,
 We marshalled our forces in line,
And took Uncle Samuel's lieutenant,
 And made him a Colonel so fine.

The picked men, the wise, the respected,
 The flower of the country were there;
From these with great care was selected,
 The staff of the brave General Thayer.

Their merits were tested severely;
 They were men from whom foes never ran;
But, to give you my meaning more clearly,
 I will say, "the subscriber was one."

We had great men, but some didn't know it—
 Men of mark with the sword and the pen—
The statesman, the scholar, the poet,
 And candidates—say about ten.

Were we pained with bruise, or a felon,
 The belly-ache, or a stiff neck
We had only to call on McClellan,
 Or our own faithful surgeon, Doc. Peck.

There are many of water suspicious,
 Especially if it be cool,
Let such quaff a potion delicious,
 Like us, from the green mantled pool.

'Midst the slime where the buffalo wallows,
 Let him stoop, the potion to draw,
And reflect, while the foul draught he swallows,
 On the julip, the ice and the straw.

At meals, 'mid confusion and clatter,
 When halting at night, or at noon,
Some five of us ate from one platter,
 And ten of us licked at one spoon.

Our eyelids were strangers to slumber,
 We heeded not hunger or pain,
While we followed them, days without number,
 Over sand hill, and valley, and plain.

No false one his treason was showing,
 No timid one wished to turn back,
While along the dark trail we were going,
 We watched for the moccasin track.

At length, far away in the valley,
 The light of their camp-fires appeared,
And the bugle notes, bidding us rally,
 With joyful emotions were heard.

Like Pat, on a peck of perates,
 Like Diedrick, on cabbage or kraut,
So we, on those dangerous traitors
 Descended and put them to rout.

Like rats, from a ship's conflagration,
 Like fleas, from a well littered stye,
So scattered the whole Pawnee nation
 At the sound of our rallying cry.

And now, when the wars are all over,
 And peace and security reign,
Let us bring forth the big bellied bottle
 And drink to the Pawnee campaign.

In the early part of 1861 there were wild rumors of invasions of Omaha contemplated by the secessionists of Missouri, when Colonel Miles, of the Second United States Infantry, came in from Fort Kearney, in April, with Companies E and F of that regiment on their way South; the command was encamped here several days, awaiting transportation down the river. The Omaha *Telegraph*, of April 25th, says: "As the Omaha is almost hourly expected the two companies now here will probably join the four expected from Fort Randall, and it is hardly to be supposed that six full companies, well drilled and equipped, commanded by a brave and gallant officer, will allow themselves to be trifled with, or their orders go unfulfilled, in their own land by a parcel of rebellious rowdies of no patriotism and less judgment. We had the pleasure of meeting Colonel Miles, now in command of the two companies here, and who will be by seniority of rank in command of the united six; and from his personal qualities and past history we would caution the people of St. Joseph against meddling with him or his men. Considerable excitement prevails in the city to learn what has been really the fate of the Omaha, and what is to happen at St. Joseph to the troops on their way down the river. It is reported that the St. Joseph people will endeavor by mob violence to prevent the soldiers from obeying their orders and from garrisoning Fort Leavenworth, upon which point, we take it, the Missourians have an eye for plunder. We believe that the people of St Joseph will not prove such desperate fools as to attempt so hazardous an undertaking, for we feel sure that mob violence, opposed to the drill of the regulars, must in any case result greatly to the damage of the former, and would be but amusement for the latter."

On the 28th Colonel Miles and his command embarked on the steamer West Wind, and, in order to avoid anticipated trouble at St Joseph, left the boat at Forest City, Kansas, and marched across the point, re-embarking below St Joseph, at Palermo. May 3d the steamer Omaha went down the river with the heavy baggage of Companies C, E and I, of the Fourth Artillery (from Fort Randall), but the soldiers were marched overland across Iowa, to Eddyville, the terminus at that time of the Des Moines Railroad. The soldiers were banquetted in fine style by the citizens of Council Bluffs, May 4th, upon starting out on their march.

In this connection it may be mentioned that on the 10th of May ten twelve-pound howitzers were spiked at Fort Kearney by Captain C H Taylor, Second Dragoons, then commanding that post, who claimed that he feared they would be taken by a mob and turned against his command. He had previously received orders to send the guns to Fort Leavenworth, but chose to disregard those orders, alleging lack of adequate escort, and deliberately destroyed them instead. His explanation as to where the mob was to come from in that early day, when the nearest settlements (and mere hamlets at that) were two hundred miles distant, would be of interest.

May 18th, Governor Alvin Saunders issued the following order

"WHEREAS, The President of the United States has issued his proclamation, calling into the service of the United States an additional volunteer force of infantry and cavalry to serve for a period of three years unless sooner discharged, and the Secretary of War having assigned one regiment to the Territory of Nebraska, now therefore I, Alvin Saunders, Governor of the Territory of Nebraska, do issue this proclamation and hereby call upon the militia of the Territory immediately to form in the different counties volunteer companies, with a view of entering the service of the United States under the aforesaid call. Companies, when formed, will proceed to elect a captain and two lieutenants. The number of men required to each company will be made known as soon as the instructions are received from the war department, but it is supposed now that it will not be less than seventy-eight men. As soon as a company is formed and has elected its officers the captain will report the same to the adjutant general's office.

"Efforts are being made to trample the stars and stripes, the emblem of our liberties, in the dust. Traitors are in the land, busily engaged in trying to overthrow the government of the United States, and information has been received that these same traitors are endeavoring to incite an invasion of our frontier by a savage foe. In view of these facts I invoke the aid of every lover of his country and his home to come promptly forward to sustain and protect the same."

Nebraska furnished, to aid in putting down the rebellion, one regiment of infantry, the First Nebraska, which was mustered in at Omaha during June and July, 1861, as the various companies were filled by Lieutenant Lewis Merrill, Second United States Cavalry, was transferred into the mounted infantry service by special orders from the headquarters at St. Louis, Department of Missouri, October 11, 1863, and assigned to duty on the plains, re-enlisted for another term of three years July 22, 1864, and was mustered out at Omaha July 1, 1866, having remained in the service more than a year after the close of the war. During its term of service the following named constituted the list of commissioned officers:—

Colonels—John M. Thayer (promoted to brigadier general of volunteers, October 4, 1862) and Robert R. Livingstone.

Lieutenant-Colonels—Hiram P. Downs, William D. McCord, Robert R. Livingstone and William Baumer.

Majors—William D. McCord, Robert R. Livingstone, William Baumer, Allen Blacker and Thomas J. Majors.

Adjutants—Silas A. Strickland (afterwards colonel of the 50th Ohio Infantry and brevet brigadier general), Francis I. Cramer and Francis A. McDonald.

Quartermasters—J. N. H. Patrick, John E. Allen and Charles A. Thompson.

Commissary—John Gillespie.

Surgeons—Enos Lowe, James H. Seymour and William McClelland.

Assistant Surgeons—William McClelland, Napoleon B. Larsh and George Wilkinson.

Chaplain—Thomas W. Tipton (afterwards elected United States Senator from Nebraska).

Sergeant-Majors—William I. Whitten, William W. Ivory, John P. Murphy, Andrew C. McMaten, Abijah S. Jackson and Edwin R. Capron.

Quartermaster-Sergeants—John Gillespie, Edwin R. Capron and John M. Robinson.

Commissary-Sergeants—Charles Schmidt, Charles Thompson, Stephen W. Moore and John Gillespie.

Hospital Stewards—Edward Donovan, George Shultz and John M. Stewart.

Principal Musician—Robert A. Collins.

Chief Buglers—John Y. Hooper, Henry Voght.

Saddler—Carl Lindell.

Company A: Captains—A. F. McKinney, Neal J. Sharp, John McF. Hagood, Martin B. Cutler; First Lieutenants—Robert R. Livingstone, A. F. McKinney and Lee P. Gillette; Second Lieutenants—Neal J. Sharp, John McF. Hagood and John G. Whitelock.

Company B: Captains—William Baumer, Charles E. Provost; First Lieutenants—Peter Walter, Ernest Bimmerman, Theodore Lubbee; Second Lieutenants—Henry Koenig, Theodore Lubbee, Anton Althaus.

Company C: Captains—J. D. N. Thompson, Thomas J. Majors, Thomas H. Griffin; First Lieutenants—Thomas J. Majors, Reuben C. Berger, Thomas H. Griffin, William W. Ivory, David W. Smith; Second Lieutenants—Reuben C. Berger, Thomas H. Griffin, William W. Ivory, William A. Polack, Wilson E. Majors.

Company D: Captains—Allen Blacker, John C. Potts; First Lieutenants—Lee P. Gillette, John C. Potts; Second Lieutenants—Charles E. Provost, Elias M. Lowe, John C. Potts.

Company E: Captains—William G. Hollins, Sterrit M. Curran; First Lieutenants—Sterrit M. Curran, William S. Whitten, W. H. B. Stout; Second Lieutenants—J. N. H. Patrick, William S. Whitten, George W. Reeves, Abijah S. Jackson, Louis J. Boyer.

Company F: Captains—Thomas M. Bowen, George W. Burns, Lyman Richardson, Henry Kuhl, Edward Donovan; First Lieutenants—George W. Burns, Alexander Scott, John P. Murphy, William M. Alexander; Second Lieutenants—Alexander Scott, John P. Murphy, Fred. Smith, Merrill S. Tuttle, William R. Roper.

Company G: Captains—John McConihie, Thomas J. Weatherwax; First Lieutenants—John Y. Clopper, Thomas J. Weatherwax, Morgan A. Hance; Second Lieutenants—Thomas J. Weatherwax, Morgan A. Hance, John S. Seaton.

Company H: Captains—George F. Kennedy, William W. Ivory; First Lieutenants—Lyman M. Sawyer, Silas A. Strickland, William T. Clark, William R. Bowen; Second Lieutenants—Silas A. Strickland, William T. Clark, Stephen W. Moore, James N. Nosler.

Company I Captains—Jacob Butler, John P. Murphy, Henry H Ribble, First Lieutenants—Henry H Ribble, Francis I. Cramer, John Talbot, Emery Peck, Second Lieutenants—Francis I Cramer, Emery Peck, Francis A McDonald, George P. Belden.

Company K Captains—Joseph W Paddock, Edward Lawler, Henry F. C Krumme, Lewis Lowry, First Lieutenants—Robert A Howard, Edward Lawler, Edward Donovan, James Steele, Second Lieutenants—Edward Lawler, Edward Donovan, Lyman Richardson, Louis Lowry, Alfred Roudibaugh

### SECOND NEBRASKA CAVALRY

This regiment was mustered in for nine months' service, the date of muster-in extending from October, 1862, to March, 1863, the various companies being discharged during the months of September, October, November and December, 1863 The following named were the officers

Colonel—Robert W Furnas.
Lieutenant-Colonel—William F Sapp.
Majors—George Armstrong, John Taffe (afterwards congressman), John W. Pearman
Surgeon—Aurelius Bowen
Assistant-Surgeons—William S Latta, H G. Hanna.
Adjutant—Henry M Atkinson
Quartermaster—Josiah S McCormick
Commissary—John Q Goss
Sergeant-Major—W N McCandlish
Quartermaster-Sergeant—Zaremba Jackson
Commissary-Sergeant—Charles H King
Hospital Stewards—Charles Powell, Samuel G Latta

Company A Captain—Peter S Reed First Lieutenant—Silas E. Seely; Second Lieutenant—Elias H Clark.

Company B Captain—Roger T. Beall, First Lieutenant—Charles D Davis; Second Lieutenant—Charles F. Porter

Company C. Captain—Thomas W. Bedford; First Lieutenant—James W. Coleman, Second Lieutenant—Henry M Atkinson, Jacob R Berger.

Company D Captain—Henry L. Edwards, First Lieutenant—Henry Gray, Second Lieutenant—Wilbur B Hugus.

Company E Captains—Robert W. Furnas, Lewis Hill, First Lieutenant—Lewis Hill, John H Mann, Second Lieutenant—John H Mann, Alexander S Stewart.

Company F Captain—Dominie Laboo, First Lieutenants—Charles W Hall, Robert Mason, Second Lieutenants—Robert Mason, Henry Newcomb

Company G Captain—Oliver P Bayne, First Lieutenant—Chauncy H Norris, Second Lieutenant—Joseph S Wade

Company H Captain—John W Marshall, First Lieutenant—Isaac Wiles, Second Lieutenant—Abraham Deyo

Company I Captains—John Taffe, Silas T Leaming; First Lieutenants—Silas T Leaming, Moses H Deaming, Second Lieutenants—Moses H Deaming. Jacob H Habock

Company K Captain—Edwin Patrick, First Lieutenant—William B James, Second Lieutenant—Phillip P Williams

Company L Captain—Daniel W Allison, First Lieutenant—John J Bayne, Second Lieutenant—Daniel Reavis

Company M Captain—Stearns F Cooper, First Lieutenant—Obadiah B Hewett, Second Lieutenant—Francis B. Chaplin

### CURTIS HORSE

Nebraska furnished four companies of cavalry for service in the Southern States, first attached to a command designated "Curtis Horse," but which was consolidated with other battalions at Benton Barracks, St Louis, in December, 1861, and was thereafter known as the Fifth Iowa Cavalry, the Nebraska companies being A, B, C and D., of which regiment General W W. Lowe, of Omaha was colonel The first named company was mustered in September 14, the second September 21, the third September 19 to October 3, 1861, at Omaha, Company D being mustered in at Benton Barracks November 13, following. The battalion served until the 11th of August, 1865. It was officered as follows:

Company A: Captains—M. T. Patrick (afterwards promoted to lieutenant-colonel of the 5th Iowa), William Kelsey, John J. Lower, Samuel Paul, Marion A. Hinds; First Lieutenants—William Kelsey, John J. Lower, Horace Walter, Thomas W. Ritchie, Marion A. Hinds; Second Lieutenants—John J. Lower, Horace Walter, Fred. A. Williams, Marion A. Hinds.

Company B: Captains—John T. Croft, Erastus G. McNeely; First Lieutenants— Milton S. Summer, Erastus G. McNeely; Second Lieutenants—Jeremiah C. Wilcox (afterwards major 5th Iowa Cavalry), Erastus G. McNeely, Douglas H. Stevens, James H. Wing.

Company C: Captains—J. Morris Young, Alfred Matheas, Charles A. B. Langdon; First Lieutenants—Alfred Matheas, Charles A. B. Langdon, William T. Wilhite; Second Lieutenants—Charles A. B. Langdon, William T. Wilhite.

Company D: Captains—Harlan Baird, William Curl, William C. McBeath; First Lieutenants—William Curl, William C. McBeath, Joseph S. Rich, John S. Lemmon; Second Lieutenants—William Aston, William W. Buchanan, William C. McBeath, Joseph S. Rich, John S. Lemmon.

FIRST BATTALION NEBRASKA VETERAN VOLUNTEERS.

During the year 1864 a battalion of four companies of cavalry was organized, the date of muster of the various companies ranging from January 14 to August 31, of that year, for services in the West, which battalion was consolidated with the First Nebraska Infantry in July, 1865. The following named were the officers:

Company A: Captains—George Armstrong (afterwards major of the regiment), Charles F. Porter; First Lieutenants— Charles F. Porter, John Talbot; Second Lieutenants—Henry F. C. Krumme, Merrill S. Tuttle.

Company B: Captain—Jerembe Jackson; First Lieutenants—Joseph N. Tutwiler, W. H. B. Stout; Second Lieutenants—Joseph N. Tutwiler, W. H. B. Stout, James M. Nasler.

Company C: Captain—Henry Kuhl; First Lieutenant—Martin B. Cutler; Second Lieutenant—George P. Belden.

Company D: Captain—F. C. Kumme; First Lieutenant—William R. Bowen; Second Lieutenant—Samuel A. Lewis.

In these various organizations Omaha was well represented, furnishing more than her quota of men in those trying years. It is to be regretted that the official records in the office of the adjutant-general of the State are of the most incomplete character, as to showing the part borne by this then young territory in the suppression of the rebellion. A compilation from these records was made in 1888 by Lieutenant Edgar S. Dudley, of the regular army, by the authority of the Governor, but it consists only of the roster of "Nebraska Volunteers from 1861 to 1869," giving no information whatever as to the various engagements in which those volunteers participated, general or special orders concerning them, or any of the details as to their service. The work, however, reflects credit upon Lieutenant Dudley, as it is evident that he has carefully arranged and presented all the material then available.

MILITIA ORGANIZATIONS.

In August, 1864, a company of mounted militia was organized in Omaha and mustered into service on the 30th of that month, being discharged November 13, 1864. Of this company John R. Porter was captain, Allen F. Riley, first lieutenant, and Martin Dunham, second lieutenant. August 30, of

## MILITIA ORGANIZATIONS AND OFFICERS 157

the same year, an artillery detachment was sworn into service, enlisting for sixty days, of which Edward P Child was captain and James M Johnson, first lieutenant and Martin Dunham, second lieutenant At that time a general uprising of Indians throughout the West was anticipated and militia companies were organized and mustered in in various cities and towns of the territory In addition to the companies above named, and previous to their being formally sworn into the service of the territory, four home guard companies were organized Of these Roger T Beall was captain, George C Gates, first lieutenant, and J H Barlow, second lieutenant, of Company A, John Taffe captain, Edwin Patrick, first lieutenant, and Abraham Deyo, second lieutenant, of Company B, Charles S Goodrich, captain, Martin Dunham, first lieutenant, and David T Mount, second lieutenant, of Company C, and Jesse Lowe, captain, E Estabrook, first lieutenant, and O B Selden, second lieutenant of Company D

On the 10th of July, 1861, the First Nebraska Infantry was banqueted at the capitol building in fine style by the citizens of Omaha, and on the 25th the officers of that regiment gave a supper at Keith's Hotel, complimentary to Lieutenant Merrill, on which occasion they also presented him with a handsome sword

In 1873 there were two military companies in Omaha, the Guards and the Rifles

During the year 1879 Companies G and H of the State militia were organized in Omaha The former was mustered into the service with fifty-four men George H Crager was captain, John King, first lieutenant, J Ed. Smith, second lieutenant, and E H Lawton, first sergeant It was disbanded, after nearly three years' service, on account of lack of support from the State It was composed of a fine body of men and was a very popular organization, and so well drilled that it carried off four prizes offered on various occasions for proficiency in drill and discipline

Company H was organized shortly after Company G and had a membership of sixty-eight Its first officers were Edward Simmonds, captain, Henry Bolln, first lieutenant, F B Angel, second lieutenant, and John Casey, first sergeant It was composed almost entirely of enterprising young mechanics, and when the Smelting Works strike occurred they very seriously objected to taking an active part in its suppression, believing the workmen had right and justice on their side Lieutenant Bolln, with about twenty men, were on duty at the Smelting Works, however, for four days The company was mustered out early in 1882, at which time Henry Bolln was captain, Edward Fee, first lieutenant, James Donnelly, Jr, second lieutenant, and D C Miller, first sergeant Companies G and H were armed by the State, but provided their own uniforms

The Edward Creighton Guards was the name of a local military company which was organized as a part of the military force of the state, was mustered in on the 3d of December, 1887, and discharged in September, 1889 Immediately after its organization Lieutenant L W. V Kennon, of General Crook's staff, took charge of the company and soon brought it to a high state of proficiency in drill and discipline. At the State Encampment, held nine months after its organization, the company was complimented in general orders read in presence of the entire brigade Its officers were C J Smyth, captain, George J Paul, first lieutenant, Edward J McVann, second lieutenant, and John J. Mullen, first sergeant

The Omaha Guards, organized October 4, 1887, with about sixty members, is not a part of the State militia The company is armed with Springfield rifles, owns a fine Gatling gun, has a first-class armory and is handsomely uniformed Its first officers were. A. H Scharff, captain, Jesse Lowe, first lieutenant, Charles A. Harvey, second lieutenant, Henry B. Mulford, third lieutenant, W. A. Webster, first sergeant, S. B. Reed quartermaster-sergeant, and Nat M. Brigham, color sergeant. The following named are the officers now serving: F. E. Bamford, captain; H. B. Mulford, first lieutenant; C. H. Wilson, second lieutenant; A. P. Cone, first sergeant; Eli Hodgins, quartermaster; W. B. T. Belt, third sergeant; Wm. B. Ten Eyck, fourth sergeant; T. D. Daken, fifth sergeant; F. S. Knapp, S. F. Mills, B. L. Searle, corporals; H. M. Murray, lance corporal; C. H. Gardner, chaplain, E. W. Lee, surgeon. June 1891 the Guards participated in an inter-State drill at Kansas City, and brought home the first prize offered for the best drilling shown by companies which had never before competed. To Sergeant Foye was awarded the gold medal offered for excellence in drill shown by the first sergeants of the various companies.

January 11, 1891, a branch of the Union Veteran Corps was organized in Omaha, and named in honor of the late Colonel James W. Savage. The following named were elected officers: J. A. Bartlett, colonel; J. S. Miller, lieutenant-colonel; E. A. Shaw, major; L. B. Edmunds, adjutant; C. W. Allen, chaplain. Fifty names were enrolled as charter members.

Fort Omaha, located three miles north of the business portion of Omaha, but now within the city limits, was established in 1868 as Sherman Barracks. In 1869 "Omaha" was substituted for "Sherman" and in 1878 the name of the post was changed to Fort Omaha. In August, 1869, Ellen J. Seymour and husband, Emerson Seymour, conveyed to the United States by warranty deed the north half of the southeast quarter of the northwest quarter of section thirty-three, township sixteen, range thirteen, the twenty acres adjoining on the north being conveyed to the government by Charles B. Wells and wife, September 4th following. May 27, 1868, Augustus Kountze purchased the twenty acres adjoining on the south, the twenty acres which the Seymours subsequently deeded to the government, and also twenty-two and a half acres of the northeast quarter of the northwest quarter of section four, township fifteen, range thirteen, which tract of forty-two and a half acres he leased to the United States in September, 1868, for a period of ten years, the government having the right to renew at the termination of the lease for another term of ten years, the land reverting to Kountze in case the military post was abandoned before the expiration of the term specified. October 2, 1868, a new lease was made for ten years, without the privilege of renewal. By a conveyance dated June 4, 1868, William D. Hall and Henry Hickman each acquired title from Kountze to a one-seventy-ninth interest in the forty-two and a half acres.

August 10, 1880, Augustus Kountze filed a petition in the District Court for Douglas County against Stevens & Wilcox, Gilbert H. Collins, John S. Collins, Samuel E. Rogers, William D. Hall, Henry Hickman and others, reciting that, for the purpose of securing the location of a permanent military post adjacent to the City of Omaha, and the purchase of lands necessary therefor, the said Kountze, and seventy-nine other persons and firms, contributed one hundred dollars each, in 1868, for the purpose of conveying land by deed or lease to the government, and made their petitioner their trustee; that petitioner had so purchased the land described, had given to each of his associates a certificate showing their respective ownerships of an undivided one-seventy-ninth interest. The petition recites the fact of the leasing to the government, in 1868, and a renewal by the government, in 1878, for one year, and again in October, 1879, for a term of twenty years, with the privilege of a renewal for an indefinite term, and then sets up the fact that a permanent military post cannot be established upon ground which the United States does not own in fee simple, and petitioner prays for a decree by the court directing the said Kountze to convey said land to the government by absolute conveyance. March 18, 1882, default was entered against all of the defendants and ten days later a decree as prayed for was entered. Under this decree said Kountze conveyed the forty-two and a half acres to the government by deed dated April 17, 1882.

When the proposition was made, a year or two since, to secure another location for Fort Omaha, it was claimed that the tract deeded by Kountze would revert to the original owners in case the property was abandoned for military purposes. The foregoing statement is based upon information derived from the records of the Midland Guarantee & Trust Company, of this city, and may be relied upon as correct with respect to the manner in which the government became possessed of the land the fort has occupied for more than twenty years, and which is now of great value.

The following named have been commandants of the post at various dates: Brevet Major William Sinclair, captain Third Artillery, assigned December, 1868; Brevet Brigadier General L. P. Bradley, lieutenant-colonel Twenty-seventh Infantry, assigned January, 1869; Brevet Lieutenant-Colonel Henry Haymount, captain Twenty-seventh Infantry, assigned April, 1869; Brevet Brigadier-General James N. Palmer, colonel Second Cavalry, assigned April, 1869; Brevet Major-General John H. King, colonel Ninth Infantry, assigned September, 1872; Brevet Major-General Jeff C. Davis, colonel Twenty-third Infantry, assigned September, 1874; Brevet Major-General John H. King, assigned 1876; Brevet Major-General William P. Carlin, colonel Fourth Infantry, assigned 1882; Brevet Major-General Frank Wheaton, colonel Second Cavalry, assigned 1886.

It being deemed desirable by the government to secure more extensive grounds for a military post, Senator Manderson introduced the following bill December 13, 1887:

"*Be it enacted by the Senate and House of Representatives of the United States of America in Congress assembled,*

"That the Secretary of War is hereby authorized to sell the military reservation known as Fort Omaha, near the City of Omaha, in the State of Nebraska, and such of the buildings and improvements thereon as can not be economically removed to the new site herein provided for. In disposing of said property the Secretary of War shall cause the grounds to be platted in blocks, streets, and alleys, if in his judgment it would inure to the benefit of the government in making sale of said site, having due reference to the requirements of the houses and buildings located on said grounds, in such cases as they may be sold with the ground. The Secretary of War shall also cause the lots, lands, and buildings to be appraised and sold at public or private sale, at not less than the appraised value, having first been offered at public sale. The expense of advertising, appraisement, survey, and sale shall be paid out of the proceeds of said sale, and the balance paid into the Treasury of the United States.

"SEC. 2. That the Secretary of War is authorized and shall purchase suitable grounds, of not less than three hundred and twenty nor more than six hundred and forty acres in extent, to be situate within a distance of ten miles of the limits of said City of Omaha, in the State of Nebraska, and construct thereon the necessary buildings, with appurtenances, sufficient for a ten-company military post, to be known as Fort Omaha, in accordance with estimates to be prepared by the War Department; and a sufficient sum of money, not exceeding two hundred thousand dollars, is hereby appropriated, out of any money in the Treasury not otherwise appropriated, to enable the Secretary of War to comply with the provisions of this act: *Provided*, That the title to the lands authorized to be purchased under the second section of this act shall be approved by the Attorney-General: *And provided further*, That not more than one-third of said sum shall be expended in the purchase of a site; and the whole expenditure for site and improvement shall not exceed the sum of two hundred thousand dollars.

"Sec. 3. That section one of this act shall be of effect when the purchase of a new site provided for in section two shall have been effected."

This bill passed and became a law July 13, 1888. Bids were advertised for and in response thirty-one tracts of ground were offered the government, at various prices. These proposals were all examined by the Secretary of War and Quartermaster General and referred to General John R. Brooke, commanding the Department of the Platte, who personally viewed the various sites offered and recommended the one known as the H. T. Clarke tract, lying contiguous to the town of Bellevue, six miles due south of the southern boundary of Omaha. This recommendation being forwarded to Washington, the land was inspected in May, 1889, by Secretary of War Proctor and General Schofield, with a party of military and civil officials, all expressing approbation of the judgment of General Brooke, the result being that this site, embracing 543 acres, was purchased by the government at a cost of $66,666 and as soon as the necessary buildings can be erected will be occupied as a military post. Doubtless additional appropriations will be made by the government, in order to properly develop the property, and in course of time it will certainly become one of the handsomest military stations in the West. The department rifle range is located adjacent to this tract and it is generally believed that it will be converted into a national range, the ground being admirably adapted to the purpose.

In February, 1891, Congress changed the name to Fort Crook and appropriated $500,000 for improvements.

The headquarters of this military division, now known as the Department of the Platte, were located at Omaha soon after the beginning of the war of the rebellion. The department comprises twelve posts in Nebraska, Iowa, Utah, Montana, Wyoming and Idaho. At the intersection of Twentieth Street and the Union Pacific tracks is located the Quartermaster's Depot, from whence are distributed all the supplies used by the troops in this command. Five acres of land, purchased in 1880 by a number of public-spirited citizens of Omaha for this purpose, are covered with buildings and general facilities necessary for the transaction of the immense amount of business here transacted. The army headquarters occupied for several years a building erected, for the government's uses, by John and Richard Withnell, at the southwest corner of Harney and Fifteenth Streets, afterwards known as the *Herald* building. Then the government leased buildings to be erected for office purposes at Fort Omaha, but this was found to be an undesirable location and the headquarters were removed to the Strang Building, corner of Tenth and Farnam. In 1889 another change was made to the present location, the fifth floor of the Bee Building. Brigadier-General John R. Brooke is the commander of the department and the following named constitute the department staff:

Major Michael Sheridan, assistant adjutant-general; Major John M. Bacon, acting inspector-general; Captain P. Henry Ray, acting judge-advocate; Lieutenant-Colonel William B. Hughes, chief quartermaster; Major William H. Bell, chief commissary of subsistence; Lieutenant-Colonel Dalles Bache, medical director; Lieutenant-Colonel Thaddeus H. Stanton, chief paymaster; Captain James C. Ayres, chief ordnance officer; Major Daniel W. Benham,

WITHNELL BUILDING—HEADQUARTERS DEPARTMENT OF THE PLATTE—1876.
FIFTEENTH AND HARNEY STREETS.

LOOKING NORTHWEST FROM TWELFTH AND FARNAM STREETS, 1867.

## DEPARTMENT OF THE PLATTE OFFICERS 161

inspector of small arms practice, First Lieutenant C C. Worden, acting engineer officer. The general staff officers serving in the department are Captain John Simpson, assistant to the chief quartermaster and in charge of the quartermaster's depot at Omaha, Captain Charles F Humphrey is assigned to duty upon the construction of building, etc , at the new Fort Omaha, First Lieutenant Fayette W Roe, Third Infantry; and First Lieutenant Charles M Truitt, Twenty-first Infantry, aides

It is expected. when the United States Custom House and Post-office building shall have been completed, and the courts, post-office, and federal offices removed into it, the present government building will be remodeled for use as the permanent military headquarters for the Department and that it will thereafter be occupied for this purpose for many years to come.

In concluding this chapter, it will not be out of place to say that the selection of the more extensive grounds for Fort Omaha, at a greater distance from the city, was made on the recommendation of General Sheridan and other eminent military authorities, that there should not be so many military posts in the country, but they should be much larger, that they should be further from the large cities, and yet close enough to make available the railroads centering there

The people of this city are to be congratulated upon the fact that, with the whole West to choose from, and many rival cities struggling for the location of this important post, the military authorities decided upon Omaha as the best point for the purpose

# CHAPTER XVII.

NOTABLE PERSONS VISITING OMAHA — PRESIDENTS, PRINCES AND POTENTATES — HOW THEY WERE RECEIVED.

January 12, 1872, the Grand Duke Alexis, of Russia, was publicly received in Omaha, taking in this city on his journey from St. Louis to the plains, where he proposed going on a buffalo hunt with General Sheridan. He was met at the depot by that officer, General Ord and General Palmer, commanding the Department of the Platte and at Fort Omaha, respectively. The three officers were accompanied by their aides in full uniform, and there was also a citizens' committee present. The party proceeded from the depot direct to the residence of ex-Governor Saunders, a large and handsome building which occupied the ground, then some thirty feet higher than the present grade, upon which the city hall has been erected. Here an elaborate dinner was served, to which the leading people of the town were invited. At 4 o'clock, P. M., the Grand Duke and his suite departed for the West, accompanied by General Sheridan and his staff.

King Kalakaua, of the Sandwich Islands, arrived in Omaha on the 21st of January, 1875, on his return home from an extended visit to the United States. He was accompanied by Governor John O. Dominis and Governor John M. Kapena, of Honolulu, Colonel William M. Wherry, of the United States Army, H. A. Paine, of Boston, and Colonel A. C. Dawes and Colonel James N. Brown, of St. Joseph, Missouri. The party had dinner at the Grand Central, and in the afternoon a drive about the city was taken; a tour of the High School building was made, and the day closed with a reception in the parlors of the Grand Central. The party proceeded westward the following day.

November 1, 1875, President U. S. Grant visited this city, accompanied by Mrs. Grant and Fred. Grant and his wife. Private Secretary Babcock, ex-Secretary of the Navy Borie, Secretary of War Belknap, General Alvord, General McFaley, General Vincent, General Wm. Myers, General A. J. Myers, Colonel Benjamin and Colonel Crosby were also with the President, who came to Omaha from Des Moines, Iowa. From that city, General George Crook, then commanding the Department of the Platte, General Perry, General Ruggles, Colonel Litchfield, General Manderson, General Thayer and A. S. Paddock had escorted the party, and were joined at the transfer by an Omaha committee consisting of Mayor C. S. Chase, Ezra Millard, Colonel R. E. Wilbur, Senator Hitchcock, S. H. H. Clark, J. E. Boyd, J. C. Cowin, E. A. Allen. An artillery salute was fired as the train rolled into the Union Pacific depot, in which building the famous Twenty-third Infantry Band was stationed, discoursing well selected music. A long line of carriages conveyed the party up Tenth and Farnam to the Grand Central Hotel, where a brief halt was made. Thence the procession proceeded to the High School grounds, where were assembled the pupils of all the city schools. Here President Grant was introduced by the Mayor. In response, the President made one of his brief, modest speeches to the thousands of children, saying, "I am pleased to stand beneath the

Looking North from South Eighth Street 1875.

shadow of this building which is so well calculated to prepare you for useful occupations and honorable stations in life His Honor, the Mayor, has said that I am in favor of free speech, and therefore I want other people to do the talking " From 12 until 1, p. m , a reception was held in the judges' chambers of the Custom House building, the rooms having been handsomely decorated with flowers and flags by Mr James T. Allan, of the post-office, and his assistants. Then dinner was taken at the Grand Central and the party resumed their journey to the West in the evening

Dom Pedro II, of Brazil, accompanied by three of his officials, visited Omaha April 26, 1876 He was traveling through the United States in a quiet manner, as Mr D Pedro de Alcantara The party were met at the transfer depot by Mr L M Bennett, then superintendent at this point of the Pullman Palace Car Company, in obedience to a telegram from the headquarters of the company in Chicago. Carriages were taken on this side of the river and a tour of the city made At the High School a piano duet was played by Miss Blanche Deuel and Miss Nelia Lehmer At the smelting works the Brazilian monarch manifested more interest than at any other point in the city.

November 3, 1879, General and Mrs. Grant reached this city over the Union Pacific, on their return from their journey around the world A large delegation of citizens met them at the depot and escorted them through the streets in the following order of procession (1) A battalion of the Ninth United States Infantry, (2) the Ninth Infantry Band, (3) a battery of artillery, (4) Company G, State Militia, (5) Union Pacific Band (6) City Fire Department; (7) Brandt's Band, (8) Lyran Singing Society, (9) Union Pacific shopmen, (10) civil societies, (11) Mænnerchor singing societies, (12) University Cadets, from Lincoln, (13) Grand Army posts; (14) city band, (15) Company H, State Militia, (16)

trade representatives. The line of march was north on Tenth to Harney, east to Ninth, north to Farnam, west to Fifteenth, north to Dodge, and west on Dodge to the High School, where addresses of welcome were made by Governor Nance and Mayor Chase, a brief response being made by General Grant The column soon after marched in review past a platform erected on Farnam and Fourteenth, on which were stationed the General and a number of military officers and citizens. In the evening there was a banquet at the Withnell, then the chief hotel of the city The next day was Sunday, and General Grant attended services in the morning at the First Methodist Church, a small frame building on Davenport, near Seventeenth, the sermon being preached by Rev J B Maxfield, from II Corinthians, xviii, 4 General and Mrs Grant were the guests of General George Crook, at Fort Omaha, during their stay, proceeding eastward on Monday, accompanied by their son, Colonel Fred Grant, and wife, who had arrived in Omaha on Sunday, coming from Chicago.

President R B Hayes visited the West in the fall of 1880, arriving in Omaha on the morning of the 3d of September, and was welcomed at Council Bluffs by a delegation consisting of Mayor Chase, General Williams, Colonel Ludington, Major John V. Furay, General John King, Senator Saunders, Congressman E K. Valentine, General C F. Manderson and John C. Cowin, Esq The President was accompanied by Mrs Hayes and two sons, Secretary of War Ramsey, General W T. Sherman, General McCook and others The party visited Fort Omaha and other points of interest, including the High School, where they climbed into the tower, at the suggestion of Mrs. Hayes, obtaining thereby a view of Omaha and surroundings which could be gained in no other way. At 1 o'clock in the afternoon they returned to the depot and proceeded westward

In October, 1881, King Kalakaua again visited Omaha, the guest for two days of James M. Woolworth, Esq., at whose home a reception was given in his honor, which was attended chiefly by young people of the city. Previous to this Miss Woolworth and Miss Butterfield had visited the Hawaiian Islands and received many courtesies and kind attentions from the King, and the first opportunity which was offered for a return of these courtesies was improved by Mr. Woolworth and his family. On the same day the Marquis of Lorne, then Governor-General of Canada, passed through the city on his way East, with his suite, making only a brief stop at the depot.

The following year, September 8th, the Marquis of Lorne, this time accompanied by his wife, the Princess Louise, visited Omaha. The party were met at the transfer depot by General O. O. Howard, then commanding the Department of the Platte, Thomas L. Kimball, John C. Cowin and others, by whom the Marquis and the officers with him were escorted to Fort Omaha and other points of interest, the Princess remaining in her car at the depot. In the afternoon the train proceeded westward.

October 12, 1887, President and Mrs. Cleveland spent a few hours in Omaha, arriving at 9:50 in the morning, accompanied by the President's private secretary, Daniel S. Lamont, his former law partner, Colonel Bissell, of Buffalo, New York, and Postmaster General Vilas. They were met at the Northwestern Railroad depot in Council Bluffs, and escorted to this city by a committee composed of James M. Woolworth, Dr. George L. Miller, Senator Charles F. Manderson, George W. Holdrege, Congressman John H. McShane, General George B. Dandy, Max Meyer, James E. Boyd, Charles H. Brown and J. H. Millard. Arriving at the Omaha depot the party were joined by acting-Mayor William F. Bechel, Governor John M. Thayer and Senator A. S. Paddock. Carriages were in readiness, and a tour made of the principal portions of the city. At Sixteenth and Farnam a triumphal arch had been erected and handsomely and richly embellished. A detachment of the military from Fort Omaha was present, flags and banners abounded, there was a number of fine brass bands in attendance, and the city presented a very attractive appearance. Calls were made upon the President for a speech, but he declined, pleading lack of time. Upon leaving Omaha the party proceeded southward.

December 24, 1890, Henry M. Stanley, accompanied by his wife, visited the city and was met at the depot by a delegation consisting of Mayor Cushing, Governor Thayer, Major T. S. Clarkson, Dr. G. L. Miller, E. Rosewater, Edward P. Roggen, G. M. Hitchcock and Thomas Swobe. Twenty-three years previously he had been a resident of Omaha, being at that time western correspondent for the New York *Herald* and St. Louis *Republican*, and his subsequent achievements as an explorer were watched with the closest interest by the people of this city. The following sketch, which he published in the New York *Herald*, under date February 4, 1867, is now of local interest: " Omaha City, the capital of Nebraska and terminus of the Union Pacific Railroad, is beautifully located on a high, level plateau, forty feet above the highest water mark, on the west bank of the Missouri. A low range of hills, gradually rising to an elevation of eighty to one hundred feet above this plateau, and about one mile from the river, affords fine locations for private residences. On one of these hills is the territorial Capitol, surrounded by a park six hundred feet square. The panoramic view from these hills, and especially from Capitol Hill, is rarely if ever surpassed in picturesque beauty, and even grandeur. Below the city, with its wide, regular streets, business blocks, churches and buildings, there the railroad, winding from huge machine shops around the city, then cutting through the hills, passes on its way mills, warehouses and gardens. The eye then takes in the darkly-colored river, making a great bend of ten or fifteen miles around Iowa Bluffs, the steamboats coming, going, or unloading freight and passengers on its banks, here and there a raft or log carried down by the swift current of the river. Three miles back of the river, directly east of Omaha, Council Bluffs, half hidden among the ravines, leans up against the high walls of the green bluff. This charming view of the river and city, hill and plain, affords a never-ending source of pleasure to the *beholders. Omaha is situated very nearly on an air line and almost half way between New York and San Francisco. Her commanding position as terminus of a railway destined to carry the great traffic between the Atlantic and Pacific, probably to revolutionize the Chinese and Japan trade of the world, gives her commercial advantages which, in the last twelve months, have doubled her population, and which, sooner or later, will make her one of the leading cities of the Great Northwest. Preparations for building business blocks, churches and private dwellings next season are being made on a large scale, and, although hundreds of mechanics are expected to arrive here in the spring, I doubt whether the supply will be equal to the demand."

On the 13th of May, 1891, President Harrison accompanied by the Hon John Wanamaker, postmaster-general, Hon Jerry Rusk, secretary of the Department of Agriculture, Mrs. Harrison, Mis McKee, Mrs. Russell Harrison, and others, visited Omaha, and were the guests of the city for six hours. At just 11 40 A M an engine, profusely decorated with flags and bunting, came, drawing the presidential train into the depot, and it had hardly come to a stop when cheer after cheer burst from the thousands of throats of the waiting crowd which had gathered to welcome the party. As soon as the carriages which were in waiting had been entered, the line of march was taken up Tenth Street to Farnam and up Farnam to Seventeenth, where a speaking platform had been erected for the occasion. The procession was headed by the Omaha Guards, followed by the Second Infantry, from Fort Omaha, and the carriages containing the presidential party and the various committees and municipal officers. As the line started, a salute of twenty-one guns was fired from the battery, stationed on South Twelfth Street.

It was one continuous ovation from the depot to the speakers' stand. The sidewalks were filled to overflowing, and along much of the route the dense crowds encroached on the passageway that was with difficulty kept open by the police. It was absolutely impossible to keep the crossings of the side streets clear, and the attempt to do so was soon given up.

Every window had from three to a dozen occupants, and housetops and balconies could scarcely contain the thousands of eager ones who sought some vantage from which to view the distinguished party that was passing below.

Arriving at the stand Mayor R C Cushing delivered an address of welcome, to which the President briefly responded. Short addresses were also made by Postmaster-General Wanamaker and Secretary Rusk. The party then repaired through the dense crowds to the Bee Building, where a reception was held in the rotunda, being probably the first time a presidential reception was ever held in a newspaper building. Carriages were then entered by the distinguished guests and a large number of the leading citizens and a drive was taken through the principal streets, stopping at the High School (where President Harrison addressed the children), and Creighton College, and ending at the hospitable home of ex-Senator Saunders, on Sherman Avenue, where Mrs. Harrison and the ladies of the party held a reception. At 6 o'clock the party was driven to the train and departed eastward.

It is doubtful if there ever were so many flags and so much bunting displayed in Nebraska as on this occasion, and it seemed as though each person was determined to make the most show of patriotism possible.

In May, 1892, the General Conference of the Methodist Episcopal Church met in Omaha, and, necessarily, the leading men of this denomination from all over the world visited this city, where they remained nearly a month; but, as the Conference is more particularly referred to in another chapter, they will not be especially mentioned here.

In 1891, and again in 1892, the city officials of Boston visited Omaha and were entertained by the city officers and members of the council.

In addition to the above, there are many of the notable people of the country who make occasional visits to this city, including Jay Gould, of New York, Mr. Fred Ames, of Boston, George Francis Train, Sidney Dillon, and many others.

Being located on the principal lines of transportation to California, Omaha is peculiarly situated, and therefore receives many more notable visitors than she otherwise would; and it is to her credit that she has never failed to extend to all the most unbounded hospitality. The citizens have ever entertained with a lavish hand, and few who have partaken of their hospitality will ever forget it.

# CHAPTER XVIII.

### The Press of Omaha — Newspapers now Published — A List of the Dead and Buried.

The Omaha *Arrow*, ostensibly the first newspaper published in this city, was really printed in Council Bluffs. It had a brief existence, the first issue being dated July 28, 1854, and the last November 10th of that year. It was a weekly published by J. E. Johnson and John W. Pattison, Mr Pattison being the editor. In 1858 the latter was associated with W. W. Wyman for a few months in the publication of the Omaha *Times*. During the war he was proprietor and editor of a paper at Sidney, Iowa, and after the war was in the employ of the St Louis *Republican* for several years as a court reporter. The *Arrow* was an enthusiastic advocate of everything calculated to advance the interests of Omaha. The *Palladium*, published in 1854, at Bellevue, insisted that that town was the only town in the Territory suitable for the building of a great city, and affected to sneer at Omaha's prospects, to which the *Arrow* responded with zeal and vigor in defense of its own location. A Muscatine Iowa, paper, publishing a paragraph making a sneering reference to Omaha as "a city with six houses," the *Arrow* retorted. " Why, St Nicholas, N Y., is not a circumstance for comfort, ease and cheap living to its namesake in our city. Here you may get venison, fowl, bird, or fish cooked in any manner you please You may smoke in the parlor, put your heels upon the sideboard without injury to the furniture, or for variety may spread your buffalo on the green grass, and take a comfortable smoke without fear of being run over by a score of woolly-headed servants

Omaha *City*, indeed Why, we have editors, squatters, deer, turkeys, grouse, and other 'animals' a plenty, and will soon show you that Omaha City will be one of *the* cities of the West" It is unfortunate that a paper so zealous and enthusiastic in its championship of the new town could not have received adequate support. Mr Pattison came West as a correspondent of the New York *Herald*, and was a writer of more than average ability. Mr. Johnson was a Mormon, and at one time published a weekly paper at Wood River Crossing, Neb, when the settlement consisted chiefly of his own residence and a small water-mill He afterwards drifted out to Salt Lake

The *Nebraskian*, Democratic in politics, was established in 1854, by Bird B Chapman, Nebraska's second delegate to Congress Four years later he sold it to Theodore Robertson, and, in 1860, it was purchased by M. H. Clark, in 1863 it was sold by Mr. Clark to Alfred H. Jackson, and in June, 1865, its publication ceased In 1859, Mr. Robertson and General John M. Thayer became involved in a heated political controversy, which resulted in the distribution of handbills, printed in the largest and blackest type to be found in the city, wherein each characterized the other as possessing, in an infinite degree, all of the qualities which tend to make men infamous General Thayer was challenged to mortal combat by Mr Robertson, who was represented by Captain W E. Moore, but better counsel prevailed, and the difficulty was bridged over A gentleman of this city has copies of these handbills, which are somewhat interesting, as indicating the character of the political controversies of that period.

The *Times*, also Democratic, was founded in 1857, by Wm. W. Wyman, the first issue being dated June 11th. In 1858, during a session of the legislature, a daily edition was published for a short time, but proved unprofitable; and in 1859 the publication of the weekly edition was also discontinued. Mr. Wyman was a newspaper man of experience, and a gentleman of high character, who commanded the respect and confidence of the community to an unusual degree. For a number of years he was postmaster of this city.

The Omaha *Democrat* was established in 1858, by Hadley D. Johnson, one of the leading citizens of the town, and an active politician, but the paper was short lived.

The *Telegraph* was established as a daily, in September, 1860, Major Henry Z. Curtis, son of General Samuel R. Curtis, being the editor and proprietor. Mr. Charles Goodrich, ex-city comptroller, and Charles W. Sherman, now proprietor of the Plattsmouth *Journal*, did the type-setting on the *Telegraph*. It was an evening paper and boasted largely of its dispatches "by the Missouri & Western Telegraph, Stebbins' Line," though said dispatches were extremely brief. In the fall of 1861, the proprietor of the *Telegraph* discontinued its publication and entered the Union army, serving with distinction upon the staff of General Samuel R. Curtis.

The Omaha *Republican* was first issued as a weekly, May 5, 1858. Edward F. Schneider and Harrison J. Brown were the first proprietors, soon succeeded by Dr. G. C. Monell. In August, 1859, it was purchased by E. D. Webster, a protege of Thurlow Weed, and he gave the paper a standing and reputation throughout the country. In 1861, Colonel Webster sold the paper to E. B. Taylor and E. A. McClure (the latter still a resident of Omaha), and during the war Colonel Webster served the country as private secretary to Secretary Seward. Messrs. Taylor & McClure converted the paper into a tri-weekly, and in January, 1864, commenced the publication of a daily edition. Since that date, the paper has had varying fortunes, and many owners. In 1866, Major St. A. D. Balcombe purchased the *Republican*, and in 1871 sold a half interest to Waldo M. Potter. About this date a consolidation with the Omaha *Tribune* was effected, and for nearly two years the paper was called the *Tribune and Republican*, the "*Tribune*" portion of the name being dropped in January, 1873. In 1875, the *Republican* became the property of a stock company, with Casper E. Yost as business manager, and Isaac W. Miner as secretary. In 1881 Mr. Yost and Fred Nye bought the paper, and in the fall of 1886, sold it to S. P. Rounds, Sr. (recently public printer at Washington), and Cadet Taylor, for the very handsome sum of $105,000. The death of Mr. Rounds, a year later, plunged the paper into fresh difficulties, and in December, 1888, Mr. Yost again took charge of the *Republican*, this time as receiver, appointed by the court to protect the interests of the various stockholders, Messrs. Rounds & Taylor having organized a stock company to conduct the affairs of the paper. Early in 1889, Mr. Nye again became interested in the ownership of the *Republican*, this time with Frank B. Johnson as a partner. In October, following, Major J. W. Wilcox, of the *Evening Dispatch*, purchased the *Republican*, the job department connected with the paper being retained by Messrs. Nye & Johnson. Major Wilcox, finding the longer publication of the paper unprofitable, gave up the contest, and the daily *Republican* ceased to exist July 29, 1890. It is now published as a weekly.

The Omaha *Daily Herald*, Democratic, was established by Dr. George L. Miller and Daniel W. Carpenter, in 1865. Three years later the paper was purchased by Lyman Richardson and John S. Briggs, though Dr.

THE BEE BUILDING.

Miller retained the editorship, and soon after bought Mr. Briggs' interest, and the firm of Miller & Richardson, as proprietors, continued until March, 1887, when they sold the paper to John A McShane, who controlled it for a year, and it then passed into the management of R A. Craig, and in March, 1889, the paper was purchased by G M Hitchcock Under the management of Miller & Richardson, though published in a State that was overwhelmingly Republican in politics, the *Herald* took high rank, and attained great popularity Indeed, its popularity was not confined to Nebraska, or the West, but assumed a national character Dr Miller was a writer of unusual vigor, and possessed strong convictions on all important topics, with a courage to declare them The *Herald* was an earnest and persistent advocate of the benefits of tree culture in Nebraska, and to its efforts in this direction is due much of the development that has been made in forest culture in Nebraska during the past twenty-five years

The *Daily Evening Tribune* was the outcome of a desire on the part of certain citizens of Nebraska to defeat General John M Thayer in his aspirations for re-election to the United States Senate in 1871 The first issue appeared July 20, 1870, the necessary funds being furnished chiefly by John I Redick, Wallace R Bartlett, Clinton Briggs, Charles F Hickman, and Phineas W Hitchcock, small amounts being subscribed by a large number of Omaha people of both political parties, though Mr Redick was the main promoter of the enterprise Mr. Hitchcock, being elected to the senate in January, 1871, defeating General Thayer, was induced, soon afterwards, to take $20,000 worth of stock in the paper The *Tribune* was a handsomely printed, spirited publication, edited by C B Thomas, who came from the East to take charge of that department of the paper It was said that he had formerly been a clergyman, but that fact was never betrayed by the character of the editorial columns of the paper. Joseph B Hall was president of the Tribune Company, and brought with him, from the State of Maine, the greater part of his working force. The paper was Republican in politics, and waged bitter warfare upon the *Daily Republican*, which was responded to in kind, but that fact did not interfere with the consolidation of the two papers in 1871.

The first issue of the *Evening Bee*, Republican in political faith, appeared June 19, 1871, starting out with the bold announcement in the first issue, that it was "the best advertising medium in the city." H H Geralde was the ostensible editor and proprietor July 27, the following editorial was printed "The popular favor heretofore accorded the *Bee* as a gratuitous advertising medium, and the general desire expressed by a large number of our citizens for its enlargement as an evening journal, warrant the hope of its future success as a thoroughly fearless and independent exponent of public opinion Mr Harry Geralde will continue as the editor-in-chief, assisted by gentlemen of journalistic experience It will be the aim of the publisher, from the outset, to make the *Bee* a newspaper in the true meaning of the word" This was signed by Edward Rosewater, as publisher and proprietor The growth of the paper from that date, has been continuous and rapid, though many were the obstacles with which it was forced to contend Starting as an evening paper, it has, for many years, printed a morning edition also In 1878, a stock company was formed to manage the business, Mr Rosewater retaining the controlling interest and remaining in charge of the editorial department In June. 1889, the establishment was moved to the new building erected by the Bee Building Company, on Farnam and Seventeenth Streets, seven stories high, and covering an area of 132 feet square, the largest newspaper building, as to ground covered, in the world It is a strikingly handsome and substantial structure, costing nearly half a million dollars, and is one of the chief points of interest pointed out to strangers visiting the city. Edward Rosewater is president of both the Bee Publishing Company and the Bee Building Company, George B. Tzschuck being secretary and treasurer of the first named organization, and N. P. Feil, a son-in-law of Mr. Rosewater, secretary and treasurer of the second company.

The publication of the *Evening World* was commenced in August, 1885, G. M. Hitchcock, Frank J. Burkley, Alfred Millard, W. F. Gurley, and W. V. Rooker being the proprietors, with the first named as editor-in-chief and principal stockholder, Mr. Burkley, business manager, and Mr. Rooker as managing editor. In March, 1889, the *Herald* was purchased, and the two papers merged under the name of *World-Herald*. A building on Farnam Street, between Fourteenth and Fifteenth, three stories high, was purchased in 1889, and fitted up in the most convenient manner for a first-class newspaper office. The paper is now in a strong financial condition, is ably edited, and rapidly increasing its subscription list. Mr. Hitchcock is still the chief owner, with Mr. Burkley in charge of the business department, and Mr. Robert B. Penttie as managing editor.

October 27, 1888, Major J. C. Wilcox began the publication of the *Evening Dispatch*, a Republican paper (or, rather, resumed its publication, as he established a paper by that name in 1873, but discontinued it after a few months' experience). October 13, 1889, he purchased the Omaha *Republican*, and for a time continued both publications, but in December, 1889, he ceased publishing the *Dispatch*, and gave his entire attention to the *Republican*. On the 1st of July, 1890, the paper announced itself as favoring the adoption of the constitutional amendment prohibiting the manufacture and sale of intoxicating liquors in Nebraska, which announcement created a decided sensation throughout the State, as the paper had previously opposed the amendment, and the question at issue was one which was then attracting great attention.

The Omaha *Democrat*, an evening paper of Democratic faith, is the successor of the *Inter-State Herald*, formerly the Council Bluffs *Herald*, which latter paper was established in Council Bluffs by R. E. Ingraham, S. T. Walker, and W. A. Spencer, in 1882. It was purchased by W. R. Vaughan, October, 1888, and was at once removed to Omaha, where its publication was continued for a time as the *Inter-State Herald*, then as the *Inter-State Democrat*, and on October 1, 1889, the name was changed to the Omaha *Daily Democrat*. It was owned by a stock company, M. V. Gannon being president, W. R. Vaughan, vice-president and managing editor, William McHugh, treasurer, and B. A. Fowler, secretary. They suspended publication early in 1891.

The Nebraska *Tribune* is a German daily and weekly which has built up a large circulation. It was established eight years ago by F. C. Festner, recently deceased, and was for many years edited by Frederick F. Schnake. Otto Kinder and Joseph Wortenberger are the present editors.

The *Danske Pioneer* is a Scandinavian weekly of much influence with that class of citizens. It has a large circulation, and is ably edited by Mr. Sophus F. Neble, the present owner. The paper was established in 1871, by Mark Hansen.

The *Pokrok Zapadu*, edited and owned by John Rosicky, is a weekly printed in the Bohemian language. The paper has been under the control of Mr. Rosiscky for many years, and has attained a wide circulation. It was founded in August, 1871, by Edward Rosewater, and published bi-monthly.

The Swedish *Tribune* and Swedish *Post* are both well conducted weeklies, which circulate extensively among the Swedish people. The former is edited by Claes Algotelmen, and the latter, by C. A. Jacobson.

The *Westliche Courier*, a German weekly, edited by Mr. Bruno Tzschuck, formerly Secretary of State for Nebraska, and, later, Consul to Vera Cruz, Mexico, after several years' existence, was sold to Mr. Frederick F. Schnake, formerly of the Nebraska *Tribune*, who changed its name to the Nebraska *Banner*, and still publishes it.

The *Dannebrog*, a Danish weekly, is edited by Otto Wolf.

The Omaha *Weekly Mercury* was established by F. M. MacDonagh, at Plattsmouth, Nebraska, in 1871, under the name of Nebraska *Watchman*, and moved to Council Bluffs in 1878, and to Omaha in 1879. Mr. MacDonagh died in this city, June 5, 1885, and the following year the paper was purchased by A. L. Pollock, who sold it to John T. Bell in the latter part of 1888. In January, 1890, Messrs. Victor E. Bender and Frederick W. Taylor purchased the paper, the latter selling his interest to Mr. Bender in May, 1890. It is devoted more to the legal interests than any other, and is the recognized organ of the bar of this city.

The Omaha *Excelsior* was established as an amateur paper about fifteen years ago, by Clement C. Chase, then a boy at school. It has since developed into a paper of considerable influence, under the management of its founder, and is the chief society paper of the city. It is published weekly, and has connected with it a valuable job printing establishment, of which Mr. Chase and George B. Eddy are proprietors.

The *Railway News and Reporter*, Daniel B. Honin, editor and proprietor, is a weekly, devoted especially to the interests of railroad men.

The Omaha *Times*, a weekly, published by Blackman & Garton, H. G. Boluss, editor, was established in September, 1890.

*Progress* is the name of a weekly published by the colored men of Omaha, and which shows considerable ability. The first issue appeared during the latter part of 1889.

*United Labor* is a weekly publication, which was commenced in October, 1890. It is devoted to the interests of the local labor associations. William S. Sebring is the business manager.

The *Knights' Jewel* is published in the interest of the Knights of Pythias, by Will. L. Scism.

The *Omaha Original*, Mrs. Helen A. Van Camp, publisher, is a weekly family paper which made its first appearance on Easter day, 1891.

There are several trade papers published in Omaha, among them being *The Omaha Furniture Journal*, a monthly, devoted, as its name implies, to the interests of the furniture and kindred trades, edited by Mr. A. Spitko; the *Western Merchant*, owned by Mr. A. H. Comstock; and the *Western Printer*, published by the Great Western Type Foundry in the interest of their business.

The Western Newspaper Union, George A. Joslyn, manager, supplies "ready prints" to over three hundred outside papers, and this matter is ably edited by Mr. Cal. Shultz, an experienced newspaper man who has been connected with the Omaha press for nearly a quarter of a century. The *Auxiliary*, a monthly publication issued from this office, is a very handsome publication, devoted to furthering the interests of the house. The American Press Association, M. G. Perkins, manager, also does a large business in furnishing stereotyped matter for weekly papers.

Omaha, like all other cities, can point to a long list of newspaper wrecks: The *Nebraska Daily Statesman*, which was born July 17, 1864, and died three days later; the *Evening Times*, started in 1869, as the result of a printers' strike, by Charles Collins, P. F. O'Sullivan, William E. Cook and John Howard, and which lived about six months; the *Daily Union*, also the outgrowth of a printers' strike in 1873, and which publication was discontinued after ten months on the part of Cal. D. Shultz, Billy Edwards, Thomas Wolf, George W. Frost, E. N. Sweet and others; *The Independent*, which T. H. Tibbles commenced to publish in September, 1877, and which lived less than half a year; the *Commercial Exchange*, published for a year or two by W. C. B. Allen previous to 1880; the *Evening News*, established by Fred Nye in May, 1878, and discontinued in June, 1880; the *Evening Telegraph*, by S. F. Donnelly and H. S. Smith, which lived for nearly two years from May, 1880; *Center-Union Agriculturist*, published by George W. Brewster, discontinued about 1882; the *Agriculturalist*, published for many years by Jeremiah Behm and discontinued about fifteen years ago; *Nebraska Journal of Commerce*, Taylor Bros., proprietors; *The Vesten*, published by O. R. Nelson and Halfdan Jacobson previous to 1882; the *Omaha Post*, by Charles Bankes, discontinued about 1884; the *Evening Dispatch*, first known as the *Union*, was a printers' paper, afterwards owned by Frank Sweezey and Leonard Livesey and, later, by George C. and Robert Wallace, was established in the fall of 1883, and lived about a year; the *Sunday News*, owned and edited by Harry Merriam, was established May 10, 1885, and survived for ten months; the *Sunday Mirror* was owned by Daniel Shelley and Frederick Benzinger, but they discontinued its publication after issuing half a dozen copies, in 1889; the *Chronicle*, Thomas Cotter, proprietor, and G. M. Crawford, editor, was published for several months in 1887 and 1888. The foregoing list of newspaper enterprises which have not proved profitable is not given as a complete list, but it is sufficiently extended to show that the business is a precarious one, in which the failures far exceed the successes.

The *High School Journal* was first published, commencing December, 1872, by an association of pupils of the High School, styling themselves the High School Publishing Association. Henry D. Estabrook was editor-in-chief; Miss Stacia Crowley, assistant editor; Miss Kate Copeland, "culling" editor; Charles R. Redick and John Creighton, local editors; Miss Josie Ord, and Lucius Wakeley, exchange editors; Martha Crary, Frederick Knight and George Jewett, business managers; Arthur C. Wakeley, Miss Etta Hurford, Miss Claire Rustin, Miss Blanche Deuel, Arthur Remington and Cassius Gise, directors. Although it was issued only once a month, the work evidently proved too much for this editorial and business force, for within half a year the paper passed into the management of James F. McCartney (afterwards city clerk), who ceased its publication in December, 1881, having in the meantime changed the name to the *Omaha Home Journal*. Mr. McCartney died September 4, 1883, at Denver.

In 1876, Henry D. Estabrook and James Ross began the publication of a monthly, styled the *Miscellany*, which was soon afterwards purchased by John H. Pierce, and the name changed to the *Western Magazine*. It was a publication of decided merit but succumbed to financial pressure after a year's experience.

In 1888, the *Rising Tide*, afterwards the *Omaha Leader*, was established as the organ of the temperance associations. It suspended in the fall of 1890, upon the defeat of the prohibition amendment. George H. Gibson was editor and proprietor.

With respect to the first issue of a morning paper in Omaha the following account, from the pen of Mr. Cal. D. Shultz, editor of the publications of the Western Newspaper Union of this city, was printed in the *World-Herald* March 2, 1891. Mr. Shultz has been connected with the Omaha press for a quarter of a century and is excellent authority on newspaper matters. He says:

"In a recent issue of the *World-Herald* reference was made to its being the oldest paper in the city and some interesting reminiscences given of its pioneer days and its perplexities and difficulties under which it labored at that time. In the article alluded to no reference was made to the fact that the *World-Herald* printed the finest morning daily ever given out in Omaha, as well as that it is now the oldest paper in the city. Its old-time manager and editor, Dr Miller, made this claim some months ago, in a series of articles contributed to the *Omaha Bee* on the subject of early journalism in this city, and the writer hereof adds his testimony to the correctness of the doctor's conclusions John S Briggs, who is still a resident of Omaha, could tell the story about the first morning daily publication in the Nebraska metropolis, as its writer heard him tell it nearly twenty-five years ago He was an important factor about the *Herald* building, on the corner of Thirteenth and Douglas in those early days He it was, I think, who officiated as 'make up' of not only its first daily, but the first weekly forms of what has now grown to be a powerful and widely circulated journal in this prosperous and progressive city But not to digress from the original thought—that of the first morning daily paper in Omaha—the fact is now recalled that the *Republican* appeared as a morning daily the same day the *Herald* did, but its inspiration came from the indomitable energy and push of the editors and managers of the democratic paper, who were constantly on the alert for new fields to conquer, and, as a consequence, was a little behind that sheet in getting before the public in its new form, accompanied with the announcement that it would hereafter issue in the morning instead of evening Both the *Republican* and *Herald* had for many months been putting forth daily evening editions, but Dr. Miller, alive to the signs of the times, saw there was a demand for later and more satisfactory news, such as could only be secured and properly put in shape in a daily morning edition. The thought came with such force that the doctor at once determined upon the change

"The contemplated new departure was communicated to Foreman Briggs, and that gentleman, after the evening edition had gone to press, notified the compositors (of which there were less than half a dozen in those days) to be prepared to represent their cases at an early hour in the evening, explaining that the *Herald* henceforth and hereafter was to be a morning daily In the meantime arrangements for lighting had been perfected, the pressman notified of the new order of things and other preliminaries arranged for inaugurating the change that was about to take place in publication hour It is surmised, too, that the foreman cautioned the printers not to mention out of the office the information that had been communicated to them. There is good ground for the supposition, for the proprietor of the *Herald* had in view the surprising of the public, as well as the publisher of the *Republican*

"The scheme worked well enough so far as readers of the paper were concerned, but Major Balcombe 'got onto the racket,' so to speak, either by seeing operations going forward in the *Herald* building, or through information communicated to him by some of his printers, who had been given a 'pointer' by brother workmen doing the night act on 'the sheet over the way' Then there was a hurrying to and fro, printers were hunted up in various parts of the city, some of them called out of bed, it may be, and told to present themselves at the office without delay They obeyed promptly, and thus the *Republican* was enabled to present a morning daily on the same date of its contemporary, though, perhaps, not as early in the day or in quite as good shape It is due to say of the *Republican*, however, that it 'got there' in very good shape, for Major Balcombe, although not the aggressor in journalistic innovations, was capable of doing some tall rustling when about to be distanced by some rival paper.

'Thus was inaugurated daily morning journalism in Omaha, and credit must be given the *Herald* and its energetic publishers of that day, not alone for having issued a little in advance, but for having furnished the inspiration that called two Omaha morning dailies into the field almost simultaneously. The *World-Herald* is still on the ground, being now issued every day in the year, instead of six days in the week, as was the case when the change was made and for many years thereafter."

The *Trade Journal of the Business Men's Association of Nebraska*, which was published for a couple of years as a small paper, has recently been enlarged to a twenty-eight page royal quarto, and is published weekly. It has a large circulation. It is devoted to the interests of the business men of the State, and gives very full market quotations.

# CHAPTER XIX.

### The Liquor Traffic — Early Prohibition in Nebraska — The High License Law of 1881 — Prohibition Battle of 1890.

In these later days of prohibition, it is interesting to note that the first Territorial Legislature passed an act prohibiting, absolutely, the manufacture and sale of intoxicating liquors. Following is the full text of the law:

SECTION I. Be it enacted by the Council and House of Representatives, of the Territory of Nebraska: That from and after the first day of April, A. D., 1855, it shall not be lawful for any person to manufacture, or give away, sell, or in any way, or by any manner or subterfuge, traffic, trade, exchange, or otherwise dispose of, any intoxicating liquors within this Territory, to be used as a beverage.

SECTION II. The places commonly known as dram shops are hereby prohibited and declared public nuisances, and their establishment shall be presumptive evidence of a sale of intoxicating liquor, within the provisions of the foregoing section.

SECTION III. The establishment, or the keeping of a place of any description, whatever, within or without a building, coming within the spirit and intent of this act, and the establishment, or the keeping a place of any description where other persons are accustomed to resort, providing their own liquors, of the prohibitory character, purchased elsewhere, and drinking the same there, shall be taken to be within the meaning of this act.

SECTION IV. Every person engaged in any of the acts above prohibited, or in any way aiding or assisting in such illegal acts, whether as principal or clerk, bookkeeper, or otherwise, shall be subject to the penalties herein provided.

SECTION V. Courts and juries are required to construe this act so as to prevent evasion and subterfuge, and so as to cover the act of giving, as well as of selling, in the places above prohibited.

SECTION VI. Whoever is guilty of violating any of the provisions of this act, on conviction thereof, shall be fined in a sum not less than ten, nor more than one hundred dollars, or be imprisoned in the county jail not more than ninety days, or both, in the discretion of the court; and may be prosecuted therefor either by indictment or by information before a justice of the peace; the punishment shall be fine only.

SECTION VII. Any person being convicted for a second or any subsequent violation of this act shall be fined in a sum not less than one hundred dollars, or be imprisoned not more than one year, as provided in section six of this act.

SECTION VIII. An information or indictment under this act may allege any number of violations of its provisions, by the same party, and he may be found guilty of, and punished for, each offence, as under separate information or indictment, but a separate judgment must be entered in which a verdict of guilty is found.

This act was approved March 16, 1855, and was so completely and absolutely ignored by the residents of the Territory that the fact that such a law was passed is probably not remembered by a score of the oldest of Nebraska's old inhabitants. In no portion of the Territory was the slightest attention paid to its provisions, and on the 4th of November, 1858, a license law was approved by the Governor, which repealed the act of March 16, 1855, and provided for the issuance by county commissioners of licenses to sell malt, spirituous and vinous liquors to responsible applicants, upon payment of a fee of not less than twenty-five dollars, or more than five hundred dollars. A bond of not less than five hundred dollars, or more than five thousand dollars, was required; the selling to Indians, minors, idiots and insane persons was prohibited, and liquor dealers were held responsible for the support of all persons who became a public charge in consequence of intemperate habits. Suits for liquor sold in quantities of less than five gallons, except in cases where it was used for medicinal, mechanical, or sacramental purposes, could not be instituted. Cities and incorporated towns were authorized to increase the amount of the annual license fee to one thousand dollars.

In 1881 the Nebraska legislature passed what has since been known as the "Slocumb" law, for the regulation of the traffic in intoxicating liquors. This law was the outcome of strong efforts which were made at that session of the Legislature, and the session of 1879, to pass a prohibitory law. In the preparation of the Slocumb bill some of the best legal talent of the State was employed, and in its operation the law has so commended itself to all but uncompromising prohibitionists that it has served as a model for many other States in legislating upon this subject. Briefly stated, the law provides as follows:

Section one provides that the county board of each county may grant licenses for the sale of malt, spirituous, and vinous liquors, if deemed expedient, upon the application, by petition of thirty of the resident free-holders of the town, if the county is under township organization. The county board shall not have authority to issue any license for the sale of liquors in any city or incorporated village, or within two miles of the same.

Section two provides for the filing of the application, and for the publication of the application, for at least two weeks before the granting of the license.

Section three provides for the hearing of the case if a remonstrance is filed against the granting of a license to the applicant.

Further sections provide for the appealing of the remonstrance to the district court; the form of license; the giving of a five thousand dollar bond by the successful applicant for the license.

Sections eight, nine and ten make it an offense, punishable by a fine of twenty-five dollars, for any licensed liquor dealer to sell intoxicating liquor to minors or Indians.

Section eleven provides that any person selling liquor without a license shall be fined not less than one hundred dollars, nor more than five hundred dollars, for each offense; and section twelve provides for the trial of such offenders.

Section thirteen makes it an offense, punishable by a fine of one hundred dollars and a forfeiture of license, for any licensed liquor vender to sell adulterated liquor.

Section fourteen makes it an offense, punishable by a fine of one hundred dollars, for any person to sell or give away any liquor on Sunday, or on the day of any general or special election.

Sections fifteen to twenty-three, inclusive, define the liability of saloonkeepers for damages sustained by anyone in consequence of the traffic, and provide the steps necessary to collect such claims.

Section twenty-four relates to the issuance of druggists' permits.

The local option feature of the law is contained in section twenty-five, the salient part of which reads: "The corporate authorities of all cities and villages shall have the power to license, regulate and prohibit the selling or giving away of any intoxicating, malt, spirituous, and vinous liquors, within the limits of such city or village. This section also fixes the amount of the license fee, which shall not be less than five hundred dollars in villages and cities having less than ten thousand inhabitants, nor less than one thousand dollars in cities having a population of more than ten thousand.

Sections twenty-six and twenty-seven relate to druggists' registers and penalties for violation of the rules governing the same.

Section twenty-eight makes drunkenness an offense, punishable by a fine of ten dollars and costs, or imprisonment not exceeding thirty days.

Section twenty-nine provides that the doors and windows of saloons shall be kept free from screens and blinds.

Under this law, the license to sell liquor in Omaha was fixed at one thousand dollars. At that time there were one hundred and sixty-five saloons in the city, with a population of about thirty-two thousand. The number was largely reduced by the operation of the new law, the license having previously been only one hundred dollars a year; but with the growth of the city the number of drinking places gradually increased, but not in like ratio. For the year ending April 1, 1886, there were 143 licenses issued; during the next year, 176; for the year ending April 1, 1888, 223; for the year following, 262; from April 1, 1888, to January 1, 1890, 247; and for the year 1890, 240; the population having increased in the mean time from 32,000 to 142,000. In 1891 there were 247, and in 1892, 237. The number of licenses referred to includes those issued to drug stores, wholesale dealers, and all places where liquors are sold.

The attempt to enforce the provisions of high license, just after its passage, excited the most intense opposition on the part of the saloon men of this city. Among those who took an active interest in carrying the law into effect, was Colonel Watson B. Smith, clerk of the United States courts, and this activity resulted in his receiving numerous anonymous letters and postal cards of a threatening character; and at various times, it was reported, he was followed by one or more persons as he returned to his home in the evening after office hours. On the morning of the 5th of November, 1881, he was found lying dead in the hall of the third story of the custom house and postoffice building, in front of his office door. The body was lying in a pool of blood, with a bullet hole through the head, and on the door casing was found a mark made by the ball after it had accomplished its fatal work. Colonel Smith had been detained at the office until a late hour the night before, and it was evident that he had reached the hall and was about to lock the office door for the night, when he met his death. He had, in consequence of the receipt of the letters referred to, been carrying a revolver for self-protection, and this weapon, with one empty chamber, was found lying near the body, as was also a bundle of letters and papers which he had apparently had under his arm as he attempted to lock the office door.

As the news of the killing was spread over the city, great excitement prevailed, the general supposition then being that the liquor interests of the city were responsible for a cowardly assassination. An inquest was held by the coroner, the jury returning the following verdict: "The jury find that the deceased came to his death at the door of his office, in the United States court house and postoffice, in the City of Omaha, Nebraska, after 10 o'clock and fifteen minutes, on the night of November 4, 1881, by a gunshot wound through the head, inflicted by some person, or persons, unknown, and we do further find that the killing was premeditated murder." A citizens' mass meeting was held in the afternoon, at the Academy of Music, and $4,500 subscribed as a reward for the apprehension of the murderer (afterwards increased to $5,000); the liquor dealers of the city—then organized as "The Merchants' and Manufacturers' Union"— offered a reward of five hundred dollars; the Good Templars' societies, two hundred dollars; and Governor Nance added the two hundred dollars which the State is authorized to offer under such circumstances; making a total of $5,900. Extraordinary efforts were made to capture the guilty party, or parties, but to no purpose, and to this day the mystery of Colonel Smith's death remains unsolved. December 15, 1881, one August Arndt was arrested on the charge of threatening the life of E. S. Dundy, United States District Judge, and it was then thought that he was implicated in the killing of Colonel Smith, but sufficient proof to warrant his indictment was not obtained. He was tried before Judge Foster, of Kansas, on the charge of threatening the life of Judge Dundy, convicted, and sentenced to a confinement of three months in the Douglas County jail, which sentence was carried into effect. The threats referred to were alleged to have been made in consequence of certain rulings by the court in connection with a land suit Arndt had had in Judge Dundy's court with the Union Pacific Railroad Company.

The prohibition sentiment having largely increased in Nebraska, the Legislature of 1889 passed the following act:

*Be it enacted by the Legislature of the State of Nebraska:*

SECTION 1. That, at the general election to be held on the Tuesday succeeding the first Monday of November, A. D. 1890, there shall be submitted to the electors of this State, for approval or rejection, an amendment to the Constitution of this State in words as follows: "The manufacture, sale, and keeping for sale of intoxicating liquors as a beverage are forever prohibited in this State, and the Legislature shall provide by law for the enforcement of this provision." And there shall also at said election be separately submitted to the electors of this State, for their approval or rejection, an amendment to the Constitution of the State in words as follows: "The manufacture, sale, and keeping for sale of intoxicating liquors as a beverage, shall be licensed and regulated by law."

SEC. 2. At such election, on the ballot of each elector voting for the proposed amendments to the Constitution, shall be written or printed the words: "For proposed amendment to the Constitution, prohibiting the manufacture, sale and keeping for sale of intoxicating liquors as a beverage;" or "Against said proposed amendment to the Constitution, prohibiting the manufacture, sale and keeping for sale of intoxicating liquors as a beverage." There shall also be written or printed on the ballot of each elector voting for the proposed amendment to the Constitution the words: "For proposed amendment to the Constitution that the manufacture, sale and keeping for sale of intoxicating liquors as a beverage in this State shall be licensed and regulated by law;" or, "Against said proposed amendment to the Constitution that the manufacture, sale and keep-ing for sale of intoxicating liquors as a beverage shall be licensed and regulated by law."

SEC. 3. If either of the said proposed amendments shall be approved by a majority of the electors voting at the said election, then it shall constitute section twenty-seven (27) of article one (1) of the Constitution of this State.

In the fall of 1889 those favoring prohibition in this city organized for work. The members of the Woman's Christian Temperance Union, the Good Templars, Non-Partisan League and the Prohibition Club formed a combination for the campaign, with John Dale, president; W. N. McCandlish, secretary; Charles Watts, Luther A. Harmon and Mrs. George W. Clark, executive committee. In order to secure the support of the city churches the following was printed as a circular and thoroughly distributed:

"*To the Pastors and Officers of the Churches in Omaha:*

"DEAR BROTHERS—A meeting was held in the First Baptist Church, in this city, October 21, 1889, in response to a call signed by about thirty pastors, with a number of other temperance workers.

"The object of the meeting, as presented in the call by its originator, Mr. L. L. Abbott, is briefly summed up in the necessity for the immediate organization of a Gospel Temperance Union, through which could be secured the united efforts of all Christians and moral people in opposition to the rapidly growing power of the rum traffic. Also:

"*a.* That this Union work should be built upon the teachings of the Bible:

"1. That we are our brother's keeper.

"2. Cursed is he that giveth his neighbor drink.

"3. No drunkard shall inherit the Kingdom of Heaven; and

"4. I will not be with you except ye destroy the accursed thing from among you.

"*b.* That this work should be upon a line that will unite all who love our Lord, and others who, through love of humanity and our nation, desire to labor for the protection of our youth and homes from the Great Destroyer—Intemperance.

"c. That to do this successfully the workers should invite the men, women and children of our State, without regard to religious or party affiliations, to unite in one grand effort to OUTLAW THE LIQUOR BUSINESS, and thus speedily drive it from the land.

"This is not a secret society, but an open union in which all can unite and work.

"The fact may not be recognized by all that the struggle only one year ahead of us in Nebraska will probably concentrate more money and effort on the part of the liquor interests than any other place or period in the past.

"The times demand a fearless ministry and people in battling with the rum traffic, and it is within the power of the professing Christians in this State to close every saloon, and in neglecting to do so they are and forever will be held responsible.

"At the meeting alluded to the undersigned were appointed a committee to suggest plans for action until a more formal organization shall supplant them. We come to you with these proposals:

"1st. That a public gospel temperance service be held every Sunday afternoon, at Boyd's Opera House, whereat, perhaps, the churches by turn may principally conduct the services.

"2d. That in each church such a service be held one Sunday evening each month. That these for greater interest and union be inter-denominational, in that the speakers at the meeting in a Methodist Church, for instance, come from a Presbyterian Church, and so on—urging each pastor to call out his lay talent to assist him.

"3d. That a Union be organized in each church, to render more effective the work of all, and such Union appoint one representative to the central organization.

"Will you kindly express your views on this subject to the chairman or secretary at as early a day as convenient? Earnestly implore the guidance of the Holy Spirit in this matter."

Boyd's Opera House was occupied on Sunday afternoons during the fall and winter. Then the Exposition Building was occupied for a short time and in the spring the old Acadamy of Music—which had degenerated into a variety hall known as the "People's Theatre"—was leased and fitted up, at considerable expense, for the purpose of holding public meetings. Large sums of money were raised in various parts of the country, and sent to Omaha and other portions of the State to aid in carrying the prohibition amendment. Rev. Dr. Thomas, of Chicago, ex-Governor St. John, of Kansas, Dr. Kynett and other speakers of prominence delivered addresses at the theatre, and a large tent was erected in a grove at the intersection of Twenty-Eighth and Mason Streets, and here public meetings were conducted during the summer, under the auspices of the Good Templars, where addresses were made by a dozen or more speakers, hailing from various States of the Union, and so generally bearing the title of "Colonel" that that distinction was applied in derision to all prohibition orators, by the opposition, during the closing months of the campaign.

### THE JOINT DEBATES.

June 5th and 7th a debate was held at Beatrice, in the presence of nearly six thousand people, Professor Samuel Dickey, of Michigan, chairman of the executive committee of the National Prohibition party, and Rev. Sam. Small, of Utah, appearing as advocates of the prohibition cause, and Edward Rosewater, editor of the Omaha *Bee*, and John L. Webster, Esq., of Omaha, as defenders of the high license system. A full shorthand report was made of this debate, printed in the *Bee* and sent broadcast over the land. In September a similar discussion was held at Grand Island, ex-Governor Larrabee, of Iowa, and ex-Attorney-General Bradford, of Kansas, representing the prohibition cause and Messrs. Rosewater and Webster, the high license doctrine. Complete shorthand reports were also made of these speeches and published in the *Bee*, with a view of giving the widest circulation to the arguments on both sides of the question. The Grand Island debate was noticeable for the valuable mass of information on this important subject presented by the speakers. The exponents of the high license system had made a close and careful study of the question, its history in the various States where prohibitory laws had been enacted, with the practical results arising therefrom. This fact, together with the official positions recently occupied by the champions of prohibition in their own States, in one of which statutory, and in the other constitutional prohibition had been the law of the land for nearly a decade, gave character and force to the arguments advanced.

In addition to their services on these occasions Messrs. Rosewater and Webster spoke in various towns and cities throughout the State against the prohibitory amendment, Mr. Webster making thirty speeches, and Mr. Rosewater nearly as many, during the closing weeks of the campaign.

In the meantime the friends of the amendment were very active. To Rev. M. L. Holt was given charge of the organization of the Omaha churches in behalf of the cause, and a very active campaign was made. The local press, with the exception of the *Leader*, a weekly paper of limited circulation, opposed the amendment, but the city was flooded with copies of a New York weekly called the *Voice*, which claimed to be the organ of the National Prohibition party, and the *Lincoln Call*. The publishers of the *Voice* devoted a great deal of space to the Nebraska campaign and many thousands of copies of the paper were distributed gratuitously throughout the State. They also undertook the collection of a fund in aid of the amendment, and a sum variously estimated at from $15,000 to $40,000 was thus secured and sent to Nebraska, the contributions coming from every State in the Union. The interest of the children and youth was elicited by means of contests for Demorest medals of silver, gold and diamonds, offered as prizes for distinction in oratory, the selections being confined to a book of essays detailing the evils of intemperance. During the month of October an entertainment of some sort could be found at the old Academy of Music (which had been re-christened "Amendment Headquarters") nearly every evening. Mrs. Helen Gougar, Miss Frances E. Willard, Mrs. Mary Lathrop, Mrs. Russell, ex-Governor St. John, of Kansas, and other speakers of like prominence, followed each other in rapid succession. On the Sunday immediately preceding election day Governor St. John was billed to appear, in the following sensational manner: "Free Grand Barbecue at Amendment Hall next Sunday Afternoon! Ex-Governor St. John will Roast Editor Rosewater and Eat Him in the Evening!" A challenge to St. John was thereupon printed in the *Bee* by Rosewater, and the Coliseum Building, capable of seating eight thousand people, was secured for a meeting at 2 o'clock Sunday afternoon, on which occasion at least five thousand people assembled to hear the anticipated discussion; but Mr. Rosewater was the only speaker. At the afternoon meeting at Amendment Headquarters, Governor St. John announced that upon arriving in Omaha that afternoon he learned that he had been challenged by Rosewater; but, in view of the fact that a large package of that morning's issue of the *Call* of Lincoln (a prohibition paper) had just been distributed among those present, containing an interview at Lincoln held the night before with St. John, who then refused to accept Rosewater's challenge, which was the subject of the interview, many of his hearers declined to accept the inference he plainly meant to convey, to-wit: that he had not heard of the challenge until he arrived in

Omaha. He made a brief address that afternoon and in the evening spoke at length, but distinctly declared that he had no intention of participating in barbecues or posing as a cannibal.

The last few weeks of the campaign were especially exciting, as the impression generally prevailed that the vote would be close. Those who favored the amendment began the campaign early in the spring, and every hamlet in the State was visited by their speakers. Their opponents began their task later on, and, in many sections of the State, no anti-amendment speeches were made. However, a great deal of literature, tending to show the discouraging features of the prohibitory law in States where it had been adopted, with facts and figures as to the remarkable development of Nebraska under the high license system, was circulated, chiefly by an organization, composed of leading business men of the State, known as "The Bankers' and Business Men's Association," and called by the prohibitionists "Bummers' and Boodlers' Association." Edward P. Roggen, of Lincoln, ex-Secretary of State, was put in charge of the anti-amendment work, by this association, and devoted all his time for several months to the task. An organization called "The Personal Rights League," of which Louis Heimrod, of Omaha, was president, composed mostly, if not entirely, of foreigners, or those of foreign parentage, canvassed the State against the amendment. These two associations collected a considerable sum of money, at home and abroad, for campaign purposes.

The following address, headed, "To the Women of Nebraska," by Miss Frances E. Willard, President of the National Women's Christian Temperance Union, was given wide circulation throughout the State, dated October 1, 1890:

"*My Valiant Comrades in the Fight:*—I know 'your work of faith, and labor of love, and patience of hope.' Soon you will come even unto the last, when the ounce of power will tell beyond tons of power that have been expended hitherto. *The Brewers' Journal*, commenting upon the great decision just before you, says: 'If the Second Amendment is carried, local option will be wiped out, for it will make prohibition in the State unconstitutional.' Nothing, I am sure, has spurred you onward like this consideration. No canvass has ever been made under such pressure, for in none has the alternative been so distressing. But, on the other hand, if you succeed, you will have such promise of enforcement as has never been enjoyed, for your State will be practically surrounded by prohibition territory. To my mind, the crucial question of this campaign is, 'Will the women go to the polls?' Good and true men from all parts of the country are urging me to urge you to take upon you this final, and, as you think, heaviest cross. Go with prayer and song, with pledge and temperance literature, with coffee and sandwiches, and ballots. Establish yourselves as near the polls as practicable; embellish your headquarters with whatever can suggest the appearance of a Christian home; furnish, when you can, a buttonhole bouquet to each of those who vote for God, and home, and native land; bring out the children in battle array, with songs and banners. Sometimes they have been conveyed in wagons from one polling place to another, singing such songs as:

'Dare to do right, dare to be true;
You have a work that no other can do.'

"Two or three days before the voting, fit out every child in Sunday school and public school with an amendment ballot, asking them to see that somebody votes it for their sakes. This has been a method of great value in past campaigns. The young ladies have helped us greatly in arranging for the crusade by the children. Let the older women assemble for prayer in the church, on the principle of 'old women for council, young women for war,' and let the bells be rung every hour, when the leaders are changed in the prayer meeting. Sometimes the bells have been rung every seven minutes, as this is the interval of the passing knell of ruined lives because of drink. Let me encourage you by the statement that, having been at the polls many times, I have never found any such lions in the way as the imagination had previously contrived. Men in America, in the masses, at least, always treat women with courtesy. Their morale is excellent in this regard.

"A dignified and womanly bearing furnishes the best credentials. Read the accounts in 'Women and Temperance' of how the women went to the polls in different States, and see what a high day it was in Zion by reason of their presence. Even the conservative women of the South now, in several of the States, are habitually present when the local option fight is on. The ministers are there illustrating applied Christianity all day long, in their efforts to win votes for the home as against the saloon, and many a time, when victory turned on Zion's side, the good pastor has led the victorious group of work-a-day Christians in singing the doxology, and lifted up his faithful hands in blessing as the day's work ended. So may it be in many a hamlet, village and town throughout the great, young commonwealth whose destiny is to be decided on next November 4th, and whether you win or lose God will defend the right."

A few days before the election the Omaha friends of the amendment began the publication of a four-column, four-page paper, for free distribution throughout the city, called the *Daily Bumble Bee*, under the auspices of "The Prohibition and Non-Partisan County Central Committees," which publication was discontinued as soon as the result of the election was definitely known. Though its existence was brief, it was exciting, and the paper attracted its full share of public attention for a week. Personal feeling between the opposing factions became very bitter. In his speech at the Coliseum, November 2nd, Mr. Rosewater said he was in receipt of many threatening letters, and read the following, which he said had come to hand that day, postmarked Nelson, Nebraska: "If prohibition is defeated, four of us have decided that you must die, and Webster, too. It will take time, but we will not let you slip, nor him, either. We have children, and we know what prohibition does. If you had done as much as you could without lying, we would have let you and Webster go. We thought we would give you and him one chance for your worthless carcasses, and only one."

On election day, November 4th, the weather proved exceptionally pleasant. An earnest effort had been made in Omaha to secure a full registration of voters, and to this end large placards, ornamented with the admonition: "Register to-day!" were hung on street cars, displayed at the doors of business houses, attached to coal and lumber wagons, etc., etc., while the daily papers used every means possible to impress upon the local voter the necessity of not only registering, but of also being on hand at an early hour of the morning to cast his vote, in order to "avoid the rush" which was anticipated for the closing hours of the day. It was feared that there would be trouble at the polls, each party charging the other with premeditated outrage and violence. To guard against any thing of that kind, forty special policemen and forty-five sheriff's deputies were sworn in for special service at the polls and for a reserve at police headquarters, subject to call from any part of the city. In addition, six officers and sixty-eight patrolmen were detailed for duty at the voting places, and a force was added to the specials held as a reserve. No doubt these precautions aided in preserving order, though it is reasonable to suppose that anticipations of riot and bloodshed were largely due to the exaggerated statements of both parties. Certain it is, that Omaha was overwhelmingly opposed to the amendment, and the fact that at a few polling places those who attempted to distribute Republican, Democratic and Alliance tickets, but favoring the amendment, were so roughly treated that they were compelled to desist, has, since the election, been fully established. The contest for all of the State offices, which the leaders of the Farmers' Alliance party made, was based almost entirely upon this fact, as is shown by the following points in their notice of contest:

" That illegal combinations were organized in the city of Omaha and in the State, known as 'The Bankers' and Business Men's Association,' and 'The Personal Rights League,' whose object and purpose was to defeat and deprive voters of Omaha and the State of the right to vote freely and fully, to defeat the will of the voters, corrupting voters, and creating wholesale sentiment against a free and fair election, the boycotting and ostracizing of those who were opposed in sentiment to these societies, and the discharge of employes and threats of boycotting and discharge of all who opposed them.

" That these societies brought into the State large sums of money for the purpose of defeating a free and fair election. That these parties caused about 2,800 aliens to be naturalized, and paid fees for such naturalization in a manner that would constitute a bribe.

" That the city council of Omaha were members of this conspiracy, and, for the purpose of preventing a legal registration, appointed prejudiced and partisan persons on the boards of registration, and denied representation to other parties.

" That the county commissioners became parties to the conspiracy by appointing partisan judges and clerks of election.

" That the postmaster, and the common carriers of Omaha, were in the conspiracy and refused to deliver matter which did not agree with the views of the conspirators, and that the press co-operated by inciting a dangerous and criminal state of excitement.

" That in certain specified voting precincts in the City of Omaha the ballot boxes were not kept in view, as required by law, while the votes were being cast and counted.

" That in over thirty polling precincts, tickets bearing the name of contestant were taken from the hands of persons who were distributing them and torn up, and these men by threats and intimidation driven from the polls.

" That, by a corrupt and illegal agreement between Republicans and Democrats in the City of Omaha, it was arranged that neither Democratic nor Republican tickets should be challenged, if printed in accordance with the views of the conspirators, and that challengers from any other parties should be prevented from exercising their rights.

" That the Omaha conspiracy exists yet, and that threats have been made to prevent persons from divulging the fraudulent methods by which the election was carried.

" That in the fourth precinct of the third ward in Omaha, 150 votes cast for Powers were not counted."

The taking of testimony in the case was commenced at Lincoln, December 4, 1890. Among the witnesses who testified as to scenes of personal violence, in most of which they were the victims, were Samuel Macleod, G. W. Clark, J. Phipps Roe, L. L. Abbott, M. Osterholm, M. J. Smith, Walter B. Prugh, Rev. John H. Henderson, Charles Ellson, J. M. Taylor, Rev. Q. A. Shinn, F. A. Philleo, Silas W. Wilson, Rev. E. E. Erling, Anthony Johnson, W. H. Sherwood, Rev. P. S. Merrill, A. Thomas, W. E. Greene. These witnesses testified that they were not interfered with in casting their votes, the disturbances resulting entirely from efforts made to distribute tickets reading, " For the prohibitory amendment," which tickets otherwise followed the form of the Republican, Democratic and Alliance tickets—the voter exercising his own choice in that regard.

The last two weeks of December were devoted to taking testimony in Omaha, but here the evidence of those opposing as well as those favoring the amendment was given. Among the former were Bishop Worthington, Rev. John Williams, Rev. W. J. Harsha, Rev. C. H. Gardner, Rev. J. T. Duryea, Judges Wakeley, Doane, Clarkson and Dundy, Mayor Cushing, ex-Mayor Broatch, Police Commissioners Hartman, Bennett, Gilbert and Smith, Chief of Police Seavey, Editors Rosewater and Hitchcock, Dr. George L. Miller, Postmaster Clarkson, Sheriff Boyd, and many others, all of whom testified that the election was one of unusual quietness and good order, and that the violent telegrams sent out during the day to the effect that the city was in the hands of a mob and that the chief of police had declared his inability to maintain order were unwarranted by the facts. Some testimony of a character similar to that secured at Lincoln was also given by a few witnesses. A full State ticket had been nominated by the Prohibition party, but it received but little attention in Omaha, the main object here being to carry the amendment regardless of the party nominees.

As an offset to the claims of rioting made by the friends of the amendment, the following report, made by Police Chief Seavey to the board of fire and police commissioners, is of interest:

"I have the honor to report that during election day, the 4th inst., there were ninety-two police officers and forty-one special policemen on duty at the polls and elsewhere about the city. The policemen on day duty worked thirteen hours, those on night duty sixteen hours, and the special policemen were on duty twelve hours. I read the law governing elections to all the men and instructed them accordingly, and, notwithstanding the several complaints that the police exceeded their authority in some instances, and that certain persons did not receive police protection, I have reason to believe that the police department performed its duty thoroughly and well. Several quarrels occurred at the different polling places, which were immediately stopped by the police, thereby preventing any serious disturbance. There were thirty-one arrests made during the twenty-four hours ending at 7 a. m., November 5th, thirteen of which were for drunkenness and disorderly conduct. Two saloon keepers were found doing business on election day, namely, John Didam, at Sheely's, and F. Hunzicker, 414 South Thirteenth Street, both of whom will be prosecuted. The important and memorable election of November 4, 1890, was one of the most quiet general elections held in Omaha during my term of office. I attribute the good order of that day to the fact of the saloons being closed, the orderly conduct of our citizens and the vigilance of the officers."

During the campaign, the *Central West*, a prominent Presbyterian weekly of this city, strongly supported the amendment; hence, the following article, published as an editorial, after considerable testimony had been taken in Omaha, may be considered a fair summing up of the situation:

"In its issue immediately after the late election, the New York *Voice* published a dispatch from Omaha, the gist of which is contained in the following extract:

"'The whole city is given entirely over to the whisky mob. There is riot and bloodshed in nearly every ward. Men, ladies of the Woman's Christian Temperance Union, are being insulted, mobbed, and driven from the polls by the drunken rabble. Ministers of the gospel are slugged, beaten, and dragged from the polls and compelled to flee for their lives.'

"This dispatch shows upon its face that it was sent while the election was in progress. It was evidently not based upon a calm and complete review of the situation, and is open to the suspicion of being part of a preconceived plan to throw discredit upon the election in this city. It has laid the foundation of the assaults upon Omaha which have appeared in religious and other journals.

"This paper has taken occasion to say that such representations were not warranted by the facts. The investigation which has been conducted in this city and at Lincoln has sustained this opinion. A large amount of testimony has been taken. A considerable part of it, however, is worthless as evidence, unless the recognized laws of evidence are to be ignored. A number of the witnesses testified as to their opinions, and what they thought, and what they feared. The witnesses who were so free in expressing their opinions, on cross-examination, testified to a state of facts which materially discounted the value of their opinions. For instance, on their examination in chief, several witnesses declared that the election was not a fair one, while on cross-examination the same witnesses testified that no one was prevented from voting as he saw proper.

"The testimony shows that, while there were individual instances of bad treatment, there was no such state of affairs as the *Voice* correspondent represented. The city was not given over to the whisky mob. There was no mob, neither was there any riot. There is not a particle of evidence that there was bloodshed in any ward. There is no evidence that 'ministers were slugged, beaten and dragged from the polls,' or that anyone had reason to flee for his life. Moreover, there is not a syllable of evidence to the effect that any minister was ridden on a rail. That some men, and even ladies, were insulted, we do not undertake to question. These are the acts of a low class of men to be found in all cities. Their conduct admits of no apology, and deserves the severest reprobation.

"The matter of interference with ticket peddlers figures quite largely in this testimony. It is a noticeable fact that every man who claims to have experienced any ill-usage was peddling tickets of all parties. Upon its face this seems to have been a disinterested course to pursue, but in reality it was not. For example, among other tickets peddled by them was one which was headed 'Democratic Ticket.' Below the names on the ticket were the words, 'For the Prohibition Amendment,' etc. Now the State Convention of that party had squarely pronounced against the prohibitory amendment. The authorized ticket of that party was made up in accordance with this declaration. Under the laws of Nebraska the ticket so presented was the only regular ticket. Of course it was the privilege of any Democrat who wished to vote for the amendment to substitute in writing the word 'for' for the word 'against.' But neither he nor any set of men could print a ticket which in a material point differed from the ticket prepared by the authorized committee of that party. The laws of Nebraska recognize a 'regular ticket,' and they make it a misdemeanor to offer a ticket which contains a printed alteration of any name which appears upon the regular ticket. In view of the fact that the statute uses the phrase 'regular ticket,' the interpretation would doubtless hold that no departure in a substantial particular from the regular ticket would be admissible. At all events this opinion was generally held, and hence all other tickets were regarded as bogus. The fact that such tickets were circulated largely contributed to irritate the situation. It was, so far as results were concerned, an attempt to mislead voters. The caption, which presumably defined the character of the ticket, led some voters to suppose that the whole ticket was what it purported to be, when in fact it was not. There was no propriety or wisdom in resorting to such tactics. It was the trick of a ward politician. More than fifteen hundred votes were cast in favor of the amendment, and the testimony fails to show that anyone experienced ill-usage in casting his vote.

"Men of the highest standing, like Judges Wakeley and Clarkson, Rev. Drs. Duryea and Harsha, Bishop Worthington and Rev. John Williams, testified to the orderly and peaceable character of the election in Omaha. Their testimony was direct and positive, being based upon their own observations and also upon their knowledge of previous elections, and should carry conviction to every fair-minded person.

"It seems strange to us that there are Christian people, and even ministers, who have shown a disposition to resent any attempt to deny or disprove these charges. The *Central West* gave the amendment an honest and consistent support while it was pending, but it by no means follows that it is the duty of this paper to countenance or endorse all the tactics of those who claim to be prohibitionists. We aim at all times to speak the things that we believe to be true. The commandment, 'Thou shalt not bear false witness against thy neighbor,' covers the community as well as individuals. Those who bear the name of Christ should, of all others, evince a spirit free from censoriousness, and a positive reluctance to believe evil of an individual or community until it has been fully and irrefutably established."

The result of the election was a surprise to both parties, the amendment receiving but 82,390 votes as against 112,043. As a majority of all the votes cast was necessary for the adoption of the amendment, it was defeated by a majority of 50,277, though the majority of votes cast in opposition was only 29,653. Douglas County polled 1,555 votes for the amendment and 23,918 against it. The amendment to make the licensing of saloons a constitutional measure was also defeated, the vote being 75,515 for and 91,035 against, Douglas County casting 22,786 for the proposition and 1,940 against it. The prohibition vote in Omaha was materially affected by the practical effect of the law in Iowa, as witnessed in Council Bluffs, where, for nine years the efforts made to carry out the law had proven futile, the result being that that city had last year and still has a much larger ratio of saloons to population than Omaha, run in utter and open violation of law by men of no financial responsibility. Contrasted with this the Nebraska high license law has secured a comparatively strict regulation of the saloon business and greatly reduced its evils.

A quarter of a century ago the Good Templars' organization was very popular in Omaha. A number of lodges were organized, and the membership included a large proportion of the young people of the city, but the interest gradually decreased, and, for a dozen years past, the order has not been active in Omaha. Life Boat Lodge, No. 150, meets every Thursday evening at Marathon Hall, Cuming and Twenty-Fifth Avenue, Roger Dickens, C. T.; Guy S. Andrus, P. C. T.; Miss Jessie Smith, V. T.; T. B. Barnes, L. D.; Mrs. S. L. Forby, S. J. T.; Miss Theresa Schock, R. S.; Miss Nellie Askwith, L. S.; T. L. Combs, A. S.; G. M. Frazer, Treasurer; Q. R. Shinn, C.; Edward Shinn, M.; Miss Viola M. Barnes, D. M.; Miss Rosa Dewey, G.; Lee Forby, S.

The first organization of the Woman's Christian Temperance Union in this city was effected in June, 1879, mainly through the efforts of Mrs. W. B. Slaughter, at a meeting held in the Methodist Church, on Davenport Street. At this meeting Mrs. Slaughter was elected president, Mrs. M. E. Gratton, secretary, Mrs. D. C. Sutphen, treasurer, and Mrs. W. L. Beans, corresponding secretary. The movement proved a popular one, and in a few months a great many of the ladies of the leading churches of the city were enrolled as members. The passage of the high license liquor law in 1881 gave the Union an opportunity for active work, and it bore an important part in the task of carrying the law into effect, in spite of the strong opposition of the liquor interests. In April, 1884, a restaurant was established on Fifteenth Street, near Capitol Avenue, where excellent meals were served at low prices, the main object being to compete to some extent with the free lunch business of the saloons. It was at this time that Mrs. G. W. Clark became identified with the work here, coming to Omaha from Cleveland, Ohio, armed with the experience of the famous "Woman's Crusade" of that section of the country, and from that day to this she has continued her efforts in the reformation of Omaha's unfortunates, with such rare judgment, zeal and earnestness, that she is now known throughout the length and breadth of the State. In the fall of 1884, the Union leased the notorious Buckingham Theater, on Twelfth Street, near Dodge, where a home for the needy was established, with a restaurant of the same character as that on Fifteenth Street, reading and sleeping rooms; and in the main apartment, where for years a variety entertainment of the most vicious character had been conducted, religious services were held nightly.

For two years this work was carried on, with the most gratifying results, the full extent of which will not be known until the great last day. The sale of the property compelled the ladies to vacate the building, and that class of work has not since been engaged in. In the meantime, other unions have been formed in various portions of the city. The present officers of the original Union, now known as the Buckingham, are: Mrs. Watson B. Smith, president; Mrs. M. J. Richardson, secretary; Mrs. G. W. Clark, corresponding secretary. Of the Watson B. Smith Union, of Walnut Hill, Mrs. Fannie Webster is president; Mrs. M. E. Gratton, secretary; Mrs. Marston, treasurer; Mrs. Silas Wilson, corresponding secretary. Holmes Union: Mrs. E. A. Misner, president; Mrs. Graham Park, secretary; Mrs. C. W. McNair, treasurer. Leavitt Union: Mrs. M. Rhoads, president; Mrs. F. J. Brown, secretary; Mrs. E. L. Trace, treasurer. Jennie Smith Union: Mrs. E. Jackson, president; Mrs. Mary Roe, secretary; Mrs. C. Dawson, treasurer.

# CHAPTER XX.

GOVERNOR BOYD'S ELECTION — THE CONTEST BEFORE THE LEGISLATURE — GOVERNOR THAYER'S CLAIM — THE CASE IN THE COURTS — GOVERNOR BOYD DECLARED A CITIZEN BY THE UNITED STATES SUPREME COURT — TAKES HIS SEAT.

One of the most exciting elections ever held in the State of Nebraska was the State election of 1890. There were three principal tickets in the field: the Republican, headed by Hon. L. D. Richards, of Fremont, as candidate for Governor; the Democratic, led by Hon. James E. Boyd, of Omaha; and the Farmers' Alliance, with Hon. John H. Powers at its head; and, as the result showed, the voters were very equally divided among the three parties. As noted in the preceding chapter, the question of prohibition entered largely into the campaign, as what was known as a prohibitory amendment to the constitution was to be voted on at the same election.

Each of the parties made a very vigorous canvass, and the result showed that James E. Boyd was elected Governor, receiving 71,331 votes, against 70,187 cast for John H. Powers, the Independent and Alliance candidate, and 68,878 cast for L. D. Richards, the Republican candidate. Notwithstanding the fact that Mr. Boyd was clearly elected by the returns, he did not reach the position without a contest, and was afterward ousted from the executive chair and deprived of his office for nearly one-half its term. The *World Herald* of February 2, 1892, contained the following history of the contest:

### A HISTORY OF THE CASE.

Friday, November 21st, Mr. Boyd was served with a notice of contest, served at the instance of John H. Powers, who, in his affidavit, significantly stated as his first ground of contest, to-wit:

"I was, on and prior to the 4th day of November, 1890, and am now, a qualified elector of the State of Nebraska, and was a candidate for, and eligible to, the office of Governor of this State."

Knowing ones, who, aware of a discovery made by Mr. Boyd while on a visit to his father, then residing at Zanesville, Ohio, could read between the lines that his political opponents had found a flaw in his title to citizenship, which affected his eligibility to the office of Governor. The secret was not, however, made public until later. Meanwhile the attorneys for Powers and Boyd began to hear testimony in the contest, before notaries, in the manner prescribed by the election laws of the State, and a great mass of testimony, covering a wide range of topics, was submitted, most of which was irrelevant.

The first knowledge which the public received that there was a question of Mr. Boyd's citizenship and eligibility to the executive office was obtained from a dispatch which appeared in the *World-Herald* on the morning of December 13, 1890. The dispatch was as follows:

CLEVELAND, O., Dec. 12.—A special from Zanesville, Ohio, says: A curious complication has arisen in the case of Governor-elect Boyd, of Nebraska. He was born in Ireland in 1834, and came to this city with his father, Joseph Boyd, in 1849. The father filed a notice of his intention to become a citizen, but did not take out his final papers until November, 1890. The son did not take out papers here, and it is stated that he has never been naturalized in Nebraska. The statutes provide that where the father was naturalized his sons

under twenty-one years of age are naturalized In this case the father filed his declaration in 1849, but did not take out his final papers until 1890

So important a discovery naturally caused a great deal of discussion among lawyers Henry Estabrook, Esq , in an article which appeared in the *World-Herald* of Sunday, December 8, 1890, gratuitously advanced the doctrine-of-relation argument, which he has since so sturdily maintained in both the State and National Supreme Courts Joseph H Blair, an attorney previously almost unknown in Omaha, and, as after events proved, a strong Republican partisan, combatted this and other arguments in Mr Boyd's behalf, maintaining that the Governor-elect was not a citizen, and that, neither Powers nor Richards having been elected, Govenor Thayer would hold over.

Thus matters drifted along, the taking of evidence in the Powers' contest was continued from day to day, until Monday, December 29th, but nothing affecting the citizenship question was disclosed.

When the Legislature had been organized, and both branches met in joint session, Wednesday, January 7, 1891, as required by the constitution, to canvass the returns, a hitch occurred The Independents had a majority of the membership, and undertook to abandon custom and precedent and have the Speaker act as presiding officer instead of the President of the Senate Lieutenant Governor Meiklejohn resisted this rather revolutionary proceeding, and with remarkable courage held the gavel, refusing to recognize motions to adjourn, and rapping down rebellious members who refused to recognize him as the presiding officer He maintained that the law was plain, and that the duty of the Speaker in the premises was, under the constitution, purely clerical—to open and canvass the returns as handed in by the Secretary of State. This, Speaker Elder of the House refused to do After hours of struggle a compromise resolution, submitted by Church Howe, for a recess until 10 o'clock the next morning, was accepted.

During the night a caucus of the Alliance members was held, and it was determined to take heroic measures to secure control The doors of the assembly hall were locked and strongly guarded, admission being allowed only through the cloak room, and only to those who held tickets of admission signed by Speaker Elder By this means the room was packed with partisans of the Alliance members Lieutenant Governor Meiklejohn was not permitted to stand at the presiding officer's desk, but he had brought a gavel with him, and took his station at the Clerk's desk, just in front of the Speaker, and took control of the joint convention On a suggestion from Representative Watson, of Otoe County, he addressed a note to Govenor Thayer, calling upon him for protection, and a company of militia was promptly marched into the corridors of the capitol, where a turbulent throng had assembled, clamoring for admission to the assembly hall Order was restored quickly, and meanwhile a conference committee, consisting of four Republican, four Democratic, and four Alliance members, was agreed upon, and, while the said committee was in consultation, a do-nothing status was maintained in the joint convention

The attorneys for Governor Boyd had meanwhile gone before the Supreme Court with a petition for a peremptory writ of mandamus upon Speaker Elder to compel him to canvass the returns This was granted and turned over to the sheriff of Lancaster County, who took a strong posse and proceeded to the assembly hall. Admission being denied them, the officers promptly broke in the main doors, and as promptly served the writ upon Speaker Elder. Another recess was then taken and a conference held, which resulted in Speaker Elder's proceeding to discharge his duty. The canvass of the returns was completed at 5.10 P M , Thursday, January 8th, Speaker

Elder declaring that "for Governor, James E. Boyd has received the highest number of votes, and is therefore duly elected and qualified as Governor."

Governor Boyd immediately proceeded to the Supreme Court chamber, where Judge Cobb administered the oath and approved his bond of $50,000, and the most exciting legislative episode in the history of the State was terminated.

While these exciting events were transpiring in the legislative halls, proceedings as revolutionary were being enacted in the executive department. John M. Thayer, whose term as Governor ceased when his successor had been formally declared elected and sworn in, announced that he would not vacate the executive apartments in the capitol building, asserting that Boyd was not legally Governor; that no election had taken place; and that he would, under the constitution, hold the office until his successor was chosen legally. Governor Boyd, accompanied by his attorney, called at the executive office, around which Thayer had placed a cordon of militia. He was permitted to enter. Thayer and his attorneys then formally declared that they would not surrender the apartments. Governor Boyd retired, and Thayer remained in the office all night under guard to prevent a surprise.

The other State officials, who had been declared simultaneously elected with Governor Boyd, promptly recognized him as the real Governor, and, as they constitute the State board of public lands and buildings, they assembled as such board and speedily supplied Governor Boyd with other apartments, which they officially designated the "executive offices." Governor Boyd was installed in there, the federal authorities, mail carriers, janitors, etc., recognizing him as the Governor, bringing him the executive correspondence, etc.

There were Indian troubles on the frontier at the time, and Governor Boyd appointed General Victor Vifquain his adjutant general, and placed him in charge of the militia department. General Vifquain promptly cleared the militia out of the capitol and ordered them to report for duty at Rushville, the center of the Indian troubles.

Meanwhile Thayer and his attorneys had applied to the Supreme Court on Friday, January 9th, for a writ of *quo warranto* to compel Boyd to desist from acting as governor. Leave to file the petition was not granted until Tuesday, the 13th. Judge Cobb, C. J., in making the ruling, said:

"Last Friday morning application was made to file information in the nature of a *quo warranto* by John M. Thayer against James E. Boyd. We have been given an opportunity for consultation and consideration of this matter. But, as time is passing, and these matters are of great importance to the parties in court, as well as to the people generally, we have concluded, as a mere matter of form and proceeding, and as a matter of notice, as well as jurisdiction, to indicate that a summons may be issued, returnable according to the statutes governing the issuance of summons in the district court here. And we have determined in consultation that I should say that, if it should appear at any time in the course of these proceedings that the person who was elected Lieutenant-Governor at the last election should desire to intervene in this proceeding, in view of a decision in a certian way as to the eligibility of the present incumbent of the executive office, that the Court will allow such intervention, and, furthermore, while it may seem somewhat out of place that what I am about to say should come from this place, we have deemed it advisable that it should be said that, during the pendency of these proceedings, so far as the matter may ever be decided by this Court, unless we should be advised differently from what we now are, that the relator will lose nothing by a quiet and orderly submission to the present order of things growing out of the recognition of James E.

## THE LEGISLATURE RECOGNIZES GOVERNOR BOYD. 191

Boyd as the legal Governor, as now recognized by this Court and all departments of the State government."

Despite this plain appeal to Thayer to vacate the rooms he was occupying in the capitol, he refused to surrender; so on the following day the board of public lands and buildings made a formal demand upon him to leave. At 11 o'clock the next morning, Thursday, January 15th, Thayer, under this order, vacated, and Governor Boyd was promptly installed.

Some of the Alliance leaders in both branches of the Legislature were still disposed to refuse recognition to Governor Boyd, pinning their faith to the contest, which they expected to result in displacing Boyd with Powers. On Friday, January 16th, however, a motion was passed in the Senate, by a vote of fourteen yeas to thirteen nays, recognizing Boyd as Governor.

Monday, January 19th, John M. Thayer, by his attorney, filed an affidavit of notice of application for a restraining order on January 29th, claiming in the affidavit that he (Thayer) had been unlawfully ejected from the Governor's office by one James E. Boyd, etc. When the 29th arrived, the application was not called up, it being regarded as ridiculous.

Thursday, January 22d, the Supreme Court decided that the House having refused to recognize Governor Boyd, all joint proceedings must be annulled until resolutions, bills, etc., are approved by the Governor.

Thayer delivered his closing message to the Legislature, Thursday, February 5th; a resolution having been passed, the House, by a vote of fifty-four to forty-six, decided to recognize Boyd as Governor that day. The message of Governor Boyd was read to both Houses the following day.

Monday, February 16th, Governor Boyd's attorneys filed a motion to dismiss the *quo warranto* proceedings begun by Thayer. Accompanying the motion was a demurrer, setting forth that Thayer, not being a party in interest, was not concerned in the citizenship question. This motion was argued before the Court on Wednesday, March 4th, and the following day a decision was handed down overruling the demurrer and fixing Tuesday, March 16th, as the date when Governor Boyd must answer to question of citizenship.

Thursday, March 12th, the case was argued before the Supreme Court, the counsel for Governor Boyd making a splendid showing. Counsel maintained:

First. That the Court has no jurisdiction to determine this contested election.

Second. That Thayer is not eligible.

Third. That James E. Boyd is a citizen of the United States as fully as any native born citizen, not only since he took out the papers on the 16th of December, but ever since the year 1867, when the State of Nebraska was admitted to the Union.

Arguing the latter vital points, his counsel held in these words:

" I assert that James E. Boyd is a citizen of the United States. It is conceded by all that James E. Boyd is competent and capable under the laws of the United States to become a citizen without any act on his own part. It does not come under the category of those who have an act affirmatively to perform. When he was a boy of nine years the constitution was such that it was competent for Mr. Boyd to become a naturalized citizen without any affirmative act on his part. A great many rights are given to persons as citizens after they have taken out their first papers. The rule has been adopted that a person who has taken out his first papers is entitled to the protection of the Government, and it has never been questioned, unless under some treaty between this Government and the original country from which the party came. But this is not the point I was going to make. Let me refer to another matter. They say in our answer that we state on information and belief that

Joseph Boyd took out his papers. 'Why did you not name the court?' they say. The information that came to me was that Joseph Boyd's vote was challenged, and that he qualified himself—that was after he took out his first papers; that some of the records of the court are burned. These are matters that we ascertained, and I would not permit it to be put in that he had done it, but it was our information and belief. Joseph Boyd is an old man nearly eighty years old to-day. If he took out his final papers, it was nearly forty years ago, and he might have forgotten whether he had taken them out or not. He supposed he had. The Supreme Court of the United States has decided that it is not necessary to have a judge of the court admit a person to citizenship. They say, 'Why did you take out your papers on the 16th of December?' There was a question about these matters, and, as Mr. Boyd was elected Governor of this State, he wanted to place himself in a position that there would be no question about his citizenship at the time that he entered upon the duties of his office, although we concede that that may have no bearing upon his eligibility; but at least he is a citizen now, and has been a citizen beyond question from the time that he took out his papers. That is the reason that this was done. I will venture the assertion that there are thousands of instances where the papers are taken out the second time. They tell us there are only two ways of acquiring citizenship, and that is naturalization and native born. I say no. There are very many ways of acquiring citizenship. It may be by treaty, by general law, as has been in this case. The position I take, in my opinion, cannot be gainsaid. It is incontrovertible. On the admission of the State of Nebraska into the Union in 1867, every *bona fide* inhabitant of that territory became, by that union, a citizen of the State of Nebraska and of the United States. The organic act providing for the organization of the territory provided, among other things, for the qualification of voters, and the only thing that can be urged against it is that there is the qualification with respect to voters, and it was not intended that any other persons should be citizens. After the organic act it was competent for the Legislative Assembly to adopt any rules which it saw fit, with respect to the eligibility of persons to hold office and vote — to give the right of franchise to residents of one, two, three months, or six years.* The right to citizenship and the right to vote have nothing in common, as a general thing. Persons may be citizens and not have the right to vote, and vote and not be citizens. The restriction with respect to the elective franchise has nothing to do with the question of citizenship. All women born or married here are citizens. The children are citizens. The question of the restriction of the elective franchise has nothing whatever to do with the question of citizenship. Under the act of 1864 this State shall be admitted on an equality with the original thirteen States.

When Massachusetts was formed into a State, the people of the State of Massachusetts, every *bona-fide* inhabitant of the State, were clothed with the inalienable right of citizenship. The question of the admission of the older States has exactly the same conditions, and it is the inalienable right of all parties in the territory to become citizens. I assert that every State that comes into the Union, leaving out of consideration the condition of the rebel States, comes in with every *bona-fide* inhabitant as a citizen of that State, on an equality with the inhabitants of the original States. Congress, by the enabling act, called upon the actual inhabitants, the men out upon the frontier, to form a government for themselves. They promised them if they would do so acceptably to Congress, they should be admitted into the Union, in conformity with the rights of the original States, in all respects whatsoever. The right of citizenship, under

OMAHA AS SEEN FROM EAST SIDE OF MISSOURI RIVER—1889.

OMAHA & GRANT SMELTING AND REFINING WORKS.

the constitution of the United States, and the constitution and laws of the several original States, was a right not conferred by the original colonies upon the organization of the several States, nor was it a right conferred by the constitution of the United States, nor any laws enacted thereunder, but the fact is that citizenship in the original colonies, upon organization into States, was one of the inalienable rights of man as a member of the society organizing a civil community, a State, and every State was an organization of the inhabitants thereof. And the Nation was an organization of the inhabitants thereof, as well as the constituted States. And, upon the formation of the general government, every State that was admitted into the Union carried with it the right of citizenship to every *bona-fide* inhabitant of the several original States, not by virtue of any law, but by virtue of the inalienable right of man in his association with others to form a government. Therefore, every *bona-fide* inhabitant of the original States, on the admission of such States into the Union, became *ipso facto* citizens of the United States. Every new State that has been admitted into the Union has been admitted into all the rights, privileges and immunities awarded to the original States. And I claim for Nebraska, as a constituent member of the great Union, and for every one of its *bona fide* inhabitants, the same rights granted by the enabling act of Congress that belonged to the inhabitants of Massachusetts, New York, South Carolina, and every other original State, making every one of our *bona fide* inhabitants citizens, upon admission to the Union. To deny us this right is to deny us that grand right of equality with the other States.

"After the war with England, of 1812, a law was enacted in the Territory of Orleans, being a portion of the Louisiana grant, providing that all foreigners should become naturalized within a certain time, under the laws of Congress, providing a uniform rule of naturalization, and on failure to do so they should be considered alien enemies and liable to arrest and punishment. After the admission of the Territory of Orleans into the Union, in 1812, as the State of Louisiana, a large number of persons, claiming to be British subjects and aliens, were arrested as aliens who had failed to become naturalized. Several of them were discharged by the Supreme Court of the State of Louisiana, on the ground that they were not aliens, though they had never been naturalized under the naturalization laws of Congress. So great was the excitement concerning the matter, that several cases were transferred to the Federal Court to obtain the opinion of that tribunal on the question of citizenship. The United States Court held that, as these persons, though never naturalized under the naturalization laws of Congress, were *bona fide* inhabitants of the Territory of Orleans at the time the territory was admitted into the Union as the State of Louisiana upon terms of equality with the original States, which was the exact language of the admission act of the State of Nebraska, they became, the Court declared, by that act of admission, *ipso facto* citizens of the United States and of the State of Louisiana."

The Court reserved its decision until after the Legislature adjourned, it being openly charged that the majority of the Court, being in sympathy with the railroads, was holding the decision over the Governor's head as a club to intimidate him against approving any legislation inimical to the railroad interests. It is a fact that the railroad regulation measure, known as the "Newberry Bill," did pass both houses and was vetoed by Governor Boyd, April 3, stirring a furious storm of indignation among the people of the State, and it was stated that, the evening previous to affixing his veto, the syllabus of an opinion by one of the justices was shown him. It was favorable to the

Governor, but the judge, who it was alleged wrote it, cast the balance of power in the Court against him.

Tuesday, May 5, 1891, just one month after the adjournment of the Legislature, the Supreme Court handed down a decision adverse to Governor Boyd. The following is the syllabus:

State *ex rel.* John M. Thayer *vs.* James E. Boyd. *Quo warranto* judgment of *ouster.*

The Supreme Court has jurisdiction to entertain proceedings by information in the nature of *quo warranto*, instituted for the purpose of determining the rights of persons claiming the office of Governor.

Second. Under the provisions of Section 2, Article IV, of the constitution, no person is eligible to the office of Governor who has not been a citizen of the United States, and of this State, for at least two years next preceding the election at which such officer is to be chosen.

Third. Where a plurality of votes are cast for a person for a public office who is ineligible, the election is void.

Fourth. Under the fourth section of the act of Congress, entitled "An Act to Establish a Uniform Rule of Naturalization," approved April 14, 1802, the child of an alien under twenty-one years of age, though born in a foreign country, becomes a citizen by the naturalization of his parent, if dwelling within the United States at the time the parent is admitted to citizenship, but it does not have that effect if the child is over twenty-one years old at the time the parent is naturalized.

Fifth. The order of a court admitting an alien to citizenship is a judicial act, in the nature of a judgment, and can be proved only by the record.

Sixth. The fact that an alien has, for many years, voted at the elections held in this State, and filled important public offices, does not establish that he is a citizen of the United States.

Seventh. Where an alien is naturalized under the naturalization laws, his citizenship dates from the time the order of the Court is made admitting him to citizenship.

Eighth. The alien inhabitants of the Territory of Nebraska, at the time of its admission as a State, did not become citizens of the United States by virtue of the act of Congress admitting the State into the Union.

Ninth. The words, "Citizens of the United States," as used in Section 2 of Article IV of the State constitution, are construed to mean a person who is an American citizen by birth, or a person of foreign birth who has been duly naturalized under the provisions of the uniform rule of naturalization established by Congress.

Tenth. Under Section 1 of Article V, of the constitution, a person elected to the office of Governor is entitled to discharge the duties and receive the emoluments of the office, for the term of two years, from the first Thursday after the first Tuesday in January, following his election, and until his successor is duly elected and qualified.

Eleventh. When the person receiving the highest number of votes for the office of Governor is ineligible, under the constitution, to be elected, the then acting Governor holds over.

Twelfth. The duties of the chief executive office of the State devolves upon the Lieutenant-Governor, in certain contingencies, among which are the failure of the Governor-elect to qualify, and the disability of the Governor. It cannot be said that there has been a failure to qualify where no person has been constitutionally elected to the office.

Thirteenth. The words, "Other disabilities of the Governor," appearing in Section 16, Article V, of the constitution, have no reference to the ineligibility of the person to be elected. But these words cover any disability of the Governor not specifically enumerated in the Section, after the commencement of his term of office occurring.

Fourteenth. Held, that, when the non-election of a person to a public office is ascertained by the proceedings in *quo warranto*, the person entitled to hold over must then re-qualify.

The opinion was written by Judge Cobb, Judge Norval assenting, Judge Maxwell dissenting, holding that, when a Territory is admitted to Statehood, the enabling act so operates as to make every resident of the Territory a citizen of the State, just the same as though it was a foreign territory acquired by the United States.

The opinion was handed down at 4:30 in the afternoon, and the Court immediately adjourned. At 5:15 Governor Thayer entered the executive chamber and demanded that the office be turned over to him, under writ of ouster, which had been procured to head off any motion for stay of proceedings, pending an appeal to the Federal Supreme Court. Governor Boyd quietly yielded the office to him, and the great wrong was accomplished.

Governor Boyd's attorneys at once began to prepare an appeal to the Supreme Court at Washington, and on Friday, May 15th, Justice Brewer, for the Court, granted the application for a hearing on a writ of error.

When the Supreme Court met, after the summer recess, application was made for its advancement on the docket, and it was granted, the arguments being listened to by the full bench on Tuesday, December 8th.

On Monday, February 1, 1892, the United States Supreme Court handed down its opinion in the case, fully sustaining the position of Governor Boyd's attorneys. Below will be found the syllabus of the Court:

BOYD v. STATE OF NEBRASKA *ex rel.* THAYER. February 1, 1892.

JURISDICTION OF SUPREME COURT — FEDERAL QUESTION — CONSTITUTIONAL LAW — NATURALIZATION.

1. A decision, by the Supreme Court of a State, that a person, born in a foreign country, and claiming to have become a citizen of the United States by the operation of its laws and constitution, is not such a citizen, and therefore not eligible to the office of Governor, under the requirements of the State constitution, involves the denial of a right or privilege claimed under the constitution and laws of the United States, and is reviewable in the Supreme Court thereof. Field, J., dissenting.

2. In a proceeding to oust a person from a State office, on the ground that he is not a citizen of the United States, a demurrer to an answer which set up facts alleged to show a naturalization necessarily presents a federal question, which is reviewable in the United States Supreme Court. Field, J., dissenting.

3. Congress has plenary legislative power over the Territories of the United States and their inhabitants, and, upon the admission of a Territory into the Union, may, if it so desires, effect a collective naturalization of its foreign born inhabitants as citizens of the United States.

4. When a State is admitted into the Union upon an equal footing with the original States, all residents thereof, who are endowed by Congress with political rights and privileges, or who, with the consent of Congress, are permitted to participate in the formation of the new State, become citizens of the United States by adoption, even though, being foreigners, they have never complied with the requirements of the naturalization laws.

5. The Nebraska Enabling Act (13 U. S. St. p. 47) declared that all persons qualified to vote for Representatives of the Territorial Legislature should be entitled to vote upon the acceptance or rejection thereof, and should be eligible to election as members of the convention. By the existing laws of the Territory, foreigners who had declared an intention to become citizens were entitled to vote at elections, and this provision was carried into the constitution of the new State, as ratified by Congress. *Held* that, upon the admission of the State into the

Union, all persons of this class became citizens of the United States.

6. When a foreigner takes the oath declaring an intention to become a citizen of the United States, his minor sons thereby acquire an inchoate *status* as citizens; and, if they attain majority before their father completes his naturalization, that *status* is capable of being converted into complete citizenship by other means than the direct application provided for by the naturalization laws.

7. Where a foreigner takes the oath declaring an intention to become a citizen, while his son is yet a minor, and the son, on coming of age, votes at an election under the erroneous belief that his father has completed his naturalization, and soon afterwards removes to a distant territory, and for many years endures all the privations and dangers of frontier life, votes at elections, is elected to office, takes an oath to support the constitution of the United States, and takes part in the formation of a State constitution and government, he is entitled to the benefit of his father's declaration of intention in the same manner as if he himself had made the declaration; and, where the Territorial laws and the new State constitution, with the sanction of Congress, confer political privileges upon foreigners who have made such declaration, he will be considered as belonging to that class, and on the admission of the State will become a citizen of the United States.

8. When no record can be produced showing the naturalization of a foreigner, naturalization may be inferred from the fact that for a long time he voted, held office, and exercised all the rights and privileges of a citizen.

9. On an information to oust from office a foreign born person, on the ground that he is not a citizen, an answer, upon information and belief, that the respondent's father completed his naturalization before respondent reached his majority, and prior to that time exercised all the privileges of citizenship, is admitted by a demurrer, and is sufficient to show that respondent himself is a citizen.

48 N. W. Rep. 739, reversed.

John L. Webster, John H. Blair, Omaha, G. M. Lambertson, O. P. Mason, Lincoln, and Judge Dillon, of New York, appeared for Governor Thayer. John C. Cowin, John D. Howe, Henry D. Estabrook, Omaha, represented Governor Boyd, assisted by ex-Attorney General Garland, of Washington, and Charles Ogden, of Omaha.

One curious circumstance in connection with this case was the fact that the Washington correspondents, by some means, obtained, and published to the world, a synopsis of the Supreme Court's decision several weeks before it was handed down by the Court.

Notwithstanding there had been much speculation as to the course Governor Thayer would pursue, he very gracefully surrendered the office to Governor Boyd, who took possession on the afternoon of February 8, 1892.

The event was duly celebrated at Lincoln, on Monday, February 15th, large delegations visiting the capital city from all parts of the State.

GLIMPSES OF OMAHA.

# CHAPTER XXI.

NAVIGATION—THE FIRST STEAMER ON THE MISSOURI—SCENES OF LATER YEARS.

Before the era of railroads, Omaha depended upon the Missouri River as a "base of supplies," and for several years the "levee"—now within the boundaries of Iowa—presented a lively scene upon the arrival or departure of the steamers then plying the river. The steamboat first venturing to ascend the Missouri was the Independence, Captain Nelson, of Louisville, which left St. Louis May 15, 1819, with passengers and a miscellaneous cargo for the thriving town of Franklin, Howard County, Missouri, the site of which town was long since swept away by the changing stream. Among the passengers on this pioneer steamer was Major J. D. Wilcox, father of Captain Wm. P. Wilcox, of this city. The occasion was a memorable one in the history of that section, and a dinner, in honor of that event, was tendered Captain Nelson and the passengers, by the delighted citizens of Franklin, when the following toasts were presented and properly responded to: (1) "The Missouri River; its last wave will roll the abundant tribute of our region to the Mexican Gulf in reference to the auspices of this day." (2) "The memory of Robert Fulton, one of the most distinguished artists of the age; the Missouri River now bears upon her bosom the first effect of his genius for steam navigation." (3) "The memory of Franklin, the philosopher and statesman; in anticipation of his country's greatness, he never imagined that a boat at this time would be propelled by steam so far westward to a town bearing his name on the Missouri." (4) "Captain Nelson, the proprietor of the steamboat Independence; the imaginary dangers of the Missouri vanished before his enterprising genius." (5) "Louisville, Franklin and Chariton; they become neighbors by steam navigation." (6) "The republican government of the United States; by facilitating the intercourse between different points, its benign influences may be diffused over the continent of North America." (7) "The policy resulting in the expedition to the Yellowstone." (8) "South America; may an early day witness the navigation of the Amazon and La Plata by steam power, under the auspices of an independent government." (9) "International Improvements; the New York Canal, an imperishable monument of the patriotism and genius of its proprietor." (10) "The Missouri Territory; desirous to be numbered with the States on constitutional principles, but determined to never submit to congressional usurpation."

The expedition to the Yellowstone referred to in the foregoing, for which we are indebted to an old copy of the *Missouri Intelligencer*, was a government undertaking. Major S. H. Long, of the United States Topographical Engineers, was in command of the party, which left Pittsburg, Pennsylvania, May 3, 1819, on the steamer Western Engineer. Proceeding down the Ohio and up the Mississippi to the mouth of the Missouri, the expedition reached the town of Franklin on the 13th of July, to a description of which place considerable space is given in an interesting account of the trip, published by Edwin James, geologist and botanist of the expedition. The members of this party were also hospitably entertained by the citizens of Franklin, and it is interesting to note the following comments upon the prospects of the settlement, by Mr. James: "It is doubtful whether the present site of Franklin will not, at some future day, be occupied by the river, which appears to be at this time encroaching upon its bank. Opposite Franklin is Booneville, containing, at the time of our visit, eight houses, but having in some respects a more advantageous situation, and probably destined to rival, if not surpass, its neighbor."

In this connection it may not be improper to give space to a story of Indian warfare, as related by Mr. James: "Mr. Munroe, a resident of Franklin, stated that, being on a hunting expedition in 1816, on a branch of the Le Neine River, he found the relics of the encampment of a large body of men, whether of white troops, or Indian warriors, he could not determine. Not far from this encampment he observed a recent mound of earth, about eight feet in height, which he was induced to believe must be a cache, or place of deposit for the spoils which the party occupying the encampment had taken from the enemy, and which they could not remove with them on their departure. He opened the mound, and was surprised to find in it the body of a white officer, apparently a man of rank, and which had been interred with extraordinary care. The body was in a sitting posture, upon an Indian mat, the back resting against some logs placed around it in the manner of a log house, enclosing a space about three by five feet, and about four feet high, covered at the top with a mat similar to that beneath. The clothing was still in sufficient preservation to enable him to distinguish a red coat, trimmed with gold lace, golden epaulettes, a spotted buff waistcoat, finished also with gold lace, and pantaloons of white nankeen. On the head was a round, beaver hat, and a bamboo walkingstick, with the initials "J. M. C." engraved upon a golden head, reclined against the arm. On raising the hat it was found that the deceased had been hastily scalped. In elation to this story, General Smith observed that, when he commanded the United States troops in this department, he was informed of an action that had taken place near the Le Neine, in the autumn of 1815, between some Spanish dragoons, aided by a few Pawnee Indians, and a war party of Sacs and Foxes. In the course of this action a Spanish officer had pursued an Indian boy, who was endeavoring to escape with a musket on his shoulder, but who, finding himself nearly overtaken, discharged the musket behind him at random, and had killed the officer on the spot. The skirmish continuing, the body was captured and recaptured several times, and at last remained with the Spanish party."

On the 19th of July the expedition resumed its course up the river, the Western Engineer thus being the first steamboat to ascend the Missouri River above the town of Franklin. September 15th, the mouth of the Platte River is reached, and two days later "the trading establishment of the Missouri Fur Company, known as Fort Lisa, and occupied by Mr. Manuel Lisa, one of the most active persons engaged in the Missouri fur trade." The position selected for the establishment of winter quarters for the exploring party was "on the west bank of the Missouri, about half a mile above Fort Lisa, five miles below Council Bluffs, and three miles above the mouth of Boyer's River," which location is but a short distance above the site of Florence, and in the immediate vicinity of where the reservoirs are located from which Omaha is now supplied with water. This point was reached September 19, 1819. On the 3rd of October the party were visited by a band of Otoe and Iowa Indians, for the purpose of holding a council. A dance was given by the Indians, with a recital of their martial deeds, the latter exercise being preceded by the respective narrators' striking a post with a stick, indicating that what he was about to say would be "the truth, the whole truth and nothing but the truth." Of this part of the enter-

View of the Levee before the Construction of the Union Pacific Bridge.

tainment, Mr James says "Ietan went on to narrate his martial exploits He had stolen horses seven or eight times from the Konzas, he had first struck the bodies of three of that nation slain in battle He had stolen horses from the Ietan nation, and had struck one of their dead He had stolen horses from the Pawnees and struck the body of one Pawnee Loup He had stolen horses several times from the Omawhaws and once from the Puncas He had struck the bodies of two Sioux On a war party, in company with the Pawnees, he had attacked the Spaniards and penetrated into one of their camps, the Spaniards, excepting a man and boy, fled, himself being at a distance before his party, he was shot at and missed by the man, whom he immediately shot down and struck Little Soldier, a war-worn veteran, took his turn to strike the post He had struck dead bodies of individuals of all the nations around, Osages, Konzas, Pawnee Loups, Pawnee Republicans, Grand Pawnees, Puncas, Omawhaws, Sioux, Padoucas, La Plais or Bald Heads, Ietans, Sauxs, Foxes and Ioways, he had struck eight of one nation, seven of another, etc He was proceeding with his account when Ietan ran up to him, put his hand upon his mouth and respectfully led him to his seat This act was no trifling compliment paid to the well-known brave It indicated that he had still so many glorious acts to speak of that he would occupy so much time as to prevent others from speaking, and put to shame the other warriors by a contrast of his actions with theirs"

Mr James gives many interesting details of their experiences at this point during the winter "Mr Fontenelle," the father of Logan Fontenelle, visits the camp and states that the Omawhaws (Omahas) "had been much necessitated for food, subsisting for some time upon the fruit of the red haws, which the squaws sought for under the proper trees, beneath the snow" The Sioux, he reports, are suffering from the mumps, after having had a scourge of small-pox Big Elk, the famous Omaha chief, also pays his respects to the explorers "He observed that we must think them strange people to be thus constantly wandering about during the cold of winter, instead of remaining comfortably housed in their villages 'But,' said he, 'our poverty and necessities compel us to do so in pursuit of game, yet we sometimes venture forth for our pleasure, as in the present instance, to visit the white people, whom we are always delighted to see'  Then he warned the party against Indians of other tribes, who made false protestations of love; the Omawhaws alone, of all the Indian nations in the land, had never stained their hands with the blood of the white man. He added a strong expression that, such was his attachment to us, he believed he should, at a future day, be a white man himself"

The river is measured just below and above the camp, and found to be, at those points, 100 and 277½ yards, respectively. A measurement of the current shows a velocity of 1,324½ feet per hour on the surface, and of 2,680 feet per hour at a mean depth of ten feet  In June, 1820, the camp called Engineer Cantonment was broken up, the exploring party proceeding westward up the Platte River, by land, and the steamboat was sent down to the Mississippi River

Captain La Barge, who was at Omaha with his steamboat, the John M Chambers, in 1877, assisting in the rebuilding of the railroad bridge, made his first trip up the Missouri in 1827, when a lad thirteen years of age, going up to the mouth of the Yellowstone in a steamer completed at Pittsburg that year for the American Fur Company's service  La Barge spent the winter of 1827 with Cabanne, a trader, located in the vicinity of the former site of Engineer Cantonment  In 1834 a new boat, the Assinniboyne, was put in service on the Missouri by the Fur Company, which boat was burned to the water's edge in 1835, the company losing about $75,000 worth of furs.

For many years there was a lively traffic carried on by steamers on the Missouri River as far north as Fort Benton. Among the vessels engaged in the business after the founding of this city were: The West Wind, Lizzie Bayless, E. A. Ogden, D. A. January, T. C. McGill, Omaha, Watossa, E. M. Ryland, Platte Valley, Hattie Florence, May Little, Martin Graham, Denver, Sam. Getty, Chippewa, Spread Eagle, St. Mary's, Admiral, Fanchon, Fannie Tatum, Katie P. Kountze, Kate Kinney, J. H. Lacey, Only Chance, Yellowstone, Deer Lodge, St. Johns, Prairie State, Effie Deans, Montana, Spray, A. B. Chambers, Fontenelle, Kate Howard, Camilie, Monongahala, Sultan, Polar Star, J. M. Converse, Morning Star, J. H. Lucas, New Lucy, David Tatum, Emma, Star of the West, Wm. Campbell, F. X. Aubrey, Australia, Cataract, Edinburg, Emigrant, Hannibal, T. E. Tutt, Carrier, D. E. Taylor and Amazon.

In 1857 there were fifty boats regularly employed on the Missouri, running as far north as this city. For many years the firm of Porter & Deuel—John R. Porter and Harry Deuel, the latter now city passenger agent for the Union Pacific—carried on a business as steamboat agents which amounted to a million dollars annually. John A. Horbach also did a heavy business as steamboat agent here for many years.

In 1849 Captain W. P. Wilcox, for many years a resident of Omaha, and known all over the West as a member of the firm of Stephens & Wilcox, was clerk of the steamer El Paso, which was engaged for two weeks in ferrying California emigrants across the Missouri at this point.

Captain W. W. Copeland, of this city, spent the period between 1860 and 1867 on the river, running between Vicksburg and Fort Benton, a considerable portion of which time was given to the service of the St. Joseph and Omaha line. On the Fourth of July, 1861, the West Wind, of which he was clerk, was tied up at St. Joseph. The Second Iowa Infantry, encamped in that city, discovered a peculiar looking flag floating from the flag-staff of the steamer, and Captain Clautman was sent with his company, K, to secure its prompt removal, under the impression that it was a "rebel rag." Captain Copeland, happening to be the only one of the boat's officers on board at the time, was directed by Captain Clautman to at once "haul down his colors," which command was received with considerable surprise. Explanations followed, and the patriotic contingent from the Second Iowa were soon convinced that the colors in question were not the emblem of treason, but a flag used by the steamer before the passage of South Carolina's ordinance of secession. This was the last anniversary of the Nation's independence Captain Clautman was permitted to witness. On the 16th day of February, following, confronted by genuine rebel flags, with volleys of rebel musketry and cannonading shaking the ground beneath his feet, the air thick with sulphurous smoke, his life was willingly yielded up by him in order that victory might be achieved by his comrades on the bloody field of Donelson.

# CHAPTER XXII.

BENEVOLENT AND CHARITABLE INSTITUTIONS — NEBRASKA INSTITUTE FOR THE DEAF AND DUMB — ST. JOSEPH'S HOSPITAL AND SIMILAR INSTITUTIONS — DOUGLAS COUNTY HOSPITAL AND POOR FARM.

In the way of institutions to aid the sick and unfortunate, Omaha is far behind many cities of less population and importance. The needs in this direction are fully appreciated by the better class of citizens, and, doubtless, the next five years will witness great advances in this line.

Northwest of the business portion of the city, now within the municipal borders, is located the State Institute for the Deaf and Dumb, opened for the admission of pupils in April, 1869. The act of the Legislature authorizing its establishment was approved February 7, 1867.

The first efforts for the establishment of this institution were those of Rev. H. W. Kuhns, then a member of the Omaha School Board, to whom the parents of Kate Callahan, a little deaf mute of this city, made application to have her educated at the expense of the State. Mr. Kuhns saw the necessity for a State institution for the purpose of educating the deaf, and agitated the question of having one provided. The subject was taken up by other citizens and the newspapers, and the act of the Legislature authorizing its establishment was approved February 7, 1867, and in April, 1869, the institution was opened for the admission of pupils. The law required the location of the asylum to be within three miles of Omaha. The first board of officers were: John S. Bowen, Blair, president; Joseph H. Millard, Omaha, treasurer; Rev. Henry W. Kuhns, Omaha, secretary; Dr. G. C. Monell and Rev. Henry W. Kuhns, Omaha, executive committee; John S. Bowen, Blair, E. H. Rogers, Fremont, Dr. Aurelius Bowen, Nebraska City, Dr. G. C. Monell, Omaha, Dr. Abel L. Child, Plattsmouth, and Dr. John McPherson, Brownville, directors. Prof. W. M. French, a deaf mute, was the first superintendent, and his sister, Mrs. Jennie Wilson, was the first matron. In their first report, dated December 1, 1869, the directors speak as follows with respect to the opening of the institution: "No sooner was the principal, W. M. French, appointed, than, with the concurrence of the Board, he issued a circular, and engaged in correspondence, inviting all the deaf mutes of the State, of suitable age, to the institution. A building sufficient for the immediate requirements of the pupils was obtained and supplied with the necessary furniture, and the little family of the first pupils gathered to their temporary home. They came tardily. Parents could not spare them; some could not afford the expense of such clothing as they deemed needful; the institution was new and untried; but gradually the number of pupils has increased, and at the date of this report thirteen pupils are regularly entered."

An additional hindrance was that these children were generally the objects of solicitude to their parents, because of their affliction, and it was, therefore, with great unwillingness that they were entrusted to the care of strangers.

The citizens of Omaha donated ten acres of ground, and in 1871 an appropriation of $15,000 was made for the erection of more suitable buildings, and a brick structure, 44x60 feet, three stories high, was completed and ready for occupancy January 1, 1872. In the meantime Professor R. H. Kinney and wife had succeeded Professor French and Mrs. Wilson, who had resigned, and Mrs. Mason, and two assistant teachers, Miss Maggie Bickford and Miss Gertrude Jenkins, were employed.

The act of 1867 made no appropriation of funds to begin work, and much difficulty was experienced in getting the enterprise established. A small building located in the woods south of St. Mary's Avenue was first rented, and this was occupied until the building north of the city was completed. There was great rejoicing on the part of the friends of the institution when the appropriation of $15,000 was secured, the money being carried up from Lincoln by Secretary Kuhns.

In 1875 another appropriation of $15,000 was made by the Legislature, and a second building was erected. In the meantime, an additional ten acres of land had been purchased, trees planted, a substantial barn erected, the grounds fenced and the property put in excellent condition. In the latter part of 1876 the buildings and land were valued at $40,000. September 1, 1878, Professor J. A. Gillespie, the present incumbent, was appointed principal of the institution, in the management of which he is assisted by Mrs. Gillespie. At this date there were fifty-two pupils, and the following named officers: J. A. Gillespie, principal; J. A. McClure, F. L. Reid and Mrs. M. T. Benson, teachers; Mrs. S. A. Thompson, matron; Dr. J. C. Denise, physician; and S. F. Buckley, foreman of the printing office. Professor McClure was connected with the institute for fifteen years, resigning some three years since on account of failing sight. For many years the pupils have printed a paper, *The Mute Journal*, first as a monthly and afterwards as a semi-monthly publication, and have made it a very spicy and interesting journal. The institute is now a credit to the State, and has become, under the faithful and efficient management of Professor Gillespie, the agency of great good to the unfortunate class it was designed to aid. The status which the Nebraska home for the deaf and dumb has attained, in the estimation of those who make the care and instruction of these unfortunates a specialty, is shown in an interview with Professor Alexander Graham Bell, on the occasion of a recent visit to Omaha by that gentleman, as printed in the *Bee*. Professor Bell said: "The Nebraska institute is celebrated the world over for its progress in the matter of teaching the deaf to hear. The method in use here was originated by Professor Gillespie, and is revolutionizing the manner of instructing these unfortunates. For a number of years teachers in these institutions have been accustomed to summon their pupils by ringing a dinner bell, but it never seemed to occur to any one that a child who could hear a bell might be taught to hear speech. It remained for Professor Gillespie to do this, and he has demonstrated that fully sixteen per cent. of our deaf mutes may be taught to hear and speak; and, when you consider that the census of 1880 reports about thirty-four thousand deaf mutes in this country, you see how important this matter is. A child which is born deaf never learns to speak because it does not hear any one else speak, but the organs of speech are not defective, and the so-called dumb may be taught to speak. The method pursued by Professor Gillespie is to form those pupils who can hear any loud noise, such as a dinner bell, into classes, and teach them to articulate, thus transforming them from deaf mutes into ordinary deaf people. This method has been thoroughly tested, and is now in practical use in three institutions beside the one here. These are the State institutes of Arkansas and New York, and the Voice and Hearing school, in Englewood, near Chicago. The latter is a private institution, conducted by a former instructor in the Nebraska institute. While I was in

Europe I was questioned very closely about the Nebraska institute and the work it was doing, but was unable to give a very extended idea of the matter, as I had never visited it; so I resolved to avail myself of the first opportunity and investigate the method fully. Professor Gillespie has gained a reputation in this thing, which is world-wide, and has done more to change the general idea regarding this subject than any one ever dreamed of."

He has also introduced into this school a method of presenting language to the deaf, which, though in use but a short time, gives evidence of being a reformation in this line of work. It is simply to present language to these pupils in the form of complete thoughts, instead of in simple ideas. They, having no language of their own, are dependent upon their teachers. By the method here introduced the teacher will supply the smoothest idiomatic expression for the thought presented, and the pupil, after giving this expression, written on the blackboard, a moment's attention, is required to reproduce it, and it thus becomes his own. Many of the difficulties met with by the deaf to master the English language are thus overcome.

The institute now has 130 pupils. The following named persons constitute the board, officers and teachers: J. A. Gillespie, A. M., principal and steward; T. F. Moseley, A. M., R. E. Stewart, A. B., C. C. Wentz, A. M., Mrs. T. F. Moseley, Miss Ella M. Rudd, teachers; W. E. Taylor, A. M., Mrs. W. E. Taylor, Mrs. C. E. Comp, Mrs. C. C. Wentz, oral and aural teachers; Miss May Murray, art teacher; Mrs. J. A. Gillespie, matron; J. C. Denise, physician; Miss Helen McCheane, clerk; Mrs. Anna Richards, nurse and supervisor of large boys; Miss Mamie Sutter, seamstress; Miss Lelia Foote, supervisor of girls; C. E. Comp, foreman of printing office; D. J. Richards, foreman of carpenter shop.

The Woman's Christian Association is an incorporation formed by a number of the ladies of Omaha for benevolent purposes. An organization was effected December 4, 1883, and three small rooms were rented in the old City Hall building, which were occupied for more than a year. No. 1606 Farnam Street, a small frame building, was then secured, and during the year practical assistance was rendered to more than two hundred women and children, and from that date the work of the association has steadily increased. A building on Burt Street, No. 2718, was purchased in 1887 for $5,000, the money being raised by subscriptions to make the first payment of $1,500. Here a permanent home for aged women and a transient abode for destitute women and children has been successfully conducted since October, 1887. E. A. Benson gave the association two lots on Dodge and Forty-first Streets, in 1887, and there it is proposed to erect a spacious and handsome building in the near future. In November, 1887, arrangements were made for establishing a home for young women who were endeavoring to support themselves, the object being to afford to this class comforts and conveniences which would otherwise be beyond their reach, and at the same time throw about them protection and care. A three-story building on Dodge Street, near Nineteenth, was secured and soon filled with young women employed in offices and stores. This home is now at 109 South Seventeenth Street, Mrs. E. J. Evans, superintendent. In April, 1888, a Woman's Exchange was established at No. 1617 Farnam Street, where various articles of home manufacture are sold. All of the enterprises of the association are supported by donations and subscriptions, which fact renders their success much more creditable to the association. Following named are the officers: Mrs. P. L. Perine, president; Mrs. H. M. McCague, Mrs. J. B. Jardine, Mrs. M. A. Elliott, Mrs. H. Ludington, vice presidents; Mrs. Ida C. Tilden, treasurer; Miss Hattie Collier, corresponding secretary; Mrs. L. L. Boltz, recording secretary. Mrs. H. M. McCague is at the head of the executive committee for the management of the Burt Street Home, and Mrs. Ida C. Tilden for that of the Young Women's Home.

St. Joseph's Hospital, formerly Mercy Hospital, Twelfth and Marcy Streets, was first opened for the reception of patients September 1, 1870, a two-story frame building, containing two wards and ten rooms, having been erected by the Order of the Sisters of Mercy, at a cost of ten thousand dollars, the money being obtained by personal solicitation by the Sisters. Two years later the capacity of the building was doubled, at an outlay of fourteen thousand dollars, the money being secured in the same way as before. April 10, 1880, the management passed into the hands of the Order of Sisters of St. Francis. In 1882 these Sisters rendered the city efficient service by taking charge of a temporary smallpox hospital provided by the Council to treat several cases which made their appearance here. For two months this service continued, at the close of which, James E. Boyd, then Mayor, sent the Sisters his personal check for a handsome sum, in recognition of their self-denying work. It was suggested that the Council appropriate a reasonable sum to the hospital in this connection, but the suggestion was not adopted. The growth of the city having rendered the late location of the hospital undesirable for that purpose, a building to accommodate four hundred patients has been erected on a beautiful site, consisting of four lots, at Tenth and Castellar, donated by John A. Creighton, whose wife, recently deceased, bequeathed fifty thousand dollars to aid in the erection of the new edifice. It has a frontage of two hundred feet on Tenth, with two wings extending eastward one hundred and fifty feet. It is built of brick, three stories high, and basement, and cost one hundred and fifty thousand dollars.

The institution is known as "The Creighton Memorial." The corner stone was laid on November 23, 1890, with impressive ceremonies, conducted by Bishop Scannel, of Concordia, Kansas, and the building completed and occupied June, 1892.

It is proposed that the building lately vacated shall be occupied by the J. A. Creighton Medical College, an institution that has been lately projected.

The Immanuel Hospital and Deaconess' Institute is located in Monmouth Park, in the northwest portion of the city. The plan of the building is quite extensive, only the south wing being completed at this time. It occupies a very commanding position, the grounds comprising half a block—twelve lots—and cost eight thousand dollars. The purpose of the founder of this institution includes also the building up of a Deaconess' Institute, for the training of Protestant women to engage in services similar to those performed by the Sisters of Charity of the Catholic Church. In 1879, the founder of this hospital, Rev. E. A. Fogelstrom, came to Omaha and took charge of the Swedish Lutheran Church, of which he was pastor for ten years, during which time he erected the present handsome church building, at the corner of Nineteenth and Cass Streets, at a cost of $30,000. He has been actively engaged in enlisting the interests of the citizens of this place in this enterprise, and securing the necessary funds to carry it out. In both these respects he has been wonderfully successful, as is attested by the magnificent building recently completed. In January, 1890, an incorporation was effected, in order to hold the property, under the name of "The Evangelical Immanuel Association for Works of Mercy," with eleven incorporators, including Dr. George L. Miller, Fred. Drexel, Alfred Millard, Wm. L. McCague, G. A. Lindquest, John Johnson, Guy C. Barton, Anthony Johnson and Joseph Barker. Rev. E. A. Fogelstrom is manager, and Wm. L. McCague, treasurer. Up to January 1, 1891, forty thousand dollars had been expended in improvements, with only one-third of the building, contemplated in the plans, completed. On the date named the institution was opened for the reception of patients.

The Deaconess' Home was erected as a separate institution, in 1891, on the block east of the hospital, at a cost of $5,000. It is a two-story building, with room for thirty sisters.

The Creche, or day nursery, for the care of children of women who are compelled to go out from home to work, is the outgrowth of a suggestion made by the late Mrs. Orpha C. Dinsmoor to a society of ladies called the "Unity Club." September 20, 1887, an organization was effected with Mrs. Dinsmoor as president; Mrs. H. C. Aiken, vice-president; Mrs. T. M. Orr, secretary; Mrs. G. A. Joslyn, treasurer; Mrs. T. L. Kimball, Mrs. H. C. Aiken, Mrs. E. D. Van Court, Mrs. W. E. Burlingim, Mrs. Ada T. Walker, Mrs. L. A. Groff, Mrs. Alma E. Keith, Mrs. G. A. Joslyn and Mrs. T. M. Orr, trustees. An incorporation under the name of "The Omaha Charity Association" was perfected, and a lease for twenty-five years, at a nominal rental, was made with the city for a lot at the northeast corner of Harney and Nineteenth Streets. For a year an old frame building, previously used for a tool house by the city, and which occupied the rear of the lot, was used; but on Washington's birthday anniversary, 1889, the ladies threw open to the public their new brick building, just completed at a cost of about nine thousand dollars, two stories high, containing twelve rooms. The funds necessary were obtained from donations, and from two charity balls, held in the Exposition building. The enterprise has proven a success in every respect, and it is the purpose of the ladies to add to the building so as to provide room for a kindergarten and a training school for servants. The present officers are: Mrs. T. L. Kimball, president; Mrs. James Van Nostrand, vice-president; Mrs. Ada T. Walker, treasurer; Miss S. J. Barrows, secretary.

The Bishop Clarkson Memorial Hospital, formerly the Child's Hospital, located at number 1716 Dodge Street, was established in December, 1881, through the efforts of Bishop Robert Clarkson. Miss Sarah Mattice, of New York City, who had had considerable experience in similar institutions in the East, came to Omaha in the fall of 1881, and rendered most efficient service in the most trying period of the history of the hospital. She solicited funds, gave practical assistance in designing the building, and was manager of the hospital until March 10, 1884. The work was first carried on in a little, old frame building which occupied the ground now covered by the present brick structure, and the first money deposited in the bank, to the credit of the enterprise, was fifty dollars sent by Mrs. John Jacob Astor. Soon afterwards Mrs. Ogden, of New York, sent Mrs. Clarkson five thousand dollars. The further sum of three thousand dollars was raised, mainly in Omaha, by donations, and the substantial brick building now used was put up, at an original cost of eight thousand dollars, which has since been increased to twelve thousand, and opened for the receipt of patients just previous to the death of Bishop Clarkson, which occurred on the 10th of March, 1884. Miss Mattice was matron, as well as manager, until that date, and was succeeded as matron by Mrs. Maria Belt, who served in that capacity for three years, when the present matron, Mrs. F. A. Moore was installed. Mrs. Robert Clarkson was elected member for life upon the death of her husband. Mrs. A. J. Poppleton is secretary. The property is owned by the Trinity Cathedral Chapter.

The Open Door is an establishment conducted under the auspices of Buckingham Union of the Women's Christian Temperance Union, for the reception and reformation of young girls who have gone astray. A comfortable building, number 2630 Capitol Avenue, was secured and opened for boarders in the summer of 1888, and from that date the capacities of the institution have been taxed to the utmost. Later better quarters were secured on North Twentieth Street, opposite the Coliseum, and January 1, 1892, the establishment was moved to 1607-9, Lathrop Street. Mrs. G. W. Clark, an active member of the State Board of Charities, has had the management of the institution from the first, and has devoted to the service all her time and energies. In fact, the Open Door was established at her suggestion, and she has been the chief factor in the collection of means for its support. In the collection of money she has been greatly assisted by Mrs. Watson B. Smith. The following named constitute the board of managers: Mrs. G. W. Clark, Mrs. Watson B. Smith, Mrs. M. J. Richardson, Mrs. L. C. Blackman, Mrs. A. S. Potter. The physicians of the city have rendered their services gratuitously to the inmates of this institution.

The County Hospital, first occupied December 22, 1890, will afford accommodations for one hundred and sixty-five patients. In addition, provision is made for fifty-six insane patients in pavilion number two, and eighty-five in pavilion number four, a total of three hundred and six. Arrangements are made for classifying the patients according to their needs and condition. There are also administration buildings, work shops, and buildings for the domestic department, all arranged for adding increased facilities for the care of patients, as the needs arise. The estimated total cost is as follows: administration buildings, $35,000; domestic buildings, $27,000; boiler house, $15,000; isolated pavilion, $23,000; medical pavilion, $37,000; insane pavilion, $40,000; isolated insane, $23,000; corridor, $3,000; total $213,800. The contract price was $120,033, but several changes in the plans were made, and during the progress of the work complications with the contractors, Edward Walsh and Jerry Ryan, and the architect, E E. Myers, of Detroit, arose, causing long delays and great additional expense. The building has a frontage of three hundred feet, and extends back a distance of four hundred and ten feet, exclusive of engine and boiler rooms. Its general appearance is not so attractive as might have been expected from so large an outlay, and during the erection of the building the local press had much to say in condemnation, not only on account of the delays, but also of the character of the work. The interior arrangements, however, are convenient and well planned, so that the inmates will be made as comfortable as can well be, provided it can ever be made substantial enough to be safe. The building is located on the west side of the county farm, surrounded by a tract of several acres of land set aside for the purpose, and the development of the grounds will add much to the appearance of the institution.

As the Douglas County hospital and poor farm have ever been a source of great expense to the county, and have probably caused more trouble to the people of the city and county than any other one thing, the following history from its inception to the present time is given:

During the early days of 1859 the county commissioners, James H. McArdle, Sylvanus Dodge and Harrison Johnston, conceived the idea that it would be a capital plan for Douglas County to have a poor farm. They spent several weeks in looking for a site and in getting prices, but were unable to find anything that just suited. At the meeting held on March 1st of that year, H. Z. Chapman, long since deceased, appeared before the board and made a proposition to sell the county 170 acres of ground, it being the northeast quarter of section 29, township 15, range 13, the tract being what is now known as the county poor farm. He wanted $6,000, $1,000 in cash, with the balance to be paid as follows: $1,100 in one year,

$1,200 in two years, $1,300 in three years, $1,400 in four years, which amounts were to include principal and interest at the rate of 10 per cent. per annum.

Action upon this proposition was deferred until March 4th, when the county commissioners again met, and, after some discussion, made the purchase, giving Mr. Chapman $2,000 in county warrants, put in at fifty cents on the dollar, and their own personal notes for $4,000, due in one, two, three and four years, drawing interest at the rate of 10 per cent. per annum. To secure the payment of these notes, they, as county officials, mortgaged the land, giving Chapman the first lien.

For just one year everything was serene, but at the end of that time Mr. Chapman wanted his money which was due upon the first note. When he made the demand the three commissioners told him to whistle—that his claim was not worth the revenue stamps that were upon the mortgage. They told him in addition to this that there was a territorial law forbidding county commissioners from mortgaging county property. Mr. Chapman hoped that the three gentlemen would do a little considering, but he hoped in vain, for they proposed nothing of the kind, and when the last note was due he went into our courts and was knocked out, the judge deciding that the commissioners had exceeded their authority in executing the mortgage, and that the county was not liable. General Experience Estabrook defended and there won his spurs.

Chapman was not discouraged, but at once appealed to the supreme court of the State. In due course of time a trial was reached and the decision of the lower court was sustained. Then he gave up the fight and left the State. The disappointment was too much, and in a few years he died.

The old debt remained until about 1878, when Attorney Bonney from Chicago, representing the Chapman heirs, appeared upon the scene to demand the payment of the notes, together with the accrued interest, or the return of the land, which in the meantime had become valuable.

Elated by former victories, the commissioners told Mr. Bonney to try his hand at collecting, and advised him to sue for the money.

Bonney said that he would do that very thing, and immediately brought suit in the United States circuit court.

As upon former occasions, the county won, the court holding that the commissioners had no authority to mortgage county property, and that in doing so the creditor should have to look to them and not to the county for payment.

Bonney was not to be bluffed, and at once he appealed to the United States Supreme Court. J. M. Woolworth was employed and paid thirteen hundred dollars to assist J. C. Cowin, who was then county attorney. In November, 1885, a final decision was reached, and the judgment of the court was that the County of Douglas was liable for the whole debt, both principal and interest, amounting to $14,732.07. At that time the county was short of funds, but on July 3, 1886, the Chapman heirs were paid $9,500, and fifteen days later the balance.

About this time the commissioners, R. O'Keefe, F. W. Corliss and George W. Timme, were convinced that there was an urgent demand for a county hospital and a poor farm, as the old Hascall building, which had been occupied as a poor house, was altogether too small.

How to raise the money to erect a new building was the question. But a real estate boom was at its height that year, and the commissioners thought that by platting fifty acres of the poor farm and selling the lots, a fund could be created. The longer they thought the more determined they became, and at last they decided to lay out and sell 235 lots.

Commissioner Corliss, of Waterloo precinct, fathered the resolution and it went through. The land was platted by the county surveyor, and on November 3, 1886, the proposition to sell was submitted to the voters of the county, but unfortunately it was not carried by a two-thirds majority, and, as a result, parties who purchased lots at the subsequent sale have brought suits against the county aggregating something over $100,000, asking for the return of their money, on the ground that the election was void and that the sales were illegal.

On February 26, 1887, J. H. McCulloch, who was then county judge, appointed John Rush, Chris. Hartman and John L. McCague to appraise the lots which were to be sold. On March 3rd they took the oath of office and the proceedings were reported to the county commissioners. Mr. McCague was absent from the State, and on April 8th William Gibson was appointed to fill the vacancy.

These appraisers visited the premises, and on April 13th reported under oath that the lots were worth $206,450, or an average of $878.51 per lot. These lots were in that portion of the farm known as the east fifty acres.

About that time the commissioners adopted a resolution that the proceeds of the sale should be appropriated to the erection of a suitable building for the care and protection of the county poor and insane.

In April, of 1887, after duly advertising the event, a public sale was held. Thousands of persons followed a brass band and journeyed to the poor farm. The auctioneer, Thos. Riley, mounted a dry goods box, and offered lot one, block one, for sale. After some spirited bidding it was knocked off to W. I. Kierstead at $2,650, and after the disposal of the 235 lots the commissioners found that they had a hospital fund of $330,480 on hand, $191,035.16 of which was cash and the balance was notes secured by mortgages on lots sold.

Shortly after this the commissioners took steps looking to the construction of a building. Architect E. E. Myers, of Detroit, was employed to prepare the plans and the detailed drawings, and upon these a number of parties bid. Ryan & Walsh were the lowest bidders, and were awarded the general contract at $106,937.34, while J. S. Pope & Co. were awarded the steam heating contract at $25,519.

Dan. L. Shane was employed as superintendent at one hundred dollars per month. Work upon the building commenced and proceeded until the structure was up as high as the water tables. Then it was ordered stopped by Mr. Shane, he declaring that poor material, such as would not pass inspection, was being used by the contractors.

A short time thereafter Mr. Shane was retired and a Mr. Ross appointed to fill the vacant place. As time rolled along, the fact of poor material having been used became apparent, and not only that, but evidence of poor workmanship was visible. A section of the south wing, being unable to sustain its own weight, tumbled out and fell to the ground. Shortly after the roof had been raised the corridor arches of the north wing gave way and fell, nearly wrecking that portion of the building.

Other evidences of poor work were visible on every hand, and it was not until after two coats of mineral paint had covered the exterior of the hospital that it had anything like a presentable appearance.

During the progress of the work, the newspapers were very severe in their denunciation of the character of the work done by the contractors, and also of the action of the architect. That they had sufficient grounds for their condemnation has since become apparent. Early in the morning of the 12th of May, 1892, Superintendent of the Poor Mahoney arrived at the court house and reported that the building was settling rapidly. The trouble was in the north wing, which was 160 feet long and three stories high. Mr. Mahoney reported that just after midnight his family were awakened by a loud sound, like unto the report of a cannon. He hastily dressed himself and went on a tour of inspection, but discovered nothing wrong. In the morning, however, feeling that there must be something wrong, Mr. Mahoney arose early and began a more thorough investigation, and was not long in discovering that the unoccupied north wing of the structure had settled during the night, and that the interior and exterior walls were badly cracked from the roof to foundation. Superintendent of Buildings Tilly at once made an inspection and immediately ordered all the inmates out of that part of the building, and directed that the doors be locked. It was estimated that the amount that would have to be expended to save the building would be at least $25,000. The county commissioners found themselves in a dilemma. The hospital fund was exhausted, and would not possibly have any money available until July, 1892. The general fund was in a depleted condition, as were all the other funds except the bridge fund. Notwithstanding this condition of affairs, the board at once took measures to prevent any further damage. They employed Mr. Richard Smith, a contractor, to go out with Inspector Tilly to ascertain what was necessary to save the building. An account of the visit which these gentlemen made was published in the Omaha *Bee*, of May 13, 1892, and is, with slight correction, as follows:

"The commissioners instructed Inspector Tilly to employ an expert to ascertain what was needed to save the building. Acting under these instructions, Contractor Dick Smith's services were secured, and together the two men journeyed to the hospital. They had inspected the exterior walls and gone through the basement, first and second story corridors. Then they were about to go into the garret, under the roof, along the center to the north end, but, on account of the lack of light, an attendant was sent after a lantern, when, a moment later, and without any warning, the corridors fell with a loud crash, filling the place they occupied with dust and debris. A second later there was another crash, as the floor below was too weak to stand the strain.

"The whole mass fell to the main floor, and for a moment it sustained its load, but finally broke, and the whole mass of brick, mortar, wood and iron went into the basement. The corridor walls swayed back and forth, but at last they straightened up, and are now standing, although bulged and twisted out of shape.

"The men hurriedly left the building, expecting that the outer walls and the roof would go next, but they stood the strain, though they look as if a cyclone had passed over that section of the country.

"The slate roof has cracked and in some places sunk down a foot, while the walls, from the water tables to the eaves, have sprung out in places at least eight inches.

"Inspector Tilly states that the entire wing will have to be torn down. To do this, it will be necessary to prop all of the partition walls to hold them from falling. Then the outer walls will have to be braced, in order to prevent the roof from dropping in. After this is done, the roof will have to be taken apart and the entire wall pulled down, brick by brick.

"This is not the worst thing that is liable to happen. The walls of the south wing have commenced to crack, and to-day a crack in the ceiling of the floor of the corridor of the south wing extends from the main building to the south end. While this work is not such as to cause any alarm, it is as large as the cracks in the north wing were when the building was visited by a *Bee* reporter yesterday.

"An attempt will be made to save the south wing. Contractor Smith has been instructed to employ a force of men and work night and day until this portion of the building is in a safe condition. He stated that he would put iron rods through the building at intervals of ten feet, and if this could be accomplished before an accident occurred the structure could be saved.

"If the south wing should fall without a moment's warning, as did the corridors of the north wing, the loss of life would be great, as the administration rooms, the insane and sick wards are all in that portion of the building.

"The falling of this wing is attributed to two causes, the first and principal one being poor construction by Ryan & Walsh, the contractors. The second cause was that for months water had run down the eave spouts and into the ground around the foundation walls, causing them to settle. By the settling, the walls had been drawn apart, leaving nothing to support the brick arches over the corridors.

"The falling walls this morning nearly resulted in a panic among the inmates, but by the coolness and presence of mind of Mrs. Mahoney several serious accidents were prevented.

"When the arches went down, all the steam pipes in that portion of the building were broken, and great clouds of steam hissed through the south corridor, where the insane congregated. As this steam enveloped them, they made a wild dash for the south windows, preparatory to jumping to the ground, twenty feet below. Mrs. Mahoney, although frightened nearly to death, rushed down the corridor and was the first person to reach the windows. There she held them back, and, by her nerve and coolness, held them at bay until the steam was shut off and until assistance arrived."

During the construction of the building, from common reports, it was almost impossible for the contractors to keep the walls standing; and, as there was a large bill for extras, we give herewith a few of them:

After the north wing had been repaired, Ryan & Walsh put in a bill of $5,880 for 196 beam arches, $7,840 for turning the brick over the same, $130.90 for tearing out those portions of the arches that did not fall, $165 for putting the material back, $432 for seventy-three yards of cement placed in the floor that was broken, $152 for lumber used in the new floor and $50 for nails. Then there was another bill for extras for making the same repairs. These figures were $1,890 for sixty-three center beams, $2,520 for turning the brick arches, $182.12 for brick used in the gable and $386.10 for extra brick used in repairing the walls of the corridors.

These bills of extras were not all, by any means. They kept on until they had piled up to the enormous sum of $50,612.49 over and above the price at which Ryan & Walsh contracted to erect the building. Messrs. Coots and Shane, the superintendents, allowed, after a careful inspection, $7,852.82 of the bills, rejecting $42,759.67. Then the balance went before the commissioners, where it was again rejected, after which Ryan & Walsh brought suit in the district court for the full amount. The case was tried and a verdict rendered in favor of the county. An appeal was taken to the supreme court, where the decision of the lower court was set aside. The supreme court issued its mandate, instructing the county to pay Ryan & Walsh $37,000, but it is doubtful when the judgment will be paid, as suit has now been brought against the contractors and the bondsmen to recover, and hold them for the damage to the hospital caused by the recent falling of the corridor arches.

On the night of May 17, 1892, a heavy wind also wrecked the new brick barn at the poor farm, and so frightened the inmates of the hospital who were in the south wing, that they remained up all night, expecting the remaining portions of the building to collapse at any moment. Fortunately, the iron rods which had been put in so strengthened the structure that it remained uninjured.

When the Convent of St. Mary's was sold in 1888, the proceeds were used to erect the building at the corner of Fifteenth and Castellar, known as the Convent of Mercy Orphanage. It is a substantial structure, supplied with all recent improvements for buildings of its character, with ample play rooms, school rooms, dormitories and chapel. It is also the mother house of the Sisters of Mercy in Nebraska. But a more retired situation is now deemed necessary, and ground was broken in July, 1890, for another orphan asylum on a much larger scale, at Benson Place, where a tract of ten acres has been secured, and will be handsomely developed. There are many private charitable organizations connected with the Catholic Churches, notably, the St. Vincent De Paul's, the Catholic Knights of America, the Catholic Mutual Benefit Association, and the Catholic Young Men's Union.

The Methodist Episcopal Hospital and Deaconess' Home Association, at Omaha, was organized March 3, 1891, and soon after incorporated with Rev. J. W. Shank as president, J. J. McLain, vice-president, and J. E. Cowgill, secretary. The constitution declares that the purpose of the association is to care for the sick, regardless of race, color, or religious belief. Free membership tickets are to be given bishops, elders, and the editors of religious papers, but a membership fee of ten dollars a year is charged other applicants, the payment of two hundred and fifty dollars securing a life membership, and all members of the association not in arrears for dues to receive free treatment at the hospital. A suitable building was purchased, and furnished, on Twentieth Street, between St. Mary's Avenue and Harney Street, and the institution opened on the 28th of May, 1891. During the first year 243 patients were treated, fifty-seven of whom were charity patients. The following named persons are the officers for the present year: president, J. W. Shank; vice president, J. J. McLain; secretary, H. R. Day; treasurer, S. W. Lindsay; auditor, W. C. White. The trustees are B. R. Ball, Rev. G. M. Brown, S. W. Nicholson, S. W. Lindsay, J. J. McLain, F. W. Hills, Rev. H. A. Crane, John Dale, Rev. A. Hodgetts. Miss Pfrimmer is matron.

The Presbyterians of the city, in 1890, established a hospital at 1626 Wirt Street, with accommodations for a limited number of patients. Dr. W. O. Henry is the medical superintendent, and the following are the board of trustees: Robert McClelland, C. A. Starr, W. R. Drummond, Colonel Charles Bird, Lew Anderson, L. B. Williams, J. L. Welshans, G. W. Hervey, M. M. Van Horn, W. C. McClain, Alex G. Charlton, Z. T. Lindsay, J. C. Denise, Harry Lawrie and Frank Koze. The following rules govern the institution: Five thousand dollars will endow one bed permanently; $300 will support one bed one year; $20 will support one bed one month; $7 will support one bed one week. Permanent endowment of one bed entitles the donor to name the bed. Churches, Sunday Schools, societies, or individuals who make donations as above, will receive a certificate from the Presbyterian association of Omaha. Donations of all kinds of hospital supplies and medicines are solicited and will be thankfully acknowledged. Charity patients will receive medical and surgical attention free. Paying patients occupying a general ward will be charged $10 per week. Patients occupying private rooms will be charged $15 per week. Medical and surgical attendance to paying patients will be the usual fees, or as per agreement. All regular physicians in good standing have equal privileges in access to the hospital. It was incorporated as the Presbyterian Hospital in Omaha, May 2, 1892, with the following incorporators: C. A. Starr, R. McClelland, J. C. Denise, S. M. Ware, and W. G. Hervey. The hospital has a large and talented medical staff.

The Omaha City Mission was organized under the name of the Christian Workers' Association, October 22, 1875, the object being to advance the interests of the Christian religion by active work. In November of that year it was resolved that a Sunday School should be established for the benefit of newsboys, boot-blacks and other children of the more neglected class. C. E. Brewster was elected superintendent and R. J. Wilbur and T. W. Lemon assistants. In order to reach the children, a grand dinner was given them on Thanksgiving Day in a vacant store-room in the Visscher Block, which occupied the present site of the Millard Hotel. At this spread the boys and girls of the class it was desired to reach showed their appreciation of the efforts made in their behalf, by responding to the invitation to the number of more than three hundred. The purpose of the proposed Sunday School was explained to them at length, and with full hearts (and stomachs) they voted unanimously in the affirmative, when asked if they would all be present at the Second Baptist Church building, on Harney Street near Fifteenth (now used as a blacksmith shop), on the following Sunday afternoon, when the opening session of the school would be held. The hour having arrived witnessed the sad spectacle of an attendance of four of the three hundred and over who had partaken, with so much zeal and enthusiasm, of the society's hospitality but three short days before. However, the superintendent and his two assistants divided these four—all boys—among them, as best they could, without resorting to Solomon's proposition for securing an absolutely equal division, gave them much sensible and seasonable instruction and told them to come again, with judicious hints as to May day festivities the following spring. As events indicated, these four lads were present, evidently, as spies sent out to inspect the land, and that their report was favorable was evidenced by the largely increased attendance the following Sunday. In a short time more room was found necessary, and this was secured in the quarters then occupied by the Y. M. C. A. Later on the school was held in the Academy of Music, and then in Gise's Hall, in the Caldwell Block. In January, 1876, an industrial school for the instruction of girls in habits of industry was established, with Mrs. J. B. Jardine as superintendent. During this year a building on Eleventh Street, formerly used for public school purposes, was offered the association free of charge, by the city authorities, and the free lease of a lot by Dr. G. C. Monell, in the same block, on Tenth Street, was promptly accepted. A number of citizens contributed to a fund to pay for the removal of the school building on to this lot, and there it has since remained. At the annual meeting in October, 1876, a change to the Omaha City Mission was made, in the name of the association. Three departments have been successfully conducted by the mission for many years: The industrial school, Sunday School and a relief department. By means of the latter, charity work is done during the entire year, but especially in the winter months, on an extensive scale and in a thoroughly practical way. In the two schools the attendance averages about the same—one hundred and twenty-five. In connection with the mission the Provident Dispensary was instituted in March, 1892, and Dr. E. T. Allen, who had done much for the work, was made physician in chief of a corps of about forty physicians. Here indigent persons may receive treatment for ten cents a visit, including medicine. The officers of the association are: A. P. Hopkins, president; J. A. Gillespie, first vice-president; E. T. Allen, second vice-president; Miss Mary Goodman, secretary; Alfred C. Kennedy, treasurer; P. S. Leisenring, superintendent Sunday School; Mrs. A. P. Hopkins, superintendent industrial school; Mrs. J. B. Jardine, chairman relief committee; Rev. A. W. Clark, missionary; J. B. Jardine, Thos. Kilpatrick, C. F. Goodman, W. J. Broatch, Wm. McCague, and George O. Calder, trustees.

Looking Northwest from South Ninth Street, 1876.

# CHAPTER XXIII.

FINANCIAL FACTS — PUBLIC AND PRIVATE IMPROVEMENTS — GRADING DOWN HILLS AND FILLING DEPRESSIONS — PRESENT CITY OFFICIALS.

Omaha's increase in population and commercial importance has been rapid. In ten years, 1880 to 1890, she has advanced from the sixty-fourth place in the list of American cities to twenty-first place. The first years of her history were marked by wild speculations which the financial panic in 1857 suddenly blasted, and business depression followed. Then the gold discoveries at Pike's Peak, and in the sands of Cherry Creek, in 1858, resulted in this city's becoming an outfitting and freighting point. The inauguration of the Union Pacific Railway enterprise, in 1864, with Omaha as the initial point, gave the town a new impetus. The financial crash of 1873 was damaging to Omaha, as it was to all western towns, and for three years thereafter real estate could be bought for a song; and, in view of the enormous increase in city property since, it is surprising that no one took advantage of the prices quoted in those days of depression. Lots fronting east on Pleasant Street, now a choice residence location, were offered at $300 each, with no takers; east front lots on Twenty-fourth, between Farnam and Dodge, were offered at from $500 to $800; and in Byron Reed's Addition, west of the High School, lots now worth thousands of dollars were offered in vain at from $300 to $400 each. In the spring of 1877 there was a slight demand for Omaha real estate, which, steadily increasing from that date, has resulted in the general up-building of the city. Additions have been made north, south and west, until the city contains twenty-five square miles of territory within her borders.

In 1860 Omaha had a population of 1,861; in 1870, 16,083; in 1880, 30,518; in 1885' 61,835; in 1886 (estimated), 70,410; in 1887 (estimated), 96,717; in 1888 (estimated), 121,112; in 1890 (United States census), 140,452, an increase of 358 per cent. in ten years. The present growth of the city is all that could be desired. In the business portion, substantial blocks are being erected, in many instances by eastern capitalists, and in the residence localities thousands of workmen are engaged building homes for a prosperous, enterprising people.

An insight into public receipts and expenditures in the early history of Omaha is shown by a report made by an auditing committee at the council meeting held March 23, 1859. For the year preceding, the expenses of the city clerk's office were $12,593.48, but disbursements were made by that office in those days of a character not now within its province, as is shown by the following "bill of particulars."

EXPENDITURES.

| | |
|---|---|
| Pre-emption cases | $ 382 15 |
| Capitol Building | 6,998 09 |
| Scrip (bill for printing) | 95 00 |
| Elections | 14 00 |
| Repairs | 90 50 |
| Printing | 50 00 |
| Rent | 81 73 |
| Stationery | 46 64 |
| Solicitor | 253 00 |
| Recorder | 531 50 |
| City Physician | 100 00 |
| Treasurer | 43 75 |
| Street Commissioner | 152 00 |
| Marshal | 468 60 |
| Collector | 192 35 |
| Assessor | 153 00 |
| City Engineer | 134 00 |
| Protection of the Poor | 331 59 |

Criminal Proceedings ............... 100 00
Improvements...................... 1,153 67
Incidental Expenses................ 1,221 41

RECEIPTS.

The total amount returned by
  ccity ollector was............$ 3,901 45
Scrip received for taxes........ 1,658 94
Warrants received for taxes.... 1,678 26
Cash ........................... 561 20
                                 ———
                                 $7,799 85

The receipts of the treasurer's office were $5,875.89, as follows:

Scrip............................$ 2,767 89
Warrants ....................... 2,169 64
Cash ........................... 938 36

The disbursements for the year footed up $5,806.07, leaving the magnificent total of $69.82 in the city treasury.

The report of the city assessor, dated November 22, 1858, fixed the assessed valuation at $202,074; personal property, $178,362; total, $1,491,114. On this amount a tax of five mills was levied, which would make the city revenue from this source $7,455.51, for the fiscal year ending March 10, 1859. To the above amount was added $347.50 derived from licenses, and $39.84 received by the mayor in the deeding and redeeming of city lots; and, as the total expenditures were $12,593.48, the committee found a deficit of $4,750.57. They took a cheerful view of the situation, however, saying: "As a large portion of the expense was to defray the liabilities of the city on account of the capitol improvements, which will not again occur, and as other items of expenses can be dispensed without detriment to the general prosperity of the city, it is hoped that, by a judicious and economical administration of the city finances, the receipts will defray the expenses of the present fiscal year, and perhaps cancel a portion of the city debt." The amount of scrip issued to that date, $60,000, warrants then outstanding, $12,414.14, and a floating debt of $275.45, brought the total liabilities up to $72,689.59. To offset this large sum, the committee presented the following as assets:

Taxes due the city...................$ 3,554 12
Amount received at tax sales......... 1,286 03
Bond and mortgage of Hotel Company, 15,000 00
City engineer's instruments, etc .....    200 00
Scrip on hand redeemed...............  2,868 68
City warrants redeemed...............  3,130 39
Cash in treasury... ..................     69 82
Balance in collector's hands .........     88 03
Four lots in block H, estimated value..  3,000 00
Eight lots in block D, estimated value.  3,000 00
Two lots in block G, estimated value.    1,000 00
Fifty-six lots in J, K, L, M, N, O, P, estimated value.......... ..........   5,000 00
Four lots in block 128, estimated value  5,000 00
Eight lots in Jefferson Square.........  4 000 00
Twenty lots in Market Square.........   1,000 00
Interest in court house, say............ 3,000 00

Total............................$51,197 07

These represent a total of $51,197.07, which left a balance of $21,492.52 on the wrong side of the ledger. The committee close their report by recommending that the city property be sold in order to cancel the debt.

The financial standing of Omaha in the money centers of the East is now so well established that for several years past her bonds, bearing but five per cent. interest, have commanded a handsome premium. The bonds sold during 1890 bore interest at but four and one-half per cent, and sold for a premium of three per cent. The assessed real estate and personal valuation for taxation for 1891 was $20,000,176.50, though the actual value of real estate alone is conservatively estimated at ten times that amount. The tax levy for city purposes for the year 1891 was $761,128.34. The total collections from all sources, for the year ending December 31, 1891, were $1,595,038.83. January 1, 1892, the city's bonded debt was $2,036,109, while the value of the real estate owned by the city is $1,792,255, and of personal property, $95,904.91; total $1,888,159.91. In 1860 the revenue from taxes was $5,299; in 1870 it was $134,446; in 1880, $177,478; in 1885, $374,773; in 1886, $475,932; 1887, $625,000; 1888, $739,331; 1889, $994,881. The increase in the city debt has been as follows: 1879, $200,000; 1880, $228,900; 1881, $328,900; 1883, $528,900; 1884, $698,900; 1885, $848,900; 1886, $1,048,900; 1887, $1,223,900; 1888, $1,458,500; 1889. $1,661,100. There is an additional amount of $1,614,450 of bonded indebtedness, but this is not a city obligation, proper, but represents bonds issued on account of paving, curbing and guttering, which amount is taxed up against the abutting property, and is paid for by yearly installments, extending over a period of ten years. The paving at intersections of streets and alleys is paid for by the city.

Omaha now ranks seventeenth in the list of clearing house cities, and the banks showed aggregate deposits, March 1. 1892, of $20,109,563.97, distributed as follows: nine national banks, $16,623,467.99; nine savings banks deposits and two State banks, $3,486,095.98. The aggregate capital of the national banks is $1,000,000; of the savings banks, $625,000; and of the two State banks, $104,000. The clearing house, W. H. S. Hughes, manager, was established in 1885, for which year the clearings were $61,384,000; 1886, $93,793,000; 1887, $147,714,000; 1888, $175,714,000; 1889, $208,790,000; 1890, $255,557,652; 1891, $214,758,386, with some of the banks not reporting through the clearing house. In addition to the figures given above, the South Omaha banks, of which three are national, are really a part of the Omaha banking system, and make quite an addition to the capital and the business of the city. During this period the percentage of annual increase has varied from nineteen to fifty-two.

The public improvements carried on by the city were insignificant in extent, until about 1882, when the necessity therefor became so apparent that a general system of grading, sewerage, and paving was inaugurated. In January of that year, a board of public works was appointed by the mayor and council, consisting of James Creighton, chairman, Joseph Barker and John Wilson. The first meeting of the board was held January 22d. In July, 1884, Mr. Barker was succeeded by Clark Woodman, and in March, 1885. Fred. W. Gray was appointed as the successor of Mr. Wilson. In July, 1885, J E. House was appointed chairman of the board in place of Mr. Creighton, resigned, and in October of that year T. C. Brunner succeeded Mr. Gray. Mr. Woodman resigned and Albert Schaul was appointed to fill the vacancy November 22, 1885, and in September of the following year Henry Voss succeeded Mr. Brunner. In 1887 the board was legislated out of existence by the new charter, and in May a new one was appointed by the mayor and council, consisting of St. A. D. Balcombe, for three years; C. E. Mayne, two years; and Louis Heimrod for one year; the first named being designated as chairman. In October, 1888. John B. Furay succeeded Mr. Heimrod and William I. Kierstead was appointed to fill the vacancy caused by the resignation of Mr. Mayne; he was re-appointed in July, 1889, for three years, and resigned January 13, 1891. A. A. Egbert was appointed to fill the vacancy, February 17, 1891.

Previous to the appointment of this board, a very considerable sum had been expended by the city, under direction of the street commissioner, for grading, and Farnam Street had been macadamized from Ninth to Fifteenth at a cost of $25,000; but general improvements were conducted so loosely that the aggregate amount thus expended cannot now be ascertained. The work done on Farnam proved a useless expenditure, and a few years later that street was paved with Sioux Falls granite in the most substantial manner. Originally the Waring system of sewerage was adopted, but that also proved to be a costly experiment, the remarkable growth of the city since not having been anticipated or provided for when the sewers were built, and they were soon found to be entirely inadequate.

At the close of the year 1888, the Board of Public Works reported (including an estimated expenditure for 1882) a total outlay by the city for public improvements, from 1882 to 1888, inclusive, of $5,035,518.07, but did not take into account sundry expenses, inspection, etc., which would amount to nearly $60,000 more. The Eleventh Street viaduct cost $95,734.92, and that on Sixteenth Street, $38,793.05, both being built in 1887. The foundation for the city hall, practically lost by the change of plans in 1888, cost $38,650.95. With the close of the year 1888, there were forty miles of street pavements laid and sixty-six miles of sewers constructed. Previous to 1882, $50,000 had been expended on sewer construction, which amount is included in the total given above. The material used for paving is Sioux Falls granite, Colorado sandstone, asphaltum, cedar and cypress blocks, and vitrified brick. In addition to the outlay by the city, the street railway companies have expended many thousands of dollars in paving their right-of-way on various streets.

During the year 1889 the Board of Public Works expended $846,665, paying $77,415 for nineteen miles of curbing; $103,668 for six and seven-tenths miles of sewers; $183,482 for eleven miles of paving; $182,000 for twenty-two miles of grading. The cost of sidewalks (taxed against property owners) laid during the year was about $112,000. The sum of $55,000 was expended in park improvements by the South Omaha Company, and about $20,000 by the Omaha Park Commission. Since January 1, 1883, fifty-one miles of streets had been paved, at a cost of $3,182,952, the largest disbursement for this purpose having been made in 1888, when $1,000,464 was expended. There had been nineteen miles of stone curbing laid, at a cost of $77,415; over seventy-two miles of sewer built, costing $1,217,172; and one hundred and three miles of streets graded, making a total outlay for this class of public improvements to January 1, 1890, of $6,540,472. June 25, 1890, P. W. Birkhauser succeeded St. A. D. Balcombe as chairman of the board.

In the paving contracts let since 1890, wooden blocks have not been considered, the experience of the past in that regard having proven unsatisfactory. During the year 1890 nine and one-fifth miles of streets were paved at a cost of $506,480, making the total mileage of paved streets a trifle over sixty-one miles. Street curbing was done to the extent of nineteen and one-fifth miles, at a cost of $72,355. Twelve miles of sewers were constructed, costing $112,430, making a total of eighty-five miles of sewers. Twenty-two and one-half miles of streets were graded, at an outlay of $208,253. Thirty thousand dollars was expended in building twenty-two miles of sidewalks, in addition to an expenditure of $22,000 by property holders. The total outlay for public improvements during the year, including county expenditures, on city streets, was $32,350; bonds voted for the Tenth Street viaduct, $150,000, and $200,000 expended on the city hall foot up $1,377,317.

The following information on the improvements of the city is obtained from the city engineer's report for the year ending December 31, 1891: There was expended for sewers, $70,376.03; for curbing, $16,562.71, for about five miles; grading, $150,868.85; paving, $136,531.16. The total mileage is as follows: sewers, 92.11 miles; curbing, 117.64 miles; grading, 136.6 miles; paving 64.22 miles. The total amount expended for these improvements during the nine years ending June 1, 1892, was: for sewers, $1,412,334.50; for curbing, $609,996.32; for grading, $1,154,990.54; and for paving, $3,796,662.66.

In 1889 new plans for a city hall were adopted, Messrs. Fowler & Beindorf, of Omaha, being the successful architects in a competitive examination, and the building is now in course of erection on the site chosen by the voters of Omaha, in 1882, and again at an election held in the spring of 1889, the northeast corner of Farnam and Eighteenth Streets. John F. Coots, the builder of the Douglas County Court House, was awarded the contract for the building, which cost about $550,000. The corner stone was laid June 19, 1890, with appropriate ceremonies, by the Grand Lodge of Masons of Nebraska, which happened to be in session in Omaha on that date. An interesting feature of the occasion was the presence of ex-Mayors A. J. Poppleton, George Armstrong, B. E. B. Kennedy, Charles H. Brown, Joseph H. Millard, Champion S. Chase, James E. Boyd and Wm. J. Broatch. Following is the address of Mayor R. C. Cushing:

"*Fellow Citizens of Omaha, Gentlemen of the Common Council and of the Masonic Fraternity:* We are assembled to-day to deposit a block of enduring granite stone which will, we trust, uphold years after all present shall have departed, a fabric devoted to our city's business.

"To its sealed recesses we confide such evidences of our city's present size and prosperity as may serve to interest the busy populace of some future generation, when these firm walls shall have crumbled and the secrets of this corner stone shall have been brought to light.

"The pyramids and sphinx of the Nile tell to-day an Egyptian tale better than the ashes of the great Alexandrian library. The ruins of our ancient cities, for instance, the Coliseum of Rome, speak louder in the descriptive than the scribes of that day. Therefore, it is altogether fitting that such memorials of our day should be entrusted to the strong guardianship of stone.

"Here and there, even at this time, as our hills are leveled, or our foundations laid, the busy spade of the workman exhumes, from its long forgotten grave, Indian relics, some domestic utensil, or some weapon of war, upon which we gaze with absorbing interest as the sole histories of nations long vanished.

"In their rugged outlines we may venture to read something of their wars, their daily pursuits, and their homes, which, but for these recovered implements of stone, would have been a blank forever.

"To the people of some long distant day, we offer a more legible story, and one which, we believe, is more in accord with the spirit of the present age. From this recess, hereafter, will be taken no weapon of death, no evidence of barbaric wars, but tokens only of peace and prosperity, which have hitherto blessed this city, and which we devoutly hope may continue to bless it for ages yet to come.

"Upon the stone now to be placed will rise, we hope, a structure which will be an honor to our city and a satisfaction to its inhabitants. Within its walls, we trust that no ignoble motive, no corrupt suggestion, may ever find a place, and that it may be not only an edifice for the transaction of the city's business affairs, but also a temple of integrity, justice and patriotism. And may the figure which the architect has designed for its summit look down for many years upon a community happy, united, prosperous, honest and charitable.

"To you, gentlemen of the Masonic Fraternity, I now extend my most hearty thanks for your interest in the occasion, and turn over this block to be fitted in its place by your skillful and experienced hands."

It is only within a few years past that there have been erected in Omaha business houses of any considerable size or cost. Boyd's Opera House, built in 1881, cost $125,000; the Ware Block, built in 1885, cost $86,000; the Omaha National Bank building, erected in 1882, and added to in 1889, cost about $140,000. The Nebraska National building was erected in 1883 at a cost of $65,000. The First National Bank building, costing $250,000, the Merchants' National, costing $180,000, and the United States National, costing $150,000, were all completed in 1888.

The New York Life Insurance Company building, ten stories high, cost about $900,000, and was completed in 1889, as was also the magnificent structure erected by the Bee Publishing Company at a cost of $500,000. The Paxton Block was completed in 1888 at an expense of $361,000; the Barker Block, finished the same year, cost $70,000; the Granite Block, erected by William A. Paxton, who also built the Ware and Paxton buildings, cost $40,000; the Withnell was built by John and Richard Withnell, in 1887, at a cost of $40,000; the Karbach, completed in 1892, and owned by Charles J. Karbach, cost $150,000; the Ramge, the property of Frank J. Ramge, finished in 1888, and cost $100,000; the Sheely was built in 1887-8 by Joseph Sheely, and cost nearly $100,000; the Commercial National Bank building, built in 1890, cost about the same amount; the Murray Hotel, built by Thomas Murray, cost $140,000; the Dellone, built by Frank Dellone, cost $100,000; the Paxton Hotel, built by Charles W., James B. and Richard Kitchen, cost $275,000; the Millard Hotel, built by the Millard Hotel Company, cost $200,000; the Woolworth Block, on Howard Street, built by James M. Woolworth, cost about $100,000; the Dr. S. D. Mercer Blocks on the same street, cost $250,000; the Fred Ames buildings, corner of Eleventh and Howard and Sixteenth and Farnam, each cost about $100,000; the buildings owned by the Ezra Millard estate, located on both sides of Harney, corner of Eleventh, cost $204,000; Dewey & Stone's building, on Farnam near Twelfth, cost $40,000; the Chamber of Commerce building cost $100,000; the Exposition building, with alterations, cost $113,000; the Strang building, erected by A. L. Strang, cost about $35,000; the Union Pacific Headquarters building cost $200,000, and the Burlington & Missouri River building, about half that sum; the buildings used by Mr. Fred Krug, for brewery purposes, cost $150,000; J. J. Brown's building, corner of Sixteenth and Douglas, $100,000; the Kirkendall building corner of Sixteenth and Dodge, cost $50,000; the American National Bank cost $120,000; Charles Turner's business block on Tenth and Harney cost $36,000, and his residence on west Farnam Street a like amount; the Rector & Wilhelmy building, Tenth and Jackson, cost $25,000; the Smith building, corner of Harney and Twelfth, cost $40,000, and the W. H. Cremer building, adjoining on the west, $30,000; the W. J. Broatch building, on Harney, near Thirteenth, cost $25,000; the John McCreary building, on Douglas, east of the Millard Hotel, cost about $50,000; the Hellman Block, corner of Farnam and Thirteenth, about $40,000; the Young Men's Christian Association building, Douglas and Sixteenth, $90,000; A. S. Paddock's building, corner of Douglas and Twelfth, $90,000; the Pacific Express Company's building, Fourteenth and Harney, $130,000; the First Methodist Episcopal Church, Davenport and Twentieth Streets, $95,000; Parlin, Orendorf & Martin building, Ninth and Jones, $30,000; the Max Meyer & Brothers' building, Farnam and Eleventh, $45,000; the McGavock building, $40,000; the New St. Joseph Hospital, $150,000; the J. L. Byers' Block, Douglas and Fifteenth, $122,000; the Estabrook Block, Sixteenth and Chicago, cost $60,000; the J. W. Lytle Block, on Farnam between Eleventh and Twelfth, cost $35,000; Trinity Cathedral, $100,000; First Congregational Church, $60,000; and many others.

The building of handsome and attractive residences in all portions of the city has also been a marked feature of Omaha's progress during the past few years.

The conversion of the village of Omaha into the present city has involved the removal of a vast amount of earth, in the grading down of hills and the filling up of ravines. In its earlier stages this work of transformation, now so gratifying to behold in its results, caused much bitterness of feeling on the part of old-time friends and neighbors and damage suits without number against the city. This era of street improvement dates back to 1873, when a radical grade was established for St. Mary's Avenue, or, rather, a grade then considered radical, but which in these latter years adjacent property holders would reject as not providing for a sufficient filling in of the low ground and cutting down of the hills. But the grade then proposed for that street met with indignant opposition from heavy property owners on both sides of that then important thoroughfare, and a compromise grade was finally accepted, the result being that the avenue has lost its prominence, and adjacent streets have absorbed its business.

Farnam Street has had three changes of grade, involving a cut of forty-five feet at the intersection of Seventeenth, and a fill of quite that much between Twentieth and Twenty-fourth. Previous to this the block bounded by Farnam, Harney, Seventeenth and Eighteenth had been purchased by the county commissioners as a court house site, on account of its commanding elevation. Anticipating a reduction of the grade on Farnam, the commissioners removed considerable earth from the court house block, and complaints were freely made that that beautiful site was being destroyed by a lot of men who had no eye for the picturesque. But those whose business requires them to climb the long flights of steps now reaching to the building from the street level do not complain because a few feet of earth were scaled off of the top of the hill by the county board, "but, on the contrary, quite the reverse." This improvement of Farnam Street also caused the destruction of the handsome and expensive residence Governor Saunders had built at the northeast corner of Farnam and Eighteenth, the present site of the city hall. West of Twenty-fourth the cuts and fills were not so radical, which fact people owning the abutting property have already lived long enough to regret.

Cuming Street has been converted from a hilly country road into a magnificent street, with an ascending grade westward so slight that it is scarcely perceptible. The creek, through which a sluggish stream flowed eastward along the line of Nicholas Street, breeding pestilence and death in the hot summer months, has been filled up and in its place are now the sites of substantial brick structures. Directly north of this stream, on Sixteenth Street, was formerly a hill of considerable steepness on which, west of the road, stood the "claim shanty" in which Mr. John A. Horbach lived when he perfected his entry of eighty acres of land, paying therefor the government price of a dollar and a quarter an acre. On the Sixteenth Street bridge, by which the stream was crossed, a well-known citizen, Henry Durnall, was killed late one night by being thrown from his buggy by his runaway horse. This bridge was afterwards purchased by the county commissioners and placed across a stream near Florence.

South Sixteenth and South Eleventh Streets have been improved at great expense to the city and lot owners. At the intersection of Jones, the former street has been cut about fifty feet, and Eleventh Street, at the intersection of Pierce, was cut sixty-six feet. Jones Street was formerly the bed of a stream called Otoe Creek (afterwards South Omaha Creek), and property in that vicinity was of little value. East of Eighth Street, from this creek northward to Farnam, was a high bluff under which, just south of Farnam, was for many years a large pond which was used for skating purposes in the winter by the giddy youth of that period. The bluff has been graded down, the low levels raised, and a net work of iron placed thereon to accommodate the immense railway business of which Omaha is now the center.

But the greatest change, perhaps, is that which has been wrought on Leavenworth Street. A dozen years ago it had five distinct and separate names — Leavenworth,

Plum, Sherman, Grant and Third—the various parties platting additions which extended the street westward fixing such names to the portions thus platted as suited their exuberant fancy. At one point the street was only about forty feet wide, while high elevations and deep ravines characterized it from one end to the other. For two years a bitter warfare waged, with the proposed improvement of this street as the bone of contention. Petitions and remonstrances by the dozens were sent in to the council. Various boards of appraisers were appointed and their reports rejected. Meetings of interested property holders were held and enlivened by loud talk and personal abuse. Some of the heaviest property holders on the street opposed the enterprise most strenuously, and on one occasion Mayor Boyd (during whose last term the fight occurred) remarked to a delegation which waited upon him in that connection that the council had devoted more time during the year preceding to Leavenworth Street than to any other half dozen streets in the city. However, the progressive element succeeded; twenty-foot cuts were made, ravines filled, narrow places widened and one name given the street for its entire length. It is now one of the most promising east and west thoroughfares in the city, is paved for a distance of over two miles, has a double-track electric motor line, and the solid business blocks completed, or now being built, along the street prove the wisdom and prudence of those who advocated the improvement of the street. And a similar experience has followed in all portions of the city where first-class grades have been established, regardless of public and private expense. In every case the property affected has been largely increased in value, and substantial and expensive improvements have resulted.

An immense amount of eastern capital has sought investment in this city, chiefly through the local loan associations, the principal of which are: The American Loan & Trust Company, O. M. Carter, president, capital $400,000; the Omaha Loan & Trust Company, A. U. Wyman, president, capital $350,000; the Union Trust Company, W. A. Paxton, president, capital $300,000; the Anglo-American Mortgage & Trust Company, L. W. Tulleys, president, capital $300,000; the Equitable Trust Company, Lewis S. Reed, president, capital $200,000; Home Investment Company, Edwin S. Rowley, president, capital and surplus $280,000; McCague Investment Company, John L. McCague, president, capital $200,000; Mutual Investment Company, W. H. Russell, president, capital $75,000; Globe Loan & Trust Company, H. O. Devries, president, capital $300,000; Mead Investment Company, W. D. Mead, president, paid in capital and surplus $80,000; Omaha Mortgage Company, Thomas Brennan, president, capital $100,000. Many of the leading money syndicates of the East also have resident agents in Omaha.

# CHAPTER XXIV.

### BENCH AND BAR—PERSONAL MENTION OF MEMBERS OF A DISTINGUISHED PROFESSION—ORGANIZATION OF TERRITORIAL AND STATE COURTS.

[As is well-known, Judge Savage was first selected to write this chapter, as well as others, but his untimely death rendered it necessary for some other person to perform that duty, and, at the request of the executors of the late judge, the writer consented to prepare these pages, knowing full well the loss to the profession, as well as to the publication, in that Judge Savage had not completed his task. But having accepted the office, I trust that I have given such attention and consideration to the subject as it deserves, and that it will be satisfactory to the members of the bar, as well as to the public generally GEO W AMBROSE]

Personally, I deem the subject of this chapter an important one, and I trust my view of it is not exaggerated "Mine office" must not be magnified, however, but those who come after us may care to know something of the order of men with whom the meanest as well as the greatest of individuals have to deal. The legal profession, it is said, "is a republic open to all," and from among its members are taken those, who, in a large degree, make as well as administer the law, and each, in the eloquent words of Bishop Horne, "when he goeth up to the judgment seat, puts on righteousness as a glorious and beautiful robe, and to render his tribunal a fit emblem of the eternal throne of which justice and judgment are the habitation."

The bar of Omaha has always been a prominent one in the territory as well as in the State. The writer recollects that, in the early seventies, at one time when Associate Justice Miller, of the Supreme Court of the United States, was in attendance in this city, holding the circuit court, that he remarked that nowhere in the eight states then composing this circuit was there an abler bar than in Omaha, and such has been its reputation, not only in the State, but in the surrounding states as well. In the early territorial days the membership of the bar included many who are not here now, and it has been impossible for the writer to obtain some of their names, but Thomas B Cuming, afterwards secretary and acting governor of the territory, together with one Turk, were in 1858, a leading firm, conducting a general business, and it is said that Governor Cuming especially was a silver-tongued orator of great ability Jonas Seely, now dead, was then a resident of Omaha, engaged in the general practice, and John I Redick and Clinton Briggs were then, as for many years thereafter, a prominent firm of attorneys, and, together with Poppleton, Lake, Woolworth, Brown, Kennedy, Little, Richardson, Estabrook, Hitchcock and Daniel Gantt, formed a combination of brains and pluck and push — all of them good lawyers, and all of them rose to eminence in their profession in later years None of us who knew him could forget Daniel Gantt, a thorough chancery lawyer, imbued with great love for his profession, nothing so delighted him as to have fall into his hands an intricate and complicated case in chancery He was the last United States District Attorney of the Territory Soon after the admission of the State he removed to Nebraska City and was afterwards made Chief Justice, and died in office in 1878 No purer man or brighter legal mind has ever adorned the bench of Nebraska The personal mention of others of the territorial bar will be made under the proper head, in comments upon the bar of the city.

## TERRITORIAL DAYS.

The organic act under which Nebraska was created a territory was passed by Congress in May, 1854. Under that act, on the 29th day of June, 1854, President Pierce commissioned Fenner Ferguson Chief Justice, and Edward R. Hardin and James Bradley Associate Justices, of the Supreme Court. These judges came to Nebraska in the fall of that year, Chief Justice Ferguson taking the first judicial district, consisting of Douglas and Dodge Counties, Judge Hardin the second district, comprising the territory south of the Platte River, and Judge Bradley the third district, which embraced Washington and Burt Counties. These assignments were made by Hon. Thomas B. Cuming, secretary of the territory, who, by reason of the death of Governor Burt, was the Acting Governor. The first term of the Supreme Court was fixed for the third Monday of February, 1855, at Omaha, and the first term of the District Court for this district was assigned to be held on the second Monday in March, 1855, at Bellevue, which was then a part of Douglas County. February 10, 1855, the Supreme Court was organized at Omaha, in the Hall of Representatives, in the old State House, on Ninth Street between Farnam and Douglas Streets. There were present Chief Justice Ferguson; Judge Hardin; Experience Estabrook, United States Attorney; and J. Sterling Morton, clerk.

There was nothing done at that term, except to take an adjournment until the June following, when the court again convened with the same judges and the district attorney present. At this term there were admitted, upon motion of General Estabrook, O. D. Richardson, A. J. Poppleton, A. J. Hanscom, Silas A. Strickland, L. L. Bowen, A. D. Jones and Samuel E. Rogers, as members of the bar, and their admission constituted the only business transacted at that term of court.

By an act of the Territorial Legislature, passed March 16, 1855, terms of the Supreme Court were appointed to be held at Omaha on the second Tuesday of December, and the second Tuesday in June, of each year. There were no other terms of the court held from June, 1855, until June, 1857. Judge Ferguson held his first term of District Court for this district at Bellevue, March 12. 1855, at which time the only business transacted was the appointment of Silas A. Strickland as clerk of the court.

On the 12th of April, following, the court met, but immediately adjourned until October 16, 1855, at which term Allen Root and O. P. Mason, who have become historic characters in this State, were admitted as attorneys.

October 22, 1855, the first grand jury of the territory was convened, and consisted of the following named persons: R. Hogeboom, I. P. Halleck, Sylvanus Dodge, Jesse Lowe, foreman, A. Davis, J. F. Kimball, H. Johnson, A. W. Trimble, S. Driskall, J. C. Reeves, J. Sailing. P. Cassidy, H. H. Smith, W. H. Smith, and J. R. Allen. The first indictment for murder was returned by this jury, Mr. Henry being the accused. He was defended by A. J. Poppleton and O. P. Mason, and was acquitted.

In 1856 Judge Bradley resigned, and returned to La Porte, Indiana, and Judge Eleazer Wakeley, of Wisconsin, was appointed by President Pierce in January, 1857, to fill the vacancy; which position Judge Wakeley occupied until soon after the inauguration of President Lincoln, in 1861, when he returned to Wisconsin, again locating in Nebraska in 1868.

Judge Ferguson, the first judge of this district, was elected a delegate to Congress in 1857, serving two years, and was succeeded on the bench by Hon. Augustus Hall, of Iowa. Judge Ferguson was born in Columbia County, New York, in 1814. He studied law in the office of Koon & Bramhall, at Albany, was admitted as an attorney in 1840, and as a counselor in 1843. His residence in Nebraska was at Bellevue, then the trading post of the American Fur Company under the agency of the famous Peter A. Sarpy. The death of Judge Ferguson occurred there November, 1859, at the age of forty-five, where his family continued to reside for many years.

Augustus Hall was appointed judge of this district in 1857. He died in 1861 at the age of forty-seven years. His residence was at Bellevue. He continued to act as judge until his death. His widow and son, Richard S. Hall, now of the firm of Hall, McCulloch & English, still reside in Omaha. Judge Hall was succeeded by William Pitt Kellogg, of Illinois. The last territorial judge of this district was William Kellogg, who was also of Illinois, and was the immediate successor of William Pitt Kellogg. The latter went into the army of the rebellion, and after the war removed to the State of Louisiana, where he subsequently became known through the offices which he held as Governor of Louisiana and as Senator of the United States. Judge Wakeley was succeeded by William F. Lockwood, who held the office until the admission of the State, in March, 1867. A very pleasing incident may here be noted. The territorial judges, Ferguson, Hall and Wakeley, have each sons in the active practice of the law in Omaha. Arthur Wakeley, Richard S. Hall and Arthur N. Ferguson (Mr. Ferguson having, as noted elsewhere, been appointed judge), also Experience Estabrook, the first United States Attorney, has a son, Henry D. Estabrook, engaged in the practice—all of them "chips of the old blocks."

One of the institutions of those early days, and which has since become historical, was an organization known as the Omaha Claim Club. This organization was composed of about two hundred individuals who were among the earliest settlers of Omaha and the surrounding community. The land laws of the United States permitted every person who came within their terms to settle upon 160 acres of government land, and perfect his title and secure his patent; but the early settlers thought that, because they came here in an early day, they had acquired superior rights to even the laws of Congress upon the subject of the location of government land, and so this organization was for the purpose of protecting any of its members in pre-empting and holding 320 acres of land; and no person who came upon this soil, and sought to locate in the exact terms of the law upon government land, was permitted to enjoy the fruits of his labor, but whenever he attempted it he was waited upon by a committee and informed, under certain pains and penalties to be administered by the club, that he must deed his land to the member of the club desiring it. If not, at times he was ducked in the Missouri River; at other times his little shanty, located upon his government land, was burned down; or perhaps a stray shot would " wing " him; and at last he would be driven from the land, if he was so contumacious as not to comply with the requirements of the club.

This organization became a fruitful source of litigation in this community, not only during the territorial days, but in the days of Statehood: but the majority of the members of the Claim Club were enabled to hold their lands by some means, and many of them, who have since become rich and honored in the community, have become so because of their membership in this club. Many a case has gone through the courts of the territory, as well as through the courts of the State, involving the history and action of this Claim Club, and two notable ones were decided by the Supreme Court of the United States; one, the case of Pierce vs. Brown, in 7th Wallace, 214, the other, Alexander H. Baker vs. William S. T. Morton, et al., decided in 12th Wallace, 150.

Mr. Baker, who was for a great many years a well-known citizen of this city, and who is now a resident of Grand Island, located upon 160 acres of land in what is known as Orchard Hill, and Brown located upon the adjoining 160 acres. Neither Brown nor Baker were members of the Claim Club, but Pierce was, and he feasted his greedy eye upon those choice 320 acres, and set about to obtain them; and he did, as is alleged in the case, with other persons who were members of the club, procure a deed both from Baker and Brown for their pre-emption claims after the title had inured to them under the land laws of the United States. This was brought about by Pierce, with other members of the club, going to these two gentlemen and threatening to take their lives by hanging or drowning them, or in such other manner as the agents of the club might think fit and proper to employ.

This was in 1857; and, upon their acquiring the pre-emption title from the government, these threats were about to be carried into execution, when these gentlemen conveyed to Pierce their pre-emption entries. Afterwards, bills in equity were filed in the territorial courts, alleging these threats, and that the conveyances were obtained by duress. The courts of the territory, as well as the Circuit Court of the United States for this district, decided against the gentlemen and sustained the conveyances thus obtained. Upon appeal to the Supreme Court of the United States, that court made very swift work of setting aside the decrees of the Circuit Court of the United States, and held that the conveyances were obtained by duress, and reinstated Mr. Baker and Mr. Brown in their titles.

The attorneys who were instrumental in obtaining the decision of the Supreme Court were Messrs. Redick and Briggs, while the attorney who contended for Pierce and Morton was Mr. Woolworth. The records of the testimony in those two cases are still extant, and the student who desires to become acquainted with the modes and operations of the early settlers in Nebraska Territory will find very choice reading by consulting those printed records.*

## DAYS OF STATEHOOD.

Nebraska was admitted as a State March 1, 1867. The constitution was adopted in 1866 by a vote of the people, at which time William A. Little was elected Chief Justice and George B. Lake and Lorenzo Crounse Associate Justices. Mr. Little died before having qualified for the office, and Governor David Butler appointed O. P. Mason, of Nebraska City, to fill the vacancy. The State then consisted of but three districts. Judge Mason was assigned to the first district, Judge Lake to the second, and Judge Crounse to the third. These judges, under the constitution, were judges of the Supreme Court, with power to hold the courts of the three districts, and twice a year they met as a Supreme Court to listen to appeals and writs of error, the judge from whom the appeal or writ of error was taken not sitting in the appellate court. This condition of things continued until the adoption of the constitution in 1875, when they ceased to hold the district courts, the State having been re-districted and other judges elected for the district courts. The first term of the court for this district, the second under the State constitution, was held at Omaha, April 16, 1867, Judge Lake presiding, with George Armstrong, clerk, Andrew Dellone, sheriff, and George W. Doane, prosecuting attorney. The members of the bar, then engaged in active practice here, were James M. Woolworth, A. J. Poppleton, John I. Redick, Clinton Briggs, George W. Doane, John R. Meredith, Charles H. Brown, Experience Estabrook, Albert Swartzlander, George H. Roberts, Silas A. Strickland, J. C. Ambrose, John D. Howe, George C. Hopkins, George M. O'Brien, Ben. Sheeks and Charles P. Burkitt.

*The writer wishes to acknowledge the receipt of valuable information, concerning those early days, from Charles P. Birkett, and from Hon. James M. Woolworth in his article in Volume IX of Magazine of Western History.

That term was held in the old court house, then standing at the corner of Sixteenth and Farnam. Upon the assembling of court that morning, the writer, having arrived in Omaha the month previous, walked into the court room for the first time, and his recollection of its surroundings are quite vivid. The judge's raised desk was at the south end, in front of which sat the clerk. The bar was fenced off with a wooden railing, and on either side were the petit and grand jury boxes, on raised seats. Two old-fashioned heating stoves warmed the room, the space outside of the railing being allotted to witnesses and spectators.

Time has made wonderful changes since those days. Old age, with its gray hairs and wrinkled brows, has taken the place of youthful activity. Wealth has favored some, and the plodding of everyday life still exists with the many. But, with all this, let a plurality of those wise, gray heads and (by no means few) bald-heads get together, and the live scenes of our court room enactment are still the subject of much merriment.

Upon the opening of court, James W. Savage, John C. Cowin, Champion S. Chase, and the writer were admitted to the bar. Of these four, James W. Savage has been the first to solve the mystery of the Infinite; and, of those who were then active practitioners, Clinton Briggs, John R. Meredith, Silas A. Strickland and George M. O'Brien have died. The balance of those then present are still here, with the exception of George H. Roberts, George C. Hopkins, Ben. Sheeks and J. C. Ambrose, either engaged in the active practice of their profession, or retired upon a competency. The business of the court, after the admission of the gentlemen named, proceeded in the usual way, with a call of the docket and the answers of attorneys who were fortunate enough to have any business. There were then no printed dockets, and the writer recollects that the clerk had prepared his docket for the use of the court, from which the attorneys had abstracted their cases, in little pass books, and, as the judge made the call, notations were entered in these little books as to the disposition of the various suits. The first jury case, in the second district, taken up at this first term of court under the State government was entitled, "State of Nebraska vs. Ottway G. Baker, for murder," and the first jury called consisted of the following named persons: James Slightman, Wm. T. Clark, Charles Powell, Edward Whitehorn, Tholemiah A. Megeath, Wm. Neighly, Dorland L. Clapp, Enos Scherbe, James L. Hawkins, Wm. H. Lawton, James M. Parker, and Milton C. Outhwaite. The history of this trial is referred to elsewhere.

The district court continued to be held by Judge Lake as associate justice of the Supreme Court until the adoption of the present constitution in 1875. In November of that year, James W. Savage was elected judge of this district, now become the third under the re-districting of the State, and composed of the counties of Sarpy, Douglas, Washington and Burt. He was nominated as a Democrat, in a district supposed to be overwhelmingly Republican, his competitor being John M. Thurston, to whom it was no reproach to be defeated by Judge Savage, under the circumstances, for the latter was much more generally known throughout the district, was more advanced in years and practice, and possessed great personal popularity. Mr. Thurston has since achieved such distinction that his defeat at that time has been to him a subject of congratulation. In November, 1879, Judge Savage was re-elected for another term of four years, but resigned in 1882, when James Neville was appointed to fill out his unexpired term.

In 1879 Judge Savage's competitor was Charles A. Baldwin, Esq. The Legislature of 1883 having made provisions for two judges of this district, Hon. Eleazer Wakeley was appointed by Governor Dawes to serve with Judge Neville. Although a Democrat of pronounced views, Judge Wakeley was unanimously selected by the bar of the district to fill the position, and was also heartily endorsed for the appointment by the citizens of the district generally, irrespective of politics. In the fall of that year these two judges were elected for a term of four years, at the end of which period Judge Neville announced his decision to retire from the bench. In the meantime there had been such an increase in the business of the court that the Legislature of 1887 passed an act providing for four judges for this district, and Governor Thayer appointed Lewis A. Groff, Esq., of this city, and M. R. Hopewell, Esq., of Burt County, as the two additional judges. Just previous to the election in November, 1887, at a meeting of the bar of the district, Judges Wakeley, Hopewell and Groff were unanimously endorsed for renomination. The two latter being Republicans left the fourth place to be filled by the Democratic convention, which placed in nomination the name of W. A. Stowe, of this city, who was entirely acceptable to the bar. The nomination was made on Saturday, and on the Tuesday following, while attending a case in the Supreme Court at Lincoln, Mr. Stowe was stricken with apoplexy, and died a few days later.

The members of the bar then, in a petition universally signed, requested Hon. George W. Doane to allow his name to be used upon a ticket with the other three judges, as a non-partisan, to which he assented, and the four gentlemen named were all elected, notwithstanding an exciting political contest, the Republican party having placed in nomination for the position four lawyers belonging to that party. In September, 1889, Judge Groff resigned to accept an appointment as commissioner of the general land office, tendered to him by President Harrison. As his successor, at a bar meeting held for that purpose, Joseph R. Clarkson, Esq., was selected, and again the Republican party placed its own candidate in nomination, in the person of Herbert J. Davis, Esq., who was appointed by Governor Thayer to serve until the general election, in November following. Mr. Clarkson was elected by a decisive majority and served until March, 1891, when he resigned the position.

In 1891 an act was passed by the Legislature providing for three additional judges for this district, on account of the remarkable increase of business, and the bar again convened for the purpose of making nominations for judges, three to comply with the provisions of the act, and one to fill the vacancy caused by the resignation of Judge Clarkson. The meeting was held March 28, 1891, when Herbert J. Davis, Frank J. Irvine, Lee S. Estelle and Arthur N. Ferguson were chosen, and on the 31st of March they were appointed by Governor Boyd. In November, 1891, the following judges were elected by vote of the people: George W. Doane, M. R. Hopewell, C. R. Scott, A. N. Ferguson, W. W. Keysor, Frank Irvine, H. J. Davis.

As illustrative of the growth of the legal business of this county, it may be stated that the first printed docket, dated November, 1871, contained 409 cases; the docket of the June term following contained 321 cases; that of the June term, 1880, contained 418 cases; the docket of the May term, 1888, contained 1,389 cases; and that of the February term, 1891, contained 2,407 cases. In these dockets only civil cases appear, no attention being paid to printing the docket of the criminal calendar.

In the first printed bar docket for this county, appear the names of fifty-six attorneys, while on that of the docket for the February term, 1891, are the names of 350 attorneys.

The space allotted will allow personal mention of but a few of the large number of attorneys now in active practice, and the writer has been under the necessity of con-

## DOUGLAS COUNTY BAR MEMBERSHIP.

fining himself to such of the older class of lawyers as, by their years and prominence in the profession, would seem to require more than a mere mention in the general list.

The following is the present membership of the Douglas County bar, June 1, 1892:

Abbott, L. I.; Adams, Ben. S.; Adams, Isaac; Ambrose, Geo. W.; Anderson, Gustave; Anderson, W. A.; Andrews, I. R.; Anstine, S. R.

Bachelor, I. C.; Baker, Ben. S.; Baird, William; Baldridge, Howard H.; Baldwin, Arthur E.; Baldwin, Charles A.; Balliet, C. H.: Barnard, J. C.; Bartholomew, W. O.; Bartlett, Edmund M.; Baxter, Irving F.; Beckett, William D.; Beekman, W. H.; Benson, H. H.; Benson, N. I.; Bertrand, George E.; Bevins, Andrew; Birkett, Charles P.; Blair, Joseph H.; Bloom, Simeon; Boucher, J. J.; Bowman, G. G.; Bradley, Edgar S.; Bradley, L. H.; Breck, C. H.; Breckenridge, C. F.; Breckenridge, R. W.; Breen, John P.; Brodérick, T. S.; Brogan, F. A.; Brome, H. C.; Brown, Charles H.; Brown, George F.; Bryant, James S.; Burbank, B. G.; Burgner, John Q.; Burnham, Leavitt.

Calder, George O.; Capek, Thomas; Carr, James W.; Carr, John L.; Carroll, W. J.; Cartan, D. L.; Cathers, John T; Cavanagh, J. A.; Charlton, Paul; Chase, Champion S.; Christofferson, George; Churchill, A. S.; Clair, W. J.; Clapp, Charles E.; Clark, C. H.; Clarkson, J. R.; Cobb, Silas; Cochran, B. F.; Cochran, H. E.; Congdon, Isaac E.; Connell, W. J.; Cooley, Julius Smith; Cooper, George W.; Copeland, L. B.; Cornish, Edward J.; Corson, W. A.; Cowherd, William M.; Cowin, John C.; Covell, George W.; Cralle, C. K.; Crane, Herbert; Crane, Thomas D.; Crofoot, Lodowick F.; Cromelien, John F.; Crosby, S. M.; Crow, Joseph; Crow, William H.; Crowell, Edward; Curtis, W. S.

Daniels. Edward; Davis, H. J.; Davis, John P.; Day, Curtis L.; Day, George A.; Day, H. L.; De Bord, W. A.; DeFrance, W. H.; DeLamatre, C. W.; Detwiler, J. O.; Dick, R. A. L.; Dillon, John T.; Doane, George W.; Doane, William G.; Dolan, Bernard; Donovan, D.; Duffie, E. R.; Dunn, I. J.

Edgerton, J. W.; Elgutter, C. S.; Eller, J. W.; Elliott, Clarence D.; Elmer, W. D.; English, J. P.; Estabrook, H. D.; Estelle, Lee; Evans, J. W.

Farnsworth, E. T.; Fawcett, Jacob; Felker, W. S.; Ferguson, A. N.; Fitch, F. W.; Foster, W. A.; Fowler, C. A.; Fraser, A. A.; French, E. R.

Gannon, M. V.; Garton, A. E.; Gaylord, R. E.; Gilbert, George L; Giller, W. M.; Gilmore, George F.; Godwin, Parke; Goss, Charles A.; Green, Alex.

D.; Greene, C. J.; Gregory, D. D.; Griffith, J. C.; Grossman, J. H.; Gurley, William F.

Hale, L. F.; Hall, M. A.; Hall, R. S.; Haller, C. W.; Halligan, C. P.; Halligan, J. J.; Hamilton, James W.; Harrison, C H.; Harrigan, J. D.; Hawes, Pat. O.; Hawley, J. B.; Healey, Wm. E.; Heller, Frank; Helsley, Lee; Herdman, W. H.; Herdman, R. E. L.; Hitt, H. C.; Holden, S. E.; Holland, John S.; Holmes, Louis D.; Holsman, H. B.; Horton, Richard S.; Houder, J. W.; Howe, John D.; Hubbard, N. M.; Hunt, George J.; Hyde, M. D.

Ives, W. C.; Irvine, Frank; Irwin, H. B.

Jeffrey, George; Johnson, D. L.; Johnston, John W.

Kaempfer, Charles F.; Kaley, J. L.; Kauffman, E. N.; Keller, Charles B.; Kelly, W. R.; Kennedy, B. E. B.; Kennedy, Howard, Jr.; Kennedy, E. L.; Kent, L. H.; Keysor, W. W.

Lake, George B.; Lander, Dana S.; Lane, E. C.; Langdon, Martin; Lapsley, D. L.; Learned, M. L.; Ledwich, James; Lee, Charles C.; Legge, George; Lindsay, M. S.; Lunt, A. J.; Lytle, John W.

McCabe, James; McClanahan, A. A.; McCloud Imri L.; McCoy, F. L.; McCulloch, J. H.; McDuffie, Robert A.; McGilton, E. G.; McHugh, W. D.; McIntosh, James H.; McWilliams, H. L.; Macfarland, J. M.; Macomber, J. H; Mahoney, T. J.; Magney, George A.; Marple, C. H.; Maxwell, H. E.; Meikle, James B.; Mercer, D. H.; Merrow, D. W.; Miles, Charles V.; Minahan, T. B.; Montague, R. V.; Montgomery, C. S.; Montgomery, Eugene; Morearty, E. F.; Moriarty, J. T.; Morris, W. R.; Morris, L. M ; Morrow, M. Henry; Morsman, W. W.; Morton, James F.; Munn, F. E.; Murdock, A. H.; Murdock, L. H.

Nelson, William T.; Neville, James; Nevin, J. E.

O'Brien, George M., Jr.; O'Brien, Moses P.; O'Connell, Daniel; O'Connor, J. J.; Offutt, Charles; Ogden, Charles; O'Hollaren, F. C.; Olmsted, R. H.

Page, E. C.; Parish, J. W.; Parker, F. A.; Patrick, Robert W.; Pennock, Henry W.; Peart, W. L.; Perley, Lyman O.; Piatti, L J ; Pilcher, J. D.; Place, George H.; Points, J. J.; Pope, O. G.; Poppleton, A. J.; Poppleton, W. S.; Powell, Clinton N.; Powers, H. E.; Powers, James A.; Poynton, G. W.; Pratt, E. D., Jr.; Prichard, George A.; Pritchett, G. E.

Ransom, F. T.; Read, A. C.; Read, Guy R. C.; Redick, W. A.; Rich, Edson; Richards, David H.; Richardson, R. W.; Richmond, R. M.; Riley, A. K.; Ritchie, A. S.; Robbins, J. James; Robbins, Silas; Robertson, Bernard N.; Rogers, J. W.; Rood, E. S.;

Roudebush, J. W.; Rush, S. R.; Rutherford, G. A.

Saunders, W. A.; Schomp, John.; Scott, C. R.; Scott, E. H.; Scott, Edward Harlan; Sheean. J. B.; Shields, George W.; Shoemaker, W. S.; Simeral, E. W.; Simeral, William; Slabaugh, W. W.; Smith, Ed. P.; Smith, George S.; Smith, Howard B.; Smyth, C. J.; Stoddard, H. P.; Strawn, Wm. S.; Strickler, V. O.; Sturdevant, F. M.; Sturges, Hiram A.; St. Clair, L. E.; Sues, G. W.; Swartzlander, Albert; Swezey, Field W.; Switzler, Warren.

Talbott, John F.; Taylor, J. W.; TenEyck, W. B.; Thomas, B. F.; Thomas, Dexter L.; Thomas, E. E.; Thomas, E. G.; Thompson, H.; Thurston, John M.; Tiffany, F. B.; Tipton, J. G.; Tooley, T. J.; Townsend, George W.; Trauerman, Moses R.; Troup, A. C.; Tunnicliff, N. H.; Turkington, George E.; Tuttle, Charles F.

Van Dusen, J. H.; Van Etten, D.; Van Gilder, W. C.; Vinsonhaler, D. M.

Wakeley, A. C.; Wakeley, E.; Walker, Will I.; Wappich, W. F.; Ware, J. D.; Weaver, F. L.; Webster, John L.; Webster, John R.; Wessells, Frank W.; West, Joel W.; Wharton, J. C.; White, B. T.; White, John F.; Winter, Phil. E.; Wilcox, Seymour G.; Williams, John T.; Williams, William N.; Wittum, George F.; Wolcott, E. C.; Wood, E. C.; Woolson, J. L.; Woolworth, J. M.; Wright, L. R.

Yeiser, John O.

Of the members of the Douglas County bar, many have received distinction at the hands of the people, and also by appointment from the President of the United States. P. W. Hitchcock served as delegate to Congress in the territorial days. He was United States marshal for Nebraska, and served as United States senator for six years. Charles F. Manderson is now serving his second term in the United States Senate. William J. Connell has just concluded a term as congressman. John I. Redick was appointed one of the judges of New Mexico by President Grant. James W. Savage served several terms as one of the government directors of the Union Pacific Railway, by appointments from President Cleveland and President Harrison. Experience Estabrook, Silas A. Strickland, James Neville, and George E. Pritchett have each served as United States attorney for the district of Nebraska. Mr. Barnes, William H. Morris, and William Gaslin were elected judges of other districts in this State. Eleazer Wakeley, Experience Estabrook, James M. Woolworth, Clinton Briggs, Charles F. Manderson, George B. Lake, Isaac S. Hascall, John L. Webster, Silas A. Strickland, and Charles H. Brown were members of the constitutional conventions of 1871 and 1875. A. J. Poppleton, George Armstrong, Clinton Briggs, B. E. B. Kennedy, George H. Roberts, Charles H. Brown, and Champion S. Chase have served as mayors of the city. Watson B. Smith was for many years clerk of the United States Circuit and District Courts of Nebraska. Howard B. Smith and George I. Gilbert have each served as members of the fire and police commission of Omaha, by appointment from Governor Thayer.

Since the admission of Nebraska as a State, taking into account the large number of lawyers that have been in Omaha and are still residents of the city, there have not been as many deaths as one would at first imagine; but Clinton Briggs, Silas A. Strickland, E. F. Smythe, General George M. O'Brien and Judge James W. Savage have died. I mention these out of the number because of their particular prominence. The writer of this chapter can not forego passing some slight eulogy upon the character of Clinton Briggs, both as a lawyer and as a man. He was one of the most genial, pleasant-spoken gentlemen who ever traveled the streets of Omaha. He was everybody's friend. In a long and intimate acquaintance with him, the writer never knew him to speak ill of man or woman. He was, in fact, beloved by everybody. As a lawyer, he was consulted upon the gravest questions which have ever arisen in this State. His acquaintance extended to every county, and his advice was sought by men in every walk of life, in every part and section of the State of Nebraska. He was not an orator. He disliked talking to juries, but with his

pen and paper, in the solitude of his office, he could prepare an argument equal to any that was ever submitted to any court. He was deeply interested in the litigation which sprang up in the early seventies in Nebraska between the Union Pacific and the Burlington & Missouri River Railroad Companies and the counties in the State, in relation to the question of taxation of land obtained by those roads from the government to aid in their construction. A case had gone up from the State of Kansas, involving the rights of the counties of Kansas to tax the lands of the Kansas Pacific Railroad. The decision of the Supreme Court of the United States was against the right of taxation. Based upon that decision, the attorneys of the two roads in Nebraska filed a large number of bills, enjoining every county in the State through which these two roads ran, from collecting the taxes which had been assessed upon their lands. Judge Briggs, among others, was retained by the counties to aid in the defense of those suits. The case was tried before John F. Dillon in the Circuit Court of the United States, and, upon an appeal to the Supreme Court of the United States, Judge Briggs made the argument; the result of that argument, and the consideration given to it by that august tribunal, gives to Judge Briggs the high distinction of being the first man in the United States to cause the Supreme Court to reverse itself. Judge Briggs' biography will appear elsewhere in this book, and it is unnecessary for the writer to enter into any specific account of his character, or of minute details of his life. Judge Briggs had a large clientage in this city, where he was actively engaged in the practice of his profession from the year 1856 to the day of his death.

James W. Savage came to Omaha in April, 1867, having practiced law in the city of New York prior to the war; and, after having done honorable service as colonel of a regiment of New York cavalry, had gone to Mississippi to engage in the raising of cotton; and, finally, desiring to resume his profession, came here. The writer never will forget the first time that he met Judge Savage, which was two days after his arrival in the city. From that time until his death they were friends, and in a somewhat active professional life to both there never was any necessity of a written stipulation as to the conduct of any law suit. His term upon the bench, of seven years, was important, in that he was the first judge in this district under the constitution of 1875, and many questions arose before him which were new, and which had not been passed upon by the Supreme Court. He was painstaking and patient as a judge, always pleasant and affable, and very considerate, especially of the feelings of younger men at the bar. The full history of Judge Savage's life is written elsewhere. The writer, at the memorial services held by the bar at his death, took occasion to speak of him:

"It is a great mistake to think that the best thoughts of man find utterance in human language. They come to us all in silent meditations and adoration, and no ear ever hears, and no heart is ever gladdened, except the heart of Him who is the Father of us all. The nature of Savage was spiritual, earnest, highly poetic and sympathetic; and, if the incandescent light of the past could be turned on, the glow would reveal that the unuttered thoughts of him we mourn were far brighter than any of those which have pleased us when we heard them. Savage was a copyist. Did you ever view the paintings of the old masters, side by side of which hung the copy? Go, look, if you never have, and observe that, while the old is perfect and massive, the new, touched by a master hand as well, is resplendent with roseate hues and a newer life, touched with the ever present. In such a sense he was a copyist. His mind was stored with the lore of the masters of literature. He made large drafts upon them, but what he brought to us from them was tinctured with a newer life and a holier purpose.

"'Noise and heat are born of earth, and die with time;
The soul, like God, its source and seat, is solemn, still, silent, sublime.'

"So with our brother."

Silas A. Strickland was a native of the State of Ohio, and, in the early days, under Judge Ferguson, served as a clerk of the District Court of this district. His residence was at Bellevue, which was at that time in Douglas County. He served in the Legislature of the Territory for many terms. He was an important factor in the legislative assemblies. He always fought against Omaha and for Bellevue becoming the capital of this State. Upon the breaking out of the war, General Strickland entered as a private of the First Nebraska Infantry and was soon promoted to adjutant, and resigned in 1862. He was then mustered in as lieutenant-colonel of the Fiftieth Ohio Volunteer Infantry, and was afterwards, in 1865, promoted brevet brigadier-general. He was a distinguished officer and served with credit to himself and his country. Upon the admission of Nebraska as a State, he was appointed by General Grant as United States attorney for this district and returned to Omaha with his family, which consisted of his wife and one child, who still survive him, and are residents of this city. General Strickland served as United States attorney for four years. In politics he was an ardent, hard-working Republican; he was a man who was always a friend to those who had befriended him. No more genial gentleman ever graced this bar; and no one was ever listened to with keener delight than was General Strickland. He was an impassioned orator, and after his retirement from the office of United States attorney his practice was confined almost exclusively to criminal business. As an illustration of his style the writer remembers a defense made by him of a criminal in the District Court of the United States for Nebraska, but the character of the offense is forgotten; but, when General Strickland had completed his argument and left the court room, the writer, together with General Manderson, picked up a sheet of foolscap upon which were entered in the general's handwriting the heads of his argument. The face of the sheet of foolscap was covered with his notes, in the logical order of the facts, as presented; and, ending up in large letters in lead pencil, underscored, were these words, "then a blaze of glory;" and Strickland might be called a "blaze of glory" whenever he was at his best. The effect of those words can be imagined better than described. General Strickland died in this city some twelve years or more ago, and his memory is still fresh among those who knew him.

Edwin F. Smythe was a native of New York and came to Omaha in the early seventies. He married the only daughter of the late Jesse Lowe, who is mentioned elsewhere as the first mayor of the city. In many respects Mr. Smythe was a remarkable man. He was in no sense a student, but his intuitive perception of the law was very great. He had a fine, retentive memory and a great adaptability to the circumstances with which he was surrounded. It is no slur upon other members of the profession to say that there is no lawyer who has ever practiced at this bar who had the number of clients that Mr. Smythe had. By his genial nature, and right adaptation to the circumstances, he had a large circle of friends and acquaintances, who, notwithstanding the vicissitudes of his life, never deserted him. He was a friend to everybody and everybody was his friend. He died in the prime of life, leaving a wife and one daughter.

General George M. O'Brien was an Irishman by birth, and served in the army of the late rebellion as brigadier general. His service was mostly confined to the western territory, but that service was an honorable one to him and a credit to his country. In

1866 he commenced the practice of law in Omaha, and continued until his death in 1885. Mr. O'Brien was a painstaking lawyer and had the confidence of a large clientage. He was a great friend and admirer of General Logan, and the writer remembers that the death of the lamented Logan was learned in Omaha on Sunday night. General O'Brien then heard of his death and returned to his home greatly shocked and depressed at the death of his favorite general. Very soon thereafter he was taken sick. He said to his wife when first taken, "Mother, I am called." General O'Brien was held in esteem by a large circle of friends and acquaintances, and died in the prime of his life, leaving a large family; his two sons, Moses P. and George M. O'Brien, succeeding him as lawyers in his practice, and are now prospering beyond most young men of their years.

Hon. James M. Woolworth has been a resident of Omaha since the 31st of October, 1856. He was born in Onondaga County, New York, in 1829, and was educated at Hamilton College, graduating with distinction in 1849. He was admitted to the bar two years before locating here, and has followed that pursuit from the date of his admission. He served as the first city attorney of Omaha, and was also a member of the Legislature in the territorial days, and was a member of the Constitutional Convention of 1871. In 1873 he was the Democratic nominee for chief justice, but the overwhelming Republican majority which characterized Nebraska in those days prevented the election of any of the Democratic candidates. He has been prominently identified with the advancement of the interests of the Episcopal Church in this city, and was for a quarter of a century a vestryman of Trinity Church. He contributed generously to the erection of Trinity Cathedral, but soon after its completion severed his connection with that society, and organized the All Saints' Church Society, bearing a very heavy portion of the financial obligations connected therewith, and taking an active part in the church management. For several years he has held the position of chancellor of the diocese of Nebraska; is a trustee of Racine College, Wisconsin, and of Brownell Hall, in Omaha, which former institution conferred the degree of LL. D. upon him, in 1875. He was one of the projectors of the Union Stock-yards Company, one of the original trustees of the South Omaha Land Syndicate, and is a director of the South Omaha Land Company, counsel of the Stockyards Company, and a director of the First National Bank. His professional practice has been for many years confined to important cases, and, as a chancery lawyer, he enjoys the distinction of standing at the head of his profession in the West. He has been identified with many important cases in which the Union Pacific Railroad Company was a party, notably the legal battle which resulted in transferring the "initial point" of the Union Pacific Road from the Nebraska to the Iowa side of the Missouri River. Mr. Woolworth has always held large real estate interests in this city, which have contributed to make him one of the wealthy men of Omaha.

General Experience Estabrook, the first United States Attorney for Nebraska, appointed by President Pierce, came to Omaha in April, 1855, from Geneva Lake, Wisconsin. During the summer of 1855, he brought his family, consisting of Mrs. Estabrook, a daughter Augusta, now Mrs. Robert Clowry, and son, Henry D., a prominent member of the Douglas County bar. General Estabrook was born in Lebanon, New Hampshire, April 30, 1813, and just previous to coming to Nebraska filled the position of attorney general of Wisconsin, thus being a member of two administrations in the conduct of public affairs, in speaking of which, recently, he said that he had learned upon investigation that of all of the officials forming those administrations he was the only one yet living. In 1855 he helped General Curtis prepare the first bill for a Pacific railroad charter which was passed by any legislative body, being the bill passed by the Nebraska Legislature, in February, 1855. The draft of this measure was made in the office of Dr. Lowe, then receiver of the land office in Council Bluffs. General Estabrook was retained as attorney by the Council Bluffs & Nebraska Ferry Company, and, in part consideration of his services, was given the block upon which he has resided for thirty years, bounded by Chicago, Cass, Sixteenth and Seventeenth Streets, now valued at over $300,000. He was a member of the Constitutional Convention of 1871, and of 1875, and has always taken, until recent years, a lively interest in State politics, though never in any sense an office seeker. He has been recognized during all of his residence in Nebraska as a lawyer of decided ability, though he has not made the efforts to distinguish himself at the bar which have characterized many of his associates in that profession who located here at an early period.

Hon. Andrew J. Poppleton, one of Omaha's pioneers, located here October 13, 1854. He was born at Troy, Michigan, July 24, 1830, graduating from Union College of Schenectady, New York, in July, 1851. In October, 1852, he was admitted to the practice of law by the Supreme Court of Michigan, and soon after entered upon the practice of that profession in Detroit, which pursuit he has followed during all of his residence in this city. He was a member of the first territorial Legislature, which assembled January 16, 1855, and also of the sessions of 1857 and 1858. The location of the territorial capital was a subject of paramount importance to be considered by the first Legislature, and it was only by the most careful management on the part of the Omaha members, of whom Mr. Poppleton was the leader, that this city secured the prize, by a majority of one vote. His services in this connection are more particularly referred to elsewhere in these pages. In 1858, Mr. Poppleton was elected mayor of Omaha, and in 1867, and again in 1868, was the choice of the Democratic party of Nebraska for congressman; but the Republicans, being in the majority, succeeded in defeating the Democratic nominees. December 3, 1863, he was appointed attorney for the Union Pacific Railroad, which position he retained until 1888. During this period he had charge of the company's interests in litigation in Nebraska, Colorado, Wyoming, Kansas, Utah, Idaho, Montana, Oregon and Iowa, appearing frequently in cases before the Supreme Court at Washington. His connection with the hearing in that tribunal of the vexed question of the eastern terminus of the Union Pacific Railroad is set out in detail in the chapter relating to the location of the Union Pacific bridge. Mr. Poppleton has always stood at the head of the Nebraska bar, and is widely known for his ability as a public speaker, though he has confined himself exclusively to the practice of his profession. In 1879, he represented, in the United States Court here, a party of Ponca Indians who appealed to that court for protection in certain legal rights then, for the first time in the history of this country, claimed by the red man. The questions involved were novel and, of course, with no precedent to guide in their determination. In this litigation, Mr. Poppleton attracted national attention from all classes of people, and succeeded in putting the Indians upon a higher plane, with respect to their relations with the government, than they had ever before occupied. This service was rendered a defenceless people, without hope of fee or reward, though it involved much hard labor projected into a life already one of unusual activity and mental strain. In 1887, the degree of LL. D. was conferred upon Mr. Poppleton in recognition of his unusual attainments in a literary way. Upon resigning the position of general attorney of the Union Pacific, it was Mr. Poppleton's inten-

tion to refrain from active pursuits; but the charms of his profession were not to be resisted, and, when he was offered the position of city attorney by Mayor Cushing, in January, 1890, he accepted, to the decided satisfaction of all classes of Omaha people, who felt that their interests could not be in better hands in litigations in which the city might be a party.

Hon. John R. Meredith, for many years a prominent lawyer of this city, was born at Gettysburg, Pennsylvania, April 15, 1820, but soon after moved with his parents to Pittsburg. He used to say, in a joking way, that his grandfather was in the revolutionary war, his father in that of 1812, and he in the war of the rebellion, Mr. Meredith having been one of the guards at the White House in the early days of 1861, sleeping beside General Hunter, on the floor of the east room. A certificate of this service was afterwards sent him, and is now in the possession of the family. Mr. Meredith secured a classical education, in spite of financial difficulties, and was admitted to the practice of law at Steubenville, Ohio, in 1848, where he served for some time as prosecuting attorney, and while filling this position was successful in a famous criminal case, where the prisoner was defended by Edwin M. Stanton. He located in Omaha with his family in 1858. In 1867, Mr. Stanton, then Secretary of War, telegraphed Mr. Meredith at Omaha, as follows: "You are appointed on the board of examiners at West Point." But this honor Mr. Meredith declined, and about this time Salmon P. Chase wrote him that he would be appointed judge of the first district of Nebraska, if he would accept, but this position was also declined. He was urged for the chief justiceship of the territory by the lawyers of both parties, and it is known that Mr. Lincoln had determined upon his appointment, but was overruled in that matter by the influence of Mrs. Lincoln and her friends, and the place was given to William Pitt Kellogg, then

colonel of an Illinois regiment. After the death of Mr. Meredith, October 21, 1880, there was found among his papers a letter from Mr. Stanton, stating that he would gladly appoint Colonel John M. Thayer, of the First Nebraska Infantry, a brigadier-general, as a personal favor to him. About 1865, he formed a law partnership with George W. Doane, which continued for five years, during which period Mr. Meredith was for some time collector of internal revenue for this district. In the fall of 1871 he was stricken with paralysis, which necessitated his retirement from active business. He was an elder in the Second Presbyterian Church (now known as the First) and contributed liberally toward the erection of the building at the corner of Dodge and Seventeenth Streets. A man of winning, lovable character, Mr. Meredith was universally esteemed. He was active in all good works, honorable in all his dealings, and of the highest Christian character. December 30, 1852, he was married to Miss Annie M. Collier, of Philadelphia.

Judge George W. Doane located at Decatur, Nebraska, April 18, 1857, and three years later moved to Fort Calhoun, coming to Omaha in the fall of 1864. He represented Burt, Washington and Sarpy Counties at the fifth session of the legislative assembly, and Douglas County at the twelfth. He also represented this county in the State Senate at the regular session of 1881 and the special session of 1882. In August, 1857, after a residence of but four months in the territory, he was elected district attorney of this judicial district, and re-elected in 1859. In 1865, he was elected prosecuting attorney of Douglas County, and during the term prosecuted and convicted Ottway G. Baker for the murder of Woolsey D. Higgins, being the second conviction under which a legal execution took place in Douglas County. In 1887 he was elected one of the judges of the third judicial district for a term of four years. He was re-elected in

November, 1891, for four years. Mr. Doane while at the bar always convinced the court and opposite counsel that there was a lawyer trying his side of the case. As a judge, he is always prompt in attendance, decisive in his judgment and makes a model trial judge.

Judge George B. Lake was born in Saratoga County, New York. He came to Omaha November, 1857, from Elyria, Ohio, and has made this city his home since that date. He has had various professional partnerships in the meantime, the first being with A. J. Poppleton, under the firm name of Poppleton & Lake; the second was with George I. Gilbert, as Lake & Gilbert; the third, with Charles H. Brown, under the style of Lake & Brown; the fourth, with James W. Hamilton, formed in January, 1888; and the fifth and present, being styled Lake, Hamilton & Maxwell, Henry E. Maxwell, a son of Chief Justice Maxwell, of the Supreme Court, having been recently admitted to the firm membership. Upon the admission of Nebraska to the Union, Mr. Lake was elected one of the three judges then composing the Supreme Court, the State being divided into three judicial districts, and he was assigned to the district which included Douglas County, with nine others, and held in Omaha, in April, 1867, the first term of court held in Nebraska under State government. In 1870 he was elected chief justice for a term of four years, and four years later was again elected, drawing by lot the short term of two years, as the result of which he became chief justice for that period. In 1877, he was elected associate justice for a term of six years, under the constitution of 1875, the last two years of which term he was the presiding judge. He declined re-nomination in 1883, and since the first of January, 1884, has been engaged in private practice in this city. He has always taken an active interest in matters of public concern. For years he served with credit to himself and advantage to the city upon the school board, under the old system, and was elected a regent of the high school, in 1871. He was four times elected a member of the territorial Legislature, and represented Douglas County in the constitutional convention of 1871. He was appointed by Judge William Pitt Kellogg to assist Prosecuting Attorney Charles H. Brown in the trial of Cyrus D. Tator, the first man legally executed in Douglas County, and as judge of this district tried and sentenced to death Ottway G. Baker, the second criminal hanged in this county by process of law. Judge Lake has four children: George E., Carrie J. (Mrs. Jay Morton), Mary (Mrs. Charles Deuel) and Fred.

Hon. Phineas W. Hitchcock located in Omaha in 1857 and engaged in the real estate and insurance business, and was, soon after his arrival here, admitted to the bar, but never engaged in active practice. His native place was Lebanon, New York, his birthday being November 30, 1831. He graduated in 1855 at Williams College, Massachusetts. Mr. Hitchcock was a delegate from Nebraska to the Chicago convention which nominated Mr. Lincoln, in 1860, and was appointed United States marshal for the territory in 1862, and held that office two years. In 1864 he was elected a delegate to Congress. In 1867 he was appointed Surveyor General of Nebraska, and was elected to the United States Senate in 1871. He was married to Miss Annie Monell in 1857. His only surviving son, Gilbert M. Hitchcock, is the editor and chief owner of the *World-Herald*, of this city. As a lawyer he never took front rank, but as a politician he was a success, and one of the chief elements of that success was that he never forgot or forsook a friend.

Hon. Charles H. Brown was elected mayor of Omaha in 1867, six years after first becoming a resident of the city. His early life in the West was spent on the plains and in aiding in the construction of the Union

Pacific Railroad. He was elected prosecuting attorney of Douglas County in 1862, and was re-elected in 1863. In 1864 he was elected a member of the constitutional convention and a member of the territorial House of Representatives, being re-elected to the Legislature in 1865, in which year he was also elected a member of the city council and re-elected in 1866. In 1875, he was a member of the convention which drafted our present State constitution, and in 1876 was elected to the State Senate, re-elected in 1878, and again in 1882. While prosecuting attorney of this county, he convicted Cyrus Tator of the crime of murder, this being the first case where a man was legally executed in the territory. Mr. Brown was born at Stephentown, New York, and was admitted to the bar of New York in 1860. In 1884 he was the Democratic nominee for Congress, and was defeated by 650 votes, in a district of about eight thousand Republican majority. As mayor, Mr. Brown was ex-officio justice of the peace, and as such did the entire magistrate business of the city, then containing ten thousand people. It is a remarkable fact that, during the year he held this office, trying a multitude of cases, both civil and criminal, he had but one case appealed from his court, and that was dismissed before reaching a decision in the district court. Mr. Brown has a logical, judicial mind, but, having no particular ambition in that direction, and no need to struggle for the almighty dollar, he has kept himself in later years, especially, from advancement at the bar. He retired from active practice some years since.

Hon. George I. Gilbert located in Omaha in 1857, and the following year was elected city attorney. In 1860 he formed a law partnership with George B. Lake, and the following year was elected prosecuting attorney for Douglas County; in 1862 he located in Washington Territory, and in 1863 was appointed by the territorial Legislature as probate judge of a county which embraced the southern half of what is now the State of Idaho. During the five years he spent in Washington, he was largely interested in mining. In 1867, he went to Chicago and engaged in the commission business as a member of the firm of Gilbert, Wolcott & Company. In 1869 he returned to Omaha, and in April, 1875, formed a partnership with B. E. B. Kennedy, which still exists. He was appointed by Governor Thayer, in 1887, a member of the fire and police commission, which position he still holds. He was married several years ago to Miss Cornelia Richardson, daughter of the late Governor O. D. Richardson.

Elmer S. Dundy was appointed judge of the Supreme Court of Nebraska Territory by Mr. Lincoln, in 1863, and again on the 20th day of January, 1864, which office he held until the admission of Nebraska as a State in 1867. In April, 1868, he was commissioned judge of the United States District Court for the district of Nebraska by President Johnson, and has held that office ever since; and now in his old age he is enjoying life and still holding court nearly the year around. Judge Dundy for many years resided at Falls City, Richardson County, Nebraska, but some ten years ago removed to Omaha, where he with his family still continues to reside. Judge Dundy has made an able, upright judge; has administered the law, as he has seen it, in a dignified and impartial way; and is one of the most pleasant and affable gentlemen to associate with that there is within the boundaries of the State. A man who is sentenced for a crime by Judge Dundy feels as though a favor has been conferred upon him, from the urbane manner and kindly spirit in which the sentence is pronounced.

Hon. B. E. B. Kennedy, who located in Omaha, September, 14, 1858, was born April 20, 1827, at Bolton, Vermont, He was admitted to the bar in 1853, and was married August 4, 1858, to Miss Frances Nims. He served as mayor two terms, being re-elected in 1863, and as city attorney in 1866 and 1867. He was a member of the house of Representatives, in 1864, and of the territorial council in 1865 and 1866. He served as a school director, under the old system, from 1864 to 1872, and was a member of the city council in 1862, and of the house of representatives in 1879. He has been a member of the normal school board of the State since June, 1872, and of the State fish commission since June, 1882. Mr. Kennedy has one son and two daughters, his youngest daughter being Mrs. Will. S. Poppleton. The writer can say of Mr. Kennedy that he is absolutely without stain in his private character, fair in his dealings with men generally, and in the trial of causes always open, winning no case by tricks, and earnest but not eloquent. His success has been in the domains of real estate and probate law; and he is withal a kindly, affable gentleman.

Judge Eleazer Wakeley came to Nebraska early in 1857 as associate justice of the territory under appointment of President Pierce, and was assigned to the third district, embracing all the northwestern portion of the territory, then unorganized into counties, with the exception of Washington and Burt, and a few others, and comprising an area of about three hundred and fifty thousand square miles. He first took up his residence in De Soto, then a promising young "city" in Washington County. He was re-appointed by President Buchanan, but, on the Republicans coming into power under President Lincoln, he returned to Wisconsin and resumed the practice of law at Madison, representing that district in the Legislature in 1866 and 1867, returning to Omaha in the last named year, where he at once entered upon the practice of his profession. In 1871 he was a member of the Nebraska constitutional convention, and in 1883 was appointed district judge of the third district by Governor Dawes, of the opposite political party, in deference to the unanimous application of the Douglas County bar, and that fall was elected for a term of four years, and at its expiration in 1887 was re-elected. Judge Wakeley was born at Homer, New York, in 1822, and was admitted to the bar in 1844, at Elyria, Ohio. In 1845, locating at Whitewater, Wisconsin, he served as representative in the Legislature in 1847 and as State senator in 1851 and 1855.

Judge Wakeley left Madison, Wisconsin, to return to Omaha, in November, 1867; and his reputation as a lawyer having been such, during his administration as judge in the territory, that within two weeks after his leaving Madison he was assisting Judge Doane in the trial of a contested and important jury case, so that he was not long in giving himself a status at the bar. From 1871 to 1878, he was the assistant attorney of the Union Pacific Railroad Company, having special charge of its Nebraska litigation, then very large and important. During all the years from 1867 to 1883, the time of his appointment as judge, he was very busy as a lawyer; and the reports, from the first to the fourteenth, opening with the January term, 1883, of the Supreme Court, contain many cases argued by him, embracing a vast range of subjects, including the law in relation to the service of process upon managing agents of corporations, questions of corporation law, grading taxes, the right to enter salt lands under the statutes of the United States, the right of husband's courtesy in real estate, the right to forfeit land grants of the Union Pacific corporation, the liability of stockholders in railroad corporations, the liability of sureties for tort of an officer. and the right to levy upon property in the hands of an administrator for taxes. All these questions, and many more, were litigated by him in the courts of the State. In the United States Circuit and Supreme Courts, he was engaged very largely in the preparation of arguments which were made in cases involving various rights of the Union Pacific Rail-

road Company. Among these, were the cases against Durant and the Wyoming Coal Company and Polk County, the right of the Union Pacific Railroad Company to mortgage its land grant, as well as many others of national importance.

Judge Wakeley has a fund of humor in his composition, much more than one would imagine, to see him administering equity law from the bench. He is also very quick in repartee. When he and Judge John I. Redick, noted for his ready wit and keen hits, met, as they frequently did in contested cases, they seldom failed to give and take sharp thrusts, and he who had the last word was apt to get the best of the encounter. Several such passages at arms are current in local legal gossip. As illustrating Judge Wakeley's fund of humor I give the following very spicy correspondence, relating to that subject which is the bane of every lawyer's life, that of borrowing books:

"OMAHA, September 13, 1875.
"HON. E. WAKELEY, CITY.

"*Dear Judge:*— I hold your receipt for Abbott's Third National Digest, which was taken by you some four months ago. If you have no further use for the book I should like it. I often wish to consult it, but still, if you are not through reading it, I can get along without it.

"Yours truly, G. W. AMBROSE."

"LAW OFFICE OF E. WAKELEY,
"OMAHA, September 14, 1875.

"*Dear Ambrose:*— I herewith comply, under protest, with your untimely request that I should return your book.

"You remark that you have held my receipt for it some four months. This is probably true. But if you will read the statute of limitation of Nebraska, you will observe that it does not bar a claim, under any written instrument, until the lapse of five years, leaving you about four years and eight months still to reclaim your book. Why, then, this undue precipitancy?

"Will you permit me, as a searcher after legal knowledge, respectfully to inquire if you can refer me to any respectable authority requiring the borrower of a law book to return it within four months? I have read a large number of cases in my time, and I do not remember one in which such a proposition is advanced, although there may be an occasional dictum to the effect that the borrower is under a moral obligation to return the book as soon as he becomes able to buy one for himself.

"Considered upon principle and without reference to authority, how would the proposition stand? Is it reasonable to suppose that a man engaged in a somewhat active practice can find time in four months to read through all the books he borrows, besides perusing the daily papers, answering dunning letters, and keeping up with the Beecher-Tilton literature? That case, you will remember, was going on for some two months after I got your volume.

"You remark that you often wish to consult the book. I highly commend that resolution. You would certainly find it beneficial to occasionally read some law, and, if you should become accustomed to it, you would find it comparatively easy; only, don't overdo it at first.

"The only thing I object to in that paragraph is an implication that I would not allow you to consult the book at my office. This is unjust. I have never refused the owner of a book that privilege, even when it has occasioned inconvenience to myself.

"In conclusion, permit me to suggest that, if you really can not afford to keep law books, for other practitioners to use, it would be a philanthropic thing for you to sell them to some one who can.

"Gratefully yours,
"E. WAKELEY."

Judge John I. Redick came from Lansing, Michigan, to Omaha, arriving October 27, 1856. He was born in Wooster, Ohio,

July 29, 1828, and just previous to his locating here had been admitted to the bar, and in February, 1857, formed a partnership with James G. Chapman, under the firm name of Redick & Chapman, which partnership was not of long duration. In 1859, he entered into partnership with Clinton Briggs, which continued for ten years. In 1887, he formed a partnership with W. J. Connell, which existed for about a year. In 1876, he was appointed by President Grant United States judge for New Mexico, which position he retained for a year and a half, and then served the Union Pacific Railroad Company, as attorney, at Denver, Colorado, for one year. In January, 1887, he located at Los Angeles, California, where he became actively engaged in real estate transactions, and served for nearly two years as president of the Southern California National Bank. In the fall of 1889, he returned to Omaha, and will make it his permanent home. He has been largely interested in real estate in this city since the date of locating here, and has thereby amassed a handsome fortune. In 1869, he was one of the seven men who built the Omaha & Northwestern Railroad, and was also one of the builders of the Grand Central Hotel. He was chairman of the Nebraska delegation to the Baltimore convention which nominated Lincoln and Johnson, and also chairman of the delegation from this State which nominated Grant for his second term, at the Philadelphia convention. Mr. Redick was first married to Miss Mary E. Digby, in 1855, of Pittsburgh, Pennsylvania, his wife dying in this city, in 1865. Two years later he married Miss Mary E. May of Omaha. He has seven sons, Charles R., William A., John I., Jr., Clarke, Chatham, George M., and Elmer. No man at this bar ever enjoyed a more prominent place as a jury lawyer than Mr. Redick. He had his own original methods in the trial of causes, and great tact in the presentation of the facts to a jury, and was very generally successful, with his partner, Judge Briggs, to look after the law of the case.

Charles P. Birkitt, Esq., is one of Omaha's oldest lawyers, locating here June 1, 1856, coming from New York. He served three terms in the city council, and was extensively engaged for a number of years in the practice of his profession. In 1872 he was appointed agent for the Ponca Indians, at that time established on their reservation in Dakota, twenty-seven miles below Fort Randall. This responsible position he filled for three years, and for several years thereafter was established in Washington City. Mr. Birkitt was married in Omaha, in 1860, to Miss Mary A. Neale, and has three children living.

Charles A. Baldwin was born near Utica, New York, October 8, 1825. Seven years later the family removed to Geauga County, Ohio, where he assisted his father in clearing a farm in the woods. At the age of eighteen, after receiving a good common school education, he entered the Western Reserve Academy, at Farmington, Ohio, a branch of the famous Oberlin College, where he attended during three summers, teaching school the intervening winters. In 1846, his health not being good, he abandoned his plan for a collegiate course and returned to his father's farm. Taking up the study of law, he engaged in regular practice in 1854. In 1859, he located in Akron, Ohio, and formed a law partnership with General L. V. Bierce, who had a national reputation as a criminal lawyer, which fact aided in giving Mr. Baldwin a preference for that class of practice; and, for many years after locating in Omaha, which event occurred in November, 1868, he devoted himself almost entirely to the defense of persons charged with criminal offenses. The first case of that character with which he was connected here was that of the State against Hernandez, indicted for an assault upon his wife with intent to kill. The defendant was a member of Selden Irwin's dramatic troupe then, in November, 1868, performing at the Academy of Music. Mrs. Hernandez was a sister of Mrs. Irwin, and a ten-year-old daughter of the defendant, who was an important witness for the State on the trial, afterwards became the wife of the famous John Dillon. Various circumstances combined to make this case one of unusual prominence, and it proved an excellent introduction to Mr. Baldwin in a professional way. Later on, his practice called him into other portions of the State, appearing for the defense in notable criminal cases in North Platte, in Dakota County, in Custer County and elsewhere. He successfully defended James Davis and wife, of this city, who were indicted for the killing of Jerry McCormick, a western cattleman, who assaulted them with a revolver; and, in 1889, he assisted John C. Cowin in the defense of Lizzie Beechler, who was tried for the killing of Harry King, at the Paxton Hotel, in this city. In 1870, he assisted United States District Attorney Strickland in prosecuting four Pawnee Indians for the murder of Edward McMurty in the unorganized territory in the western part of the State, May 8, 1869, when a conviction was secured; but Judge Dillon afterwards decided that the United States Court had no jurisdiction of the case. The prisoners were then tried in the district court at Lincoln, but on account of the impossibility of securing the attendance of witnesses they were finally discharged from custody. A very important civil case with which Mr. Baldwin was connected was that of Franklin Robinson vs. A. D. Jones, et al., involving the title to Omaha real estate, valued at $200,000, recently decided in favor of Mr. Jones, whom Mr. Baldwin represented, having pitted against him at various stages of the case, Judge Doane (previous to his going upon the bench), A. J. Poppleton, John W. Lytle and Patrick O. Hawes. Mr. Baldwin was married in 1848 to Miss M. Isidore Gridley, who, by the way, was a schoolmate of Mrs. Garfield, widow of President Garfield. Mr. and Mrs. Baldwin have had three children, one dying in infancy. The others are Leona, now Mrs. Frederick Mertzheimer, and Frank, who died at Denver, in 1883, while in the employ of the Union Pacific Railway Company.

George W. Ambrose has been a resident of Omaha for nearly a quarter of a century, engaged in all these years in the active practice of his profession. He is now upwards of fifty years of age, and, while he is the writer of this chapter, the bar will perhaps excuse that he personally mentions himself very slightly, as a full history of his life is written by another hand and printed in its proper place in this volume. Mr. Ambrose has been connected from the early history of this State with the important questions that have been determined by the courts. In all questions of taxation and constitutional law, he has been in a great degree the forerunner, and has been connected with cases in which these questions have been definitely settled and determined by the Supreme Court. He was the city attorney and argued the case on behalf of the city in the case of Bradshaw against Omaha, reported in I Nebraska Reports, which was argued at the first term of the Supreme Court held in the State; afterwards, the case of Turner against Althause, involving the same question, was decided and is reported in VI Nebraska Reports. The report of the two cases shows that Mr. Ambrose enjoys the distinction of being upon both sides of the same question in the two cases and beaten in both instances, which was no surprise to him.

John L. Webster has been an active practitioner at this bar for the last twenty years or more, and, as a lawyer, citizen or friend, is worthy a place in any community. Mr. Webster, upon whatever subject he may be called to address the courts, is always prepared. He makes a very fine legal argument. He is a student of books, and he draws very largely for what he has to say upon what is contained in the books which he reads. Mr. Webster, as well as others who are in this personal mention, are more accurately and thoroughly described in their proper place in this book. Mr. Webster has lately rendered great service to the State in his advocacy of the question of high license, as against prohibition, and he is entitled to deserving mention among those who fought a very severely contested battle in the late election. He was selected as one of the four delegates at large to the Republican national convention at Minneapolis.

John M. Thurston removed to Omaha from the State of Wisconsin, in 1869, where he commenced the practice of law. He served acceptably in the city council of the city and as city attorney, and was elected to serve a term as a member of the lower house of the Legislature of the State. He was soon thereafter selected by Mr. Poppleton as the assistant general attorney of the Union Pacific Railroad Company with headquarters at Omaha. Mr. Thurston at a very early date established his reputation as an orator; and, upon the retirement of Mr. Poppleton as general attorney for the Union Pacific, Mr. Thurston was selected by the management to that position, and is now the general solicitor of that great corporation. Mr. Thurston has been an important factor in the trial of cases in this State, one of which was the great criminal case of the State against Olive, who, with others, was indicted for the burning of three men in the western portion of the State, and the trial of which was transferred to Adams County. The killing of these men caused such a feeling in the State that the Legislature passed a special act authorizing the governor to appoint counsel to assist in the prosecution. Governor Nance appointed Mr. Thurston as one of such counsel. The defendants were convicted before a jury, but were released upon an appeal to the Supreme Court. Mr. Thurston's connection with the case ceased after the trial in the lower court, and, although he has never been specially engaged in the criminal practice, he has defended fourteen men for murder, and secured acquittal of them all. In some instances, his clients have been convicted upon first trial, but the verdicts in every instance were set aside, as notably that of Lauer, at Omaha, for the murder of his wife. Mr. Thurston has had equally good success in the civil branch of the law. He was a member from Nebraska of the Chicago Republican national convention, in 1888, and as temporary presiding officer of that convention made a national reputation as an orator, which he now enjoys, and always, whether at the bar or on the lecture platform, he acquits himself to the satisfaction of all his friends.

William J. Connell came to the city of Omaha as a young man and engaged as a clerk in the store of the old firm of Tootle & Maul. Afterwards, he took up the practice of law and was admitted to the bar, in 1870, and at once, by his indomitable push, made himself felt as a lawyer. Mr. Connell has had a marked experience at the bar. He has been extremely fortunate in the trial of his causes. He is well read, and is a hard fighter, and as city attorney of this city for a number of years has established a reputation as a lawyer of great ability. In 1888, he was elected as a representative from the first Congressional district a member of the lower house of Congress, and served for two years; having been defeated in a contest by his Democratic competitor, in the fall of 1890, and, as he has returned to the practice of his profession with his accustomed vigor, he will meet with undoubted success. He was again appointed city attorney for Omaha in January, 1892.

Judge H. J. Davis came to Omaha about ten years since and soon proved himself to be a lawyer of ability. He attracted the attention of Judge Savage, and in 1885 the latter took him into partnership, under

the firm name of Savage, Morris & Davis, Mr. Morris being a step-son of Judge Savage: the firm, as thus constituted, made a good working team. In 1889 Judge Davis accepted the nomination at the hands of the Republican party as its candidate for judge to fill the vacancy of Lewis A. Groff, who had resigned. Upon his nomination, Governor Thayer appointed him as judge of the district court, and he served in that capacity for a few months, having been defeated at the polls for election by Judge Joseph R. Clarkson. He then returned to his place in his old firm, where he continued until the death of Judge Savage, when the firm became Davis & Morris. Upon the creation of three new judges by the legislature of 1890, in obedience to the wish of the bar, he accepted a nomination at its hands, and in March, 1891, was appointed by Governor Boyd as one of the judges of the district court of this district, and elected by the people in November, 1891. Judge Davis, while upon the bench, has evinced qualities which go to make a good judge, and there is no doubt that, with the opportunity now presented to him, he will fulfill his ambition to become an excellent judge rather than a great lawyer.

Judge Arthur N. Ferguson is the son of Chief Justice Fenner Ferguson, the first judge appointed in the territory of Nebraska. He is about forty-nine years of age, and for the last twenty years has been a resident of the city of Omaha, where he has practiced his profession in a quiet, unostentatious way. Judge Ferguson, in March, was appointed by Governor Boyd one of the judges of the district court, to fulfill the requirements of the act of 1891. He was selected by the bar without any personal solicitation upon his part, but simply because of his calm, judicial temperament and his well-known upright character and his good standing as a citizen, as well as a lawyer. He was elected for four years, in November, 1891. Judge Ferguson married Miss Sears, a sister of Mrs. Andrew J. Poppleton, and his family reside in a comfortable, unpretentious home, in the northern part of the city, respected by all who know them.

Judge Lee S. Estelle served one term as judge of the District Court of Douglas County. Mr. Estelle, as prosecuting attorney for the third judicial district, established for himself a reputation as a criminal lawyer, and is very fond of the practice, and from choice was assigned the criminal docket. Since his retirement from the office of prosecuting attorney, and during the last six years, he has had to do with the defense of most of the important criminal cases that have been tried, and has uniformly been very successful. He is a good talker and a painstaking lawyer. Prior to his elevation to the bench he was the attorney of the school board of the city. Judge Estelle is a pleasant, affable gentleman, and has a great ambition to make his mark as a criminal lawyer, and he will have abundant opportunity to develop himself in that regard. He is about forty years of age, and has a quiet, pleasant home, where he resides with his wife and family, an honored husband and father. Judge Estelle was defeated for re-election in November, 1891, and has again resumed the practice of his profession.

Judge Lewis A. Groff came to Omaha about 1880 and at once entered into partnership with Mr. C. S. Montgomery. The firm soon established a reputation as collecting lawyers, and acquired a large and lucrative business in that line. In 1886, he was appointed one of the judges of the district court by Governor Thayer, which position he resigned in 1889 to accept that of commissioner of the general land office, tendered him by President Harrison. Judge Groff, while upon the bench, gave good satisfaction; but the labor was great and the pay small, and it was not long until it became apparent to himself, as well as his friends, that his health was failing him. As a commissioner of the general land office, Judge Groff established a great reputation throughout the entire country. He was a most valuable officer in that department, and especially to the settlers of the Northwest he has endeared himself; and all classes of people were sorry to know that his continued failure of health rendered it necessary for him to resign and seek another clime. Judge Groff is an honorable and upright man and an esteemed citizen, and Omaha regrets to lose him; but the loss of Omaha will be the gain of California, to which State he has now removed.

Hon. C. F. Manderson came to Omaha some twenty years since from the State of Ohio, and formed a partnership with the late Judge Savage, which partnership continued until Judge Savage went upon the bench, of which fact mention has been made elsewhere. His biography is written in its appropriate place in this book, and it is needless here to recur to his career as a soldier in the late war, or as senator of the United States. Mr. Manderson, soon after coming to Omaha, established a decided reputation as an orator. He is a pleasant, smooth speaker, having a fund of wit and sarcasm in his nature which he enjoys displaying, and he displays it to good advantage. He served a term of four years as city attorney and was an acceptable officer. If there is one thing that he enjoys more than another, it is telling a good story. He is an adept in that art. While at the bar in this city, he displayed great aptitude in the preparation and presentation of his cases to the jury.

Judge James Neville came to Omaha from the State of Illinois, having graduated from the law department of Michigan University; and, after having practiced law for some years, was appointed by General Grant, through the instrumentality of Senator Hitchcock, District Attorney of the United States for the district of Nebraska, which office he held for eight years. Upon the appointment of his successor, he returned to the bar, and was soon after appointed judge of the district court of this district, to succeed the late Judge Savage who had resigned from that position. Judge Neville held the office of judge for eight years and declined a re-election. He has amassed, in this city, a comfortable fortune, and is of that nature and disposition capable of enjoying easy life.

Hon. George E. Pritchett is a native of the State of New York; and came to Omaha about twenty years ago, and soon thereafter formed a partnership with Mr. J. S. Spaun, under the firm name of Spaun & Pritchett. Mr. Pritchett has served the city as city attorney; he was elected in 1876 one of the members of the Legislature in the lower house, and served his constituents acceptably. He was appointed by Grover Cleveland as United States District Attorney for the district of Nebraska, which office he held for some four years, and was succeeded by Benjamin S. Baker, upon the incoming of President Harrison's administration. Mr. Pritchett is one of the most thorough lawyers we have at the bar, and enjoys the confidence of a large clientage and has amassed considerable wealth. He is now mostly engaged in the business of looking after the legal affairs of the Omaha Street Railway Company and the Merchants National Bank.

Richard S. Hall is the son of Associate Justice Augustus Hall, and was five years of age at the time of the death of his father. Mr. Hall resided at Bellevue in this State with his mother, now Mrs. Stephen D. Bangs, until in his early manhood, when he came to Omaha and commenced reading law in the office of George W. Doane. He has been a practitioner for some fifteen years. He was formerly associated with John M. Thurston, as the junior partner. He is now the senior member of Hall, McCulloch & English. Judge McCulloch was formerly county judge of this county for two years, and the firm is considered one among the leading

firms of the city, and has acquired wealth and reputation in the practice of the law. Mr. Hall is now one of the attorneys for the Missouri Pacific Railway. He is an aggressive and hard fighter, and loves a good story as well as a good fee in a law suit.

The particulars of Mr. John C. Cowin's life appear elsewhere in this history. The writer has been associated with him from the first organization of the courts of this State, in 1867. He is a man of great native force of character, of great forensic ability, and he is in earnest in the prosecution or defense of his cases. One thing may always be said of John C. Cowin, and that is, he has never been known to forget the interests of his clients. As a prosecutor for four years in his early history, he established a reputation as an orator and as a lawyer. He has ever been a diligent student, and has had to do with very large interests in this city. His business has become very extensive, and he enjoys the trying of a good law suit as well to-day as he did a quarter of a century ago. Perhaps the bar will pardon the writer, but, whether it does or not, it is nevertheless true that, in the discussion by Mr. Cowin in what is known as the street car cases, in the circuit court of the United States, of the principle of exclusive privilege, which was asserted by the defendant street horse railway company, he displayed an ability and research that placed him in the front rank of lawyers in this country. The question is regarded by those who are at all conversant with the subject as one of the most difficult of solution in the whole range of subjects to which the courts have given any attention. In the contested election case of Thayer vs. Boyd, the argument made by Mr. Cowin, upon the question of who is a citizen of the United States in order to hold office within the State, the writer believes to be one of the most masterly discussions of that question that has ever been made by a lawyer within the last century.

Leavitt Burnham commenced his career in 1870, by clerkship in the office of Watson B. Smith, clerk of the United States circuit and district courts, where he was employed for some considerable time, and commenced there the reading of law. He performed the duties of his position in a very acceptable manner, both to the bench and the bar, and was afterwards permitted to practice, after reading for some considerable time in the office of Hon. A. J. Poppleton. Upon his admission to the bar, he still remained in Mr. Poppleton's office, and was engaged for a long time in giving attention to legal matters in the State connected with the Union Pacific Railroad outside of Omaha. He left the Union Pacific service in 1877 and went into private practice. In 1878 he was appointed land commissioner of the Union Pacific Railroad Company, having charge of their large land interests in Nebraska until January, 1886, when he resigned and again resumed the practice in 1890. Mr. Burnham is a citizen of probity, and has endeared himself to a large circle of friends, and is a lawyer of more than ordinary acumen and ability.

John Schomp was born in New Jersey and is forty years of age. He was admitted to the bar in 1868. He removed to Omaha in 1888, and is now engaged in the practice of law as the senior member of Schomp & Colson. Mr. Schomp is a very large man physically, and is equally so mentally. He is a gentleman in every sense of the term, and one whom every lawyer is glad to meet wherever he may.

Warren Switzler is about thirty-seven years of age and was born in the State of Missouri. He commenced life in a newspaper office, setting type. Having been admitted to the bar, he removed to this city in 1877, where he has established a reputation as a careful and painstaking lawyer, and the firm, as now composed of Switzler and J. H. McIntosh, under the firm name of Switzler & McIntosh, is one of the prominent firms of the city. He has always taken an active part in religious matters, being a devout member of the Presbyterian Church. In the fall of 1890, he was elected to the State Senate, where he served his constituents in a very acceptable manner and added to his already established reputation as an honorable gentleman and a good citizen.

T. J. Mahoney was born April 17, 1857, in Crawford County, Wisconsin, of Irish parentage. He removed to Iowa in 1864 and remained there until 1885. He was educated at the University of Notre Dame, Indiana. He taught school for eight years in Guthrie County, Iowa, the last three of which were spent as instructor in Latin and mathematics in the county high school of Panora. In 1881, he was elected county superintendent of schools of Guthrie County and served two years. In 1885, he graduated from the law department of the Iowa State University, and in the same year settled in Omaha and commenced the practice of law. In 1888, he was elected county attorney of Douglas County and re-elected in 1890. In politics, Mr. Mahoney is a Democrat. He is the senior member of one of the leading law firms of the city, Mahoney, Minnehan & Smyth, and is regarded very highly as a lawyer and citizen by the profession.

Judge George W. Shields is essentially a selfmade man. He started out in life in this city as a newsboy, at one time delivering the entire circulation of the Omaha *Herald*, the chief organ of the Democracy of this State. For a time he was peanut boy upon the Union Pacific Railroad, and, after having lost his left arm while engaged in working at a brick machine, he attended the high school of this city, from which he graduated with honors and commenced the study of law. Ever since his admission to the bar he has acquitted himself well, and in the fall of 1887 was elected county judge and re-elected in 1889, and administered the affairs of the office with great credit to himself and satisfaction to the litigants.

Charles Ogden is a native of Louisiana and came to Omaha a young man, just starting out in his profession, some twelve or fifteen years since. He is a pleasant, genial gentleman of the pure Southern type. He has long been connected with the Fremont, Elkhorn & Missouri Valley Railroad Company as its local attorney, and in which capacity he has been very successful. He is one of the old-fashioned kind of Democrats and enjoys the confidence of his party, and is considered one of its chief advisors in this State. Mr. Ogden is a student, and enjoys having the walls of his office literally lined with books. His library is of very great value, and contains many rare volumes.

William R. Kelly and John Schomp constitute the physical heavy weights of the Omaha bar. Mr. Kelly came to Nebraska at an early date and located at Lincoln. Soon thereafter, he became the local attorney of the Union Pacific Railway Company, not only for Lancaster County, but for all of the counties in the southwestern part of the State, and, after the appointment of Honorable John M. Thurston as general solicitor of the road, he was called to Omaha to take the position of assistant general solicitor, as well as general attorney for the State of Nebraska. Mr. Kelly is not only a genial gentleman but a good lawyer, thoroughly versed in corporation law and well adapted to manage and control intricate corporation cases, which work he performs the greater portion of. Mr. Kelly is about forty-two years of age and enjoys a wide acquaintance, and has thoroughly established his reputation as a lawyer.

Charles J. Greene has been a resident of this city for many years, where he has taken front rank as a lawyer and as an orator. Mr. Greene is local attorney for the Chicago, Burlington & Quincy Railway Company in this city, and his time is altogether taken up with corporation law. At the last national convention held in Chicago, he was one of the delegates from the State of Nebraska, and acquitted himself with great credit. Mr. Greene has never been an office seeker, except for such as might be ornamental, and in that respect he has been remarkably successful. Mr. Greene was a great admirer of Roscoe Conkling in his lifetime, and his friends think that he has many of the characteristics of that great orator. There is no more genial companion than Charlie Greene. He enjoys his life and the work of his profession in the highest degree.

Henry D. Estabrook is essentially an Omaha boy. He was born in the State of New York, coming to Omaha at an early age, where he has grown to manhood, receiving his education in her schools, and graduating with distinction from the St. Louis Law School. He is the son of General E. Estabrook, and inherits to a great degree the legal ability of his father, while there has been eliminated from his composition many of his father's idiosyncrasies. Mr. Estabrook has established a reputation as a lawyer and orator, and has acquired both fame and money in the practice of his profession.

Judge Edward R. Duffie was born in the State of New York and is about forty-eight years of age. He removed to Sac County, Iowa, when about twenty-three years old, and soon thereafter commenced the practice of law in northwestern Iowa. He served a term of eight years upon the bench in his district and established a reputation second to none in the State as a jurist. He removed to Omaha in 1887, where he has continued to reside with his family, and where he has established an enviable reputation as a lawyer.

Hon. George W. Covell was born in the State of New York and is some fifty-five years of age. Upon his removal from New York he went to Missouri, where he studied law and was admitted to the bar in 1860. During the war he was in the rebel army, after which he removed to Nebraska City, and in 1886 came to Omaha. Mr. Covell held many positions of trust in Nebraska City, and in 1876 was elected a member of the State Senate, where he served with great acceptability to his constituents, and endeared himself by his manly and upright conduct to his associates. He is one of the stern kind of Democrats in politics. He is a hard fighter and a good lawyer.

Isaac E. Congdon is the senior member of the oldest firm of lawyers now engaged in the practice in Omaha. The firm consists of Mr. Congdon, Judge J. R. Clarkson and George J. Hunt. Mr. Congdon was a member of the firm of Manderson & Congdon, he then having just graduated from the university as a lawyer; afterwards, upon the election of General Manderson to the Senate of the United States, Mr. Congdon formed a connection with the firm of Clarkson & Hunt, as it had theretofore been existing. All of these gentlemen, in their several departments, are model lawyers. Judge Clarkson has lately resigned a seat upon the bench, to which he was elected after a very sharp contest about a year ago, but he liked the contest at the bar, together with its remuneration, better than a prosy seat upon the bench.

C. F. and R. W. Breckenridge, father and son, have been residents of Omaha for about ten years, and are engaged in the practice of law together. They are well adapted as members of the firm, C. F., the father, having had years of practice and experience at the bar, and his son, R. W., being a young man full of vim and push, have made the firm one of considerable pecuniary profit as well as importance in the administration of justice in this city.

Joseph H. Blair is the only really cosmopolitan lawyer we have amongst us. He is well-known throughout the United States, having practiced law before all the courts in some eight different States. He is a man well along in the fifties, is still active in his profession, and there is only one thing that he loves better than the law, and that is to sit upon the edge of a brook with a fish-hook and line in his hand and plenty of fish in the stream.

Judge William O. Bartholomew came to Omaha in 1868, and has been a continuous resident ever since. In 1878, Mr. Bartholomew was elected County Judge of Douglas County, serving two years and being re-elected for another term; but before the completion of his second term he was compelled, on account of ill-health, to resign his office. A misfortune to him as well as to the balance of the bar of the city is, that Judge Bartholomew has never yet regained his health. While at the bar, he displayed remarkable judgment, and received from the judges of the Supreme Court the highest encomiums respecting an argument which the writer believes is the only one he ever made before that body. Judge Bartholomew still graces the court room with his presence daily, taking much part in conversation and reminiscences, but is unable to do any active work.

Judge Charles H. Breck became a member of this bar in the fall of 1889, at which time he removed to Omaha from Richmond, Kentucky, where he was born, and had always resided. He is the son of the late Judge Daniel Breck, so well-known in the judicial and political annals of Kentucky, as a judge of the Court of Appeals and a member of Congress. He came highly commended by the bench and bar of his native State as a man of ability and experience and culture in his profession, and has so proved himself. He is about fifty years of age. For many years he was upon the bench and connected judicially with the affairs of his native county. He was induced to remove from where he had lived a life of great activity and usefulness, and to sever his old associations, by the desire to be with his large family of sons, who had preceded him to this city.

William F. Gurley was born in Davenport, Iowa, and is now twenty-nine years of age. He came to Omaha in 1881, and entered the employ of Louis Bradford, the well-known lumber merchant of this city. Soon afterwards he was appointed clerk of the county court, which position he held for several years, and then entered the office of Thurston & Hall, attorneys of this city, where he performed the duties of clerk. In 1884 he was appointed private secretary to Senator Manderson, which position he held until the winter of 1885, when he engaged for a short time in the real estate business. In June, 1886, he first threw out his shingle to the breeze. Later, for one year, he held the position of assistant county attorney, under E. W. Simeral. In 1890, he was a candidate for the office of State Senate upon the Republican ticket of Douglas County, and was defeated. Mr. Gurley is a fine talker and holds a high place among the younger lawyers of the city.

M. V. Gannon came to Omaha some five years ago from Des Moines, Iowa, where he had established a reputation as a lawyer and as a prosecuting officer of some considerable extent. Mr. Gannon is an Irishman by birth, strongly and thoroughly imbued in the principles of the Irish cause; as an orator, he is in large demand at all gatherings where the woes of Ireland are to be discussed. In 1891, he was elected president of the Irish National League, which position he still fills.

Francis Albert Brogan was born in Dewitt, Iowa, December 6, 1860, and lived on a farm in that locality until his fourteenth year. In 1875, he moved with his parents to Hartford, Kansas. He was educated in St. Benedict's College, Atchison, Kansas, and in Georgetown University, Washington, District of Columbia, graduating from the latter institution with highest class honors, in 1883. During the winter of 1884 and 1885, he read law in the office of Judge T. A. Hurd, in Leavenworth, Kansas, and the following year took a course at the

Harvard law school. In June, 1885, he was admitted to the bar at Emporia, Kansas, and began the practice of his profession there, being associated in practice with C. N. Sterry, one of the leading railroad lawyers in the State. In 1886, he entered the race for county attorney, as the Democratic candidate, but, although receiving the highest vote cast for any nominee on his ticket, he was defeated, his party being in a hopeless minority. From 1886 to 1888, he was in the employ of the Atchison, Topeka & Santa Fe Railroad Company as one of its assistant attorneys, and was connected with much of the important litigation of that company. In July, 1888, he removed to Omaha and began practice here, associated with M. V. Gannon, under the firm name of Gannon & Brogan. The partnership was dissolved the following year, Mr. Brogan retiring from the firm. Mr. Brogan was married October 17, 1888, at Emporia, Kansas, to Miss Maude H. Perley, of that place. In politics, he has always been a Democrat. He was raised and educated a Roman Catholic.

John Paul Breen was born of Scotch-Irish parentage on the 20th day of April, 1856, on a farm near the little village of Lockport, in the State of Illinois. In the spring of 1857, his parents moved to the then wild and unsettled portion of western Iowa, and located on a farm near Fort Dodge, at that time a small garrisoned fort for the protection of the early settlers in that part of the State from Indian attacks and depredations. At an early age he commenced to attend the winter terms of school in the rude, rough log school houses of that part of western Iowa, frequently walking a distance of two or three miles through severe winter storms and deep snows to enjoy the meagre opportunities afforded by these schools for an education, in the summer time working on the farm. From the log school house of the country district, he went to the village high school. At nineteen, he passed the school board examination for a teacher's certificate, and at twenty commenced to teach school near his old home at Fort Dodge, Iowa, and continued to teach for the next four years. In 1879, while principal of the Dayton, Iowa, school, he commenced, unaided and alone, the study of the law, and, in connection with his duties of school teacher, kept up the study until 1882, when he was admitted to the bar at Fort Dodge, Iowa. In that year he was elected to the office of county recorder in his home county, and served in that office two years. He then opened a law office in Fort Dodge, but soon removed to Cedar Rapids, Iowa, seeking a wider field for operations. In 1884, under the auspices of the Republican State campaign committee, he "stumped" the State of Iowa for "Jim." Blaine and glory. In 1886, he removed to Omaha and commenced the practice of the law here. He is a pronounced cosmopolitan, in respect to all national distinctions, social prejudices and religious creeds.

Hon. Frank Irvine, one of the judges of the district court of the fourth judicial district, became a member of the Douglas County bar in 1884. His experience in the practice of his profession at that time was limited. He had served an apprenticeship of three years in the office of George B. Corkhill, United States district attorney for the District of Columbia, and assisted in the preparation of the trial of the Giteau case, filling the position of assistant attorney for one year thereafter. Having in 1883 graduated from the National University, he took up his residence in Omaha in 1884. Mr. Irvine soon gained an enviable reputation as a lawyer of unusual ability. In 1886 he associated himself in the general practice of the law with Henry D. Estabrook, under the firm name of Estabrook & Irvine. Later, Mr. Charles E. Clapp became a member of the firm. In 1891, the number of the judges of the district court for the fourth judicial district having been increased by law, the bar of the district held

one of the jury dockets. He has developed a great capacity as a judge, his literary learning, as well as his legal training, having demonstrated that he has great capacity and that he is a man who will grow as a judge as he has grown upon his fellow members of the bar, as a man and lawyer, during his residence in this city. He has a calm, judicial temperament, and a very discerning mind; he acts with great moderation; he does not arrive at a point so quickly as some others, but when he has arrived at a conclusion is firm and decisive. He is very much liked upon the bench; his companionship is sought after and enjoyed by very many. His habits are domestic and retiring, and in the years to come the writer bespeaks for him a full measure of usefulness and honor in his profession.

Edward W. Simeral, a native of Steubenville, Ohio, has made Omaha his home since 1869. Selecting law as his profession, he studied with Silas A. Strickland and John L. Webster, and was admitted to the bar in 1876. He was elected as the first county attorney of Douglas County, in 1886, holding the office for two years. Since his retirement from office he has attended strictly to his private practice, which now requires his undivided attention. He is attorney for the Bee Publishing Company, the Millard Hotel Company, and other corporations, and is recognized by his professional brethren, and the public at large, as a worthy and intelligent representative of the Omaha bar.

The following have been officers of the United States Courts for Nebraska:

United States Marshals.—C. E. Yost, May 10, 1867; Joseph T. Hoile, January 25, 1870; William Daily, July 13, 1872; Ellis L. Bierbower, December 11, 1880; Brad. D. Slaughter, June 17, 1889.

United States Attorneys.—S. A. Strickland, June 15, 1867; James Neville, May 20, 1871; G. M. Lambertson, December 22, 1882; George E. Pritchett, February 24, 1887; Benjamin S. Baker, February 4, 1890.

Clerks United States Circuit Court.—E. B. Chandler, May 9, 1867; Watson B. Smith, May 30, 1868; E. D. Frank, November 21, 1881.

Clerks United States District Court.—Watson B. Smith, June 1, 1868; E. D. Frank, March 23, 1880; E. S. Dundy, Jr., November 23, 1882.

The following constitute the judges of the probate and the county court, with the dates of their service: Judge Scott was first probate judge, but there are no records of his proceedings; Clinton Briggs, 1857 to 1860; George Armstrong, 1860 to 1863; Hiram M. Dickinson, 1863 to 1865; Isaac S. Hascall, 1865 to 1867; Benjamin Shecks, September, 1867, to December 9, 1867; R. J. Stuck, December 9, 1867, to December 21, 1868; J. R. Hyde, December 21, 1868, to November 8, 1869; L. B. Gibson, November, 1869, to November, 1871; Robert Townsend, 1871 to 1873; William L. Peabody, 1873 to 1876; C. H. Sedgwick, 1876 to 1877; W. O. Bartholomew, July 28, 1877, to January 29, 1881; Howard B. Smith, January 29, 1881, to September 6, 1881; A. M. Chadwick, September 6, 1881, to February 20, 1884; J. H. McCulloch, February 20, 1884, to January 5, 1888; George W. Shields, January 5, 1888, to January 5, 1892; James W. Eller, January 5, 1892, elected for two years.

The bar in the last few years has received many notable accessions from Iowa, in the persons of John P. Breen, D. D. Gregory, E. R. Duffle, W. S. Strawn, W. W. Morsman, A. S. Churchill, M. V. Gannon, Judge I. H. Macomber, and E. G. Thomas; from Illinois: John C. Wharton, William Baird, Jacob Fawcett, Louis D. Holmes, and L. H. Bradley; from Kentucky: Judge Charles H. Breck and Charles Offutt. All these gentlemen brought with them reputations as good lawyers, which have been fully sustained, and are each and all of them considered expert in the various branches to which they devote themselves.

The bar of Omaha has been exceedingly

blessed in its officers. In the more than a quarter of a century, there has been no officer connected with the courts against whom there has been the slightest suspicion of dishonesty. The sheriffs of Douglas County have been uniformly able and honorable gentlemen, never shirking their duty, and among those who have filled that office the writer can not refrain from mentioning the name of Henry Grebe. He was first elected sheriff in November, 1869, which office he held for four years, and has been for the last eleven years deputy sheriff under the gentlemen who have at various times held that office, making a continued service of fifteen years. Henry Grebe is a well educated man of German descent, and is one of the pioneers of Nebraska. He is by trade a mechanic. He served in the constitutional convention of 1875. During his term in the sheriff's office, there never was a jar or discrepancy in the service of process by him, and the courts of Douglas County will be very barren when he shall cease to be a participant in the administration of justice; and the writer knows that he but echoes the universal voice of this bar, when he says, "May Henry Grebe's German accent sound in our ears for many years yet to come."

In the clerk's office, we have had, in the United States Courts, Watson B. Smith, who died an untimely death, whether by accident or by murder, never yet has been determined, which occurred in November, 1881. He was a conscientious and faithful officer, and was succeeded by Elmer D. Frank, the present clerk of the circuit court. Elmer D. Frank is an affable gentleman, enjoys the taxing up of costs, as well as the hunting of bear.

In the District Court of Douglas County, we have had Armstrong and Ijams, and now Frank E. Moores, who is an abbreviated edition of the Star Spangled Banner, and who keeps himself very busy in his polite attention to the seven courts, enjoying the large revenue he derives from his office. He makes a good clerk, and always has a salutation for everybody.

This chapter has not been written as a homily upon what the profession should be, nor as an eulogy of the few who have been mentioned. We speak of the orators of ancient Greece, but there were no orators in Greece except at Athens. Not so here; there are orators at this bar who have not been mentioned as such.

My work is done. It is submitted to the candid judgment of the profession, hoping that it may be considered in some slight degree meritorious.

# CHAPTER XXV.

### HOTELS OF EARLY AND MODERN DAYS — CHANGES OF MANAGEMENT AT THE HERNDON — HOW THE GRAND CENTRAL WAS NAMED.

Omaha's first hotel was a log building, sixteen by eighteen feet, one story, bearing the high-sounding title of "The St. Nicholas." It was put up by the Nebraska & Council Bluffs Ferry Company, and was occupied first by the family of William P. Snowden (afterwards city marshal). It was located on the corner of Twelfth and Jackson Streets.

The City Hotel, a small frame structure at the southwest corner of Harney and Eleventh, was built in 1854.

The Douglas House, a large two-story frame structure, at the southwest corner of Thirteenth and Harney Streets, was built in 1855. The rear portion was made of cottonwood slabs, set up and down, and Mr. A. J. Poppleton, who was a boarder at the Douglas at that time, says the building was a very cold one in winter. For several years it was a leading hotel, however, and maintained a high tariff as to prices. Wells Brothers were the first proprietors.

The Farnham House, recently torn down to give place to the brick block on the north side of Harney between Thirteenth and Fourteenth, was built by W. A. Gwyer, in 1858. St. John Goodrich, father of ex-City Comptroller Goodrich, was one of the early proprietors.

The Tremont was built in 1856, on the south side of Douglas Street, between Thirteenth and Fourteenth, and was opened for business in October of that year by Wm. F. Sweesy and Aaron Root, who were the proprietors until 1865, when the building was moved to the southeast corner of Sixteenth and Capitol Avenue.

The Union Hotel was built in 1860 by William G. Florkee. It was a two-story frame house, on the northwest corner of Dodge and Fifteenth Streets.

The Pacific House, a frame building on Tenth between Capitol Avenue and Davenport, was built in 1866, by David T. Mount.

The Metropolitan Hotel, Douglas Street, near Twelfth, was built in 1868 by D. A. Van Namee.

The Wyoming and the Cozzens were built in 1867, the former by Dr. Isaac Edwards and the latter by George Francis Train. Senator Paddock was the proprietor of the Wyoming for several years. When first opened, this house was called the Edwards House. The cost of erection was $21,000, and the first proprietor was Mr. Godfrey, who afterwards platted Godfrey's Addition. The building was framed in Chicago. While owned by Dr. Edwards, Messrs. Davis and Nicholas were at one time in charge of the hotel, both of whom were drowned in 1889, at the Johnstown, Pennsylvania, flood. In 1869 the name of the house was changed to the Casement, in honor of the contractors who built the Union Pacific, and in 1870 was again changed and for many years was known as the Wyoming. Then as the Canfield House it built up a great custom, under the management of George Canfield. Recently the name was changed to Hotel Faris, S. J. Faris, proprietor. S. H. H. Clark is the present owner of the property.

The Herndon House, built in 1856-7 by Dr. George L. Miller and Lyman Richardson, now a portion of the building used as general offices by the Union Pacific Railroad

Company, was the first hotel of any size erected in Omaha. The first landlord was Mr. M. W. Keith, and he was succeeded by two or three others until finally it fell into the management of Mr. James T. Allan, by whom it was first conducted as a high-toned boarding house, and afterwards as a hotel. Meanwhile it became the property of Dr. G. C. Monell, and he leased it to Mrs. Bronson. Mr. Allan was disposed to hold on to the possession, and considerable difficulty followed, which Mr. Silas Seymour, engineer of the Union Pacific, thus refers to in a letter written in October, 1866: "We found that the Herndon, of Omaha, was in a sort of transition state, and its guests, as farmers say, 'between hay and grass.' Our longtime friend and distinguished host, Mr. Allan, had been called upon by Dr. Monell, the landlord, to surrender its use and occupation into the hands of Mrs. Bronson, who had recently leased it and stood ready to enter upon the duties of hostess as soon as Mr. Allan could find it convenient to vacate the premises, all of which the said Mr. Allan seemed in no haste to do. An entire week had been spent by the parties in strategy and legal skirmishing, during which it was not unusual for Mr. Allan to visit the kitchen in the morning and find Mrs. Bronson's cooking stove standing in the place of his own, which had been thrown over the adjoining fence during the night, and not infrequently were the guests of the house stopped in the middle of a meal (while waiting, perhaps, for more warm cakes) by the intelligence that the stove had just been thrown out of the kitchen. Fortunately for us, however, Mrs. Bronson's stove was outside the fence when we arrived, and remained there during the following day and Sunday." The Omaha *Times*, of February 4, 1859, gives this account of "A Pleasant Occasion," which occurred the week previous:

"At dinner last Thursday the guests of the Herndon House, at the invitation of Hon. Wm. A. West, prolonged their sitting for the purpose of testing the quality of a couple of baskets of excellent champagne. A number of toasts were proposed, among which were the following, quoted from memory:

"'Our Entertainer, Marshal West; may a long time elapse before his official connection with the people of Nebraska shall be severed.' Drunk with all the honors.

"'Our Hosts of the Herndon.' Response by Doctor Miller, in a few feeling and appropriate remarks.

"'The Ladies of Omaha.' Responded to by Sydney Paddock, with his usual suavity of manner, in the course of which he paid a graceful compliment to the ladies of Omaha, so well represented by the brilliant array at the table.

"'The Judiciary of Nebraska.' Response by Judge Wakeley, whose neat and well-turned remarks were received with applause;

"'The Veterans of the Fontenelle War; they who shed their blood in the defense of their country deserve well of that country in the time of security.' To loud calls, Captain Moore responded in some forcible remarks, giving some striking reminiscences of those 'times that tried men's souls.'

"'The Lady of the Present Day; she wants but little on her head, but much below to make a spread.' To this toast Mr. McConihie was called upon to respond, and volunteered a song, which was rendered with effect and received with applause.

"'The Bar.' Jonas Seely was loudly called for, and responded very briefly.

(By a lady guest) "'The Omaha Bachelors; there is but one thing needful—take unto yourselves wives.' Responded to by J. W. Paddock, in behalf of the brotherhood of which he was so lately a member, and exhorting them to 'be wise in time, 'tis madness to defer.'

"'The Navy of the United States.' Responded to by Captain Curtis, of the Ferry Company's Steamer, Nebraska.

"'Woman; in view of the space she occupies, with truth may she say: 'No pent up sidewalk can control our powers, but the boundless street we claim for ours.'" Response by Joseph Millard, with song. 'I See Them on Their Winding Way.'"

The Hamilton House, a brick building still standing, in a re-organized shape, on the south side of Douglas, between Fourteenth and Fifteenth, was built in 1856, by C. B. Smith and C. W. Hamilton, H. M. Judson and —— Burnham being the first proprietors, who opened the house for business in August 1856. Mr. Judson bought the furniture in St. Louis, and on his return brought up on the steamboat half a dozen colored people as servants. Among the early boarders at the house were United States Marshal B. P. Rankin, Governor Cuming, Governor Richardson, John M. Thayer, and other well-known people. The upper part of the house was one large bedroom, filled with bedsteads ranged against the walls, and about once a week this room was cleaned out for ball-room purposes. On these gala occasions the music was furnished by Byron Reed, Aaron Cahn, Frederick A. Schneider and Washington Griffith, the last named a resident of Council Bluffs.

Referring to the hotel accommodations of that period, Mr. James M. Woolworth, in a pamphlet entitled "Omaha City, the Capitol of Nebraska," which he published in 1857, says: "A company of twelve gentlemen, largely interested in the town, have recently purchased, for $15,000, a steamboat of the first-class—the Washington City—which is moored at the landing and used as a hotel. Cheap and comfortable accommodations are thus afforded to 250 persons. The necessity of large hotel accommodations may be inferred from the fact that there are now one thousand people in Omaha over our population of last March. It is reasonable to expect this number will be considerably increased in two months."

The Grand Central was the first large hotel built in Omaha. It occupied a quarter of a block, 132x132 feet, at the southwest corner of Farnam and Fourteenth Streets. The building was of brick, four stories high. It was commenced in 1871, the money being raised by stock subscriptions representing about a hundred different individuals and firms. The outlay exceeded the anticipations of these contributors, the work dragged and many discouragements were met with. The house was completed in the fall of 1873, receiving its first guests in October. About this time there was a lively discussion with respect to the name of the hotel. The name, "Grand Central," had been generally agreed upon but a change was made and the building was called the Pullman House. This change did not meet with public favor, and the newspapers were filled with protests and suggestions. One writer, disguising his personality under the classic *nom de plume* of "Hash," inquired: "Why not name it the 'Buchu House?'" and added, "certainly Hembold has done as much for Omaha as Pullman. Or why not name it the 'Georgefrancistrain House?' There is a name whose owner has advertised Omaha more than any other man." Then L. M. Bennett, superintendent of the Pullman Palace Car Company, called attention to the fact that in 1863 Mr. Pullman had built a very fine car and christened it "Omaha," which communication was followed by one signed "Modesty," who suggested that there might be objections to specially honoring Mr. Pullman in the way proposed, but there could be none with regard to the local superintendent of the Pullman Company, and that the title, "The Bennett House," would just about fill the bill. The Omaha *Herald* thought that it would be a very neat thing to name the new hotel in honor of Mr. Duff, of the Union Pacific Road, which suggestion was endorsed by a correspondent who added that his first preference as to a name was "The Credit Mobilier." Thereupon Mr. George P. Bemis stated, through the public prints, that as early as 1871 George Francis Train had, in his publication styled the "Train Ligue," christened the building the "Omaha House." It was finally agreed the hotel should be called "The Grand Central;" and, it may be, the fact that a number of persons who had subscribed to a fund for the formal opening declared that they would not pay their subscriptions, if the name "Pullman House" was insisted upon, had some bearing in settling the question. There was much litigation in the courts in connection with the erection of the building, many of the stockholders refusing to pay their subscriptions, for various reasons. A loan of $100,000 was made the company by Messrs. Edward Creighton, A. J. Poppleton, and others, who took a mortgage on the property as security; and this mortgage it was found necessary to foreclose in 1878. April 18th, of that year, the sale took place, and the property was purchased by Augustus Kountze for $120,000, the total indebtedness at that time being $190,000, no interest having been paid on the loan since March 2, 1872. There was also due Withnell Brothers and McCafferty, the builders, the sum of $10,000 principal, and $5,000 interest. Mr. George Thrall was the successful bidder for the lease of the hotel, and conducted the business in a manner profitable to himself and satisfactory to the public until the spring of 1878, when he gave up the hotel to go into other business. It was then leased by the Kitchen Brothers—Charles W., James B. and Richard Kitchen. They immediately began extensive improvements, including the putting in of an elevator. A large sum was expended for furniture, which was being delivered at the house when at half past six o'clock on the evening of September 24, 1878, fire was discovered in the elevator shaft in which workmen were employed that day up to six P. M., and it is the general belief that the flames caught from a lighted candle they had been using in their work. There was a story circulated at the time to the effect that one of these men was eating supper at a restaurant when the fire alarm sounded and the announcement was made that the Grand Central was burning, and that he jumped up and rushed out, exclaiming: "And I left a burning candle in the elevator shaft!" The building was entirely consumed, and with it were burned to death five brave firemen—Lewis Wilson, Alonzo Randall, John A. Lee, William McNamara and Henry Lockfield, who had succeeded in gaining an entrance to the third floor of the building with a hose, when the floors all gave way and were instantly a mass of flames. The disaster was keenly felt by the people of Omaha, for the Grand Central had been the boast of the city from the time of its completion, and the prospect for its rebuilding was then exceedingly doubtful. The house had been closed for three months and was to have been re-opened five days later. The Kitchen Brothers secured the building at the southwest corner of Fifteenth and Harney Streets, owned by the Withnell Brothers, and formerly occupied as headquarters for the military of the Department of the Platte. (This property was afterwards purchased by Miller & Richardson, for the *Herald* newspaper and job offices.) The building was fitted up for hotel purposes, christened the Withnell, and here the Kitchens received their patrons and made them as comfortable as circumstances permitted, until October, 1882.

The Paxton Hotel, now occupying the ground on which the Grand Central formerly stood, was built by the Kitchen Brothers, the former lessees of the Grand Central, at a cost of $275,000. The ground, 132 feet square, cost them $30,000; it is now worth a quarter of a million. The building, five stories, is solidly built of brick and iron, lighted by an electric plant which cost $10,000, and is fitted with all the requirements for a first-class hotel. The property is owned by the Kitchen Brothers Hotel Company, and is leased. On the night of April 12, 1891, this building also caught fire, inflicting a damage of about $25,000, and causing the death of

Michael Carter, captain of No. 2 Hose Company, who with pipemen Martin Mulvihill, Peter McGuire and Thomas Downs, was crushed by the falling of a brick wall upon them as they were ascending a long ladder, the accident occurring upon almost the same spot where the five firemen were killed, in September, 1878, when the Grand Central was destroyed. The three pipemen were all severely bruised, but escaped with their lives.

The Paxton had been leased to different parties for several years, but, after considerable litigation, the proprietors regained possession in May, 1892, and are at this time conducting it.

The Millard Hotel, occupying an area of 132 by 200 feet at the northeast corner of Douglas and Thirteenth, was built in 1882 by a syndicate, composed of Samuel Sheavs, J. E. Markel, Thomas Swobe, Ezra Millard, J. H. Millard and George Giacomini. It is a substantial brick structure, five stories high, and, with improvements made at various times, cost over $200,000. For many years the business was conducted by Messrs. Markel & Swobe, but the former retired in March, 1891, leaving the latter as sole manager.

For a quarter of a century Thomas Murray devoted a lot, 66 x 132 feet, which he owned at the northwest corner of Harney and Fourteenth, to a variety of purposes, resulting in a general collection of all sorts of worthless "plunder." The ground is now of great value, and thereon he erected a hotel building which was first opened for business under the name of the Murray, in September, 1888. It is a substantial brick structure, six stories high, 60 x 132 feet, located at the northwest corner of Harney and Fourteenth, and cost, with the furniture, $140,000. The hotel has achieved great popularity under the management of Mr. Benton Silloway.

The Mercer is a new six-story hotel which was completed and opened in June 1892. It is located on the corner of Howard and Twelfth Streets, and was built and is owned by Dr. S. D. Mercer. It contains 150 rooms and is under the management of Don H. Porter, a well-known and experienced hotel man. It cost $200,000. It deservedly stands well up in the list of Omaha's first-class hotels. Mr. G. S. Erb, of Salt Lake City, has leased this hotel for five years from the first day of August, 1892.

The Hotel Brunswick was opened in 1892 by Hon. W. F. Sweesy, who had built it in the fall of 1891. It is located on the corner of Sixteenth and Jackson, and is one of the handsome buildings on that thoroughfare.

The Hotel Dellone recently completed by Mr. Andrew Dellone, at the southwest corner of Capitol Avenue and Fourteenth, at an expense of $100,000, Chauncy Reed lessee and manager, is one of the handsomest and most substantial buildings in the city.

The Barker, on Thirteenth and Jones, Mr. George Van Oman, proprietor; the Merchants', on Farnam, between Fifteenth and Sixteenth, Nat. Brown, proprietor; Hotel Casey, 1213, 1215, 1217, Douglas, J. Casey, proprietor; the Grand Central Hotel, Fifteenth and Jackson, Peterson & Son, proprietors; Hotel Esmond, Drexel & Hart, proprietors; the Metropolitan, 1122, 1124, Douglas, Gay & Hoar, proprietors; the Windsor, Tenth and Jackson, Schlank & Prince, proprietors; Union Depot Hotel, Mason and Eleventh, W. M. Walker, proprietor, with many others of lesser note, now afford excellent accommodations for the traveling public.

Probably there are more historical facts connected with the hotel now known as the Jennings House than with any other building now used as a hotel in Omaha. It was built by George Francis Train, in 1867, being erected in sixty days, and was opened by the Cozzens, of West Point, New York, who conducted it for a year. Mr. Philo Rumsey took it then, and had charge of it for three years, closing out in the fall of 1871. It then stood vacant for a number of years, being opened about 1880, and conducted by different persons, but not successfully. Later Mr. Philo Rumsey again returned to the city, took hold of the house, and was doing a very good business when, in trying to save the life of a little girl in a hotel fire in Buffalo, New York, he lost his life. The late Dr. J. W. McMenamy purchased the property and used it for a medical institute until his death, after which time it was run by a Mr. A. T. McLaughlin as a medical institute; but, by reason of the attacks of newspapers because of some questionable transactions, its reputation failed, and the house was again closed. After remaining closed for some months it was again named, this time the Jennings, and is now doing a fair business under the management of Mr. Edwin Jennings.

In concluding this chapter it may not be out of place to refer to some of the hotel schemes which have originated, been canvassed among the people, and then, just as everyone expected to see reared skyward the towering buildings, there has been a hitch, and the scheme collapsed. At different times there were to be hotels on the corner of Tenth and Farnam, where the excavation was made; on the corner of Farnam and Twentieth; on Sixteenth and Harney; and at various other places. The probabilities are that most of these schemes were more in the nature of real estate speculations, with a view of benefitting surrounding property, than for the purpose of meeting the demands for hotel accommodations. There are, at the present time, prospects that at least one more large hotel will be erected in Omaha, and that a start will be made this summer (1892) on the work.

# CHAPTER XXVI.

LIBRARIES — EARLY EFFORTS IN THIS DIRECTION — THE GREAT PUBLIC INSTITUTION OF TO-DAY — PRIVATE COLLECTIONS OF BOOKS — BYRON REED'S BEQUEST — THE LIBRARY BUILDING.

To Mrs. Mary Allan Bock, who was for several years the efficient librarian of the public library, the editors of this work are indebted for the following very interesting chapter.

The libraries of Omaha, both public and private, are institutions to which her citizens may point with pride.

Not until 1871 was there any movement to establish a circulating library. In the latter part of that year, as the result of the efforts of John T. Edgar, Nathan Shelton and A. M. Henry, articles of incorporation of the Omaha Library Association were adopted and signed by the following: T. E. Sickles, St. A. D. Balcombe, H. W. Yates, Herman Kountze, George L. Miller, J. T. Edgar, Ezra Millard, Albert Swartzlander, Nathan Shelton, C. H. Brown, P. H. Allen and A. M. Henry.

The first meeting of the stockholders was held at the rooms of the Board of Trade, December 30th. The first board of directors was then chosen, as follows: A. J. Poppleton, St. A. D. Balcombe, H. W. Yates, J. T. Edgar, J. Patrick, A. Swartzlander, S. S. Caldwell, G. L. Miller, J. W. Gannett, N. Shelton and A. M. Henry. January 3, 1872, the election of officers took place, the result being: president, A. J. Poppleton; vice president, N. Shelton; treasurer, S. S. Caldwell; secretary, A. Swartzlander; corresponding secretary, A. M. Henry. At the same meeting steps were taken toward the collection of books. The donation by John T. Edgar of one thousand volumes, and the purchase of eight hundred volumes from O. E. Crosby, of Fremont, formed the nucleus of this library.

In 1872, the city received from J. M. Pattee a collection of books which, under certain conditions, were given the association, making a total of 2,600 volumes. These were catalogued and numbered, a room rented in the second story of the Simpson Block, on Fourteenth, between Douglas and Dodge Streets, and May 1, 1872, the room was opened, with Mrs. Aliman as librarian. An annual fee of three dollars was required to become a member. The first catalogue was issued in the same year.

Mrs. Aliman served but a few weeks and was succeeded by Miss Louise Honey, a former teacher in the public schools. She held the position until September 1st, 1872. Upon her resignation Miss Delia M. Sears was elected to fill the vacancy.

In 1874 the library was moved to the second story of the Marshall building, on the north side of Dodge, between Fourceenth and Fifteenth Streets, where it occupied the whole floor. This gave the association very pleasant rooms and it was hoped the list of subscribers would rapidly increase.

On the resignation of Miss Sears, in December, 1876, Miss Jean M. Allan was elected to the position.

At the thirteenth special session of the Nebraska State Legislature, a bill was introduced in the Senate by T. B. Kennard, January 16, 1877, entitled: "A Bill for an Act to Authorize Cities to Establish and Maintain free Public Libraries and Reading Rooms."

This bill was referred to the judiciary committee, who reported the same back, with the recommendation that said bill be passed, with the recommendation to "Amend the title of the bill so as to read, 'incorporated towns and cities.'"

The amended bill was passed in the Senate February 8, 1877, by a vote of 31 to 19 and in the House February 15, 1877, the vote being 49 to 29.

The fees charged and the proceeds from entertainments were the only source of income. Among some old papers the following tickets were found by the writer:

HOME LECTURE COURSE OF 1876.
OMAHA LIBRARY ASSOCIATION.

J. M. WOOLWORTH, December 8th—"An Afternoon in the Houses of Parliament."
A. J. POPPLETON, December 15th — "Edmund Burke."
JOHN D. HOWE, December 22d—"Frauds."

LECTURE COURSE OF 1877.

RT. REV. JAMES O'CONNOR, Bishop of the Catholic Church, January 31st.
DOCTOR E. B. FAIRFIELD, Chancellor, University of Nebraska, February 8th.
RT. REV. ROBERT H. CLARKSON, Bishop of the Episcopal Church, February 15th.

After struggling until June, 1877, the directors, convinced that with its prospective income it would be impossible to longer keep open its doors, adopted this resolution:

"WHEREAS, it is evident that this association is not able to keep the library and reading room open with its present and prospective income, be it

"Resolved, That the president pro tem. appoint a committee of three to consult with the city council of Omaha and inquire whether it will establish and maintain a public library and reading room for the use of the inhabitants of this city, under the act of the legislature approved February 17, 1877."

By an ordinance approved June 12th, the city signified its willingness to maintain such an institution, to be known as the Omaha Public Library, and elected the nine directors, namely: W. Wallace, N. T. Spoor, L. S. Reed, A. Rosewater, Lyman Richardson, Mrs. O. N. Ramsey, J. H. Kellom, J. M. Thurston and H. J. Lucas.

To maintain the library, a tax of one-fourth mill was levied, ninety per cent. only, being available. This gave an income of $1,274.80. At the first meeting of the directors, J. H. Kellom was elected president, Lewis S. Reed, secretary, and Miss Jean M. Allan, librarian.

August 6, 1877, the board received from Leavitt Burnham, secretary of the Omaha Library Association, a certificate, dated August 4th, being a transfer of the books and property of the said association to the Omaha Public Library Board; this was read and placed on file. With the assurance of a settled income, the library awoke to a new life; its success was certain and its growth rapid and uniform. In January a room was secured on the second floor of the Williams Block on the northeast corner of Dodge and Fifteenth Streets, the accommodations being a large reading room with an alcove for the books.

Owing to the rapidly increasing number of book borrowers, it was found necessary to change the system used by the association, and blanks, methods of circulation, etc., similar to those used in the Chicago Public Library, were adopted. The library was opened to the public in its new rooms in February, 1878. On the opening day over two hundred cards were issued, showing that the citizens fully appreciated the institution. The first finding list, numbering seventy-four pages, was published by private parties, every alternate page being used for advertisements. With the increased list of newspapers and periodicals, the reading room soon became a popular resort. The income being small, it was not until the latter part of April that the first installment of books was purchased.

In 1878 the library tax levy was increased to one-half mill, amounting to $2,782.09, thereby allowing a sum sufficient to make additions, both to the library and reading room. Among them were many juvenile publications, a class that had been somewhat neglected, and, as a result, this brought to the rooms many young people who never before had known that there was such an institution in the city.

There was no change in the board of directors until August, 1879, when the council elected C. V. Gallagher and H. H. VonRaven to succeed those whose terms had expired.

February 2, 1880, the librarian tendered her resignation, Mary P. Allan being elected to fill the position.

The death, March 5, 1880, of H. J. Lucas, caused a vacancy in the board, which was filled by the appointment of F. R. McConnell.

Early in the year the first finding list published by the library was issued. This contained forty-seven pages and sold readily.

June, 1880, J. H. Kellom, president, resigned, also F. R. McConnell. These places were filled by the election of J. W. Savage and J. M. Ross. Wm. Wallace was elected president.

In October the work on the accession catalogue was commenced, there being, up to that time, no complete record of the books.

This year had seen such a decided growth that it was necessary to find larger quarters. The rooms on the same floor, vacated by F. C. Currier, were secured, giving much more space, better light and ventilation. Through the courtesy of United States Senator Paddock, the library was made a depository of congressional documents from November, 1880. Senator Manderson has also used his influence to the benefit of the library.

The next change of directors occurred in July, 1881, W. A. L. Gibbon and John T. Bell being elected, vice A. Rosewater and Lyman Richardson, whose terms had expired.

Until this time all the work had been done by the librarian; but the increasing borrowers, and the additions of new books, required another pair of hands; and, in December, 1881, the first assistant was employed.

The increased expenses compelled the directors to petition the council for a levy of three-fourths of a mill, which was given, increasing the income to $4,847.12.

C. D. Hine and W. A. L. Gibbon resigned from the board, Miss E. E. Poppleton and H. P. Lewis filling the vacancies thus caused.

In 1882, L. B. Williams, requiring for his business the rooms occupied by the library, fitted up others on the same floor for its use. These were held until the addition of a third story, when the institution was enabled to secure nearly the whole of the additional room, and for the first time possessed accommodations in any degree commensurate with its needs. Though on the third floor, and lacking an elevator, the library was thronged with borrowers and the reading room overcrowded.

The experiment of having boys as runners was tried here, but was not a success, so another assistant was procured. In only two years the library had outgrown rooms that had seemed spacious, and compelled another change. After careful consideration of the rooms offered, those owned by N. B. Falconer were deemed the best. These rooms were situated on Douglas, between Fifteenth and Sixteenth Streets, and consisted of the second and third floors. These, while objectionable in many respects, were such an improvement over the old quarters that the disadvantages were overlooked. Here the reading room was on the third floor and the circulating department and the reference room on the second. This was the first effort toward a reference room proper. It was so well patronized by young and old that additions were rapidly made to its shelves, and it gave promise of becoming a valuable addition. Two new directors were elected: E. Dunn and J. P. Metzger, John Wilson succeeding Mr. Metzger in 1887.

In May, 1886, another change was made in the office of librarian, Miss Jessie Allan, the assistant librarian, assuming charge. In 1887 it was decided that the system in use since the beginning had proved entirely inadequate for a large and growing library. As the force was too small to attempt alone the extra work, the services of Mr. Charles Evans, formerly librarian of the Indianapolis Library, was secured. April, 1887, the reorganization was begun. The entire library, then numbering about fifteen thousand volumes, was re-classified, re-numbered, and the majority of these books card catalogued; at the same time a new finding-list was being completed, and was published in April, 1888. It contained 252 pages and was admirably classified and indexed. To this list has been added three supplements, it being the plan to publish such an additional list once a year. On the resignation of H. P. Lewis and John T. Bell, in 1887, Miss Claire Rustin and T. K. Sudborough were elected members of the board.

When the building, corner Douglas and Fifteenth Streets, occupied by N. B. Falconer, changed hands, Mr. Falconer required all of his own building. This prospect of another move brought up the subject of a permanent library building. October 31, 1887, there was received from the city clerk a resolution adopted by the city council on the 18th of October, 1887, of which the following is a copy:

"*Resolved*, That the directors of the Public Library submit to the council plans for a library building to be located on Jefferson Square, with an estimated cost of same."

The special committee was directed to present to the city council an estimate of $80,000 for a building, with the request that the council submit to the electors a proposition to vote bonds for that amount. This failed to pass the city council, and for a time the subject was dropped.

January 21, 1888, found the library established on the third floor of the Paxton Block, on the corner of Sixteenth and Farnam Streets, its present quarters. Here is space enough for a large reading room and a reference room distinct from the other departments.

The largest number of books purchased at one time was in August, 1889, when the library of the late O. F. Davis was bought. This contained about eight hundred volumes, of which 327 were afterwards sold to the Kearney, Nebraska, Library.

In 1888 the tax levy was increased to one mill, making an annual income of $16,429.16.

The vacancy caused in August, 1890, by the resignation of John Wilson was filled by the appointment of W. S. Curtis.

November 21, 1890, the library sustained a loss in the death of Judge James W. Savage, the president of its board of directors. At a special meeting of the directors these resolutions were passed:

"The directors of the Omaha Public Library, in expressing their deep sorrow on account of the death of the Honorable J. W. Savage, wish to show their high esteem for his rectitude of purpose, faithfulness to duty and kindly disposition, not only in all the relations of life, but especially in the discharge of all the labors pertaining to the work of our board. His enlightened and enthusiastic interest in the library work during a long period as director, and including nine years' service as our president, has raised a debt of gratitude which the community can never discharge; therefore be it

"*Resolved*, That we hereby testify to his worth as a citizen, a neighbor, a friend, as a member of this board; and we tender to his relations our heartfelt sympathy; and, further, that, as a testimonial of our appreciation, it is ordered that his portrait be procured and hung in the library to the end that all may bear witness to our appreciation."

A. J. Poppleton was elected to fill the vacant membership.

January 3, 1891, Mr. Poppleton introduced the following resolution, which was unanimously adopted:

"WHEREAS, The City of Omaha has power (under the charter for metropolitan cities and the general laws of this State) to purchase or lease grounds for a library, and to erect thereon 'an appropriate building for the use of such library,' and also power 'to establish and maintain public libraries,' and to provide the necessary grounds or buildings therefor; and

"WHEREAS, Said city has also power to issue bonds for the erection of 'needful buildings for the use of the city,' upon approval of two-thirds of the electors of said city; and

"WHEREAS, The present quarters of the library are unsafe and inadequate, and the provision made therefor in the city hall will be inadequate; therefore

"*Resolved*, That a committee of three, of this board, be appointed by the president, with power and authority to confer with the city council, or such committee as it may raise for that purpose, with instructions if possible to agree upon and report a plan for the selection and acquirement of a suitable site for such library building, with a view to the erection thereon, as soon as funds can be provided by law, of a suitable, indestructible, fire-proof library building.

"*Resolved*, That it is the sense of this board that, in view of the fact that the library now contains books, publications, and manuscripts (many of them of great and exceptional value) to the number of over 33,000 volumes, the time has come for effectual measures for its preservation, and also for rendering the use and enjoyment thereof convenient and accessible to the people at large as well as to such persons as may be engaged in special investigation or general literary work."

As will be seen the foregoing preamble and resolutions were adopted by the library board in January, 1891, but, before the city council took any action on the matter, an event happened which located the library and provided a site for the building. The late Byron Reed, who had devoted much time and expended considerable money in gathering together one of the most valuable collections of coins, books, periodicals and newspapers, bequeathed the whole collection to the City of Omaha, and also gave to the city a lot upon which to erect a library building. The fifth, sixth and seventh clauses of his will are as follows:

Fifth—I hereby give and devise to my son, Abraham L. Reed, a lot of land, at the southeast corner of Harney and Nineteenth Streets, in the City of Omaha, and State of Nebraska, 88.5 feet front on Harney Street, by 93.8 feet on Nineteenth Street, in trust, to be by him conveyed to the City of Omaha, provided said city accept the same, subject to the following conditions, to-wit: That said city erect a first-class fire proof building thereon, covering the whole of said lot, and at least four stories high, suitable for a public library, or art gallery, the erection of said building to be commenced within one year from the day this will is admitted to probate, and to progress so far as to be under roof within two years after it is commenced. As soon as said building is enclosed the trustee above named is directed to execute and deliver to said City of Omaha a deed for said lot. Conditioned that said premises shall ever be used for the benefit of the public as a public library and art gallery and for such other purposes as may be necessary or incidental thereto. The management of said institution shall be conducted and directed by said City of Omaha, and shall be wholly in the interest and for the benefit of the public.

Sixth—In case said lot of land, with the conditions thereto attached, as aforesaid, be accepted by said City of Omaha (and not otherwise), and such acceptance be in writing and filed with this will within one year from the day this will is admitted to probate, then I do hereby give and bequeath to said City of Omaha my private library of books, documents, manuscripts, pamphlets, files of newspapers and other periodicals, autographs, and literary relics, together with my collection of coins, medals, paper money, bonds, drafts and currency, and the cases in which they are contained. This gift shall not take effect until the building above provided for shall be fully completed and ready to receive the same; and, in case the City of Omaha shall decline to accept the devise of said lot at the corner of Harney and Nineteenth Streets, with the conditions thereto attached, as aforesaid, then this gift of said library and coin collection shall be void, and of no effect. In case the above conditions be complied with by the City of Omaha, so that this gift is made effectual, then said library and coin collection shall be placed in said building, and forever thereafter be used and displayed for the benefit of the public, under such reasonable rules and regulations as may be provided therefor by the City of Omaha, one of which shall be that no books or other articles shall be taken outside the building by any person wishing to read or examine the same; and another rule shall be that, for at least a portion of the time (if not all the time), the public shall be admitted free of charge to all the benefits of said library and coin collection, under reasonable rules and regulations. In selecting and delivering said library and coin collection, my executor is directed not to include any book or other literary property a duplicate of which is at the time in the Omaha Public Library; and, in selecting and delivering the collection of coins, medals, and paper money, bonds, drafts and currency, he is not to deliver any duplicate pieces, nor any pieces that have no numismatic value.

My said executor, knowing my wishes in this matter, is constituted the sole judge as to what pieces and articles to deliver and to retain, under this, the sixth, clause of my will.

Seventh—In case the above described lot at the corner of Nineteenth and Harney Streets be not accepted by said City of Omaha, with the terms and conditions thereto attached, as hereinbefore set forth, and within the time limited, as aforesaid, then the devise of said lot, together with all the gifts and bequests contained in the fifth and sixth clauses of this, my will, are hereby revoked and made null and void, and said trustee above named shall convey said lot to my residuary devisees, and all the real and personal property described in said fifth and sixth clauses hereof shall be included with the other property of my estate, and shall be disposed of according to the residuary clause of this, my will, omitting the fifth and sixth clauses thereof.

Subscribed June 4, 1891.

Filed June 13, 1891; G. W. Shields, County Judge.

In accordance with the provisions of Mr. Reed's will, the city council submitted a proposition to the citizens authorizing the issuance of bonds to the amount of $100,000, for the purpose of erecting a building on the lot. The bond proposition was carried by a large majority, and the bonds issued by the city and sold, and the money turned into the library building fund. On the 8th day of December, 1891, the city council passed an ordinance formally accepting the bequest, under the conditions of the will. The library board also purchased additional ground, had plans prepared for a building, which were adopted, and the work of construction is now going on. It is estimated that, exclusive of the lot, the Byron Reed gift is worth $50,000.

The directors of the public library submitted to the city council the following statistics for the year ending December 31, 1891:

In the showing, where any comparative statements are made, they are for the whole of the year 1891, as compared with the year ending May 31, 1891:

Total number of volumes in accession catalogue, 36,274; volumes added since last report, 2,631; total accession for 1891, 5,051; total accession for the year of the last report, 6,004; number of book borrowers' cards issued during year, 4,269; number of book borrowers' cards issued during year of last report, 3,757; number of cards in use at end of year 1891, 10,080; number of cards in use at end of last report, 9,275; number of books issued for home use during year 1891, 175,-102; number of books issued for home use during year of last report, 162,702; number of books issued for use in reference room during 1891, 21,420; number of books issued for use in reference room during year of last report, 16,342; total amount of money expended by the board for year 1891, $25,-257.93; total amount expended for year of last report, $20,971.73.

The above amount, $25,257.93, includes $6,000.00 recommended by the board to be applied as a first payment upon the purchase of land to be used for a library building.

The foregoing statistics show substantial growth in the use of the library, and a slight falling off in the rate of book accessions.

In closing this brief history of the Omaha public library it is interesting to note that two directors, Messrs. L. S. Reed and William Wallace, have served continuously. It must be a source of gratification to these gentlemen to have witnessed the growth of this institution from 2,600 to 40,000 volumes, with a home circulation of 200,000.

Miss Jessie Allan has charge of the city library and is assisted by the following named: Miss Maggie O'Brien, Miss Blanche Allan, Miss Edith Tobitt, Miss Theodora Burstall, Miss Cora McCandlish, Miss Mary Devitt.

Through the generosity of the New York Life Insurance Company one of the finest law libraries in the West was brought here. It was placed in rooms in their building, northeast corner Seventeenth and Farnam Streets, and opened in October, 1889, for the free use of the tenants of said building.

There are at present eight thousand volumes in the library, embracing English, Scotch and Irish reports, the State and territorial reports, complete to date, and all the leading text books, covering every branch of the law. The sum of forty thousand dollars was expended for this collection. To maintain and keep it supplied with leading law periodicals and publications requires from four thousand dollars to five thousand dollars yearly. The librarian is Mr. E. E. Willever, who has been in charge since its organization.

The Omaha Law Library Association owes its inception to the disinterested efforts of some of the oldest members of the Douglas County bar. Organized in December, 1871, it has had a somewhat migratory existence. It occupied at first, as a sort of a joint tenant with the Omaha Library Association, rooms of the latter in Simpson's building on Fourteenth Street. Soon after, however, the library was moved to rooms over the Omaha National Bank, then situated on the southwest corner of Thirteenth and Douglas Streets. These quarters adjoined the law office of the Honorable E. Wakeley, the first president of the association, and he undertook the charge and general supervision of the library. About the year 1877 the library was again moved to the Monell building on Douglas between Fifteenth and Sixteenth Streets. Here it remained for several years, and, when the present court house was completed, the county commissioners placed at the disposal of the association the northwest court room, better known as "No. 3," and occupied more especially of late by Judge Melville R. Hopewell as a court room. Elaborate bookcases and suitable furniture were also furnished by the commissioners, and those of the association who had followed the library in its peregrinations supposed that here, at last, a fixed anchorage had been found. Not so, however. Lawyers and legal business and cases in court grew and multiplied with the growth and expansion of Omaha's other business. In brief, the association was compelled to find another home. At this juncture W. A. Paxton, who had just completed his magnificent block on the corner of Sixteenth and Farnam, having always in view the wishes and convenience of his tenants, many of whom were lawyers, offered to the association, rent free, for a term of five years, suitable rooms upon the fifth floor of his block, the single proviso being that the library would occupy and maintain the same, a request which it is, perhaps, needless to say met with a speedy compliance upon the part of the board of directors. Thus it was that on January 1, 1889, the library was moved from the court house to its present quarters in the Paxton Block.

Although its officers consist now, for the most part, of younger members of the bar, the older practitioners have always taken a deep interest in it. Twenty years ago law libraries in Omaha were the rare exception, and the scarcity of text books and reports of the different States emphasized to those who controlled the business of the bar the necessity of such an organization as this. The association held its first meeting in December, 1871. It was called to order by Charles F. Manderson, and A. J. Poppleton was elected temporary chairman and John L. Webster, temporary secretary. Upon motion of John I. Redick the association proceeded to a permanent organization. The following gentlemen were then elected directors for the first year: E. Wakeley, A. Swartzlander, C. F. Manderson, George Armstrong, and A. J. Poppleton, and the following officers were elected: president, E. Wakeley; vice-president, A. Swartzlander; treasurer, W. J. Connell; secretary, J. L. Webster. The original subscribers to the stock of the library, and those who may be termed its founders, were the following: J. M. Woolworth, C. S. Chase, A. Swartzlander, A. J. Poppleton, J. W. Lytle, G. Armstrong, C. Wiltse, J. C. Cowin, G. B. Lake, E. Wakeley, W. J. Connell, G. I. Gilbert, B. E. B. Kennedy, James Neville, G. W. Doane, J. L. Webster, F. W. Wessells, Robert Townsend, John Taffe, C. F. Manderson, A. M. Henry, J. W. Savage, C. A. Baldwin, George M. O'Brien, J. E. Kelley, T. W. T. Richards, J. R. Meredith, J. I. Redick and C. Briggs. These are names for the most part well-known, not only in Douglas County, but throughout the entire State, whither the vicissitudes of business frequently called the old-time practitioners. Some of these death has claimed; many have long since retired from practice; while not a few still reap a harvest, well earned by two decades of faithful labor, many hours of which have been spent in communion with the silent volumes upon the shelves of the association.

Additions have from time to time been made to the library, and it now includes United States Supreme Court Reports; English Common Law Reports; English Chancery Reports; Vesey's Chancery Reports; Condensed English Chancery Reports and also English Law and Equity Reports. It includes also reports of the following states: Alabama, California, Connecticut, Illinois, Indiana, Iowa, Kansas, Kentucky, Maine, Massachusetts, Michigan; Law and Equity Reports of Mississippi, Minnesota, Nebraska, New Hampshire, New Jersey, New York, including Cane's Cases; Cane's, Johnson's, Cowan's, Wendall's, Hill's and Denio's Reports; those of the Court of Appeals, and Chancery Reports; Ohio, Pennsylvania, Rhode Island, South Carolina, Tennessee, Texas, Wisconsin and Bigelow's Insurance Reports. The board of directors for the present year are George B. Lake, B. E. B. Kennedy, C. S. Chase, H. J. Davis, C. W. Haller, Isaac Adams, W. W. Keysor, F. L. McCoy, E. W. Simeral, J. W. Carr and A. C. Wakeley. The officers are: president, C. S. Chase; vice president, E. W. Simeral; secretary, A. C. Wakeley; treasurer, J. W. Carr. librarian, Miss Bessie C. O'Brien.

THE LATE BYRON REED'S LIBRARY.

There are two Catholic libraries in the city, both being at the college (Twenty-fifth and California Streets) and known as the Creighton College Libraries. The first is for reference and for use by the priests and professors of the college, only. It was begun in 1879, by the Jesuits, when they assumed control of the college. There are at present about 7,200 volumes in the collection. It has no printed catalogue as yet. Its manuscript list embraces the best works in Catholic theology, moral, dogmatic, and Scriptural; besides works in Philosophy, history, literature, law, medicine, natural sciences, mathematics and ancient classics.

The collection is valuable not only for authors in varied fields of human knowledge, but also for old and rare books of the fifteenth, sixteenth and seventeenth centuries. Among these might be mentioned DeSyra's notes on the Bible, published at Cologne, in 1478, bound in thick oak, capitals illustrated by hand, and one of the first books from the press of the famous Koelkoff, of Lubeck; Servius' edition of Virgil's works, published at Basle, in 1547, by Seb. Henricpetri; the Aldine of Thomas Campegius, on the authority of the Roman Pontiff, a valuable work from the famous Aldine press 1555; Anderson's large folio edition of Cook's voyages, published in London, by Alexander Hogg, a curious, rare edition, with 150 full page etchings of the last century.

The nucleus of this library was purchased from Bardstown College, Kentucky, an institution which was closed after the civil war. When it was offered for sale, in 1879, Rev. Roman Shaffel, S. J., of Creighton College bought three thousand volumes for three thousand dollars, of which two thousand dollars came from John Creighton, the remainder from the Jesuit community. Having no endowment fund it depends altogether on donations.

The Students' Library was organized in April, 1880, by a number of the students, under Rev. Austin Beile, S. J., the first president.

As no library fund exists, upon which the association can draw, the books have been purchased by monthly fees contributed by the members, donations of friends, and also from the proceeds obtained by entertainments given by the association. This collection now numbers about 11,000 volumes.

The Masonic and Odd Fellows orders have libraries in their halls of several thousand volumes each.

Swedish, Danish and Bohemian societies have each fine libraries, which are well patronized and added to year by year.

Among the private libraries of the city that of Byron Reed is the largest and most unique. It contains 4,500 volumes, not including 1,000 bound magazines and newspapers. For many years Mr. Reed has spared neither time nor expense to place his collection in the place it holds to-day. Among the sets worthy of mention and seldom to be found in a private library are: The complete files of the New York *Daily Times*; Philadelphia *Enquirer*, *Harper's Weekly*; *Niles' Weekly Register* 1811-1848; Richmond *Sentinel* (the organ of Jefferson Davis); complete sets of the State Journal from 1855; complete sets of the Omaha directories; Statutes at Large of the Confederate States, also of the State of Virginia —this is particularly valuable, there being but three sets in existence. Among the histories of the northwest are first editions of Lewis and Clarke's Expedition, Carver's Travels, DeSmet's Western Missions and Missionaries, also a volume containing an account of the first steamboat up the Missouri to Omaha, published in 1819.

A volume that attracts attention is a choir book of Gregorian chants, a large book bound in copper, heavily studded with spike-like projections, the initial letters being richly illuminated. Another work, and one of peculiar interest in Omaha, where a cloister is established, is a book of regulations for the Order of Poor Clare. It was wrought at Milan, in the fifteenth century.

Mr. Reed's collection of coins stands among the three or four most valuable and complete in the United States. It includes specimens of all the coins struck in the United States, as well as the trial pieces. His collection of the coins of foreign countries is quite complete. A numismatist grows enthusiastic over these and the ancient coins dating back to the seventh century B. C. The collection—books, coins, manuscripts and autographs—is valued at nearly $50,000.

The library of J. M. Woolworth, the oldest in the city, is devoted mainly to law.

That of the late James W. Savage has a fine collection of Shakespeariana.

William Wallace makes a specialty of publications on the civil war.

A. J. Poppleton has one of the finest miscellaneous collections in Omaha.

These are only a few of many private libraries that would be a credit to older cities.

# CHAPTER XXVII.

OMAHA'S SYSTEM OF WATERWORKS — THE CONTEST IN THE CITY COUNCIL — DESCRIPTION OF THE METHOD NOW USED.

Very early in the history of Omaha was the necessity for a system of waterworks, especially for protection from fire, recognized. In April, 1857, the city engineer was instructed to ascertain and report to the city council "whether it will be practicable to bring the water from Omaha Creek, west of the capitol, by means of a syphon, to the principal streets, to be conveyed into cisterns, to use in case of fire, and the probable cost of the same," which examination was made by the city engineer at once, and an adverse report made by him at the next meeting of the council.

In March, 1864, the city engineer was instructed to "examine and report whether there are any springs within the city limits from which water may be brought into the city for the purpose of extinguishing fires, and, if not, that he be requested to report some other feasible plan to supply the city with water;" and a few days later a committee was appointed to "ascertain the cost of a fire engine and apparatus, and a suitable number of cisterns to afford adequate protection against fire." If either the engineer or committee presented a report on these subjects, the city clerk forgot to mention that fact in his minutes of the council proceedings.

A few years later cisterns were built in the business portion of the city, and supplied with water from the river by pumping with the fire engines, but these proved entirely inadequate on several occasions, and the necessity for something better adapted to the needs of the city soon became apparent. In April, 1870, Mr. Flagler, president of the Holly Waterworks Company, of Lockport, New York, addressed the council upon the subject, urging the advantages of the Holly, or direct pressure, system as being superior to all others. On this occasion, Mayor Ezra Millard presented to the council letters from the mayors of various eastern cities endorsing that system. A vote of thanks was returned to Mr. Flagler by the council, and there the matter rested for several years. In the latter part of 1873 the council advertised for bids for the boring of an artesian well, 2,000 feet deep. W. E. Swaim, of Joliet, Illinois, proved the lowest bidder, and he proposed to bore and case a well of six inches diameter in the clear for $6 per foot for the first 500 feet, $8 per foot for the second 500 feet, $9.50 per foot for the third 500 feet, and $10.50 per foot for the fourth 500 feet, with a rebate of $2.40 per foot for each foot not cased. The proposition to vote bonds to an amount necessary to do this work failed to carry, and the scheme to obtain water in that way was abandoned. In March, 1874, a resolution was adopted by the council authorizing the issuance of bonds to provide for the building of waterworks, and W. W. Marsh, J. H. Congdon, J. E. House, J. E. Boyd, Jonas Gise, John A. Horbach, Alvin Saunders, Herman Kountze and James Creighton were appointed a committee to visit various eastern cities and inspect the different systems of waterworks, but no practical results were reached.

In February, 1878, Alderman C. V. Gallagher offered a resolution, which was adopted, instructing the committee on public property and improvements "to inquire into the feasibility and expediency of establishing a system of waterworks, and also to investigate and advise the council as to the propriety of submitting to a vote at the spring election the question of voting bonds for that purpose." A month later the committee referred to presented a report to the effect that the financial condition of the city did not, at that time, warrant the outlay necessary to establish a system of waterworks, and recommended that the city attorney advise the council " what proceedings, legislative or otherwise, are necessary to enable the city to raise the funds required to procure a permanent system of waterworks." This report was adopted.

July 9, 1878, an ordinance was passed by the council, on first and second readings, authorizing the entering into a contract by the city with S. L. Wiley & Co. for the construction and maintenance of a system of waterworks. This was the beginning of a local fight which lasted a year, raging at times with great violence, the majority of the council, then composed of twelve members, favoring the letting of the contract to the Holly Manufacturing Company, of Lockport, New York, who used the direct pressure system, public sentiment generally favoring the reservoir and gravitation system. The last named company made a proposition to construct waterworks at Omaha, July 23d, through its agent, Dr. J. T. Cushing, and this gentleman five days later took Councilmen Jones, Hascall, Stephenson, Kaufman, Labagh and Redman to Ottumwa and Burlington, Iowa, in order that they might compare the Holly and Wiley systems, the former having been adopted by the Burlington people, and the latter being in operation at Ottumwa. A general invitation was extended to the council as a body to go, but it was accepted only by those named. In the meantime the subject was being discussed in the daily papers, the *Herald* and the *Republican* favoring the Holly system, and the *Bee* opposing it. Mass meetings were held at various times in the court house, and considerable bad feeling manifested. In the council the Holly system was endorsed by Councilmen J. D. Jones (president), Isaac S. Hascall, Charles Kaufman, G. F. Labagh, Joseph Redman, Fritz Riepen, Bernard Shannon and Felix Slaven; Councilmen Thomas A. Dailey, James Stephenson, Levi Kennard and O. G. Dodge opposing the adoption, aided by the mayor, C. S. Chase, who vetoed in regular order the various ordinances which the " solid eight " drafted and passed in the Holly interests.

August 20th, Dr. Cushing was arrested upon complaint of Edward Rosewater, editor of the *Bee*, on the charge of " bribery and attempting to bribe" members of the city council. An investigation was had before Justice Powell, District Attorney A. N. Ferguson appearing for the prosecution and John C. Cowin for the defendant. Several witnesses were examined, and an effort was made to show that one of the councilmen favoring the Holly system had been tempted by the offer of a suit of clothes to change his views as to the merits of the two systems, but this attempt failed, as did also the efforts to fasten upon Dr. Cushing the crime charged against him. August 8th, an ordinance based upon the Holly proposition was passed on third reading by the council, by a vote of eight to four, and was vetoed by the mayor. On the following day application was made to Judge James W. Savage, of the district court, for an injunction to restrain the city authorities from taking further action with respect to entering into a contract for the construction of waterworks under that ordinance. The petition was signed by James E. Boyd, James K. Ish, William A. Paxton, O. C. Campbell, and Lewis Brash, who were represented on the hearing of the case by George W. Doane, John D. Howe, and Edward W. Simeral, the city council being represented by E. Wakeley, J. C. Cowin and George E. Pritchett. The petitioners claimed that the ordinance was unconstitutional; that it granted exclusive privileges; that the law authorizing the construction of waterworks intended that the city should be the owner thereof; that the ordinance was unreasonable and necessarily void, first, because it granted exclusive privileges to one company without allowing for competition, and, secondly, because it was prejudicial to the city and favorable to the waterworks company, in not providing for a limiting of the franchise in price, and in not providing that the city might purchase either the franchise or the works at the expiration of twenty-five years; that the ordinance was not passed in accordance with the rules of the council, or parliamentary rules; and that the necessary expenses of the city already provided for would more than consume the amount of the tax levy for that year. The case came up for argument September 6th, and two days were occupied with the hearing. September 13th Judge Savage gave an elaborate decision in favor of the petitioners and on the same day a special meeting of the council was held, at which was passed substantially the same ordinance to which objection had been made, but the word "exclusive" was stricken out as previously applied to the franchise. This ordinance was vetoed by the mayor, and on the 17th, passed over his veto by a vote of eight to three, Stephenson, of the opposition, being absent.

Recourse was again had to the district court on injunction proceedings, and Judge Savage again decided adversely to the solid eight of the council, and on the 14th of October an ordinance was introduced authorizing the city to contract with any responsible person or corporation to construct waterworks. To this various amendments were offered favorable to the Holly system, and the ordinance, as amended, passed over the veto of the mayor, and in February, 1880, a contract was entered into by the council, without the mayor's signature, for the construction of a system of waterworks.

Large quantities of pipe for mains were at once brought to Omaha by the Holly people and distributed along many of the principal streets of the city, and in March a tract of ground was secured in Hanscom Place Addition, directly north of Hanscom park, as a site for reservoirs or settling basins, and the work of excavating commenced. The election of April 6th, however, put into the city council several new members who had taken an active part in opposing the Holly system, including James E. Boyd, which gave the opposition a decided majority. At a meeting held April 16th, the city attorney was requested to state "the present status of the contract between the city and the Holly company," and at a meeting held four days later an ordinance was introduced repealing the Holly ordinance. At this meeting was read an opinion on the subject, given by A. J. Poppleton, Esq., in response to an application made by councilman Stephenson, which held that the Holly ordinance had not been legally passed; that there was no such corporation in existence; that it was not authorized to contract; its acceptance and bond were without effect; that no lawful record had been made, because its alleged articles of incorporation had not been acknowledged; the ordinance passed was to the effect of granting illegal, exclusive franchises; that the bond claimed to have been filed by the waterworks company was without date and not legally filed; that the acceptance of ordinance 412 was void for want of an acceptor authorized to make contracts; that the mayor, in his official capacity, is a necessary party to the valid contract in respect to waterworks. The repealing ordinance was then passed under a suspension of the rules, and, on the 22nd day of April, J. D. Cook, an engineer of Toledo, Ohio, was employed by the council to prepare plans for a system of waterworks for Omaha. An ordinance was drafted, based upon the requirements of Mr. Cook's plans, which provided for reservoirs for storage and settling purposes, and passed without a dissenting vote. The city clerk was directed to advertise for bids for the construction of waterworks in accordance with the ordinance; and on the 20th of July a year and nine days after the date of the introduction in the council of the first ordinance on the subject, the contract to construct waterworks for the city was awarded to a company of Omaha men, consisting of Samuel R. Johnson, Sidney E. Locke, Charles H. Dewey, John T. Clark, Nathan Shelton, and Milton Rogers, under the style of "Sidney E. Lock and Associates;" but an organization was perfected soon afterwards as the "City Waterworks Company." The contract, which was for twenty-five years, required the completion of the work in two years, but the water was flowing through the pipes early in September, 1881.

Originally only seventeen miles of pipe were laid, but additions were constantly made as the growth of the city required it. The system adopted was a combination of the gravity and direct pressure systems. The original plant consisted of one five-million gallon pumping engine, delivering, through twenty miles of pipe, to storage reservoirs of ten millions capacity, situated on Walnut Hill, the flow line at the reservoir being 305 feet above low water line of the Missouri River. July 1, 1886, the City Waterworks Company sold its stock to a Boston syndicate represented by S. L. Wiley, himself being purchaser of a large portion of the stock, for the sum of $1,300,000. Mr. Wiley thus became the manager of the business, and immediately arranged to carry into effect a plan he had contemplated when he put in a bid to construct the works in 1878, i. e., the establishment of pumping works and settling basins above Florence. The preliminaries for this had all been settled when the property and franchise were transferred, July 1, 1887, to the American Waterworks Company, of Chicago, with $4,000,000 capital, who owned and operated the works up to September, 1891, when the works were sold to the American Waterworks, of New Jersey. The New Jersey corporation was incorporated with ten million dollars, and consisted of the entire waterworks plant of Omaha and the entire Denver waterworks plant of Denver, Colorado. Additional pumping engines and settling basins were added from time to time, until the present pumping capacity of ten million per day was reached. Owing to the rapid growth of the city, and sufficient ground suitable for the settling basins not being obtainable, and the danger of contamination of the supply from sewerage, it was decided, in 1888, to move the pumping plant six miles up the river, to Florence, where it had been contemplated to locate the works in S. L. Wiley's plan, which was submitted to the city ten years previously, by S. L. Wiley & Co.

The formal opening of the new works, August 1, 1889, was an event long to be remembered by the citizens of Omaha. Early in the morning a special train carried over five hundred invited guests, including county and federal officers, heads of wholesale and manufacturing enterprises, professional and newspaper men, to the scene. A thorough inspection of the plant was made, followed by speech making. Then Acting Mayor Lee, of Omaha, formally started the pumps amid much enthusiasm, and the guests sat down to a sumptuous lunch, supplemented by speech making and congratulatory remarks. Among the speakers were the president of the American Waterworks Company, Mr. W. A. Underwood, Hon. T. T. Flagler, president of the Holly Waterworks Company, Mr. W. I. Kierstead, of the Board of Public Works, Mr. George Barker, president of the Bank of Commerce, Councilman I. S. Hascall and ex-Mayor Chase. Resolutions were presented by Congressman W. J. Connell which were unanimously adopted, thanking the company for their hospitality and congratulating both the

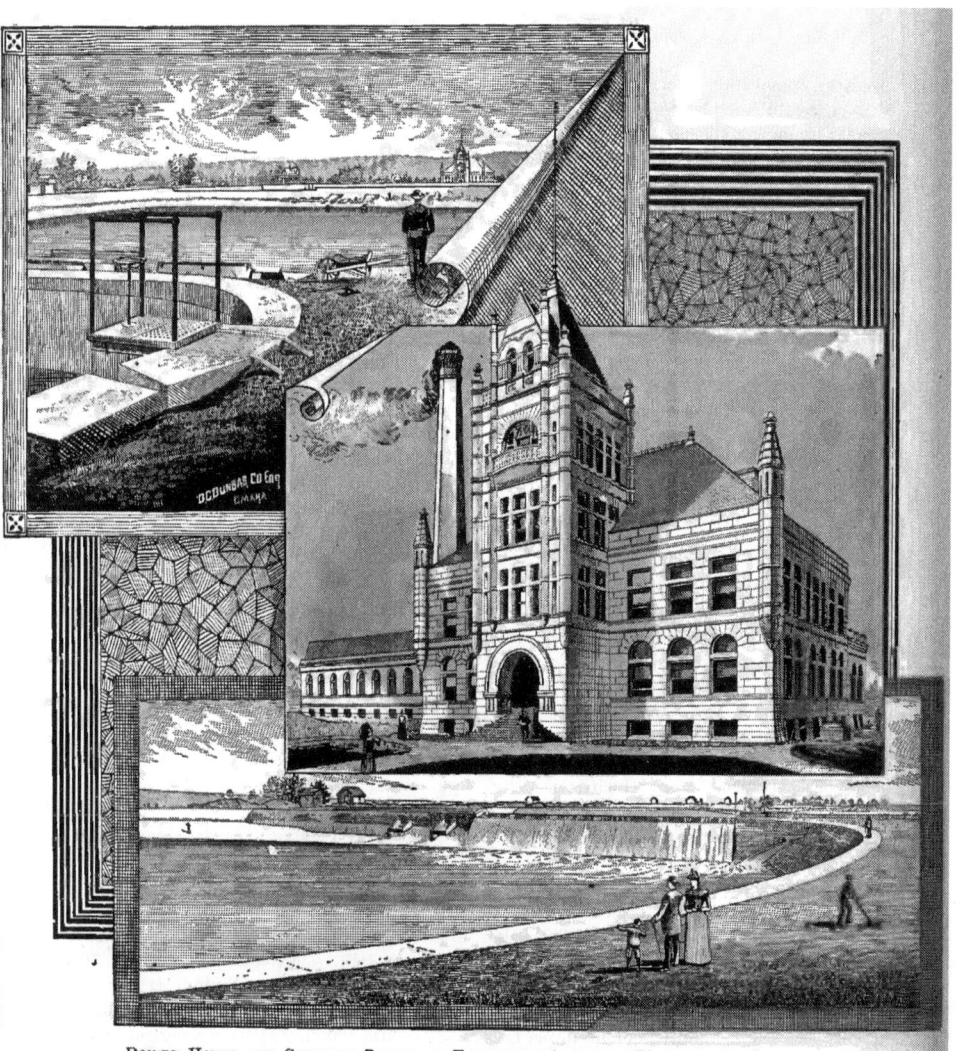

POWER HOUSE AND SETTLING BASINS AT FLORENCE—AMERICAN WATERWORKS COMPANY.

company and the citizens of Omaha over the successful completion of the enterprise.

The pumping station, built of Warrensburg sandstone, size 120 x 160 feet, is the finest and most complete building of its character in the country. It will be lighted by electric incandescent lights. The boiler plant consists of six upright boilers, and Butman furnaces. The pumping engines are the Allis low service and the Gaskill high service, each of a capacity of fifteen million gallons per day. The most complete modern machines of the same pattern as those used at Chicago and Buffalo have been provided. The supply is taken from inlet cribs, and delivered by the low service pump to the last of the series of five settling basins, which have a capacity of one hundred million gallons. These basins are constructed with stone retaining walls, and lined throughout with concrete and cement. Valves operated by hydraulic pressure are located in the bottom of the basins, for the purpose of emptying the contents into a drain tunnel, leading to the river. The top strata of water flows over a wire, with a current of air underneath, from each basin to the next, through the five basins, till the last one is reached, from which it is delivered by a high service pump for consumption through a thirty-six inch main pipe to the city.

The company also maintains a separate direct pressure system for that portion of the city located on high ground. This being largely a residence district, a domestic pressure of forty pounds is maintained, except upon receipt of fire alarm, when it is increased to one hundred pounds direct pressure. The water supply for the City of South Omaha, and the Union Stock Yards, is also furnished by this company. The water mains are of standard weight, cast iron pipes, of large diameter. The total mileage, January 1, 1891, was 158 miles, with 1,344 fire hydrants of the standard Matthews and Gaskill patterns. Ludlow valves are used. The entire construction of the works has been done in the most substantial manner, the aim of the company being to have the best works in the United States. The number of consumers is nearly seven thousand. The daily consumption in 1884 was 1,200,000 gallons, and the present consumption is about 17,000,000. There are now over seven hundred metres in use.

The company supply South Omaha, and the high ground on the south side, by direct pressure, and for this service purchased an eight million gallon triple-expansion Gaskill pumping engine, and placed it in a pumping station recently erected at the corner of Twentieth Street and Poppleton Avenue. The building is of brick, 76 x 124 feet, and thirty feet high in the clear. The cost of this improvement is about $45,000. Room is provided for an additional engine of like capacity. A powerful Allis pumping engine has recently been placed in position at Florence, with a capacity of eighteen million gallons every six hours. Plans are perfected for the construction of another large reservoir on the high point northwest of Walnut Hill, to be supplied by a forty-eight inch main with a capacity of ninety million gallons in twenty-four hours. This reservoir will be 310 feet above the pumping station at Florence. The combined daily capacity of the entire system November 1, 1890, was as follows: Florence, 48,000,000 gallons; the lower city stand, 28,000,000 gallons; Poppleton Avenue, 8,000,000 gallons; Walnut Hill, 6,000,000 gallons; total, 70,000,000 gallons. The Walnut Hill reservoirs are 210 feet above low water mark.

A contest having arisen among the stockholders for control of the company, Mr. Underwood resigned the presidency and from the board of directors, and shortly afterward the Denver Waterworks Company, the Denver City Waterworks Company and seven stockholders went into the United States District Court, at Lincoln, and asked for the appointment of a receiver, on the ground that the affairs of the company were being manipulated by Mr. C. H. Venner in such a manner as to defraud them. Upon a hearing, Judge Dundy rendered a decision on February 11, 1892, and appointed Mr. Ellis L. Bierbower receiver, with Alonzo B. Hunt as receiver to take charge of the mechanical department, on the ground that there were no legal officers to take charge of the affairs of the company. The business of the company has been conducted without a stoppage and is still in charge of the receivers, and outside of the court proceedings, the articles which have appeared in the newspapers, and the presence of Mr. Bierbower in the office, there has apparently been but little change in the personnel and conduct of the management of this great, beneficial and necessary institution.

# CHAPTER XXVIII.

### INDIANS AS LITIGANTS—STANDING BEAR SUEING FOR HIS RIGHTS—SUBSEQUENT SUITS IN THE UNITED STATES COURTS.

On the 23d of March, 1879, twenty-nine Ponca Indians, men, women and children, with Chief Standing Bear in charge, were arrested at the Omaha Indian reservation, by Lieutenant Carpenter and a squad of soldiers sent out from Fort Omaha for that purpose by General Crook, under orders from Washington. Two years previously the Ponca tribe had been taken from their reservation in southern Dakota and located in the Indian Territory. Here they endured privations and suffered extremely. A large proportion of their number died, and, becoming desperate, the party in question left their new home in midwinter, determined to make their way back to the reservation from which they had been removed without their consent, and where they had been prosperous and contented, and had made considerable advance in agriculture. Upon reaching the Omaha reservation, they were heartily welcomed by the Omahas and furnished with the supplies so much needed. Their captors started to take them back to the Indian Territory, stopping over a few days for rest at Fort Omaha. Late Saturday night, Mr. T. H. Tibbles, then assistant editor of the Omaha *Herald*, heard of the arrival of the Indians at the fort, and on Sunday went up to see them. Hearing their story, and being touched by their miserable condition, he returned to the city and visited a number of churches that night and induced the ministers to make some remarks to their congregations with regard to the case. He published in the *Herald* an extended report of what he had seen and heard. Rev. W. J. Harsha, of the Presbyterian Church, Rev. E. H. E. Jameson, of the Baptist Church, Rev. A. F. Sherill, of the Congregational Church, and Rev. H. D. Fisher, of the Methodist Church, joined heartily with Mr. Tibbles in espousing the cause of the Indians. A. J. Poppleton, Esq., and John L. Webster, Esq., were consulted by Mr. Tibbles as to the legal status of the case and as to whether or not the release of the Indians could be secured by means of a writ of *habeas corpus*, though never before in the history of this government had such a course been attempted with the red man. After a full consideration of the matter, these gentlemen volunteered their services and General Crook was cited to appear before Judge E. S. Dundy, judge of the United States District Court, and show cause why the Indians should not be released from custody. The petition was as follows:

"In the District Court of the United States, for the District of Nebraska:

"Ma-chu-nah-sha (Standing Bear) versus George Crook, a brigadier-general of the army of the United States and commanding the Department of the Platte.

"The petition of Ma-chu-nah-sha (then followed the names of all the Indians under arrest), who respectfully show unto your Honor that each and all of them are prisoners, unlawfully imprisoned, detained, confined and in custody, and are restrained of their liberty, under and by color of the alleged authority of the United States, by George Crook, a brigadier-general of the army of the United States and commanding the Department of the Platte, and are so imprisoned, detained, confined and in custody, and restrained of their liberty, by said George Crook, at Fort Omaha, on a military reservation under the sole and exclusive jurisdiction of the United States, and located within the territory of the district of Nebraska. That said imprisonment, detention, confinement and restraint by said George Crook, as aforesaid, are and were done by him, under and by virtue of some order or direction of the United States, or some department thereof, and which order or direction is not more particularly known to these complainants, whereby they are unable to more particularly set the same forth, save that the complainants are informed and believe that said order or direction is to the effect that these complainants be taken to the Indian Territory as prisoners.

"These complainants further represent that they are Indians of the nationality of the Ponca tribe of Indians, and that for a considerable time before and at the time of their arrest and imprisonment, as herein more fully set forth, they were separated from the Ponca tribe of Indians, and that so many of the said Ponca tribe of Indians as maintained their tribal relations are located in the Indian Territory.

"That your complainants at the time of their arrest and imprisonment were lawfully and peacefully residing on the Omaha reservation, a tract of land set apart by the United States to the Omaha tribe of Indians, and within the territory of the district of Nebraska, and were so residing there by the wish and consent of said Omaha tribe of Indians, on lands set apart to your complainants by said Omaha tribe of Indians.

"That your complainants have made great advancement in civilization, and at the time of the arrest of your complainants some of them were actually engaged in agriculture, and others were making arrangements for immediate agricultural labors, and were supporting themselves by their own labors, and not one of these complainants was receiving or asking support of the government of the United States.

"That your complainants were not violating, and were not guilty of any violation of, any law of the United States for which said arrest and imprisonment were made.

"That, while your complainants were so peacefully and lawfully residing on said Omaha reservation, as aforesaid, they were each and all unlawfully imprisoned, detained, confined, and restrained of their liberty, by said George Crook, as such brigadier-general, commanding the Department of the Platte, and as such prisoners were transported from their said residence at the Omaha reservation to Fort Omaha, where they are now unlawfully imprisoned, detained, confined, and restrained of their liberty, by said George Crook, as aforesaid:

"Wherefore, these complainants say that their imprisonment and detention are wholly illegal, and they demand that the writ of *habeas corpus* be granted, directed to the said George Crook, brigadier-general of the United States, commanding the Department of the Platte, commanding him to have the bodies of (here followed the names of the complainants) before your Honor, at the time and place therein to be specified, to do and receive what shall then and there be considered by your Honor concerning them, together with the time and cause of their detention, and that the complainants may there be restored to their liberty."

General Crook being cited to appear, and the preliminary proceedings having been disposed of, the case came on for hearing in the United States court room, at Omaha, April 30, 1879, the lawyers above named appearing for the Indians, and United States District Attorney G. M. Lambertson for General Crook, the point to be decided being whether the complainants had dissolved their tribal relations and were "persons" within the meaning of the law. One evening and two day sessions of the court were occupied with the case, Judge Dundy deciding it in favor of the complainants, holding

"First. That the Indian is a person, within the meaning of the laws of the United States, and has therefore the right to sue out a writ of *habeas corpus* in a federal court, and before a federal judge, in all cases where he may be confined, or in custody, under color of authority of the United States, or where he is restrained of liberty in violation of the constitution or laws of the United States.

"Second. That General George Crook, the respondent, being commander of the Military Department of the Platte, has the custody of the relators, under color of authority of the United States, and in violation of the laws thereof.

"Third. That no lawful authority exists for the removal by force of any of the relators to the Indian Territory, as the respondent has been directed to do.

"Fourth. That the Indians possess the inherent right of expatriation, as well as the more fortunate white race, and have an inalienable right to life, liberty, and the pursuit of happiness, so long as they obey the laws and do not trespass on forbidden ground.

"Fifth. Being restrained of liberty, under color of authority of the United States, and in violation of the laws thereof, the relators must be discharged from custody, and it is so ordered."

A few days later General Crook received orders from the War Department to release the Indians, and they at once returned to the Omaha reservation, Standing Bear presenting to Mr. Poppleton a war bonnet of historic value, to Mr. Webster a tomahawk, and to Mr. Tibbles a handsome pair of beaded moccasins, in appreciation of the great service they had rendered him and his people.

April 5, 1880, John Elk, an Indian, presented himself for registration before Registrar Charles Wilkins, of the fifth ward of this city, with a view of voting at the local election the following day. The officer refused to put his name upon the list, and, thereupon, Elk brought suit for damages in the sum of six thousand dollars, claiming that he had abandoned his tribal relations and that, under the fourteenth and fifteenth amendments to the constitution of the United States, he was a citizen and entitled to all the rights of citizenship. The suit was brought in the United States Court, before Judges McCrary and Dundy, Messrs. Poppleton and Webster appearing for Elk, and District Attorney Lambertson for Wilkins. The case was decided against the complainant, on a demurrer filed by Lambertson setting forth: (1) That the petition did not state facts sufficient to constitute a cause of action; (2) That the court had no jurisdiction of the person of the defendant; and (3) That the court had no jurisdiction of the subject of the action. An appeal was taken to the Supreme Court of the United States, and the decision of the lower court was sustained, Justices Harlan and Wood dissenting.

In the spring of 1888, a suit was brought in the circuit court of the United States for Nebraska, by the heirs of Sophia Felix, a half-breed Indian of the Sioux nation, claiming title to 120 acres of land now included within the city limits of Omaha, and of immense value. The land had been deeded by Sophia Felix to M. T. Patrick, in 1860, which deed, complainants claimed, had been obtained by "wicked devices and fraudulent means." The heirs set out in their petition that it was only within two years prior to bringing the suit that they had been entitled to bring such an action, for the reason that until August, 1889, they had maintained their tribal relations as members of the Santee band of the Sioux nation. They were represented on the hearing by a great array of legal talent, including John C. Cowin and Charles Ogden, of Omaha; Shipman, Barlow, Larocque and Choate, of Boston; and J. H. Parsons, of Birmingham,

Alabama. A. J. Poppleton, George W. Ambrose and John L. Webster appeared for the defendant, and gained the suit. On the trial of the case, Mr. Ambrose made a pertinent reference to the famous Dred Scott decision, wherein Judge Taney held that the negro had no rights which a white man was bound to respect. Mr. Ambrose insisting that, if the rule contended for by the complainants should obtain, the white man had no rights which an Indian was bound to respect. An appeal was taken to the United States Supreme Court, where it was decided in favor of Mr. Patrick, May 16, 1892, on the ground that the plaintiff had waited too long before beginning the suit. The hearing at Omaha was before Judges Brewer and Dundy. Judge Brewer was soon afterward appointed to the United States Supreme Court.

In the two cases last mentioned, that of Standing Bear figured prominently, as establishing a precedent in legal proceedings where Indians were parties.

# CHAPTER XXIX.

COUNTY FAIRS — DRIVING PARK ASSOCIATION — BOARD OF TRADE — REAL ESTATE EXCHANGE — REAL ESTATE OWNERS' ASSOCIATION — MANUFACTURERS' AND CONSUMERS' ASSOCIATION.

On the first and second days of October, 1858, Douglas County made its first public display of agricultural products, at which time a fair was held at Saratoga. Among the prominent exhibitors were Joel T. Griffin, Hadley D. Johnson, O. P. Hurford, A. J. Simpson, J. W. Tousley, Peter Windheim, Moses Shinn, Edwin Patrick, Jesse Lowe, and C. Davidson; Mr. Griffin exhibiting thirty varieties of vegetables. The premiums offered ranged in value from fifty cents to five dollars. J. W. Tousley was awarded the last named sum for his fine display of hogs, and also received a premium of one dollar for his superior skill in the ambrotype line, which shows that Tousley blended the practical with the artistic and æsthetic while aiding in the development of the boundless West.

The Omaha *Times* thus describes one of the main features of this occasion: "The fair closed with a specimen of equestrianism by ladies, although we were informed it was not down on the bills. The ladies entering for the prize, a beautiful side saddle, were Mrs. E. V. Smith, Mrs. Boyd, and Miss Augusta Estabrook. The course chosen for the exercise was far too small, being but two hundred feet square. The horses were put under a full run, and in the short turn, both horses and riders, to maintain an equilibrium, were going at an angle of forty-five degrees. To say the least of it, the race was exciting. Miss Estabrook, upon her little pony, calm and collected, was loudly cheered by the spectators, as also was Mrs. Smith, upon a white pony. Mrs. Boyd also was entitled to her share of the award of praise. The falling from her horse at the close of the race, while it resulted in no material injury, was a subject of regret by all. The champions for the prize seemed to be Miss Estabrook and Mrs. Smith — more graceful riders than all three would be hard to find — and we are informed that the committee awarded it to Miss Estabrook. That little pony and cool little rider, under full run, have been flying around the race course of our brain ever since." The successful competitor was the daughter of General Estabrook, and is now the wife of Colonel Clowry, the well-known Western Union official.

From that date county fairs were annually held here, with more or less success, for a number of years. In 1875, Messrs. Al. Patrick, M. T. Patrick, A. H. Baker, James Stephenson and Dr. J. P. Peck, bought the forty acres of land north of the city on which the fairs had generally been held and organized the Omaha Driving Park Association, erected buildings, fenced in the grounds and constructed a splendid track for racing purposes. In 1880 they sold out their interests to an association composed of J. J. Brown, Charles H. Brown, Chris. Hartman, D. T. Mount, George Canfield, Benjamin Wood, John D. Creighton, W. A. Paxton, and James E. Boyd, each owning one-tenth of the stock, and the remaining one-tenth being the undivided interest of the association. The officers are as follows: Joseph Garneau, Jr., president; Charles A. Coe, vice-president; H. K. Burket, secretary;

Frank D. Brown, treasurer; Thomas Swobe, William Krug, George W. Ames, directors. This company expended about fourteen thousand dollars in putting up additional buildings, making it more suitable for the purposes of the State fair, which was held at Omaha for several years thereafter, as it had also been previously. A few years later the property passed into the ownership of J. J. Brown, Charles Brown and John D. Creighton, and the Omaha Fair and Exposition Association was formed, composed of about fifty of the enterprising citizens of Omaha, which association leases the grounds and buildings and gives annual displays of the highest order of merit, bringing to Omaha visitors from all parts of the United States. The premium list for 1889 amounted to about twenty thousand dollars. The officers of the association are as follows: D. T. Mount, president; Churchill Parker, vice-president; Hugh G. Clark, treasurer; J. H. McShane, secretary; D. T. Mount, Churchill Parker, Hugh G. Clark, J. H. McShane, M. T. Patrick, J. H. Hungate, and J. J. Brown, directors: J. H. Hungate, J. J. Brown, and M. T. Patrick, executive committee.

Just previous to the organization of the exposition association, the buildings on the ground were nearly all destroyed by a tornado, and, in the fall of 1887, more extensive structures having been erected in the meantime by the present association, a very considerable loss was inflicted by fire which, it is claimed, was caused by sparks from a passing engine on the Belt Line Railway. A suit was brought against the Missouri Pacific Railway Company, the owners of the Belt Line, for the sum of eighteen thousand dollars damages, the plaintiffs being the Fair and Exposition Company and an insurance company which paid out about half that amount on account of the fire. The case was tried in the district court in December, 1889, and decided in favor of the railroad company.

The Douglas County Agricultural Society was re-organized in 1882, with D. T. Mount as president, George N. Crawford, secretary, and J. J. Brown, treasurer. The following year George N. Crawford was elected president, John Baumer, secretary, and J. J. Brown, treasurer. In 1884, John T. Paulsen was elected president, Henry Eicke, vice-president, John Baumer, secretary, and Henry Bolln, treasurer, and were all re-elected in 1885, with the exception of Henry Eicke, Elijah Allen being elected vice-president in his place; and the board thus formed was re-elected in 1886, and the two succeeding years, with the exception that Mr. Paulsen was succeeded in 1887, as president, by Daniel H. Wheeler, Sr., and who was also re-elected to that position in 1888. An allowance of fifteen cents per voter is drawn from the State treasury annually, in aid of county agricultural associations, which gives Douglas County, this year, $3,252. The membership fees amount to about one hundred dollars annually, and there is something additional received from advertisements printed in the premium lists. Space is rented of the Fair and Exposition Association at a nominal figure. The county society is well managed, and its annual displays attract much attention. The present officers of the association are: H. G. Clark, president; Frank B. Hibbard, vice-president; John Baumer, secretary; Henry Bolln, treasurer; and these, with Henry Eicke, J. W. Agee, M. D., Jno. F. McArdle, Oscar J. Pickard, E. H. Walker, G. R. Williams, Richard Engelmann and Julius Treitschke, constitute the board of directors.

A re-organization of the Omaha Driving Park Association was effected during the year 1890, with W. H. S. Hughes as president, Richard S. Berlin, secretary, and W. S. Rector, treasurer. A tract of land was secured, about a mile west of the city limits, and a large force employed erecting buildings and constructing a mile track, one hundred feet wide. It is the design of the association to expend a large sum of money in the improvement of their property for racing and county and State fair purposes. Thomas Swobe, Joseph Garneau, J. H. Birkett, Richard S. Berlin, Dr. J. M. Swetnam, William Krug and D. S. Mercer, constitute the present board of directors.

Omaha's first Board of Trade was organized in 1865, with Augustus Kountze as president, and E. P. Childs, secretary. For a few years it flourished, after a fashion, and then passed out of existence. In 1877 (March 12th), through the efforts of W. C. B. Allen, now of Idaho, another organization was effected, of which he was secretary and A. J. Poppleton, Esq., president. The following year John Evans was elected president and Mr. Allen re-elected secretary. In 1879, W. J. Broatch was elected president and Thomas Gibson secretary; in 1880, and again in 1881, James E. Boyd, president and Mr. Allen, secretary; in 1882, Hugh G. Clark, president, and Thomas Gibson, secretary; in 1883, C. F. Goodman, president, and Mr. Gibson, secretary; in 1884, N. B. Falconer, president, and Mr. Gibson, secretary; in 1885, Max Meyer, president, and Mr. Gibson, secretary, but the latter resigned before the close of the year and was succeeded by Frederick B. Lowe; in 1886, and again in 1887, Max Meyer, president, and G. M. Nattinger, secretary; in 1888, P. E. Iler, president, and G. M. Nattinger, secretary; in 1889-90-91, Euclid Martin, president, W. N. Nason, secretary. Henry Pundt was the treasurer in 1865; C. C. Housel, in 1877-78-79-80-81; W. J. Broatch in 1882-83-84; J. A. Wakefield in 1885-86-87-88, and Hugh G. Clark in 1889-90-91. The present officers are: Euclid Martin, president; Max Meyer, first vice-president; S. A. McWhorter, second vice-president; C. F. Goodman, treasurer, and W. N. Nason, secretary. E. E. Bruce, C. H. Fowler, Joseph A. Connor, H. G. Clark, James Stephenson are directors—all re-elected January 12, 1891.

The Board of Trade building, with a frontage of 132 feet on Sixteenth Street and 66 feet on Farnam, was commenced in 1884, the lot having been bought of the city for thirteen thousand dollars, and finished the following year, at a cost of nearly one hundred thousand dollars. It is five stories high and a very handsome structure. The lot is now worth one hundred thousand dollars. To Mr. Thomas Gibson, now of Los Gatos, California, is due the chief credit for the purchase of the lot and erection of the building. He was then secretary of the board, and through his efforts the money was raised to secure the lot at the remarkably low price asked for it. At his suggestion, the membership fee was increased to one hundred dollars for those then belonging to the organization (having previously been but twenty-five dollars), and to $125 for new members, a large additional membership being secured through Mr. Gibson's personal and persistent efforts. The foundation of the building, costing ten thousand dollars, was paid for out of funds belonging to the board and the property bonded for sixty thousand dollars, all of which sum was carefully and judiciously expended on the building, the erection of which added much to the prestige of the board. The fee has been gradually raised from twenty-five dollars to five hundred dollars, and the board has now 235 members, 250 being the limit of membership allowed by the constitution. This organization has been an active force in advancing the interests of Omaha.

The Omaha Real Estate Exchange, organized in November, 1886, was a very important factor in the development of the public interests of the city. The original members were The Omaha Real Estate & Trust Company, Marshall & Lobeck, Bell & McCandlish, Hartman & Gibson, Mead & Jamieson, Gregory & Hadley, W. G. Shriver and M. A. Upton & Company. Additional members were admitted afterward, including Clark & French, John B. Evans & Company, Ballou Brothers, George N. Hicks and George P. Bemis. The first officers elected were: Alvin Saunders (of The Omaha Loan & Trust Company), president; John T. Bell, vice president; David Jamieson, secretary; J. W. Marshall, treasurer; J. S. Gibson, W. G. Shriver, Frank L. Gregory, executive committee. It was the design at first to limit the membership to twenty-five, but this number was increased to fifty a few months later. The admittance fee was fixed at ten dollars and the members were assessed afterwards for whatever money was required to meet expenses. A large room was fitted up at No. 1519 Farnam Street, these quarters being changed afterwards to a room in the Board of Trade building, and for two years the members derived much benefit from the association. In the fall of 1889, a re-organization was effected, a spacious room on the first floor of the New York Life building was secured, and here, for many months, daily meetings were held from 11 to 12, attended by all classes of citizens. From 11:30 until noon, there was an open call of real estate offered for sale and on Saturdays a public auction was held, and all kinds of public enterprises were discussed by the exchange, and encouragement, in a practical, substantial way, given those who showed themselves worthy of endorsement. An extensive correspondence was carried on with people in all parts of the country who sought information respecting Omaha and its opportunities for the investment of capital in manufacturing enterprises, the loaning of money on real estate securities, the purchase of property, etc., etc. While the Real Estate Exchange did good work for Omaha during its existence, it gradually dwindled, its members lost interest and it disbanded in 1890.

Pursuant to a call made by D. Farrell & Company, the P. J. Quealey Soap Company, the Rees Printing Company, and the W. A. Page Soap Company, a meeting of the manufacturers of Omaha was held in the office of the Real Estate Owners' Association, in the New York Life building, for the purpose of taking steps to form an organization for their mutual benefit. Mr. Samuel Rees was made chairman, and Mr. L. M. Rheem, secretary. Hon. J. M. Thurston, on invitation, made an appropriate address, and, after considerable discussion, a resolution was adopted instructing the chairman to appoint a committee on permanent organization, and the meeting adjourned to meet September 26th, when the report of the committee was adopted. The association was named "The Manufacturers' and Consumers' Association of Nebraska," the object being to make it a State organization. Mr. W. A. Page was elected president; Mr. I. S. Trostler, vice-president; Mr. A. J. Vierling, treasurer; and Mr. H. J. Pickering, secretary. Mr. Pickering soon resigned and Mr. A. D. Bradley was elected as his successor. The association has been very successful in its undertakings, and held the most popular exposition ever held in the State, in June, 1892.

In May, 1892, the association was regularly incorporated under the laws of the State, with the following officers and directors: W. A. Page, president; I. S. Trostler, vice-president; A. D. Bradley, secretary; A. J. Vierling, treasurer. Directors — Beatrice, A. R. Dempster, A. C. Scheiblich; Fremont, T. F. Hummel; Hastings, G. H. Edgerton; Kearney, J. J. Bartlett; Lincoln, H. J. Hall; Nebraska City, Carl Morton; J. T. Robinson, J. H. Barrett, D. Farrell, Jr., Samuel Rees, H. B. Mulford, Charles Metz, W. R. Drummond, I. S. Trostler, C. P. Gedney, E. P. Davis, P. J. Quealey, Charles Coe, M. C. Peters, W. C. Smith, A. H. Rawitzer, J. F. Murphy, A. J. Vierling, J. H. Evans, Aaron Chadwick, W. A. Page, W. W. Cole, R. F. Hodgin, George M. Tibbs, C. W. Thompson, H. F. Cady, Omaha.

In June, 1891, the Real Estate Owners' Association was formed. It has for its object the upbuilding of the interests of the city, and has already done a great amount of very valuable work in this direction. It not only encourages the location of manufacturing and other business interests in Omaha, but has devoted no little attention to looking after the political interests of the city and county, more from a business than a political point of view. The following constitute the officers and board of directors: George H. Boggs, president; John T. Cathers, vice-president; George P. Bemis, secretary; Cadet Taylor, treasurer; St. A. D. Balcombe, A. L. Reed, Jeff. W. Bedford, George N. Hicks, J. H. Dumont, C. R. Scott, E. A. Benson. The following are the advisory board: Herman Kountze, S. D. Mercer, Max Meyer, O. M. Carter, Samuel E. Rogers, A. J. Simpson, John A. Horbach, Lew W. Hill, E. Rosewater, C. S. Chase, F. Krug, R. N. Withnell, J. B. Kitchen, Benjamin F. Smith, L. S. Reed, H. Pundt, A. P. Wood, G. W. Lininger, Warren Switzler, Chris. Hartman, C. C. George, W. J. Connell, W. A. Paxton, F. E. Bailey, Norman A. Kuhn, Joseph Barker, T. C. Bruner, W. W. Lowe, Thomas J. Rogers, P. L. Perine, Thomas Swobe, John Steel, E. Wakeley, J. N. Cornish, W. V. Morse, A. P. Hopkins, F. P. Kirkendall, A. Hospe, Jr., W. F. Allen, Henry J. Windsor, G. C. Towle, Henry A. Thompson, William H. Crary, S. K. Spalding, Martin Ittner, C. O. Lobeck.

# CHAPTER XXX.

BRIDGES AND VIADUCTS—ENORMOUS EXPENDITURE IN THEIR CONSTRUCTION—MARVELS OF ENGINEERING SKILL—THE NEBRASKA CENTRAL.

The Union Pacific bridge is one of the most substantial in the country. Work upon it was commenced in the spring of 1869, and the formal test as to its capacity was made March 14, 1872, when two flat cars loaded with stone, weighing six hundred thousand pounds, were pushed across the structure by an engine, upon which Superintendent Sickles, who had charge of its construction, rode across the bridge, thus backing his faith in its soundness by risking his life upon it. Bonds to the amount of $2,500,000 were issued for the erection of the bridge, but the cost, it is stated by competent authority, did not exceed $1,750,000. The contract price was $1,089,500, the Boomer Bridge Company, of Chicago, being awarded the contract September 4, 1868. During the night of August 24, 1877, the two eastern spans were completely wrecked by a cyclone. John Pierson, a watchman who occupied a little house which stood on the eastern span, was the only witness of the disaster. He went down with the wreck and barely escaped with his life, being caught in such a way by the bridge timbers that he was unable to release himself for some time. He then managed to cross over to the Nebraska side of the river just in time to prevent the destruction of a freight train which was on the point of pulling out of the depot to cross the river. A temporary bridge was put in, the space formerly covered by the first span was covered by an extension westward of the Iowa approach, and the second span replaced in a most substantial manner. The "Queen of Decatur," a flat-bottomed ferry boat, was brought down from Decatur, Nebraska, and used for ferrying purposes for a month. Regular crossings on the bridge were resumed September 19, 1877. In 1886 and 1887 the bridge was practically re-built. New stone piers, laid to bed-rock, with the deepest pier eighty feet below high water mark, were built, affording a secure resting place for the spans, four of which are two hundred and fifty feet long, and six one hundred and twenty-five feet, and the width of the bridge increased to fifty-six and one quarter feet to provide room for a roadway on each side of the double track for pedestrians and street cars. The bridge will stand a pressure of four tons to the square foot. While the construction of this bridge was in progress many lives were lost, the sinking of the immense iron caissons preparatory to building the stone piers being attended by great risk to the workmen.

The Omaha and Council Bluffs Railway & Bridge Company was organized in this city April 1, 1887, by J. H. Millard, Frank Murphy and Guy C. Barton, of Omaha, and John T. Stewart, Thomas J. Evans, and George F. Wright, of Council Bluffs. The original capital stock was $750,000, increased at the present time to $1,500,000. The present list of officers are: John T. Stewart, president; Guy C. Barton, vice-president; J. H. Millard, treasurer; and George F. Wright, secretary. The company's bridge and motor line were completed and opened for traffic November 1, 1888. The cost of the bridge, approaches and viaduct was $750,000. It is built of iron, is thirty-three feet wide and fifty-four feet above high water mark. The length of the main line between the cities of Omaha and Council Bluffs is five miles of double track or ten miles of single track railway, of standard gauge and weight. The total trackage, including leased lines composing the Council Bluffs Street Railway, amounts to twenty miles. The power is electricity, and the equipment consists of four two hundred-horse power, compound engines, ten eighty-horse power boilers, seven seven hundred-horse power electric dynamos, seventy-five Pullman passenger cars, and fifty ten and fifteen-horse power motors. One hundred trains are run over the main line between the two cities of Omaha and Council Bluffs, daily. The bridge, with its approaches, is nearly a mile long.

The Nebraska Central Railway Company was voted bonds December 3, 1889, to the amount of $250,000, by Douglas County, to aid in the construction of a third bridge across the Missouri at this point. It is to be built pursuant to an act of Congress which provides that it shall be accessible to all railroad companies desiring to use it, upon fair and equal terms. Among the most prominent and active men in the company are John A. McShane, John H. Dumont and W. A. Underwood, the latter being president of the American Water Works Company. The bonds were voted on condition that the bridge be completed by June 22, 1892.

The railway tracks crossing Eleventh Street are spanned by an iron viaduct built by the Morse Bridge Company in 1886-7, at an expense, including damages to adjacent property holders, of $98,528.92. Three-fifths of the cost of the viaduct was paid by the Union Pacific and Burlington & Missouri River Railroads. The main roadway of the structure is twenty feet wide with a six-foot sidewalk on each side.

The same railway tracks at the intersection of South Sixteenth Street are crossed by a wooden viaduct built by Raymond & Campbell, of Council Bluffs, the plans being drawn by Andrew Rosewater, who was city engineer at the time. It, as well as the Eleventh Street structure, is about a quarter of a mile long, with a twenty-foot roadway and two six-foot sidewalks. The total cost was $42,732.99, and it was completed early in 1887. Both of these viaducts afford motor line connection with the southern part of the city by means of double tracks.

January 1, 1891, the Tenth Street viaduct, built by the Union Depot Company, was opened for traffic. It is one of the largest ever built, being 1,520 feet in length—two hundred feet over a quarter of a mile—and is eighty feet wide. The roadway is sixty feet in width and on each side is a ten-foot artificial stone sidewalk. It is a substantial steel structure, with the supports resting on stone foundations. On the east side connection will be made with the second floor of the new union depot, now in course of erection. To aid in the construction of this viaduct and the depot, bonds to the amount of $150,000 were voted by the city November 30, 1889. The total cost of the structure was $215,000 besides damages to abutting property, which were assessed upon property owners, to the amount of $37,550. Engineer Smead, of the Union Pacific offices, drew the plans for the viaduct and Chief Engineer Doran of the Union Depot Company had charge of its construction. This viaduct proved to be the subject of considerable litigation. The property owners south of the railway tracks and within a certain distance of South Tenth Street were assessed to pay the damages awarded to the owners of property which was injured by the building of the viaduct, to which assessment they objected, chiefly on the ground that it was an improvement which benefitted the public at large, hence the assessment should be levied upon the entire city. Finally an injunction suit was brought in the district court by Augustus Kountze and others to restrain the collection of the tax by the city. The case came up for hearing before Judge Doane in January and on the fourteenth of that month a decision was rendered to the effect that it was the duty of the Union Depot Company to pay the damages resulting to abutting property by the construction of the depot. The amount assessed had been, in fact, paid in to the city treasury by the depot company before the work was commenced, and the court held that the property owners in that taxing district could not be required to pay that assessment.

December 30, 1890, Ernest Stuht, a tax payer, sued the City of Omaha, Richard C. Cushing as mayor, Charles Goodrich as comptroller, Thomas H. Benton as auditor of public accounts of the State, Alvin Saunders, trustee, the Union Depot Company and Thomas L. Kimball, president of the Union Depot Company, to restrain the delivery of the viaduct bonds to the Union Depot Company, pursuant to its demand. This petition set up several points, the principal one being the claim that by a collusion between the depot company and the Union Pacific Railroad Company the latter was endeavoring to prevent the Chicago, Milwaukee & St. Paul Railroad Company from entering the city, via the Union Pacific bridge, thus indicating a purpose to not carry into effect the condition in the proposition upon which the bonds were voted by the citizens of Omaha, allowing all railroad companies so desiring it free access to the passenger depot, to aid in the construction of which the bonds were to be given. The connection of ex-Governor Saunders with the case was by reason of his having been deeded certain lands in the early history of the Union Pacific Road to aid in building a passenger depot, and State Auditor Benton was made a party from the fact that the bonds had been sent to that official for registration a few days before the suit was brought. A temporary injunction was granted by Judge Doane, and January 13th an amended petition was filed by Mr. Stuht and John D. Howe, Esq., which set forth that the voting of the bonds on Thanksgiving Day was illegal; that there was a general election only three days later; that at the special bond election, November 30th, only thirty per cent. of the electors voted; that the city authorities were not authorized, either by the charter or by the law relating to voting bonds for the works of internal improvements, to submit such a proposition; that the ostensible purpose named in the proposition was to vote a donation for a union depot, whereas the real purpose was to pay for the building of the viaduct; that the railway companies that destroyed Tenth Street were in law required to pay the cost of the viaduct, but by collusion between the city officers and the railroads it was endeavored to practice a fraud on the law by throwing the burden on the taxpayers and taking it from the railroads; that the depot enterprise was a private investment for speculative purposes for the pecuniary benefit of a few individuals; that the Union Depot Company had been recently organized and expected to secure practically all of its capital stock by gifts of real estate and bonds by the City of Omaha, which real estate covered about twenty acres at the west end of the bridge and was of the value of many hundreds of thousands of dollars; that said depot company proposed to lease said property to a large number of railroad companies as tenants, requiring of each of them the payment of large rentals, so as to secure from said property enormous revenues for stockholders, thereby rendering the depot property oppressive and burdensome to the railroad tenants, for whose use in fact nearly all of said real estate was donated by Omaha. Further, that the conditions precedent had not been performed by the depot company; that the size of the building had been changed; that it did not agree with the proposition; that the plans were changed after the election had adopted them, which was illegal; that only some $40,000 had been spent, instead of $150,000; also that the two eastern railroads, the Milwaukee and Rock Island, for whose benefit in part the city devoted the twenty acres of land, had been prevented from coming upon the said grounds; that the city authorities were about to deliver conveyances to the depot company, conveying all its property rights to the depot grounds, with the effect of relinquishing all the trusts upon which said property was conveyed to the Union Pacific in 1872; the said real estate was bought with $200,000 of city bonds in 1872 for the Union Pacific, on condition that it should construct its bridge across the river at Omaha; that the eastern terminus should be at Omaha; that the company should upon said grounds make up all of the west bound passenger and freight trains; that all trains coming from the East on all railroads should be transferred upon said grounds; that said company should expend $100,000 in depot buildings on said grounds; that all its machine and repair shops should be erected and maintained at Omaha; and that eastern railroads should have the right to use its bridge for reasonable compensation. All of which things the said company has failed and refused to do. That neither of the $200,000 bonds had yet been delivered to the city by the depot company.

January 12th an answer had been filed by Mr. Kimball, on behalf of the Union Pacific Depot Company, to a petition previously filed by Messrs. Stuht and Howe, which answer stated that the mayor and council were duly authorized by law to pass an ordinance calling for the viaduct bonds, and had acted legally when the proposition was submitted to the people who ratified it by their votes. It denied that the Union Depot was a private venture gotten up for speculative purposes, but that on the other hand it would prove a great benefit to the traveling public and the citizens of Omaha generally. It claimed that up to that time the Union Depot Company had spent more than one hundred and fifty thousand dollars, the amount stipulated, and had, in every detail, followed out the original contract; that the company was then ready to proceed to comply strictly with the ordinance, and that the viaduct had been completed and turned over to the public use. The answer also denied that the Union Pacific had refused to permit trains of other roads to cross the bridge into the Union Depot, and stated that the depot company was ready to comply with the ordinance and erect a magnificent structure; but that if the injunction was granted the company would be compelled to abandon its organization as a depot company and to permit the premises set apart for a depot to revert back to the original owners, and thus prevent for years the construction of a union passenger depot, much to the detriment of the people.

City Attorney Poppleton filed an answer January 31st on behalf of the city, setting out that the bonds and deeds, conveying to the Union Depot Company the lots and lands previously voted to the Union Pacific Railroad Company, for depot purposes, had been drawn up in proper form and delivered to the trustees, to be by them delivered to the depot company when so ordered by the city authorities, and a trial of the case before Judge Doane was reached February 4th. John M. Thurston appeared for the depot company, Mr. Poppleton for the city, and John D. Howe and John C. Cowin for Messrs. Stuht and Howe. The hearing of the case occupied two days, and on the 21st of March Judge Doane rendered a decision sustaining the injunction and holding that the conditions upon which the bonds were to be delivered had not been complied with. The court found that the plan of the depot had been materially changed; that the amount required to be expended by the company on the depot before the delivery of the bonds had not been expended; that the company had not delivered to the city its bonds for $200,000; and that other roads had already been denied access to depot privileges, in violation of the terms of the bond proposition.

November 30, 1890, the Inter-State Bridge and Street Railway Company filed its articles of incorporation, which set forth the following as the purpose of the organization: "The general nature of the business to be transacted by this corporation shall be to construct, maintain and operate a bridge across the Missouri River, at and near the lands owned by the East Omaha Land Company, in the States of Iowa and Nebraska, and also to construct, maintain and operate a steam, electric, motor, horse, elevated, cable, or other line of railway, and a public way across said bridge and within the counties of Douglas, Nebraska, and Pottawattamie, Iowa. with the termini thereof in the said cities of Omaha and Council Bluffs." John A. Creighton, Andrew J. Poppleton, Henry W. Yates, Richard C. Cushing, James M. Woolworth and Arthur S. Potter were the incorporators, and the capital stock was fixed at $2,500,000. One of the last acts of the session of Congress which terminated March 4, 1891, was to grant a charter to this company for the construction of its bridge. Comparatively nothing was done toward the construction of this bridge at the time the proposition of the Nebraska Central Railway Company, in June, 1892, was submitted to the people. This latter proposition having carried, by vote of the people, the Inter-State bridge was rendered unnecessary, and the probabilities are that it will not be built.

As previously stated the Nebraska Central Railroad Company had been voted bonds in December, 1889, to the amount of $250,000 to aid in the construction of a bridge across the Missouri. Owing to the fact that two of the eastern railroads—the Rock Island & Pacific, which had been expected to use the Nebraska Central bridge, and the Chicago, Milwaukee & St. Paul—shortly after made contracts with the Union Pacific Railway Company for the use of its bridge, and the extreme stringency of the money market, nothing was done toward the construction of this bridge.

On the 2d day of May, 1892, through Mr. J. H. Dumont, vice-president, and Mr. John L. McCague, secretary, the Nebraska Central Railroad Company made another proposition to the county commissioners for the issuance, by Douglas County, of $500,000 to aid in the construction of a railroad bridge, with approaches and connections, giving outlets to the South, to the West and to the North. At the same time the same company made a proposition to the city council for the issuance by the City of Omaha of $250,000, to aid in acquiring depot grounds and constructing one hundred miles of railroad into the State of Iowa, for the purpose of connecting with all railroads which might be within connecting distance of Omaha. These propositions were fully discussed before the respective bodies, and, after being amended so as to more effectually protect the interests of the public, were submitted to the voters of the city and county at a special election held June 16, 1892, and were carried by a large majority. Mr. John D. Howe was especially active in looking after the interests of the people, appearing before both the county commissioners and the city council. As the Nebraska Central propositions are considered among the most important which have ever come before our people, the city proposition is given here in full, and so much of the county proposition as materially differs from that of the city. The proposition to the city is as follows:

The amended proposition of the Nebraska Central Railroad Company to the City of Omaha, Nebraska:

"*To the Mayor and the City Council of the City of Omaha, Nebraska:*

"The undersigned, the Nebraska Central Railway Company, proposes to acquire and take possession of, for railway purposes, that certain tract of land, located within the district bounded by Fifteenth Street, Chicago Street, Eleventh Street, California Street, and the right of way of the Omaha Belt Railway Company, except the south half of block thirty-eight, lots three and four; block twenty-eight, lot one; and north one-half of lots two and three, block twenty-seven; and to erect thereon a union passenger depot on the corner of Fifteenth and Chicago Streets, to cost, including the other railway improvements on said grounds, not less than four hundred thousand dollars.

"Provided, the City of Omaha, in Douglas County, Nebraska, will donate to the said Nebraska Central Railway Company two hundred and fifty thousand dollars of its four per cent. bonds, one hundred thousand dollars thereof to be dated January 2, 1893, and one hundred and fifty thousand dollars thereof to be dated January 1, 1894, to become due and payable twenty years from their respective dates, with interest payable semi-annually, all payable at the fiscal agency of the State of Nebraska in the City of New York.

"Said bonds to be of the denomination of one thousand dollars each, and each thereof to recite:

"'This bond is one of a series of two hundred and fifty bonds of like amount and tenor, which are issued by the City of Omaha, in Douglas County, Nebraska, to the Nebraska Central Railway Company, to aid it in acquiring land in the City of Omaha for union depot and terminal purposes, and in the construction of a union railway passenger depot upon said ground, and its railway tracks, side-tracks, turnouts, switches and approaches leading thereto, and other railway improvements therewith connected.'

"Said bonds to be executed and registered at, or immediately after, the dates thereof, and immediately thereafter delivered to the First National Bank of Omaha, Nebraska, trustee, to be held in trust for delivery to the Nebraska Central Railway Company, its successors or assigns, by said trustee, in inatallments as hereinafter provided.

"The said Nebraska Central Railway Company plans to construct, or cause to be constructed, a line of railway in the State of Iowa, not less than one hundred miles in extent, from the east approach of a bridge, which the said Nebraska Central Railway Company has also planned to construct over the Missouri River, intersecting or connecting with, or reaching, the lines of two or more of the following railway corporations, viz.:

The Illinois Central Railway Company, the Winona & Southwestern Railway Company, the Minneapolis & St. Louis Railway Company, the Chicago, St. Paul & Kansas City Railway Company, the Chicago, Fort Madison & Des Moines Railway Company, the Atchison, Topeka & Santa Fe Railway Company, the Baltimore & Ohio Railway Company, the Ohio & Mississippi Railway Company, the Keokuk & Western Railway Company, the Quincy, Omaha & Kansas City Railway Company and the Iowa Central Railway Company.

One hundred thousand dollars of said bonds shall be delivered by said trustee to said Nebraska Central Railway Company, its successors or assigns, when it or they shall have acquired and taken possession of that certain tract of land located within the district bounded by Fifteenth Street, Chicago Street, Eleventh Street, California Street and the right of way of the Omaha Belt Railway Company (except the south half of block thirty-eight, lots three and four, block twenty-eight, lot one, and the north half of lots two and three, block twenty-seven).

"Provided, that the said one hundred thousand dollars of said bonds shall not be delivered until after the said Nebraska Central Railway Company, its successors or assigns, shall have constructed the said line of railway in the State of Iowa.

"One hundred and fifty thousand dollars of said bonds shall be delivered by said trustee to said Nebraska Central Railway Company, its successors or assigns, when it or they shall have completed the erection of a union passenger depot upon said tract of land above described, to cost, including the other railway improvements on said grounds, not less than four hundred thousand dollars. proof of such cost to be made by the sworn statement of the president and treasurer of said railway company, filed with the city clerk of Omaha, accompanied by certificate signed by the city attorney and city engineer that in their opinion such amount has actually been expended.

"Provided, that, if the said Nebraska Central Railway Company, its successors or assigns, shall fail to acquire and take possession of said land, it shall not be entitled to receive any part of said one hundred thousand dollars installment of bonds; and, further provided, that none of said one hundred and fifty thousand dollars installment of bonds shall be delivered until at least one railway company in addition the Nebraska

Central Railway Company shall be actually using said union depot, and

"Provided, further, that the mayor and the city council shall, by resolution, upon the full performance of the undertakings on the part of said railway company herein contained, order the delivery of said bonds at the times aforesaid; and

" Provided further, that all matured coupons shall be removed and canceled by said trustee before the delivery of the bonds to which they are attached; and,

"Provided, further, that the mayor and city council of the city of Omaha shall cause to be levied on the taxable property of said city an annual tax sufficient for the payment of the interest on said coupon bonds as it becomes due, and after the expiration of ten years from the date of said bonds the mayor and city council of said city shall cause to be levied in addition to all other taxes on the taxable property of said city an amount of tax sufficient to create a sinking fund for the payment at maturity of said bonds (the amount of tax to be levied for such sinking fund not to exceed twenty-five thousand dollars in any one year); said tax to be continued from year to year until the said bonds are fully paid.

" The acquirement of the said lands and improvements herein contemplated, including the said railroad in Iowa, shall be begun within one year from May 1, 1892, and be pushed to completion without unnecessary delay, and shall be completed within three years from the first day of July, 1892.

" In case any of the terms, limitations, conditions or provisions proposed herein, relating to the beginning, progress and completion of said improvements are not complied with (unless delay is directly and necessarily caused by injunction or other judicial proceedings, or by unavoidable accident or act of Providence), the said company shall not be entitled to receive said bonds, or any thereof, even though the electors of said City of Omaha shall have by their vote authorized the issuance of said bonds; but all right to said bonds shall by such default and without any judicial determination become forfeited.

" Provided, however, that if the beginning, progress or completion of said improvements shall be delayed or obstructed by any of the aforesaid causes, the times herein allowed for the progress and completion of said improvements shall be extended to the extent of such delay or obstruction; and, should a dispute arise between the said City of Omaha and the said Nebraska Central Railway Company with respect to the cause or extent of any such delay, the same, at the election of said Nebraska Central Railway Company, shall be referred for determination to a board of arbitrators, to be appointed as hereinafter provided.

" In consideration of receiving the proposed subsidy, the Nebraska Central Railway Company agrees to allow all railway companies the following rights: The right to run their locomotives, passenger and freight trains over its main and passing tracks within the City of Omaha; and over its proposed bridge and approaches, the right to use such portion of its terminal grounds, depots and facilities as may be necessary and proper for the conduct of the business of such roads, including any enlargement of its depot and depot grounds; the right to have their cars switched and delivered by the Nebraska Central Railway Company upon all of its switch tracks; the right to connect their roads at any point within one hundred miles of said City of Omaha with any line of railway which the Nebraska Central Railway Company, or its successors or assigns, may construct or cause to be constructed east of the Missouri River, and to run their locomotives, passenger and freight trains over the main and passing tracks of said railroad; it being hereby agreed that in case the Nebraska Central Railway Company shall construct its proposed line east of the Missouri River, through the agency of any other corporation or party, it will cause such corporation or party to execute and deliver to the City of Omaha a good and sufficient instrument, binding it or him to abide by the terms, conditions and provisions of this proposition, the same as the said Nebraska Central Railway Company would have been bound if it had built the same, before delivery of the aforesaid one hundred thousand dollar installment of bonds.

" Provided, that the use and enjoyment by such railway companies of each and every of said rights shall be upon just and equal terms and the payment of just and fair compensation to the Nebraska Central Railway Company, its successors or assigns, and subject to such operating rules and regulations of the Nebraska Central Railway Company, its successors or assigns, as shall be necessary and proper, just and reasonable.

"And the said Nebraska Central Railway Company will submit any dispute arising between it and such other company or companies, as to the use and enjoyment of any rights under this proposition, or as to the terms, compensation, operating rules and regulations relating thereto, to a board of arbitrators, to be made up of three persons who are judges of the State district court, or its successor, of the district embracing the County of Douglas, to be selected by a two-thirds vote of all the persons who are district judges of said court.

"Provided that any such railway company, other than said Nebraska Central Railway Company, its successors or assigns, shall have the election to submit any such dispute to arbitration or to pursue any other remedy.

"Wherever arbitration is provided for by this proposition, the party desiring to submit any matter to arbitration shall cause to be served upon the other party a written notice which shall set out the matter in dispute to be submitted, and the time proposed for the hearing, which shall not be less than thirty days after the time of service; and thereupon the adverse party shall, within twenty days after such service upon it, serve its answer, if any it have, upon the party demanding the arbitration.

"The board of arbitrators, when organized, shall have power to fix the time of hearing and to adjourn the same from time to time, and to make all necessary rules and regulations for the production of testimony in the possession of either party, and otherwise to compel a fair and speedy trial; the decision of a majority of the board shall control, and the final determination of the board shall be final and conclusive upon the parties, of all matters submitted and decided.

"Wherever arbitration shall be resorted to, such arbitration shall be the exclusive remedy of the parties (except as herein elsewhere provided), as to the matters and things involved and decided therein.

"Said Nebraska Central Railway Company, its successors and assigns, shall transport freight (including transfer of freight and all charges incidental to said transportation) over any bridge and approaches, as well as over any railway it shall construct, within one hundred miles of the Missouri River within the State of Nebraska, for just or reasonable rates or charges; and, in case of difference as to what constitutes just and reasonable rates or charges under this paragraph, the mayor and city council, or said railway company, may submit the same to arbitration in the manner and to the arbitrators above provided for; but this paragraph respecting freight charges shall not become operative or in force until five years from the date of the delivery of the last installment of the bonds hereinbefore referred to.

"It is further proposed that said bonds shall be delivered to the Nebraska Central Railway Company, its successors or assigns, only upon the execution, by the said Nebraska Central Railway Company, or its successors, and delivery to the city of Omaha, of an undertaking in writing to the effect that the principal depot of said railway company, its general offices and principal machine shops when built, shall be located and maintained within the corporate limits of the City of Omaha, and that a violation of the terms of said undertaking by the said Nebraska Central Railway Company, or its successors or assigns, shall render the said Nebraska Central Railway Company, or its successors, indebted to the said City of Omaha in the full amount of said bonds, and interest thereon.

"This proposition shall, after being duly acknowledged by the Nebraska Central Railway Company, be recorded in the office of the register of deeds of Douglas County, Nebraska, and, for a period of twenty years from and after this date, shall be referred to by giving the book and page wherein the same is recorded, in any mortgage, deed of trust, deed of conveyance, or lease, of said depot or depot grounds, with the statement that the said Nebraska Central Railway Company, its successors and assigns, are bound by the terms, limitations, provisions and conditions of this proposition which are hereby made its covenants, that attach to, and run with, the said property into whosoever hands it may come.

"Provided, that the city council of the City of Omaha, the mayor approving in due form, shall enact a certain ordinance, which, at the date hereof, is pending consideration before said council, entitled, 'An ordinance granting permission and authority to the Nebraska Central Railway Company, its successors and assigns, to construct railroad tracks along, across, over and under certain streets and alleys in the City of Omaha, subject to certain conditions, and to vacate parts of certain streets and alleys in the City of Omaha upon compliance with certain other conditions.'

"And it is also provided, that if said Nebraska Central Railway Company shall not, within forty-five days of being notified by the city clerk of the adoption of this proposition at the election held to vote upon the same, file with the said city clerk its written ratification of this proposition, under its corporate seal, none of said bonds shall be issued, and all the terms and provisions of this proposition shall be held for naught.

"The Nebraska Central Railway Company agrees, before an election's being called, to submit to the voters of the City of Omaha this proposition: that it will execute and deliver to said city a bond, with good and sufficient sureties, in the sum of five thousand dollars, and five thousand dollars cash, conditioned upon the payment of the expenses of said election.

"This proposition and acceptance thereof by the City of Omaha, and the ratification of this proposition by said Nebraska Central Railway Company, or its successors or assigns, as herein provided, shall be construed and understood to constitute a contract between the said Nebraska Central Railway Company, its successors or assigns, and the said City of Omaha, and all the terms, conditions, agreements, and provisions made on the part of the Nebraska Central Railway Company in this proposition contained, are hereby made the covenants of the said Nebraska Central Railway Company, its successors and assigns, which shall attach to and run with all of its said property, and be binding upon any party into whose hands it, or any of it, may come.

"In witness whereof the said Nebraska Central Railway Company has caused these presents to be executed, this 16th day of May, A. D. 1892.

"NEBRASKA CENTRAL RAILWAY COMPANY."

Signed by J. H. Dumont, vice-president, and attested by John L. McCague, secretary.

In the proposition to the county the Nebraska Central Railway Company "proposes to build a double track steel railway bridge across the Missouri River, at the location shown upon the plans for said bridge, which has been approved by the honorable, the secretary of war of the United States, and also a double track railroad from the west approach of said bridge through the City of Omaha, to a connection with the tracks of the Union Stock Yards and Railway Company at South Omaha, and also to project a line of railway from the west approach of the aforesaid bridge into the interior of the State of Nebraska, and to construct that portion thereof extending (as nearly as practicable) in a westerly direction from a point on the main line of said railroad north of Mount Pleasant or Pacific Street, in the City of Omaha, Nebraska, to a point on the Little Papillion Creek in section twenty-five, township fifteen, north of range twelve, east of the sixth principal meridian, and also to construct a line of railway from a junction with the main line of said railroad near the intersection of Fourteenth Street and Izard Street, northerly to Grace Street in said city, both of said lines or portions of railroad to be constructed and completed simultaneously with the construction and completion of the aforesaid bridge and tracks to the track of the Union Stock Yards and Railway Company at South Omaha; provided the County of Douglas will donate to the Nebraska Central Railway Company $500,000 of its four and one-half per cent. coupon bonds, dated July 1, 1892, due and payable twenty years from January 1, 1894, with interest payable semi-annually, from January 1, 1894, on the first day of January and the first day of July in each year, principal and interest payable at the fiscal agency of the State of Nebraska in the City of New York; said bonds to be of the denomination of one thousand dollars each, and each thereof to recite as follows: 'This bond is one of a series of five hundred bonds of like amount and tenor which are issued by the County of Douglas, in the State of Nebraska, to the Nebraska Central Railway Company, to aid it in the construction of a railway bridge across the Missouri River at Omaha, Nebraska, and a double track railway from the west approach of said bridge through the City of Omaha to a connection with the tracks of the Union Stock Yards and Railway Company at South Omaha, and its side tracks, turnouts, switches and other railway improvements therewith connected;' all of said bonds, in case the issuance of said bonds be authorized by vote of the electors of Douglas County, to be executed and registered on the first day of July, A. D. 1892, and to be immediately after registration delivered to the First National Bank of Omaha, Nebraska, to be held in trust for delivery to the said Nebraska Central Railway Company, its successors or assigns, in installments as follows:

" One-half when said bridge and its approaches are completed, and the remaining one-half on the completion of said railway lines; all matured coupons to be removed from said bonds before delivery by the said trustee, who shall deliver the said bonds to the Nebraska Central Railway Company or its order, after the board of county commissioners, or its successors, shall by resolution order said trustees to make delivery thereof, which resolution shall be adopted when said bonds have been earned by said railway company as herein contemplated, but not before. The improvements herein contemplated shall be begun within one year from the first day of May, A. D., 1892, and be pushed to completion without unnecessary delay; and not less than $500,000 shall be expended in actual construction of said bridge and railroad within a period of nine months from the commencement of said work (said sum to include the cost of materials paid for and delivered upon the ground, but not to include the cost of right-of-way or real estate), proof of said expenditures to be filed with the board of county commissioners in the form of a sworn statement by the president and treasurer of said Nebraska Central Railway Company; work on said proposed improvements not to cease for a period exceeding ninety consecutive days before the expenditure of a sum not less than two million dollars has been made thereon, and all of said work shall be completed and in operation within three years from and after the first day of July, 1892."

It also provides for arbitration in case of disputes, similar to that contained in the proposition to the city; for the use of its tracks and bridge at a reasonable charge by all other railroads; that the Nebraska Central Railway Company shall relinquish all claims to the $250,000 in bonds voted on the third day of December, 1889, upon the voting of this subsidy.

Before the expiration of the forty-five days provided for in the proposition, the Nebraska Central Railway Company notified the city and county authorities of its acceptance. Surveys are being made, and it now appears as though not only Omaha's eastern connections were provided for, but her terminal facilities settled for many years to come.

The following are the officers of the Nebraska Central Railway Company: J. H. Dumont, president; O. M. Carter, vice-president; F. A. Nash, second vice-president and general manager; John L. McCague, secretary; A. U. Wyman, treasurer.

# CHAPTER XXXI.

### The "Initial Point" — The Legal Battle — Bridging the Missouri.

It is difficult at this time to appreciate the intense interest which was taken for many years by the people of this section, with respect to the "initial point" of the Union Pacific Railway. As to whether the road should be built from the west bank of the Missouri River, or from the Iowa side, was a question over which the citizens of Council Bluffs and of Omaha waged bitter warfare for many years, the Council Bluffs people believing that if that question were decided in their favor material advantage to their city would result. In the spring of 1875 the matter finally reached a legal hearing in the United States Circuit Court, at Des Moines, Iowa, before Judge John F. Dillon, two citizens of Council Bluffs—Samuel E. Hall and John W. Morse—having applied to that court for a writ of mandamus to compel the railway company to operate the Missouri River bridge as a part of its line, and to make up its freight and passenger trains on that side of the river. They were represented by Hon. John N. Rogers, of Davenport, Iowa, the Union Pacific Railway being represented by Hon. A. J. Poppleton, the citizens of Omaha taking part in the conflict and being represented by Hon. James M. Woolworth. There were other lawyers taking minor parts in the trial, but the gentlemen named bore the brunt of the fight. The case was decided by Judge Dillon in favor of the Council Bluffs interest, and was appealed to the United States Supreme Court by Mr. Poppleton, and was heard at the October term, 1875. A clear idea of the points involved may best be gained by quoting these proceedings.

Mr. Poppleton urged in the Supreme Court hearing that the lower court had erred in holding that Hall and Morse could lawfully become relators on behalf of the public in this suit, without the assent or direction of the attorney-general of the United States, or of the United States district attorney, for the district of Nebraska; that the court erred in holding that the lawful eastern terminus of the Union Pacific was on the Iowa side of the Missouri River; that the court erred in holding it to be a duty obligatory upon the Union Pacific Railway to run its through freight and passenger trains to and from the Iowa side of the river; that the court erred in holding that to operate said railroad and its branches as a continuous line is to operate said company's main trunk and each branch as a continuous line; that the court erred in holding that the fourth section of the act of Congress of March 3, 1873, is applicable to the facts appearing from the alternative writ and return thereto, and authorized and justifies the granting of the relief prayed for; that the court erred in holding the bridge, erected and maintained by the railroad company at Omaha, a part of the railroad of said company, and that it should erect, maintain and operate the same; that the court erred in holding that the act of Congress of July 1, 1862, and the acts amendatory thereof, empowered the said railroad companies to build, maintain and operate a railroad within the boundaries and jurisdiction of the State of Iowa; and that the court erred in awarding the peremptory writ and ordering the issue of the same.

He quoted the orders of President Lincoln with respect to locating the initial point of the road, the first being dated November 1, 1863, in which he said: "I, Abraham Lincoln, President of the United States, do hereby fix so much of the western boundary of the State of Iowa as lies between the north and south boundaries of the United States township, within which the City of Omaha is situated, as the point from which the line of railroad and telegraph * * * shall be constructed." The second order, dated March 7, 1864, uses this language: "I, Abraham Lincoln, President of the United States, do, upon the application of the said company, designate and establish such first above named point on the western boundary of the State of Iowa, east of and opposite to the east line of section ten, in township fifteen, north of range three, east of the sixth principal meridian, in the Territory of Nebraska." This left a line of one mile, north and south, upon which the railroad company could fix their initial point to build from, westward.

Mr. Poppleton also quoted the various acts of Congress relating to the establishment and construction of the Union Pacific Railroad, among them that of February 24, 1871, authorizing the issuance of bonds for the building of the Union Pacific bridge at Omaha, using this significant language: "Provided that nothing in this act shall be so construed as to change the eastern terminus of the Union Pacific Railroad from the place where it is now fixed, according to law." He also quoted the debates in Congress with respect to the Union Pacific Railroad, all tending to show that Congress at no time claimed the right to charter corporations for the construction of railroads within the limits of a State, and that the purpose was to authorize the construction of a railroad from the Missouri River through the various territories to the east line of the State of California; that the initial point, as fixed by the railroad company, based upon the orders of President Lincoln, was on the east line of section ten, where it touches the west bank of the river, and that from this point the road was located, and the location was approved by the president; that from this point it was built and accepted by the government, and its bond subsidy delivered, and land grant adjusted and administered. He said that to contend that Congress and the president intended to fix the terminus on the Iowa shore is to contend that Congress had the power to charter a corporation to build and operate a railroad within State limits. The bill, as originally offered, fixed the eastern terminus of the main trunk within the State of Kansas, and of the Omaha line within the interior of the State of Iowa; but, the objection being made that Congress lacked power to authorize the building of a railroad within State limits, the eastern terminus of the main trunk was fixed in the Territory of Nebraska, and of the Omaha branch on the western boundary of Iowa. The official reports of Secretaries of the Interior Usher, Harlan and Browning were quoted from, and also the official reports of the government directors of the Union Pacific Road, in which the initial point at Omaha was referred to repeatedly; and Mr. Poppleton stated that for eight years, in all the official acts and declarations with reference to the road, Omaha has been treated as the eastern terminus.

He held that there could be no better evidence of the intentions of Congress not to grant the power to bridge the Missouri, in the act of 1862, than the fact that this authority was given in express words in the act of 1864. The bridge to be built was to enable the Union Pacific, and other roads terminating on the Nebraska shore, and roads terminating on the Iowa shore, to maintain "a more perfect connection" with each other, and with roads to be built on either side of the river in the future. If the bridge is an extension of the railroad, and the initial point is in Iowa, east of and opposite to section ten, the bridge should have been constructed at that point. If established there, as claimed; when and how was the terminus changed? When the president fixed the eastern terminus, his power was exhausted. If the company is bound to run its trains to the terminus, and it is established at the point contended for by the defendants, the mandamus could only lie to compel the operation of the road to a point nearly three miles north of the bridge in controversy.

A franchise to build a bridge, or establish a ferry, granted to a railroad company, does not constitute said bridge or ferry a part of its railroad any more than a franchise to erect a rolling mill, or work a coal mine, would constitute such mill or mine an extension of its railroad.

Referring to the demand that continuous trains be operated across the bridge, Mr. Poppleton said that, at the time the law was passed, it was safe to say that such a feat as running a single train three thousand miles had never been attempted. It was intended that the line was to be connected and continuous in the sense that the trains of different companies were to be run in close connection with each other. The change of trains at the foot of the mountains may be more economical for the Union Pacific Company, and safest and best for passengers and freight; but, in the theory of the defendant, the duty is imperative to run the same train from one end of the road to the other.

No sane railroad manager would care to have his motive power and rolling stock massed on the east side of the Missouri River when the bridge may be disabled by accident, or its approaches swept away by the ice gorges and floods which are the regular spring product of that capricious stream, and an embargo placed upon business more lasting and effectual than mountain snows. These things may seem trivial to a "citizen of Council Bluffs," anxious to take the train or ship a package of merchandise on the Iowa shore, but to the company, which has forty thousand dollars a day at stake, they are considerations which have dictated the establishment and retention of terminus, trains and works, on the west bank of the Missouri River for the ten years in which the company has been engaged in construction and operation of their roads. It lies upon the very surface of this case that it originates in a neighborhood contention, rather than a public and national grievance. The real parties responsible for the maintenance and continuance of the bridge transfer are those railroad companies which refuse to use it and the legislation which has compelled this refusal. Aside from the prohibitory legislation of Iowa, and this suit, the vexed transfer question would have been long ago solved by a general use of the bridge by all railroads having termini on the Missouri River at or near Omaha and Council Bluffs. To lay upon the Union Pacific Railroad Company alone the burden of operating this bridge, with all its through trains, in addition to its transfer business, to cause the destruction and removal of its works and headquarters, built up on a construction of the law now sought to be overturned, to the injury and ruin of a community of twenty thousand people, from whom it has received large donations and benefits, would be to inflict on it and them a great injustice. But to do it in the face of ten years of construction, declaration and action of all the officers and agents of the United States, establishing and executing the law in direct opposition and conflict with the interpretation contended for by defendant, may well be regarded as a calamity by both road and people.

Mr. Rogers, on behalf of the citizens of Council Bluffs, made an elaborate argument. He said that the purpose of the government was to construct a line of road west from the one hundredth meridian and connecting with the Missouri River by three trunk lines: one south of the Kaw, in Kansas; one from the western boundary of Iowa; and the other at Sioux City, Iowa. A fourth branch, to run from St. Joseph, provided the consent of the State of Kansas could be first secured, was also authorized. Mr. Rogers quoted President Lincoln's message to Congress, dated March 9, 1864, in which the following language was used: "I deem it proper to add that, on the 17th day of November last, an executive order was made upon this subject, and delivered to the vice-president of the Union Pacific Railroad Company, which fixes the point on the western boundary of the State of Iowa, from which the company should construct their branch roads to the one hundredth degree of west longitude, and declared it to be within the limits of the township in Iowa opposite to the town of Omaha, in Nebraska." Congress had authorized the construction of the bridge, and the operation of a continuous track in connection with their road. Transfer grounds had been secured and used in connection with said track, and the whole owned and operated by the company; but, instead of using the bridge as a part of its line and as a means of connecting its road with the Iowa roads terminating at Council Bluffs, it had, under the unauthorized name of "The Omaha Bridge Transfer," undertaken to interpose the bridge and its approaches as an independent and distinct line of travel and transportation between the Iowa roads and the Union Pacific Railroad, effecting the connection by means of distinct trains, a distinct time table, and a distinct tariff of fares and rates, ten dollars per car being charged on freight, and fifty cents per passenger for transportation across the bridge.

The act of 1862 fixed the point of intersection of the northernmost branch of the Pacific Railroad at Sioux City, on the east side of the Missouri, and the southern branches at St. Joseph, Missouri, also on the east side of the river, and at Kansas City, Missouri, where the river turns eastward, and provided that the central branch should begin " at a point on the western boundary of the State of Iowa to be fixed by the president." By law, the western boundary of the State of Iowa, south of Sioux City, is coincident with the middle of the main channel of the river; but Congress did not intend to make this line, in the middle of a navigable river, the actual starting point of the railroad, but meant a point on dry land, either on the Nebraska or Iowa shore. If they meant the Nebraska side, why was Iowa referred to at all? Why not say " a point on the eastern boundary of the territory of Nebraska," or, " a point on the western shore of the Missouri River, opposite Iowa?" The language used must mean a point on the Iowa shore as nearly as practicable to the actual boundary of the State of Iowa. The word " on " in our language, designating the situation of a place, often means " near," " at," or " by." If the question were asked, " What is the western boundary of Iowa? " the answer would be, " The Missouri River." " A point on the western boundary of the State of Iowa" means a point in Iowa on the Missouri River: *i. e.*, the Iowa shore of the river. If Congress had meant the Nebraska shore, they would have said so. Did Congress intend to leave the transit of the Missouri River wholly unprovided for, or did they mean to impose the duty of providing the means of said transit upon the Union Pacific Railroad Company? Clearly, the latter. Congress had in contemplation a great, continuous, trans-continental highway from the Atlantic to the Pacific. This proposed national highway is intersected at the western boundary of Iowa by a great, navigable river, difficult of passage. The Iowa lines of railway formed the next link in the chain east of the river, and terminated on the eastern shore. Did Congress intend to leave here a hiatus in the line? They provided against this at the terminus of the other branches, at Sioux City, St. Joseph, and Kansas City. Did they intend to leave this vitally important river transit liable to fall into the control of third parties, to be managed for selfish and speculating ends, without the least regard to the public interests? Can it be that a matter of such great moment, so clearly provided for in fixing the starting points at the northern and southern branches of the road, was totally neglected as respects the central and principal branch? The terminus of the central branch was intended to be on the eastern side of the river.

The acts of 1862 and 1864 are to be considered together. We have, then, an act providing for a line of railway which must necessarily cross the Missouri River, and requiring it to commence "at a point on the western boundary of the State of Iowa" (which boundary is the Missouri River), and, further, in order " to make convenient and necessary connections with other roads * * * * to establish and maintain all necessary ferries upon and across the Missouri River, and other rivers which its road may pass in its course;" also, " to construct bridges over said Missouri River, and all rivers, for the convenience of said road, provided that any bridge or bridges it may construct over the Missouri River, or any other navigable river on the line of said road, shall be constructed with suitable and proper draws," etc., etc. What room is there for doubt that Congress regarded the Missouri River as a river which the road must pass "in its course" and because its starting point was fixed on the Iowa side? If there was doubt as to the right of the company to pass beyond the middle of the river and come to the Iowa shore in the original charter of 1862, that doubt is set at rest by the ninth section of the amended charter of 1864, which, in terms, authorizes the company to construct a bridge over the Missouri River, which presupposes that the eastern end of it shall rest upon the Iowa shore, and this is done " to enable the Union Pacific Railroad to make convenient and necessary connections with other roads," not to enable " other roads " to make connection with the Union Pacific, by running their trains across the bridge of the latter company.

The second order of President Lincoln fixed the initial point "on the western boundary of the State of Iowa, east of and opposite to the east line of section ten, in township fifteen, north of range thirteen, east of the sixth principal meridian, in the Territory of Nebraska." The words, "in the Territory of Nebraska," evidently referred solely to the location of the said section ten. In the executive message of the president, he declares the point in question to be within the limits of the township in Iowa opposite to the Town of Omaha, in Nebraska, the second order having been made at the request of the railroad company for the purpose of fixing the starting point more definitely and precisely. If the point fixed be on the Nebraska side, it must be in section ten, a fractional section, bounded on the east by the river. The point described in the order cannot be found anywhere except on the Iowa shore, or in the middle of the river.

The action of the president, in approving the map or location of the route filed in the interior department, was an entirely distinct act from his designation of the point from which the road should commence, in which he gives his sanction to the point on the western shore of the river, at which the route laid down on the map begins, as the " precise point of departure of their said branch road from the Missouri River." Since the road was to be in fact built westward from the Missouri River, the "point of departure" from the river had to be fixed on, and so necessarily to be shown in the map of the route. The construction of the road was commenced on the west side of the river, and prosecuted westerly to completion before the bridge was begun and before its location had been fixed. The track laid down from that point in section ten was never used and never intended to be. After it had served its purpose of lengthening out the first forty miles of road, the track was taken up, and all pretense of running the road to said initial point was abandoned. Their actual stopping place is in the immediate vicinity of the west end of the bridge, from which the track runs continuously across the bridge into Council Bluffs. Mr. Rogers quoted from the official reports of Second Comptroller Broadhead, Chief Engineer G. M. Dodge, and Government Directors Wilson, Wade, Price, Harrison, Ruddock, and others, to the effect that the bridge was a part of the line of the road, the report of the second comptroller being with respect to the extra charge made by the Union Pacific Company in its bills for transportation for the government, on account of the bridge, the comptroller holding that it should be operated as a part of the road.

As to the claim that Congress had no right to invade the State of Iowa with a railroad charter, Mr. Rogers referred to the fact that Congress had granted authority for the building of the Union Pacific bridge and its eastern approaches on the solid ground of Iowa, and that the Texas Pacific Road ran across nearly the whole of the State of Texas, and entirely across California, which road had been chartered by Congress. "Can it be maintained," he asked, "that, in providing for the great national trans-continental highway for purposes of inter-state and international commerce, and as a means of conveying government mails, troops and munition of war, Congress is precluded from enabling it to cross a State line in order that it may connect with another link in the chain of communication, terminating on the other side of said line?" The debates in Congress referred to occurred upon the act of 1862; two years afterwards the amendatory act was passed, conferring in express terms the power of the company to bridge the Missouri, and, if necessary, to pass State boundaries for that purpose.

Mr. Rogers proceeded at great length, going over all the points involved with careful minuteness. The case was taken under advisement by the supreme court, and a decision rendered affirming the decision of the lower court, which fixed the eastern terminus of the road on the Iowa side of the river, and holding that the writ of mandamus granted by Judge Dillon was properly granted. Mr. Justice Bradley, however, dissented from the opinion rendered by his associates, in the following terms: "I am obliged to dissent from the judgment of the court in this case. The Missouri River is, by common acceptation, the western boundary of Iowa, and the fair construction of the charter of the Union Pacific Railroad Company, which adopts that boundary as its eastern terminus, is that the road was to extend from the Missouri River westwardly. The subsequent express authority given to construct a bridge across the river, in my judgment, confirms this view of the subject; and, as a mandamus is a severe remedy, requiring a clear right and clear duty to support it, I think it ought not to be granted in this case, especially as it requires the company to use the bridge as a part of their continuous line with all their trains, which may impose much inconvenience on them, without corresponding benefit to the public."

The majority decision of the supreme court was, at the time, considered by many of the citizens of Omaha a great disaster. Certain it was that the transferring of passengers and baggage on the Iowa side of the river was for many years a great source of annoyance to the traveling public; and Omaha's reputation was so intimately connected therewith that an injury was thereby inflicted the extent of which it would be difficult to estimate. A large sum of money was expended by the railroad company in the erection of a depot, round house, hotel, platforms, etc., etc.; and for ten years the "transfer," situated three miles east of the river, presented a busy scene. In the meantime the Chicago & Northwestern Road had secured entrance to Omaha from the north, by way of its own bridge at Blair, and the

Chicago, Quincy & Burlington had completed its bridge at Plattsmouth; so that two of the four trunk lines connecting Omaha with Chicago were no longer dependent upon the Union Pacific bridge, and the transfer gradually lost its importance. One of the conditions of the voting of bonds in 1889 to aid in the erection of a union depot and a viaduct on Tenth Street was that all eastern roads should be granted access, upon reasonable terms, to said depot when completed; and, as contracts have since been made with several roads by which their trains cross the bridge, it is safe to say that within a short time the transfer question, once so important, will cease to vex or worry either the people of Omaha or the general commercial public.

# CHAPTER XXXII.

### The Union Depot — Legal Complications — Eastern Railroad Connections and Terminal Facilities.

Beyond doubt, the passenger depot building which was to have been erected on the site of the old Union Pacific depot would have been a substantial, convenient and costly structure. The plans and specifications called for a building having no superiors in its line in this country, and the estimated cost was one million dollars. The work was being done by a corporation styled the Union Depot Company, composed of officials of the Union Pacific and Burlington & Missouri River Railway Companies, the funds being provided by those railway companies. It was expected that the building would be completed by July 1, 1891, to an extent to admit of its being used, but that it would not be entirely finished until a year and a half after that date. It was to cover, with its train sheds, nearly three and a half acres of ground. The main building would have had a frontage of 160 feet on Tenth Street, with a depth of 140 feet, and was to be constructed of pressed brick and stone, and furnished with all modern conveniences. The plans showed the main building four stories high, with an ornamental tower 260 feet high. There was to be, to the east of the main building, three train sheds, built of iron, one, seven hundred and fifty feet long, over the main tracks, and two, over the stub tracks, to be between five hundred and six hundred feet in length. The entrance to the main building was to be at the west end, on a level with the Tenth Street viaduct, twenty-five feet above the track level. The southwest corner of the building was to be thirty feet east of the east side of the viaduct and the northwest corner seventy-five feet, connected by a covered approach for carriages. A separate building, 180 feet long, for express and baggage purposes, was to have been erected to the east of the depot, in the basement of which were to have been located the electric, heating and ventilating plants. Everything necessary to make this one of the most complete and convenient depots in the country was to have been provided. It was estimated that the cost of the building and the viaduct would reach one and a half million dollars, which expense was to have been shared equally by the two railroad companies. All the Iowa roads were to have been admitted to bridge and depot facilities, so that the transfer delays and difficulties would be done away with. The following named were the officers of the Union Depot Company: Thomas L. Kimball, president; George W. Holdrege, vice-president; and J. G. Taylor, secretary and treasurer. These gentlemen, with W. H. Holcomb and Erastus Young, of the Union Pacific, and W. P. Durkee, of the Burlington & Missouri, constituted the board of directors.

The lack of adequate depot facilities, and the delay in transferring to other railways on the eastern side of the Missouri, had long been sources of annoyance to the citizens of Omaha. The depot building which the Union Pacific Company erected in the seventies had never been an object of pride with the people, but, on the contrary, the railroad company had been accused of not fairly carrying out its obligations in that regard; hence, when city bonds to the amount of $150,000 were asked for in the fall of

1889, to aid in the erection of a new depot and the necessary viaduct, strict pledges were demanded, as follows:

" Provided, however, that said bonds shall not be issued until there shall have been executed and delivered to the City of Omaha, two certain bonds, as follows, to-wit:

" First. The written bond of the said Omaha Union Depot Company, in the sum of $200,000, as liquidated and agreed damages, to be also signed by the Union Pacific Railway Company and the Chicago, Burlington & Quincy Railroad Company, as sureties for said Omaha Union Depot Company, conditioned for the construction and maintenance of said union depot by said Omaha Union Depot Company in the manner and form as above specified, with the necessary tracks, side-tracks, turn-outs, switches and approaches, including the said viaduct or approach over and upon Tenth Street, in a good, workmanlike manner; said viaduct or approach to be completed on or before January 1, 1891, and said union depot to be opened for use on or before January 1, 1892, unless the construction of such structures, or either of them, shall be delayed by strike or strikes, or by injunctions or other judicial proceedings. To the extent of such delays the last named times shall be extended.

" Said bond to be further conditioned that any and all railroad companies that desire the privilege shall have the right to run passenger trains into and from said union depot upon just and equitable terms, to be agreed upon between the said Omaha Union Depot Company and the railroad company making application therefor. And, in case the said companies are unable to agree as to what are just and equitable terms, the question shall be submitted to three arbitrators, one to be chosen by each of said companies, and the two thus selected to choose the third, the decision of any two of said arbitrators to be binding upon both companies.

" Second. The written bond of the Union Pacific Railway Company, to the sum of two hundred thousand dollars, as liquidated and agreed damages, conditioned that any and all railroad companies that may desire the privilege shall have the right to run their passenger trains over the Missouri River bridge and approaches thereto of said Union Pacific Railway Company, using therefor its tracks from the union transfer at Council Bluffs, Iowa, to and from the said Omaha union depot, upon just and equitable terms, to be agreed upon between the Union Pacific Railway Company and the railroad company making application for such use of said railroad tracks and bridge; and, in case the said companies are unable to agree as to what are just and equitable terms, the question shall be submitted to three arbitrators, one to be chosen by each of said companies, and the two thus selected to choose the third, the decision of any two of said arbitrators to be binding upon both companies. Upon the execution and delivery of said bonds to the City of Omaha, the mayor thereof shall deposit the coupon bonds of the city, herein provided for, with the banking firm of Kountze Brothers, who shall deliver them to the Omaha Union Depot Company on January 1, 1891, or as soon thereafter as they are presented, with a certificate from the president of the Omaha Union Depot Company, attested by the mayor of the city of Omaha to the effect that the viaduct in this proposition mentioned has been opened for use, and when not less than one hundred and fifty thousand dollars shall have been expended on construction of said depot as evidenced by vouchers and contracts for material therefor."

The bonds required of the depot company and the railroad company were given, the city bonds voted November 30th, and the viaduct was completed and opened for traffic on the date specified; but new complications arose, in consequence of Mr. Jay Gould's having obtained control of the Union Pacific Railroad, in December, 1890.

## THE UNION DEPOT.

April 30, 1890, while the Union Pacific was under the management of Charles Francis Adams, an agreement was entered into by the officials of that road with the officers of the Chicago, Milwaukee & St. Paul Railroad Company, by which the latter company secured the right, for a term of 999 years, to move its trains, both passenger and freight, on the Union Pacific tracks as far as South Omaha, to stand its cars on certain tracks, and to use such portions of track as permitted it to get its cars on to the river bottoms. For the use of these tracks, over which it was allowed to transfer its cars by its own motive power, the Milwaukee company was to pay a rent of forty-five thousand dollars per year, in monthly payments.

May 1, 1890, a like arrangement was made with the Chicago, Rock Island & Pacific Railroad Company, but, in addition to the use of the tracks between Council Bluffs and South Omaha, with depot facilities, the Rock Island company also acquired the right to use the Union Pacific tracks between Lincoln and Beatrice, making connection at the latter point with its main line to Denver. During the summer of 1890 the Rock Island company built a line from South Omaha to Lincoln, and would thus become, in effect, a competitor with the Union Pacific for Denver business, when it would enter upon the use of its new line, which it expected to do January 1, 1891. The Milwaukee company, by the terms of its agreement, became a competing road with the Union Pacific for South Omaha business.

This state of affairs was evidently not satisfactory to Mr. Gould, and he took measures to break the agreements, under which the Milwaukee company had been operating for several months. December 27, 1890, the latter company was prevented from crossing the bridge to Omaha by the Union Pacific company's locking its switches at the transfer. Four days later the Milwaukee officials applied to Judge Doane, of the district court, for an injunction to restrain the Union Pacific company from interfering with the running of the trains of the Milwaukee company. A temporary injunction was granted, but the Union Pacific company transferred the case to the United States Court, and Judge Dundy decided that he would not interfere in the case without having all the points fully presented. January 5th the parties appeared in court, the Milwaukee company being represented by A. J. Poppleton, James M. Woolworth, and C. S. Montgomery, of this city, John T. Fish, the company's general solicitor at Chicago, and John W. Carey, the company's solicitor at Milwaukee, though the last two named took no active part in the proceedings. The Union Pacific was represented by John M. Thurston and E. P. Smith, of its law department, and Bailey P. Waggener, general attorney for the Missouri Pacific, which road was also under the control of Mr. Gould.

The position taken by counsel for the Union Pacific was: The agreement made April 30th was in the nature of a lease, and that it could not be legally made without the assent of the stockholders of the road; that the rights of the general government were jeopardized in its character as chief creditor of the company, in consequence of the earnings of the road being largely reduced if the agreement was carried out; that the charter of the Union Pacific Road prohibited a leasing of its lines, and if a mile of the road could be leased the entire road could be; that the United States supreme court had decided that the Missouri River bridge was a portion of the main line and must be operated as such. Mr. Thurston stated that he had serious doubts as to the legal right of the Union Pacific Company to enter into a contract with the City of Omaha to allow the eastern roads to run their trains into the new depot with their own engines, as provided for when the viaduct bonds were voted.

Counsel for the Milwaukee insisted that the agreement in question was not a lease, as the Union Pacific retained full control of the premises; but that it was a contract which the officials of the Union Pacific Company had a right to make, and that similar contracts were now in operation at other points, to which the Union Pacific Company was a party, among which were cited the use of the Union Pacific line between Omaha and Valley by the Omaha and Republican Valley Railroad Company, the running of Pullman cars over the line, the use of the Union Pacific Road between Omaha and Granger by the Oregon Short Line, and the use of the Union Pacific tracks between Topeka and Kansas City by the Rock Island Company. They claimed that public interests demanded that parallel railway lines be avoided wherever it was possible to do the necessary business over one road. As to the bridge charter, they insisted that the act of February, 1871, required the Union Pacific Company to grant other roads the use of the bridge on fair and reasonable terms.

The arguments in the case occupied two days. Judge Dundy then requested a filing of the authorities presented, and on the 30th of January announced his decision to the effect that the bridge was a public thoroughfare and that the contract with the Milwaukee company, if shown to have been made by the proper authorities, on behalf of the Union Pacific, would be binding, upon a suitable time table being arranged. Judge Dundy also held that other roads may also be allowed the use of the bridge upon payment of a reasonable toll.

January 8th the Rock Island company also secured from Judge Doane a temporary injunction to restrain the Union Pacific company from interfering with the running of the trains of the petitioner.

The case was taken by the Union Pacific attorneys to the court of appeals at St. Paul, Minnesota, and that court sustained the opinion of the United States court at Omaha.

Prior to these legal complications the Union Depot Company had entered into contracts for the erection of the main building, and its construction had proceeded until the walls had reached a level with the Tenth Street viaduct. On December 30, 1890, Mr. Ernest Stuht, a tax payer, brought suit to restrain the delivery of the viaduct bonds and also to restrain Alvin Saunders, who for years had held the title as trustee to a portion of the land upon which the Union Depot was to be erected, from delivering the deeds to the property. result of the trial is fully set forth in the chapter on bridges and viaducts. As a result of this litigation, work was stopped on the building, and the question at this writing, August, 1892, appears to be no nearer solution than it did seventeen months ago.

In the meantime there have been several meetings of the citizens; committees have been appointed to wait upon the depot company, and steps taken looking to the completion of the depot; but so far without result.

# CHAPTER XXXIII.

THEATRES AND OPERA HOUSES — THE COLISEUM — SOME NOTABLE ENTERTAINMENTS.

The Academy of Music was the first building erected in Omaha for theatrical purposes. Its first season opened in the winter of 1866-7. The building was owned by Colonel John G. Clopper and S. S. Caldwell, forming part of the block on the south side of Douglas Street which extends from Thirteenth to Fourteenth Street, and which was considered, at the time of its erection, a business block of magnificent proportions and striking architecture. For several years the theatre was managed by Henry Corri, who maintained there one of the best stock companies in the West, and which supported at various times the leading stars of the country. The property afterwards passed into the hands of John I. Redick, and of late years has been run as a variety theatre. During the summer of 1889 it was used as a headquarters by the liquor Prohibition party of Omaha.

In 1870, Mr. Redick built at the northwest corner of Farnam and Sixteenth Streets a large, frame structure, the upper portion of which he designed for an opera house. The first entertainment within its walls was a lecture by Mrs. Livermore, the audience being kept waiting a couple of hours in consequence of a delayed train. During the wait the gas had been turned down, and when Mrs. Livermore finally made her appearance the footlights were turned on first, and, in the effort to give the audience the full benefit of the five large reflectors in the ceiling, those lights were turned off entirely, in the hurry and confusion, the result being that the lecture was delivered with only the footlights burning. The building did not fasten itself in the regards of the public as a place of amusement, and a few years later, having passed into the hands of J. M. Pattee, of lottery fame, was rented to the city for council chamber and city offices. In 1889 it was torn down to give place to the handsome buildings of the Commercial National Bank and F. L. Ames.

Early in 1878, an effort was made to erect an opera house, and so general was the interest manifested that the prospect appeared very encouraging. Mr. James E. Boyd offered to sell, for that purpose, his lot at the northeast corner of Farnam and Fifteenth for $20,000, and take stock in the enterprise to that amount, the total cost of the building to be not less than $40,000. General W. W. Lowe offered to sell to an opera house company a lot 66x132 feet, on the southeast corner of Dodge and Sixteenth, for $12,000, or one of the same size at the southwest corner of Harney and Sixteenth for $7,000. S. E. Rogers offered a lot, 44x132 feet, at the northwest corner of Douglas and Twelfth for $6,000, and Joseph Barker offered his lot, 44x132 feet, at the northwest corner of Farnam and Fifteenth, for $10,000, on twenty-five years' time, with interest at ten per cent. It is interesting to note the increased price these various lots would bring now (1892). It is safe to say that the Boyd lot would bring $150,000; the Dodge Street lot, offered by General Lowe, is worth $100,000, and his Harney Street lot $60,000; the Rogers' lot would probably sell for $45,000; and the Barker lot would be a good investment at $132,000. It was the design to have the proposed structure a chamber of commerce building and an opera house combined. The enterprise was taken in hand by the board of trade, and Messrs. J. I. Gibson, C. C. Housel, W. J. Broatch, G. W. Lininger and Edward C. McShane were appointed a committee to canvass the city for the sale of stock. The city press "boomed" the project, and the committee worked faithfully in its behalf, but failed to secure sufficient pledges to carry out the scheme, and it was given up.

Boyd's Opera House was built by James E. Boyd, at a cost of ninety thousand dollars, and was first thrown open to the public on the night of October 24, 1881, on which occasion the Fay Templeton troupe presented the play of "Mascotte" to an audience which filled the building in every part. At the conclusion of the first act, General C. F. Manderson made a short address and presented the following:

"*Resolved*, That this complete building, resting secure upon its solid foundations, with its thorough protection from danger by fire, its ample means of ingress and egress, its supply of stage conveniences, its artistic decorations, its luxurious comforts for its patrons, and its perfection in every detail, supplies a long felt want of Omaha. We, in common with the people of this community, most heartily appreciate the generous enterprise of our fellow townsman, the Honorable James E. Boyd, and congratulate him upon the great success attending the opening of this beautiful temple of the Muses."

The motion to adopt the resolution was seconded by Hon. Ezra Millard, followed by suitable remarks, and the resolution was then adopted by a hearty vote, to which Mr. Boyd responded in a short address. The next day a valuable silver service was presented Mr. Boyd, inscribed: "Citizens of Omaha to James E. Boyd, October 24, 1881." On the evening of the 27th he was tendered a banquet at the Withnell Hotel. Soon after its completion the opera house passed into the management of Mr. Thomas Boyd, who conducted the business until the close of the season in 1891 with profit to the owner and satisfaction to the public. During the summer of 1889 the property was sold to a syndicate, consisting of Mr. O. M. Carter and others, for $235,000, and leased for a term of two years to Messrs. Thomas Boyd and D. W. Haynes.

The opera house was leased in the summer of 1891 by Mr. L. M. Crawford, who had formerly conducted the Grand Opera House in the Exposition building, and was opened as a popular priced house. Mr. Crawford intended that it should continue to be called Boyd's Opera House, but Governor Boyd objected, on the ground that it would interfere with the business of his new theatre which he was then erecting on the corner of Harney and Seventeenth Streets. The matter was carried to the courts and Mr. Crawford was compelled to change its name, which he did, calling it the "Farnam Street Theatre." The house is managed by Mr. W. J. Burgess.

On the 20th of April, 1885, Max Meyer, Frederick W. Gray, William Wallace, John A. McShane, J. A. Wakefield, C. E. Squires, I. W. Miner, B. F. Smith and Louis Mendelhson organized a company for the erection of an exposition building. The south half of the block, bounded by Capitol Avenue, Davenport, Fourteenth and Fifteenth Streets, was leased of A. J. Poppleton for a term of thirty years, and on this ground was put up a brick building with a frontage of 266 feet on Capitol Avenue and a depth of 120 feet. Mr. Meyer was elected president of the association, Mr. Gray, vice president, Mr. Wallace, treasurer and Mr. Miner, secretary, of the association, and to those offices these gentlemen have been elected annually since. The design was to put up a building to cost about $25,000, but the outlay soon reached double that amount. On the evening of February 18, 1886, there was a formal opening of the building, on which occasion there were about five thousand people present. The musical orchestra band, comprising sixty pieces, furnished the instrumental music, and there were solos, duets, quartets, and choruses, with an address by A. J. Poppleton, Esq., reviewing the growth of Omaha from the date he had built his home on that identical ground, a quarter of a century before, with a view of getting away from the turmoil of the business portion of the town. In the fall of 1886, the Exposition Company leased a lot adjoining their building on the north, and built an addition of 120 feet on Fourteenth Street and sixty-six feet on Davenport. In the main building and annex was held that fall a very successful exposition. In June, 1886 a grand musical festival was held, under the management of C. D. Hess, of Chicago. All sorts of entertainments have been given in the building since that date: contests on roller skates and bicycles; sparring exhibitions by John L. Sullivan; Patti has sung there to an eleven thousand dollar house; two great religious revivals were held in the building, one of them being under the management of Rev. Sam Jones; a meeting of the general assembly of the Presbyterian Church, in 1887; charity balls, from which thousands of dollars were realized; a season of American opera; city, county and State conventions. Varied and extensive have been the attractions which have drawn the public to the Exposition building during the past six years. The annex was leased by the city in 1887, and re-arranged for the purpose of council chamber, police court, police station, and city offices, vacated by the city May 1, 1890. In the same year, L. M. Crawford leased the western portion of the main building for opera house purposes, with Mr. I. W. Miner as manager. The amount expended in fitting the building for this purpose, and for changes made since, brings the total outlay of the Exposition Company up to $113,000. There being a general desire, in 1889, to establish a public market for the sale of vegetables, fruits, meats, etc., in some central locality, the Exposition Association offered to sell the building to the city for that purpose, fixing the very low price of sixty thousand dollars upon the property. A vote was taken upon the proposition, but it failed to secure the necessary majority. In February, 1891, the property passed into the possession of Mr. Poppleton.

The Eden Musee was established in 1887, by William Lawler and J. E. Sackett, in a three-story building at the northwest corner of Farnam and Eleventh Streets, in what had formerly been Creighton Hall. It proved a very profitable as well as a popular enterprise. A considerable sum of money was expended in fitting the building for the purpose, and the management has been characterized by a spirit of enterprise and liberality from the outset. It took fire on March 6, 1892, and was completely destroyed, the loss being about twenty thousand dollars. With characteristic enterprise the managers at once leased the Grand Opera House, re-arranged it for the purpose, and opened it March 14, 1892, with new attractions throughout. It continues to be a very popular place of entertainment.

Governor James E. Boyd, in 1890, purchased of General W. W. Lowe a beautiful site for a new opera house, at the southeast corner of Seventeenth and Harney, with a frontage of one hundred and fifty-two feet on the former street and eighty-eight on the latter, and erected thereon Boyd's New Theatre. It is five stories high, built of stone, iron and pressed brick, with a fire-proof protection of the auditorium from the stage, a seating capacity of two thousand, and possesses all the modern appliances and improvements for buildings of this character, it being one of the best theatre edifices in America. The house was opened Thursday evening, September 3, 1891, by Mr. Thomas Boyd, the lessee, a large and fashionable audience being present. Augustus Thomas' American play, "Alabama," was presented by A. M. Palmer's company. Governor Boyd was called before the curtain, when he made a short address in regard to the progress of Omaha, and alluding to the work which he had undertaken, all modestly put and well delivered. When the applause had subsided Hon. J. M. Thurston was called for, and spoke in praise of the man whose capital had gone into the building. "Whoever causes a smile to ripple upon the lips, whoever causes a gleam of joy in the eye where a tear drop is about to fall," said Mr. Thurston, "has done something for the good of humanity."

The estimated cost at the outset was $150,000, but nearly $100,000 additional was expended on the building in carrying out the desires of Governor Boyd to make it the equal of any theatre in the country.

In the early history of Omaha the Herndon House dining room, the main room of the old court house, and a hall on the third floor of the J. J. Brown building, at the southeast corner of Fourteenth and Douglas, were utilized at intervals for theatrical purposes. The place last mentioned was fitted up with a stage, curtain and footlights, and for some months was known as "Potter's Theatre." There have been various places of amusement of a lower order, but were usually managed in such a way as to excite the hostility of the authorities in a few months after opening, so that their existence has been short-lived. M. B. Leavitt, now somewhat famous as a manager, at one time conducted a place of amusement on lower Farnam Street, in company with the late Frank Walters.

A portion of the Goos Hotel building, erected some five years ago, was fitted up for theatrical purposes, and here plays were presented in the German language, for three years, and for many years a stock company did a successful business in the old Stadt Theatre on Tenth Street. At Kessler's Hall on Thirteenth Street is a Bohemian theatre. In various portions of the city are halls fitted up with stage and accessories for amateur theatricals and concerts.

In 1888, there was erected at the intersection of Twentieth and Lake Streets a large frame structure, 200x300 feet, with a seating capacity of eight thousand, and standing room for nearly as many more. It was designed for bicycle races, running races, walking contests, conventions, concerts, etc., and was built at a cost of forty-five thousand dollars, by a stock company, of which Samuel E. Rogers, Julius Meyer, William Mardis, E. S. Flagg and John S. Prince were the incorporators. The last named was given the management of the enterprise, and many notable entertainments have been given in the building; but it has not proven a financial success, and during the summer of 1890 there was considerable litigation with regard to the property. One of the most noted entertainments given at the Coliseum was on the afternoon and evening of March 4, 1890, when Patti appeared in grand opera, with her famous troupe, before an audience of 8,500 people. On this occasion Patti was on her way from San Francisco with one date unfilled. Proposals were made by her manager to Omaha, Kansas City and Minneapolis, for this date, but Omaha was the only city of the three which accepted the required condition, that a fund of $13,500 be placed in the bank as security against loss by the troupe, this money being raised by the Coliseum Company without appealing to the citizens for help. A further sum of $2,500 was expended in fitting up the stage and in making necessary changes in the building. The event was a success in every particular, the afternoon and evening performances being each attended by so large an audience that the Coliseum Company made money by their enterprise. A grand Merchants' Exposition, which was held in the building in October, 1889, was also a satisfactory experiment financially, and added much to the popularity of the management with the people of Omaha. Probably the most surprising exhibition ever held in the Coliseum was that of the Manufacturers' and Consumers' Association, of Nebraska. The exhibits were confined wholly to goods manufactured in the State, and the result was a surprise to all, even to the manufacturers themselves. There were exhibitors from the several cities in the State, and the people of Omaha were much pleased by the display made by their own manufacturing concerns, and equally so by the showing from Lincoln, Beatrice, Nebraska City, Fairmont, and other cities of the State. The exhibition opened June 11, and closed June 22, 1892, and was attended by about fifty thousand people, every one of whom gave evidence of gratified surprise at the magnificent showing. One other gratifying fact in connection with the exposition was, that after all expenses were paid there was a handsome balance to be placed to the credit of the association.

The Coliseum building was utilized in July, 1892, for the holding of the People's Party Convention, which nominated General Weaver, of Iowa, for the presidency, and General Field, of Virginia, for the vice-presidency of the United States.

While the enterprise has not been a financial success, the people of Omaha have on many occasions found the Coliseum building a very convenient thing to have in the city.

# CHAPTER XXXIV.

EDUCATIONAL — DISTRICT AND PRIVATE SCHOOLS — THE PRESENT PUBLIC SCHOOL SYSTEM.

To Miss J. Adelaide Goodwill, now Mrs. Allen Root, is to be awarded the distinction of teaching the first school in Omaha. She began a term, July 1, 1855, in a room of the old State House, on Ninth Street, with forty pupils, among whom were: Carrie E. Goodwill, Elizabeth Davis, Emma Logan, Maggie Gilmore, Lizzie Jones, Katie Davis, Annie Davis, Enos Johnson, Benjamin Johnson, James Johnson, Ewing Armstrong, Robert Armstrong, C. D. Jones, Willie Gilmore, Justin Davis, James Peterson, Willie Brown, Nancy Peterson, Mary Peterson, Sarah Peterson, Nellie Brown, Emma Peterson, Mary Ryan, James Ryan and James Ferris. This school was successfully conducted by Miss Goodwill until about the middle of December, when she was required to vacate the building, which was then fitted up for the assembling of Nebraska's second legislature, which was convened that month. Mrs. J. P. Manning was also connected with a school established soon after this date.

"Simpson University," for which a site was selected on the high ground just northwest of what is now known as Shinn's Addition, was chartered by the legislature of 1855, with the following named incorporators: Rev. W. H. Good, J. H. Hopkins, W. D. Gage, Charles Elliott, Moses F. Shinn, Thomas H. Benton, Jr., O. B. Selden, John B. Robertson, Mark W. Izard, Thomas B. Cuming, Charles B. Smith, William N. Byers and J. R. Buckingham. In his message to the legislature, two years later, Governor Izard refers to this educational institution as being " permanently located," and adds that " donations of a considerable amount have been received " in aid of the erection of buildings. February 10, 1857, the legislature memorialized Congress to grant to Simpson University land to the amount of " not less than ten thousand acres." This memorial was, no doubt, consigned to the waste basket when it reached Washington; certain it is the grant was never made and no buildings were erected; and both history and tradition are silent as to what became of the "donations of a considerable amount," which Governor Izard referred to. Possibly the expression was a mere figure of speech indulged in by the governor to round out a period in his message.

The legislature of 1857, by virtue of an act approved February 11th, incorporated another institution of learning, to be located at Saratoga, two miles north of Omaha, the incorporators of which were: Joseph S. Grimes, L. M. Kuhn, George J. Park, B. B. Barkalow, William Hamilton, J. Allen, C. D. Martin, Samuel Gamble, John Hancock, Thomas Officer, William Young Brown, Reuben Gaylord, Thomas M. Chestnut, N. L. Rice, John H. Kellom, N. M. Giltner, Cortland Van Rensselaer, Fenner Ferguson, William L. Plumer, O. F. Parker and LeRoy Tuttle. Mr. Kuhn is the only one of the above named who is now a resident of Omaha. Mr. Officer was at that time, and is yet, a resident of Council Bluffs. This had the same experience as Simpson University, so far as practical results were concerned.

October 23, 1857, Mr. John H. Kellom, superintendent of public instruction, published a card in the Omaha *Times*, recommending J. S. Burt as " a teacher of a select school," and trusted that " the citizens of

Omaha who had children to educate would give him liberal encouragement to open a good school in the city." Evidently Mr. Kellom's suggestion was not generally heeded, for it is a matter of history that Mr. Burt did not linger long in Omaha, but went out to the rival town of Fontenelle, in 1858, and there taught a term of school in the winter of 1858-9, with Miss Sarah Gaylord, now Mrs Sardis Brewster, as his assistant.

Early in 1858 it was known that a bishop of the Catholic Church would be sent to Omaha, and the following interesting report was made to the city council by a committee appointed to consider that important event "In view of the great importance of the location of the Roman Catholic See at this point, the measure of which we can best appreciate by reference to Dubuque, Chicago, Cincinnati, Cleveland and numerous other places, which will readily occur to the consideration of the council, your committee feel assured that what at first sight would appear to be great liberality would be justified by the result. In Dubuque alone the expenditures of the church have already reached something more than half a million dollars, resulting in improvements of such a character as to minister to the pride and gratification of her citizens The schools established under the auspices of the church have given her a wide educational celebrity, bringing scholars from all parts of the State, as well as Minnesota Wisconsin and Illinois Of her ten thousand Catholic citizens known for their wealth sobriety and industry, it cannot be doubted but a large portion have been attracted by the same influences your committee are anxious to add to those which have already made Omaha the metropolis of Nebraska, which influences will follow the settlement of the bishop at this place

"Your committee beg leave to suggest that it is only by combining all and every influence in our power that we can hope to make Omaha a great centre of population; that the two great elements, capital and labor, must be induced by every motive we can bring to bear to join hands for our advantage Your committee is satisfied that immigration and capital will at once follow the announcement by the bishop of his determination to settle here, and, believing that the city will be repaid ten-fold for its liberality, they recommend that the city deed to the bishop the following lots 1 in block 21, 1 in 142, 2 in 172, 7 in 203, 7 in 219, 6 in 25, 3 in 67, 5 in 204, 8 in 219, 4 in 26, 6 in 169, 1 in 173, 3 in 229, 8 in 218, and 2 in 232, out of the lots already offered for sale; or they would suggest that, if this proposition should not suit a majority of the council, the thirteen lots claimed by Mr. Bird, and now belonging to the city, with eleven of the best lots remaining in the possession of the city, making in all twenty-four lots, shall be deeded to him The following are the twenty-four Lot 1 in block 5, 8 in 23, 3 in 216, 1 in 250, 9 in 180½, 1 in 203, 3 in 11, 3 in 114, 1 in 229, 5 in 351, 9 in 182½, 8 in 203, 2 in 21, 4 in 166, 4 in 232, 1 in 163 and 4 in 4 "

At a meeting held a few days later the following was adopted

"*Resolved*, That there be donated to the Catholic bishop twenty-four of the best lots of those not advertised, or claimed, or called for "

The matter resulted in no lots whatever being deeded by the city, the bishop, James M O'Gorman, who located here in the spring of 1859, declining to assume any responsibility as to permanent improvements here by the church

November 10, 1859, witnessed the inauguration of the public school system of Omaha as on that day Mr Howard Kennedy, brought from New York State under contract for one year, at a salary of one thousand dollars, began his school in the old capitol building Messrs A. D. Jones, J H.

Kellom and Dr. G. C. Monell composed the district school board. In this building a graded school was then established, with a high school department.

In a report made to the territorial commissioners of schools, dated January 2, 1861, and signed by Dr. Monell, Jesse Lowe and J. H. Kellom, this language was used: "One male teacher was employed to teach the higher studies and superintend the subordinate teachers in the different schools. One principal and three subordinate departments do not sufficiently accommodate all the scholars. Though the average attendance is about sixty scholars to a teacher, yet eighty or ninety were often present."

The charge for instruction in Latin, Greek, French, German, surveying, chemistry and belles-lettres, was fixed at three dollars per quarter; for the common branches, including philosophy, book-keeping and elementary algebra, the charge was two dollars per quarter, one dollar per quarter for small scholars, and double these rates were charged non-resident pupils. The territorial and county fund for the support of Omaha schools for the year ending December 31, 1860, was $1,246.50. Licenses and fines added $656.60, making a total of $1,903.10.

The report thus explains the fixing of these rates: "Four subordinate schools are really needed, but even these cannot be sustained the coming year without more funds. The value of real estate being generally reduced at the last assessment, and the reduction of the school tax last winter to one mill on the dollar, instead of two mills as heretofore, will reduce our public school fund to about one-fourth or one-third the amount of the last year. This reduced revenue would easily support a single school in this city. Two plans suggest themselves to the directors to supply the deficiency: First—To lay on the city a sufficient tax; and, second—to charge each scholar a moderate tuition." They chose the latter.

"The schools will therefore be conducted as heretofore, except that a small price will be charged each pupil attending school. This will combine the advantage of free schools to a sufficient extent to secure their permanence, with a charge for tuition so moderate as to be within the reach of all."

Appended to this was a report of the school examiner, George I. Gilbert, as follows: "We, the undersigned examiner, found the following named persons to be of good moral character, and qualified to teach orthography, reading, writing, arithmetic, geography and English grammar, and have granted them certificates accordingly, for the term of one year, to-wit: Howard Kennedy, J. J. Monell, Mrs. Isabella Torrey, Miss F. Seymore, Miss Smiley, Edward Kelley, H. Davis, Mrs. Mary P. Rust, Mrs. Nye, Miss A. Hayes and Miss Hamilton."

William E. Harvey was territorial school commissioner at that time, and in his report for 1861 states that there were then 571 children in this district, between the ages of five and twenty-one, of which 456 were attending school.

The first territorial school law was passed at the session of 1858-9, and it was under its provisions that Mr. Howard Kennedy was employed to take charge of the schools of Omaha. Edwin Loveland was then a member of the board of directors (the others being A. D. Jones and Dr. Monell), but resigned soon after, and was succeeded by Jesse Lowe. Messrs. George I. Gilbert and P. W. Hitchcock constituted the examining board. For lack of school buildings the two-story brick structure on Ninth, between Douglas and Farnam, first used as the territorial capitol, was used, and in addition there was a small building near the intersection of Thirteenth and Douglas, which was occupied by a primary school. Besides having a general supervision of the educational interests of Omaha, Mr. Kennedy taught a high school department, Mrs. Rust, Mrs. Nye, Mr. and Mrs. Shimonski and Miss Abbie Hayes (now Mrs. Judge Lake) were Mr. Kennedy's assistants. The desks and seats for these first schools were made by Mr. H. H. Visscher. In April, 1860, there was a fine school exhibition given at the Methodist Church, on Thirteenth Street, the present site of the Omaha National Bank building.

As late as 1864, according to Mr. B. E. B. Kennedy, an excellent authority on this subject, Omaha owned no school buildings, but depended upon renting quarters. At the date last named the control of the schools was lodged in a board consisting of B. E. B. Kennedy, Esq., Judge George B. Lake and Colonel Lorin Miller.

In 1860-61, Mr. Kellom, then a member of the board of directors, taught several classes in the old State House, Miss Smiley being one of his assistants. Mrs. Torrey taught a school near the old military bridge, probably in her own house, and Miss Sarah Gaylord taught some classes in the basement of the Congregational Church, at the corner of Farnam and Sixteenth Streets, about the same period. In 1861, Mrs. Shimonski, Mrs. J. H. Kellom and Mrs. James W. Van Nostrand, were occupied in teaching. In April, 1861, Professor S. D. Beals established in the north half of the old State House what was known for several years as the Omaha High School, which was removed that fall to the old Hamilton House, on the south side of Douglas, between Fourteenth and Fifteenth Streets. The school had then from eighty to ninety pupils. Mrs. J. W. Van Nostrand was Professor Beals' assistant. In 1862 the school was removed to the First Baptist Church and two rooms of an adjoining building called Case's Row,on the north side of Douglas, between Fifteenth and Sixteenth. At this time Mrs. Charles R. Turner was assistant teacher, succeeded soon afterwards by Miss Emma Beals. A year later the church building was bought by Professor Beals, and by him removed to the southeast corner of Fifteenth and Capitol Avenue, and here a prosperous career was entered upon and continued for several years, the school including in its list pupils from Sarpy, Nemaha, Washington, Dodge and Burt Counties. In the first year's register of Professor Beals' school are found the names of Miss Lizzie Davis, now Mrs. Herman Kountze; Miss Gussie Estabrook, now the wife of Colonel Clowry, of the Western Union Telegraph Company; Miss Emma Lehmer, now Mrs. W. V. Morse; Miss Laura Lehmer, now Mrs. A. H. Cooley; Miss Helen Ingalls, now Mrs. Flemon Drake; Miss Lizzie Jones, now Mrs. V. M. Mackey; Miss Melissa Perkins, now Mrs. Byron Reed; Ralph E. Gaylord; Frederick W. Davis; Jeff. Megeath; Julius Roeder and Andrew McAusland. Later on appeared the names of Miss Bertha Isaacs, now Mrs. Frederick A. McConnell; Miss Carrie Loveland, now Mrs. A. S. Van Kuran; Miss Frank Crawford, now Mrs. E. K. Valentine; Miss Ella Cole, now Mrs. C. E. Squires; Miss Alzina Scott, now Mrs. Thomas Swobe; Miss Kate McAusland, now Mrs. John R. Manchester; Miss Georgia Hanscom, now Mrs. George E. Pritchett; Miss Jennie Brown, now Mrs. James Forsythe; Archie Powell; Frank Kennard; Thomas Rogers; Alfred Millard; Edward Peck; Robert Livesey and many others, now well-known residents of Omaha.

In 1862 a school was opened on upper Harney Street by Mr. Littlefield and his wife, which school was continued for about a year; and about the same time a German-English school was maintained on Farnam Street, near Tenth, by a German named Wurtz. In the same vicinity Rev. O. C. Duke, an Episcopal clergyman, established a parochial school for boys, which was succeeded by a school on the north side of Dodge Street, between Fourteenth and Fifteenth Streets, styled the Collegiate Institute, under the charge of Dr. Rippey.

In 1863 a school was taught in a building on Jefferson Square, in which school Miss Celestial Parker, afterwards Mrs. Joel A. Griffin, was one of the teachers. Miss Burkeley, daughter of Mr. Vincent Burkeley, was also one of the teachers about that date, her school being in a building on Howard and Eighth Streets. In 1865 the frame structure on Jackson and Eleventh Streets was built; in 1866 another at Burt and Twenty-third was erected; and in 1868 the Pacific Street building was put up at a cost of twenty-three thousand dollars, including the purchase price of the lot. The erection of the Izard Street building, costing thirty-five thousand dollars, followed, and then the Pleasant Street building, which with the lot cost seven thousand dollars. In the meantime the Jefferson Square building had been moved over to Cass Street, where the brick structure now stands, which latter building was put up about 1875, the Dodge Street building being erected about the same time. Mr. B. E. B. Kennedy was a school director continuously from 1863 to 1872; Judge Lake, Colonel Lorin Miller, John Evans and Andrew J. Simpson being associated with him on the board at various times.

By an act of the legislature of 1869, the governor of the State was directed to transfer to the City of Omaha for school purposes the grounds known as the capitol grounds, and the buildings thereon, and also provided for a board of regents to have the management of the same. The following preamble set forth the reasons for such enactment:

WHEREAS, The capitol grounds heretofore occupied by the State of Nebraska were originally conveyed to the Territory of Nebraska by said City of Omaha; and

WHEREAS, After the erection of a capitol building thereon had been commenced by the government of the United States, the appropriation therefor was found to be insufficient; and

WHEREAS, After the suspension of the construction of said buildings, for the reason aforesaid, the people of the said City of Omaha contributed the sum of sixty thousand dollars to complete the same; and

WHEREAS, The State of Nebraska has ceased to use said capitol grounds and buildings for the objects originally contemplated; and

WHEREAS, The said capitol building is now in a condition to require the expenditure of a large sum of money before the said building can be safely used by the State of Nebraska for any purpose; therefore be it enacted, etc.

The bill provided for the deeding by the governor, on or before the first day of April, 1869, bound the city to use said property for educational purposes only, and prohibited the city from conveying, leasing, or in any manner encumbering the property. Alvin Saunders, George W. Frost, Thomas Davis, John H. Kellom, Augustus Kountze and James M. Woolworth were constituted by the bill the board of regents, the first two named to serve for three years, the two next named to serve two years, and the two last named to serve one year, so that two regents were to be elected annually, commencing with the municipal election of 1870.

The board thus appointed held its first meeting April 13, 1869, and perfected its organization by electing Alvin Saunders, president; Augustus Kountze, treasurer; and James W. Van Nostrand, secretary. Application was at once made to Governor David Butler for the deed of the capitol square, to which he replied that "the original files of the laws passed at the last session of the legislature have been sent away by the secretary to have them bound," and that as soon as they were returned he would make the deed asked for. If such conveyence was made by Governor Butler it was mislaid, and never recorded, which fact seems to have been overlooked until the meeting of the legislature of 1889, when application was made to that body for the conveyence authorized by its predecessor of twenty years previous. The result was the deed was prepared, signed by Governor Thayer, and at once properly placed upon record.

It was at first supposed that the old capitol building could be used for high school purposes, and a committee of experts, Jonas Gise, John H. Green, and John D. Jones, was employed to thoroughly examine the structure and report as to its condition. They evidently made a favorable report, for on the 4th of May, 1869, Mr. Frost was directed by the board to employ an architect at an expense of not exceeding $250, and Secretary Van Nostrand was directed to make a ground plan of the building. G. R. Randall, of Chicago, was employed upon recommendation of Mr. Frost and another inspection of the building was made, Mr. Randall reporting it insecure " in construction and inferior in material." It was then resolved to remove the old building and put up an entirely new one on plans to be furnished by Mr. Randall. The sum of $20,000 was turned over to the board of regents by the " board of trustees of school district No. 1, of Douglas County "—the Omaha district— and bonds to the amount of $100,000 in aid of the erection of the new building were voted and the work entered upon with commendable vigor. Mr. A. C. Dort was employed to superintend the tearing down of the old capitol and removing the material, and as soon as the ground was cleared the laying of the foundations of the handsome building which now graces that magnificent site were commenced. The work was carried on with earnestness and zeal, and the building finally completed in the latter part of 1872 at a total cost, including the heating apparatus, of $225,000. During this time changes were made in the board of regents. Thomas Davis resigned and C. W. Burt was elected to fill the vacancy, W. W. Lowe, George B. Lake and Eleazer Wakeley also serving as regents, in addition to those appointed, being elected by the people.

By an act approved June 6, 1871, to take effect January 1, 1872, the board of trustees of school district No. 1, and the board of high school regents were both legislated out of existence, though each "continued business at the old stand" until the latter part of May, 1872. By the act referred to, the control of the schools of the district named passed into the control of a board of education, consisting of two members from each ward of the city, which made a total membership of twelve, one-half of which number were to be elected for a term of one year, and the remainder to serve a term of two years, those elected annually thereafter to serve a term of two years. A small portion of the city was then included in school district No. 2, but was afterward brought under the control of the board of education, so that the entire city was included in one district. The first board elected consisted of Alvin Saunders, Dr. Theodore Baumer, Vincent Burkeley, Adolph Boehne, Charles M. Connoyer, Flemon Drake, C. W. Hamilton, Joseph Redman, James Creighton, John T. Edgar, Thomas F. Hall, and Howard Kennedy, and the first meeting was held April 8, 1872. Mr. Edgar was elected president, and Mr. Drake, secretary. Among the first resolutions introduced was one by Mr. Hall, which provided that " there shall be no religious services of any kind or nature performed in any of the public schools, and that the reading of the Bible, prayers, singing of hymns or psalms are considered in the category of religious services, and that the superintendent and teachers of the public schools are hereby directed to conduct the schools so as to prevent the performance of any of the above services." On motion of Mr. Kennedy action upon the resolution was postponed until the adoption of rules and regulations for the schools came before the board for consideration, and the resolution was never voted upon.

Prof. A. F. Nightingale was the first superintendent of public schools elected under the present system, the board of education choosing him for that place at their meeting of June 3, 1872, for the period of one year, fixing his salary at $2,400, and other salaries were established as follows: Principal of the high school, $1,800; principals of the graded schools, $1,500; first assistant teachers, $750; second assistant teachers, $650; and third assistant teachers, $550. At this time the property, assets and liabilities of the board of trustees of school district No.

1 and of the board of regents were turned over to the board of education. Up to that date the total receipts of the board of regents amounted to $183,024.48, and their disbursements to $174,852, leaving a balance on hand of $8,172.48, with outstanding obligations to the amount of $23,894.76. The first issue of school bonds was dated July 1, 1871; the amount was $100,000, running twenty years and drawing ten per cent interest. The credit of Omaha in eastern money centers was not as well established then as now, and only $96,150 were realized on this issue. The following year an additional amount of $50,000 was voted in aid of schools, but owing to legal defects these bonds were destroyed in March, 1873, having been replaced by another issue of the same amount, bearing date February 15, 1873. The rate of interest on these bonds was also fixed at ten per cent. In 1888 school bonds to the amount of $200,000 were voted, but the rate of interest was reduced to five per cent.

In 1876 the first class was graduated from the high school, and was composed of the following persons: Stacia Crowley, Blanche L. Deuel, Ida M. Goodman, Addie H. Gladstone, Fannie E. Wilson, Esther Jacobs, Bertha M. Isaacs, Margaret M. McCague, Nelia Lehmer, Alfred Ramsay, Henry C. Curry. Of these Miss Stacia Crowley and Miss Ida M. Goodman are still connected with the schools in the capacity of teachers. Addie H. Gladstone was married to Mr. D. Gross; Fannie E. Wilson, to Mr. S. F. Woodbridge; Bertha M. Isaacs, to Mr. F. R. McConnell; Nelia Lehmer, to Mr. Richard Carrier, and are all residents of Omaha. Esther Jacobs was married to Mr. A. Rosenberg, and removed to Schuyler, Neb.; and Margaret McCague, to Rev. Albert M. Gordon, and resides at Alliance, Neb. Miss Blanche L. Deuel, who was Mr. Harry P. Deuel's daughter, was, at the time of her graduation, quite a talented musician, and was deservedly popular among all classes of people in Omaha. She died within a year or two after graduating, and her loss was almost universally mourned.

This district is now called the Metropolitan School District and contains fifty-two buildings. The board consists of fifteen members. Teachers to the number of 298 are employed, receiving salaries ranging from $400 to $1,500 per annum, principals being paid from $800 to $1,400 each. The principal of the high school is paid $2,600 The total value of school buildings and real estate is about $1,250,000. For the year ending July 13, 1891, $215,191.08 was paid out for salaries. The money received by the city from licenses and fines goes to the school fund and the amount derived from these sources during the school year ending July 1, 1891, was $280,851. In 1891 14,093 pupils were enrolled. In the high school building a manual training department has been successfully maintained for several years. This department was for several years in charge of Mr. A. M. Buman, who is entitled to much credit for the successful introduction and operation of this branch. In 1891 Mr. Buman resigned his position and removed to Des Moines, Iowa, to take charge of the manual training department of the public schools of that city. He was succeeded by Mr. John E. Wigman, who was for many years a pattern maker for the Union Pacific Railway Company. The course includes mechanical and architectural drawing, wood turning and joining, metal moulding, etc. During the winter of 1888 a cooking department was also conducted in that building, a class of over one hundred girls being instructed by a teacher of skill and experience. This department proved to be thoroughly practical, and the prospect for continued and permanent usefulness was very encouraging; but the failure to secure general public favor, together with a combined attack made upon the innovation by the city press, led to a discontinuance of the department at the end of the year. During the past three winters

High School Building

night schools have been conducted in a large number of school buildings, with a large attendance of pupils and most gratifying results. The school population of Omaha, July 1, 1891, was 27,280.

The public schools of Omaha are not surpassed by those of any city in the United States, and are the subject of much favorable comment in the leading educational journals of the country. So efficient and popular have they become that private schools in Omaha have been practically abolished. The present superintendent, Mr. Frank A. Fitzpatrick was elected to fill that responsible post in July, 1891, succeeding Henry M. James, who held the position nine years, succeeding George B. Lane, who succeeded Prof. S. D. Beals, who took charge of the schools in 1874. Prof. Nightingale was his predecessor.

An annual enumeration of the school children of Omaha is taken in April, and the following figures show the steady increase in this regard for the past ten years: April, 1880, the number was 6,468; 1881, 7,184; 1882, 8,104; 1883, 8,921; 1884, 10,167; 1885, 11,202; 1886, 11,831; 1887, 14,889; 1888, 19,260; 1889, 20,243; 1890, 24,520; 1891, 27,281. The average attendance at the public schools during the year 1891 was 9,715. To this may be added 2,500 pupils who attend parochial and private schools. The total revenue for public school purposes for 1891 was $407,634.23, and the total expenditures $372,826.36. At the close of the school year, June, 1892, there were twenty-two brick and thirty-nine frame buildings in use for school purposes, a total of sixty-one.

The first secretary of the board of education was Flemon Drake, who resigned before the expiration of his second term. His successors were: C. K. Coutant, W. H. S. Hughes, Thomas J. Staley and C. D. Woodworth. Charles Conoyer served from 1880 until 1887, when he was succeeded by J. B. Piper, who served until 1890, when Mr. Conoyer was again elected, and is still serving. The following figures are taken from the secretary's report for the school year 1891-92: Average attendance, 10,879; total revenue (1892), $396,206.56; total expenditures (1892), $387,119.24; valuation of school houses, $661,785; valuation of school sites, $577,000; salaries (1892), males, $14,261.75, females, $208,910.11; fines (1892), $15,986; licenses (1892), $271,593.90; pupils enrolled, 14,525; high school enrollment (1892), 747; high school graduates (1892), sixty-five.

When the high school building was erected there was much more room than necessary for the high school classes, and the board of education maintained in the building a graded school known as the Central School. This school was maintained without question for about fifteen years. The high school, however, continued to grow and to encroach on the rooms which had been used for the graded school, until, in 1887, it was found necessary to transfer the seventh and eighth grades from the high school building to other buildings. This created quite a stir among the people in the neighborhood, but, as it was the only feasible thing to do at that time, it was finally acquiesced in. Ever since the growth of the high school has continued, and the prospects were that the Central School would be completely crowded out and dispersed. Upon the question as to what should be done, the people living in the neighborhood were much divided; some of them wanted a separate building on the high school grounds; some, and apparently the majority, were in favor of an addition to the high school building; while others were in favor of another site and a separate building for the graded school. Many of the citizens who had children in the lower grades were much opposed to the transfer of the lower grades from the building and brought the weight of their influence to bear on members of the school board to have them still maintain all the grades there, even if it was necessary to divide the high school in order to do so. In the meantime, those who were opposed to the presence of the lower grades were not idle, and one of them, Dr. S. R. Towne, in the fall of 1891, instituted suit in mandamus to compel the vacation of the rooms by the lower grades, the building at the time being overcrowded, there being 1,066 pupils. The case was heard by Judge Irvine in the district court, who decided that the pupils of the grades complained of had no legal right in the building, but were there on sufferance; but the testimony failed to show that the high school was suffering hardship from said occupancy by said lower grades sufficient to call for the power of the court to eject them. The court also decided that the contention of the defendants was not supported, *i. e.*, that the rooms were not, under the terms of the grant, intended to be occupied by the lower grades, but, on the contrary, were to be occupied by the grades named, or higher grades, and decided further that injunction was the proper remedy. After much discussion the board of education, in 1890, submitted to the electors a proposition to issue bonds for several school buildings, among them $75,000 for an addition to the high school. A very light vote was polled, and the proposition failed to carry, owing to the activity of those who were opposed to any additional building on the high school ground. In the meantime the question arose as to the title of the high school grounds, and a committee of the board was sent to Lincoln for the purpose of having the legislature direct the governor to make a deed to the board of education, as the legal successors of the board of regents, the former deed never having been recorded. The committee was not successful in its mission, some of the leading citizens making it their business to go to Lincoln to oppose the action. The legislature, however, directed the governor to make a deed of the grounds to the City of Omaha, which was done, and the deed duly recorded. The demand for room was urgent, and the board, as a last resort, adopted a resolution to erect a temporary four-room building on the grounds in the rear of the present building. For some reason the city council was much opposed to this action, and, before anything had been done toward the erection of the structure, it passed an ordinance extending the fire limits so that they took in the high school grounds. This, of course, made it unlawful to erect a frame building. The board of education then changed its plans to a brick building, and the city council ordered Mr. Whitlock, who was superintendent of buildings, to refuse a building permit for the erection of the building on the high school grounds, claiming that they were deeded for high school purposes only. The attorney for the board, Judge Lee S. Estelle, applied to the courts for a writ of mandamus to compel the superintendent of buildings to issue the permit. By direction of the city council Mr. Poppleton, then city attorney, appeared for Mr. Whitlock. The case was carried to the Supreme Court of the State, and the application for mandamus denied, the court in its opinion distinctly ruling that the grounds could not be used for any educational purpose lower than for a high school. Thus was finally determined a question which had for years been a source of vexation and annoyance to the members of the board. The action of the legislature and the decisions of the courts render it almost certain that the grounds will never be used for anything except for the Omaha High School. Another question has arisen, however, and that is as to whether the board of education or the city council shall make provisions for the payment for improvements, such as pavements, sidewalks, etc. This question is now being discussed.

At the election held in November, 1891, a proposition was submitted to the electors of the city providing for the issue of bonds to the amount of $385,000, for the purpose

Brownell Hall.

of purchasing sites and erecting buildings. Among them was a site and building for the Central School. The proposition was carried by an overwhelming majority. A site was purchased on Dodge Street, opposite the southwest corner of the high school grounds, upon which a building is now being erected.

Upon the re-opening of the schools in the fall of 1890, a Normal school department was added to the system, with Mrs. Grace Sudborough (for many years connected with the schools) in charge, and Miss Helen L. Wyckoff and Miss Emma R. Rugh, as training teachers. The school commenced work November 17, 1890, on which date twenty-five graduates of the high school were enrolled as pupils. A number of Omaha young ladies who were attending the State Normal School returned home in order to attend the school here. In the employment of teachers for the city schools, preference has always been given to residents of Omaha, and the material from which to select teachers hereafter will be largely increased by the establishment of the Normal school department. There were twenty-one graduates from this department in 1891.

The present school board is composed of the following: S. K. Spalding, president; W. N. Babcock, vice president; Charles Conoyer, secretary; Emma C. Monzingo, clerk; F. A. Fitzpatrick, superintendent; Ed. O. Hamilton, superintendent of school buildings; Irving Baxter, attorney. Members— C. E. Babcock, W. N. Babcock, H. B. Coryell, C. S. Elgutter, W. S. Gibbs, R. W. Gibson, C. L. Jaynes, Euclid Martin, Morris Morrison, J. J. Points, W. S. Poppleton, Clinton N. Powell, C. J. Smyth, Charles Wehrer.

Brownell Hall, an Episcopalian school for young ladies, was established in 1863, by Bishop Talbot, in a building erected at Saratoga, three miles north of Omaha, for a hotel. It was supposed that the mineral springs located under the bluffs at that point would become popular as a health resort, and a large hotel building was erected by the Saratoga Town Site Company, about 1858, to accommodate the expected guests. The enterprise proved a failure, however, and the building was disposed of at much less than cost. In 1868 the school was incorporated by Bishop Clarkson, Samuel Herman, J. M. Woolworth, C. S. Chase, W. H. Van Antwerp, George W. Doane, Dr. G. C. Monell, Col. Benjamin Alvord R. C. Jordan, John I. Redick, and H. W. Yates. The first principal was Rev. O. C. Dake, and the first board of trustees consisted of the following named: Bishop R. H. Clarkson, Rev. George C. Betts, Rev. Samuel Herman, R. C. Jordan, Dr. G. C. Monell, John I. Redick, J. M. Woolworth, H. W. Yates, C. S. Chase, Col. Benjamin Alvord and G. W. Doane, all of Omaha; J. A. Ware, Nebraska City; G. F. Blanchard, Fremont; E. S. Dundy, Falls City; and Charles R. Dakin, of Decatur. Bishop Clarkson was president of the board and R. C. Jordan, secretary. Under this management Rev. Samuel Herman was the first rector and principal, to be succeeded in 1869 by Bishop Clarkson, as rector, and by Miss Elizabeth Butterfield, as principal. In 1867 and 1868 a large building was erected on Sixteenth Street, corner of Jones, on two lots, one of which was donated by Mr. Herman Kountze and the other sold by him to the trustees for $1,600 (in 1887 this ground was sold to W. F. Lorenzen for $25,000). The school was then moved down from Saratoga, and in 1871 Mrs. P. C. Hall became principal. In 1876 Rev. Robert Doherty was elected rector and principal, which positions he still retains. In 1880 a building was erected for a primary school, and in 1881 the rector put up a building on a lot, purchased by himself, adjoining the hall, and used it as an annex to the school. In 1886 Mr. Herman Kountze donated to the school a handsome site on South Tenth Street, and gave liberally to the building fund, to which a large number of people also contributed. On this site a large building, in three parts, each 40 x 100 feet and joined in the form of the letter H, was erected in the most substantial manner, of stone, brick and iron. It is admirably adapted to educational purposes and draws its pupils from all parts of the West. The following named are the officers and faculty: Visitor, the Rt. Rev. George Worthington, S. T. D.,LL.D.; rector, the Rev. Robert Doherty, M. A. of Trinity College, Toronto, S. T. D. of Hobart College, Geneva; secretary and treasurer, Mr. A. P. Hopkins; lady principal, Mrs. S. H. Windsor, seventeenth year in the school; vice principal, Miss K. T. Lyman, B. A. Vassar College, twelfth year in the school; mathematics, Rev. Robert Doherty, M. A., S. T. D., Miss Ethel Davenport, Miss Lucy E. Burgess; natural science, Miss K. T. Lyman, B. A.; English literature and composition, Miss L. C. McGee, Ph. M.; lectures in geology, Mr. William Cleburne, of Trinity College, Dublin; Latin language, Miss K. T. Lyman, B. A.; modern languages, Miss J. M. Young; conchology, Miss Emma Doherty; instrumental music, Miss M. E. Wallace, Miss Lucy E. Burgess; vocal music, Mrs. J. W. Cotton; art, Mrs. J. M. Yonng; preparatory department, Miss F. D. Wall, Miss Cora B. Clark; gymnastics, Miss C. B. Clark; housekeeper, Miss Mary Bradley; chemistry, F. M. Mueller, A. S.

In 1868 the first class was graduated, the only two members of which were Helen Ingalls, now Mrs. Flemon Drake, and Helen Hoyt, now Mrs. Horace Burr. They were the first graduates from a school of this rank in Nebraska.

There is also a school on Nineteenth Street, near California, conducted under the auspices of the Episcopal Church, which has two teachers.

At No. 1003 South Twentieth Street, is a German Lutheran school, with two teachers, where both German and English are taught. It has an attendance of about one hundred and twenty-five pupils. A branch of this school is maintained on north Twenty-sixth Street, and another at South Omaha.

On Harney Street, near Nineteenth, a large brick building, costing twenty-five thousand dollars, was erected in 1883 by German citizens, to be used for a German-American school, a gymnasium and for social purposes. For several years an excellent school was maintained, but was abandoned in 1889, as the public schools of the city have grown in efficiency and popular favor to such an extent as to render private schools almost superfluous.

There are two commercial colleges in the city: the Omaha Business College, established by George R. Rathbun, in May, 1873, now located in a large brick building at the southeast corner of Twenty-fourth and Paul Streets, of which Mr. Rathbun is still the proprietor; and the Omaha Commercial College, M. G. Rohrbough, G. A. Rohrbough and L. J. Rohrbough, proprietors, located in the Boston Store block, corner of Douglas and Sixteenth Streets. Both institutions are well patronized and are deservedly popular.

The Presbyterian Theological Seminary at Omaha, Nebraska, was organized in the spring of 1891, by a convention of the representatives of the Presbyterians in the large region contiguous to this city.

Articles of incorporation were adopted and a board of directors, numbering forty was elected to manage the institution.

A most generous offer of twenty-five acres of land, located in Seymour Park, was made by Dr. George L. Miller, upon the only condition that the main seminary building, to cost not less than $20,000, should be erected thereon, and that its foundations should be laid within three years from the date of his offer. Almost the whole of the four hundred acres of the beautiful lands of Seymour Park were thrown open to the management from which to select its twenty-five acres for the seminary site. Seymour Park is about five miles from the business center of Omaha, and is

reached at present by two lines of railway, with suburban trains, also by beautiful driveways. Street car lines are expected in the near future. It is one of the most beautiful sites in the West, with its knolls, valleys, and groves, its sightliness and extended views.

The board of directors unanimously accepted Dr. Miller's generous offer, and took immediate steps for organizing and starting the work. The following faculty was elected and has served very efficiently during the past year: Rev. William W. Harsha, D. D. LL. D., professor of didactic and polemic theology; Rev. Stephen Phelps, D. D., professor of ecclesiastical, homiletical and pastoral theology; Rev. John Gordon, D. D., professor of biblical and ecclesiastical history; Rev. Matthew B. Lowrie, D. D., professor elect of new testament literature and exegesis; Rev. Charles G. Sterling, Ph.D., instructor in Hebrew; Rev. Thomas L. Sexton, D. D., lecturer on home missions.

The seminary was opened in the fall of 1891, with nine students in the junior class, only the one class being organized. The recitations were conducted in the parlors of the Second Presbyterian Church. At a meeting of the board of directors at the close of the seminary this spring, plans were approved and adopted for a seminary building to cost forty thousand dollars. Work is now being done preparing the stone and other materials for the structure. The stone for the building is generously donated by the Evan's quarry, in the Black Hills, South Dakota, while the Northwestern and Burlington & Missouri River railways generously transmit it to the park free of charge.

Professor John H. Kellom, so prominently connected with the public school system of Omaha in its earlier history, and in whose honor one of the schools was named, died at Tustin, California, March 17, 1891, and, as a fitting close to this chapter, we give the following beautiful tribute to his character, written by one of his old pupils, Henry D. Estabrook, Esq., for the *World-Herald:*

"When the capitol was removed from Omaha it was replaced by the high school —a profitable exchange. And there the noble structure has remained, and will remain, the sign-manual of Omaha's true greatness. It was important that no mistakes should be made in the beginning of the enterprise. The original impulse must be strong and in the right direction. John H. Kellom consented to act as principal, choosing as his assistant Mr. Ralph E. Gaylord, of this city. Prof. A. F. Nightingale was called as superintendent. Three men never associated in a common cause better adapted to the work in hand and personally more congenial. Mr. Kellom was a man of means and of wide influence. He had held offices of public trust; he had refused a nomination for congress. The emoluments of a teacher's position offered no temptation. He accepted the place through a sense of duty, and in response to the universal popular demand.

"Mr. Kellom was a born teacher. In the first place he was a Christian gentleman, in the non-theological meaning of the phrase, a happy optimist, all-charitable, all-loving Christian, whose rules of governing were in the beatitudes, whose approving smile was itself a benediction. In the next place he was a profound scholar. The older I grow and the more I try to learn, the more I appreciate his wisdom and erudition.

"Up to that time our public schools had been governed on the theory that to spare the rod was to spoil the child. I know this to be a fact, for I had matriculated in nearly every school in Omaha, and had been kept from spoiling by being most effectually tanned. Mr. Kellom inspired his scholars to govern themselves through the approval of their own conscience. This was a new invention. It was a wonderful discovery. At the risk of appearing indelicate, I will illustrate my meaning by a personal reminiscence. I had committed some trespass which I knew merited a castigation, the which I fully expected to have administered. When Prof. Kellom requested me to step with him into an adjoining room, I received the pantomime commiseration of my mates and hurled back a wink intended as defiance. But the bastinado was never mentioned. In the space of ten minutes, I learned more about American institutions and a democratic form of government than I had ever known before. What my teacher endeavored to impress upon me was the fact that I was a part of these institutions and of this government, and responsible primarily to myself for my own conduct; that the public school was, perhaps, the most important feature of all our institutions, conferring benefits gratuitously, which were inestimable to every person willing to do his part in the world; that fun was fun, and he delighted in it as much as anyone; but lawlessness was treason, and hurt no one half so much as the one guilty of it; that he felt sure that all I needed was to be reminded of these things, and my own conscience would tell me what was right and manly and—that was all.

"Many persons well-known in Omaha were charter members of the high school. Without the roster before me, I am able to recall the following: Arthur C. Wakeley and his brother Bird, Frederick Millard, William McCague, George Jewett, Charles Sweesey, Charles J. Emery, Frederick Knight, Nathan Crary, George Shields, William R. Redick, Charles R. Redick, Martin Cahn, Albert Cahn, William Nash and his brother Samuel, Henry Sharpe, Arthur Huntington, John Creighton, Cassius Gise, Charles Saunders, George Lake, William Wilber, Ferdinand Streitz, Kate Copeland, Claire Rustin, Ida Doolittle, Stacia Crowley, Salina Jones, Addie Gladstone, Esther Jacobs, Bertha Isaacs, Julia Knight, Clara Campbell, Nelia Lehmer, Carrie Wyman, Elta Hurford, Jessie Rodis, Miss Schaller and Bessie Cleveland.

"None of the men mentioned has disgraced himself that I know of, and many of them have won places of influence and distinction. Many of the women mentioned may not recognize their maiden appellations —it is so long since they have heard them; but in the heart of every one of us the name of John H. Kellom will remain always a hallowed and grateful memory.

"Mr. Kellom was a man who loved to see things grow, and to assist in the process. When his age and infirmities admonished him that to teach the young idea how to shoot had become too arduous and confining, he took to growing oranges in the mellifluous climate of California. Only a year ago my wife visited him and Mrs. Kellom at their home in Tustin. It was her first visit to the golden State; and, as the train came down out of the mountains, where snow and clouds seemed piled upon each other—it was all so high and cold and white—into the gorgeous valley of the Sacramento, with its riotous roses and carnival of vegetation, the change was like the thrilling transition of a dream. One day was devoted to a pilgrimage to Tustin. It was a joyous, tearful meeting between the old professor and his former pupil. Towards evening Mr. Kellom insisted upon showing her the beauties of his orange groves. Leaning upon his arm, together they wandered through long vistas of trees laden with their yellow fruit, each tree trained in the way it should go (of course!), perfect in its symmetry, like a huge bouquet, erect, luxuriant, with an individuality of its own. The groves were filled with Mexicans, picking and packing oranges, and their swart faces and fantastic costumes added piquancy to the scene. As they looked the sun went down in a perfect explosion of colors, the clouds fairly dripping their crimson light, the very air incarnadined. She left him and his wife standing in this mellow glow, their venerable heads crowned with a radiance not of earth, their faces bathed with the golden mist—left them among their books and flowers, in an Arcadia of their own. And now God hath taken him out of Eden to usher him into Paradise. Well, it was an ideal life, without fret or friction, and yet too useful to be selfish. Our old professor teaches us something even in his death."

When the board of education was considering the plans for a school building to be erected on the Paul Street school site, they gracefully honored the memory of Prof. Kellom, by giving to the new building his name. Mr. F. R. McConnell, who was at that time a member of the board, and who had been a pupil of the public schools under Mr. Kellom, made the motion to name it the Kellom School, and the motion was unanimously adopted. As an acknowledgment of the honor Mrs. Kellom presented the school with a beautiful American flag, which was raised upon the school building for the first time on the day of the formal opening of the school.

# CHAPTER XXXV.

CHURCH ORGANIZATIONS — YOUNG MEN'S CHRISTIAN ASSOCIATION — PERSONAL SKETCHES OF BISHOPS AND PIONEER CLERGYMEN.

Omaha has ninety-two church organizations—eighteen Methodist, fifteen Presbyterian, twelve Congregational, nine Baptist, nine Catholic, eight Episcopal, eight Evangelical Lutheran, three United Presbyterian, three Jewish, three Evangelical, two Christian, one Unitarian, one Universalist and one Latter Day Saints. The first sermon preached in this city was by Rev. Peter Cooper, a Methodist minister of Council Bluffs, in August, 1854. The St. Nicholas Hotel, then occupied by Mr. and Mrs. William P. Snowden, being utilized for church purposes on that occasion. Services were held the following year in the capitol building on Ninth Street, by Rev. Isaac F. Collins, also a Methodist preacher, and in September, 1855, he organized a church society. In 1857 there were seven churches in Omaha, viz: Trinity (Episcopal), Rev. George W. Woten, rector; St. John (Catholic); Congregational, Rev. Reuben Gaylord; Methodist, Rev. J. M. Chivington; Baptist, Rev. J. W. Leach; Presbyterian (old school), Rev. W. W. Bergen; Universalist, Rev. Mr. Merritt.

The First Methodist Church was organized in September, 1855, by Rev. Isaac F. Collins, and the following year a small brick building was erected, at a cost of $4,500, on the present site of the Omaha National Bank. This building was occupied about five years, and then gave place to a two-story business house built by the church society, and a brick chapel building erected in 1868, on Seventeenth Street between Dodge and Capitol Avenue, it being the design of the society to construct a large and expensive church edifice in connection therewith, at the southeast corner of Seventeenth and Capitol Avenue. Financial difficulties ensued, however, and the plan was not carried out, the church society practically losing this property and also the property on Thirteenth Street. A frame edifice was erected in 1876, on Davenport just west of Seventeenth Street, which was occupied until June 8, 1890, when the basement of the new building at Davenport and Twentieth was occupied for the first time. The new edifice is of stone and brick, solid and massive, and imposing in appearance. The brick used in the walls are dark red, twelve inches long, and of less thickness than ordinary brick. The tower is 125 feet high, adding greatly to the appearance of the building. The interior is finished after the latest designs in church architecture. The auditorium seats twelve hundred people. The church is lighted by electricity, with combined lights in the basement. The cost of the building was about $100,000, and it was dedicated May 24, 1890. The original church records have disappeared, the earliest date now accessible being that of May 15, 1862, when the following named were the board of trustees: George W. Homan, P. A. Demarest, John Ritchie, Edwin Loveland, George C. Ritchie, J. W. Tousley, N. P. Isaacs, George W. Forbes and Samuel Burns, the last two named still being residents of this city. Following is a list of the pastors in their order: Isaac Collins, J. M. Chivington, J. W. Taylor, W. M. Smith, H. T. Davis, David Hart, T. B. Lemon, W. M. Smith (second term), W. B. Slaughter, H. C. Westwood, G. W. DeLamatyr, G. W. Gue, Clark Wright, L. F. Britt, H. D. Fisher, J.

B. Maxfield, J. W. Stewart, Charles W. Savidge, R. N. McKaig, T. M. House and P. S. Merrill. Rev. Frank Crane, of Bloomington, Ill., succeeded Rev. Mr. Merrill, September, 1892. During the war Mr. Chivington served on the plains as colonel of a Colorado regiment and attacked an Indian village with his command, on one occasion, under circumstances which excited much unfavorable newspaper comment. Mr. DeLamatyr was elected to Congress from Indiana, a few years ago, on the Greenback ticket.

The South Tenth Street Methodist Church was organized by Rev. J. M. Adair, who, in the summer of 1872, held meetings in the grove at Tenth and Pierce Streets. The lumber used for seats was paid for by a Sunday collection and Mr. Paul Harmon made the seats gratuitously. In November of that year a little church building on the east side of Tenth Street, between Pierce and Pacific, then owned by Rev. Thomas McCague, was purchased and used for several years. Rev. T. H. Tibbles succeeded Rev. Adair in the pastorate, in 1874, and during his two years' service a parsonage was erected on the same lot with the church. Rev. J. P. Roe was appointed pastor in 1876, serving two years, one year without pay. In 1878, Rev. P. C. Johnson was assigned to this church and was succeeded the following year by Rev. D. Marquette, who secured a lot at the corner of Tenth and Pierce Streets on which a new

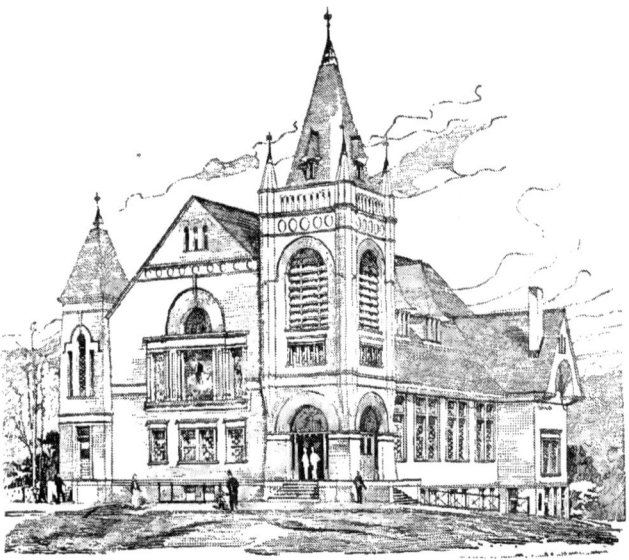

HANSCOM PARK M. E. CHURCH.

building was erected and dedicated on the 10th of July, 1881. Rev. J. W. Stewart succeeded Rev. Marquette in 1882, and remained two years, to be followed in 1884 by Rev. Edward G. Fowler. In 1886, Rev. T. C. Clendenning took charge of the church and was succeeded in April, 1888, by Rev. C. N. Dawson. Rev. A. Hodgetts is the present pastor. The church property is valued at $15,000.

Seward Street Methodist Episcopal Church was formerly known as the Eighteenth Street Methodist Episcopal Church, the change of location being made in 1884. At that time the membership was only thirty, Rev. R. L. Marsh was pastor. Rev. Charles W. Savidge assumed the pastorate September 9, 1885, and remained three years, during which period the membership reached nearly one hundred, and an addition to the building was found necessary. Rev. W. M. Worley succeeded Mr. Savidge in 1888, and remained one year, to be followed by Rev. H. A. Crane, who went as a missionary to dedicated, March 6, 1887. This was occupied till the fall of 1892, when a new building costing $20,000 was erected on the same site. The property is now worth $30,000. Rev. H. H. Millard was the first pastor, and was succeeded in September, 1887, by Rev. G. M. Brown, who served till September, 1892, when he was succeeded by Rev. William P. Murray.

Trinity Methodist Episcopal Church, located at Twenty-first and Binney Streets,

TRINITY M. E. CHURCH.

Bombay, September, 1892, and was succeeded by Rev. D. K. Tindall.

The Hanscom Park Methodist Episcopal Church owes its existence largely to Mr. John Dale, who succeeded in raising the funds necessary for the work in 1886. The society was organized in October of that year, with twenty-two members, seven of whom were members of Mr. Dale's family. A lot was purchased at the corner of Georgia and Woolworth Avenues, and a church and parsonage erected, the former being was organized in 1887 with sixteen members, and a building costing $16,000 was dedicated in October, 1888. Rev. Alfred H. Henry was appointed pastor in October, 1887; Rev. J.W. Robinson succeeding him in September, 1888. In September of the following year the present incumbent, Rev. W. K. Beans was appointed pastor and is now serving his fourth term with this church. The present membership is two hundred.

The Newman Methodist Church purchased, in 1889, the building vacated by the

## CHURCH ORGANIZATIONS.

St. Mary's Avenue Congregational Church in November, 1888, the first pastor being Rev. J. E. Ensign, who remained a year and was succeeded by Rev. Charles W. Savidge, at which date the membership of the society was one hundred and forty. This church was never regularly organized and in the fall of 1891 the property was turned over to those from whom it had been purchased and the society disbanded.

The following named have served as pastors: Rev. John P. Nulter, 1858; Rev. Henry Meyer, 1859; Rev. August Macke, 1861; Rev. Henry Muhlenbrock, 1862; Rev. Henry C. Dryer, 1864; Rev. Henry Brinkmeyer, 1865; Rev. William Gemeck, 1866; Rev. P. J. May, 1867; Rev. J. J. Faust, 1870; Rev. J. L. W. Pauli, 1872; Rev. Daniel Welter, 1874; Rev. C. Brugger, 1877; Rev. H. Bruns, 1881; Rev. H. Krueger,

CONGREGATIONAL CHURCH.—FIRST PROTESTANT CHURCH BUILT IN OMAHA.
Located at Sixteenth and Farnam Streets.

The German Methodist Episcopal Church erected its first house of worship on Davenport, near Fourteenth Street, in 1860, but incurred so heavy an indebtedness that it was found necessary to dispose of the property, and a lot on the corner of Jackson and Tenth Streets was secured and a small building erected thereon. In 1886 this property was also sold and a more commodious edifice built at Eleventh and Center Streets.

1884; Rev. C. G. Becker, 1887; Rev. J. H. Hilmes, 1889.

An organization of the Swedish Methodist Episcopal Church was perfected December 3, 1882, with twelve members, and the church building on Eighteenth Street, between Cass and California, formerly occupied by a society known as the Eighteenth Street Methodist Church, was purchased for three thousand dollars. The present membership is one hundred. The first pastor was Rev. H. L. Lindquest, the second, Rev. J. O. Alven, the third, Rev. Olin Swanson and the fourth, the present pastor, Rev. P. J. Berg.

Rev. Reuben Gaylord secured the building, in 1856, of the First Congregational Church edifice, a small brick building facing east, on Sixteenth, opposite the present site of the Paxton Block. The society was organized May 4th, of that year, with nine members. He remained pastor of that church until 1865, when he was succeeded by Rev. William Rose, who remained two years. Rev. E. S. Palmer then became the pastor, and was succeeded by Rev. A. F. Sherrill, D. D., in 1869. Rev. Joseph T. Duryea, of Boston, became Dr. Sherrill's successor, in 1889. In the meantime the first building was sold and another erected, at the corner of Nineteenth and Chicago, in 1870, which was occupied for sixteen years. In 1888 the spacious building on Davenport, now occupied by the society, was completed, at a cost of about sixty thousand dollars.

The Second Congregational Church Society, known as "St. Mary's Avenue," was incorporated March 7, 1882, its membership being composed chiefly, at the outset, of former members of Dr. Sherrill's church. A lot on St. Mary's Avenue, just east of Twenty-seventh Street, was purchased for $1,200, and thereon was erected a small frame building, at a cost of $3,175, which was dedicated October 29, 1882. Rev. Willard Scott, of New York, preached his first sermon in the building December 10th, following, and was at once engaged as pastor. It was not until May 8, 1883, however, that he was installed, the church being formally

FIRST CONGREGATIONAL CHURCH.

organized on that date, with a membership of sixty-five. An addition to the building was soon found necessary, but the continued increase of membership demanded still more room, and two lots directly opposite, with a frontage of 128 feet on the avenue, were bought for fourteen thousand dollars, in 1887, on which was built the house now occupied by the society, costing, furnished, and including organ, thirty-three thousand dollars. It is 65x96 feet, with pews for seven hundred in the auditorium, with chapel rooms on the first floor with seating capacity for 550. The first floor was first occupied on Thanksgiving day, 1888, and the main floor, March 10, 1889. Up to the present time about five hundred members have been received. With a present membership of nearly four hundred, it is the largest of that denomination in Nebraska. Mr. Scott resigned the pastorate here in November, 1891, and now fills the pulpit of the South Congregational Church, Chicago. Rev. S. Wright Butler, of Port Chester, New York, accepted a call from this church and entered upon his duties as pastor here, May 1, 1892.

Plymouth Congregational Church began its work as a Sunday School, January 6, 1884, conducted by members of the First Congregational Church, with some assistance from the Young Men's Christian Association, the church society being formed March 1, 1885, with sixteen members. The first pastor was Rev. George S. Pelton, who resigned November 30, 1886, and was succeeded by Rev. Alford B. Penniman, November 21, 1888; he resigned and the present pastor, Rev. Dr. A. R. Thain, assumed charge, February 2, 1889. The first church building was erected in 1884, at the corner of Spruce and Nineteenth Streets, at a cost of about three thousand dollars. The property was sold to the board of education in 1887, for seven thousand dollars. Two lots in Kountze Place were then donated the society by Mr. Herman Kountze, and on those a building was erected, at a cost of eighteen thousand dollars, with a parsonage adjoining, costing $3,556. The present membership is 135.

Rev. George S. Pelton, pastor of the Third Congregational Church, organized the Saratoga Congregational Church, January 24, 1886, and for nearly a year thereafter services were held in the Saratoga school house, Rev. John A. Milligan being chosen pastor in March 1887. In the fall of that year a lot at the corner of Ames Avenue and Twenty-fifth Street was bought, at a cost of $1,100, and a chapel erected thereon, costing five hundred dollars. In June 1888, Rev. F. S. Forbes became pastor of the church, to be succeeded in 1889 by Rev. H. N. Smith, pastor. Rev. George A. Conrad, the present pastor, has been in charge since the early part of 1891.

The Hillside Congregational Church was organized November 30, 1886, with a membership of twenty-two and Rev. H. C. Crane as pastor. Since that date two hundred additional members have been received. The Sabbath School, held in a grove in 1886, has an enrollment of four hundred. The Christian Endeavor Society of the church has a membership of one hundred, and there is also a society for the encouragement of culture connected with the church, forty-five members of which are pledged to graduate at some educational institution. In 1887 an addition to the church was built and also a parsonage, and the property, corner of Thirtieth and Ohio Streets, is valued at $10,000. Rev. Dr. Sherrill and his church and Rev. J. L. Maile, superintendent of Home Missions, were active in the establishment of the Hillside Church. Rev. H. H. Morse was pastor for a few months in 1890, and was succeeded in June, 1892, by Rev. G. J. Powell.

Park Place, or Eighth Congregational Church, of Omaha, has its place of worship at No. 3029 California Street, and the parsonage joins it on the east, the two buildings, which were erected in 1887, costing about four thousand dollars. The society was organized December 27, 1887, with only ten members. The present membership is ninety-five. The Sunday School of this church has been made an important feature and has nearly 250 pupils enrolled. Rev. M. L. Holt was the pastor from its organization until August, 1890, when he resigned to to take charge of the prohibition work in zation consisted of Samuel Moffat, senior warden; Charles W. Hamilton, junior warden; Thomas B. Cuming, A. J. Hanscom, Jonas Seeley and A. F. Salisbury, vestrymen. Until July, 1860, Rev. G. W. Watson, of Council Bluffs. officiated as rector. A lot at the southwest corner of Farnam and Ninth Streets was leased for a term of years,

TRINITY CATHEDRAL.

Omaha. Rev. William S. Parke has been pastor of this church since the autumn of 1891.

Trinity Cathedral, Episcopal, as Trinity Church, was organized July 13, 1856, by Bishop Kemper, of Wisconsin, who, during that summer, visited Omaha in company with Bishop Lee, of Iowa, and Rev. W. N. Irish, of Missouri. The first parish organi- and a small brick church built thereon. This building became the property of the lot owner in 1869, and has been used since that date, in conjunction with the grounds surrounding, for a natatorium. In 1867, the church society erected a large frame building, at a cost of fifteen thousand dollars, on the corner of Eighteenth and Capitol Avenue. November 10, 1869, this building was

burned down, and a temporary structure erected on the site. A handsome stone cathedral now occupies this ground, costing about one hundred thousand dollars. The following named have been the rectors of this church: Rev. George W. Watson, Rev. John West, Rev. O. C. Dake, Rev. William H. Van Antwerp, Rev. George C. Betts, Rev. John G. Gossman, Rev. A. C. Garrett, Rev. John D. Easter, Rev. Frank R. Millspaugh, Rev. Charles H. Gardner. Mr. Henry W. Yates has been a vestryman of this church continuously for twenty-five years.

St. Barnabas Episcopal Church was organized in June, 1869. It has now a handsome church edifice and commodious rectory at the corner of 19th and California Streets, the total value of ground and building amounting to about twenty thousand dollars. The original membership of twenty has grown to two hundred and fifteen. The first rector was Rev. George C. Betts, who was succeeded in 1873 by Rev. Hammond, who remained two years, and for the two years following the pulpit was vacant. Rev. John Williams became rector in June 1877, and still retains that position.

St. John's Episcopal Church was organized in June, 1885, by Rev. William Osgood Pearson, with twelve members. The following year a church building was erected at the corner of Franklin and Twenty-sixth Streets, at an expense of six thousand dollars, including furniture. There are ninety-one communicants. Rev. Mr. Pearson resigned in 1890, and was succeeded by Rev. J. O. Feris, the present rector.

All Saints Church (Episcopal), corner of Howard and Twenty-sixth, was organized in November, 1886, by members of Trinity. The society, now numbering 190, owns a handsome property, with church building and rector's residence, costing about eighteen thousand dollars. The former residence of James M. Woolworth, a substantial building which stood for many years on Howard Street, near Twelfth, was moved to the lot adjoining on the south the one occupied by the church building, and practically rebuilt for a parsonage. Rev. Louis Zahner, the first rector, resigned in the spring of 1891, and later was succeeded by Rev. T. J. Mackay, the present pastor.

Rev. Henry W. Kuhns, D. D., still a resident of Omaha, came here in 1858 as a missionary in the service of the Alleghany (Lutheran) Synod of Pennsylvania. Finding some Lutherans in the town, he organized nine of them into a congregation, and held services first in the Methodist Church, on Thirteenth Street, and afterwards in the Congregational Church, on Sixteenth. In 1860, two lots on Douglas Street, now a part of the site of the Millard Hotel, were bought for church and parsonage purposes, upon which a brick church was erected that year and a parsonage the next year. In the belfry of this church was placed the first church bell brought to Omaha. Dr. Kuhns remained pastor of this congregation for fourteen years, and was succeeded by Rev. Billman, who remained but a year. Rev. W. A. Lipe was the next pastor, and remained until 1879. Rev. H. L. Baugher, D. D., succeeded Mr. Lipe, but returned to the East in 1880. At this time the Douglas Street property was sold, and two lots at the northeast corner of Harney and Sixteenth Streets were bought for $3,500—now worth $100,000—and a proposition made by Augustus Kountze, of New York, to duplicate any amount the congregation might raise towards the erection of a building was promptly accepted. The result was the erection of a handsome brick building at a cost of fifty thousand dollars, named the Kountze Memorial Church, in honor of the deceased father of Mr. Kountze. Upon the completion of this building Rev. George F. Stelling, D. D., became the pastor. He died in January, 1884, and was succeeded by Rev. J. S. Detweiler, D. D., who resigned the pastorate recently, Rev. A. J. Turkle being his successor.

330    HISTORY OF THE CITY OF OMAHA.

St. Mark's Evangelical Lutheran Church, located at the corner of Twenty-first and Burdette Streets, was organized December 12, 1886, with twenty-four members, the church building being dedicated June 12, 1887, with Rev. George H. Schnur as pastor. August 1, 1889, he resigned, and January 1, 1890, Rev. J. G. Griffith, took charge, and in the summer of 1892 he was succeeded by Rev. J. S. Detweiler, D. D. The present membership is ninety, with over one hundred members of the Sunday School.

KOUNTZE MEMORIAL ENGLISH LUTHERAN CHURCH.

The Shull Memorial Lutheran Church, also known for a time as the Southwestern Lutheran Church, was organized April 7, 1889, and incorporated on the 17th of that

## CHURCH ORGANIZATIONS.

month. On October 12, 1892, this church re-incorporated, and the name was changed to Grace Lutheran Church. The two handsome and valuable lots on which the present chapel stands were donated by the Shull heirs for church purposes in 1887, and are valued, with the building, at $11,000. The congregation was organized by Rev. Luther M. Kuhns, born in Omaha, a son of Dr. Henry W. Kuhns, the first pastor of the Douglas Street Lutheran Church. Rev. Luther M. Kuhns enjoys the distinction of being the first Lutheran minister born in Nebraska. The present church council consists of: Rev. Luther M. Kuhns, chairman; August Engel, secretary; W. H. Koenig, treasurer; L. H. Korty and L. P. Norberg, elders; and J. A. Swobe and R. W. Dyball, Jr., deacons.

In 1855 Rev. William Leach located in Omaha as a missionary for the Baptist Church denomination, and held services, more or less regularly, in the old capitol building, but it was not until 1859 that a minister of this denomination was regularly established here In that year Rev. Barnes organized the First Baptist Church, and a small building was erected on Douglas Street between Fifteenth and Sixteenth. Three years later the society disbanded and sold its property, but in 1866 a re-organization was effected and Rev. W. J. Kermott engaged as pastor, and services held in the court house for several months. The brick church, one of the best buildings for this purpose in the city, was erected in 1870, but for several years only the lower portion of the building was used. The following named have served as pastors since the resignation of Rev. W. J. Kermott: Rev. J. W. Daniels, Rev. E. C. M. Burnham, acting pastor, Rev. J. W. Donnelly, Rev. O. T. Conger, Rev. E. H. E. Jameson, Rev. J. W. Harris, Rev. A. W. Lamar, since December, 1891, pastor of the First Baptist Church, of Galveston, Texas. August 1, 1892, Rev. W. P. Hellings, D. D., became pastor of the church.

The Calvary Baptist Church organization dates from November 25, 1886, when forty-nine persons, most of whom were from the First Church, banded together to build up a church society in the northwest part of the city. At the beginning, a mission chapel on Saunders Street, near Cuming, was used for holding services. Then a lot at the southwest corner of Seward and Twenty-sixth Streets was bought, at a cost of $5,700, the chapel being sold two years later to the Welsh Presbyterians, for six hundred dollars. A building on the Seward Street lot was completed in December, 1888. During the next year Central Park Mission was organized, taking away many active members of the Calvary Church. Rev. A. W. Clark was the pastor from the time the church was organized in 1886, till 1891. Rev. S. K. Wilcox was pastor during a part of 1891, and until June, 1892.

The Beth-Eden Baptist Church, located on Park Avenue, near Leavenworth, was organized in November 1886, and in March 1888, the church building, costing twelve thousand dollars, was dedicated. Rev. H. L. House was pastor from the organization till April, 1891, and was succeeded (July, 1891) by Rev. E. N. Harris, of Milwaukee, who assumed the pastorate in October of that year. The present membership is 160.

The Immanuel Baptist Church had its origin in the North Omaha Baptist Mission Sunday School, established in October, 1887, at No. 2409 Saunders Street, in an old storeroom. The Sunday School grew rapidly in membership, but the organization of the Trinity M. E. Church, the Knox Presbyterian and St. John's Episcopal Church, in the immediate vicinity, reduced this membership considerably, and the Baptist people concluded that they had built up a mission school for other denominations as well as their own. The church was organized April 30, 1888, with forty-four members, and a building was erected at Twenty-fourth and Binney Streets the following year, being dedicated December 15, 1889. The present membership is 125. Rev. Frank W. Foster, the present pastor, has served the church from the beginning. The church property is valued at $6,500.

The Olivet Baptist Church was organized in October 1889, and in the summer of 1890 a church edifice costing two thousand dollars was erected. Rev. Thomas Stephenson, now pastor of a Baptist Church in South Omaha, was pastor till September, 1891, and was followed by Rev. Geo. P. Peck.

December 1, 1884, the First Danish Baptist Church, of Omaha, was organized by Rev. H. A. Reichenbach, of Council Bluffs, Iowa, who afterwards preached for the new society, consisting of thirteen people, on Sunday afternoons, in a private house, until February 28, 1888, when he moved to Chicago to take editorial charge of a church paper. A small building was put up for church purposes, costing $523, on a lot at No. 2511 Decatur Street, leased at an annual rental of sixty dollars. May 2, 1890, a lot at the northeast corner of Twenty-seventh and Seward Streets, was bought for $3,500, on which it is the purpose of the society to build a comfortable church in the near future. Rev. N. Madsen was the second pastor of the church, remaining until July 25, 1889, and was succeeded by Rev. J. A. Jensen.

The German Baptist Church, corner of Seward and Twenty-sixth Streets, was organized May 30, 1886. It has now a membership of ninety-three. The church building was dedicated in October, 1888, and the building and lot are valued at six thousand dollars. The first pastor was Rev. A. Genius, the second Rev. H. G. Carstons, and the third Rev. H. Schroeder.

The First Presbyterian Church was organized by Rev. George P. Bergen, in June, 1857, with a very small membership. In 1859 he was succeeded by Rev. George Webster, who left the following year, after which the society had no services. In 1860, Rev. F. M. Dimmick established the Second Presbyterian Church, and in 1868 the congregation took possession of their new building, still standing, but much enlarged and improved, at the northwest corner of Seventeenth and Dodge Streets. Rev. George D. Stewart succeeded Mr. Dimmick in 1870, and, in 1877, was himself succeeded by Rev. W. J. Harsha, who was remarkably successful in his work. Mr. Harsha resigned to accept a call to the Second Collegiate Reformed Church, New York, in the spring of 1892. The church has now a membership of over five hundred, and, in the meantime, under Mr. Harsha's pastorate, has aided in establishing half a dozen other societies of the same denomination, and furnishing a large portion of the membership. Some four years since, in view of the fact that it was the oldest existing Presbyterian society in the city, the number was changed to the first.

The Second Presbyterian Church — first called the North Presbyterian Church—was organized on the 27th of February, 1881, in the Saunders Street Mission Chapel, near the northwest corner of Cuming and Saunders Streets, by a commission of the Presbytery of Omaha. It was organized with forty-four members, seventeen of whom united on profession. The mission chapel was used as a place of worship until October, 1882, when the church took possession of the present edifice. The first pastor was Rev. F. S. Blayney, who served the church faithfully for five years, his pastorate closing in December, 1885. During his ministry, the present edifice, costing five thousand dollars, was erected and dedicated, clear of debt. Rev. William R. Henderson took charge of the church in February, 1886, and remained its pastor until May, 1890, resigning to give his entire time to the *Central West*, a strong Presbyterian paper of which he was editor until the latter part of 1891. During his ministry the church grew from a membership of seventy-four to two hundred and forty, the present membership, with about 160 more which were received and dismissed to other churches. The present pastor, Rev. S. M. Ware, was given a call June 11, 1890, and took charge July 13th. The church building is located near the corner of Twenty-fourth and Nicholas Streets.

The Southwest Presbyterian Church, corner of Leavenworth and Twentieth, was organized October 4, 1882. A mission Sabbath School had been established in July, 1881, utilizing a small frame building about sixteen feet square, which occupied the site of the present church, and was owned by Ezra Millard, who had a short time previously platted ten acres of land lying south of Leavenworth and west of Twentieth Street. No rent was charged for the building, which was subsequently moved a block further south and considerably enlarged. Rev. William McCandlish, now deceased, was particularly efficient in the conversion of this mission school into a church organization, as he was in everything tending to advance the cause of religion wherever and whenever he found opportunity in the course of a busy and useful life of seventy-four years. Among those who joined the church at the date of organization were: Mr. and Mrs. James France, Mr. and Mrs. Joseph L. Welshans, Mr. and Mrs. J. R. Hardenbergh, Mr. and Mrs. Howland Dailey, Mr. and Mrs. J. S. Ramsyer, Mr. and Mrs. David R. Loring, and E. J. Brenton. Rev. Frank H. Hays was the first pastor, remaining about a year, and, on the 19th day of August, 1883, was succeeded by Rev. Thomas C. Hall, a son of Rev. Dr. John Hall, of New York, the ordination sermon being preached by Dr. Hall. The charge to the people was delivered by Rev. William McCandlish, and the charge to the pastor, by Rev. W. J. Harsha. The present church building was erected in 1884. In July, 1886, Rev. Hall resigned and removed to Chicago, and Rev. David R. Kerr became pastor of the church April 1st of the following year, resigning in the fall of 1889.

He is now president of the Bellevue, Nebraska, college. Rev. R. V. Atkisson was then pastor for one year. The present pastor is Rev. Dr. Shields, from St. Louis.

The Castellar Street Presbyterian Mission was organized in September, 1883, and a lot on Sixteenth and Castellar purchased for $1,100. In December of that year the church building was completed and occupied, Rev. Thomas Hall preaching on Sunday afternoons until December, 1885. June 16, 1886, the church society was organized with nineteen members, and soon after Rev. J. M. Wilson became the pastor, which position he still holds.

The Westminster Presbyterian Church, southwest corner of Mason and Twenty-ninth Streets, was organized in 1887, with forty-seven members. Work on the church edifice was commenced that year and completed in 1888. The ground and building are valued at $25,000. Present membership two hundred. The first and only pastor, to this date, is Rev. John Gordon, D. D. This is one of the very few churches west of the Missouri River which has been self-sustaining from the outset.

October 13, 1887, the Knox Presbyterian Church was organized with thirteen members. At first meetings were held in a vacant store-room on Lake Street between Nineteenth and Twentieth, but in a short time a little mission building was purchased, and this gave way, in about a year, to a commodious building on the corner of Nineteenth and Ohio, which will seat about four hundred people. The present membership is 150. Rev. Paul Martin served as pastor from May 10, 1888, to February 28, 1889, and was succeeded by the present incumbent, Rev. Asa Leard, who was installed July 14, 1889. The society has property valued at nine thousand dollars, and is practically out of debt.

The Lowe Avenue Presbyterian Church, recently organized, is located at Lowe Avenue and Nicholas Street. Its present pastor is Rev. C. G. Sterling.

The First German Presbyterian Church, located at the corner of Eighteenth and Cuming, was organized December 20, 1880, with twelve members, and two years later a church was built, the sum of $3,300 being paid for a lot and small building used for a parsonage, and $1,700 for the church edifice. The society also owns a lot in South Omaha, on which a church is to be built at some future date. The society now has eighty members. Rev. F. H. W. Bruechert was the first pastor and remained until 1883, when he was succeeded by Rev. John G. Schaible, who is now in charge.

The First United Presbyterian Church dates its organization back to January, 1868, as the result of the missionary labors of Rev. Thomas McCague, known throughout the country for his zeal, earnestness, ability and Christian character, who began his church work in Omaha in July, 1867, in a school building then standing on the southeast corner of Capitol Avenue and Fifteenth. In September, 1872, Rev. James Duncan became the pastor, and so continued for one year, during which period the congregation purchased the Baptist Tabernacle, on Eighteenth Street near California. Mr. McCague took charge of the church again in 1873, and served till 1878, with the exception of the year 1876, during which Rev. Joseph McCarthy was pastor, and was succeeded by Rev. D. R. Miller, who was pastor for two years, to be succeeded by Rev. E. B. Graham who served for eight years and resigned to devote his entire attention to the publication of a denominational paper, the *Midland*, of this city. December 8, 1890, the society dedicated a handsome and convenient church building on Emmet and Twenty-first Streets, costing fourteen thousand dollars, with a seating capacity of seven hundred. Rev. John M. French is the present pastor.

The Park Avenue United Presbyterian Church was organized October 30, 1886, the first pastoral settlement being effected the 1st of April, 1887, Rev. John A. Henderson taking charge of the young congregation, and is still the pastor. At the date of organization there were twenty-six members. The church is located at the corner of Park Avenue and Jackson Streets, on a lot donated by Mr. Joseph Bell, deceased. The cost of the building was about three thousand dollars, and of the parsonage adjoining $2,600. The property is now valued at sixteen thousand dollars. A Sabbath School was organized in 1885, with W. M. Lorimer as superintendent, he retaining the office until April 1, 1890, when he was succeeded by Mr. H. W. Spaulding.

The Central United Presbyterian Church was organized May 23, 1887, with thirty-six members. The chapel building on Seventeenth, between Dodge and Capitol Avenue, which the Swedish society had bought of G. M. Hitchcock, and which had been built by the First Methodist Church people, was purchased for eleven thousand dollars, and services have been held there regularly since. In 1889 the block in which the property is situated was condemned by the general government for a postoffice site, and the church received nineteen thousand dollars for its interest. Rev. John Williamson, of Bellefontaine, Ohio, is the only pastor the church has had. The present membership is about two hundred. A flourishing mission Sunday School has been built up at the corner of Cass and Twenty-sixth Streets. A handsome stone church of modified Gothic architecture, 69x85 feet in size, is now in process of construction, on the northwest corner of Dodge and Twenty-fourth Streets. The cost will be over thirty thousand dollars.

The First Christian Church was organized in 1868, with Rev. J. W. Allen, now of Chicago, as pastor. The first church building still stands, on Harney, between Fourteenth and Fifteenth, and is used as a blacksmith shop. In 1878 the church was re-organized by Elder B. B. Tyler, of New York City, and for a time worshiped in the Methodist Chapel, on Seventeenth Street, near Dodge. The society now owns a good building at the corner of Capitol Avenue and Twentieth Street, which is worth, with the lot, twenty-five thousand dollars. A branch society has been established at Walnut Hill. The following named have served as pastors of the First Church: Rev. J. W. Ingram, Rev. D. R. Lucas, Rev. R. H. Ingram, Rev. J. H. Fay, D. D., Rev. C. B. Newman, Rev. A. Martin and Rev. T. E. Cramblet.

The Walnut Hill Christian Church was recently organized, and has not a large membership, and, thus far, no pastor. Services are held in a building at the corner of Nicholas and Dale Streets.

The First Free Evangelical Church (German) was established August 22, 1886, with eighteen members. The building, Twelfth and Dorcas Streets, was completed in December, 1886, and the following year a parsonage with ten rooms was erected adjoining. The property is valued at $8,000. Rev. F. H. W. Bruechert is the pastor, and the present membership is fifty.

Zion's Church of the Evangelical Association was organized in November, 1888, with twelve members. The church building, corner of Twenty-fifth and Caldwell Streets, was erected at that time and cost $3,500. Rev. W. F. Schwerin was the first pastor, and the present incumbent, Rev. W. H. Althouse, the second. The services are conducted in the German language.

The Swedish Evangelical Mission Church, corner Twenty-third and Davenport Streets, is the outgrowth of a work begun in 1880, by the present pastor, Rev. J. A. Hultman, who came to Omaha in that year as a member of a concert company then giving entertainments through the United States. Becoming interested in the work of starting a Swedish mission here, he gave up his occupation as a singer and organized the mission with twenty-four members. For the first month he worked gratuitously; the next month he received a salary of fifteen dollars, and later, for some time, only twenty dollars a month. When first organized, the services were held in the old Tenth Street mission. Two years later the brick church, on the east side of Seventeeth Street, between Dodge Street and Capitol Avenue, was purchased. Five years later the present church was built, the lot costing $11,000 and the church building $15,000. There is now a debt of $8,000 upon the congregation, the balance of the expense of lot and build-

SWEDISH MISSION.

ing having been paid off—mostly by contributions of laboring men and women who attend the church. The present membership is six hundred. The church is fitted up with an inclined floor and opera chairs, with seating capacity of fifteen hundred, which is usually fully occupied. In connection with the church there is a roomy parsonage. Rev. Mr. Hultman is the only pastor the church ever had.

The First Unitarian Church was organized by Rev. H. F. Bond, and incorporated August 22, 1869. A lot at the southeast corner of Cass and Seventeenth was then purchased and a brick chapel erected at the south end of it, with a view of having the main building joined to it on the north. For various reasons, this improvement was postponed from year to year, but recently the original design has been carried out. Rev. W. E. Copeland succeeded Mr. Bond and was the pastor for many years. In 1888 Mr. Copeland took up his residence on the Pacific coast, and the present incumbent, Rev. Newton M. Mann, took charge of the church in September, 1889.

The People's Church was organized and the attendance of a large number of people secured of a class seldom seen in the churches. The expenses were borne by contributions, chiefly from business men of the city, who recognize the peculiar fitness of Mr. Savidge for this work. A large choir, led by Mr. Frank S. Smith, had charge of the music, adding much to the attractiveness of the service. In June 1890, the ser-

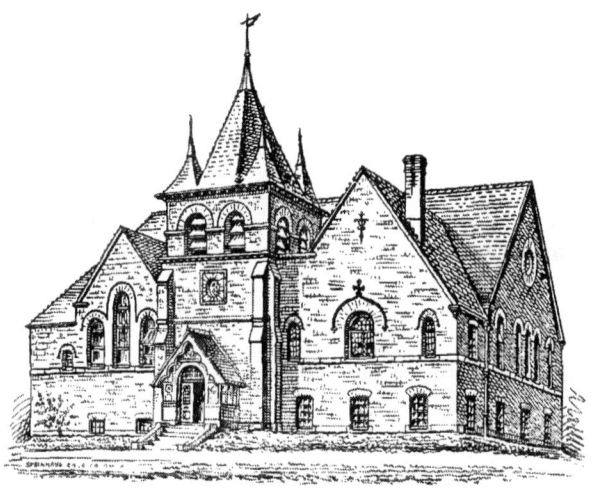

FIRST UNIVERSALIST CHURCH, KOUNTZE PLACE.

The First Universalist Church is of recent origin, and for a time held services in Goodrich Hall, on Saunders Street. Rev. Q. H. Shinn was pastor till October 1891, when he resigned to take up the missionary work in the field extending from the Missouri River westward. His successor is Rev. W. Franklin Smith, of Galesburg, Illinois. A brick church building was recently completed, at the corner of Lathrop and Nineteenth Street:, which cost about fifteen thousand dollars.

For about eight months, commencing early in the fall of 1889, religious services were held by the Rev. Charles W. Savidge, in Boyd's Opera House. A society known as

vices were discontinued. Commencing October 30, 1881, the opera house was used for church purposes for several weeks by the Lutheran Church, Rev. Dr. Stelling, pastor, pending the building of their handsome church edifice, the Kountze Memorial. In June, 1890, Mr. Savidge became pastor of the Newman Methodist Church. October 12, 1891, he purchased the church building on Eighteenth Street, between California and Webster, formerly occupied by the United Presbyterians, having no money to devote to that purpose—not a member, nor a person pledged to attend. It was filled with hearers almost at once, and

## CHURCH ORGANIZATIONS.

in twenty-one weeks $2,100, the amount required for purchase and repair, was paid up. The People's Church, as the name implies, is for the people not usually church goers, and is not denominational. A flourishing sewing school is conducted by Mrs. Savidge; poor children attend, and are given the garments they make. A rescue home for boys, under the management of James A. Kellar, who is himself one of the boys, rescued in New York City, has been established, and homeless and tramping boys are cared for, fed and supplied with places to work, mostly on farms in the country. Two persons are also employed in visiting from house to house to relieve, so far as can be done, the sick and poor.

The Salvation Army has been established in this city for five years. The number of persons now connected with it as workers is sixty-five, with headquarters at the old First Methodist Church, on Davenport Street, between Seventeenth and Eighteenth Streets, and a branch on North Twenty-fourth Street. The army has accomplished a good work among those who were beyond the reach of the established churches. Three services are held daily, and the average daily attendance is three hundred. The army is supported by donations and by contributions from persons many of whom are in good circumstances and give considerable amounts. If the collections exceed the expenses the officers of the army in charge of the work are allowed out of the collections an amount, not to exceed seven dollars each, per week, for their entire support. If the expenses equal or exceed the amount collected weekly, the officers receive nothing. A number of persons connected with the army work without pay.

The Seventh Day Adventists have but one church society in Omaha, organized in February, 1890, with Elder H. A. Hennig as pastor. It has a membership of thirty, and services are held in a church on Eighteenth near Cuming Street, the society having no church building of its own.

N. I. Benson, Esq., now a member of the Douglas County bar, formerly a rabbi of the Jewish Church, furnishes the following information with respect to the religious organizations of the people of his faith: The history of the Hebrews, as a religious body in this city, must be traced back to 1868, when services were held in the old Masonic Hall on Fourteenth Street, where for four years services were held on Jewish holidays, speakers being chosen from those in attendance. In 1872 another step was taken by the few leading Hebrews then here, to make the organization more permanent. It was the purchase of five acres on Pleasant Hill, to be consecrated as the Hebrew cemetery. Meanwhile the only religious services held were during the holidays at the Max Meyer building on Farnam and Eleventh Streets. Mr. L. Abraham, now dead, was the efficient reader of the congregation during these years. In 1874, the congregation, now fully organized, though not yet incorporated, purchased a piece of property on Cass, between Sixteenth and Seventeenth, for twelve hundred dollars. This property was sold several years later, and the present site of the temple on Harney Street was bought for $4,400. In 1875, Rev. David Stern was called to take charge of the pulpit, the congregation having about twenty members, and remained about eight months. In 1883 Rev. Mr. Saft was called to take charge of this pulpit and teach the Sabbath school. His charge of the pulpit ended at the expiration of his first term of office. During the years which intervened between 1875 and 1883, the congregation not having the expense of paying a spiritual guide, a sinking fund of several thousand dollars was accumulated for the purpose of erecting a synagogue, and the synagogue on Harney Street was the result. It was erected at an expense of between four thousand and five thousand dollars, and was dedicated in the fall of 1886 by the Rev. E. H. Harfeld. At the expiration of his term, Rev. N. I. Benson, of Owensboro, Kentucky, was chosen rabbi and he took charge in the fall of 1885, and remained four years, leaving the church with a membership of about 120. He was succeeded by Rev. William Rosenau, a graduate of the Hebrew Union College of Cincinnati. In addition to the Congregation of Israel there is another Jewish body in this city named Chebra Bikur Cholim, organized about four years ago and originally intended as a society for relieving the sick and burying the dead. But the scope of its usefulness did not end there, as ever since its organization religious services have been held every year during the holidays at the Unitarian Church. Recently, this society rented the Garneau Church and furnished it. It is intended to have regular Sabbath service and a Sabbath school for poor Jewish youth was opened for the admission of pupils February 23, 1890. The Bnai Israel, or Sons of Israel Church was started ten years ago, the first place of worship being at a house rented for that purpose on Thirteenth Street, between Dodge and Capitol Avenue. Mr. Cohen was the first rabbi and he remained until the latter part of 1882. Rabbi Leeveen succeeded him, but remained only a few months. In 1883 Rabbi Bramsan took charge of the congregation, and still ministers to its spiritual wants. In September, 1890, the members of the congregation purchased a building on South Thirteenth Street, near Williams, as a place for holding services. The Russian Bnai Israel Congregation was organized eight years ago. The society has passed through various vicissitudes, but has become quite strong within the last two years. In 1889 a temple was built on Capitol Avenue, between Thirteenth and Fourteenth, at a cost of six thousand dollars. Max Berlin is reader for the congregation at present and L. Catlin is president. The Bnai Jacob Congregation was organized in 1889, and M. Goldstein secured as rabbi, but dissensions arose in the church concerning the doctrines advocated by the rabbi, and the result was the dissolution of the congregation. A large number of the members then joined the Russian Bnai Israel. Rev. Mr. Rosenau was called to occupy the pulpit of Dr. Szold, of Baltimore, September 1, 1892, and was succeeded by Rev. L. Franklin, the youngest graduate from the Hebrew Union College, of the class of '92.

There are four church organizations and two missions supported by the colored people of Omaha. St. John's A. M. E. Church was organized about 1870 and a substantial brick building erected at the corner of Webster and Eighteenth Streets, on which $18,000 has been expended. It has a membership of 250. The following named have served as pastors: Rev. John M. Hubbard, Rev. W. B. Ousley, Rev. George W. Gaines, Rev. James W. Braston, Rev. Ben Watson, Rev. W. L. Harard, Rev. Foushee, Rev. Ricketts, Rev. Burrell Mitchell, Rev. P. A. Hubbard, Rev. Wm. A. Moore and Rev. H. B. Parks, late of Topeka, Kan. A Baptist Society was organized in 1889. The present pastor, Rev. T. H. Ewing has had charge for the past four years. The society has recently completed a substantial building at the corner of Grant and Twenty-third Streets, known as Zion Church. The Christian Church, in the southern part of the city was established in 1889, under the auspices of the mission board of that denomination, under the pastorate of Rev. Hancock. St. Paul's A. M. E. Church, Nineteenth and Center Street, was organized in 1889. A lot and small dwelling house were recently purchased by the society, in which building services are held. Rev. J. H. Wilson, Rev. M. Green and Rev. W. D. Venable have been pastors. St. Phillips Mission, on Twenty-first Street, between Nicholas and Paul, was established in 1881 by Dean Millspaugh, of Trinity Cathedral, but since 1885 Rev. John Williams, of St. Barnabas Episcopal Church, has had charge of the work. Rev.

## CHURCH ORGANIZATIONS.

John A. Williams, a young colored minister of education and theological training, became the pastor in June, 1891.

Mt. Pisgah Baptist Church is located at 1216 Dodge Street, where the members of this congregation have worshiped since the summer of 1891. There are one hundred and fifty members, and the congregation is usually large. Rev. J. R. Richardson is pastor.

The Young Men's Christian Association of Omaha, was organized in 1865, with Thirteenth, and then a change was made to a frame building on Farnam which occupied the present site of M. H. Bliss' crockery establishment. In a short time better quarters were secured in Mr. Poppleton's building, corner of Tenth and Farnam. Some two years later the association moved up town again and for a time was quartered in a building occupying the present site of the Barker block, Farnam and Fifteenth. The re-organization of this building necessitated another move and rooms in the L. B.

YOUNG MEN'S CHRISTIAN ASSOCIATION BUILDING.

Watson B. Smith, president; Wm. Fleming, treasurer and Dr. J. C. Denise, secretary. A two-story building, on Twelfth Street between Farnam and Douglas, was erected at a cost of $2,600, with a very good library and reading room on the first floor and a room for public services on the second. In the course of a few years the organization ceased to exist and the property was devoted to other uses. In 1877 a re-organization was effected and the association put upon a more substantial basis. Rooms were secured over Huberman's jewelry store, corner of Douglas and William's building, corner of Dodge and Fifteenth, were secured and here the association remained until July, 1888, when possession was taken of the four upper floors of the substantial association building at the corner of Douglas and Sixteenth Streets, completed at a cost of $90,000, including heating and furniture. The lot cost $25,000, in 1866, and is now valued at $100,000. The association now stands upon a substantial basis. All of the modern improvements are found in the building and the social, religious, athletic and educational features of the association's management have brought under its influence hundreds of young men who might not have been reached otherwise. In the success which has been achieved during the past few years the late Pierce C. Himebaugh is entitled to unlimited credit. He contributed liberally of his means to secure the purchase of the ground and erection of the building and devoted years of earnest, personal effort to the details of the work, imbuing others with his own zeal, enterprise and unflagging courage in the midst of great financial difficulties.

On September 15, 1891, Frank W. Ober became General Secretary of the Association and since that time the institution has enjoyed a season of prosperity. The current expenses of the Association and improvements were $11,231.11 the past year.

The secretary's report shows the following receipts from May 1, 1891, to May 1, 1892: Memberships, $5,304.50; subscriptions, $4,520.57; rent of halls, $824.50; Star course, $262.71; miscellaneous, $346.02. Total, $11,258.30. Receipts from rentals of stores, $8,675.00.

The above amount has been applied to the payment of interest on mortgage, taxes, repairs, insurance, improvements and $1,500 towards the payment of old floating indebtedness, none being available for use in current expenses.

The treasurer reports that on May 22, 1891, from the best figures then obtainable, the floating indebtedness was $8,302.71. "If we add to our present bills payable, (viz., notes for $2,300) the note of $3,500 given for old indebtedness contracted principally in finishing the building and to be paid out of the balance received from rentals of building, our present floating indebtedness is $5,800, being a reduction of $2,502.71 in the past year. There are also pledges on the books, most of which are good, for $2,800. As far as known every outstanding bill against the association has been met in full."

The membership November 1, 1892, was 775, and rapidly increasing. A number of leading young men of the business and social circles of the city are members.

The officers of the association are: A. P. Tukey, president; C. A. Starr, Esq., vice-president; William H. Russell, treasurer, Charles E. Williamson, recording secretary. The executive officers are: Frank W. Ober, general secretary; Otto D. Heissenbuttel, assistant secretary; Frank R. Roberson, assistant secretary; W. S. Sheldon, physical director.

Bishop James O'Gorman, who was so closely identified with the interests of the Catholic Church throughout the west, was consecrated vicar-apostolic of this See May 8, 1859, and removed to Omaha immediately afterwards. He was born in the County Limerick, Ireland, in 1809, and at the age of nineteen entered the Monastery of Mount Melarry, joining the Trappist order, though his family were generally Protestants. In due time he was ordained priest and in 1830 was sent to America to establish a branch of the order at Dubuque, Iowa, to which he gave the name of the New Melarry. It was owing to his efforts that the Mercy Hospital (now St. Joseph's) was established and that the St Mary's Convent was built. He did not exhibit the business enterprise which characterized his successor, Bishop O'Connor, but was a very popular man with all classes of people and especially beloved by those of his religious belief. He died July 4th, 1874, and his remains were buried under the altar of St. Philomena Cathedral.

Bishop Robert Clarkson (Episcopal) was appointed missionary bishop of Nebraska and Dakota in 1865, and was consecrated November 15. He was born in Gettysburg, Pennsylvania, November 19, 1826, and educated at Pennsylvania College, Gettysburg, graduating in 1844. Four years later he was married at Hagerstown, Maryland, to Miss McPherson and removed at once to Chicago, where he became rector of St. James Episcopal Church, where he remained seven

## CHURCH ORGANIZATIONS.

teen years. In 1857 he received the degree of D. D. from Pennsylvania College and in 1872 the degree of LL. D. was conferred upon him by the Racine, Wisconsin, College, and also by the Nebraska University. Coming to Omaha in 1865, Bishop Clarkson made this city his home until the day of his death, March 10, 1884, beloved and honored by the entire community. His remains are buried in the shadow of the beautiful Trinity cathedral, whose building was largely due to his efforts, in a spot he had selected for that purpose.

Bishop James O'Connor was consecrated bishop of Dibona and vicar-apostolic of Nebraska August 20, 1876, at St. Charles Seminary, near Philadelphia, and located in Omaha the following month, accompanied by Arch-Bishop Ryan, of Philadelphia, who preached the installation sermon. Bishop O'Connor's diocese included Nebraska, Wyoming, that portion of Montana which lies east of the Rocky Mountains and the part of Dakota which lies west of the Missouri River. He died in this city May 27, 1890. During his life here he was recognized as a man of the highest personal character, of broad and liberal views and possessed of a remarkable knowledge of men and affairs. His popularity was not confined to those of his own faith, and he was universally respected and esteemed. Bishop O'Connor was born in Queenstown, Ireland, September 10, 1823, and came to America at the age of fifteen, in company with his brother, Michael O'Connor, afterwards bishop of Pittsburg. A few years were spent in study at St. Charles Seminary, Philadelphia, and he was then sent to Rome, where he was ordained priest in 1845. Returning to this country he was appointed president of St. Michael, Pennsylvania, in 1857, and in 1864 was transferred to St. Charles Seminary, Philadelphia. In 1872 he was appointed pastor of St. Dominic's Church, Holmesburg, Pennsylvania, and in 1876 was made a bishop.

Bishop R. Scannell, recently appointed to the See of Omaha, was born in Cloyne, County Cork, Ireland, in 1845. He was ordained in 1871 and came to America the following year, locating at Nashville, Tennessee, where he was assistant pastor at the cathedral for two years and then took charge of a church in West Nashville. Later he was appointed vicar-general of that diocese. In 1883 he secured the erection of St. Joseph's Church, in West Nashville, and organized a prosperous congregation. In December, 1888, he was consecrated Bishop of Concordia, Kansas, and on the 21st of March, 1891, was appointed to his present position. The installation services, held on the 12th of April, at St. Philomena's Cathedral, were of the most solemn and impressive character. The closing address was made by Bishop Hennessey, of Wichita, Kansas, in the course of which he said: "Thirty years ago the saintly Bishop O'Gorman received episcopal consecration. As a child I knelt at his side and held the crozier. He came here to an almost trackless desert, suffering the inconvenience, almost of a rudimentary civilization. He was succeeded by the amiable, the gentle, the intellectual James O'Connor, whose noble qualities added lustre to the higher art of America, while his grand administrative abilities give this See of Omaha an importance second to none in the west."

Bishop John P. Newman was born in New York City, September 1, 1826, and educated at Cazenovia Seminary, New York. In 1849 he became a minister in the Methodist Church. The years 1860-61 he spent in European travel, passing some time in Palestine and Egypt. In 1869 he was installed pastor of the Metropolitan Church in Washington, where he remained until 1874, to which church he returned in 1876 and served three years, again returning in 1884 and serving as pastor for another term of three years. From 1869 to 1874 he was chaplain of the United States Senate, and in the latter year was sent abroad by President Grant, as Inspector of Consuls. He was appointed by his church denomination, in 1876, one of the commissioners to adjust the differences between the northern and southern branches of the Methodist Church, and in 1881 was a member of the Ecumenical Council, which assembled in London, England. The degree of D. D. was conferred upon him in 1863, and that of LL. D. in 1887. At the general conference of 1888 he was elected bishop and Omaha was selected as his episcopal residence, in September of that year. October 8th, of that year, he was tendered a public reception in the First Methodist Church, where addresses of welcome were delivered by John M. Thurston, Esq., and Governor John M. Thayer. A banquet at the Paxton Hotel followed and was rendered a memorable occasion. Bishop Newman's reputation is national, and he has long been considered one of the most distinguished men of his denomination. He spent part of the year 1890 in establishing missions in Japan.

On Christmas Day, 1855, Rev. Reuben Gaylord arrived in Omaha with his family. He came to make the new settlement his permanent home, and to aid in building up a religious sentiment in the West. He was a pioneer by instinct, having located at Jacksonville, Illinois, in 1835, and at Danville, Iowa, in 1844, when those sections of country were wild, and settlers few and widely scattered. He came to Nebraska in the service of the American Home Missionary Society, Congregational, and was paid a salary of only fifty dollars per month, though the cost of living here was so great as to render that amount entirely insufficient to support his family. He went to work with energy and zeal, however, preaching Sunday afternoons in the old State house; services being held in the same building in the forenoon by Rev. Isaac F. Collins, a Methodist clergyman, and at night by Rev. William Leach, of the Baptist denomination. In 1856 Mr. Gaylord succeeded in securing the erection of a small brick church, which fronted east on Sixteenth Street, between Farnam and the alley just north. It had seating capacity for 225 persons, and cost $4,500. On the 17th and 18th of June, 1857, a fair was held by the ladies to get money enough to furnish the church, and in this way raised about four hundred dollars clear of expenses. Mr. Gaylord's work extended throughout the eastern part of Nebraska. He organized churches at Fontenelle, Fremont, Bellevue, Florence, Calhoun, Decatur, Brownville, and other places, besides devoting much time, in 1859, to collecting funds in the East, to aid in the carrying forward of an enterprise to establish a college at Fontenelle. He was the pastor of the First Congregational Church of this city until 1864, when he resigned to accept the agency of the American Home Missionary Society for Nebraska and Iowa. At the time of his death he was in charge of a church at Fontenelle, the second of his denomination organized in Nebraska. He died January 10, 1880, and was buried at Prospect Hill Cemetery. His widow and son, Ralph E., reside here, and a married daughter, Mrs. S. C. Brewster, lives at Irvington, Nebraska.

The late Rev. William McCandlish was a clergyman who will long be remembered throughout the West. Bishop Clarkson was accustomed to say of him that he "ought to have been a bishop." His residence in Nebraska dated back to the fall of 1858, when he located at Fontenelle, but a few years later he became a citizen of Omaha and so remained until his death in 1884. The house he built in 1868, at the head of St. Mary's Avenue, is still standing. Mr. McCandlish was born in Kirkcudbrightshire, Scotland, September 12, 1810, and came to this country with his parents when he was seven years old, locating at Newville, Pennsylvania. He was educated at Washington and Jefferson Colleges, graduating in 1834, and the last journey of his life was made in June, 1884, when he attended a meeting at the old college, of his classmates, who had separated half a century before. He pursued his theological course at the Allegheny Seminary, Pennsylvania, and in 1837 was ordained a minister in the Presbyterian Church. September 10, 1838, he was married at Allegheny City to Miss Maria Howells, a cousin of W. D. Howells, the author, and took charge of a church at Wooster, Ohio. A few years later he moved to Illinois, and for a time was pastor of a church in Quincy, of which O. Browning, of President Lincoln's cabinet, was one of the supporters. For thirteen years he was superintendent of the American Bible Society, in Nebraska, Colorado and Wyoming. Dakota and Utah being also included in his territory a large portion of that time. The last act of his life, August 5, 1884, was to carry a bible to a neighbor a few blocks from his home. Returning, he said he would lie down for a short time, as he felt chilly. An hour later his wife visited his room to find that in that brief interval the last great change had come, and that an earnest, loyal Christian soul had assumed immortality. Mr. McCandlish was a man of the highest integrity, devoted to the advancement of the Christian religion, but allowing, in his dealings with men, for those differences in opinion which circumstances and early associations naturally create. His manners were simple and unaffected, commanding respect and esteem from all with whom he was brought in contact. Three of his six children are still living: W. N., Isabella S. and Robert C. Mrs. McCandlish died in this city December 28, 1887.

Rev. Thomas B. Lemon came to Nebraska in 1856, with a view of practicing his profession as a lawyer, locating at Bellevue, where he was admitted to the bar. Two years later he entered the ministry of the Methodist denomination and until his death, in March, 1890, was a zealous, earnest preacher of the gospel. A man of commanding influence and force of character and, withal, eloquent and gifted of speech, and of winning manners. As one of the early pastors of the First Church of Omaha and, later, as presiding elder of this district, he bore an active part in pioneer Christian work in this section of Nebraska. At one time he held religious services in the Academy of Music, soon after that building was completed, and thereby reached a class of people that never visited the churches. Just before leaving Maryland he was married to Miss Margaret B. Waters, who survives him and is yet a resident of Omaha. Their family consisted of Thomas B. W., A. R., Maggie E. (now Mrs. A. B. Smith) Della M. (now Mrs. J. W. Maynard) and Walter W.

Rev. Thomas McCague was the pioneer minister of the United Presbyterian Church here. He was born in Ripley, Ohio, in 1825, and has the distinction of being the first American missionary in Egypt, to which country he was sent in 1854, remaining six years. In July, 1867, he came from Nebraska City to Omaha by direction of the board of missions of his denomination, to organize a church here. This he did, services being first held in what was known as Beal's School House, corner of Fifteenth and Capitol Avenue. At the end of the year the board decided to suspend work in Omaha, and then Mr. McCague took the matter in his own hands, put up a small church building on South Tenth Street, in one corner of the lot his home occupied, and for four years struggled along without any financial aid from the board. His earnestness as a pastor and high character as a citizen secured hosts of warm personal friends, and he has lived to see his denomination well established and prosperous in every way. He was married in Warren County, Ohio, to Miss Henrietta M. Lowes, in July, 1854. Mr. and Mrs. McCague have nine children: John L., Margaret M., (now Mrs. Albert Gordon) William L., Thomas H., Josie M. (now Mrs. J. H. McCulloch), Annie N.,

Lydia S., George S. and Brower E., all residents of Omaha except Mrs. Gordon, whose husband is pastor of a church at Alliance, Nebraska.

Of the Lutheran church in Omaha, the Rev. Henry W. Kuhns is the pioneer, in fact he was the first of his denomination to locate in Nebraska, coming here in 1858 as a missionary, with a commission which described his field as including Omaha, and adjacent parts, and really embracing a large scope of country west of the Missouri River, in which there are now about three hundred Lutheran ministers, with a membership of over nine thousand. Mr. Kuhns began his work in this city on a salary of five hundred dollars a year. Services were first held in the Methodist Church, on Thirteenth Street, and then in the Congregational Church, on Sixteenth Street. In 1860 a small brick church building was erected on a lot on Douglas Street, which is now a portion of the site of the Millard Hotel. Owing to ill-health Mr. Kuhns resigned his pastorate in 1872, and for several years resided in the southern States, returning to Omaha in 1887 to live a quiet, retired life, but still continuing in the ministry. In the early history of the Nebraska Deaf and Dumb Institute Mr. Kuhns was closely identified with it, serving five years as secretary of the directory, and it is chiefly due to his efforts that the institution was located here. He was born August 23, 1829, at Greensburg, Pennsylvania, and was educated at Gettysburg. October 18, 1860, he was married to Miss Charlotte J. Hay, of Johnstown, Pennsylvania. They have three children living: Luther M., pastor of the Grace Lutheran Church of this city, Paul W. and John H.

# CHAPTER XXXVI.

CATHOLICISM IN OMAHA — CHURCHES AND SCHOOLS — CREIGHTON COLLEGE.

[Miss Stacia Crowley furnished the facts as set forth in this chapter.]

On or about May 15, 1855, in the court room of the old State House, then standing on the west side of Ninth Street, between Farnam and Douglas, was celebrated the first church services, in Nebraska, according to the rites of the Roman Catholic Church.

The celebrant was Rev. Father W. Emonds, who had been brought here from St. Joseph by Mr. Jeremiah Dee, when he visited that city for supplies. A temporary altar was draped, and Mrs. Thomas O'Connor, still a resident of this city, brought from her home near by, a pitcher of water to be used during the service. Mr. John Kelley, now living in Washington County, served at this mass. Father Emonds remained a short time, and funds were collected toward the erection of a church.

There are still many men living in Omaha who remember with a smile and a sigh, the thrill and excitement of the day when it was announced, in the vocabulary of the times, that "the Irish are jumping the park!" A strip of ground a block in width, extending from Jackson to Davenport Streets, had been set aside by the founders of the town for park purposes. The men who were engaged in digging the foundations for the first Catholic Church were thought to be encroaching upon this territory. Every man in the population, and a great many of the women, were soon on the grounds, and what affords many rather laughable stories to-day, threatened to be a very serious matter then. It was, however, decided that the trenches were dug outside of the park and on lots donated to the church people by the Council Bluffs & Nebraska Ferry Company.

In the spring of 1856 the contract was let for the building of the first church edifice in Nebraska. It was erected where the excavation had been made, on the northeast corner of Eighth and Howard Streets. It was a brick building twenty-four by forty feet. The stone foundations were laid by Ferry & Jenkinson, who also laid the foundations of the capitol building. The stone was brought from Lutz's quarry at first, but some of it came from J. B. Mold's and some from John Green's. The brick work was done by Bovey & Armstrong, also builders of the capitol, and to Mr. Henry Livesey belongs the distinction of having laid the first brick in the first church building erected in Nebraska. The carpenter work was done by Wolfel & Baker, of Columbus.

While this building was under way, Father Scanlan, of St. Joseph, arrived and celebrated the second mass, in the parlor of Governor T. B. Cuming, whose beautiful and cultured young wife was a zealous Catholic. This quaint and picturesque old house is still standing, surrounded by a spacious lawn and orchard, on the southwest corner of Dodge and Eighteenth Streets. Having been completed, the church was dedicated "St. Mary's" by Rev. Father Scanlan, in August, 1856. On this same day, by way of a beginning, the reverend gentleman administered the sacrament of baptism to fifteen babies. Some of the families connected with the opening of the old church, were the Begleys, Burkleys, Corrigans, Cassidys, Creightons, Dees, Ferrys, Gradys, Hughes, Hickeys,

Holmes, Kelleys, Kenelleys, Murphys, McGoverns, McArdles, McDonalds, O'Connors, Ryans, Rileys, Swifts, Suttons, Tiernans and Toners.

For some time services were conducted by visiting priests, and not until the fall of 1857 was the first regular pastor appointed. There is no official record of the pastors, but as nearly as can be learned from regular attendants of this church, they came in the following order: Fathers Kavanagh, Powers, Cannon, Dillon, McMahon, Lawrence, Kelley, Hayes, Daxacher, Greenabaum, Egan and Curtis. The first organist was Miss

St. Mary's Roman Catholic Church.
First Catholic Church in Omaha.

Celia Burkley, and the principal members of the choir were Mr. and Mrs. Vincent Burkley and Mr. and Mrs. Bremer.

In the winter of 1858 the vicarate of Kansas and Nebraska was divided, and Rev. James O'Gorman, of the Trappist Monastery near Dubuque, Iowa, was appointed vicar apostolic of Nebraska, and titular Bishop of Raphanea. He was consecrated at St. Louis, May 10, 1859, and came to Omaha the latter part of the same month. One of the first ceremonies in which he assisted after his arrival was the ordination of Rev. William Kelley. This took place in the church on Eighth Street, June 25, 1859. Father Kelley was therefore the first priest ordained in the diocese. He is still connected with the cathedral, and for the past few years it has been a common request at weddings that Father Kelley may be allowed to officiate, the request being usually supplemented by the explanation: "He married my father and mother."

When Bishop O'Gorman arrived in Omaha he found only two Catholic clergymen ministering to about three hundred families scattered all over the territory. He decided after some hesitation to locate here; but for some reason did not accept the title to sixty-three full lots offered by way of inducement. Had he done so, the church in Omaha would have been the richer to-day by a few millions. He first resided in a white frame house on the southwest corner of Harney and Eighth Streets, vacated for that purpose by Mr. Thomas O'Connor. Later he purchased from the father of Mr. Lyman Richardson, the property on which St. Philomena's Cathedral now stands, on Ninth and Harney Streets. On this property Mr. Richardson had erected a house, which was for many years the bishop's residence. Within its walls this venerable and beloved prelate breathed his last, July 4, 1874. It served as a residence for the priests connected with the cathedral until 1889, when it was taken down and the present handsome brick structure took its place. After the coming of the bishop, the little church on Eighth Street, with its unpainted wooden cross, was elevated to the dignity of a cathedral.

In 1867, on the completion of the Harney Street Cathedral, the old building was used as a school and placed in charge of the Sisters of Mercy. In 1882, the ground upon which it stood was condemned and bought by the Burlington & Missouri River Railroad, and this old landmark disappeared for-

St. Mary's Convent, Twenty-fourth Street and St. Mary's Avenue—1868.

ever. With the dedication of the new cathedral, St. Philomena's, began a new era for Catholic Omaha. This structure cost upward of fifty thousand dollars, and was furnished with the first pipe organ ever brought to Omaha. An exquisite marble altar, the work of foreign sculptors, was presented by Mrs. Edward Creighton; and back of this was placed a triple window, of what is still one of the richest and most artistic designs in stained glass in this city. Three acres of land were purchased and a boarding school for young ladies built by the Sisters of Mercy. This building stood on the north side of what was named, from the convent, St. Mary's Avenue. The land was purchased from Harrison Johnson for $150, and in 1887 it was sold for $82,000. Adjoining this purchase was the first Catholic cemetery, located between what is now Twenty-first and Twenty-fourth Streets and Harney and St. Mary's Avenue. Not a trace remains to-day of graveyard, convent or hill. The grader has done his work, and paved streets and elegant residences have made strange these once familiar places.

The pastors of the cathedral have been Fathers Curtis, Byrne, Jennette, O'Brien, McDermott, Riordan, English, O'Connor and McCarthy, the present incumbent. Under his able administration many improvements have been made. St. Philomena's continued to be the only Catholic Church until 1868, when Father Greenabaum organized the few German families in the congregation and built St. Mary Magdalene's, on Douglas between Sixteenth and Seventeenth. There were not more than a dozen families; among them were the Kosters, Frenzers, Wassermans' Rebhausens, Mergens, Bedessems, Roblings and Kaufmans. In 1887 Father Glauber, the second and present pastor, purchased a site on the corner of Center and South Seventeenth Streets and erected thereon the Second German Church. This was dedicated St. Joseph's, September 12, 1887. When Father Glauber selected this site, he met with considerable opposition, the general feeling being that it was too far out. He persisted, however, and assured his people

ST. PHILOMENA CATHEDRAL.

that their suburban lots would be city property within five years. If you visit that part of the city to-day, you will find viaducts and motor lines have been built, the surrounding streets graded and paved, gas, water and sewerage connections made, and the site could be sold to-day for at least four times the purchase money.

On the death of Bishop O'Gorman, in 1874, Rt. Rev. James O'Connor, D. D., was appointed Vicar General of Nebraska and titular Bishop of Diboua. Bishop O'Connor was really the first bishop of Omaha, but could not claim that title until 1885, when this city was made a See. He was called upon to preside over a bishopric including Nebraska, Dakota, Wyoming, and the eastern part of Montana, the most extensive territory under any Catholic bishop on this continent. He was a ripe scholar and a man of fine literary attainments, and as such was respected by the ablest men of all denominations. He was a pious and zealous priest; and, while the spiritual welfare of his people was always nearest his heart, he was at the same time an able man of business, and much of the great material prosperity of the church in Omaha, is due to his prudence and foresight. In death he was most sincerely mourned; and the old cathedral, already dear to Catholic Omaha, has become still dearer since his body has been placed in the vault under the high altar, where Father Curtis, the first pastor, and Bishop O'Gorman had already been laid. At the time of his coming the cathedral and the German Church were found sufficient. Since that time seven new parishes have been created in Omaha, two in South Omaha, and the congregation of the cathedral is still as large as it was on his arrival. This is, in some respects, a very remarkable congregation. You may see at the same service, Indians, Chinamen, Negroes, Arabians, Poles, Bohemians and Italians, many of them still wearing the costumes of their native country.

The Holy Family parish was created in 1877. The first church was a small frame building, formerly used as a school house. The present edifice is a handsome brick, combining church and school. The first pastor's were Fathers Quinn and Curtis. Later the church was placed in charge of the Jesuit fathers. The pastors of that order have been Fathers Shaffel and Hillman. St. Peters is a duplicate of the church of the Holy Family, and is located on West Leavenworth Street. This prosperous parish was in charge of Rev. Father Boyle, who has been succeeded by Father Conway.

In December, 1883, was dedicated St. Patrick's, located on Fifteenth and Castellar. The growth of this parish has been phenomenal. Rev. John Jennette, the first pastor, is still in charge. When the parish was organized it was found to contain fifty-two Catholic families, residing in town and country. The country in this case included the farms upon which South Omaha has since been built. Father Jennette's circumstances were soon similar to those that embarrassed the famous old lady in the shoe, but he was relieved by the creation of a new parish. He began nine years ago with fifty-two families. The overflow from his congregation fills two large churches in South Omaha, and he has still three hundred families left. On the same block with St. Patrick's Church, school and residence, is located the orphanage conducted by the Sisters of Mercy.

In 1879 a Bohemian Catholic Church was organized. It is known as St. Wenceslau's and is on the corner of Fourteenth and Pine Streets. The church building cost nine thousand dollars, and there is besides a fine residence and school. The pastors have been Fathers Kozarink and Klima. The present pastor, Rev. William Choka, is also vicar general of the Diocese of Nebraska.

St. Cecilia's, on Walnut Hill, is a new parish. The appointments of this church are very dainty and elegant, but it is already too small for the congregation. The first pastor was Rev. Father O'Callaghan, and the second, Father Smith. The present pastor is Father Carroll. A new parish, including old Fort Omaha and Kountze Place, was created in 1890, and is known as the Sacred Heart. It is in charge of Father Smith.

The first school connected with the Catholic Church in Omaha, was taught by Miss Joanna O'Brien, and later by Miss Celia Burkley, now Mrs. Burkhard. It was a small frame building, south of the Eighth Street Church, and accommodated both sexes. A larger frame was soon erected and set

CATHOLICISM IN OMAHA. 349

apart for boys. The first teacher in this school was a Mr. Webster. It was, according to all accounts, a very lively place. A strip years later, so successful as county superintendent, and enabled him still later to fill many other important public offices so ac-

ST. JOHN'S COLLEGIATE CHURCH.

of pine shingle was the board of education, and it must have been in this school that Mr. John Rush, who took charge in 1866, gained the experience that made him, some ceptably. Among the boys who began their education in this school are many well-known citizens; notably, Hon. John Mulvihill, Jeremiah Mulvihill, Patrick and John Swift,

Frank Burkley, Jeremiah Linahan, Terence and John Mahoney, Thomas and John Garvey, and the McGovern brothers. In 1877 this building was moved to the northern part of the city and used for a church.

The first boarding school for young ladies was St. Mary's, on the hill, in charge of the Sisters of Mercy. It was a very popular school in its day; and its annual commencement exercises, held in the hall of the old county court house, were looked upon as the social event of the year. There are now three convent schools in Omaha where a thorough education in all the higher branches of study can be had. The Convent of the Sacred Heart, a select boarding school for young ladies, is located at Park Place, in the northwestern part of the city. It is a commodious brick structure with beautiful lawn and gardens. Many of the pupils come from the far East as well as the far West. Madame Conway is the mother superior, and the enrollment for the present year was 128. The ladies of this order also conduct a private day school for girls at Twenty-seventh and Leavenworth. Nine teachers are employed, and the building is a fine three-story brick. Madame Tobbits is the superior. St. Catherine's Academy, at Eighteenth and Cass, is a well patronized private school conducted by the Sisters of Mercy. Mother Leo is the principal. There are eight parochial schools. Of these, St. Philomena's Holy Family, St. Patrick's, St. Stanislau's and St. Wenceslau's are in charge of the Sisters of Mercy. St. Joseph's and St. Mary Magdalene's are German Schools, and are in charge ot the Sisters of the Precious Blood. St. Peter's is in charge of the ladies of the Sacred Heart. The total attendance at these schools is 1,500.

But the school in which Catholic Omaha takes most pride is Creighton College. This is the only endowed Catholic College in the United States. It was the dying request of Mr. Edward Creighton that his wife, the late Mrs. Mary Creighton, should endow a free college in Omaha for the education of youth without regard to creed or color. His wish was complied with, and Creighton College is the result. It was incorporated by an act of the legislature in 1879, with power to " confer such degrees as are usually conferred by colleges and universities in the United States;" and in the same year was entrusted by Bishop O'Connor to the Fathers of the Society of Jesus, by whom it is conducted.

The grounds are six acres in extent, the building being located upon a hill which commands a magnificent view for miles in every direction. It is of striking appearance and when the left wing is added will have a total frontage of 250 feet. Mr. John A. Creighton has supplied the college with one of the most complete astronomical and chemical outfits in the West. There is also a college library of six thousand well selected volumes. Students are admitted without regard to their religious convictions and the catalogue for 1890 contains a list of 220 names. Rev. James Hoeffer, S. J., is president and prefect of studies. Connected with this institution is St. John's Collegiate Church, one of the most beautiful church edifices in the city. It is built of gray stone and in the Romanesque style of architecture. Many of its interior decorations, stained glass windows, altars and the organ, have been placed as memorials for various members of the Creighton family. The High Altar, artistic in design and execution, was erected by Hon. John A. McShane as a memorial of his wife, Mary Lee McShane. This is not a parish church, but is the Chapel of Creighton College, and the officiating priests are those in charge of the college.

The Poor Clares, a cloistered order of nuns, have a fine building with extensive grounds on West Hamilton Street. The Catholic population of Omaha, is estimated at seventeen thousand.

CREIGHTON COLLEGE.

# CHAPTER XXXVII.

CEMETERIES — BURIAL PLACES OF EARLY DAYS — THOSE OF LATER YEARS.

In 1858 Moses F. Shinn set apart ten acres of his pre-emption northwest of the city for cemeterial purposes. The first burial was that of Alonzo F. Salisbury, a member of the council, representing Douglas County in the third session of the territorial Legislature. His death occurred in March, 1858. The second was that of J. L. Winship, in June, 1858. Adjoining this ten acres on the south, Jesse Lowe devoted a tract of land to the same purpose, on which a number of burials were made; but the title of the land was retained by Messrs. Shinn and Lowe. The ground was unfenced and cattle roamed over it in droves. In 1859 Byron Reed purchased Mr. Shinn's ten acres and tried to organize a company to convert the property into a first-class cemetery, but failed, and he was compelled to undertake it himself. He then purchased fifteen acres of Mr. Lowe, and, of the twenty-five acres, dedicated fourteen for cemetery purposes with reversion to himself or heirs, when the ground ceases to be used for cemeterial purposes. For twenty years the cemetery (which he christened Prospect Hill Cemetery) had been managed by Mr. Reed, during which time his outlay had exceeded the income about five thousand dollars, until, in 1885, he turned the management over to the Forest Lawn Cemetery Association. In the spring of 1890 an organization of the lot owners, known as Prospect Hill Cemetery Association was effected, with C. A. Baldwin as president and C. F. Catlin as secretary, assuming control and management of the cemetery and improving and beautifying it very much since that time. The association has recently acquired from the estate of Mr. Reed, land lying between that portion of the cemetery now occupied and Parker Street, and extending from the east line of the cemetery to Thirty-third Street on the west.

In the early settlement of Omaha, about five acres of land, on the crest of a beautiful elevation in what is now Shull's Addition, were used for burial purposes, practically "without leave or license." The improvements made recently in that locality, resulting in the exposure of the remains buried here long years ago, caused the Messrs. Shull to set apart two lots to be used for a re-interment of these remains, which property has been deeded to the Lutheran Church. In this old burial ground, used for only a few years, Governor Cuming was buried, but the body was afterwards removed to Prospect Hill Cemetery, where it now reposes. Recently, in excavating for a building, an expensive iron casket, with heavy plate glass, was unearthed, and near by there was brought to the surface a coffin in which was the body of a man encased in a soldier's overcoat, with buckshot in the pockets. A pistol was also found in the coffin.

Early in the sixties a tract of several acres of land was purchased for cemeterial and school purposes by the Catholic Church, north of St. Mary's Avenue and east of what is now Twenty-fourth Street. In the northwest corner of this tract a considerable space was used for burial purposes for a few years, during which period the body of General E. O. C. Ord's father was buried there. The encroachments of the city caused an abandonment of this cemetery about 1869, and the bodies have since been re-interred in the Holy Sepulchre Cemetery, chiefly. This burial place contains forty acres—though but one-fourth of that amount has been dedicated to cemeterial purposes—and is located on the north side of Leavenworth Street, about two miles west of the city limits. St. Mary's and Cassiday's Cemeteries are situated far outside the city limits, to the southwest, and have been used for many years by the Catholic denomination. They each contain about twenty acres, and in neither has there been much attempt to adorn, by the planting of trees or shrubbery, or in laying out the grounds in an artistic manner. The same may be said of the Holy Sepulchre Cemetery. The land now comprised in Cassiday's Cemetery was entered at the government land office by one Sullivan, who used a land warrant belonging to James Ferry, father of Mrs. John Rush. The tract comprised 120 acres, one-half of which was deeded by Sullivan to Bishop Meigs, of Leavenworth, for cemeterial purposes. Thomas O'Connor furnished the money to pay Mr. Ferry for his warrant, with the understanding that it would be promptly refunded by the Catholics of Omaha, a subscription paper having been previously signed for that purpose. But money was scarce in those days, and considerable time elapsed before Mr. O'Connor was able to collect the amount he had paid out.

In 1885 an act was passed by the Legislature increasing the amount of land which could be owned by cemeterial associations, and the Forest Lawn Association was at once formed and a half section of land purchased of John H. Brackin at one hundred dollars per acre. It is situated seven miles northwest of the business center of the city, is admirably adapted to the purpose, with commanding heights, lovely glades, a variety of natural forest and a never-failing stream of water. Mr. Brackin was very active in securing the necessary legislation, and in forming the organization afterwards, and it is a curious fact that the first burial in Forest Lawn was that of Mr. Brackin, September 1, 1886, his death having occurred in California and the remains being brought to this city for interment. About half of the 320 acres have been platted into lots and the grounds handsomely improved under direction of skilled landscape gardeners. Up to October 1, 1892, there had been 2,829 burials. A section is owned by Douglas County, in which there are 755 bodies buried. The Grand Army of the Republic, the Free Masons, and the Omaha Typographical Union also own burial places in the cemetery. Following named are the officers of the association: J. J. Brown, president; S. T. Josselyn, treasurer; James Y. Craig, superintendent; H. I. Plumb, agent; J. C. Denise, C. H. Brown, S. T. Josselyn, James Forsythe, Herman Kountze, M. H. Bliss, F. B. Lowe, O. S. Wood, C. H. Brown and A. P. Wood, trustees.

The Mount Hope Cemetery Association—P. W. Birkhauser, president; H. H. Benson, treasurer; F. L. Blumer, secretary; and F. W. Melcher, agent—owns 128 acres of ground about the same distance from the city as Forest Lawn, but farther west, in what is known as the Benson tract. The association was formed in 1888. A considerable sum of money has been expended in improvements, which have already added much to the appearance of the property.

North of the city, near Forest Lawn, is the Jewish Cemetery; and southwest, on the line of the Missouri Pacific, about three miles from the business portion of the city, is the Bohemian Cemetery; and on the Military Road, west of Fort Omaha, are Evergreen and Springwell Cemeteries—the latter owned by a Danish organization. All of these are small tracts, where but little has been done in the way of improvement or development.

## CHAPTER XXXVIII.

THE MEDICAL PROFESSION — PRACTITIONERS OF THE DIFFERENT SCHOOLS — MEDICAL COLLEGES.

[The following sketch of the regular physicians of the city is from the pen of Dr. W. F. Milroy.]

The space in this work allotted to a history of the medical profession of Omaha renders it impossible to present a biographical sketch, even though brief, of all those who have been identified with the growth of the city as practitioners of medicine. It will therefore be the aim of the writer to view the profession collectively, for the most part, restricting his narrative to such matters as have been of interest to Omaha's physicians as a whole.

Those who were first to locate in Omaha as qualified physicians were young men, carried hither by an ambition to gain a livelihood, while at the same time putting themselves in a position to receive the advantages to come from the development of a new country. Like others who constituted the community to which they came, they lived not so much in the present as in the future. At the close of the late war several who had been in the medical service of the government located here. In later years, when the fame of Omaha went abroad, and her splendid future began to be apparent, with the influx of business men of every variety the physician came also. Among these later arrivals were some who came directly following their graduation, and many who, having been in active practice for a shorter or longer period, had felt the need of a wider field for the exercise of their powers than was afforded by their residence in smaller towns.

The physicians of Omaha have, to a good degree, been alive to their position and opportunity, and have kept well abreast of their day, in respect to those discoveries and inventions in medical and surgical science which have been so fruitful of blessing to the race, in procuring a greater degree of health and duration of life. Omaha need feel no shame as she considers her representation in the medical world.

The first physician to locate in Omaha was Dr. George L. Miller, who came from Syracuse, New York, in the fall of 1854, and practiced his profession until 1856, when he turned his practice over to Dr. A. Chapel, who located in Omaha that year. These gentlemen were both graduates of the New York College of Physicians and Surgeons. Dr. James H. Seymour, Dr. W. R. Thrall, Dr. William McElwee and Dr. B. T. Shelley — the latter the founder of the town of Niobrara, Nebraska — located in Omaha in 1855, but none of them became permanent residents. Dr. James P. Peck established himself here in 1856, and for more than thirty years was actively engaged in the practice of his profession, dying in 1889 universally esteemed. His son, Edward Peck, is connected with the Omaha Elevator Company. Dr. Gilbert C. Monell, father of John J. Monell, and Dr. William McClelland became citizens of Omaha in 1857. The latter was surgeon of the First Nebraska Infantry during the war. Dr. Monell went out of practice about 1870. Both of these gentlemen died several years ago. Dr. C. A. Henry, though not a graduate of any medical school, enjoyed a considerable practice in that line in 1855-6, owing to the lack of physicians and the fact that he was a druggist. He was an important citizen in many respects in those early days, and put up the first three-story business house in Omaha, the Pioneer Block on lower Farnam Street.

March 25, 1855, the "Nebraska Medical Society" was incorporated by the following named physicians: George L. Miller, B. T. Shelley, M. H. Clark, Henry Bradford, J. C. Campbell, Joseph Venable, Josiah Craine, Samuel Wilson and James Stokes. They were authorized to establish county and district societies and also to appoint an inspector "to examine and determine the quality and purity of all drugs and medicines offered for sale in the territory." This association evidently did not materialize, for two years later the legislature chartered another "Nebraska Medical Society," naming as incorporators: A. Chapel, W. R. Thrall, J. P. Peck, A. McElwee and George L. Miller, of Omaha; A. B. Malcolm, of Florence; John C. Campbell and A. Bowen, of Nebraska City; Andrew S. Holliday, of Brownville; and E. A. Donelan, of Plattsmouth. These gentlemen evidently realized the magnitude of the task of having an inspector examine all the drugs and medicines offered for sale in Nebraska, for the authority to appoint such an official was not given by their charter.

The first meeting of the physicians of Omaha was held about 1857 or 1858 to adopt a fee bill for mutual protection; and the first meeting looking toward an organization of a medical society was held June 14, 1866. At this time Omaha had begun to attract attention in the States east of the Missouri, and as a result immigration was drawn to this point, and with it the physicians rushed in. The first to come were young men, who had in some capacity been engaged in the army, and after the disbandment in 1865 had resumed the study of medicine and been graduated the following year. Of these Dr. R. C. Moore and I. N. Rippey came in the fall of 1865; Drs. C. H. Pinney, S. D. Mercer, and George Tilden in 1866; Dr. V. H. Coffman in 1867. Dr. J. H. Peabody was stationed in Omaha as an army surgeon in 1863, and returned to permanently settle in 1866.

The Omaha Medical Society was organized, with a constitution prepared to meet every emergency which might arise in the next fifty years, August 1, 1866, with the following membership: Augustus Roeder, I. N. Rippey, J. H. Peabody, C. H. Pinney, R. C. Moore, S. D. Mercer, L. F. Babcock, J. R. Conkling, J. P. Peck, William McClelland, E. H. Den, Enos Lowe, G. C. Monell. The following were the first officers, who were chosen November 12, 1866: President, Dr. Peck; vice-president, Dr. Roeder; secretary, Dr. Rippey; treasurer, Dr. Peabody.

At the preliminary meeting held June 14, 1866, Dr. Enos Lowe was chairman and Dr. Rippey acted as secretary. The following preamble and resolution was adopted:

"WHEREAS, the regular practitioners of medicine in the City of Omaha, Nebraska, feel the importance of some organization for the advancement and promotion of medical science, as well as for the mutual protection and welfare of its members; be it

"*Resolved*, that we, the undersigned, do agree to form among ourselves (and the regular practitioners of medicine who may from time to time be admitted) an association to be known as the Omaha Medical Society, of Omaha."

December 17, 1866, a very comprehensive fee bill was adopted, not only setting forth the prices to be charged for ordinary professional services, but also naming the remuneration to be demanded for the various simple surgical operations and venereal diseases. No mention was made of the capital operations, or other operations requiring abdominal section. It was a very sensible fee bill and a very important factor in binding together the profession for mutual protection. The fee for services for opinion upon life insurance was set at five dollars, which has

still continued to be the fee demanded by the physicians in this city, and paid by all reliable companies which have done business in Omaha. At that time the usual fee in the eastern States was from two to three dollars. This bill established the fees for professional services at that early day in our city, and by common consent has been accepted by both regular and irregular physicians from that time to the present. Those doctors of Omaha's younger days had a very slippery sort of men to deal with, and the fee bill was generally looked upon as the only means of self protection.

At a meeting held February 10, 1868, preliminary steps were taken to organize a State medical society, which in the following June culminated in perfecting the association. To-day this association is in a most flourishing condition, having held annual meetings up to the present time, having a constantly increasing membership, and ranking with the best State organizations of this character in the Union.

A special meeting was held February 12, 1868, to take measures for procuring the body of Ottway G. Baker, who was to be hanged for murder February 14th. A committee was appointed to petition the judge of the district court for the purpose. On the 24th, this committee made quite a voluminous report, setting forth that the judge first acceded to their request, but later, on account of the strenuous opposition of the Catholic priest who was Baker's spiritual advisor revoked the order. The society coincided with the committee in condemning the action of the judge, who thus denied to science an opportunity to investigate a very important matter, by his vacillating course. The priest also was quite severely criticized. On March 9, 1868, this society voted twenty-five dollars to defray expenses incurred in the interest of members of the society, on condition that a certain skeleton should, as soon as convenient, be turned over to the society. What connection this action may have had with the removal of the body of Baker, which the society claimed, or the bones of some other individual, there is nothing in the transactions of the society to indicate. The crime which Baker expiated upon the gallows was one of the most cold blooded and atrocious which has ever occurred in the history of this city, and, since several members of the medical profession were more or less intimately connected with the prosecution, from the finding of the body of the victim in a burning building to the expiation of the crime on the gallows, they very naturally felt greatly aggrieved at the action of the court in this matter.

The meetings of the Omaha Medical Society were held with considerable regularity, and the scientific work accomplished was quite commendable, up to about 1877, when, through internal dissension and the withdrawing of the more active members, it became practically moribund, and finally expired about 1881. The last meeting was held July 18, 1881, and an effort was made toward another meeting, September 5, 1881, with the result as recorded, "no quorum."

Following this date, a period of nearly two years rolled by before the restless spirit of organization again aroused itself in the medical profession of Omaha. Upon the evening of April 11, 1883, Drs. James Carter, J. M. Swetnam, J. B. Ralph and George B. Ayres met at the parlors of the Creighton House, for the purpose of taking steps looking to the organization of a county medical society. A committee was appointed to draw up and publish a call to the physicians of Douglas County to meet for the above purpose. In response to this call, twenty-eight of the physicians of this county met at the Millard Hotel on April 18, 1883, the organization was perfected with the following officers: president, Dr. H. Link, first vice-president, Dr. J. M. Swetnam, second vice-president, Dr. J. H. Peabody, secretary, Dr. James Carter, treasurer, Dr. L. B. Graddy, board of censors, Drs. G. B. Ayres, J. B. Ralph, L. A. Merriam, R. C. Moore and A. A. Parker. The charter members were, in addition to those mentioned above, Drs. V. H. Coffman, Ewing Brown, C. T. Wood, S. K. Spaulding, L. F. McKenna, P. S. Leisenring, R. W. Colville, W. O. Bridges, P. Grossman, S. D. Mercer, Joseph W. Search, W. S. Gibbs, Harry Durham, M. A. Rebert, H. P. Jensen, J. C. Denise and J. M. Woodburn.

During almost three years succeeding this organization, meetings of the society were held semi-monthly or monthly and great interest prevailed. Many papers of value were read and the work of the members was highly satisfactory. In the spring of 1884, the Nebraska State Medical Society held its annual meeting in Omaha and was entertained at a banquet by the Douglas County society, the sum of $360.00 being collected for that purpose. The officers of the society in 1884 were: president, Dr. J. H. Peabody; first vice-president, Dr. G. B. Ayres; second vice-president, Dr. G. A. Arbuckle; secretary, Dr. James Carter; treasurer. Dr. M. A. Rebert; censors, Drs. W. O. Bridges, L. A. Merriam, S. K. Spaulding, L. B. Graddy, J. M. Swetnam.

In 1885 the officers were: Dr. James Carter, president; Dr. J. B. Ralph, first vice-president; Dr. W. P. Wilcox, second vice-president; Dr. W. O. Bridges, secretary; Dr. M. A. Rebert, treasurer; Drs. L. A. Merriam, L. B. Graddy, J. M. Swetnam, W. O. Bridges and E. E. Womersley, board of censors. In 1886 Dr. R. C. Moore was chosen president; Dr. E. E. Womersley, first vice-president; Dr. Eleanor S. Dailey, second vice-president; Dr. E. A. Kelly, secretary; Dr. L. A. Merriam, treasurer; and the board of censors were: Drs. J. M. Swetnam, James Carter, L. B. Graddy, M. A. Rebert and E. A. Kelly.

During the early part of 1886, the attendance upon the meetings was very small. Some had withdrawn, owing to their having taken offense at remarks made in discussions of the papers. From various causes others had lost interest. Many of the older practitioners had allowed their business affairs to so interfere with their duties in the society that they were rarely present. In short, a process of disintegration had been under way for some time, and had arrived at such a stage of advancement that at the meeting of May 4, 1886, at which the above officers were elected, a motion was carried "that, when we adjourn, we adjourn *sine die.*" Notwithstanding this action, meetings were held from time to time through the year, and in the fall a strong effort was made to revive the declining vigor of the organization.

Perhaps the greatest obstacle met with was the impossibility of dropping a large number of members who were so in name only. This was owing to the fact that to do so a larger number of voters must be present, under the constitution, than were able to be obtained. After several ineffectual efforts at re-organization, the final meeting of the society occurred on March 1, 1887, at which "no essayist responded to the call" and the society adjourned. The experience of the Douglas County Medical Society was, during the greater portion of its history, one of success, and yet it contained within itself the elements of decay, as the event proved.

The Omaha Medical Club was the next society organized among the Omaha doctors. The most striking characteristic of this infant organization was simplicity. During the first year succeeding January 4, 1888, the date of its birth, it possessed no written constitution or laws of any description whatever. It was mutually agreed among its members that it existed for scientific work solely, and that the discussion of all personal differences and of all questions of medical ethics should be prohibited. Membership in this club was open to any reputable graduate of any "regular" medical college, but no one was regarded as a full-fledged member until he had read a paper

Yours Fraternally
James H. Peabody

before the club upon some subject relating to the practice of medicine. The meetings were held at the office of the essayist of the occasion, who was also the presiding officer at that meeting. Throughout the whole period of the existence of this organization meetings were held semi-monthly, except during July and August. There was never a failure to secure a quorum, seven members, and on only one occasion did the essayist fail to do his part. The following is a list of the physicians who became members during the first year: A F Jonas, R M Stone, J E Summers, Jr, H Gifford, S R Towne, A B Somers, H W Hyde, W F Milroy, L A Merriam, W L Ross, Eleanor Dailey, B F Crummer, C M G Biart, Mary Strong, James Carter, Robert Gilmore, L B Graddy.

At the completion of the first year of existence, a discussion was had by the members of the club upon the general good of the organization. It was thought that there was a possibility of error on the side of extreme simplicity of organization as well as in the opposite direction. It was therefore thought best to formulate in writing the hitherto unwritten regulations of the club, which was done in a series of twenty-three rules. These rules included a statement of the points already referred to, and further specified that a failure to provide a paper, at the time such paper shall be due from any member by regular rotation, shall terminate the membership of the individual thus delinquent, as shall also his absence from four consecutive meetings, sickness or prolonged absence from the city alone excusing, that candidates for membership shall have been residents of Omaha for at least one year, unless a full-fledged member can vouch for his previous good character, and two negative ballots shall exclude from membership. Other minor matters were also touched upon.

The papers produced by the members of the club were, as a rule, very meritorious

and the discussions spirited and interesting. At the termination of the second year of work, in January, 1890, an evening was devoted to a banquet at the Murray Hotel, which proved an enjoyable affair. The following physicians were members in addition to those already mentioned: Clark Gapen, H C Van Gieson, W H Slabaugh, M Helfritz Jonas, J P Lord, A W Riley, W H Christie and J F Presnell.

The conditions which surrounded the Omaha Medical Club were not favorable to its ever securing a large membership, nor was this the design of its originators. Owing to these facts, and possibly, in some degree, to a healthy spirit of rivalry, a new society appeared to contest the field early in 1888. This organization, called the Omaha Academy of Medicine, was perfected in May of the above year. Its organization was modeled after that of the New York Academy of Medicine, with the following officers: President D C Bryant, M D, first vice-president George B Ayres, M D, second vice-president, James H Peabody, M D, secretary C P Harrigan, M D, treasurer, Ewing Brown, M D, board of trustees, Drs John C Jones, A P Ginn, W F Milroy, J P Lord, and Charles Rosewater. The membership of this academy was limited to thirty and constituted, in addition to the officers, as follows: B F Crummer, A W Edmiston Wm H Galbraith, Oscar Hoffman, M A Hughes, H P Jensen, P C. Keogh, W G Kemper, R C Moore. L. F. McKenna, W L McClannahan, A A Parker, J B Ralph. George Tilden W C Reeves, J E Summers, Jr, H C Van Gieson, J H Vance E E Womersley. During a few months following the organization, the regular semi-monthly meetings were held, though a quorum, ten members, was seldom present. From its inception, the Adademy of Medicine appeared never to have rightly secured a hold upon life; and, having struggled through a sickly existence of one years duration. it fell into a quiet sleep from which no one has had the heart to awake it. *Requiescat in pace.*

A feeling existed in the profession, even prior to the date of organization of the two societies last described, that there should be, in a city of the size and importance of Omaha, a medical society that might include within its membership all practitioners within the city who deserved to be recognized as regular and reputable. Such an association was in demand; first, to give tone and standing to individual practitioners; secondly, to promote a feeling of harmony and community of interest among all members of the profession and discourage hurtful rivalries; thirdly, to take cognizance of the enforcement of such laws relating to the practice of medicine as existed, and endeavor to improve these where they were found deficient; and fourthly, and most important of all, to stimulate to scientific work the members. This feeling continued to gain ground, notwithstanding the organizations of 1888, it being alleged that they were exclusive and did not meet the demand. Accordingly, in response to an invitation by postal card, a meeting was held at the Paxton Hotel on March 18, 1890. About sixty-five of the leading physicians were present and effected a temporary organization by the election of Dr. B. F. Crummer, chairman, and Dr. Charles Rosewater, secretary. After a general discussion of the considerations involved, a committee to draft a constitution and by-laws was appointed, and the meeting adjourned for one week. At the appointed time the committee reported, and the organization was perfected with the following officers: President, W. F. Milroy, M. D.; first vice-president, B. F. Crummer, M. D.; second vice-president, A. F. Jonas, M. D.; secretary, Charles Rosewater, M. D.; treasurer, S. K. Spaulding, M. D.; board of censors, Drs. D. C. Bryant, W. H. Christie and J. P. Lord.

The following is a list of physicians who have become members of this society: Dewitt C. Bryant, C. M. G. Biart, Bennett C. Anderson, Frederick Bacon, W. O. Bridges, H. L. Burrell, Benjamin F. Crummer, E. W. Chase, Howard Cook, W. H. Chritsie, J. C. Denise, A. W. Edmiston, Harold Gifford, Clark Gapen, Robert Gilmore, W. S. Gibbs, C. P. Harrigan, H. P. Hamilton, H. P. Jensen, A. F. Jonas, M. Helfritz Jonas, John C. Jones, L. J. Kohnstamm, P. S. Leisenring, J. P. Lord, W. F. Milroy, L. A. Merriam, Joseph Neville, A. A. Parker, Alfred Raymond, M. A. Rebert, M. O. Ricketts, A. W. Riley, Charles Rosewater, A. B. Somers, S. K. Spaulding, John E. Summers, Jr., S. R. Towne, H. C. Van Gieson, W. P. Wilcox, George P. Wilkinson, E. E. Womersley, E. E. Sloman, R. C. Moore, R. S. Knode, S. B. Gillett, J. C. Aiken, W. R. Lavender, J. T. Presnell, Eleanor S. Dailey, F. E. Coulter, John D. Peabody, Mary Strong, Robert McDonald, W. O. Henry, J. A. A. Kelley, Thomas Kelley, W. L. Ross, Hannah C. McCahan, E. Holovtschiner, Paul Grossman, W. O. Rodgers, J. T. Mathews, H. W. Hyde, Andrew Crawford, Wm. M. Davis, G. S. Milnes, A. H. Jago, C. C. Allison, Gertrude Cuscaden, W. M. Brown, H. M. McClanahan, C. F. Clark, C. Riis, W. M. Barritt, L. F. McKenna, T. S. Owen, Sherman Van Ness, Joseph McDonnell, B. F. Whitmore, Fred Swartzlander, J. E. Claussen, H. L. Hewetson. From its beginning the Omaha Medical Society has gone steadily forward with its scientific work, in a manner highly creditable to the profession it represents. It also took an active part in the labor of securing the enactment of, and putting in force, the medical law of 1891.

The plan of this organization is simple, yet comprehensive, and it would seem that the time has come when the profession of medicine in Omaha is big enough, in respect both to numbers and spirit, to effectually frown down any internal convulsions that may threaten to disrupt the new society; that

there are, in other words, enough physicians among its members who place in higher estimation their divine art than the prosecution of personal animosities. Thus, there may be a grand future in store for this new association. Out of its labors may develop results great enough to shed the brightness of their influence, not over this city and State alone, but around the very world. Let it not be understood from these animadversions that the physicians of Omaha have been, as a profession, given over to petty contentions and petty jealousies. It is a thread-bare topic—the alleged unfriendly feeling among doctors. The failure to perpetuate the various associations which have been from time to time inaugurated in Omaha by no means demonstrates the truth of this. The temporary character of some of these has been due to causes already referred to. No profession or association of human beings, of whatever sort, can hope to escape the infliction of one or more mischief makers among their number, and the medical profession of Omaha is, alas! no more fortunate than others.

In the spring of 1869 the first school of medicine in the State of Nebraska was organized in the City of Omaha, under the name of the Omaha Medical College. The college was incorporated under the laws of the State with the following individuals as trustees, viz: J. P. Peck, M. D.; S. D. Mercer, M. D., J. C. Denise, M. D.; H. P. Mathewson, M. D., and James H. Peabody, M. D. The incorporation took place May 22, 1869. The following are the chairs which were established and the gentlemen who were chosen to occupy them: Anatomy, descriptive and surgical, H. P. Mathewson, M. D.; physiology and histology, Richard C. Moore, M. D.; principles and practice of surgery and clinical surgery, S. D. Mercer, M. D.; principles and practice of medicine and clinical medicine, J. P. Peck, M. D.; materia medica and therapeutics, James H. Peabody, M. D.; chemistry and toxicology, George Tilden, M. D.; obstetrics and diseases of puerperal women and children, V. H. Coffman, M. D.; general pathology and morbid anatomy, C. H. Pinney, M. D.; medical and surgical diseases of women, Jacob C. Denise, M. D.; physical diagnosis and diseases of the chest and throat, vacant, and medical jurisprudence, James W. Savage, Esq.

A good deal of work was done by the trustees in arranging the preliminary details looking to the opening of the college, but, owing to various obstacles in the way, and a growing feeling among those thus occupied that the enterprise was premature, it was abandoned.

In 1880 was organized the Nebraska School of Medicine, Preparatory. The following statement, taken from the records of the institution, expresses briefly the object and aim of the institution.

"It is the mature judgment of our leading physicians, as well as prominent citizens of other business pursuits, that the time has arrived for the establishment of a medical school in our State. After deliberate consultation as to demands and the available means of conducting such an enterprise, the school has been organized under the name and title of the Nebraska School of Medicine, and located at Omaha, a city of upwards of 32,000 inhabitants, and growing rapidly, supported by a State with 500,000 people, and with well established commercial relations existing between it and adjoining States and territories.

"The school for the present will be preparatory simply, but the instruction given will be thorough in all branches. Each chair will be represented by a man of experience and ability in his respective department. A number of eastern schools of medicine have established graded courses and allow students who are far enough advanced to enter higher classes, hence, students in the West can attend our school for one or two terms and then be admitted to advanced classes of other schools, when their proficiency will warrant such advancement."

The course of instruction continued for twenty weeks, beginning the middle of October. The instruction was by didactic, clinical and practical work. The following prominent physicians constituted the faculty: R. R. Livingston, M. D.; S. D. Mercer, M. D.; A. S. v. Mansfelde, M. D.; George B. Ayres, M. D.; J. C. Denise, M. D.; P. S. Leisenring, M. D.; Richard C. Moore, M. D.; and W. S. Gibbs, M. D. The school opened as proposed, and had in attendance fourteen students, of whom two were women.

The success of the Nebraska School of Medicine encouraged those engaged in it to go a step farther, and they organized, upon this foundation, the Omaha Medical College. A board of trustees was elected, consisting of the following physicians: R. R. Livingston, V. H. Coffman, G. B. Ayres, S. D. Mercer, P. S. Leisenring, J. C. Denise, R. C. Moore, G. H. Peebles and W. S. Gibbs.

At the request of those interested in the establishment of this college, the stockholders of the Omaha Medical Society, incorporated in 1869, surrendered their charter and the same name was assumed by the new corporation. The incorporation of the present Omaha Medical College was effected on the 14th day of June, 1881. The professorships established were: Dr. R. R. Livingston, principles and practice of surgery; Dr. V. H. Coffman, principles and practice of medicine; Dr. George B. Ayres, anatomy, descriptive and surgical; Dr. S. D. Mercer, clinical surgery; Dr. P. S. Leisenring, obstetrics and diseases of women; Dr. G. H. Peebles, diseases of children; Dr. J. C. Denise, physiology, ophthalmology and otology; Dr. R. C. Moore, materia medica and therapeutics; A. S. v. Mansfelde, histology and general pathology; Dr. James Carter, chemistry and toxicology; Dr. H. P. Mathewson, diseases of the mind; Dr. W. S. Gibbs, demonstrator of anatomy; and J. C. Cowin, Esq., medical jurisprudence.

Two lots were purchased at the corner of Eleventh and Mason Streets, and upon these a building was erected at a cost of about $4,500. The most serious obstacle that appeared in the way of success was found to be the lack of clinical material. To meet this difficulty an arrangement was effected with the management of St. Joseph Hospital, whose property was immediately adjoining that of the college, by which the students of the college were admitted to the wards of the hospital.

As is almost universally true in the history of cities whose growth is so phenomenal in its rapidity as has been that of Omaha, the citizens are so engrossed in the development of such private and public improvements as are absolutely essential to the comfort of the productive portion of the community, that the establishment of hospitals, asylums and eleemosynary institutions in general does not keep pace with the growth of the city's population. In Omaha this has been true. The want of hospital facilities has been seriously felt by the community at large. Those medical colleges which have the most extensive clinical facilities, up to a certain point, are, at the present day, regarded as being better equipped for furnishing a thorough and practical medical education. In the growth and prosperity of this city, the Omaha Medical College would be naturally expected to share, by reason of extended clinical facilities. However, owing to the fact just alluded to, material which would have been available in abundance for clinical instruction, had there been suitable hospitals, has been of no benefit to the college until recently.

It has therefore been with the odds strongly against it that whatever growth the college has experienced has been attained. In spite of these untoward circumstances, continued and substantial progress has been

made. This has been most marked in respect to the character of the instruction given, the improvements in the college building and the elevation of the standard of requirements demanded for graduation. For several years past a large majority of those graduated have attended during three full sessions of the college, and with the session of 1891-2 the graded course, occupying three years, became obligatory.

In 1887, the college building was removed to the corner of Twelfth and Pacific Streets, where it now stands. It was also much improved and enlarged by the construction of an additional story.

Numerous changes have occurred in the personnel of the faculty from time to time since the establishment of the college. In 1882, Donald Macrae, M.D., of Council Bluffs, became a member of the faculty as professor of gynecology, and has remained in various capacities to the present time. In 1883, Ewing Brown, M. D., was elected to the position of demonstrator of anatomy, and in the following year was made professor of anatomy, which chair he continues to occupy. In 1884, Dr. L. F. McKenna became a member of the faculty, as professor of clinical medicine, which position he held until 1889, when he resigned to be succeeded by Dr. W. O. Bridges. In 1884, also, Dr. W. F. Milroy accepted the position of demonstrator of anatomy. He occupied this position during two sessions of the college, after which he was transferred to the professorship of histology, general pathology and hygiene. In 1891 he was assigned to a new chair of clinical medicine, retaining the subject of hygiene. General pathology and histology were given in charge of Drs. H. L. Hewetson and W. R. Lavender respectively. Dr. L. D. Abbott, of Fremont, Nebraska, was in 1884 elected professor of theory and practice of medicine, and occupied that position two years. In 1886, Dr. Joseph Neville was elected professor of clinical surgery. In 1887, Dr. J. E. Summers, Jr., was elected to, and still occupies, the chair of principles and practice of surgery.

In 1890, a number of changes were made. Dr. W. H. Christie was elected to the chair of materia medica and therapeutics, made vacant by the resignation of Dr. Carter, Dr. H. C. Van Gieson was chosen professor of physiology, while Dr. Gibbs was associated with Dr. Macrae in the chair of theory and practice of medicine. Dr. C. M. G. Biart was appointed lecturer on dermatology, and Dr. Harold Gifford, lecturer on bacteriology. Laboratories were established this year, also, for the purpose of affording practical instruction in histology and pathology.

In 1891, by a mutual agreement between the parties interested, the Omaha Medical College became the medical department of the University of Omaha, the chancellor of the university thereby becoming an officer of the medical college.

This year also witnessed material changes in the faculty of the college. Dr. George Wilkinson succeeded Dr. Van Gieson in the chair of physiology; Dr. F. S. Thomas, of Council Bluffs, having previously assisted Dr. Macrae, was elected professor of diseases of the mind, and Dr. Oscar Hoffman assumed the duties of the chair of dermatology.

In 1892 three of the incorporators of the college who, throughout its history, had been among its most active workers, withdrew from the faculty. These were Dr. R. C. Moore, Dr. P. S. Leisenring and Dr. G. H. Peebles. They were succeeded respectively by Drs. H. M. McClanahan, E. W. Chase and Sherman Van Ness. These changes came about, not through any unfriendly feeling on the part of college or professor, but because of circumstances in each case on account of which each wished to be relieved of his duties to the college.

Further alterations were effected in the assignment of Dr. Wilkinson to the new chair of electro-therapeutics, Dr. C. C. Allison assuming that of physiology; Dr. A. F. Jonas succeeded Dr. Neville as professor of clinical surgery; Dr. Gifford, in addition to bacteriology, was made clinical professor of ophthalmology and otology, and Drs. D. Y. Graham and C. L. Mullins were made assistants to the demonstrator of anatomy.

It thus appears that by making the numerous changes in the faculty that have been enumerated, and adding from time to time those having made a special study of the several departments of medical science, who have made Omaha their home, the college has acquired a corps of instructors who are competent to furnish a medical education broad and deep.

The completion of Immanuel Hospital, an institution most excellent in its management and equipment, which is under the exclusive medical control of members of the staff of this college; the well known good character of the Clarkson Memorial Hospital, which also derives its medical service from this faculty; the large aggregation of the sick in the Douglas County Hospital; and the Methodist Hospital, whose good character is attested by its constant inability to accommodate the applicants requiring its service—both practically under the above medical management—all combine to give the college every desired clinical advantage.

It thus appears that Omaha, as the metropolis of a vast territory, offers the residents thereof facilities for securing a medical education that are unsurpassed.

On May 30, 1892, was founded the John A. Creighton Medical College, being the medical department of The Creighton University. The following physicians constitute the faculty of this institution:

A. W. Riley, Paul Grossman, W. J. Galbraith, B. F. Crummer, P. S. Keogh, H. P. Jensen, J. P. Lord, J. H. Peabody, D. C. Bryant, H. L. Burrell, S. K. Spaulding, W. R. Martin, C. Rosewater, F. E. Coulter, W. M. Barritt, J. D. Peabody, A. Johnson, G. H. Brash, together with Mr. W. S. Robinson.

As yet this faculty has not had the opportunity to demonstrate its right to exist. It surely is not, however, too much to expect that a body of men of such eminent ability, laboring together under the auspices of so important an institution of learning, will do much to advance the interests of medical science, and to establish the importance of Omaha as a centre of medical education, of the most thorough character.

It is to the periodical literature that we must look for the general diffusion of knowledge in medicine, as well as in other departments of thought. With competent observers the experience of all is equally valuable and it is the record of this experience that, taken together, comprises the sum of knowledge.

In March, 1887, Mr. H. J. Penfold established the *Omaha Clinic*, a monthly periodical designed to further the interests of medicine in this portion of the west. Through the difficulties of its early struggle for existence the *Clinic* was successfully lead by Dr. J. C. Denise, as editor. The *Clinic* is now edited by Dr. George Wilkinson, under whose management it has made steady advancement in excellence.

In April, 1892, the Omaha Microscopic Society was formed. Its membership consisted almost entirely of physicians, and its object was the perfecting of its members in the use of the microscope in the study of normal and diseased structures in connection with the practice of medicine. Its membership has reached about thirty, and it gives every evidence of enjoying a long and useful life.

Prior to 1891 all efforts to secure the legislation necessary to protect the people of Nebraska from being a prey to medical quacks had been of little avail. The consequence was that Nebraska occupied a position in the rear of the states in their progress in this direction.

In the spring of 1890, agitation was commenced with renewed energy to secure the much needed legislation. While notable service was rendered in this work by a num-

ber of physicians, not residents of the city, Omaha may fairly lay claim to the credit of the splendid results which were achieved. The funds needed for pushing the work were contributed mainly, though not entirely, by Omaha physicians, and a great amount of effort was given by them. Attorneys were employed to draft a bill. Candidates for the legislature were interviewed and pledged to the support of adequate medical legislation, in case of their election. Physicians were present continuously, during the session of the legislature, to resist the efforts, thoroughly organized, to defeat the measure. In short, it was only by the most untiring vigilance and earnestness of effort that the law of March, 1891, was secured.

This much having been accomplished, in order that the law might not join the throng of "dead letters" upon the statute books, the Douglas County Medico-Legal Association was organized in Omaha on July 31, 1891. The officers of the association were: Dr. Joseph Neville, president; Dr. E. E. Womersley, vice-president; Dr. George Wilkinson, secretary, and Dr. C. G. Sprague, treasurer.

This association was not intended to take the place of the authorities established by the new law for its enforcement, but only to second their efforts. Shortly before the enactment of the new law, a strong effort had been made by the Omaha Medical Society to enforce the then existing law of 1881 and 1883. It was the special design to ascertain, by its practical application, wherein this law was defective. The result of this effort was that many of the quacks were driven from the State; and yet many points were discovered at which there was great room for improvement in the laws. After the organization of the medico-legal association, the work of the Omaha Medical Society in this direction received the attention of the former organization. It was through its agency that proofs were furnished and prosecutions carried to successful issue in Omaha, and the army of quacks completely routed.

Mere show of force was in many cases enough, others fought it out and were defeated.

No effort was made in this bill to create a sanitary board in the state board of health, as a concentration of effort upon the one question—the regulation of the practice of medicine—was thought to promise better results. It is true that, in most of the states, sanitary measures have preceded the medical practice act, but the course adopted here was so successful that the law which now governs the practice of medicine in Nebraska is superior to that of any state in the Union.

It is frequently remarked that large cities are a detriment to the State in which they are found, but in this instance at least, Nebraska owes to Omaha her heart-felt thanks.

It should be added that the work of the medical profession above described was earnestly seconded by the homeopathic and eclectic schools in the State.

The medical profession of Omaha needs no apologist. Contentions and cut-throat methods and misunderstandings there may have been in years gone by, but, like the city itself, the profession having come to maturity, has put away such childish things as these. It is pervaded, to a marked degree, by a spirit of harmony and of earnest work for the advancement of medical science and the honor of the profession. The standard of attainment of its representatives is an elevated one, and Omaha may well take pride in her medical sons and daughters, as also may any man or woman feel honored in being known as an Omaha physician.

[Dr. W. H. Hanchett contributes the following sketch of the homeopathic practitioners of Omaha.]

Homeopathy in Nebraska has had a happy growth. This school of medicine, born with the immortal Hahnemann, in 1755, may be likened unto this beautiful State—though in existence for past ages, yet unknown to man and only a waste; but, when discovered, at once blooming into beauty and usefulness. The soil in this young State seemed fertile for the thrifty plant of the new school, and it has grown commensurate with Nebraska's wealth and population.

Homeopathy was very fortunate in having for its first representative here Dr. A. S. Wright, now of Santa Rosa, California. Dr. Wright came to Omaha when it was the capital of the territory, in 1862. He was a bright, ambitious young physician of more than ordinary ability, a graduate of the Pulte Medical College of Cincinnati. After practicing a short time in Indiana, he came to the then young and prosperous City of Omaha to cast his lot and fortune with those sturdy young men who had the eye of faith to see that the little city of 2,000 or 2,500 souls would be multiplied by hundreds in the near future and that the "star of empire" would surely "westward take its way." The homes that were visited by the doctor were among the comfortable ones of the city and the names enrolled on his ledgers have played prominent parts in the history, not only of the city, but of the State. Dr. Wright was among those who bought property in these early times, and we are glad to know that a man who has borne his burden so successfully, so manfully, can rest in a competency in his declining years.

Homeopathy then, even in those early days, had a strong exponent in Dr. A. S. Wright, and he laid a firm foundation for the wonderful popularity which has ever characterized the school in Omaha and Nebraska. From 1862 to 1868 he was the only homeopath in the State, and the only homeopath in Omaha till 1868. In that year came Dr. W. H. H. Sisson from New Bedford, Massachusetts, a man of fine presence and genial nature, bringing with him the attainments of a first-class surgeon. He died in Omaha in 1873.

Following Dr. Sisson, in 1868, came Dr. O. S. Wood, who is with us yet. To Dr. Wood the school of homeopathy owes much. He has "borne the burden and heat of the day" in advancing the interests of its work in the State, and is still in active practice. Drs. Earhart and Manden came in the following year from Philadelphia. They formed a partnership and built up a lucrative practice. However, Dr. Earhart, through the influence of friends, moved to Fremont, in this State, where he afterwards gained a fine practice. Dr. F. Saxenberger came to Omaha in 1871, where he lived four years, afterwards leaving on account of his health. In the next year Dr. E. F. Hoyt came from Grand Rapids, Michigan, remaining in the city a short time in partnership with Dr. Wood. In 1874, Dr. J. M. Borglum, a student with Dr. Sisson, after graduating at the St. Louis Homeopathic Medical College, began practice in Omaha. He afterwards removed to Fremont; but, feeling that Omaha was to be the western commercial center, came back to the city and is in practice here at the present time. In 1875 came Dr. H. C. Jesson, from Chicago, and Dr. H. A. Worley, from Davenport. Dr. Worley came from a partnership with his father—who had done pioneer work for the school in Iowa—remained till 1879, when he returned to Davenport and staid there till the death of his father, when he again came to Omaha and entered partnership with Dr. C. M. Dinsmore. In 1878 Dr. C. M. Dinsmore, who died December 8, 1890, came to Omaha from Missouri. To no physician in the State is more credit due for earnest, effective work in furthering homeopathic interests in the matter of medical legislation.

In this same year came Dr. John Ahmanson, who, though he took up the study of medicine in later life, thoroughly mastered his profession. He was a member of the State Legislature in 1871, and enjoyed a lucrative practice till his death in August, 1891. In 1880 Miles B. Gifford came from New York and entered into a partner-

*Amelia Burroughs*

ship with Dr. Dinsmore, where he remained one year, returning to New York. The same year Dr. C. L. Hart came to our city. During the brief existence of the medical department of the State University of Nebraska, Dr. Hart occupied the chair of materia medica. In the succeeding years came Drs. G. H. Parsell, Francis M. Jackson, E. Stillman, B. Spencer, Amelia Burroughs, W. H. Hanchett, R. W. Connell, Mary J. Breckinridge, H. S. Knowles, C. G. Sprague, E. T. Allen, W. H. Parsons, Emma J. Davies, G. W. Williams, W. B. Willard, C. W. Hayes, E. L. Alexander, C. M. Campbell, J. W. Barnsdall, Mrs. H. B. Davies, Freda M. Lankton, W. A. Humphrey, D. A. Foote and H. P. Holmes. Among these are men and women who are ambitious, hard-working physicians, bearing in their hands diplomas earned by years of hard and patient work in the best colleges of our country; men and women who are abreast with the times; men and women who are not only practitioners, but standards; men and women who are to-day entering the households of the intelligence and wealth of this beautiful city.

The organization of a flourishing State medical society is largely due to Omaha physicians. In 1873 Dr. A. S. Wright gathered together eight physicians who met at Lincoln on the 2d day of September. Dr. E. M. Hurlbut was elected president and Dr. A. S. Wright first vice-president. Among Omaha physicians who have been president of the State society, and have done efficient work in furthering the interests in the State, are A. S. Wright, O. S. Wood, C. M. Dinsmore, C. L. Hart. The present officers of the society are: president, W. H. Hanchett, of Omaha; vice-president, W. A. Humphrey, of Plattsmouth; secretary, Willis Buck, of Minden; treasurer, O. S. Wood, of Omaha. Omaha has a successful local society, whose officers are: president, C. G. Sprague; vice-president, G. H. Parsell; secretary, Freda M. Lankton; treasurer, D. A. Foote.

Homeopathy has nothing to fear for the future. It is no longer a question whether it is a success or not. Hospital wards and sick rooms speak with no uncertain sound. It is known by its fruits, and demands at least the tolerance of all fair minded men and women. As to its future in Omaha, we may, at least, predict a continuance of the wonderful growth of the last few years. Men of scholarship and ripe learning are coming into its ranks every day, and find enough, and more than enough, for all to do.

Since writing the foregoing many changes have taken place in the local societies of Omaha and Nebraska, but the period has been one of prosperity and continued growth. A law was passed by the Nebraska State Legislature in 1891 with a view to the regulation of the practice of medicine in the State of Nebraska. One of the requirements of the law was that there should be four members of the State Medical Board of Health, two of which were to be appointed from the allopathic school, one from the homeopathic and one from the eclectic. Dr. E. T. Allen, of Omaha, was honored by the Governor of the State with the appointment of the secretaryship for the homeopathic school and he has done much towards the advancement of the interests of the homeopathic school. It may be remarked with a feeling of pride that this medical board recognize the diplomas of every homeopathic medical college in the United States, thus showing that our schools of medicine are thorough in the requirements of their graduates.

It may also be said that recently several members of the homeopathic school have been appointed to important positions on the staff of the Douglas County Hospital, which is supported by public tax.

# CHAPTER XXXIX.

DENTISTRY IN OMAHA—THE PIONEERS IN THAT LINE—IMPROVEMENTS OF LATER YEARS.

The first dentist locating in Omaha, was Rev. William Leach, who organized the first Baptist church; but he followed the business only to the extent of eking out his salary, somewhat, as a minister. Mr. Leach came here in 1855, remaining only a short time. Dr. Benjamin Stickles, the first fire warden in Omaha, located in this city in 1858, and had an office and residence on Harney Street just west of Twelfth; and, until 1866, he and a Dr. L. G. Canfield were the only dentists in the town. In 1866, Dr. Stickles, a strong, robust man, sold out his business to Dr. J. S. Charles, and went to New York State for the benefit of his wife's health, as she was an invalid. For several years he was employed as conductor on the Schenectady Railroad, and then died, his invalid wife surviving him. In the latter part of 1866, a Dr. Smith opened a dental office in a frame building on lower Farnam Street, used by Dewey & Stone as a furniture store, which building had been moved down from Florence. But he remained only a few months, and all of the dentistry business of Omaha was attended to by Dr. Charles and Dr. Canfield for two years, the former having his office in the Visscher Block, and the latter in the second story of what was then known as the Commercial Block, on the southwest corner of Douglas and Fourteenth, and later on, in the Cahn building, northeast corner of Farnam and Fourteenth. Then Dr. C. H. Paul and Dr. J. P. Porter came to divide the patronage, and Charles and Paul formed a partnership which continued for several years. In 1869, Dr. Bond, a son of Rev. Bond, the Unitarian clergyman, located here and had an office in the Commercial Block, but left the city in 1871. Dr. F. W. Thompson came to Omaha from Leavenworth, Kansas, in 1869, and in 1871 removed to Chicago. Dr. Thomas M. Barton established himself in business, in 1871, in an office in the Visscher Block, but did not remain long; and in the same year Dr. Robert H. Bohn opened an office at 181 (old number) Farnam Street. This number was on the north side of Farnam, between Thirteenth and Fourteenth, in which block several dental establishments were located, during a long period, and the name "Dentist Row," was given that locality. Dr. A. S. Billings came in 1873, and Dr. A. W. Nason the following year; and in 1875 the two formed a partnership under the name of Billings & Nason, which continued for half a dozen years or so. In 1874, Dr. Edward Neve, who had been a watchmaker with John Baumer, on lower Farnam Street, hung out his sign as a dentist at 171 Farnam (between Thirteenth and Fourteenth), after having qualified himself for that pursuit by a course of study. In 1879, Dr. A. P. Johnson, a student in the office of Charles & Paul, established himself in business on his own account, in "Dentist Row," where he has since remained. In April of that year Dr. G. W. Wertz located in Omaha, in a frame building standing where Mr. Samuel Burns' crockery store is now located. In December, 1881, he came near losing his life by a fire which destroyed a clothing store adjoining his office on the east. The stock in this store had been heavily insured a short time before, and an investigation made by the authorities resulted in one of the most noted criminal trials ever witnessed in this country. The insurance companies interested employed John M. Thurston, Esq., to assist District Attorny N. J. Burnham in prosecuting the case, the result being that two men served a term in the penitentiary for the crime of arson. Frank Currier, a well-known and popular photographer, occupied the upper floor of the building fired, and was asleep at the time in a room opening into his picture gallery. It was by the barest chance that he escaped with his life, losing all of his furniture, material and personal effects. He was never able to recover from this disaster, as he had no insurance; and, after a few years of struggles and disappointments, death came to his relief under circumstances which led to the belief on the part of his friends that it had not come unsought.

Omaha has now twenty-two dentists, the majority of them quartered in elegant offices, provided with all of the latest appliances and inventions in the dental line, and in this direction the inventive genius of the country has not been idle. Hence, though the extracting of molars has not yet become a luxury to be eagerly sought after, the operation is shorn of many of its old-time terrors; and the filling of dental cavities is now much more quickly and substantially done than in the days of Dr. Benjamin Stickles, the pioneer dentist and fireman of Omaha. The State boasts a dental association which holds annual meetings, and the Omaha members do their share in making those meetings profitable and interesting. It is the outgrowth of the Missouri Valley Association, organized some fifteen years ago, of which Dr. A. S. Billings was secretary several terms. The Nebraska Dental Association was organized in 1879.

Among the improvements in the dental business which have come into use in this city during the past few years, may be mentioned the dental engine patented by S. S. White, by means of which cavities are bored out in much less time than formerly. It is said that this invention was first applied to shearing sheep by an Ohio man, who was discouraged when he found that it clipped off the hide of the sheep as well as the wool, and that he then threw the machine aside as worthless. The idea was then elaborated by Mr. White, who secured a patent, and has made fame and fortune thereby. Gold crowns and enamel facings, now so common, were not known in Omaha dentistry of the early period, and the laboratory work of those days received no aid from the electrical apparatus now used. The electric mallet, by which two thousand strokes per minute may be given in driving the filling into a cavity, has supplanted the tedious process of former years, and in every particular the dentists of this city have kept pace with their brethren of the eastern cities.

# CHAPTER XL.

POLICE AND FIRE DEPARTMENTS — GREAT RESULTS FROM SMALL BEGINNINGS — THE PRESENT SYSTEM.

The police force of the city was organized in March, 1866, and consisted of four men. In March, 1868, the council concluded that "the wearing of some uniform dress by members of the police would give very general satisfaction," and the policemen were directed to provide themselves with "dark blue, single-breasted coats, trimmed in dark buttons, with pants of the same material, and caps with brass plate in front marked with the words 'city police,' said suits to be worn when the policemen are on duty."

The following year the force consisted of eighteen men, three for each ward and elected by the council. Maurice Sullivan was captain and Rodney Dutcher, lieutenant. The former resigned soon afterwards and Lieutenant Dutcher was promoted to the vacant position and A. P. Sanders elected lieutenant. In December, 1870, the city marshal recommended a reduction of the force, by the discharge of six men and the lieutenant, which recommendation was adopted by the council, an ordinance to that effect being passed January 31, 1871. Of the twelve men then constituting the force, ten were assigned to night duty and two to day service.

October 9, 1871, Mayor Caldwell sent to the council a message calling attention "to the probability of the personal property of our citizens being without the protection of insurance, in consequence of the unprecedented conflagration now raging in Chicago, involving the destruction of nearly the entire city, bankrupting, as it doubtless will, all the insurance companies of the city." As a measure of present safety, he recommended that the city marshal be instructed to employ a special police of night watchmen "to serve until the insurance of our people can be examined and re-adjusted, say ten days, or two weeks." The recommendation was adopted and a night force of twelve men appointed to serve two weeks.

In June, 1874, the office of captain of police was abolished and the force put under direct control of the city marshal, and so remained until 1887, when a law was passed by the legislature, creating a board of fire and police commissioners; early in May of that year Governor Thayer appointed as such board, L. M. Bennett, Christian Hartman, George I. Gilbert and Howard B. Smith, the mayor serving as a member ex-officio. Messrs. Bennett and Hartman were appointed for four years, and Messrs. Gilbert and Smith for two years, but were reappointed for four years in May, 1889.

The members of the board filed their oaths of office on the 10th day of May, met for the first time on the 11th, and on the 16th day of May adopted "rules and regulations governing the appointment, promotion, removal, trial and discipline of officers and men of the police department of Omaha" and filed the same with the city clerk on that day. On the 19th the board met to appoint a chief of police. There was quite a number of applicants for the position, but Webber S. Seavey was chosen.

Thus far there had been no conflict between the city council and the commission; but, immediately upon the appointment of Chief Seavey, a serious difficulty began. May 21st, Chief Seavey filed a bond in the sum of ten thousand dollars with the board, although there was no ordinance providing for such a bond, and although the act creating the commission had not provided for a bond. The bond was approved on that date by the board and was afterwards filed with the council. On the 25th of May, Chief of Police Seavey entered upon the duties of his office, ex-Marshal Cummings vacating. May 28th, the board appointed J. J. Galligan chief of the fire department.

On the 7th day of June, the majority of the committee on judiciary of the city council submitted the following report: "The judiciary committee, to whom was referred the pretended official bond of one Seavey, together with the report from the police committee, have had the same under consideration and report thereon as follows:

"First. That the board of fire and police commissioners, without the necessary rules and regulations to be prescribed by ordinance, have no authority to make any such appointment; and, as the ordinance to prescribe rules is under consideration by the council and has not passed, the pretended appointment is premature and uncalled for.

"Second. That no authority exists at the present time for the presentation of the pretended bond to the city council, and the same is not in form prescribed by any law now in existence. For these reasons we recommend that the pretended bond be rejected." This report was signed by I. S. Hascall, M. Lee and Leavitt Burnham; the minority of the committee recommended that the bond be accepted.

On June 14th, the city attorney gave an opinion in which he substantially approved the action taken by the board. On the 15th, the city council passed an ordinance requiring each commissioner to give a bond in the sum of five thousand dollars, which was done. The bonds of Commissioners Bennett and Hartman were approved by the council August 9, 1887, but the bonds of Commissioners Gilbert and Smith were rejected, for the reason that the names of the sureties who had signed the bonds, respectively, did not also appear in the body of those instruments as well. Therefore Gilbert and Smith filed new bonds, and presented them to the city council August 30th, which bonds the city council neglected either to approve or disapprove.

June 28th, the board appointed all the members of the fire department to the positions they had held before the existence of the board, and July 26th the board met for the purpose of examining applicants for positions on the police force, among whom were all the members of the old force, and July 28th appointed forty-two men, part of whom had been on the old force and part of whom were new men. July 29th, the board notified fourteen of the old members of the force that their services were no longer needed.

The city council had, from the first, refused to recognize Chief Seavey in his official capacity and had refused to pay him. The council now refused to recognize or to pay any of the appointees of the board who had not previously been on the force. The position taken by the board was, that the rules and regulations adopted by them would not have the force and effect of ordinances, unless approved by the city council, but would still have the force of rules and regulations which could, at any time, be repealed or modified by the board itself.

On the 1st of October, 1887, the board passed the following:

"WHEREAS, There is a dispute between the city council of the City of Omaha and the board of fire and police commissioners as to the duties and power of this board, and

"WHEREAS, This board is advised by its counsel that it has not the power to bring such a suit in the supreme court as will promptly and finally settle the relative powers and duties of this board and of the city council, and

"WHEREAS, the city council can do so; therefore

"*Resolved*, That the board respectfully

requests the city council to instruct the city attorney to request the attorney general of the State of Nebraska to bring an action to test the title of Webber S. Seavey, chief of police.

"WHEREAS, This board did, on the 30th day of August, 1887, approve the pay roll of the members of the police department for the month of August, 1887, and transmit the same to the council through the comptroller, and

"WHEREAS, The city council has refused to pay the salaries of certain of said police officers, due for the month of August, and

"WHEREAS, Some of said officers and their families are suffering for the necessities of life; and

"WHEREAS, Said men have faithfully served the city, and have given up other positions to accept the duties and responsibilities of police officers, to protect the life and property of the citizens of Omaha; therefore be it

"*Resolved*, That we respectfully but urgently request the city council to pay said men out of funds specially provided and available for that purpose."

No attention was paid to this request, and the council still refused to recognize Chief Seavey and the new appointees of the board, and still refused to pay their salaries. An indignation meeting of the citizens was called to meet at the board of trade rooms. There was much excitement, and resolutions were passed condemning the action of the city council. An association was formed, called the "Policemen's Relief Association," for the purpose of raising money to pay the salaries of the police until the city council should do so.

For a period of several months this association continued to pay the salaries of the chief of police and the policemen. Finally, Edward W. Simeral, county attorney, instituted suit in the supreme court to test by a proceeding in *quo warranto* the title of Chief Seavey to his office. Thereupon, the city council employed J. C. Cowin and G. W. Ambrose to represent the city, and filed an amendment to the petition in the supreme court, and also caused a proceeding in *quo warranto* to be instituted against the commissioners, to test their title to office.

These cases were argued together in the supreme court, George B. Lake appearing for Chief Seavey and the commissioners. The opinion of the supreme court is found at page 454 of volume 22, of Nebraska Reports. It sustains fully the legality of Chief Seavey's appointment and his title to his office, as well as the title of the commissioners. During all this time the city council had not paid the salaries of the commissioners. Thereupon, suit was begun in the district court against the city by the commissioners for their salaries, and judgment was rendered in their favor. The money advanced by the "Policemen's Relief Association" was also recovered in an action against the city in the district court.

The force, as now organized, is made up of a very superior body of men and is under excellent discipline, Chief Seavey having served during the late war as an officer of the Fifth Iowa Cavalry. On the 31st of December, 1891, the force consisted of eighty-eight men, viz.: one chief, two captains, one chief of detectives, three sergeants, four detectives, one court officer, two jailers, two patrol drivers, two patrol conductors, one sanitary officer, four mounted men and drivers and sixty patrol men.

In presenting his report for 1890, Chief Seavey made the following suggestions to the board of commissioners:

"First. That the honorable mayor and city council be requested to take action toward building a workhouse for this city.

"Second. That the police force be increased to one hundred and twenty-five men, and that two sergeants and two more detectives be appointed to go on duty May 1, 1891.

"Third. That an amount of money, not to exceed five hundred dollars, be set aside to be placed at the disposal of the chief of police for detective services, subject to the approval of the mayor and the finance committee of the board of fire and police commissioners.

"Fourth. That an examining board, consisting of the committee on men and discipline and the city physician, meet during the month of April in each year and examine every member of the police department as to his mental, moral and physical condition, and general fitness for police service, and report the result of their investigation to the board of fire and police commissioners.

"Fifth. That on the 1st day of May of each year the board of fire and police commissioners grade the police force as follows: Officers of the first grade to receive seventy-five dollars per month; officers of the second grade to receive seventy dollars per month; officers of the third grade to receive sixty dollars per month."

The amount paid policemen between December 31, 1890, and December 31, 1891, was $77,926.39.

There is a great deal of work done by the police. The sanitary and other police officers have served 5,000 notices, and abated 3,000 nuisances.

There have been 17,260 meals furnished to prisoners, sick, injured and destitute persons who have been brought to the station during the year, the expense of which amounts to $2,350.68.

Males arrested during the year, 6,386; females, 895. Number of days lost by policemen caused by sickness and accidents, 1,307; boys arrested under sixteen years, 145; accidents reported, 184; burglars frustrated, 6; attempted suicides, 3; dead bodies taken to morgue, 34; destitute persons cared for, 86; disturbances suppressed, 11; fire alarms recorded, 206; fires attended by police, 115; intoxicated persons arrested at home, 1; lodgers accommodated, 2,760; lost children found and sent home, 121; calls for patrol wagon, 3,140; nuisances and dead animals reported, 4,311; packages stolen property recovered, 259; prisoners taken to county jail, 1,280; runaway horses stopped 122; sick and injured persons taken to station, hospital or home, 169; suicides reported, 13.

The first reference made in the records of the city clerk's office with regard to providing for protection against fire appears under date of October 27, 1857, when Bovey, chairman of the fire committee, recommended the formation of a hook and ladder company and the purchase of two twenty-foot ladders, one forty-foot ladder and one sixty-foot ladder, which report was adopted. In November, Messrs. Schneider and Hurford submitted to the council a proposition to sell to the city a fire engine for $1,500, on one and two years time, but the proposition was rejected and Alderman Visscher appointed a committee to procure at once the hooks and ladders recommended by the fire committee. June 25th, 1860, the following communication was presented to the council:

"To the Hon. Mayor and City Council of Omaha: The undersigned officers of Pioneer Hook and Ladder Company No. 1, respectfully show to your honorable body that the said company is fully organized; that they have under contract and nearly completed a truck with the necessary hooks and ladders; that the whole will be complete and in running order on the 1st day of July, 1860, and that they are without a place to keep same. We therefore respectfully ask your honorable body to procure for us a proper place to keep the same." Signed by Benjamin Stickles, foreman; J. S. McCormick, first assistant foreman; W. J. Kennedy, treasurer; James W. Van Nostrand, secretary. Henry Gray, Henry Z. Curtis, M. H. Clark, A. J. Simpson and P. W. Hitchcock were also members of this company at the date of its organization. The constitution of the company was also presented and accepted and the clerk directed to issue certificates of membership to the officers and men. The communication was referred to the fire committee, who soon afterwards reported that they had secured a building for the use of the company on Twelfth Street. The following November Benjamin Stickles was elected fire warden of the city. Of the four persons named above all but Stickles are still residents of Omaha. In the summer of 1862 the city purchased of Redick and Briggs part of lot 1, in block 121, corner of Douglas and Twelfth, with a small building thereon, for $215 cash, for the use of the hook and ladder company. It is noted that this was a cash transaction, for in that early period in Omaha's history, in most of the deals in which the city was a purchaser, there was no cash available.

The first bell used to sound the alarm of fire in Omaha was that of the Lutheran Church, then situated on the site now occupied by the Millard Hotel, and very near the location of the hook and ladder company's house. As there were objections to having the church entered and the bell rung by persons not connected with the church, the pastor, Rev. H. W. Kuhns, then living close by, used to ring out the alarm. This bell was rung for every fire for several years, and until after the department had one of its own.

A special election was held May 25, 1862, to vote upon the proposition for the city to borrow eight hundred dollars to be used in buying a fire engine. There were only thirty-five votes cast at this election, all but one being in favor of plunging the city into debt to the amount stated, but evidently the credit of the city was not sufficiently established in the financial centers to secure a loan for that amount, for nothing was done in the premises until March, 1864, when the council appointed a committee " to ascertain the cost of a fire engine and apparatus, and a suitable number of cisterns to afford adequate protection against fire," and there the matter rested for a year and a half. In September, 1865, a council committee of three was appointed to solicit subscriptions for the purchase of a fire engine. This scheme evidently failed, for seven days later a special election was called for, October 14th, to vote for or against the city's making a loan of three thousand dollars in order to buy a fire engine, hose and hose cart. On this occasion 132 votes were cast and all in the affirmative, which shows that the residents of Omaha were a unit in recognizing the need of better facilities for subduing fires. In December following the mayor was authorized to contract with the Amoskeag Manufacturing Company for the purchase of a number three steam fire engine, hose carriage and 1,500 feet of hose at a price not exceeding eight thousand dollars. Two months later Alderman Charles H. Brown offered a resolution, reciting that the city's finances were in such condition that it would not pay more than five thousand dollars for a fire engine and that, "present and future expenses being considered, it will be wiser and more economical to rescind all action relative to the purchase of a steam fire engine and contract in place thereof for a good, smart, hand fire engine to cost not over the sum first herein mentioned." The resolution was adopted and the mayor was directed to telegraph the Amoskeag Manufacturing Company, rescinding the order to build a steam fire engine and to have the message repeated to insure certainty of transmission, which was done, at a cost of $14.92 for telegraph tolls. An effort was made to have the city purchase a hand engine which the hardware firm of Schneider & Hurford had brought to Omaha, but was not successful.

The following month, March, 1866, a special meeting of the council was held to consider a petition signed by two hundred citizens of Omaha, praying for the purchase by the city of a steam fire engine, and remonstrating against the purchase of any other. A resolution was adopted instructing the mayor to purchase a steam engine, at a cost not exceeding eight thousand dollars, providing the citizens of Omaha would take the three thousand dollars of city bonds previously voted, and also guarantee the payment of the remaining five thousand dollars. Four days later Alderman Andrew J. Simpson reported that, under the authority of the city, he had purchased a hand fire engine at Davenport, Iowa, and a resolution appropriating eight hundred dollars to pay for the same was adopted. At this meeting of the council the mayor was instructed " to confer with Messrs. Button and Blake, of Watertown, New York, in relation to the purchase of hose and a hose carriage, and report to the council as soon as possible." In May, 1866, Hook and Ladder Company No. 1 was directed to take charge of the " Fire King Engine," on its delivery at the levee, and on the 12th of July Fire Engine Company No. 1 was accepted as an organization by the council, and the Fire King engine was turned over to that company, which, with the hook and ladder company, was authorized to elect a chief engineer, who was to have control of both organizations. In August arrangements were made to purchase of Aaron Cahn lot one, block 140 (the lot now occupied by the Chamber of Commerce building and worth over $100,000), for $2,500, of which amount one thousand dollars was to be paid in cash, $750 in six months and the balance in one year, the deferred payments to bear ten per cent. interest. The following year a building was erected on this lot for engine purposes, by H. H. Visscher, at a cost of $4,241.61, for which he received city bonds, payable in one year. An effort had been made in the spring of 1867, to borrow $12,000 on the city's credit, for developing the fire department, but the council committee of three appointed for that purpose reported that the only offer they had was one from Mr. Edward Creighton to loan the city half the amount needed, taking city bonds at ninety cents on the dollar, the city to pay twelve per cent. interest on the face value of the bonds. [In this connection it is gratifying to note that Omaha city bonds, sold in April, 1889, bearing only five per cent. interest, brought a premium of eight and a quarter cents.]

In 1870 a second-class rotary steam engine and a thousand feet of rubber hose were bought of H. A. Silsby for $5,500, the price of the hose being two dollars per foot. At that time Omaha considered the city on the shore of Lake Michigan as a model, and upon receipt of the new engine christened it the " New Chicago No. 2."

From these beginnings have grown the splendid fire department possessed by Omaha. In 1870 the city was supplied with an electric alarm system, put in by Gamewell & Co. at a cost of five thousand dollars, with ten boxes and seven and a half miles of wire. There are now eighty-four alarm boxes, fifty miles of wire and four circuit repeaters. There are twelve engine houses which are fully equipped, eighty-eight men and twenty-five horses, three engines, twelve hose carts, two hook and ladder trucks and two chemical engines. The yearly expenses of the department are ninety-seven thousand dollars. In 1885 the change was made from a semi-volunteer to a full-paid department. Andrew J. Simpson, still a resident of Omaha, was one of the first officers of the department, having been elected chief in 1866. He was succeeded in that position in June, 1869, by Joseph F. Sheely, and he in turn by J. E. Markel, in 1871. In August, 1872, Charles Simpson was elected chief and was succeeded by Stephen N. Mealio, who was elected in March, 1874, but resigned soon after, and John J. Galligan was elected chief and held the place until April 15, 1877. The position was then filled for about eighteen months by Frank Kleffner. In October, 1878, occurred the disastrous Grand Central Hotel fire, and a few days thereafter the council again elected Galligan chief. April 18, 1882, John H. Butler was elected to the place, to be succeeded by Galligan in July, 1886, who, at this writing (August, 1892), still fills this important position, to which he was three times elected, and any attempt to supplant him would rouse a storm of opposition on the part of a community he has served for so many years with courage, zeal, and rare ability.

The following named have served as assistant chiefs: O. P. Ingalls, August von Windheim, Joseph F. Sheely, S. N. Mealio, Charles Hunt, Solomon Prince, James France, Harry Taggart, Charles Schlanck, John Galligan, Charles Salter and J. J. Barnes.

Upon the recommendation of the police and fire commissioners, the city council recently authorized the purchase of an improved water tower, which will enable the department to flood the top stories of high buildings. It is expected that this water tower will add materially to the already efficient apparatus of the department.

The Durant Fire Company was organized in 1867, by the Union Pacific Railroad Company, for the protection of its own property, with a membership of forty-two, but the number has been gradually reduced until it has now but twenty-three men. The railway shops have been fitted up with hydrants, standpipes, electric fire boxes, ladders, fire buckets, etc., in the meantime, to such an extent that the present force is more efficient than was the much larger one of twenty years ago. The Durants have a fire steam engine, one large and two small hose carts, and are abundantly supplied with everything required to fit out a first-class fire company. In the yards, conveniently located, are sixteen hydrants owned by the railroad company and three belonging to the city. There are fifteen electric signal boxes connecting with the central station, and from that, connection is had with the headquarters of the city's fire system. In former years the Durants seldom turned out for service outside the grounds of the railway company, but it is now subject to the call of the chief of the city department, and when the services of this model company are required they are promptly and cheerfully given. The following named have served as foremen of the Durants since the organization in 1867: William Fassett, two years; A. A. Gibson, one year; S. Courtney, one year; John Curtis, two years; W. Gushart, two years; John Clair, one year; Thomas Meldrum, one year; Michael Lawless, one year; Charles Fisher, one year; Thomas Cummings, one year; Thomas Meldrum, one year; John McDonald, two years; Peter Dowdel, one year; Charles Fisher four years.

A notice of the Omaha Fire Department would be incomplete without special mention of W. J. Kennedy and Joseph F. Sheely, to whose untiring zeal, enthusiasm and excellent judgment much of the present efficiency of the department is due. For thirty years these gentlemen gave valuable time and services to the fire department, and were particularly active in the early days, when it was composed of volunteers and when their services were of special value in organizing and rendering efficient when means and facilities were woefully lacking. Augustus von Windheim, the organizer and foreman of the first hand engine company in Omaha, was also an efficient and enthusiastic fireman. In the Union Pacific Fire Department Mr. Charles Fisher has been likewise valuable, bringing to the sevice of that department rare judgment and skill. Recognizing his superior fitness he has had charge of the fire system of that company at various times since its organization.

In 1890 lots were purchased by the city for six new engine houses, to be located as follows: corner of Eighth and Pierce, Thirtieth and Spaulding, Creighton Avenue and Twenty-ninth Avenue, Thirty-sixth and Jones, Vinton near Twentieth, and Hamilton, near Lowe Avenue. Bonds to the amount of fifty thousand dollars had previously been voted to provide for an extension of the fire department. A trifle over fourteen thousand dollars was paid for these lots, leaving thirty-five thousand dollars to be used in the erection of buildings this year, and it is proposed to add twenty-five men to the force.

June 25, 1890, there was a State Firemen's Tournament at Plattsmouth, in which the Omaha Veteran Fireman's Association contested for, and won, a prize banner valued at three hundred dollars to be awarded to the best drilled and best marching company. The following named constituted the veteran association: William Shull, J. F. Sheely, John Banmer, Charles Fischer, Max Meyer, J. J. Galligan, Daniel W. Shull, Ed. Maurer, Henry Pundt, Ed. Wittig, Solomon Prince, Louie Faist, H. Berthold, Joseph Tehon, A. P. Hopkins, P. Besen, Charles Schlank, H. Kunda, Judge Beneke, L. Kroitzsch, J. A. Lichtenberger, C. V. Gallagher, P. Windheim, F. Schmidt, J. J. Donnelly, Jr., P. J. Karbach, John A. McShane, Harry Taggart, Frank X. Dellone, M. Hellman, Aaron Cahn, Sr., F. H. Kosters, F. P. Hanlon, J. E. Markel, J. H. Butler, Julius Treitschke, Joseph Rotholz, John F. Behm, A. H. Sander, Phillip Dorr, William Mack, W. H. May.

# CHAPTER XLI.

LABOR DISTURBANCES — DAYS OF ANXIETY AND DREAD — WISE AND MODERATE COUNSELS FOLLOWED.

There have been several labor disturbances in this city, of more or less prominence, the first of any moment, perhaps, being that of the printers, in 1869, which resulted in the establishment of the *Times* newspaper, referred to more at length in another chapter. In 1874 there was another printers' strike, and the *Union* newspaper was the result. Since that date there have been various differences between the newspaper printers and their employers, but no strikes of special importance.

In June, 1877, Superintendent S. H. H. Clark, of the Union Pacific Railroad, received direction from his superiors to make a considerable reduction in the wages of the company's employes. A resistance to this order was made, not only in Omaha, but all along the line, and it was deemed advisable to withdraw the order. In the meantime, the railroad workmen on the east side of the river were holding meetings at Council Bluffs, and on the 23d adopted the following:

"*Resolved*, That section men, car cleaners and laborers do not work for less than $1.50 a day; and if their demands are not acceded to by the railroad companies by Tuesday noon, they should strike."

"*Resolved*, That all laboring men within the city, including brick-layers and others, should not labor for less than $1.50 a day."

On the 25th, about 150 track repairers on the Kansas City, St. Joseph & Council Bluffs Railroad struck, and were joined shortly afterwards by numbers of brick-layers and others. It was feared an attempt would be made to destroy the Union Pacific bridge (the great strike of railroad men in Pennsylvania occurred that year), and a guard of fifty men was organized to protect it and other property of that company. Traffic between Omaha and the East was seriously interfered with, and for a time all of the freight cars of the Union Pacific were kept on this side of the river, but there was no strike in this city.

November 1, 1877, the men employed at the smelting works struck on account of a proposed reduction of their pay to $1.75 for twelve hours' work. Two or three days later the difficulty was adjusted, and the men returned to work, their wages being fixed at $1.25 for nine hours' work. In May, 1880, there was another and much more serious strike of smelting works' employes, and about one hundred colored men were shipped in from Kansas and Missouri to take their places. While on the cars en route to Omaha, they were supplied with arms and ammunition, as it was supposed they would be assaulted when they attempted to go into the works. Great excitement prevailed, and when the party reached the city, on the morning of the 21st, crowds of people were found gathered near the buildings. Inside these, and about the grounds of the smelting works company, were stationed armed men. During the day, means were found by the strikers and their friends to reach the imported laborers and induce them to agree to return to their homes, a fund of about three hundred dollars being raised to pay their railroad fare, the negroes claiming that they did not know at the time of their employment that there had been a strike on the part of the company's employes. The officers of the company, becoming seriously alarmed, telegraphed Governor Nance for aid, and two companies of the State militia were at once ordered to Omaha—Company I, of Columbus, Captain John N. Lawson and Captain C. M. Copp's Company, of Wahoo. Company G, Captain Crager, and Company H, Captain Bolln, of Omaha, were also directed to report to the officers of the smelting company. The last named command, being composed almost entirely of young mechanics, and sympathizing with the strikers, declined to serve on such duty, and only fifteen of their number could be induced to respond to the call. For three days this military force was stationed in and about the smelting works. On the 24th, the matters in dispute were amicably arranged by arbitration, and peace was once more restored.

In March, 1882, occurred a labor strike which will long be remembered in the history of Omaha. The Burlington & Missouri River Railroad Company was making extensive improvements on "the bottoms," which necessitated the removal of a large amount of earth east of Eighth Street and between Howard and Farnam, the bluff being cut down and a pond of considerable size filled up. The contract had been let to James Stephenson, of this city, and he had been at work but a short time when he announced his intention to reduce the pay of the workmen twenty-five cents per day, which left their daily wages $1.25, instead of $1.50, as at first paid. General dissatisfaction was expressed by the men, and a strike followed. Stephenson then proposed to pay $1.40, but that proposition was rejected, and the former price of $1.50 insisted upon. Meetings were held, the strikers marched through the streets, and in front of Mr. Stephenson's livery establishment, on Harney Street, hung in effigy a man of the sort supposed to be willing to work for $1.25 a day. Bands were secured, speeches made, funds raised for the strikers, and a state of general excitement and anxiety prevailed. It was resolved by the striking laborers to demand $1.75 a day, and to stand by that demand to the last. Jefferson Square was utilized as a meeting place, and here thousands assembled daily to listen to addresses; and in the evenings similar meetings were held at the Academy of Music, Metz's Hall, and other places. Stephenson was waited upon by a committee, and he then agreed to pay $1.50 a day for a time, and, as soon as the weather became sufficiently settled to warrant it, to raise the wages to $1.75 per day, and also agreed to pay the men every Monday night. The committee reported in favor of accepting this proposition, but the strikers rejected it. The railroad company then took charge of the work with a force of laborers from Plattsmouth, bringing the men up in the morning and returning in the evening. At a meeting at Metz's Hall, March 7th, Mayor James E. Boyd was present by invitation and addressed the strikers, urging them to either return to work or to refrain from molesting other men who were willing to work for the wages offered. He referred to his own experience as a mechanic, early in life, when he said he had worked in Omaha for much less pay than that which the striking laborers had refused. On the 9th, a procession of twenty-five hundred men marched through the streets, and finally passed down Farnam Street to the locality where the laborers from Plattsmouth were at work, under the protection of an armed special police. A rush was made by the marching column, the men were driven from their task, and their spades, shovels, and wheeled scrapers were thrown into the pond. Several shots were fired and three men of the assaulted party injured.

On the night of the 8th a special train took Superintendent Holdrege, of the Burlington, and a party to Lincoln to interview Governor Nance with respect to the situation, and on the 9th the following was sent that official, signed by Mayor Boyd and

Sheriff David N. Miller: "A mob of three thousand or four thousand men drove the laborers from their work on the Burlington grounds and seriously injured three men. We are powerless to keep the peace, and call upon you to enforce the laws and protect peaceable laborers from mob violence. We are of the opinion that United States troops are absolutely necessary to restore quiet and that the militia would be insufficient. We have just been informed that to-day notice is to be served on all manufacturers that their men must join in the strike and remain idle until the difficulty is settled, and we fear danger." In addition telegrams and letters of the same general import were sent by several business men of the city.

Upon receipt of the foregoing official demand for aid, the governor telegraphed President Arthur, requesting that the troops at Fort Omaha be placed at the disposal of the authorities at Omaha, and the various companies composing the First Regiment, Nebraska National Guards, were directed to be in readiness to come to this city on short notice. Companies C and E, Fifth United States Cavalry were sent to Omaha from Sidney, Nebraska, and on the following day Companies A, B, D, F, G, H, I and K, of the First Regiment, State militia, arrived at Omaha, under command of Colonel Colby, and encamped on the grounds of the Burlington company, where the men were at work, most of the soldiers being quartered in the old Catholic Church building. The regulars were also stationed in the same vicinity, with a Gatling gun and a howitzer. Sunday afternoon, March 12th, while the regulars were at Fort Omaha for the day, a large crowd assembled near the grounds to witness the dress parade of the militia regiment, and much throwing of missiles at the guards was indulged in, chiefly by a party of boys. One George P. Armstrong, a man about sixty years old, attempted to pass along Eighth Street, but was pressed back by a sentry, who pointed a bayonet toward him. Mr. Armstrong attempted to thrust the bayonet aside, and a scuffle ensued. Several guards ran to the spot, and in a moment the old gentleman fell, with a bayonet thrust through the body. He was carried into the camp and the excitement of the citizens allayed by the statement that his injuries were slight, and when the parade was concluded the crowd dispersed. That night Mr. Armstrong died from his injuries; and when that fact became known great excitement prevailed, and a general demand was made for the surrender of the soldier who had inflicted the fatal injury. Police Judge Beneke issued a warrant for his arrest, in the name of "John Doe," but the officer attempting to serve it was refused admittance to the camp, whereupon Sheriff Miller and his deputy, Edward Crowell, went to the camp and made a search of the soldiers' quarters, but were unable to identify the man they sought, and hence made no arrests. The funeral of Mr. Armstrong, which occurred the following Sunday, was one of the most imposing ever witnessed in Omaha.

A special grand jury was sworn to take action in the matter of the strike, and Daniel O'Keefe, John Quinn, Bernard Shannon, Edward Walsh, George Grooms and —— Van Orman were indicted on the charge of "assault with intent to kill," the charge having reference to the occasion when the rush was made on the laborers, and their tools thrown into the pond. All of these men were arrested, but gave bail and held themselves ready to appear for trial whenever needed. A continuance was had until the next term of court, and that practically ended the matter. March 20th several of the militia companies left the city for their respective homes, and the excitement died out, the Burlington & Missouri River Company completing the work of grading without further molestation.

July 19, 1883, occurred the great strike of telegraph operators, which extended all over the land, and was inaugurated at noon of that day by the sending out from the headquarters of the order of the message, in cypher (previously agreed upon as a signal), "General Grant dropped dead!" At that time Mr. L. M. Rheem was manager of the Western Union office here, employing thirty-two operators, twenty-three of whom quit work, although first-class men were then earning from $110 to $150 per month, $75 per month being the lowest wages paid. There was then an organization known as the Telegraphers' Brotherhood, and the refusal of the telegraph companies to recognize this organization in the settlement of differences was the cause of the strike. On the 21st of August, the Brotherhood gave up the contest, and soon afterwards ceased to exist.

In 1883, and again in 1884, there were printers' strikes, but they were of short duration; and in March, 1886, occurred the great strike among the employes of the Texas Pacific and Missouri Pacific systems, which was so disastrous to the West and Southwest. From the 5th day of that month until the 1st day of April, not a car was permitted by the Knights of Labor to leave Omaha over the Missouri Pacific road. The history of that great struggle between organized labor and organized capital remains to be written. In its bitterness and disastrous results, it has been equalled, thus far, only by the railroad strike in Pennsylvania in 1877. Its effects were but slightly felt in this city, however, and no violence or destruction of property occurred.

The Legislature of the State, at its session in 1891, passed a law making eight hours a day's work, for all except farm hands and domestics, throughout the State, and provided that the law should go into effect on the first day of August, 1891. The result of this law was to force all employers to hire their employes by the hour. There was, however, much dissatisfaction among some of the workingmen, and several strikes occurred, the principal ones in Omaha being of the smelting works' employes and job printers; neither one of which was successful. For the purpose of testing the constitutionality of the law, Samuel Rees, at the request of the Central Labor Union, employed men by the hour for more than eight hours a day and by the month, and had them work more than eight hours per day, and had a test suit brought. The case was heard by Judges Wakeley, Doane and Davis, and the decision of the court was that, while the law was constitutional, there was nothing in it to prevent a man's entering into a contract to work as many hours as he saw fit; that, when men were hired by the month, eight hours would constitute a day's work, and they would be entitled to reasonable compensation for overtime, if they worked more than eight hours. Judge E. R. Duffie argued the case on behalf of Samuel Rees. Hon. J. L. Webster appeared for the smelting works, and Hon. C. J. Smyth, appeared for the Central Labor Union. Before long everything had settled down to its regular condition, and nearly all the workingmen are working by the hour, and the number of hours varies in different trades from eight to ten per day.

# CHAPTER XLII.

GRAND ARMY POSTS — WOMAN'S RELIEF CORPS — THE LOYAL LEGION.

The first post of the Grand Army of the Republic, established in Omaha, was instituted January 26, 1867, with George Armstrong as post commander, R. A. Bird, assistant commander; E. K. Valentine (late Sergeant-at-Arms of the House of Representatives), adjutant, and F. W. Becker, quartermaster. W. J. Hahn was appointed aide-de-camp to Gen. S. A. Hurlburt, then commander-in-chief of the Grand Army, and in consequence of this appointment Captain Hahn was the temporary commander of the Department of Nebraska, the first to fill that position. He was succeeded by Gen. S. A. Strickland, who appointed Captain John C. Cowin as adjutant; J. E. Philpot, of Lincoln, succeeded General Strickland as department commander, in 1868, but the order was not put upon a permanent basis, or any progress made in the establishment of posts. In 1874 Paul VanDervoort was appointed provisional commander of Nebraska; and, when he had succeeded in establishing enough posts to form a department, was elected department commander, with Lee Estelle as adjutant. W. H. Wilbur was the next department commander; William Coburn, adjutant, and he was succeeded by Col. James W. Savage, with Capt. S. Wood as adjutant.

The headquarters of the Department of Nebraska Grand Army of the Republic are located in this city at 219 South Fourteenth Street. T. S. Clarkson is department commander; Joseph Teeter, S. V. C.; Willis Gossert, J. V. C.; John B. Sawhill, A. A. G.; Charles L. Howell, A. Q. M. G.; P. H. Steele, A. I. G.; Rev. W. E. Kimball, chaplain; W. H. Johnson, M. D.; Chas. E. Burmester, senior aid and chief of staff.

Phil. Kearney, Post, No. 2, Fort Omaha, was the first post organized here, January 1, 1876, being the date of its muster, with a membership of seventy-six; but by March 1, there were 120 comrades enrolled. The first officers were: Joseph Dreschlinger, commander; Hugh Kerr, S. V.; James Begley, J. V.; Elbert H. Dunwardin, adjutant; Michael Coady, Q. M.; Frank A. Bradbury, Surgeon; George W. Thompson, Q. M. S.; Charles Reis, O. G.; Benjamin Harris, O. D.; Alfred F. Moore, S. M.; Patrick Russell, I. G.; Thomas Mungen, S. The present officers are: John Reagan, commander; Gregory Farrell, S. V.; Jacob Theurer, J. V.; Robert Gruner, adjutant; James Davidson, Q. M.; Andrew Mayewski, surgeon; William L. Allison, chaplain; Perry A. Lyons, O. D.; Henry Keeler, O. G.; John S. Wood, S. M.; John Scanlan, Q. M. S.

U. S. Grant Post, No. 110, was organized as Omaha Post, August 18, 1882, the name being changed January 12, 1886. The charter members were as follows: Charles F. Manderson, David E. Kimball, Samuel B. Jones, A. D. Morris, Wm. Coburn, Charles E. Burmester, C. H. Frederick, W. F. Bechel, James S. France, J. C. Holtorf, C. F. Goodman, E. A. Parmalee, M. R. Risdon, C. E. Squires, Victor Landergren, W. J. Broatch, J. S. Caulfield and Mark Hansen. The post has now a membership of 105, with the following named officers: C. S. Chase, commander; R. S. Wilcox, S. V.; H. H. Benson, J. V.; Q. H. Shinn, chaplain; William H. Christie, surgeon; John Jeffcoat, adjutant; D. M. Haverly, Q. M.; Lafayette Anderson, O. D.; M. McMahon, O. G.; Simeon Bloom, P. M.; S. Adamsky, Q. M. The shortest term of service rendered by a member of this post was one month and two days, and the longest, thirty years and twenty-three days. The membership of the post includes one United States senator and two brigadier generals. One member, Capt. C. H. Kettler, served in the Texan War, the Mexican War, and the War of the Rebellion.

George A. Custer Post, No. 7, was organized June 7, 1876, with the following named charter members: William Coburn, W. T. Rogers, Charles J. Greene, Paul Van Dervoort, John S. Wood, M. R. Risdon, James S. France, E. Schlick, R. H. Wilbur, C. L. Bristol, H. Geiscke, Charles E. Squires. Silas A. Strickland, A. H. Scott, H. Kensley. O. Steen, I. N. Parker. The record of the first list of officers elected was not preserved. The following named is the present list of officers: Charles L. Thomas, commander; Fritz Wirth, S. V.; George H. Rhodes, J. V.; J. P. Henderson, Q. M.; William P. Brown, adjutant; Dr. H. C. VanGeison, surgeon; O. G. Decker, chaplain; Charles Henn, O. D.; F. Garrity, O. G.; Jerome Potter, S. M.; William L. Lindley, Q. M. S.

George Crook Post (formerly Gate City Post, and then Phil H. Sheridan Post), No. 262, was instituted April 6, 1888, the following named being the charter members: L. F. Maginn, J. B. West, G. C. Bonner, George R. Rathbun, John B. Furay, J. G. Willis, W. S. Askwith, William Stuart, A. K. Rhoades, W. C. McLean, D. O. Clements, S. K. Jackson, S. K. Spaulding, Levi Grate, P. Flanagan, J. Bliss. Following named were the first officers: J. G. Willis, commander; L. F. Maginn, S. V. C.; George R. Rathbun, J. V. C.; S. K. Spaulding, surgeon; W. S. Askwith, Q. M.; W. C. McLean, O. D.; D. O. Clements, O. G.; J. B. West, chaplain. The present officers are: George C. Bonner, commander; B. R. Ball. S. V. C.; J. B. West, J. V. C.; A. K. Rhoades, Q. M. S.; S. K. Spaulding, surgeon; L. F. Maginn, O. D.; T. L. Hull, O. G.; D. O. Clements, S. M.; Charles Kohl, Q. M. S.

Omaha has the distinction of furnishing the only member of the order who, having served only as a private during the war, reached the honorable position of grand commander of the United States. To Paul Van Dervoort was awarded this distinction, at the meeting of the grand commandery in 1882, at Baltimore. He was very active with Gen. John A. Logan, in perfecting the organization that year of the National Woman's Relief Corps, which now has a membership of over eighty thousand, and was elected in 1884, an honorary member, the only person ever elected to that position. He was also presented with a handsome gold badge by this large, patriotic and influential association, at Portland, Maine, in 1885.

There are three posts of the Woman's Relief Corps in this city. George A. Custer Post, No. 82, holds meetings at 2:30 p. m. on Thursdays, at the G. A. R. Hall, No. 116 North Fifteenth Street. Mrs. A. Henderson is president; Mrs. Dora Green, vice-president; Mrs. Mattie Rhoades, junior vice-president; Mrs. Louisa Kirby, treasurer; Mrs. Angelina Whitmarsh, secretary; Mrs. Sophia Rawitzer, chaplain; Mrs. Anna Crawford, conductor; Mrs. Mary McKinney, guard. George Crook Post, No. 88, meets on the second and fourth Friday evenings of each month, at Goodrich Hall, on North Twenty-Fourth Street. Mrs. Anna E. Askwith is president; Mrs. Anna Tule, senior vice-president; Mrs. Amelia E. Drake, junior vice-president; Mrs. E. A. Hull, chaplain; Mrs. Sophia M. Bennett, treasurer; Miss Nellie Askwith, secretary; Miss Mamie Mulhall, conductor; Mrs. Nellie Clements, assistant conductor; Mrs. Addie M. Rhoades, guard. U. S. Grant Post, No. 104, meets on the second and fourth Tuesday afternoons of each month, at Clark's Hall, 107

South Fourteenth Street. Mrs. Ella S. Collins, president; Mrs. Eliza S. Adamsky, senior vice-president; Mrs. Juliette A. Rhoades, junior vice-president; Mrs. Roanna E. Benson, secretary; Mrs. Sarah M. Christie, treasurer; Mrs. Helen B. Jeffcoat, chaplain; Mrs. Laura Landergren, conductor; Miss Nettie Haverly, guard; Miss Emma Adams, assistant conductor; Miss Alice A. Sreeves, assistant guard.

George A. Crook Camp No. 1, Division of Nebraska, Sons of Veterans, meets on the first and third Mondays at G. A. R. Hall. W. K. Jacobs is captain; John L. Gideon, first lieutenant; C. E. Burmester, second lieutenant; John B. Cultin, first sergeant.

Thurston Division, No. 2, O. R. T. of N. A., meets at G. A. R. Hall, 114 North Fifteenth Street, on the second and fourth Saturdays of each month. J. H. Flannagan, C. T.; E. C. Mangrum, secretary and treasurer; W. E. Travis, A. C. T.; A. M. Wood, P. C.; N. Crenshaw, S. T.; W. G. Meelens, J. T.; Charles L. Pond, I. S.; A. L. Beechler, O. S.

The Nebraska Commandery of the Military Order of the Loyal Legion of the United States has its headquarters in Omaha. It was organized at the Paxton Hotel, December 17, 1885, a charter having been obtained by a number of residents of Nebraska, who were admitted to membership August 5, 1885, in the California Commandery. The following named were elected to fill the various official positions, and served without change until May 4, 1887: Commander, Col. James W. Savage; senior vice commander, Capt. William J. Broatch; junior vice commander, Gen. Amasa Cobb; recorder, Major J. Morris Brown; registrar, Capt. William H. Ijams; treasurer, Lieut. William Wallace; chancellor, Capt. Frank E. Moores; council, Lieut. E. S. Dundy, Capt. Henry E. Palmer, Capt. Church Howe, Ensign W. H. Michaels, Capt. George M. Humphrey. The membership November 1, 1892, is 153. The officers elected at the annual election, 1892, were: Brevet Maj. Gen. John R. Brooke, commander; Lieut. John B. Furay, senior vice commander; Brevet Major Chas. W. Pierce, junior vice commander; Major Horace Ludington, recorder; Capt. H. E. Palmer, registrar; Capt. Jas S. France, treasurer; Lieut. Jas. T. Kinsler, chancellor; Capt. E. C. Jackson, Lieut. W. F. Bechel, Lieut. Geo. E. Pritchett, Lieut. Thos. Swobe, Brevet Brig. Gen. V. Vifquain, council.

This order is composed of three classes of members: the first being those who served as officers during the war of the rebellion, in the union army; the second are members by inheritance; and the third is composed of those who distingushed themselves in civil life by services rendered the government during the war. Of the latter class, but one is admitted for each thirty-three first class members. Thus far only four have been admitted members of Nebraska Commandery.

# CHAPTER XLIII.

MASONIC HISTORY — INDEPENDENT ORDER OF ODD FELLOWS — KNIGHTS OF PYTHIAS.

[The following chapter of the history of Masonry in Omaha, is contributed by William R. Bowen. John Evans is the author of the article on Odd Fellows, and Egbert E. French of the one on Knights of Pythias.]

FREEMASONRY.

The first record of this society in Nebraska bears the date of 1854.

It is asserted by men competent to determine, and of unquestioned veracity, that Freemasonry existed among the Indians when white men first crossed the plains of Nebraska; that the mysteries of this society were known to the "medicine men" of several Indian tribes, and were by them handed down from generation to generation. In the early sixties Major Frank North found Masonry among the Sioux; a party en route to California in 1849, wintered in the Black Hills, and preserved their cattle by branding them with the square and compasses, an emblem so respected by the red men that the cattle were neither disturbed nor permitted to stray far from the camp. The sun dance, modernized as it is, has characteristics familiar to every Masonic student. The Mormons carried a pseudo-masonry to Utah from their lodge at Nauvoo, which lodge was organized for sinister purposes under authority obtained from the Grand Lodge of Illinois in 1841.

Coming down to matters of record, we find that the first lodge of Freemasons in Nebraska was created by the Deputy Grand Master of Illinois, the authority being dated early in February, 1855, permitting the establishment of a lodge at Bellevue, Douglas (now Sarpy) County. This lodge still exists as Nebraska Lodge, No. 1, having been moved from Bellevue to Omaha in 1888. While at Bellevue there were connected with it: Ansel Briggs, ex-governor of Iowa; James M. Gatewood and George Hepner, Indian agents; the pioneer, Peter A. Sarpy, Leavit L. Bowen, Addison R. Gillmore, Henry T. Clarke. Silas A. Strickland, Augustus Hall, Thomas Clifton, Louis F. Bartels, Charles D. Keller, Joseph M. Whitted, Stephen D. Bangs, and others who took prominent parts in the early days of Nebraska. Here, as elsewhere, the Freemasons lodge was the very first social organization wherein men could safely lay aside their "armed neutrality" and with confidence enjoy fellowship with one another.

The second lodge in Nebraska was created May 10, 1855, by the Deputy Grand Master of Missouri, and took his name, "Giddings" lodge. It was located at Nebraska City, Otoe County, and remains there, bearing upon its rolls the names of the leading citizens of that locality.

Capitol Lodge, No. 3, at Omaha, was created January 9, 1857, by the Grand Master of Iowa. Its meetings were first held in the east third of Pioneer Block, now No. 1108 Farnam Street, then in the third story of No. 1313 Farnam Street, and May 10, 1877, it moved to Freemasons Hall, at the northwest corner of Capitol Avenue and Sixteenth Street.

Among the early members of this lodge were: Robert Shields, William H. Demorest, Samuel E. Rogers, Charles W. Hamilton, John R. Porter, John M. Chivington, Mark W. Izard, Addison R. Gillmore, Aaron Cahn, Charles Turner, George Armstrong, Alfred D. Jones, John Reck, Joel T. Griffen, Elias

Hicks Clark, Oscar P. Ingalls, Joseph P. Manning, John M. Thayer, William Cleburne, Lorin Miller, John Logan, Robert C. Jordan, Philip ("Peter") Windheim, Meyer Hellman, Henry H. Visscher, George L. Miller, Alfred Sayre, William N. Byers, James E. Boyd, Dr. Augustus Roeder, Augustus A. Egbert, John H. Green, James G. Megeath, Rev. Henry W. Kuhns, Dr. William McClelland, Charles Bremer, William Ruth, James K. Ish, Harry P. Deuel, Byron Reed, Phineas W. Hitchcock, Matthew C. Wilbur and Henry Grebe. The first petitioners were Alfred D. Jones, John Reck and Joel T. Griffen, and the first Master Mason was made by Robert C. Jordan. This lodge has held a leading position in Nebraska Freemasonry.

These three lodges, in 1857, formed the Grand Lodge of Nebraska, which now has about two hundred lodges and about ten thousand members.

The first Royal Arch Chapter in Nebraska was organized under the leadership of Robert C. Jordan, November 21, 1859, and is known as Omaha Chapter, No. 1. In 1867 the Grand Chapter of Nebraska was organized. It now has over fifty subordinate chapters in Nebraska, with a membership of upwards of three thousand.

In 1867, Omaha Council No. 1, of Royal and Select Masters was organized by A. T. C. Pierson. The Grand Council of Nebraska has ten subordinate councils.

In 1865 Robert C. Jordan, Dr. George B. Graff, Herman Kountze and Robert W. Furnas, formed Mount Calvary Commandery, No. 1, Knights Templar, an organization that has flourished until the Grand Commandery of Nebraska has twenty-two subordinate commanderies, with a membership in the State of about twelve hundred.

In 1867 the Ancient and Accepted Scottish Rite of Freemasonry was established in Nebraska, four bodies of which exist in Omaha.

In addition to these pioneer bodies, there have since been established in Omaha, Covert Lodge, No. 11, created July 24, 1865; and Saint Johns Lodge, No. 25, created May 28, 1869. Nebraska Lodge, No. 1, has been moved from Bellevue to Omaha; Bellevue Chapter, No. 7, Royal Arch Masons, has been removed to Omaha.

All the Masonic bodies of Omaha meet in Freemasons Hall, Omaha, a valuable property owned entirely by the bodies above mentioned. There are about eight hundred Freemasons in Omaha who are members of these bodies, and as many more who retain membership in eastern lodges. The Omaha bodies are wealthy and contented, having as much or more work than is desirable.

In this brief sketch only those individuals have been named who were connected with Nebraska Freemasonry during or prior to 1862.

### ODD FELLOWS.

On Friday, February 1, 1856, there assembled at the old Capitol building, situated on the west side of Ninth Street, between Farnam and Douglas, Brothers Alfred D. Jones, Taylor G. Goodwill, Hadley D. Johnson, George Armstrong and A. S. Bishop, who had solemnly pledged themselves to unite their energies in the organization and maintenance of a lodge of Odd Fellows and to bring other good men within their fold, and, by union of effort, increase their power for good, and the promotion of the general welfare within the sacred precincts of their lodge room, and as good and useful members of the community.

Upon their petition, the Grand Lodge of the United States granted a charter by the authority of which these brothers were constituted a lodge to be known and hailed as Omaha Lodge No. 2, I. O. O. F. The first lodge in Nebraska was instituted at Nebraska City, but it has since been merged with another lodge at that place, so that No. 2 now stands at the head of the list. The following officers were elected and duly installed by D. D. Grand Sire, J. P. Cassidy, of Council Bluffs; N. G., Alfred D. Jones;

V. C., Taylor G. Goodwill; R. secretary, A. S. Bishop; P. secretary, George Armstrong; treasurer, Hadley D. Johnson.

These brothers were thus entrusted with the responsibility of a great and sacred trust, and from the subsequent events they and we may feel proud of their work. There were present on the occasion, participating in the ceremony, the following named visiting brothers: C. C. Van, of Ft. Des Moines Lodge, No. 25; Godfrey Hattenback, of Franklin Lodge, No. 25; Abram Hecht, of Cincinnati, Ohio; —— Murh, of Green Mountain Lodge, No. 7, and Brothers Milton Rogers, J. D. Test, M. W. Robinson, John A. Lafferty, George Daugherty, J. J. Martin, J. S. Hootun and E. R. Robinson, of Hawkeye Lodge, No. 49, of Council Bluffs, Iowa.

This lodge was called into being contemporarily with the founding of this beautiful city, whose name it bears. The five noble brothers whose names are graven in the charter, and those who joined them in their grand work, met with the many discouraging difficulties and trials incident to the establishing of civil societies in all new countries; but they successfully maintained their purpose, and their lodge became an acknowledged factor in the influences for good during the formative period of society in this city. Hence, I deem it of peculiar interest to the present membership to know who were the immediate recruits of our founders, and the material of which they were made. I will therefore recall the names of those admitted during the first two years of the life of the lodge, and relate some of the incidents which transpired during that period.

The records show that at the second meeting, February 8, 1856, the N. G., Brother A. D. Jones, made the remarkable announcement that, owing to want of members, he would postpone the appointment of his supporters and other subordinate officers; and the V. G. made a similar announcement as to his supporters. At this meeting, the lodge adopted the constitution of Council Bluffs Lodge, No. 49, for the temporary government of the lodge. At the third session, February 15, Mr. H. C. Anderson was initiated (the first new member) and was then appointed warden. At the fifth session, February 29, the Rev. Wm. Leach and the Rev. J. F. Collins were initiated, the former being appointed chaplain, and the latter, conductor. In consideration of their prospective valuable services as clergymen, the admission fees of these brothers were remitted. At the sixth session, March 7, the first absentees were noted, being Jones, Johnson, Armstrong and Leach. This must have been an election night. At the fifteenth session, four applications for membership were presented; and at the twentieth session, June 13, 1856, Brothers John Ricks, J. W. Richardson and G. W. Hepburn, were admitted to membership on card, and, at the following session, Brother D. D. Carr was admitted in the same way. July 4, 1856, officers were elected as follows: N. G., Taylor G. Goodwill; V. G., John Ricks; secretary, George Armstrong; treasurer, J. F. Collins; and at the meeting of July 18, they were installed by D. D. Grand Sire Holley, assisted by Brothers Decker and Brown, of Nebraska City, with the following additional officers: Warden, Hadley D. Johnson; conductor, George Armstrong; O. S. G., A. D. Jones; I. S. G., A. D. Jones; R. S. to N. G., H. C. Anderson; L. S. to N. G., H. C. Anderson; R. S. S., A. D. Jones; L. S. S., G. W. Hepburn; R. S. to V. G., William Leach; L. S. to V. G., D. D. Carr. We have frequently heard of persons making themselves scarce when wanted, but here is a remarkable instance of a person making himself very numerous when wanted, as the foregoing record shows Brother Jones to have been installed into three offices. On motion of Brother Jones, the fees for the five degrees conferred upon Brothers Leach and Collins were remitted, which would indicate that the clerical services and good influences of these brothers were fully appreciated by Brother Jones and the lodge. The degree of Rebekah was conferred on the wife of Brother Collins.

For several months following but few meetings were held. During this time, however, Dr. George L. Miller, H. W. Tuttle, John Y. Clopper and J. B. Allen were initiated, and Jeremiah Cassidy, Asa Hunt, John R. Porter and G. W. Crowell were admitted to membership by card. November 1, the acquisition of new members enabling a revision of the appointive officers, appointments were made as follows: Warden, John R. Porter; conductor, D. D. Carr; O. S. G., J. Cassidy; I. S. G., H. C. Anderson; R. S. to N. G., Asa Hunt; L. S. to N. G., G. W, Crowell; R. S. S., George L. Miller; L. S. S., George Armstrong; R. S. to V. G., H. W. Tuttle; L. S. to V. G., G. W. Hepburn. November 21, I. E. Allen was initiated, and on the 28th H. B. Porter elected on card. At this meeting the lodge resolved to lease the upper story room of J. M. Thayer's building for one year, at three hundred dollars per annum, which action displayed great nerve and faith in success of their enterprise on the part of this plucky little band. In January, 1857, John Logan, George W. Crowell and James L. Wheeler were admitted to membership; in February, Byron Reed, George A. Graves and Oscar Wolcott; in March, E. F. Cook and John M. Thayer; in April, J. D. Kellogg; in May, John McCormick and Silas E. Hall were admitted. June 26th, the following officers were elected: N. G., Asa Hunt; V. G., W. Leach; secretary, G. W. Crowell; treasurer, Byron Reed. From this date forward initiations were quite frequent. At the meeting of December 11, the proposition was made that, in view of the hard times resulting from the panic of the previous September, city scrip be received for dues, and the matter was left to the discretion of the secretary; but at the following meeting he was relieved of that discretion and instructed to receive scrip. January 5, 1858, at a special meeting of the lodge, arrangements were made for a public ball, the price of the tickets being placed at four dollars each, and later on it is discovered that a net profit of $60.35 was realized from this ball. At this date, the membership has reached a total of thirty-nine, with a loss of one member by death and another by withdrawal.

The membership roll of the lodge shows that from its organization to the present time 671 have been admitted, of which number the lodge has lost by death thirty-three, and by withdrawal 412, leaving the membership July 1, 1890, 226. During this period 1,142 degrees have been conferred by this lodge upon its members, which has entailed a vast amount of labor upon its officers. The amount of revenue received by the lodge has been $46,362.69, and the amount paid for the relief of its members and families, and burying the dead, is $11,144.90. The lodge now possesses available assets to the amount of $29,579. This lodge has also aided in vitalizing and fostering other subordinate lodges in this city, having an aggregate membership of 674, making the total number of active membership in this city of not less than 900. Its moral influences have not been confined to this city, but apply to every portion of the state, which now has within its bounds 180 lodges with 8,000 active members. This lodge has furnished to the order at large four grand masters—Asa Hunt, Alfred D. Jones, Alvin Saunders and St. John Goodrich; three deputy grand masters—Asa Hunt, Alvin Saunders and John Evans; three grand secretaries—Byron Reed, St. John Goodrich and John Evans (furnishing the grand secretary for fifteen years); seven grand treasurers—John R. Porter, Alfred D. Jones, Asa Hunt, D. C. Sutphen, A. J. Simpson, Martin Dunham and Alvin Saunders; five grand representatives to the Sovereign Grand Lodge—St. John Goodrich, Alf. D. Jones, John Evans, C. C. Housel and F. B. Bryant. It has also furnished two United States Senators—John M. Thayer and Alvin Saunders, both of whom have also served Nebraska as Governor.

The lodge met for some time in the old Capitol building, and then moved to a small wooden building at the corner of Eleventh and Dodge, where the Third Ward School building now stands. Its next meeting place was in a house occupied by Reverend Leach, on Dodge Street, near Twelfth, where it is said that in the winter water would freeze beside a red-hot stove. The old Western Exchange building, Farnam and Twelfth, was next occupied for lodge purposes, at which time the entire effects of the lodge were kept and carried back and forth from his residence in Park Wilde, by Alf. D. Jones. Next, a lodge room was found in the residence of George Armstrong, and then in a brick building on the North side of Dodge just east of Fifteenth. The old Pioneer Block next afforded quarters for the Lodge, and then a removal was made to the third story of a building on Farnam Street, occupied by G. H. and J. S. Collins, and here the lodge remained until 1874, when it was removed to its present quarters, the building erected by the Odd Fellows at the northwest corner of Dodge and Fourteenth, which was erected at a cost of $27,000.00, the lot having been donated to the order by the Town Site Company. To Alf. D. Jones belongs the credit of retaining this lot, as he kept the taxes paid for many years when the Lodge was short of funds.

## KNIGHTS OF PYTHIAS.

The order of the Knights of Pythias was introduced into Nebraska by Col. George H. Crager, a member of Rising Sun Lodge, No. 26, of Philadelphia, Pennsylvania, who, after an honorable service of four years in the army, during the war of the rebellion, removed with his family to Omaha, and entered the service of the Union Pacific Railway Company, where he has held positions of responsibility and trust for twenty-four years. Feeling a deep interest in the order of the Knights of Pythias, and finding no lodge organization in his adopted city, he enlisted the co-operation of friends, and, after securing a commission as deputy grand chancellor, entered upon the work of organizing the first lodge west of Pennsylvania. Conspicuous among those who rendered assistance, were John Taylor, Dr. L. F. Babcock, J. E. Neal, Edwin Davis, Edwin Stanton, George S. Markham and Charles Skinner. Several preliminary meetings were held, appropriate paraphernalia secured and on the 23d of November, 1868, the deputy grand chancellor instituted Nebraska Lodge, No. 1, at Omaha, and installed as first officers the following: George H. Crager, venerable patriarch; Edwin Davis, worthy chancellor (presiding officer); Charles Skinner, vice chancellor; L. F. Babcock, recording scribe; Edwin Stanton, financial scribe; Thomas C. Brunner, banker; J. E. Neal, guide; H. A. Monier, inner steward; John Taylor, outer steward.

The meetings of the lodge were held in a rear room in the third story at No. 1319 Douglas Street. The new order was deservedly popular, and the lodge increased in membership rapidly. In the course of a few months some of its active members, among whom were E. E. French, Rev. E. V. Glover, Henry Fulton, E. S. Seymour, George E. Powell, W. H. Jackson, E. W. Caldwell and John J. Curtis, conceived the idea of organizing another lodge. A petition was circulated and numerously signed by well-known citizens, and with the approval of the Supreme Chancellor, Damon Lodge, No. 2, was instituted at Omaha, by Deputy Grand Chancellor Crager, on the 29th of April, 1869.

Following this, on the 25th of August, 1869, Planet Lodge, No. 4, composed exclusively of Germans, and working in the German language, was instituted by the deputy grand chancellor. Prominent and active in the organization of this lodge were Andrew Zimmerman, A. B. Huberman, Charles E. Bruner, J. F. Kuhn, Joseph Rosenstein, Henry Leisge, Emil Faust, Charles Hollo.

On the 19th of September, 1869, after the fifth lodge had been instituted in the State, a meeting of past chancellors was held at Pythian Hall, southeast corner of Fourteenth and Douglas Streets, in Omaha, for the purpose of arranging for the organization of a Grand Lodge of the Knights of Pythias for Nebraska. At this meeting David Carter acted as chairman, and E. E. French, secretary. The sum of $105 was subscribed toward defraying the expenses incident to the organization of a grand lodge, and the meeting adjourned to October 1st. At the second preliminary meeting, held October 1st, officers for the proposed grand lodge were chosen as follows: Grand venerable patriarch, George H. Crager; grand chancellor, David Carter; grand vice chancellor, John Q. Goss; grand recording and corresponding scribe, E. E. French; grand banker, T. C. Brunner; grand guide, William L. Wells; grand inner steward, John F. Kuhn; grand outer steward, John Taylor.

On the 13th day of October, 1869, agreeable to previous notice, the past chancellors and representatives of the subordinate lodges, assembled at Pythian Hall, No. 515 Fourteenth Street, in the City of Omaha. Samuel Read, of Mount Holly, New Jersey, the supreme chancellor of the Supreme Lodge Knights of Pythias of the World, being present, accompanied by Henry Simons, deputy grand chancellor for the Territory of Wyoming, and George H. Crager, deputy grand chancellor for the State of Nebraska, the Grand Lodge Knights of Pythias of Nebraska was formally instituted, and the officers selected at the preliminary meeting of October 1st duly installed.

Damon Lodge, No. 2, after one year of prosperity, began to decline; many of its members who were railroad employes were transferred to other localities, and the general stagnation of business which followed the completion of the Union Pacific Railway interfered with the growth of the order to such an extent that in the spring of 1871 the lodge found its membership reduced to barely a quorum. Becoming discouraged and disheartened, the few members remaining surrendered the charter to the grand lodge at its session in July of that year, and the lodge became extinct. For ten years following the demise of Damon Lodge, the order made little if any progress in Omaha. The result of the election of officers in Planet Lodge, No. 4, in December, 1880, being unsatisfactory to a portion of its membership, fourteen withdrew and petitioned the grand chancellor for a charter to organize a new German lodge. The petition receiving the approval of that officer, Omaha Lodge, No. 26, was instituted by district deputy grand chancellor John F. Kuhn, on February 8, 1881, with thirty charter members.

April 3, 1884, Myrtle Lodge, No. 2, was instituted at Omaha by Grand Chancellor J. G. Jones, assisted by J. S. Shropshire, E. E. French, S. M. Willox and A. F. Borden. This lodge (which received the number formerly held by the extinct Damon) started with a charter membership of sixty and increased rapidly.

April 8, 1886, Triangle Lodge, No. 54, was instituted by District Deputy Grand Chancellor Alfred D. Jones, with a charter membership of fifty-four. This lodge, being the first one located remote from the business center of the city, has enjoyed unusual prosperity. Its meetings were held in the Toft Block, corner of Saunders and Charles Streets for a time, and subsequently moved to Wolff's Hall, on Cuming Street, where it is now located. Its membership exceeds that of any other lodge in the city.

June 1, 1886, Pythagoras Lodge, No. 59, organized by Kt. Charles L. Connors, was instituted in Cosmopolitan Hall, on South

Thirteenth Street, by District Deputy Grand Chancellor Alf. D. Jones, assisted by members of the various city lodges, with a charter membership of twenty.

March 9, 1887, Park Lodge, No. 69, with thirty-four charter members, was instituted by District Deputy Grand Chancellor John E. Smith.

March 16, 1887, Mt. Shasta Lodge, No. 71, was instituted by District Deputy Grand Chancellor John E. Smith, assisted by officers and members of the various sister lodges of the city, with a charter membership of 58.

April 20, 1887, Oriole Lodge, No. 76, organized by Kt. Harry Merriam, of Nebraska Lodge, No. 1, was instituted by District Deputy Grand Chancellor John E. Smith, with a charter membership of 107.

June 8, 1887, Viola Lodge, No. 80, organized by Capt. J. C. Laing, of Nebraska Lodge, No. 1, was instituted by District Deputy Grand Chancellor John E. Smith, with a charter membership of thirty-two.

June 9, 1887, Marathon Lodge, No. 82, organized by Kt. J. E. Smith, Jr., of Park Lodge, No. 69, was instituted at the Castle Hall of Triangle Lodge, with a membership of twenty-nine. The work of instituting was done under the direction of Gen. John E. Smith, D. D. G. C., assisted by members of Triangle Lodge.

June 28, 1887, Forest Lodge, No, 84, was instituted at Madson's Hall, corner of Sixth and Pierce Streets, by John W. Lounsbury, special district deputy, with a charter membership of thirty.

March 7, 1888, Virginius Lodge, No. 95, was instituted at Goodrich Hall, on Saunders Street, by District Deputy Grand Chancellor H. C. Cole, with a charter membership of thirty-eight.

February 23, 1888, Good Samaritan Lodge, No. 97, organized by N. J. Edholm, of Nebraska Lodge, No. 1, was duly instituted by District Deputy Grand Chancellor H. C. Cole, with a charter membership of thirty.

On the 17th of November, 1888, Jan Hus Lodge, No. 5, organized by Kt. Frank Vodicka, was instituted by H. C. Cole, D. D. G. C., with a charter membership of thirty. This lodge is composed of Bohemians, and the work and business of the lodge is conducted in that language.

May 9, 1890, Franklin Lodge, No. 123, was instituted by the district deputy grand chancellor, W. L. Scism, with a charter membership of thirteen. The membership of this lodge is composed exclusively of printers.

On the 21st day of May, 1890, Rathbone Lodge, No. 126, organized by Kt. H. A. Porter, was instituted by the grand chancellor, Macfarland, with a charter membership of sixty.

June 10, 1890, Mars Lodge, No. 130, was instituted by the district deputy grand chancellor, Will L. Scism, with a charter membership of twenty-two. The meetings of this lodge are held in the extreme northern part of the city, adjacent to Fort Omaha. At the close of the year 1891 there were eighteen lodges of the Order of the Knights of Pythias in the City of Omaha, whose aggregate membership exceeded fifteen hundred. March 31, 1891, Good Samaritan Lodge, No. 97, consolidated with Nebraska Lodge, No. 1, and on April 1, following, Virginius Lodge, No. 95, also consolidated with Nebraska Lodge.

On April 21, 1891, Park Lodge, No. 69, consolidated with Marathon Lodge, No. 82, and on May 27, 1891, Viola Lodge, No. 80, also consolidated with Marathon Lodge.

On May 16, 1891, Mt. Shasta Lodge, No. 71, Oriole Lodge, No. 76, and Franklin Lodge, No. 123, consolidated under the name of Triune Lodge, No. 56.

February 3, 1892, Rathbone Lodge, No. 126, consolidated with Nebraska Lodge No. 1, thus reducing the number of lodges in Omaha to eleven, whose aggregate membership June 30, 1892, was 995.

There are two sections of the Endowment Rank in the City of Omaha, officered as follows: Section No. 95, Joseph Rosenstein, president; Jacob Frank, secretary and treasurer. Section No. 735, James Donnelly, Jr., president; George W. Sabine, secretary and treasurer.

The Uniform Rank of the Order of the Knights of Pythias in Omaha, comprises seven active divisions, constituting what is known as the Omaha (Second) Regiment.

Among those who have attained prominence in the order in Omaha, by reason of long and active service, none are more deserving of special mention than J. S. Shropshire, who was initiated in Damon Lodge, No. 2, in 1869. Afterwards transferring his membership to Nebraska Lodge, No. 1, with which he is still connected. He has occupied every official position in the subordinate lodge, and on January 18, 1871, received the rank of past chancellor in the grand lodge, and at the annual session held in October, 1875, was elected to the office of grand chancellor. November 28, 1881, he was appointed representative to the supreme lodge of the world to fill vacancy, and at the expiration of his term of office, was elected for the full term of four years. He has distinguished himself in the councils of the supreme lodge as an able debator, parliamentarian and jurist. He is the author of " K. of P. Common Law," a book with an extensive circulation, and considered excellent authority as a digest of Pythian law.

Egbert E. French was initiated in Nebraska Lodge, No. 1, December 24, 1868, and at the organization of the grand lodge, was elected to the office of grand recording and corresponding scribe, (the title of the office was afterwards changed to grand keeper of records and seal.) At each subsequent annual session he was re-elected, and held the office of grand keeper of records and seal continuously for twenty years. At the session of the grand lodge, in January, 1872, he was elected supreme representative, and by subsequent re-elections held the office for six years, his service terminating at the session of the supreme lodge, held in 1878, at Indianapolis. A vacancy occurring in the office of supreme representative, he was, on March 12, 1890, appointed by Grand Chancellor, Macfarland to fill same, and attended the biennial session recently held in the City of Milwaukee.

John J. Monell united with Nebraska Lodge, No. 1, in 1873, by card from St. Albans Lodge, No. 17, of Council Bluffs, Iowa. He received the rank of past chancellor in the Grand Lodge of Nebraska, February 4, 1874, and in August of the same year was elected to the office of grand chancellor. At the annual session in October, 1875, he was elected representative to the supreme lodge for the term of two years, and at the session of October, 1877, was unanimously re-elected for four years, and again in 1881 for four years. The first movement in the direction of a higher rank in the order, was inaugurated in the supreme lodge by Representative Monell at the session of 1876, resulting later in what is now known as the uniform rank.

Alfred D. Jones was initiated in Nebraska Lodge, No. 1, in 1869. He was admitted to the grand lodge November 25th, of that year. At the annual session in January, 1871, he was elected representative to the supreme lodge and served for the term of two years. At the same session he was also elected grand vice chancellor, which position he resigned at the semi-annual session in July following.

To the energetic work of the four individuals last above mentioned, in connection with Col. George H. Crager, is due the preservation of what, for thirteen years, was the only American lodge of the order in Omaha. While hundreds of others who obtained membership, worked for awhile, became weary in well-doing and dropped out, these brothers have labored unceasingly for twenty years, and now have the satisfaction of seeing the order they love so well permanently established and occupying a leading position among the cryptic societies.

Yours truly,
Jno. M. Thurston

# CHAPTER XLIV

### TRANSPORTATION LINES—EARLY HISTORY OF THE UNION PACIFIC—OTHER RAILWAY LINES

#### THE UNION PACIFIC

Closely allied in their prosperity are the Union Pacific Railroad—the pioneer railway line—and the City of Omaha, and a history of the latter would be incomplete that did not include that of the former. With respect to the earlier stages of work on this great line of railway no man is able to speak more intelligently than Hon Peter A Dey, its first engineer, now a member of the Railroad Commission of Iowa. On this subject he writes the authors of this work as follows

"During the year 1853 I was entrusted by parties interested in the construction of the Rock Island Railroad, with making surveys for a line of railway across the State of Iowa General Dodge, J E House, of Omaha, and George C House, of Iowa, were members of the corps. After reaching the Missouri River, we made a survey of that stream from the mouth of the Boyer to the mouth of the Platte, with a view of selecting the most available point for bridging the river

"About the first of December we crossed into Nebraska and over into the Platte Valley The breadth of the valley, and the knowledge that it extended to the base of the mountains, and that the branches reached to the divide of the continent, lead us to the conclusion that if a Pacific Railroad was ever constructed, the six hundred miles or more of this valley would be utilized

"For a number of years following, whenever opportunity offered, I had, from the surveys made by the general government and all other available sources, attempted in theory, at least, to extend a line across the continent that would be available for construction

"During the next ten years the growing importance of California and Oregon, with the gold discoveries in Colorado and the industrial development of Utah, attracted public attention to the necessity of connecting by some internal way the Mississippi Valley with the Pacific States and Territories This matter gained importance after the war began, and the possibilities of disintegration developed with the unsatisfactory results of the first year This resulted, in 1862, in the passage of the act making a grant of lands and a subsidy, which would be a first mortgage on the road, of sixteen thousand dollars per mile on that portion of the road on the plains, thirty-two thousand dollars per mile on four hundred miles of the more expensive road, and forty-eight thousand dollars per mile on one hundred and fifty miles of the mountainous work In 1862 the company was organized temporarily at Chicago, William R Ogden being selected as President, and Mr Orcutt, of Albany, New York, as Treasurer and Henry B Poor, Secretary For a year following nothing further was done except to make some reconnoisances with a view of selecting the data for subsequent surveys

' After the adjournment of this convention, at the solicitation of Henry Farnam, then president of the Rock Island Railroad, I examined most of the then known passes through the mountainous range west of Denver I then followed north, examining the Black Hills, and from there went west crossing the divide of the continent and down the Echo Canon to the Weber River, and then down the Weber River to the Salt Lake Valley I also examined a route up the Weber River from the mouth of the Echo to Kansas prairie, and then down the Timpanoges River to Provo The result of this was a report to Mr. Farnam, in which I stated that any line crossing the mountains west of Denver, and for a long distance north or south, was impracticable with the maximum grade of 116 feet to the mile, fixed in the act of Congress I took a copy of Stansbury's map of Salt Lake, and on it traced the line of road that in my judgment was the most practicable. This left the Missouri River in the vicinity of Omaha, reaching the Platte Valley near Elkhorn, and followed up the Platte to the mouth of Lodge Pole, then up this stream until its bend to the south, where a tunnel was proposed, then crossing the Laramie Plains, reaching the Salt Lake Valley as above indicated. The matter rested for a year without anything further being done, but a small portion the stock required by law having been subscribed.

"In the summer of 1863 Thomas C. Durant, as I learned, individually subscribed a sufficient amount of stock to effect the permanent organization, and under his instructions, during the years 1863 and 1864, surveys were made from the Missouri River to Salt Lake. Messrs. J. E. House, Samuel B. Reed, James A. Evans, Percy T. Brown and Ogden Edwards had charge of different parties in running preliminary lines and making locations. Mr. Reed made the surveys from Salt Lake to Green River; Mr. Evans from Green River to the eastern base of the Black Hills; Mr. House the eastern end of the line and Messrs. Brown and Edwards the intermediate region. The main difficulties to be encountered were crossing the Black Hills, the divide of the continent, and the rim of the Salt Lake basin, and reaching the plains below with the gradients allowed. These, however, were accomplished with a reasonable degree of success, with perhaps the exception of the Black Hills, this, however, future surveys and examinations made practicable.

"There were three lines of railway under construction from the east, crossing the State of Iowa; the Northwestern, the Rock Island, and the Burlington, with a view, probably, of fixing a terminal point that would be reasonably accessible to the three. Mr. Durant determined upon making Omaha the initial point, and although the surveys developed a much easier and more practical line in the vicinity of Bellevue, and also further north, he adhered with great tenacity to this point. Afterwards Silas Seymour, who, I think, was appointed consulting engineer, solved the problem of cheap construction, by practically adopting the Bellevue line, after reaching Mud Creek, some three miles west of the Missouri River. This was accomplished by an increase of distance of nine miles, in going fourteen miles west from the point of divergence. The Northwestern or the Burlington now occupies nearly the line of the original survey for some distance west. My impression is that each goes over part of the ground covered by the original survey. There was considerable discussion at the time of the change of the line, and it was thought it meant an abandonment of the initial point. This, however, was saved, and the general government advanced to the company, what was probably the ruling consideration for the change, sixteen thousand dollars per mile for each of the nine additional miles, when the estimated cost of the fourteen miles was as great as the twenty-three.

"The discussion of this question was, to a great extent, confounded in the public mind, with the Hoxie contract, executed September 23, 1864. This contract practically conveyed to Hoxie all the interest of the company in the first mortgage for 100 miles, which was made by the amendment of 1864, a lien on the road prior to the lien of the general government, the bonds furnished by the government, a land grant mortgage of the same amount, and stock to the amount of five thousand dollars per mile. Mr. Hoxie was to build the road for the first hundred miles at fifty thousand dollars per mile. The engineer's estimate for this hundred miles, with the limitations in the contract, was less than thirty-thousand dollars per mile. The sidings were limited to six per cent of the length of the main line, the grades were subject to the control of the contractor, limited only to the grade of the New York Central out of Albany. The cost of station buildings, machinery, machine shops, tanks, equipment, etc., was limited to five thousand dollars per mile. The cost of iron delivered at Omaha was limited to one hundred and thirty dollars per ton. Mr. Hoxie was to pay for the first mortgage and government bonds, eighty per cent of their par value, and seventy per cent for the land grant bonds, or, he took $48,000 of bonds on the road and paid for them $37,600.

"The rate these securities were disposed of, a government six per cent. bond, and a mortgage that was prior to it at eighty cents on the dollar, seems extraordinary, yet this contract had the approval of five directors, who were specially selected to protect the interests of government, and a secretary of the interior, whose attention was called to the terms of the contract. This contract became the basis of the Credit Mobilier, and its iniquities have become so generally public property, and destroyed the reputation of so many statesmen, that it is not necessary to pursue it further. The motive for making these contracts has not generally been appreciated. At that time it was generally believed that two hundred miles west of the Missouri River was the limit of arable lands, except where irrigation was available, and that it was thought the entire country, on account of the absence of rain, would ever remain a desert. There can be but little doubt that the motive influencing Mr. Durant, if not his associates, was to realize from the contract for construction all the profit possible, and turn the property over to the government to operate, under the conviction that it could never earn its expenses. His conduct is consistent with this theory, for he gave personal attention to the construction, until the tracks of the Union and Central Pacific Roads were connected at Promontory, and left for New York, never seeing the road afterward. The extraordinary earnings and the property of the road for the first few years after its completion, though loaded down with an indebtedness that should have bankrupted it, made a later and further depletion possible. My sympathies are strongly enlisted with Mr. Adams, who has, in a straight-forward, honest way, sought to rescue the property from the mis-management of his predecessors, and with his effort to have Congress so arrange the maturity of the indebtedness that the earnings of the road will eventually be able to put it in a position where it can be paid. Had such a management as he brought to the road been applied to the construction, and maintained in its operation, the Union Pacific stock, notwithstanding the competition, in my judgment, would be the best railroad property in this country."

Mr. Dey was so opposed to the conditions of the Hoxie contract, and the price at which the construction of the road was fixed under that contract, that he not only resigned his position as engineer, but set out his reasons therefor in two letters. The first is addressed to Thomas C. Durant (then the master mind of the railroad company, though his nominal position was that of vice president), and was as follows:

ENGINEER'S OFFICE,
UNION PACIFIC RAILWAY,
OMAHA, Dec. 7, 1864.

*Dear Sir:*—I hereby tender you my resignation as chief engineer of the Union Pacific Railway, to take effect December 30, 1864, one year from the date of my appointment. I am induced to delay until that time that I might combine the results of surveys of the present year and present them to the company and to myself in a satisfactory manner. My reasons for this step are simply that I do not approve of the contract made with Mr. Hoxie for building the first hundred miles from Omaha west and I do not care to have my name so connected with the railroad that I shall appear to indorse this contract. Wishing for the road success beyond the expectation of its members.

" I am respectfully yours, etc."

He wrote General Dix, president of the road, on the same day, as follows:

"OMAHA, Dec. 7, 1864.

*Dear Sir:*—With this I send in my resignation as chief engineer of the Union Pacific Railroad Company. My reasons I have given. I received the contract nearly a month ago. When I first read it I felt that it was made against my known views and I could not be held in any measure responsible for it, but it has since been a constantly recurring subject of thought to me and I am not now satisfied that I shall be able to acquit myself of all blame if I become an instrument of its execution. You know the history of the M. & M. Road, a road that to-day could be running to this point if its stock and bonds only represented the amount of cash that actually went into it. My views of the Pacific Railroad are perhaps peculiar. I look upon its managers as trustees of the bounty of Congress. I cannot willingly see the repeat of the history of the M. & M. by taking a step in the incipiency of the project that will, I believe if followed out, swell the cost of construction so much that by the time the work reaches the mountains the representative capital will be accumulated so much that at the very time when the company will have need for all its resources as well of capital as of credit its securities will not be negotiable in the market. From my boyhood I have associated Mr. Cisco and yourself with Mr. Bronson and Mr. Flagg, men whose integrity, purity and singleness of purpose have made them marked men in the generation in which they lived. Of course my opinion remains unchanged. You are doubtless uninformed how disproportionate the amount to be paid is to the work contracted for.

I need not expatiate upon the sincerity of my course when you reflect upon the fact that I have resigned the best position in my profession this country has ever offered to any man.

"With Respect, etc."

On the 30th of November, 1863, Messrs. Peter Dey, A. J. Hanscom, John McCormick, George H. Mills, E. B. Taylor and Augustus Kountze addressed the city council on the subject of "granting the Union Pacific Railroad Company certain rights and privileges on the levee," and the matter was referred to the judiciary committee, which committee, through George B. Lake, chairman, presented the following at a meeting of the council held December 7th, 1863:

"WHEREAS, The Union Pacific Railroad Company is desirous of obtaining the right of way over all that certain piece or parcel of land situated in the City of Omaha, in the Territory of Nebraska, lying along the bank of the Missouri River and designated on the lithographed plat of said city made and published by Poppleton & Byers as 'Levee,' for the purpose of constructing, maintaining and operating three or more tracks of said railroad over the same, with the required side-tracks, switches, water stations, warehouses, wharfs and appurtenances and whatever else may be necessary to the operation, maintenance and security of said railroad, its property and business, and,

WHEREAS, The first grant of such rights and privileges to said company will be of great benefit and advantage to said city so long as the same shall be used by the said company, therefore:

"*Resolved*, By the city council of the City of Omaha, that the mayor of said city be and is hereby authorized, empowered and required to make, execute and deliver to the said Union Pacific Railroad Company, their successors, assigns and grantees, in accordance with the charter of said city, and the ordinances in such case made and provided, a deed of grant of said city and the corporate authorities thereof of the right of way over, upon and through the said premises, with the free and uninterrupted liberty of laying out, locating and constructing, maintaining, operating, furnishing and enjoying three or more tracks of said railroad over the same, with the requisite side-tracks, turnouts, switches, water stations, warehouses, wharfs and appurtenances, and whatever else may be requisite and necessary for the location, construction, operation, maintenance, enjoyment and security of said railroad and its appurtenances and business, with free ingress, egress and regress upon, through and over the same to and for the said company, its successors, assigns, grantees, servants, tenants, occupiers and possessors—its property, trains, passengers and freight, so long as the same shall be used, occupied and enjoyed for that purpose by the said company, its successors and assings. And it is further

"*Resolved*, That the rights and privileges hereby granted shall not be so construed as to conflict with or impair any privilege heretofore granted to any person or persons, or bodies politic or corporate whatsoever, in or to the aforesaid ground. That suitable crossings shall be made and provided by said company at all public streets crossed by any of the said railroad tracks, which it is necessary for the public to use to enable them to reach the ferryboat and steamboat landings, so as not to obstruct travel to or from the ferry or steamboat landings, and that the right of the public to travel over and enjoy said ground shall be unimpaired only so far as the reasonable exercise of the privileges hereby granted shall abridge the same and that the substance of this last resolution be incorporated in said grant by way of limitation of the privileges of said company."

This resolution was adopted as was also the following, offered by Judge Lake:

"*Resolved*, By the city council of the City of Omaha, that the mayor of said city be and he is hereby authorized, empowered and required to make, execute, acknowledge and deliver to the Union Pacific Company a deed of conveyance in fee simple of the fol lowing described pieces or parcels of land, situated in the County of Douglas and Territory of Nebraska, to wit: Blocks L, N, O, P and Q, in said city, as designated on the lithographed map thereof made and published by Poppleton & Byers, said conveyance to contain a proviso that in case the eastern terminus of the Union Pacific Railroad on the Missouri River shall not be located and continued within one and one-quarter miles of Farnam Street in said City of Omaha, then and in that case the premises hereby conveyed shall revert to and become re-invested in the said City of Omaha."

December 2, 1863, there was a formal breaking of ground for the railroad, at a point on the river considerably above the present site of the shops. It was an eventful occasion, and enthusiastic addresses were made by Governor Saunders, Mayor B. E. B. Kennedy, Dr. G. C. Monell, Judge A. V. Larimer (of Council Bluffs), Judge George B. Lake and George Francis Train, interspersed with firing of cannon.

January 15, 1864, the following was presented and adopted:

"*Resolved*, That the mayor be and he is hereby directed to convey, by deed in fee simple, to the Union Pacific Railroad Company, the following described lots in the City of Omaha, on condition that the principal depot grounds of said railroad be located on the eastern border of the City of Omaha, between the bluff and Missouri River, and that the route of said railroad be westerly from said city, within one and one-fourth miles of Farnam Street, leaving township 15, range 13, from the western border of the same, to-wit: Lot 8, block 2; lots 5 and 6, block 3; lot 4, block 4; lot 7, block 35; lots 5 and 8, block 65; lot 1, block 66; lots 3 and 4, block 67; lots 7 and 8, block 69; lots 1 and 4, block 94; lots 2 and 7, block 96; lot 8, block 99; lots 5 and 6, block 126; lot 5, block 127; lot 5, block 130; lot 1, block 156; lot 3, block 157; lot 5, block 307; lot 6, block 308; lot 6, block 310; lot 5, block 312; lot 6, block 313; west half lot 7, block 315; lot 3, block 316; lots 1 and 6, block 317; lot 2, block 318; lot 1, block 319; lot 7, block 322; lot 8, block 323; lot 7, block 326; lot 2, block 327; lots 2, 5, 6, 7 and 8, block 328; lot 3, block 331, and lot 3, block 333."—44½ lots.

On the 23d of March, 1864, Alderman Vincent Burkley, as chairman of a committee to whom the matter had been referred, presented the following, which was adopted:

"Your committee, to whom was referred the relation and resolution presented by Augustus Kountze on behalf of the Union Pacific Railroad Company, relative to donating certain lots belonging to the city for other lots owned by individuals, which are required for the use of that corporation, beg leave to report that in their opinion the additional donation of city property asked for in the petition is not demanded by the interests of the city at the present time, and your committee would recommend that until the Union Pacific Railroad Company can exhibit satisfactory evidence to the city council that the additional donations are desired by the citizens of Omaha, the petition and resolution lie on the table."

September 11, 1865, the following petition was presented and the mayor instructed to make the grant asked for:

"*To the Honorable the Mayor and Common Council of the City of Omaha:*

"Your petitioner, the Union Pacific Railroad Company, respectfully represents that it is desirious of obtaining the right to use and occupy, for the purpose of building thereon its depots, machine shops, engine houses, work shops, freight houses and appurtenances, all that portion of the following described streets in the City of Omaha marked and designated on the accompanying plat, and including within the blue line marked thereon, to-wit: Capitol Avenue, Davenport Street, Chicago Street, Cass Street, California Street, Webster Street, Burt Street, Seventh Street, Eighth Street, Ninth Street, Tenth Street and Eleventh Street.

"Your petitioner further represents that the same are the only suitable and practicable grounds for the erection of said buildings in said city, and that they are necessary for the building of the same.

"Your petitioner, therefore, prays that all such portions of said streets may be vacated and a grant thereby made to your petitioner for the uses aforesaid, and also that lots of the said city lying within the same limits may be granted said company for the like purposes."

In the proceedings of May 1, 1866, is found the following entry; relating to a matter of the greatest importance to the city in view of the present business character of the street referred to. "On leave A. J. Poppleton, Esq., attorney for the Union Pacific Railway Company, made a few remarks, stating that owing to the late high water in the river it was necessary to have other tracks running through the city besides the one on the bottom, and he asked on behalf of the company that they might be permitted to lay a track along Fourteenth Street.

"Mr. Reed, engineer of the company, submitted a profile of said street.

"After remarks upon the subject by several citizens and some discussion by the council, the following resolution was, on motion of Alderman Ingalls, adopted:

"'Resolved, That the right of way be granted to the Union Pacific Railway Company over Fourteenth Street, for a double track, with the usual restrictions common to railroad companies in other cities, and that the mayor be authorized to execute a conveyance accordingly.'"

On the following day the deed provided for by the foregoing resolution was signed by the mayor, Lorin Miller, and in view of the present importance of this street, and the character of the business houses erected thereon, the exact terms of this deed become matters of interest. After reciting the authority under which the conveyance is made, it continues, as follows:

"Now therefore, in consideration of the premises, and the sum of one dollar lawful money of the United States unto the said party of the first part well and truly paid by the said party of the second part, at and before the ensealing and delivery thereof, is hereby acknowledged, the said party of the first part hath granted, bargained and sold, and by these presents both grant bargain and sell unto the said party of the second part, its grantees, successors, and assigns, the right of way over, upon and through all that certain piece and parcel of land situate in the City of Omaha, and Territory of Ne-  , designated on the lithographed map of said city, made and published by Poppleton & Byers, as Fourteenth Street, from the northern to the southern corporate limits of said city, with the free and uninterrupted liberty and privilege of laying out, locating, constructing, maintaining, operating, furnishing and enjoying, a double track of said railroad over and upon the same, with free ingress, egress and regress upon, to and over the same, to and for the said party of the second part, its grantees, successors, and assigns, tenants, servants, occupants, and possessors, its property, trains, passengers and freight.

"To have and to hold all and singular, the said rights and privileges as aforesaid, unto the said party of the second part, its grantees, successors and assigns, so long as the same shall be used, occupied and enjoyed for the purpose aforesaid by said party of the second part, its grantees, successors and assigns. And the said party of the second part, its grantees, successors and assigns shall provide suitable and sufficient crossings at all public streets crossed by said railroad tracks; shall not move their trains along through said Fourteenth Street at a rate of speed to exceed five miles per hour; they shall, in laying, locating, constructing and operating their said tracks over and upon said Fourteenth Street, conform as near as practicable to the grade of said street, and they shall not use said street as a standing place for cars, so as to obstruct the travel and passage of persons, property and freight, across, over and along the same."

Those were the days in which the Union Pacific Company received everything it asked for, and it was not backward in preferring its requests. August 22, 1866, the company "respectfully represented" that in order to properly carry out its purpose of "building, and maintaining depots, machine shops, engine-houses, work-shops, freight houses, side-tracks, switches and other structures, with their appurtenances necessary and convenient for the use of its road in said City of Omaha" it was necessary that the company be granted a right of way over the following named streets: Seventh, Eighth, Ninth, Tenth, Eleventh, Twelfth, Thirteenth, Fourteenth, Capitol Avenue, Davenport, Chicago, Cass, California, Web-

ster, Burt and Cuming, within an area specified on a plat submitted. The petition was granted, of course, and the mayor directed to execute the proper conveyance.

Under date of February 20, 1867, the council records show that the following action was taken with respect to the locating of the Union Pacific bridge, at this point. A resolution passed at a meeting of the citizens of Omaha, held a few days previously, was presented, requesting the council to appoint O. P. Hurford, A. S. Paddock and George L. Miller, a committee to proceed to New York immediately to confer with the company proposing to erect a bridge across the Missouri River, and that said committee be authorized to pledge any sum not exceeding one hundred thousand dollars, if the same be necessary, to secure the location of the bridge at Omaha. Two days previously, a legislative act had been approved authorizing the City of Omaha to raise the amount of money above named for the purpose in question. Alderman Birkett offered this resolution, which was adopted:

"*Be it Resolved*, By the city council of the City of Omaha, that the mayor of said city be and he is hereby directed to subscribe for and in behalf of said city, to the capital stock in any company or corporation that now is or may be hereafter organized for the purpose of constructing a railroad bridge across the Missouri River at Omaha, to any amount in his discretion, not exceeding the sum of $100,000.00, and that he be further authorized and empowered to guarantee the feasibility of said bridge at said point against the encroachments of the Missouri River, and to hypothecate and pledge the whole or any part of the stock so by him subscribed to make good such warranty, and further, that said mayor be, and he is hereby authorized and empowered to guarantee the payment by said City of Omaha, of any sum not exceeding $100,000.00, in lieu of a subscription to the stock of said company in case he shall deem it necessary so to do, in order to secure the location of said bridge at Omaha, or to secure its permanency after said location, and said mayor is hereby authorized to appoint any suitable person or persons to proceed to the City of New York to act in his behalf, in all respects, the same as he might do in person."

Dr. Miller having signified his inability to act as a member of the proposed committee, the following named were appointed: Ezra Millard, O. P. Hurford, B. E. B. Kennedy, A. S. Paddock, James Creighton, Augustus Kountze and Frank Smith, and the mayor was authorized "to telegraph to persons named in the foregoing committee to any extent he may deem necessary for the purposes contemplated."

January 8, 1868, a resolution was adopted by the council whereby the city assured all the expense of securing to the railroad company "free of cost the right of way for a track from the bridge crossing of the Missouri River known as 'Line No. Two,' or 'Lower Omaha Crossing,' to its intersection with the track already built, and also a track from said crossing to the machine shops and depot of said road, and also such grounds for depot purposes as may be deemed necessary by the chief engineer of said road, and being about twelve acres as shown on the maps in the engineer's office; and in case the upper crossing shall be adopted and the bridge located at or near that point we pledge the like aid, and that the mayor be and he is hereby authorized and directed to call an election for the purpose of deciding whether or not a loan shall be made by the city of a sum sufficient for that purpose."

March 4, 1868, Alvin Saunders, Augustus Kountze, O. P. Hurford, Ezra Millard, Enos Lowe and Dr. George L. Miller were appointed by the council, or committee, "to represent the interests of the City of Omaha before the board of directors of the Union Pacific Company, in New York, and other railroad companies in any matters arising before said companies involving the interests of said city."

The following month an agreement was entered into, as follows:

"OMAHA, April 27, 1868.

"Memorandum of agreement between Thomas C. Durant and Sidney Dillon, on the part of the Union Pacific Railroad Company, and Dr. Enos Lowe, O. P. Hurford, Ezra Millard and A. Kountze, committee on the part of Douglas County, have this day agreed on the following terms touching the erection of a bridge over the Missouri River at Omaha. First. That $250,000 bonds are to be issued by Douglas County, to run twenty years and bear seven per cent. per annum interest, payable semi-annually at New York. Second. Said bonds are to be delivered to the said railroad or bridge company from time to time as the construction of the bridge progresses. Third. The interest on the bonds shall accrue to said bridge company only at the date of delivery. Fourth. Proper trustees shall be appointed on the part of the railroad company, and acting in behalf of Douglas County, who shall hold the bonds and make delivery of the same in accordance with the agreement.

"Signed by: Thomas C. Durant, Sidney Dillon, Enos Lowe, O. P. Hurford, Ezra Millard, A. Kountze, Omaha committee."

(The original of this agreement, from which the above was copied, is among the papers of the late Mr. Byron Reed, of this city.)

A special election was held July 13th, following, to vote upon the proposition to issue city bonds to the amount of $150,000, "for the purpose of paying for the necessary right of way and depot grounds in said City of Omaha, required by the Union Pacific Railroad Company in connection with its bridge across the Missouri River.

The bonds were voted, and at another special election, held January 18, 1869, the rate of interest was fixed at ten per cent. and an additional fifty thousand dollars voted for the same purpose as that for which the original issue had been voted, viz: To secure right of way and depot grounds, which proposition also carried, making a total sum of $200,000 of city bonds, authorized to be issued in aid of the company, in addition to the twelve acres of land on the table land and various lots in other localities.

In the meantime the County of Douglas was doing its share toward aiding the railroad company, and on the 13th of July, 1868, a county election was held to pass upon this proposition, and which was carried by a heavy majority: "Shall the County of Douglas, for the purpose of securing the location and aiding in the construction of a railroad bridge across the Missouri River, between the Union Pacific Railroad and such other railroads as may seek connections therewith, at Omaha City, in said county, contribute thereto in county bonds the sum of $250,000, payable in twenty years from date, bearing seven per cent. interest per annum, payable semi-annually in the City of New York * * * * One hundred thousand dollars to be issued and delivered to the Railroad Bridge Company whenever it shall properly appear to the county commissioners of said county that said company have in good faith expended $300,000 in the construction of said railroad bridge; the said bonds to bear date upon the delivery thereof; * * * and the further sum of $100,000 of county bonds to be issued and delivered to the Railroad Bridge Company whenever it shall properly appear to the county commissioners of said county that said company have in good faith expended $600,000 in the construction of said railroad bridge * * * and the further sum of fifty thousand dollars of county bonds to be issued and delivered to the said Railroad Bridge Company whenever it shall properly appear to the county commissioners of said county that said company has in good faith completely constructed and erected said railroad bridge so as to be in good and sufficient order for the use contemplated," etc.

On the 4th of March, 1871, a statement was made to the county board by Superintendent T. E. Sickles, of the Union Pacific Railroad, to the effect that there had then been expended in the construction of the bridge the sum of $325,674.02, and hence the first installment of $100,000 in county bonds was due the company; and on the 22d of November, 1874, application was made by the railroad company for the final installment of fifty thousand dollars, from which it may be inferred that the bridge was then considered completed.

During that year the city acquired possession, from the individual owners, of the various lots and parcels of ground desired by the railroad company, which property was transferred to the company by Alvin Saunders, (in whose name it had been taken in trust) by the following conveyance:

"This indenture, made this 20th day of January, 1872, by and between Alvin Saunders, trustee of the City of Omaha, in the State of Nebraska, party of the first part, and the Union Pacific Railroad Company, party of the second part, witnesseth:

"WHEREAS, The real estate and premises hereinafter described were conveyed to said party of the first part by divers persons under the direction of a commission, or board of adjustment, appointed by the City of Omaha to make settlement with the owners of certain lots and lands required by the said party of the second part for depot and transfer grounds and for right of way connected with its bridge over the Missouri River, all of which lands and premises were paid for by the said City of Omaha and conveyed to the said party of the first part as aforesaid, to be by him held in trust for said city during the time required to make such settlement or adjustment and afterwards to convey the same to the said party of the second part hereto, when directed so to do by said City of Omaha, with such restrictions and limitations as might be deemed necessary to protect the interests of said city, all of which will more fully appear on reference to a certain instrument in writing containing a formal declaration of said trust, executed by the said Alvin Saunders on the 31st day of August, 1869, in book 7 of deeds, at page 277 of the records of Douglas County, in the State of Nebraska; and whereas the city council of said City of Omaha, by resolution passed on the 2d day of January, 1872, did direct the said party of the first part to make, execute and cause to be delivered to said party of the second part a deed to said real estate and premises hereinafter described, subject to the terms, conditions and restrictions of a certain contract of which the following is a copy, to-wit:

"'Agreement made this first day of January, in the year of our Lord one thousand eight hundred and seventy-two, by and between the Union Pacific Railroad Company, authorized by law of Congress, to build a bridge across the Missouri River at or near Council Bluffs, Iowa, and Omaha. Nebraska, and the County of Douglas, in the State of Nebraska, parties of the second part, witnesseth: That, whereas the parties hereunto desire to arrange for the more perfect connection of any railroads that are or shall be constructed to the Missouri River at or near Council Bluffs, Iowa, and Omaha, Nebraska, now in consideration of the premises and of the receipt by the party of the first part of the bonds of said Douglas County, to the amount of $250,000, and in further consideration of the receipt by the party of the first part of a deed from said city of Omaha to certain real estate in said city, known as the depot grounds and right of way, the party of the first part for itself and its successors, covenants and agrees to, and with the said County of Douglas and the said City of Omaha as follows, to wit:

"First. That it will construct, complete and maintain a railroad bridge over the Missouri River at said City of Omaha.

"Second. That the eastern terminus of the Union Pacific Railroad shall be and remain at said City of Omaha.

"Third. That after its Missouri River bridge at the City of Omaha, is completed and ready for use, the Union Pacific Railroad Company will make up all its regular west-bound passenger and freight trains on the grounds, which the people and the City of Omaha propose as above to deed to said Union Pacific Railroad Company, and as is already mapped and planned, that is to say all passengers and freights coming from the east on all lines of roads seeking a connection with said Union Pacific Railroad at its eastern terminus shall be delivered and transferred to the Union Pacific Railroad Company upon said depot grounds, where the Union Pacific trains shall be made up for the west, and that said party of the first part will, after such bridge completion, transfer upon said grounds to the various railroads that do or may begin or end in Council

Bluffs or Omaha, all its passengers, baggage, express matter, mails and freight north, east, or south bound.

"Fourth. That the said Union Pacific Railroad Company will, within one year from the date hereof, expend in improvements in the building of passenger and freight depots, general passenger and freight offices, land offices, transfer and telegraph offices, upon said grounds, a sum that shall not be less than $100,000, and to maintain these buildings and offices thereon.

"Fifth. All machine and car shops and other manufactories required for the use of said company at its eastern terminus, all permanent offices for the company required for the transaction of its business, including the land department, general superintendent's office, general passenger and freight offices, warehouses for the company's use, etc., shall be erected and maintained at Omaha.

"Sixth. That under proper rules for their regulation, to be prescribed by the said party of the first part, the trains, cars and engines of all railroads now or hereafter running into Omaha and Council Bluffs, shall have unobstructed access and transit to and over said bridge and its approaches, and such roads shall have the right to take, or cause to be taken, their trains, cars and engines with their freight and passengers, over and across said bridge and its approaches at reasonable compensation without discrimination, hinderance, preference or delay; *Provided*, however, that the Union Pacific Railroad Company shall in all cases have the option of substituting its own engines for those of such other railroads in the operating of its said bridge, receiving reasonable compensation therefor, the object of this clause being to make a virtual and operating connection upon said transfer grounds between all the railroads desiring such connection which do or may begin or end in or pass through Omaha or Council Bluffs, and trains and business of other railroads.

"In witness whereof the said party of the first part has caused these presents to be executed in triplicate, by its vice president, hereby binding said Union Pacific Railroad Company, and its successors, to the covenants and agreements herein contained, and the parties of the second part by their authorized officers, have hereunto set their hands in triplicate, the day and year first above written.'

"Which said contract was duly executed and delivered by the triplicate parties thereto. Now, therefore, in consideration of the premises, and the sum of one dollar in hand paid, the receipt of which is hereby acknowledged, the said party of the first part does hereby grant, sell and convey unto the said party of the second part and its successors, the following described real estate, situated in the City of Omaha, County of Douglas and State of Nebraska, and bounded and described as follows, (here follows a lengthy description of the property conveyed) hereby limiting the use of all said premises to the legitimate purpose of depot and transfer grounds and grounds for right of way and approaches to said Missouri bridge, subject to the conditions and restrictions contained in the contract above recited, and provided further, that in case said premises, or any part thereof, be abandoned or disused, or converted to any other than the uses and purposes hereinbefore limited, then the same shall revert to and become the property of the City of Omaha."

This deed was signed by Ex-Governor Saunders, witnessed by W. R. Bend and A. J. Poppleton, and acknowledged before W. R. Bend as notary public, the date of the acknowledgment being January 26, 1872. It is recorded in book twelve of deeds, at page 220, Douglas County records. The contract which is embodied in the foregoing instrument, has appended, the following:

Signed by: "Union Pacific Railroad Company, by John Duff, vice president. Executed in presence of A. J. Poppleton. Attest: R. H. Rollins, Secretary Union Pacific Railroad Company. E. A. Allen, President City Council and Acting Mayor of Omaha; C. L. Bristol, City Clerk, per I. Usher, Deputy; the County of Douglas by M. W. E. Purchase and James H. McArdle, Commissioners; William H. Ijams, County Clerk."

The intention of having all transfers of passengers and freight made on the Omaha side of the river did not prove one of easy enforcement, however, and on the 13th day of March following, this entry appears in the city records:

"WHEREAS, It is reported by good authority to this council that the superintendents of the several roads passing through Iowa and terminating in Council Bluffs, and at the Missouri River, have positively refused and declined to transfer their westerubound passengers and freight across the Missouri River Bridge between Omaha and Council Bluffs, and have, in fact, refused to even allow their cars to be crossed over said bridge, intending, evidently, by such action, to compel the Union Pacific Railroad Company to make their transfers on the east side of the river and at a great distance from its terminus, therefore be it

"*Resolved*, By the city council of the City of Omaha, that the officers of the Union Pacific Railroad Company are hereby respectfully requested not to go beyond their terminus in Omaha to discharge their passengers and freights, and we further request that if any third party has to be employed temporarily to assist in making their transfers said party shall be the representative of the eastern roads, and not of the Union Pacific Railroad Company"

Several prominent citizens addressed the council, the resolution was adopted, and a copy thereof and also of the preamble, ordered sent to Superintendent Sickles

In February, 1873, the Union Pacific Company took a train of cars over the bridge into Iowa, which action called forth the following at the first meeting of the Omaha city council thereafter

"WHEREAS, It has come to the knowledge of this council that the Union Pacific Railroad eastward-bound train was, on Sunday afternoon last, taken across the bridge at this point, and the transfer of passengers and freight made on the Iowa side of the Missouri River, contrary to the stipulations of a contract existing between the Union Pacific Railroad Company and the City of Omaha, therefore be it

"*Resolved*, By the city council of the City of Omaha, that a committee of three be appointed whose duty it shall be to call on Superintendent Sickles and ascertain the cause of the violation of the said contract as herein set forth, and whether it is the intention of the said Union Pacific Railroad Company to continue to make such transfer on the east side of the river, said committee to report to the council at the next meeting the result of its inquiries"

The committee was appointed and at the next meeting of the council reported that Superintendent Sickles "explained the case to their entire satisfaction, and that the Union Pacific Railroad Company are disposed to and will keep in good faith their part of the contract"

The year within which buildings for general offices, a depot "to cost not less than $100,000, etc , etc , were to be erected, passed without a compliance on the part of the railroad company with that clause of the contract, and in September, 1873, an extension of ten months from September 9th was granted the company by the council to complete, on lots 1 and 2 block 231 (southwest corner of Tenth and Mason Streets) "a building for its general offices according to, or equal to the general plan adopted by the company at the same time, and shall maintain the said buildings and offices on said grounds respectively," such acts would be accepted by the city as a compliance with the fourth clause of the contract, and Ex-Governor Saunders, as trustee, was empowered and directed to execute the proper instrument to carry the agreement into effect. In June of the following year a further extension was granted the company by which the depot was to be completed by November 1, 1874, according to the plan adopted by the company August 18. 1873, "as modified by resolution of the executive committee of said company, passed May 25. 1874, at a meeting thereof in the City of Boston," and the office building, it was provided, was to be under roof by January 1, 1875

The foundation for the building for office purposes was laid in the most substantial manner, and with that the work stopped In July, 1875, Mr Sidney Dillon, president of the railroad company, was waited upon at the Grand Central Hotel, during a visit in Omaha, by a committee of the council, to learn why the said building was not being completed. Mr. Dillon stated, in response, that the railroad company had been short of funds, but was now in position to go on with the work; that it was extremely desirous of carrying out to the letter, its contract with the County of Douglas and City of Omaha; that Dr. G. C. Monell had offered to sell the Herndon House, corner of Ninth and Farnam, to the company for the purposes of a general office building, and that if the county commissioners and city council would permit it, the company would buy said building and expend fifteen thousand dollars in putting it in proper condition. These facts were reported to the council by the committee, with the recommendation that the railroad company be held to the original agreement with respect to the office building. The matter was finally adjusted, however, and the Herndon House purchased and enlarged at various times since that date, at a total expenditure of about $200,000, and it is now one of the most convenient and extensive railroad offices in the United States.

The shops of the Union Pacific Company, now covering nearly forty acres of ground, were established in 1865, in a very small way. They are now noted all over the West for their extent and completeness, two million dollars having been expended in buildings and machinery. There are now operated from Omaha, by this company, 8,471 miles of road. More than fourteen thousand persons are employed, the monthly pay roll amounting to nearly one million dollars.

Following are the executive officers and their assistants, who have their headquarters in Omaha:

Executive Department.—S. H. H. Clark, president and general manager; E. Dickinson, assistant general manager; Frank D. Brown, local treasurer.

Law Department.—John M. Thurston, general solicitor; W. R. Kelly, assistant general solicitor; W. J. Carroll, assistant to general solicitor; W. R. Kelly, general attorney for Nebraska and Iowa; Edward P. Smith, assistant general attorney for Nebraska.

Claim Department.—John R. Manchester, general claim agent.

Land Department.—B. A. McAllaster, land commissioner.

Accounting Department.—Erastus Young, auditor; F. W. Hills, assistant auditor; R. Anderson, auditor of disbursements; A. S. Van Kuran, freight auditor; W. S. Wing, auditor of passenger accounts.

Traffic Department.—E. L. Lomax, general passenger and ticket agent; J. N. Brown, acting assistant general passenger and ticket agent; J. A. Munroe, freight traffic manager; Elmer H. Wood, assistant general freight agent; C. J. Lane, division freight agent.

Operating Department.—E. Dickinson, assistant general manager; P. J. Nichols, general superintendent Nebraska division; R. Sutherland, superintendent Nebraska division; E. Buckingham, superintendent car service.

Mechanical Department.—J. H. McConnell, superintendent motive power and machinery.

Telegraph Department.—L. H. Korty, superintendent of telegraph.

Coal Department.—G. W. Megeath, superintendent.

Supply Department.—J. W. Griffith, general purchasing agent; J. H. Stafford, general storekeeper; A. E. Hutchinson, stationer.

Miscellaneous.—F. Washburn, superintendent hotel department; A. W. Scribner, tax commissioner; W. J. Galbraith, M. D., chief surgeon.

In 1866 a special election was held, July 30th, to vote upon a proposition for the issuance of bonds by the city to the amount of forty thousand dollars, in aid of the Cedar Rapids & Missouri River Railroad Company "payable in three years from the 1st day of April, 1867, or, from thirty days after the said railroad be built to the east bank of the river, opposite Omaha," said bonds bearing interest at the rate of ten per cent. The vote at this election was exceedingly light, there being but 357 ballots cast in favor of the proposition, and fourteen against it. The mayor was authorized, August 29, 1866, to issue the bonds. Of this amount thirty thousand dollars was to be given to the company, and the remainder used in securing a right of way grant to the ferry landing, opposite the city, for the ferriage of said railroad company's business across the river.

On the 2d of January, 1867, Gen. G. M. Dodge, W. W. Walker, O. P. Hurford and S. S. Caldwell, appeared before the council and stated that only $22,500 in notes had been realized from the thirty thousand dollars of city bonds previously issued, and asked that bonds to the amount of ten thousand dollars additional be issued, to comply with the proposition previously made by the railroad company. Action upon this matter was postponed a few days, when a special meeting was held, and a resolution adopted to the effect that in the issuance of its bonds to the amount stated, the city had fully complied with the terms of the proposition in question.

### THE OMAHA & SOUTHWESTERN AND THE OMAHA & NORTHWESTERN.

November 30, 1869, a resolution was adopted by the county commissioners, calling a special election to vote upon the proposition to issue bonds to the amount of $350,000, to be dated January 1, 1870, and run twenty years, at ten per cent. semi-annual interest, the county reserving the right to redeem any portion of said bonds after the expiration of five years, in aid of two railroads. To the Omaha & Southwestern Railroad Company $150,000, " to aid in constructing a railroad from Omaha in a southerly direction, by way of Lincoln, to the southern boundary of Nebraska, in Gage County," and to the Omaha & Northwestern Railroad Company $200,000, " to aid it in constructing a railroad from the City of Omaha in a northwesterly direction to the mouth of the Niobrara River, upon such route as said companies have respectively adopted." The election was held December 30, 1869, and the issue of bonds authorized by a vote of 1,655 in the affirmative to 176 in the negative. Evidently these companies lost no time in applying to the county commissioners for aid, the Omaha & Southwestern having organized November 27, 1869, and the Omaha & Northwestern, November 30th—the date of calling the election. The incorporators of the first named company were: S. S. Caldwell, Francis Smith, John T. Clopper, A. S. Paddock, Henry T. Clarke, Alvin Saunders, Thomas Malloy, Henry Gray and Clinton Briggs. Messrs. John A. Horbach, Ezra Millard, John A. Morrow, Edward Creighton, James E. Boyd, Herman Hountze, Jonas Gise, Joseph H. Millard, C. H. Downs, William A. Paxton and Joseph Boyd, signed the incorporation papers of the Omaha & Northwestern Company. Augustus Kountze, John I. Redick and others, were included in the list of stockholders of the latter road.

The Omaha & Southwestern was built to the Platte River, where passengers were conveyed across by means of a flat-boat ferry, and then connection was made, at first by wagon and afterwards by rail, with the Burlington & Missouri River Railroad, a mile or so distant from the ferry.

In 1871 the last named railway company secured possession of the line of the Omaha & Southwestern Company and thereby gained an inlet to Omaha.

The Omaha & Northwestern Company pushed the work on their line up through Washington County, first to Blair and then to Herman, later on Tekamah, in Burt County, was reached and then Oakland. In 1878 the road was sold under foreclosure proceedings, was reorganized as the Omaha & Northern Nebraska Railway Company, and the line extended to Oakland, Burt County. In 1879 the St. Paul & Sioux City Railroad Company became the owners of this line and sold it two years later to the Chicago, St. Paul, Minneapolis & Omaha Railroad Company, who now own and operate it.

### THE BURLINGTON ROUTE.

The Burlington Route (Burlington & Missouri River Railroad in Nebraska), has its headquarters here for the operation of all lines belonging to the Chicago, Burlington & Quincy Railroad Company west of the Missouri River. The construction of the Burlington & Missouri River Railroad in Nebraska, was commenced in 1869, and in July, 1871. a connection from Plattsmouth, on the Missouri River, was made with Omaha through the acquisition of the Omaha & Southwestern Railroad.

There are now operated from the Omaha office of the Burlington route, 3,320 miles of railroad. Of this amount, 2,253 miles are in Nebraska, 260 in Kansas, 366 in Colorado, 219 in Wyoming, and 169 in South Dakota, with about fifty-three miles in Iowa and Missouri; and connecting all of the principal Missouri River termini in the East with the cities of Denver, Cheyenne, Deadwood and Sheridan in the West, and branches have recently been constructed to the coal and oil fields of Wyoming. That portion of the road which is in the State of Nebraska, reaches nearly all important points in the State.

All trains of the Burlington system arrive at and depart from the Union Depot in Omaha, crossing the Missouri River at Plattsmouth over the steel bridge which was completed August 30, 1880. This company has expended in Omaha, for improvements, including the lines to the stock yards at South Omaha, $880,783.43. The number of employes in Omaha is about 450, and the monthly pay roll amounts to about $30,000.

This road has been a powerful factor in the development of that portion of the State known as "the South Platte country." Its land department has been admirably managed and every inducement possible offered to secure a settlement upon the valuable agricultural and grazing lands of the company, of an industrious and enterprising people. The result has been most gratifying and has fully demonstrated the wisdom shown by the company in the adoption of a liberal system in disposing of its lands, furnishing free transportation to land-seekers, loaning to destitute settlers seed sufficient for their first planting, extending the time of payment on land contracts, and in many other ways aiding the people who were seeking homes in that portion of the State.

The road is managed by the following named:

General Officers.—C. E. Perkins, president, Burlington, Ia.; J. C. Peasley, first vice president, Chicago; L. O. Goddard, assistant to first vice president, Chicago; Geo. B. Harris, second vice president, Chicago; T. S. Howland, secretary, Boston, Mass.; T. M. Marquett, general solicitor, Lincoln, Neb.; J. W. Deweese, solicitor. Lincoln; W. W. Baldwin, land commissioner, Burlington, Iowa; C. J. Ernst, assistant land commissioner, Lincoln, Neb.; J. C. Bartlett, superintendent Burlington voluntary relief department, Chicago; C. H. Williams, assistant superintendent Burlington voluntary relief department, Chicago; R. D. Pollard, tax agent, Omaha.

Treasury Department.—J. C. Peasley, treasurer, Chicago; J. G. Taylor, auditor and assistant treasurer, Omaha; D. T. Beans, cashier, Omaha; J. G. Floyd, paymaster, Omaha.

Accounting Department.—W. P. Durkee, assistant auditor, Omaha; H. D. Allee, assistant auditor, Omaha; Edward O. Brandt. assistant auditor, Omaha; W. Randall, freight and ticket auditor, Omaha.

Operating Department.—G. W. Holdrege, general manager, Omaha; T. E. Calvert, general superintendent, Omaha; Geo. H. Crosby, general freight agent, Omaha; Allen B. Smith, assistant general freight agent,

Omaha; J. Francis, general passenger and ticket agent, Omaha; Arthur B. Smith, assistant general passenger and ticket agent, Omaha; T. Marsland, general baggage agent, Lincoln; Geo. Hargreaves, general purchasing agent, Chicago; Geo. Yoemans, assistant purchasing agent, Chicago; E. J. McClure, consulting engineer, Chicago; I. S. P. Weeks, chief engineer, Lincoln, Neb.; D. S. Guild, supply agent, Plattsmouth, Neb.; J. W. Bell, stationer, Lincoln, Neb.; C. E. Yates, superintendent telegraph, Lincoln, Neb.; M. McKinnon, car accountant, Lincoln, Neb.; D. Hawksworth, superintendent motive power, Plattsmouth, Neb.; Geo. H. Ross, superintendent car and special freight service, Chicago; E. S. Grensel, master mechanic, Plattsmouth, Neb.; J. C. Salsbury, master mechanic, Lincoln, Neb.; A. B. Pirie, master mechanic, Wymore, Neb.; R. B. Archibald, master mechanic, McCook, Neb.; J. P. Reardon, master mechanic, Alliance, Neb.

### THE KANSAS CITY LINE.

The Kansas City, St. Joseph & Council Bluffs Railroad Company, now operating a road between Kansas City and Omaha, was organized July 11, 1870, and holds its property by the consolidation of several companies which were, originally, as follows:

The Platte County Railroad Company, incorporated February 24, 1853, and its name changed March 23, 1863, to the Platte County Railroad, which was sold to the State of Missouri, February 12, 1864. The Atchison & St. Joseph Railroad Company, incorporated December 11, 1855. The Weston & Atchison Railroad Company, incorporated April 22, 1859. The Missouri Valley Railroad Company, created by a change of name of the Atchison & St. Joseph Railroad Company and the consolidation with it of the Weston & Atchison Railroad Company, by legislative authority, March 8, 1867. Under an act of the legislature of the State of Missouri, dated February 18, 1865, the Platte County Railroad was turned over to the Weston & Atchison Railroad and the Atchison & St. Joseph Railroad Companies. The St. Joseph & Council Bluffs Railroad Company, incorporated July 16, 1867, and consolidated April 7, 1869, with the Council Bluffs & St. Joseph Railroad Company, the consolidated company taking the name of the St. Joseph & Council Bluffs Railroad Company, which was organized under the general laws of Iowa, to build from Council Bluffs to some point on the Missouri State line, to connect there with a railroad from St. Joseph to said line. The Missouri Valley Railroad Company and the St. Joseph & Council Bluffs Railroad Company were consolidated July 11, 1870, under the name of the Kansas City, St. Joseph & Council Bluffs Railroad Company. The northern terminus of the track owned by this company is at Council Bluffs, but its passenger trains reach Omaha over the Union Pacific Bridge, or via Pacific Junction and the bridge at Plattsmouth.

Until the completion of this railroad, the choice of passenger travel from St. Joseph to Omaha lay between steamboat and stage, and of freight transportation by either river or wagon. A line of steamboats, making two departures a week during the season, was run for several years between St. Joseph and Omaha. The delays and dangers caused by high winds, the swift current and shifting sand bars, the numerous snags, and other impediments to navigation, made the river journey long and monotonous, but was preferable to the still more wearisome trip by stage, through mud, snow and swamp, which had to be endured when navigation closed on the first appearance of winter.

It was therefore with a feeling of great relief that the completion of the road in 1868 was hailed, not only by the traveling community, but still more to the merchants and shippers, to whom it brought much greater advantages, by giving them facilities during the whole year, which they had enjoyed only during the season of navigation.

That Omaha, for her early prosperity, is largely indebted to the completion of this railroad, there can be no doubt. The means it afforded for the transportation of material, contributed to the early completion of the Union Pacific, and the opening of the first trans-continental railway. Great difficulties and delays had occurred in the prosecution of that work because of the lack of adequate transportation, the line of boats from St. Joseph being barely able to carry the freight offered by the merchants during the busy season, and the added demands for the moving of the enormous quantities of material used on that great work, taxed to the utmost every available means of conveyance.

There can be no doubt then, that the Kansas City, St. Joseph & Council Bluffs Railroad contributed largely to the facilities required for the completion of the Union Pacific, and its opening in 1869, to which time may be traced the beginning of Omaha's thrift, and her rapid increase in wealth, population and commercial prosperity.

### THE CHICAGO, ROCK ISLAND & PACIFIC RAILWAY.

The Chicago, Rock Island & Pacific Railway Company, now operating a road between Chicago and Denver, Colorado Springs and Pueblo, via Omaha with numerous branches both east and west of Omaha, among which is a line reaching from Davenport, in the State of Iowa, via Kansas City and St. Joseph to Topeka, southwest and south respectively to the southwestern corner of the State of Kansas and through Indian Territory into the State of Texas, with such connections between these latter lines and the lines via Omaha as relate them intimately, also to the City of Omaha, is a consolidated corporation. The parent or original company was the Rock Island & LaSalle Railroad Company, organized in 1847, to construct a railroad from Rock Island to the Illinois River, at the termination of the Illinois and Michigan Canal. Its powers were subsequently enlarged so that it might project its railroad by the way of Ottawa and Joliet to the City of Chicago, and its name was changed to the Chicago & Rock Island Railroad Company. In 1854 this line was completed from Chicago to Rock Island and was the first railroad connecting the lakes with the Mississippi River. In 1856 there was constructed, under the auspices of this company, the first bridge across the Mississippi River. Prior to that time, and in 1852 a line was surveyed for a railroad from Davenport, Iowa, westward, which should be an extension of the above mentioned line. This extension was the old railroad originally known as the Mississippi & Missouri Railroad, to which was granted by the State of Iowa, a portion of the land grant given by Congress to that State to aid in the construction of sundry lines of railroad across the State of Iowa. The Mississippi & Missouri Railroad was, through many difficulties, completed to a point somewhat east of the center of the State of Iowa where, by reason of financial difficulty, the enterprise was delayed. Subsequently, mortgages executed by that company conveying its line of road and land grant to secure bonded indebtedness was foreclosed, and the road and land grant sold to a corporation known as the Chicago, Rock Island & Pacific Railroad Company, incorporated under the laws of Iowa for the purpose of acquiring the property under said foreclosure. Subsequently this company and the Chicago & Rock Island Railroad Company, of Illinois, were consolidated; the company to be known as the Chicago, Rock Island & Pacific Railroad Company, and the road was completed to Council Bluffs, Iowa, in 1869, since which time it has been closely and intimately related in matters of transportation with the City of Omaha, and the great State lying west of it. By subsequent consolidations the title of the company was changed to the Chicago, Rock Island & Pacific Railway Company, and such company became thereby the owner of a main line from Chicago to Council Bluffs, together with numerous short branches in the State of Iowa, and one considerable branch extending from the City of Washington, in the State of Iowa, southwestwardly to Kansas City, except that the southwestern end of said branch was and is a leased line. Later, under the auspices of that company, a system of railroads was projected and constructed westward from the Missouri River across the State of Kansas, in part through portions of the State of Nebraska, westward to the City of Colorado Springs, in the State of Colorado, with leased branches to the Cities of Denver and Pueblo in said State; extending also southwestwardly to the southwestern corner of the State of Kansas and to the State line of Kansas a little south of the City of Wichita. In 1890, by contract with the Union Pacific Railroad Company, there was acquired by it the right to use the Union Pacific branch for the operation of its trains into the City of Omaha and about the same time, there was constructed by it a line of railroad reaching from Omaha to Lincoln, Nebraska, and by means of this and a leased line, its was enabled to reach its own line from Omaha at Beatrice, Nebraska.

At the present time it is extending its line south from the southern point below Wichita through the Indian Territory into the State of Texas. At the date of its last annual report, in April, 1892, this company was operating 3,455 miles of railroad, of which it owned 2,725 miles; used under long leases 352 miles and enjoyed trackage rights over 377 miles. The company operates, via Omaha, fast passenger trains, finely equipped, between the City of Chicago and important points in the State of Colorado. By means of them, as also by means of other trains operated by the company between Omaha and points west, the people and business men of the City of Omaha are enabled to reach many points to the west of the city not previously accessible at all, or if accessible, not so directly. The like is true of points to the east, and the business interests of Omaha may well appreciate the advantages and opportunities which the 3,500 miles of this great system bring to the doors of the chief City of Nebraska.

SIOUX CITY & PACIFIC RAILROAD.

The following items of information have been kindly furnished by one of the officers of the road:

The Sioux City & Pacific Railroad as to Iowa, was organized August 1, 1864, and the "Northern Nebraska Air Line"—the Nebraska portion of the present Sioux City & Pacific Railroad—was organized June 7, 1867. The two companies were united by articles of consolidation made September 15, 1868, the consolidated company taking the name of "Sioux City & Pacific Railroad Company."

Construction was commenced in 1867, and the first portion, viz: from Missouri Valley, Iowa, to California Junction, Iowa, was completed—5.84 miles—August, 1867. From California Junction to Sloan—49.5 miles—was completed in December, 1867. From Sloan to Sioux City, Iowa—20 miles—was completed in March, 1868. From California Junction to Fremont, Nebraska, —32.08 miles—was completed in February, 1869, making a total of 107.47 miles, 80.47 miles being in Iowa, and 26.95 miles in Nebraska. This company received land grants through acts of Congress July 1, 1862, and July 2, 1864.

Connecting at Missouri Valley, Iowa, with the Cedar Rapids & Missouri River Railroad (now the Chicago & Northwestern Railway), this line succeeded the old stage line from Council Bluffs to Sioux City, Iowa, and was for many years the only line of communication between Sioux City, on the north, and Council Bluffs or Omaha on the south, and continues to be the connecting link in the through train line between Kansas City and St. Paul, Minnesota.

#### FREMONT, ELKHORN & MISSOURI VALLEY RAILROAD.

The Fremont, Elkhorn & Missouri Valley Railroad Company was organized under the general laws of Nebraska, January 20, 1869, and construction was commenced from Fremont northward the same year, resting at a point about ten miles from Fremont until 1870, when it was extended and completed to West Point, county seat of Cuming County. In 1871 it was completed to Wisner, 16.72 miles farther. Here it rested until 1879, when it was extended 58.56 miles to Oakdale. In 1880 it was completed to Neligh; also a branch from Norfolk to Plainview. In 1881 it was extended to O'Neill, and from Plainview to Creighton. In 1881 the line was extended to Long Pine. In 1882 it was completed to Thacher. In 1883 to Valentine.

In January, 1885, the company acquired the right to extend into Dakota. January 20th, by act of Congress, the right-of-way was granted through the military reservation at Fort Robinson, and in August, 1885, the line was completed to Chadron. December of the same year it was completed to Buffalo Gap, Dakota. June, 1886, it was completed to Rapid City, South Dakota, and September 1, 1886, it was completed from from Dakota Junction to the Wyoming State line. February 28, 1887, Congress gave the right-of-way through the military reservation of Fort Mead, and November 21st, it was completed to Whitewood, South Dakota. December 29, 1890, the line was completed to Deadwood, the mining centre of the Black Hills. The same year a branch was built from Whitewood to Belle Fourche, South Dakota.

In 1891, there was built a system of narrow gauge lines to the mines in Ruby Basin and the Portland mines.

In October, 1885, the Wyoming Central Railway was organized under the law of Wyoming, and in 1886 this line was completed from Wyoming, Nebraska State line, to Douglas, Wyoming. In 1887, from Douglas to Glen Rock, and in 1888, from Glen Rock to Casper, and June 4th was consolidated with and merged into the Fremont, Elkhorn & Missouri Valley Railroad Company.

In 1886 a branch line was built from Fremont through Wahoo, in Saunders County, to Lincoln, the capital of Nebraska. The same year a branch was built from Scribner, Nebraska, to Lindsey, Nebraska. In 1887, a branch was built from the Fremont-Lincoln line, from Platte River to Linwood, Nebraska; also from Platte River to Hastings, Nebraska. Also a line from Arlington, Nebraska, to Omaha; also a line from Irvington to South Omaha, and from Lindsay, Nebraska, to Oakdale, Nebraska. In 1888 the branch from Norfolk to Creighton was extended to Verdigre, Nebraska. In 1887, the line resting at Linwood was extended to Geneva, and in 1888 to Superior. In 1890 from Buffalo Gap to Dakota Hot Springs.

TOTAL MILES IN THE SYSTEM:

Sioux City & Pacific Railroad in
  Iowa ........................ 80.47
Sioux City & Pacific Railroad in
  Nebraska .............. 26.95    107.42
Fremont Elkhorn & Missouri Valley Railroad in Nebraska ... 985.19
Fremont. Elkhorn & Missouri Valley Railroad in Wyoming ... 180.46
Fremont Elkhorn & Missouri Valley Railroad in South Dakota. 184.88   1,300.53

Total number of miles ....... 1,300.53  1,407.95

It affords access to the Omaha markets from four States, and the best of passenger through car service from Omaha to St. Paul and Minneapolis. Omaha to Dakota Hot Springs. Omaha to Deadwood. Omaha via Fremont and Superior to Newton, Kansas. Omaha to Hastings, Nebraska, and as a system, is one of the most important feeders Omaha has.

## MISSOURI PACIFIC RAILWAY.

The Missouri Pacific Company made a connection with the Union Pacific line at Papillion, fifteen miles west of Omaha, about 1882, reaching this city by using the track of the last named road, until it completed the Belt Line, in the winter of 1885 and 1886. It affords the people of this section direct access to St. Louis and the South. Its Omaha officers are T. F. Godfrey, city passenger and ticket agent; H. B. Kooser, city freight agent; G. E. Dorrington, traveling passenger agent, and J. O. Phillippi, assistant general freight and passenger agent. Since the completion of the Belt Line the business of the Missouri Pacific has increased rapidly in this section. S. H. H. Clark, first vice president and general manager of the Missouri Pacific, who has lately become president of the Union Pacific, has his headquarters in Omaha. The company has recently completed a branch line which leaves the main road at Union, Nebraska, and reaches Omaha by way of Plattsmouth. There has been much speculation of late years as to which of the roads entering this city would extend a line to Yankton, Dakota, an important railway connection, and the general supposition has been that this work would be undertaken by the Missouri Pacific Company. Two passenger trains, each way, per day, are run on this road.

## THE BELT LINE.

The Belt Line, which encircles the city, extending from Webster and Fifteenth Streets to South Omaha, was a Union Pacific enterprise originally. In 1883 and 1884 that company commenced to secure the right-of-way by regular condemnation proceedings and made considerable progress when, for some reason not made public, the enterprise was abandoned. At that time Mr. S. H. H. Clark was general manager of the Union Pacific, but resigned soon after and was employed by Mr. Jay Gould to carry out the Belt Line scheme, ostensibly as an independent line of railway but in fact in the interests of the Missouri Pacific Road, which then ran its trains into Omaha over the Union Pacific lines from Papillion. Injunction proceedings were commenced in the United States Court by the Union Pacific Company to prevent Mr. Gould from carrying his purpose into effect, and a considerable delay resulted. A compromise was effected, however, Mr. Gould paying to the Union Pacific people about $70,000 and then the securing of the right-of-way and construction of the road was pushed rapidly. From a point near the crossing of Farnam Street extension a branch line to Papillion was built, thus giving the Missouri Pacific direct access to Omaha as well as securing to that company the advantage over all competitors of having a line which practically enclosed the city. The wisdom shown by Messrs. Gould and Clark in this enterprise is now apparent and the Belt Line is already worth many times its cost. The entire expense of the construction of the two roads, including money paid for right-of-way, was about $700,000, but that investment has been increased largely since by general improvements. Harry Gilmore is the local superintendent of the road. During 1890 there was a large sum expended at the South Omaha end of the road in the way of switches, double trackage, etc. Six daily trains each way afford transportation to suburban residents along the line. The monthly pay roll amounts to $10,000.

## CHICAGO, ST. PAUL, MINNEAPOLIS & OMAHA RAILWAY.

The Chicago, St. Paul, Minneapolis & Omaha Railway Company gained an entrance into Omaha in 1881, by purchasing of the St. Paul & Sioux City Company the line of road built originally by the Omaha & Northwestern Company, and have since that date expended a large amount of money in the erection of a depot building, corner of Webster and Fifteenth, and constructing a commodious freight yard one1 one mile in length and five hundred feet wide, north of Webster Street; also a fifteen stall round house, water tank, coal sheds and other conveniences for the proper handling of its large business.

The general officers of this road are: Marvin Hughitt, president, Chicago; Martin L. Sykes, vice president, treasurer and assistant secretary, New York; Samuel O. Howe, assistant treasurer, New York; Edwin E. Woodman, secretary, Hudson; William H. Phipps, land commissioner, Hudson. The following officers have headquarters in St. Paul: Edwin H. Winter, general manager; Thomas Wilson, general counsel; Walter A. Scott, general superintendent; James T. Clark, general freight agent; Thomas W. Teasdale, general passenger agent; Charles W. Johnson, chief engineer; Lewis A. Robinson, auditor; Robert W. Clark, local treasurer; William H. S. Wright, purchasing agent; Edwin E. Woodman, right of way and tax commissioner; Henry C. Hope, superintendent of telegraph and signals; Edmond L. Poole, claim agent; Alexander Drezmal, car accountant.

H. S. Jaynes is superintendent of the Nebraska division; Wm. B. Fordyce, train dispatcher; Lyman Sholes, division freight agent; and Richard Dodd, traveling auditor. This division extends from Omaha to South Sioux City, opposite Sioux City, with branch lines running from Wakefield to Norfolk, Concord to Hartington, Wayne to Bloomfield, and from Coburn to Ponca. Great improvements are made by this company annually, in all branches of its business. Its suburban train service is being constantly expanded and improved, and a considerable sum of money is expended each year in extending its depot facilities. Its track is laid with steel rails on oak ties, well ballasted. Five thousand cars of live stock per year are brought to Omaha over this line, and its direct connection with the lumber regions of the great lakes gives it an importance in that respect which is not shared by many railway lines. Half a million dollars is paid out annually in Nebraska to employes. Over one billion pounds of freight is handled yearly at its Webster Street depot. The following shows the number of miles in the Nebraska division:

| | |
|---|---|
| Missouri River to Omaha | 123.06 |
| Sioux City Union Depot to bridge track, (leased) | 50 |
| Sioux City Bridge Company's track | 3 90 |
| Coburn to Ponca | 16.33 |
| Emerson to Norfolk | 46.50 |
| Wakefield to Hartington | 33.76 |
| Wayne to Bloomfield | 48.14 |
| Total | 267.19 |

It is rumored that an extension will be built by the company early in 1893, from Ponca to Newcastle, Neb. The Omaha and Winnebago reservations, through which the line runs, are being rapidly put under cultivation. It is estimated that nearly 100,000 acres were broken by the plow. on this line in Nebraska, in 1892.

This road, which is called in Omaha " the St. Paul," is known in St. Paul and on Wall Street as " the Omaha." The Chicago, St. Paul, Minneapolis & Omaha Railway, the Chicago & North-Western, the Sioux City and Pacific, and the Fremont, Elkhorn and Missouri Valley, form the " Great North-Western Line," of which Marvin Hughitt is president.

### OTHER RAILROAD SCHEMES.

In November, 1875, the Board of Commissioners of Douglas County adopted a resolution calling an election to be held November 30th, to decide whether or not county bonds should be voted, to the amount of $125,000, to be dated July 1, 1876, bearing seven per cent. semi-annual interest, and to run twenty years, but redeemable at the expiration of five years, at the option of the county; said bonds to be given to the Nebraska Central & Black Hills Railroad Company. This donation was upon condition " that the said company shall grade, tie, iron and construct, or cause to be constructed, a first-class narrow-guage road from Omaha, the initial point to be within a mile and a half of the court house, and run in a westerly direction through Douglas County, thence through Saunders, Butler and Polk Counties. It shall bridge the Platte River, provide also a wagon bridge, free of charge to the public, and have trains running into Saunders County by September 1, 1876." This proposition was defeated at the polls by the small majority of 250 votes.

In February, 1888, a resolution was adopted by the County Commissioners requesting the Omaha, Yankton & Northwestern Railroad Company (consisting of Nathan Shelton, A. A. Egbert, Charles T. Taylor and R. C. Patterson) to file a plat of the survey of their proposed line of railway, as a condition precedent to the calling of a special election to vote upon the proposition to aid that company to the extent of $300,000 in the construction of their road. Considerable time was occupied with negotiations, but the company failing to comply with this requirement of the Commissioners, the matter was referred to the judiciary committee of the board, which reported adversely to calling an election on the ground that "the proposition does not properly guard the interests of the tax payers of Douglas County." The report was adopted, and the business was in that way disposed of.

The Chicago, Milwaukee and St. Paul; Chicago & Northwestern; Chicago, Burlington & Quincy; Chicago & Rock Island; Wabash & Kansas City; St. Joe & Omaha lines afford direct connection with the north, east and south. Offices are also maintained in Omaha by the Atchison, Topeka & Santa Fe Railroads; Baltimore & Ohio; Chicago, St. Paul & Kansas City; New York, Chicago & St. Louis; Pennsylvania lines; Toledo, St. Louis & Kansas City.

# CHAPTER XLV.

STREET RAILWAYS — EARLY LEGISLATION — RECENT COURT PROCEEDINGS.

At the session of the territorial legislature of 1867, an act was passed incorporating the "Omaha Horse Railway Company," with Alfred Burley, Ezra Millard, George W. Frost, Joel T. Griffin, J. W. Paddock, C. S. Chase, George M. O'Brien, J. R. Meredith, R. A. Bird, E. B. Chandler, John McCormick, Augustus Kountze, William Ruth, J. Frank Coffman, A. J. Hanscom and David Butler as incorporators. The act required that the company should have one mile of properly equipped road in successful operation within two years, and granted the company the right to lay out, construct, maintain and operate a single or double track railway, "in, on, over and along such street or streets, highway or highways, bridge or bridges, river or rivers, within the present or future limits of Omaha, or within five miles adjacent thereto, as said company may order or direct, for the uses herein specified; but said company shall not build a track through, or occupy, except for crossing purposes, Fourteenth Street, or any other street through which any other railroad company has already obtained the right of way."

The capital stock of the organization was fixed at $100,000; the use of steam as a motive power was prohibited; exclusive right to the use of the streets of Omaha, and for five miles adjacent thereto, for horse railway purposes, was granted the company for a term of fifty years from January 1, 1867, and at the end of that period the entire property of the company was to revert to the city.

The first line built extended from Ninth and Farnam to Cuming and Twentieth Streets, and a ten cent fare was charged, though tickets good for eight rides could be bought for fifty cents. There were a great many stockholders, at first, all of whom rode free, and until 1873 the income of the road was about equalled by the expenses. In the early part of 1872, fare boxes were put on the road, the conductors taken off, and the fare reduced to five cents. About January 1, 1873, A. J. Hanscom bought a majority of the stock and controlled and operated the road till July 1, 1873, when he sold his interests to W. W. Marsh. In 1878 the property was sold to the highest bidder, for cash, by the sheriff, in consequence of the foreclosure of mortgages which had been given in the meantime, and the highest bidder was W. W. Marsh, who secured the entire plant for about $25,000. He added largely to the property, and built the St. Mary's Avenue, Sixteenth and Eighteenth Street lines. In 1883 S. H. H. Clark, Guy Barton and Frank Murphy each bought one-fifth interests in the property, on a basis of a total valuation of $500,000, and a new company was formed. Then the lines on Twenty-fourth, Thirteenth, Cuming and Leavenworth Streets were built, and the Farnam and Cuming Street lines extended so that on the 1st of April, 1889, there were thirty miles of road in operation, and the property was valued at a round million dollars.

The session of the Legislature of 1888 and 1889 passed an act authorizing the consolidation of street railway companies, and on the 1st day of April, 1889, the Omaha Cable Tramway Company and the Horse Railway Company were consolidated under the name of the "Omaha Street Railway Company," with a capital stock of four million dollars. The following named were elected directors:

S. R. Johnson, W. V. Morse, Charles B. Rustin, Benjamin F. Smith, A. S. Paddock, Frank Murphy, W. W. Marsh, Guy Barton and W. A. Smith; Frank Murphy was chosen as president; S. R. Johnson, vice-president; and D. H. Goodrich, secretary and treasurer.

The Cable Tramway Company of Omaha was incorporated in June, 1884, by the following named: Samuel R. Johnson, Charles B. Rustin, Isaac S. Hascall, Casper E. Yost and Fred. Drexel. There was a re-organization effected December 4, 1888, under the style of the Omaha Cable Tramway Company, a new franchise having been secured in May, of that year, granting broader privileges, and giving the company the right to run its cars on all the streets of the city, and allowing it to use cable, electricity, or such other motive power as might be deemed advisable. The capital stock of the company was fixed at two million dollars. The operation of the line was commenced December, 1887, and soon thereafter four and a half miles of double track were in use. A splendid power-house, 132 by 140 feet in size was built in 1887, at the intersection of Harney and Twentieth Streets. The incorporators of the company, when re-organized, were S. R. Johnson, L. B. Williams, C. B. Rustin, W. V. Morse, B. F. Smith and S. D. Mercer. The following named were the officers of both of these companies: S. R. Johnson, president and treasurer; L. B. Williams, vice-president; C. B. Rustin, secretary.

The Omaha Motor Railway Company was organized in the spring of 1887, by Dr. S. D. Mercer, S. S. Curtis, C. E. Mayne, C. B. Brown, J. F. Hertzman, H. J. Davis and E. L. Stone, all of whom, excepting Mr. Stone (who was also a stockholder in the cable company), were members of the first board of directors. The first work was done by employes of the cable company; and, as their services could not be had in the day time, work was done at night. In fact, owing to injunctions, and other obstructions, a large share of the construction of the motor line was done at night, chiefly on Saturday nights, after midnight. The night, in July, 1887, on which the work was inaugurated, nearly a mile of track was laid. It was commenced at the corner of Davenport and Fourteenth Streets, extended north on Fourteenth to Cass, west to Seventeenth, north to Webster, west to Twenty-second, north to Burt, and west on Burt to Twenty-sixth. The work was but of a temporary character and hastily performed, to get over as much ground as possible before being stopped by opposing companies. The portion of the track laid on Webster Street was soon after removed to Burt Street, and the light "T" rails replaced along the entire line by rails of the most substantial character. In a short time seven miles of road were built, exclusive of two and a half miles in South Omaha, and the company acquired a portion of the Benson line. During the following winter Dr. Mercer purchased almost the entire stock of the company, selling about a quarter thereof in February, 1888, to John A. and P. W. Horbach, but buying back their interests the following January (1889), and selling three-fourths of the stock to a syndicate consisting of J. H. Millard, J. J. Brown, E. W. Nash of Omaha, and N. W. Wells of Schuyler. During 1888 work had been pushed at all possible points, and in November, 1888, the company had been granted permission, to a limited extent, by the council, to erect poles, in order to run cars by electricity by means of overhead wires. Great opposition was at once met with, as the citizens generally were opposed to the erection of these poles, and the stringing of wires, which the overhead system involved. The district court was appealed to, the horse car and cable companies taking an active part in the contest in seeking to prevent the motor company from carrying out its purpose. The case was heard before Judges Wakeley, Doane and Groff, sitting as a court of equity, and depositions and affidavits almost innumerable were presented by the parties in interest. Testimony as to the comparative merits of the overhead, underground, and storage systems were taken in Boston, Chicago, New York, Washington Territory, Richmond, Scranton (Penn.), and other points. The litigation terminated in favor of the motor company. Previous to this there had been various injunction proceedings had in the district court, the other street railway companies trying to prevent the motor company from occupying various streets, in which proceedings the latter company was generally upheld by the court, in some cases being required to share with its rivals the use of a joint track. The capital stock of the motor company was half a million dollars, all paid in. It erected a power-house at the corner of Nicholas and Twenty-second Streets. The officers of the company were: S. D. Mercer, president; E. W. Nash, vice-president; W. B. Millard, secretary and treasurer. Directors: J. H. Millard, S. D. Mercer, E. W. Nash, J. J. Brown and W. B. Millard. Attorneys J. C. Cowin, W. J. Connell and H. J. Davis represented the motor company in its various legal complications of its earlier history. John D. Howe fought the battles of the motor company from the reorganization. William L. Adams, for many years connected with the civil engineering department of the Union Pacific Railway, and chief engineer of the Belt line, was chief engineer of the motor company.

The Benson Motor Company was organized in the winter of 1886-7, by E. A. Benson, C. E. Mayne and W. L. McCague. Three and a half miles of road were built the following spring, from the corner of Lowe and Mercer Avenues, to the center of a large tract of ground platted as "Benson Place" during that winter. At first the cars were operated by means of a steam dummy, but this proved very objectionable to farmers, and others, whose horses were frightened thereby, so that application was made to the county commissioners to declare it a nuisance, and the engine was finally removed and horses were substituted as a motive power. Later still, the motor has given place to electricity. The company is called the Benson and Halcyon Heights Railway Company.

The Omaha and Southwestern Street Railway Company was organized in the summer of 1887, with S. J. Howell, Cyrus Morton, J. T. Paulsen, Henry Ambler and C. F. Harrison as the incorporators, who built about three miles of road that fall. The cars were moved by horses. By means of this line, Windsor Place, Howell Place, Ambler Place, Eckerman Place, Shriver Place and West Side were reached. The eastern terminus of the road was the northwest corner of Hanscom Park.

The Council Bluffs and Omaha electric motor line, connecting the two cities, was completed in the fall of 1888. It is owned chiefly by Council Bluffs capitalists. This company also owns the Missouri River bridge, over which their cars pass, on which provision is also made for teams and pedestrians. The bridge is of steel and wrought iron, has a river span of four hundred feet, and is of a total length, including approaches, of 2,700 feet. The cost of the bridge and five miles of track was about $750,000.

During the spring of 1889 efforts were made to consolidate the Mercer motor line and the Omaha Street Railway Company, and in the month of November this was accomplished by the purchase of the former by the latter, who increased their capital to five million dollars to effect the purchase. On the first of January, 1890, the new company thus formed owned and operated thirty-six and one-half miles of horse railway tracks, nine and one-half miles of cable lines, and forty miles of electric motor tracks, making a total of eighty-six miles of street railway in actual operation, with a full equipment of everything necessary for a first-class system. Since this time more than half of the horse lines have been changed to electric lines. Following named are the officers for the year 1892: Frank Murphy, president; Guy C. Barton, vice-president; W. W. Marsh, treasurer, D. H. Goodrich, secretary; W. A. Smith, general manager; F. A. Tucker, general superintendent.

The United States census for 1890 shows that the increase in street railway transportation in Omaha, during the past ten years, is 998 per cent., which is by far the largest percentage of any city in the country. Boston is the only city that has more miles of electric motor line than Omaha.

In the spring of 1891 the Metropolitan Street Railway Company built what is popularly known as the Dundee line, now extending from Forty-first and Farnam Streets north and west to the residence of J. N. H. Patrick, on Wilson Street, the length of the line being 7,500 feet, 1,200 feet having been added in the spring of the present year. On the latter date the horses previously used gave place to electricity as the motive power.

On the 3rd of July, 1891, the Inter-State Bridge and Street Railway Company began running cars on their electric motor line to East Omaha. The line is about two and a quarter miles long, running from the intersection of Sherman Avenue and Locust Streets, east on Locust Avenue, in East Omaha. The line is well equipped with Westinghouse, single reduction motors. There is a fifteen minute service, and transfers are made to and from the Sherman Avenue Line of the Omaha Street Railway.

# CHAPTER XLVI.

### Telegraph and Telephone—Electric Light System.

The telegraph line from Omaha to Sacramento, California, was completed July 4, 1862, a California company, which had already constructed a line between San Francisco and Sacramento, building to Salt Lake, and the Pacific Telegraph Company completing the connection between Omaha and Salt Lake. The work for the last named company was done by the late Edward Creighton, of Omaha, who was superintendent of the company. The enterprise was carried on in the face of great dangers and hardships. The through line was first called the Pacific Telegraph. In connection with this great enterprise, the late Colonel A. C. Boone, of Denver, for fifty years Indian trader and agent, used to tell of the strong opposition made by the Sioux to the extension of the line through their country. He was present at a council held with that tribe, at one time, by representatives of the government, when the importance of the enterprise was set out in glowing terms by one of the latter, who stated that when the line was completed the Great Father, at Washington, could talk over the wire with a man on the Pacific coast. At this one of the head chiefs was observed to draw his blanket over his face; and, when asked why he did this, responded, "I am ashamed." "And what are you ashamed of?" was asked. "I am ashamed of that big lie!" he replied.

But the first line to reach Omaha was one from St. Louis, called the "Missouri & Western Stebbins' Line," completed in 1860. This was also built by Mr. Creighton. The *Omaha Telegraph* was the first daily paper printed here, with the exception of a brief experiment in that line attempted by Mr. Wyman with the *Times*, and it boasted much of its few and brief dispatches received over this line. In March, 1861, the receipt of these dispatches was interrupted by an ice gorge in the Platte River, whereupon the *Telegraph* promptly announced that Operator Peck had gone down to attend to the matter, and that "he will cross from side to side in a skiff, forming his connections with the wire on either side, and through Mr. Byron Reed, at Omaha, will keep up the transaction of public and private business, as heretofore." The following issue of the paper declared, with all the additional horror to be given the announcement by large type, "Mr. Peck Probably Drowned!" and also published the following messages:

"North Bank Platte River, March 1, M. *Dear Reed:* Have just arrived. Platte River flooded and running full of ice. Think it very dangerous to cross, but will make the attempt.—Peck."

"Omaha, 12 M. *Dear Peck:*—Leave all your valuables on this shore, so that if you are drowned the loss may be as light as possible.—Reed."

Fortunately, Peck was not drowned, though his escape deprived the *Telegraph* of a sensation which it would doubtless have made the most of, judging from its startling head line, based evidently, upon the assumption of Mr. Peck that the crossing was dangerous.

Direct eastern telegraphic facilities were afforded Omaha in 1861, by the construction of the Illinois & Mississippi Valley line. Robert C. Clowry had charge of the first office opened in Omaha, the Missouri & Western Company, in 1861, which company formed a combination with the Pacific Company, in 1862, for terminal business. The latter company employed Charles E. Pomeroy as manager until October 1, 1863, when he was succeeded by Edward Rosewater, who held that position until 1869, when he resigned and took charge of the Atlantic & Pacific and Great Western offices, in 1870. He gave up the position in September, 1871, to assume the management of the *Bee*, the publication of which he commenced in June of that year. In 1870 a line was built from Chicago to Omaha and called the Great Western, whose Omaha business was in charge of Mr. Rosewater, but this line was soon absorbed by the Western Union, which last named company also absorbed the Pacific line in 1866, and has now a splendid office in the Omaha National Bank building, occupying the entire fifth floor and a portion of the basement floor. There are 208 names on the pay roll, requiring a weekly disbursement of two thousand five hundred dollars for salaries. There are 112 circuits outside the city, covered by the Omaha office, involving the use of 9,500 cells of battery. W. W. Umsted is the local manager. The third district, comprising Nebraska, Wyoming, Colorado, Utah, Idaho, Indian Territory, Arizona, Kansas, Montana, New Mexico and a part of Iowa, Missouri and Texas, has its headquarters in Omaha. J. J. Dickey is superintendent and Charles B. Horton assistant superintendent. During 1892, more than six million messages were handled by the Omaha office, and five thousand miles of new wire were strung in the district.

In 1885 the Pacific Telegraph Company built a line to Omaha from St. Joseph, Missouri, established an office here, and built up a lucrative patronage, with twenty offices in Nebraska, and afterwards sold the line to the Postal Telegraph Company, whose business at Omaha is in charge of W. S. Dimmock. The office in this city employs forty men. The company built nearly seven thousand miles of new lines throughout the country in 1890. This company has succeeded to the territory formerly covered by the Baltimore & Ohio Telegraph Company.

The Nebraska Telephone Company is the successor of the Omaha Electric Company, organized in May, 1879, of which C. W. Mead was president, J. J. Dickey, vice-president and general manager, L. H. Korty, secretary and treasurer. In addition to the above named, the following were interested as stockholders: S. H. H. Clark, W. A. Paxton, J. T. Clark, J. W. Gannett, Thomas L. Kimball and H. E. Jennison. In July, 1882, the present company was incorporated, with S. H. H. Clark as president; Mr. Korty, secretary and treasurer; Mr. Dickey, vice-president; and Flemon Drake, general manager, which officers have charge of the affairs of the company at this time, with the exception that Casper E. Yost is now president and general manager and Mr. Drake is no longer connected with the company. The Nebraska Telephone Company secured from the American Bell Telephone Company a perpetual and exclusive franchise for Nebraska and Pottawattamie County, Iowa, and in May, 1883, bought all the property owned by the Omaha Electric Company. The incorporation was effected with a capital stock of $250,000, which has since been increased to $700,000. Beginning business in May, 1883, with 323 subscribers and 160 miles of wire, steady and rapid progress has been made by the company since that date. November 1, 1892, there were over fifteen hundred miles of line within the city limits, and nearly seventeen hundred subscribers. The present system of the company supplies the telephonic demands of 4,500 subscribers, requiring the use of 2,859 miles of wire. For the city business an average of 235 men are employed, to whom $7,200 is paid monthly. The exchange was first located in the Union Block, on Fifteenth and Farnam, a removal to the Ramge Building, Harney and Fifteenth, being effected July 1, 1887, which change involved an outlay of over twenty thousand dollars, and an immense amount of tedious and vexatious work. In the Ramge Building eighteen rooms on the fifth floor, a large portion of the basement, and an adjoining building in the alley, are occupied. Upon getting into more convenient quarters, which gave the necessary space for the increased demands of the business, the company entered upon a system of improvements, regardless of expense, one feature being a new switch board, made of solid mahogany and costing $32,000. This has a capacity for 4,500 subscribers, which can be increased by adding sections of a capacity of two thousand each. The placing of this board in position involved much labor, there being over thirty-seven thousand soldered connections. The "clearing off" method of this switch board is a great improvement on those formerly used, and in this respect the Nebraska company was a pioneer. Their example was soon after followed by the Liverpool, England, company, and more recently by various exchanges in this country. The company purchased a lot, 66x132 feet in size, at the southwest corner of Douglas and Eighteenth, paying therefor $31,500, and in the spring of 1891 proposed to begin the erection of a three-story brick building, sixty-six feet square, with high basement, and to adopt the underground system for wires in the business portion of the city. By this means a great saving on repairs would be gained and the unsightly and dangerous masses of wires which now disfigure the main business streets removed from sight, and the risk to life greatly reduced. Sleet and hail storms always inflict much damage to the overhead wires, one storm, in March, 1889, imposing an expense of $4,400 upon the Omaha company for repairs. A sleet storm in March, 1892, cost the company over twelve thousand dollars for repairs. It is said that on one occasion a storm at Kansas City damaged the telephone system to the extent of twenty thousand dollars. The Nebraska Telephone Company has recently adopted what is known as the long distance telephone system in connecting its various exchanges throughout the State.

By reason of two changes of grade of Douglas Street, the erection of the building proposed on the corner of Eighteenth and Douglas Streets has been delayed; but, now that these changes have been made, the building will soon be constructed. One hundred and fifty thousand feet of duct have just been laid, which is equal to three miles of trench or completed conduit. This will lessen the amount of wire now strung on poles about seven hundred miles. The building and conduits will be occupied June or July, 1893.

The American District Telegraph Company was organized in June, 1883, with an authorized capital of $100,000. The incorporators were M. H. Goble, J. J. Dickey, L. H. Korty, L. M. Rheem and Flemon Drake; L. H. Korty, president; M. H. Goble, vice-president; L. M. Rheem, secretary and treasurer. The office was first located at 209½ South Thirteenth Street, but was soon afterwards moved to the present location, number 1304 Douglas Street. There were but eight messengers at first, but the company have now fifty-three employes in the Omaha office and fourteen in the South Omaha branch. The cab and parcel delivery business has been added, and the company has also established a system of private watchman service, by which reports are received at stated intervals, more or less frequent, from the watchmen engaged in the various large manufactories of the two cities, by means of electric gongs. They have also a system of automatic fire alarms, by which the exact location of fires in any part of a building may be ascertained. The value of the watchman service may be shown by an instance where the watchman in one of the chief hotels of the city failed to ring in his report one night. A messenger was sent at once to ascertain the reason, and found the watchman lying intoxicated in the basement of the hotel, with an overturned lantern, still burning, on the floor beside him. The present officers of the company are: L. H. Korty, president; J. J. Dickey, vice-president; L. M. Rheem, secretary, treasurer and general manager; James Donnelly, Jr., superintendent.

The Northwestern Electric Light Company was organized in 1883, and established its first power-house in the Strang building, on Farnam and Tenth Streets, but afterwards moved to the Woodman Linseed Oil Mills. The power is now furnished from the power-house of the Thomson-Houston Company. The present officers of the Northwestern Company are: Henry T. Clarke, president; Nathan Merriam, secretary; John T. Clarke, treasurer and manager. This company was the first in Nebraska to operate arc and incandescent lights.

The Sperry Electric Light Company, organized in 1883, with a capital of fifty-six thousand dollars, of which amount fifteen thousand dollars was paid for the patents of the Sperry company, for Nebraska. A brick building, now used as a steam laundry, was put up by the company on Dodge Street between Eleventh and Twelfth. It was the intention of this company to supply buildings with light by the storage system, but this was found to be impracticable. Among those who took stock in the enterprise were Guy Barton, A. J. Simpson, Churchill Parker, W. A. L. Gibbon, Dr. V. H. Coffman, George C. Ames, John A. McShane, George W. Ames, J. H. Dumont and George Armstrong. The investment proved unprofitable, and a consolidation was effected with the New Omaha Thomson-Houston Electric Light Company.

The Thomson-Houston Electric Light Company was organized September 26, 1885, the following named being the incorporators: J. C. Reagan, J. E. Riley, J. W. Paddock, George W. Duncan, C. G. Reagan, George Canfield, Alfred Shroeder, M. A. McMenamy. The business has since passed into other hands—the New Omaha Thomson-Houston Electric Light Company—with S. L. Wiley as president and manager and H. E. Chubbuck, secretary, treasurer and superintendent. The new company has a capital of $600,000, and operates seventy miles of wire. The power-house, situated at the foot of Jones Street, is 118x135 feet, three stories high, built of brick in the most substantial manner. From this, power and light are furnished for manufactories in all parts of the city, day and night, in addition to the general business of the company. More than $300,000 was expended in improvements and extensions in 1890.

The Omaha Illuminating Company was incorporated November 16, 1886, and leased for ten years all the rights and interests of the Northwestern Electric Light Company. The incorporators were: Pierce C. Himebaugh, C. C. Warren, Henry T. Clarke, Frank Warren and Ralph Breckenridge, with a capital of twenty thousand dollars. The present officers are: S. L. Wiley, president; Henry T. Clarke, vice-president; R. V. Montague, secretary and treasurer. The power is furnished by the new Thomson-Houston Company.

# CHAPTER XLVII.

GRAIN ELEVATORS — FIFTEEN YEARS' DEVELOPMENTS IN THIS LINE — STORAGE CAPACITY FOR MILLIONS OF BUSHELS.

In 1875 John McCormick, David S. Barriger and Fred H. Davis erected, at the corner of Jones and Seventh Streets, the first elevator built in Omaha. At that time the wheat shipments from Nebraska amounted to only a few hundred cars per annum, and the oat crops were insufficent to supply the home demand. More attention was given to corn by Nebraska farmers, but the export from this section was so limited that when these gentlemen built their elevator its capacity of but 200,000 bushels was deemed sufficiently large for all practical purposes. The Chase patent was used, and the building was 80 by 132 feet on the ground and 80 feet high. Including the outlay for offices, a warehouse for sacking purposes, and cribs, the sum of forty thousand dollars was expended. The following winter the Omaha Elevator Company was organized, with Mr. McCormick as president, Mr. Barriger vice-president and Mr. Davis secretary and treasurer, with a paid up capital stock of fifty thousand dollars. In July, 1879, the buildings were all destroyed by fire, entailing a loss of one hundred thousand dollars, three-fourths of which amount was covered by insurance. Before the smoking ruins were fairly removed, Mr. McCormick commenced the erection of a temporary building on the ground for warehouse purposes, in order to continue the business, and Mr. Barriger was planning for the construction of the immense elevator now standing near Spoon Lake, on the Council Bluffs side of the river, which was completed in 1883, at a cost of $280,000, with a storage capacity of over one million bushels. The business was conducted by the officers of the Omaha Elevator Company until Mr. McCormick's death, in 1885, when the Omaha Elevator and Grain Company was organized, with H. W. Rogers as president, Mr. Barriger, vice-president and Mr. Davis, secretary. In August, 1889, a consolidation was effected with the Union Elevator Company.

In June, 1877, C. W. Lyman and P. C. Himebaugh started, under the firm name of C. W. Lyman & Co. Soon afterwards Nathan Merriam was admitted to the firm, and in the following August, on the retirement of Mr. Lyman, the firm became Himebaugh & Merriam. They engaged in the grain business with a capital of $25,000, the building erected that year having a capacity of thirty thousand bushels. A few years later the large building east of Twelfth Street, on the Union Pacific Railroad, was erected. In August, 1889, a new company was formed by the consolidation of the Himebaugh & Merriam Company and the Omaha Elevator and Grain Company, and styled the Omaha Union Grain Company, under the following management: H. W. Rogers, president; P. C. Himebaugh, vice-president; Nathan Merriam, general manager; David S. Barriger, assistant general manager; Edward P. Peck, secretary; S. B. Cochran, treasurer. In consequence of the death of Mr. Himebaugh, in April, 1890, other changes were made and the Omaha Elevator Company was organized and purchased the entire elevator property and plant of the Omaha Union Grain Company. The present officers are: F. H. Peavey, president; A. B. Jaquith, vice president and manager; C. T. Peavey, treasurer; and E. P. Peck, secretary. These officers, with F. H. Davis, E. C. Michener and C. M. Champlin constitute the board of directors.

The Omaha Elevator Company owns and operates the elevator east of Thirteenth Street, known as "Elevator A," which has a capacity of two hundred thousand bushels, and leases the elevator east of "A," known as "Elevator B" (which is owned by the Union Elevator Company), with a capacity of 750,000 bushels. Seventy other elevators in this State, owned and operated by the Omaha Elevator Company, have a combined capacity of 1,000,000 bushels.

The Fowler Elevator Company erected a small building in June, 1888, and commenced business in a modest way. The following year a stock company was formed with a capital of fifty thousand dollars, and the storage capacity increased to 200,000 bushels. B. Fowler is president; C. T. Brown, secretary, and C. H. Fowler, treasurer of the company, with offices in the First National Bank Building, the elevator being located at the intersection of North Tenth and Charles Streets. This company owns and controls twenty elevators in Nebraska. It has recently built nine elevators on the Kearney and Black Hills branch of the Union Pacific Railroad.

The elevator built during the year 1890 by the Woodman & Ritchie Company, has a capacity of 600,000 bushels, and was opened for business September 1, 1890. It is constructed after the most improved methods, with abundant facilities for the storage of grain. The company was organized with Clark Woodman, president; Frank E. Ritchie, vice-president and Charles L. Harris, secretary, in 1890, with a paid up capital of $500,000. The amount invested in ground and building is $250,000. The elevator is 60 feet wide, 264 feet long and 140 feet high. It is located just across the alley from the Woodman Oil Works, with convenient railway trackage. Upon the death of Mr. Woodman, which occurred in Chicago, in August, 1891, Mr. Ritchie was made president.

# CHAPTER XLVIII.

BANKS AND BANKING — THE GROWTH OF THESE INSTITUTIONS — EXPENSIVE AND ATTRACTIVE BANK BUILDINGS.

[Mr. A. P. Hopkins, president Commercial National Bank, is the author of this chapter.]

The history of banking in Omaha seems to naturally divide itself into two periods, the first period commencing with the year 1855 and ending with 1863. The second period commencing with 1863 and extending down to the present time. During the first period the banking system of the country changed from the State bank system to the National. At the commencement of our history the State bank system was at its height. "Banks of Issue" under State charters were multiplying with great rapidity, especially in the new and growing West. The abuse of this system in the West became so great that the name "wildcat banking" has been used as descriptive of the operations of this period. The panic of 1857 was so severe and far-reaching in its effects that a very large majority of the banks throughout the country went down in the general crash. The methods continued, however, until displaced by the National system, in 1863. The banks of Omaha, during this time, were not by any means the worst of their kind, but were really better than the average.

The first office opened in Omaha for the transaction of a general banking business was in the spring of 1855, by the Western Exchange Fire & Marine Insurance Company, at the southwest corner of Twelfth and Farnam, the site now occupied by the United States National Bank. This company was the first financial institution established in Nebraska under a charter from the legislature. Thomas H. Benton, Jr., a son of Senator Benton, was president, Leroy Tuttle, cashier, and A. U. Wyman, teller. The latter two gentlemen have, each, since occupied the honorable position of treasurer of the United States. The Western Exchange Fire & Marine Insurance Company from its organization was aided greatly by the government deposits, and did a large and flourishing business, until its failure, September 23, 1857.

The next in order was the Bank of Nebraska, organized June 7, 1856, and located at the southeast corner of Farnam and Twelfth Streets. Its officers were: B. F. Allen, president; Samuel Moffatt, cashier. This bank issued thirty-seven thousand dollars in currency under the management of Allen & Moffatt, which was redeemed in full. B. R. Pegram, of Council Bluffs, Iowa, bought the bank and became its president in 1858, and D. C. DeForrest was made cashier. The bank went out of business in 1859.

From a history of Omaha, written by James M. Woolworth, and published in 1857, we take the liberty to quote, regarding the two banks just referred to: "The charters of these institutions are of the most liberal kind. No public securities are required, no control over them is exercised by the government, they might issue their bills to any amount, without one dollar of gold with which to redeem them. It would be hard for the public to protect themselves against fraud, should the officers please to close the institution, but the public hold a strong protection against such a course in the character and worth of the gentlemen who own the banks. Not only is their moral character above suspicion of such a gross act of public injury, but their business interests and relations are too dear and extended thus to be sacrificed. Indeed so careful have these gentlemen been to protect themselves individually, and the public from the possibility of such an act, that they did, on organizing their two institutions, place in the banks, gold and securities exceeding the amount of money issued by them. The consequence has been that their bills have been and are regarded as a safe circulation both at home and abroad. But so large are the advantages which these banks secured and yielded to the stockholders that at the last session of the legislature, the government was importuned for other similar charters for institutions like these all over the territory, by parties whose responsibility was doubted. The legislature passed acts chartering eight of these banks, but the governor vetoed all the bills. The house passed two over his veto, the others were lost. The excitement both in and out of the territory, was very great, in so much that Nebraska money fell into disrepute, and both banks in Omaha, thereupon began to draw in their circulations, and they have redeemed nearly all of it. Hereafter they will bank on some other circulation than their own."

The Omaha & Chicago Bank was granted a charter February 10th, 1857. H. B. Sackett, now a resident of Council Bluffs, was president and J. V. Schell, cashier. Its place of business was in the Western Exchange Fire & Marine Insurance Company Building, southwest corner of Twelfth and Farnam Streets. This bank was in existence between five and six years, W. J. Kennedy closing up its affairs in 1864.

In the history of Omaha already referred to, appears an advertisement of "William Young Brown, real-estate agent and exchange broker. Money loaned for capitalists." This party, in 1858, brought the head office of the bank of Tekamah to Omaha. This was a chartered institution, and its failure a little later is said to have entailed more loss on the general public than any other of the early banks of Omaha.

In the first issue of the *Omaha City Times*, June 11, 1857, is found the following advertisement: "Gridley & Co., F. Gridley, J. H. Kellom—new banking house—The subscribers having, formed a copartnership for the purpose of conducting a general banking business at Omaha, would respectfully give notice that while awaiting the erection of their banking office, they can be found at the office of O. D. Richardson, Esq., first office west of the Pioneer Block. We respectfully ask of the business men and citizens of Omaha and vicinity, generally, a due share of their deposits and business. Money Loaned. Drafts on New York, St. Louis, and all of the Eastern cities; gold and silver bought and sold on reasonable terms. Collections made and remitted for at current rates of exchange." This firm was in business for about three years.

John McCormick was in business in 1857 at the present site of the Arcade Hotel, on Douglas Street just east of Thirteenth Street, and continued to do a money-loaning business for four or five years. It is said that he had more money than any one else in Omaha at that time.

Samuel E. Rogers, now vice-president of the Merchant's National Bank, was a banker and real-estate broker, with an office at the corner of Douglas and Eleventh Streets, in 1857. H. C. Rariden & Co., were bankers and land-agents, with an office on Harney Street, in 1857 and 1858. The Nebraska Land & Banking Co., Fleming Davidson, president, R. C. Shain, cashier, were in business February 1, 1858. G. C. and J. J. Monell, under the firm name of Monell & Co., carried on a business as bankers and land agents in 1857. Their advertisement also appears in the *Omaha Times* of date August 12, 1858. Artemus Sahler & Co., bankers, dealers in Eastern exchange, land warrants and real estate agents, were in business in 1858. Smith & Parmalee were also in the business of loaning money during the years above named.

Two firms who started prior to some of those named above, outlived the first period of Omaha's banking history—Barrows, Millard & Co., and Kountze Bros. The former started a land agency on Harney Street, in 1855, the firm consisting of Willard Barrows, of Dubuque, Ezra Millard, of Sioux City, and J. H. Millard, of Omaha. From the locating of land warrants and handling of exchange the firm gradually drifted into regular banking. In 1860 Smith S. Caldwell joined the firm, and in 1862, J. H. Millard withdrew. There was no further change in this firm until after the close of the first period of this history.

Kountze Bros. started December 10, 1857, just after the panic of that year, Augustus Kountze having been previously the president of the Bank of Dakota. The firm originally consisted of Augustus and Herman Kountze, but a few years later included also two other brothers, Luther and Charles. Their first banking house consisted of a small one-story building of but a single room on the north side of Farnam between Twelfth and Thirteenth Streets, larger quarters being afterwards secured in a building which stood near the corner now occupied by the Nebraska National Bank. W. H. S. Hughes, now manager of the Omaha Clearing House, entered the service of Kountze Bros., as book-keeper, December 26, 1859, and remained in the employ of that firm and its successor, the First National Bank, for more than a quarter of a century. In the rear of Kountze Bros'. banking room stood a big safe, fastened by means of hasp and staple and a padlock. The purchase and sale of gold, mined in Colorado, was a considerable part of the business transacted by the bank in the early days, and the shelf extending along the east side and north end of the building was frequently covered with tin pans filled with the precious metal. Mr. Hughes and Luther Kountze slept in the bank as a guard. Upon the occasion of the burning of Lawrence, Kas., during the war by the infamous guerilla, Quantrell, it was reported that he and his band contemplated a raid upon Omaha, and in order to secure additional protection for the bank, the windows were provided with heavy iron bars. The Kountze Bros. established a branch bank in Denver in 1862, under the management of Luther and Charles—now the Colorado National Bank, and five years later established the New York Banking House of Kountze Bros., of which Augustus Kountze was long the head, his brother Luther being associated with him in the management. Charles Kountze is president of the Denver bank. Herman Kountze has long had the management of the Omaha establishment.

At the commencement of the second period of this history, in 1863, there were but two banking houses in Omaha—Barrows, Millard & Co. and Kountze Brothers—both located at Twelfth and Farnam Streets. The former occupied a portion of the first floor of the two-story and basement brick building that stood at the southwest corner of Twelfth and Farnam, and was a landmark of the city until torn down, in 1886, to make room for the present United States National Bank building. Willard Barrows withdrew, and the firm name was changed to Millard, Caldwell & Co., in 1864, C. W. Hamilton, who had been with the firm as bookkeeper since 1861, being then admitted as a partner. May 1, 1868, Ezra Millard retired from the firm, and the name was changed to Caldwell, Hamilton & Co., Mr. M. T. Barlow being admitted a partner. In 1883 another re-organization was effected, and

THE UNITED STATES NATIONAL BANK

started with a paid up capital of $100,000 which, in 1886, was increased to $250,000. The following year the magnificent stone structure now occupied by the bank was erected on the site of the old building. It has a frontage of sixty-six feet on Farnam Street and a hundred and thirty-two on Twelfth, is

five stories high, and is fitted up with all the modern improvements for bank and office buildings. The present officers of this bank are: Charles W. Hamilton, president; Milton T. Barlow, cashier; C. Will Hamilton, assistant cashier. The present capital stock of the United States National is $400,000. Mr. Caldwell died June 26, 1884.

THE FIRST NATIONAL BANK.

August 26, 1863, the First National Bank, of Omaha, opened for business, with a capital of fifty thousand dollars, Edward Creighton, president; Herman Kountze, vice president; Augustus Kountze, cashier; H. W. Yates, assistant cashier; and succeeded to the business of Kountze Brothers. This was the first bank to organize under the national banking law, in Nebraska, and among the earliest in the country, its charter number being 209. It occupied for its first banking house the one-story frame building at the northwest corner of Twelfth and Farnam, formerly occupied by Kountze Brothers.

The building was about twenty-two by fifty feet, with a square front. On its windows were the legends: "Gold Dust and Government Vouchers Bought," "Exchange Bought and Sold." The bank occupied these humble quarters until the fall of 1866, when it moved to the southeast corner of Thirteenth and Farnam, occupying what, at that time, seemed palatial quarters in a two-story brick building, which it continued to occupy until torn down in 1886 to make way for the present five-story and basement brick and stone fire-proof structure, which ranks as one of the best and most convenient office buildings in the West, and cost about $300,000. The banking room takes up the greater portion of the main floor, and is all that can be desired in the way of appointments and conveniences. The building is sixty-six by one hundred and thirty-two feet, with a banking room sixty-two feet wide, ninety feet long and twenty-one feet high. The present officers of the bank are: Herman Kountze, president; John A. Creighton, vice president; Frederick H. Davis, cashier; W. H. Megquier and H. E. Gates, assistant cashiers. The capital stock has been increased to $500,000.

THE OMAHA NATIONAL BANK.

In 1866, Mr. Ezra Millard, at that time senior member of Millard, Caldwell & Co., organized the Omaha National Bank, with a paid up capital of $50,000, Ezra Millard, president, and Joseph N. Field, cashier. Mr. Field came to Omaha and signed the first currency of the bank, but never actually filled the position of cashier, which was practically vacant until January of 1867, when it was filled by the appointment of J. H. Millard. The Omaha National opened for business July 1, 1866, in a one story frame building about twenty by forty, located in the street at the northwest corner of Douglas and Fourteenth. The bank room was about twenty by thirty, separated by a board partition from the parlor in the rear, which was also used as a bedroom. The counter, which extended from the front window to within about two feet of the partition, was of pine boards painted white in the front, the top covered with black oil cloth. A large fire-proof safe, with a burglar proof chest in the bottom, was conspicuous against the white partition in rear of the banking room. The furniture was marked by its simplicity rather than its elegance. The safe was not considered trustworthy enough to leave a very large amount of money in it over night. It was customary for one of the bank employees, before the day's business began, to secure a good sized bundle of currency from the more secure vault and burglar proof safe of Millard, Caldwell & Co., and, having disguised it by wrapping it in an old newspaper, to walk unconcernedly through the streets from Twelfth and Farnam to Fourteenth and Douglas, as though carrying a bundle of old clothes. The package seldom contained less than $20,000; when business was over for the day, the ceremony of the morning was again gone through with, to get the funds of the bank to a place of safety for the night. This was kept up until January 1, 1867, when the bank occupied its elegant and commodious, and for those days, extravagant quarters, at the corner of Thirteenth and Douglas, now occupied by the Omaha Savings Bank. The working force of the bank during the first six months consisted of the president, the book-keeper (who was also general all round office man) and the teller, who was also messenger boy, janitor and general assistant. From an old book used as a blotter on the counter of the Omaha National Bank the first six months, an idea may be gained of the amount of the clearings of the Omaha banks in the fall of 1866. October 25th, the settlement of checks for that date showed the Omaha National had checks on the First National Bank amounting to $5,561.63, and the First National had checks on the Omaha National to the amount of $405.25, leaving a difference of $5,156.28 in favor of the Omaha National. On the same day, the Omaha National had checks on the firm of Millard, Caldwell & Co., to the amount $314.92. In contrast with this may be given the business of October 25, 1892, when the Omaha National had checks against the First National to the amount of $129,840.30, and the First National had checks drawn on the Omaha National to the amount of $195,695.07, leaving a difference of $65,855.77 to be adjusted. On the same day the Omaha National cashed checks on the United States National (the successor of Millard, Caldwell & Co.) to the amount of $22,295.96, and the United States National took in checks on the Omaha National to the amount of $85,790.80. The capital stock of the Omaha National has been increased to $1,000,000. Joseph H. Millard is president; W. B. Millard, vice president; William Wallace, cashier; Richard Carrier and Edward E. Balch, assistant cashiers.

The Central National Bank of Omaha was organized in April, 1868, with a capital of $100,000, John McCormick, president; James G. Chapman, vice president; James M. Watson, cashier; Ben B. Wood, teller. This bank went into voluntary liquidation in January, 1871, its business being merged with that of the Omaha National, Mr. Watson, the cashier, taking a position with the Omaha National, which he held for a number of years.

MERCHANTS NATIONAL BANK.

In the fall of 1866 J. A. Ware & Co. opened a banking office at the northwest corner of Thirteenth and Farnam. The firm consisted of J. A. Ware, a banker of Nebraska City; Posey S. Wilson, who had been Mr. Ware's cashier for two years, and John W. Hugus, of Omaha. The capital employed was between $40,000 and $50,000. The business was successful, and a deposit account of $100,000 to $200,000 secured. In November, 1867, Mr. Wilson went to Cheyenne, W. D. Morton, a brother of J. Sterling Morton, taking his place at Omaha. In July, 1868, Mr. Wilson sold his interest in the firm of J. A. Ware & Co. to Mr. Ware and Mr. Hugus, and they in turn sold out to Governor Alvin Saunders, Ben B. Wood and others, who started the State Bank of Nebraska, succeeding to the business of J. A. Ware & Co.

The State Bank of Nebraska started with a paid up capital of $50,000: Alvin Saunders, president; J. R. Porter, vice president; Ben B. Wood, cashier. The capital was afterwards increased to $100,000. Mr. Saunders retired from the presidency in 1876 and was succeeded by Frank Murphy. The State Bank of Nebraska was succeeded by the Merchants National Bank of Omaha, October 2, 1882, with a paid up capital of $100.000: Frank Murphy, president; Samuel E. Rogers, vice president; Ben B. Wood, cashier; Luther Drake, assistant cashier. August 10, 1885, the capital was increased to $200,000; to $300,000 April 26, 1887; to $400,000 May 5, 1887, and to $500,000 May 3, 1888. Its building, at the northeast corner of Farnam and Thirteenth, erected in 1888, at a cost of $180,000, is one of the landmarks of the city.

### OMAHA SAVINGS BANK.

In 1882 there was organized in this city the first exclusively savings institution in Nebraska—the Omaha Savings Bank, which began business September 4th of that year in the Millard Hotel building, but moved into the quarters vacated by the Omaha National Bank, at the southwest corner of Douglas and Thirteenth, when that institution took possession of its fine structure on Thirteenth Street. The first officers of the savings bank were: James E. Boyd, president; William A. Paxton, vice president; Charles F. Manderson, managing director; John E. Wilbur, cashier. The present officers are: Charles F. Manderson, president; L. M. Bennett, vice president; Francis W. Wessells, managing director; John E. Wilbur, cashier. The capital stock is $150,000. From the date of its establishment this bank has had the confidence of the public to a marked degree, and its deposits have long since passed the million dollar mark.

### NEBRASKA NATIONAL BANK.

In the spring of 1882, Henry W. Yates, who had been for nineteen years connected with the First National Bank, first as assistant cashier and afterwards as cashier, severed his connection with that institution, and with A. E. Touzalin organized the Nebraska National Bank, which opened for business April 27, 1882, with a paid up capital of $250,000—the largest capital, at that time, of any bank in the State. Its present capital is $400,000. It occupied as temporary quarters a frame building, moved from the permanent site into the street for that purpose, formerly occupied by Brash's clothing store, and here the bank remained until its new building, costing sixty-five thousand dollars, was completed, July 1, 1883. The site, at the northwest corner of Twelfth and Farnam, adjoins on the east that formerly occupied by Kountze Brothers, with whom Mr. Yates commenced his banking career in 1863. The first officers of the bank were: Samuel R. Johnson, president; A. E. Tonzalin, vice president; Henry W. Yates, cashier. Mr. Johnson retired from the presidency in November, 1883, and was succeeded by Mr. Yates, June 7, 1887, Mr. Touzalin was made second vice president, Lewis S. Reed being promoted from a directorship to the active vice presidency of the bank. Mr. Touzalin died September 12, 1889. May 25, 1885, W. H. S. Hughes, who has probably seen more continuous bank service than any other person in Omaha, was appointed cashier, leaving the First National Bank, of which he had been bookkeeper since its organization, to go back to the locality where he commenced bank life over twenty-five years before. This was the first bank in Omaha to adopt the Corliss safe. At the beginning of the present year (1892) W. H. S. Hughes retired from the cashiership of the bank and was succeeded by Lewis Reed, R. C. Cushing becoming vice president.

### THE COMMERCIAL NATIONAL BANK.

The Commercial National Bank of Omaha was organized by Mr. Ezra Millard, who had been associated with banking in Omaha from 1860; first as senior partner in the firm of Millard, Caldwell & Co., and later as organizer of the Omaha National Bank, in 1866, and its president from that time until January, 1884.

The meeting for organization was held

April 7, 1884, in room 109 of the Millard Hotel. The capital stock was placed at $250,000. The first board of directors consisted of the following named gentlemen: Ezra Millard, Wm. G. Maul, Clark Woodman, L. B. Williams, James W. Garneau, Samuel R. Johnson, A. P. Hopkins. The bank opened for business on May 1, 1884. At a special meeting of the board of directors, held June 23, 1884, it was voted to increase the capital stock $50,000, making its paid up capital $300,000. This additional capital was paid in July 15, 1884. At the annual meeting in January, 1885, the board of directors was increased from seven to nine members. In August, 1886, Mr. Ezra Millard, the organizer and president of the bank, died at Saratoga, N. Y. This was a serious loss to Omaha, and was especially severe on the bank. Mr. Millard's long and honorable connection with banking in Omaha made him a power in the business community and a tower of strength to the bank. In July, 1888, the board of directors, who had, ever since the organization of the bank, been discussing a permanent location, purchased the northwest corner of Sixteenth and Farnam Streets for $92,000. The directors next turned their attention to improving their purchase, and the fall of 1888 was taken up with the discussion of plans of bank buildings. In December, 1888, a plan was agreed upon. In January, 1889, it was decided to increase the capital of the bank $100,000, and to have it called in by April 15, 1889.

The contracts for the new building were let in March, 1889, and the bank occupied its present beautiful and convenient quarters, May 1, 1890. The building is a landmark in the city, and is distinctively a bank building. In August, 1890, Mr. Andrew Henry, who was connected with the bank since its organization, serving most of the time as a director, died at Columbus, Neb., the bank thus for a second time losing a valued counselor by death.

Its present board of directors is as follows: E. M. Morsman, E. M. Andreesen, Charles Turner, Wm. L. May, Wm. G. Maul, Edwin S. Rowley, Charles E. Bates, Alfred Millard and A. P. Hopkins. A. P. Hopkins is president, Wm. G. Maul vice president, Alfred Millard cashier.

THE AMERICAN NATIONAL BANK AND THE M'CAGUE SAVINGS BANK.

The business of McCague Bros. was founded in March, 1880, at which time John L. McCague opened a real estate office upon the southeast corner of Fifteenth and Douglas streets. Six weeks later the office was removed to the second story of the Frenzer Block, opposite the postoffice, at which place the real estate business was continued for two or three years. In 1881, William L. McCague became identified with the business, as did also Alexander Charlton in 1882. September 1, 1883, the firm of McCague Bros. announced that from that date they would engage in banking. As soon as ground floor quarters could be secured in the Frenzer Block the business was removed, this removal taking place in the fall of 1883. During 1884 Mr. Thomas H. McCague became a member of the firm, the members then being John L. McCague, William L. McCague, Thomas H. McCague and Alexander G. Charlton. From the date of the establishment of the bank to August, 1889, the business grew steadily until the McCague Bros. bank became recognized as one of the solid banking institutions of the city. August, 1889, in order to accommodate the rapidly increasing needs, the banking business of McCague Bros. was divided into two institutions, viz: The American National Bank, with a paid up capital of $200,000.00, and The McCague Savings Bank. The officers of The American National Bank are: John L. McCague, president; A. R. Dufrene, vice president; Henry F. Wyman, cashier; E. C. Brownlee, assistant cashier, and the directory: John L. McCague, A. R. Dufrene, E. M. Morsman, R. S. Hall, W. S. Poppleton,

Alexander G. Charlton and Thomas H. McCague. The McCague Savings Bank has a capital of $200,000.00, of which $50,000.00 is paid up. The officers of this institution are: W. L. McCague, president; John L. McCague, vice president; Alexander G. Charlton, cashier; and the directory: John L. McCague, William L. McCague, Thomas H. McCague, Alexander G. Charlton and J. H. McCulloch. Since August, 1889, to the present time, the growth of the business has been very rapid. Both of the above institutions occupy elegant and convenient quarters in the new building constructed for their use on the northwest corner of Fifteenth and Dodge.

### THE BANK OF OMAHA.

The organizers of the Bank of Omaha were A. Henry, of Columbus, Neb., and Thomas H. McCague, of this city, beginning business on Thirteenth Street near Jackson, under articles of copartnership dated October 15, 1885. Mr. McCague remained with the bank only one year, and in September, 1888, Mr. Henry sold the business to Frank Wassermann, Charles P. Needham and Peter Goos, of Omaha, who conducted a general banking business in the same building until June 5, 1889, when an assignment was made, sheriff William Coburn being appointed assignee to wind up the affairs of the bank.

### UNION NATIONAL BANK.

The Union National Bank, of Omaha, began business July 1, 1886, with a paid up capital of $100,000. The following named gentlemen constituted the first board of directors: W. W. Marsh, J. W. Rodefer, Thomas Irwin, Wm. A. Smith, Wm. Fleming. The officers were: W. W. Marsh, president; J. W. Rodefer, cashier. The latter was succeeded November 25, 1889, by Charles E. Ford. This bank was first located in Masonic Block, on Sixteenth Street, and on November 25, 1889, moved to its present location at the southeast corner of Dodge and Sixteenth Streets, occupying the quarters especially prepared for the Douglas County Bank, the business of which was absorbed by the Union National. The first six years of its existence this bank developed only a very moderate growth. On July 1, 1892, it increased its capital to $250,000. Mr. G. W. Wattles, of Carroll, Iowa, was at the same time elected vice president, in place of Mr. David Bennison, resigned. Mr. Wattles is active in the management of the bank. The changes last referred to seem to have been of substantial benefit to the bank, its business and deposits more than doubling between July 1 and December 1, 1892. Its present board of directors consists of: W. W. Marsh, David Bennison, Wm. Fleming, W. A. Smith, Charles E. Ford. The officers are: W. W. Marsh, president; G. W. Wattles, vice president; Charles E. Ford, cashier; Charles Marsh, assistant cashier.

### THE NATIONAL BANK OF COMMERCE.

The Bank of Commerce was the outgrowth of a private bank establishment, started by Frank B. Johnson and Robert L. Garlichs, in May, 1885, under the firm name of Garlichs & Johnson. Their place of business was on the west side of Sixteenth, between Cass and California Streets, capital fifty thousand dollars. September 1, 1886, they organized the Bank of Commerce—with George E. Barker, president; Robert L. Garlichs, vice president; and Frank B. Johnson, cashier—with a capital of $100,000, which was increased July 1, 1888, to $500,000. At this date the bank was removed to the Barker building, corner of Farnam and Fifteenth Streets, and at the next election of officers Ellis L. Bierbower was elected vice president, to fill the vacancy caused by the retirement of Mr. Garlichs. April 14, 1890, the business was reorganized under the national banking act, as The National Bank of Commerce, of Omaha; president, J. N. Cornish; vice president, George E. Barker; cashier, Ellis L. Bierbower; assistant cashier, W. S. Rector.

## DOUGLAS COUNTY BANK.

The Douglas County Bank was established in 1885, as a private institution, by C. S. Parrotte, at the northwest corner of Sixteenth and Chicago Streets; the capital stock being increased to $100,000 upon the incorporation of the bank soon afterwards, at which time Mr. C. S. Parrotte was elected president; J. H. Parrotte, vice president, and Samuel E. Sample, cashier. In 1889 the bank removed to the Kirkendall Building, southeast corner of Dodge and Sixteenth, and on the 25th of November, of that year, wound up business by going into voluntary liquidation.

## NEBRASKA SAVINGS AND EXCHANGE BANK.

Nebraska Savings Bank commenced business October 3, 1887, in the Board of Trade Building, at the southwest corner of Sixteenth and Farnam Streets, with an authorized capital of $400,000, and a paid in capital of $100,000. John L. Miles, president; Andrew Rosewater, vice-president; Dexter L. Thomas, cashier; T. J. Mahoney, attorney. The first board of directors consisted of the following named gentlemen: John L. Miles, Dexter L. Thomas, Samuel Cotner, James Thompson, Alvin Saunders, John Rush, Andrew Rosewater, Samuel D. Mercer, J. H. Evans, Erastus A. Benson, Morris Morrison, George E. Barker, F. B. Johnson, Peter Glandt, Nathan Merriam.

November 21, 1887, W. A. L. Gibbon was appointed assistant cashier, and was placed in charge of the branch office at South Omaha, which was at this time opened. January 15, 1889, Andrew Rosewater was succeeded in the vice-presidency of the bank by Samuel Cotner, who served until January, 1892. At the annual meeting in January, 1890, the name of the bank was changed from the Nebraska Savings Bank to the Nebraska Savings and Exchange Bank, and in the following July the South Omaha branch, with the building that had been erected there, was sold to the Packers National Bank of that place.

On December 8, 1891, Mr. John L. Miles, who had been president of the bank since its organization, and who had been for a long time in poor health, resigned his position, and Mr. John Rush was elected president. Mr. Miles died the same month, on Christmas day, at his home in this city.

The present officers are: John Rush, president; Clinton Orcutt, vice-president; Dexter L. Thomas, cashier. The directors are: John Rush, J. H. Evans, E. Rosewater, E. A. Benson, Clinton Orcutt, L. G. Kratz, James Thompson, David Anderson, Alvin Saunders, Geo. E. Barker, Andrew Miles, Dexter L. Thomas, N. A. Kuhn, W. S. Gibbs.

The authorized capital has been reduced from $400,000 to $200,000, and the paid up capital has been increased from $100,000 to $150,000, from the earnings of the bank. October 6, 1892, the deposits of the bank were $117,100. Number of accounts opened since commencement of business, 3,926. The bank has made 6,068 commercial loans and 520 real estate loans.

## THE STATE NATIONAL BANK.

The State National Bank, which opened for business in the spring of 1887, at the northwest corner of Harney and Fifteenth, with a capital of $100,000, was a short-lived institution. Its chief stockholder was E. L. Lyon, who came here from Marshalltown, Iowa, where he had been engaged in the banking business for some time. He was president of the bank and A. A. McFadden, cashier. A few months later Mr. Lyon sold his stock to Mr. E. E. Whaley, of Loup City, Nebraska. An inspection by Bank Examiner Griffith, disclosed the fact that a considerable portion of the bank's assets consisted of Mr. Whaley's paper, which had been received in payment of Mr. Lyon's interest, and the directors were notified that this paper must be converted into cash within twenty-four hours or he would be compelled to take charge of the bank. Within the time specified the directors adopted a resolution to close up the business, which was done. Some three months later, Mr. Lyon, having returned to Omaha from California, repurchased his interest from Mr. Whaley, and permission was obtained from Washington to resume business, but the experiences it had passed through were so demoralizing in their effects that the efforts to re-establish the business was unsuccessful, and in a few weeks the doors of the bank were closed.

### THE OMAHA BANKING COMPANY.

The Omaha Banking Company began business in the summer of 1887, with a capital of fifty thousand dollars, at No. 320 South Fifteenth Street, removing a year later to the corner building previously occupied by the State National Bank. Clifton E. Mayne was president, Patrick Ford, vice president, and J.W. Gross, cashier; the latter being succeeded by Hartford Toland, and he by Thomas F. O'Brien. The business proved unprofitable and the directors closed it up June 30, 1889.

### MECHANICS' AND TRADERS' BANK.

The Mechanics' and Traders' Bank began business March 1, 1888, at No. 318 South Fifteenth Street; authorized capital $250,000, with fifty thousand dollars paid in. Richard C. Patterson and Frank Barnard were the main stockholders. The bank voluntarily closed its business February 1, 1890.

### GERMAN-AMERICAN SAVINGS BANK.

The German-American Savings Bank, located in the Commercial National Bank Building, was established in 1889, with an authorized capital of $250,000, and a paid in capital of $25,000; Jefferson W. Bedford, president; J. R. Harris, vice president, and J. W. Harris, cashier. It is, at this date, November, 1892, winding up its business and turning over its deposits to the American Savings Bank.

### ANGLO-AMERICAN MORTGAGE AND TRUST COMPANY.

The Anglo-American Mortgage and Trust Company, opened a banking house in 1888, at No. 405 South Fifteenth Street; capital stock $300,000; L. W. Tulleys, president; J. N. Brown, vice president; J. V. McDowell, secretary, and E. B. Walters, treasurer; has since gone out of business.

### THE GLOBE LOAN AND TRUST COMPANY SAVINGS BANK.

On March 25, 1890, the Globe Loan and Trust Company Savings Bank was organized, with the following officers and board of directors: President, H. O. Devries; vice president, Cadet Taylor; cashier, W. B. Taylor; assistant cashier, Charles E. Williamson. Directors: W. J. Broatch, Hugh G. Clark, B. S. Baker, J. B. Dennis, D. H. Wheeler, E. M. Stenberg, H. K. Burket, D. T. Mount, John Jenkins, and the above officers.

It opened for business April 1st, at 307 South Sixteenth Street. The subscribed capital is fifty thousand dollars, with twenty-five per cent. paid in, and seventy-five per cent. subject to call by the board of directors.

The Globe Loan and Trust Company, which has a paid-in capital of $200,000, owns the controlling interest, and the bank is managed by the same officers. The growth of this institution during the first year convinced the board of directors that they must provide a permanent home of their own. The ninety-nine year ground lease, and Globe Building, southwest corner of Dodge and Sixteenth Streets, was purchased in November, 1890, and fitted it up expressly for the accommodation of the savings bank and trust company business, and was occupied in April, 1891.

Since the organization of the Globe Loan and Trust Company Savings Bank there has not been a single change among its officers, and the same is true of the Trust Company. The Boards of Education of Omaha and

South Omaha designated this Savings Bank as the school savings depository, and the system was introduced in May, 1890. The schools savings system has the cordial support and co-operation of parents, pupils, teachers and public school officials, and its beneficial influence upon the rising generation is conceded by every one conversant with the workings of the system. The total school deposits are about $7,400, and there are about 4,800 school children who are depositors.

This bank has had a continuous growth. It began business in the midst of the dull period and financial stringency of 1890, and yet it has grown steadily from the first. It does no commercial, but a strictly savings bank business, and loans only on first real estate mortgages, or approved collaterals. The deposits the first day were $1,564.14. The semi-annual growth has been as follows:

| | |
|---|---|
| May 6, 1890. | $ 2,208.10 |
| November 6, 1890 | 11,010 17 |
| May 6, 1891 | 30.006.60 |
| November 6, 1891 | 53,884.13 |
| May 6, 1892 | 84,976.67 |
| July 6, 1892 | 99,460.94 |
| November 1, 1892 | 109,958.80 |

The number of accounts, November 1, 1892, were 7,442.

### DIME SAVINGS BANK.

The Dime Savings Bank, of Omaha, is the outgrowth of the savings department of the the Mutual Investment Company, the first institution west of Chicago to receive deposits of less than one dollar. The bank was incorporated under the new banking law of the State, March 1, 1890, with a paid up capital of $25,000. It had at that time deposits amounting to $16,154, and accounts to the number of 681.

| | |
|---|---|
| March 1, 1891, its deposits were | $35,742 |
| Number of accounts | 1,956 |
| March 1, 1892, deposits | 77,156 |
| Accounts | 4,888 |
| Deposits now (October, 1892) about | 90,000 |
| Accounts | 6,009 |

Its first board of directors was: P. C. Himebaugh, W. H. Russell, G. H. Payne, F. H. Taylor, W. A. Goddard, G. M. Nattinger, Hon. Alvin Saunders, F. W. Hills, Nathan Merriam, J. A. Gillespie, W. F. Allen. And its officers were: P. C. Himebaugh, president; W. H. Russell, vice president; G. H. Payne, cashier.

Its present officers are: W. H. Russell, president; W. F. Allen, vice president; J. G. Cortelyou, cashier.

The increase of its business has been such that at a late meeting of the directors it was decided to double its paid up capital, making it $50,000.

### THE GERMAN SAVINGS BANK.

The German Savings Bank commenced business June 2, 1890, in the building at the southeast corner of Thirteenth and Douglas, which the Commercial National Bank had just vacated. The authorized and subscribed capital is $500,000. The paid in capital is $100,000. The board of directors consists of Frederick Metz, Sr., Frederick Krug, Henry Bollin, Charles J. Karbach, Henry Meyer, George Heimrod, L. D. Fowler. The officers are: Frederick Metz, president; Charles J. Karbach, vice president; L. D. Fowler, cashier. December 24, 1891, the bank moved from Thirteenth and Douglas to its present beautiful and convenient office, in the Karbach Block, at the corner of Fifteenth and Douglas. The business of the bank has steadily grown, as evidenced by the following figures:

| | |
|---|---|
| June 21, 1890, the deposits were | $ 57,114.49 |
| June 30, 1891, the deposits were | 333.547.56 |
| June 27, 1892, the deposits were | 635.558.60 |
| July 12, 1892, the deposits were | 650,563.42 |

### THE CITIZENS BANK.

December 7, 1886, W. G. Templeton and A. D. King, from Fremont County, Iowa, where Mr. Templeton had served as county clerk four years and Mr. King as county treasurer six years, established, at 2408 Cuming Street, the Citizens Bank, with a capital of $10,000. Mr. King was at the same time the president of the Hitchcock County Bank, of Culbertson, Nebraska, where he now (October, 1892) resides, having disposed of his Omaha interests.

The bank was incorporated September 1, 1888, with an authorized capital of $100,000; paid in capital, $25,000, and within six months from its incorporation $27,500, additional capital was paid in, raising the paid up capital of the bank to $52,500. The first board of directors consisted of W. G. Templeton, Isaac Johnson, J. A. Patrick, George E. Draper, A. H. Sanders, George A. Day, James Hendrickson. The officers were: George E. Draper, president; F. C. Johnson, vice president; W. G. Templeton, cashier; J. A. Patrick, assistant cashier. On July 1, 1890, W. G. Templeton accepted the cashiership of the Midland State Bank, on Sixteenth street. Mr. J. A. Patrick, the assistant cashier, was in charge of the bank until September 2, 1890, when he was elected cashier in place of Mr. Templeton, resigned. W. R. Roberts was at the same date elected assistant cashier, and in September, 1891, was elected cashier.

At the annual meeting, September, 1892, the present board of directors was elected, consisting of W. G. Templeton, George E. Draper, F. C. Johnson, A. H. Sanders, Martin Tibke, James Hendrickson, W. R. Roberts. The officers are: George E. Draper, president; F. C. Johnson, vice president; W. R. Roberts, cashier. The deposits of the bank at the date of its organization as a State Bank, September, 1888, were $22,375. The deposits on October 7, 1892, were $65,700. The bank occupied its present attractive quarters, at the corner of Twenty-fourth and Cuming Streets, on Thanksgiving Day, 1890.

### AMERICAN SAVINGS BANK.

This is an outgrowth of the savings department of the American Loan and Trust Company. It was incorporated June 22, 1888, with a paid in capital of $100,000. The officers and directors were: O. M. Carter, president; C. S. Montgomery, vice-president; Philip Potter, treasurer; A. C. Powell, cashier; H. R. Gould. It occupied the basement under the United States National Bank, at the south-west corner of Twelfth and Farnam Streets, until January, 1890, when it was moved to the Opera House Building, corner Fifteenth and Farnam. On December 15, 1892, it moved into spacious and elegant quarters on the main floor of the New York Life Building, at the corner of Seventeenth and Farnam. This bank has lately absorbed the deposits of the German American Savings Bank, retired from business. The American Savings Bank is conservatively managed and has had a steady and healthful growth. No changes have ever occurred in its officers or board of directors, which remain the same as at its incorporation, in 1888.

### OMAHA LOAN AND TRUST COMPANY SAVINGS BANK.

This institution is an outgrowth of the savings department of the Omaha Loan and Trust Company. The department had been started as a branch of the business of the Trust Company, in 1888. It was regularly incorporated under State law in October, 1889, with a capital stock of $100,000, of which $50,000 was paid in. The first board of directors consisted of the following prominent business men: J. H. Millard, J. J. Brown, E. W. Nash, Thomas L. Kimball, Guy C. Barton, George B. Lake, A. U. Wyman.

The officers were: A. U. Wyman, president; J. J. Brown, vice-president; W. B. Millard, treasurer. There has never been any change in the board of directors. The present officers are: A. U. Wyman, president; J. J. Brown, vice-president; W. T. Wyman, treasurer; Frank Brown, cashier. The bank, at the date of its incorporation, occupied quarters in the Millard Hotel Block, at Thirteenth and Douglas Streets, but upon the completion of the J. J. Brown Block, at the corner of Sixteenth and Douglas Streets, the bank moved to that location, where it occupies a handsome and convenient banking room on the main floor.

The bank, as previously stated, was incorporated in October, 1889. Its deposits December 31st of that year, amounted to $282,000. On December 31, 1891, the open accounts on the books of the bank numbered 967, averaging $341 apiece, or a total deposit, exclusive of certificates, of $506,000.

Mr. A. U. Wyman, the president of the bank, was for a number of years the treasurer of the United States, and has a national reputation. Added to this the directorate is especially strong in men of well known financial ability. The success of the institution is therefore assured.

### MIDLAND STATE BANK.

Midland State Bank was organized July 1, 1890, succeeded to the business of the Sixteenth Street branch of the National Bank of Commerce, which in turn had succeeded to the business originally started in this neighborhood, by Garlichs & Johnson. Its authorized and subscribed capital is $100,000; paid in capital fifty thousand dollars. The first board of directors consisted of the following persons: F. C. Johnson, W. G. Templeton, J. N. Cornish, Allen T. Rector, George Draper, George A. Day, George E. Barker and H. N. Wood. January, 1891, the directorate was increased to ten by adding Lee W. Spratlin and William Sievers. The first officers of the bank were: F. C. Johnson, president; Allen T. Rector, vice president; W. G. Templeton, cashier. On April 1, 1892, the number of directors was reduced from ten to five. The present board is as follows: F. C. Johnson, C. A. Sharp, W. G. Templeton, William Sievers and W. R. Roberts. The officers are F. C. Johnson, president; C. A. Sharp, vice president; W. G. Templeton, cashier.

### SOME OMAHA BANK STATISTICS.

DEPOSITS OF THE OMAHA CLEARING HOUSE BANKS FOR YEARS ENDING

| | |
|---|---|
| October 2, 1890 | $18,382,618 |
| September 25, 1891 | 14,739,860 |
| September 30, 1892 | 18,196,422 |

AGGREGATE DEPOSITS OF OMAHA BANKS ON JULY 12, 1892.

| | |
|---|---|
| National Banks | $19,626,213 |
| State Banks | 1,130,081 |
| Savings | 2,855,764 |
| | $23,612,058 |

EXCHANGES OF OMAHA CLEARING HOUSE SINCE ITS ORGANIZATION.

| For Year Ending. | Amount | Per Ct. of Increase. |
|---|---|---|
| September 30, 1885 | $51,428,609 | ..... |
| September 30, 1886 | 82,690,570 | 60.04 |
| September 30, 1887 | 137,220,534 | 65.09 |
| September 30, 1888 | 166,007,003 | 20.09 |
| September 30, 1889 | 201,250,166 | 21.02 |
| September 30, 1890 | 245,062,456 | 21.07 |
| September 30, 1891 | 221,128,895 | *9.07 |
| September 30, 1892 | 272,939,692 | 23.04 |

*Decrease

# CHAPTER XLIX.

### Omaha's Park System—The Struggle for Jefferson Square—Boulevards.

In platting Omaha a reasonable provision was made for public parks, considering that in 1854 very little attention had been given by eastern cities to a matter now deemed of the utmost importance by all enterprising communities. The seven blocks bounded by Eighth, Ninth, Jackson and Davenport Streets had been set aside for that purpose. The block bounded by Fifteenth, Sixteenth, Farnam and Douglas was christened Washington Square, and at first designed for public uses, but was within a very few years deeded to the county as a site for a court house.

### JEFFERSON SQUARE.

Jefferson Square was also platted as a park, and is the only spot left to the public within the boundaries of the city proper for park purposes, and from the earliest history of Omaha an almost continuous struggle has been maintained to convert it to other uses. In 1858 a resolution was offered in the city council providing that lots 3, 4, 5 and 6, in that block be set apart for school purposes. The same year a proposition was made to sell the square but City Solicitor George I. Gilbert, to whom the matter was referred, reported that the council could not make a legal transfer of public grounds. Afterwards a school building was erected on this block and in October, 1867, a special council committee reported, recommending that said building be at once removed, which report was adopted.

In January, 1868, one J. L. Williams proposed to lease Jefferson Square for market house purposes, and the council committee to whom the matter was referred reported that they " had conferred with many prominent property holders of the city, and that they were all in favor of the proposition," hence the committee recommended that the proposition be accepted, reserving to the city the right to purchase the market house at the end of six years, at a fair valuation. The report was laid upon the table, and the council, in " the rush and hurry of business," forgot to take it up again. Six months later the board of school directors made a proposition to lease the ground for a term of twenty-five years for school purposes, and a resolution was offered in the council directing the mayor to make a lease with the directors of " School District No. 1," for said term, on condition that the school board erect a three-story brick building, on the square, to cost not less than $40,000, and to be completed by the 1st of October, 1869; the block to be enclosed by "a substantial and comely paling; the grounds laid out and ornamented with trees, etc., under the direction of a competent landscape gardener," and conditioned further: "That at the expiration' of the said term of twenty-five years said city shall either purchase, at a fair appraised value, the improvements on said square, or extend and continue the duration of said lease on such terms and for such length of time as the parties thereto may agree upon, the choice of the alternative to rest with the city.'' The report of the committee was adopted, but for some reason not appearing of record, the scheme was not carried into effect.

In 1870 Lyman Bridges made a proposition to the council to build a market house on Jefferson Square, but the committee to whom the matter was given for consideration and investigation reported in favor of an indefinite postponement of the subject, which report was adopted. In 1872 a resolution was adopted by the council offering the block to the general government as a site for headquarters buildings for the Department of the Platte, and a special committee appointed to bring the matter to the attention of General Ord, then commanding said military department. That officer passed the proffer along to his superiors, through the regular, red tape channels, and there the matter ended. In 1877 an effort was made in the council to provide for the establishment of two market houses, one to be located on Jefferson Square, and the other south of Farnam Street, but failed to secure enough votes and the following spring the ground was graded, seeded down, fenced, and trees planted in the square and on the curb line of the streets by which it was bounded, by Mr. James T. Allan.

But this did not end the struggle to divert the property from the purposes to which it had been dedicated more than a score of years previously. In April, 1878, the judiciary committee of the council and the city attorney were directed to "inquire into the right of the city to Jefferson Square, with a view to having Douglas County and the city put up a building, or buildings, for the joint use of the county and city, and to fix a value upon the property." These officials reported that the city council could not convey to the county any title to the property; that the erection of a joint building by the county and city would be carrying into effect the public purposes for which the ground had been dedicated, and that the value of the property was $16,000, and a few days later a resolution was adopted offering the ground to the county commissioners "as a site upon which to erect, jointly with the city, public buildings for the use of the city and county, subject to the valuation as fixed by the city council, to-wit: $16,000, two-thirds of that amount to be allowed to the city by the county for the privilege of the joint occupancy of said square." This generous proposition was not accepted by the commissioners, who were, at that time, negotiating for the purchase of the block upon which the court house now stands. In May, 1882, Mr. Webster Snyder presented to the council a scheme by which he was to furnish a city hall free of expense to the taxpayers. He proposed to erect, at an expense of $100,000, a building on Jefferson Square; of generous dimensions, the lower story of which was to be used as a market house, and the second story for city offices and council chambers. There was much discussion of this proposition, but it was suffered to drag along for a year, and was then finally rejected by the council.

In May, 1887, a resolution was introduced in the council by Alderman Bailey, authorizing the sale to the government for a postoffice site, of the west half of the square, for the nominal consideration of one dollar, the sale of the remainder for what it would bring in the market for business or residence purposes, and the purchase, with the money thus received, of the block known as the Governor Izard block, or some other square, in that vicinity, for park purposes. The resolution was rejected by the council.

In the latter part of 1888 a strong effort was made to have the site of the city hall—located by a vote of the citizens at the northeast corner of Farnam and Eighteenth Streets two years previously—relocated and Jefferson Square used for that purpose. The proposition was submitted to a vote in February, 1889, and overwhelmingly decided in the negative. Then a few weeks later the property was included in a large list of sites proposed for the new postoffice building, for which an appropriation of $1,200,000 had recently been voted by Congress, but was not considered desirable for that purpose by the treasury department, whose agent was sent to Omaha to select a suitable site. On this occasion the value of the ground was fixed at $400,000—certainly a handsome increase over the figure given eleven years previously, and affording a fair indication of the changes wrought in the value of Omaha real estate, by the wonderful growth of the city during that period. It will be seen that this small spot on the earth's surface has had a remarkable history, and it is a matter of surprise that it still remains free to the public. The trees which were planted in the spring of 1878 have attained considerable size, and now afford abundant shade. The square was improved considerably in 1889 by the park commission.

### HANSCOM PARK.

In October, 1872, a tract of ground, covering fifty-seven and a half acres, was offered the city for public park uses, by two of the earliest settlers in Omaha—Andrew J. Hanscom and James G. Megeath. The tract is situated in what was then the extreme southwestern part of the city; was covered at that time by a thrifty growth of young trees, and was in many ways specially adapted to that purpose. No charge was made for the property, but the gift was upon condition that the city expend in improving it the sum of three thousand dollars in 1873, four thousand dollars each year for the three years following, five thousand dollars in 1877, and the same amount in 1878; to forever keep the property in good order, and to grade and keep in good repair at public expense the streets by which the tract was bounded. The donation was accepted on these conditions, the property christened "Hanscom Park," and for ten years past has been a popular resort for all classes of people. The tract is now of great value, and its donors will ever be held in grateful remembrance for their generosity, foresight, public spirit and enterprise. In the earlier years of the history of this park the city was in financial straits, and considerable management was required to provide funds to carry out the necessary improvements. Indeed, it is well known that the conditions in that respect were not literally fulfilled, owing to a lack of money, but Messrs. Hanscom and Megeath, realizing the situation, displayed commendable forbearance in not insisting upon a strict performance of all the conditions embraced in the deed of gift.

### THE PRESENT PARK LAW.

At the session of the legislature of 1889 a law was passed providing for a general system of parks, for all cities of the metropolitan class (Omaha being the only one in the State), and the appointment by the Judges of the District Court of a board of five commissioners, to have control thereof. Following is the full text of the law:

"In each city of the metropolitan class there shall be park commissioners, who shall have charge of all the parks and public grounds belonging to the city, with power to establish rules for the management, care and use of public parks and parkways; and it shall be the duty of said board from time to time to devise and suggest to the mayor and council a system of public parks, parkways and boulevards within the city and within three miles of the limits thereof, and to designate the lands and grounds necessary to be used, purchased or appropriated for such purpose; and thereupon it shall be the duty of the mayor and council to take such action as may be necessary for the appropriation of the lands and the grounds so designated, and for the purpose of making payments for such lands and grounds assess such lands and grounds as may be specially benefited by reason of the appropriation thereof, for such purpose, and issue bonds as may be required in excess of such assessment. Said board shall be comprised of five members, who shall be resident freeholders of such city, and who shall be appointed by the judges of the judicial district in which such city shall be situated.

"The members of said board shall be appointed by said judges, a majority of said judges concurring, on the second Tuesday of May, 1889, or on the second Tuesday of May following the creation of this act of any city of the metropolitan class, one for the term of one year, one for the term of two years, one for the term of three years, one for the term of four years and one for the term of five years; and after the appointment of said five members it shall be the duty of said judges, a majority concurring, to appoint or reappoint one member of said board each year on the second Tuesday of May. A majority of all the members of the board of park commissioners shall constitute a quorum. It shall be the duty of said board of park commissioners to lay out, improve and beautify all grounds now owned or hereafter acquired for public parks and employ a secretary and also such landscape gardeners, superintendents, keepers, assistants, or laborers, as may be necessary for the proper care and maintenance of such parks, or the improvement or beautifying thereof, to the extent that funds may be provided for such purposes. The members of the board at its first meeting each year after the first Tuesday in May shall elect one of their members as chairman of such board. Before entering upon their duties each member of said board shall take an oath to be filed with the city clerk that he will faithfully perform the duties of his appointment, and in the selection or designation of land for parks or boulevards and in making appointments he will act for the best interests of such city and the public, and will not in any manner be actuated or influenced by personal or political motives.

"The chairman of such board shall receive a salary of six hundred dollars per annum and the other members of said park commission shall receive a salary of two hundred dollars per annum.

"For the purpose of paying such salaries, providing funds for laying out, improving or benefiting parks and public grounds and providing for the salaries and wages of employes of said board the mayor and council shall each year at the time of making the levy of taxes for general city purposes make a levy of not less than one and a half mills and not exceeding three mills on the dollar valuation on all the real and personal property within the corporate limits of such city taxable according to the laws of this State; and such fund to be known as the park fund, the warrants thereon to be drawn only in the payments of accounts or claims audited by the said board of park commissioners."

## THE PARK COMMISSION.

Under the provisions of this law the judges, May 14th, 1889, selected the following named as a board of commissioners: George L. Miller, for the term of five years; George W. Lininger, for the term of four years; Augustus Pratt, for the term of three years; George B. Lake, for the term of two years; Alfred Millard, for the term of one year. A three mill levy was made by the mayor and council and a fund of about $62,000 raised for the use of the board during the remainder of the year.

The first meeting of the board was held May 15, 1889, when Dr. Miller was elected president, and Guy R. Doane, secretary. Correspondence was had with leading landscape gardeners of St. Louis, Minneapolis, St. Paul, Chicago and Cincinnati, resulting in the employment of Mr. H. W. S. Cleveland, of Minneapolis, to prepare plans for the use of the commission and to superintend the improvement of the public grounds of Omaha. In June a visit was made by the Board to Minneapolis and Chicago, to view the public parks and gain information as to the methods pursued in those cities for their development. The work thus far done here has been under the superintendency of William R. Adams, William L. Adams having charge of the surveys. He was succeeded by J. E. House, civil engineer, in 1892. During the year and a half ending January 1, 1891, the board expended $70,738.22. May 14, 1890, Alfred Millard was re-appointed a member of the commission for a term of five years; May 14, 1891, Geo. B. Lake was re-appointed, and on May 14, 1892, Thomas Kilpatrick was appointed in place of Augustus Pratt, who declined.

The legislative session of 1891 gave to the park commissioners somewhat increased powers and provided that, "the mayor and council are authorized to negotiate for and purchase such lands as may be designated by the park commission within the limits designated, notwithstanding said limits include land within the boundaries of other cities or villages, and if such lands are in the limits of other cities or villages, said cities or villages shall cease to have jurisdiction over said land after it is acquired for park purposes, by gift, purchase, condemnation or otherwise, and the park commission is given power to purchase or condemn land in cities or villages within the three mile limit. For the purpose of paying for and improving the same the mayor and council may appropriate money from the general fund or issue bonds to an amount not to exceed $500,000 within three years from the passage of this act, and thereafter not to exceed $50,000 per year. Said bonds shall not be issued, however, until authorized by a two-thirds vote at a general election. Improvements upon streets abutting upon parks or similar grounds shall be paid for from the 'park' fund hereafter provided. The board of park commissioners shall be composed of five resident freeholders, to be appointed by the judges of the District Court on the second Tuesday in May, and they shall hold office five years. The chairman shall be elected at the first meeting after the first Tuesday in May each year and he shall receive a salary of $600 per year. The other members shall receive a salary of $200 per year. For the purpose of providing funds for the park commission the council shall each year make a levy of not less than $1\frac{1}{2}$ mills and not exceeding three mills on the dollar valuation on all real and personal property within the corporate limits; provided, that when the total valuation of taxable property exceeds $25,000,000 the rate of levy shall be reduced in proportion to the increase of valuation."

### THE NEW PARKS.

Acting under the provisions of the act of the legislature, in November, 1891, on the recommendation of the park commissioners the city council submitted to the voters of the city a proposition providing for the issuing of bonds to the amount of $400,000, to be used in purchasing tracts of land for park purposes. The proposition was carried by an overwhelming vote, and the bonds were issued and sold for a premium of $26,728. The park board recommended to the city council the purchase of the following tracts of land:

*The Parker Tract.*—The south half of the northeast quarter, of section 33, township 16, range 13, eighty acres, for seventy-five thousand dollars. The recommendation was approved by the city council, and the property will be bought as soon as title can be procured from the heirs, who now hold it. It is situated just northeast of Fort Omaha.

*The Distin Tract* was bought for ninety thousand dollars. It contains 110 acres, and is situated in the angle of Ames Avenue and Forty-eighth Street.

As heretofore mentioned the Bemis Park Company, in 1889, donated to the city a narrow strip of land about two hundred feet wide, extending from Thirty-third Street on the east to Thirty-sixth Street on the west, being mostly a narrow, deep ravine. The park commission then recommended the purchase of the ground lying between the donated strip and Cuming Street, making the park contain about ten acres, at a cost of thirty thousand dollars. This purchase was also made.

### ELMWOOD PARK.

Fifty-five acres of this park were donated in 1890, by Lyman Richardson, John T. Bell, Leopold Doll and others. The board realized that this was where the large park of the city could be made, and recommended the purchase of the remainder of the quarter section, in which most of the donation was located, being the southeast quarter of section 24, township 15, range 13. The remainder of the quarter section, about 115 acres, and twenty acres in the section on the west of it, have since been purchased for nine hundred dollars per acre; also twenty acres of ground northeast of said park, and extending north to Dodge Street, was purchased for twelve thousand dollars. This park contains about 210 acres, and has cost the city, by purchase, about $135,000.

Of the $426,000 received from the sale of bonds there remains a balance of about ninety-six thousand dollars, which it is intended to use partially, or wholly if necessary, to purchase land for park purposes in the southeast portion of the city.

### BOULEVARDS.

It is the intention of the park commission to eventually connect all the parks in the city by handsome, wide boulevards. Lands for this purpose have been donated in various localities. One of these will run from Ames Avenue north to the Parker tract, and thence north to connect with the Forest Lawn Cemetery boulevard, which will be turned over to the city. This boulevard will be one hundred to one hundred and twenty feet wide. Most of the land has been donated by property owners. There are a few persons having small holdings who have not donated. The city attorney has begun proceedings to condemn the tracts not donated.

The engineer of the park board is making a final survey of a line from a point near Hanscom Park, southwest, running to Ruser's Shooting Park, and from thence to Elmwood Park, for a boulevard two hundred feet wide.

As the boulevards will add greatly to the value of property where they are located, there is scarcely a doubt but that most of the land necessary for them will be donated by property owners, and that it will not be many years until the city will be well supplied with these beautiful drives.

Up to October, 1892, the following amounts had been expended on the various parks by the park commissioners since the work came into their hands. The amounts cover all expenses, including improvement, maintenance, etc.:

| | |
|---|---|
| On Hanscom Park | $72 850 47 |
| On Capitol Avenue Park, between Eighteenth and Twentieth Streets | 1 481 91 |
| On Jefferson Square | 6 453 32 |
| On Bemis Park | 758 90 |
| On Himebaugh Park (formerly Belt Line Park), a strip of land dedicated to the city in platting Saunders & Himebaugh's addition | 42 00 |
| On Elmwood Park, including bridges | 22,295 58 |

In addition to the above, there has been a small sum expended on boulevards.

### SYNDICATE PARK.

Syndicate Park, owned by the South Omaha Land Company, adjoins Omaha on the southeast. It contains 108 acres, with an abundance of forest trees and never-failing springs of water. The company has expended about $30,000 in improving the park.

A strong pressure has been brought to bear upon the park commissioners to induce them to purchase Syndicate Park, for the southeast park, but up to the present time it has not been done, there being much division of sentiment among the people in the southern portion of the city as to the best location for a park in that section, many urging that Syndicate Park is in South Omaha, and object on that account. Some of the influential property owners and citizens claim that Syndicate Park can never be diverted to any other than park purposes, as the surrounding property was sold by the original owners with the understanding that it should be a park, and that this being the case it is unnecessary for the city to purchase it. A great many recommended a location further east for the public park, and favored purchasing what is known as the Clark tract, on the bluffs, overlooking the river. The question has not yet been decided.

In October, 1892, Syndicate Park was enclosed with a high board fence, and watchmen placed in charge, to keep the public off the property, the owners thus giving notice that it was considered by them to be private property. If the people desire to use the park, the company which owns it demands that it shall be paid for by Omaha or South Omaha.

LOOKING NORTHWEST FROM FOURTEENTH AND FARNAM STREETS—1873.

LOOKING NORTH FROM FOURTEENTH AND FARNAM STREETS—1873.

# CHAPTER L.

THE POSTOFFICE — CUSTOM HOUSE — INTERNAL REVENUE DEPARTMENT — EXPRESS COMPANIES.

### THE OMAHA POSTOFFICE.

The Omaha postoffice was established May 6, 1854, by the efforts of Hon. Bernhard Henn, then a member of Congress from Iowa, who also secured the appointment of A. D. Jones as postmaster. The first building used for postoffice purposes was a small house on Thirteenth Street, directly in rear of the Douglas House. David Lindley, who conducted the hotel, taking charge of the mail as Mr. Jones' deputy. Mr. W. W. Wyman was then appointed postmaster, and a building at the corner of Eleventh and Harney was occupied as the postoffice. Mr. Wyman erected a two-story brick at the northwestern corner of Thirteenth and Douglas, using the first floor for a postoffice and the upper floor as a printing office, he being then the publisher of the *Omaha Times*. Mr. Wyman was a democrat and in consequence of Mr. Lincoln's election lost his official position and George Smith became postmaster of Omaha. The office was then moved to the building at the northeast corner of Farnam and Fourteenth. A few years later it was moved to the store room under the Academy of Music, on Douglas Street, and here for a year or two John H. Kellom was postmaster. In 1871 Joel T. Griffin was appointed postmaster, and the office was moved to the A. J. Simpson building on Fourteenth Street. Then Casper E. Yost became postmaster and, following the example of all his predecessors, secured a removal of the office, this time to a store room in the Creighton Block, on Fifteenth Street. The present postoffice building, which cost $300,000, was commenced in 1870, and when it was completed, in 1874, the office was moved into it. In 1876 Thomas F. Hall succeeded Mr. Yost as postmaster, and at the close of his term he was succeeded by C. K. Coutant. When the democrats came into power, in 1885, C. V. Gallagher was appointed by President Cleveland, and was succeeded in the fall of 1890 by T. S. Clarkson. For twenty years James I. Woodard, the present deputy postmaster, has been connected with the office in various capacities. In 1873, when the delivery system was established, there were but six carriers, and the business for that year was as follows: Stamps sold, $31,860.10; box rent, $1,103.50; unpaid postage collected, $18.54; waste paper sold, $20.00; Money order business, $1,053,458.20; total, $1,089,660.34. In contrast with this may be given the business of 1889 and 1890, as follows: Stamps sold 1889, $228,108.47; 1890, $260,394.18. Box rent 1889, $2,036.00; 1890, $2,030.00. Total 1889, $230,204.47; 1890, $262,424.18; increase over 1889, $32,219.71. Money orders paid 1889, $90,958.00; 1890, $101,238.00; increase over 1889, $10,280.00.

There are now sixty-seven carriers regularly employed and seven substitutes. Eight of the carriers are mounted. There are also forty-five clerks. One hundred and eleven mails are received daily. During 1890 there were 19,935,834 pieces handled. The office expenses for the year were $76,481.94. There are 212 letter boxes distributed about the city for the receipt of mail. Joseph E. Cramer is superintendent of mails.

For the year from July 1, 1891, to July 1,

1892, the following is the amount of business which was done by the Omaha postoffice: Stamps and envelopes sold, $277,740.95; box rents received $2,076.75. Number of mails received, 111; number of mails dispatched, 111; annual allowance for office expenses, $37,800; cost of free delivery, $57,807.67; salaries railway postal clerks, $100,285.74; making a total of $195,893.41 for expenses. Number of male clerks, thirty-seven; number of female clerks, eight. Total number of street letter boxes, 212.

### THE NEW POSTOFFICE.

In 1889, chiefly through the efforts of Senator Manderson and Congressman McShane, a government appropriation of $1,200,000, was secured for the erection of a new postoffice building the cost of the site not to exceed $400,000, the present building proving entirely too small for even present needs. Of course there was much strife by property owners in particular and the public, in a general way, to secure the location of this building so as to best advance special interests. Various sites were offered, the choice finally narrowing down to the block bounded by Farnam, Douglas, Eighteenth and Nineteenth, and the one bounded by Dodge, Capitol Avenue, Sixteenth and Seventeenth, a second visit to this city by the agent of the government being necessary to settle the matter. The Farnam Street ground had the advantage of being much higher, thus affording a much more prominent and striking position for the handsome structure it is the purpose of the government to erect, while the Dodge Street site was considered easier of access. The latter was finally selected and the various interests therein adjusted by a board of appraisers, appointed by Judge Dundy, of the United States District Court, the wife of ex-President Cleveland being the owner of a valuable portion of the block. The total valuation of the various subdivisions of the property was fixed by these appraisers at a trifle less than the allowance of $400,000.

The bill for the new building was approved by the President of the United States on January 21, 1889. It provided for an appropriation of $1,200,000 for the purchase of a site and the erection of a United States custom house, a court house and postoffice, an amount not exceeding $400,000 to be paid for the site, and no plan of a building to be approved by the secretary of the treasury which should exceed in cost of erection $800,000. The bill also provided that upon the completion of the new building, the present government building should be turned over to the secretary of war for use as offices for the headquarters for the Department of the Platte. Since the passage of the original bill, Senator Manderson has succeeded in having a bill pass the United States Senate increasing the appropriation to $2,000,000. The matter is now awaiting action by the house of representatives at Washington.

In the spring of 1892 the contract for the basement was let to O. J. King, of Omaha, and the work has progressed until this part of the building is now nearly completed. It is expected that the contract for the superstructure will soon be let, and that the work will be pushed until the building is finished. The plans of the new building contemplate its erection on the eastern portion of the block, so that if the additional appropriation is made the structure will be extendeded to Seventeenth Street without changing the plans of the building under the present appropriation. Mr. W. H. Alexander was appointed disbursing officer for the new building, and Mr. Charles F. Beindorf was appointed superintendent of construction.

The style of architecture of the new building is the Romanesque. The basement and first story are to be constructed of St. Cloud pink granite, finished in natural rock face, with joints, corners and jambs dressed. The three upper stories are to be of sandstone. The main entrance is from Sixteenth Street; it is approached from a loggia fifteen feet wide and fifty long, surrounded by a balustrade. It is composed of a facade of five arches springing from massive piers. These are embellished on each side by groups of polished granite columns with carved capitals. The carving is continued on the soffit of the arches. Three doors give access to the interior from this loggia.

Over the center of the loggia is a magnificent tower rising to a height of 190 feet, with a large clock and dial on each of the four sides.

To the right and left of the loggia, are gables, projecting toward the street, with grouped triple windows, surmounted on the roof with handsome double dormer windows and produce a charming effect.

The entrances on Dodge Street and Capitol Avenue are emphasized by very handsome gables, presenting the feature of triple grouped windows before mentioned. On the first floor, entrance is had through a facade of three arches, the door being recessed. The gables extend into the roof, which is hipped, and which is further broken up by dormer windows grouped to the best advantage.

### PLAN OF THE BUILDING.

The basement is devoted to a heating and ventilating plant, elevator and electric light machinery, and offices on Sixteenth Street (not assigned), and storage purposes.

The first floor is very conveniently arranged; entering from Sixteenth Street into a large vestibule and thence into the office proper, where you stand before the private boxes, of which there are fifteen hundred; on either side are the various deliveries. To the right of the entrance are the elevators, of which there are two. Around these are the main stairs, leading by easy stages away up into the tower.

Following the wide corridor to the right, on the northeast corner are a suite of offices, not assigned; passing these is the Capitol Avenue entrance. Directly west of this are the postmaster's and assistant postmaster's offices, toilets, etc. At the end of the corridor is a large shaft, with stairs leading above the roof, for the use of the mail superintendent and signal service inspectors.

To the left of the Sixteenth Street entrance and up to the Dodge Street entrance are quarters for the money order department, toilet rooms, etc. West of the Dodge Street entrance are the rooms of the registry department. The first story is 22 feet in height and over the working department on a line with the screen, is a skylight 100x100 feet in size, assuring ample light.

On the second floor to the right of the elevators are rooms for the internal revenue department; west of these are lawyers' consulting rooms and library, with toilets, etc. To the left of the elevators, facing Sixteenth Street, are large quarters devoted to the customs' department. West of these, facing Dodge Street, are postoffice inspector's and witness rooms with all conveniences; these are all reached from a large, well-lighted corridor. The inside is devoted to a court over the skylight before mentioned.

On the third floor to the right of the elevators, facing on Sixteenth Street, are the United States marshal's quarters, with rooms for deputy, clerk, etc. On the northwest corner is a large court room with two private rooms for judges on the east of same. To the left of elevators, facing Sixteenth Street, are rooms for the district attorney, clerk of court and grand jury; next to them on the west are two judges' rooms and on the southwest corner is a large circuit court room, with private stairway leading to witness rooms on second floor.

The north half of the fourth floor is arranged for the signal service bureau, with all appliances and conveniences. The south half is intended for dormitories of mail clerks.

## U. S. CUSTOMS OFFICE.

[W. H. Alexander, surveyor of the port of Omaha, contributes to this work the following article on the subject:]

Omaha was made a port of delivery by act of Congress approved July 7, 1870. Mr. S. A. Orchard was the first surveyor appointed. In those days there were few importations, and such articles as were bonded to Omaha were examined and the duties fixed upon them at the port of original entry, so that the surveyor's part in the transactions here was largely clerical, delivering the goods upon receipt of the duties specified in the transportation papers. There were more steamboats on the Missouri then than now, however, and as owners are required to enroll their boats at the customs office in the district where they operate, the surveyor must furnish enrollment papers, licenses, certificates and such other documents as are required by law. For several years, too, it was a part of the surveyor's duty to collect marine hospital dues, a contribution of thirty cents per month from every man employed on the river boats, to a fund held by the government for medical treatment and care of any who should become disabled in the service, provided applications for aid were made within one year from the date of retirement.

It will be seen, therefore, that the early surveyors were not entirely free from labor on government account.

There was no federal building here during Mr. Orchard's term, his office being located in a little building belonging to the postmaster, facetiously alluded to by the surveyor as "the hut."

Mr. H. K. Smith succeeded Mr. Orchard, serving nearly two years, and after him came W. W. Copeland, the present Omaha agent of the "Red Line" freight route. During Mr. Copeland's term of office the United States custom house and postoffice building was completed and placed in his charge as custodian.

The next surveyor appointed was Mr. John Campbell, who held the office two terms. Business had materially increased before Mr. Campbell retired, though a glance through the records brings to mind some rather diminutive footings, and once (in January, 1884) no transactions at all were reported. Nor was the February following particularly conspicuous for activity, the total receipts being only one dollar. Business revived, however, in March, and the handsome sum of $2,200 came in from customs.

Further along in this article a comparative statement of receipts for the several years intervening between 1872 and 1892 appears, which will doubtless be of interest to many.

In the fifth year of Mr. Campbell's service, the appointment of a deputy surveyor was authorized, and Capt. James N. Phillips was given the position.

On June 10, 1880, Congress passed an act which conferred upon Omaha, and several other ports, the privileges of immediate transportation, that is, collectors at ports of first arrival were authorized to forward merchandise in bond, without appraisement, leaving the examination and assessment of duties, for surveyors at the ports of final destination. This method of forwarding is of great advantage to the importer, as it does away with the breaking of packages for inspection, while enroute, which often results in material damage through imperfect repacking, and it saves considerable time between shipment and delivery. There was a proviso in the bill, however, that proper officers and facilities for the performance of the new requirements must be present, and the Secretary of the Treasury, in whose discretion the matter rested, withdrew the privilege almost immediately, because the scheme was not then considered practicable for Omaha.

In 1886 the office of deputy surveyor was abolished, and Capt. Phillips was left, like Othello, without an occupation.

Mr. Robert C. Jordan was appointed in the same year to succeed Mr. Campbell as surveyor. He undertook to perform the duties of the office alone, but it became apparent before very long that one man was not equal to the requirements, and the department restored the office of deputy and authorized the appointment of a clerk. These new positions were filled by Mr. Vincent Burkley and Mr. E. J. Murphy, respectively.

In February, 1888, through the efforts of Senator Manderson, the privileges of immediate transportation were re-conferred upon Omaha, and from that time on imported merchandise has been examined, appraised and duties fixed at this port.

Mr. Jordan retired from office December 1, 1889, and was succeeded by W. H. Alexander, the present surveyor.

At this point it may be proper to explain two or three official terms which appear ambiguous to many, and about which considerable inquiry has been made:

First. As to the character of the several customs districts. A port of entry is the place of first arrival of imported merchandise. There it is entered, either for consumption, warehousing, or immediate transportation to some other customs point. A port of immediate transportation is the place to which merchandise can be re-shipped after arrival entry, without examination or appraisement. A port of delivery is the place to which merchandise, after being examined, appraised and duties fixed at the port of entry, can be sent in bond, to be released when the specified duties are collected. New York is a port of entry, St. Louis and Omaha are ports of immediate transportation, and Council Bluffs is a port of delivery.

Second. At the larger seaports, where the duties are multiplied and more varied, the chief officers are a collector, naval officer, and a surveyor. At seaports of less importance and at the larger border ports, there is a collector, and a surveyor. At all interior ports the chief officer is the surveyor, but all the functions lodged in a collector which are requisite for the transaction of business, are bestowed upon the surveyor, so that he is really a collector. The old official designation will doubtless be changed before long, now that interior ports have an individual character, and the term collector be used altogether as the chief officer's title. Surveyor Alexander's assistants are Capt. J. N. Phillips, deputy; H. C. Crumb, chief clerk and inspector, and G. L. Laws, immigration agent.

Two things in particular, that have been of great advantage to importers, are the bonded warehouse, furnished by Mr. William Bushman, and a commodious examination room. At this date Omaha is thoroughly equipped for every branch of customs service made possible by law. It is the chief port within the circle of St. Paul, Chicago, Kansas City and Denver, and most of the importations except for Sioux City and Lincoln, within a wide circuit, are made through the Omaha office. The following comparative table of duties collected since Omaha was made a port, shows the remarkable increase of recent years, and gives Omaha a place among the first forty of the 130 customs districts of the United States:

| | |
|---|---|
| 1872 to 1881, 10 years | $ 10,080 08 |
| 1882 | 2,940 81 |
| 1883 | 3,403 44 |
| 1884 | 6,201 82 |
| 1885 | 9,125 23 |
| 1886 | 19,588 53 |
| 1887 | 22,240 48 |
| 1888 | 29,854 69 |
| 1889 | 68,238 92 |
| 1890 | 67,189 26 |
| 1891 | 93,350 06 |
| 1892 | 127,962 56 |

Since the beginning of 1888, business at this office has rapidly increased. Pains have been taken by the customs officers to familiarize merchants and manufacturers with the details of importing, and the advantages of direct shipment to Omaha, in bond, and to give the office here the prominence it deserves. Surveyor Alexander has been ably assisted in his plans for developing facilities for increased business, by Senator Manderson, and has received at all times the most courteous and encouraging consideration of his requests from the department.

INTERNAL REVENUE DEPARTMENT.

[Gen. J. B. Dennis, chief deputy collector, furnishes the following in regard to the Internal Revenue Department:]

The Internal Revenue District of Nebraska was organized in August, 1862. At this time the department had assessors as well as collectors.

The first appointment was J. H. Burbank, assessor, August 26, 1862, who served to July 1, 1865. C. H. Norris, probably his deputy, was acting assessor from July 1, 1865, to July 31, 1865. T. W. Tipton was then appointed, and served from August 1, 1865, to November 1, 1866. A. S. Holiday was appointed November 1, 1866, and served until April 1, 1867. F. Renner was then appointed and served from April 1, 1867, to May 6, 1869. T. J. Majors was appointed May 6, 1869, and served until May 20, 1873, when the office was abolished.

From the organization of the revenue service, up to May, 1873, the office of assessor was a very important, as well as a very laborious one. At this time the government levied a tax on all incomes over one thousand dollars, on all business and trades, as well as professions.

A doctor could not write a prescription without paying a special tax for the privilege; a dentist could not pull a tooth without paying a special tax; a lawyer could not prepare a brief without paying special tax; a notary could not put his jurat to an instrument without paying special tax; a tailor could not make a suit of clothes without paying special tax; a barber could not draw his razor across a face without paying special tax. All legal instruments had to bear a tax stamp, all notes, bills of exchange, drafts, checks, receipts, invoices, bills of lading, deeds, proprietary articles of all kinds, had to bear a tax stamp, and a druggist filling a prescription, had to put upon the prescription; bottle or package, a revenue stamp. Even matches had to pay their share of the running expenses of the government.

Spirits were taxed two dollars on each gallon manufactured, malt liquors one dollar per barrel; manufacturers of tobacco paid twenty-four cents per pound, cigars twelve dollars per thousand, snuff sixteen cents per pound, cigarettes six dollars per thousand.

Each stallion, jack or bull, kept for use had to contribute to the general fund. The assessor and his deputy had to ride over the country making assessments, and when his list was made up, he turned it over to the collector, taking his receipt for the full amount assessed.

Since the abolishing of the office of assessor, and the cutting off of the collections from many sources, the collector's lists have been made up by the collector, and the commissioner of internal revenue makes the assessment. The first collector was J. Sweet, who served from September 16, 1862, to August 4, 1866. Joseph E. Lamaster was appointed August 4, 1866, and served until December 2, 1872; Henry A. Newman served from December 2, 1872, to August 1, 1878; Fleming W. Robb, appointed August 1, 1878, served until March 6, 1879; Henry A. Newman, from March 6, 1879, to March 15, 1879; Lorenzo Crounse, appointed March 15, 1879, served to April 1, 1883; George W. Post, served from April 1, 1883, until November 1, 1886.

On the 20th day of August, 1883, the collection district of Dakota was consolidated into the district of Nebraska, since which time the collection district of Nebraska has comprised Nebraska, North and South Dakota. George W. Post served as collector until the 1st day of November, 1886; Simon H. Calhoun was appointed collector on November 1, 1886, and continued in office until June 26, 1889, when the present collector, John Peters, was appointed.

The collections have increased nearly every year from $12,338.45 in the fiscal year ending June 30, 1863, to the enormous sum of $4,889,588.65 in the fiscal year ending June 30, 1892. The collections for fiscal year ending:

| | |
|---|---|
| June 30, 1863 | $ 12,338 45 |
| June 30, 1864 | 26,795 91 |
| June 30, 1865 | 57,818 75 |
| June 30, 1866 | 100,874 78 |
| June 30, 1867 | 107,975 84 |
| June 30, 1868 | 127,735 11 |
| June 30, 1869 | 161,388 48 |
| June 30, 1870 | 308,501 51 |
| June 30, 1871 | 224,368 92 |
| June 30, 1872 | 195,698 91 |
| June 30, 1873 | 242,962 38 |
| June 30, 1874 | 276,886 52 |
| June 30, 1875 | 292,472 30 |
| June 30, 1876 | 502,395 59 |
| June 30, 1877 | 602,743 36 |
| June 30, 1878 | 699,821 37 |
| June 30, 1879 | 876,309 81 |
| June 30, 1880 | 912,734 86 |
| June 30, 1881 | 962,064 86 |
| June 30, 1882 | 1,108,191 15 |
| June 30, 1883 | 1,320,517 24 |
| June 30, 1884 | 1,519,643 63 |
| June 30, 1885 | 1,971,296 12 |
| June 30, 1886 | 1,674,013 12 |
| June 30, 1887 | 2,393,404 70 |
| June 30, 1888 | 2,778,269 38 |
| June 30, 1889 | 2,248,624 19 |
| June 30, 1890 | 2,969,745 17 |
| June 30, 1891 | 3,255,331 93 |
| June 30, 1892 | 4,889,588 65 |

The revenue force in this district consists of John Peters, collector; John B. Dennis, chief deputy, with two office deputies, and three clerks, while the outside force is one stamp deputy at Nebraska City, Neb., ten division deputies, ten storekeepers and eight gaugers. The offices of the Internal Revenue Department were first, and for some years afterward at Nebraska City, and were removed to Omaha about the year 1872.

EXPRESS COMPANIES.

On the 3d day of August, 1857, was established the first express office in Omaha, the United States Express Company being the pioneer in that line. Mr. J. Shepard, now assistant manager of that company, opened the office. Mr. C. C. Woolworth, brother of Hon. J. M. Woolworth, was the first agent. He was succeeded by David Moffatt, now of Denver, late president of the Denver & Rio Grande Railroad Company. The Barkalow Brothers and Mr. E. M. Morsman have also acted as local agents for this company.

The United States Express Company reached Omaha via Western Stage Company, from Iowa City, and in 1858 extended their service over the same stage line from Omaha to Fort Kearney, John Heath being the first agent at that place. He was succeeded by Dr. G. L. Miller.

The United States Express Company was the first company operating the Union Pacific Railway, sending out a "run" July 1, 1866, to Columbus, Nebraska, that being the western terminus of the railway; E. M. Morsman was express messenger. This company has had an office in Omaha all the time since 1857, and now has a joint office with the Pacific Express Company, S. A. Huntoon, agent. They traverse the Chicago, Rock Island & Pacific Railway, with other important systems, aggregating twenty-five thousand miles.

About 1864 the American Express Company opened an office in Omaha, reaching it via stage from Chicago & Northwestern Railway. They also occupied the Union Pacific Railway for a short time, and up to its completion to Grand Island. It now operates on the Chicago, Burlington & Quincy; the Chicago & Northwestern, and the Kansas City, St. Joseph & Council Bluffs lines of railways, having close connection with New York by means of an exclusive train. The superintendent of the western department, L. A. Garner, has his office in this city. Charles S. Potter is the local agent.

The Holiday Overland Mail and Express succeeded the American, on the line of the Union Pacific Railway and Wells, Fargo & Company succeeded them, being a continuation of the company with a change of name. Wells, Fargo & Co., occupied the Union Pacific Railway—Omaha being the eastern terminus of their routes until 1869.

Wells, Fargo & Company have their headquarters, middle department, here, employing a general superintendent and six division superintendents, with a territory extending from the Missouri River to the Rocky Mountains and from the Gulf to the Canadian border. The local force consists of thirty-five men. Dudley Evans is the general superintendent and Chas. S. Potter the local agent.

The Union Pacific Railway Company organized an express department called the Union Pacific Railway Company's Express, which went into operation September, 1869, Wells, Fargo & Co. retiring from that line. Subsequently the Union Pacific Railway Company's Express was extended over the Kansas & Pacific Railway and branches, and in November, 1879, the business was incorporated (in Nebraska) under the name of the Pacific Express Company—J. W. Gannett, A. J. Poppleton and E. M. Morsman, incorporators. Sidney Dillon was the first president of the Pacific Express Company. The Pacific Express Company was extended from time to time, until it now covers about 24,000 miles of railway; has its general executive and financial offices in Omaha, having built an expensive and commodious building to accommodate that business. It has about 120 employes in Omaha. The present officers are: E. M. Morsman, president and treasurer; O. W. Mink, vice-president; W. F. Bechel, secretary and auditor. Capital, $6,000,000.

The Adams Express Company came to Omaha November 15, 1888, via the Chicago, Milwaukee & St. Paul Railway, and has since maintained an office here. R. B. Reeves is the local agent.

The Merchants' Union, now the American, was represented here by John A. Horbach in 1866 and 1867. There was a lively competition in those days for business, and Mr. Horbach says he stood ready to receipt for anything, from a gold pen to a steam boiler. Rates were "knocked endways" and for a time were but little in advance of freight bills.

# CHAPTER LI.

### ART IN OMAHA — EARLY ORGANIZATIONS OF ARTISTS — WESTERN ART ASSOCIATION — ART EXHIBITIONS — PRIVATE COLLECTIONS OF PICTURES.

[A chapter from the pen of Joseph T. Duryea, D. D.]

During the autumn of 1877 an effort was made to interest and assist all those who were disposed to devote themselves to the study and practice of art, which resulted in the formation of a "Sketch Class," by Mrs. Charles F. Catlin.

Mrs. Catlin had been residing in the City of New York for nearly a year, in order to the enjoyment of the advantages of membership in the Art Students' League, an association of artists and art students. The opportunity for study and tuition was inviting, but the chief attraction was found in daily companionship with artists who were full of enthusiasm, and earnestly devoted to their work, many of whom became noted in after years, such as F. S. Church, Walter Shirlaw, Turner, Weir, Van-Boskerck, Kelley and Hirschberg. Under the impulse in this manner received, Mrs. Catlin endeavored to excite in her friends a desire for the best possible incentives and helps to improvement in knowledge and skill. Among them were Mr. Charles S. Huntington, Mr. Frederick Knight, Mr. William R. Morris, all well known for their high attainments.

With the aid of such associates the Sketch Class was started in October, and continued its work two evenings a week for the two years following, with a recess during the summer months. The large dining room in Mr. Catlin's residence was used as a studio, and so great was the success of the movement, that it was soon filled to the utmost extent of its capacity.

The work of the class was entirely in white and black, from original figures, each member in turn posing for the benefit of the rest of the members.

The following are the names of a few of the members of the class. The Misses Fanny Butterfield, Woodie McCormick, Selma Balcombe, Christina Ross, Gwynnie Gwyer, Carrie Wyman; Messrs. Frederick Knight, Charles S. Huntington, William R. Morris, Lieutenant Schuyler, U. S. A., and Professor Landeryou.

In 1879, the ladies of Trinity Church, formed a temporary association for the purpose of presenting an art loan exhibition, with Mrs. Bishop Clarkson as president, Mrs. A. J. Poppleton as secretary, Mrs. Lyman Richardson as treasurer, and Mrs. Charles F. Catlin as superintendent of the gallery. If it were practicable to transfer the pages of the catalogue to this chapter, it would not only illustrate the judgment and taste of many of the citizens of Omaha of that early period in the life of the city, but also reveal the degree of wealth already attained by many, and the measure of cultivation and refinement expressed in the elegance of their homes and the abundant means of mental improvement and æsthetic enjoyment.

The exhibit comprised: 232 oil paintings, water-colors, and etchings; 273 specimens of bric-a-brac and household decorative art; 192 ceramics and pottery; 167 lace and textile fabrics; 73 ancient jewelry; 256 mineral and geological curios; 58 Indian relics; 236 ancient books and manuscripts; a collection of ancient coins belonging to Mr. Charles Ogden.

The earnestness of the exhibitors and the extent of their labors may be known, from the fact that there were upon the several committees and in charge of the various departments, 151 ladies and gentlemen. The distribution of the objects throughout the homes of the city may be learned from the fact that the number of those who loaned them were 219. The exhibition continued for three weeks, and during the entire period the building in which it was presented was filled with visitors, both day and night. Critics of good judgment regarded it as a success, from an artist's point of view, and the general appreciation of its excellence was evident from the fact that it was financially a success. No one of the many visitors now surviving, can fail to recall it with lively and pleasant recollections.

In the year 1881, a number of women expressed, one to another, a desire to provide for themselves facilities for instruction and training in the principles and practice of art. They had already attained some proficiency in drawing and painting in oils and water-colors. In the month of November they resolved to invite such of their friends and neighbors as they supposed might be in sympathy with their aim, to meet for consultation. They were assembled at the residence of Mrs. James W. Van Nostrand. Among those who were present were Mrs. Frank Colpetzer, Mrs. Mary S. DuBois, Mrs. Robert Doherty, Mrs. G. I. Gilbert, Mrs. Hume, Mrs. J. J. L. C. Jewett, Mrs. R. C. Moore and Mrs. Clark Woodman.

It was decided to form an association to be styled "The Social Art Club of Omaha." A committee was appointed to draft a simple plan of organization and report at an adjourned meeting. It consisted of the following named persons: Mesdames Jewett, Moore and Doherty.

At a meeting held at the residence of Mrs. Gilbert, a constitution and by-laws were adopted. The design of the association was stated in a preamble, to be "mutual improvement through instruction and practice in all artistic industries." The officers were elected as follows: President, Mrs. James W. Van Nostrand; vice president, Mrs. Robert Doherty; treasurer, Mrs. George I. Gilbert; secretary, Mrs. J. J. L. C. Jewett.

The executive management of the club was entrusted to a board of managers. Under their direction and by their judicious and vigorous efforts the association entered upon a period of prosperity and usefulness, which continued about three years, with a maximum membership of seventy-five.

Two ample rooms were secured and properly prepared and furnished and a practical school of painting in oils and water-colors was opened, with Mrs. Cram as teacher in oils and Miss Lizzie Pennell in water-colors. A sketch class was formed under the supervision of Mr. Charles Huntington and Mr. William Morris, who had valuable assistance from Mr. Diederick Parker.

Twice each year the work of the members was presented for inspection by an exhibition and offered for sale to those who might be disposed to make purchases. During the period of its existence, the club made no appeal for pecuniary assistance, but maintained its expenses by the contributions of its members and by the proceeds of occasional entertainments, which were generally regarded as well worth the price of admission. Under its auspices Mr. Oscar Wilde was secured as a lecturer, in March, 1882. When the time came to disband, in order to make way for a larger organization, on a broader basis, the society was free from debt and held valuable materials, plaster casts, etc. Specimens of the work of the members of the club may be seen upon the walls in the houses of many of our citizens to this day.

THE WESTERN ART ASSOCIATION.

In June 1888, Mr. C. H. Kent, through the daily papers, issued a call for a meeting of persons interested in the study and practice of art, with a view to the formation of an art association. In response, about twelve assembled at Meyer's Art Rooms, on Sixteenth and Farnam Streets. After consultation, it was agreed to appoint a committee to visit the artists resident in the city and endeavor to interest them in the movement, and engage them in the endeavor to further it. This committee was composed as follows: Mr. Charles H. Kent, chairman; Mrs. Frances Mumaugh, Miss M. F. Murray, Miss Maggie Roeder, Miss May Willmasser.

The committee performed the service and issued circulars calling a meeting at Meyer's Art Rooms, on Sixteenth and Farnam Streets. At that time about fifty were present. They were addressed by Mr. George W. Lininger, who explained the general object of the proposed association and the measures and means through which it might be accomplished, and also set forth the benefits it might render to the members and to the community. There was a free and full discussion of these topics and the conclusions were reached which found expression afterward in the constitution adopted:

"The object of the association shall be to advance the knowledge and love of the fine arts through the exhibition of works of art, the acquisition of books and papers for the purpose of forming an art library, lectures upon subjects pertaining to art, receptions given to men or women distinguished in art, and by other kindred means, to promote social intercourse among its members."

It was at this meeting Mr. Lininger made known his intention of building and furnishing an art gallery contiguous to his residence, and his desire to place it at the disposal of the members of such an association as was proposed for the purpose of study, and also of practice in copying under reasonable restrictions. In order to afford additional encouragement, Mr. Adolph Meyer offered the use of Music Hall, without cost, for the first exhibition, and Mr. Clement Chase engaged to furnish the catalogues without charge to the association. A resolution was passed that a temporary organization be made and a committee appointed to prepare for a permanent organization by framing a constitution and by-laws. This was carried into effect by the selection of Mr. George W. Lininger, as president; Miss M. F. Murray, vice president; Miss Kate M. Ball, secretary; Mr. C. D. Kent, assistant secretary; Miss Maggie Roeder, treasurer. The president appointed as the committee: Mr. C. D. Kent, chairman, Mrs. Thomas M. Orr, Mrs. Frances Mumaugh, Mrs. George I. Gilbert, Mr. Robbins, Mr. Hyde.

On September 20th, at Meyer's Hall, the committee reported at a full meeting, the constitution and by-laws were adopted, and a board of managers was selected, consisting of Mrs. Frances Mumaugh, Mrs. T. M. Orr, Mrs. M. S. Silkworth, Mrs. J. M. Woolworth, Miss E. J. Shultze, Mr. Louis Mendelssohn, Mr. Clement Chase, Mr. Adolph Meyer, Mr. J. K. O'Neil, Mr. W. V. Morse. The officers of the temporary organization were made permanent.

ART EXHIBITIONS.

In the year 1886, in connection with the Inter-State Exposition, there was an exhibition of works of art, under the direction of a special organization consisting of Mr. G. W. Lininger, manager; Mr. C. K. Collins and Mrs. J. S. Briggs, assistants; J. D. Bailey, custodian; and Mesdames Samuel Burns, Frank Colpetzer, P. E. Iler, G. W. Lininger, J. M. Woolworth, committee.

Mr. Lininger loaned from his collection sixty-four pictures, ten pieces of statuary, several antique vases, and a specimen of Aubesson tapestry. The general loan collection contained more than three hundred paintings, some of which were of great merit. There were also collections of works in water colors, pastel, crayon, etchings, engravings and photographs. There were specimens of taxidermy, needle work and fine cabinet work.

The first autumn exhibition of the Western Art Association was held at the Lininger Gallery, November 15 to 17, 1888. It consisted of oil and water color paintings (on canvass, plaque and panels) original and copied, pastel, crayon and charcoal, India ink, and several architectural drawings, in all, 333 numbers, with thirty-five sets of decorated china.

In this and the subsequent exhibitions the works presented were from the members of the association exclusively, and these only were offered in competition for honorable mention and later for premiums. The first premiums were offered at a meeting of the association in April, 1889, and were as follows:

For oil painting—first premium, $25.00; second, $15.00; third, $10.00. Water colors —first premium, $15.00; second, $10.00. Porcelain—first premium, $10.00; second, $5.00. Pottery, $5.00; clay modeling, $5.00.

On November 5, Mr. Lininger offered a medal for the best work in water colors; Mr. Frederick Knight a medal for the best work in china. In October, 1890, Mrs. Emma H. Thayer offered a medal for approved work in water colors, and Mr. Lininger's medal was awarded for excellence in still life.

The progress manifested from year to year will be partly evident from the following statistics:

At the spring exhibition, May 15 to 20, 1889, there were oil paintings, 206; water colors, 44; crayon and pastel, 31; china, 33 sets; architectural drawings, 8.

At the fall exhibition of the same year, oil, 201; water, 41; pastel, 2; black and white, 11; china, 26 sets; and a specimen in clay modeling.

In the fall of 1890, oil, 217; water colors, 70; black and white, 12; china, 25.

In November, 1891, oil, 147; water colors, 99, black and white, 15; china, 55.

It will be noticed that the increase in the number of works presented is chiefly in the list of water colors and china. The decrease in the number of oil paintings is due to the steady elevation of the standard of excellence and the taste of the people generally.

In the year 1890, a number of gentlemen united to form the Omaha Art Exhibition Association, the object of which was to collect works of art of the first rank and present them to view for the benefit of the people of the State, to whom otherwise they would never be within view. As a result of their efforts there was gathered one of the very finest collections ever exhibited in this country. Some idea of the quality of the collection may be formed from the values set upon the pictures, several of which were estimated in sums approaching $1,000, and a few ranging from $1,000 to $10,000, one at $12,000, one at $18,000 and one at $50,000. There were seventy-two water colors, most of which were of a very high degree of merit. The etchings numbered forty-seven, and the fac simile reproductions of oil and water color paintings of well known artists 166. There were 119 specimens and collections, large and small, of antiquities and curios, which furnished instruction and entertainment seldom available in one place and at one time save in the instance of great national exhibits.

## THE LININGER GALLERY.

Mr. G. W. Lininger came from Illinois to Council Bluffs, and thence, after a short period of residence in that city, to Omaha, in 1873. During the intervals of occupation, in the management of an extensive business, he had devoted himself to the study of art. As his means were increased, he began to make careful and judicious selection of paintings and other works, with a view to the establishment of a gallery, which should represent the various schools of ancient and modern art. So far as he was able, he determined to procure original works, but meanwhile to secure the very best copies to fill out the schedule of schools and masters.

The nucleus of his collection was exhibited

The Lininger Art Gallery

## ART IN OMAHA.

in 1886, at the Inter-State Exposition, of which mention has been made.

In October, 1888, he accepted plans for the gallery, which stands at the rear of his residence and in immediate connection with it, so that from within it appears to be an extension of the parlors It is of brick and terra cotta, with beltings of grey stone, in the Italian renaissance style, with exterior niches for statues The dimensions are thirty-five by seventy, the height of the walls twenty feet, skylight fourteen by forty-four feet The floor is tiled, the wainscotting of marble with trimming of mahogany and bronze, the walls in rough plaster finish, the roof of red Spanish tiles The cost of the building was fifteen thousand dollars. The present contents are valued at $200,000 There are 60 old oil paintings, 162 modern oil paintings, 15 water colors, 22 statues and busts 8 bronzes, over 50 vases, plaques and porcelains

In the first class there are represented Guido Reni (3), Francesco Solimene (2), Guercino, Luca Giordano (8), Rossi Rembrandt, Jordaens, Albini (3), Zurubaran, Fra Angelico, Forma, Guylenburch, Francis Bouchei (2), Raphael, N Viso (2), Nani, Angelica Kauffman (2). Andrea DelSarto, Francesco DeRosa, Anton Raphael, Mengs, Martorelli, Donzello, Megnaid.

Among the modern painters are. Louis B. Hurt, Makovski, Aug Muller, Lacitti, Petruolo, Peluso, Maldarelli, G Fougi, J Daubeil, C P Ream (4), C Moll, P. Aldi, F Ricci (3), Nakken, F Martin, Cosroe Dusi, J Vogl, Colle Sione, Einst (2), L. Legat, F L. Guyot (2), Louis Plas, T. Sidney Cooper, J F. Herring Sr, Van Abbu, C Bomblid, C Hunt, E Lugo, C Del Morici, F F Spohler, W Keiremans, G Abbati, G Armando, Jacovacci, Koelman, Perez, W L Anderson, Kuwasseg, Scarpinate, Schroyer, Petruolo, Mazzoni, J Cook, C Cattelh, H DeLorme, G Bellei (2), Mollica (2), R Navarro, E. Rau, C Ceci, F Franchi, Claudia Rinalda, Mavozof, Adolph Domini, C. Padia, F. Paola, Ernst Bandini, H A. Bothast, Fichel, Maul.

Among American painters there are. J. G Borglum (8), Mrs J G Borglum (8), A Rothery (2), Mrs F. Mumaugh, J. L. Wallace, Robert Shade, F. W. Wood (2), G. H Smilie, C A Sommer, David Huntington, C Heyd, Harry Eaton

Mr and Mrs Borglum have been residents of this city, and at several exhibitions their work has been presented to the public. They have exhibited in the Paris salons, and their pictures have attracted the attention of the critics of the leading French journals

Mr Borglum was educated in Nebraska He began to draw when a boy. Following his bent he early made a choice of his profession He studied for a time with Mr Harry Aberly, then removed to California, where he continued his studies with Miss Jaynes Putnam and at the Art School in San Francisco, with Mr Virgil Williams as preceptor Mr G W Lininger sent him abroad for further instruction, where he remained for three years Both these artists give abundant promise of distinction

PRIVATE COLLECTION OF MR J M WOOLWORTH

This includes a work of Herring, the distinguished English painter of domestic animals, a fine work of Corot, one of Rousseau, one of the Impressionist Renou, and one of the well known American fruit painter, M. Rienes These are all small. The larger pieces are A Camp of Gypsies on the Danube, by Golsoule, and a Marine View off the Coast of Britain, by Colbach In addition there are portraits of several members of the family and of Mr. Justice Miller, by LeCleie, which merit notice as fine specimens of this department of art

A visitor at the residence would not fail to view an excellent copy of the Renus of the Pitti Palace in Florence, and a pair of Sevres vases of the time of the French Revolution, thirty inches, and one of Dresden workmanship of larger size In the library of between four and five thousand volumes, besides the standard works with the variety of titles, there are examples of the best editions and of the more rare and curious works, and also interesting manuscripts among which are reproductions of a part of Domesday Book and of early English charters and legal documents. There are besides engravings and etchings of great beauty.

PRIVATE COLLECTION OF MR. J. N. H. PATRICK.

These have not been made for the ends of the connoisseur in art, but solely with a view to the enrichment of the home and the enjoyment of the members of the family and their friends. The several works are distributed throughout the apartments in such a manner as to give the best general effects.

The visitor upon entering the great central hall of the house sees the well-known Storm on the Matterhorn, by Bierstadt, six by seven feet; and on the other side of the great window, The Fisherman's Daughter, by Jameson; just below, two fine examples of the work of Bradford. On the east wall are fine specimens of the work of Pelouse, of Pezyant, of Britcher, of Walter Crane, and on the opposite wall, a large and beautiful work by P. A. Gross. There are also fine examples of the work of DeBerg, Verron, Beard, Gelebert, Petitjean and Gross.

In the drawing room may be seen excellent examples of the work of Dupres, of George Innes, William Hart, Bougniet, Langre, Bierstadt, Gross and Petitjean.

There is in the dining room a work in still life by Fouace, there are two of Jeannin's flower pieces, and a work of Gripp and Vanseverdonk. In the breakfast room is a fine flower piece by Abbott Graves; in the blue room an excellent Bristol, and a water-color of the Italian school, by Franz; in the library another Bristol and two panels by Maurice Blum. Here and there are set many fine bronzes and Sevres vases. One of the most attractive objects is the statue, life size, of Jael, by Baldi, of Rome, in conception, design and finish, entitled to high rank in its department. The Italian Fisher Boy, by Andrioni, of Rome, in marble, is worthy of careful attention, as also a superb bronze by Dubucand.

There are in the city other fine collections of works of art, and curios in private residences accessible to those who desire to view them. Mr. Herman Kountze has several paintings of the modern schools and many fine prints, and a Gobelin tapestry valued at eight thousand dollars. Together with other objects of interest, fine paintings are to be seen in the homes of Mr. Samuel R. Brown, Mr. Guy C. Barton, Mr. Thomas R. Kimball and Mrs. B. D. Crary. Mr. W. F. Parker has, at his country residence at Florence, copies of the exhibits of the salons and academies, engravings, prints, etchings, photographs and photogravures.

The Omaha Academy of Fine Arts is the successor of the Omaha College of Fine Arts, which began its existence in May, 1891, and was soon after abandoned on account of financial difficulties. The Western Art Association, which had taken a deep interest in the institution, in order to continue a school of this kind, then instituted the present academy in the fall of the same year. The object is to afford facilities and instructions equal to those of the leading cities. The school is kept open from September to June, and carries on its rolls the names of more than seventy-five students, but it has not been a financial success. Mr. J. Laurie Wallace, a graduate of the Philadelphia Academy of Fine Arts, and formerly president of the Chicago Society of Artists, is the director in art. This institution, incorporated in January, 1893, with a capital stock of $25,000, seems to be in a fair way to succeed.

In the coterie of artists in Omaha, there are several who have shown talent much above the ordinary. Among those who have done meritorious work are J. Laurie Wallace, Albert Rothery, Miss Tenic Snowden, Mrs. Mumaugh, J. K. O'Neill and others.

# CHAPTER LII.

East Omaha — Its Manufacturing Interests — What has been Done — Enterprises now There — Omaha Bridge and Terminal Railway.

### EAST OMAHA.

The City of Omaha is mostly built upon hills and bluffs, having within its limits but a small territory of level land available for trackage purposes. When the late Mr. A. E. Touzalin and associates, C. E. Perkins, G. W. Holdrege, H. W. Yates, and others were seeking trackage room for the Burlington Road, their attention was called to a large tract of level land lying northeast of the city. They at once realized that it would be desirable to secure this territory and set about it. Piece after piece of land was purchased until they had control of over a thousand acres. The possession of so large a body of fine territory caused them to enlarge their plans concerning it, and instead of land simply for trackage purposes, they conceived the idea of organizing a corporation, adding still further to the possessions. For this purpose the East Omaha Land Company was incorporated on the 15th day of February, 1887, with the following officers: Richard C. Cushing, president; George W. Holdrege, vice-president; Henry W. Yates, secretary and treasurer.

On June 1, 1887, the officers of the company asked Mr. Arthur S. Potter to join them and requested him to assume the management of their property, and formulate plans for its proper development. This he consented to do, and from that time to the present he has acted as general manager of the company. Mr. Potter believed that to attain the greatest success in handling of the company's property, and also to have the company's action be of the greatest benefit to the City of Omaha, was to retain the lands in a body and not sell any of them for a period of several years, but to develop a plan of improvement under which development there would be established upon the grounds a manufacturing city. He therefore outlined such a system of improvements which was accepted by the officers and stockholders alike of the company, and from that time to the present, the improvements have followed along the line so laid out.

After Mr. Potter assumed the management of the company some time was occupied in perfecting titles to the lands already secured and purchasing others adjacent until the company was possessed of about two thousand acres. The first work was to cut out roads through the forest and turnpike them. In this way, the company laid out over seventy-seven miles of streets, but the land itself was covered with willows, brush and trees. These were all cleared away, the land was plowed, dragged smooth, leveled and seeded down. Here and there a nicely trimmed tree was left to relieve the landscape from monotony. To protect its property the company concluded to fence in every lot. It has thus built many miles of characteristic fence of half round cedar posts painted red and four barbed wires.

The turnpike roads suggested graded streets and the company decided to have them. It constructed a railroad from the centre of its land to a point near Florence put it into the hands of a contractor, and engaged him to deposit on its streets a million yards of earth. This piece of work cost the company $300,000. Between the "Island," that is the lands of the East Omaha Land Company and the City of Omaha, lies "Cut-Off Lake," and a low marshy tract, half a mile wide. Over these, on Locust Avenue, the company constructed a bridge, which, though much better than any owned by many ambitious cities, did not seem to this company to be in harmony with the solidity, magnitude and permanence of its other plans. It has therefore been removed, and a grade, one hundred feet wide has been filled in over both lake and bottoms, connecting the lands of the company and the paved streets of Omaha by a splendid drive. The company also arranged to grade Avenue H into Omaha by way of Eleventh and Nicholas Streets. The latter thoroughfare has been paved at a cost of nearly one hundred thousand dollars, so that now one can drive from the city hall in Omaha to the Carter White Lead Works in East Omaha, over continuously paved streets.

To provide trackage for manufacturers, a system has been devised which is unequaled in any other location. Around the territory extends a Belt Line. From this main track, branches extend north and south through the alleys. These are thirty-eight feet wide having a main side track down the middle from which side tracks branch off to every lot, so that every industry located on these lands has a private side track in its rear. No tracks are on the streets, which will be paved. To supply homes for working men, the company has arranged for the erection of dwelling houses of various sizes and styles. They are being built as rapidly as demanded. The streets of the residence portion of the tract are broad and clean. The grass plots about the houses are kept in order by the company, and everything connected with this portion of the grounds presents a picture of beauty and of health.

The American Water Works Company of Omaha, has engaged by contract to lay fifty miles of water mains in the streets of the company and erect seven hundred hydrants. This waterworks system will give to the dwellings and the industries an abundant supply of the best water. The contract when completed will cost the company $40,000 per annum, for hydrant rental alone. A sewer system has been adopted and is in course of construction which will cost half a million dollars.

There has already been located upon these lands a number of important manufactories and others are now negotiating for sites. In order that there might be nothing wanting to render East Omaha complete, as a future manufacturing city, the managers of the company determined to provide transportation for working men to and from their labor, and afford better railroad facilities. They organized the Inter-State Bridge and Street Railway Company, which constructed a street car line on Locust Avenue, from Sixteenth Street, Omaha, for a distance of two and a half miles east, past the factories and homes in East Omaha. This street car line has been in operation for over a year. Under a contract with the Omaha Street Railway Company, a system of transfers has been entered into by means of which a passenger can ride from any part of the city of Omaha or South Omaha, into East Omaha, or from East Omaha to any part of Omaha or South Omaha, for five cents. It was the design of this company to also build a bridge across the Missouri River by which railroads could enter East Omaha directly from the east. While the enlarged plans of the Omaha Bridge and Terminal Railway Company have greatly extended its territory of operation and the business it will transact, viz: furnish terminal facilities for all Omaha, South Omaha and Council Bluffs, the center of operation of that company will still be East Omaha. Here its bridge will be located. Close by will be its Omaha freight depot, and from East Omaha as a center will radiate to all parts of the two counties its terminal lines. So that while the business of the bridge company will be much larger than East Omaha, into East Omaha it will come, and to the growth of East Omaha it all will contribute. It will thus be seen

that what South Omaha has become towards the south of the main city, East Omaha may be to the north It is probably destined to become one of the largest and most prosperous manufacturing centers of the west

OMAHA BRIDGE AND TERMINAL RAILWAY

The origin of this important undertaking is closely connected with the history of East Omaha In 1890, Mr Arthur S Potter, general manager of the East Omaha Land Company, became impressed with the belief that the interests of that company demanded better railroad facilities, and especially shorter connection with the eastern railroads terminating in Council Bluffs He conceived the project of organizing a new company and constructing a bridge across the Missouri River, and presented his views to the leading members of the East Omaha Land Company. They were favorably received, and it was determined to go ahead with the scheme Under Mr Potter's management the new company was organized, with the name of Inter-State Bridge and Street Railway Company The intention of its promoters was to construct and operate a street railway connecting East Omaha with Omaha and Council Bluffs, for the purpose of affording transportation to the workmen engaged in the factories located in East Omaha, also to construct a bridge across the Missouri River, between the lands of the East Omaha Land Company and the city of Council Bluffs, Iowa This bridge was to afford the railroads easy access to East Omaha from the east

After receiving from the City of Council Bluffs, a franchise to operate a street railway in that city, on the 14th day of January, 1891, an application was made to Congress for a charter to build a bridge across the Missouri River, and though it was most earnestly opposed by those who thought it in conflict with their interests, the charter was granted and approved on the 13th day of February, 1891

Up to this time the whole design and expectation of Mr Potter, and his associates, was only to advance the interests of the East Omaha Land Company A later and clearer comprehension of the railroad situation, induced him into the conclusion that there was an opportunity here for a terminal railroad, which should possess and operate a full equipment of depots, yards and rollingstock, and which should construct terminal and side-tracks, for the use of manufactories and other industries, into every portion of the cities of Omaha, South Omaha and Council Bluffs. Such enlarged purposes of the company called for a more extended legal authority, increased capital, and a wider range in the business to be transacted The articles of incorporation were therefore amended The new name, Omaha Bridge and Terminal Railway, identifies the company intimately with the city The capital stock was increased to $7,500,000, and the nature of the business to be transacted no longer confines it to the street railway and a bridge, but empowers the company to carry on all the business transacted by a railroad, while it is absolutely independent of any railroad company All of its property is located in the City of Omaha and vicinity Its interests are identified with those of the city, and its object is to foster and build up commercial and manufacturing interests here

Through the banking houses of Drexel & Company and John Lowber Welsh, of Philadelphia, the company has negotiated a loan of five million dollars This money will be expended as needed in carrying out the purposes of the company

Contracts have recently been let for the bridge, which is to be a doubled track steel structure with sufficient capacity for railroads, street cars, vehicles and foot passengers. It will be a low bridge, and therefore must be furnished with a draw. This draw is one of the longest, if not the longest in the world It will be 520 feet long. But few boats of any kind now navigate the Missouri River, therefore it will not be necessary to frequently open the draw, but as a boat may appear and demand passage at any time, the company must always be prepared to open the draw on short notice. To accomplish this at a minimum expense and a maximum speed, an electric motor has been devised, which will always be ready to begin operations at a moment's notice, yet which, when not in operation, will not consume power and fuel. One span of the bridge will be 560 feet long. This is the longest fixed span in the world. Besides these unique characteristics, it is said that this bridge will be the heaviest, the largest, and the most expensive bridge across the Missouri River. Four contractors are now actively at work in the construction of this bridge About two hundred men are employed by these contractors, pushing the work on both sides of the river as rapidly as possible. The false work, or temporary structure, is nearly completed, and a large force of men is engaged in sinking the heavy caisson for the pivot pier of the draw. A contract has been let, and the work is now in progress, for constructing a dyke on the Nebraska side from the bridge site 2,500 feet up the river, in order to permanently keep the channel under the draw. The character of all the work is of the most solid and enduring kind, indicating that the company is building for the future as well as the present.

Terminal lines of railroads will extend on both sides of the river, from either approach of the bridge, to connect with all the railroads now terminating in the cities of Omaha and Council Bluffs, and also to furnish connection and passage through the cities for any railroad which in the future may build to them. The Union Land and Improvement Company recently secured from the city council of Council Bluffs a franchise for a railroad right of way over the levee and certain streets and alleys in that city. Under this franchise a railroad has been laid from the bridge site, connecting with all the railroads now entering Council Bluffs. This franchise and railroad has been purchased by the bridge company, and will give them excellent terminal facilities in that city. On the west or Omaha side of the river, there will be two distinct lines of road. One for freight and the other for passengers.

The freight line will run along the surface of the ground and into a union freight depot to be located in the vicinity of Thirteenth and Nicholas Streets, Omaha. About this depot site the company has secured some one hundred acres of land. This territory will afford ample room for tracks, yards and storage, also for the erection of private freight depots for any railroad companies which, though using the lines of the terminal company, may desire to have separate freight depots. The terminal grounds acquired by the company comprise a tract north of Nicholas street, in the city, extending along the west side of Eleventh Street to a point north of Grace Street. From this point the tract extends forty rods on each side of Eleventh Street, north to Locust. In all, 99.24 acres of land have been deeded to Messrs. Anthony J. Drexel and Edward T. Stotesbury, for the terminal company. The sale of this tract of land constitutes the largest single transfer of real estate in the history of the city, the aggregate price paid being $674,100, as follows: The Byron Reed estate, $310,000; Sylvester Cunningham and William Thompson, $162,500; Chas. H. Brown and John J. O'Connor, $48,000; Benj. S. Allison, $60,000; John A. Horbach, $88,400; Clarence S. Joy, $2,500; Lewis S. Wallace and Fred B. Bollard, $2,700. For a number of weeks prior to the commencement of 1893, the Potter & George Company, of Omaha, had the negotiations for the transfer of these lands in charge, and by the successful termination of the negotiations, have placed upon the public records an item of historic interest, not only to the parties directly concerned, but one marking the beginning of a new epoch in the railroad situation of Omaha. One of the advantages of the low bridge and surface freight line will be that all the local freight for the thousands of manufacturing industries which must be ultimately located upon the lands of the East Omaha Land Company and adjacent territory on the same level, will be delivered to them at their doors at the lowest possible expense without the cost of lifting over a high bridge.

The line for passengers and traffic through the city will be entirely separate from that used for local freight. Free from freight cars and the switching, its entire capacity can be utilized for through business. At a short distance west of the bridge, this line will begin to rise on a trestle on which it will run to the level of Sixteenth Street, thence southwest through the city it will reach South Omaha and Sarpy County.

### PASSENGER DEPOT

On this line in a location convenient to the city, and past which several of the most important street car lines now run, will be located a site for a union passenger depot. Several acres of land will be required to carry out the designs of the company regarding this depot. The structure itself is expected to cost half a million dollars and will be of a size and design commensurate with the importance of the city and of a capacity sufficient for all the prospective needs of the business.

The officers of the company are Richard C Cushing, president, George W Holdrege, vice president, Henry W Yates, treasurer, Arthur S Potter, secretary and general manager

# CHAPTER LIII.

COMMERCE — SOME EARLY MERCANTILE HOUSES — ENTERPRISES OF THE PRESENT TIME.

As every large city in the history of the world has been noted as a commercial center, and by reason of its favorable location as a distributing point, has become distinguished for its mercantile establishments, no history would be complete without a sketch of the leading houses in this line. The story of some of the

EARLY COMMERCIAL HOUSES

exhibits to some extent the kind and amount of business formerly transacted here.

Among the first mercantile ventures in Omaha, was that of Tootle & Jackson, in 1854 or 1855, whose store stood on the corner of Tenth and Farnam Streets. Mr. M. Tootle, of this firm, was a resident of St. Joseph, Missouri, and a pioneer in many enterprises in the then new country opening for settlement west of the Missouri River. He became sole owner of the business here in 1859. In 1862 W. G. Maul succeeded to the management of the business and remained in business until the death of Mr. Tootle, in January, 1887. The first stock brought here consisted of only a few wagon loads of merchandise, sufficient no doubt for the few people gathered here, and of the usual assortment of dry goods, boots, shoes, crockery, etc. By 1880 this enterprise had developed into a strictly wholesale dry goods business, filling five floors 44x132 feet at the south-west corner of Eleventh and Harney Streets, and with customers from Iowa, Nebraska, Colorado, Wyoming, Montana, Utah and Idaho. In the earlier years of the business, quite an item of it was in Indian goods, which were sold to traders who had permits to trade at the different trading posts. The Kilpatrick-Koch Dry Goods Co. succeeded to this business in 1887.

Vincent Burkley established the first store in Omaha devoted exclusively to the sale of clothing. That was in May, 1856, and the stock of goods, which cost about $8,000, was shipped by boat from Cincinnati. In connection with the clothing business, Mr. Burkley had a tailoring department. This establishment ceased to exist in the winter of '57 and '58.

M. Hellman and Aaron Cahn were attracted to Omaha in the fall of 1856, and immediately after their arrival secured a small one-story frame building of twenty-two feet front and forty feet in depth, on the northwest corner of Thirteenth and Farnam Streets, and opened a retail clothing, furnishing and merchant tailoring business, under the firm name of M. Hellman & Co. In 1857 the firm bought a ready-framed store in Cincinnati and had it sent here by boat and erected on the lot next to the southwest corner of Thirteenth and Farnam Streets. This building was twice as long as the first, but of the same dimensions otherwise. Ten years later the present double five-story structure was built, the lower floors of which were occupied by Mr. Hellman. From 1865 to 1884 a wholesale department was run in connection with the retail trade. The tailoring business was continued till 1890. Wishing to retire from business, Mr. Kahn sold his interest in 1885. After that time Mr. Hellman was the sole proprietor till his death, in March, 1892. This was probably the oldest retail clothing house between the Missouri River and the Pacific, north of Kansas, at the time of Mr. Hellman's demise. August 1, 1892, the Columbia Clothing Company— M. H. Cooke, proprietor—succeeded Mr. Hellman, and carries on business at the old stand.

Megeath & Co. carried on a large mercantile business in Omaha in the early days, a distinguishing feature of their trade being the Mormon patronage, of which they had a very large share. At the close of the annual migration westward, generally about the last of July, the last train out (called the Church train) used to take the balance of the entire stock of Megeath & Co. This firm had several portable warehouses that they kept at the end of the Pacific Railroad during its construction, and thus carried on a thriving business. Their trade with the Mormons amounted to between one and two million dollars per year.

J. H. Lacey and John McCormick, under the firm name of Lacey & McCormick, opened the first wholesale grocery house in Omaha, in 1859. They had a good share of the Pike's Peak trade, and did a very large business for several years. Their store was located at what is now known as 1306 Farnam Street.

Another of the representative houses in its line was that of William Stephens and Capt. William P. Wilcox, who, as Stephens & Wilcox, began business in 1865, with a stock of general merchandise, at what is now 1309 Farnam Street. The building they first occupied, a little frame, was found too small at the end of the first year, and their stock of groceries and boots and shoes was disposed of to make room for a department of Indian goods, robes and furs. The destructive fire of 1867, which consumed nearly all the buildings in the block on the south side of Farnam, between Thirteenth and Fourteenth Streets, gave Stephens & Wilcox an opportunity for putting up a fine building such as Omaha had never seen before, and they and other merchants moved their stores into the street, and the ground they had lately occupied was soon covered by Central Block, in which this firm had, what was then said to be, the finest dry goods store in the West, something considered to be too fine for those days, when mahogany counters were not the fashion. Their immense stock of Indian goods then became a prominent feature of the trade. Beads, Iroquois jewelry, hatchets, knives, hand mirrors, blankets, Indian cloth, hair oil, Jamaica ginger, vermillion, and jewelry were standard goods, and sales thereof were large. For a number of years Indians came to Omaha to trade, and large consignments of goods were sent up the river. The Indians were good judges of what they most needed, and seldom bought anything but the best class of merchandise, and as this was the only house in this portion of the West then carrying these goods, the sales were large, the Sioux, Pawnees, Winnebagoes and Omahas being the principal customers. Large delegations of Sioux chiefs and warriors, on their way to see the Great Father at Washington, generally stopped at Omaha, and while here made the store of Stephens & Wilcox their headquarters, holding their councils on the second floor, sitting on rolls of carpet. Red Cloud, Spotted Tail, Red Dog, Blue Horse, Big Foot, Young-Man-Afraid-of-His-Horses, and other well-known warriors were among them. On one of these occasions Red Cloud presided, as great chief, sitting in an arm-chair and dressed in a black frock coat and trousers and soft hat, furnished by Stephens & Wilcox. Red Dog, the second chief, a large, fat Indian, became jealous of Red Cloud's fine clothes and raised a disturbance which stopped all further proceedings until he had been similarly attired, when he looked upon himself with great complacency, though his limbs protruded through his garments in a manner that was amusing to see. The Indian trade was very profitable, and at one time, rather than miss the profits to be made on an immediate consignment of goods, two thousand dollars expressage was paid to have them in Omaha in time to be sent west on an Upper Missouri River boat. The amount of robes and furs handled was very large, and a day's sales sometimes amounted to ten thousand dollars, and the annual volume of business to $300,000. This firm ceased to exist at the death of Mr. Stephens in 1881.

The firm of Smith & Hopkins, composed of H. K. Smith and A. P. Hopkins, started in 1867 as agents for the O line of steamers and general commission and forwarding agents, on Thirteenth, between Farnam and Harney Streets, occupying a building that had formerly been a flour mill. In 1868 the firm became Smith, Hopkins & Housel, and continued under that style till the fall of 1871, when C. C. Housel assumed control of the business, which later fell into the hands of a Mr. Troxel, then Troxel & Williams. The house of Smith & Hopkins took entire charge of steamboat cargoes sent here, and after paying freight charges, often amounting to from one to five thousand dollars, held them for the consignees. A large part of the goods were shipped west overland. The O line steamers, which ran between St. Louis and Omaha, made tri-weekly trips, and were capable of carrying from 1,500 to 3,000 tons burden. The average at this port was a steamer a day, but as many as fourteen steamers are said to have been tied up at the levee at one time. Light stern-wheel steamers ran from Pittsburg, Cincinnati and St. Louis to Fort Benton, carrying great quantities of dry goods, groceries, hardware and general supplies for Montana points, as well as provisions for Upper Missouri government posts, and trinkets, beads, paints and blankets. Many of the boats from Ohio River points came to Omaha loaded almost entirely with nails and heavy hardware. The government business on the steamboat lines to this place was very large. Tens of thousands of bushels of corn, worth a dollar a bushel, often lay on the levee, consigned to posts in the far west. Occasionally whole boat loads of government goods, consisting of bacon, side-meat and cords of canned goods, consigned to Forts Bridger, Laramie, Kearney and other points, came at one time. Merchants doing business in Omaha in the years from 1865 to 1869, still have vivid recollections of the Omaha levee during the boating season. It was no uncommon sight to see the levee from the present Union Pacific Bridge north for the distance of a mile or more, covered with great piles of corn, railroad ties, iron and miscellaneous freight of all kinds; the more perishable freight being covered with white tarpaulins to protect it from the weather. The channel of the Missouri being so changeable the boats could not land at any given point, but were obliged to land and discharge their cargoes where they could. This gave to the Omaha levee of that period a very busy and at the same time a picturesque appearance. Steamboating on the Missouri in those days was hazardous business, as many voyagers found to their cost. The steamboat Marietta sunk at the foot of Farnam Street in 1868 or 1869, and lies there yet, and the Benton was snagged and sunk some distance above the city, near Decatur. She was on her way to the upper river agencies and a large part of her cargo was lost.

MERCANTILE FIRMS OF THE PRESENT TIME.

DRY GOODS AND CLOTHING.

The Kilpatrick-Koch Dry Goods Co., of which Thomas Kilpatrick is president; Allen Koch, vice-president; Robert Cowell, second vice-president and treasurer, and James Risk, secretary, importer and jobber of dry goods, notions, and men's furnishing goods, is located at 1101 to 1105 Harney Street, and in 1887 succeeded Tootle, Maul & Co., who had been in the wholesale dry goods business for many years. After occupying for two years, the store used by its predecessors, this company found it necessary, to accommodate its growing business, to pierce the partition wall and occupy the adjoining store, thereby adding nearly fifty

per cent. of space to the store and making an establishment four stories high, one hundred and thirty-two feet deep, with a frontage of sixty-six feet. This firm started on a capital of $250,000, which has been increased to $300,000 fully paid in, with a surplus of $15,000. Forty-two persons are employed, of whom eleven are commercial travelers. The trade covers western Iowa, Nebraska, Colorado, Wyoming, Idaho and Utah, and amounts to $1,100,000 or $1,200,000 per year.

The firm of M. E. Smith & Co., importers and jobbers of dry goods, furnishings and notions, is composed of Monroe E. Smith, Arthur C. Smith, George M. Tibbs and Walter D. Smith, and moved to Omaha from Council Bluffs in 1886, locating at the corner of Eleventh and Douglas Streets. Having outgrown the accommodations there, the business was moved January, 1890, to the present quarters, 1101 to 1107 Howard Street, corner of Howard and Eleventh, which had been built for the special occupation of this firm, where more than twice the former amount of room is occupied, using, in fact, seven floors 66 feet wide by 132 long. The number of traveling representatives has been increased from six, the number first employed, to eighteen, who now traverse the territory from Western Iowa to Portland, Oregon. Since 1889 one story of the establishment has been devoted to the manufacture of pants, overalls, jumpers, duck-lined goods and all kinds of shirts except white. The capacity of the plant has been enlarged from year to year and during the last twelve months has been doubled and one hundred and fifty persons, mostly women, are employed, using, one hundred, and twenty machines, operated by electric power and turning out one hundred dozen garments daily when running at full capacity. It gives a better idea of the magnitude of this industry to say that enough goods are actually manufactured by this firm each year, to furnish every male citizen in Omaha over ten years old, a complete suit of clothes in addition to a duck overcoat, a jumper and a pair of overalls. Twice a year several trains, often containing twenty or thirty cars, loaded exclusively with this firm's goods, arrive from New York, where, in order that the firm's purchasing interests may be properly attended to, an agent is constantly kept. Besides the hands in the factory, forty other persons are employed about the store, and the whole number of employes is over two hundred. The business of 1892 amounted to $1,500,000.

N. B. Falconer is a dealer in dry goods. In 1868 a small one story frame building, on the corner of Fourteenth and Farnam Streets, was occupied by Ross & Cruickshank, with a stock of dry goods and notions, which was the origin of the present establishment of N. B. Falconer, who, three years later, bought out Ross and became the principal partner in the firm, which took the name of A. Cruickshank & Co., thus putting his capital against his partner's experience in business. After occupying a building on the corner of Fifteenth and Farnam six years, Mr. Falconer, in 1877, erected a two-story brick building on the corner of Fifteenth and Douglas, where now Browning, King & Co. are located, and there did business for ten years. In 1883 he became sole proprietor, and in 1887 built, at 1505-7 Douglas Street, the double three-story structure he now occupies, to which, in 1891, he added No. 1509, and connected it with the building already occupied. A select retail trade in fine dry goods is the principal business of this house. A wholesale business is also transacted, and goods of various kinds imported directly from England and France. In addition to the dry goods trade, a book and a toy department are maintained. From seventy-five to eighty-five persons are employed. A stock varying in value from $250,000 to $300,000 is carried, and the annual sales reach half a million.

The Morse Dry Goods Company, which

does a wholesale and retail business in dry goods, carpets, draperies, etc., was organized and began business in 1877, with S. P. Morse president and W. V. Morse vice president, the capital stock being $250,000. The building occupied by this company is one of the handsomest mercantile structures in the city, with a five-story front on Farnam Street and six stories on Sixteenth Street, occupying the ground upon which stood the first Congregational church erected in Omaha, and also a part of the ground occupied later by the Redick Opera House, which, in its day, was the favorite histrionic resort of the elite of Omaha. Each story of the building contains ten thousand square feet of flooring. All modern mercantile conveniences, including one freight and two passenger elevators, cash system, etc., are in use. The average stock of goods is valued at $250,000, conveniently arranged in twenty-eight departments, each complete in itself. The trade amounts to a million dollars annually, and two hundred persons are employed in the transaction of the business.

Kelly, Stiger & Co. opened a dry goods house in Omaha in 1886, at the corner of Fifteenth and Dodge Streets, where they succeeded in building up a very successful and profitable business. In 1890 they re moved to the southwest corner of Fifteenth and Farnam Streets, where they occupy a large amount of floor space and carry a large stock of goods.

Thompson, Belden & Co., dry goods merchants, carry a large stock at the corner of Sixteenth and Douglas Streets. These gentlemen opened a store here in 1886, and have been in their present quarters since March, 1890. From the first this has been a "cash" house. Although warned against beginning a business here on that plan, they promptly adopted it, and find that plain figures, one price and pay down have succeeded. Besides being the first cash house, this firm was the first in Omaha to issue an illustrated catalogue of dry goods. This firm employs fifty persons and does a business of $250,000 annually.

Bennison Brothers deal in dry goods and carpets, at 1519-21 Douglas Street, where they occupy a three story building and employ from fifty to seventy persons.

Browning, King & Co., manufacturers and retailers of fine clothing, have one of their numerous branch stores in Omaha, southwest corner Fifteenth and Douglas, employing twenty-five persons. This branch was started in 1889, and on April 14, 1890, the entire stock was destroyed by fire, entailing a loss of $64,000, on which there was an insurance of $40,000. The house was immediately rebuilt and the business enlarged.

Freeland, Loomis & Co. are proprietors of the Continental Clothing House, corner of Fifteenth and Douglas Streets. This is one of the four houses of which this firm is proprietor, the others being in Boston, and Des Moines and Newton, Iowa. This branch was established here in 1887, and now employs thirty or forty persons, occupies over seventeen thousand square feet of flooring, carries a stock of $100,000 value, and claims to be the largest clothing house in Nebraska. On the night of December 27, 1892, a fire, which broke out in the carpet store of S. A. Orchard, destroyed the upper portion of the Continental Block, and the stock of the Continental Clothing Company was very badly damaged by water. The block is expected to be rebuilt at once, and will again be occupied by this company.

M. Levy, M. Strasburger and H. Cohn are the Nebraska Clothing Company, at Douglas and Fourteenth Streets. They started in 1886.

S. Arnstein is proprietor of the People's Clothing House, 1303 Douglas Street. He has built up a trade since 1885, and now occupies a three-story building and employs seven clerks.

Albert Cahn, exclusive gentleman's furnisher, 1322 Farnam Street, has been in business since 1884.

D Altman deals in fine clothing and gentlemen's furnishing goods, at 617 North Sixteenth Street. His business dates from 1877.

Blotcky Brothers' Company, importer and jobber of notions and furnishing goods, is a corporation recently formed by uniting the firms of Blotcky & Cohen, of Omaha, Blotcky Bros, late of Des Moines, Iowa, and C E. Williams and John Davis, of the same place. They will operate on a capital of $120,000, fully paid in, and occupy the four-story building at 1114 Harney Street. The members of the company are Jos Blotcky, president; M I Blotcky, vice president, Sol Blotcky, secretary, C. E. Williams, treasurer, and John Davis.

Levinston Brothers are wholesale dealers in dry goods, notions, furnishings and jewelry, at 313 South Thirteenth Street

The Boston Store, at the northwest corner of Sixteenth and Douglas Streets, is one of the late handsome additions to the mercantile structures in this city. It is occupied by J L Brandeis & Sons, who carry a very heavy stock of dry goods, millinery, etc. Mr Brandeis began business in Omaha in 1883, with a small jobbing trade, which he carried on for a while, and then embarked in the present line. This firm now employs one hundred persons, and sell goods of the value of $400,000 annually.

Gilmore & Ruhl are wholesale clothiers, at 1109 Harney Street. This house was established here in 1887, employs eighteen persons, and does a business amounting to $400,000 per year

H R Baldwin sells dry goods and notions and carries a side line of crockery, tinware, etc., at 1307-9 North Twenty-fourth (formerly Saunders) Street. In 1887 the business was begun, occupying the front half of 1309 only. Attention to business has been rewarded, and for two years the space in two numbers has been well filled with goods

Mr Baldwin carries a stock of $13,000, employs five clerks, and sells a large amount of merchandise

The firm of Stephens & Smith dealers in men's furnishings, 109 North Sixteenth Street, is composed of Lucien Stephens and Fred L Smith. They began business in April, 1891, and have a trade that steadily increases

### HATS AND CAPS

C H. Frederick & Co, hatters, are engaged in business at 120 South Fifteenth Street, in the Creighton Block. Mr Frederick entered into business in Omaha January 1, 1871, to which he has continuously devoted his attention since, and being a practical hatter he has built up a flourishing and constantly increasing trade

Pease Brothers are hatters and men's furnishers, at 122 South Fifteenth Street. They have been in business since 1885.

L O Jones ("Jones of Omaha"), deals in hats and men's furnishings, at 115 South Sixteenth Street. He began business in 1885

The Gate City Hat Company consists of Alexander Gunther, president and treasurer, Herman Drishaus, vice president and secretary, Edward J Roe, manager. This house carries hats, caps and straw goods, at 1023 Harney Street, where a large business is done, occupying a four-story building. The authorized capital stock is fifty thousand dollars, of which thirty thousand dollars is paid in. In May, 1890, the present firm succeeded Parrotte, Scripps & Co, who had been in the business about ten years. Nine traveling men represent the firm abroad

W. A. L Gibbon, wholesale dealer in hats, caps and straw goods, succeeded Darrow & Logan October 1, 1891. Mr Gibbon employs six commercial men and his trade covers the usual tributary territory

### MILLINERY AND NOTIONS

I Oberfelder & Co are importers and jobbers of millinery and notions. The business was established here in 1881. This firm occupies the five-story building, 208 to 212 South Eleventh Street, and extends its trade to Utah and Oregon.

Mrs. J. Benson deals in fancy dry goods, notions, etc., at 210-212 South Fifteenth Street. She began business in 1887.

### RUBBER GOODS.

The Omaha Rubber Company deals in rubber goods. Their present place of business is 1520 Farnam Street. O. H. Curtis is president and J. Hurd Thompson secretary and treasurer. Their store-room is unusually large and well filled. Eighteen or twenty persons are employed in various capacities about the place, a part of them being engaged in manufacturing and repairing.

### TOYS, TENTS.

H. Hardy & Co. are jobbers of toys, dolls, albums, fancy goods, house-furnishing goods, etc., of which they carry a crowded stock, at 1319 Farnam. This firm began business in 1877, and, with some changes, has continued till now. Four traveling men solicit trade abroad.

The Omaha Tent and Awning Company, A. H. Rawitzer, manager, began business in 1886, and now employs twenty persons.

### FURNITURE AND CARPETS.

Business was begun, at 1115-1117 Farnam Street, where the Dewey & Stone Furniture Company is now located, early in the sixties. Louis Hax, a resident of St. Joseph, Missouri, then had a furniture store there, conducted by John Trimble. The building, a two-story frame, had been moved from Florence when that place began to decline and Omaha took the lead in mercantile matters. In 1865, C. H. Dewey and John Trimble formed a partnership and bought out Mr. Hax. In 1866, E. L. Stone purchased an interest in the business, and the firm became Dewey, Trimble & Co. In 1870, Mr. Trimble sold his interest in the business to his partners, and the firm became Dewey & Stone, which so remained until December, 1888, when a stock company, with an authorized capital of half a million, was formed, known as the Dewey & Stone Furniture Company, William Gyger and William I. Kierstead, who had long been in the employ of the house, becoming stockholders in the new corporation, whose officers were: C. H. Dewey, president; E. L. Stone, vice president; William Gyger, secretary; George E. Crosby, treasurer; and William I. Kierstead, manager. In August, 1890, Mr. Dewey's death occurred. At the beginning, and for some years afterward, the partners did most of the work incident to the business, which, however, after a time rapidly expanded, and now occupies a four-story brick building on Farnam Street, built by the company in 1876, a five-story brick building on Harney Street, built in 1882, and a large warehouse on Leavenworth Street. This house has done the longest continuous and uninterrupted business in the same location of any in the city. From a small local retail trade the business has come to extend across the continent to the Pacific Coast, and amounts to half a million per year, employs fifty-five persons, and in length of time in business and amount of trade, is not exceeded by any house of the kind west of Chicago. The building on Farnam Street was the first four-story business building, and that on Harney Street the first five-story building, erected in the State of Nebraska. The premiums paid by the present company and its predecessors for insurance against loss by fire would amount, at 7 per cent. compound interest, to more than $150,000.

In 1877, before Omaha had attained much size, and while the bulk of the business of the town was considerably nearer the river than now, S. A. Orchard and Samuel Bean, under the firm name of Orchard & Bean, opened a carpet store at 1113 Farnam Street, occupying a single story, and carrying a stock of goods proportioned to the demands of the trade as it then existed. This store was next east of Dewey & Stone's. By 1882

the commercial portion of the city had extended westward so far that the corner of Fifteenth and Farnam Streets became a desirable location, and to that point the business was moved, occupying the corner where Kelley & Stiger now are, the building having been built purposely for S. A. Orchard, his partner, Mr. Bean, having died in 1881. In the summer of 1890, Mr. Orchard had built, for his especial occupancy, at 1414 to 1418 Douglas Street, the handsome and commodious five-story building he lately occupied, into which he moved in September, adding furniture to the line of carpets he had formerly carried. This business, which, at the outset, gave employment to only three persons, required twenty-five in 1892, and amounted to $200,000. Among the buildings removed to make room for this was the old Marble Hall, a wooden structure, which, in its palmy days of '65 and 66, was a popular resort, where many business men spent their evenings, and where music and refreshments attracted large crowds of pleasure seekers, who wanted plenty of company and entertainment. On the night of December 27th, 1892, a fire broke out in Mr. Orchard's store, which, together with the entire stock, was soon consumed. The loss on stock and fixtures amounted to about $120,000, the insurance to about $85,000.

The Omaha Carpet Company began business in 1884. The officers are H Duneker, president, J H Tiorlicht, vice president, D D Miller, secretary and treasurer, and Fred Sunder, superintendent. The business includes both wholesale and retail branches, and extends over the territory naturally tributary to Omaha. It now employs ten persons and occupies three stories of the building 1511 Douglas Street.

Charles Shiverick & Co , the junior partner being Arthur Shiverick, are located at 1206 to 1210 Farnam Street. This business was established in 1871. They have a fine store, and occupy five floors with their trade in furniture, carpets, etc.

The Omaha Furniture Company does business at 1207 Farnam Street. In 1882 H J Abrahams started the business, which, with some changes, has continued to the present time. Seven persons are employed and the business is confined to the retail trade.

Chamberlain, Anderson & O'Connell are dealers in furniture and bedding at 208 to 212 North Sixteenth Street, where they have been in business since the spring of 1886. Since opening, however, the stock and trade have increased largely, and what was but a small business at first, has necessitated considerable enlargement of the space formerly occupied.

The People's Mammoth Installment Company is the latest house established in the furniture, carpet and tinware line, having opened a business at 1315 and 1317 Farnam Street, the 1st of September, 1891. It is a corporate concern with B Rosenthal, president and manager. The place is well fitted up and attractive.

I Brown deals in furniture, carpets and stoves, at 1205 Douglas Street. The business was begun in 1879, and has steadily grown to occupy four floors. In 1889 Mr Brown built the building he now occupies, at a cost of $15,000. He does a retail business only.

J. M Young succeeded the firm of Hill & Young, dealers in furniture, stoves, carpets and house furnishing goods, at 1211-1213 Farnam Street in July, 1892. Hill & Young commenced business in the autumn of 1884. Mr Young occupies a building four stories in height and averages from twenty to twenty-five employes. The business runs to $100,000 annually.

### BOOTS AND SHOES

The Morse-Coe Shoe Company began its existence October 1, 1891, when the firms of W V Morse & Co and Charles A Coe & Co united and incorporated. W. V Morse & Co were engaged in the wholesale and retail trade as far back as 1869, and built up a large business. In 1889 the company began the manufacture of boots and shoes, with a capacity of four hundred pairs per day. Charles A. Coe & Co. embarked in the wholesale boot and shoe trade in the early part of 1890. Since the consolidation of the two firms the building occupied by Morse & Co. has been used for manufacturing purposes, and the business incident to the wholesale trade transacted at the Coe & Co. store. This company is now erecting, at the corner of Twelfth and Howard Streets, a brick factory of five stories and basement, 66 by 88 feet on the ground, which will have a capacity of one thousand pairs of shoes daily, employing, at the start, from 150 to 200 persons. Twenty salesmen are employed, who sell goods in western Iowa and through the entire western country to the Pacific Coast. The officers of the company are: W. V. Morse, president; Charles A. Coe, vice president; and E. E. Hastings, secretary and treasurer.

W. N. Whitney came to Omaha in 1865, and soon after went into partnership with O. P. Ingalls, the pioneer maker of and dealer in boots and shoes, who started in business here in the fall of 1854. Two years later a dissolution of the partnership occurred, and since that time Mr. Whitney has conducted a retail boot and shoe store, generally carrying a stock of about twenty thousand dollars value. He is now located at 103 South Fifteenth Street.

A. D. Morse does a large retail shoe business at the corner of Fourteenth and Farnam Streets. He succeeded W. V. Morse, who had carried on the shoe business at this stand at the time the lots opposite were prairie and bare of buildings.

George W. Cook & Son now occupy one of the stores in the new Karbach block, where they carry a large stock of boots and shoes, the present stock being valued at about forty thousand dollars, the year's sales amounting to sixty-five thousand dollars. The senior member of the firm began business in Omaha in 1883. The present partnership was founded September 1, 1891.

The firm of Drexel & Rosenzweig is composed of John C. Drexel and R. Rosenzweig, who are successors of Henry Dohle, at 1419 Farnam Street. They have a busy trade.

Norris & Wilcox deal in boots and shoes, at 1517 Douglas Street, and have been in business since July, 1887. They carry a large stock and do a good business.

J. W. Schoelply deals in fine footwear, at 1415 Douglas Street.

The firm of Kirkendall, Jones & Co., formerly Reed, Jones & Co., of Columbus, Ohio, located a branch house here in 1879. They are manufacturers of boots and shoes and cover thirteen states and territories with their business—a large trade being established in the Pacific states. The manufacturing, which is done at Columbus, is managed by Mr. Jones, and the western trade, centering at Omaha, is managed by Mr. Kirkendall. The firm occupies a large four-story store at 1102 to 1106 Harney Street, and carries a very large and complete stock of goods—one not exceeded in size by any in the West. Thirty persons are employed at the store, and sixteen commercial men represent the house abroad.

The American Hand Sewed Shoe Company, manufacturer and jobber of boots and shoes, occupies 1204 and 1206 Harney Street, carrying a full line of leather and rubber goods, occupying seven floors. Fifteen or twenty persons are employed, five of whom are traveling salesmen. The trade of this house extends as far west as Utah.

The Williams-Hayward Shoe Co., incorporated, is a manufacturer and jobber of boots, shoes and slippers, at 1212 Harney Street, occupying a large four story building. Its business is in Nebraska, Colorado, Utah and a portion of South Dakota and Iowa. The house has been established since 1887.

Z. T. Lindsey is a wholesale dealer in rubber boots and shoes and rubber and oiled clothing, at 1111 Harney Street. This business was started in 1886, and now requires from twenty to thirty people—six to ten salesmen traveling through the territory naturally tributary to Omaha. The annual business is not less than $200,000.

### DEPARTMENT STORES.

The W. R. Bennett Co. is a "wholesale and retail dealer in everything useful, ornamental and staple," occupying a four story building at 1502 to 1512, Capitol Avenue. The firm's origin dates back to 1878, when the two partners and a single assistant were enough to do the business. They now employ one hundred people. The business is mostly retail. The members of the firm are W. R. Bennett, president; F. W. Brown, vice-president; S. F. Bennett, secretary and treasurer.

William and Edward Hayden, who constitute the firm of Hayden Brothers, established themselves in business at 116 South Sixteenth Street, in May, 1888. One year later they moved into the handsome building, 102 to 112 South Sixteenth, where they occupied a five story building, seventy-six feet deep with a front of 132 feet. In the summer of 1891, finding their accommodations too small, Hayden Brothers built for themselves an addition on Dodge Street 66 by 132 feet in width and depth, and five stories high, so that now the amount of floor space used amounts to over two acres. This firm now has twenty-eight different departments, each complete in itself, and can supply clothing, all things used about a house for food, household furniture and utensils, musical instruments, etc. In addition to the retail trade a fair wholesale trade is sustained. The cash system has been in use since the firm began business. The number of employes, at first about fifty, is now 275 or 300. A marked feature of this firms business, was its gift sale. Between September 1, 1891, and February 25, 1892, each purchaser of fifty dollars worth of goods, received a card entitling him to a gift. The aggregate amount of the value of these gifts, distributed at the latter date, was $57,494.50, and included a great variety of articles ranging from a carriage whip to a $1,100 piano.

The Bell Department store opened April 2, 1892, with a complete stock in over twenty lines, amounting to $100,000, and occupying four floors at Dodge and Fifteenth Streets. The proprietors are H. C. Moody, A. S. Ackerman and L. B. Williams. From fifty to seventy-five clerks and other persons are employed about the store.

### JEWELERS.

The Max Meyer & Bro. Company is the oldest firm in their line in Omaha, the business having been begun in May, 1866, by Max Meyer, who conducted it alone in a small frame building on the south side of Farnam near Eleventh Street, carrying a stock suited to the demands of the limited trade of the times. In 1869 two brothers were associated in the business, and after occupying several places that soon proved too small to accommodate the trade, they obtained a portion of the Paxton Block, taking fifty feet on Farnam Street and running back 132 feet, making one of the finest corners obtainable. Here the growth of the trade has continued, until no house in the West does a larger business. A stock of $250,000 is carried, from which they sell at wholesale and retail. Fine jewelry is manufactured, a designer and several manufacturing jewelers being employed the year round. Diamonds are imported, and once in two years a member of the firm goes to Europe to purchase diamonds and other goods—their imports amounting to from $20,000 to $50,000 annually. The stock of sheet music, books and musical instruments is large and fine. In all, fifteen departments are operated, each complete in itself. Twelve commercial men travel west to the mountains and north to Dakota. Seventy-five persons are employed, and the annual business is $750,000. The company, incorporated in 1890 with a capital stock of $250,000, is composed of Max Meyer, president; Adolph Meyer, vice president; Moritz Meyer, secretary and treasurer, and others who hold smaller amounts of stock.

John Baumer heard of the attractions of Omaha while in London, England, in 1867, and decided to make this city his future home. In July, 1867, he began business on Farnam Street, with a small stock of watches, clocks and jewelry. The traffic the first year amounted to $2,000, and he did not require any assistant in transacting it. The trade for each of the past two years has exceeded $50,000, and the number of persons employed is eleven. Since 1879, Mr. Baumer has been located at 1314 Farnam Street.

C. S. Raymond has been established in the jewelry business in Omaha since 1884. In the summer of 1891 the building he occupied, at the corner of Fifteenth and Douglas Streets, was torn down to make room for the fine structure known as Karbach Block, into which he moved, occupying new quarters on the old lot, a few months later. Mr. Raymond's present business place is, therefore, the newest in the city, and the large and complete stock of diamonds, watches, jewelry and other valuables is displayed in a very attractive manner, the furniture and appointments all being of a beautiful and costly character. The basement is used for an art room. Mr. Raymond employed four persons when he began business in this city, and now has twenty.

S. Bank has been in the business of selling jewelry and musical instruments since 1887, at the Golden Eagle Store, at 114 South Sixteenth Street.

Joseph P. Frenzer, jeweler, has an attractive store in the Frenzer Block, Fifteenth and Dodge Streets, where he located in July, 1890.

The Sol Bergman Jewelry Company began business June 1, 1891, and now occupies number 313 South 16th Street.

MUSICAL INSTRUMENTS.

The Mueller Music Company deals in pianos, organs and other musical instruments, at 107 South Sixteenth Street. This company was established at Council Bluffs in 1859, and the Omaha branch in 1886. Mueller & Schmoller are managers.

BOOK STORES.

The Megeath Stationery Co., wholesale and retail bookseller, stationer and printer, has been recently formed and combines and represents the business lately carried on by J. S. Caulfield, the Omaha Book and Stationery Co. and the type writing and stationery house of Joseph P. Megeath, and occupies the store at 1304 Farnam Street. The officers are Jos. P. Megeath, president; John L. Gideon, vice-president; Frank J. Coates, secretary and treasurer. S C. Abbott began the book, stationery and wall-paper business in 1866, and was succeeded in 1876 by John S. Caulfield who continued the book and stationery business till the month of December, 1892, when the Megeath Company took charge.

The firm of Chase & Eddy, number 1516 Farnam Street, composed of Clement Chase and Geo. B. Eddy, does a general retail book business and handles, in addition to books, a large number of accessories. This firm dates from 1875. They use the first floor of their building for a book store and the second floor for a job printing office, where they do fine printing and copperplate engraving, employing eighteen persons.

In the fall of 1878 A. Shonfeld opened an establishment called the "Antiquarian Book Store" where a large stock of both new and second hand books are displayed for sale— many of them quaint and rare tomes that seldom appear in public. Attention to business and the increasing demands for books by a reading public have built up a good trade, and to supply it Mr. Shonfeld finds frequent and large importations of books from Europe, and a visit thither once in three or four years absolute necessities. The last year's importation, selected in Europe by Mr. Shonfeld himself, was 10,000 volumes.

Barkalow Bros. are railway news agents. April 4, 1865, with Dr. Geo. L. Miller, who furnished the capital, a partnership was formed, and a book and stationery store was opened. When the Union Pacific Railroad reached Columbus this firm started in the railway news business and put boys on the trains of that road. As the road has extended, this firm's traffic has grown, and now it controls the news business on the Union Pacific to San Francisco, California and Portland, Oregon, and has the privileges of the union depot at Denver. The firm also does the news business on the Chicago & Alton, from Chicago to St. Louis and Kansas City and has branch establishments at Chicago, Kansas City, Denver, Ft. Worth, Ogden and Portland, and employes about one hundred agents. The business at Omaha is managed by S. D. Barkalow and the Denver branch by D. V. Barkalow. Dr. Miller's connection with the firm ceased about the time that the news business was begun.

The Omaha News Company, a branch of the American News Company of New York, began business here in 1881, and is now located at 1417 Davenport Street, where it occupies a two-story brick building, twenty-two feet wide and over a hundred feet long. This company supplies books, periodicals and newspapers to newsdealers and stationers, in Nebraska, Western Iowa, South Dakota, Wyoming, Idaho and Northern Kansas. The stock carried is valued at twenty thousand dollars, and the annual sales amount to $150,000. Twelve persons are employed. William D. Bancker, Jr., has occupied the position of manager for three years past; William Schulze is foreman.

### PAPER DEALERS.

The Carpenter Paper Company, corner of Howard and Twelfth Streets, has a corporate existence dating from February, 1888, with a paid up capital of seventy-five thousand dollars, and a wholesale trade extending from the Mississippi to the Rockies.

The King Paper Company, 1406-1408 Howard Street, is one of the firms that have lately begun business. The trade is mainly confined to Nebraska and Iowa.

### WALL PAPER DEALERS AND DECORATORS.

T. J. Beard & Brother are interior decorators and dealers in paper hangings, at 1410 Douglas Street. T. J. Beard's residence in Omaha dates from 1869, when he began the business of painting and decorating. In 1879 the firm of Beard Brothers put in a stock of paper, and became the first exclusive wall paper house in this city, and absorbed this trade, which previously had been carried on in connection with other lines of business. This firm now occupies a large, two-story building, employs from twelve to fifty men and does a business of fifty thousand dollars annually.

Henry Lehmann does a large business in paper hangings, window shades and art mouldings, at 1508 Douglas Street.

Henry A. Kosters, 109 South Fourteenth Street, is one of the old landmarks in the commercial history of Omaha. He is now engaged in the business of decorator and dealer in paper hangings, in which he has had many years' experience, having first started here in this line in 1856, and after an intermission of some years, taken it up again.

Henry Osthoff deals in wall paper and window shades, and does house and sign painting, at 519 North Sixteenth Street. The business is managed by Charles L. Hunt.

### ART GOODS.

A. Hospe, Jr., is a wholesale and retail dealer in art and musical goods, at 1513 Douglas Street. He began business in 1874, in a little room ten by eighteen feet in size, with a small stock of pictures, mouldings and looking glasses. The first year's sales amounted to about $1,200. From such a beginning the business has grown to its present proportions, occupying now four floors at No. 1513 and two floors in No. 1515, requiring the services of twenty-two persons, and amounts to $100,000 annually.

Rose's Art Store, J. M. Rose, proprietor, dates from October, 1880. This enterprise was also instituted on a limited capital, and has enlarged with the growth of the city until now a handsome stock is carried.

H. P. Whitmore is the successor in business of Hoglen & Whitmore, dealers in fine art goods and importers of works of art in oil and water colors, who entered this business in 1889, occupying four floors at 1519 Dodge Street. The second floor of the establishment is used as a gallery for the exhibition of pictures of all kinds, many of which are fine works of art imported by the firm from England and the countries of continental Europe. The number of employes is eight, and the value of the stock carried is $15,000.

The Heyn Photo-Supply Company is successor to S. Heyn, jobber in supplies, mouldings, pictures and frames. The business was initiated in 1884, and the company was incorporated in January, 1891.

The increased demand for art goods in Omaha is probably due to the growth in population mainly, but the change from cheap chromos and prints to statuary, fine oil paintings and the most expensive and artistic frames, indicates a vastly greater appreciation of the beautiful in art on the part of purchasers, as well as a greatly augmented ability to buy them.

#### CROCKERY AND GLASSWARE.

The crockery, glass and chinaware trade is in the hands of the following named parties: Samuel Burns, at 1318 Farnam, the oldest dealer in the city in this line, whose business dates back to 1861. His store is large and the display of goods is costly and handsome.

M. H. Bliss is successor to Bliss & Isaacs, importers and jobbers, whose business was established in 1875, as Brown & Bliss, and became Bliss & Isaacs in 1878. Three years ago, on the retirement of Mr. Isaacs, M. H. Bliss became sole proprietor. His business now covers Nebraska, Wyoming, Dakota, Idaho, and requires two or three commercial travelers.

W. L. Wright is a wholesale dealer, at 1207 Howard Street.

A. A. Stewart & Co. deal in bar glassware, at 1405 Jackson Street.

Gatch & Lauman, wholesale and retail dealers in china and glassware, are the successors of the firm of Perkins, Gatch & Lauman, which began business in Omaha five years ago. In 1891 Mr. Perkins retired from the firm, and C. L. Garrison was admitted into it. This house occupies No. 1516, in the Paxton Block, on Farnam Street, in addition to which they have a warehouse at Ninth and Jones Streets. All the country between Omaha and Oregon is included in this firm's territory.

Charles A. Harvey's store is located at 1514 Farnam Street, where tiles, terra cotta, mosaics, stained glass, and goods of like character are carried in stock.

#### BILLIARD MERCHANDISE.

The Brunswick-Balke-Collender Company, one of the largest dealers in billiard merchandise in the world, located one of its thirty-five branches in the United States here about fifteen years ago, with J. C. Selden, who has been with the house twenty-seven years as manager. Four years ago the company built a substantial four-story brick building, at 407-409 South Tenth Street, three floors of which it occupies, and does a business of about $85,000 yearly.

The Gate City Billiard Table Company has lately succeeded the Garden City Billiard Table Company, which began business about two years ago. The company does a wholesale trade, and employs two commercial travelers.

### GUNS AND SPORTING GOODS.

The Cross Gun Company is the successor of Frank Cross and J. W. Dunmire, who constituted the Cross & Dunmire Gun Company, at 1512 Douglas Street. J. J. Harden was the originator of the business, in 1886, and was succeeded by Gwin & Dunmire in 1889, which firm, after several changes, retired from the business. The present firm began business in August, 1892, and is managed by W. D. Townsend.

The Collins Gun Company, is the sign under which Frank S. Parmalee does business. The house was originally Collins & Petty, started in 1878. In 1885, the successors of Collins & Petty assumed the name of the Collins Gun Company, the partners then being J. S. Collins and F. S. Parmalee. Mr. Collins retired from the firm in 1890. This house does a wholesale and retail business in firearms, ammunition, etc., at 1312 Douglas Street.

### PLUMBERS' SUPPLIES.

J. L. Welshans & Co., 1416-1418 Harney Street, have been in business as sanitary plumbers and dealers in plumbers' supplies since 1881, and are the successors of Hamilton & McEwan. The firm has a well-stocked store and employs from fifteen to fifty men.

The Hussey & Day Company, 409-411 South Fifteenth Street, is a corporation, with N. B. Hussey, president; F. B. Hussey, secretary and treasurer; Frederick Arnd, vice president. This house began to do business here in 1887, in steam-heating, gas-fixtures and plumbing, and now has a large trade.

### IRON AND HARDWARE.

W. J. Broatch started in the wholesale iron, steel and heavy hardware business, in Omaha, in the spring of 1874, and is therefore the oldest merchant in the hardware line in the city. The building first occupied was a little, old structure, opposite his present location, 1209-1211 Harney Street, and his help was a boy. His only competitor in business then was J. T. Edgar & Co. After twice out-growing the buildings he occupied, Mr. Broatch, in 1880, built the commodious four-story brick building he now occupies. The business has kept pace with the growth of the city and State, and now requires the labor of fifteen persons to carry it on.

The Baum Iron Company was incorporated in 1888, with a paid-up capital of $100,000. This house does a wholesale business in iron, steel and heavy hardware, at 1208 and 1210 Harney Street, where it occupies a five story building and employs sixteen people, five of whom are on the road as commercial travelers. The trade of this house extends through Nebraska, Colorado, Wyoming, Utah. Idaho and parts of Iowa and Kansas.

The Lee-Clarke-Andreesen Hardware Company does business at 1219 to 1223 Harney Street and handles hardware, cutlery, nails and tinware. This company was incorporated in January, 1888, succeeding Lee, Fried & Co., who had been in business since 1880. The company has an authorized capital $300,000, of which $200,000 is paid in. Ten salesmen make frequent visits to the principal towns in Nebraska, Wyoming, Idaho, Utah, western Iowa, and parts of Colorado and Dakota. The officers of the company are H. T. Clarke, president; H. J. Lee, vice-president; E. M. Andreesen, treasurer; and C. H. Clarke, Secretary.

The Rector & Wilhelmy Co. filed its articles of incorporation in 1884, and is composed of the following named persons: P. C. DeVol, president; F. B. Hochstetler, vice-president; Allen T. Rector, treasurer; W. S. Wright, Secretary; and J. F. Wilhelmy. It has a capital stock of $125,000 fully paid in. The company erected the structure it now occupies, a fine brick establishment sixty-six feet by one hundred feet and four stories high, at the corner of Tenth and Jackson Streets, in 1889, at a cost of $39,000. Thirty persons are employed, eight of whom are commercial travelers.

The James Morton & Son Company is at

1511 Dodge Street, where a wholesale and retail hardware trade is carried on. James Morton is president and treasurer and C. W. Morton, secretary.

Lobeck & Linn, successors to E. T. Duke, are wholesale and retail dealers in builders hardware, cutlery and tools, at 1404 Douglas Street, where they have been established since May, 1891. As a commercial house this reaches back to quite early times. Mr. Duke, the predecessor of this company, who took charge of the business in 1876 was himself preceded by J. T. Edgar, who, after running the business some years, died while consul at Beirut, Syria.

The Crane Company is a branch of the Chicago house of the same name, dealer in wrought iron pipes, boiler tubes, malleable and cast iron fittings and a multitude of other things of a kindred nature. The office and store is situated at 922-924 Farnam Street and the warehouse on Douglas Street. The business of the past year has crowded a million closely. Twenty persons are in the employ of this branch, five of whom are salesmen on the road. Mr. H. T. Lally, who was the manager of this company several years at Omaha, took charge of the company's business at San Francisco, California, April, 1892, and was succeeded by H. H. Deane, senior member of the firm of Deane & Horton of Lincoln.

The U. S. Wind Engine and Pump Company, 916-918 Jones Street, is one of the branches of the house whose factory is at Batavia, Illinois. G. F. Ross manages the Omaha business. This branch, which was started here five years ago, now affords employment to four travelers and fifteen other persons.

Previous to removing to this city, in 1886, the Churchill Pump Company had been in business four years at Council Bluffs. In January, 1889, the company became corporate with E. V. Lewis, president and treasurer; W. H. Rayner, vice-president; and A. S. Cost, secretary. The company is a jobber of steam, water and plumbers' supplies with an authorized capital of fifty-two thousand dollars. On account of increase of business this firm has lately taken enlarged quarters at 1014-1016 Douglas Street.

Fairbanks, Morse & Co. have a branch house in Omaha, at 1102-1104 Farnam Street, with a large warehouse and boiler platform on the railroad. They are dealers in scales, engines, steam pumps, boilers and a large list of other things. Five traveling salesmen and fifteen other persons are employed by the firm which does a business of $200,000 annually. F. C. Ayer is manager.

The firm of A. L. Deane & Co. is composed of A. L. Deane, J. W. Donnell and M. DeCasky and they handle Hall's patent safes and bank locks at 321-323 south Tenth Street. This firm succeeded P. Boyer & Co. four years ago. Their trade covers Iowa, Nebraska and the southwest.

PRINTING MATERIAL.

The Great Western Type Foundry, 1114 Howard Street, is a branch of the Chicago house, established here in December, 1887, W. A. Potter, manager. The business occupies six floors and employs fifteen or twenty persons. The trade is mostly retail, but some goods are sold to dealers. This firm does a large electrotype and repair business, and buys and rebuilds machinery.

In 1885, Marder Luse & Co., of the Chicago Type Foundry, established a branch of their house here, under the name of the Omaha Type Foundry, which was managed by H. J. Pickering and H. P. Hallock. In January, 1891, Messrs. Pickering and Hallock withdrew, and Mr. Hallock established the Atlantic-Pacific Type Foundry. In January, 1893, most of the type foundries having been consolidated under the name of the American Type Founders' Company, these two houses were united, with H. P. Hallock in charge. The name is now Marder Luse & Co. Foundry, Omaha Branch, and the place of business is 1118 Howard Street.

### STOVE STORES.

The firm of Milton Rogers & Sons, dealers in stoves, ranges, mantels, etc., at 1321-1323 Farnam Street, is probably the oldest house of the kind in the State of Nebraska, and was established here by Milton Rogers in June, 1855, as a branch of the tinware and stove store he had opened, some years before, in Council Bluffs. The first building occupied by Mr. Rogers was of one story, twenty feet front and forty feet deep, built of cottonwood, and stood on the north side of Farnam Street between Ninth and Tenth. In 1860 Mr. Rogers bought a lot on the corner of Fourteenth and Farnam Streets, and built a one-story frame, covering the lot. Later he joined the other property holders, when the entire south side of Farnam Street, from Thirteenth to Fourteenth, was built up solid with three-story buildings. He occupied his new store in January, 1868. In the year 1884 the firm became Milton Rogers & Son, by the admission of Thomas J. Rogers to an interest in the business, and in 1884 the present firm name was assumed, when Warren M. Rogers became a partner in the business. This house carries a large stock, and employs from fifteen to thirty-five men.

Robert Uhlig is proprietor and C. M. Eaton manager of the Omaha Stove Repair Works, 1207 Douglas Street. This enterprise was started in 1884, but Mr. Uhlig has been connected with it only since 1889. This house claims to carry repairs for 40,000 different stoves, and is said to have the most complete stock of the kind in the west—having on hand four hundred tons of castings, and doing a business of $75,000 yearly.

The Great Western Stove Company, of Leavenworth, Kansas, has a branch at 909 Jones Street, Omaha, which has been operated since 1888. E. A. Trussell manages the Omaha trade.

Wm. Lyle Dickey & Co. do a large retail business in stoves, ranges and furnaces, at 1403 Douglas Street, where they have been established since 1888.

John Hobrecker, Jr., is western agent for numerous stove manufacturing companies, at 1009-1011 Jones Street, where a large stock of goods is carried. Mr. Hobrecker has been engaged in this line here for the past three years.

### FARM MACHINERY, VEHICLES.

As this city is the center of a large agricultural district tributary to it, the increased tillage of late years, necessarily causes a greater demand for farm machinery; this being the case, it is easy to judge of the demands of agriculture in this district by the number of agricultural implement houses and the amount of machinery distributed from here.

G. W. Lininger is the oldest implement dealer in Omaha. He came to Council Bluffs in 1868 and together with E. L. Shugert started as a pioneer in this line in that city. In 1873 Mr. Lininger removed from Council Bluffs and began business in Omaha as G. W. Lininger & Co. In 1879 he sold out his business. Two years later was organized Lininger, Metcalf & Co., incorporated with a capital of $100,000, with the following named stockholders: G. W. Lininger, president; J. M. Metcalf, vice-president; H. P. Devalon, secretary and treasurer; Thomas Metcalf and Mrs. Lininger. Since then Thomas Metcalf has withdrawn from the business and F. L. Haller has been added to the firm. The history of this house is the same old story of industry, energy and honesty that characterize the growth of other successful business ventures. In the first year Messrs. Lininger and Devalon managed to get along very well with the assistance of one helper. Times have changed since then. After occupying and outgrowing several buildings, the company bought the property formerly occupied by the Bemis Brewing Company on Sixth and Pacific Streets, which was remodelled at a cost of seventeen thousand dollars. There the establishment now covers three acres, with sixty-five thousand square feet of flooring under metal roof.

This is one of the largest jobbing implement houses in the world, having eighteen branch houses in the State, employing four traveling men and from seventy-five to one hundred other men at headquarters. The business requires an active capital of about a half million dollars.

The Parlin, Orendorff & Martin Company, of Canton, Illinois, does a jobbing business in farm machinery. The business was begun in the fall of 1882, as Parlin, Orendorff & Martin, and incorporated under the present style, in 1887. This company owns and occupies, at the corner of Ninth and Jones Streets, Omaha, a large, five-story brick building, has five traveling salesmen, and does a business of between three and four hundred thousand dollars yearly. Euclid Martin is treasurer and manager.

The Omaha branch of the Avery Planter Company, of Peoria, Illinois, is located at Eighth and Pacific Streets, and is managed by F. P. Day. It was started here in 1882, and now sends out from three to six traveling men. Among other things, this branch sells one thousand planters and two thousand cultivators, and does a business of $200,000 annually.

The Aultman & Taylor Company, manufacturers of threshers and other machinery, is represented here by F. L. Loomis, who is located at Tenth, and Farnam Streets. This company has had a representative here for ten or twelve years.

William Deering & Co., of Chicago, have sold binders, reapers, and other machinery, at their branch house here, since 1880. This branch has twelve traveling men, and occupies a building, the property of the company, fifty feet wide, one hundred and twenty feet long, and seven stories high, at 801-803 Capitol Avenue, which was erected in 1890. The last year's business amounted to three-quarters of a million dollars. Thomas Blenkhorn is the general agent.

The McCormick Harvesting Machine Company, of Chicago, has had a branch here for several years. Employment is given to twenty men, and a large amount of machinery sold and distributed throughout the State. W. G. Sawyer is general agent, with office and warehouse at 808 to 812 Leavenworth Street.

The Nebraska Moline Plow Company began business in this city in July, 1892, at the corner of Ninth and Leavenworth Streets. This is a branch of the Moline Plow Company of Moline, Illinois, and is managed by Theo. Starks. This company was formerly represented here by the Moline, Milburn-Stoddard Company.

Kingman & Co. are dealers in farm machinery, buggies and wagons at Ninth and Pacific Streets. A. L. Carson is local manager. This is one of several houses established by this company in leading cities along the Mississippi and Missouri Rivers, and began business in July, 1892.

T. G. Northwall is general agent for the Skandia Plow Co., Craner, Steel & Austin, and the O. S. Kelly Co., and handles a general line of farm implements and machinery. The agency was established in 1889.

Major George Armstrong and his son, E. L. Armstrong, as Armstrong & Co., were in the agricultural implement business in this city from January, 1886, to January, 1891. At the latter date E. L. Armstrong became sole proprietor of the business. He occupies a large three story building, and sells, at wholesale, implements and vehicles, the manufacture of more than twenty different companies. The trade extends west to Wyoming and north to Minnesota. The office and warehouse are at 1308 to 1312 Izard Street.

The Winona Implement Company is another enterprise started here in 1886. Location, Fourteenth and Nicholas Streets. T. O. Eichelberger is general manager.

W. T. Seaman owns and occupies a building of sixty feet front and one hundred and fifty feet depth, five stories high. This is filled with all sorts of vehicles from the heaviest farm wagon to the finest buggies and carriages, which, as a retail stock, is rarely exceeded in the United States. His place of business is 1331 to 1335 North Sixteenth Street.

The Columbus Buggy Company of Columbus, Ohio, has one of its branches at Omaha, which does a wholesale and retail business under the management of G. D. Edwards. One hundred styles of vehicles are displayed. A building five stories high, 66 by 132 feet on the ground, occupying numbers 1610 to 1614 Harney Street, was occupied by this company in January, 1893. The two lower stories will be used for repository or show rooms, and the remainder for storage.

Sutphen & Son, proprietors of the Sutphen Fine Carriage Repository, have been established in Omaha since March, 1890, and now are located at 2020 Farnam Street, doing a wholesale and retail business.

A. H. Perrigo & Co. are dealers in bicycles and tricycles at 1406 Dodge Street. They have been in business since 1889.

### STORAGE.

W. M. Bushman does a storage business and maintains a receiving, forwarding and financial agency, at 1013-1015 Leavenworth Street, where he has fine trackage. Mr. Bushman also has the government bonded warehouse in his building, which is 44x128 feet on the ground, with five stories and basement. He has been engaged in this line in this city for five years past.

The Western Cold Storage Company occupies a large building on Ninth and Davenport Streets. The officers of the company are: P. A. English, president; C. Murray, vice president; A. E. English, secretary and treasurer.

The Nebraska Cold Storage Company, a receiving and forwarding institution, occupying five floors at 815-817 Howard Street, has storage capacity for eighty carloads of produce, forty of which are dry storage. It is well provided with trackage. The officers of the company are: L. Kirschbraun, president, and E. Lowenstein, secretary and treasurer.

### GROCERS.

"Henry Pundt, teas and groceries; founded 1856," is the legend inscribed on the three-story building, 1218 Farnam. At the beginning of its existence this house was Pundt & Koenig, occupying a two-story brick building on Thirteenth and Farnam, where the Merchants National Bank now stands. That store was then one of the finest in the city, and the firm sold great piles of groceries, liquors and provisions, hardware, boots and shoes, to outfitters and emigrants to California, and other points in the West. On the death of Mr. Koenig, in 1863, Mr. Pundt assumed the firm name and style of H. Pundt & Co., the company being nominal. From 1874 to 1879, Pundt, Meyer & Raapke were engaged in the jobbing and retail grocery business. Since the latter date Mr. Pundt has done an extensive business in the retail grocery trade, carrying also a large stock of liquors.

D. M. Steele & Co., are wholesale grocers and importers of teas and cigars. The present firm is the successor of Steele, Johnson & Co., who began business in Council Bluffs in 1867, and, attracted by the rapid growth, commanding position and numerous western railway connections, moved to this city in 1872, and occupied a three-story building on the corner of Thirteenth and Harney Streets, having, at that time three or four men in the field. In February, 1885, the firm of D. M. Steele & Co. succeeded the old firm, the new company being composed of Dudley M. Steele, Dudley Smith and John M. Steele. As the trade increased, larger accommodations were demanded, and a five-story building, 132 feet deep, with sixty-six feet front, was erected in 1890, for the firm's special use, at the corner of Twelfth and Jones Streets, which was immediately occupied. Into this building tracks run connecting with all the railroads entering the city, making it easy for the employes of the house to load and unload goods without interference or expense on the part of the railroad companies. All large consignments received or sent out are handled in this way. They import large quantities of tea direct from Yokahama, Japan, and cigars from Cuba. They are also agents for some of the largest cigar manufacturers in the world. The twenty-one salesmen employed by this house visit the principal towns in Nebraska, Western Iowa, Northern Kansas, South Dakota, Colorado, Wyoming, Montana, Idaho and Utah. A branch warehouse for staple goods, is located at Salt Lake City, which supplies the far west trade in the district tributary to that point.

The McCord-Brady Company, successor to McCord, Brady & Co., wholesale grocers, was incorporated January 1, 1891, with James McCord, president; William H. McCord, vice president; John S. Brady, treasurer; Frank J. Hoel, secretary. The original firm was established here fourteen years ago and built up a trade which now reaches out over Nebraska, Kansas, South Dakota, Wyoming, Colorado, Utah, Montana, and as far west as Idaho, Nevada and Oregon. This company has all the conveniences of storeroom and trackage to facilitate and expedite business. The triple five-story brick building now occupied was constructed in 1883.

Paxton & Gallagher (W. A. Paxton and Ben Gallagher), grocers, have in their employ fifty-five persons, twenty-one of whom are commercial travelers. This house, which dates from 1879, does a general grocery business, imports large amounts of tea and cigars, and extends its trade to the Pacific States. The business occupies a large three-story building at 707 to 711 South Tenth Street.

Meyer & Raapke style themselves "The Pioneer Grocery House of Omaha," having been established in 1868. At that time they did only a retail business, amounting to about $20,000 annually. In 1872 it became a wholesale traffic, Mr. Meyer doing all the traveling for the house for two or three years. The business now occupies a four-story building, at 1403 to 1407 Harney Street, and the trade amounts annually to half a million dollars, and keeps six men on the road. In 1887 a tussle with fire and water cost $20,000.

Allen Brothers, who were in the retail trade from 1881 to 1883, entered the wholesale business at the latter date. They began with two men on the road, and now have seven. They occupy a four-story building, at 1108-1110 Harney Street.

Sloan, Johnson & Co., wholesale grocers, have been in business in Omaha since 1886. They employ twenty-five persons.

The Union Pacific Tea Company has one of its two hundred branches at Omaha, under the management of John Nevin, 204 North Sixteenth Street. The business is strictly a cash trade, and confined mainly to tea, coffee and spices. It was established in 1887.

T. S. Grigor & Co. have been established in the tea, coffee and spice trade here since 1884.

Sommer Brothers established a staple and fancy grocery business in 1885, which is now carried on at 2723 Farnam Street and 1302 North Eighteenth Street.

P. M. Back keeps a general stock of goods at 1120 to 1124 South Seventh Street, where he began work as a penniless clerk in 1875. After serving several years as clerk, he became a partner in the business, and later became sole proprietor.

Little & Williams, grocers, are located at 1407 Douglas Street. They have done business in this block since 1871.

William Gentleman, whose cognomen seems to have been appropriately bestowed, is a grocer at 501-503 North Sixteenth Street. He started in business in 1877.

A. H. Gladstone has been in the grocery business in Omaha since 1869, and was originally located on a portion of the ground

occupied by the Millard Hotel. The present firm of Gladstone Brothers has existed since 1886, employs about fifteen people, and handles groceries, wines, liquors and cigars, at 1308-1310 Douglas Street.

In September, 1888, the Clarke Coffee Company and the firm of Gates, Cole & Miles united and formed the Consolidated Coffee Company, importer and jobber of teas, coffees, spices and cigars, with a capital stock of $130,000, one-half being paid in. Forty men are employed, ten of whom are on the road as commercial travelers. The amount of sales is half a million yearly.

The firm of Bates & Co. consists of J. E. and C. R. Bates, whose business dates back to 1886, when the commission house was started, to which a wholesale grocery trade has since attached. They do a business of $100,000, and keep three commercial men in the field.

A branch house of the A. Booth Packing Company is located in Omaha, and does a business in oysters, fish, etc., that compares favorably with that done by branches of the house in other cities.

The Platt Company, packers of the tiger brand of oysters, have had an agency in Omaha for ten years past, but it was not till the fall of 1889 that the business done here was sufficient to justify the establishment of a branch house. In addition to the oyster business, a large stock of fresh fish and celery are also carried. Two commercial men solicit orders outside, and four within the city, and twenty persons are employed in the work incident to the business in Omaha, which is managed by L. E. Wettling, who has had charge of the business since June, 1892. The firm's Omaha headquarters is at 701 South Thirteenth Street.

## WHOLESALE FLOUR DEALERS.

William Preston has been a dealer in flour in Omaha for about twenty years. His first location was at the corner of Sixteenth and Douglas Streets, where the J. J. Brown Block now stands, where he conducted a wholesale and retail trade in flour and feed. In 1880, George Richardson and Charles L. Todd were associated in the business, and the firm became William Preston & Co., wholesale dealers in flour. Mr. Todd retired from the firm in 1884, and Mr. Richardson in June, 1891, since which time Mr. Preston has conducted the business, with the assistance of his sons, Alfred A. and Walter G. Preston. The annual sales of flour amount to $250,000, and the trade covers Nebraska and adjoining states.

Since December, 1889, the R. T. Davis Mill Company, of St. Joseph, Missouri, has had a branch house at 802 Jackson Street, which does a large flour business.

C. E. Black manages the wholesale flour business of S. F. Gilman, 1013 to 1017 North Sixteenth Street. The enterprise was started in the fall of 1887, with one carload of flour, and now that amount is disposed of daily. Since August, 1891, the trade has been carried on in a house built purposely for this firm. Mr. Gilman is a resident of Davenport, Iowa, and the business, since its institution, has been in the charge of Mr. Black.

George Richardson, a former employe of William Preston & Co., has, since September 1, 1891, conducted the business of wholesale dealer in flour, grain and hay, at 1207 to 1211 South Twentieth Street, employing six persons.

## DRUGS.

The Richardson Drug Company, wholesale druggist at 902 to 906 Jackson Street, was established in January, 1887, as a branch of the well-known St. Louis house of the same name, and succeeded to the wholesale business of the Goodman Drug Company, on Jones Street. The building which this firm now uses is sixty-six feet wide, 132 feet long, and five stories high, with double basement, all of the space in the house being occupied. The business, which at first gave employment to four traveling men and twenty persons at the house, now requires nine men on the road and forty-seven persons at the house. The first year's business was over half a million dollars, and the trade has steadily grown each year since. The extensive laboratory is a prominent feature of the institution. The goods sold by this house are sent to all parts of the west, northwest and southwest. Since the burning of the establishment at St. Louis, the Omaha house has been the working center of the business. The officers of the company are: J. C. Richardson, president; C. F. Weller (president of the Chemical Bank of St. Louis), vice president and manager of the Omaha business, and Amos Field, secretary and treasurer.

The wholesale drug house of Blake, Bruce & Co., importers of druggists' and stationers' sundries, is the successor of the H. T. Clarke Drug Company. This house has done business here since January, 1887, and is located in the double four-story brick building, corner of Tenth and Harney Streets. They do business on a capital of $150,000. The members of the company are: C. F. Blake, E. E. Bruce, W. B. Goodall, C. E. Bedwell. The trade extends into Western Iowa, Nebraska, Missouri, Kansas, South Dakota, Wyoming, where the firm's commercial travelers visit, and to points farther west by mail orders.

In November, 1883, J. A. Fuller and J. H. Dumont enlisted in the drug trade, under the firm name of J. A. Fuller & Co. They are located at 1402 Douglas Street, and are engaged in the usual prescription business and in jobbing of heavy goods.

The Goodman Drug Company is the successor of C. F. Goodman, who started where the company now does business, 1110 Farnam Street, in April, 1868. Mr. Goodman bought the realty and stock, succeeding E. A. Allen, and engaged in the wholesale and retail drug trade, in which he continued till January, 1886, when he organized the Goodman Drug Company, of which C. F. Goodman is president and O. P. Goodman treasurer. The wholesale department was moved to Jones Street, between Tenth and Eleventh Streets, where it continued a year, and was then sold to the Richardson Drug Company. The retail business was continued at the old stand, and physicians' supplies and surgical instruments added to the usual line of goods. In 1877 the Pioneer Block, in which the company was located, burned, the store, warehouse and stock being a total loss, amounting to $50,000. The re-establishment of the business was quickly accomplished, and the jobbing and retail trade amounts yearly to $100,000. Mr. Goodman was sole representative in this line of business when he engaged in it twenty-three years ago.

The Kinsler Drug Company began business in 1887. In November, 1889, it was incorporated, with a capital stock of $30,000. The officers are: J. T. Kinsler, president; M. J. Kinsler, vice president; J. C. Kinsler, secretary and treasurer. This firm first started in business in a nicely fitted up store at 1307 Farnam Street, succeeding Cheney & Olsen. In May, 1892, Hullinger & Railey bought this stock, and now occupy the store. In June, 1890, a second store was opened, on the corner of Sixteenth and Farnam Streets, in the Commercial National Bank building. This store is well fitted up, and has the finest marble soda fountain and counter in the central west.

McCormick & Lund are prosperous druggists at Fifteenth and Farnam Streets. In January, 1891, they succeeded D. W. Saxe, who had done business here for eight or ten years. The members of the firm are John McCormick and John G. Lund.

The Aloe & Penfold Company commenced business here in March, 1891, as a branch of A. S. Aloe & Co., of St. Louis, Missouri, with a capital stock of $10,000. Its trade in instruments, supplies, optical goods, drugs, etc., extends from the Missouri River to the Pacific Coast. The officers of the company are,

A. S. Aloe, St. Louis, Missouri, president; E. E. Muffitt, vice president; H. J. Penfold, secretary and treasurer. Place of business 114 South Fifteenth Street.

Charles R. Sherman and A. B. McConnell are manufacturing and prescription pharmacists at 1513 Dodge Street, under the firm name of Sherman & McConnell. They have a neat store, and do a wholesale and retail business in homeopathic supplies, in addition to the usual line of traffic. They have been in business since 1889.

Leslie & Leslie, proprietors of the "Central Pharmacy," have been engaged in the drug business here since 1884.

James Forsyth came to Omaha in the spring of 1864, and after long service as a clerk in the drug business, opened a store on his own account, in 1877, on the corner of Fourteenth and Douglas Streets. Three years later he bought the branch store of C. F. Goodman, on the corner of Capitol Avenue and Sixteenth Street, where he is now located.

Norman A. Kuhn (Kuhn & Co.), started in the drug business in April, 1879, at Fifteenth and Douglas Streets, and has built up a brisk business.

John W. Bell, druggist, is located at the corner of Eleventh and Mason Streets. He came to Omaha in 1870, and conducted a branch store for Ish, on Twelfth and Douglas Streets, till 1876, and soon after started in the drug business for himself, on Tenth, between Leavenworth and Marcy. In 1880 the block he was in, burned, and his loss was total; including stock, books, accounts, and all. Insurance $1,500. The fire occurred May 1st, and on June 1st Mr. Bell had completed and occupied a new structure on the site of the one burned. The building of the viaduct necessitated a removal, and in January, 1891, he moved to present location.

R. H. Blose, a former employe of Kuhn & Co., opened a drug store at 1101 North Eighteenth Street, in January, 1889. which he conducted till September, 1892, when he disposed of his interest, and the establishment took the name of the Palace Pharmacy, under the management of C. Bartels, a native of Hanover, who received his education for this line of business in the old country. This house has a well-established suburban trade.

The Hunter Homeopathic Pharmacy Company, established February, 1892, is composed of J. P. Hunter, president; Herman Luyties, Jr., vice-president, and E. Irene Hunter, secretary. The establishment does both wholesale and retail business and is the only exclusively homeopathic pharmacy in Omaha. The trade extends throughout Nebraska and into surrounding States.

### COMMISSION HOUSES.

Peycke Brothers, Ernest and Julius, do a large commission business in fruit and produce, at the corner of Eleventh and Howard Streets. Ernest and Edmund Peycke began the business on Farnam Street in 1870, and later Julius was admitted as a member of the firm, and in 1884 the manufacture of confectionery was added to the business. Since January, 1891, Peycke Brothers have conducted the commission business, and Edmund Peycke has been proprietor of the candy manufacturing business. The commission trade amounts to a large figure yearly and keeps a large force of hands busy.

Porter Brothers' Company, commission merchants, of Chicago, Illinois, have a branch house here, managed by P. W. Butts, 801 to 811 Jones Street, which was established May, 1890, employing fifteen persons. The fruit received is almost entirely in car load lots from California, a portion of which is disposed of in Omaha and the remainder shipped to towns in Iowa, Nebraska, Dakota and Kansas. Trackage accommodations permit the unloading of three cars at once greatly facilitating the disposal of consignments. The business is extensive and increasing.

Branch & Co. are wholesale commission merchants at the corner of Harney and Thirteenth Streets. The business, which is flourishing, was established in 1883, and embraces fruits, produce and oysters.

Kirschbraun & Sons have one of their three produce commission houses in Omaha, located here in 1884, at 1209 Howard Street. The business is managed by Louis Kirschbraun.

The remainder of the produce and commission business is divided up among the following named companies, some of which do a large business:

Robert Purvis, 1220 Harney Street, established 1870.

Schroeder & Co., 423 South Eleventh Street; in business since 1887.

The Iowa and Nebraska Creamery Company, 309 South Twelfth Street, began business December, 1890. The members of this company are N. F. and P. C. Storey.

Ribbel & George, 1207 Howard Street, established 1888.

Williams & Cross, 1214 Harney Street, began business in 1890.

Mullin & McClain, 415 South Eleventh Street, started in 1888.

Riddell & Co., 1104-1106 Howard Street, whose business dates back to 1885.

S. I. Valentine & Co., 307 South Twelfth Street, are a later accession to the commission business.

John A. Krug & Co., 1011 Howard Street, established 1889.

L. M. Leslie, 1015 Howard Street, have been in the commission business since 1889.

J. H. Feilbach & Co., 1017 Howard Street, date back to 1887.

Icken & Wohlers, 1205 Howard Street, have been in business since January, 1891.

### SEED HOUSES.

John Evans, now doing business at 1406 Dodge Street, is the proprietor of the original seed house of Nebraska, having started the business in 1867, in connection with groceries. He does a jobbing business that extends to the Pacific Ocean, and has a large retail trade in Omaha.

Phil Stimmel is a grower and jobber of Nebraska and Northern seeds. He occupies a four-story building at 911 Jones Street, and has three traveling salesmen. The house was opened in 1885.

The Nebraska Seed Company has lately succeeded the Emerson Seed Company, at 421-423 South Fifteenth Street. This company also has three traveling salesmen, and employs from five to fifteen men. Mrs. Philip Windheim is the proprietor of the business, and Richard Engelmann manager.

### SADDLERY, LEATHER AND HIDES.

L. C. Huntington engaged in the hide and leather business in 1861. As L. C. Huntington & Co. the business continued till 1875, when his son took the place of the company. This was the first house of the kind in Omaha. Since 1886 C. S. and A. S. Huntington, the sons of the founder of the house, have carried on the business at 1114 Jackson Street, where they employ nine men.

G. Brandenburg & Co. are wholesale leather dealers at 1012 Farnam Street. This house was established in 1884.

C. D. Woodworth & Co., retail dealers in harness and saddles, have been in business since 1885, at that time succeeding L. Woodworth, who had been in the carriage and harness business since 1861. In March, 1892, Woodworth & Co. bought out Welty & Guy, and occupied that firm's late quarters at 1316 Farnam Street.

Collins & Morrison are successors to G. H. & J. S. Collins, wholesale dealers in saddlery, 1316 Douglas Street, where the business was begun May 1, 1864. In the palmy days of the former firm's existence it sold large amounts of goods for stocking western military posts in the Department of the Platte, and when the Union Pacific was built, construction companies and graders were extensive purchasers, whose trade left a large margin of profit in the dealers' hands. In 1880 G. H. Collins died, but the business continued under the firm name till February, 1890, when John Morrison, who had been in the firm's employ for a long time, became a partner in the business, the partnership name becoming Collins & Morrison. From 1871 to 1880 the business was carried on at 1315 Farnam Street. At the latter date a fire destroyed the building this company occupied, and $20,000 worth of stock. Immediately after the fire the present three-story brick building was erected, and, on its completion, was occupied with a stock of saddles, harness and adjuncts of the trade. A large portion of the goods they handle are manufactured here. Twenty-five persons are employed, and goods are sent all over the northwestern country.

George Oberne & Co., of Chicago, dealers in hides, wool, etc., have five branch houses in western cities. The Omaha branch, managed by F. S. Bush, is located at 513 South Thirteenth Street, and has existed in Omaha since 1868. Four or five traveling men are employed, and the same number about the house.

J. S. Smith & Co. are in the same business as the foregoing, and are also a branch of a Chicago house. Mr. Ed. Perry has had charge of the business since it was opened here in 1885. The combined annual business of these two firms is nearly half a million dollars.

### OIL, LEAD, PAINTS, AND GLASS.

The Consolidated Tank Line Company, of Cincinnati, established a branch here in 1879, which handles all the products of petroleum, and also linseed oil, turpentine, and axle grease. The company's office is in the Merchants' National Bank, the works at Thirteenth and Locust Streets, and occupy three acres of ground. Forty men are employed outside, and twelve in the office; 125,000 barrels of coal oil are handled, and the aggregate of the business is $900,000. The company does its own cooperage, and turns out at its works in this city over three hundred barrels daily. Alex McDonald is president of the company, John B. Ruth is manager for the Omaha branch and its agencies, and L. J. Drake is general manager, with headquarters at Omaha, having charge of Iowa, Nebraska, Dakota, Missouri and Kansas.

The Fidelity Oil Company, R. C. Baughman, proprietor, wholesale dealer in illuminating and lubricating oils, located at South Twentieth Street and Union Pacific Railroad tracks, began business here in 1886. The amount of sales of oil annually is 27,000 barrels. Employment is furnished to twenty-seven persons.

A branch house of Scofield, Shurmer & Teagle, refiners of petroleum and its products, of Cleveland, Ohio, is located at Tenth and Clark Streets, having been established in 1890. Twelve men are employed, and the business is growing. T. S. Waltemeyer is manager.

Since the spring of 1890 the St. Louis Lead and Oil Company, the Collier White Lead and Oil Company, and the Southern White Lead Company, of St. Louis, Missouri, have been represented here by E. E. Brando. Two men travel from here for these firms. Between 800 and 1,000 tons of lead are annually sold.

The Omaha Oil and Paint Company sells paints and art glass at wholesale, at 1402 Dodge Street. The paint is manufactured at Lincoln.

The Kennard Glass and Paint Company has been in the import, jobbing and retail trade since 1887. The members of this firm, L. J. and F. B. Kennard, are among the old merchants of the city, having been in the dry goods trade in the latter part of the sixties, and conducted a wholesale drug business from 1875 to 1883. They employ ten persons, and do a business extending as far west as Utah.

Harry T. Warner, corner of Twentieth and Cuming Streets, has dealt in paints, oils and wall paper since April, 1888. Since March, 1889, the manufacture of paste has been carried on, in connection with the other business, and a sufficient quantity is made to supply the city trade, and places easily accessible in Nebraska and Iowa.

TOBACCO AND CIGARS.

Max Meyer & Co., the junior partner being Moritz Meyer, who has charge of the business, are wholesale and retail dealers in tobacco and cigars, at 1522 Farnam Street. They carry a very large stock of goods, and import cigars largely from Cuba and tobacco from Austria. Five salesmen sell their goods in the territory west of the Missouri River tributary to Omaha.

Henry Langstadter, successor to Erlich & Langstadter, 116 South Fifteenth Street, has dealt in cigars, tobacco and smokers' articles in Omaha since 1889.

E. L. Robertson & Bro., 216 South Fifteenth Street, deal in cigars and tobaccos, at wholesale and retail, and rank among the first dealers in the city in amount of business done. They have been in business here about three years.

H. Rosenstock & Co. are importers and dealers in leaf tobacco, at 1104 Douglas Street. They succeeded, September, 1891, Wedeles & Co., who had been in business five years. Rosenstock & Co. do a strictly wholesale business.

WHOLESALE LIQUOR STORES.

The oldest house in this line is that of Riley Brothers, who do a wholesale liquor and cigar business at 1118 Farnam Street. This firm, which now consists of Andrew, E. F. and Bernard Riley, began business on Twelfth and Douglas Streets in October, 1877, as A. Riley & Co. Since that time some changes have occurred in the membership, Mr. Dillon, a former member, retiring and the present partnership beginning in 1888.

The firm of Frick & Herbertz, composed of Andrew Frick and Charles Herbertz, began business in 1885, which has proved satisfactory. They are located at 1001 Farnam Street.

John Boekhoff, of 1210 Douglas Street, has been in the liquor business since 1885, when a partnership was formed by Boekhoff & Mack, which existed till 1889. Since then Mr. Boekhoff has carried on the business alone.

M. Wollstein & Co. first opened a liquor store on Thirteenth and Jackson Streets in 1881. The Chicago Liquor House, on Sixteenth and Davenport Streets, was started in 1884, and the Eagle Liquor House, at 2224 Cuming, early in 1891.

L. Kirscht and E. Durr have carried on a liquor business in Omaha since 1887, although the present house was established in Council Bluffs in 1861, as Groenewig & Kirscht, becoming L. Kirscht & Co. on the retirement of Mr. Groenewig, in 1879, and Kirscht & Durr in 1892. They are located at 407-409 South Tenth Street.

Adler & Heller, jobbers in liquors and cigars, at 1114 Farnam Street, first began business here in 1877. The monotony of commercial routine was varied in 1888 by a fire, which, with water, damaged them to some extent.

Henry Hiller, proprietor of the Family Wine and Liquor House, began in 1890, and does a wholesale and retail business at 616 North Sixteenth Street. Number of employes, five.

J. A. Wood & Co., liquor merchants, are located at 213 South Fifteenth Street. This firm, which has been established four years, imports fine foreign goods specially for its own trade. The members of the firm are: John A. Wood and E. E. Whitmore.

William Darst, importer and wholesale and retail dealer in wines and liquors, began business in Omaha in 1886, carrying a good stock, and having a trade extending west to Ogden, Utah, and into Montana. Mr. Darst was succeeded in July, 1892, by the Los Angeles Wine, Liquor & Cigar Co., which

was incorporated with L M. Darst, president, M J. Manix, vice president William Darst, secretary and treasurer, with a paid up capital of $25,000 This is probably the only absolutely cash liquor house in Nebraska The business occupies numbers 116 and 118 South Sixteenth Street

Ike New, wholesale dealer in wines and liquors, opened a store in the city January 1, 1892, at Thirteenth and Douglas Streets

C. B Connor is a wholesale dealer in foreign wines, liquors and cigars, at 1409 Douglas Street He opened this house at the beginning of the year 1892

McGuire & Co , wholesale liquor dealers, opened a store at 216 South Fourteenth Street, in March, 1892

Grotte & Co , successors to R R Grotte, conduct a wholesale liquor store at 1020 and 1022 Farnam Street

### WHOLESALE DEALERS IN BEER.

The Anheuser-Busch Brewing Association, of St Louis, Missouri, established a branch business here in 1874, shipping in car load lots of beer, Her & Co being the Omaha representatives till 1879, at which time the company established itself in quarters on Capitol Avenue In 1887 the company, having outgrown its accommodations, erected at the corner of Thirteenth and Jones Streets, a refrigerator capable of holding ten cars of beer, also a stable with accommodations for fifteen horses, an office, and a bottling department, for its business, and a three-story pressed brick building which is rented The company employs ten men, and disposes of eighteen or twenty thousand barrels of beer and six thousand casks of bottled beer, annually, in Omaha The business is under the efficient management of General Agent George Krug, assisted by Julius Bursler.

The Joseph Schlitz Brewing Company, of Milwaukee, has a branch house here, at South Ninth and Leavenworth Streets, John Marhover, agent. The wholesale business of this firm is handled by R R Grotte This company is now erecting, on the lot facing Sixteenth Street, and south of the Board of Trade Building, a structure to cost $100,000 when completed

W J Lemp, of St Louis, established an agency here in 1887, from which the city trade and a small portion of this State and Iowa are supplied with beer The amount handled here is nine thousand barrels annually Seven men and four teams are employed The sub-agencies through the State are not supplied from here, but from the brewery in St Louis In 1888 a brick office, storage-room and stable were erected at 1517 Nicholas Street, where the Omaha headquarters are located P J Boysen is city agent

### LUMBER

Although the City of Omaha is built very largely of brick and stone, and other imperishable materials, yet, its rapid growth in the last six years, from 40,000 to 140,000 inhabitants, and the large number of buildings necessary to shelter the increased population, have required the erection of a very large number of structures of wood As a consequence of the demand for material of this kind, both for the city retail trade and for the wholesale business in the State, a large trade in lumber has developed. Following is some account of the firms engaged in the lumber trade

George A Hoagland has been in the wholesale and retail lumber business, in this city, since 1861 In the spring of that year the present business was started, George T. Hoagland and George Bebbington, of St Joseph, Missouri, forming a co-partnership as George T. Hoagland & Co , and making use of the opportunity offered to ship a sufficient quantity of lumber to Omaha on the steamer Lizzie Bayliss, afterwards used as a ferry-boat between Council Bluffs and Omaha, to start a yard, of which Mr Bebbington took charge The stock did not amount to more than five or six car loads, but it was enough to inaugurate a fully equipped yard in the then little village of Omaha. The site for the business was on Visscher's property, where the Millard Hotel now stands. The office occupied a small room in the second story of Visscher's carpenter shop. George A. Hoagland came to Omaha in the fall after the yard was started and became an employe of the firm. In the year 1865, Mr. Bebbington retired from the partnership, which then became George T. Hoagland & Son, and so continued till January, 1874, when George A. Hoagland purchased his father's interest, and became sole proprietor of the business. Mr. Hoagland has had some experience with both fire and flood. On Christmas night, 1870, an employe, who slept in the office at the lower yard, allowed it to take fire and burn up, destroying about three thousand dollars worth of property. An examination of the locality after the fire revealed the charred remains of the unfortunate employe, who had, himself, perished in the flames, the victim of his own carelessness. In the spring of 1881, the great flood swept over Mr. Hoagland's yard and damaged the stock to the extent of ten or twenty thousand dollars. In the days of steamboat navigation on the river, the lumber was unloaded from the boat close to the water's edge, and it was often necessary to work men and teams day and night to save the lumber from falling into the river, which undermined and swept away the banks to a great extent in a very short time. In the spring of 1867 the river was so high that the only available landing place, along the Omaha river front, was where the original waterworks pumping engine was afterwards located, and from that place to the mainland lumber had to be towed on a flatboat, made for the purpose. The first shipments of lumber, at wholesale, directly from Omaha, were made by George A. Hoagland in 1871-2. Previous to that time these shipments had been made from Chicago and other points east. The little country yard, which this was, in its early days, requiring only one or two men to do the work, has now become an establishment requiring eight or nine clerks, and from fifty to one hundred other persons at the Omaha yards alone. Mr. Hoagland has a capital of $500,000 in the business. The main yards, at the foot of Douglas Street, cover five acres of ground, with a branch yard and business office at the corner of Ninth and Douglas, a large wholesale and retail yard at Council Bluffs, and nearly twenty branches in the larger towns of this State, which do a retail business. The stock of lumber carried will average ten million feet.

H. F. Cady, the successor of Cady & Gray, has a large planing mill and sash and door factory located at the foot of Farnam Street, with an extensive lumber yard adjoining it on the north. The business was established in 1867, by Harris & Foster. The death of Mr. Harris left the business in the hands of Wm. M. Foster, until January 1, 1875, when the firm of Foster & Guiou was formed, Mr. Charles H. Guiou becoming Mr. Foster's partner. This arrangement continued for one year, and then Mr. Foster conducted the business alone until January 1, 1880, when Mr. Gray became a partner, the firm becoming Foster & Gray, and two years later, he purchased Mr. Foster's interest, and managed the business under his own name until January 1891, when H. F. Cady was associated in the business, the firm name becoming Cady & Gray. On January 1, 1892, Mr. Gray retired from the firm, and H. F. Cady became sole proprietor. The planing mill was built in March, 1889, and during that year Mr. Gray paid out over $100,000 in wages and salaries. Mr. Cady has the contract for supplying the lumber for the building for the electric exhibit at the Columbian Exhibition, at Chicago, in 1893, which will cover nine and three-fourth acres of ground, and require seven hundred car loads of lumber in its construction. All the mill work is prepared and sent from Omaha. About five acres of ground is occupied by the yard and mills. One hundred and fifty men are steadily employed. The trade, which is almost exclusively wholesale, amounts to $750,000 per year, and extends over large portions of Nebraska, western Iowa, South Dakota and Colorado.

The Chicago Lumber Company, F. Colpetzer, manager, Charles H. Guiou, assistant manager, conducts an extensive business on Fourteenth Street, near the Union Pacific Railway. The Omaha business was established in 1876, and there are thirty-two branch yards in this State. The total capital used for the Nebraska business is $1,300,000, and the annual sales amount to $2,500,000.

John A. Wakefield, located on Pierce Street, from Seventeenth to Eighteenth, has a capital of $150,000, invested in the business, and his annual sales amount to $500,000. He deals in lumber, wholesale and retail, and began business in this city in January, 1880. Three acres of land are included in the yard, a peculiar feature of which is a substantial roof, covering the entire area and keeping the whole stock dry. There is not another yard of this size under one roof in the United States.

Louis Bradford, the proprietor of a large lumber yard on Douglas Street, in this city, and other yards at various places in the state, does an extensive wholesale and retail business. This establishment dates from 1879.

C. N. Dietz has been in the lumber business in Omaha since 1881, and has branch yards at Lincoln, Hastings, Aurora, Bromfield and Trumbull. The Omaha yards are located at Thirteenth and California Streets.

Rittenhouse & Embree, successors to the Omaha Lumber Company, are located at South Eighteenth Street and Union Pacific track. The present firm began business in March, 1891.

The Star-Union Lumber Company, has existed about three years. The business is both retail and jobbing. Yards at Tenth and Nicholas Streets, and office at 627 Paxton Block. John R. Davis is president; Renfrew Stevenson, vice president, and A. J. Whidden, secretary and treasurer.

The Wyatt-Bullard Lumber Company does a wholesale and retail business, at Twentieth and Izard Streets. It began business in September, 1890.

F. C. Colpetzer and C. H. Guiou employ seven men at their lumber yard on Eighteenth and Nicholas Streets, where they occupy half a block. The business has been running since 1886.

The Hampton Lumber Company incorporated and began business in January, 1890. E. G. Hampton is president and treasurer, and W. T. Robinson, secretary.

C. L. Chaffee, wholesale dealer in lumber, engaged in business here in 1877, and built up a trade in this line, and in July, 1891, purchased the stock and business of the Howell Lumber Company, which he combined with his own, thereby making a business second to none of this kind in the West. The yards are situated on Twenty-sixth Street and the Union Pacific Railway, and have an area of fifteen acres. The office is located on the main floor of the New York Life Building. Fifty men are employed in the yards, where from five to eleven million feet of lumber are piled.

Charles R. Lee deals in hardwood lumber. He has been in the present business since February, 1885, and occupies half a block at southwest corner of Ninth and Douglas Streets. He is the only dealer in hardwood lumber, exclusively, in the city.

## COAL.

C. B. Havens, G. W. McGeath and John McGovern formed a copartnership under the style of C. B. Havens & Co., dealers in coal, in 1886, which continued till May, 1891, when Mr. McGeath retired from the business and a new company was formed and incorporated under the same name, with C. B. Havens, president and treasurer; H. F. Lemist, vice-president; G. P. Cronk secretary; and John McGovern. The principal office is at 1506 Farnam Street, with branches at Lincoln, Nebraska and Atchison, Kansas. This firm handles as much as fourteen thousand car loads annually.

The Nebraska Fuel Company was incorporated in August, 1883. The officers are: George C. Towle, president; George Paterson, vice president and treasurer, and F. H. Blake, secretary. The company does a wholesale and retail business, in coal, coke, etc.

The Omaha Coal, Coke and Lime Company, was organized in 1883. The present officers are: J. A. Sunderland, president; L. T. Sunderland, secretary, and J. F. Pollock, treasurer.

P. H. Mahoney & Co., do a wholesale and retail coal business, at 813 North Sixteenth Street, and corner of Tenth and Douglas Streets. This firm, of which Louis Bradford is junior partner, has existed since 1889. This company also does a large amount of contract business in grading and hauling.

Johnson Brothers are engaged in the retail coal business to some extent, but their business is mainly teaming. The two employments requiring about thirty men.

The Nebraska Coal and Lime Company. E. A. Blum, president and treasurer, and H. B. Morrill, secretary, has existed since 1887, and does a jobbing and retail business.

D. T. Mount and J. H. Griffin, as Mount & Griffin, employ thirty men in furnishing fuel to Omaha consumers. For ten years this firm has sprinkled the city's streets, and for two years have employed twenty-five teams on the contract for street sprinkling, in Salt Lake City, Utah.

Coutant & Squires succeeded Foster & Gray, as dealers in hard and soft coal, in 1884, and now carry on a busy trade.

Jeff. W. Bedford, deals in coal and other kinds of fuel, lime and other constructive material.

## ICE.

The large demand which the various industries and domestic occupations make for ice, has caused the formation of several ice companies here whose facilities and appliances for harvesting annual crops of a superior quality of ice, are second to those of no other city on the Missouri River. One of the oldest of these companies is the "Arctic Ice Company," which was incorporated in January, 1888, with a capital of $30,000, of which $20,000 is paid in—David Talbot, president and Henry J. Cole secretary and treasurer. The company's ice houses are located at the foot of Jones Street and below the Pacific railroad bridge. In summer, twenty men and twelve wagons are required to deliver ice. In winter, 150 men are usually kept busy four or five weeks cutting and storing the amount necessary for the next season's trade. The business is largely wholesale. Last year there were shipped to South Omaha, Kansas City and other points, over ten thousand tons. The annual business is $50,000.

The Crystal Ice Company was incorporated in January, 1889. The officers are William Fitch, president and secretary, and John P. Bay, treasurer. The capital stock is $60,000, fully paid up. This company is the result of the consolidation of the former firm of Fitch & Bay, The Kimball Ice Co., and Kennedy & Newell, the latter of which had been in business for twenty years. Fifty men and fifteen or twenty wagons are employed in summer, and in winter, for three or four weeks, from 150 to two hundred men are kept busy. One ice house is located on the corner of Fourth and Pierce Streets, one on Eighth and Nicholas and another at Cut-Off Lake. The capacity of these houses is twenty thousand tons. A large part of the business is supplying railroads, breweries, etc. Ice is obtained from Cut-Off Lake, the water works basin and the Missouri River. This Company deals in coal also. The yard is situated at Twelfth and Nicholas Streets. This branch of the business was added two years ago.

The Kimball Ice Company does a local

business only. J. H. Hungate is one of the veteran ice dealers of Omaha. After many years of service in this line of trade, both alone and as a partner, he bought out Mr. Kimball, his associate, in the fall of 1890, since which time he has been *de facto* the Kimball Ice Company. The ice houses are on Fifteenth and Grace Streets, where the capacity is fifteen thousand tons and at the reservoir, at the foot of Webster Street, where the capacity is seven thousand tons. The amount annually handled is about fifteen thousand tons. Twenty men and eight teams are employed in summer; and for six weeks in the winter, about eighty men are required to secure the crop.

H. C. Bostwick and J. C. Sharp with numerous partners, started a limited business in 1886, as the South Omaha Ice Company. In 1888 the company was incorporated with A. C. Foster, president, H. C. Bostwick, treasurer, and J. C. Sharp, secretary. The capital stock is ten thousand dollars, fully paid in. The ice it handles is obtained from Swift & Company, of South Omaha, the company not cutting any itself. During the warm season thirty men and eleven teams are employed, and fifteen thousand tons of ice disposed of. J. A. Doe is manager.

F. L. Cotton, dealer in ice, as well as coal and lumber, has been in the ice business for three years past, and handles in the city trade eight thousand tons per year. His ice is cut on the Florence and Walnut Hill reservoirs.

### LIVERY STABLES

James Stephenson is the proprietor of "Stephenson's Superb Stables," at 1001 Harney Street. In 1869 he bought a livery business and outfit from Dr. Pinney, of Council Bluffs, which he conducted in a small wooden building at the southeast corner of Tenth and Harney Streets. He built the present handsome brick structure in 1880, at a cost of $35,000, putting into it seventy-five horses, which, with the rolling stock, constitute a finely equipped stable. He owns another large stable on Nineteenth and Nicholas Streets, which he uses exclusively for sheltering two hundred mules and horses, which constitute his grading stock, with which he does a large amount of contract work. Stephenson & Williams are proprietors of the Omaha Cab Company.

J. T. Withrow & Co. have done a livery business at 1307 to 1311 Harney Street since 1885. In June, 1891, a fire destroyed all their carriages. They keep about twenty horses.

J. W. Cotton's livery and sale stables are located at the corner of Fifteenth and Cass Streets. He keeps twelve or fifteen livery horses and boards about forty.

Flanagan & Heafey conduct the "Buckeye Stable," at 418-420 South Nineteenth Street.

At the corner of Seventeenth and Davenport Streets is located the "Palace Stable," a structure 92 feet wide, 130 feet long and four stories in height. It was erected by E. H. Sherwood and completed in November 1887. Alex Benham occupied it a short time only. Mr. Sherwood then took the Benham stock and consolidated with it the livery outfit of James McShane and ran the business till 1890, and then Dr. V. H. Coffman became the owner of the horses and carriages, which he sold to C. T. Taylor, the present proprietor, a year later. There are now in the stable one hundred and five livery horses and from fifty to ninety boarders and one hundred vehicles.

The Jefferson Square Stable, 420 North Sixteenth Street, is conducted by L. Kroner. He keeps twelve or fifteen horses. The building is one of the early structures.

C. H. West is proprietor of a nicely fitted up little stable on the corner of Twenty-eighth and Leavenworth Streets, where about thirty-five horses are boarded. He also keeps a few teams for hire.

G. and L. St. Julian are the proprietors of "The Little Gem Stable," at 1718 Cass Street, which is a very handsome little structure, built by Mrs. S. R. Myers, in 1890. It has a capacity for accommodating forty-eight horses, and has been occupied by the present management since June 1891.

Edward Baumley, successor to Charles Baumley, has a small stable on St. Mary's Avenue and Seventeenth Streets.

### EXPLOSIVES.

Hugh G. Clark was in business in Omaha from 1876 till his death in December, 1892. Beginning in 1876, he was in the general merchandise business until 1884, when he sold out, retaining the agency for various powder and dynamite companies only, which of late years has developed into a large business itself. In connection with a branch, conducted by his son, in Denver, Mr. Clark's business extended as far west as Nevada, and north to Montana. Since Mr. Clark's death the business has been in charge of his son, Walter G. Clark.

### LAUNDRIES.

J. H. Evans bought a half interest in the City Steam Laundry of H. L. Wilkins, in 1878, the firm name then becoming Wilkins & Evans. In 1885 Mr. Wilkins withdrew and Mr. Evans took the business. In 1891 it was incorporated as a stock company, with a paid up capital of $100,000.00, Mr. Evans being president. This company owns and operates five large laundry plants, situated in the following named cities: Council Bluffs, Iowa, Lincoln, Omaha and South Omaha, Neb., with main offices at Omaha. These laundries contain the latest improvements in machinery and represent a capital of $250,000.00. Over three hundred hands are employed in them.

The Frontier Steam Laundry has been in operation since 1884, when it was started by J. C. Estel, who was succeeded the following year by M. Collins, who still operates it, occupying two stories and a basement, 22x130 feet in size, at 1542 Howard Street, and employing thirty-one persons.

The Nebraska Steam Laundry has been running since 1885, when it was put in operation by C. S. Poor and S. F. Henry, the latter of whom, still runs it. Fifteen persons are employed.

The Gate City Steam Laundry, situated at 207 North Seventeenth Street, is operated by Truman Brothers, who have been in the business since May 1890. They employ thirteen persons.

There are thirty-eight other laundries enumerated in the city directory, of various pretentions, tapering down to those of Sim Jin and Yee Sang Charlie.

### UNDERTAKING.

M. O. Maul is successor to Drexel & Maul, undertakers and embalmers, 1417 Farnam Street. In the spring of 1865 Jacob Gish, the first regular undertaker in Omaha, established himself in business and some years later was succeeded by John G. Jacobs, who disposed of the business to Drexel & Maul in December, 1883. This firm was dissolved in 1888, Mr. Maul becoming sole proprietor. Since 1865 Jacob Gish and his successors in business, have occupied the same lot, number 1417 Farnam street.

Heafey & Heafey carry on business at 218 and 220 South Fourteenth Street. This house was established about 1877, by McCarty, Donnelly & Co., and, after some changes of proprietorship, came into the hands of Heafey & Heafey in 1884. In addition to undertaking, a stock of church goods is carried.

H. K. Burket, funeral director and embalmer, 113 North Sixteenth Street, came to Omaha in 1883, since which time he has been in the present business, in which, he is the longest established director in this city.

Swanson & Valien, corner Seventeenth and Cuming Streets, have been in the undertaking business since October, 1888.

Taggart & Co. are undertakers and embalmers, at 207 North Sixteenth Street. They have been in business in Omaha six years.

The following list comprises the principal trades now represented in Omaha, and gives a close estimate of the capital invested at the close of 1892:

| Class | Capital Invested |
|---|---|
| Coal, lime, etc. | $ 255,000 |
| Rubber goods | 110,000 |
| Guns and sporting goods | 49,000 |
| Seeds | 50,000 |
| Safes, scales, etc. | 38,000 |
| Steam, water and railroad supplies | 275,000 |
| Sash, doors and blinds | 65,000 |
| Wall paper | 16,000 |
| Drugs | 455,000 |
| Crockery | 158,000 |
| Produce and fruits | 172,000 |
| Butter and eggs | 24,000 |
| Shelf hardware | 300,000 |
| Harness and saddlery | 210,000 |
| Hats and caps | 85,000 |
| Agricultural implements and carriages | 910,000 |
| Iron, steel and heavy hardware | 170,000 |
| Jewelry | 155,000 |
| Lumber | 1,810,000 |
| Liquors | 610,000 |
| Millinery | 55,000 |
| Notions | 62,000 |
| Paints and glass | 121,000 |
| Oysters and fish | 45,000 |
| Photograph supplies | 40,000 |
| Paper | 70,000 |
| Artists' materials | 10,000 |
| Books and stationery | 70,000 |
| Boots and shoes | 560,000 |
| Tea, coffee and spices | 90,000 |
| Confectionery | 195,000 |
| Cigars and tobacco | 255,000 |
| Dry goods | 700,000 |
| Flour | 100,000 |
| Furniture | 360,000 |
| Groceries | 1,490,000 |
| Syrups | 45,000 |
| Clothing | 155,000 |
| Carpets | 35,000 |
| Barbers' supplies | 10,000 |
| Electric supplies | 10,000 |
| Printers' supplies | 40,000 |
| Leaf tobacco | 20,000 |
| Surgical instruments | 30,000 |
| Stoves | 90,000 |
| Leather and shoe findings | 20,000 |
| Toys | 25,000 |
| Twines and cordages | 20,000 |
| Butchers' supplies | 10,000 |
| Oils | 340,000 |
| **Total** | **$10,920,000** |

The trade of the wholesale houses in Omaha during 1892 was unprecedented. The rush of orders was so great as to overtax many houses, and necessitated many enlargements of capital and capacity.

Below is a close estimate of the business done in leading lines by the wholesale houses during the last year, as given by Bradstreet:

| Class | Aggregate Sales |
|---|---|
| Groceries | $10,400,000 |
| Wines and liquors | 2,900,000 |
| Dry goods | 2,750,000 |
| Boots and shoes | 2,600,000 |
| Shelf hardware | 2,200,000 |
| Heavy Hardware | 370,000 |
| Leather and shoe findings | 100,000 |
| Harness and saddlery | 500,000 |
| Hats, caps and gloves | 400,000 |
| Clothing | 550,000 |
| Produce and fruits | 1,900,000 |
| Seeds | 200,000 |
| Rubber goods | 550,000 |
| Printers' supplies | 190,000 |
| Paper | 500,000 |
| Paints, oils and glass | 430,000 |
| Drugs | 1,800,000 |
| Millinery goods | 140,000 |
| Confectionery | 600,000 |
| Agricultural implements | 8,500,000 |
| Flour | 1,200,000 |
| Lumber | 5,500,000 |
| Wall paper | 75,000 |
| Steam, water and railway supplies | 2,000,000 |
| Photograph supplies | 70,000 |
| Guns and sporting goods | 175,000 |
| Cigars and tobacco | 1,785,000 |
| Coal, coke, cement, etc. | 1,440,000 |
| Safes, scales, etc. | 285,000 |
| Crockery | 350,000 |
| Furniture | 1,090,000 |
| Oysters and fish | 350,000 |
| Stoves | 215,000 |
| Jewelry | 700,000 |
| Notions | 150,000 |
| Twines and cordage | 140,000 |
| Tea, coffee and spices | 675,000 |
| Oils | 750,000 |
| Sash, doors and blinds | 140,000 |
| Books, stationery and periodicals | 700,000 |
| Barbers' supplies | 36,000 |
| Butchers' supplies | 85,000 |
| Carpets | 75,000 |
| Leaf tobacco | 90,000 |
| Toys | 90,000 |
| Surgical instruments | 45,000 |
| **Total** | **$56,091,000** |

# CHAPTER LIV.

Manufacturing Interests — Their Growth and Present Condition — A Gratifying Array of Facts.

It is only within a few years past that the manufacturing interests of Omaha have assumed importance, which fact is due, chiefly, to the lack of cheap fuel. The development of coal mines in Iowa, Kansas and Missouri, with the gradual reduction of freight rates by the railroad companies and the introduction of electricity as a motive power for manufacturers, has produced great and most gratifying results in this connection, and now Omaha occupies a high station as a manufacturing center, the total capital invested at the close of 1892 being $12,267,600.00.

Manufacturing began with the beginning of Omaha, and the first thing attempted in this line was the making of brick on the block bounded by Fourteenth, Fifteenth, Leavenworth and Marcy Streets. Here, in the summer of 1854, Ben Winchester, the contractor for brick for the territorial capitol, prepared a kiln for burning and covered it with canvas to protect it from rain. The canvas was stolen (whether by Indians or whites, tradition saith not) and a heavy rain falling at night reduced the shapely parallelopipeds to a formless pile of clay. Thus ended the first attempt to manufacture in Omaha, and the bricks for the structure were brought from the Iowa side of the river. A little later O. B. Selden, the pioneer blacksmith, erected his forge on the north side of Howard between Thirteenth and Fourteenth Streets, where he became an important adjunct to Omaha's incipient greatness.

In the same year a saw mill was established by Thomas Davis at the corner of Ninth and Jackson Streets. This was close to the corner of the present Union Pacific freight depot. In 1855 Smith & Salisbury erected a saw mill on the bank of the river about 200 yards above the spot where later stood the old water works pumping station. To this mill logs were rafted down from points higher up the river. These mills were kept busy and the lumber was not generally allowed to remain long on the yard. In order to get lumber it was often necessary to have a team ready to haul it away as soon as it was sawed, for the rule, first come, first served, applied, and he who waited to allow others to be first supplied, often went away empty handed. The demand for lumber and fuel soon caused the destruction of the forest about Omaha and with it the mills also disappeared. It was not till 1858 that a permanent factory was established and then the first of the

### CARRIAGE FACTORIES

was erected and business began by Andrew J. Simpson, who has the oldest established carriage manufactory in Nebraska. He engaged in that business in this city in that year, coming from Sacramento, California, and opening a small shop on Douglas Street, near Fourteenth, but for many years his business has been conducted in a three-story brick building, erected by himself, on Dodge Street, west of Fourteenth. He employs thirty-five men.

Frost & Harris—Harry Frost and L. D. Harris—both former employes of Andrew J. Simpson, began business for themselves in

May, 1889, at the corner of Twenty-third and Izard Streets, and now employ twenty-five men, doing an extensive business in carriage manufacturing and repairing.

William R. Drummond & Co., located in a three-story brick building, on Eighteenth Street, near Farnam, have twenty-five thousand dollars capital. Their business as carriage manufacturers was begun in this city in 1885. They employ twenty-eight workmen.

E. D. Meadimber is the successor of the firm of Meadimber & Dally, which began the business of carriage making in 1875, on the corner of Sixteenth Street and Capitol Avenue, employing two men. In 1881 that partnership was dissolved. In July, 1890, the factory then occupied by Mr. Meadimber, on the corner of Sixteenth and Chicago Streets, burned, entailing a loss of thirty-five thousand dollars, but Phœnix-like he rose from the ashes, and within twenty-four hours from the time the fire broke out he had an awning stretched over the hardly-cold brick walls of his late factory, and a portion of his men were at work as usual, and within forty-five days from the time of the fire he had erected a substantial brick factory at 1513 and 1515 Chicago Street, forty-four feet wide, 132 feet long and four stories high, with modern machinery and run by electric power. Fifty men are now employed and all sorts of carriages are made.

William Suyder began the business of carriage manufacture in 1879. The work of the first year was done by himself. Since then he has gradually increased the number of his employes, having at the present time twelve men. He makes a specialty of fine carriage work. The factory is located at the corner of Fourteenth and Harney Streets.

B. H. Osterhoudt is proprietor of the Cass Street Carriage Works. The business was begun in 1887.

The Cuming Street Carriage Works are operated by F. W. Simpson. The business was started in 1886.

The carriage works of William Pfeiffer are located at the southwest corner of Twenty-eighth and Leavenworth Streets.

### IRON WORKERS.

P. J. Karbach is one of Omaha's old settlers. In 1858 he was in the employ of his brother, Charles J. Karbach, blacksmith, who then had a shop on Douglas Street, where Beard Brothers are now. For two years following 1866 the brothers were partners in business. Then P. J. Karbach opened a shop, and in 1870 added wagon making, which he has continued till the present time. He is now located at 1312 Howard Street, where he has a substantial brick building of three stories, and employs eight men.

W. Boehl, proprietor of the Acme Iron and Wire Works, has been in the business since 1869. After experiencing some reverses he finally built the establishment he now occupies at 512 South Sixteenth Street.

T. M. Trevett, machinist, established himself in the locksmith and repair business on Douglas Street in 1869. Later he was burned out. In 1888 he removed to his present place, 714 South Fourteenth Street, where he manufactures elevators and does a general manufacturing and repair business, employing seven hands.

E. P. Davis is president, J. B. Cowgill general superintendent and H. S. McDonald secretary of the Davis & Cowgill Iron Works, manufacturers and jobbers of machinery. They employ fifty men and are extensive manufacturers of electric street railroad cut gearing. Their machinery finds a market throughout the west from British Columbia to Texas and as far east as Indiana.

John McLearie and E. Oehrle are the proprietors of the Phenix Foundry and Machine Company, which arose from the ashes of a business of the same kind carried on by these gentlemen at Twenty-fifth and Patrick Streets until burned down in 1889. They now employ twenty-five men at the works on Pinkney Street and Belt Line.

Wearne Brothers are proprietors of a foundry at 1409 Jackson Street. The business dates from 1880. Fifteen men are employed, and their castings are sent over the entire north-west.

The Mid-Continent Boiler Works, corner of Pierce and Nineteenth Streets, Wilson & Drake, proprietors, carry on an extensive business in the line of boilers, tanks, etc., with $30,000 invested. The establishment employs thirty men.

Carter & Son have been engaged in the manufacture of boilers, tanks, smoke stacks, etc., in Omaha since 1888, on the B. & M. railway tracks at the intersection of Twentieth Street. Twenty men are employed by this firm.

C. Specht is proprietor of the Western Cornice Works, which were started up in Omaha in 1880, with four or five men, now employing fifty to seventy. Mr. Specht has done an extensive business during the late building era, having done the work in his line on many of the finest buildings in the city.

The Eagle Cornice Works, John Epeneter, proprietor, are situated at 1110, 1112 Dodge Street, having been moved from Council Bluffs in 1885. Thirty men are employed. Ornamental stamping is done here, these being the only works where this kind of work is done west of Chicago.

McBrien & Carter are manufacturers of sheet metal cornice work, etc., at 110 South Eleventh Street. They employ five men and have been established here since 1889.

J. J. Leddy is proprietor of the Champion Iron and Wire Works, at 403 South Fourteenth Street, which have been in operation since 1887, employing ten men.

The Omaha Machine Works were located in Omaha in 1888, and give employment to fifteen men. The proprietors are C. O. Michaelson and C. F. Jorgenson.

The Omaha Safe and Iron Works of G. Andreen, at 610, 612 South Fourteenth Street, have been operated since 1875. Mr. Andreen is an inventor and has three patents on articles of his manufacture. In July, 1892, Earl W. Gannett purchased an interest in these works, of which G. Andreen is president and manager, and Mr. Gannett secretary and treasurer. Fifteen men are employed.

John Pabian has machine works at 1209 South Thirteenth Street. The business was started in 1890.

The Omaha Manufacturing Company was established here in 1891. Wrought iron and steel ribbon fencing are manufactured. Wm. C. Smith and Isaac N. Hamilton are the proprietors.

The Martin & Morrissey Manufacturing Company, of East Omaha, manufactures feed steamers, tank heaters and special machinery, and also does all kinds of casting. This company began business in Iowa in 1888 and accepted the inducements offered by the East Omaha Land Company and located in East Omaha in July, 1890, being the second manufacturing company there. The building occupied is forty by ninety feet in size, part of it being two stories. Work is given to a number of men varying from twelve to twenty.

The Paxton & Vierling Iron Works, capital $125,000, corner of Seventeenth Street and the Union Pacific Railway, are the outcome of a small establishment located on Cass Street a dozen years ago, known as the Cass Street Foundry, of which T. W. T. Richards and L. G. Heybrook were the proprietors. The destruction of the building by fire caused a removal of the business to the present site, and in 1886 it passed into the ownership of Wm. A. Paxton, Robert Vierling, Louis Vierling and A. J. Vierling, who now occupy the positions of president, vice president, secretary and treasurer, and manager, respectively, in the order named. Great success has attended the enterprise, and the establishment is now favorably known all over the west. Two hundred and fifty men are constantly employed. The manufactured product of these works amounts to $300,000.00 annually. The company owns four acres of land, so that there is abundant room for growth.

The manufacture of barbed wire for fencing purposes was inaugurated in Omaha by Thomas Gibson while secretary of the Board of Trade. He commenced in a small way at the foot of Capitol Avenue in 1880. A few years since M. M. Marshall, O. N. Ramsey, W. J. Broatch and others purchased the plant, and it was by them removed to the corner of Fourteenth and Nicholas Streets, where $50,000 was expended in ground and buildings. Employment was given to one hundred men, the manufacture of wire, nails and wood fence pickets was added and the business largely increased. The company was later styled the Omaha Barb Wire Fence and Nail Company. The officers were: Jeff W. Bedford, president; Thomas H. Taylor, manager; Charles Burmester, secretary and treasurer; the capital being $150,000., and the annual product of barbed wire four or five thousand tons—enough to encircle the world once or make a five wire fence long enough to inclose twice the amount of land in the States of North and South Dakota, Nebraska and Kansas, and then have some to spare. The company was unable to compete with the larger factories of the kind, and closed down in the fall of 1892.

Nail works were established in this city in the spring or 1878, a temporary building being erected on the north side of the Union Pacific track between Sixteenth and Seventeenth Streets. Machinery to the value of $14,000 was put in and work carried on quite actively for a time. John A. Creighton was president of the company; G. T. Walker, vice-president and superintendent; James Creighton, secretary and treasurer; John A. McShane, assistant secretary and treasurer; and Robt. W. Wilson, assistant superintendent. The company had a paid up capital of $50,000. During 1879 40,000 kegs of nails were made and an additional outlay of $12,500 made, in providing more machinery and extending the buildings. Legal complications arising, work was suspended for several years, but in 1886 Mr. Walker re-organized the company, his associates being W. H. Havens, W. N. McCandlish and George C. Towle. A considerable sum of money was expended during that year and the year following in improvements, and a quantity of nails were manufactured. It was then decided to remove the works to some locality where more ground could be secured and re-built on a much more extensive plan, and the company concluded to accept a very generous offer made by certain property owners at St. Joseph, Mo., and in 1888 the plant was removed to that city.

UNION PACIFIC RAILROAD SHOPS.

When the Union Pacific Railroad Company began the construction of its road, shops were established here in a small way. The investment has been gradually increased, as the needs of the road required, until $2,510,-000 have been expended in machinery and buildings, and now about sixty acres of ground are covered by the buildings, in which are carried on all the industries connected with shops of this character; the plant being the largest and most complete of its kind west of Chicago. The number of men employed, January 1, 1893, was 1,385, and the average number for the year 1892 was 1,318. The wages paid during the year to employes of the shops was $1,377,226, an average per month of nearly $115,000. The value of the output will aggregate more than $3,750,000, which includes the building of sixteen locomotives and the repairing of 250; the building and repairing of 5,911 freight and 250 passenger cars. Over 6,000 tons of castings were made, used and shipped to the other shops of the railroad system. The furnaces used 12,150 tons of coal during the year. J. H. McConnell is the superintendent of motive power and machinery; J. H. Manning, division master mechanic; A. M. Collett, general foreman car department; O. E. Gugler, foreman of the shops; Edward Richelieu of the foundries, and A. A. Gibson of the blacksmith shop. The location of these shops at Omaha adds fully 7,000 persons to its population.

### TINWARE FACTORIES.

The Western Tinware Manufacturing Company—M. M. Gowdy, C. G. Newell and M. G. Kibbe—began business January 1, 1890. Twenty-five persons find employment in the manufacture of pieced ware. The company also handles stamped and japanned tinware. On account of the growth of this industry this firm moved, January 1, 1892, from its former quarters at 614-18 South Eleventh Street to 1211 Harney Street, where increased facilities afford the requisites for increased production.

The Omaha Tinware Manufacturing Company — William Wallace, president; Frank P. Hanlon, vice president; Lewis Ley, manager; and C. Wright, superintendent — commenced business January 1, 1890, having been organized the year previous. The business is conducted at Nos. 1316-18 Jones Street, and employs seventy-five hands. The manufactured articles, among which are one million cans, being sold throughout Iowa, Nebraska, South Dakota, Wyoming and Colorado. Four car loads of tin plate per month are used.

### SHOT WORKS.

The Omaha Shot and Lead Works, formerly the Northwestern Shot and Lead Company, have been in successful operation for twelve years, the first location being on South Twenty-fourth Street, in Wilcox's addition. New works of a solid and expensive character were built in 1890, on Seventeenth Street near Mason. F. B. Lawrence is president and T. H. Merriam secretary of the company.

### SMELTING WORKS.

The Omaha & Grant Smelting Company was organized October 15, 1870, by C. H. Downs, Wm. H. Pier, John A. Horbach and W. W. Lowe, with a capital stock of $60,000, which amount was expended in construction within a year or two. In its early history A. L. King, Leopold Balbach, C. W. Mead, C. B. Rustin and E. W. Nash were identified with the company, Mr. Nash being the only one of all of the above named who is now connected with it. Mr. Charles Balbach was superintendent of the works from 1871 to 1888. In August, 1882, the Grant Smelting Company, of Denver, Colorado, was consolidated with the Omaha company and a re-organization was effected with a capital of $2,500,000.00 fully paid in. The present officers are: Guy C. Barton, president; James B. Grant, vice-president; E. W. Nash, secretary and treasurer; Edward Eddy, general manager. The money invested in buildings and machinery at Omaha and Denver foots up something over $1,000,000. The business for the year 1892, amounted to $21,354,000. More than one thousand men are employed at Omaha and Denver by the company—now the largest of its kind in the world—and over $70,000 per month is paid out for salaries and wages. The buildings are of the most substantial character, and those in this city, with the yards, cover about twenty-five acres of ground. The establishment handles silver, lead and copper ores from the western States and territories, Mexico and the British possessions. The following is a statement of the product of the business for 1892:

48,000 tons lead, valued at ................... $ 3,840,000
17,000,000 ounces of silver, valued at ..... 14,716,550
123 000 ounces of gold, valued at ......... 2,534,800
1000 tons copper and sulphate, val. at ... 263 500

Total value ........................................ $21,354,850·

### WHITE LEAD WORKS.

The Carter White Lead Company is the successor to the Omaha White Lead Company, which established in Omaha the first white lead works west of Chicago and St. Louis and started them up about the first of August, 1878. The original stockholders

THE SMELTING WORKS DURING THE FLOOD OF 1881.

RUINS OF THE GRAND CENTRAL HOTEL, BURNED SEPTEMBER, 1878.

were Wm. A. Paxton, Levi Carter, C. Hartman, W. B. Royal, C. W. Mead, N. Shelton, D. O. Clark and S. E. Locke. The company was organized with a capital stock of $60,000, with C. W. Mead, president; N. Shelton, secretary and S. E. Lock, manager; the capacity of the works being about 1,000 tons per year, and the working force numbering about twenty. In 1881 the capacity of the works was increased to fifteen hundred tons per year and the, capital to ninety thousand dollars. The business flourished for two or three years and then, on account of the low price received for the manufactured product during the last part of 1885, the affairs of the company were brought to a close. In January, 1886, the works and business were sold to Mr. L. Carter, who organized the Carter White Lead Company, with a capital of $150,000, with L. Carter, president; H. W. Yates, vice-president, and S. B. Hayden, secretary. In 1889 the capital was increased to $500,000, Mr. Yates selling his interest to Messrs. Carter and Hayden. In the latter part of 1889 improvements costing sixty thousand dollars, and increasing the capacity of the plant to over four thousand tons per year, were added, and the working force increased to about fifty men. On June 14, 1890, the works were completely destroyed by fire and on the 15th of July the company commenced the erection of new works, costing nearly $200,000, and having a capacity of ten thousand tons per year, at East Omaha, and by the first of December, of the same year, they were completed and in operation. There are now employed at the works from sixty to seventy-five men, and the weekly pay-roll amounts to from $650 to $800. During the year 1892 the company's sales amounted to seven thousand tons, or fourteen million pounds of pure white lead, of the value of one million dollars. All the pig lead used is bought from the Omaha and Grant Smelting and Refining Company. The increasing business of these works, now among the largest in the country, is expected to require their enlargement during the coming year.

GAS WORKS.

January 15, 1868, two petitions were presented in the City Council praying for authority for the supplying of Omaha with gas—one by George B. Groff and others, on behalf of "The Omaha Gas Company," and the other by Enos Lowe and others, representing "The Omaha Gas Manufacturing Company." The petitions were referred to a special committee, which afterwards presented a favorable report, which was adopted, and the proper ordinance drafted and also adopted. The first named company did not prosecute the work, however; but Dr. Lowe's company perfected its organization and went about their task with considerable enthusiasm. Two lots were leased to the company by the city for a term of thirty years from February 19, 1868, at the nominal rental of five dollars a year, the city having the right to buy the works at an appraised value at the end of fifteen years. In November, 1869, the Gas Company reported to the Council that the total number of consumers of gas was 198. One year later there were only one hundred street lamps in the city. From these small beginnings the business has steadily increased. Employment is now given to 125 men, to whom $6,000 is disbursed monthly. The works were extended during the year 1890 at an outlay of $100,000, including $60,000 paid for a new gas holder at the corner of Twentieth and Center Streets, since which time about $25,000 has been annually paid out for repairs and extensions. The company has now nearly 4,000 patrons, and there are nearly 800 street lamps. Five thousand tons of coal are consumed yearly, brought chiefly from Pennsylvania. Three-fourths of the block bounded by Jones, Leavenworth, Eleventh and Twelfth Streets is covered by the buildings of the company, but it is purposed to remove the manufacturing plant to the tract of three acres owned by the company at Twentieth and Center Streets. The three gas holders have a capacity of 900,000 feet. There are eighty-five miles of mains. Frank Murphy is president of the company, George E. Barker secretary and Isaac Battin treasurer and superintendent. The company has a capital of $500,000, with a funded debt of $300,000. During 1890, $52,000 was expended in additions and improvements.

### STONE CUTTING.

Fred Drexel and John M. Drexel, cut stone contractors, began business here in 1859, at the corner of Eighth and Jones Streets, and continued as partners one year. Fred Drexel has been in the business continuously since that time. The firm of Drexel & Foll, of which he is senior partner, was formed in the fall of 1884. H. P. Drexel became a partner in the firm in 1885. The saw mill and yard are located at the corner of Fifth and Jones Streets, where the company have the latest improved machinery, and employ an average of seventy-five men throughout the year. The trade of this company extends into Iowa on the east and as far north and west as Dakota and Western Nebraska.

On the 20th day of November, 1892, the stone saw mill, together with all the machinery in it, was wholly destroyed by fire, the loss being about $8,000. The mill will be rebuilt immediately.

Benjamin Melquist has been in the cut stone business since the spring of 1883, when he started with three employes. His large yards are situated at 501 Jones Street. He now employs twenty-five men.

Schall & Hering are also cut stone contractors, with mill and yard on Jones between Fifth and Sixth Streets. They employ from twenty to forty-five men.

The principal part of the building stone used in the construction of buildings here is brought from other states. Gray sandstone from Warrensburg, Missouri; Oolitic limestone from Bedford, Indiana; blue sandstone from Cleveland, Ohio; red sandstone from Portage, Wisconsin, Colorado Springs, Colorado, and from Arizona and Wyoming; white limestone from Joliet, Illinois; brown stone from Ashland, Wisconsin, and pink and white sandstone from Kasota, Minnesota.

### PLANING MILLS.

A. Moyer is proprietor of the Gate City Planing Mills, at 106, 108, 110 South Ninth Street. He built a one story wooden building on the site of the present mill in 1877, employing four men at the beginning. In 1884 the finishing rooms burnt, involving a loss of $7,000; insurance, none. A second fire broke out in the main building in the spring of 1886 and destroyed nearly the whole building, involving a loss of five thousand dollars, with precisely the same amount of insurance he had at the first fire. He immediately rebuilt the factory, making it two stories and put in new and improved machinery. The number of employes is now generally from fifteen to twenty-five.

F. H. Miller began the manufacture of sash, doors, blinds, etc., at the corner of Twenty-ninth Street and Belt Line Railway, in August, 1887. The following February he took as a partner G. M. Gunderson, and the firm of Miller & Gunderson was formed. The factory is two stories high and eighty-six by one hundred feet in terrestrial dimensions. This business employed ten men at the outset and now employs from twenty to fifty.

M. A. Disbrow & Co., corner of Twelfth and Izard Streets, are wholesale manufacturers of sash, doors, blinds, etc. M. A. Disbrow, of Lyons, Iowa, is president, and M. B. Copeland, of Omaha, is secretary and treasurer. The business was begun here in 1886. Fifteen men are employed. The main office and factory are at Lyons, Iowa.

A. Rosenberry, whose extensive planing mill is located at the corner of Fifteenth and Marcy, began business in 1879, in a small way. He now employs fifty men and has one of the best equipped establishments in the West.

John F. Coots, one of the most extensive contractors in the West, has a large planing mill at Sixth and Jones Streets.

Richard Stevens & Sons' planing mill occupies Nos. 214 to 220 North Twenty-eighth Avenue, and gives employment to twenty shop men and twenty to forty men on building contracts, paying out $6,000 a month for wages.

### BOX FACTORIES.

Frank R. Heft manufactures cigar boxes at 1501 Jackson street. In 1884 he started on Capitol Avenue in a 12x14 room, and made boxes by hand. In 1889 he took possession of his present quarters, where he turns out 90,000 cigar boxes annually, with the aid of five people. Mr. Heft has the best of modern machinery and finds a market for his products throughout the central west.

J. J. Wilkinson is proprietor of the City Box Factory, at 1110 Douglas Street. F. C. Feckenscher began the business, and after running three or four years succeeded by Mr. Wilkinson, who assumed control of the business in May, 1891. About fifteen persons are employed, most of whom are girls.

The Consolidated Box Manufacturing Company was, at the beginning of the enterprise, Vogel Brothers. In August, 1889, L. D. and J. W. Vogel leased an acre of ground on Twenty-Sixth and Walnut Streets and erected a planing mill of one story, sixty by eighty feet in size. In September, 1890, they added a large box factory and a lumber shed. In May, 1891 this firm became stockholders in the Consolidated Box Manufacturing Company, with factories at St. Louis, Denver, Muscatine and other places, putting the factory into the combination and taking stock to the amount of the property contributed. Thirty-five men are employed here, and packing boxes of all kinds are manufactured, consuming in the business over two million feet of lumber annually.

H. B. Mulford & Co. are the proprietors of the Omaha Box Factory, at the corner of Twenty-first Street and Avenue H, East Omaha. The factory is one hundred feet wide and 190 feet long and two stories high, contains four sets of saws and has a capacity of five thousand boxes per day. The product is mostly packing boxes, of which 300,000 were made in 1891, and the output for 1892 was nearly 800,000. The dovetailing machinery is a duplicate of that of the well known Paepcke & Co., of Chicago, and is the only duplicate of their machinery ever made or sold by that firm. The factory began operations January 1, 1891, and employs sixty-five men. Most of the manufactured product is sold in this city, but some of it is sent to points in Iowa, Nebraska and Kansas.

In connection with the above, F. S. Knapp conducts the Omaha Kindling Factory. Acting upon the universally applicable principle, " Let nothing be wasted," Mr. Knapp has the refuse of the factory collected and prepared for sale. The kindling is sold in bundles or wagon loads; the sawdust is sifted and sold by the barrel for packing purposes and for spreading upon floors. The business amounts to about $400 per month.

The Omaha Paper Box Factory—John L. Wilkie, proprietor—has been established ten years. This industry was begun by the proprietor, aided by one assistant. At the end of a year he employed five hands, and now employs twenty. The business occupies two rooms twenty by eighty feet in size, with basement, at 1822 and 1824 St. Mary's Avenue. All kinds of paper boxes are made. Seven carloads of strawboard were used last year. From twelve to fifteen hundred boxes are made daily, mostly for the candy, cracker and shoe trade.

The Omaha Basket Manufacturing Company, of which Oscar J. Pickard is president, G. E. Ferry, vice president; C. J. Roberts, superintendent, and G. D. Keller secretary and treasurer, has a capital of $20,000, and furnishes work for twenty-five employes. The business was established in November, 1888, the factory being located at Westlawn and the office at 1318 Jones Street.

The Omaha Casket Company began business in the fall of 1887, in a large factory at the intersection of North Twenty-ninth Street and the Belt Line. The business is now owned by Messrs. McClatchen & Andrews, who have recently made extensive additions to the plant.

### FURNITURE FACTORIES.

Murphy, Wasey & Co. are manufacturers of chairs, wire mattresses, spring beds and cots. The business, which was established by this company in Detroit in 1872, was begun here in 1889. Land was purchased on Spaulding Street at the corner of the Belt Line Railway, and a factory sixty by one hundred and fifty-three feet on the ground, and three stories high, a ware room one hundred and twenty feet square and five stories high, and an engine room, were erected. 25,000 spring beds are manufactured annually. 270,000 chairs manufactured at Detroit are sold here to supply the trade naturally tributary to Omaha. From ninety to one hundred and ten persons, many of them boys and girls, are usually employed. The business here is run on a paid up capital of $150,000. The officers of the company are: M. J. Murphy, president; Geo. E. Wasey, secretary and treasurer, Detroit; James F. Murphy, vice-president, and Henry Whitney, assistant treasurer, Omaha.

The Beebe & Runyan Furniture Co. was incorporated in February, 1891; capital stock $100,000, of which $50,000 is paid in; officers, C. A. Beebe, president; E. Beebe, secretary; W. Runyan, treasurer; and W. Beebe, manager. The factory and warehouse, a large three story building, is located on Thirteenth and Grace Streets and is isolated, in fact, away out on the bottom, as it might be expressed, where, however, there will be many more busy factories in the near future, as the mechanical industries of Omaha are fast spreading in that direction. Twenty-five persons are employed. The company manufactures mattresses and does a jobbing business in furniture in the states contiguous to Nebraska, and in the territories.

The E. M. Hulse Company was incorporated in January, 1889, and is the successor of the E. M. Hulse Mattress Company. E. M. Hulse is president; W. C. Hayner, secretary; H. A. Shipman, treasurer. The factory is of two stories, sixty-six by one hundred and thirty-two feet. at 1307 to 1311 Nicholas Street, and gives employment to sixty men in the manufacture of lounges.

The firm of Billow & Doup is composed of N. K. Billow and L. G. Doup. They manufacture mattresses and pillows at Fourteenth and Davenport Streets, where the business has been carried on since January 1, 1891. They employ fifteen people and manufacture five thousand dollars worth of goods monthly, which are sent to all parts of the West.

The Omaha Upholstering Company manufacture parlor furniture at 1302-1306 Nicholas Street, and has been in operation two years. From twenty to twenty-five hands are employed. The officers of the company are: A. Lehman, president; H. L. Axtater, secretary; H. A. Shipman, treasurer.

The Omaha Mattress Company manufactures mattresses and comforters, occupying a portion of the above mentioned building. It began business in March, 1890, succeeding to this line of manufacturing, which the E. M. Hulse Company then discontinued. Ten persons are employed. H. Jenter is president, and O. B. Anderson is secretary and treasurer of this company.

Frederick Krause owns and operates the Nebraska Broom Factory, at 1317 Chicago Street. In the fall of 1880 he began business at 1101 South Third Street, succeeding

## MANUFACTURING INTERESTS.

August Pandow. The factory, with the entire plant, stock and manufactured goods, was destroyed by fire in October, 1883, involving a loss of six thousand dollars, upon which there was not a cent of insurance. Financially crippled, but not discouraged, he rebuilt at his present location, at a cost of four thousand dollars, putting in the latest improved machinery. The factory now employs eleven persons, uses electric power and turns out eight or nine thousand dozen brooms annually, which amount would be doubled if " home industries " were properly patronized.

### LINSEED OIL WORKS.

In the spring of 1872 the oil mills now operated by the Woodman Linseed Oil Company were established by M. H. Harris, Robert K. Taft and Clark Woodman, under the firm name of Harris, Taft & Woodman, with a capital of $40,000 invested in grounds, buildings and machinery, and an additional fund of about $75,000 for operating expenses. The company loaned out to the farmers of Nebraska that spring 2,000 bushels of flax seed in order to encourage the growth of that staple, resulting in the marketing, the following fall, of about 20,000 bushels of seed, which was converted by the company into oil and oil cake, and thus was laid the foundation for a business which has since grown into enormous proportions. The death of Mr. Harris left the style of the firm Taft & Woodman, and so it continued until December, 1880, when Mr. Taft withdrew from the firm, removing to San Jose, California, soon afterwards, where he is now successfully engaged in fruit culture. The early years of the business were marked with difficulties and discouragements, but these were overcome, the buildings added to from year to year, and improved machinery introduced. The company now employ sixty men, paying out for wages over $3,000 monthly, and the sales for 1892 footed up $1,500,000. Since the death of Mr. Woodman the business has been managed by Frank E. Ritchie.

### PRINTING.

On the 1st day of May, 1880, Samuel Rees purchased the plant of the printing office and bookbindery of the Omaha Book Company. Mr. Rees had been superintendent of the job department of the Omaha *Republican* office for four years, previous to this time. He conducted the business alone until 1884, when the Rees Printing Company was organized, the principal stockholder, beside Mr. Rees, being Mr. John F. Fairlie, who had been for years connected with the business, and who had conducted the bindery of the Omaha Book Company, and formerly the bindery of Fairlie & Monell, of which he was the senior partner. Constant additions were made to the machinery, type and working force until 1887, when the company purchased the lithographic and printing office of the Omaha Lithograph and Stationery Company. Mr. Edward Haymaker had been the practical manager and one of the leading stockholders of the latter company, and became one of the stockholders in the Rees Printing Company and superintendent of the lithographic department. Though only a small office when Mr. Rees purchased it, the plant has become one of the largest in this line in the western country. Its present officers are: Samuel Rees, president; John F. Fairlie, vice president; Edward Haymaker, secretary.

The Festner Printing Co., 1307 Howard Street, is composed of Julius T. Festner, August Droste and Geo. B. Tzschuck. This firm is the successor of F. C. Festner, who began the business in October, 1872, as a bookbinder, occupying a small room on the corner of Twelfth and Farnam Streets. In 1876, printing in a small way was added. In 1882 the *Nebraska Daily Tribune* (German) was started. In 1887 the present four story brick building, 33x100 feet, was built.

Mr. F. C. Festner died in 1890, and the present company succeed to the business the following November.

The Western Newspaper Union, auxiliary publishers or printers, whose business is that of supplying country and other weekly newspapers with "ready prints" containing general news and miscellaneous reading, is the most extensive printing establishment of its kind in the United States. It is the outgrowth of the Iowa State Printing Company, of Des Moines, Iowa, which was organized in 1872. In the year 1879, through the efforts of George A. Joslyn, who had recently become connected with the enterprise, the company was reorganized as the Western Newspaper Union, the intention being to supply partly printed sheets to country newspapers in the territory lying between the Ohio River and the Rocky Mountains. Since its reorganization the company has greatly increased its business and at the present time has plants in twelve cities, with sixty large fast cylinder presses, and over thirty newspaper folding machines. The number of newspapers printed by the company is over 1,900. The Omaha house was started in the spring of 1880, and now employs thirty-eight persons. Seven cylinder presses, three newspaper folders and two complete stereotyping outfits are kept constantly at work supplying about 250 newspapers. In addition to supplying these, their office does the local presswork for nearly all of the papers printed in Omaha, outside of the large dailies. The work here is under the immediate supervision of Mr. Joslyn, the president of the company, who is assisted by Col. H. C. Akin, who has been connected with the office for several years.

Omaha Republican Printing Company has existed since 1884, and now employs about seventy-five persons. This company, besides the usual job printing, does a large amount of work for county officers, binds books, makes electrotypes and deals in stationery and supplies of various kinds. The officers of the company are: A. H. Comstock, president; Ray Nye, vice president; C. E. Brown, secretary and treasurer. The capital stock is $100,000, of which $65,000 is paid in. The four story building at the corner of Tenth and Douglas Streets, occupied by this company, was burned on the night of January 5th, 1893, the loss to the company amounting to $50,000, insurance $45,000.

The American Press Association has one of its numerous branches at Omaha, which was established here in October, 1886, with M. G. Perkins manager, who still retains that position. The Omaha branch employs from twenty-five to thirty men and furnishes stereotype plates to newspapers in Iowa, Kansas, Nebraska, Missouri, Colorado, Wyoming and Utah.

Ackerman Bros. & Heintze are railroad and book printers, binders and electrotypers at 1116 Howard Street, where they occupy a five story building, fully equipped with the machinery incident to their business, employing from fifty to seventy persons. This house started in a small way in October, 1887. The firm uses, as one of the items in its business, twelve carloads of railroad manilla paper annually.

The firm of Klopp, Bartlett & Co., printers, binders and blank book makers, 1114-1116 Farnam Street, is composed of C. H. Klopp, E. W. Bartlett and A. T. Klopp, who started in May, 1885, with a capital of $6,000, using foot power presses and employing a very small number of hands. The firm now employs thirty persons, using four cylinder and two job presses run by a gas engine. The capital now employed is $28,000.

Fleming & Black are proprietors of the Western Stereotyping, Electrotyping and Plating Works, at 1112-16 Dodge Street, where they employ seven men. This business was established in 1890.

The Burkley Printing Company was incorporated October 1, 1891, with F. J. Burkley, president; D. C. Shelley, vice president; H. V. Burkley, secretary and treasurer, and

V. Burkley. Previous to incorporation the company had existed a year and a half, the Burkleys being the members of the company. The amount of capital stock is twenty thousand dollars, paid up, and the number of employes sixteen. Eight presses are run.

E. P. Walker is the successor of Tagger & Walker, book-binders and blank-book makers, 1121 Farnam. The business was begun in 1884. Six persons are employed.

### CLOTHING AND BAG FACTORIES.

The Katz-Nevens Company, of which Charles F. Nevens is president and Samuel Katz secretary and treasurer, manufactures pants, shirts and overalls. This business was begun in 1884 by the Canfield Manufacturing Co., which was bought out by the present company in 1889. The employes are mostly girls and number about 125. The annual product of this factory is about 13,500 dozen garments.

The increasing business of the last two years has compelled this factory to seek more commodious accommodations and January 1, 1892, the plant was removed from the Bemis Omaha Bag Factory building to Eleventh and Douglas Streets.

The Robinson & Stokes Company succeeded the J. T. Robinson Notion Company, January, 1892. The former company began the jobbing business in 1885 and in 1889 bought out the DeGraff Manufacturing Company's plant and began manufacturing overalls, work shirts, jumpers and pantaloons, employing 125 persons, six of whom were traveling salesmen. Receiving encouragment to locate at East Omaha, this company erected a commodious brick factory there of fifty feet front, one hundred and fifty feet deep and four stories high, specially adapted to the needs of the business, with dynamo for electric light, elevator, etc., and accommodations for one thousand operatives. In the autumn of the same year this company failed, for want of sufficient capital to run the business, and, in January, 1893, was succeeded by the Kilpatrick-Koch Dry Goods Co., who added the manufacture of clothing to their former business.

About April 1, 1892, F. S. King and J. P. Smead, formerly with Frank Howard & Co., of Atchison. Kansas, began the manufacture of pants, shirts and other clothing in Omaha. The firm of King & Smead now employs seventy operatives and three traveling men and turns out forty-five dozen garments per day.

An account of the manufactory of M. E. Smith & Co., is given in chapter on Commerce.

The Omaha National Knitting Factory is located at the corner of Fifteenth and Howard Streets, Bilz Brothers, proprietors. It has been in operation since 1885, employs eight persons and turns out various kinds of knit goods.

The Bemis Omaha Bag Co., manufacturer of burlaps and cotton bags, and dealer in grain bags and twines, located here in the spring of 1887, with a capital of $750,000, and erected a large five story brick building on Eleventh Street, at the north end of the viaduct. A business of more than $700,000 was transacted during 1890. Among other items one hundred car loads of flour sacks and fifty of burlap bags were made and sold. At the start about twenty-five hands were employed, and now (December, 1892) one hundred persons are employed, and 12,000 tons of material have been handled during the present year. The trade extends from the Missouri River to the Pacific coast, a large amount of goods being consigned to the latter region. The members of this company are: J. M. Bemis, president, Boston; S. A. Bemis, secretary, St. Louis, and M. C. Peters, local manager at Omaha.

B. Gotheimer, 1314 Farnam Street, shirt manufacturer, employs fifteen hands; has been in business ten years.

G. E. Cutts, successor to William H. Harrison, 1114 Farnam Street, shirt manufacturer, who had been in business here for ten years, employs ten hands.

Lewis Baer, shirt manufacturer, 1505 Howard Street, has been in business two years, and employs fifteen hands.

### MERCHANT TAILORS.

Frank J. Ramge started in business, in Omaha, in the spring of 1864, and is now the senior draper and tailor in the city. For a short time he did all his work himself. He has never been in partnership, except a short time with J. H. Stein. His experience with fire has been somewhat unique. Although a fire has never originated on his premises, and his goods have never been damaged by fire, yet, on five different occasions it has consumed adjoining buildings and compelled him to remove his stock. In 1887 Mr. Ramge erected the handsome Ramge block, sixty by one hundred and thirty-two feet, five stories high, at the corner of Fifteenth and Harney Streets, in which his extensive tailoring establishment is located.

C. J. Canan and J. J. Heller do business at 1302 Douglas Street as C. J. Canan & Co. Mr. Canan has been in the tailoring business for a long time, and his business is the next oldest in this line, in Omaha.

Helin & Thompson are located at 1612 Farnam Street. John F. Helin, the senior partner has been in business in Omaha since 1874, at which time he was associated with G. A. Lindquist. In 1887 the present partnership with C. W. Thompson was formed. In connection with their trade this firm carries a stock of furnishing goods.

Helin, Thompson & Co. are importers and jobbers of woolens and tailors trimmings. George E. Warner is the junior partner. This firm has existed since 1889.

"Ed. Hart, the tailor," is located at 210-212 South Sixteenth Street, where he began business in 1890. This is one of a number of establishments he has in the larger cities of the northern States. The business compares favorably with others in this line.

Nicoll the Tailor, whose establishments are located in ten large cities, including New York and Chicago, has also a house in this city at 207 South Fifteenth Street, in the fine and newly completed Karbach block. The stock carried is large, and the furnishings and appointments of the store are on a scale of elegance very pleasing to look upon.

Thomas Tallon came to Omaha in 1867, and for three years was a member of the firm of Jones, Price & Tallon, merchant tailors. From 1875 to 1890 Mr. Tallon was in the employ of M. Hellman & Co., since which time he has conducted business for himself.

Frank Vodicka, fashionable tailor, is located at 312 South Twelfth Street, in the United States National Bank building. He learned his trade years ago in Frank Ramge's establishment, and began business in 1883 in company with Joseph Papaz, the partnership continuing two years. Since that time he has conducted the business alone. Besides the city trade, of which he has a good share, he fills orders from western points.

R. Kalish began the tailoring business in Omaha in December, 1882, with just one nickel in his pocket. He has recently moved into a handsome store in the Callahan block, where he has a handsome stock of goods. Attention to business and real estate speculations have been profitable.

C. E. Shukert, furrier, at 407 South Fifteenth Street, initiated his business in this city in July, 1887, with himself and one assistant as a working force. His trade has greatly increased since, and he now employs on an average, fifteen people.

### BUTTON FACTORIES.

The making of pearl buttons is an industry of recent growth in Omaha, brought about by the immigration to this country of Bohemian button makers, who had been thrown out of employment in their native land by the action of the American tariff law on this class of manufactures. Anton Masilka started the business here in August

1890, and now employs nine men. The annual output of buttons is from eight thousand to ten thousand gross, all of which is taken by the Kilpatrick-Koch Dry Goods Company.

In November, 1891, the Western Button Manufacturing Company, Frank J. Kaspar, president, and John P. Ribyl, secretary, began business, employing twenty one and now over thirty men, and turning out a large number of buttons, which are sold throughout the West. This company at first operated on the system in use in the "old country" but now uses improved machinery.

### MANUFACTORIES OF FOOD SUPPLIES.

The Glencoe Mills were put in operation in November, 1880, by William Marsh and W. A. Smith, first as a flour mill but later the product has been confined to feed mostly.

The Omaha Milling Company built their steam mills at 1313 North Sixteenth Street, in 1887, and opened for business in March of the following year, with a capacity of 350 barrels daily. The company is composed of J. N. Paul, president; Aaron Chadwick, secretary and treasurer, and C. T. Boudinot, vice president. The authorized capital is $100,000, and the company employs twelve men.

The American Cereal Company, successor to the Pearl Hominy Company, filed its articles of incorporation in June, 1891. The capital is $100,000, of which fifty thousand is paid in. The incorporators are Dudley Smith, president; Edgar Allen, vice president; Charles L. Saunders, secretary and treasurer; Daniel Farrell, Jr., and William J. Cartan. The mills are in operation at East Omaha and have a capacity of two hundred barrels daily, of pearl flake hominy and corn meal, which find ready sale in the North and West and in the southern States. Employment is given to fifteen persons.

The New York Biscuit Company, successor to the McClurg Cracker Company, is located at Ninth and Leavenworth Streets, the business being established in 1885. The establishment has a capacity of 150 barrels of flour daily, and 102 hands were employed until it shut down, the early part of 1892.

The Garneau Cracker Company, established in St. Louis in 1832, located a branch house in Omaha in 1883, erecting a large three-story brick building at the corner of Jackson and Twelfth and filling it with the latest improvements for a wholesale bakery business. The business, under the management of Joseph Garneau, has grown so that a branch bakery for bread and cakes has been established at the corner of Thirteenth and Mason. The firm employs 105 persons. The business has been conducted, since July, 1890, by the American Biscuit and Manufacturing Company, incorporated under the laws of Illinois, with a capital of ten million dollars, with headquarters in Chicago and branches in all of the leading cities of the West and South. Joseph Garneau, Jr., remains as manager here.

The Haarmann Brothers are proprietors of the Omaha Vinegar Works, 1714 to 1718 South Twentieth Street. They built the present factory about five years ago and have been engaged in the manufacture of vinegar in Omaha since 1870. They employ eight men.

The Omaha Consolidated Vinegar Company has a factory at 1124 South Fiftieth Street, formerly known as the West Side Vinegar Works. This company is composed of J. H. Barrett, president; P. Schwenk, vice-president, and A. D. Slater, secretary and treasurer. It was incorporated in 1889, and operates on a capital of $25,000, employing eight persons.

The product of the two factories, amounting to 25,000 barrels of vinegar annually, is sold by the Haarmann Vinegar Company formed in 1891 and composed of F. Haarmann, J. H. Barrett, C. Haarmann and A. B.

Slater. Six thousand barrels of vinegar go to South Omaha to be used for pickling purposes by the packers.

The Gedney Pickle Company has $20,000 invested in plant and buildings, at the corner of Eleventh and Grace Streets, in what was formerly the Gedney Company's packing house, which has been remodeled, enlarged and fully stocked with machinery and implements necessary to the present business. Eighteen people are employed at the factory and three salesmen travel abroad. The product of 250 acres of land is put up in the form of pickles, catsups, sauce, etc., in 5,000 wooden packages and 10,000 dozen bottles, and sold through the West. The The officers of the company are W. W. Marsh, president, C. B. Gedney, vice-president and manager, and J. L. Pickering, secretary and treasurer. The factory has been in operation since July, 1890.

Kopp, Dreibus & Co., manufacture confections, and do a jobbing trade in cigars and fruits. The members of the firm are Michael Kopp, Anton Dreibus and Jacob Kopp. This industry was started in 1884. The number of employes is from thirty-five to forty-five, and the number of traveling salesmen is ten. The business amounts to $175,000 annually. This is the first steam candy factory in the State. One thousand barrels of sugar per year are used.

Vogele & Dinning are manufacturing confectioners and wholesale dealers in fruits, at 1110 Howard Street. The business was begun in 1884. They employ thirty people in the business.

Ed. Peycke and M. S. Van Deusen constitute the Peycke Candy Company, manufacturing confectioner and wholesale dealer in cigars, with a capital stock of $50,000. This company has a good share of the business in this line, and its trade extends to the Pacific slope.

Farrell & Co., manufacturers and refiners of syrups, molasses and vinegar, established themselves in business here in June, 1887.

They occupy a large brick building at the corner of Eighth and Farnam, have one hundred employes, and sell their manufactured goods throughout the entire west. The company possesses abundant capital and enterprise. The annual sales amount to nearly half a million dollars.

Grant & Sons, located at 109 South Sixteenth Street, established their business as manufacturers of confectionery in 1888, with a capital of $5,000. They have six employes.

The German Yeast Company's factory is located at Twenty-eighth and Boyd Streets and the office at 1414 Harney. The manufacture of yeast was begun in 1888, and gives employment to twenty-two persons. The officers are: W. E. Clarke, president; W. W. Cole, vice president; J. B. Miller, secretary.

Fleischmann & Co., compressed yeast manufacturers, have a branch in this city, Elmer E. Bryson being agent.

BREWING,

which is now one of the leading industries in Omaha, had an humble beginning in 1859. In that year Frederick Krug erected the first brewery within the State of Nebraska. The great number of people who passed through Omaha, then a village of perhaps fifteen hundred, on their way to Pike's Peak, and the Mormon emigration to Utah, demanded a great deal of stimulant, and the difficulty and expense of obtaining a supply of beer from eastern points, hastened the erection of a brewery here, which Mr. Krug began in the spring of 1859 and completed in six weeks The building was a one-story frame, twenty-two by forty feet in size, at what is now 1013 and 1015 Farnam Street, the site occupied by the Vienna cafe. The work of erecting the building was mainly done by Mr. Krug himself, who took as a partner a shoemaker named Rudolph Selzer, and the firm started out as Krug & Selzer, the former attending to the work of brewing and delivering the beer and the latter taking charge of

a room in the front part of the building where beer was retailed. The brew was from twelve to eighteen barrels weekly, which supplied the three saloons then running and the Mormons at Florence, who were the brewer's best customers. In 1860 Mr Krug purchased his partner's interest and became sole proprietor. The business increased during the second year so much that from the occasional aid of a single assistant, steady employment was given to two. In 1863 a malt house was built on Eleventh and Jackson Streets, and in 1867 the whole plant was removed there and a brick building about forty-four feet wide and eighty feet long, one and one half stories in height, was erected and employment given to six men, two hundred and fifty or three hundred barrels of beer manufactured monthly, and small shipments made to Bellevue and Fremont. Since that time an annual increment in buildings and improvements has been made until the present time, when the establishment, which is of solid brick buildings, occupying almost an entire block, has cost $500,000, and gives employment to about sixty men, and produces fifty thousand barrels of beer annually. January 1, 1892, Frederick Krug was succeeded by the Frederick Krug Brewing Company, with a capital of $1,000,000. The officers of the company are Frederick Krug, president, William Krug, vice president and general manager, Conrad Wiedemann, treasurer and assistant manager, M Thomas, secretary; C. F. Boufflei and Edward Krug, directors—the officers being also included in the directorate. A tract of eighteen acres of land was purchased by Mr. Krug on South Twenty-fourth Street, near Vinton, at a cost of $150 000, upon which a new brewery is now in process of erection. It consists of two principal buildings, one fronting on Green Street (a continuation of Vinton Street), the outside dimensions of which are 81 by 165 feet, with height varying from one to six stories, the other is 110 by 318 feet, the different portions varying from one to six stories in height and fronting on Boulevard Street, with railway trackage between them. The cost of the present buildings and machinery is about $500,000, and $250,000 more will be expended to erect other necessary buildings. The entire establishment is of brick and iron, the outside of stock or pressed brick, with stone and copper trimmings. Capacity 200,000 barrels per year.

Metz & Brothers, brewers, a firm composed of Frederick, Sr, Charles and Frederick Jr, own and operate one of the oldest establishments in Omaha, at Sixth and Leavenworth Streets, occupying three-fourths of a block. This brewery was established in 1861, by one McCumbe, and was afterwards sold to Joseph Baumann and John Green. After changing ownership several times it became the property of the present proprietors in 1864, for the purchase price of $6,500. Since that time it has been rebuilt and is now a valuable, commodious and substantial establishment. The output, which is 30,000 barrels annually, is equal to its capacity. The pay roll is $2,500 monthly and forty men are employed. Fred Metz Jr, is the business manager.

In 1865 Joseph Baumann began the business of brewing in a small way on Sherman Avenue, conducting the business with one assistant. In 1876, on the death of Mr. Baumann, his widow succeeded to the business, with Gottlieb Storz as foreman, who conducted the business until 1884, when Mr Storz and J. D Iler purchased the property, and as Storz & Iler carried on the brewing business, enlarging and improving the buildings and machinery and greatly increasing the output.

In May, 1891, Mr. Iler sold his interest and the Omaha Brewing Association, a corporation, was formed, with G Storz, president, Frederick Stubbendorf, vice president, Louis Schroeder, secretary and treasurer, capital stock, one million dollars, thirty per cent being paid up. Fifty men are employed and forty-five thousand barrels of beer annually made, which is mainly sold in Omaha, about one-fourth going out into the State of Nebraska. The buildings and appurtenances occupy two acres of ground. Ninety thousand bushels of barley are used annually. The bottling department of the Omaha Brewing Association is at 1421 Sherman Avenue, where the business is conducted by I. and M. Kahn. Last year the business amounted to twelve thousand cases, or twenty-four thousand dozen bottles. This company is now erecting, on Sherman Avenue between Clark and Grace Streets, a new brewery of brick, iron and cement, with stone trimmings and latest improved machinery, to cost, when complete, about $500,000. The front on Sherman Avenue will be two hundred feet, and the building, a portion of which is to be six stories high, will run back to the railroad tracks in the rear, where all the conveniences for receiving and shipping merchandise will be provided. The capacity of this new plant will be 150,000 barrels or more annually. It is expected to be ready for occupancy in the autumn of 1893.

MALT, SODA WATER, WEISS BEER.

The Gate City Malt Company is composed of R. Peterson, P. S. Boien and A. Blum, who bought the building formerly occupied by the N. K. Fairbanks lard refinery, a three story building 66x100 feet in size, to which a four story addition forty feet square was made in the fall of 1891, in the latter part of which year malting was begun, the capacity of the plant being six hundred bushels daily and the actual output four hundred bushels. The amount of trackage (nearly three hundred feet) in front of the malt house, corner Second and Pine Streets, and a total of eight hundred feet capable of being utilized, make the location desirable. The use of steam power for moving all grain and the arrangement for storing, steeping, sprouting and drying are of the most convenient character. The kilns occupy two floors forty feet square and the growing room two floors 66x100 feet. The malt is principally consumed in the manufacture of beer in Omaha.

Pomy & Segelke, manufacturers of soda water, dealers in mineral waters and bottlers' supplies, began business in 1869, at the corner of Eleventh and Leavenworth Streets, in a small one story brick building, which they occupied till 1884, when they erected and moved into their present commodious brick factory at 1114-16-18-20, corner of Tenth and Pierce Streets.

Gustav Pomy began on a small scale and conducted the business alone the first year and then associated William Segelke with him. The firm now employs at different seasons of the year from fifteen to thirty men and sends goods to all parts of the west, as far as Oregon and Washington.

E. Engeler began weiss-beer brewing in 1868. Since 1871 he has been located at 1110 North Eighteenth Street. Competition between him and other manufacturers (no less than fourteen having attempted to compete successfully with him and failed) has rendered the business unprofitable. He employs one man and the product is limited to three hundred barrels.

H. W. Snyder manufactures soda and mineral water at 1512 Grace Street. He employs from eight to fifteen men. The business was started in 1880.

DISTILLING.

The Willow Springs Distillery was formerly located in Council Bluffs, where it was known as the McCoy Distillery, and brought to Omaha in 1866 by James G. Megeath and Samuel D. Megeath, who purchased it at a government condemnation sale. Peter E. Iler & Co., consisting of Peter E. Iler, Joseph D. Iler and Marsh Kennard, were taken into partnership, and in the course of a few years became the sole owners, the Megeaths selling their interest. The company was incorporated in 1872. It is now the third largest establishment of the kind in the United States, the plant, including ten acres of ground, being valued at a million dollars. The distillery output in 1891 was 2,412,784 gallons of spirits, alcohol and whiskey, on which a revenue tax of $2,161,505.60 was paid, and the sales amounted to $2,847,812.15. During the year there were used 559,500 bushels grain, 4,000 tons hay, 11,500 tons coal, 31,463 barrels, 3,500 head of cattle were fattened, and the wages paid out were $70,168.80. The figures for 1892 are as follows: Sales of manufactured product, $3,346,690; internal revenue tax paid on same, $2,589,160.60; paid employes (wages), $70,421.63; number of barrels made and used, 35,505; tons of coal consumed as fuel, 12,500; tons of hay fed to cattle, 4,000; number of head of cattle fed, 3,500; number of bushels of corn used, 547,540; number of bushels of rye used, 30,970; number of bushels of barley used, 75,674; number of bushels of oats used, 35,000. The manufactured product is sold in the country west of the Mississippi River, a large part of it going to the Pacific Coast. On two occasions the distillery has been damaged by fire, the first in November, 1884, when property of the value of $50,000 was destroyed, and the second in July, 1886, when an equal or greater loss occurred. The business is now managed by Peter E. Iler and Henry Suessenbach.

### MANUFACTURING PHARMACIST.

The Mercer Whitmore Co., manufacturing chemist and pharmacist, occupies six floors in the Mercer Building, Twelfth and Howard Streets, each 125 feet deep, and fitted up with the latest improved machinery and appliances for the manufacture of nearly every form of preparation in which medicine is now exhibited. This establishment, which has but just begun business, has twenty thousand dollars invested in machinery, and starting with eighteen workmen, is expected soon to employ from seventy-five to one hundred persons, and turn out a large amount of manufactured goods. This company was incorporated January 1, 1893, with a capital of $100,000. The parties chiefly interested in this enterprise are: Dr. S. D. Mercer, president and treasurer; Geo. W. Mercer, secretary; Dr. B. F. Whitmore, vice president and general manager. The foregoing and E. W. Marsh, of Omaha, and J. W. Deweese, of Lincoln, constitute the board of directors. A. L. Johnson, lately with Parke, Davis & Co., has charge of the manufacturing interests.

### SOAP FACTORIES.

In 1869, P. J. Quealey, with very little capital, began the manufacture of soap at his present location, Twenty-sixth Street and U. P. Railway. By industry and energy he made his way against the competition of rival factories and was getting along well when, in 1879, his factory was burned to the ground. He immediately began to replace his building and soon had it almost completed when, by a defect in a chimney, the structure again took fire and was entirely consumed. There was no insurance and he suffered a total loss. Undaunted he bought a kettle on credit, hung it on a tripod formed of green saplings, and by the side of the still smoking ruins of his late establishment, he set about making another kettle of soap, and sent word to his creditors to decide what should be done. They came, viewed the primitive process of soapmaking, commended his pluck and extended his credit. Another building soon occupied his former factory site and business was resumed. In 1889 a stock company was formed with W. F. Roskie, president; P. J. Quealey, vice-president, and J. B. Huse, secretary; capital stock $25,000, of which $6,000 is paid in. Various brands and qualities of hard soap are manufactured, as well as soft soap for families. From five to twenty persons are employed, mostly boys and girls.

The W. A. Page Soap Co., is a corporation, the officers being W. A. Page, president; C. H. Wagner, vice-president; Alex G. Charlton, secretary and treasurer. The capital stock is $50,000, paid in. The factory has been in operation since May, 1888, at 115-123 Hickory Street. The business has increased rapidly and thirty-three people are employed. The business of the present year amounts to $140,000. The coarser grades of soap are made of pure tallow, obtained from the packing houses of South Omaha, and the finer grades from cocoanut oil from the "South Sea," and the traditional odor of a soap factory does not exist here. Thirty different brands of soap are manufactured, aggregating something like six million bars for the year's business. Ogden is a distributing point, where a resident agent attends to the trade south and west. Six traveling salesmen are employed.

### CIGAR FACTORIES.

Joseph B. West and Charles L. Fritscher formed a co-partnership, in March, 1867, as manufacturers of fine cigars and wholesale dealers in leaf tobacco, in Omaha, which lasted twenty-five years. They were the pioneer cigar manufacturers, and for a long time the leaders in this line, but the business ceased to be profitable on account of strikes and difficulties with the Cigarmakers' Union, and West & Fritscher closed their factory in 1891.

O. K. Dellecker, manufacturer and jobber of fine cigars, at 1408 Douglas Street, began business in 1883. Since 1887 he has carried on the business alone. He employs eleven hands, and the number of cigars manufactured amounts to 500,000.

Joseph Beckman manufactures cigars at 1611 Farnam Street. He has been in the business since 1875, and employs seven persons. Annual product about 250,000.

J. H. Richards is located at 1017 Farnam Street. He employs five persons and manufactures 250,000 cigars annually. Has been in business since 1890. Like the other manufacturers, his goods are chiefly consumed in Omaha.

H. C. Hartry has manufactured cigars at 1116 Farnam Street since 1886, and employes from three to six men.

Other manufacturers are H. Beselin, 2409 Patrick Avenue; B. Trosler, 1105 Farnam, who employ a small number of hands. Cigars are also made by others, but in small quantities and with few workmen. This fast decaying industry, in Omaha, which once employed two hundred persons, now scarcely gives work to fifty.

### ASPHALT PAVING.

The officers of the Grant Asphalt Paving and Slagolithic Company, which was organized under the present name, January 1, 1891, are: John Grant, president and general manager; E. W. Nash, secretary; and Guy C. Barton, treasurer. Crushing works, for crushing slag obtained from the smelting works, to be used for paving instead of stone, are located at the corner of Sixth and Davenport Streets. These works have a capacity of 150 tons per day. Buildings and machinery for preparing asphalt for use in the construction of pavements and walks have lately been erected near Paul and Eleventh Streets. Their capacity is 1,600 yards of asphalt pavement per day. This company's muster roll depends upon the amount of paving being done, and contains from 30 to 350 names. Mr. Grant has devoted a great deal of time to the study of pavement and the material therefor, and has three patents on slagolithic pavement.

The Barber Asphalt Paving Company, C. E. Squires, general western agent; P. W. Henry, superintendent, and C. O. Howard, cashier, has plants at East Omaha and at South Fifth and Jones Streets. This company has paved a very large portion of the street area of Omaha, and now employs a large force of men.

## MARBLE WORKS.

The Omaha Marble Works were established in 1868, by M. J. Feenan, and at that time supplied the local demand for monuments and tombstones, and later did work for points as far as one hundred miles north and fifty miles south of this city. Ten years ago the works were moved from the business portion of the city to their present location, 2212 Poppleton Avenue. Mr. Feenan claims that these are the oldest marble works in Nebraska.

W. Y. Teetzel is the proprietor of the Omaha Monumental Works, Eighteenth and Cuming Streets, where he began business in August, 1890, employing ten men.

## SADDLERY.

Marks Brothers' Saddlery Company began business in Omaha in 1885. They do a wholesale business in saddlery and harness, occupying four floors at 1215 Harney Street. In 1891 they finished and occupied their new three story brick factory at East Omaha, where they do a large manufacturing business, employing seventy-five men.

Welty & Guy are manufacturers and wholesale dealers in saddlery hardware, harness and saddles, at 1316 Farnam Street.

## BRICK MANUFACTURERS.

There were, during the year 1892, only about fifteen manufacturers actively engaged in making brick in Omaha, several yards, which had heretofore done a large business, being idle during the year. The product for 1892 was about 45,000,000 brick. To make these required the labor of something over three hundred men. During the great building era in Omaha there were fifty-two brick manufacturers, turning out 150,000,000 brick annually. Among the principal manufacturers at the present time are: Martin Ittner, who has made brick in Omaha for the past fourteen years, and averages annually over five million brick, at his yards located at Thirtieth and Lake Streets and Twenty-sixth Street and Creighton Avenue; Richard Smith, who began business here in 1886 and established the first machine yard in the city, and now makes 4,000,000 brick per year; Rocheford & Gould; the Grand View Brick Company; G. W. McBride; John P. Thomas; The Omaha Standard Brick Company; Hermann Deiss; Ittner & Cassell; R. Peterson; John Withnell, and Withnell & Smith. John and Richard N. Withnell were pioneer brickmakers in Omaha and have been engaged in this line ever since brick began to be used in the city. Henry Livesy, Arthur Johnson & Brother, Lars Johnson, Bailey & Olsen, Rasmus Hansen, The Omaha Standard Brick Company, John Cremer, George H. Youngerman and others, have contributed largely to the brick supply.

## MISCELLANEOUS

The Adamant Wall Plaster Company was incorporated in March, 1889, and is the successor of the Nebraska Adamant Wall Plaster Manufacturing Company, which, until the time of the incorporation of this company, was located at South Omaha. The works are now located at East Omaha, where ten men are employed. The annual product is 24,000 barrels.

Carson & Banks are manufacturing jewelers, at room 30 Barker Block. The individual partners are W. F. Carson and W. A. Banks. This industry was initiated in 1890. Six persons are employed.

The Omaha Art Stained Glass Company, G. H. Heckerman, president, and T. T. Wilson, secretary, manufacture stained glass windows, etc., at 1012 Farnam Street. This industry was started in 1888, and the present company incorporated in 1891, with a capital stock of $10,000 paid in, and employing from eight to fifteen men. The company sends work to Texas and west to the Pacific.

John Power, manufactures all kinds of tanks and dairy cooperage, at Fourth and Jones Streets. The industry was begun sixteen years ago. Eight men are now employed.

The number of men employed in the industrial establishments of Omaha is about 7,500.

Bradstreet furnishes most of the following statement as showing the amount invested in the leading manufacturing industries in Omaha for the year ending December 31, 1892;

| Class | Capital Invested |
|---|---|
| Asphalt | $ 60,000 |
| Bag factory | 150,000 |
| Basket manufacturers | 10,000 |
| Boiler works | 28,000 |
| Bottling works | 65,000 |
| Boot and shoe factory | 110,000 |
| Box factories, etc. | 49,000 |
| Breweries | 850,000 |
| Brick | 365,000 |
| Brooms | 20,000 |
| Buttons | 17,000 |
| Canning and preserving | 10,000 |
| Carriage tops | 6,000 |
| Carriages and wagons | 225,000 |
| Chairs and furniture | 200,000 |
| Cigar manufacturers | 50,000 |
| Coffee, baking powder, etc. | 95,000 |
| Collars and cuffs | 3,000 |
| Confectionery | 155,000 |
| Cooperage | 14,600 |
| Cornice | 46,000 |
| Crackers | 200,000 |
| Distillery | 400,000 |
| Fence works | 10,000 |
| Flags, awnings, tents, etc | 10,000 |
| Flour and corn mills | 90,000 |
| Foundries and machine shops | 250,000 |
| Hominy | 10,000 |
| Horse and cattle food | 49,500 |
| Laundries | 198,000 |
| Linseed oil | 450,000 |
| Malt house | 32,000 |
| Manufacturing chemists | new |
| Mattresses | 20,000 |
| Overalls | 130,000 |
| Planing mills | 190,000 |
| Plating works | 2,500 |
| Printing, blank books, etc | 500,000 |
| Saddlery | 77,000 |
| Safe and iron works | 30,000 |
| Sash, doors and blinds | 275,000 |
| Shirt factories | 14,000 |
| Shot and lead pipe | 200,000 |
| Show cases | 4,000 |
| Smelting works | 3,600,000 |
| Soaps | 80,000 |
| Soda water | 40,000 |
| Syrup refiners | 40,000 |
| Tinware | 65,000 |
| Trunks | 16,500 |
| Union Pacific shops | 2,620,000 |
| Vinegar and pickles | 60,000 |
| Wall plaster | 24,000 |
| White lead | 500,000 |
| Wire works | 9,500 |
| Yeast | 15,000 |
| Total | $12,740,600 |

## THE MANUFACTURERS' AND CONSUMERS' ASSOCIATION OF NEBRASKA.

The Manufacturers' and Consumers' Association of Nebraska was organized September 26, 1891. Its object is to promote home industry by encouraging the purchase of Nebraska products and manufactures. The members of the association take the ground that factories will increase both in size and in number when they are given a good market for their products, and that if the people of Nebraska wish to see manufacturing industries of the state developed they must patronize the factories that are already located in their midst. By keeping this truth before the people a strong sentiment has already been worked up in favor of Nebraska goods, and it is the object and aim of the association to strengthen this sentiment. The officers of the association are: W. A. Page, president; L. L. E. Stewart, vice-president; O. C. Holmes, secretary; A. J. Vierling, treasurer; and thirty-three directors. The only paid officer is the secretary who devotes his entire attention to the work of the association, spending half of his time in Omaha and the balance of his time in visiting the retail merchants throughout the State in the interest of Nebraska manufacturers. The association numbers about 150 active members who are all engaged in manufacturing, and about 80,000 general or honorary members who have pledged themselves to give preference to Nebraska made goods. The great exposition of Nebraska manufactured goods, held in June, 1892, in Omaha, was so marked a success that it has been determined to hold one every year. A monster building suitable for exposition and convention purposes is projected and will probably be erected during the coming year. It is safe to say that the Manufacturers' and Consumers' Association is to-day the most active and aggressive commercial organization in Nebraska, and is destined to play a most important part in the development of the State.

# CHAPTER LV.

SOME EVENTS OF 1892 — THE NATIONAL DRILL — GENERAL CONFERENCE OF THE M. E. CHURCH — NATIONAL CONVENTION OF THE PEOPLE'S PARTY — IMPERIAL COUNCIL MYSTIC SHRINERS — PUBLIC IMPROVEMENTS AND STATISTICS.

As one of the youngest cities of the United States in the class to which she belongs, Omaha was, during 1892, recognized by the remainder of the country as a place of importance, far beyond what she had ever been. Her citizens had attempted to secure the holding of the National Republican Convention here, and although not successful, they felt very well satisfied to think that the West had been strong enough in the councils of that party to bring the convention to Minneapolis. There were, however, three gatherings of national importance held here during the year—the National Competitive Drill, the General Conference of the Methodist Episcopal Church, and the National Convention of the People's Party; each of them bringing to this city visitors and delegates from almost every part of the United States.

### THE NATIONAL DRILL.

The National Competitive Drill of the militia companies of the United States took place in June, opening Monday. the 13th, and continuing eleven days. The following companies were present, in camp, which was located on the fair grounds, in the northern part of the city: Branch Guards, St. Louis, Mo.; Sealey Rifles, Galveston, Texas; National Fencibles, Washington, D. C.; Belknap Rifles, San Antonio, Texas; Indianapolis Light Artillery, Indianapolis, Ind.; Zollinger Battery, Fort Wayne, Ind.; Cincinnati Light Artillery, Cincinnati, Ohio; Omaha Guards, Omaha, Neb.; Dallas Light Artillery, Dallas, Texas; McCarthy Light Guards, Little Rock, Ark.; Chicago Zouaves, Chicago; Hale Zouaves, Kansas City, Mo.; Devlin Cadets, Jackson, Mich.; Lima City Guards, Lima, Ohio; University Cadets, Lincoln, Neb.; Fletcher Rifles, Little Rock, Ark.; Governor's Guards, Denver, Colo.

On Tuesday, June 14, 1892, the companies were drawn up on the parade ground, and Governor Boyd and Mayor Bemis delivered addresses of welcome. A large crowd was present, including many ladies. Tuesday evening a grand parade was made down Sixteenth and Farnam streets, which was a beautiful sight, and which was reviewed from the balcony of the Paxton House, by General Brooke and staff, Governor Boyd and staff and Colonel Waldron, commander of the militia of Arkansas.

On Wednesday, June 15th, a sham battle was fought at the camp, which drew as spectators what was said to have been the largest crowd ever on the grounds. Every day there were competitive drills between the companies.

The camp was named Camp Brooke, in honor of Brig. Gen. John R. Brooke, U. S. A., commanding department of the Platte. Capt. Wm. V. Richards, 16th U. S. infantry, was commandant of the camp. The following prizes were awarded:

### NATIONAL INFANTRY DRILLS.

National Fencibles, Washington, D. C..... $5,000
Sealey Rifles, Galveston, Texas........... 2,000
McCarthy Light Guards, Little Rock, Ark. 1,000

### MAIDEN INFANTRY DRILL.
| | |
|---|---|
| Co. A. Neb. Cadets, Lincoln | $1,500 |
| Lima Guards, Lima, Ohio | 750 |
| Governors Guards, Denver, Colo | 500 |

### ZOUAVE DRILL.
| | |
|---|---|
| Hale Zouaves, Kansas City, Mo | $1,500 |
| Chicago Zouaves, Chicago, Ill | 750 |

### ARTILLERY DRILL.
| | |
|---|---|
| Indianapolis | $1 000 |
| Dallas | 500 |
| Zollinger, Ft. Wayne, Ind | 250 |

### GATLING GUN DRILL.
| | |
|---|---|
| Cincinnati | $500 |
| Omaha Guards | 250 |

Individual prizes were awarded as follows: Captain making best score in National Drill, Captain Downs, sword; same, Maiden Drill, Capt. W. F. Bell, sword; best drilled soldier, Durand Whipple, McCarthy Light Guards, medal; company ranking highest in camp discipline, Governor's Guards, Denver, flag; most popular company in camp, Chaffee Light Artillery, cup.

The prizes were all raised by subscription by the citizens of Omaha.

THE GENERAL CONFERENCE OF THE M. E. CHURCH.

Probably there never was so truly an extended recognition of that great section of our country, known somewhat indefinitely, as the West, as was that made by the Methodist Episcopal Church, when it decided to hold in Omaha its Twenty-first General Conference. Never before had this body met so far west, and but once had it met so far west as Chicago, and that was in 1866. The conference was composed of delegates from the district conferences of this great denomination from all parts of the civilized world, the number of persons in attendance being about five hundred, and although the conference assembled on Monday, May 2, 1892, and held sessions every week-day until Thursday, the 26th of May, the entire body was entertained by the people of Omaha —the sum of $50,000 having been raised for that purpose. There were present in Omaha, at some time during the session of this body, nearly every man who has attained prominence in that denomination. The proceedings of the conference were printed daily, the church authorities issuing a 56 column paper every week-day for that purpose. On the evening of May 3, 1892, the mayor and city council tendered a reception to the bishops, delegates and friends of the general conference, at the Exposition Hall. The reception was largely attended, many of the prominent citizens and families being present to welcome the visitors. Addresses were made by Mayor George P. Bemis, Mr. E. P. Davis, president of the city council, Mr. Henry D. Estabrook, Judge Jacob Fawcett, Bishop Thomas Bowman and Bishop Newman, after which refreshments were served, and the citizens and visitors presented to each other. The conference passed by unanimous rising vote a resolution of thanks to the municipal authorities for this reception. Before adjourning the conference expressed its hearty appreciation of the many courtesies received by its members. To many of the visitors, especially those from the far East, Omaha was a revelation. While some of the members of the general committee had expressed doubts before the assembling of the conference in regard to the ability of Omaha to entertain the delegates and visitors, there was no question about it when the adjournment came. The conference held its sessions in the Exposition Hall, which was fitted up and decorated for the occasion. One unpleasant feature was the weather, as it rained nearly every day during the session of the conference.

THE NATIONAL CONVENTION OF THE PEOPLE'S PARTY.

Following closely upon the General Conference of the Methodist Episcopal Church, came the National Convention of the People's Party, which was the first National convention of any political party ever held west of the Missouri River.

At the Coliseum building, at 10 o'clock

on the morning of Saturday, July 2, 1892, Chairman Taubeneck, of the national committee, rapped with his gavel upon the speaker's desk, and called to order the first National Convention of the People's Party. Prayer was offered by Rev. Benjamin F. Diffenbacher, chaplain of the Nebraska legislature of 1891. Hon. Geo. P. Bemis, mayor of Omaha, delivered an address of welcome to the convention, which was responded to by the Hon. Ben Terrill, of Texas. The national committee selected as temporary officers, C. H. Ellington, of Georgia, as chairman, and J. B. Hayes, of New York, as secretary, which selection the convention ratified by acclamation. The usual committees were appointed, and the convention adjourned over Sunday, to meet again Monday morning. On the morning of the 4th, H. L. Loucks, of South Dakota, was elected permanent chairman and J. B. Hayes, secretary.

On the morning of July 5th, at 3 A. M., the convention nominated as its standard bearer, James B. Weaver, of Iowa, for president of the United States, and James G. Field, of Virginia, for vice-president. This convention brought to Omaha many men who have been prominent in the politics of the country for years.

### THE MYSTIC SHRINERS.

The Imperial Council of the Noble Order of the Mystic Shrine met in Omaha on the 15th and 16th of August, 1892, and were entertained by the local body. For two days the city was given up to the illustrious nobles of this mystic organization, and they made the most of the freedom of the city, which had been presented to them. There were coaching parties and excursions to South Omaha, to Florence, to the Smelting Works and to Council Bluffs; an evening parade by the Shriners, in their full dress suits and fez caps, with many noteworthy features, including some live camels; a reception by Governor Boyd and Mayor Bemis at the Paxton Hotel, and a banquet at the Millard. Refreshments were also served at the rooms of the local temple.

### THE OMAHA AND PLATTE RIVER CANAL.

In the year 1887, Mr. S. L. Wiley, while manager of the American Water Works Company, of Omaha, was examining the sources available for water supply for the city, and found that a phenomenal head of about two hundred feet existed between the waters of the Platte River south of Fremont, and the City of Omaha, and after making one survey, concluded to get an act through the legislature that would authorize and facilitate the construction of the canal now about to be built. With the help of Mr. Henry St. Reyner, of Sidney, the act was passed.

Mr. Wiley then began the surveys in earnest, and after four years of planning and personally spending over four thousand dollars in the work, he succeeded in interesting some of the leading citizens of Omaha in the enterprise, which culminated in the organization of a company called the "Omaha Canal and Power Company," with an authorized capital of three million dollars. The following gentlemen were recently elected officers of the company for the first year: Herman Kountze, president; H. T. Clarke, first vice-president; Dr. George L. Miller, second vice-president; Frank Murphy, treasurer; S. L. Wiley, secretary.

The final surveys and location of the canal are now being made under the management of Mr. Wiley, assisted by R. B. Howell, C. E., and Andrew Rosewater, consulting engineers.

This project contemplates the bringing of the Platte River to within six miles of Omaha, by a canal thirty-five miles long, which will have a capacity sufficient to furnish a volume of water capable of producing over twenty-five thousand horse-power—the largest water power in the United States except Niagara Falls—and which it is anticipated, will make Omaha the great milling center of the West, as well as the greatest manufacturing town west of Chicago.

The power proposed will be developed in the Papillion Valley, under about 145 feet head, and, under the favorable conditions existing, shows a maximum two-thirds greater than St. Anthony's Falls at Minneapolis. This development under such high heads presents new phases in engineering, and a most careful examination for the works to be constructed is now being made by engineers of national reputation.

The canal will be nearly all in Douglas County, which it will traverse from the northwestern to the southeastern portion. The works will necessarily be of a most substantial character, built of masonry backed by earth. The waters of the Platte will be taken from the river by the building of a low dam. It is proposed to carry the power by electricity under high voltage into the center of the city, where a large building will be located from which the power will be distributed to every portion of the city to supply light, power and heat. It is expected the company will reduce the price to the users of power to the lowest possible rate.

### THE HANGING OF DIXON.

On the evening of September 30, 1891, at Fort Niobrara, Nebraska, Clinton E. Dixon, a trumpeter of the Sixth Cavalry, shot and killed Corporal John R. Carter, of troop F, of the same regiment. The history of the case was this: Corporal Carter had been instructed by the commanding officer of the fort to drive away from the post two notorious negro women. The corporal was obliged to use force in his efforts to rid the garrison of the objectionable women, and thus aroused the bitter animosity of Dixon, who went to the quarters of the troops and asked Carter to step outside, as he wished to speak to him. An instant after, the soldiers within the barracks were startled by the report of a revolver just outside the door.

Rushing out they found Carter on his knees with his arms around Dixon's waist, and Dixon trying to free himself from Carter's hold. "For God's sake, don't let him get away," called Carter, "he has shot me." Dixon, who still held the smoking revolver in his hand, threw it away when the other soldiers rushed upon him. He was overpowered and placed in chains. Carter died about midnight, but before dying left an ante mortem statement, as follows: "I was foully murdered by Clinton E. Dixon and after he shot me, I bit his thumb."

Dixon was tried at Omaha in the United States district court; found guilty of murder in the first degree, and sentenced by Judge Dundy to be hanged on April 22, 1892; but on the failure of the commissioners of Douglas County to assent to the execution within the precincts of the court house and jail of the county, the President of the United States, " in consideration of premises and divers other good and sufficient reasons thereunto moving," respited the execution until May 20, 1892. On account of the sessions of the Methodist Conference sitting at the date of May 20, 1892, the execution was again postponed until June 17, 1892. June 17th was the day for the assembling of the Grand Lodge of Master Masons of Nebraska, and as United States Marshal B. D. Slaughter was grand master of that body, the president again granted a respite until June 24, 1892. Persistent efforts were made to have the sentence commuted, but without success, and Clarence E. Dixon paid the penalty of the law at Douglas County jail. He left a confession, claiming, however, that the killing was done in self defense.

### POLITICAL NOTES.

In November, 1892, occurred the general election in Nebraska, for presidential electors, governor and other state officers, for members of congress, for members of the legislature, and in this county and city for county attorney, for three county commis-

sioners, and for nine ward councilmen for the several wards of Omaha. There were four parties in the field, the Republican, the Democratic, the Independent or People's and the Prohibition. While the Democratic party had held its convention and nominated a full ticket, many of the leaders openly advocated and advised the voting for the Independent electors, with a view of throwing the State of Nebraska to General Weaver, and prevent its electoral votes being cast for General Harrison. It was hoped by the Democratic leaders that in the event of a very close election, every western state could be carried for the Independent candidate, General Weaver, by the help of Democratic votes, to prevent the Republican candidate, General Harrison receiving a majority of the electoral votes—and thus throw the election of president into the National house of representatives at Washington, which was largely Democratic and would insure the election of Grover Cleveland. The movement in Nebraska was not a success, as there were 25,344 persons who voted for the Democratic electors, and the Republican electors carried the presidential ticket by 4,823 plurality. The general result throughout the nation was such a triumph for the Democratic ticket, however, that the action in Nebraska made little difference.

On the state, county and city tickets each party made an independent fight, there being no coalition between the Democratic, Independent or Republicans.

Another element, entering largely into the contest for the local offices, was the American Protective Association, a recent political organization, made up of those who were opposed to Catholics holding offices. This association made no nominations outside of the regular political parties, but endorsed such candidates on the other tickets as were in sympathy with the objects of their organization. In this way they were able to elect nearly every candidate whom they endorsed.

David H Mercer, one of the young men of the city, Republican nominee, endorsed by the American Protective Association, was elected to Congress from this district his opponents being Judge George W Doane, Democrat, of Omaha, Rev Robert L Wheeler, Independent, of South Omaha, and R W Richardson, Prohibitionist.

The following senators and representatives to the state legislature were elected. Senators—C. O Lobeck, W. N Babcock, Charles L Clarke. Representatives—Thomas D Crane, W N Nason, Charles H Withnell, M O Ricketts, Charles A. Goss, George W Ames, J H Kyner, August Lockner and A L Sutton. Contest proceedings were commenced by the defeated Democrats for the seats given to the two Republican senators, and seven Republican representatives, but they were not successful.

In Omaha the nine members elected to the city council to serve for two years, one from each ward, were as follows: I S Hascall, first ward, Peter Elsasser, second ward, A. B McAndrews, third ward, D H. Wheeler, fourth ward, W A Saunders, fifth ward Christ Specht, sixth ward, C. L Thomas, seventh ward, Charles E Bruner, eighth ward, and Churchill Parker, ninth ward. There were also elected by the city at large, five members of the board of education, to serve for three years, as follows Henry C Akin, J F Burgess, B F. Thomas, Henry Knodell and Rev J T Duryea. Three new members of the board of county commissioners Henry Livesey, J. W. Paddock and G R Williams were also elected. Jacob L Kaley, the Republican nominee, was elected county attorney.

In connection with the election of county commissioners, a question has arisen under the Australian ballot law, which was adopted by the legislature in 1890. It appeared that in the official ballots provided for under this law, an error was made in those which were sent to Valley precinct, in this county.

After the name of William Olmstead, the Democratic nominee, the word "prohibitionist" had been printed. Mr. Olmstead was defeated by five votes, and he claims that this error in the ticket deprived him of some votes to which he was clearly entitled, and has begun contest proceedings for the seat.

SOME STATISTICS.

The deposits in the nine National banks of Omaha were on December 2, 1891, $14,288,206, and on December 9, 1892, $16,582,656, showing an increase of $2,300,-000. These deposits were much greater at the close of the year than ever before in the history of the city.

The savings banks' deposits also showed a very large increase; at the close of 1891, the deposits in all the savings banks amounted to $2,978,651, and at the close of 1892 to $3,883,260, showing a gain of about $900,000 during the year.

The State bank deposits also increased during the year from $137,300 at the close of 1891, to $149,858 at the close of 1892.

The total deposits in the banks of Omaha at the close of 1892, as compared with 1891, is shown in the following:

|  | 1891. | 1892. |
|---|---|---|
| Nine National banks | $14,288,206 | $16,582,656 |
| Eight Savings banks | 3,001.651 | 3,883,260 |
| Two State banks | 137,300 | 149,858 |
|  | $17,427,157 | $20,615,774 |

This shows an increase for the year of over $3,000,000.

The reports of the clearing house also show a very heavy gain for the year, the total clearings for 1891 were $215,103,314; for 1892 they were $295,026,585, or an increase of nearly $80,000,000.

PUBLIC IMPROVEMENTS.

Notwithstanding there was great delay in starting on the public work in the spring of the year, $675,000 were expended for public improvements during 1892. Asphaltum, stone, and brick were the materials used for paving, and the following shows the amount of paving done with each material and the cost of the same:

| Material. | Sq. yds. | Cost. |
|---|---|---|
| Asphaltum | 34,692 | $ 91,000 |
| Stone | 64,827 | 118,857 |
| Brick | 56,257 | 112 513 |
| Total | 155,776 | $322,370 |

During 1892, sixteen miles of wooden sidewalk were laid at a cost of $27,316. Permanent sidewalks costing $19,461 were also laid, making the total expended for sidewalks during the year $46,777.84.

Eleven miles of curbing, costing $36,520, were also put down in 1892, making the total curbing in the city 130 miles which has cost $670,452.

As a means of comparing the relative progress of four of the great western cities for 1892, the amount expended for new buildings for the year is here given: Omaha, $3,718,000; St. Paul, $2,200,000; Kansas City, $1,269,934; Minneapolis, $4,815,220.

The real estate transfers for the year amounted to $13,465,308, while in 1891 they were $15,969,674.

In 1892 there were 1,226 couples married in Omaha, an increase of fifty-seven couples over 1891.

# CHAPTER LVI.

### Some of Omaha's Representative Citizens.

GEORGE W. AMBROSE.—The bar and the courts of Nebraska know and honor the legal record of Geo. W. Ambrose, of Omaha. Personal hard work and fair dealing through twenty-five years, have written his name very large and legible in the annals of State litigation, and with frequent final hearing at Washington.

Several issues, as the Slocum law, the taxation of railways, damages for original street grades, etc.,—issues of great social and economic importance in the State—through his clear view of the principles of law and clear statement of the same, have been made precedents of national value.

And yet but few friends, even at the bar, who know the lawyer well, know anything of the upcome, the biography of the man. He is the second son of Ruel and Rebekah Ambrose, who were pioneers in Michigan, his father being a merchant in Detroit, where Mr. Ambrose was born October 5, 1836.

He is of Puritan stock, his father's mother, Sallie Eaton, being a great-granddaughter of Francis Eaton, a passenger in the Mayflower. Soon after the boy's birth, his father pushed sixty miles into the woods of Michigan, opening a general store and bank in Sharon, Washtenaw County; and in 1842 journeyed into Illinois with the lad, who wore out the six following years with losing his shoes in the mud streets of Chicago, helping his father build a flouring mill at Elgin, and beginning school days.

The family then returned to the Sharon homestead, where George passed his youth in farming and in the old school house on the hill; at sixteen swinging the cradle through six acres of good grain in a day. He was a good boy, beloved of parents, and favored by those who knew him.

His upper schooling was gathered at Kalamazoo College, the State Normal School at Ypsilanti, the law office of Judge F. C. Beaman of Adrian; and in April, 1863, he graduated from the law department of Michigan University, at once opening office at Ann Arbor.

But the stars move westward, and in March, 1867, Mr. Ambrose became a resident of Omaha; the friend of all Nebraska, in law, politics and social welfare.

He soon secured a good practice, increasing from year to year in variety and importance of causes, until he stands, in the judgment of the profession and the public, in the front rank of able and successful lawyers. His experience during those years had covered a wide field of legal research, bringing him frequently into causes of more than ordinary magnitude, many of them involving novel and unsettled questions. Some of these were leading cases in Nebraska, in which constitutional construction or fundamental propositions of law were to be, for the first time, settled.

Among them may be noted the Pleuler case, reported in 11 Nebraska, 547, involving the constitutionality of the Slocum or high license law, then recently enacted. Those interested in the liquor traffic opposed it as too stringent, and on the ground, among others, of conflict with the constitution. A test case soon arose in which Mr. Ambrose made the brief and the principal argument in favor of the validity of the act. It was sustained, when it reached the Supreme Court, largely upon his line of argument,—the court holding it in all respects valid and constitutional; and it has proved an effective and popular statute for regulating the liquor traffic.

In Hanscom vs. The City of Omaha, 11 Nebraska, 37, involving the principle upon which special taxes may be assessed, he was one of the counsel for the city, and successful in the district court; but, on account of the peculiar facts in the case, the judgment was reversed on appeal.

Harmon vs. The City of Omaha, 17 Nebraska 548, was the first case presenting the question whether, under the constitution of 1875, damages, caused by grading in front of lots, could be recovered from the city. Mr. Ambrose successfully maintained the proposition that such damages were included in the provision that property shall not be "damaged for public use without just compensation therefor." Establishing a principle of great and lasting importance in this state.

His special strength as a lawyer is shown in a clear perception of the pivotal question upon which his cause will turn; preparing it with that in view; and in the lucid and logical presentation of his points, carrying conviction to the minds of the jury and the court. This is aided by the research which brings to the aid of the court adjudicated causes bearing closely upon the question in review; and the discrimination which eliminates all foreign elements from the discussion; and in this he has had marked success. It is not his habit to seek notoriety by sensational or clamorous demonstrations before a jury, but in that field of labor he addresses their reason and understanding, appealing to their sense of justice, fair play and right between litigants, whether persons or corporations. As a specimen of his style of legal argument, I give an extract of his brief in the case of Felix (half-breed Indian) vs. Patrick, et al., in the United States Supreme Court, upon the right of Indians to maintain suits in the courts of the country:

"Is an Indian a person? If he is, then the courts are open to him and he is bound, like any other person, to all provisions of law which apply to litigants. If he is not a person then the rule of the Dred Scott case is reversed, and the rule of decision here must be that a white man has no rights which Indians are bound to respect. Is such a rule to obtain? Hardly. At the time of the discovery of this continent, Columbus, and those with him, thought that the land upon which their eyes rested was located beyond the Ganges, and vaguely known to him as the Indies. He found here a race of people inhabiting the country and gave to them the name of Indian, because of their supposed location in the Indies. By all literary, as well as law writers, this race has, from time immemorial, been considered free persons, living together in a state of nature. They have been so recognized by every act of congress relating to their interest, and by every court which has been called to pass upon their property rights. They have never been considered in a state of vassalage, or chattelized; they have been treated with as persons capable of receiving the title to property, to hold property, to use property, varying in this as to the status of the negro race. The negro race were chattels in the eyes of the law, incapable of holding property, owing to their masters entire subservience. Not so with the Indian. The various tribes of Indians in this country have been considered by the highest courts of the land as nations, governing themselves by their own law, usages and customs without interference in that regard by other persons inhabiting this continent. Every case which in this argument will be referred to, these people have been considered and treated as so many independent nations, composed of individual persons. It will not do to say that they were not such. In every aspect of our civilization, they have been so treated; in every tribute which has been paid to their bravery, their courage and fidelity, they have been treated as persons capable of exercising every attribute which belongs to our common humanity."

In the case of the State ex rel, the Attorney General vs. The Nebraska Distilling Company in the Supreme Court, the validity of the anti-trust statute was drawn in question. Mr. Ambrose made the brief and argument for the Distilling Company, and took occasion then (1890) to lay before the court the same lines of argument, relating to the labor organizations, as obnoxious trusts, if their objects became perverted, as were used by Judges Taft, Ricks and others in the late railroad strike decisions, and as given by Associate Justice Brewer in his great paper upon "The Movement of Coercion" in January, 1893. Mr. Ambrose said:

"The greatest trusts that this world has ever seen have been the labor organizations of this country. It is a trust which controls, makes and unmakes corporate bodies. It controls the price of labor and the price of material; and every day adds action and life to this human anaconda, called labor unions.

"Both labor and capital are necessary for the continuance of this country; but to say that one shall be fostered at the expense of the other is demagogism; and still the politicians of the country, not because of their love for labor, but because of their love of place and power, pander to labor, and howl themselves hoarse as against capital.

"If a law should be passed by the legislature of Nebraska which should attempt to dissolve these labor organizations now existing, and prevent the formation of others in the future, and this court should, by its decree, sustain such legislation as competent, I apprehend that the cyclones which sometimes sweep over the country, devastating everything in their path would be mild and gentle as a summer's breeze in comparison to those which would unseat your honors from the wool-sack which you now so gracefully occupy. But the time will come when some judge in his majesty will arise and in no uncertain terms rebuke the organizations which are now exempted from the operation of this act of the legislature, and which exemption renders the legislation of Nebraska obnoxious to the constitution."

And that he has borne his legal lances and duties in strong arms, let me say that Judge Lake, then of the Supreme Bench, once remarked:

"There is no lawyer in the State whose briefs the supreme court finds more satisfactory, than those of Ambrose."

I need not lengthen this sketch with the further history of his great or noted cases, but an inspection of the dockets of the district, supreme and United States courts of Nebraska, will assure all that he is at the large end of the large cases in the State; and if you poll the clients of many years, you will find the verdict on the side of the clients' abiding faith in the attorney, and warm friendship between the two.

But once has he touched politics, being elected to the State senate in 1876, and serving the State with a firmness above price. Twice wedded, and of several children born to him, one daughter remains, Mrs. Mamie Ambrose Rivinius, of Boston. He has one brother, James Clement Ambrose, the platform lecturer of Chicago, and one sister, Emma O. Ambrose, now twelve years a Baptist Missionary in Burmah, India.

GEORGE B. AYRES was born in Olmsted county, Minnesota, June 15th, 1856, and entered the high school at Rochester, that state, at the age of fourteen, where he finished in 1873. During the last three years of his high school education he also studied medicine with his uncle, Dr. Galloway, and entered the medical department of of the University of Michigan in the fall of 1873, where he remained at close application to his study for one year, but finding that he would be too young to graduate at the end of his period of study, he decided to go one year to Carleton College at Norfield, Minnesota, after which he returned to the University of Michigan, in 1875, took his second course in medicine, and in the spring of 1876, accompanied Prof. Ford to Long Island College Hospital, where he took the summer course in medicine and a degree of Doctor of Medicine, in the fall of 1876 before he was twenty-one years old.

He again returned to Ann Arbor in the fall of 1876, took the degree of Doctor of Medicine from that institution in the spring of 1877, after which he was elected as assistant professor of anatomy there, which position he filled with honor and dignity for three years, and acted as secretary of the faculty of the medical department the last year of his stay.

Dr. Ayres came to Omaha in the fall of 1880, and with Dr. Mercer, started the Omaha Medical College; for three years he filled the chair of anatomy and afterward, for several years, clinical surgery, with much credit to himself and honor to the institution. During the first five years, from 1880 to 1885, he was assistant to Dr. Mercer, and assistant surgeon of the Union Pacific Railroad, and also the last few years was division surgeon of the Missouri Pacific.

In 1888, Dr. Ayres was appointed medical director for the Mutual Life Insurance Company of New York, and had charge of the State of Nebraska, North and South Dakota, Wyoming, Idaho, and a portion of Montana and Kansas, and filled the position with credit to himself and satisfaction to the company.

As a private practitioner, Dr. Ayres was assiduous, sagacious, and excelled in nearly every department, although surgery was his favorite practice. He had located for life in Omaha, and to be near him, his parents, who had no other children, removed to Douglas County and settled near Omaha, where they now live.

He was married February 7th, 1885, to Miss Agnes Hoyt, of Omaha, who still resides in this city. In all the social and professional walks of life where Dr. Ayres was known, he was respected and loved. His gentle manners, brilliant intellect and active disposition brought him friends and success everywhere, and his untimely death, August 19, 1890, was considered a great loss to the profession and to the society of Omaha.

SAMUEL DeWITT BEALS was born in the village of Greene, Chenango County, New York, on the 10th day of January, 1826. His father's father, Capt. William Beals, master of a merchant vessel, put out from Stonington, Connecticut, just before a severe storm, and was never after heard from. His father, at that time a lad of eight years, was "bound out" as an apprentice to an uncle, Joseph Smith, to learn the carpenter's trade, and with him, afterward, went to the Chenango valley, New York.

His mother's father, Samuel Martin, of Coventry, New York, went from Connecticut to Chenango on horseback, taking all his earthly goods, and his young wife, Phœbe Goodrich, with him on one horse. This young woman had seen greater hardships of a similar kind. When a mere child, her father fled with her in his arms and with an older sister (all on the same horse) from the atrocities of the Indians and the flames of their burning home, fired by the noble (?) red men of the Mohawk Valley, at the burning of the village of Schenectady, in 1790. His father, Henry Beals and his mother, Ruth Martin, were married at her father's home in Coventry, in 1823. To them were born five children, three sons and two daughters, of whom only two survive, Susan Maria Stoddard, of Coventryville, New York, and the subject of this sketch.

DeWitt attended the village schools until 1840, when he was sent to a much-praised private school in Coventry. In 1842-3, his father had retired from his business as architect and builder, and lived on a farm of six hundred acres, on the crest of the divide between the Chenango River and the Genegantslet, one of its tributaries on the west.

Rural life at that time did not offer sufficient attractions to the son, and he bargained with his father to pay for his time and all his expenses while attending school, which he could do from a bequest from his mother's mother, (of which his father was guardian). In 1842-3 he attended the academy, at Oxford, and in 1844-5, the academy at Norwich, New York—the late Benj. F. Taylor being principal. While there, after a vigorous wrestling-match with his room-mate, he took cold that resulted in pneumonia, and threatened quick consumption.

His father would never after allow him to attend school away from home, and he was obliged to finish his school-work with the Rev. Dr. Azariah G. Orton, of the Presbyterian Church, and Rev. Dr. John V. Van Ingen, of the Episcopal Church, as tutors. His private studies, however, have never been abandoned and his library now numbers upward of three thousand volumes.

At the age of seventeen, he became a member of the First Congregational Church, of Greene. This church was connected with the Presbytery of Chenango, on what was known as the "plan of union." He was chosen several times as lay delegate to the Presbytery, and once to represent the church at the Synod of Susquehannah, at Walton, Delaware County, N. Y. The Presbytery, at a session held in Norwich, N. Y., chose him as its lay commissioner to the general assembly of the Presbyterian Church at St. Louis, Mo., in 1857. At the Synod he took an active part in the discussion of the right of synod to put any other construction on the act of the Presbytery of Chenango, in the "Norwich Church case," than the specific interpretation of the Presbytery itself. The Synod might pronounce the act of Presbytery unwise or unconstitutional, it could not give it an other interpretation. At the general assembly, although strongly opposed to slavery, he voted with the minority, against sending a committee to the Southern States to spy out slave holders in the church.

In 1848 Mr. Beals' father gave him a farm, which after a few years, on account of ill health he was obliged to give up. In 1858, he accepted an unsolicited offer of the principalship of the Union school, in his native village.

On the 28th day of June, 1847, he was married to Miss Grace Elizabeth Williams, daughter of Samuel and Sarah Williams, of Greene, N. Y., who has shared his sorrows and joys, his disappointments and successes, through the varied experiences of forty-six years. They have had two children, Emma Elizabeth Beals, born at Greene, July 4th, 1848, and Clara Williams Beals, born in the same town, September 28, 1851. Both died in Omaha, while yet young; the former at the age of twenty-two, on December 8, 1870, and the latter on the 15th day of January, 1869, at the age of 17. Their mortal remains rest in Prospect Hill Cemetery.

Mr. Beals came to Omaha in 1861, reaching here on April 5th. On the 22d of the same month, he opened a private school in the old State House on Ninth Street. This school was known for upward of six years as the Omaha High School. It opened with seven pupils, but before the end of the year the enrollment exceeded ninety, and two assistants became necessary. Pupils came from the adjoining counties and from the valley of the Platte, a hundred miles away, to attend this institution. It was well sustained, but on account of high rents and cost of living it did not prove to be profitable. He closed the school in May, 1867, and was immediately appointed clerk by the Hon. Thos. P. Kennard, secretary of state and *ex-officio* state librarian, who, residing at a distance from the capital, could not attend to the clerical duties of these offices.

In 1868, Governor David Butler appointed Mr. Beals his private secretary, and for the following year the clerical duties, and often more than these, devolved upon him.

Mr. Beals was appointed State Superintendent of Public Instruction by the governor, Febrnray 23, 1869. In this office his duties were difficult and arduous. The general tax for schools had been retained in the counties and towns where collected, and its distribution by the commissioners had been little more than in name. He secured their full payment into the State treasury and made the first equitable distribution in the following December. He visited nearly every organized county in the State, holding teachers' institutes, making addresses, and counselling with county superintendents and district boards, concerning the county organization of districts and the management of district affairs. He advised the officers of counties which were only partly settled, to include the whole county in the organized school districts, even to include the whole county in one district, and to build school houses as they should be required in different neighborhoods, taxing the whole county for the erection of every building, and in this way lighten the burden of the first settlers in all parts of the county, and compel non-resident land holders to contribute so far to the prosperity of the settlers, on whose labors they depended for profits by the increase in values. In many counties this policy to some extent was adopted. In Hall County it was fully carried out, and with best results.

In compliance with the law he designated the text books to be used throughout the State, and, notwithstanding the strenuous opposition of disappointed publishers, gained their general adoption. Some of the State officers proposed to make money out of the recommendation. One of them was dispatched to Chicago, but the same train that carried the State official carried also a private messenger, sent by the superintendent to inform the publishers, that the list of books would not be changed so long as the superintendent held his office; that their money, or want of it, would have no influence to change the list. He regarded a public office as a public trust; no man could make him swerve from faithfully performing every public duty, without regard to partisan or private interests. He raised the standard of teachers' qualifications by preparing and sending questions for the examination of teachers to the county superintendents, and receiving the answers submitted in return. To this thorough supervision and unselfish administration at the beginning, Nebraska owes much of her educational prosperity.

At the close of his term in 1871-2, he examined and graded the Omaha schools according to a course of study which he, assisted by Lyman Hutchinson, had prepared for them in 1870. In 1872-3, he held a principalship in one of the schools. In the fall of 1873, both political parties nominated him to the office of county superintendent of public instruction, for Douglas County. He was, of course, elected, and while in office revised the records of the district boundaries and their past changes, made new plats of all the districts, and devised a simple and complete method of keeping records of all future changes in boundaries, so that they could be seen at a glance. He prepared a graded course of study to secure uniformity of work and to prevent much of the unreasonable delays caused by change of teachers. His certificates gave full confidence to school directors as to the qualifications of the teachers presenting them. He resigned in July, 1874, to take the superintendency of the Omaha schools. To this office the board of education elected him six years in succession.

In the management of these schools he accomplished what few would have the courage to undertake. He prescribed methods for doing the work in all subjects, in all classes and grades, from the lowest in the primary, to the highest in the grammar department. It was not uncommon for him to take a class out of the teacher's hand, and give a practical illustration of the methods he recommended. To young and inexperienced teachers he gave particular attention, leading them to practice the best methods, at the same time explaining the reasons for their use, that they might be in full sympathy with the work.

In each of the first four years, he made nine entirely new monthly written examinations, preparing all the questions in all the subjects, for all the grades. He carefully examined the standing of all the pupils except the first primaries, and made all promotions. Such was the system in the work that similar classes in different parts of the city, on any given day, were rarely more than one or two lessons apart. Yet there was no unnatural strain, no nervous anxiety, save in a few instances that were traceable to the teacher and not to the school work. Men, who had for years been engaged in educational work — practical teachers from the extreme East, as well as from the West — after visiting them, pronounced the Omaha schools among the best in the country; some frankly said they had never seen such good work anywhere.

Since the expiration of his last term as superintendent, Mr. Beals has taught in the Omaha high school, where he is now engaged.

GEORGE PICKERING BEMIS.—The ancestry of the subject of this sketch were of English origin. The earliest mention of any member of the family in the United States is that of Joseph Bemis, who was born in 1619 and was in Watertown, Massachusetts, as early as 1640; was selectman in 1648, 1672 and 1675, and died August 2, 1684. In the fifth generation from him was Jonas Bemis, born December 21, 1766, and died July 7, 1841. His son, Emery Bemis, (the father of the present George Pickering Bemis, of whom we write), was born June 30, 1800, in Lincoln, Massachusetts, and died in Cambridge, same State, November 28, 1882.

George Pickering Bemis was born in Boston, Massachusetts, March 15, 1838, and few Americans during the active period of their lives have seen so much of the world; have come into intimate contact with so many people of all classes and conditions of society, at home and abroad; have been identified more or less closely with so many and varied enterprises, social, commercial and political, as Mr. Bemis. His given name was from the Rev. George Pickering, the grandfather on the mother's side, who at the time of his death, was the oldest effective Methodist minister in the world, having been a preacher for fifty-seven years. Inheriting from his father a considerable fortune, principally in slaves, Rev. Pickering refused to receive them or any profit from their sale or labor, and they were freed; he also declined to be made a bishop. He died December 8, 1846, in his seventy-eighth year.

When thirteen years of age Mr. Bemis removed with his parents to New York, he having previously attended the grammar schools of his native city, and for one year a school in Maine conducted by Alexander Hamilton Abbott. Although his father was a merchant in affluent circumstances, young Bemis, before he was fourteen, commenced his business career by engaging with a retail grocery on Eighth Avenue, New York, to open and close the store at $2.50 per week. About a year later he was employed with the shipping house of Wm. Whitlock, Jr., trading to Havre, France, and other countries, with packet and clipper ships. Four years later Mr. Bemis engaged with the extensive produce commission house of Finch & Hill, as head clerk, where he remained two years and then joined his father, who was doing an extensive business in the wholesale leaf tobacco trade in Boston for one-half a century.

In April, 1861, after the breaking out of the civil war and the Sixth Massachusetts Regiment had been fired upon in Baltimore, Mr. Bemis enlisted in the second battalion of light infantry, Boston Tigers, of Boston, expecting to go to Baltimore, but was ordered instead to Fort Warren, in Boston harbor, where he was the first guard, and remained about a month, after which he was on escort duty in the city for six months, when George Francis Train, who was in London introducing street railways, sent for him. On his arrival in that city he took charge of Train's business affairs, and also became general manager of the only American newspaper in Europe, *The London American*, at the solicitation of George Peabody, Charlotte Cushman and other prominent Americans who had raised a fund for the support of the paper. During the years 1861, 1862 and 1863, this paper had an extensive circulation in London, Paris and other European cities, and did effective service in the Union cause, while at the same time a rebel paper, the *Index*, was established within a couple of doors, advocating the cause of secession.

In 1863, Mr. Bemis returned to New York and established himself in the brokerage business in Wall street. In 1864 he again joined Train and helped to organize the *Credit Mobilier* for the purpose of building the Union Pacific Railway, and in 1865 assisted in organizing the *Credit Foncier* of America under charter from the Territory of Nebraska, of which Train was president, and Bemis secretary, the purpose being to build up towns and cities along the line of the Pacific Road. In 1868 Mr. Bemis came to Omaha, which has since been his place of residence, although during the time when Mr. Train was so extensively engaged in lecturing throughout the country he was his constant companion and business manager. In 1870 he accompanied Mr. Train on that gentleman's second tour around the world, visiting Japan, China and India, returning by way of the Red Sea and Suez Canal, to Marseilles in October, where Train organized a following of 80,000 of the *Commune*, the *International* and *Ligue du Midi*, while Paris was being besieged by the Prussians, and for a short time held possession of the city by a *coup d'etat*.

After Mr. Train retired from public life, Mr. Bemis devoted himself, until 1887, to the real estate and loan business in Omaha, where he has large interests.

The Bemis Park Company was organized and incorporated October 4, 1889. The officers elected were George P. Bemis, president; E. W. Nash, vice-president; J. H. Dumont, secretary and treasurer. The directors were the three officers named; also Dr. S. D. Mercer and E. L. Bierbower. This company was formed for the purpose of platting a sixty-acre tract; forty-eight acres and a half, known as College Place, belonging to Mr. Bemis, and eleven acres and a half being a part of Mercer Park, and belonging to Dr. Mercer.

The Bemis Park proper was dedicated to public use on the day of the recording of the plat of the sixty acres, October 23, 1889. It was laid out by Alfred R. Edgerton, landscape architect, of Syracuse, New York. It contains six acres and forty-four hundredths. Since then the city has purchased three acres additional, on the south side, giving it nearly a thousand feet south frontage on Cuming Street.

Mr. Bemis was nominated October 17, 1891, by the Republicans of Omaha for the office of mayor,—Henry Osthoff being selected the same day as the nominee of the Democrats. The nomination of Mr. Bemis was wholly unsolicited by him. His election on November 3, following, was by the largest majority ever given to any candidate for that office, being 4,484 votes over his opponent. "Mr. Bemis," said the *Bee* of the next day, "has reason to feel proud of this manifestation of popular confidence in his integrity, ability and fidelity to the material interests of this city. At no time in her history has Omaha been as much in need of a vigilant, energetic and devoted executive head of her municipal government. Mr. Bemis is not a politician. He is the creature of no cabal or political combine. He has not sought the office, but the office has sought him. His highest ambition will be to serve Omaha and merit the esteem and confidence of her best citizens."

The inaugural address of Mayor Bemis gave abundant evidence of the determination on his part, to use every legal means, to the extent of his power, in guarding honestly and economically the best interests of the city. "In accordance with the provisions of the charter," said he, "I will, from time to time, avail myself of the right conferred, to communicate to you such information and recommend such measures as may tend to the improvement of the finances, police, health, security, ornament, comfort, and general prosperity of the city. I shall endeavor also, as required by the charter, to be active and vigilant in enforcing all laws and ordinances of the city and to cause all subordinate officers to be dealt with promptly for any neglect or violation of duty. I am fully determined, to the limit of my power, that every department of the city shall be conducted honestly and economically, and with a view solely to the best interests of the public." That these pledges were carried out by the mayor cannot be gainsaid.

It has fallen to the lot of Mayor Bemis to welcome, since he became chief executive of Omaha, many gatherings from abroad, to the hospitalities of the city. In these public addresses he has evinced great versatility, a profound knowledge of men, and an unusual degree of that peculiar tact necessary in successful off-hand speeches. To the quadrennial general conference of the Methodist Episcopal Church, his greeting was peculiarly happy. Among many other of his good words on that occasion were these:

"We fully realize and appreciate the grand life-work which you have chosen in elevating mankind morally, mentally and spiritually; and we feel confident that your sojourn with us will ever be remembered as influencing us for good during the remainder of our lives. What a noble ambition for our young men to emulate, to follow in the footsteps of representatives of such a great organization.

"What a field there is for action," added the mayor, "in the way of home missionary work in the slums and amongst the poor and lowly in our cities. I sometimes wonder if our churches are not tending too much in the direction of social clubs; whether too much money is not going into great church edifices and not enough into the moral, mental and social elevation of the poor, forsaken mortals that seem to be doomed to the 'wallows' of our cities. It seems to me that we need more 'Peoples' Churches,' more 'Boys' and Girls' Industrial Homes,' more 'Homes of Shelter' more 'Open Doors,' more out-door preaching and teaching, more hospital, jail and poor-house visitations, and better sanitary work in the squalid and criminal districts. Our missionaries should become neighbors to the poor and destitute, and not merely visitors. The poor are inevitably better for close association with whole-souled men and women working for them in methods that do not permit a suspicion of sham."

The welcome of the mayor to the National Convention of the People's Party, July 1, 1892, was of a character well calculated to bring out his best thoughts upon matters appertaining to proper legislation—to a sound currency—and to correct relations as between capital on the one side and labor on the other. It was received as a more than ordinary non-partisan effort. Its patriotism was unmistakable : "Some may differ with you," said he, "as to how the country should be governed ; but we will not forget that we are all brothers, all citizens of this great nation. We are all Americans—not enemies, but friends—all anxious, in our way, to labor for the welfare or our glorious Union, which has no equal, and which, we sincerely hope and pray, will continue free and prosperous forever."

The address of Mayor Bemis to the representatives of organized labor, September 5, 1892 ("Labor Day") was especially characteristic of one who has always been known as the friend of the working man, and met with the hearty approval of the thousands of the honest sons of toil who had assembled to do honor to the day. Among other things, the speaker said: "The great body of the American people are right. In heart and in purpose, they are with the cause of labor. All that is lacking is the full appreciation and proper recognition of the reasonable demands of labor. How is this to be brought about? By violence? No. By anarchy? No. By riot and turbulence and bloodshed? No. It is to be brought about only in the manner we witness to-day—by peaceable agitation, and by orderly proceedings. It is by these means the working men of this country propose to demonstrate the justness of their cause, and to prove not only that 'the laborer is worthy of his hire,' but is entitled to such compensation for his labor, and to such reasonable hours of toil, as will enable him to support a family comfortably and decently and live like a man among men, with some of the comforts and pleasures of life."

There was much to be commended in his welcome to the Grand Lodge I. O. O. F., October 19, 1892; also, in his greeting, on behalf of the City of Omaha, to the members of the Head Camp of the Modern Woodmen of America; in his address to the Illustrious Nobles of the Imperial Council of the Mystic Shrine; to the Nebraska State Underwriters' Association at its second annual banquet; and to the many other of the numerous addresses he has been called upon to make, in his official capacity.

JAMES E. BOYD was born in County Tyrone, Ireland, September 9, 1834, and came to Belmont County, Ohio, with his parents in June, 1844. In 1847 he went with his father to Zanesville, in the same state, where he lived until 1856. There he worked three years in a provision store when he began carpenter-work. On the 19th day of August, of the year last mentioned, he reached Omaha, with his brother, John M. Boyd. At first, the two carried on the carpenter and joiner business. James was elected county clerk of Douglas County in 1857, but subsequently resigned the office. On the 22d of August, 1858, James was married in the Pacific House, Council Bluffs, Iowa, to Anna H. Henry, a native of Hamilton, Madison County, New York. She had a few months previous arrived in Omaha. Afterwards, the two went to Wood River, Buffalo County, (near the present town of Gibbon), Nebraska, the husband opening a stock farm. They remained there nine years. Mr. Boyd also engaged in merchandizing at Kearney City, two miles west of Fort Kearney, and in 1866, for the first time, contracted with the Union Pacific Railroad Company to grade a portion of their road, grading in four years over three hundred miles. Previous to this and while living at Wood River, he engaged in freighting across the plains. This was in the summer of 1865.

While residing in Buffalo County, Mr. Boyd was elected to the legislature—the first one that assembled after Nebraska became a State. It convened July 4, 1866.

After the completion of the Union Pacific Railroad (in working upon which, Mr. Boyd laid the foundation of his fortune) he moved back to Omaha. This was in February, 1868. He soon after purchased a controlling interest in the Omaha Gas Works and in 1868 and 1869 was manager of the plant. In the winter of 1869–70, he organized the Omaha & Northwestern Railroad Company, and was elected its first president. He built the road from Omaha to Blair. He put into the undertaking one-sixth of the money required to complete it to Tekamah. This road has since become an important part of the Chicago, Minneapolis, St. Paul & Omaha line.

In 1870, he helped to organize the Central National Bank of Omaha, and he was also president, for some time, of the Omaha Savings Bank.

In 1871, he was elected to the constitutional convention which framed a constitution that year to be submitted to the people of the state for adoption or rejection. It was rejected. While a member of this convention, the following was published of Mr. Boyd:

"J. E. Boyd, the young railroad king of Nebraska, has one of the most perfect physical organizations of the convention. A well balanced brain, supported by a strong, vigorous, and active physical constitution, gives him the peculiar elements essential to success. All the qualities of his mind are centered in financial issues. He is a good liver and enjoys a square meal. Given to a lymphatic temperament, he takes the world easy and meets the business of the future with mathematical calculations. He is neither miserly or lavish with his means, but must see first a necessity and then he will supply it. He would make a good lawyer, a better judge, but could become eminent only as a financier. He did faithful service as a member of the constitutional convention."

Mr. Boyd was also a member of the constitutional convention of 1875, and was chairman of the committee on railroads — not only in this convention, but in that of 1871.

In 1872, Mr. Boyd commenced pork packing in Omaha. The next year his buildings were considerably enlarged and the business increased to 13,450 head. The succeeding year the grasshopper ravages were such as to cause much of the live stock of Nebraska to be sold outside the state, and the number of fat hogs was much lessened. In consequence the packing for 1874–5 amounted to only 11,420. For 1875–6, Mr. Boyd still further enlarged his plant, and packed 15,042 hogs. The year 1876 was a favorable one for Nebraska farmers, who secured a large crop of corn and the packing season, which opened November 1st, was almost double that of the preceding year. In anticipation of this, Mr. Boyd erected extensive additions to his packing house, which then had a capacity for handling 40,000 head. The works represented an outlay of $33,000 and were equal in every particular to any similar establishment, at that date, in the west. In 1877, there were packed 40,000 hogs; in 1878–9, 60,000. The destruction of his establishment by fire January 18, 1880, was followed by a reconstruction of his premises on a larger scale and at a cost of $50,000. In 1886, he killed 141,000 hogs. He continued the business until the summer of 1887, when he sold his establishment.

In 1880, Mr. Boyd was one of the councilmen of Omaha, and on the 6th of April of the next year was chosen mayor of the city, receiving a majority of 1,939 votes in a total of 4,300. He served the full term of two years. He was at that date extensively interested in stock raising in Wyoming, near Fort Fetterman. The next year he was president of the Omaha Board of Trade. He was again elected mayor in 1885 by a large majority, proving himself, while in office, an able and efficient executive officer.

In 1881, during his first administration as mayor, the high-license law went into effect in Omaha and was enforced, although with much difficulty. He visited Detroit, during the same term of office, and made a careful investigation of its law with respect to paving and other public improvements; and it was at his suggestion that the city charter was amended so as to provide that paved intersections of streets and alleys should be paid for by the city, and the property holders should have five years in which to pay for the remainder. The present system of paving, curbing, guttering, and sewerage was adopted while he was mayor.

In politics, Mr. Boyd is a democrat. In the senatorial campaign of 1883, he received the vote of the democrats in the legislature for United States Senator, when Mr. Manderson was elected by the republican majority.

In the presidential campaign of 1884, he was a delegate to the convention which nominated Grover Cleveland, for whom he cast his vote. He was selected a member of the national democratic committee, and was a delegate to the national democratic convention of 1888. He was at this period head of the Chicago commission firm of James E. Boyd & Brother, and a member of the Chicago Board of Trade, also a member of the New York Stock Exchange.

As long ago as November 1880, Mr. Boyd laid the foundation of "Boyd's Opera House," on the northeast corner of Farnam and 15th Streets; and he had the structure completed and opened for business October 24, 1881; It had a seating capacity, all told, of 1,700. It was an expensive building for that time, and is still used as a theater, but is owned by other parties.

In 1890, Mr. Boyd began the erection of his new opera house on the southeast corner of Harney and Seventeenth Streets, an imposing structure five stories in height and having a seating capacity of two thousand. It was opened Thursday evening, September 3, 1891. The entire cost of the building was nearly $250,000.

In 1890, Mr. Boyd was nominated by the Democratic State Convention as candidate for governor, and was elected; on the 6th of February he sent his message to the legislature. It was an effort of more than ordinary importance:

"Assembled here," said the governor in the opening paragraph, "by the direction of the people of this great and growing commonwealth of Nebraska, to promote their interests and render obedience to their expressed will, I hope that in all things concerning the dignity of citizenship, and the public weal we may go hand in hand toward the faithful fulfillment of our accepted trust, guided by our best wisdom, ambitious in the performance of our labors, and at all times true to the honor and the escutcheon of the State. We meet here, instructed by the public voice, you in your sphere and I in mine, different in action, yet the same in end. As public servants, with express commands, we shall be held to strict account by those who sent us here. Subterfuges and strategies and weak expedients will all be swept away when we are called upon to explain the record made within these walls. Our principles abandoned and our pledges unperformed, the people disregarded and the State betrayed, means tomorrow as it meant yesterday, swift and complete political death. In all that pertains to blooming fields and prosperous homes; in all that brings the people of the prairies in close alliance with the people of the towns; in the promotion of their welfare; in the protection of their rights; the redress of their wrongs; in lifting their burdens and the speedy granting of their appeals; and finally in strict and even-handed justice to all, I herewith extend you my hearty approval in advance."

The governor then briefly presented for the consideration of the legislature a few suggestions of what appeared to him to be essential to the welfare and contentment of the people of the State. (1) He urged strict economy in public affairs; (2) he thought it a duty to lessen, if possible, the hardships of excessive taxation, wherever it existed; (3) he recommended an ample law concerning usury; (4) the public schools he spoke of as a source of great utility; (5) a reform in the system of voting was recommended; (6) prohibition he declared was dead, and should be allowed to rest in peace; (7) he thought the supreme judiciary should be relieved, and that a new constitution for the State was needed; (8) he entered pretty fully upon the question as to what legislation was needed concerning railroads; (9) the World's Columbian Exposition he spoke highly of, and recommended a reasonable appropriation by the State for an exhibition therein of its natural wealth and its resources, its material prosperity and the advanced industries of its people ought, he thought, to be exhibited to the world at large; (10) he spoke of the drouth of the preceding summer, and of the calling out of the national guards in the recent troubles with the Indians on the northern border of the State; (11) he recommended the election of presidential electors by districts; and (12) he asked for a close communion between the legislative and executive branches of the State government.

The governor concluded his message in these happy words: "Let us be distinguished in our labors for the good of our fellows and the glory of the State by that exalted ambition which rises above party affiliations and party strife; and when at last we part and go out from the scenes of our public service let us bear away with us that high consideration and respect, each for the other, that endearing remembrance of our public and social relations, and that sterling confidence in the sincerity and honor of us all, without which official life loses its most pleasing charm."

On the 6th of May following he was ousted from his office by a decision of the supreme court of Nebraska, Thayer, the previous governor, being given the place by that tribunal. However, on the 8th of February, 1892, he was reinstated as governor, under the ruling of the Supreme Court of the United States, and served the remainder of the term for which he had been elected. As chief executive of Nebraska, Governor Boyd performed his duties with credit, reflecting honor upon himself and the State.

CLINTON BRIGGS.—One of the pioneers of Nebraska, who has passed to that "undiscovered country from whose bourne no traveler returns," but whose memory is cherished by thousands, was Clinton Briggs, for many years one of the leading citizens of Omaha.

Mr. Briggs was born in Washtenaw County, Michigan, on the ninth of September, 1828. He studied law with Lathrop & Duffield, at Detroit, having, previous to 1850, received an academic education. He was admitted to the bar by the supreme court of his native state in 1853, soon after which he entered the law office of William H. Seward, of Auburn, New York, and the next year, on examination, was admitted to practice in the supreme court of that State. The year following, he was married to Miss Emily Manley, of Skaneateles, New York, an accomplished and estimable lady.

Mr. Briggs, on going to the West, began the practice of his profession in Omaha, he having settled here as early as the nineteenth of November, 1855, which gave him, properly, the title of "pioneer." He was soon elected county judge for a term of two years, before the expiration of which he was chosen a member of the legislature of the territory. He subsequently assisted in framing the present code of civil procedure of the State. Continuing in his law practice at Omaha, he formed a partnership with John I. Redick, and for ten years, and until the dissolution of the firm, they had a large and leading practice.

In 1860, Judge Briggs was elected mayor of the City of Omaha, on the republican ticket. His term in that office was distinguished by the establishing of telegraphic communication between Omaha and New York, and between the city first named and San Francisco. He had the honor of sending the first congratulatory messages to those cities. He was afterwards a member of the constitutional convention, in 1875, of Nebraska, and assisted in framing the present State constitution. The prominent position taken by the judge on the important questions which came before that body, added much to his reputation.

During the fifteen years following 1860,

Judge Briggs was engaged in an extensive practice, which frequently required him to prosecute cases in the supreme court of Nebraska, and the United States courts. His health becoming impaired, he abandoned the general practice, confining himself to a few important suits. In 1877, he was a candidate for the United States Senate, his name having been brought forward by his friends and his candidacy urged by them in recognition of long, persistent and successful efforts to compel two leading railroads of Nebraska to pay taxes on their immense land grants; but he was unsuccessful in the senatorial race.

In 1878, Judge Briggs traveled extensively in Europe, with advantage to his health, and upon his return he continued his journeyings in California and other western States and in the Territories. He aided, during his residence in Nebraska, various public enterprises, both in Omaha and the State at large, among which was the construction of the Omaha and Southwestern Railroad. At the time of his death, which occurred on the sixteenth of December, 1882, he was still employed in a number of important law cases.

Mr. Briggs had, in a marked degree, that intuitive perception of right and justice, that nice discrimination, that power of distinguishing between reported cases, that ability to eliminate the essential facts from the often confused narrations of clients, that readiness to discover the point really involved in a mass of testimony, which, when united, we are in the habit of denominating a legal mind. He was a logical reasoner, with excellent powers of analysis. Thus it happened that his counsel was eagerly sought after and implicitly followed by men of large means and representatives of important interests.

He was not what is ordinarily termed an eloquent man, nor was he fond of addressing juries; but when he did so, his character as a fair, honest and impartial man was frequently quite as effective as the most impassioned oratory would have been. He had a way of stating his opponent's case in what appeared to be the most disinterested manner, giving to him the benefit of all doubtful testimony and then demolishing the fabric he had erected, which was at once ingenious and successful.

But it was in courts of equity and before appellate tribunals that his abilities were most manifest. The early reports of the State, and those of the United States Supreme Court, when Nebraska was a Territory, bear witness alike to his industry and success. For ten or fifteen years of his residence in Omaha, the firm of which he was a member had a practice more varied, if not more extensive, than any other in the State. By it, and by successful investments in real estate, he had amassed, at the time of his death, a considerable fortune, which has now grown into a large and valuable patrimony.

His life was gentle, his manner quiet, his voice low, and his habits rather retiring than aggressive. Conspicuous among his characteristics was an evident unwillingness to wound the feelings of anyone, even his antagonists. With the younger members of the bar he was always a favorite, and for them he invariably had some kindly word of advice or congratulation. So it came to pass that the sudden and mysterious catastrophe which terminated his life found him with hardly an enemy in the world. He left one child—a son, Clinton Henry Briggs —born February 9, 1867, who, with the mother, still survives.

WILLIAM JAMES BROATCH, the subject of this sketch, was born in Middleton, Connecticut, July 31, 1841, where he attended the public and high schools at intervals until the age of seventeen years. Losing his father at twelve, and being the eldest of a family of five children—four brothers and one sister—he was obliged to secure employment in order to support the family. From twelve to fourteen he lived upon a farm—rough and incongenial as the labor upon a New England farm was to him,—yet the experience was invaluable in after life, and aided him greatly in the charge of the Yankton Indian Agency, a position afterwards held by him,—the reservation then consisting of four thousand acres, where the Indians were taught to till the soil and acquire the habits of civilized people.

From fourteen to seventeen he was employed, when not in school, in various manufacturing establishments, where he learned to forge a piece of iron or run a lathe, as well as to manage the machinery in general use in a machine shop. During this period he attended school in winter, and at other times prosecuted a course of study and reading during evening hours. It was his ambition to take a collegiate course, but in this he was destined to disappointment. At seventeen he went to Hartford and there entered a store as a clerk, where he remained until the breaking out of the war of the Rebellion, which occurred just before he had attained his majority. During these years he still kept up his educational desires, and associating other clerks with him, formed a class for evening study.

Mr. Broatch was always a strong abolitionist and took a deep interest in everything relating to the question of slavery. He felt that, all other means failing, a war for the liberation of the slaves would be justifiable. From the time that the *Star of the West* was fired into, December, 1860, he saw that war was inevitable, and in order to accustom himself in some slight degree to the hardships incident to campaign life, he forsook his bed and slept upon the floor. When the first call for troops was made, he volunteered in Captain (afterward Senator) Hawley's company, but being a minor, was rejected. In September, 1861, having come of age, he enlisted in Company A, Eighth Connecticut Volunteers, at Hartford; and, with that regiment, he served in the Burnside expedition on the coast of North Carolina, being present at the battles of Roanoke Island and Newbern, and at the siege of Fort Macon. He was also in the naval engagement at Roanoke Island, February 7, 1862, on board the gunboat *Chasseur*, which was used as a transport for a part of his regiment and by some mistake took part in the engagement. He was promoted to second lieutenant in March, 1862, and to first lieutenant in the following September.

After McClellan's failure on the peninsula, Burnside's command was hurriedly sent to the James River, and there Lieutenant Broatch was detailed for recruiting service in his native State. A portion of the time he was stationed at Fort Trumbull, assisting in the care of recruits and in making frequent trips to the field with detachments, which were assigned to regiments. Fort Trumbull was the headquarters of the Third United States Artillery and the Fourteenth United States Infantry. Becoming acquainted with many regular officers, Lieutenant Broatch determined to enter the regular army. He accordingly resigned his commission in October, 1863, and in November following enlisted in the Fourteenth United States Infantry. He went to the field at once and joined his regiment on the Rappahannock. He subsequently took part in the Mine Run campaign which, though brief, was distinguished for hardship and the extremely cold weather, rather than military results. During the winter of 1863-64, he was called before a board of examination, composed of a detail of officers from Syke's division of regulars, and, passing, was recommanded to the secretary of war for a commission in the regular army. At this time he was first sergeant of Company F, Second Battalion of the Fourteenth Infantry. In February, 1864, the secretary of war convened a board of regular officers at Washington, before which he appeared, and, passing a satisfactory examination, he soon had the satisfaction of knowing that President Lincoln had sent his name to the senate for confirmation as a second lieutenant of infantry. He was appointed sergeant-major of the Third Battalion, Fourteeth Infantry, and served as such until the 14th of May, 1864, when notice of his confirmation had been received. He was in the Fifth Army Corps and present in all its battles and skirmishes, commencing the fifth of the month last named, beginning with the Wilderness on that day and ending with the Chapel House in October following—including besides the two just mentioned, those of Spottsylvania, Tolopotomy, Petersburg and Weldon Railroad. He was brevetted first lieutenant in the month last mentioned for gallant and meritorious service at the battle of Chapel House and assigned to the Tenth Infantry, leaving the field late in the month, his regiment being reduced to sixty-five muskets. He acted as aide-de-camp on the staff of General Hayes, commanding a regular brigade at the battle of Weldon Railroad, and was assistant adjutant general of the regular brigade under General Stone and Colonel Wintrop, his staff duty commencing with August and ending with October, 1864.

Lieutenant Broatch was ordered, afterwards, to Fort Porter, Buffalo, where, after a short stay, he was ordered upon recruiting service in New York City and Brooklyn. He remained in these cities until the spring of 1865, when he was ordered to a similar duty at Harrisburg, Pennsylvania. In the autumn following he was ordered to the general depot of Governor's Island, New York Harbor, and in December thereafter, with a company, joined his regiment at Jefferson Barracks, Missouri.

In March, 1866, Lieutenant Broatch was appointed an aide-de-camp on the staff of Brigadier General Philip St. George Cooke, and came with him to Omaha, the headquarters of the Department of the Platte, which had just been created. On the 28th of July, following, he was commissioned a captain in the Fortieth regiment of infantry, joining it at Alexandria, Virginia.

Captain Broatch, in March, 1867, embarked with his company on the steamer *Flambeau*, for Fort Fisher, North Carolina. Arriving off the entrance to Cape Fear River, they were stranded on a sand bar and wrecked, losing nearly all their personal effects. He served in North Carolina during the reconstruction period. He subsequently went to New Orleans with his regiment,—asking, finally, to go upon awaiting orders, which was granted, and he went to Ohio. Afterwards he was detailed to take charge of the Yankton Sioux Indians, and having served as Indian agent for a year, during 1869–70, he again went to Ohio on awaiting orders. Finally, he resigned his commission in the army, to take effect December 31, 1870.

Captain Broatch settled in Omaha in March, 1874, and engaged in the iron and heavy hardware trade, which he has ever since followed. He was a member of the Nebraska legislature in 1881, and took an active interest in the passage of the high license law. The bill, as introduced, made the license five hundred dollars. He amended it in committee of the whole and made it one thousand dollars. He was a member of the Missouri River Commission, being appointed by President Arthur at the time of its creation; and he served upon it until his resignation in March, 1891. He has also been a member of the Omaha Board of Trade since its re-organization in 1877, and was a member of its board of directors in that year and in the one following, and was its president in 1879.

In May, 1887, Mr. Broatch was elected to the office of Mayor of Omaha. During his term, the high license law, in its entirety, was, for the first time, enforced in the city. He endeavored and fully succeeded in administering affairs of his office in a conservative manner and in the interest of good government. There were many abuses which he made it his aim to correct —one at a time—and in such a way as to produce the least possible friction. He was the first mayor under the new charter. This charter brought with it enlarged powers and increased responsibilities, and Mayor Broatch did not shrink from them, but pursued his official career within the law, being determined that his administration should be clean and in the interest of the property owners and tax payers.

As Mayor of Omaha, Mr. Broatch was frequently called upon to address assemblages of people from abroad and sometimes he was asked to speak to his fellow citizens. In all these efforts he acquitted himself with credit. Some of his efforts deserve especial mention. In the dedication of the Jewish Synagogue, July 1, 1889, are a few words on religion, of which any of our most learned theologians might be proud:

"Every effort to establish religious worship is consistent with the best interests of society and should be encouraged. Religion is a necessity, and every human being is happier with a well grounded faith. In our hours of adversity, when abandoned by former friends, we turn to our God and religion and there find a consolation which nothing else affords. The Indian has his religion, primitive though it be, and

" 'Sees God in clouds, or hears Him in the wind.'

"He, in his way, looks forward to the time when he must pay that debt to nature which none can escape, and hopes by his deeds on earth to obtain a happy place in the hunting grounds of the spirit land. He has no conception of a spiritual existence such as we believe in, yet he believes in immortality and is happy in his religion. Go wherever you will, where you find the synagogue, the cathedral, or the church, you will find a people prosperous and happy, obedient to the laws, and advancing in all that contributes to the amenities of life and makes it worth having."

His speech on behalf of the city to the convention on Charities and Reform; his address to the A. O. U. W., when they dedicated their new hall; his remarks at the opening of the Hebrew Charity Fair; his address on the opening of the Inter-state Bridge across the Missouri; and the words spoken by him upon the dedication of the Y. M. C. A. building, were all able efforts.

Mr. Broatch was unanimously nominated at the Republican State Convention, in 1892, as an elector-at-large on the Republican ticket, and was elected on the 8th of November following. He has always been an ardent Republican, and regrets that his vote will not avail in the choice of a president. He favors the principle of protection, and believes in that of reciprocity. He never has, however, believed in a protection which will admit of the formation of great trusts, or allow manufacturers to amass colossal fortunes.

Mr. Broatch was married January 21, 1869, at Canton, Ohio, to Julia F. Schneider. Two sons have been born of this union, one only now living—James Wallace Broatch—who is a graduate of Yale College, and is at present engaged with his father in the hardware business in Omaha.

AMELIA BURROUGHS.—The parents of the subject of this sketch, Peter Milestone and Nancy Parsons Milestone, are both natives of England, the first of Yorkshire, and the latter of Southampton. They came to America about forty-three years ago, the father settling in Medina and the mother in Cleveland, Ohio. They were married in July, 1857, and now reside in Omaha.

Amelia is the eldest of the family of five children, having been born in Wellington, Ohio, on the 22d of June, 1852. Her earliest education was obtained at home and at the district schools of her native place. The parents having moved to Cleveland in 1860, the daughter, thereafter, had the advantages of public and select schools, attending among others those of Humiston Institute and Woodland Avenue Seminary.

Miss Milestone was married in Cleveland October 8, 1873, to Edgar W. Burroughs of Greenwood, Michigan, where the two resided for two years. One child, a son—Will Bliss—was born there September 14, 1874, and is still living.

Mrs. Burroughs had, from an early age, a desire to study medicine, and this was gratified by her entering upon a course of reading, in 1877, with her aunt, Dr. Kate Parsons, of Cleveland, having previously studied at her home, and acting as assistant physician at the women's dispensary in connection with the Cleveland Homeopathic Hospital College. In the fall of the year last mentioned, Mrs. Burroughs entered this college as a regular student, graduating in 1881, acting as dispensary physician the second year of her course in that institution, and having under her care over a thousand patients.

After this, in 1881, Dr. Burroughs came to Council Bluffs (where her husband had located meanwhile) and opened an office in the practice of her chosen profession. In 1883, she located in Omaha, where she has since lived.

Dr. Burroughs is a member of the Nebraska State Homeopathic Society, the Northwestern Academy of Homeopathy, and the American Institute of Homeopathy.

ROBERT HARPER CLARKSON was born at Gettysburg, Pennsylvania, November 19, 1826. He was of an old and honored family. His grandfather, Rev. Joseph Clarkson, D. D., was rector of St. James Church, Lancaster, Pennsylvania, until he reached a great age. The father of the subject of this sketch was, during his son's boyhood, a man of extensive business and was always held largely in public esteem. During the latter part of his life he lived in retirement. He died in Omaha. His wife was Priscilla Harper.

Robert's academic education was received at Pennsylvania College, in his native place, where he graduated in 1844. Shortly afterward he became tutor at the College of St. James, in Hagerstown, Maryland. While there he studied theology, and was ordained deacon, June 18, 1848. He was married May 8, 1849, in the place last named, to Meliora McPherson.

On the day of their wedding, before the sounds of festivity were over, the young couple took up their long and weary way to Chicago—he, while yet in deacon's orders, to be rector of St. James Church, in that city. For the seventeen years in which he held the position, "by his untiring efforts, his urbane manners, his loving interest, his wise administration," he so managed the affairs of the parish that it became the leading one in the diocese. He was ordained priest January 5, 1851. In 1857 he received his doctorate in divinity from his *alma mater*, and also from

Racine College. The University of Nebraska, in 1872, conferred upon him the first of its degrees of doctor of laws.

In 1865, the subject of this sketch was elected missionary bishop of Nebraska and Dakota by the general convention of the church. On the 15th of November, of that year, in his own church edifice, in Chicago, he was consecrated to that office. He first visited Omaha the next month, and shortly after became a resident of this city. In 1868, Nebraska was erected into a diocese and he was unanimously elected its first bishop. He retained jurisdiction in Dakota for some years, when the western part of that territory was detached and made a separate district with a bishop of its own. In the fall of 1883, at his own request, he was relieved of his missionary jurisdiction, the work having outgrown his strength; and he then looked forward to years of effort to be given wholly to Nebraska. But the future was not unveiled before him; his labors were nearing their end. He died in Omaha on the 10th of March, 1884, and was buried on the 13th in the cathedral yard, in a spot which he had selected, south of the south transept of the building.

His widow survives him, and she is still a resident of Omaha. Their children are Mrs. Mary McPherson Millspaugh and Nellie Clarkson Davis.

The record of Robert Harper Clarkson, as rector and bishop in the Episcopal Church, is one of more than ordinary interest. Upon his arrival in Chicago, the zeal and enthusiasm of his nature, at once began to stimulate the efforts of his parishioners, and the parish soon felt the influence of his energy and devotion. Additional accommodations were shortly needed for the increasing congregation—the members of which he gathered from all sorts and conditions of men. The little edifice at Cass and Illinois Streets soon proved quite inadequate for the number of people that frequented the services, and a new and larger building was demanded. The lot on which the present church stands was purchased, and the corner stone of the new structure laid in the spring of 1856. The edifice was a fine one, but was destroyed in the great fire; but the debt of $30,000 upon the premises, owing to the energy and tact of Dr. Clarkson, had previously been cancelled. The history of the parish under his rectorship of seventeen years, was one of great unity and increasing prosperity.

When Dr. Clarkson was made missionary bishop, Nebraska was not the pleasant diocese it now is. It had no delightful residences like Omaha with its fine buildings and its cultivated society. There was no stately cathedral, no lovely bishop's house, no Brownell Hall with its crowding scholars. The bishop's trials and perils, by land and water, by flood and tempest, by heat and cold, during the early years of his episcopate, would, if truthfully and minutely related, shock the nerves of sensitive persons. He lived to see the State of his adoption rise to power, in population and in wealth. He lived to see the few struggling missions, which, far scattered, were all he could call his own when first he came, expand into flourishing diocese with its fine churches, its schools, its colleges and its hospitals.

As a man, as a citizen, as a priest, as a bishop, Robert Harper Clarkson played well his part. He had a ready wit; was fertile in resources and quick in perception. Few men have lived who surpassed him in nobleness and generosity. He could not resist the appeal of distress. His purse, his home, his pen, his influence, were always at the command of his friends. "Anger passed out of his heart and resentments faded from his memory as the cloud fades from the limpid waters."

In the school, which Bishop Clarkson provided for the daughters of Omaha and the West; in the beautiful charity for little children which he planted and built up in this city; and in the catheral here, which he toiled so incessantly to complete; in these and in many more achievements, he has erected unto himself a monument that will tell, to future ages, in unmistakable language, of his purity, of his goodness, and of the nobility of his Christian charity.

VICTOR H. COFFMAN, M. D.—From the genealogical leaflet of the Coffman family, compiled by Isaac Fenton King, a member of the family, we learn that the ancestors of Victor H. Coffman, the subject of this sketch, were originally from Woodstock, Virginia. William Coffman, the father of him of whom we write, was born at Zanesville, Ohio, June 8, 1807, and died at Indianola, Iowa, April 8, 1888. On December 10, 1835, he married Mary Gates, who died at Indianola, Iowa, February 2, 1868. Victor H. Coffman was born September 10, 1839, near Zanesville, Ohio, where he spent his early childhood. When in his fourteenth year his parents moved to Indianola, Iowa. Soon afterwards he entered the Iowa Wesleyan University, at Mount Pleasant, continuing his course till the senior year. He then began the study of medicine with Dr. C. W. Davis, under whose instruction he advanced rapidly during the period of study. He was, of course, called upon many times to witness and assist in various surgical operations, at which times he became almost disheartened with the profession, the sight of mangled limbs being almost too much for his sensitive nature and too sympathetic heart; but the encouragement of his sister and the determination of Dr. Davis, who recognized marked ability in his young student, he is indebted for his future surgical career. In 1859 the young surgeon entered the Chicago Medical College, attending the regular lectures during that year and the one following. When the war began, General George W. Clark, a warm personal friend, who was recruiting a regiment for the field, advised him to go before the army medical board for examination, promising, if he passed the required examination, to have him commissioned as a medical officer in his regiment. He reported immediately at Keokuk, Iowa. After going through the examination, Dr. Hughes, chairman of the board, stated he would take great pleasure in recommending the young man to Governor Kirkwood for a commission, and, although only nineteen years of age, he was commissioned assistant surgeon, September 16, 1862. General Clarke, with his officers, requested that he be assigned to the Thirty-fourth Iowa infantry, and ordered to report at once at Camp Lauman, at Burlington, Iowa, where his regiment rendezvoused. On his arrival, he relieved Dr. Horace Ranson, who was in charge. The acquaintance there begun with Dr. Ranson, has continued with warm friendship to the present. Dr. Coffman accompanied his regiment to Helena, Arkansas, there joining the fleet which transported the army to attack Vicksburg. From Vicksburg (still on duty with the regiment) he went to Arkansas Post, participating in the battle and capture of that place, and accompanied his regiment, which escorted the prisoners captured there through to Chicago. The medical experience of that voyage is indescribable. Small-pox broke out among the prisoners; the cold weather was fatal to many; the dead were buried at every landing; and at Arsenal Island, near St. Louis, all the sick were put in a small-pox hospital. Between Alton and Chicago the faithful hospital steward was taken with the disease and died at Camp Douglas. Returning to Benton Barracks, St. Louis, Dr. Coffman reported the entire regiment disabled and ordered them into the hospital and convalescent camp. When the regiment was recruited, it returned to engage in the siege of Vicksburg. The sickness endured by the command was most appalling, and the death rate so great that it came near decimating the entire army.

Though Surgeon Coffman made many amputations to save life, in order to transport the wounded to the hospitals, it would have been unnecessary, in many cases, had these patients been where their shattered limbs could have been cared for.

When ordered to the first charge at Walnut Hill, an old friend, Lieutenant Fitzer, of the Fourth Iowa, received a slight wound in the head, so trifling in appearance that he thought it looked cowardly to leave the field. Dr. Coffman insisted he should go at once to the hospital steamer, and maintain perfect quiet; if not, he would be in great danger, as he believed the wound sufficient to rupture the vessels of the brain. True to his predictions, the lieutenant died of that wound, and his bravery was confirmed.

It was in this campaign when Dr. Coffman, with Surgeon Burke, General Sherman's medical director, entered a field hospital where some old surgeons were operating on a soldier, attempting to remove an arm with a tourniquet applied, the hemorrhage was uncontrolled. Dr. Coffman seeing the peril, stepped up, and placing his thumb over the subclarian artery, compressed it, telling the surgeons to remove the tourniquet and proceed with the amputation, which they did. Upon this incident, the medical director at once issued an order assigning him as *chief* of the operating staff, which honored position he always filled with honor at every succeeding engagement during the war. When General Sherman called for volunteers, through the officers of his command, to run the batteries at Walnut Hill, the Thirty-fourth Iowa responded, knowing that the passage before the batteries meant almost instant death. Dr. Coffman was consulted, stating he would accompany them on the transport to the bottom of the Yazoo River, where they were all destined to land, fortunately the order was rescinded, and the brave soldiers were saved from destruction, as the river was full of torpedoes.

On the 26th of November, 1863, Dr. Coffman was honored by receiving promotion to the office of surgeon of the regiment. The duties of regimental surgeon he performed faithfully, till he was assigned to duty on the staff of General C. C. Andrews, commanding one of the divisions of the Thirteenth Army Corps, as his chief medical officer. At the siege of Mobile, he was at the operating table, where he worked for forty-eight hours continuously without rest. He was also on duty for a term with General Steel, as his medical officer. Dr. Coffman was always a favorite with his superior officers, never failing to obey an order.

On the 13th of March 1865, was dated his commission, from the President of the United States, as brevet lieutenant colonel, for meritorious services rendered during the Mobile campaign, he having been recommended by General C. C. Andrews, with whom he was serving. When not on other duty, the doctor continued with his regiment through the different campaigns. He was with the fleet which encountered such a fearful storm on the Gulf of Mexico *en route* to the mouth of the Rio Grande, after which he was with General G. Ransom, who was the commander of the forces on the Texas coast, and of whom he speaks with the greatest praise. At the close of the war he was ordered to proceed north to Davenport, Iowa, where his regiment was mustered out of service in 1865. The doctor never had been off duty or on a leave of absence during the war. Upon leaving the army Dr. Coffman went to Philadelphia, obtaining the degree of doctor of medicine from the Jefferson Medical College, thence returning south, he went to Houston, Texas, taking the position of acting surgeon. He was assigned to duty with the Seventeenth Infantry, Major Lathrop's command, serving with them till the fall of that year, when he returned to New York, entering the College of Physicians and Surgeons, at Bellevue Hospital, spending the winter there, from whence he came to Omaha to visit a sister, and thinking this a good field, decided to locate. He arrived in April, 1867, on a stage coach, with Judge Savage as a fellow passenger.

The history of the Iowa troop, in commenting on the 34th Iowa Infantry, refers to Surgeon Victor H. Coffman as one of the best and bravest of surgeons, and best of men. Since the close of his army service, he has always been willing to aid the invalid soldiers, and soldiers' widows, to obtain pensions whenever it is in his power. The doctor has continued in general practice since he first located in Omaha. He applied the first plaster of paris dressing for spinal curvature in Nebraska, his patient being a little child of Captain Spencer, late of the Confederate navy. The first operation of ovariotomy in Nebraska was performed by Dr. Coffman, in St. Joseph's hospital, since which time he has many times performed the same successfully. One of his recent operations was one of the most brilliant ever performed in this country, being the removal of a tumor of the thyroid gland, an operation never before performed in this country. It was performed in the presence of all the most prominent physicians and surgeons of Omaha, not one of whom believed the patient could survive; yet this did not deter Surgeon Coffman. The patient fully recovered and is still a resident of Omaha. This operation is seldom performed even by Billroth, of Vienna, who has only performed it four times and not always with success. Dr. Coffman's operations have always been characterized by conservatism. Whilst partial to operation surgery and bold in its execution, he has a dislike to fractures, preferring to pay the fee to another surgeon to attend cases of this kind, rather than perform the operations himself. His obstetric practice has been very extensive and most successful, but his preference is to treat disease. He has the reputation of being most remarkable in his faculty to diagnose diseases. In disposition he is kind, considerate, and most generous, never losing an opportunity to render assistance to young and less favored men in his profession. He is a descendant of a long line of professional men, among whom have been those devoted to law, medicine, theology and letters. He is a first cousin to

Rev Dr William King of the Methodist Episcopal Church, holding the honored position of president and professor of Greek and Latin of Cornell College for the past twenty years.

Dr Coffman was married on the 10th of September, 1879, by the Rt Rev Daniel Riordan, in the city of Chicago, to Miss Rose Devoto, a young lady of many accomplishments and rare gifts, a graduate of the famous school, St Mary's Academy, Notre Dame, Indiana, where she is remembered as one of the brightest students

Her name is still a household word in her loved alma mater, spoken with affection by tutors and students She is a native of Ohio, though born of Italian parentage. She inherits a voice of rare sweetness which has received much cultivation Of this union there have been four children Weis D Coffman, born August 8, 1880, Augusta Marie, born December 6, 1882, Rose Lyle, born July 1, 1886 Thecla Ione born January 11, 1892, died, March 11, 1892

* Doctor fairly worships his children. They have been baptized in the Catholic Church, and his greatest pride is in their little devotions He believes in educating children in faith and belief and observance of a religion, and an obedience to the laws of God and man Dr Coffman is a member of the State Medical Society, also a member of the American Medical Association He was one of the organizers of the Omaha Medical College and was chosen professor of theory and practice, which position he held for a term of years, during which time he was also elected president, resigning his chair on account of over-work in his profession, he having probably the most extensive practice in the State, during several years past, his book accounts and cash receipts amounting to thousands of dollars yearly. His devotion has been to the practice and not to collections, as his unpaid book accounts attest After having been in practice twenty-five years in Omaha, his unpaid accounts amount to over one hundred and fifty thousand dollars He has always been most kind to the poor, and more considerate to them in his attentions than to the wealthy He keeps pace with his profession, is a keen observer, a special diagnostician, and withal a very successful practitioner Socially he is "a hale fellow well met" with all, is widely known in his profession from ocean to ocean, and is recognized by the ablest men as at the head of his profession He has a great reverence for religious belief, and during the earlier part of his life was a member of the Methodist Episcopal Church

THOMAS B. CUMING.—The subject of this notice was born in Genessee County, New York, December 25, 1828 His father was Francis H Cuming, born in Connecticut, an Episcopal clergyman, who officiated first in St Luke's Church, in Rochester, and subsequently in St Mark's Church, Grand Rapids, Michigan His mother's maiden name was Caroline A Hulbert, who died when Thomas was a child, and the father again married—the second time to Charlotte Hart The boy became one of the family of Rev Dr Penny, a Presbyterian preacher, in Rochester He afterwards returned to his father (whose home was then in Michigan) under whose care he was prepared for college

In his boyhood, he enjoyed a training of the highest character His father instilled into his young mind, with all a parent's anxiety and care, those habits of laborious study—of thorough mastery of whatever engaged his attention — which eminently fitted him for an honorable career in life Especial care was taken as to his religious culture He entered the first freshman class of the University of Michigan—an institution then just put into operation The student-life of the young man was a commendable one, and, although the youngest of his class when graduated, he received the honors of the faculty, evidenced particularly in the university, by his delivering the Greek oration

Removing with his father's family to Grand Rapids, he began teaching, following that occupation until the commencement of the Mexican war, when he enlisted, and, after many hardships, reached the scenes of conflict, and was soon the recipient, by post, of a lieutenant's commission Contracting disease, he was compelled to return to his own country from the army He was afterwards "carried away" with the California gold fever, but he got no farther west on his journey than St Louis, where he was prevailed upon to accept the position of telegrapher Although entirely unacquainted with telegraphing, in three weeks he mastered "the magnetic mysteries of lightning printing," and was subsequently placed in charge of the Peru and Keokuk offices. This brought him finally to the last-named place as a resident—fortunately.

But the occupation of the young man did not wholly engage his mind. He wrote an anonymous article to the *Dispatch*, a paper published in Keokuk. It arrested attention; he wrote another—curiosity as to who was its author was excited; another and another appeared, and curiosity increased more and more. One person and another to whom they were first attributed disclaiming their authorship, they were at last traced to the young telegraph operator. The ability which they displayed was not to be lost, and he was immediately placed in charge of the paper. It soon came to be the leading journal in the State—hardly ever did a country newspaper exercise such large influence.

On the 6th of December, 1853, Mr. Cuming and Miss Marguerite Carleton Murphy, a most intelligent and beautiful lady, of Keokuk, were married. The wife, a Catholic in her religion, is a descendant of some of the first settlers of Maryland and Virginia, of which last mentioned State she is a native; and she is still living in Omaha, highly respected, the sister, it may be said, of Frank Murphy, the well-known capitalist of the city.

It was while in charge of the *Dispatch*, in 1854, and somewhat in reward for the valuable services rendered by him to the democracy, that he was appointed Secretary of Nebraska, by President Pierce, under the act of congress organizing the Territory, approved May 30, of that year. The officers appointed were, Samuel Burt, of South Carolina, governor; Thomas B. Cuming, of Iowa, secretary; Fenner Ferguson, of Michigan, chief justice; James Bradley, of Indiana, and Edwin R. Hardin, of Georgia, associate justices; Mark W. Izard, of Arkansas, marshal; and Experience Estabrook, of Wisconsin, attorney. Governor Burt reached Bellevue, the only village in the Territory worthy of the name of one, on the 7th of October, 1854, and the next day came Secretary Cuming and his lady. The governor was soon taken sick, but notwithstanding the fact, took the oath of office on the 16th. Two days later he died.

The vacancy in the executive office caused by Governor Burt's death, was filled by Secretary Cuming, who, *ex officio*, became acting governor. The first act requiring his signature in an official way, was his transmitting the intelligence of the governor's death to President Pierce, by telegraph and letter.

The acting governor's first official act, which was the first one performed in the Territory by its chief executive, was the issuing of a Thanksgiving proclamation, October 18, 1854.

The second official act of the acting governor was a proclamation, issued in pursuance of the requirements of the organic act, giving notice that there would be an enumeration of the inhabitants of the territory. It was dated October 21, 1854, and announced that the enumeration would commence in three days thereafter, under officers, instructed to complete the same, if possible, in four weeks. Immediately after the completing of the census (which showed a population of 2,732, including 13 slaves), notices were distributed for the election of a delegate to congress and a territorial legislature. The election was held December 12, 1854, resulting in the election of Napoleon B. Gidding, as delegate. Upon the basis of 2,732 inhabitants, Governor Cuming apportioned the number of councilmen and representatives among the eight counties of the Territory he had created under the organic acts as follows: Douglas County, four councilmen, eight representatives; Pierce County, three councilmen, five representatives; Burt County, one councilman, two representatives; Washington County, one councilman. two representatives; Dodge County, one councilman, two representatives; Cass County, one councilman, three representatives; Forney County, one councilman, two representatives; Richardson County, one councilman, two representatives.

The location of the capital of the Territory was another of the important acts devolving upon Governor Cuming. It was given him by the organic act and he had to determine and fix the time and place when the first session of the legislative assembly should be held. He fixed the date to be January 16, 1855, and the place Omaha City, by a proclamation issued December 20, 1854.

At ten o'clock A. M., on the day fixed by the proclamation just mentioned, the legislature of the Territory assembled at "Omaha City," consisting of thirteen councilmen and twenty-six representatives, the number designated in the act of congress creating the Territory, and to this body on that day Governor Cuming delivered his message.

It may be mentioned that even before the assembling of the legislature, Omaha was the scene of intense excitement. "Men disappointed in their cherished hopes at the failure to secure the location of the capital in their respective 'towns,' filled the streets, and vowed that the session should not be held." But the decision of the governor was finally sustained without bloodshed.

A successor to Governor Burt in the person of Mark W. Izard, of Arkansas, having been appointed by the president, that officer was formally presented to both houses of the territorial legislature by Acting Governor Cuming, on the 30th of February, 1855, and was heartily welcomed. He responded in a neat but very brief speech. On the 23d he took the oath of office and the acting governor at once assumed the duties of secretary only. Governor Izard delivered his first formal message on the 27th.

From the date of Secretary Cuming assuming again the duties of his office until the resignation, in November, 1857, of Governor Izard, when he again became acting governor, he discharged them faithfully.

His message as acting governor to the territorial legislature at its fourth session, which began December 8, 1857, and was delivered the next day, recommended an application to Congress for a grant of land to assist and encourage railroad enterprises, especially for a Pacific railroad through the route by the valley of the Platte, arguing that to be the most feasible and natural route. The subject of banking was next mentioned; he advocated a monthly or at least quarterly inspection of them. He informed the legislature that the United States wagon road from the Platte River, by way of the Omaha reserve, had been constructed to the Running Water, a distance of one hundred and three miles; and that the military road to Fort Kearney was nearly finished. He also mentioned that there had been preempted in the Territory, during the year 1857, 402,349 acres of land; that 339,131 acres had been secured on warrants; and that 63,218 acres had been purchased with cash. It was, by odds, the ablest executive paper that had yet made its appearance in Nebraska.

"Peace and good order," said the governor, "practical vigor and manly observance of constitutional obligations have characterized the conduct of our people. No dangerous agitations or political heresies have been permitted to take root; but the seeds of industry, education and law, planted at the commencement by enterprising and practical men, have yielded the legitimate fruit of safe and efficient self-government. Under such circumstances, and inhabiting a country of such vast extent, natural beauty and productive wealth, . . . we may well congratulate each other upon our verification of the political truth—'Happy is that people, whose annals are tranquil'."

But "peace and good order" did not long prevail among the members of the legislature. The cause, as already explained in this history, was the attempt to remove the sitting of the legislature from "Omaha City" to Florence; but the firm attitude of the acting governor for the month that he still remained in office, helped in no small degree to thwart the plans of the malcontents.

The third governor of Nebraska Territory was William A. Richardson, who relieved the acting governor on the 10th of January, 1858, and the latter again resumed his duties as secretary. He was, soon after, paid a merited compliment by one of Omaha's most talented speakers: "The executive energy which in stormy times organized this Territory; the rich, full, nervous rhetoric which captivated the people on more than one occasion; the rare, curious, thorough learning on the ' philosophies,' which, a year ago, charmed and astonished this auditory; the hearty grasp of the hand; the generous warmth of the heart; the decision which even in sickness withstood the Florence recusants;—all these qualities characterize the man, who seems to me a striking example of western character."

This was the tribute paid by James M. Woolworth to the secretary as acting governor; and time has only made more emphatic its justice. Mr. Woolworth referred to the sickness of the secretary. It began even before the renewal of his gubernatorial duties and unfortunately did not end with them.

Thomas B. Cuming died on the morning of the twenty-third of March, 1858. As Governor Richardson had been absent from the Territory some weeks, the secretary had up to the time of his decease again been, for that period, acting governor. His funeral was on the twenty-fourth, and his remains were deposited in their final resting-place in Omaha, on that day. They were followed to the grave by many hundreds. Minute guns were fired by the Omaha Light Artillery; and the Council Bluffs Guards, with muffled drums, shrouded colors, trailed arms and heavy hearts, participated in the obsequies.

In stature, the subject of this sketch was rather below the medium height. He was compactly built; his complexion swarthy; his hair black as the plumage of the raven; his eye-brows heavy; his eyes deep-set, restless, dark and flashing.

Neither the lapse of time, nor thronging events can efface the memory of the gifted and generous Cuming from the minds of those still living, who knew him. No more gifted person has ever lived in Nebraska.

CHARLES H. DEWEY, for twenty-five years was an important factor in the business interests of Omaha. Locating here in 1865, he bought a small stock of furniture and formed a partnership with Mr. John Trimble, now a resident of San Jose, Cal., the firm being Dewey & Trimble. The business was conducted at that time in a small frame building on Farnam Street, and the entire stock did not exceed $3,500 in value. The ground upon which the building stood is now a portion of the site occupied by the four story brick structure in which the business of the Dewey & Stone Furniture Company is conducted. Certainly no other firm in the city can say their business has been conducted on the same spot of ground continuously for twenty-eight years. Previous to locating in Omaha, Mr. Dewey's life had been full of adventure and varied experiences. He was born in Kennebec County, Maine, September 28, 1828, his mother, Sallie Williams, being a direct descendant of Roger Williams. When he was two years old the family moved to Amherst, Massachusetts, thence to Binghampton, New York, and from there to Cashocton, Ohio, where all his early associations were centered. There he learned the furniture trade with his father. Ex-Governor Stone of Iowa, now assistant United States land commissioner at Washington, lived in the family, and the two boys painted chairs together.

In the spring of 1849, Mr. Dewey crossed the plains to California, walking every step of the way from Independence, Missouri, pursuant to a determination formed upon starting, to make the journey in this way, following the wagon filled with supplies. In those early days the country swarmed with hostile Indians, and the trip was marked with hardships and thrilling adventures. The succeeding seven years were spent in California, a large portion of the time in the mining camps on Feather River, Clear Creek, Trinity River, Yuba Bar and other famous localities. In 1854 he located in Sacramento, and the following year rented a building at the corner of K and Sixth Streets, and established a carriage business with Mr. Andrew J. Simpson, now of Omaha, as a partner. Two years later he returned to the States and engaged in the furniture business, being located at different periods for a short time, in Davenport, Iowa, South Bend, Indiana, Nashville Tennessee, Denver Colorado, and a portion of the time in Kentucky. Mining excitements retained their charms for him, however, and in 1862 he went to Pike's Peak and, later, spent some time in the newly discovered gold fields of Montana and Idaho, returning East with an ox team in 1865. Reaching Omaha, he camped at the corner of Fifteenth and Capitol Avenue, where he found an abundance of prairie grass for feed. He was impressed by the prospects of Omaha, in a business way, and concluded to locate here. His career in this city was marked by an unusual degree of financial prosperity and a personal popularity perhaps unequaled by that of any other resident of Omaha. Generous and free-hearted, enterprising and of an unusual business sagacity, he occupied a prominent position in all of the relations of life during his long residence here. He was often urged to accept political office, and on more than one occasion was importuned by the leaders of the Republican party to allow his name to be used for the position of mayor, but he had no taste for politics and always refused these opportunities for political preferment. In 1884, however, he accepted the nomination for elector-at-large on the Blaine ticket. In 1878 he was appointed by President Hayes commissioner to the Paris Exposition.

During the past twenty years Mr. Dewey spent a considerable portion of his time in travel, visiting Europe first in 1870. In 1881 he made a trip around the world, sailing from San Francisco and visiting every divison of the globe—Europe, Asia, Africa, North and South America, Australia, China, Japan and the Sandwich Islands.

In August, 1866, Mr. E. L. Stone became a partner in Mr. Dewey's business which was for sometime conducted under the style of Dewey, Trimble & Co., and upon the retirement of Mr. Trimble a few years later the business was conducted for many years under the firm name of Dewey & Stone. During this period their four-story building on Farnam Street, Nos. 1115 and 1117, was erected, as was also their five-story structure south of it, fronting on Harney Street. The first four and five story business buildings built in this state. In 1888, the business had grown to such an extent that a stock company was organized, with a limit membership, under the style of The Dewey & Stone Furniture Company, and it is now the oldest and largest estabiishment of its kind in the West.

Mr. Dewey was married May 16, 1866, to Miss Sarah J. Bell, of Bellville, Ohio. They have one daughter, Belle. On the 27th of August, 1890, Mr. Dewey died at Battle Creek, Michigan, his health having gradually failed for a year or so preceding. The death of any man occupying a prominent place in public esteem always attracts attention, but in this instance there was an element of warm personal regard on the part of the citizens of Omaha which rendered his taking off a matter of individual sorrow and sincere regret. His charity was unbounded, and in many of the humble homes of Omaha his name will be cherished with feelings of gratitude for kindness rendered in times of distress. Unobtrusive and thoughtful in his deeds of benevolence, it was not, until after his death, generally known how extended and far reaching had been his acts of beneficence. For many years to come the name of Charles H. Dewey will be cherished by the people of this city he so dearly loved, as an honorable, upright, enterprising, conscientious man.

GEORGE W. DOANE.—The subject of this sketch was born in Circleville, Ohio, in December, 1824. He received a liberal education, and graduated from Marietta College, in 1845. He subsequently read law with his father, and was admitted to the bar in *court in banc*, at Columbus, in January, 1848. He then commenced the practice of his profession in his native place, but realizing that, by the organization of the new Territories of Kansas and Nebraska, a broader and more promising field would be presented to the young practitioner, started, in the early spring of 1857, on a prospecting tour through the then new West. After visiting some of the embryo cities of Kansas and forming the acquaintance of some of the mild-mannered gentlemen, dubbed, politically, "border ruffians," as well as some of the opposite party, whose leaders were "Jim" Lane and John Brown, he pursued his journey to the more inviting, because more peaceable, shores of Nebraska, and landed at Omaha on the 18th day of April, of the year last mentioned.

After casting about for a location, Mr. Doane, joined a party of young men who were going into Burt County to locate and lay out a town site, and there he made his first settlement upon one of the most beautiful tracts of land on the Missouri slope, which he immediately improved and pre-empted. After he had been a resident of the territory for *full three months*, he was prevailed upon to submit his name as a candidate for district attorney of the third judicial district of the territory, which extended from Douglas County to the British possessions,—the Territory of Dakota not having then been formed. At the election, which occurred in August, he was successful against four competitors, although it required three months to ascertain the result, on account of the wide extent of the district and the imperfect means of communication.

Immediately after the election, and before the result was known, he returned to Ohio to close up his law business there, with a view to his permanent location in the Territory of his adoption. It was while there, and about three months after the election, that he first learned of his election. In the spring of 1858, he returned to Nebraska and entered upon the duties of his office, which required his attendance upon all the courts in the organized counties of the Territory north of Douglas County, and over which Judge Wakeley was the presiding judge. At that early day there was not a court house in the whole district, and improvised temples of justice were established in hotel bar-rooms, store-rooms temporarily vacated for the purpose, or such other quarters as could be found of sufficient capacity to accommodate the crowd which is usually attracted to the county-seat of a pioneer community at a term of court. It goes without saying that the accommodations provided were, as a rule, entirely inadequate, and as a consequence, some ludicrous incidents occurred in the administration of justice.

At the election in August 1858, Mr. Doane was elected to the territorial council from the district composed of Burt, Washington and Sarpy Counties, receiving a majority in each county and the unanimous vote of Burt County, where he then lived. During his service as a member of the council, and of the judiciary committee of that body, he prepared, and was mainly instrumental in having adopted, a code of civil procedure, which has remained in force substantially as originally framed, to this day, and which was based upon the code of Ohio, his native state.

After the expiration of his term as district attorney in 1859, he was re-elected to that office, and continued to perform its duties in the third judicial district, until the office was superseded by that of prosecuting attorney, for each county.

On the 25th day of October, 1859, Mr. Doane was married to Emily R. Greenhow in Keokuk, Iowa, by whom he had a family of seven children, of whom five are still living. In his family relations, he has been exceptionally happy, his wife having proved not only a loving helpmeet, but an accomplished and graceful mistress of his household.

After completing his term of service in the council, he located with his wife in Fort Calhoun, Washington County, in June, 1860, —that being the nearest town to Omaha in the third judicial district, and the law requiring him to reside in the district. After the office of district attorney was abolished by the creation of that of prosecuting attorney in each county, in 1862, during the disturbance occasioned by the civil war in all classes of business, and in none more than in the legal profession, he returned temporarily to Ohio; but after the proclamation of President Lincoln in 1864, locating the initial point of the Union Pacific Railroad on the section immediately opposite that upon which Omaha was built, he returned to Nebraska, locating permanently in Omaha, where he has since resided. In 1865, he was elected prosecuting attorney of Douglas County, the one in which Omaha is located; and during his term of office, he prosecuted and secured the conviction of Baker for murder, which, on account of the atrocious circumstances attending it, became a *causa celebre*; and the criminal's subsequent execution is the more noteworthy, as being, with one exception, the only legal one which had up to that time, ever occurred in this county, if not in Nebraska.

In 1866, Mr. Doane was again elected a member of the territorial council, and served in that body at the last session before the State organization. He has also served as a member of the State senate from Douglas County during the sessions of 1881 and 1882.

At the election of judges of the third judicial district, embracing the counties of Douglas, Sarpy, Washington and Burt, in the year 1887, Mr. Doane was placed in nomination by a spontaneous call of the bar and citizens, as a non-partisan candidate for one of the positions on the bench of the district; and with the other three who were placed in nomination on the same ticket, he was elected by a large majority.

Upon the expiration of his first term as judge, in 1891, the number of judges having been in the meantime increased by the legislature to seven, Judge Doane was again placed in nomination, this time as one of the candidates of the Democratic party for the same position and was re-elected by the largest vote given to any candidate for the office, or for that matter, by the largest vote given to any candidate for any office voted for at that election in Douglas County.

While in the performance of his judicial duties, in September, 1892, he received the unanimous nomination by the convention of the Democratic party of the second congressional district, as the candidate of the party for congress, and, having accepted the nomination he resigned his position on the bench, in October, and entered actively in the canvass. The election resulted in his defeat, although he ran about a thousand ahead of his ticket—the partisan majority in the district being too great to overcome.

On the occasion of Judge Doane's retirement from the bench, a formal leave-taking was indulged in, and a number of complimentary speeches made by the bar of his judicial district. It took place on the twenty-second of October, 1892. Among other features of the occasion was the presentation of a beautiful dish, to ornament his table, appropriately inscribed as the gift of the bar.

As a citizen, Judge Doane is one of the best which any community can furnish—honest, honorable, just, liberal according to his means, and of unblemished character,—always on the side of good morals and of public and private rectitude. His family and his home life are his chief pleasure.

ROBERT DOHERTY.—On the 9th day of March, 1844, Robert Doherty—now the Reverend Robert Doherty, Doctor of Sacred Theology, Rector of Brownell Hall, and Canon Residentiary of Trinity Cathedral, Omaha, Nebraska,—was born at Tiergormly, County Cavan, Ireland, one of the small estates his father then owned, the other being Dumbarlain, in the same county. Robert was a family name both on the paternal and maternal sides, and, he being the firstborn, was baptized by that name.

Robert's forefathers were anciently lords of the great Barony of Inishowen, in the County Donegal, a huge peninsula, enclosed on one side by Lough Foyle, and on the other by Lough Swilley—both salt water lakes. Four miles from the city of Londonderry, there is a hill 802 feet high, from the top of which can be seen a vast extent of country, strewed with ruined castles and strongholds of the O'Doherty. In 1608 the name was the watchword of Ireland. In that year, one of the lords of Inishowen, Sir Caher O'Doherty, the latest and among the greatest of the Irish chiefs, headed a movement to break the English yoke and drive out the hated invaders and heretics. Sir Caher is described as a man to be marked in a thousand, the loftiest and the proudest in bearing in the province of Ulster. His Spanish hat and heron's plume were the terror of his enemies and the rallying point of his friends. He defeated and slew Sir George Pawlett, the vice provost of Derry, and laid the city in ashes. He was the Scotchman's scourge, and yet his uprising was mainly the cause of the settlement of Ulster by the Scotch in the reign of James the First of England and Sixth of Scotland. He was waylaid and murdered by a Scotchman named Sandy Ramsay, who shot him through the head from behind a ledge of rocks. Sir Caher was a devoted son of the Roman Catholic Church.

More than two centuries later, the father of Robert, whose name was John Doherty, an ardent member of the Church of England in religion, and a tory in politics, married Isabel Harman, a descendant of one of those hated Scotch heretics; but, for many generations, the ancestors of Robert had accepted the reform faith, and with that acceptance had become supporters of British connection.

Robert was the son of his father's old age, the latter being seventy at the date of his son's birth, and living to be eighty-four when he was "gathered to his fathers." The old man's means seemed, as age grew upon him, to melt away, so that when he died, the wife, the son Robert, and three sisters younger than he, were left with scarcely anything for their support; but the aged parent did leave a " pearl of great price " in an honorable name, and in the priceless example of a pious, pure and manly life, for which the son has always been thankful. His prayers, precepts and truthful, honest ways, made an indelible impression on the young son's mind, which, under Providence, has since had much to do, doubtless, in determining the latter's course of conduct and the choice of his calling.

At the age of sixteen, Robert emigrated to Canada, arriving at Hamilton, September 18, 1860, with good health and great hopes, and with half a crown in his pocket. He worked on a farm three years, studying in all his leisure moments. At the end of that time, with the money he had saved, he paid his way to the high school, in the town of Brantford, for another three years. At this school he completed a course in Greek, Latin, mathematics, physical science, history and other branches, and carried off first prize as head boy of the institution in these studies. In Trinity University he matriculated, in 1866, at the examination, taking the Strahan prize of $130 for general proficiency. In the following year he won the Burnside prize of $180 for general proficiency in classics, mathematics, science and literature. In the middle of the next year he was attacked with nervous prostration, resulting from too close application, and was obliged to leave the university and abandon all study

544   HISTORY OF THE CITY OF OMAHA.

and reading for three years. Meanwhile he was examined before the education board of examiners and obtained a first-class ("A") certificate, permanently good, and authorizing him to teach anywhere in the Province.

The young man immediately obtained a school with a good salary. The occupation helped to chase away melancholy thoughts and to hasten his recovery, and the income gave him a living and something to lay by, with which to complete his course in the university as soon as a renewal of health would permit. His work in the school was very successful. He established a reading club and a literary society among the young people, and founded a circulating library by subscription. He returned to college in 1869 and took a double course in arts and divinity, graduating in the former in 1871; in the latter, in 1872.

Mr. Doherty was ordained a deacon, June 29th, of the year last mentioned, in St. James' Cathedral, Toronto, by Rt. Rev. A. N. Bethane, and a priest, at the same place, and by the same prelate, on St. Luke's day, 1873. He was appointed to St. John's Church, Huston, and completed and furnished the building that year,—presenting in the first eleven months of his pastorate, eighty-four persons for confirmation—the largest that year in the diocese of Toronto.

In the summer of 1874, he came to Nebraska and took charge of St. Stephen's Church, Grand Island, but at Christmas of the same year he was transferred by the late Bishop Clarkson, to Omaha as assistant at Trinity Cathedral and professor of science in Brownell Hall, with the title of "Bishop's Chaplain." He opened a mission service in the Cass Street school-house and worked assiduously.

In 1875, on nomination of the bishop and the dean, the subject of this sketch was elected a Residentiary Canon of Trinity Cathedral. At Easter, 1876, on the resignation of Dean Easter, the bishop nominated the Reverend Mr. Doherty as his successor in the cathedral. He was also elected rector of Brownell Hall the same year by its board of trustees. He accepted the place and at the same time agreed with the vestry of Trinity Cathedral to take charge of the church until they could obtain a dean. He taught in the school, and conducted the services of the cathedral from April 1st to October 1st, of that year.

He was married August 1st, 1876, in Trinity Cathedral, by Bishop Clarkson, to Emma Windsor, a native of Maryland, daughter of the late Rev. John Henry Windsor, a descendant of the Windsors, barons of Huel Grange and earls of Plymouth. During the Rev. Doherty's rectorate at Brownell Hall, which thus dates from June 1876, all the property belonging to the institution has been acquired. The hall had an old wooden building, one hundred feet of land, and a debt in excess of the value of both, at the time he became rector. The present school is the product of the work done; for the institution did not get money from the East to build with, except $2,500.

The reverend and worthy gentleman has been for seventeen years examining chaplain of the diocese, and has been thrice elected to represent the church in the general convention which meets once in three years.

The Reverend Doherty is the oldest resident Episcopal clergyman, except one, engaged in work in Omaha, and has, perhaps, the longest residence in the city of any other of the religious denominations. The influence and confidence enjoyed by him among the people of Nebraska, both inside and outside the church, must conspire, in a marked degree, to make him feel satisfied and happy.

HENRY D. ESTABROOK was born in Alden, New York, on the twenty-second of October, 1854. He is the son of Hon. Experience Estabrook* and Caroline Augusta Maxwell Estabrook. Through his grandmother (whose maiden name was Hibbard) on the paternal side, his genealogy is traced to John Alden and Precilla Mullen Alden, from one of whose sons the town of Alden was named. With his parents and sister, Caroline Augusta, now Mrs. Robert Clowry, whose husband is vice-president and general superintendent of the Western Union Telegraph Company, the subject of this sketch came to Omaha, in 1855, when of course, he was a mere child, and here he has lived ever since.

Henry's education was received in the public schools of this city, except a year or two in Washington University, St. Louis His first distinctive employment was on the Omaha *Bee* and *Herald* as reporter, distin-

---

*For a brief biographical sketch of Hon. Experience Estabrook, see pages 231, 232, of this History.

guishing himself the first week of his engagement on the paper first named, by getting its editor involved in a twenty thousand dollar law suit for libel, which, however, was subsequently dismissed. He afterwards studied law, graduating with distinction from the St. Louis Law School, in 1876.

But the young man came near being a professional musician. He studied both vocal and instrumental music all through his youth, continuing it while in St. Louis, in which city he took part as a soloist in the Oratorios of Messiah and Sampson. He paid his way through the law school by singing in Dr. Goodall's church—Pilgrim Chapel (Congregationalist). He has taken part in numerous operettas and concerts, and at the age of eighteen wrote a libretto to "The Joust," music by his sister, which was published in Chicago. He has, ever since old enough to sing in public, held choir engagements, and does so still.

During the same year of his graduation from the St. Louis Law School, Mr. Estabrook was admitted to practice, in Omaha, in all the courts, State and Federal, having since established a reputation as a lawyer and orator of which he may well feel proud. His first partnership was with R. S. Hall, Esq.; his second, with Earl B. Coe, Esq., now of Denver, who is many times a millionaire; his third and last, with Hon. Frank Irvine, late one of the judges of the district court in Omaha, now a supreme court commissioner. Mr. Estabrook is now alone in the practice. He was married on his twenty-fifth birth-day, to Miss Clara C. Campbell, a school-mate in the Omaha High School, and daughter of O. C. Campbell, formerly assistant postmaster. They have one child, a daughter, Blanche Denel Estabrook, born January 1, 1881

It is not too much to say that Mr. Estabrook "bounded" into a national reputation as a lawyer by his connection with the celebrated case in the Supreme Court of the United States, entitled "James E. Boyd, plaintiff in error, vs. State of Nebraska, ex rel. John M. Thayer, defendent in error." This is the well-known case of "Thayer vs. Boyd," a contest for the governorship of Nebraska.*

Before the hearing of this case by the Supreme Court of the United States, every lawyer knew, of course, something about the *Doctrine of Relation;* but it was reserved to Mr. Estabrook to use it with great power in what may be set down as the most important of all judicial cases hitherto tried, to which the doctrine is applicable. He confined himself briefly to a consideration of what the doctrine of relation really is, and then to its application to the case before the court. As presented, the arguments on that legal principle clearly overshadowed what he had to say upon all other points, notwithstanding his elucidations of the conscription laws were full, and his references many and of high authority; and it is not too much to say it helped materially in securing a favorable decision for his client, although, evidently, it ran counter to opinions previously formed by some of the justices sitting in the case.

This is what the *World-Herald's* Washington correspondent, of December 8, 1891, said: "His [Estabrook's] argument brought forth many inquiries from the bench, evincing a keen interest in the unique line of thought. When Estabrook entered the ground where he held that the son brought up from boyhood in Nebraska, naturally believed, with his father, that his relationship to the country and its upbuilding gave him citizenship, Justice Field and others of the associates asked many questions, which showed the argument took root. The statement made a profound impression and lead to a new line of research, not exactly statutory or constitutional law."

But law is not the only field in which Mr. Estabrook has acquired a national reputation; indeed, his fame as an orator has now quite eclipsed his prestige as a lawyer—not, however, to his disparagement, but rather to the aggrandizement of his professional calling. For a number of years he had been considered in his own city and State a public speaker of much ability—that was all; but suddenly, even more rapidly than his advancement in law, he stepped into the front rank of American orators. The secret was this: the occasion came; *he was equal to it;* and now the world (as it should) applauds him.

But a city—a State—reputation is one thing; quite another is one which has reached to the "utmost bounds" of a whole country. Now, this is what the *World-Herald* said February 19, 1891: "At the time our brilliant townsman, Henry D. Estabrook, came

*See Chapter XX of this History.

forward to defend the citizenship of James E. Boyd, when it was assailed over a year ago, he little thought that he was laying the foundation for his own reputation as an orator. His plea before the Supreme Court of the United States, however, attracted the attention of many persons, and was the cause of his selection to respond to the toast 'The Mission of America,' at the Marquette Club banquet, in Chicago, a week ago, [February 12, 1892]." The occasion was the annual banquet of the Marquette Club, at the Auditorium Hotel, in Chicago, upon the anniversary of the birth of Abraham Lincoln. Mr. Estabrook accepted the invitation—he was to make his debut outside of Nebraska, and he was to contend with such champions as Shelby M. Cullom and Benjamin Butterworth.

Cullom spoke first, to the toast, "Abraham Lincoln." His effort was a powerful one. Then followed Mr. Estabrook, speaking to the toast, "The Mission of America."

"Of course," said the speaker, "our destiny as a nation is in the hands of the Almighty, and we can only surmise what His intention is concerning us, and the mission we are to fulfill among the nations of the earth, by a careful persual of His word."

Mr. Estabrook then spoke of ancient times, when the earth was first peopled, and of the confusion of tongues which followed, and of its effects upon the world in the course of ages; then of the promise of the Saviour that all nations should again be united; then of the discovery of a new continent, of the Mayflower, of Plymouth Rock, of the Declaration of Independence, of the Revolution, of Lincoln and the Rebellion, and of Grant, Sherman and Sheridan. And then, with wonderful effect, he gave utterance to these and other impassioned words:

"Citizens: America, the tower and bulwark of human liberties, is still in process of erection. It was our fathers' task to die for it; he ours the harder task to live for it. We will not survive to see it finished; God forbid that we should survive to see it perish!

"We are responsible for the acts of our own generation and for the education of the next. Shall our institutions endure and for how long?

'How long, good angel, oh, how long?
Sing me from heaven a man's own song?
Long as thine art shall love true love,
Long as thy science truth shall know,
Long as thine eagle harms no dove,
Long as thy law by law shall grow,
Long as thy God is God above,
Thy brother every man below—
So long, dear land of all my love,
Thy name shall shine, thy fame shall glow.'"

"Long before the audience arose at the end of his oration," said the Chicago *Times*, the next day, "to wave their napkins and give three cheers for the young orator from Nebraska, they were looking from one to another in admiring astonishment at his fervid eloquence and simple and impressive style of oratory." And thus the *Inter-Ocean* (after giving his words in full): "Mr. Estabrook finished amid applause, the audience rising to their feet, waving their handkerchiefs and giving three cheers. He was repeatedly interrupted by loud indications of his auditors' appreciation, sometimes almost tumultuous."

On this "Mission of America," Mr. Estabrook has received many congratulatory letters; among others, one from Lady Henry Somerset, another from Frances E. Willard. One of Minnesota's poets—a lady—has paraphrased it in rhyme. In that masterly effort there can be no doubt he had ascended to a dizzy height. Would he in the future sustain himself? We shall see.

At a reunion dinner of the High School Debating Club, in Omaha, March 12, 1892, Mr. Estabrook spoke on "Our Society." It was an eloquent effort.

And again, at the opening exercises of the Kellom School, in Omaha, May 6, 1892, upon the offering of a flag by Mrs. Kellom and her daughter, and which was accepted by Mr. Estabrook on behalf of the teachers and pupils of the public schools, he delivered a most patriotic apostrophe to the stars and stripes — to "the proud emblem of our national freedom."

On the 2d of May, 1892, Mr. Estabrook spoke words of welcome (along with the mayor of Omaha, and others) to the general conference of the M. E. Church, assembled in the city, during the delivery of which, he gave "voice" to a brief sermon (and that, too, to ministers and bishops, laymen and D. D.'s) that will long be remembered.

But, abroad, could "Nebraska's young orator" sustain himself? Could he again "duplicate," as it were, his signal triumph at the Marquette Club? It was not long before he was called upon to make the trial.

The Union League Club, of Chicago, was to have a Washington Day banquet in the February just passed, and Mr. Estabrook was invited to speak. His topic was, "The Vengeance of the Flag." He began by referring to February as the "holy month"—that gave birth to Washington and Lincoln; then he related how he had clasped hands with a Kentuckian at the foot of Liberty's great martyr, in Lincoln Park; then he dwelt at length upon the assassination of the president; then finally he reached the point where the assassin was caught, upon the stage, in the folds of the flag.

"It was no accident but a miracle of gratitude—the vengeance of the flag! * * * The flag was the captor—the flag was its country's Nemesis! All hail the flag! our proud and happy flag! radiant in its beauty, sparkling with its stars, conscious of itself, its God, and its America! Look up, my countrymen: look up, poor human race, look up to it in reverence and with a prayer of gratitude! Behold it unfurled above the nations of the earth, the splendor of its sheen as lambient as the sunlight that plays upon it; its undulations as billowy and voluminous as the clouds of heaven: its gorgeous colors painted upon the air, as impalpable as the rainbow—Hope's phantom flag!"

Here is what, among other things, the *Inter-Ocean*, on the 24th of February, said:

"Does any one who was present at the Washington Day banquet of the Union League Club know that an epic poem was there recited that memorable evening? Or, rather, let it be asked if every heart of that brilliant concourse of exceptional men did not thrill with the consciousness of a poem's melody, and beauty, and power, and inspiration when Henry D. Estabrook delivered his monograph on 'Lincoln and the Flag?' This speech was one of those rare orations not intended to be subjected to criticism through the medium of the eye, but which when uttered by the voice vibrant with emotion, passionate with enthusiasm, fire the souls of men, and quicken the dullest sensibilties into an ecstacy of profound emotion. It was as much a poem as if it had been written to the rules of scansion, in the very vein and spirit of poetry, free rein given to the fancy, and unchecked freedom to the fervor of the writer; an epic, not an oration; an apostrophe, not an address; and as the vivid sentences poured eloquent from a passionate heart rather than escaped from the cunning of a clever brain, it was no wonder that the listeners sat spell-bound until feelings no longer to be repressed were vented in mighty enthusiasm. No such thing was ever heard at a banquet board before."

On "The Vengeance of the Flag," Mr. Estabrook has been the recipient of commendatory letters, some from as far south as Alabama; but, besides this (and what is a sure test of success), he has received several applications from school teachers for copies for purposes of recitation.

The very latest of Mr. Estabrook's oratorical displays was in Lincoln, Nebraska, before the Young Men's Republican Club, in an address on "Parties."

And this is what the *Capital City Courier* says: "When *The Courier* promised a rare treat in Mr. Estabrook's address on 'Parties,' it knew that the fulfillment would fill up and overflow the promise—and it did most effectually. Mr. Estabrook's speech was delivered to the young men surrounded by the four walls of the Windsor dining hall, but in reality he spoke to the entire city of Lincoln. The papers, notably the *State Journal*, gave admirable reports of his address, but the electric effect of his peroration was communicated by the banqueters to those on the outside, and that's the way Henry Estabrook's magnificent effort has become the talk of the town. A reporter with the celerity of chain lightning, the care of an old maid, and the amiability of an angel, couldn't reduce one of Estabrook's speeches to paper and half do him justice. His subtlety of expression, grace of manner, splendid delivery, a voice that rises and falls in musical cadence in correspondence with the rhythm of his words, all these are lost in the printed report. Cold type congeals the fire of passionate eloquence, and deadens the finer qualities of speech, leaving but a bare outline of a form full of beauty—a colorless photograph of a brilliant bouquet.

"Estabrook is a scholarly man, and his mind is not muddy. He has a keen wit and is a master hand at sarcasm. His address on 'Parties' was an ideal banquet talk, a speech with real thought in it, polished off with a delicacy and wit that made it sparkle with brilliancy."

N. B. FALCONER was born in the City of Glasgow, Scotland, in the year 1835. His father was the principal dry goods merchant in the city. He died when the subject of this sketch was only eight years of age, leaving his affairs to his oldest son, with whom, at the age of fourteen, the boy went to learn the business. After four years, not being taken in partnership with his brother, he left him to learn the embroidery manufacturing business with D. and J. MacDonald, the greatest manufacturers of embroideries, at that time, in the world. Within three years they gave the young man the management of the principal department of the house, where he sold for them in the first year over four hundred and fifty thousand dollars' worth of goods.

The next year, Mr. Falconer was offered the management of the Glasgow offices of a large New York house. He accepted it, but at the end of one year he left the firm and commenced for himself in Glasgow, as an American commission merchant; that is, buying goods for New York houses. In this business, he was quite successful until the fall of Sumpter and the commencement of the war of the Rebellion. All trade for the time ceased, as the banks had all suspended and nearly all the business people failed.

Mr. Falconer spent a year in New York collecting what he could of what was owing him; and in 1862, he commenced the importing business in that city, and by 1865 had become the largest importer of alpacas in the United States—his sales, in that year, amounting to over six hundred thousand dollars. But the government continued to increase the duties on that class of goods from thirty-four per cent, when he began importing, to one hundred and twenty per cent on all but the finest varieties, so that all the houses in that trade in the city were driven out of business and he at last also had to retire.

Some years before, he had bought out the business of Ross & Cruickshank, in Omaha, paid out Mr. Ross, and paid Mr. Cruickshank a salary and a small part of the profits, to run the store.

Mr. Falconer now determined to push this business, and came out here and built the brick building on the corner of Fifteenth and Douglas Streets, which was the commencement of the boom for Omaha. At that time, this city and Council Bluffs were about equal in population, but Council Bluffs had the best thus far. Upon the opening of the new store his trade grew rapidly, his patrons coming largely from Council Bluffs and the nearer towns in Iowa, and from the west for hundreds of miles, till now he has over five thousand customers out of the city, and his retail sales alone are over five hundred thousand dollars a year, and are steadily increasing.

During his career as an importer, he crossed the Atlantic seventy-three times and visited nearly every country in Europe. His knowledge of the markets, of course, has given him a great advantage in his present business, as he knows exactly where to get all his goods at first hands.

Mr. Falconer had the honor to represent the State of Nebraska as commissioner at the Exhibition at Paris, and was president of the Omaha Board of Trade for one term. But the exigencies of his large and rapidly growing business prevent him taking as much part in public affairs as he would like. At the last election he was strongly pressed to run for congress by the populist party, with whose principles he has much sympathy, but his business affairs would not permit.

FENNER FERGUSON.—The subject of this sketch was born in Rensselaer County, New York, in the year 1814. He was the youngest of nine children. His father, Stephen Ferguson, was born in 1772, in Dutchess County, New York, and moved with his parents, at the age of four years, to Rensselaer County, where he continued to reside until his death, in 1852, at the age of eighty. His mother's maiden name was Dorothy Palmer.

The old homestead is still occupied by the Ferguson family, and has been without a break since the beginning of the war of the Revolution.

Fenner Ferguson obtained his early education in the district schools, and finished the same at the Nassau Academy. He completed his legal studies with the law firm of Coon & Bramhall, of Albany, and after his admission to the bar became a member of that firm.

For a number of years he had an extensive practice in Albany, and in the eastern part of the State extending to practice in the courts of New York City. One of the most important cases he had was that known as the "Patroon Giant," being extensive grant of land from the English crown prior to the Revolutionary war.

His health failing, he removed to Michigan about the year 1845 and located at Albion, Calhoun County. While there, he held several important offices as well as being in full and successful practice. He was appointed master in chancery, was elected prosecuting attorney, and later on member of the legislature, the State capital being at Lansing.

He was appointed on October 12th, 1854, by the president of the United States, chief justice of Nebraska, under the provisions of the Act of Congress, approved May 30th, 1854, establishing the territories of Kansas and Nebraska. At this time there were no railroads in the far West, and the journey was made by way of Chicago to St. Louis, and from thence up the Missouri River by steamboat. He arrived in Nebraska in the month of November, 1854. Council Bluffs was then known as Kanesville, and Judge Ferguson and his family remained there two weeks before finally moving to Bellevue, now in Sarpy County. This was the only inhabited part of the territory north of the Platte River. At this point Peter A. Sarpy had a post of the American Fur Co., and the government agency buildings for the Otoes, Pawnees, Poncas, and Omahas, were also located here. Judge Ferguson and his family occupied one of the agency buildings as their home.

Upon the convening of the legislature, by Acting Governor Thomas B. Cuming, Judge Ferguson assisted in the recommendation of the laws to be adopted, and organized and opened the courts, thus starting and establishing the rule of law and order, which has continued with increasing prosperity up to the present time.

In 1857, during President James Buchanan's administration, he was elected as delegate to the Thirty-fifth Congress, which position he occupied for two years. He returned from Washington in the summer of 1859, and after a short illness died in November of that year, at the age of forty-five.

He was a man of fine physique, being slightly over six feet tall, and weighing full two hundred pounds. He was kind and considerate to all, a man of deep learning and a close student. Especially was he kind and considerate to the younger members of the bar, who were then entering the territory.

He was married in 1841 in Albany to Helena E. Upjohn, he had four sons, Arthur N., now of Omaha, A. G., of Vancouver, B. C., S. W., of Idaho, and Charles Fennel. The latter died in intancy in Michigan. His widow survived him many years, dying in 1888.

ARTHUR NORTHCOTE FERGUSON was born October 4, 1842, in Albany, N. Y. His father was Fennel Ferguson, then a practicing lawyer of that city, his mother's maiden name was Helena E. Upjohn. Both are now deceased. The family moved to Calhoun County, Mich., when the subject of this sketch was a small boy, where they resided until the fall of 1854, when they came to Nebraska—the father having been appointed chief justice of the territory by President Pierce, he having continued the practice of law with marked success while living in Michigan.

On reaching Nebraska, Judge Ferguson located at Bellevue, where the Omaha Indian agency building—a log structure—was fitted up as a residence. Not only the Omahas, but the Pawnees, Poncas and Otoes had their agency buildings there. Adjoining the residence first mentioned was one occupied by J. Sterling Morton and wife, who had just married and come West. Peter A. Sarpy (after whom Sarpy County was named) had, at this time, his post at Bellevue, as agent of the American Fur Company.

Mr. Ferguson's playmates for a considerable time after the family settled in Bellevue, were Omaha Indian boys. He remembers well when the first newspaper actually printed in Nebraska was first issued. It was called the *Nebraska Palladium*, and Arthur was present when, late in the fall of 1854, the first impression was taken off. A man by the name of Reed was editor.

In Michigan, the subject of this sketch attended the district school, but in Bellevue, as common schools had then no existence in the territory, the boy, then in his thirteenth year, was a scholar in a private school taught by Mrs. Nye.

Fennel Ferguson, the father, in 1857, was elected delegate to congress from Nebraska, having previously resigned his seat upon the bench. While at Washington, he sent his son to school at Alexandria, Va. This was a noted institution for the exclusive education of boys, under the leadership of Benjamin Halliwell. The school was attended by pupils from various parts of the country. Here he remained for a portion of two years, afterward attending Kinderhook Academy, in Columbia County, N. Y., leaving that school in the fall of 1859.

Three years subsequent to that date, Mr. Ferguson and his two brothers, A. G. and S. W. Ferguson, were engaged as civil engineers in the location and construction of the Union Pacific Railroad, continuing in that service from the commencement until the completion of the road, in 1869.

The subject of this sketch entered the University of Iowa, after finishing his work upon the Union Pacific Railroad, entering the law department of that institution, and graduating therefrom in June, 1870, with the degree of LL.B. His preceptors there were: Chancellor Wm. G. Hammond; John F. Dillon, United States circuit judge, and George G. Wright and C. C. Cole, judges of the Supreme Court of Iowa.

Mr. Ferguson commenced the practice of law in Bellevue, Neb., in July, 1870, continuing there until 1872, when (in April) he moved to Omaha, where he has ever since been in the practice of his profession. He first formed a partnership with Hon. John I. Redick, and subsequently with Hon. William Neville, now a district judge in Nebraska.

In 1877, Mr. Ferguson was elected a member of the State senate for the counties of Douglas and Sarpy. In 1879, at the ending of his term as senator, he was elected district attorney of the third judicial district, composed of the counties of Douglas, Sarpy, Washington and Burt, serving two years. He was then elected for two years a member of the board of education for the City of Omaha.

On the 30th of March, 1891, the subject of this sketch was appointed one of the judges of the fourth judicial district of Nebraska, by Governor Boyd, to hold the office until January, 1892; but in the fall of the year after his appointment, he was elected to the same office by the people, for a term of four years, which office he now holds.

He was married April 15, 1879, at Omaha, to Miss Delia L. Sears, of this city, sister of Mrs. A. J. Poppleton. Of this union two children have been born—Alice S. and Elizabeth F. Ferguson.

As a lawyer, he was studious and extremely careful, and his judgment always reliable; as a judge, he enjoys an excellent reputation as conscientious, industrious and exact in his conclusions. As a citizen, his example is excellent, with great integrity of character—always seeking to be right rather than great or brilliant.

JOSEPH WARREN GANNETT was born June 5, 1831, in Sharon, Norfolk County, Massachusetts. He came of good Puritan stock, counting among his ancestors, Matthew Gannett, who came to Massachusetts soon after the settling of the colony and settled at Hingham; also Governor Wm. Bradford, Miles Standish, and others known in the early history of the colony. His grandmother, Deborah Sampson Gannett, was notable as one of the few examples of a woman-soldier, having regularly served for a year and a half in the Continental Army during the Revolutionary War without her sex having been discovered. She was honorably discharged by General Knox, and received a pension granted by congress. She married Benjamin Gannett, of Sharon, and their son, Captain Earl Bradford Gannett, was the father of Joseph W. Gannett.

The subject of this sketch was educated in the schools of his native village, finishing at a neighboring academy. He went early in life to Boston and engaged in business. He became a member of the firm of Brett, Gannett & Co., doing a large general dry goods business. He was afterward connected for a number of years with the mercantile house of James M. Beebe & Co., and a member of the succeeding firm of J. C. Burrage & Co. until July, 1870, when he was appointed auditor of the Union Pacific Railway to take charge of the accounts and financial affairs of the operating department of the company, in which position he remained until 1883. After his retirement from that office, on account of ill-health, he did not again engage in active business but was vice-president of Omaha Savings Bank, and was interested in a number of enterprises in Omaha and the West, until the time of his death, July 29, 1889.

Mr. Gannett was secretary and treasurer of the Omaha & Republican Valley Railroad Company, also of the Utah & Northern

Railroad Company, of the Echo & Park City Railroad Company, of the Salt Lake & Western Railroad Company, of the Greeley, Salt Lake & Pacific Railroad Company, and several other railroad companies; also of the Pacific Express Company, and treasurer of the St. Joseph Bridge Company. He was elected regent of the University of Nebraska in 1875, and was re-elected in 1879. He was also elected a member and State councilor of the American Institute of Civics, in 1886.

April 19, 1866, he married, in Boston, Miss Frances R. Josselyn, daughter of Nathan Josselyn, for many years a large ship-builder of Quincy Point, Massachusetts. There is one son, Earl W. Gannett.

W. A. L. GIBBON.—The father of the subject of this sketch was Myles Gibbon; his mother, Celia Lennon Gibbon. Their ancestors came from Ireland and settled in Delaware County, New York, in the early part of this century. The son was born at Griffin's Mills in the county just mentioned, June 6, 1839. He removed with his parents to Kenosha County, Wisconsin and subsequently to the town of Kenosha. As his parents were poor, the family suffered the usual privations of early settlers, and the boy was compelled to assist his father in earning a livelihood. He attended the public schools in Kenosha and graduated at the high school there, at the age of seventeen. He contemplated taking a university course and then to study law; but the death of his parents and lack of funds prevented the consummation of his plans.

Mr. Gibbon afterward removed to St. Louis. This was in 1856. There, he attended the law school for a short time and again endeavored to prepare himself for entering the legal profession, but was a second time obliged to abandon the undertaking for lack of means; so he resolved to follow some commercial pursuit.

He moved to Chicago in 1858, and shortly thereafter to Michigan where he was engaged in the capacity of clerk in the employ of the Detroit & Milwaukee Railroad Company. He returned to Chicago in 1861, and accepted an inferior clerkship in a wholesale hat, cap and millinery house, where he advanced, step by step, from clerk to proprietor. At the time of the great fire he lost, through bankrupt insurance companies, $35,000.

Mr. Gibbon subsequently returned to St. Louis, where his life was, financially, a struggle, caused largely by his Chicago losses. In 1878, he came to Omaha without money and a stranger, to take charge of the finances and credits of one of the largest wholesale grocery houses in the city; entering that service on a salary, and at the end of seven years withdrawing as a partner.

After retiring from the grocery business, Mr. Gibbon organized and became one of the firm of Edney & Gibbon, in the wholesale hardware business in Omaha. Ill health and final death of Mr. Edney terminated the partnership after a duration of about three years. Mr. Gibbon, soon after, organized the Nebraska Savings and Exchange Bank at South Omaha, and became its cashier and manager. A large and successful business was built up, and at the end of four years the bank was sold to the Packers National bank, Mr. Gibbon withdrawing. By economy and wise investments in Omaha real estate, he has accumulated considerable money and valuable property—making himself easy in a financial way. In October, 1891, he returned to his early love by embarking in the wholesale hat and cap business in Omaha, under the firm name of W. A. L. Gibbon & Co., which house is now one of the largest west of Chicago.

While Mr. Gibbon has given the best of his life to business pursuits, he takes a lively interest in all public matters touching Omaha's commercial needs as a distributing center. He is at present president of the Board of Trade and chairman of the executive committee of the Omaha Commercial Club; was a member of the board of education for three years; is the owner of a large private library; and, as far as business will admit, is an extensive reader and close student, and has considerable ability as a public speaker.

The honesty as well as determination and perseverance of Mr. Gibbon in business matters are the prime factors in his success, to which is properly added a clear insight of the laws of trade. He was married to Miss Nellie Mack on January 16, 1869, in Chicago. Their children are: Chas. B., Ella, William, May, Celia, Pauline, Clare, Walter, Gervaise.

JOHN ANDREW GILLESPIE is of Scotch-Irish descent. His ancestors were early settlers in Pennsylvania, in what is now known as the Cumberland Valley; and there many of the family still reside. The father of John—Samuel Laird Gillespie—was a fuller by trade; he was also a teacher. The mother's maiden name was Elizabeth Stewart. She was of an English family, who moved to this country about the beginning of the last century.

The subject of this sketch was born at Newville, Cumberland County, Pennsylvania, June 5, 1845. He was reared according to the code of a Scotch Presbyterian. He is the sixth of a family of seven. He attended the common schools of his old mountain home in his boyhood. In 1860, the family moved to Cedar County, Iowa. At the commencement of the Rebellion, his two eldest brothers enlisted to serve under the old flag, leaving him as the "man of affairs" at home for a time; then he followed their example, enlisting in Company G, of the Second Iowa Volunteer Cavalry. He served with the regiment until the close of the war, being in every battle and skirmish in which the company was engaged, from the time he enlisted until he was mustered out of the service. When the war was over, he returned to his home in Iowa, and entered the Iowa State University, graduating in 1870, with the degree of B. D. He afterwards taught school a year in Illinois and was then called to take a position as teacher in the Iowa school for the deaf and dumb at Council Bluffs, where he remained six years.

While in the university, Mr. Gillespie formed the acquaintance of Helen Zimmerman, to whom he was married in 1874. This excellent and talented woman has been a true helpmeet to her husband, in every word and work since their marriage.

Mr. Gillespie was appointed superintendent of the Nebraska school for the deaf and dumb in 1878, taking charge of the institution on the first day of September, of that year, where he still remains, and where most of his work for the deaf has been done. It was through him that the idea of developing the latent hearing remaining to many of the deaf was first brought about. Through his method, many children who would otherwise be deaf and dumb are simply hard of hearing. His latest scheme in connection with the education of that class of pupils is the devising of a plan of presenting language to them, which he calls "the complete thought method;" which is found to be a very satisfactory plan of work for deaf and dumb children.

The subject of this sketch has been more or less connected with organized charity work of Omaha. He has been corresponding secretary of the National Conference of Charities and Corrections. He is a Grand Army man, a Presbyterian and a Republican. Under his administration, the institution over which he presides has ever sustained an enviable reputation as progressive and original as to methods, and in a marked degree has been successful as to results.

GEORGE PAUL ALBRECHT GROSSMANN.—The father of the subject of this sketch was Julius Grossmann, a descendant of a long line of successful merchants, who were aldermen in a Silesian city when Columbus discovered America. He purchased an extensive estate in Upper Silesia, in 1827, after finishing his studies at the University of Breslau, Germany. In 1830, he led to the altar Miss Emilie Hoefer, the eldest daughter of a wholesale merchant of a large neighboring city.

Paul was born in Silesia, on the 2d day of October, 1846, and was the youngest of the family. In 1848, his parents moved to Breslau, where the children were sent to the best schools in that place. Paul received his instructions at the St. Elizabeth and St. Mary Magdalene's College, of Breslau, and finished the necessary examinations for entering the university, in the spring of 1866.

Shortly after being matriculated in the medical faculty of the University of Breslau, the Austro-Prussian war broke out, and the young man entered the army service as a one-year volunteer, taking artillery for the troop of his choice. When the year of service was passed, he underwent the required examinations to become an officer of the troop mentioned, in case further service became necessary. Then he returned to his studies, and finished in the next two years (that is, in the spring of 1869) the first terms of his medical education. So, being a candidate of medicine, his father sent him to the University of Wurzburg, then the very best medical school in existence.

After the first casual examination, the late famous Professor Scanzoni took a personal interest in him, and opened the sick rooms of his clinic for his visits and instructions at any spare time. Professor Munde, now of New York, was Scanzoni's assistant then. In 1870, in March, he returned to Breslau. Professor Spiegelberg gave him the use of the obstetrical department of the university clinic to write an essay on "The Changes of the Infant's Skull in Passing through the Pelvis during Childbirth." This essay gave him the degree of Doctor of Medicine, *magna cum laude*, on the 20th of July, 1870. On this very day he was to enter the army, with the rank of first sergeant of the artillery. He reported himself as M.D., and offered his services in that capacity. He was advised that he would be shortly reclaimed to the medical staff, but somehow matters were delayed, and he marched to France as a soldier. His captain had no physician to his company of field artillery, and asked him to perform the duties of a company surgeon. After the battles around New Breisach, the chief surgeon of his corps wanted him to join his medical staff, but he preferred the excitement of the active service, that enabled him to do medical work on the battle-field. Many a night, after a day of severe fighting, he stood on the battle-field until dawn, bandaging the wounded of his company to prepare them for transportation to the nearest hospital. His company belonged to the corps of the famous General von Werder, who commanded in Alsace and Lorraine, and fought against Generals Garibaldi and Bourbaki.

During the four days' battle around Belfort, his company was very severely attacked by French infantry, and the doctor was sent to look for the ammunition that stood sheltered behind a hill, when suddenly an orderly appeared, calling for ammunition, as the French had approached very close, and there were no shells in the ammunition boxes of the guns. There was one long safe road around the hill, and a short one in the line of the French artillery. Shell after shell was thrown in that road and exploded. Then he chose this road, and without losing a man or horse, arrived in time to have the attack repelled. His part in this battle was the means of his being awarded the order of the "Iron Cross," the second in his family, as a brother of his father received it too, in 1813, in the war against the first Napoleon. Shortly after, the doctor was promoted to a lieutenancy of artillery.

When the war closed, Dr. Grossmann was ordered back to Germany, and was given charge of eight hundred French prisoners of war. After sending those men back to France, he was discharged and returned to Breslau, where Professor Spiegelberg offered him the place of second, or house assistant in his clinic. After holding this position for nine months, and passing the examination ordered by the government, the doctor was made first assistant surgeon of Spiegelberg, who was then the leading gynæcologist and obstetrician of Germany. During the time—three years and three months—that he held this position, he contributed frequently to medical journals and had access to the large material in the different departments of the clinics of the university hospitals, where thousands of sick were every year attended by the staff of surgeons. During his stay in the lying-in hospitals in Wurzburg and Breslau, he had the opportunity of witnessing and attending over 3,000 cases of confinement.

In 1875, in the fall, the doctor concluded to find a place on the globe where medical services were better paid than at home. He started out with the ships of the Hamburg-American Steamship Co. to the United States, and, later on, to the West Indies and Central America, where he was offered an opening with good prospects. On his way there he wanted to visit the United States, and landed in New York City, in March, 1877. Before starting on his journey, Dr. Grossmann was married, in England.

He arrived at Omaha in March, 1877, and being delayed here, began to practice. It proved to him a good field of work and he stayed. In 1880, on January 1st, he took charge of a department of the St. Joseph's Hospital, and has held it since. In May, 1882, he performed a Cæsarian section, after Porro's method—the sixth operation of this kind made in the United States, and the thirty-sixth made altogether. In 1883, the doctor was offered the chair of surgery in the medical faculty of the State University, at Lincoln, but his lectures there demanded two days of each week, and, on account of his practice in Omaha, he resigned this position, as it interfered to much with his work in this city.

In May, 1885, he was married to Mrs. Amalia von Platen-Taylor, the second daughter of B. B. von Platen, then a colonel of Charles XV Prince Hussars. The von Platens are of German descent, who took up possessions in Finland, in the thirteenth century, dating their ancestry prior to the eleventh century, and were known among the crusaders. Amalia von Platen received her education at home, by the best of instructors, in science, music, literature and fancy needle-work, finishing her course of education in the best convent school that then existed, in Copenhagen, Denmark, and afterwards at Hanover, Germany. Mrs. Grossmann is quite an accomplished linguist, being able to converse fluently in five languages.

In 1890, Dr. Grossmann was offered and accepted the position of local surgeon of the Missouri Pacific Railway, and, in 1891, he was appointed consulting surgeon of the Union Pacific System.

When, in 1892, the Creighton University opened a medical department, he was chosen professor of clinical medicine and medical director of the new Creighton memorial hospital (St. Joseph's), one of the largest and best equipped hospitals west of Chicago. He is a member of the Omaha Medical Society and of the National Association of Railway Surgeons.

The only son of the doctor is now finishing his medical course in the University of Pennsylvania. Dr. Grossmann's only brother, Julius Grossmann, Ph.D., is librarian and counsellor of archives of the Emperor of Germany, and is considered an eminent authority on modern history, throughout the continent.

DR. WILLIAM HENRY HANCHETT was born in Illinois, near the city of Chicago, in 1854, being the second of five sons, four of whom are homeopathic physicians.

His father, David Hanchett, was born in Hartford, Connecticut, and is able to trace his family history back for many generations in America. John Hanchett was one of the men who founded the city of Boston, and from him down the doctor has the record of the birth and death of all his ancestors since that time. Among his ancestors in New England were prominent officers in the Revolutionary War. It is with pride that Dr. Hanchett traces his ancestry back to the energetic people of that favored land. His mother, Fayetta Churchill, was born in New York. Her father, Alfred Churchill, was prominent among the early settlers of Chicago. She is a very charitable woman and of beautiful character. From this ancestral stock, the doctor has inherited a personal energy, which has characterized his professional life and made him successful in what he has undertaken.

He graduated at the Chicago Homeopathic Medical College in 1879. After practicing several years in the East, he located in Omaha in 1884. At this time there were few homeopathic practitioners in this city, and it gave him an ample field for work. His energy and success in the treatment of the sick soon won for him a large and lucrative practice, until to-day he enjoys the reputation of being one of the most successful physicians in the West. He is often called long distances in consultation with physicians not only throughout Nebraska, but oftentimes to other states.

His skill and judgment in medical matters have been acknowledged in many ways by the physicians of the West. He is at present president of the Nebraska State Homeopathic Medical Society which, under his direction, has had a remarkably prosperous year in its growth. He has also held the office of secretary and vice-president of this same society, and has had much to do with the moulding of this great organization for homeopathy in the West. In political and civic societies he has held important positions, and wielded an influence of much force. For three years he held the office of surgeon-general of the State of Nebraska for the order of the Knights of Pythias.

He has for the past five years been editor of the general practice department of the *Medical and Surgical Record of Nebraska*, and his editorials and articles have been of a peculiarly practical turn, for which characteristic he is noted as a physician.

Dr. Hanchett is a member of the American Institute of Homeopathy, and for years has attended the meetings of this national society of the homeopathic school as a delegate from his state.

The doctor is a thoroughly Western man and has unbounded faith in the resources of this great country, and especially, has been a hard worker for the up-building of Omaha. He has always taken a live interest in the improvements of this city. He has recently built one of the finest homes in Omaha, where he now resides, and where he greatly enjoys entertaining his friends with true hospitality.

His wife, Ida McMicken, was born in Illinois, and is of Scotch descent. She was educated at Vassar College, and is a woman of remarkable intelligence and generosity. To no woman of Omaha can more credit belong, for the organization and development of literary work and true refinement. Several years ago Mrs. Hanchett organized a reading club, at her home, especially for the benefit of young women. From that small beginning has grown the Cleofan, with its two chapters. Chapter I is organized for the married women of Omaha, and its members are among the brightest women of the city. Chapter II is for young women, and especially in this society, Mrs. Hanchett has done much for those employed in offices and stores, as well as for many of the teachers of the city. Her services have always been gratuitous, and her work has been for the good she could do others.

The doctor has two children—a son and a daughter — Reid Churchill Hanchett and Hope Hanchett.

Since writing the above, Dr. Hanchett has been honored by an appointment on the staff of visiting physicians to the Douglas County Hospital, and also on the medical staff of the Methodist Hospital, also the Presbyterian Hospital of Omaha. He has recently been elected president of the Omaha Homeopathic Medical Society.

E. T. ALLEN, M. D.

PIERCE C. HIMEBAUGH was born January 9, 1840, in Erie, Erie County, Pennsylvania. His father's name was Mathias Himebaugh. Both his parents died when Pierce was but a small boy, in the town where he was born. An older brother, Orlando, was appointed his guardian. This brother settled near Geneva, Illinois, soon after, taking his young ward with him. Pierce was educated in the common schools of the neighborhood for several years, when his guardian moved to Nebraska, about ten miles north of Fremont, taking his young brother with him. Here the latter lost his health and returned to Illinois, making his home at Sycamore, where, at the age of twenty-four, he began his business career, by conducting a flour mill, which he continued for several years—also one in Rochelle, Illinois, for six years.

In 1869, Mr. Himebaugh went to Chicago and was engaged in the grain commission business until 1875, when he sold out and engaged in the grain business in the firm of Wanzer & Co. He was connected with that firm about a year.

Mr. Himebaugh came to Nebraska in 1876, located in Omaha, and engaged in grain business in connection with the firm of Wanzer & Co., of Chicago, which he continued for about eighteen months. He then formed a partnership with C. W. Lyman in the same business; the style of the firm was C. W. Lyman & Co. This firm built the Union elevator "A" in sixty days. Mr. Lyman's interest in the firm was then purchased by N. Merriam, and the firm name was afterward changed to Himebaugh & Merriam. The elevator "A," which the firm owned, had a capacity of 200,000 bushels, and the elevator "B," which the firm leased, but in which they had an interest of thirty-five per cent, had a storage capacity of 700,000 bushels and cost $125,000. As early as 1881, the firm employed twenty men and handled at the rate of about 3,000,000 bushels of grain a year. The trade had increased to that extent, from the shipment of one car load a day, when they began business, to eighty-five car loads, at the date just mentioned. Afterwards the business largely increased. The firm had large warehouses and elevators in other parts of the State, down to the date of Mr. Himebaugh's decease.

Mr. Himebaugh was president of the Y. M. C. A., of Omaha, seven years and vice-president one year. He donated to the society, while he was president, more than $12,000, which was put into their fine building in the city. He was married at Sycamore, Illinois, December 6, 1864, to Annette C. Johnson, a native of Vermont. There is one child, Grace L., of this marriage living.

Mr. Himebaugh died in San Jose, California, April 1, 1890. The funeral took place at 3 p.m., the third day. The services were held at the Hotel Vendome, where he breathed his last, by Rev. Dr. Wakefield, the Episcopal clergyman of San Jose. His remains were interred temporarily, pending arrangements for their removal to Omaha.

He was a member of the Congregational Church and gave one-tenth of all his income to religion and charity. He was always spoken of as a man of great liberality and benevolence, and was well known for his generosity, which continually endeared him to all who came in contact with him. No man who has ever lived in Omaha was more noted than he for absolute purity of principle and excellence of character.

GEORGE A. HOAGLAND has been well known in commercial circles, and connected with one of the principal mercantile establishments of Nebraska since as a boy, more than thirty years ago, he came to Omaha, where he has since continuously resided.

His father, George T. Hoagland, a native of New Jersey and now a prominent citizen of St. Joseph, Missouri, soon after his marriage with Miss Nancy A. Gale, of Massachusetts, removed to Boonville, Missouri, where George A. Hoagland was born May 20, 1843. The family moved to St. Joseph in 1852, where the elder Hoagland engaged in the lumber business, and the son acquired the rudiments of an education which was supplemented with a year's study at Weston, Missouri, and another year spent at the college at Liberty, Missouri, from which he returned at the breaking out of the war of the Rebellion, when the practical work of education in that state was suspended. Accepting his father's offer of a situation as clerk in the lumber business, which had been established the spring previous, he came to Omaha in August of 1861 and assumed the duties of the position. The firm name was Geo. T. Hoagland & Co., the junior partner being George Bebbington, and the business was carried on upon the ground now occupied by the Millard Hotel, the office being in a small room over Visscher's carpenter shop, which stood in the yard.

George liked the business, soon learned it and concluded to make Omaha his future home. On May 22, 1864, George A. Hoagland and Ianthe C. Wyman, daughter of W. W. Wyman, Esq., a prominent journalist of this city, were married. Of this marriage seven children have been born, of whom five are still living, viz: Emma Bell, Laura Maria, William Wyman, Paul Ingalls and Helen Lemon. The two oldest of these have lately visited Europe and the West Indies to complete their education with a sight of foreign lands; the oldest son is engaged in business with his father, and the others are at school.

In the year 1865 Mr. Bebbington sold his interest, and the firm name became George T. Hoagland & Son, George A. becoming resident partner and manager. The construction of the Union Pacific Railroad which soon after followed, gave a great impetus to trade in Omaha, and especially to the lumber business, large demands for lumber being frequently made, and a thorough acquaintance with the class of material demanded and having it constantly in stock, enabled this firm to fill large orders. It was no unusual thing for G. W. Frost, then purchasing agent for the Union Pacific, to drive over to the Hoaglands' place of business and ask how much of a certain kind of lumber they had in stock, and on learning the amount, without stopping to ask the price, to say: "All right, send it down right away." An order of this kind often amounted to $15,000 or $20,000, and $50,000 or $60,000 worth of lumber was often supplied within sixty days. The country trade, too was good, and as this was the point from which supplies were transported westward by wagon, it frequently happened that parties hauled lumber as far west as 100 or 150 miles, and large lots went to Columbus, 93 miles from Omaha, in this way. It is no unfrequent thing now for Mr. Hoagland to meet men in his trips out into the state who remind him of the purchases they made from him "away back in the sixties" and hauled across the prairies to build their houses and other buildings. It was in 1871 or '72 that Geo. A. Hoagland determined to change the method of doing the wholesale lumber business which had before been done at Chicago and other eastern centers, and make Omaha a wholesale place from which shipments should be made direct. In this he was warmly opposed by Chicago merchants and others who ridiculed the idea, but the present immense business in this line done here thoroughly vindicates Mr. Hoagland's judgment.

In January, 1874, Geo. A. Hoagland purchased his father's interest and became sole proprietor of the business, which moved along very smoothly until 1881, when the great flood in the Missouri River made the bottom lands, occupied by the lumber yards, navigable for steamboats and ruined a great amount of lumber, Mr. Hoagland's loss on this occasion amounting to $20,000.

With the building up of this city this business has greatly increased. Not only is a large business done in Omaha, but about twenty branches for the retail trade have from time to time been established on the Union Pacific and Burlington & Missouri River roads in Nebraska, and also a yard at Council Bluffs, where Mr. Hoagland does the leading business.

George A. Hoagland's success in life illustrates the old proverb: "Keep your shop and your shop will keep you." No merchant in Omaha has attended more closely to business than he. The result of this is that the capital now employed is $500,000, and the annual sales which during the first year did not exceed forty or fifty car loads, have recently amounted to 60,000,000 feet in one year, enough to load 4,500 or 5,000 cars, which would make a solid train over thirty miles in length, or long enough to reach from Omaha to Valley station on the Union Pacific road. The shrewdness, foresight and winning qualities which made him successful in business have often created opportunities for Mr. Hoagland to become a candidate for political offices, but his natural modesty, conservatism and freedom from political ambitions have never permitted him to accept such offers, and he contents himself with the discharge of his duties as a private citizen, unassuming kindness to those in need, and to the management of his own affairs.

JAMES KERR ISH was born January 10, 1836, in Alde, Loudoun County, Virginia. His father was John Ish, who was the real builder of the town, and was in active business for many years, afterward moving to Harper's Ferry, where the mother of the subject of this sketch, formerly Miss Batson, of Virginia, died—the father going thence to Galveston and ending his days there, dying with yellow fever.

James, at the age of twelve, was apprenticed to a Mr. Wiseman, in Baltimore, in the drug business, remaining with him about eight years, when he removed to St. Louis, when he was taken to Boonville by Speed & Rochelle, druggists, and given employment in a drug store of the firm as clerk. He remained there about two years, going thence to Omaha, where he arrived in 1856, still in the employ of Speed & Rochelle, who opened in the city a branch store. He was clerk for a short time longer, when he was taken in as a partner, the firm name then being changed to Speed, Rochelle & Co.

Subsequently, Mr. Ish purchased the interest of Speed, when the business was carried on in the name of Ish & Co. A few years after, Mr. Rochelle sold his interest to Mr. Ish, who then carried on the trade alone, taking in a partner (Lawrence McMahon) on the first of July, 1880, the firm conducting business under the name of Ish & McMahon.

Doctor Ish (for so he was known to all in Omaha and Nebraska) was taken sick while on a pleasure trip to the North, and returning home, died August 9, 1881, and was buried at Grass Lake, Michigan, the old family burying ground of his wife. The interest of the deceased remained in the firm until February 1, 1882, when the name was changed to McMahon, Abert & Co.

The subject of this sketch was married to Martha M. Cook, October 26, 1867, at Adrian, Michigan, his wife surviving him, and is still a resident of Omaha, a lady of more than ordinary worth and of unusual business capacity. There is but one child—James Cook Ish—of this marriage, who was born August 13, 1869, in Omaha, and is now connected with the B. & M. Railroad.

While in active life in Omaha, Doctor Ish had almost the entire control of the drug trade, doing a wholesale and retail business, but at the time of his death the firm of Ish & McMahon had given up the retail trade entirely. He was treasurer of Douglas County for two terms. He was a very prominent Mason, and was buried with the rites of that order. He was a Democrat in politics; was liberal and of a benevolent disposition; giving to religious institutions of all kinds, donating largely to public improvements, and to charitable purposes generally; and was in all respects a substantial and worthy citizen of Omaha.

BENJAMIN ELI BARNET KENNEDY —The paternal grandfather of Benjamin Eli Barnet Kennedy was John Kennedy, who was married to Hannah Barnet about the beginning of the Revolution—the husband serving in the war, and at its close the two moving into Central Vermont, then a wilderness, where, at Bolton, Chittenden County, they lived and died. Their son Samuel was born there on the fourth of May, 1789. He was married in Essex, in the same State July 22, 1816, to Hannah Mosley Morse, daughter of Elijah Morse. His wife was born February 22, 1798.

The natal day of Benjamin, the subject of this sketch, was the twentieth of April, 1827. His native place was Bolton. His father, Samuel Kennedy (already mentioned), served in the war of 1812 as a volunteer and took part in the battle of Plattsburgh, New York. His occupation was that of a farmer, but he held several positions of honor and trust—among others that of member of the legislature and judge of the *nisi prius* court of Chittenden County.

Benjamin remained at home working on the farm until of age, attending the district school in winters, except that he received a single term of academical instruction. He then commenced the study of law in the law office of Maynard & Edmunds (the latter, afterwards, United States senator), at Richmond, Vermont. He was admitted to the bar in 1853, and to the bar of the supreme court of the State in 1858, in which year he married Frances G. Nims, daughter of Reuban Nims, late of Romeo, Michigan, and removed to Omaha, Nebraska, where they arrived on the fourteenth of September, of the year last mentioned, and where they have since lived, the husband following the profession of his choice ever since, with marked success.

In 1863-4, Mr. Kennedy was mayor of the city of Omaha. He has held the office of city solicitor for one term. In 1864, and the next two years, he was a member of the territorial legislature—the first year in the house and the remaining two years in the council.* He was, in both, chairman of the judiciary committee, and in 1866, of the joint committee on revision of the statutes. The same year he was nominated by the Democratic party for the office of judge of the supreme court, but was defeated by a small majority. In 1879, he was a member of the lower house of the State legislature, and in 1864, was chosen school director of the public schools of Omaha, holding that office eight consecutive years, during which

*Ante, Chap. IX., p. 80.

time the first school buildings in the city were erected, including the high school.

Mr. Kennedy was appointed, by the governor of Nebraska, a member of the board of education of the Nebraska normal school in 1872, which office he still holds; he was also appointed a member of the State fish commission; both of these positions of honor are without emolument.

In politics, Mr. Kennedy is a Democrat. He took the freeman's oath and cast his first ballot in 1848, for Lewis Cass. In 1888, he voted for Grover Cleveland and again in 1892.

The secret of Mr. Kennedy's success as a lawyer is to be found in his strict and conscientious devotion to the interests of his clients, his undeviating rectitude, and his unvarying courtesy of demeanor. To these may be added an equable temper, which has enabled him to emerge from the forensic contests of thirty-five years with hardly an enemy or ill-wisher. He is not over-elated by signal triumphs nor overwhelmed by depression when he suffers defeat. Careful, painstaking and diligent, in the preparation of his cases, he aims to win them rather by a logical presentation of his testimony and a skillful marshaling of his facts, than by brilliant rhetoric or strategem. Thus it is, he often defeats showy antagonists, who deceived by his quiet manner and his sober, impartial opening, anticipate an easy victory. These characteristics have secured for him a large array of clients, who, once attached to him are not easily won away. In the preparation of wills, the examination of titles, and the investigation of questions relating to real estate he has but few rivals.

Mr. Kennedy has been for many years an enthusiastic hunter and an ardent lover of all sports of the field. Thus, at the close of his three and a half decades in Nebraska, he could boast, if self-laudation were possible with him, of vigorous health, of a well-earned competence, of the respect of his fellow citizens, the esteem and love of the bar, and a reputation absolutely without stain.

THOMAS LORD KIMBALL.—"Many men of a lofty grade of power and excellence have arisen in our country among a class who may be described as of Eastern blood, but Western development—growing up in the freer atmosphere, the more spontaneous life, the larger scale of being—they have, as it were, themselves enlarged in mind and have become better fitted to cope with vast executive problems." So says Mrs. H. B. Stowe, and this is peculiarly applicable to the subject of this sketch, Thomas Lord Kimball, eldest son of Amos and Johanna Kimball, who was born October 1, 1831, in Buxton, Maine, of Puritan stock, to "an inheritance of hard work" and consequent independence.

Mr. Kimball's father was a soldier of the war of 1812; a farmer; a man famed for rare mechanical skill and sound judgment. His mother was noted throughout the countryside for charitable deeds and conscientious uprightness. Their farm, which was made to produce almost everything needed for the maintenance of the large household, was among the last of these typical homes, once so common in New England.

Mr. Kimball's earliest recollection is of reading and studying by the light of pitch knots, carefully gathered for the purpose; and the knowledge thus acquired awakened in him an ambition for a broader life than that afforded by the farm. At the age of sixteen he was both farmer, teacher and pupil, fitting himself for college, where he hoped to pursue a medical course, for which he was by nature eminently fitted. An illness, by which he was confined to his house and bed for two years, frustrated this plan. Given up to die, he dismissed his doctors, and, prescribing for himself an entirely different course of treatment, was fully restored to health, thus early evidencing his leading characteristics—sound judgment and an iron will.

He apprenticed himself to the leading firm of jewelers in the neighboring town of Saco, where he was soon master of all branches of the business—that requiring artistic skill, as well as mechanical foresight and ability. So completely had he won the confidence of his employers, that at the end of his apprenticeship they established him in the town of Biddeford in like business, which he successfully conducted for several years. From the first he was foremost in accepting the responsibilities of good citizenship; "never noisy nor self-asserting," writes one of his fellow-townsmen, the editor of the *Eastern Journal*, " young Kimball was a man of broadest catholicity of spirit, yet he was, in his quiet way, chief man of his church, the superintendent of his Sunday school, an active trustee of the public schools, an attentive director of the savings bank, the alderman of his ward, consultor in all town charities, the working man on the committee for annual lyceum lectures, among the most vigorous of the temperance and anti-slavery workers—for these two great reforms were then at their height—an occasional speaker in public meetings, often a sagacious writer for the press; a man, in fact, so trusted for integrity and intelligence, that, had he remained in Maine, I may say we had no position, social or political, that would not have been open to him."

In 1857 Mr. Kimball visited Cincinnati, Ohio, and was induced to enter the service of the Pennsylvania Railway Company. That company was not long in learning that in this cool-headed resolute young man they had material for the best kind of railroad service, and they made rapid advancement in the extent and responsibility of his duties, until he was appointed general southwestern passenger agent. Mr. Kimball remained in Cincinnati four years; then was located in Chicago, in charge of all the Pennsylvania Central's passenger business west of Pittsburg. In March, 1871, Thomas A. Scott had been chosen president of the Union Pacific Railway, for years a leading spirit in the Pennsylvania Central's directory, and undoubtedly the ablest railroad man yet developed in this country. He knew Mr. Kimball well, having been associated with him for twelve years, and urged him to accompany him to Omaha, which he finally consented to do; and the two kept their union of service, where Mr. Kimball was for ten years the general ticket and passenger agent, then assistant general manager, then general traffic manager, next assistant to Mr. Potter, and at his death the acting general manager, and at the annual election was made general manager of the whole system, so remaining until Mr. Holcomb's appointment to his place, when he was made third vice-president of the railway and president of the depot company. In all these twenty years, through all administrations, through the sickness or absence of superior officers, Mr. Kimball has been much of the time the mainstay of the great railway in all its working departments, the man of large experience, stainless honor, sound judgment, tireless industry and reliant spirit, always on the ground with shoulder to the wheel in every emergency. A man of method, he was abreast of his work, and always turned a willing ear to those who sought his advice, and their name was legion. One instance occurred to the writer. I was accosted by a burly middle-aged man at one of the railway ticket conventions, of which he was a member, in this way: "Look at me; I was saved from ruin by drink through the unwearied kindness of Mr. Kimball. For years he stood by me when every one had left me. He pointed out and led me in the right way, and my family and I owe to him all we are to-day."

The duties of the day, however arduous, were never complete to Mr. Kimball until recorded in brief in his diary, which for forty years furnished a key to a most laborious and useful life — a life now in its prime, attended by the kindred blessings of health and prosperity, beloved by all who know him, a shining example to those who follow in his footsteps.

Mr. Kimball married, in 1855, Mary Porter Rogers, fourth daughter of Nathaniel Peabody and Mary Farrand Rogers, of New Hampshire. Their four children are: Frances R., now Mrs. George W. Holdrege; Thomas R., married, of the firm of Walker & Kimball, architects, Boston and Omaha; Arabel M., living with her parents; and Richard R., also married, and manager of "Riverside Farm," Mercer, Neb.

FREDERICK KRUG.—That the brewing interest is one of paramount importance in the country (look upon it as we may), is a fact that cannot be gainsaid. Take the production of the two largest breweries in the old world — those of Spaten Brau, Munich, and Dreher, Vienna — and compare them with Anheuser-Busch, St. Louis, and Best, Milwaukee, and the two last mentioned more than hold their own for production in one year: Spaten Brau and Dreher, 711,617 barrels; Anheuser-Busch and Best, 803,921 barrels. Now, while it is true that there is no brewing plant in Omaha, or Nebraska, that can make the showing of either one of the breweries just mentioned, nevertheless it is only a question of time when the Frederick Krug Brewing Company, with its capital of $1,000,000, will crowd even the most productive of these closely.

The company mentioned is an Omaha institution, of which Frederick Krug is president. He it was who, as already stated,[*] erected the first brewery in Nebraska. But his one-story frame building, on Farnam Street, of 1859, was succeeded by a brick building, forty-four feet wide and eighty long, on Eleventh and Jackson Streets, and this has finally given place to the magnificent structure, fronting on Green Street and on Boulevard, which, when finally completed and fully equipped, will be at a cost of nearly a million dollars. For each day in the year there will be a capacity of about seven hundred barrels of beer. Who shall say that the Krug Brewery is not one of the leading industries of Omaha?

As long ago as 1884, the author of *The Leading Industries of the West* wrote of Mr. Krug: "The brewery interests of Omaha are very extensive, not only because of the importance of the city as a commercial distributing point, but because the community is a liberal one and recognizes the fact that no man has a right to chain his neighbor's appetite with legislation, much less his feelings, provided he interferes with no one else. The oldest brewery now in existence in Omaha is the extensive establishment of Frederick Krug. It was commenced in a very humble way, in 1859, by the present proprietor, and under his prudent management it has become one of the most important industries of the kind in the West. The business was first commenced on Farnam Street, in decidedly unpretentious quarters, when Omaha had but one business street, we may say, and a very inferior one at that. It was removed to its present elegant location, on Jackson Street, between Tenth and Eleventh, in 1867. Enlargements and improvements have been repeatedly made since then, to satisfy the demands of trade—especially in 1883, when the brewery was made nearly double its size."

Such is the plant that is now giving way —after ten more years of prosperity—to the gigantic new one just started. Mr. Krug and his lady are estimable citizens, having a large family—five sons and three daughters.

ENOS LOWE was born at Guilford Court House, North Carolina, May 5, 1804. He was about ten years of age when his parents moved to Indiana, locating at Bloomington. When a mere boy, he began

[*]Ante, p. 506, of this History.

the study of medicine, commencing the practice in the midst of many vicissitudes and privations incident to a new, wild and sparsely settled country. Little by little the doctor accumulated enough to enable him to enter the Ohio Medical College, at Cincinnati, where he graduated with honor. He then located as a practitioner at Greencastle, and soon after moved to Rockville, continuing in active practice for some years, during which time he was sent to the Indiana Legislature.

In the fall of 1837, he moved to Burlington, Iowa, where he continued in active practice for the following ten years. He became one of the most active citizens of the place, and was one of the leading spirits in laying strong and deep the foundations of that now beautiful and prosperous city.

In 1847, Dr. Lowe received from the President of the United States the appointment of receiver of public moneys at the land office in Iowa City, to which place he removed at once. He held the office for four years. He was a member of the Iowa Legislature, and president of the senate; also a member of both constitutional conventions, and was president of the second one. In 1853, he was appointed receiver of public moneys at Kanesville (now Council Bluffs), whither he removed, holding the office two years, when he resigned.

In the mean time, he and a few friends organized the Council Bluffs and Nebraska Ferry Company, of which he became president; and he at once went to Alton, Ills., and bought the steam ferry-boat, *General Marion*, had a full cargo put on board, and brought her to Council Bluffs. From this small beginning, the ferry company, under his guidance, became a strong organization, and a most important factor in settling the great trans-Missouri country. The company built several fine steamers (some of which were destroyed by ice), and during all the period preceding the advent of railways and the building of bridges, these boats served as a most satisfactory and efficient means of communication.

About the time of the organization of the ferry company, Dr. Lowe, and a few others, obtained consent of the Omaha Indians to occupy a certain area on the west side of the Missouri. The laying out of a town immediately followed—now the site of a portion of the City of Omaha. This was done under the supervision of the doctor, as president of the ferry company. From this time he became identified with this city (and Nebraska as well), and was ever active, energetic and zealous in forwarding the interests of both. No one in the community devoted more labor or gave more time gratuitously to the public weal than Dr. Lowe. In 1866, the Old Settlers' Association was organized, and he was chosen president, holding that position for nearly four years.

At the outbreak of the Rebellion, Dr. Lowe, though somewhat advanced in years, felt that every able-bodied man should aid in stamping out the attempt to destroy the nation's life, and at once entered the service as surgeon of the 1st Nebraska Regiment, going into the field in the Department of the Missouri, under General Curtis, but he was soon after transferred to the Army of the Cumberland, with which he served as brigade and division surgeon until his health became so impaired that he resigned.

Many important industries and enterprises owe their existence to Dr. Lowe, among which may be named the Omaha Gas Manufacturing Company, the Omaha & Southwestern Railway Company, and the organization of the State Bank of Nebraska.

On July 22, 1828, the subject of this sketch was married to Kitty Ann Read, a native of Mercer County, Kentucky, who died at Burlington, Iowa, February 19, 1870. The doctor died at Omaha, February 12, 1880, leaving an only child—W. W. Lowe—now a resident of the city, and to whom the public is indebted for rescuing from oblivion many interesting facts concerning his father.[*]

There are many incidents in the career of the son, William W. Lowe, of interest to the people of Omaha,—to those of Nebraska and of the country at large. He was born in Greencastle, Putnam County, Indiana, on the 12th of October, 1831, and was a cadet at West Point from July 1, 1849, to July 1, 1853, when he graduated, being promoted in the army to brevet second lieutenant of dragoons on the same day. He served at the cavalry school at Carlisle, Penn., in 1853–54; was in garrson at Jefferson Barracks, Mo., 1855; on frontier duty at Camp Cooper, second lieutenant

[*] See *Transactions and Reports of the Nebraska State Historic Society*, Vol. I, pp. 111-114.

2d Cavalry, March 3, 1855; in Texas, 1855-56; in Fort Inge, Texas, 1856-57; at Fort Mason, same State, 1857, engaged in scouting against Indians; was promoted to first lieutenant 2d Cavalry December 1, 1856; was at Fort Mason, Texas, 1857-58; served as adjutant 2d Cavalry, May 31, 1858, to May 9, 1861; scouting, 1858; at Fort Belknap, Texas, 1858-59; Camp Cooper, Texas, 1859-60; scouting, 1860; on leave of absence, 1860-61; on frontier duty at Fort Mason, Texas, 1861; and in garrison at Carlisle Barracks, Penn., same year.

He served during the war of 1861-66: In defense of Washington, D. C., May 6 to December 10, 1861, participating (having been promoted captain 2d Cavalry, May 9, 1861, and assigned to 5th Cavalry, August 1, 1861) in the Manassas campaign of July, 1861, and engaged in the battle of Bull Run, July 21, same year; was employed in organizing his regiment, December, 1861; February, 1862, he was in Tennessee; was made colonel 5th Iowa Vol. Cavalry, January 1, 1862; he was in the campaign of February, 1862, being engaged in the attack and capture of Fort Donelson; February 13-15, 1862, was in command of that fort, and Forts Henry and Helman; February, 1862, to March, 1863, he was actively engaged in repulsing several attacks upon the works; was in cavalry operations in middle Tennessee, northern Alabama and Georgia, commanding brigade or division, March, 1863, to July, 1864, being brevetted major in the regular army, October 9, 1863, for gallant and meritorious services in cavalry engagements near Chickamauga, Ga.; brevetted lieutenant-colonel in the regular service, December 15, 1863, for gallant and meritorious service in cavalry action near Huntsville, Ala.; was employed in remounting the cavalry of the Army of the Cumberland, at Nashville, Tenn., July, 1864, to January 24, 1865; was mustered out of the volunteer service, January 24, 1865; was at Fort Leavenworth, Kan., as acting assistant provost marshal, general superintendent of volunteer recruiting service, and chief mustering and disbursing officer for Kansas, Nebraska, Dakota and Colorado, from February 14, 1865, to July 30, following; was brevetted colonel in the United States Army and brigadier-general of United States Volunteers, March 13, 1865, for gallant and meritorious service during the Rebellion; brevetted brigadier-general United States Army, March 13, 1865, for gallant and meritorious services in the field during the Rebellion; was on leave of absence July 21, 1866.

General Lowe's military services, after the close of the war, were at Nashville, Tenn., on the Pacific Coast and at New Orleans. He resigned June 23, 1869, having settled in Omaha in May, of the previous year. Since leaving the army, he has been an active business man, engaging in many undertakings of paramount importance, and has always been esteemed one of the most valuable, enterprising and energetic citizens of the city.

JESSE LOWE was born in Raleigh, North Carolina, March 11, 1814. The family soon afterward moved to Indiana. Young Jesse was educated in Bloomington College, that State; and, after leaving the institution, he studied law for some time in the office of Gen. Tilghman Howard. He did not then seek admission to the bar, but was afterwards admitted in Nebraska, although he never practiced his profession. Being in poor health, he concluded to travel; and he accordingly spent several years in the South. During this period he was engaged to a considerable extent in purchasing stock for the army. When the Mexican war broke out in 1847, he became commissary of a Missouri volunteer regiment, under Sterling Price. He was promoted to paymaster, in which capacity he served until the close of the war, when he joined his elder brother, Dr. Enos Lowe, then receiver of public money at Iowa City.

When Dr. Lowe was made receiver at Kanesville, now Council Bluffs, in 1853, Jesse Lowe accompanied him thither and assisted him in the performance of the duties of the office. One day, Jesse, looking across the Missouri, pointed to the present site of Omaha, and predicted that it was the spot for a large city. His next move was to cross the river and stake out a claim. He paddled a small skiff over the stream, accompanied by Jesse Williams; this was July 23, 1853. Each took up a claim. Mr. Lowe's was located in the vicinity of the west end of the present Cuming Street, and embraced a quarter-section of land, to which he subsequently added three other quarter-sections.

At this time, Mr. Lowe was the only person whom the agent for the Indians would permit to trade with them. Immediately upon the extinguishing of the Indian title to the land upon which Omaha is situated (which was early in 1854), a town site—the incipient city—was surveyed and platted. It is claimed the town was named by Mr. Lowe. No better or more appropriate one could have been selected. When the subject of this sketch settled here—which was not long after the place was laid out—he had, as a result of his former business enterprises and savings, considerable wealth for those days, and he established himself in the real estate business, which he continued until his death, April 3, 1868.

Mr. Lowe built the first banking house (almost the first brick building in Omaha), which, after years of occupancy by different private banking firms, became the United States National Bank, and was, early in 1887, torn down to give place to a fine modern building of stone. In 1857, the city having obtained a charter, Mr. Lowe was elected its first mayor.

The parents of the subject of this sketch being "Friends" (Quakers), his early training in the principles of that sect shaped and governed his whole life; although in his later years he became a member of the Lutheran Church. He was a man of sound judgment and excellent principles.

He was married July 3, 1856, in Burlington, New Jersey, to Sophia Happin. Four children were born of this union—Frederick Brown, Charlotte Augusta, Jesse, Jr., and Tilghman Howard.

JOHN W. LYTLE is of Scotch-Irish descent. He was born in Lower Sandusky (now Fremont), Ohio, on the 30th of June, 1838. His father and mother were Methodists, and they named their boy after John Wesley, the founder of Methodism. The father's name was Andrew Lytle. He was born on the 13th of July, 1801, at Chillicothe, Ohio. The mother's maiden name was Mary Cole. She was a daughter of one of the early pioneers of northern Ohio, and died when the subject of this sketch was about one year old.

John's early training fell into the hands of his grandmother and elder sisters. In 1838, the family moved to western Illinois, near Pittsfield, Pike County. The boy received the best common school education the place offered, and he subsequently graduated at the Griggsville Academy, attending, afterward, the State University, at Jacksonville. He commenced the study of law in the office of James Ward, a particular friend of Stephen A. Douglas. Many persons, who afterward became noted, were often in the office; and there was much discussion of the slavery question, by Lincoln, Douglas, Trumbull, Richardson, and others.

The young man (he was then twenty-four years of age) was appointed United States deputy marshal and assisted as census-taker in Pike County in 1860. In the spring of the next year, he emigrated to Kansas, where he was employed to teach the first school in Hiawatha.

In the year 1864, Mr. Lytle was engaged by Capt. James Fisk to assist in trying to open a wagon road between St. Paul and Minneapolis and Montana. There were about one hundred and fifteen persons in the party. They passed through the country about where Bismarck is now located. Just before reaching the Yellowstone Valley they came upon immense herds of buffaloes—traveling whole days without being out of sight of them. Besides these, there were numerous herds of antelope. On the 3d of October, they were attacked by a band of Uncpapa Sioux, under command of their chief Porcupine. The savages, in less time than it takes to write it, killed nine of the party.

The remainder of the white men soon placed themselves on the defense, and taught the Indians a severe lesson, whereupon the latter withdrew. However, the next day they came back in large numbers, having with them a white woman—a Mrs. Kelley—whom they had captured at Plum Creek, Nebraska. They opened negotiations with the party, offering to deliver up their prisoner upon being paid for so doing. Mr. Lytle and his associates offered the Indians two horses and harness, a wagon loaded with flour, sugar and other provisions; but the savages wanted guns and ammunition, which were refused, and the negotiations ended. Mrs. Kelley was soon after surrendered to the government.

Mr. Lytle subsequently returned to Omaha, where, on the 3d of October, 1866, he was married to Miss Anna B. La Follette. They have two children living — Edward and Emma. The former is engaged in the produce commission business, the latter is attending school at Brownell Hall, Omaha.

Mr. Lytle went with a small party to the Black Hills in the winter of 1874-75, among the very first of the gold-hunters, and built the first house in Custer City, having rived the shingles out of frozen pine timber.

Mr. Lytle was admitted to practice law in Nebraska, in 1869. He has a first-class business from a clientage of corporations and syndicates eastward of New York, in all the higher courts—State and Federal. He owns in Omaha a considerable amount of improved real estate.

Mr. Lytle has held a number of minor offices in this city, among them being that of justice of the peace and police judge. He has also been member of the board of education. He has traveled considerably, not only in his own country, but in British America and Mexico. He is looked upon as one of Omaha's substantial and reputable citizens.

WILLIAM WALLACE MARSH.—The early ancestors of the subject of this sketch were English. The first of the name to come to America was William Marsh and a brother, whose first name is unknown. These brothers settled in Connecticut. The fourth in the line of descent is William Wallace Marsh, who was born in Cuttingsville, Rutland County, Vermont, on the 14th of October, 1832. His father—his grandfather and his great grandfather, all had the given name of William—was a merchant.

The early education of William Wallace was obtained in the common schools of his native town and at Black River Academy in Ludlow, Vermont, of which institution he is one of the alumni, and is also one of its trustees. While in the state last mentioned, Mr. Marsh was a clerk in a store first in Cuttingsville, then in Ludlow. This was before he had reached his majority. He then spent two years in settling up his father's estate as assistant of one of his sisters, who was administratrix.

Mr. Marsh then went West, spending the fall and winter of 1855-56 in Galena, Illinois, and in Dubuque, Iowa. In February, 1856, he journeyed by coach from the last named place to Sioux City. Soon after his arrival there, he purchased a claim in Dakota County, Nebraska, and settled there and made a pre-emption. On the 30th of April following he left Sioux City and returned to Vermont. He closed up his business in that state and again went West, settling on his claim in Nebraska. The following year he followed the occupation of farmer, raising a fine crop of corn.

From that time until 1862, Mr. Marsh was engaged in the United States mail and stage business, quitting it in the fall of the last mentioned year. He had several routes all above Sioux City and Dakota City. The first contract ever let in the Territory of Dakota by the general government was to Mr. Marsh, and the route ran from Sioux City to Fort Randall. He made his headquarters at that time in Sioux City.

In the fall of 1862, Mr. Marsh became interested in the ferry franchise in Omaha, and was chief manager for the Council Bluffs and Nebraska Ferry Company. In the winter of 1867, he took charge, in connection with the Ferry Company, also of the Missouri River Transfer Company, overseeing its affairs. It was finally merged into the Union Pacific Transfer Company, which continued operations until the completion of the Union Pacific Railroad bridge across the Missouri, in the spring of 1871. From that date until July 1, 1873, Mr. Marsh was out of business. He then purchased an interest in the Omaha Horse Railway Company, and has ever since, through all its changes, been actively engaged in its management.

In later years the subject of this sketch has been interested in the Wyoming Stage Company, Glencoe Mills, Godman Packing Company, Gedney Pickle Company, and is now president of the Union National Bank of Omaha, and has been connected with it in that capacity ever since its organization in July, 1886.

Mr. Marsh was a member of the Omaha city council for one term (1872-73); and a member of the city school board for five years, serving as president during the last year of his membership. He was married in January, 1863, at Ida Grove, Ida County, Iowa, to Miss Flora M. Atwood, who was born in Livermore, Maine. The family consists of four sons—Charles, Frank, William and Allan.

HON JOHN A McSHANE was born August 25, 1850, in New Lexington, Perry County, Ohio His father, Thomas McShane, was a native of County Armagh, Ireland, and his mother was a native of Philadelphia Until the age of twenty-one, the subject of this sketch passed his time at work on his father's farm, and in attending the district school where he acquired his education

He went to Wyoming in 1871, and became an employe on a cattle ranch where he obtained a thorough knowledge of the stock business, and two years later invested his savings in cattle, and went into the business on his own account and made money at it, continuing to be an independent stock raiser till 1883, when he merged his interests with the Bay State Live Stock Company, one of the largest companies of Wyoming, in which he became a stockholder.

He removed to Omaha in 1874 and engaged in mercantile pursuits, which proved to be profitable, and in the year following became actively identified with many prominent enterprises both in and out of the city For several years he was general manager of the Bay State Live Stock Company, and a stockholder in the Omaha Nail Company, since removed from this city He is now president of the Union Stock Yards Company of South Omaha, also president of the Union Stock Yards National Bank of South Omaha, a director in the South Omaha Land Company and of the First National Bank of Omaha

Mr McShane's financial success, genial disposition and generosity, naturally made him popular among his fellow citizens, and a political career was opened to him upon which he entered in 1880, when he was elected to the lower house of the state legislature from Omaha He was elected to the State senate for two years, in 1882, and re-elected in 1884 During these years he was a powerful advocate of those changes in the charter of this city which increased the power of the city council, revolutionized the city government, and resulted in the public improvements which distinguish the Omaha of to-day In 1886 he was made the nominee of the Democratic party, for congress for the first district of Nebraska, which was then overwhelmingly Republican, and his election was regarded as impossible, but he made the canvass with the same judgment, skill and vigor that had previously characterized him in politics and in business, and when the ballots were counted it was discovered that he had been elected by a majority of nearly 7,000, Mr McShane thus became the first Democratic representative Nebraska ever sent to congress His record in the national legislature was excellent and satisfactory to his constituency In 1888 he was nominated for governor, but the Republican strength of the State in the year of a national election was too great to be overcome, and his opponent, Governor Thayer, was elected

John A McShane married Miss Mary M Lee, daughter of John G Lee, of Omaha, on the 25th day of April, 1876 She died April 16, 1884, leaving two children, Edward Lee and Mary Lee

Mr McShane was married again on the 11th of October, 1892, to Miss Kathryn A Lonergan, a most estimable and accomplished lady of Chicago

DAVID HENRY MERCER.—On New Year's day, 1833, in Western Pennsylvania John J Mercer first saw the light of day. He was not born in the lap of luxury, but he came of a good family,—Scotch blood predominating in his veins As he grew towards man's estate an innate desire to do something for himself prompted him to leave the old homestead. With all his belongings tied in a pocket handkerchief and buoyed up by a mother's blessing, he set out for Pittsburgh, then as now, the metropolis of Western Pennsylvania Chance and necessity anchored this boy in a blacksmith shop, where he remained until he mastered the trade "Westward the star of empire takes its way," and westward went this young man, not stopping until Benton City, Benton County, Iowa, was reached Here he formed the acquaintance of John Flora, another Pennsylvanian, a partnership was formed and the battle of life commenced in earnest. Miss Elizabeth Flora was keeping house for her brother John when Mercer arrived, but this arrangement was changed September 16, 1856, by a marriage between John J Mercer and Elizabeth Flora On July 9, 1857, there was born to them a son, the subject of this sketch, David Henry Mercer

Twelve months thereafter, this little family

decided upon a change of location, and with a team of horses, wagon and few household goods, set out for Adams County, Illinois, arriving there in the midst of winter. Good fortune smiled upon them and the future seemed secure, But as life is made up of surprises and disappointments, there was no exception in this case. Fort Sumpter was bombarded, American honor and patriotism were assaulted, and President Lincoln issued his proclamation for troops. Belonging to a family rich in military heroism, John J. Mercer knew his duty and was one of the first to answer his country's call. He volunteered as a private in Company E of the 78th Regiment, Illinois Volunteers, and left for the seat of war, leaving behind a brave mother and two children, David and sister Clara. For over three years, he battled for his country's honor, during which time he marched with Sherman to the sea, and participated in many of the most important engagements of the greatest war known in history, doing his duty so well that he soon became captain of the company in which he enlisted as a private. When the war was over he returned to his Illinois home with an undermined constitution and no plans for the future. At the earnest solicitation of his friends he was nominated for treasurer of Adams County upon the Democratic ticket, but was defeated by less than one hundred votes.

In 1866, he moved to Nebraska, then a Territory, settling at Brownville. His family soon followed. During his residence in Brownville, Captain Mercer accumulated a little property, educated his children, represented Nemaha County in the legislature, and was elected Grand Master of the Masonic Lodge of Nebraska. In 1887, Captain Mercer, wife and daughters followed David to Omaha, whither he had gone some months before. The daughters are now married— Clara, the elder, to Mr. C. H. Fowler, of the Fowler Elevator Company, now of Chicago, and Minnie to C. D. Bell, St. Joseph, Missouri. David remains in Omaha, a bachelor, residing with his parents, whom he supports in their old age.

The subject of this sketch was educated in the public schools of Brownville where he assumed a leadership among his fellows while yet a boy. He loved his books, interested himself in society work, and joined his fellows in all athletic sports. The Brownville school at this time was the best in the State, and many of its pupils are now prominent citizens of the West. During summer vacations he clerked in a clothing store, and at the age of sixteen years he taught a district school. He also corresponded for several newspapers, one of which was the *Omaha Herald*, edited at the time by Dr. George L. Miller.

In the spring of 1877, he entered the last term of the freshman class of the Nebraska State University, graduating therefrom June 9th, 1880, under the chancellorship of Hon. E. B. Fairfield. During his university career, he developed a strong aptitude for politics. He held every office within the gift of the students, and was invariably one of the leaders in all college enterprises.

Young Mercer's candidacy for editor-in-chief of *Hesperian Student*, the college paper, is part of the history of Nebraska. For six months the contest lasted. Twice was he elected, and so bitter waged the war that the faculty became involved, dividing itself equally for and against him. The plans and stratagem of this contest attracted the attention of the outside world and was characterized by the late Hon. James Laird as "a battle royal with giants on each side."

After graduation, Mercer returned to Brownville and commenced the study of law. At this time he held his first political office, that of city clerk, receiving therefor the unanimous vote of the electors, while for the other positions a most bitter contest was waged. In the fall of 1881, he entered the law department of Michigan State University, having been admitted to the bar a few weeks previous. Upon examination by Hon. Thomas M. Cooley, he was admitted to the senior class, graduating in March, 1882, with the degree LL.B.

At the end of a week's vacation he returned to Brownville and swung this shingle to the breeze: "D. H. Mercer, Attorney at Law." For three years he practiced his profession, part of the time serving as police judge and justice of the peace. He was very severe in criminal matters, and gained for himself a good reputation for enforcing the law. The last two years of his residence in Brownville, he served the Missouri Pacific Railway as local attorney.

During the Blaine campaign, having been

elected secretary of the Republican State Central Committee, a position he held two years, and refused a third, he laid aside business and devoted his time and talents to Republicanism While occupying this position he was often called to Omaha to attend meetings of the committee, and in a short time became so infatuated with the people and prospects that he determined upon a residence there During the spring of this year he was offered the mayoralty of Brownville but refused it In this connection the *Nemaha Granger*, an Independent paper, said " We have heard D H Mercer mentioned as the right man for Mayor of Brownville Mr Mercer is just the man to elect He is a young man, full of life and energy, of excellent executive ability, and prompt in the discharge of every duty He would represent Brownville creditably at home and abroad, and moreover it is time to push the young men of this community to the front The *Granger* heartily seconds the nomination of Mr Mercer and trusts that he will not hesitate to accept the position to which our citizens would be pleased to elect him "

Mercer's acquaintance with the prominent politicians of Omaha gave him an immediate prestige in Douglas County politics and he attended as a delegate the first Republican city convention which met after his citizenship in Omaha was established. This convention elected him chairman of the Republican City Central Committee He conducted this and other campaigns so successfully that he was retained in this position until he refused to have it longer

In 1891, at the urgent request of Douglas County Republicans, he accepted the position of chairman of the Republican County Committee, and managed a campaign which completely reversed the political situation in the county, electing the Republican ticket His first year in Omaha, Mercer was nominated by the Republican party for county judge, but with several other candidates on the ticket was defeated Upon Harrison's succession to the presidency, Mr Mercer occupied the position of assistant United States marshal for Nebraska, but only for a short time, as he resigned to perform the duties of special master in chancery of the United States Court In the fall of 1892, he announced himself as a candidate for congress from the second district of Nebraska, composed of the counties of Douglas, Sarpy and Washington, subject to the action of the Republican convention Under adverse circumstances and after a bitter contest, the Republican convention of Douglas County by a large majority expressed its preference for him, and sent a delegation to the congressional convention favorable to his interests The latter convention nominated him by an almost unanimous vote for this important position and the people ratified the choice at the polls on election day by the following vote D H Mercer, Republican, 11,488, Judge George W. Doane, Democrat, 10,388, Robert L. Wheeler, Independent, 3,152, and R W Richardson, Prohibitionist, 362.

Mercer waged a most remarkable campaign and by the help of the young men of the district, to whose untiring efforts is due in a great measure the credit of the victory, he defeated for congress the strongest candidate in the ranks of the democracy. The battle cry of the campaign was a quotation from Abraham Lincoln "Give the boys a chance," and it met with a hearty response

Mr Mercer is a young man of genial disposition, indomitable pluck and unflagging energy He has a remarkable memory for names and faces, and can call more people in his district by their given names than most people know by sight His friends are legion, and loyal to the core, and for them he will always fight There is not a drop of aristocracy in his blood, he knows his friends after election as well as before, and he believes that an American citizen "is the noblest work of God "

In June, 1893, President Cleveland issued his proclamation, convening in extraordinary session the Fifty-third Congress and this sketch is written while Mr Mercer is at Washington, attending to his duties as a member of this, the most important congress in years That he is meeting the expectations of his constituency is already fully demonstrated

SAMUEL DAVID MERCER was born in Marion County, Illinois, June 13, 1842. His father, Wiley Green Mercer, was born in Muhlenburg County, Kentucky, and married Miss Cynthia Huff, in Marion County, Illinois, who was the daughter of Samuel Huff, formerly of Tennessee. His grandfather's name was David Mercer, whose wife was Elizabeth Cearcy, of Madison County, Kentucky. His great-grandfather was Shadrack Mercer, who married Rhoda Price, of North Carolina; and his great-great-grandfather was Thomas Mercer, of Pitt County, North Carolina. The last mentioned emigrated from Virginia, and was the son of Edward Mercer, who was the son of Gideon Mercer, of New York and New Jersey. The family were English, but originally of Scotch extraction.

Samuel was born on a farm; there were no railroads and his home was sixty miles from the Mississippi, which was the chief artery of commerce. The home was not only a farm, but a veritable manufacturing institution as well, producing not only food for the family, but manufacturing the same by canning, drying and preserving vegetables and meats, and manufacturing the clothing of the entire family almost exclusively from the products of the farm. The wool was shorn from the sheep, washed, carded, spun, woven and manufactured into clothing on the farm, supplied with buttons of home manufacture, and colored with roots and herbs of the vicinity. Hides were tanned and manufactured into shoes, harness, etc., for domestic use; and the farm implements were often forged in the blacksmith shop, framed and made ready for use, without the expense of a dollar except labor and the purchase of the iron. This was the custom of the entire country until railroads came and made an innovation on the established practices of the farmer.

Samuel's early education was commenced by private tutors, employed on a salary, by his father with other farmers, and schools were kept in out tenement houses. Afterwards, when free schools came into vogue, he attended them until the age of sixteen, when he went, for a short time, to a select school in the village of Walnut Hill; subsequently to McKendry College, at Lebanon, Illinois.

The boy's life, when on the farm, was working with men, as all boys had to do in those days and under such circumstances. He lived with his parents in the home log house until he was old enough to aid in hewing and framing the timbers for additional houseroom.

Samuel's first business venture was that of trapping quail, mink, and other fur animals, and gathering the crude drugs of the country for sale, from which he obtained all his spending money, and accumulated enough to buy a one-third interest in a threshing machine, which, with two uncles as partners, he operated one autumn. He also planted out a large crop of fall wheat, and then taught a country school during the following winter months. The next spring, in company with Frank M. Meeker, he put in ten acres of tobacco, which yielded several thousand dollars, owing to high war prices.

During the following autumn the young man again began threshing, but, by an accident, was severely wounded in the left hand while feeding the machine; thereupon he immediately stepped from the platform, went to the village of Salem and, under the direction of Dr. William Hill, went thence to the University of Michigan to study medicine. After two years, during which he graduated from the chemical laboratory of that institution, he made an application to the board of examiners at Chicago for recommendation as assistant surgeon in the army, which was successful, and he was assigned to the 149th Regiment Illinois Volunteers. After the war, Dr. Mercer returned to the North and took a third course of lectures in the Chicago Medical College, and went thence to Berkshire Medical College, Massachusetts, where he finished his medical course and received a diploma in October, 1866. On graduation he was awarded the first premium—a case of surgical instruments—for the best thesis; subject—"Healthy Nutrition."

After this, Dr. Mercer came direct to Omaha, and has remained here ever since, never having been absent more than five weeks at any one time, continuing the practice of medicine up to 1886, during which time his labors were arduous and his practice extensive, especially in surgery.

In the winter of 1867-68 he established the first hospital in Omaha, located at the corner of what is now Cass and Twenty-sixth Streets. It was afterwards turned into a small-pox hospital purchased by the city and subsequently burned. Later on he started a private surgical hospital known as the "Omaha Medical and Surgical Institute," which he managed successfully for many years. He finally abandoned it on account of arduous duties and practice, and accepted the position of chief surgeon of the Union Pacific Railroad, establishing the system which is still in vogue, and founded, as well, the Ogden and Denver hospitals in connection with that road. He was also surgeon to the Omaha Grant Smelting and Refining Works, assistant surgeon of the Burlington & Missouri River Railroad for many years, and for ten years United States pension examiner at Omaha. During this period he was the prime mover in establishing the Omaha Medical College, in which he filled the clinical chair of surgery for four years, and delivered the following address to the first graduating class:

"Gentlemen: The degree of doctor of medicine, when properly obtained, is an honorable title. It is the legal and professional authority that admits its possessor into the ranks of the medical profession, and guarantees to him the right to practice. It also grants the privileges, immunities and honors of the profession. In addition to these honors, immunities and privileges, it brings also obligations of the most sacred and responsible kind.

"As members of the profession you are about to enter, you become the guardians of public health, and largely of individual happiness. You are to be the protectors and preservers of human life. As physicians and surgeons your decisions must necessarily often be final, a court from which there is no appeal—be the result for weal or for woe. Your duty will be to advise and protect alike the high and the low, the rich and the poor. Your authority, if judiciously directed, will be respected by all alike. In matters pertaining exclusively to your profession courts will be governed by your opinions, armies guided by your direction, and nations will submissively bow to the mandates of your authority. In private life individuals will rest their *all, even life*, with your judgment and practice. The weapons you will wield are potent for good or for evil, and upon your ability and judgment in selecting and applying, the success of your practice will depend.

"The object of your student life has been to bring about these necessary qualifications. You have gone through a full course in the several branches and passed examination satisfactory to your instructors, entitling you by right to the diploma of the Omaha Medical College, and as the chief officer of this institution, the faculty directs me, in the name of the people of the State of Nebraska, from whom this college legally received its authority to deliver to you this diploma, thus conferring upon you the degree of doctor of medicine.

"This means not only that you are qualified to commence the practice of medicine, but that your character and deportment, as *men* is such as warrants this faculty in appointing you as custodians of these important principles.

"If you would increase your knowledge, continue to be students, not as mere bookworms only, but observers of principles and facts, and reasoners from cause and effect. If you would preserve that precious jewel, 'self-respect,' remain worthy men, true to yourselves and to others. Society will then have no cause to regret your having passed the safeguards she has thrown out to protect herself from the unworthy."

Subsequently, the doctor occupied the chair of surgery for two years in the state university at Lincoln.

Dr. Mercer was seven years secretary of the State Medical Society, which was brought into existence by his own motion in 1867, and was always an active member of the same, and was president one term, and, during the last year of his practice, was vice-president of the American Medical Association, and presided part of the time at the national meeting at New Orleans.

Owing to ill-health and accumulation of many outside business affairs, Dr. Mercer retired from the practice of medicine in the autumn of 1886, just twenty years after commencing in Omaha, and during the next season embarked in the enterprise of building cable and electric railroads, but soon finding that the cable was not profitable and not adapted to cities of this size, sold his interest and put his energies into the electric plant. After three years hard struggle in fighting financial odds and opposition from opposing companies and opposing interests, he succeeded in developing the first electric railroad plant in the city, which was soon after united with that of other companies and became the principal part of the Omaha Street Railway Company, of which he is an active member and one of the directors.

During the last few years of his practice, and after his retiring, Dr. Mercer invested his surplus money largely in real estate, bought and platted that section known as "Walnut Hill," and built seventy-five houses thereon before any other settlements were made in that section, all of which were sold on small monthly payments to men desiring to secure homes. He afterwards erected several blocks of business houses in the city, including also the building known as the Mercer Hotel. He has always been an active, energetic and never-tiring worker for the interests of Omaha and Nebraska, ever showing his good faith by energy and investment of money to build up the town and the State, with a firm belief that prosperity of each should go hand in hand.

Dr. Mercer's political views are, and always have been, republican, believing firmly in the doctrines of tariff as the best means of protecting and equalizing the interests of all men, but he looks with misgiving upon the encroachments of large corporations and financial institutions organized with money to make money, sometimes without due regard to moral rights or equity among men.

In 1890, Dr. Mercer was a prominent republican candidate for governor, but was defeated in the convention, and was again spoken of very prominently as a candidate in 1892 for the same office, but refused to permit his name to go before the convention, on account of commercial reasons. He was made chairman of the Republican State Central Committee, in 1891.

In the autumn of 1892, the doctor was the prime mover in starting the drug establishment known as the "Mercer-Whitmore Co." and is also interested in several other commercial enterprises in a small way.

Dr. Mercer was married on the 12th day of November, 1870, to Miss Lizzie Covert Hulst, of Omaha, Nebraska, at the German Reform Church, in Brooklyn, New York. Miss Hulst was the daughter of Garrett Hulst, late of Alexandria, Virginia, and formerly of Brooklyn, New York, and granddaughter of Anthony Hulst, of Williamsburg, New York, and he was a son of William Hulst, who was a descendant of the original Knickerbocker family.

Dr. Mercer and his wife still live in Omaha, the home of their adoption. Their children are George W. Mercer, a graduate of Peekskill Military Academy and of Yale College; Nelson S. Mercer, a graduate of Peekskill Military Academy, and now (January, 1893,) a student at Andover, Massachusetts; Carrie L. Mercer, a student at Brownell Hall, Omaha; and Mary Mercer. The deceased members of the family are an infant daughter, and Robert L. Mercer who died at the age of four years.

As chairman of the Republican State Central Committee, Dr. Mercer, in his public utterances at the State conventions, acquitted himself with credit. In his opening address at Kearney, April 27, 1892, he said:

"Midway between ocean and ocean, on the east and on the west; and midway between the gulf on the south and the British possessions on the north; and also midway between the eastern and western boundaries of our own state, is the focal spot, the hub of the nation, the axis of the State, around which revolve all our social, commercial and political interests. Upon this spot stands the beautiful and thrifty little city of Kearney, with a people peerless in ambition, ever watchful and ready to seize the passing tide and work with a right good will to the successful finishing of every enterprise. When the republican party was born, this spot was the center of the great American desert. To-day it is the center of the nation's oasis."

\* \* \* \* \*

And again at Lincoln on the 4th of August, following, when the Republican State convention assembled to nominate candidates for State offices, the address of the doctor, was, as a partisan effort, of a high order, but reached far beyond that of the ordinary politician, as the following extracts conclusively show:

"Everywhere within the limits of our great, growing and prosperous State, there seems to be now, more than ever before, a zealous determination, touching even the deep emotions of men, to defend, to protect, and perpetuate the doctrines of the grand old Republican party.

"To-day every county, aye, every precinct, of the State is here, in convention assembled. Every caste of good society is respresented. Here in this hall labor and capital sit side by side. Here in this convention is also the buyer and the seller, the producer and the consumer—all earnestly and actively merging their interests in one common cause, and that cause is good government. Upon that condition, and that alone, we will build our platform, and through it reiterate and reconfirm to the people, the doctrines of our party, already evolved in the national platform, as established and endorsed by strong men who have successfully guided and directed the affairs of this nation for the last thirty-two years, through the vicissitudes of war and famine, peace and prosperity, until she has risen above her peers, resting now upon the very summit of success, supported by the silent powers of sixty-five millions of people.

"During these thirty-two years of republican rule, population has doubled; social and commercial affairs have increased more than a thousand per cent, while education and general growth of practical arts and sciences have kept pace with the rapid development of other departments. These results alone, ought to be enough to convince even the most skeptical, who contiually cavil about the ills of this land, and claim that there is no hope except to follow a glaring *ignis fatuus* that occasionally rises up in the midst of a mass of dark isms, from some calamity swamp.

"To-day we must make no promise which our party representatives will not faithfully keep. If we do, it will be a cause for discord; and ill results will follow evil causes.

"In fact, all things visible and invisible, palpable and impalpable, on the earth or in the heavens above, move by the incontrovertible laws of cause and effect, under the inspiration of a Diety.

"The earth revolves upon its own axis, while the sun, moon, and stars travel in their respective orbits, all with such precision and regularity, that the astronomer may calculate with mathematical accuracy the position, distance, and velocity of each. But the influence that one planet has over another, or that all have over the inhabitants of any, is a knowledge reserved to be known alone to Him who creates the cause to produce the effect.

"So it is with man; his physical power, individually or collectively, may be calculated and estimated, but the influence that one man may have over another, or that a collection of men may have over other men, is a knowledge also reserved to be known alone to the creator of the emotions of men, that spring into activity and produce effects when the cause-trigger is touched.

"Some things, however, men do know and some duties men do realize, first among which an is inalienable right to worship God according to the dictates of conscience; and, second, their intuitive duty to defend and protect personal rights, individual and collective liberty.

"It was an attempt to oppress these principles that drove the pilgrims on the Mayflower. It was an attempt to abridge these liberties that sent the tea overboard in Boston harbor. These are the kind of things that caused a mighty convulsion among the emotions of men, the effect of which was the Declaration of Independence, vouchsafing life, liberty, and the pursuit of happiness to an American people." * *

Of the particular likings of Dr. Mercer, which indicates his character more effectively than can be expressed in words, may be mentioned his love for trees and flowers (especially roses), and, it may be added, for works of art. The doctor has, also, not only strong likes but dislikes for persons, and abhors everything in word, figure or deed that is not truthful.

*Edward L. Merritt.*

GEORGE L. MILLER.—Of all the men who have been identified with the growth and progress of Omaha and have left their impress upon its history, no one has a reputation more to be coveted than George L. Miller. He was one of the pioneers, coming in 1854 to the then straggling and struggling village on the bank of the Missouri River, which had no other identity upon the map than being opposite to Council Bluffs. The latter had been a resting-place for the migrating Mormons, who were seeking a new Zion farther westward.

Dr. Miller was born in Boonville, Oneida County, New York, August 18, 1830. At the age of seventeen, he began the study of medicine in Syracuse, New York, and after five years of close application to his books, entered the College of Physicians and Surgeons in New York City, graduating in 1852. Returning to Syracuse he practiced his profession for two years, but yielding to the advice of friends he sought in the West, a wider field, coming to the extreme frontier—the "jumping off place," as it was known in those days. He arrived in Omaha when there were not to exceed twenty persons in the village, long in advance of railroads and the telegraph; and the only means of mail communications with the outside world was by stage coach to St. Joseph, Missouri, and to Davenport and Keokuk in Iowa.

He began the practice of medicine, but patients were few and the climate altogether too healthy for the amassing of a speedy fortune. Young and vigorous, with talents of a high order, he naturally took prominence in the community, where brains were at a premium, and with a natural bent for politics, he speedily became identified with public affairs. Within a twelve month of his arrival in Omaha, he was elected to the territorial legislature. He served one term in the lower house of that body. The next year he was chosen a member of the territorial council in which he served four years, and of which he was president two years.

Those were exciting days in Omaha; days when history was made, as is recounted in other pages of this work, and through it all Dr. Miller bore high rank and acquitted himself with credit.

In 1860, just preceding the war of the Rebellion, the doctor, who had gained some experience in literary work, went to St. Joseph, Mo., where, as an incident of his professional life, he wrote a series of editorial articles for the *Gazette* of that place. He was a strong unionist, and his editorials appearing in a paper published upon what was debatable ground with regard to adherance or position to slavery and the impending conflict, attracted wide attention.

Resuming his residence in Omaha, in 1861, he was appointed sutler at Fort Kearney, and remained there until 1864. The Nebraska frontier was at that time greatly menaced by the Indians and predatory raids and even battles were frequent. In the year last mentioned, the Democratic party of the Territory called upon him to run for delegate to congress, and he returned to Omaha to make it the basic point of his campaign. He was defeated at the polls, but concluded to remain in Omaha, and then associated himself with D. H. Carpenter in the founding of the *Herald*, a Democratic newspaper. Later, Mr. Lyman Richardson succeeded Mr. Carpenter as Dr. Miller's associate in editing and publishing that paper, which they continued until March, 1887.

Dr. Miller was always a man of striking personality. He possessed a strong and rugged character, with great energy and capacity for work. He was fearless in the expression of his views, yet always courteous and considerate to an opponent. He has always been devoted to Omaha and its interests; and it has been well said of him that no man has done more than he to foster the town from the days of its swaddling clothes to those of its lusty young manhood, when it has reached a population of over 150,000. He has been among the first in public enterprises, by voice and by pen urging the public good and inspiring his fellow citizens to deeds and ventures, the object and purpose of which have been the furtherance and upbuilding of the city.

Dr. Miller's strong mental acquirements and his ability as a writer, combined with the position which he achieved as a politician, soon brought him into contact with the leading men of the nation, a fact which largely advanced his capabilities for aiding the growth of Omaha. He has ever been a propaganda and the city his faith. He has always been found in the front rank among its citizens, in enticing and encouraging eastern money, seeking profitable investment in the West, to come to Omaha. Notably was this true when, after the close of the civil war, the project of a transcontinental railroad took shape. He labored hard and zealously for the building of the Pacific roads and bore a prominent part in determining Omaha as, practically, the eastern terminus of the Union Pacific. As editor of the *Herald*, he also gained distinction in his party, ranking as a leader of influence and a statesman of sound ideas.

The stand taken by him upon the great financial questions of his time deserves most earnest attention, and stamps him as worthy of a place among the soundest and best thinkers of the period upon these subjects. It also shows that he was gifted beyond ordinary writers and politicians with that prescience which enables one to see beyond the mere present, and measure, at their true value, illusory and misleading theories, which may prevail for a time and lead astray multitudes of otherwise strong and well-meaning men.

Prior to the presidential year 1876, the "greenback" or "fiat money" craze prevailed throughout the country, and especially in the western States, where it permeated all classes, composing both of the great political parties. The bonds, issued by the government for the prosecution of the war, commonly called "five-twenties," were already redeemable by their terms, and the date of maturity was not far distant when it would be necessary to either pay or refund them. The point was raised that these bonds, being payable in "dollars" without mention of "coin" or "gold," were payable in greenbacks, and the opinion was seriously upheld that instead of retiring these notes, which had been the constant effort, during the whole of General Grant's administration, a further issue should be made sufficient to pay off these bonds, amounting to nearly a billion of dollars. It was argued that this currency, going into circulation, would make money plentiful, restore business activity, and general prosperity would again gladden the land. No more pestilent theory could be conceived of, and it was now pressed at a most opportune time to do its harmful work.

The baleful effects of the panic of 1873 were still severely felt in all branches of business, and the doctrine appealed with great force to the large army of debtors who believed they would be relieved of a great portion of their burdens—as undoubtedly they would have been if such legalized robbery had been established. It, therefore, required no slight amount of moral courage to combat this theory, even if the conviction of right was surely founded.

There was, however, no hesitation on the part of Dr. Miller. He at once took his stand in uncompromising hostility to the scheme. This stand now was the more important for the reason that opinions were focusing to decide the action of the national Democratic convention, to be held the following year, to nominate presidential candidates; and it was generally thought the party would endorse the "rag money" idea, and the campaign in Ohio had already been commenced on this theory. The *Herald* teemed, during this period, with editorials, terse, strong, and vigorous, which were well calculated to carry conviction to every reader, as witness the following:

August 11, 1875.—"We did say and now repeat that if the election of Governor Allen and the Democratic ticket in the present contest [in Ohio] is to result in an alliance with the distressed states of the South to fasten the financial doctrine of inflation upon the Democratic platform next year, we hope and pray William Allen and the Democratic ticket may be defeated [in that state] by not less than one hundred thousand majority."

And the next day, Dr. Miller said: "It is rag money, irredeemable in coin that Ohio delights in * * * not the honest hard money, the world's measurer of values, by which the farmer has to buy what he consumes. But stop throwing your soft money puff-balls at Nebraska. We invite * * * attention to the latest speech of its [Ohio's] own Pendleton, who at last surrenders the monstrous heresies with which he has poisoned and polluted his State."

The doctor's vigorous efforts met with an immediate response from his own party at home, which was as surprising to the country at large as it was flattering to him. The democracy met in State convention, September 16, and unanimously adopted this resolution:

"*Resolved*, that we are in favor of a sound currency, coin, or its equivalent, as essential to stability in business and a restoration of prosperity—steps towards specie payments and no steps backwards."

And the national convention of the following year, at which Samuel J. Tilden was nominated for president by the democratic party, declared for a reform "to establish a sound currency" and protesting against the failure for eleven years "to make good the promise of the legal tender notes which are a changing standard of value in the hands of the people, and the non-payment of which is a disregard of the plighted faith of the nation."

Naturally enough, Dr. Miller became the familiar associate of the prominent men of the nation; particularly was this true with regard to Horatio Seymour, whom he held in the veneration of a foster parent. He also was very close to Samuel J. Tilden in the days of his prominence in the nation, and had Mr. Tilden occupied the presidential chair (1877-81) it is beyond peradventure that Dr. Miller would have been called to his cabinet.

Dr. Miller has never manifested any thirst for office. He has preferred to make office-holders of others rather than of himself; but he has always wielded a potential influence in politics; and when finally his party did gain ascendency in the nation and Grover Cleveland entered upon the presidency, Mr. Tilden and other prominent democrats warmly urged the appointment of the doctor as postmaster general, viewing him as a strong representative of the West, and embodying the spirit of sound democracy. Another was chosen, but the subject of this sketch was prouder of the honor gained from his endorsement, than he would have been in receiving the appointment. The recent election, for the second time, of Cleveland as president, is a source of much gratification to Dr. Miller.

When in 1887, after a long period of active life, he decided to retire from journalism, he found himself comfortably situated—possessing a competency of this world's goods. He has a fine country-seat, situated about five miles southwest of Omaha, which he has named "Seymour Park," in honor of the distinguished patron of his younger days. Here he has a domain of four hundred and sixty acres, embellished with hundreds of thousands of trees, planted by himself in early days. The whole is crowned with a costly stone mansion, supplied with all modern conveniences and comforts. His seat is of easy access to the city, two lines of railroads skirting its boundaries, each with a station upon the premises. A life of inaction was not, however, to Dr. Miller's taste. Hale and vigorous, he could not entirely relinquish labor, and he has, until recently, devoted much of his time to the general management, in the West, of a life insurance company, which has large investments in Omaha and contiguous places. He is, now, president of the board of park commissioners, a position entirely to his taste and to which he devotes much of his time in trying to secure for Omaha a system of parks—a project in which the citizens have recently aided him by the voting of $400,000 in bonds for additional sites, the improving and beautifying of which is provided for by an annual tax.

In 1890, Dr. Miller undertook to aid in the establishment of a Presbyterian Theological Seminary in Omaha. At the request of Rev. Dr. John Gordon and other clergy, he made a donation of twenty-five acres of land in Seymour Park, for that purpose, which was formally accepted by the Presbyterian body, which in turn, was endorsed by the Presbyterian General Assembly of the United States. It is expected the foundation for the main structure will soon be laid.

GEORGE MORGAN O'BRIEN was born in the County of Wexford, Ireland, on the first day of May, 1829, and died in Omaha, Nebraska, January 8, 1887. He was a direct descendant of the O'Brien family noted in the history of Ireland in her struggles for independence. The ancestral branch of his family refused to be reconciled to British rule in the Emerald Isle, and, as a punishment for their adherence to their old faith (the Roman Catholic) and their loyalty to their native land, preferring independence to British rule, were proscribed, their estates confiscated, and by a royal decree it was made lawful for any person to kill any male member of the family wherever found in the British dominions. Such treatment, instead of subduing the spirit of independence and crushing that bold family, only excited its members to renewed efforts for the liberty of their country. Under this dreadful anathema we find them earnestly resisting the regal decree and actively engaged among the leaders in the rebellion of 1798, in the province of Linster.

A grandfather was one of the leading rebel generals who fought the British forces at the memorable battles of Wexford, New Ross and Vinegar Hill. His maternal grandfather, General Martin Code was also a general who, in conjunction with General O'Brien, fought the British forces under command of General Lake, at the place last named. In this engagement General Code was taken prisoner, hung, drawn, and quartered by the British authorities * * * General O'Brien retreated with his forces and soon after fought the battle of Arkalow where he was killed; his body, being recognized, was hung upon a gibbet by authority of the British commander. The loss of the battle of Arkalow resulted in the suppression of the rebellion of 1798 and the subjugation and consequent slavery of the liberty-loving sons of the green Isle of Erin. The love of freedom was smothered for a time but not subdued. It was cherished in human souls, waiting only for an opportunity to renew the conflict and thereby take another step in the pathway of empire, destined to end in national independence. Whether among the hills of Shannon, on their way to Conaught, or enjoying the freedom of the New World, the central star of their hopes and the desire of their lives is, to witness the emancipation of their countrymen from British misrule.

For half a century, there was no opportunity offered to renew the contest; but, in 1848, the O'Briens became the moving power in another ineffectual crusade against the unwelcome bondage forced upon them. William Smith O'Brien was the leading spirit in this attempt to liberate Ireland. The subject of this sketch was then a boy of nineteen years, but with all the enthusiasm of his race, he joined the forces of his kinsman and shared in the dangers of the field in a conflict with the well-disciplined forces of gouty old John Bull. Upon the failure of that movement and the arrest of Smith O'Brien, Mitchell Meagher and other leaders, young O'Brien eluded the vigilance of the British authorities and in the spring of 1849 sailed with his father for America and settled in Wisconsin. This revolution and consequent exit from his native country prevented the consummation of his plans for a classical education, nevertheless his familiarity with the preparatory branches enabled him to take a position in this country among the leading men. For several years he was engaged as civil engineer in the Badger State, pursuing his legal studies during winter months, thus supplying the deficiency occasioned by his exile. Previous to his eighteenth year he had gained a thorough knowledge of Blackstone as the basis of future usefulness, and in after life he derived more benefit from that branch of study than from any other, and to that he attributed in a great degree his success at the bar. He thus divided his time between the law and engineering until the breaking out of the southern rebellion in 1861.[*]

In the year last mentioned, Mr. O'Brien was appointed by President Lincoln consul to Cuba, and he was in Washington, D. C., preparing for his departure for Havana,

[*] *Pen Sketches of Nebraskans*, pp. 445, 446.

when the war broke out. He immediately resigned his commission and volunteered as a private in the ranks of the National Guard, a battalion organized by Major Cassius M. Clay, for the defense of the National capital, at a time when it was in imminent danger. He rendered valuable service in the battalion until mustered out. In after years, General O'Brien prized his certificate of muster-out of service of this battalion more than all the other evidences of rank among the defenders of his adopted country, which the close of the war found him in possession of.

The subject of this sketch then received the appointment of chief clerk in the United States surveyor general's office for Wisconsin and Iowa, at Dubuque, Iowa, and discharged the duties of that position faithfully and with credit to himself, when he received a telegram announcing the death of his brother, Captain Moses O'Brien, of the Wisconsin Volunteer Infantry, who was killed at the battle of Cedar Mountain, Virginia. He immediately resigned his position and hastened to Washington for the remains of his brother, which he obtained, conveying them to Milwaukee, attending to their interment, when he returned to Dubuque, having resolved to leave his family, consisting of a wife and six children, and fill the vacancy in the number of his adopted country's defenders, caused by the death of his brother.

He obtained permission of the governor of Iowa, ratified by the war department, to raise a regiment of Irishmen at his own expense. He received his commission as colonel of the Forty-second Regiment of Iowa Infantry Volunteers on the 16th of September, 1862, and immediately entered with zeal and enthusiasm upon upon the work of raising the regiment. At that time, it was difficult to enlist men and with all his efforts and after the expenditure of a large sum of money, he failed to obtain the minimum number by the time the government required. His regiment was consolidated with the Forty-third Iowa and formed the Seventh Iowa Cavalry. In his zeal to be in the field, he consented to the consolidation and to accept the position of lieutenant-colonel of the force just mentioned, receiving the appointment by order of the governor of Iowa, January 8, 1863. The Forty-second and Forty-third Infantry made but two battalions of cavalry, in consequence of one company of the Forty-second having been transferred to the Sixth Iowa Cavalry, and a portion of the remainder to the Fourteenth Iowa Infantry. Governor Kirkwood proposed to complete the organization by the addition of a battalion of the Forty-first Iowa Infantry. Major Pattee, who was then in command of that battalion, refused to consent to the consolidation unless he could be made lieutenant-colonel. Believing it to be for the good of the service, the subject of this sketch consented to the arrangement and fell back to the rank of second major, and was mustered into that grade on the thirteenth of July, 1863. After the next month his regiment was engaged in warfare with the Indians on the plains of Nebraska and Colorado.

Major O'Brien, being an excellent engineer, constructed Post Cottonwood, Nebraska Territory, at a small expense to the government, and was for a time its commander. By his labor and ability that post afterwards became one of the best in Nebraska. On the twenty-seventh of September, 1864, the major was assigned to duty as district engineer of the district of Nebraska, and served as such until February 11, 1865, when he was relieved and given the command of his regiment and of Post Cottonwood, which position he occupied until July following, after which time he was on duty as supervising officer of the troops doing escort duty on the Overland Stage Line from Post Cottonwood to Fort Sedgwick. In frequent engagements with the Indians, he exhibited the highest qualities of a commander and proved himself an able, gallant and intrepid officer. He was afterwards brevetted brigadier-general.

In April, 1866, General O'Brien moved his family from Dubuque, Iowa, to Omaha, and after the close of the war engaged in the business of contractor, supplying materials for construction of the Union Pacific Railroad; which business not netting him expected returns, he abandoned, and settled down to a professional life, being, in 1868, appointed United States commissioner for the district of Nebraska. His knowledge of Indians and the Indian languages made him a peculiarly valuable officer, at a time when savage depredations were still of daily occurrence.

In May, of the year last mentioned, General O'Brien was admitted to practice law in the federal and State courts of Nebraska, and in February, 1873, was upon motion of Hon. Richard M. Corwin, admitted to practice in the supreme court of the United States. General O'Brien was so frequently successful in his cases that he soon became extensively known for his legal ability, his greatest successes being in the real estate and chancery branch of the practice, though the criminal dockets of this State show his connection with many of the most noted trials of that character. After his death, when the news of his illness and demise were made known to the judges of the supreme court, then holding session at Lincoln, Nebraska, they adopted resolutions commemorative of his past connection with that tribunal, and spread upon their records their regrets at the untimely death of "one of the ablest attorneys that had ever practiced in the supreme court of Nebraska since the organization of that body."

In politics, General O'Brien was an ardent Republican, having aided in the organization of that party during his residence in Wisconsin. He being one of the first Irish Republicans in America, was as a "tower of strength" in the party in the Great West.

He was married September 23, 1851, at Cleveland, Ohio, to Catherine E. Carroll, to whom he had been engaged before his enforced departure from his native land, and they raised a family of eight children, five daughters and three sons—Mary M., Kate E., George M. Jr., Margaret A., Moses P., Nicholas J., Elizabeth C., and Francis R.

George M., Jr., after a career of marked ability in railroading life, was admitted to the bar, and after his father's death filled the vacancy caused thereby in the law firm of O'Brien & O'Brien, being associated with his brother, Moses P. O'Brien, both well known for their ability in all the channels of the profession. The youngest son, Nicholas J. O'Brien, having chosen railroading as a profession is occupying a high position in the service of the Union Pacific Railway and is superintendent over the lines of that company in the State of Washington.

The record of General O'Brien and his sons is a fair reflection of their honorable ancestry. Personally, Mr. O'Brien, was quite unassuming in his manners; devoted to his profession; honest and earnest in the performance of his duty; strongly attached to friends; generally successful in his undertakings, and enthusiastically devoted to the cause of Irish freedom. His memory will ever be held dear to those who knew him.

SAMUEL A. ORCHARD, was born in Livonia, Washington County, Indiana, September 20th, 1835. His father and grandfather moved from Kentucky to Indiana soon after the admission of the latter State into the Union. His mother was a native of Virginia. He was educated in the common schools until he was sixteen years of age, and then attended Wabash College, at Crawfordsville, Indiana, for three years.

At the age of nineteen he left college, and, in company with a young man of about his own age, bought a wagon and team and traveled across the country from his home to Omaha, reaching this city in November, 1855. Realizing at once the future importance of Omaha, he immediately entered and settled on a quarter section of government land as near as possible to this place. This tract, which he cultivated and lived upon for the year following, he sold in the year 1885 for twenty thousand dollars, and it is now within the limits of South Omaha.

From 1856 to 1863 Mr. Orchard was in the produce and commission business, his store being situated on the south side of Harney Street, between Twelfth and Thirteenth Streets. During the Rebellion he was appointed assistant provost marshal under Captain O. F. Davis, which position he held until the end of the war.

Mr. Orchard and Miss Eliza A. Crawford, of Omaha, were married January 2d, 1865. The have two children, Charles Colfax and Mabel Gray.

Mr. Orchard formed a copartnership with William Preston, under the firm name of Orchard & Preston, in 1865, and engaged in the grocery and produce business. He relinquished this five years later, and accepted the appointment of surveyor of customs, opening the port here. He resigned this office in 1872, and accepted the position of assistant postmaster under C. E. Yost, which position he retained until 1877.

Immediately after retiring from this position Mr. Orchard entered into partnership with Samuel Bean, and the firm of Orchard & Bean, dealers in carpets, opened a store at 1113 Farnam Street.

In 1881 Mr. Bean died, and from that time the business has been conducted by Mr. Orchard. The demands of a constantly increasing trade caused the business to be removed first to the southeast corner of Farnam and Fifteenth Streets in 1882, and to still larger and more commodious quarters at 1414-18 Douglas Street in 1890, when a stock of furniture was added. The building on Fifteenth Street, and also the one now occupied, were especially built for Mr. Orchard, who has one of the most complete establishments in this line in the West.

Mr. Orchard has been a successful merchant and is now possessed of a comfortable fortune, and though still directing the management of the furniture and carpet business, he delegates the supervision of the details of the trade to his son Charles, and passes a large portion of his time socially with the many friends which long residence in Omaha and a companionable disposition have made him.

WILLIAM A. PAXTON.—The ancestors of the subject of this sketch were Scotch, some of whom emigrated to this country at an early day. Matthew Paxton, father of William A., was a native Virginian, born at Lynchburg, moved to Washington County, Kentucky, about sixty years ago, he having previously married Miss Cathrine Hogue, in the place of his nativity. The father was a farmer, and there was born to him five children—four sons and one daughter. Next to the eldest of the sons is the subject of this sketch, who was born January 26, 1837, in Springfield, the county and state mentioned.

William attended the schools of his native place, where the advantages of education were limited. The father, with his family, moved to Middletown, Montgomery County, Missouri, in October, 1849, and continued his occupation as a farmer.

In the fall of 1850, William left home, working at eight dollars a month farming for a year and a half, when he went to work on his "own hook," purchasing ox teams and breaking prairie. This he followed, with other jobs, until 1854, when he took charge of a farm, in Montgomery County, Mo., for the largest salary ever before paid in that region for work of that nature, getting two hundred dollars a year. This was for M. J. Ragan. He worked for him for four years.

Mr. Paxton came to Omaha, January 13, 1857, still for one year working for his old employer, as foreman in building the first bridges ever built on the military road leading from Omaha to Fort Kearney. This work he finished in December, 1857.

Mr. Paxton then returned to Montgomery County, Missouri, and married Miss Mary Jane Ware, daughter of James W. Ware, February 22, 1858. There has been born to them one son, William A., now living, and one daughter, who died in infancy.

After his marriage, Mr. Paxton employed his time for two years in farming, with poor success, coming back to Omaha in 1860, leaving his wife temporarily with her mother. He then engaged in freighting from Omaha to Denver during that year. In 1861, employed by Edward Creighton, he was engaged in building the Western Union telegraph line across the continent. In December of that year, he returned to Missouri with some capital—the result of his hard earnings—and once again attempted farming, which proved to be the wrong time—just the opening of the Rebellion—with the result of losing everything he had. He went again to Omaha, arriving there July 7, 1863, this time having with him his wife and $135, all told.

Mr. Paxton then "hired out" as foreman in a livery stable at fifty dollars a month and boarding himself, for the old firm of Wilbur & Coffman, where he worked till June, 1864, when he took charge of John McCormick & Company's teams, a freight-train freighting between Omaha and Denver and Fort Laramie.

Mr. Paxton meanwhile had purchased of Edward Creighton ("as good a man as ever lived") a team for $1,050, on four months' time, and earned the money to pay for the same with the team and his own salary. This was really his beginning financially in life. It was in 1864, in the fall of the year—his entire capital being a four-mule team and $1,800 in money. To this he added occasionally as he could until 1867, when he went to railroading, his first contract being from Julesburg ten miles west, on the Union Pacific Railroad. From there he went to Sherman, same year, and engaged in the tie business for the same road, continuing that until June, 1868. He then moved the Union Pacific forces, 6,000 men and 1,500 teams, from Rock Creek, Wyoming, to Green River; worked there grading until September, 1868, when he was sent back to Tie Siding, Wyoming, to help the railroad company out in their ties, and there, in the winter of 1868–9, he closed out his train and returned to Omaha to his family.

In May, 1869, Mr. Paxton engaged for the first time in the cattle business. In December following, he took the job of building ten miles of the Omaha & Northwestern (now the Chicago, St. Paul, Minneapolis & Omaha) Railroad, and was one of the directors and a stockholder.

In 1870, he, in company with others, went into the cattle-contracting business with the United States Government, which he followed for six years, at the same time running a cattle ranch at Ogallala, Nebraska. The cattle business he carried on actively from 1877 to 1883, when, in December of the year last mentioned, he sold out for $675,000.

Mr. Paxton was one of the original and principal promoters of the South Omaha enterprise—the organization of the Union Stock Yards Company and the Land Syndicate, now the South Omaha Land Company[*]—and has been foremost in every endeavor to uphold, in the "Magic City," the livestock and packing industry, which ranks already second (or nearly so) to Chicago in magnitude.

In 1880, the wholesale grocery house of Paxton & Gallagher was established, where the Ware block now stands, on the corner of Fifteenth and Farnam Streets, Mr. Paxton being the senior member. They have since changed their location. Their trade is now about two and a half million yearly.

In 1886, the Paxton & Vierling iron works, in Omaha, were founded, of which Mr. Paxton is also the senior member, and here, ever since, they have carried on a very successful business—now working two hundred men.

Mr. Paxton is a large owner of improved real estate in Omaha, and has extensive interests in lands and other property in the West. As a member of the house of representatives of Nebraska, he served during the twenty-fourth session, which commenced January 4, 1881. He also served as state senator during the twenty-ninth session of the legislature, convening January 1, 1889.

---
[*] See the formation and successful operations of these two companies in the History of South Omaha, following this Chapter.

# BIOGRAPHICAL SKETCHES.

JAMES HENRY PEABODY.—The subject of this sketch was born in Washington, District of Columbia, March 7, 1833; his old home was within a few blocks of the president's mansion. His ancestor, was Lieut. Francis Peabody, of St. Albans, Hertfordshire, England, who came to New England, in the ship Planter, April, 1635. He first resided at Ipswich, and in the summer of 1638 was one of the original settlers of Hampton, old Norfolk County, where he went with Rev. Stephen Bachilor and twelve others, and where he resided for several years. In 1649 he was chosen by the town of Hampton, one of three men to "ende small causes," and was confirmed in that office by the justices of that court. When the State lines were run, Hampton was found to be in Rockingham County, New Hampshire. "Being minded" as he said "to live nearer Boston" he sold his estate, March 25, 1650, and moved to Topsfield, Massachusetts. We find him thus early residing in Topsfield, Essex County, Massachusetts. He was one of the most prominent men of that town, both for property and enterprise. He married Mary Foster a daughter of Reiginald Foster. The grandfather of James Henry was General John Peabody, who was for years the principal merchant of Newburyport, Massachusetts, engaged largely in the East and West India trade. He was appointed general of the Massachusetts militia by Govenor Elbridge Gerry, one of the signers of the Declaration of Independence of the United States. In 1812 he offered his services to the United States for the war; they were, however, not accepted. He moved to Georgetown, District of Columbia, in 1812, and took with him his nephew, George Peabody, who commenced his business career with him in Newburyport, but afterwards became celebrated as the London banker and great philanthropist. General John Peabody was his guardian.

Captain John Peabody, the father of him of whom we write, was born in Newburyport, Massachusetts, but grew up in Georgetown, District of Columbia, becoming commander of some of the finest merchant ships sailing out of Richmond, Virginia, Washington and Georgetown, District of Columbia, when the commerce of the United States dotted the seas. He was for years in the Liverpool trade. He married Miss Amelia H. Cathcart, the daughter of James Leander Cathcart.

Mr. Cathcart's revolutionary war record reads like a romance. He was the son of an officer in the English army. At the outbreak of the Revolution he gave up his right in the line of inheritance to an estate in Ireland, because of sympathy with the oppressed colonies, and entered the United States navy as a midshipman and served to the close of the war. He was twice captured by the English and escaped from the Jersey prison ship once by swimming ashore and at another time on the ice. After the close of the Revolution he was taken prisoner by the Algerian pirates, taken to Algiers, where he remained virtually a prisoner for eleven years.

The Dey of Algiers, taking a great fancy to him, seeing that he was a man of talents, made him chief clerk to the regency. In this capacity he corresponded with all the foreign powers with whom the Algerines had intercourse, and was thus enabled to gain and remit to our country much valuable information.

During Washington's administration the Dey appointed Mr. Cathcart as bearer of dispatches to Philadelphia, then the seat of the United States government. General Washington treated Mr. Cathcart with the utmost courtesy, and upon the declaration of peace appointed him consul-general to the Barbary powers. After several years in Algiers he continued as United States consul to various other countries for a number of years, the greater number of his children having been born on the coast of the Mediterranean. Amelia H., the mother of James Henry, was born in Leghorn, Italy.

Captain John Peabody, father of the last mentioned, died in 1847, leaving a widow and five children dependent upon the exertions of his two eldest boys. The second son, the subject of the present article, soon obtained a position as page in the United States house of representatives, which he held for five years. This position and that of clerk in the United States pension and land offices for several years afterwards, only requiring a few hours work each day, afforded him ample opportunity to study. He occupied his leisure upon the different branches of education, reading Latin with a view of adopting, eventually, one of the professions. After his mother's death, which occurred in 1852, he commenced the study of dentistry with Dr. R. B. Donaldson, of Washington, at the same time reading medicine with Dr. Thomas J. Cathcart of the same place.

In September, 1856, he matriculated at the medical department of the University of Georgetown, Washington, District of Columbia, and had for his preceptor, Professor James E. Morgan. He continued to attend lectures and clinics here until he graduated March 8, 1860.

Whilst in the house of representatives as page, from 1847 to 1852, he formed warm attachments for several members of that body and of the senate, among whom were Andrew Johnson, General Lewis Cass and Schuyler Colfax, all of whom continued his staunch friends until their deaths.

The doctor has many reminiscences and some amusing anecdotes of events occurring from the stirring times of the Mexican war —during the repeal of the Missouri Compromise and the later sad scenes of our civil war, his fourteen years in civil service and three years in the army affording, as may be premised, many opportunities for observation.

He knew, as a boy, Clay, Webster, Calhoun and their contemporaries.

He refused an appointment of cadetship at West Point on account of his widowed mother, whose greatest support would have been cut off if he gave up his clerkship to enter the army. He had a longing desire to come west, and in 1859 was one of a company formed in Washington, District of Columbia, to explore the Black Hills for gold, having received information of that region from a Mormon, Mr. George B. Simpson, who in fleeing from Salt Lake City came through the Sioux country and brought specimens of surface washings away with him. This company had Dr. J. C. R. Clark, of Missouri, appointed by the secretary of the interior as physician to vaccinate the Indians in Nebraska and Dakota, the appointment giving him free access to the Indian country. Clark and Simpson were fitted out with hydro-oxygen blow-pipe and other apparatus for testing for gold deposits, and started out in the summer of 1859, penetrating for several hundred miles north of old Fort Laramie and well up into the Black Hills. They returned in the spring of 1860, not giving a favorable report of the richness of the deposits, although finding gold in small quantities. The civil war breaking out soon afterwards, the project was abandoned. The doctor thinks the Indians demurred at being vaccinated, although ordered by the Great Father at Washington, and refused to afford opportunities to the white medicine man to prospect for gold; at least, this was his first and last speculation in gold digging. We note this as part of the history of Nebraska.

At the outbreak of the civil war we find the doctor holding a clerkship in the United States pension office and practicing his profession before 9 a. m. and after 3 p. m., only six hours' work then being required of the clerks in government office. In the early days of Lincoln's administration the clerks in the various departments drilled in the corridors; the young Æsculapius shouldered his musket with the rest of them.

In 1862, becoming tired of civil service, the constant cannonading around Washington seemed to call him to take a more active part in the nation's struggle, he offered his services to the government and was appointed acting assistant surgeon United States Army, and continued to serve in the hospitals in and around Washington, District of Columbia. He was with the Army of the Potomac at the battle of Antietam and remained in Frederick, Maryland, in charge of the wounded after that battle, until January, 1863, when he was ordered to report to General Schofield, then in command of the department of Missouri, at St. Louis.

In March, 1863, we find him at Franklin, Tennessee, the acting medical inspector of the Army of Kentucky, under General Gordon Granger, United States Army. Here the doctor lost his younger brother, William Francis Peabody, who was killed in an engagement with Van Dorn's troops. This was a sad blow, for he loved him as a son as well as a brother, and had raised and educated this boy, who was just twenty-one when killed.

On the 20th day of April, 1863, he returned to St. Louis and was placed in charge of the United States Marine Hospital, one of the finest hospitals in that city. On August 15, 1863, President Lincoln promoted him to full surgeon United States volunteers with rank of major, and on May 24, 1864, the secretary of war ordered him to report to Major

General Curtis, in command of the Department of Missouri, at Kansas City. General Curtis ordered him to take charge of the medical department of the district of Nebraska. We find on file the following order:

HEADQUARTERS DISTRICT OF NEBRASKA,
OMAHA CITY, N. T., July 17, 1864.
[Special Order No. 69.]

Surgeon Philip Harvey, United States volteers, having been relieved, and Surgeon J. H. Peabody having reported, in accordance with special order 145, dated Headquarters, Department of Kansas, July 9, 1864, Surgeon J. H. Peabody is announced as medical director for the district of Nebraska, and will be obeyed and respected accordingly.

By command of Brigadier General Robert B. Mitchell. JOHN A. WILCOX,
Lieut. 4th Cavalry, A. A. A., General.

From this date the doctor claims citizenship in Nebraska, having invested in lands and lots in Omaha in the year 1864.

While stationed in Omaha he occupied the old state-house building (situated on the west side of Ninth Street, between Farnam and Douglas, opposite the present Union Pacific headquarters) as a hospital and medical director's office for the district of the Platte. The doctor tells some amusing stories about some Pawnee Indian scouts he had as patients during his term here and the mode of treatment which pleased them best. Whilst medical director he did quite a little practice as consulting physician with the local physicians in Omaha, and made many friendships that continue to this day. At this period he was made a Master Mason in Capitol Lodge A. F. & A. M.

He was kept very busy whilst here in supplying our troops on the plains with sanitary and medical stores, the troops at that time suffering much from the want of vegetable food. April, 14, 1865, he was relieved from duty in Omaha and ordered to Denver, but did not go on account of the extreme illness of his wife. May 15, 1865, we find him with General Clinton B. Fisk at Macon, Missouri, as medical director of the district of North Missouri. He was mustered out at Washington in August, 1865, and was breveted lieutenant-colonel by President Johnson.

Before leaving Washington he called on the president, whom he had known for years. Mr. Johnson said if he could assist him in any way he would be pleased to do it, not only for his own sake, but for the sake of the doctor's uncle, Charles Cathcart, of Indiana, who had been his colleague in congress for several years. The doctor thanked him very warmly and said as he had served his country in peace and in war for eighteen years, he believed he would take Horace Greeley's advice, "Go west and grow up with the country." The president smiled pleasantly and replied that he wished the host of office-seekers and and certain gentlemen lately in rebellion, who had been besieging him for favors since the death of the lamented Lincoln, would also take Horace Greeley's advice.

The fall and winter of 1865 and the spring of 1866 were spent by the doctor in New York at the Bellevue Medical College, the College of Physicians and Surgeons, and in the hospitals of New York city, preparing himself for a general practice in civil life. In April, 1866, he returned to Omaha and has had a very large practice ever since. He can give some interesting anecdotes of the vicissitudes of an early practitioner in and around the city, his practice in the early days extending for fifty miles around Omaha; and the bridges over the streams not being the best construction, he came near being drowned in March, 1866, by being washed off, horse, buggy and all, into the Papillion, just above Gilmore; and the messenger returning with medicine the next day to Forest City, Sarpy County, was drowned, together with his horse, by being carried under the ice in the same stream.

In 1866 he was appointed acting asssistant surgeon United States army, and placed on duty as attending physician to the officers of the United States army and their families stationed in Omaha. He continued in this office until October, 1874, when, owing to Mrs. Peabody's rapidly failing health, he gave up this position, together with a very large practice, and went to Stockton, San Joaquin County, California, remaining there until November, 1875, when he returned to Omaha.

He took an active part in the organization of the San Joaquin Medical Society whilst in California, and was elected vice president of it. In 1867 he became one of the charter members of the Omaha Medical Society, the pioneer society of the State; was elected president of the same at its second session in 1868. The State society was organized in his office, No. 325 South Twelfth Street, and he was elected president of this society at its second session in 1869. He took a very active interest in it in its early days, writing a number of articles to give interest in its proceedings. He was at various times physician and surgeon to St. Joseph's Hospital, surgeon and physician in charge of the Good Samaritan Hospital, which was burned, and consulting physician to the Child's Hospital. He has ever taken an earnest and active interest in every move that would promote the good and growth of regular medicine.

Since 1870 the doctor has been a member of the American Medical Association, the largest body of surgeons and physicians in the United States, and has contributed to its records. He also contributed a number of articles to the "Medical and Surgical History of the War of the Rebellion," and has quite a number of pathological specimens in the Army Medical Museum, at Washington, District of Columbia. He contributed an article on surgery, to the great international congress of surgeons and physicians from all nations, which met in Washington, District of Columbia, September, 1887. This congress was opened by the president of the United States and secretary of state. In September, 1876, he gave to the profession, through an article in the *Philadelphia Medical and Surgical Reporter*, his experience for sixteen years in the treatment of diphtheria and tonsilitis with oil of turpentine.

This article was copied by a number of other journals and has brought this remedy into use in this and other countries. The doctor feels justly pleased to have originated a treatment which after twelve years' trial is acknowledged to be one of the best, if not the best, mode of treating diphtheria, the deaths under this treatment being only from eight to ten per cent., whilst under all others they run from twenty to fifty. The doctor's services in consultation are often sought. Many of the younger members of the profession praise him for his uniform kindness and ethical courtesy. He is zealous for the honor of the regular profession and dislikes the name of pathist, often asserting that it should be unlawful for a physician to call himself anything but a physician, that the practice of medicine should take the whole broad field of therapeutics and not be confined to the dogma of any one. He is general surgeon of the Chicago, St. Paul, Minneapolis & Omaha Railway, Nebraska division, and consulting surgeon, Union Pacific Railway.

Doctor Peabody is a charter member of the Military Order Loyal Legion of the United States, of Nebraska, member of Custer Post, Grand Army of the Republic, vestryman Trinity Cathedral, and has taken an active interest in the promotion of the growth of Omaha, and has contributed largely for a man of his means to churches, hotels, railroads and other public enterprises in which all good citizens are interested.

The doctor has been twice married—first to Miss Mary Virginia Dent, at Louisville, Kentucky, May 26, 1859. Many of the older citizens remember her as a very lovely lady, who spent the winter of 1864 and 1865 in Omaha. She died in St. Louis, Missouri, in August 1865, leaving one son now living in Omaha, Dr. John Dent Peabody, who graduated in medicine, at Brooklyn, New York, in 1881, and in 1882 took an *ad eundem* degree from the University of Pennsylvania, at Philadelphia. The doctor was again married November 21, 1867, at Trinity Cathedral, Omaha, to Miss Jennie D. Yates, a native of Maryland. She was well-known as one of the most active workers in all good work for the city in the early days of its struggle. She was an occasional contributor, both in verse and prose, to the newspapers in the early days of Omaha.

By his latter marriage the doctor had but one child, a little girl, who died when scarcely eleven months old. His acquaintance has been prized as that of a Christian gentleman, ready to give reasons concerning his faith, and also because of his cheerful disposition and good fellowship. He is a hard worker in his profession, but sometimes feels the need of change of scene and outdoor recreation, with no anxious care to oppress him. So with dog and gun or fishing-tackle he hies him to the mountain stream or lake, and in congenial companionship spends a few days and returns with renewed vigor to what will always be his arduous pleasure—the practice of his profession.

ANDREW J. POPPLETON.—The subject of this sketch comes of a family which may be traced to an early day. An English officer of the name was in Cromwell's army which overran Ireland in 1649-50. When

## BIOGRAPHICAL SKETCHES.

the subjugation of the Island was complete he remained there. It is said that Samuel Poppleton was his grandson. Samuel Poppleton was born in Ireland in 1710, and was married to Rosanna Whaley, by whom he had four sons, Ebenezer, Benjamin, William and Samuel, the youngest of whom, Samuel, was born on Christmas day, 1750. Soon after the birth of this child the family emigrated to this country, and settled at Pownall, in the territory which now forms a part of the State of Vermont. At the outbreak of the Revolution the elder Samuel adhered to the British crown, and returned to Ireland where he died; but his four sons enlisted in the Continental Army, and were all actively engaged in the war. Samuel, the youngest, was with Ethan Allen at the taking of Ticonderoga, served under Benedict Arnold in the expedition against Quebec and at the battle of Saratoga, and subsequently came under the immediate command of Washington, and participated in a number of engagements until the close of the war. He was accustomed to say that he had been in seven pitched battles.

In 1783 Samuel Poppleton was married in Pownall, Vermont, to Caroline Osborne, by whom he had eight children, of whom William Poppleton, the father of Andrew J. Poppleton, was born in Poultney, Vermont, in 1795.

In 1811 Samuel Poppleton with his family removed to Richmond, Ontario County, New York, and in 1822 again emigrated and settled at Belleville, in Richland County, Ohio, where he died in 1833. His wife died at the same place on the 7th of November, 1842. In 1814 William Poppleton was married at Richmond, in New York, to Zada Crooks, the granddaughter of David Crooks, a Scotchman, who came to Blanford, in Massachusetts, prior to 1769, and afterwards removed to Richmond, in New York, where he died in 1820. His son David, the father of Zada Crooks Poppleton, was born in Blanford, Massachusetts, on the 2d day of December, 1769, and afterwards removed to Richmond, in New York, where he was engaged as a saw and grist miller until his death in 1812. The mother of Mrs. Poppleton was Eunice Knox Crooks, a granddaughter of William Knox, who was born in Ireland, of Scotch descent, in 1690, and came to America in 1735. She was a first cousin to Major-General Henry Knox,

Washington's artillery officer and secretary of war. She was born on the 30th of May, 1772, and died in Genesee County, Michigan, in 1863, at the great age of ninety-one. In 1825 William Poppleton and his family removed to Troy Township, in Oakland County, Michigan. He had seven children, of whom Andrew J. Poppleton, the sixth, was born in Troy Township, Oakland County, Michigan, on the 24th day of July, 1830. It is worthy of note that each generation of Mr. Poppleton's family, including himself, have been pioneers in a new country.

From Samuel Poppleton and his four sons who came to this country from Ireland and made new homes in what is now Vermont, to the subject of this sketch, all were farmers, tilling the soil with their own hands. The education of the father of Andrew J. Poppleton was limited. By his own reading and study and thought, he became a man of large intelligence, and as such and for sterling virtues was held in highest esteem in the County of Oakland. He was several times elected to local offices and once to the Michigan State Legislature.

The life of a new-comer to a Western home in the early days of the settlement of Michigan was very severe. Clearing the forests, planting a farm and building a home was a work of great privation and unremitting toil. William Poppleton passed through these days and their labors; and in his later manhood saw the State of his adoption a prosperous commonwealth, and accumulated an ample competency, living and dying on a farm which his own hands had redeemed from a state of nature.

He greatly valued the education which had been denied him, and gave to his children all the advantages in that way which the circumstances permitted. He died in May, 1869.

The boyhood of Andrew J. Poppleton was passed upon his father's farm. He inherited a love of the pursuits and association of rural life. The hay and harvest field, the ride to the mill, the orchard, the care and love of animals, the common sports of such a home came to him as natural and enjoyable exercises, and from their pleasures he has never been alienated. One of his favorite recreations in later life has been agricultural pursuits, and the breeding, raising and training of standard bred trotting horses at his Oakland Farm of some

1200 acres near Elkhorn, Neb. He has contributed a strong impulse toward the advancement of the trotting stock interests of this state.

Until 1844 he went to the country district schools; and at that time entered an academy at Romeo, a little town near by his home, where he prepared for college. In 1847 he entered Michigan University; but in the fall of 1850 he withdrew, and entered Union College at Schenectady. While he was at the latter institution the venerable Doctor Nott was its president, and Doctor Tayler Lewis its professor of Greek. Other members of the faculty left an influence upon his mind, but these two men deeply impressed themselves upon his character. As an instructor of young men, instilling into them the highest principles, and at the same time teaching them the precepts which conduct to practical success in life, Doctor Nott has been unsurpassed in this country. The nature of the country boy was open to such influences and he has carried through life what he received from the lips and from the personality of that great man. Doctor Lewis influenced the young student in another direction. A Grecian of learning and culture unsurpassed perhaps by any other in this country, he not only taught his pupils the language, but inspired in them a love of the literature of the Attic race. Mr. Poppleton graduated in July, 1851. He returned to the school at Romeo where he taught Latin and Greek until April of the next year. During the last years of his college life and while engaged in teaching, it was his ambition to be a professor of Greek in a college, which seemed to him the very highest position to which he could attain. Upon leaving Romeo, he entered the law office of Messrs. C. I. and E. C. Walker at Detroit, Michigan, then leaders of the bar of the State. He continued his studies with them until October 22, 1852, when, after a public examination by the judges of the supreme court of Michigan, he was admitted to the bar. Directly afterwards he became a student in the law school of John W. Fowler, at that time located at Baleston in New York, and afterwards removed to Poughkeepsie in that state. He enjoyed at this school the special advantages of the instruction which Mr. Fowler gave to elocution and in the related exercises. With very great gifts in public speech and trained in all of the ways of a popular orator, this gentleman was one of the most useful and successful teachers. He not only gave instruction in the exercises of declamation, but taught his pupils to think upon their feet; to prepare themselves by abundant study, and then express themselves at a moment's notice, in the presence of others and under the direction of his critical skill. Timid, hesitating, ineffective and disconnected speech was under his training developed into direct, strong, vigorous and impressive delivery, not after the pattern of his own style, but according to the natural modes of the pupil when trained and cultivated. He never had a more apt and enthusiastic scholar than Mr. Poppleton.

In April, 1853, the young man returned to Detroit and became a partner in a law firm, which was mostly engaged in a collection business, and remained there until the first of October, 1854. At this time California held out many promises to young men, and Mr. Poppleton listened to them. He turned his face to the West, and on his way reached Omaha, October 13, 1854, just about the time government was being set up in Nebraska. Omaha was just being settled; its resident population was very small; most of those who claimed citizenship really lived at Council Bluffs and in other towns in Iowa along the Missouri River. There was something interesting to the young man in the work of planting homes and the institutions of social and political order in a new country, which disposed him to remain for the winter, thinking at first that when he had seen the work completed he would continue his way to the Pacific or turn his steps in some other direction. One thing and another afterwards fell out which determined him to remain and make his home for life in the new Territory. In 1855 he married Caroline L. Sears, by whom he has three children.

The different acts of the executive in organizing the government followed one another in rapid succession. On the 21st of October, 1854, preliminary to the election of a delegate in congress and a territorial legislature, the acting governor, T. B. Cuming, issued his proclamation for an enumeration of the inhabitants. On the 26th of the same month he issued instructions to deputy marshals directing them in their duties of taking a census. On the 21st of November he sent out a set of rules for conducting the election, and, on the 23d issued a further proclamation dividing the territory into counties, apportioning the councilmen and representatives among them and ordering the election. On the 20th of December he constituted the three judicial districts, assigned the judges of the supreme court thereto, and appointed terms for the courts; and on the same day issued another proclamation convening the legislature at Omaha, on the 16th of January, 1855.

Mr. Poppleton had known and been a friend of the governor, in Michigan, and naturally was called to take part in advising the executive in these several political acts. He was elected a member of the house of representatives of the legislature. The training which he had enjoyed fitted him for these new duties. He had acquaintance with the methods and rules governing deliberative bodies; he was able to deliver himself of his views of every question no matter how unexpectedly it was presented, and he had a keen enjoyment of the excitements and contentions of the unorganized conditions of the new society. There was a good deal for the legislature to do. The whole system of laws common in an American state were to be enacted, save such as had been in outline provided by the act of congress organizing the territory. In all this work he had a large part. Besides this another matter deeply concerned every one; that was the permanent location of the capitol, which by the organic act was committed to the first legislature. Whether such a matter be considered trivial or not in a mature and settled state, it was thought to be of the first consequence at this time, because it was supposed that to the seat of government would be drawn the attention and interest of persons seeking homes in the region now first open for settlement. We cannot enter minutely into the plans, methods and influences which finally secured the location of the capitol at Omaha, but in them all Mr. Poppleton engaged with all the power of his nature; and it is not too much to say that as much as any man he contributed to the result.

From this time almost until he was stricken down by a severe sickness, judicial business in the courts was limited. There were not many controversies carried into them, and the judges were not very diligent in holding their terms. But there sprang up at Omaha as elsewhere in the territory, a popular tribunal in which there were many contentions of great interest. The public lands had not been surveyed, and no land office of the government had been opened at which titles could be secured. This state of things continued until the spring of 1857, except that government surveys of the land along the Missouri River were prosecuted to some extent. Almost everybody made a settlement upon a parcel of the public lands, and alleged a claim to it. For a variety of reasons it was impracticable for many of the settlers to remain continuously upon their claims, so that they were exposed to the settlement of a second or third comer. To protect themselves against this, they organized what were called Claim Clubs. These popular tribunals have always been found in new settlements. It naturally resulted that the owners of adjoining claims sometimes disagreed as to their dividing lines, and disputes arose between the first and subsequent claimants. Such controversies were dealt with before a meeting of all the members of the club, who were supposed to listen to the evidence and the arguments of the parties and decide according to the justice of the case. A good many controversies of this sort came before the Omaha Claim Club and were tried in this way; they gave opportunity for the gifts of the young citizen, his powers of persuasion and reasoning, and all that goes to make up a popular orator. Mr. Poppleton threw himself into the controversies in which he was engaged with all the zeal, energy and power of which he was capable. There was much that was amusing and much that was serious. The whole thing was a school in which the skill and power of the orator and lawyer were trained.

In 1857 Mr. Poppleton was a member of the state legislature which divided, a portion of the members setting up a pretended legislature at Florence. Mr. Poppleton remained at Omaha with the division recognized by the governor and was elected speaker and served in that capacity during the balance of the session.

In 1858 Mr. Poppleton was mayor of the City of Omaha, being the second person to hold that office. In the following spring after exposure in a severe storm, he suffered an attack of facial paralysis which was followed by a protracted and dangerous illness. Upon his recovery the use of one of his limbs was greatly impaired, and he never recovered its strength. He was absent from the life of the city for about eighteen months and returned to it with a vigor greatly reduced. Gradually he recovered his position at the bar, and enjoyed for many years a large measure of health and strength. He was, however, always obliged to exercise the greatest care of himself, and his habits largely upon that account have been very abstemious. During the time his strength was impaired he cultivated his love of literature and engaged in the study of the best political and philosophical works. When, in 1867, the state was admitted into the Union, he received the entire vote of the Democrats in the legislature for United States Senator; and but for methods on the part of the adverse party, which his friends have never been able to reconcile with fairness and justice, he would have been elected. In the following year he was the Democratic candidate for congress, but was defeated. He has never since taken any part in politics as a candidate for office.

Mr. Poppleton inherited from his father an uncompromising faith in the principles of the Democratic party. This faith strengthened with his strength and became a part of himself. During the war all of his sympathies, hopes and convictions were on the side of the Union, and he believed that no measure was beyond the competency of those charged with the administration which conduced to the preservation of the country. He held that the principles in which he was reared and with which he was thoroughly imbued, called every citizen to the support and maintenance of that Union which Andrew Jackson in another exigency had declared "must be preserved." The conflict once over he believed in burying all animosity. Soon after the war he obtained from an ex-Union soldier possession of a military land warrant issued to Jefferson Davis for services in the Mexican war. He returned the same to Davis at a time when the North, generally, was disposed to give the fallen chieftain very different treatment, receiving in return a letter of profound gratitude, now in his possession signed by all the members of the Davis family including the infant children whose fingers were guided to make their signatures.

It has been one of the great doctrines of Mr. Poppleton's faith that it is not the province of government to nurse by subsidies or other like aids the interests of the individual; that it is far better for every citizen to rely upon his own efforts; and as an indiscriminate charity leads its objects to depend thereon rather than upon their own industry and thrift, that the government in dispensing favors in aid of its citizens, only helped in the end to bring them into a dependent and impoverished condition. This was the fundamental principle of his political faith, and he applied it to all questions of public policy, however they arose. During this period of his life, extending from 1862 to 1878, he was devoted with all his heart, and soul, and strength, to his profession. He loved it for its own sake, and for the good it rendered to society. He held before his eye a high ideal of the lawyer, and yielded to no man in his devotion to the Law. The period which has been indicated was probably the best part of his professional life. In December, 1863, he was retained by the Union Pacific Railway Company, and continued in its service until 1888. Most of his time after 1869 was given to the company, in whose official list he bore the title of general attorney, having in his charge all its western business; that is to say in the states of Nebraska, Iowa, Missouri, Colorado, Nevada and Oregon, and the territories of Wyoming, Montana, Utah and Idaho. He conducted its important controversies in the courts personally, giving to them his best strength. After 1878, his duties became so arduous that he was obliged largely to withdraw from the courts and confine himself to the general direction of the legal business of the company.

He argued many important cases in the Supreme Court of the United States, and arrested the attention and held the highest esteem of the judges of that tribunal. His reputation was advanced to a high point not only in the West, but through the country. One of the best efforts of his was the writing of "The defence of Oakes Ames against the charge of selling to members of Congress shares of the capital stock of the Credit Mobilier of America with intent to bribe said members," which was read in the house of representatives by the clerk. It produced a strong impression and disposed the members to look upon the offenses charged against Mr. Ames in a new light. The exigency seemed, however, to call for a victim, and the result was the censure of the accused. This, however, was a favorable modification of the report of the investigating committee which recommended expulsion.

The writer of these lines has recently read that paper and has been greatly impressed by the clearness of the statement, the cogency of the reasoning and the persuasiveness of the appeal. Not long after its delivery, he was told by Mr. Sidney Bartlett, the leader of the bar of this country, that he considered it one of the best pieces of modern advocacy.

Mr. Poppleton's official connection with the Union Pacific Railway Company and his good standing and influence with the magnates in the East who controlled the destiny of that corporation, made it possible for him to continue to render the most important service to the city, of which, in 1854, he was one of the founders. By 1873, the fixing of the Union Pacific Company's terminal plant, offices and equipment at Omaha was finally decided upon and settled. In regard to Mr. Poppleton's share in this result, the most beneficial to Omaha of any event in its history, the following words from the *Omaha Herald* of that time speak:

"While we rejoice it is but proper that a few words should be said in behalf of a citizen to whom this people owe much for his intelligent, steady and well directed efforts to bring about results over which every man in Omaha is rejoicing.

"Andrew J. Poppleton is the one man who more than any other has piloted the people through these railroad complications to their present final settlement and security. We say this as a matter of sheer justice to Mr. Poppleton, without going into details to show how richly he deserves it."

Mr. Poppleton has from time to time been called upon to deliver addresses upon many interesting occasions. Among them may be mentioned a maiden address delivered before the Agricultural Society of Oakland County, Michigan, at the age of twenty-two; a lecture on Edmund Burke; an address before the general convention of the Beta Theta Pi Fraternity, at Indianapolis, September 5, 1878, on the "Unsolved Problem," having reference to the unequal distribution of property; an address on "Character," delivered before the Nebraska State University at commencement, June 27, 1877; an address before the Nebraska State Bar Association on "The Lawyer in Politics," and addresses on the occasion of breaking ground in Omaha for the construction of the Union Pacific Railway; the presentation of colors to the contingent supplied by Omaha to the Army of the Union; the laying of the corner stone of the present Douglas County Court House; the memorial meeting of citizens after the death of the Right Rev. Robert H. Clarkson, Episcopal Bishop of Nebraska; besides a large number of other addresses and speeches delivered on occasions of public or social interest. Many old residents will remember his appeal at a mass meeting of citizens for aid for those rendered destitute and homeless by the great Chicago fire. He has a full vocabulary, a glowing style, and elevated sentiments, as a perusal of these addresses will attest.

Mr. Poppleton retained his connection with the Union Pacific Railway Company until February, 1888, when he was obliged to resign on account of failing health, carrying with him from the officers and directors warm and recorded expressions of their confidence, esteem and appreciation of his long and faithful services.

During the spring following his resignation he sought recreation in travel, visiting the City of Mexico, where he was accorded the pleasureable and unexpected attention of a private and personal audience by the judges of the supreme court of that republic. Returning to Omaha, he again took up the practice of law, intending to engage only in the more important cases.

In 1890, at the earnest solicitation of Mayor R. C. Cushing, he accepted the office of city attorney of Omaha, serving therein for two years. In advising the city authorities Mr. Poppleton gave free access to all who desired his counsel, and applied to all questions democratic principles of economy and strict observance of law. During the greater part of his term he was without an official assistant, but succeeded in bringing to a final disposition in the courts 196 cases brought against the city, besides performing all the advisory duties of the office.

In 1891 and 1892 Mr. Poppleton was engaged as one of the leading counsel in behalf of the Chicago, Rock Island & Pacific and Chicago, Milwaukee & St. Paul Railway Companies in litigation before the United

States courts with the Union Pacific Railway Company, the result of which was to break down the Union Pacific bridge barrier and secure to the companies named the right to use the bridge and tracks of the Union Pacific at Omaha on reasonable terms for the purpose of bringing in and through the city their freight and passenger traffic.

On June 12, 1878, he received the degree of Doctor of Laws from the University of Nebraska.

He was one of the organizers and the first president of the Board of Trade and of the present Omaha Bar Association. He was an organizer and president of the Law Library Association, and also one of the organizers and long a director of the Omaha Public Library.

In 1879 Mr. Poppleton, in connection with Mr. J. L. Webster, made an earnest effort to secure the release, on a writ of habeas corpus, of Standing Bear, a Ponca chief, and his tribe, who had been unlawfully dispossessed by the government of their homes in Nebraska, and were being transferred to Indian Territory, under military custody. This case was exhaustively argued and is a *cause celebre*, in the history of our Indian affairs. The action of Mr. Poppleton and his associate, won the warm commendation of Helen Hunt Jackson, the author of Romona, and other humanitarians, interested in the Indian question, and secured to them the firm friendship of all Indians acquainted with the circumstances. This was the first instance in the judicial history of the United States in which the writ of habeas corpus was invoked and obtained on behalf of a tribal Indian.

In 1890 Mr. Poppleton was elected a trustee of Union College, Schenectady, New York.

In 1891, in his dual capacity of director of the Omaha Public Library and city attorney, he aided in securing the acceptance by the city of the Byron Reed bequest for public library purposes, and the voting of bonds to carry out its provisions.

Mr. Poppleton has served in many citizens' associations and committees. He has always been especially interested in questions involving the Omaha city charter, and the status and future of Omaha as a railway center and manufacturing and distributing point. A firm believer in the future of Omaha, his surplus earnings have been invested almost without exception in Omaha and Douglas County real estate, resulting in the accumulation of a large fortune.

For years he has been a stockholder and director of the First National Bank of Omaha.

About the first of January, 1892, his eyesight began to fail and in a few months was completely lost. This misfortune was accompanied during the summer by general illness.

He has since completely recovered his general health and engages in affairs as far as is possible for one suffering his affliction.

Mr. Poppleton possesses literary tastes and derives, at present, great consolation from their indulgence. He is the owner of a large and valuable private library, especially rich in historical works.

He has never been a member of any church. He has, however, continually contributed to the support of church organizations and has always possessed warm friends among clergymen.

ARTHUR S. POTTER.—The family of Arthur S. Potter is descended from Robert Potter, of Warwick, Rhode Island, who came from England in the year 1634. The grandfather of the subject of this sketch was born in 1787, in the State before mentioned, removing to Herkimer County, New York, and subsequently to Jefferson County, same State, where his son, Samuel Treat Potter, father of Arthur S., was born May 17, 1823.

Arthur S. was born in Le Ray, in the same county as his father, February 19, 1853. He has one brother and two sisters, all of whom, together with his parents, are now residents of Omaha.

His early education was at the district schools in his native town. He took his acadamic course at the Hungerford Collegiate Institute, Adams, New York, where he graduated in 1872. He then took a course in civil engineering in the Polytechnic Institute, at Troy, New York, being a member of the class of 1876. After the completion of his studies there, he removed to Michigan with his parents, spending two years in that State in the manufacturing business. He then was offered a position under the United States government, at Nebraska City, Nebraska, which he accepted in September, 1878.

On July 14, 1879, Mr. Potter was married to Miss Ella Bently, of Weedsport, Cayuga

County, New York. In October, 1879, the appropriation for the improvement of the Missouri River at Nebraska City having been exhausted, he was offered a position in the engineering department of the Burlington & Missouri River Railroad, which he accepted, and which he occupied until August, 1880. In that month, he resigned to accept a position of engineer in charge of the improvement under the United States government again at Nebraska City. This position he filled very creditably until December, 1883, when he resigned his position and came to Omaha. At this date he had accumulated by systematic saving a small amount of money, and in March, 1884, opened an office to do a general real estate business in partnership with Emory A. Cobb, under the firm name of Potter & Cobb. Although at that time not having a single acquaintance in the city and not being familiar with the business he had undertaken, he went systematically at work to accumulate the necessary knowledge to become first in his line. For three years, he worked incessantly in handling properties for other people, and was successful in that time in personally accumulating considerable means.

In 1886, a party of gentlemen, among whom were A. E. Touzalin, Chas. E. Perkins, Frederick L. Ames, G. W. Holdrege, Henry W. Yates, Thomas L. Kimball and others, collected quite a large quantity of land on the Missouri river bottoms northeast of the city, their design being to use the lands so collected for the purpose of trackage and yards, to be used by railroad companies jointly. They found upon examination, their titles to be in an unsatisfactory condition; but they had a title more or less good to about a thousand acres. On June 1, 1887, the gentlemen owning the lands above mentioned, requested Mr. Potter to take the charge of them, perfect the titles, and suggest such disposition as might be of interest to the owners. This he did, opening streets and thereby making the fact evident that the property was one of far greater value than had previously been supposed. During the next two years, he had succeeded in perfecting the title to all of the lands originally purchased, and of acquiring in all nearly two thousand acres. At this time, Mr. Potter conceived the idea of forming the lands so acquired into a permanent suburb to the city and of naming it East Omaha. He proposed a system of improvement which should cost several hundred thousand dollars, for the grading of streets, building of electric railways, and opening up in general the tract of land, which previously had been considered waste territory. He was successful in securing on the tract certain manufacturing industries, furnishing railway facilities and making other improvements. The land thus improved grew very rapidly in value. In the summer of 1890, it became to him fully apparent that the future success of the project of East Omaha for the benefit of its promoters and for the general good of the city of Omaha, should have an outlet directly across the Missouri River and that the railroads entering Council Bluffs from the east should have direct access with the East Omaha lands, by a bridge across the Missouri River. From this time on, he devoted his whole energy to the development of this project.

In January, 1891, Mr. Potter organized the company known as the Inter-State Bridge & Street Railway Company with a capital stock of $2,500,000, and in one week subscribed one-half of the stock. He at once caused a bill to be presented to congress for a charter for the construction of a low bridge across the Missouri River connecting Council Bluffs with East Omaha. On the third day of March, the bill was signed by the president of the United States and approved by the secretary of war. From that time on, Mr. Potter worked with a persistency which would not recognize the word "failure" against the most powerful opposition, until, in July, 1892, when he was successful, in company with his associates, in securing the necessary funds for the building of the bridge, completion of the Council Bluffs terminals, and the building of terminals in the city of Omaha, the whole project being on an absolutely independent basis, no railroad or railroads having any control whatever in the proposed improvements.

Mr. Potter has always, since he made Omaha his home, been broad and unbiased in his ideas and has ever had Omaha, the city chosen for his permanent residence, closest to his heart, and has demonstrated, that first, last and all the time, he is seeking that which will develop Omaha's importance in the commercial world.

LYMAN RICHARDSON was born in Pontiac, Michigan, June 6, 1834. His father was Origen D. Richardson, a native of Vermont. His mother, whose maiden name was Sarah P. Hill, was a native of Providence, Rhode Island. Mr. Richardson acquired his education in the public and private schools of Michigan, and in 1850 entered the University of Michigan, from which he was graduated in 1854. In the fall of that year he joined an engineering party engaged in surveying the lower Des Moines River for slack water navigation, and in 1855 joined his father in Omaha. He entered the office of Judge Lake, and there read law, was admitted to the bar in 1858, but not finding the legal profession attractive, he never entered the practice. In 1857 and 1858 he formed a partnership with Dr. G. L. Miller, and together they erected a large brick hotel, once known as the Herndon House, and now the Union Pacific headquarters. In September, 1860, he married Virginia Harrison Clarke, daughter of John M. Clarke then, as now, a resident of Omaha, but formerly of Richmond, Virginia. Four children have been born to them, two of whom are now living, Mary, wife of William R. Morris, Esq., and Ralph, at school in Massachusetts.

When the civil war broke out Mr. Richardson's patriotism and desire to see the Union preserved, led him to enrol his name among the foremost of those who enlisted in Nebraska. He was chosen second lieutenant of Company F, First Nebraska Volunteer Infantry, and served on the staff of General John M. Thayer until September, 1863. He participated in Sherman's first campaign against Vicksburg in the winter of 1862-3, and later in the seige and capture of that city, and was present at the battle of Chickasaw Bayou and at the capture of Arkansas Post. From November, 1863, to August, 1864, he was on the staff of General Fred Steele in charge of river and railroad transportation at Little Rock, Arkansas. In August of the latter year he resigned the captaincy to which he had been promoted, and soon after the close of the war became a cotton planter, and also engaged in lumbering in Arkansas. Convinced at the end of some three years that much more remunerative employment and a much better field for investment had developed at Omaha, then the eastern terminus of the nearly completed Union Pacific Railway, he returned to this place in 1868 and became associated with Dr. Miller in the publication of the *Herald*, which soon took a leading place among the journals of Nebraska and the West. His connection with this paper continued till March, 1887, when Miller & Richardson sold the *Herald* to a stock company of which Hon. John A. McShane was a principal stockholder. Mr. Richardson has never sought place nor political preferment, but rather has confined his efforts to the acquisition of property and the management of his private affairs. He is now one of the largest holders of real estate in Omaha, the care of which, since his retirement from the management of the *Herald*, has occupied a large part of his time and attention.

O. D. RICHARDSON.—Prominent for many years among the citizens of Omaha and Nebraska, and especially conspicuous in the early days, was Hon. Origen D. Richardson, who was born in Woodstock, Vermont, in 1796. In the war of 1812 he was a private in the volunteers of his native state, and fought at the battle of Plattsburg, New York, where General Macomb and Captain McDonough won a brilliant victory over the British September 11th, 1814.

He studied law and was admitted to the bar in 1824. Five years later he located in Michigan, where he practiced law and took an active part in that frequent concomitant of the legal profession—politics. In each of these he was successful, and soon ranked among the first lawyers, was recognized as one of the leaders of the Democratic party, and was frequently rewarded for political services with public office. He served in both branches of the legislature while Michigan was a territory, and after it was admitted to statehood. From 1844 to 1848 he filled the office of lieutenant governor. His unswerving devotion to what he believed true principles, and his unsullied integrity, gained for him the fullest confidence and respect of the people of Michigan.

In September, 1854, Governor Richardson removed to Omaha, and fitted as he was by years of political experience, at once took a leading part in territorial affairs. He was elected to the first territorial council, and in 1855 was appointed one of the commissioners to prepare a code of laws. Most of this work he did himself, and this codification is the basis of the present laws of Nebraska. He continued the practice of his profession, and was regarded as one of the leaders of the bar. The revised statutes of 1867 were prepared by Mr. Richardson, J. S. Sharp and A. J. Poppleton. Most of the work, however, was done by Mr. Richardson, who was an able jurist as well as an effective advocate. Such is the estimate of the man by Mr. Poppleton, who pays him the following tribute: "Governor Richardson—who died in Omaha, in 1876, was a clear and logical thinker, with the additional gift of a pleasing and effective style of speech. Through his strongest and most serious efforts there was apt to run an undercurrent of humor, ridicule and satire, which maintained the interest of court and auditors at the highest point; yet his chief power lay in the vigor and conclusiveness of his argument. One of Governor Richardson's best traits was his interest and sympathy with young men, students and lawyers. He was naturally genial and kindly to all, and was never too busy for a pleasant word and a hearty greeting to the young.* * * The impress of a noble character is never effaced, but becomes a guide and monitor of youth forever. His family life was singularly happy. After fifty years of domestic happiness, in which youthful vows and attachments grew stronger and more sacred with the lapse of years, husband and wife were called together—crossing the silent river, as they had so long journeyed upon earth, side by side. He left one son and two daughters, all yet living— Lyman Richardson, from its origin until very recently joint founder and proprietor and business manager of the *Omaha Herald;* Mr. Z. B. Knight and Mrs. G. I. Gilbert, all important factors in the best life of Omaha."

EDWARD ROSEWATER was born at Bukowan, a village about fifty miles south from the historical city of Prague, in Bohemia, on January 28, 1841. His elementary education was acquired in the common schools of that country where Bohemian or Czech is the prevailing language. He also received instruction in German from private tutors. At the age of eleven he was sent to an academy at Prague in which the branches taught are on about the same plane as those in American high schools.

On Christmas day, 1854, he landed with his parents in the city of New York, and thence immediately moved to Cleveland, Ohio. Owing to the limited means of his parents and the fact that he was the oldest of a family of nine children, he was at once compelled to earn his own livelihood. Having no knowledge of the English language he had great difficulty in finding something to do. The first permanent employment he was able to secure was in a wholesale tinware and stove store, where his muscles were developed in polishing stoves and in assisting journeymen tinners in manual work. By 1856 he had acquired sufficient knowledge of English to secure a position as clerk in a retail grocery store at a salary of $7 a month and board.

At the end of another year he found a clerical position in a small dry goods store at a salary of $100 a year and board. In the summer of 1857 he severed his connection with the mercantile business and took a three months course in a commercial college, from which he graduated as an alleged accountant and bookkeeper. This was a year of great financial depression, and the first and only position he secured as bookkeeper in a wholesale willow ware and basket establishment, terminated abruptly by the failure of the concern.

Unwilling to resume the drudgery of a clerk and unable to secure a position as bookkeeper, he left Cleveland in company with a young man who had been engaged as clerk in an employment office, and located in Sandusky, Ohio, where his first venture on his own resources was made under the title of "Rosewater & Warren, Intelligence Office." The partnership survived just three months. It had intelligence enough, but failed to secure employment either for its patrons or itself. Warren, the junior partner of the firm, was a telegraph operator, but had temporarily discarded his profession. It was mutually agreed that the two partners would seek their fortunes in the South, and although they had less than $5 cash when they reached Cincinnati, in October, 1858, they were not in the least disconcerted or despondent. Within twenty-four hours after landing at Cincinnati, Warren secured a temporary position as operator in the Ohio & Mississippi Railroad depot, and Rosewater at once began his apprenticeship as a telegrapher.

At the end of three months he imagined he had fully mastered the profession and accepted a position at Vincennes, Indiana, but he was chagrined when he found that he must continue "to practice" before he could hope to hold down a situation.

Returning to Cleveland in December, 1858, he completed his preliminary educacation as telegrapher within a few months, and in April, 1859, was finally assigned to Oberlin, Ohio, at a salary of twenty-five dollars a month. In June, 1859, he accepted a position as operator at Murfreesboro, Tennessee, thirty-two miles south of Nashville. Later on he was transferred to Stevenson, Alabama, at the junction of the Nashville & Chattanooga and Memphis & Charleston Railroads.

Here he remained until Alabama had seceded. In March, 1861, he accepted a position in the commercial office of the Southwestern Telegraph Company, at Nashville. After the capture of Fort Donelson and the occupancy of the city by the Union army he returned to Cleveland, where his parents still resided, and decided to enter the United States military telegraph corps. He was mustered into the service at Wheeling, West Virginia, in April, 1862, and assigned to accompany General John C. Fremont in the West Virginia campaign. On the 1st of July, 1862, he was ordered to report at Washington, where he was assigned to the navy yard, then under command of Commodore Dahlgren. When General Pope was about to enter into his famous "On to Richmond" campaign the subject of this sketch made application to the war department to accompany General Pope, and was attached to Pope's staff, to do duty in the field. He accompanied the Army of Virginia in its march to Rapidan, and its retreat across the Rappahanock, and during the three days battle near Bull Run, August 29, 30 and 31, and transmitted all of General Pope's dispatches from the battle field.

On the 1st of September, 1862, he was recalled to Washington and assigned to the war department. The members of the telegraph corps in the war department were men picked from the most skilled and trusty operators in the service, this office being the receptacle of all the dispatches directed to President Lincoln, Secretary Stanton and the general of the army.

In September, 1863, at the instance of Edward Creighton, who had the year previous built the Pacific Telegraph, he resigned his position in the army telegraph corps and entered the service of the Pacific Telegraph Company at Omaha. In the spring of 1864, he was appointed manager of the Omaha office, and continued in that capacity until January, 1870. A few months later he accepted the position of manager of the Atlantic & Pacific and Great Western telegraph lines.

While acting as local manager of the Pacific Telegraph Company he was also agent of the Associated Press and telegraphic correspondent of leading Chicago, New York, Cincinnati and St.Louis papers. Incidentally with this work he established a telegraphic correspondence bureau, which gathered important news from the Rocky Mountain region as far west as Montana and Idaho.

In the spring of 1870, he, in conjunction with others, founded the *Omaha Daily Tribune*. When the paper made its first advent on July 25, 1870, its editor-in-chief, a scholarly Massachusetts journalist, had failed to put in an appearance and his place was supplied during the first week by Mr. Rosewater, although ostensibly the editorials emanated from the pen of the gifted New Englander. This was Mr. Rosewater's first venture in journalism. *The Tribune*, although an excellent paper, was from the start a losing undertaking. Owing to differences regarding its management, Mr. Rosewater resigned his directorship in 1870, and fortunately for himself he had not severed his connection with the telegraph company, but had merely dipped into newspaper work as an amateur, with no expectation of following it as a profession.

In November, 1870, Mr. Rosewater was elected a member of the most stormy and protracted legislature that has ever been held in Nebraska. In that body he took a leading and active part in the impeachment of the governor, David Butler, and in the investigations into the management of state institutions. Among measures for which he successfully secured passage was the endorsement of the postal-telegraph system, the act regulating the practice of medicine, and the location and establishment of the state deaf and dumb institute at Omaha, and the creation of the board of education for that city. The latter measure met with strenuous opposition from the Omaha daily press.

The act creating the board of education required its submission to a ratification by the citizens of Omaha. Desiring to counteract the adverse public opinion created by the press, Mr. Rosewater started on June 19, 1871, a small paper in the shape of a theatre programme, under the heading of "*The Omaha Daily Bee.*" These sheets were given free distribution for several weeks. They contained the latest telegraphic and local news in brief, editorial comments on city and state politics.

The board of education law was sustained by the people by an overwhelming majority. Encouraged by this evidence of popular favor the paper after four weeks free distribution was enlarged and started on its career as an afternoon daily with local carrier subscriptions at twelve and one half cents per week. From the very outset the *Bee* met with the most phenomenal success. Within less than five years it outstripped the old established dailies in circulation and influence, notwithstanding the most determined and powerful opposition, both from the ruling politicians and corporate influences, which were inimical to it, owing to its vigorous antimonopoly policy.

From its inception until the present time, Mr. Rosewater has remained the chief editor and owner of *The Bee,* which for years has occupied a front rank among the great newspapers of America. Having firmly established his paper, Mr. Rosewater conceived the idea of erecting a monumental newspaper building, and this project was carried out by the erection of the Bee Building, which was begun in 1887 and completed in 1889. This structure is perfectly fire-proof and covers a larger area of ground than any other newspaper building erected on either side of the Atlantic. Its exterior is imposing and its interior is superbly fitted with all the modern appliances for the publication of a great newspaper. Mr. Rosewater was married in 1864 to Miss Leah Coleman. His family consists of two sons and three daughters.

ALVIN SAUNDERS. — The popular voice, however capricious in the beginning, is apt to place, in the long run, just estimate upon the acts of a man, whether in public or private life; especially is this true where there has not been engendered a great amount of partisan feeling in his career to antagonize his views, or to combat his doings.

The subject of this sketch is to be spoken of not only as a citizen—as a neighbor—as a father—but as a statesman. The question and its answer, by Sir William Jones as to what constitutes a state, may here properly be recalled:

"What constitutes a state?
Not high-raised battlement or labored mound,
Thick wall or moated gate;
Not cities fair, with spires and turrets crown'd;
No;—men, high-minded men."—

And one of the men such as here described, in a marked degree, ever since Nebraska was admitted into the Union, and even while a Territory, it is now conceded, has been Alvin Saunders, one of the prime factors of this trans-Missouri commonwealth.

Naturally, there is almost always in the case of a person occupying (or who has occupied) a prominent position in life, a desire by the public to know something of his early days—what were the surroundings of his youth? what the chief events of his early manhood?

Alvin Saunders was born July 12, 1817, ten miles south of Flemingsburgh, in Fleming County, Kentucky. His father, Gunnell Saunders, was a native of Loudon County, Virginia, but removed to Kentucky when a young man, locating first in Bourbon County and subsequently in Fleming; he was of English descent. His mother, Mary Mauzy, was also of Virginia birth, having been born in Culpepper County; but she was of French origin.

Gunnell Saunders was a farmer and trained his boys, five in number, to business pursuits. "When Alvin was about twelve years of age, the whole family moved from Kentucky and located near Springfield, Illinois. But little attention was then given to education in Kentucky and especially so with those in the country, or of moderate means and our hero, so long as he remained in that region, shared the fate common to all of his class; nor was his condition much improved by removal to another State, for the country where his father located was then very sparsely settled and consequently a very poor opportunity was afforded for even a common school education. A school was taught two miles distant from where his father lived for only three months in each year, and that in the winter season. The consequence was that he received only t' e first rudiments of an education, and here he would have rested his case and passed through life without further advancement had it not been for a natural taste for books and an unusual degree of ambition for improvement of the mind."*

At the age of nineteen Alvin concluded to strike out for himself could he get the consent of his father; it was reluctantly given, and the boy went "on his own hook" to what is now Mount Pleasant, Iowa, but then a part of the Territory of Wisconsin. He engaged to work with a farmer near by, but not long after became a clerk in a small dry goods store that had started up in the village. He had the will and the strength to carry on the arduous labor expected of him by the farmer who had employed him, but his tendencies—his likings—were in the direction of what is termed a "business life." He soon found that as clerk he lacked sufficient education for even his limited position. Many young men less determined and ambitious would have abandoned the attempt and returned to the farm—or hired out to become "hewers of wood or drawers of water" for others. Instead of this, he induced a resident of the place to open a night school, which he attended, and by applying himself assiduously, he was soon so far advanced in the elementary branches as to be able to hold his clerkship without difficulty. And it may here be added that as soon as he had earned sufficient money to enable him to do so, he attended an academy, and thus procured such an education as has enabled him to discharge acceptably the duties devolving upon him in his subsequent official and business career of life.

The official career of Mr. Saunders commenced by his being made postmaster of Mt. Pleasant, which he clung to for over seven years. In 1846, he assisted in forming the constitution under which Iowa was admitted as a State. It is queer that his deviation from trade into politics was the result of accidental causes. When Polk was elected president, he was ousted from the Mt. Pleasant postoffice. Concerning this, the subject of this sketch subsequently said: "The federal administration was the turning point in my life — in getting into politics. I had no particular taste then for politics and I doubt if I have ever had much since. I was raised a whig, but despite this I was appointed postmaster by Van Buren * * * the reason of my getting it being that no one else would have it, as it paid at first only about $20 a year. But it grew and when Polk was elected, our delegate to congress thought it a good thing to remember his friends, and I was removed. Thereupon my friends were indignant. They said I had been a good official, that I had been turned out unjustly; and now was the chance to get even. I suppose human nature is about the same the world over; and I did feel that I had been harshly dealt with. I entered the field as a candidate for delegate to the constitutional convention and was elected. I was the youngest man in the body, which probably gave me as much notoriety as any thing else, if I do say so."

Meanwhile, despite his mixed Virginia and Kentucky origin, Mr. Saunders became a strong opponent to the extension of slavery into the territories. Entertaining such pronounced views, an election to the senate of Iowa as a Republican was the result. This was in 1854, and he was re-elected in 1858. During his two terms of office in the State senate, he was an active and energetic member. He gave his hearty support to the election of both Harlan and Grimes to the United States Senate, and assisted in the re-election of the former at the end of his first six years at Washington. Mr. Saunders participated as a delegate in the first Iowa Republican State convention and also in the national convention which nominated Abraham Lincoln as Republican candidate for president. He was personally acquainted with Lincoln and during the presidential canvass which followed, he took an active part in advocating his election by attending Republican county conventions and urging the claims of the nominee for that high office of the republican party.

The election of Lincoln as President of the United States, and his inauguration on the 4th of March, 1861, was soon followed by the appointment of Mr. Saunders as governor of the Territory of Nebraska, a fact which serves to show that the president recognized the ability of the appointee as well as the conspicious services which he had rendered during the presidential campaign. The appointment was made March 26, 1861, and he assumed the duties of his office on the 15th of May following. It did not

*Pen Sketches of Nebraskans, p. 417.

confer on Mr Saunders a sinecure, as may be readily inferred. The civil war was already a fixed fact, and it demanded a large share of his attention, to the duties of which were added those connected with the observation and care of a large body of hostile Indians on the frontiers of the Territory. Settlers there " were subjected to the tomahawk and scalping-knife of the border savages and neither sex nor age was spared, men, women and children were alike attacked and stricken down by these inhuman beings. Whole families of frontier settlers and train after train of emigrants were either killed outright or what was worse (and particularly so with females), taken prisoners and carried out of the country. This was truly a trying time for the people of Nebraska. Nearly all the able-bodied men of the country were then in the army and were fighting in the South to save the nation from being overthrown by the rebels. But the emergency was met. The governor issued a proclamation calling on the able-bodied men of the Territory to volunteer for frontier service to protect our people from these savage foes. To this call a hearty and cheerful response was given "*

Governor Saunders had also to give attention, of course, to the ordinary affairs of the Territory—thus he was forced as chief executive officer to a triple-headed task, which required an ability—an industry—an endurance—of a high order.

Already mention has been made of the governor's giving, during the war of the rebellion, a large share of his time to that contest. As the breaking out of the conflict, Nebraska had only a small population, less in fact, than thirty thousand, yet, from this insignificant number, she sent into the field over three thousand troops, who did splendid service. As before intimated, in addition to those who went to the front against the confederates a large element was sent against the Indians, so that, in fact, the military aggregate of Nebraska at that time should include both those who went south and those who went west.

The struggle in the Territory against the double enemy was a particularly severe one, in that there was no funds in its treasury to put the forces in the field, but Governor Saunders solved the problem of how " to make something out of nothing." To care

* *Pen Sketches of Nebraskans*, p, 410

at once for national and local interests, to enact in the same moment the part of a citizen of the United States and that of Nebraska—proves conclusively that his skill, judgment, and energy were of no common degree.*

Governor Saunders was, for a number of years previous to the commencement of the Union Pacific Railroad, a zealous advocate of a trans-continental highway of the nation, and long before the bill passed congress, he had marked out in his own mind the route where it must pass. In his message to the territorial legislature of Nebraska, in 1861, he alluded to the subject. "A mere glance at the map of the country will convince every intelligent mind that the great Platte Valley, which passes through the heart and runs nearly through the entire length of Nebraska, is to become the route for the great central railway which is to connect the Atlantic with the Pacific states and territories." When the bill passed congress, authorizing the formation of the company to build the road, the governor was made one of the incorporators to give practical form to the measure. Ground was broken, in commencing operations to build the road, on the 2d of December, 1863 †

At the commencement of the legislative session of 1865, the governor, in his message, intimated he would not ask for a re-appointment to office on the expiration of his term, whereupon, on the 10th day of February, of that year, the legislature, without regard to party, passed resolutions, endorsing the general policy of his administration as chief executive of the Territory, and urgently requested the president to reappoint him for another term of four years, which was done.

One of the last public acts of President Lincoln was to sign the commission of Governor Saunder's for his second term "I saw Mr Lincoln," the governor afterwards related, "who told me to return home as it was all right, and he would attend to the commission. I started home in the morning and in the evening of the same day he was killed. I telegraphed back to find out what had become of my commission and learned that the room had not been opened. When it was opened, the commission was found on the table, unfolded with his signature at-

*See, in this connection, an article in the *Chicago Times* (supplement), of May 22 1866, entitled "An Ex-War Governor"
† Ante, p 395

tached. It was not signed by Mr. Seward. I have the commission in Mr. Lincoln's name, but, as it was not signed by the secretary of state, or sealed, it was again issued by President Johnson."

On the 27th of March, 1867, Governor Saunders having received official notice from the state department at Washington, of the president's proclamation announcing that the legislature of Nebraska, had accepted the conditions proposed by congress, and declaring the fact that Nebraska was admitted as one of the independent states of the union, the governor elect, being under the state organization then ready to take charge of the office—thereupon his duties as the chief executive of the Territory, that day ceased, when he issued an address to the people. After alluding to the proclamation of the president, declaring Nebraska's admission, he says: "I take pleasure, before retiring from this office, in availing myself of this opportunity of returning my sincere thanks to the people of the Territory for their uniform kindness, and for the alacrity and promptness with which every official demand upon them has been honored, whether in war or in peace. No period of time of the same length, since the organization of our government, has been so eventful and full of interesting history as has been the six years that I have been honored with an official connection with the people of Nebraska, and it gives me great pleasure to know that peace and general prosperity now prevail throughout our whole country; and especially to know that no country can truthfully boast of greater peace or more genuine prosperity than can Nebraska. Especially do I feel proud of the financial condition of the Territory. Six years ago, when I assumed the duties of the office, the debt of the Territory was fully two dollars for every man, woman and child in it, and the warrants on the treasury were selling at from twenty-five to thirty cents on the dollar. Now her paper is at par, and she is ready to pay every dollar of her indebtedness, of whatever character, so that the new state can commence her career without a dollar of debt hanging over her. This condition of affairs, so far as my knowledge extends, is without a parallel in the history of new states, and gives cause for mutual and general congratulation.

"While our officers and people have been so attentive to the finances of our country, they have not been idle nor wanting in other important particulars, for during the war, Nebraska furnished as many troops as any other State or Territory, in proportion to its population, and no soldier from any quarter showed more valor and made a better record for bravery or true soldierly conduct, than did those from Nebraska. So, viewing it from any standpoint, I feel proud that I have been permitted to occupy so conspicuous a position among a people so patriotic, prompt and appreciative. With my best wishes for the prosperity of the whole people of our new State and for its great success, I am, etc.,

ALVIN SAUNDERS."

In 1868, Governor Saunders was a delegate to the Republican National Convention which nominated Grant and Colfax. He then dropped politics, having already gone into business to recuperate the fortune which had been seriously impaired by the war. He devoted much of his time to banking. However, from various causes beyond his control, a financial crisis, in 1875, overtook him and he became so involved that his entire means were swept away; but, in the end, he paid off his indebtedness to the last dollar, and by devoting himself to various business enterprises in Omaha, has completely recovered from his financial embarrassments, and is again in possession of an ample competency, as the result of his sagacity and perseverance.

In the summer of 1870, Governor Saunders was first mentioned in connection with the office of United States Senator; but he was not successful in securing the position; however, in the winter of 1876-77, he was more fortunate. His term was the full one of six years. It was the time when specie payments were resumed and in this and other important measures he took an active part in carrying them forward to a successful issue. One of the principal of his official successes as senator was his securing over 600,000 acres of land for Nebraska, by the correction of the northern boundary line of the State.

The city of Omaha is much indebted to Governor Saunders for its present prosperity. He has, ever since he first became a resident of the place, taken a great interest in every enterprise of importance which, in his judgment, would, in the end, redound to its welfare. He was chairman of the bridge committee of citizens who secured to Omaha the location of the Union Pacific bridge across the Missouri, he was vice-president of the Omaha & Southwestern Railway and one of the original stockholders in the Omaha Smelting Works, and president of the board of regents of the High School, —having been largely instrumental in securing the erection of the High School building of the city The city gas works, the street railway and numerous other improvements bear witness to his zeal and generous assistance.

Four years ago, he was appointed upon the Utah Commission, which has charge of the registration and elections in Utah Territory. The law providing for this commission, which is composed of members of both the Republican and Democratic parties, and was therefore not considered as partisan, was enacted in March of 1883, and was designed to so regulate elections in that territory as to prevent all who were practicing polygamy from voting or holding elective office therein. The enforcement of this and subsequent laws on the same subject have had the effect to bring about a thorough change in the advices and teachings of the head of the Mormon Church, and it is now believed that the end is near when this relic of the darker ages shall be banished from our land The governor has recently resigned this office and is now quietly enjoying the pleasures of private life

The ex-governor "is an admirable result of a youth of hard work, a life of close and conscientious application to whatever may have demanded his attention, and an intelligent and practical comprehension of the duties which have presented themselves for his performance He is respected and popular, and will pass into the history of his State as one of the most conspicuous founders of its greatness"

Among the honors which have been justly bestowed on the subject of this sketch, and one in which he takes great pride, is the fact of his being a third class member of the "Military Order of the Loyal Legion of the United States," of which the late ex-president R B Hayes was commander-in-chief Of this class there are but few members—now numbering less than one hundred in the United States,—and these were selected because of their conspicuous loyalty to the United States government during the Rebellion Only three per cent of the members of the commandery could be admitted as members of this class, and they only upon an unanimous favorable vote taken by secret ballot No new members can now be admitted of this class, and as the members have no successors, this class will pass away at the death of its present members

It is proper to say that Mr Saunders has been in business as controller of the Omaha Real Estate and Trust Company for several years, and is now its president He is also vice president of the Mutual Investment Company, and a director in the Merchants National Bank and also in the Nebraska Savings and Exchange Bank

JAMES STEPHENSON —The energy, activity and enterprise a man displays and the amount of work he accomplishes, are, in this Western country, usually set down to his credit, and one of the reasons why the subject of this sketch enjoys a good degree of popularity is because he has strikingly developed these characteristics

James Stephenson was born October 31, 1836, on Spring Street, in New York City, when that now great metropolis was just beginning to show to the civilized world that it would one day rank among the foremost of its cities In 1853, he located at Davenport, Iowa, but only remained there a short time, removing to Newton, Jasper County, that State, where he entered the employ of the Western Stage Company Like most of his associates of that period, the desire to become suddenly rich took possession of him, and, in 1860, he turned his steps to the West, driving an ox team from Newton to Denver, Colorado, reaching there after a perilous journey of sixty-three days On the way he heard Horace Greely's memorable speech at Fort Laramie Subsequently he returned to Newton, and once more cast his fortunes with the Western Stage Company, remaining with them until he secured the contract for transporting the mails and baggage across the Missouri River from Council Bluffs to Omaha, and held this until the Union Pacific bridge was completed In 1870 he opened a livery stable in Omaha, and has continued in that business ever since, having now the finest equipped establishment of that kind in the West

Before the railroads were scattered so

thoroughly over Nebraska, Wyoming, Kansas and Iowa, Mr. Stephenson carried most of the mails, and has always been extensively engaged in staging, being one of the first to send a coach from Sidney, Nebraska, to Deadwood, Dakota, during the ever memorable year of 1877, when it was as much as a man's life was worth to venture into the Indians' country. Many, indeed, are the thrilling adventures he can relate of hairbreadth escapes from frenzied savages, and he was often an eye-witness to many small bloody encounters with them. At the time of the late trouble with the Indians at Pine Ridge agency, he had a large government contract in which two hundred teams were kept in constant employment. In 1885 he established the first cab line in Omaha, and, notwithstanding the city now enjoys excellent street railway facilities, he has always found it a paying business. In addition to this, he is an extensive railroad contractor, having done much important work for the "B. & M." and the Rock Island, and for the Union Stock Yards Company, at South Omaha.

In 1882 he removed 175,000 yards of earth on which is now constructed the Chicago, Burlington & Quincy Railway freight depot. During this contract the government troops and the State militia were called out to suppress the riots caused by one of the greatest strikes Omaha has ever seen.

Mr. Stepenson has served the City of Omaha four years as a member of the council, and he discharged his duties in that position with credit to himself and to the satisfaction of the public. He is now a prominent member of the Liverymen's Association, an active member and one of the directors of the Omaha Board of Trade, and has the street cleaning contract of the city until 1895. He is highly esteemed for his enterprise and sterling integrity.

JOHN MELLEN THURSTON. — The history of the country does not furnish a better illustration of a self-made man, than is shown by the record of Mr. John M. Thurston.

At the age of forty-three years he is general solicitor and legal adviser of the greatest railway system of the continent; has achieved a national fame as an orator second to none, and is already looked upon as one of the coming leaders of the Republican party.

What he has won has been the result of hard work, manly independence and great ability. Commencing life as a poor boy, compelled to labor with his hands for daily bread, he has risen above the circumstances of birth, and is an illustrious example of the possibilities of our civilization and free institutions.

He was born in Montpelier, Vermont, on the twenty-first day of August, 1847. His family, on his father's side, was descended from John Thurston, who came from Suffolk in England, and settled at Dedham, Massachusetts, in 1636. There were three Thurstons who arrived in New England at about the same time, and are supposed to have been brothers. From them have descended almost all of that name now living in the United States.

Mr. Thurston's mother's name was Ruth Mellen. Her family originally came from Ireland. They were among the first settlers of what was then known as the "Hampshire Grant," which is now the State of Vermont. His grandfather, John Mellen, (after whom our subject was named,) and his brother Thomas were in the battle of Bennington under General Stark. His grandfather Thurston was a soldier in the war of 1812, and his great-grandfather a revolutionary patriot, having also served as a soldier in that struggle.

Mr. Thurston's father was Daniel Sylvester Thurston. He was one of a large family born in Orange county, Vermont. One of his brothers, Elisha Thurston, worked his way through college, took up educational pursuits, was professor in various institutions of learning, and at one time was State superintendent of public instruction in Maine. About the time of the commencement of the Kansas troubles, he moved to that State, engaged in the practice of law, was very active on the side of the free-soiler, and about 1860, at the time of his death, was mayor of Manhattan, Kansas.

The father of Mr. Thurston was, for the greater portion of his life, a farmer. For a few years prior to emigrating from Vermont, he was engaged in conducting a tannery; was also for some time a member of a mercantile firm. In 1854, he moved to Madison, Wisconsin, where he remained for four years, and then went to Beaver Dam, in that State. He was a man of very great natural ability; took an active part in all public affairs, and is said by those who remember him, to have been a forcible and direct speaker, although he rarely took part in public discussions. At the inauguration of the civil war, he enlisted in the First Wisconsin Cavalry, notwithstanding the fact that he was fifty-four years of age. His enlistment as a private was made prior to the organization of the regiment, but with the promise that he should receive the appointment of regimental wagon-master. Before the regiment left the State, however, he received a commission as second lieutenant of the Seventeenth Wisconsin Infantry, generally known as the "Irish Brigade," and assisted in recruiting a company for that regiment. Before the regiment left for the seat of war, it went into winter quarters late in the fall of 1861, at Madison, the capital, where it was overtaken by violent storms and severe weather before it could be provided with the proper shelter. In consequence of this exposure, the old gentleman was attacked with congestion of the lungs, and just before the regiment departed for the front, he was carried to his home at Beaver Dam, on the supposition that his illness would necessarily be fatal. One of his last official acts before he left, was to resign his commission, so that an active man could be appointed in his place to take the field.

Recovering from his severe illness, to the surprise of every one acquainted with him, the following summer, 1862, he again enlisted as a private in the First Wisconsin Cavalry, and with that organization participated in the campaign against the "guerillas" of Missouri. He remained on duty with his company until the spring of 1863, when he was sent home in a dying condition, living but a few days after arriving there. His family at that time consisted of his wife, three married daughters, one unmarried, and the son, John Mellen, who was now compelled to support his mother and the rest of the family, as they were left almost wholly without means. The brave young fellow took hold of anything he could find to make honest wages. Every summer, from the time he was fourteen years old, he worked in the harvest fields of Wisconsin, and in the autumn hired out as an attendant to a threshing machine, receiving for his employment about thirty dollars a month.

In 1865, when but seventeen, he went to the City of Chicago to accept a situation as driver of a horse and wagon for a wholesale fruit and fancy grocery store, of which Matthew, Graff & Co., located on South Water Street, were proprietors. For this work young Thurston received ten dollars a week, out of which he was obliged to pay his board. Continuing at it for a year, he discovered that except a new suit of clothes which he did not have at the commencement of the year, he was no better off than when he began.

He returned to his mother's home at Beaver Dam, and for three winters engaged in fishing through the ice and trapping, employing a number of boys to work for him on shares, he furnishing the necessary outfit. He also drove a team over the lake twice a week, purchasing fish, which he shipped to Chicago, and during the time he was engaged in this business made it quite profitable, one winter clearing nearly one thousand dollars. During this period he attended the public schools of Beaver Dam, for a portion of the time keeping up in all the classes, though he was absent, necessarily, the greater part of the year.

In the spring of 1866 he left the public schools and entered Wayland University, an institution in Beaver Dam, which, at that time, had a full preparatory and collegiate course, ranking with the average western denominational college. This was a Baptist institution and was really a very good school. It was kept alive by that sect of Christians in Wisconsin, but it met the fate of a great many of its class. During the time young Thurston was there it was closed for want of funds to carry it on, and he was compelled to leave with the other students. This disaster occurred in the summer of 1868. He had managed to attend school about half of each school year, though he had kept up with his classes, so that when the institution was compelled to close, he had but one more year to study there to complete the full course of the college, but this collapse of the college ended Mr Thurston's school days.

He now determined to study law, and to that end he entered the office of Mr E P Smith, an eminent attorney of Wisconsin, for many years a practitioner at the Milwaukee bar, who then was a member of the Beaver Dam bar. One of the curious and pleasant changes of fortune has placed Mr. Smith under Mr Thurston's supervision as assistant general attorney of the Union

Pacific System for the State of Nebraska. On the 21st day of May, 1869, after an examination in open court, by the Honorable Alva Stuart, circuit judge in Portage, Columbia County, Wisconsin, Mr. Thurston was admitted to the bar. As soon, however, as he had passed a severe and successful examination, he found it necessary for the remainder of that summer to return to manual labor; first taking a contract to put up several miles of board fence on a large farm near the town. When the grain harvest commenced, he entered the fields as a binder, continuing at this hard labor to the end of the season. Then he prepared to move West, though he had no acquaintances in all the great domain included in that title. He procured a map and studied it carefully; for a long time he was undecided. His choice wavered between Kansas City and Omaha; but he finally decided in favor of the latter, largely for the reason that it was situated in the state from which its business must come; while Kansas City was on the Western border of Missouri, where its commercial and other relations would necessarily be more identified with Kansas affairs.

Mr. Thurston arrived in Omaha on the morning of October 5th, 1869, in company with Mr. Herman E. Luthe, now a successful attorney at the Denver bar, it being their intention to practice law together.

It is a popular belief of young attorneys that they should associate themselves together in business when they go to a new place to commence the practice of their profession. On the day of their arrival in Omaha, Mr. Thurston was possessed of about forty dollars, and he walked into the office of Mr. William H. Morris, now judge of the fifth Nebraska district, and asked him if he knew of a place where two young lawyers could get cheap office room. Mr. Morris replied he did not, but that they could put up a desk in his office if they wished and were willing to pay ten dollars a month for the privilege. Mr. Thurston immediately paid him that amount out of his forty dollars, and the young men moved in, bringing with them an old desk which had been shipped so as to be in Omaha by the time of their arrival. Then, theoretically, they commenced the practice of law. Their office was in a large room in the old Visscher block, where the Millard hotel now stands. The great room was occupied by Judge Morris as a justice office, by William Kidd, as an employment office, and by the law firm of Thurston & Luthe.

The young attorneys very soon discovered that where there is not business enough for one to live on, two must necessarily starve if they attempt to divide it between them, so Mr. Luthe, who had married just before leaving Wisconsin, and had brought his wife with him, abandoned the practice temporarily and obtained work in the Union Pacific shops as a machinist. Thus was the law firm of Thurston & Luthe dissolved. The junior member after working all winter, sent his wife back to Wisconsin, went to Denver, where he eventually succeeded in taking high rank in his profession.

Mr. Thurston, true to his characteristics of persistence, stuck to his office both theoretically and in reality. He slept on its floor at night, using for his bedding some quilts and a buffalo robe, which he had brought from his home in Wisconsin. This improvised bed was rolled up in the morning and hidden in one corner of the room. During all the period of his novitiate in Omaha, as Judge Morris very vividly recollects, Mr. Thurston was reduced to the necessity, for many considerably extended intervals of time, of living on the nutritious, but rather monotonous diet of crackers, which he was very luckily able to buy by the box from the grocery store of A. Burley, then in the Caldwell block, at wholesale prices.

Thus Mr. Thurston struggled on, varying success attending his efforts, as has been the fate of hundreds of other young men in the incipient days of their practice. In the fall of 1871, Judge Morris resigned his position as justice of the peace, and Mr. Thurston was appointed by the county commissioners to fill the vacancy. Judge Morris and himself now removed to the Caldwell Block, where they occupied two rooms, instead of one, as formerly. After Mr. Thurston's appointment as justice of the peace, the positions of the tenants were completely reversed; Mr. Morris now occupied the little desk of the lawyer, and Mr. Thurston the judicial chair.

Mr. Thurston continued to practice his profession, and "run" the office of justice of the peace, until the spring of 1873, when he resigned the latter position to form a law partnership with Hon. Charles H. Brown. The previous spring Mr. Thurston had been elected a member of the city council, from the third ward of Omaha, which office he filled for two consecutive years, acting as president of that body and also as chairman of the judiciary committee

In the spring of 1874, upon the expiration of his term as alderman, he was appointed city attorney by the newly elected mayor, Hon C S Chase, which position he filled for three years, resigning finally to accept the assistant attorneyship of the Union Pacific Railway, under the Hon. A J Poppleton, who was general solicitor of the lines of that corporation

On Christmas day, 1872, Mr Thurston was married to Miss Martha Poland, daughter of Col. Luther Poland, of Omaha, a most estimable lady, whose family were, like her husband's, originally from Vermont Her uncle, her father's brother, was the honorable and venerable Luke P Poland, for many years chief justice of the Green Mountain State, a representative in congress for several terms and United States Senator

Of five children born of this marriage, three were sons and two daughters Two of the sons died of diphtheria, leaving one son and two daughters, who now, with his estimable wife, comprise Mr Thurston's accomplished family

For fifteen years, Mr Thurston has been prominently identified with a majority of the leading cases in the courts of Nebraska Early in the spring of 1877, he was employed by the governor of the State, under authority of an act of the legislature, to prosecute the case of the State of Nebraska vs Ira P Olive This was a veritable *cause celebre*, and known to the history of western jurisprudence as the "Great Man-Burning Case" Olive and others, who were residents of Custer County, were charged with the horrible crime of not only hanging but of also burning two victims of their ferocity, named Mitchell and Ketchum, in the wilderness of that unsettled country, where their charred bodies were afterwards discovered

The trial created great excitement at the time, and was participated in by the leading lawyers of the State The cattlemen of the whole west took up the matter for the principal defendant, Olive, and for a long period there was intense excitement and grave apprehensions that there would be bloody doings at Hastings, where had assembled hundreds and even thousands of cow-boys, many of whom were supposed to have come from Texas for the purpose of rescuing Olive and his associates in the crime Mr Thurston was given the post of honor in the trial and made the closing argument for the State Olive was convicted of murder in the second degree and sentenced to the penitentiary for life He was afterwards released on a decision of the Supreme Court of Nebraska, to the effect that the laws had been so bungled, that prosecution for crime committed in Custer County could not be heard in any other county, and there was no provision of law for prosecution in Custer County

Among other notable trials in which Mr Thurston has participated was a case prosecuted in York County where two persons were arraigned for killing one William H Armstrong This was a case attended by the most romantic circumstances It grew out of a runaway match between one of the defendants and the daughter of William H Armstrong, the deceased The trouble occurred in the presence of the young woman, who was at the same time the daughter of the man killed, and the wife of one of the men who participated in the homicide Mr Thurston was the leading counsel for the defense, and after a most exciting trial the defendants were acquitted The somewhat noted Henry Clay Dean, was brought into the State by the friends of the deceased, and conducted the prosecution

Mr Thurston has also taken a leading part in a number of more or less celebrated murder trials in Nebraska, he, together with the Hon James W Savage, defended John W Lauer, whose trial, in Omaha, for killing his wife, is still of recent memory This case was one of the most celebrated criminal cases ever tried in Nebraska Public opinion was largely against the defendant The prosecution was very ably conducted by the district attorney, Mr L S Estelle, with whom was associated that prominent and successful prosecutor, John C Cowin The first trial resulted in a verdict of manslaughter, which was no more satisfactory to the public than to the defendant

The supreme court had just decided in the Bohannon case, that a defendant, at whose instance a verdict was set aside, could be again put on trial for murder in the first degree, even though on the first trial the verdict had been given of a crime of a lower degree

The defendant being fully advised of the possible result to him, insisted upon a motion for a new trial. Upon presentation thereof the motion was sustained upon the ground, as generally understood, that the defendant was certainly guilty of murder in the first degree, if guilty of anything, and that the evidence did not justify in any legal sense a verdict of manslaughter.

This seemed to be the opinion of those who had followed the course of the first trial, during the progress of which, the press had very fully printed the evidence of witnesses and arguments of counsel. Mr. Thurston was sharply criticised by the profession in the State for permitting his client to submit himself to the chances of a second trial under the lately announced rule in the "Bohannon case," and this criticism was much stronger when it was known that the second trial was to occur in Douglas County. The public interest in the case was intense, not only in Omaha, but in all that portion of the State, in which the daily papers made neighborhood items of the news of the city.

Lauer's boldness and the courage of his counsel in again going to trial before a jury drawn from a hostile and excited community compelled respect, because such a course demonstrated a consciousness of the innocence of the accused, known to him and relied upon by his counsel. It is seldom that a new trial is taken at the cost of such fearful possibilities. The result justified the act of defendant. The trial lasted three weeks, and the prosecution by the State was based mainly upon what is known as "circumstantial evidence," but it was ably presented. The effort made by the defendant was to explain the apparently incriminating circumstances, and to reconcile the whole evidence with the fact of the defendant's innocence. The arguments of counsel both for the State and the defendant may be read with profit, as models, by the criminal practitioner. Mr. Thurston, by his effort, confirmed himself in the opinion of the people and the bar as a most powerful advocate. The result was a verdict for the defendant, which was satisfactory, and the defendant was also acquitted at the bar of public opinion, before which he had been so recently condemned.

While Mr. Thurston has not devoted himself to criminal practice, but has rather avoided than sought employment in capital cases, yet he has been called upon to defend fourteen persons charged with murder, and has the almost unprecedented record of final acquittal in every case. When he became general solicitor of the Union Pacific Company, he had, perhaps, the largest practice of any lawyer in his section of the country.

Since accepting the position of general solicitor of the Union Pacific Railway Company, the responsible duties of which office he assumed on the first of February, 1888, he has retired from the general practice of the law, as the business of the railway system, which is now all under his supervision, occupies his entire time and close attention.

In 1880 Mr. Thurston was one of the presidential electors for the State of Nebraska, and was the messenger to carry the vote to Washington. In 1884 he was delegate-at-large to the Republican National Convention held in Chicago; he was the chairman of his State's delegation in the convention as well. He participated in the debates of the proceedings, and seconded the nomination of John A. Logan for the vice-presidency.

He was a member of the National Republican Convention which nominated General Harrison for president, and the temporary presiding officer of that august body. A recently published statement says of him: "Mr. Thurston has long been known as an able lawyer, but it was not until the assembling of the late Republican National Convention in Chicago, when he was made the temporary presiding officer, that he achieved a national reputation as an impressive orator. His speech, delivered upon that occasion, was one of great power, and elicited rapturous applause from the vast multitude present. Indeed, he was accorded at its close an ovation such as few speakers ever receive. He has a strong, clear, penetrating voice, and every word is uttered with the utmost distinctness; at no time is there any hesitation in his speech for the want of a proper term to express his meaning. His command of language is very unusual, while grace and polish mark every sentence. Added to these accomplishments is a splendid presence, which at once stamps him as a man of much more than average character, and as a leader of men instead of a follower.

"The record Mr. Thurston has made thus early in life is one not often met. He has not attained his present legal eminence on

account of favoring circumstances, but it is clearly the result of natural ability and close application to his profession While he has always taken an active and personal interest in political affairs, he has been thoroughly devoted to the law and has made everything else subordinate to its pursuit * * *
During the recent political campaign Judge Thurston appeared in various parts of the country in the interest of the Republican party, and everywhere met with a cordial reception from the people, and strengthened his great reputation as an orator On the night of Wednesday, October 17, 1888, he addressed the largest audience ever assembled in Chicago, up to that date, to listen to a political speech Five thousand ladies and gentlemen were crowded into Battery "D," and for two hours he held the vast assemblage as eager listeners to his splendid eloquence The verdict of the Chicago press was that Judge Thurston has but few equals in this country as a finished orator "

Mr Thurston's family and ancestors have all been believers in the orthodox religion He is not a member of any church organization, but is a very earnest believer in the general tenets of the Christian faith Five years ago, at the Chautauqua Assembly in Crete, Nebraska, he delivered an oration during the day set apart and called "Lawyers' Day," on the subject of "Law and Religion," in which he took the strongest possible ground in favor of the of the Christian belief which asserts the existence and unity of God, the resurrection and immortality of the human soul, and the atoning power of our Saviour's crucifixion

In the fall of 1875, Mr Thurston was nominated unanimously as the Republican choice for judge of the third judicial district of Nebraska, in which district Omaha is situated but was defeated at the polls by a small majority, his opponent being the Hon James W Savage

Mr Thurston is generally called "Judge," not because he ever held a judicial position, but because his friends, it is presumed, thought that when Judge Savage secured the office, his opponent was at least entitled to the brevet of that rank

It need hardly be said that Mr Thurston is a lawyer of the first class. In consultation he withholds his opinion until he is in possession of the whole case, and has looked at it from every side He examines with minutest care all the facts upon which a controversy depends, and with patience and painstaking scrutiny masters in advance all the details of the field upon which the battle must be fought He notes and strengthens the weak places in his cause, and disposes himself to parry or prevent a dangerous wound or mortal stroke at the hands of a skillful adversary He considers and adapts his plans for the impending battle, with the greatest of care he studies his adversary's case, and reasons from his standpoint as if the case were his own, and does this with such consummate skill that rarely if ever, is he surprised on the trial by the strategic measures of his opponent, or by any other mode of attack, which to others might be unexpected His self-possession is his strongest weapon, either for offense or defense His perfect work of preparation has armed him against surprises He quickly comprehends the views of others, and approves of them generously or calmly develops his objection He does not indulge in much debate Having arrived at his own conclusions, he expresses himself briefly and decisively His power and skill in the trial of cases before juries are remarkable His familiarity with the details of the controversy enables him to know just when and from what source to expect the most telling blows his opponent may give, and to know at what moment and when he may find the weak points in the harness of his adversary's cause In such matters his readiness is in no sense anything but the result of careful preparation and study of the facts and their effects He sees the case in all its aspects, appreciates the character of the witnesses, and how their testimony impresses the jury His examination and cross-examination of witnesses is direct simple and fair He has learned the art, perhaps the most difficult to acquire, of waiving cross-examination, apparently taking but little note of the matter or manner of the witness

Seldom does a party gain from Mr Thurston's course the benefit of testimony he himself could not properly produce A willful witness, however, soon finds that a firm, quiet hand is upon him, and yields to its moral power In his addresses to juries, where there is occasion, he is impassioned and persuasive, displaying the most efficient power of the advocate His method is to resolve from the testimony some one controlling theory upon which he rests his case. All the arts of advocacy to which he resorts are attacks upon such of his adversary's points as militate against his own, and to gather from the whole field the facts and circumstances which establish his contentions. In the discussion of fact he never unfairly strays from the record. In his presentation of reasons, he is facile in illustration, ready in appreciation and quick at repartee. In his treatment of parties and witnesses, he is always as generous as the nature of the subject permits. He does not seek to win by unmerited abuse or unjust ridicule. He relies upon the strength of his cause and the fairness of his reasoning, rather than upon any weakness or wickedness of the men in his adversary's camp. When confronted by a story, of the willful falseness of which he is convinced, his resort to invective, sarcasm and ridicule has proven him master of the forces of this kind of advocacy, no less than of the gentler and more pleasant arts of the profession. He enjoys the struggles and triumphs of the forum, and is not cast down by defeat. However severe the struggle, he throws into it the fullness of his strong personality and accepts the result, whatever it may be, with the consciousness that his full duty has been performed.

But it is not by the triumphs of the forum or the arts or success of the advocate that Mr. Thurston's merit as a lawyer is to be measured. In the earlier years of his practice, he diligently read and studied the works of those great commentators and authors who laid deep and broad the foundations of our common law and equity jurisprudence. He made the result of their labors his own, so that he began by becoming "well-grounded in the common law." His familiar contact with men and affairs has so ripened his judgment, broadened and quickened his powers of observation and application, that it is to his ability as a counselor that he owes his proudest success as a lawyer. The complicated questions of corporate administrations, in their legal effects, come to him almost hourly for immediate investigation and instant action. His training and habits of thought and purpose have demonstrated that the arts of the advocate sink far below the solid powers of the deliberate adviser.

Mr. Thurston has delivered many memorable addresses in different parts of the country. His oration on the centennial anniversary of constitutional independence, at Chicago, in 1889; his eulogy on General Grant, before the Union League Club; his address on Abraham Lincoln, in 1890, and his tribute to the "man who wears the button," are among the most remarkable. The press of the whole country has seemed to unite in commendation of his abilities as a powerful and eloquent public speaker. He was urged by the greater portion of the entire west for appointment as secretary of the interior in the cabinet of President Harrison, and although he made no effort to secure the position, it was at one time believed that his selection was certain. His name has twice been strongly presented to the legislature of his State for the position of United States Senator, although he has never really been a candidate for that office. Were it not for his railway connection, the people of Nebraska would insist upon his going to the United States Senate, and he has been urged by many for a still higher place. In the spring of 1889, Judge Thurston was prevailed upon to accept the presidency of the Republican league of the United States, to which he was unanimously re-elected at the annual convention, at Nashville, March, 1890. His character and ability largely contributed to making this organization very strong; but he was obliged to inform the executive committee that it was impossible for him to retain the presidency after the expiration of his second term, owing to the pressure of professional engagements, and his resignation, after his most urgent solicitation, was reluctantly accepted at the convention of the present year. He is very frequently called upon to speak in behalf of public charities and interests before moral, social, literary and political societies, to which he always responds with pleasure, and always delights and instructs. Among his fellow citizens throughout the State, but especially in the city of his home, he is held in the highest esteem, as well on account of his position and simplicity of character, as for his generous public spirit. Manly, loyal and affectionate, he enjoys in a remarkable degree the devoted love of his friends. There are many who are willing to administer to his fortunes. Besides these multitudes, there are some who are nearer to him, whom circumstances or personal relations have brought into the inner circle of his affections, whose devotion is never weary or relaxed

It is not unreasonable to expect that Mr. Thurston, still a young man, will fill other high places in the land. If he does, he will bring to the service of the country a loyalty, a devotion, a wisdom, rarely to be found amongst those who aspire to public office

The author recalls vividly the occasion of a speech by Judge Thurston at Des Moines, Iowa during the presidential campaign of 1884, when Cleveland and Blaine were the candidates. The great hall was crowded to its utmost capacity, and a surging mass of humanity seemed contending for space in which to stand. The speaker was enveloped in the enthusiasm of the cause for which he spoke, apparently oblivious to the expectancy round about him. His phraseology was charming, his delivery graceful and uniform, with the absence of tasteful mannerism, and for more than two hours the vast concourse remained spell-bound under the rich splendor of his matchless eloquence

Few men in this generation, or any other, have thrown off the circumstances of birth, and overcome the disadvantages of youth and the deprivation of early culture and education, as has Judge Thurston. To thus subdue adversity almost superior to human effort, must be experienced to be fully comprehended. To such a youth vain praise is insipid, even repulsive, but that which comes from the hearts sincerity of friend or stranger, is as efficacious to his yearning ambition as an encouraging beck from a guardian angel. To all such the gratitude of a young man of this nature is as ceaseless as the flow of a perennial fountain, even though he be not blessed with the fruits of a golden harvest, or the just plentitude of a busy and toilsome life.

GEORGE FRANCIS TRAIN.—On the 24th of March, 1829, George Francis Train was born at No. 21 High Street, Boston, Massachusetts

The ancestors of George Francis had been settled in Massachusetts for upwards of two hundred years. They came from Ireland, but there was some French blood in the family, and these facts it will be well to remember when his subsequent thoughts and acts are to be considered. A Scotch-Irishman is the embodiment of quiet resolve, a French-Irishman, of fiery zeal, but, between them, in point of brain-power, "the honors are easy."

When the boy was four years of age, his father, Oliver Train, who was born in Boston, and his mother, a native of Waltham, taking him and his sisters removed to New Orleans, at a time when the yellow fever was prevailing. Both his parents and three sisters fell a prey to the deadly scourge. Thereupon George Francis was sent back to New England. He declares his education was had in three months at a winter school. He lived until his twelfth year on the old homestead—a six-hundred-acre farm, three miles out of Waltham—under the care and teaching of his grandmother Pickering, when he found employment in a grocery store in Cambridgeport

At the age of fifteen he entered, as clerk, the house of Enoch Train & Company, Boston and Liverpool Packets. In 1849, he crossed the Atlantic and established the shipping house of Train & Company in Liverpool, and organized the prepaid passenger business (as well as that of selling small bills of exchange) throughout Europe and America, and thus, not yet twenty years old, becoming one of the principal owners and proprietors of the Diamond Line of Liverpool and New York Sailing Packets. The *Ocean Monarch*, burnt off the Welsh coast, was one of the vessels of this line. The next year he was admitted a partner of the Boston house, taking full charge of the business. On the 5th of October, of that year, he married, in Louisville, Kentucky, Miss Willie Davis, daughter of Colonel Geo. T. M. Davis, of that city

In May, 1853, Mr. Train started on a voyage to Melbourne, Australia, establishing there the house of George F. Train & Company. In the first fourteen months, this house netted $119,000 commissions. He afterward declared. "Having a fortune, I went to Australia and built the largest stores and warehouses in Melbourne. The firm of Train & Company was the largest in that city. It had branches in New York, London and Calcutta." It is needless to say, his business was a great success

A grand banquet was given Mr. Train, on the 5th of November, 1855, on his embarking on a voyage around the world, by the citizens of Melbourne. He subsequently said (in July, 1892)

"I have been around the world five times

—once in sixty days. Here is a summary of my [last] trip: I bulldozed the Mikado in Japan, frightened out of their wits the Chinese at Hong Kong, bewildered the Malays at Singapore, ran over the Singalese in Ceylon, drove the Arabs crazy at Aden, astonished the Italians, French, English and Irish, in turn, in a rapid rush through Europe, and returned to the United States."

And not long since, he declared that his "Round-the-World speeches," made on his last trip from Tacoma westward, to Tacoma from the eastward, were set up (eight columns) in the Japan *Gazette* (Yokohama) by Japanese typos; Hong Kong (China) *Press*, eight columns, by native Chinese; Singapore (East India) *Free Press*, seven columns, by Malay and East India typos; Ceylon (Colombo) *Independent*, eight columns, by Singalese compositors; *Le Phara de Porte Said* (Port Said—Suez Canal, Egypt), three pages, by Arabs. When racing around the world the other day (my fifth race), reducing time, in forty years, from two years to sixty days."

In 1857, Train commenced his career as an author. He has written, in all, the following books: "An American Merchant in Europe, Asia and Australia" (1857); "Young America Abroad" (1857); "Young America in Wall Street" (1858); "Spread-Eagleism" (1859); "Every Man His Own Autocrat" (1859); "Young America on Slavery" (1860); "Observations on Street Railways" (1860); "George Francis Train, Unionist, on Thomas Colley Grattan, Secessionist, (1861); "Union Speeches Delivered in England During the Present American War" (1862); "Speech Before the Brotherhood of St. Patrick" (1862); "Speech on Slavery" (1865); "Downfall of England" (1865); "Irish Independency" (1865); "Championship of Women" (1868).

"As agent," says Train, "for Queen Christiana, of Spain, I struck Philadelphia, in 1857, to look after her forty thousand acres of coal land." He soon engaged in building for the same royal personage, the Atlantic and Great Western Railway, negotiating the first bonds and interesting Queen Christiana, of Spain, in the scheme. His commissions in this undertaking netted him a sum that almost any capitalist would consider a handsome fortune.

The next year found him in England, as the champion of street railways (called in that country, then and now, tramways.) He endeavored "to obtain an Act of Parliament authorizing tramways in London;" failing in that, he laid tramways, by consent of the road authorties, first in 1860, at Birkenhead, and soon afterwards in London.

Says Mr. Train recently: "On my first voyage around the world four decades ago (see *Young America Abroad*), I was surprised to find that, while sewing machines, sleeping cars, steam railroads, gas lights, omnibuses, matches, pianos, Yankee notions, 'cocktails' and 'mint juleps' were evoluting our planet, there were no street railways in the old world.

"It seems to have been my destiny to introduce on land and sea, in foreign countries, new inventions promoting trade and commerce everywhere:

"I clipper-shipped the cosmos sea
And iron-railed the continent,
To introduce trade industry
From Occident to Orient."

And he also says: "New York had started the first lines and Philadelphia was busy with the new locomotion for cities, when my contractors launched my first 'tramway,' as the English say, abroad at Birkenhead, opposite Liverpool. John Laird gave me the contract, I taking all risks and agreeing to remove if the scheme proved a failure. That road was opened in August, 1859. My opening banquet had four hundred 'notables' present, Prince Albert writing me a friendly letter. The new locomotion took like wildfire. When *mirabili dictu*, Beauregard fired on Fort Sumpter and England went solid with Louis Napoleon for the South, I was furious. I thereupon played the patriot: I lost my 'tramways' but won glory."

In espousing the Union cause, Mr. Train delivered one hundred speeches for the Union and participated in as many debates. "He lectured in Great Britain and Ireland before large audiences, especially in the latter country, and, although his manner and language were singular, his sarcasm on English society were often incisive and eloquent." He also established the *London-American*, the only American newspaper in Europe, Mr. Bemis [now (May 1893) Mayor of Omaha], his private secretary, being editor-in-chief and general manager. His tramways were declared a nuisance and he was fined five hundred pounds, but refusing to pay, was thrust into a debtor's prison, where, having one Sunday, in the absence of the chaplain, preached a sermon to the inmates (among whom were editors, lawyers, and men of letters) on the "Downfall of England," the authorities concluded "to let that man out," he was "demoralizing the prisoners"

In 1862, Mr Train was in the United States He favored emancipation, but he did not believe that four millions of slaves should be immediatelly set free and become paupers on the country. He believed in the war policy of crushing the rebellion and in leaving the slavery question to some policy of gradual emancipation He undertook to 'beard the lion in his den"—to answer Charles Sumner in Faneuil Hall, when he was arrested, but soon forty thousand excited Irishmen surrounded the station house and informed the officials that "if it didn't make any particular difference to their general arrangements, they had better let that man out" He was let out

Mr Train then started on a lecturing tour through the middle and western states on his "War Policy" subject On his tour, he was shot at in Dayton, arrested and ordered out of Missouri, only escaped assassination at Alton, and was bayoneted at Davenport *

In December, 1862, Mr Train commenced the organization of the Kansas Pacific Railway and the next year he was one of the largest operators in Wall street gold market, buying and selling as high as three million in one day

We now come to the greatest business act in the career of this man, (whose life from the age of fifteen, had hitherto been, as already shown, one of most marvelous activity,) in making certain the building of the Union Pacific Railroad He was, in fact, the original organizer of the stupendous undertaking He obtained the original capital of $2,000,000. He was instrumental in getting the bill through congress which appropriated $100,000,000 of government bonds, and some 20,000,000 acres of land in furtherance of the gigantic scheme He broke ground at Omaha, on the 2d of December, 1863

In 1864, Mr Train established the *Credit Mobilier* and the next year the *Credit Foncier* of America In 1865, he invested largely in Omaha The next year he built the Cozzens Hotel in this city in sixty days at a cost of $35,000 On the 8th of January, 1868, he embarked for Europe in furtherance of matters connected with the Union Pacific Railroad, but was arrested in England for words spoken in America, but soon released, but again arrested in Ireland, where he had made speeches, suffering a much longer imprisonment, during which he was voted for by his admirers in the fifth congressional district of New York, for congress against John Morrissey, but was "counted out"

Mr Train, on the first of August, 1870, accompanied by George P Bemis, his private secretary, commenced his second voyage around the world by way of Japan, China. India, Ceylon, Arabia, Egypt, and the Mediterranean arriving at Marseilles, France, October 20, of that year He had a most remarkable experience in France, a complete record of which would fill a volume He reached New York on the twenty-first of December, of the year last mentioned Three times, since, he has traveled around the world

Mr Train has outlined his life-career in this way

"Born at No 21 High Street, Boston, 1829, residence Continental Hotel, at present—generally in some jail, color, octoroon, sex, male, height, five feet eleven inches. My father was born in Boston, my mother at Waltham, Massachusetts My room, bed. desk in our homestead, two hundred years old is still shown to visitors Married in 1851 My wife is dead My education was had in three months at a winter school I am strictly temperate; I never tasted liquor I have three grown-up children"

In conclusion, it may be said that the world has never seen but one George Francis Train, and, it may not be rash to say, it will never "look upon his like again" Eccentricity is but a departure or deviation from that which is stated, regular, or usual, and Train is spoken of as "an eccentric genius," but he is far more—he is the greatest genius of eccentricity, it is believed, that has ever lived It finds in him such an exemplification as it has never before found in any living being, and such as it will never again find, it may be safe to predict, in any sentient creature It is true that his mind frequently wanders into the "voids of space," but it has, nevertheless, an orbit

* *Pen Sketches of Nebraskans*, pp 15-17

(eccentric though it is). And that mind, on its return into the "full glare of the sun," such is its brightness, it fairly blinds the average intellect of men with its flashes.

ELEAZER WAKELEY.—The ancestors of Eleazer Wakeley, on his father's side, came from Wales to New England early in the period of its settlement. His paternal grandfather was living in Lichfield County, Connecticut, in the latter part of the eighteenth century, in which county his father, Solmns Wakeley was born, on March 17, 1794—being one of six sons, and having one sister. His mother, by maiden name, was Hannah Thompson, daughter of Henry Thompson, of Bethlehem, in the same state and county. She was born October 19, 1793.

The Wakeleys, for several generations, were mostly located in New England. They were men of rugged constitution; of mental vigor and force of character; possessing, in a marked degree, the intelligence and virtues of their times. In the maternal ancestry of Judge Wakeley's mother was some excellent New England blood—she being collaterally related, among others, to the Jonathan Edwards family of Connecticut. Her father was a volunteer in the revolutionary struggle. She had fine and strong intellectual gifts, with great fondness for reading and study, and an unusually retentive memory. Whatever inclination her son may have developed for intellectual pursuits, he attributes largely to her early training, and continual encouragement.

His father had not the opportunities of education and culture which his strong mental endowments would have justified; but he became, by reading and observation, an unusually well-informed man in current affairs, and his country's history. He held various places of public trust; was a member of the first constitutional convention of Wisconsin; and twice a representative in its legislature. He possessed strong powers of logic, and native judgment; and was a formidable antagonist in debate. As a citizen and a man, he was always high in the general esteem and confidence.

In both father and mother, the subject of this sketch had a just and warrantable pride, and an incentive to worthy effort, and an honorable life.

Born in Homer, Cortland County, New York, in 1822, he was the eldest of three sons, and had two sisters—all characterized by mental strength, studious habits, and good scholarship. His surviving brother has long been a lawyer in Madison, Wisconsin. His parents removed, soon after his birth, to Erie County, New York, where his education was begun, in a district school, at the age of four years, and continued until he was thirteen. He was considered a forward scholar at that time, when progress in public schools, although with rude surroundings, compared most favorable with that in modern institutions much more elaborate. In 1836 the family removed to Elyria, Lorain County, Ohio. Here he attended, in a desultory way, such schools as the village furnished—concluding, in the high school there, under Prof. John P. Cowles, a most learned man, then of Ohio, and afterwards prominent, for a long time, in educational work in Massachusetts. His schooling, therefore, was not very systematic, nor rounded out by a collegiate course; but he had innate love of study, and application to the duty in hand, while a student in school, and afterwards in the law. His early specialty was mathematics, for which he had a strong liking and aptitude, but which he laid aside, in after years, under the stress of a profession, which tolerates no rival in allegiance. It may be fairly said that he has kept up, to the end, the habits of close application, and of searching for the reason of things, which characterized his student life.

Having finished his education in the schools, he entered upon a thorough course of reading in the law, under Joel Tiffany, a forcible and able lawyer, and a man of marked and versatile talent. He was admitted to the bar in Lorain County, in 1844. In the fall of the following year he was nominated on the Democratic ticket for prosecuting attorney of the county, but failed of an election—the Western Reserve not being then, nor since, at all partial to Democrats.

Soon after, following his inclination for the farther West, he located at White Water, in Southern Wisconsin, in the fall of 1845, where he began the real practice of his profession. In 1847 he was elected a representative from Walworth County to the last territorial legislature of Wisconsin; and was state senator from that county from 1851 to 1855, taking an active and earnest part in legislative work and debate, and being assigned to important committees These political digressions did not interrupt an active and increasing practice from 1845 to 1857, but served, with his professional life, to make him well known throughout the State, and secure to him many valuable and life-long friendships there But a practice in the uncommercial counties of Southeastern Wisconsin was not wholly satisfying

In January, 1857, without solicitation on his part, he was appointed by President Pierce an associate justice of the supreme court of Nebraska Territory He was assigned to the third district, which included Washington, Burt, Dakota, Dixon and Cedar counties, with all the unorganized territory west and north of them to the Rocky Mountains and the British possessions It comprised an area of about 350,000 square miles, being the largest judicial district, territorially, In the United States. He resided in Washington County, and in Omaha during his official service

Prior to this time, the terms of court in that district had been held irregularly, and infrequently It was a pioneer country, so far as facilities and conveniences for court were concerned, but, thereafter, the increasing litigation was dispatched promptly, and methodically, and with such general satisfaction that the judge, at the end of his four years term, was reappointed, without opposition, by President Buchanan Soon afterwards, upon an entire change of territorial appointments, under the Lincoln administration, he returned to Wisconsin, pursuant to a previous purpose, and resumed the work of his profession, locating at Madison, the state capital Here he built up a large and successful practice in the central counties, and in the supreme court His brother, C T. Wakeley, was associated with him, and also, for a time, William F Vilas, then a young lawyer of great promise, and since distinguished in his profession, a member of the cabinet, and a United States Senator In 1883, he ran for attorney general on the Democratic State ticket of Wisconsin In 1886-7, the last year of his residence in that state, he represented the Madison district in the legislature, having in charge its large local interests. He was influential in securing the enactment of a law increasing the salaries of the judges of the supreme court In consequence of its passage while he was a member,—the Wisconsin constitution making this a disability to hold the office—he was compelled to decline the nomination for supreme judge, tendered him by a joint convention of the Democratic members of the legislature, at that session

The purpose of returning eventually to Nebraska—the *animus revertendi*, in legal phrase—had all the time a strong hold upon Judge Wakeley, and, in the fall of 1867, he returned to this State with his family, and has ever since made Omaha his home He soon secured a legal business which demanded all his time and energies, to the exclusion of other activities His practice was varied, running through all departments of the law except the criminal, for which he had an aversion In the trial courts, and the supreme court of the State, and in the federal courts he was engaged in many causes of importance, among which were several known to the profession as "leading cases" in Nebraska He had numerous corporation cases, and was for seven years assistant attorney of the Union Pacific Railroad Company In another place in this volume reference is made to his career and characteristics as a lawyer, which need not be enlarged upon here.

In Nebraska, he was a member of the constitutional convention of 1871, chosen without opposition With this exception, he has declined to be a candidate for political office, being devoted to his legal work and preferring an endeavor to "pay the debt which every man owes to his profession" He has had a busy active and successful professional life—cultivating his love of reading and study, so far as opportunity has afforded

In 1879, he was a candidate for judge of the supreme court of Nebraska, but the political majority against his party could not be overcome It has been his usual fortune to be in the political minority This alone, probably, has prevented his realizing any aspirations he may have had for such judicial preferment

In 1883, after thirty-seven years at the bar, Judge Wakeley accepted the appointment of district judge from Governor Dawes, whose action was based upon the general recommendation of the bar, and the citizens, without regard to party In the fall of the same year he was unanimously elected to the judgeship for four years, together with

"It is with but slight faith in the probability of the selection of a lawyer so far removed from Washington as John L. Webster of Omaha, for the vacancy on the supreme bench created by the death of Stanley Matthews, that *The Herald* ventures its opinion of the worth and capabilities of Mr. Webster. Feeling thus and further believing that even the remotest possibility of such a selection should be encouraged, *The Herald* unhesitatingly speaks its mind to the effect that it believes the appointment of Mr. Webster to the supreme bench would be a wise act on the part of President Harrison.

"Mr. Webster is confessedly an able lawyer, especially upon questions of constitutional law. His mental poise is excellent and the natural bent of his mind deliberative. He is from the West and uncontaminated with the influences of the eastern money-devil. He is comparatively young, in the vigorous prime of manhood and of an active blood, of such as the supreme bench needs an infusion. Though his politics should not be an element of consideration, they are in harmony with the administration. If chosen he would be an honor to the state and an acquisition to the bench."

The president recognized the demands of the west by the appointment of Justice Brewer of Kansas, whose claims to the position were unquestionably superior to those of any other candidate; but Mr. Webster had reason to feel proud and grateful for the public expression of good will which his candidacy evoked. At a meeting of the Republican league in Nashville, in 1890, he was chairman of the Nebraska delegation, and of the committee on platform. He addressed the convention on March 4th, and responded for the league to an address of welcome at Chattanooga. His speech was altogether the event of the occasion, and was received with unbounded enthusiasm.

His latest, and, perhaps, most conspicious political honor, was achieved in the state convention in April of this year (1892), where he was almost unanimously chosen as a delegate-at-large to the National Republican Convention, in the face of an opposition at once formidable and malignant.

So that to a limited extent, and somewhat in spite of himself, Mr. Webster has been prominent in Western politics. His most signal service to the State of Nebraska, however, was his contribution to the defeat of prohibition in 1890. To him, more than to any other one factor, may be attributed the result of that issue. The Beatrice Chautauqua, at this time, was the stronghold of the prohibitionists. Celebrated speakers from all parts of the country were present, and if eloquence, vociferation, and oratory, could accomplish a measure, the Beatrice Chautauqua was resolved to accomplish prohibition in Nebraska. Mr. Webster challenged their champion debaters, and in the presence of an audience of thousands vanquished and routed them.

John L. Webster was born March 18th, 1847, in Harrison County, Ohio. He served in the Union army from May to October, 1864. In the spring of 1867 he graduated from Mount Union College, at Alliance, Ohio. Shortly afterward he moved to Pittsburgh where, for the two years preceding his advent in Omaha, he studied law with the famous Tom Marshall.

What has been the secret of Mr. Webster's success? Some one has said that genius is only a capacity for hard work. Mr. Webster has worked hard, but that fact alone does not account for his steady advancement. He has so systematized and methodized his professional labors that unless one were familiar with his habits he would hardly suspect him of arduous study and unremitting toil. To see him in his office would give no indication of the multitude and importance of his affairs. He sits at a small library table, highly polished and elaborately carved. Before him, in a handsome frame, is the portrait of a young lady, whose poise of head and eye-glasses give her a Bostonese air; it is a portrait of his daughter. On the same table, in an equally attractive frame, is the portrait of his wife. His writing implements seem designed as much for ornament as for use. On one corner of the table is usually placed a vase of flowers. And these dainty articles, generally considered incongruous among the cobwebs of the law, leave no room for the accumulation of red-tape or formal documents. But there are apparently no cobwebs, red-tape, or formal documents in Mr. Webster's office. When a paper has been inspected, it is carried to some secret archive, and hidden out of sight. The room in which this lawyer works would answer to the word *boudoir*—

lambrequins and lace curtains at the windows, a Chinese screen with a golden what-is-it blazoned on its panels, a potted plant growing upon the mantel hearth, Oriental rugs, frescoed ceiling, and tinted walls—in short, a thousand and one femininities which only Webster himself would call a law office, and which only Webster's abilities could palliate. To see him sauntering down the street, a light overcoat flung over his arm, and a slender cane twirling in his fingers, you would envy him his means for leisure. He seems never in a hurry, but this is the consequence of his undeviating system of doing what he has to do. He occupies himself with one thing at a time, and does that thoroughly and well. But not even to his habit of industry, nor to his clock-work method, does he owe altogether his success. To summarize these elements in a sentence, it might be said that Mr. Webster has achieved his position at the bar, his reputation as a speaker, his recognition as one of the foremost Western men, first, by hard work systematically performed, then by a mental equipoise and an imperturbable good nature, and then—that smile! To answer an insult with a smile, instead of an oath, is sometimes heroic and always politic. Now, when you add to these elements of success, a persistent effort as un-let-upable as the force of gravity, the problem is taken out of metaphysics, and becomes a matter of arithmetic.

Mr. Webster exults in an up-hill fight. It is then that his resources, expedients, and indomitable energies have full scope. He never comes nearer being wholly and essentially great than when his opponent fancies he has him cornered.

Mr. Webster has been accused of vanity. There is a dynamic force in vanity which, however disguised, is the motive force of life. Admitting the impeachment, Mr. Webster might justify the fact.

SOLON L. WILEY was born May 31, 1840, at Cambridgeport, Vermont, where he lived until five years of age, and then moved to Greenfield, Massachusetts, where he received a common school education, and graduated at the high school there at the age of eighteen, after which he studied civil engineering and took up the branch of hydraulic engineering and made it a profession.

At the age of twenty-one the young man enlisted in the war of the Rebellion, on call of the president, serving nearly two years, in the Fifty-second Regiment Massachusetts Volunteer Infantry, in the southwest, under General Banks. He held a corporal's commission. Subsequently he held the position of purser in the merchant marine service off the eastern coast, and was at the taking of Fort McAllister. He was on the boat that made the first connection with Sherman's army on the Ogechee River.

After being mustered out of service, Mr. Wiley staid three years at Savannah, Georgia, to recuperate his health. While there, he engaged in the cultivation and manufacture of rice for the New York market.

In 1865, he married Anna C Newton, of Greenfield, Massachusetts. He went there to reside and took up the profession of engineer and contractor of hydraulic works. He continued in the business at that place for over twenty years, building twenty hydraulic works during that period. In 1875, his wife died, leaving two children—Edith A Wiley, who married William H. Sherwin, of Ottumwa, Iowa, where he holds the position of treasurer of the Iowa Water Company, and Walter S Wiley, who is, at present, superintendent of the electric light company, of South Omaha.

In 1878, Mr. Wiley was married again, to Kate M Newton, sister of the former wife, by whom he has two children—Ruth and Katharine, both living at home and attending school at Walnut Hill.

In the year 1876, Mr. Wiley purchased an interest in the City Water Works (now American Water Works Company), of Omaha, and moved to the city, where he now resides. He rebuilt the water works at Florence, and was for a number of years its manager. At present, he is the president and manager of the New Omaha Thomson-Houston Electric Light Company, and built the present works at the foot of Jones Street and throughout the city.

In religion, Mr. Wiley is a Congregationalist, in his political affiliation, a Republican. He is recognized as one of the representative men of the city—wide-awake and active, in all his business undertakings.

ORLANDO SCOTT WOOD.—It is a wise remark that "men who have achieved any worthy aim by reason of the very ability which has enabled its achievement, not only are conscious of their superiority, to those they have surpassed, but they feel the inspiration of allowing their careers to be handed down in permanent form as encouragements and incentives to others. This is true in all professions and callings." While the subject of this sketch would shrink from anything like obtruding himself upon the public, nevertheless, he does not feel himself justified, when called upon, to withhold anything that is thought conducive to the advancement of his profession or calculated to stimulate others to hold firmly to their faith and persevere in well-doing.

The father of Orlando was a shoemaker. His name was Orin Wood. The maiden name of the mother was Sally Baldwin. In the spring of 1836, the family moved from Binghamton, New York (where Orlando was born on the 27th of January, 1832), to Berrien Springs, Michigan. There the father died in October, 1838, leaving, besides the boy whose name stands at the head of this article, another and younger son. The mother and her two children had nothing left them in the way of an estate—neither money nor lands.

Until the mother could get sufficient means to take her little family East (her old home being in Pennsylvania), Orlando was sent to live among strangers, but he found kind protectors.

In the spring of 1840, Mrs. Wood, with her two children, left Michigan, journeying first to Binghamton, where she spent two weeks with her husband's relatives, and thence to her old home, in Montrose, Pennsylvania. In November, after her arrival, the subject of this sketch went to live with an uncle in South Auburn, Susquehanna County, that State; he was a farmer, and lived eighteen miles from Montrose. Orlando was a "farmer's boy" with his uncle, for seven years, working for his board and clothes. In March, 1848, he apprenticed himself for three years, to learn the carpenter's trade, at twenty-five dollars for the first year, thirty-five for the second, and fifty for the third; this included his board, of course. Up to the time of the ending of his term, he had forty dollars due him, and the following day he engaged with his employer for twenty dollars a month and board. Thus far the young man had received no education, except during three months each winter in country schools; but he thirsted for knowledge, and resolved to enter some educational institution as soon as he could save a little money.

Mr. Wood worked steadily until December, 1851, when he fitted himself out with a small amount of extra clothing, a kit of tools, and, with seventy-five dollars in his pocket, started for the Bucknell University, of Lewisburg, Pennsylvania, then presided over by Howard Malcom, D. D. He entered the academical department, and keeping his means up as well as he could, by working at his trade on Saturdays and during vacations, continued on until the close of his junior collegiate year. Then, for want of money, he undertook to work during the summer term, keep up with his class, and enter again at the commencement of the fall term, but this, as might be expected, was too much of an undertaking. He was taken with a fever, and his expenses increased so much that he was obliged to abandon, for a time, his college scheme.

In October, 1856, Mr. Wood removed to West Chester, Pennsylvania, where a friend (Reverend Robert Lowry) procured him a situation as clerk in a book store. Here he hoped to save money to finish his Lewisburg course, but was disappointed and gave up the project. He was engaged as collector and soliciting agent in Chester County during the summer of 1857, for the Chester County *Times*. In the spring of the next year he began the study of homœopathy with Dr. Joseph E. Jones, in West Chester. In 1858 and 1859, he attended his first course of medical lectures at the Homœopathic Medical College, in Philadelphia, graduating on the first day of March, 1860. At this time he was in debt sixteen hundred dollars for his education and professional outfit, which amount, he had previously arranged, was to be paid after graduation and when he had earned the money in the practice of his profession.

Dr. Wood settled in Phœnixville, Pennsylvania, on the first day of April, 1860. At that place he remained one year, when he removed to Canandaigua, New York, where he purchased the practice of R. R. Gregg, M.D. At the close of 1866, he left there, going to Philadelphia, where, for a while, he located, and in addition to practicing his profession, attended, in the winter of 1867-68, the first course of lectures in the Hahnemann Medical College, where he was again graduated, in March, 1868. In the following June he started for Omaha. He opened his office in this city, where he now resides, on the 10th of July. The doctor is a senior member of the American Institute of Homœopathy and of the Northwestern Homœopathic Medical Association and Northwestern Academy of Medicine. He was one of the charter members of the Nebraska State Medical Society, and is the only active practitioner in his State that helped to organize that institution. He has, as specialties, gynæcology, diseases of children, and rectal diseases.

In his religious belief, the doctor is a Baptist. He was baptized in 1850. He has a wife and three children—two sons and a daughter. He has been closely identified with the material interests and prosperity of Omaha every since his arrival in the city. He has stood high in the estimation of the citizens, from first to last, for his ability as a physician and his strict integrity. The Y M C A owes much to him for his wise council and hearty co-operation. He has been a member of the First Baptist Church, of Omaha, ever since he has been a resident here, and for many years has held the office of chairman of its board of trustees, and is a life deacon of his church. Through all the ups and downs of this organization of which he is a member, he has stood by it and given liberally of his means and personal assistance. But very few business men, and especially professional men, are as faithful to all the appointments of the church, and the various moral, temperance and religious organizations of the city as he. He believes it to be the duty of every man to be interested in every movement that tends to the moral welfare of the citizens of this commonwealth. The doctor has, at this time, a very extensive practice, not only in the city, but is called to different parts of the State for consultation on important cases. His success as a physician is owing largely to his thoroughness in whatever he does, and with it his having a kind heart and gentle hands.

JAMES M WOOLWORTH.—Among the crowd of bright and ambitious young lawyers who were attracted to Nebraska in its early days, there was no one who has been so thoroughly identified with the legal history of the Territory and State, so constantly engaged in laborious practice and so successful in its prosecution as the gentleman whose name heads this article. Mr Woolworth was born in 1829, in Onondaga Valley, New York. The family name is a very old one. It remains in some of the rural parts of England. In Wales is an old church dedicated to St Mary Woolworth, and formerly there was one in London bearing the same name. In recent years it has been taken down. The name was brought to this country by two brothers, Chester and Aaron, and these have been family names ever since. They settled in Connecticut, and in the early years members of the family lived in different towns of that State and Massachusetts. The immediate descendants of Chester Woolworth lived at Westfield, in the latter state. From this branch came Aaron Woolworth. His grandson, James M Woolworth has his diploma from Yale college, dated 1793 conferring the B A degree upon him, and also his diploma from Princeton, dated in 1812, conferring the degree of D D. He was an eminent Presbyterian clergyman. Dr Woolworth married Mary Buel, the daughter of the Rev. Samuel Buel, D D, another eminent minister of the same faith and at one time chaplain to Washington in the Revolutionary war.

Mr Woolworth was the second son of Samuel Buel Woolworth, LL. D. The life of this man was devoted to the cause of public education. He was a teacher in early life, and almost every town in New York sent its sons to his school, known as Cortland Academy, at Homer, in that State. For some years principal of the State Normal school at Albany, he became secretary of the board of regents of the University of the State of New York. He held this office for more than a quarter of a century, and in that and other positions did more, perhaps, for the cause of education in that commonwealth than any other one man. His name is held in Albany in most grateful remembrance.

Mr Woolworth's mother was Sophia Mickles, who came of an old Dutch family. She was a woman of great refinement, culture and beauty. Those who still remember her, delight to speak of her grace and loveliness. The son, inheriting the literary and scholastic tastes which distinguished his father, entered Hamilton College, from which institution he graduated in 1849. Betaking himself to the study of law, he was admitted to the bar in 1854, and commenced the practice of his profession at Syracuse in his native state. But the west, with its boundless possibilities, presented too tempting a field to permit him to remain long in the city of his first adoption, and he came to Omaha in October, 1856. The following extract from an address delivered by him in 1879, before the Historical Society of Nebraska, may be, to some extent, unconsciously biographical. He is speaking of the tendency to emigration in English-speaking races:

"Doubtless the charm of adventure is something; the mere fact of removal is something. The exchange of familiar and therefore tame scenes and companionships for other lands, other seas, other skies and other air, strangely quickens, freshens and stimulates the pulses, sensations, thoughts, emotions and aspirations. This is a common experience, and, touching the universal fact, is something; and yet it is inadequate to account for the sacrifice of so much that the heart loves and for the endurance of so much that the heart revolts from.

"The American has certain qualities of the Roman of ancient and the Briton of modern times—tenacity of purpose, love of dominion and aggressive egotism. Like them, he is fitted by nature for foreign enterprise. And these qualities with him are enlivened by vivacity, sensibility and emotion; he, far more than they, delights in adventure. The risks, the struggle, the promise, the freedom of colonial life, have for him, even more than for others, a charm and an attraction."

In Omaha, Mr. Woolworth took, at the very outset of his career, a leading place in the administration of the law, which he has maintained to the present day. One controlling element in his success has been his entire devotion to his business, and the firmness with which he has resisted all the allurements of political life and the temptations of public office, which a new country holds out in such profusion to young men of ability. With the exception of a seat in the State legislature at one session (perhaps hardly to be considered an exception), all the offices held by him have been directly in the line of his profession. Thus he became the first city attorney of Omaha soon after his arrival, was a member of the constitutional convention of 1871, became the candidate of the Democratic party, in 1873, for the office of chief justice of the supreme court, was one of the first regents of the high school, a trustee of Racine College, in Wisconsin, and of the female seminary in Omaha, known as Brownell Hall.

None of these positions have been allowed to interfere with Mr. Woolworth's entire devotion to the interests of his clients; and it may truthfully be said of him that no attorney in the State of Nebraska has represented so many and such varied interests, and has been employed in so many and important lawsuits, as he. It is not too high praise of him to say that no other person in the State has taken so large a part in shaping its jurisprudence and establishing its procedure. Students of "Nebraska Reports" cannot fail to notice that there is hardly an important case reported in the first volumes of the series in which Mr. Woolworth was not engaged on one side or the other. And the variety of questions argued is no less remarkable than their number. In Mattis vs. Robinson, the law of landlord and tenant was discussed; The City of Brownville vs. Middleton, and Miller vs. Finn, involved important questions of practice; Smiley vs. Sampson, and Towsley vs. Johnson, were cases in which the laws of the United States relative to preemptions were passed upon; Bradshaw vs. The City of Omaha, Poland vs. O'Connor, Sands vs. Smith, The Columbus Company vs. Hurford and McAusland vs. Pundt required the investigation and decision of multifarious questions relating to contracts, real estate agency, specific performance, practice, taxation, constitutional interpretation and others; in all of which Mr. Woolworth's ability, learning and close study are conspicuous.

Still more convincing evidence of his industry and thoroughness is to be found in the report of the United States Supreme Court for the past twenty-five years. To the bar of that court he was admitted in 1862, and since that time has argued more cases before it than any other counsel west of Chicago. Some of the leading ones, involving questions of first impression, are as follows: Sampson vs. Smiley, 13 Wallace, 91; Johnson vs. Towsley, 13 Wallace, 72.

both on the law of the public lands, Flagstaff Mining Company vs Tarbet, 98 United States, 463, on the law of mines and the location of mining claims, Union Pacific Railroad vs Durant, 95 United States, 576, on the law of trusts and the fiduciary relations of corporation officers, Wardell vs Union Pacific Railroad, 103 United States 651, on the same subject, Walden vs Knevals, 114 United States, 373, on the law of land grants to railroad company, Union Pacific Railway vs Penniston, 18 Wallace, 5, on the taxation of road-bed of company, Hunnewell vs B & M, 22 Wallace, 465, on taxation of lands granted by United States to aid construction of railroads; United States vs B & M., 98 United States, 334, constructing grants to railroads, Union Gold Mining Company vs Rocky Mountain National Bank, 96 United States, 640, on the corporate powers of national banks, Lamasters vs Keeler, 123 United States, 376 on the extent to which state laws are adapted into the practice of the federal court

The great diversity of his professional engagements is shown by a singular circumstance Within a period of ten days he argued before the Supreme Court at Washington the case of the Union Pacific Railroad Company against Penniston, before the United States circuit court at Omaha the case of Hunnewell vs the Burlington Railroad Company, and of Wade vs the Omaha Hotel Company, and before the territorial court of Utah at Salt Lake the case of Davis vs the Flagstaff Mining Company

A life of such laborious effort will never be complete and healthy without abundant recreation. This Mr Woolworth finds first, in literary studies and pursuits, and second, in his thorough devotion to the Episcopal Church Chancellor of the diocese of Nebraska, for nearly thirty years a vestryman of Trinity, a lay delegate to the general convention of the church member of the committee on revision of the liturgy, he is, by common consent, the most influential and useful layman that that church possesses in Nebraska Mr Woolworth was chosen in the vestry of Trinity Church at its first Easter election in 1857, and with brief intervals remained a member of it until the summer of 1885, when he resigned For seventeen years of this time he was its senior warden, and took upon himself the active care of its affairs. During his term of service the parish was erected into a cathedral, the principles and the details of the larger organization having been formulated by him

He has been greatly consulted by the bishops of other dioceses in the organization of their cathedrals During his service as senior warden of Trinity, the present cathedral structure was erected. He had more to do with the work than any other person Every one of the beautiful articles of furniture with which the church is filled were designed by the architect under his eye, and many of their striking features were his suggestions He and his immediate family contributed to it a number of beautiful memorials He erected the altar and reredos to the memory of his first wife The panels of the altar are five in number and are filled with bas-reliefs in bronze, illustrative of scenes in our Lord's life The bishop's throne and the annexed stalls, and the dean's and canon's stalls, were gifts of members of his family.

His work on "The Cathedral in America" is a charming contribution to a subject but little understood outside of the pale of the church, and his occasional addresses upon matters of Episcopal polity are replete with profound learning and interesting information. His addresses, essays and lectures upon general subjects have been very numerous Beginning in 1856 with a hand-book of Nebraska territory his last work was an address before the American Bar Association, at its annual meeting in Saratoga, in 1888, when he chose for his theme, "Jurisprudence Considered as a Branch of the Social Science" Between these dates he has written, compiled and published books and articles upon many topics Among these may be mentioned the first two volumes of " Nebraska State Reports," a volume of "Circuit Court Reports of the Eighth Judicial Circuit of the United States," addresses before the State University, the Bar Association of Nebraska, before the Nebraska State Historical Society, on "The Philosophy of Emigration," before his alma mater, Hamilton College, before the Iowa University Law School, the Iowa State Bar Association and at the commencement of Hobart College.

In the year 1875, Racine College conferred upon Mr. Woolworth the degree of LL D., and in 1892 the University of Nebraska conferred upon him that of LL. D. His style is concise, scholarly and polished in a high degree. His arguments in equity cases and before appellate tribunals are marked by profound learning, extensive research and logical arrangement rarely surpassed by counsel. Books are his delight; his law library is extensive, and especially rich in the works of English authors and reporters, while his collection of miscellaneous books comprises many rare editions, illustrated treasures, splendidly bound copies of English and American classics. His extensive practice in cases involving immense property interests, with corresponding emoluments, together with the rise in value of Omaha real estate, has assured to him a comfortable fortune, which his generous mode of living and his profuse benefactions to charitable objects have never been able to seriously impair. He has been twice married—his first wife having been Miss Helen M. Beggs, of Syracuse, New York, and his second, who still graces his home, Miss Elizabeth S. Butterfield, of Omaha. Of these unions three children survive. His large practice and engrossing cares have not debarred him from the enjoyment of cultured society. In his elegant residence on St. Mary's Avenue he has long exercised and still indulges a refined hospitality, which is alike alluring to the transient guest and to those who enjoy the privilege of his constant companionship. He enjoys the early history of Nebraska. In the hall of his residence is a large mantel made of brick, stone and wood taken from public buildings, all long since extinct, which were built before or shortly after the territory was organized.

# CHAPTER LVII.

JAMES WOODRUFF SAVAGE—HIS EARLY LIFE AND SUBSEQUENT CAREER—HIS DEATH IN OMAHA—TRIBUTES OF RESPECT TO HIS MEMORY

The subject of this sketch comes of a distinguished historical family. The name was brought to this country by his paternal ancestor, Thomas Savage, who landed from England in 1630, and afterwards married Faith, daughter of Anne Hutchinson. The life of this woman is familiar to every reader of colonial history. She was the famous religious enthusiast who founded the Antinomian sect, of New England. On her mother's side she was a second cousin of the poet, Dryden. In 1634, she came to Boston, Mass., to enjoy the preaching of John Cotton. Here she instituted meetings of women for the discussion of doctrinal questions, and her influence created a powerful faction and led to public disturbances. She was banished to Rhode Island, and afterwards removed to New Amsterdam, where she was murdered by the Indians, in 1643. Very eminent men of that day, among them Sir Henry Vane and John Cotton, were favorably inclined to her doctrine.

We have not space to trace the descent of the name through generations always distinguished in the annals of New England. The father of our subject was Rev. Thomas Savage, a minister of the Presbyterian denomination, who died in Bedford, N. H., in 1866, having been pastor of the church in that place for forty years.

James Woodruff Savage was born February 2, 1826, in Bedford, N. H. His early life was passed in a farming community. Its quiet and simple conditions were favorable to the formation of an ingenuous character. At the same time they were not rude. In the home of his youth there were the gravity of a minister's household, the sober faith and devout life of Christian parents, and the books and the learning and the culture of educated, gentle people. The seeds then planted have borne good fruit.

In September, 1841, the young man entered the Phillips Andover Academy, and after having been well taught at home, he began his preparation for college. In August, 1843, he entered Harvard, graduating with the degree of Bachelor of Arts, in 1847. His rank was seventh in his class. The triennial catalogue of Harvard University bears the names of fourteen of his family.

Immediately after his graduation, Mr. Savage went to St. Simons Island, which lies just off the coast of Glynn County, in Georgia, and which belongs, in large part, to the estate of T. Butler King, then a representative in congress. He was private tutor to the children of this distinguished man until July, 1848, when he returned to the North. In September of that year, he was entered a student-at-law in the office of Origen S. Seymour, at Litchfield, in Connecticut, who was his relative. At that time, Mr. Seymour was a distinguished lawyer, in large practice. He was afterwards governor and a judge of the Supreme Court of Connecticut, and took an active part in politics, as a Democrat. In order to support himself while prosecuting his law studies, in the winter of 1848-49, Mr. Savage taught a private school. In October, of the next year, he removed to New York City, where he continued his studies, in the office of George Wood. This gentleman was, at that time, at the head of the bar of the State of New York. His name may be seen very often in the State and Federal Reports, as counsel in the greatest causes.

On the 12th of February, 1850, Mr. Savage was admitted to the bar in New York City, and entered the office of his cousin, Lewis B. Woodruff, as managing clerk. Mr. Woodruff, at that time, held high rank in the profession, and his office was full of heavy business. He was a most amiable gentleman, and took a deep and affectionate interest in his young kinsman. In 1850, he was elected judge of the Superior Court of New York, and, in 1866, was promoted to a seat on the bench of the court of appeals, from which position he was removed to the office of circuit judge of the United States for the second circuit. The exclamation is natural: How fortunate were the circumstances of the early life of Mr. Savage! Above all, he had before his eyes the example of eminent lawyers and the best men, and he felt in great measure the influence of the highest professional character.

When Judge Woodruff entered upon his most useful and distinguished judicial career, his clerk commenced the practice of his profession for himself, and continued at the bar of New York City until the breaking out of the war, in 1861. It was no mean sacrifice he felt himself called upon to make for his country. He had good reason to hope for professional success in the great city, for he enjoyed associations and connections sure to bring him many and valuable engagements. Nor did he feel the assurance of high rank in the army, which stimulated the ambition of many young men. Reared in the school of the best Democrats, he valued far more than his own interests the Union which Andrew Jackson, in another juncture, had declared "must and shall be preserved." It is a part of the unwritten— the silent history of those days of doubt, that the fervor of patriotic emotion and the spirit of self-sacrifice animated the youth of the country.

On the 21st of July, 1861, Mr. Savage was commissioned a captain in the regular army, and assigned as aid-de-camp to the staff of General Fremont, and in the October following he was promoted to be major. In March, 1862, he was commissioned a lieutenant-colonel. In December, 1863, he resigned his commission in the regular army, and was mustered in as colonel of the 12th N. Y. Vol. Cav. He served until the close of hostilities, and on the 5th of August, 1865, was mustered out with his regiment.

Surely that is a happy country which can fill the ranks of her army with men of education and spirit, who will not lay down the sword until her cause is won and her honor vindicated. As long as she has such sons, however dark the clouds, the glory of the day is sure.

After retiring from military service, Colonel Savage spent a year in travel. In the spring of 1867, just after Nebraska had been admitted to the Union, he removed to Omaha, reaching this city on the 18th of April, and resumed the practice of his profession. He was, at that time, well-knit, vigorous, of dignified mien and gentle manner; a bright spirit and a kindly speech were his, so that at once friends gathered around him, and through all the years and contentions which afterward passed, he held them to him.

Colonel Savage at once took a high rank at the bar, many of whose members have attained enviable places in the country. In 1869, he became associated in practice with Charles F. Manderson, now United States Senator from Nebraska, under the style of Savage & Manderson.

The public esteem in which he was held is shown by the repeated calls of his fellow citizens for his services. In 1870, he received the nomination of the Democratic party for member of congress, but was defeated by Lorenzo Crounse. In 1873, the legislature elected him regent of the State University, which office he held until it was made elective by the constitution of 1875.

In November, 1875, he was elected judge of the third judicial district, and in 1879, was re-elected to the same office for another term. The district was largely Republican, and his election both times by large majorities bears emphatic testimony to the esteem in which he was held, and the value of his judicial services. He had the best qualities of a good judge—a vigorous administration, conscientious impartiality, a quick apprehension and a strong, native sense of justice. The business of his district very largely exceeded that of any other in the State; but fewer of his judgments were carried to the supreme court for review than those of any other judge. That court seldom reversed him. The severities of his office compelled him to resign it before the expiration of his term, his health having become seriously impaired.

In 1883, he resumed the practice of the law. With great experience, he was able to bring into the service of his large clientage wisdom, skill and abundant learning.

A vacancy occurred at this time in the chancellorship of the State University. The position was offered to Judge Savage, and the friends of the institution pressed upon him the acceptance of it, with great urgency. They felt that he had the wisdom to guide it through the troubles which then surrounded it, and bring it to that measure of success and service which other western state universities enjoy Nor did he in any measure underrate the dignity tendered him, nor what a fit man could do in it, but, greatly to the disappointment of all who hoped for good things of the young institution, he felt himself constrained to decline the honor.

At the November election, 1883, he was a candidate for judge of the supreme court, on the Democratic ticket, but was defeated by 4,250 votes, when the Republican majority in the State was five times that number He was, at his decease, one of the trustees of the Omaha Public Library, and had been since 1881 He was also a trustee of Bellevue College In July, 1885, President Cleveland appointed him a government director of the Union Pacific Railway Company, and reappointed him each year until the date of his death *

In April, 1875, he was married to Mrs Lucy T Morris, daughter of Alanson Tucker, Esq, of Derry, N H, a most intelligent and estimable lady, and an ornament to the best society of Omaha

Judge Savage, at the time of his decease, was president of the Omaha Club president of the State Historical Society, and corresponding member of the historical societies of New Hampshire, Wisconsin and Missouri For the last few years of his life, he devoted much of his time to literary pursuits and travel. He was a close student of Shakespeare, and possessed a Shakespearian library of many volumes He was also a lover of local history, writing considerable concerning the early history of the West

He died in Omaha, on the 22d of November, 1890, being, at the time, senior member of the law firm of Savage, Morris & Davis

The funeral of Judge Savage was held at his residence in Omaha, Tuesday, November 25th, under the supervision of the Loyal Legion, he having been its first commander, and was one of its charter members By an order of the department commander, the comrades of the Grand Army of the Republic were invited to be present "at the funeral exercises of past department commander and comrade, James W Savage" There

was a very large attendance of friends of the deceased, and representatives of societies, orders and associations, of which he had been a member Addresses were made by Rev Dr N M Mann, of the Unitarian Church, and Rev Wm J Harsha, of the First Presbyterian Church His remains repose in Forest Lawn Cemetery

In the federal court, C S Montgomery announced the death of Judge Savage, November 24, two days after his decease, and on the next day, a committee to draft resolutions concerning his life and character was appointed by Judge Dundy On the day first named, Judge Wakeley, of the district court, also appointed a committee to report similar resolutions, and the Bar Association, at the same time, met to memorialize his death

At the memorial meeting of the Douglas County bar, held December 6, addresses were delivered by Judge Wakeley, George W Ambrose, John D Howe, Leavitt Burnham, Henry D Estabrook, Arthur C Wakeley, W F Gurley, C. F Breckenridge, J T Moriarty, R W Breckenridge, C J Greene, Howard B Smith, W D Beckett, and Moses P O'Brien Two days after, in the federal court, remarks were made concerning the death of Judge Savage, by E B Bartlett At the Bar Association, on December 11, memorial addresses were delivered by C H Marple, J J Points and E R French An address was delivered also at the meeting of the Omaha Club, on the 28th of the previous month, by Joseph R Clarkson At the meeting of the directors of the Union Pacific Railway Company, held in Boston, November 26, 1890, President Adams announced the death of "Government Director James W Savage," in most feeling and appreciative remarks

Soon after Judge Savage's decease, the trustees of Bellevue College met and passed the following resolutions

"WHEREAS, It hath pleased Almighty God to remove from us the Hon James W Savage, who for years has been a trustee of Bellevue College, be it by us

"*Resolved,* That we place upon record our appreciation of his uniform interest and faithfulness in the discharge of his duties as a member of this board his constant courtesy, his valuable advice, and his ready liberality

"*Resolved,* That we have this action spread

* *Magazine of Western History,* Vol IX, p 295

upon our minutes, and that we furnish the same for publication in the Omaha daily papers."

The Omaha Public Library was ordered closed from 12 M. to 6 P. M., on Tuesday, November 25, 1890, the day of the funeral, and the directors passed these resolutions:

"The directors of the Omaha Public Library, in expressing their deep sorrow on account of the death of the Hon. James W. Savage, wish to show their high esteem for his rectitude of purpose, faithfulness to duty and kindly disposition, not only in all the relations of life, but especially in the discharge of all the labors pertaining to the work of our board. His enlightened and enthusiastic interest in the library work during a long period as a director, and including nine years' service as our president, has created a debt of gratitude which this community can never discharge; therefore, be it

"*Resolved*, That we hereby testify to his worth as a citizen, a neighbor, a friend, and as a member of this board, and we tender to his relatives our heartfelt sympathy; and, further, that, as a testimony of our appreciation, it is ordered that his portrait be procured and hung in the library, to the end that all may bear witness to our appreciation."

The memorial meeting of the Douglas County bar was held December 6, 1890, with Judges Wakeley, Hopewell, Tiffany and Doane on the bench. The following memorial was presented by Geo. E. Pritchett, chairman of the committee on resolutions:

"*Resolved*, That the members of the bar of Douglas County have heard with deep regret and universal sorrow of the death of James W. Savage. Identified with the administration of justice in this county for more than twenty years, he attained a position at this bar equalled by few. He was an able, learned and honorable member of the profession. His efforts were always to uphold its dignity and character, and no unworthy act could ever be charged to him in his long professional career of ever increasing honor and usefulness. His high place at the bar was obtained by the exhibition of the highest qualities of the heart and mind. In addition to his high legal attainments, he was a polished, cultured gentleman. No man came in contact with him without respecting him.

"As a judge of this court, he exhibited traits of character peculiarly fitting him for the position. Absolute integrity of purpose, a calm and dispassionate temper, great good sense and sound judgment, which, with a thorough knowledge of the law, made him a model judge.

"As a citizen, he was generous and manly, imbued with a lofty sense of honor and great dignity of character. He was as gentle in manner as he was resolute in purpose; the delight of friends, and a most welcome guest in every social gathering. His friendship was true and lasting and greatly valued by those who possessed it. He had the confidence of the people to a degree seldom attained by any man, and he discharged the duties of the many public offices which he held, with credit to himself and with satisfaction to all.

"*Resolved*, That in the death of James W. Savage this bar has lost an eminent and beloved member of this city and State, and an upright and distinguished citizen.

"*Resolved*, That we tender to the family of the deceased our heartfelt sympathy.

"*Resolved*, That these resolutions be presented to the court, with the request that they be entered upon its minutes, and a copy sent to the family of the deceased."

Said J. L. Webster, before the Bar Association, December 11, 1890:

"The Hon. James W. Savage has been disrobed of worldly life. He has become clothed with the mystic garb of immortality. His memory is dear to our affections. His character commanded our respect. His kindness secured our gratitude. His career, public and private, won our intense regard. His learning and ability challenged our admiration. He came from an ancestry historically noted in colonial times. They held distinguished place in the annals of New England. He never lowered that standard of honor and respectability.

"His youth was spent amid the hills of New Hampshire, where he acquired a sturdy and honest character, that never lessened but increased with the moving on of years. The teachings of Harvard College rounded out his early scholarship, and laid the foundation for the high literary culture and refinement that graced his after life.

"His patriotism was strong and decided. His military career, as captain and major on the staff of General Fremont—and later as colonel of the 12th New York Cavalry—was brave and distinguished If his deeds in war are not commemorated, it is only because the military exploits of so large a number of men, not less glorious, were merged in that great national achievement, so that lasting fame came only to the great leaders

"Ripened and experienced, he came to this city twenty years ago, and at once took high rank among the lawyers of this his adopted State He was a lawyer of more than ordinary talent When he addressed a court or jury, he always merited and commanded attention His energy ot manner and eloquence of speech were elements of power

"He was elected to judgeship by such a vote as told the esteem in which he was held by the people He filled the high position with becoming decorum and superior dignity When he resigned the office by reason of failing health and to seek the repose of a quiet life, it was with the regrets of an admiring constituency

"Other honors came upon him, but they were unsolicited His aspirations were high and noble, yet not controlled by selfish ambition He has left upon us a strong and lasting impression of his personality and character It was frequently said of him that he was one of God's noblemen

"His social life was without a stain His society was a delight His manners were winning and his conversation a charm We shall indulge in recollections of him because we knew him, heard him, saw him and lived with him

"As he lived beloved by all our people, we shall revere and cherish his memory Moved, as we are, by a deep and profound sensibility of his worth, we make this record of our faith in the character and manhood of the late lamented James Woodruff Savage"

The *Omaha Mercury*, of December 19, 1890, paid the deceased this tribute of respect

"Men die gloriously on the field of battle, where valorous deeds are brought into momentary relief by an advantageous background, but the glory is no less when it attaches to the death of one who has lived uprightly and conscientiously all his life, devoting that life to the attainment of what is highest and best Judge Savage was a master builder of character So assiduously had he applied himself, so symmetrically had he wrought, that he had reared a temple beautiful that was perpetually illuminated by the soul-light within He measured life by its depth, not by its extension in time With him, achievements were valued only as they augmented moral and intellectual force His rounded life touched humanity at every point, and with a quickening power'

Of the deceased, it may be recorded as has been previously of another

'He is gone from us We have laid him in the solemn calm of the grave In the springtime the melody of the birdsong and the perfume of flowers will environ it, the winter's winds will shriek above it, at night the stars will shine upon it and the nights that are starless shall shroud it in blackness Surviving affection will rear a sculptured column over it but the enduring marble itself shall crumble and decay ere his name, fame and good deeds among us shall fade from memory"

The following lines on the death of Judge Savage were written by B F Cochran

> In the sweet calm twilight
> Of a life well spent,
> Came the expected words—
> Fold thy earthly tent'
>
> Here let the record close
> It is adjudged complete—
> Of kindness failing not,
> E en in discussion's heat
>
> Of a lofty standard
> Long upborne and well,
> In war in peace in camp,
> In court, at duty's call
>
> Through a rift in the cloud of death
> Shone heaven's golden light,
> And glorified the life
> Of him who loved the right

NOTE.—The publishers, in adding the above chapter to the History of Omaha, are actuated by a desire to perpetuate in durable form, the memory of one whose life was so replete with all that constitutes the glory of our best American citizenship.

> "For still the beauty of that life
> Shines star-like on our way
> And breathes its calm amid the strife'
> And burden of to-day'

Exchange Building, Union Stock Yards, 1900.

# HISTORY OF SOUTH OMAHA.

## CHAPTER I.

### ORIGIN AND OPENING OF THE UNION STOCK YARDS

Ten years ago—that is, on the first day of January, 1883—who, of all those having the highest hopes for the future of Omaha dreamed that to the southward and southwestward, just beyond what was then its boundary lines, in the open country, where farm houses were thinly scattered over the prairie, and cornfields were plentiful, there would spring into existence, in this decade, a city of the size and importance of the one we now see — the city of South Omaha?*

To understand fully how this transformation has been brought about, an inquiry must first be instituted into the origin of the movement that led to such results The topography of this region played not a little part in the inception of the city The surface is high and rolling, the ground sloping towards the Missouri River, which washes the eastern limits of its site There is also a valley running along from northwest to southeast, through its center These topographical features make the drainage perfect Contiguity, however, to Omaha—with its financial resources, its business facilities and its railroad connections—was the more important consideration, inducing the selection of the site But a glance at what had already been accomplished in the formation of stockyards and the building of packing houses, in the City of Omaha, is important just here, to the end that the entire influences and necessities causing a change of base, may be fairly and distinctly understood

It was in 1876, that John A Smiley, of Omaha, organized, in that city, the Union Stock Yards Company, for the avowed purpose of erecting stockyards therein, or contiguous thereto A deed was made out of a valuable eighty-acre tract of land owned by him, and lying just north of the then corporate limits of Omaha. This deed was to be held until the organization of the company was perfected, when it was to be turned over to it A considerable amount of lumber, posts, and other material was purchased and shipped to Omaha, to aid the undertaking, and Philip Armour, of Chicago, and other capitalists of that city, became interested (but not pecuniarily) in the enterprise. They signified their willingness to take hold of the matter, provided the Board of Trade of Omaha, would endorse the project That body, however, declined any official aid, and the whole scheme was abandoned

"As early as 1877, the live stock committee of the Omaha Board of Trade (which Board had a few months before been organized) reported that it was impressed with the very generally expressed views of not only the business men of Omaha but of the stock raisers and shippers themselves, north, south, and west, of the importance and necessity of erecting and maintaining extensive stock yards and packing and slaughtering houses in this city [Omaha].'"

"' We have sufficient assurances,' continues the report, 'from our own personal observation as well as the opinions of live-stock men, packers and dealers interested in securing the best market for their products, that Omaha is destined to become the principal market west of Chicago for the sale of cattle, sheep and hogs'

"Then the committee further declared: 'The wealth of Nebraska, Wyoming, Dakota [North and South], Montana, Idaho, Oregon, Nevada, Utah, Colorado, and Kansas, consists, in the extent and magnificence

---

* See an *Historical Review of So Omaha* (by the author of this history), in *The Drovers Journal* of December 31, 1892

of the nutritious beef-producing grasses, the excellence of the climate, and facilities offered by a direct route of transportation to market. In the country north and south of the Union Pacific Road and its branches, it is estimated that 5,000,000 cattle can be sustained and prepared for market without difficulty, at an average expense, at present, of one dollar per head per annum each season. The drive from the Southwest is extending farther north, until, within a very short period, instead of being at the extreme northern limits, Omaha will be in the center of the great stock-growing region of the West.'

"And the committee also reported that its members had waited upon Jay Gould and Sidney Dillon, of the Union Pacific Railway, to secure the necessary franchise and privileges for the erection and maintenance of stock yards on a scale commensurate with the magnitude and growing importance of the cattle trade of Omaha. Fair promises were made, verbal pledges were given, and high hopes were raised in the minds of those interested in live stock; but 'the magnificent stock yards' did not materialize."*

The Omaha Stock Yards Company was organized on the twenty-seventh of April, 1878, its articles of incorporation being filed at three o'clock on that day, and signed by A. P. Nicholas, H. K. Smith, S. R. Johnson, J. F. Sheely, C. F. Goodman, and E. Estabrook, the first two holding 115 shares, each, of stock, the others five shares each. Another company was organized on the same day, under the same name, by J. L. Lovett, W. J. Broatch, and W. C. B. Allen; but, as they did not get their articles of incorporation on file until 4:30 P. M., the "Nicholas Company" secured the name, and the others abandoned their enterprise. On the fourth of May, following, the Union Stock Yards Company (taking the same name, it will be noticed, as the one proposed by Mr. Smiley), was organized in Omaha, by William A. Paxton, J. L. Lovett, W. J. Broatch, W. C. B. Allen, and Herman Kountze. Mr. Nicholas had previously arranged for a lease, for the term of four years, at an annual rental of about $600 a year, of a forty-acre tract of land, owned by the Union Pacific Railroad Company, just outside the city limits

*The Drovers Journal, December 31, 1892.

to the southwest, and about evenly divided by their track. Some ten acres of this ground was occupied for right-of-way and other purposes by the Railroad Company, which left thirty acres for use by the "Nicholas Company." But the yards proper were located immediately north of Wilcox' first addition to Omaha, on lot seven, lying immediately east of the railroad track and along the west side of Twenty-fourth Street. The "Nicholas Company" was to have the privilege of purchase at the termination of the lease, at the price paid by the railroad company, with ten per cent. added, this making the price about $300 an acre. [It is now (1893) worth $10,000 an acre]. But the "Paxton Company" also insisted upon having the privilege of occupying the tract, and the result was, a portion north of the railroad track was leased to that organization, and the remainder to the "Nicholas Company."

Both companies put up yards and established facilities for doing business on as extensive scale as was possible under the circumstances. In the winter of 1879 and 1880, the Union Stock Yards (the "Paxton") Company moved their business over to the Iowa side of the Missouri River. In May, of the year last mentioned, Mr. Nicholas turned his yards over to the Union Pacific Railroad Company, at a loss of sixty per cent. on his investment. These yards—usually known as the "Upper Stock Yards"—were occupied only about four years longer.

There were also other stock yards in Omaha: These were known as the "Bridge Stock Yards," and were located on the north side of the Union Pacific Railway track, nearly half a mile east of the depot of that road. They belonged to the Union Pacific Railway Company and were operated by them for the purpose of facilitating the shipment of live stock. They were vacated in 1886.

For a number of years there were incidents, events, happenings—there were reasonings, guesses, prophesyings and theories—there were, at last, firm and courageous resolves, which were to change even "the face of nature," as it appeared smiling to the southward and almost adjoining the city of Omaha. And these forecasts, these ventures, these risks, took a practical turn for the first time in 1883, when men who were ready and willing to venture upon an undertaking which seemed extra hazardous to many—who were not averse to investing largely not upon belief merely but upon then firm conviction —fixed upon the farming lands there for a "plant" (we shall see how soon it became one of sturdy growth), and gave to it not only a name but a prestige of greatness, which still excites our astonishment It is unnecessary now to mention the names of those who took an interest in the scheme; we may say, however, they were largely citizens of Omaha  The prime idea was, first, stock yards and slaughtering and packing houses; second, the laying out of a town at (or surrounding) these industries, but the two, it had already been determined, should be each an enterprise by itself, each one was to have a distinct organization—distinct officers—distinct regulations—and, in all respects, each was to control its own affairs, but it was expected the packing house interests would soon be given to others

The men who, in 1883, were interested in this gigantic undertaking, did not rush headlong into the enterprise  They took time to "post" themselves as to the movement of stock in the West  They had before them tabulated statements of live stock shipments (in car loads) over the Union and Kansas divisions of the Union Pacific railroad, also over the Burlington & Missouri River Railroad, during the years 1880, 1881 and 1882

(I) Union Pacific—Union Division

| Year | Horses | Cattle | Sheep | Hogs |
|---|---|---|---|---|
| 1880 | 612 | 7,791 | 264 | 1,606 |
| 1881 | 540 | 10 195 | 683 | 3,773 |
| 1882 | 611 | 9,833 | 922 | 3,518 |

Union Pacific—Kansas Division

| Year | Horses | Cattle | Sheep | Hogs |
|---|---|---|---|---|
| 1880 | 402 | 2,162 | 234 | 1,004 |
| 1881 | 295 | 2,737 | 184 | 2,857 |
| 1882 | 208 | 2,288 | 143 | 1 644 |

(II) Stock shipped over the B & M R R. R during the years mentioned below in car lots

| Year | Horses | Cattle | Sheep | Hogs |
|---|---|---|---|---|
| 1880 | 171 | 3 246 | 177 | 5,716 |
| 1881 | 127 | 3,710 | 314 | 6,452 |
| 1882 | 188 | 3,435 | 663 | 5,388 |

Upon these figures as a basis, it was decided that such a business as this, with its prospective increase, was a sufficient reason for undertaking the building of stock yards and packing houses on a large scale near Omaha  And this is the way they worked themselves into a conviction that prompted them to invest heavily in the undertaking.

"Omaha now is to Nebraska and the country beyond, what Chicago was to Illinois and the Great West when that city was the present size of Omaha  It is a natural law of trade that live stock will seek the nearest market, other things being equal  The creation of a market rests in a great degree with the men who have interested themselves in the stock yards, rendering such a neutral ground, where the owners of live stock may have honest, fair and proper dealings, and who are better able to support and build up such a market where they think proper, than with the foreign capitalists who now control fifteen millions of dollars in cattle on the western ranges  Is it not then interest to maintain a competing point or market on the line of the national highway whose most vital interests are identical with such an undertaking and with such decided advantages as Omaha offers? Not only must these men have a place to feed cattle, but they must have large slaughter and packing houses which are to be, and must be independent of the stock yards, where no collusion can even appear upon its face  Such is their intention, and the scheme will be carried out on the scale commensurate with their vast resources  This will in a few years render Omaha one of the largest live stock centers in the United States"

The judgment of these men was backed up by the opinion of others, who had carefully considered the subject. On November 27, 1883, Thomas L Kimball, then Assistant General Manager of the Union Pacific railway, writing from Omaha, said "On the subject of beef slaughtering and packing houses at Omaha, I have to say that it may not be out of place in this connection for me to state some of the considerations, which seem to us patent, why Omaha should be selected as the point for establishing such enterprises. Slaughtering and packing is a business which, besides calling for skilled labor and a large force of men, requires, when carried on extensively, the employment of a large capital in permanent improvement  It is therefore manifestly desirable to locate where the men can be employed, as nearly as possible, all the year round.  Here, during the months when grass-fed cattle are fat enough for beef, that class of stock could be slaughtered, and during the remainder of the year the business could be run on corn-fed cattle. The establishment of such an enterprise in Omaha would result in the shipment of Nebraska and, to some extent, Iowa corn-producing localities, of large numbers of cattle, about three years old, which had been raised to that age on western grass, for feeding a few months on corn. Corn can be had in this section of the country as abundantly and cheaply as in any part of the world; in fact, I think it no exaggeration to say that corn can be obtained here more abundantly and cheaper than elsewhere.

"By this process of corn feeding, several hundred pounds can readily be added to the weight of each animal, bringing it into prime condition for the supply of Omaha slaughtering all the year. The successful slaughtering of Kansas City furnishes us the proof of this proposition, inasmuch as that city sustains the same relations to the corn producing states of Kansas and Western Missouri, as Omaha to Nebraska and Western Iowa. No enterprise of this sort can be made equally profitable if located upon the Northern Pacific, as that line lies outside of the corn belt. Formerly there would have been an objection to this location as compared with Council Bluffs or some points on the east side of the Missouri River, on account of the arbitrary tolls charged by all bridges over that stream, but it has now become the established policy of the Iowa railways to maintain the same rates between the East and Council Bluffs and Omaha, so that it will cost no more for the shipment of the product from Omaha than from Council Bluffs. The existence of six strong eastern lines centering at this point and competing for the business of Omaha, gives all the assurance necessary that the business located here will at all times secure as favorable freight rates as may obtain at any other point in the Missouri Valley.'"

It did not require a very lengthy consideration by those determined to venture upon the experiment of establishing stock yards and packing houses near Omaha, on a scale commensurate with their ideas of what the undertaking would need, to determine upon a site for a plant and for a town as well. Simultaneously, and before any capital had been pledged for the purpose, at least two enterprising men had, without each other's knowledge, looked with "longing eyes" upon the open country immediately south of Omaha, believing it to be the point of all others suited to the purpose. And there, it may be premised, in 1884, stock yards were commenced; there afterwards, a town was platted; and there, subsequently, packing houses were established; the place, as a whole, having as early as 1883, been named by the parties most interested, "SOUTH OMAHA."* But we anticipate.

In the fall of 1882, Alexander H. Swan, an extensive cattle owner in Wyoming, decided, if possible, to establish large stock yards at or near Omaha. There was, in his mind, no doubt of the propriety of such an undertaking when viewed from a financial standpoint; and he at once proceeded to act upon his convictions. His plan was confided to Leverett M. Anderson,† who seconded, with zeal, the undertaking. The first preliminaries were arranged through a correspondence between the two. The infant plan was to secure about two hundred acres of land immediately south of the city, at what was then known as "the Summit," on which to build, not only stock yards, but packing houses and canning establishments. But soon the ideas of these men changed as to the purchase of two hundred acres; for, in May, 1883, arrangements were completed between them whereby Anderson was authorized to contract for—or rather, to secure options upon—more than eighteen hundred acres, embracing a large part of the area now constituting the City of South Omaha. Associated with him in this work was C. R. Schaller.

The land wanted, included a number of farms lying south and southwest of Omaha. The negotiations with these farmers were, necessarily, conducted with much caution, as publicity would have prevented the perfecting of the scheme. Several months were spent in details.

The farmers and other owners of this land, mostly in that part of Douglas precinct now included within the corporate limits of South Omaha, did not part with their possessions for a song. Smooth-tongued agents were not able to convince them that a good, sound price—such a price as farms well cultivated as theirs might bring if wanted by cultivators of the soil, adding to it a fair

---

*The Drovers Journal, December 31, 1892.
†Now (January, 1893) living at 1919 Burt Street, Omaha.

amount for the fact of nearness of location to Omaha—ought to be all they could reasonably ask Most (if not all) of them saw their opportunity and profited by it

By the middle of August, eighteen hundred and seventy-five acres and a fraction had been secured, for which a total price of $312,972 73 was subsequently paid—an average of $167 an acre, nearly *

So far, Mr Anderson had put up all the money—over ten thousand dollars—and assumed all liabilities, but soon Mr Swan came to the rescue, aided by a number of Omaha capitalists whom he had interested in the undertaking—prominent among them being William A Paxton,† already mentioned, and in a short time over forty thousand dollars had been paid on the various contracts with the farmers "Surely men who could pledge themselves to an outlay of so many thousands of dollars on an experiment (if experiment it was) were men who had the 'courage of their convictions.' It is just such men as these, who have followed on in the course of empire westward, and have made the West—'the vast, illimitable, changing West!'—what it is to-day"‡

Growing out of these preliminary movements was the formation of two companies, in all respects legally distinct from each other, one of which, "The Union Stock Yards Company of Omaha (Limited)," was organized in Omaha, December 1, 1883, for the purpose of establishing stock yards, such as it was thought would, in the end, answer all the needs of the market at this point, however much the business might increase

The articles of incorporation of this new stock yards company asserted, among other things "That we, Alexander H Swan, William A Paxton, John A Creighton, Peter E Iler, John A McShane, Thomas Swobe and Frank Murphy, have associated ourselves together for the purpose of being incorporated under the laws of the State of Nebraska —that is to say, subdivision entitled 'corporations' of chapter entitled 'corporations,' being chapter sixteen of the Compiled Statutes of Nebraska of 1881, and, for the purpose aforesaid, we have adopted the following articles of association First The name of this corporation shall be 'Union Stock Yards Company of Omaha (Limited).' Second The principal place of transacting the business of this corporation shall be the City of Omaha, in the County of Douglas and State of Nebraska Third. The general nature of the business to be transacted by said corporation shall be the purchase and sale, the feeding and caring for, slaughtering, dressing, packing and holding for sale, selling, and selling for others, of live stock, including cattle, hogs, sheep and horses, and shipping by refrigerator cars and otherwise, of meats and the product thereof, and doing generally the business of a stock yards and whatever is incident or in anywise related to or usually connected therewith"

The capital stock was fixed at one million dollars, which could be increased by vote of the stockholders. Business was to commence when seven hundred thousand dollars of stock had been subscribed, and as that amount was already taken it was stipulated that operations were to commence on that day (December 1, 1883) and continue until the first day of December, 1950, a period of sixty-seven years The stock was divided into shares of one hundred dollars each There were twenty-eight subscribers nine of whom held 400 shares each, $360,000, one of whom held 300 shares, $30,000, one of whom held 250 shares, $25,000, ten of whom held 200 shares each, $200,000, three of whom held 150 shares each, $45,000, five of whom held 100 shares each, $40,000 Total, twenty-eight subscribers, 7,000 shares, $700,000 *

The company immediately organized, by the election of W A Paxton, president, Alexander H Swan, vice-president, John H Donnelly, secretary, James M Woolworth, attorney The board of directors consisted of W A Paxton, A. H. Swan, Frank Murphy, B F Smith, P E Iler, John A McShane and Thomas Swobe At the election of officers for the company the next year, the following persons were chosen A H Swan, president, M A Upton, secretary;

---

*See post, Chapter III

†" In December [November], 1883, Mr Swan made overtures to William A Paxton with a view of getting him and his friends in Omaha, interested in the scheme At that time, Mr Paxton was interested in the stock yards at Council Bluffs After carefully considering the matter he concluded to go into the South Omaha enterprise and at the same time induce his friends among the wealthy men of Omaha to invest "—Sorenson's *History of Omaha*, p 317

‡*The Drovers Journal*, December 31, 1892

*" In 1883 a number of capitalists recognized that as Omaha was the center of the finest corn producing region on the continent, it ought to be a great live stock market and pork packing center They formed the Union Stock Yards Company, on a [paid up] capital of $703,000 —*South Omaha Daily Tribune*, December 31, 1892

W. A. Paxton, treasurer. For 1885, the persons elected were John A. McShane, president; W. A. Paxton, vice-president; J. C. Sharp (who had previously been appointed), secretary and treasurer. Since then, at each annual election (the first Monday in December), the gentlemen last mentioned have been re-elected.

After the organization in 1883 of the "Union Stock Yards Company, of Omaha (Limited)," one of the first things, of course, to be looked after was the purchase of suitable grounds for the stock yards. Naturally enough there was no particular haste, but due deliberation in this matter, as it was one of paramount importance. The choice was finally made and a tract purchased of Alexander H. Swan and others (who had then formed a land syndicate).* This transaction took place February 21, 1884. The land—one hundred and fifty-six and forty-eight hundredths acres—was a part of section four, in township fourteen north, of range thirteen east, of the sixth principal meridian of the government survey, all in what is now the City of South Omaha, the amount paid for the land being $78,250. The boundary lines of this tract commenced at the southwest corner of the section before mentioned, running thence north along the west line of said section four, 1,650 feet, thence east parallel with the south line of said section four, 4,060 feet, to the west line of the right-of-way of the Union Pacific Railroad Company, thence southeasterly along the west line of said right-of-way 970 feet, to a point 802 feet north of the south line of said section four, and to the south line of lands conveyed by Fred Drexel to Leverett M. Anderson; thence south 65½° west, 1,934 feet to the quarter section corner on the south line of said section four; thence south 70½° west, 980 feet; thence south 71½° west, 602 feet; thence north 23° west, 554½ feet to the south line of said section four; thence west 924 feet to the place of beginning, containing one hundred and fifty-six and forty-eight hundredths acres.†

But the first property actually purchased by the company, was the interest of W. A. Paxton in the Council Bluffs stock yards,

*A full account of this syndicate is given in Chapter III. following.

†The Union Stock Yards Company divided the payments for the tract as follows: 156½ acres land @ $500, for which they were to pay, cash $4,250; 6 notes for $12,500 each, $75,000. Total, $78,250. These notes were to be made payable one on the first day of June and December, 1884, '5 and '6.

already mentioned. Paxton, at the time just preceding the organization of the Union Stock Yards Company of Omaha, December 1, 1883, had over $100,000 interest in the Council Bluffs yards and Nelson Morris, of Chicago was also a part owner of them. It was a condition precedent to the taking stock by the former in the new Omaha company that the latter were to purchase, at a stipulated price—$110,000—his interest in the Iowa property—paying in stock $50,000 and in cash $60,000; and the stipulation was faithfully carried out.

It may seem surprising that the men who constituted the new organization should have been willing, upon what was a mere experiment, to invest so largely in the enterprise, But they understood from official reports that the number of cattle, sheep and horses, on various farms and ranges in the West, at that time, which would seek naturally, the markets of the East *largely through* Omaha, were, in—

| | Cattle. | Sheep. | Horses. |
|---|---|---|---|
| Wyoming | 521,213 | 450,225 | 11,975 |
| Colorado | 791,492 | 1,091,443 | 42,257 |
| Montana | 428,279 | 279,277 | 35,114 |
| Idaho | 191,157 | 117,320 | 24.300 |
| Washington | 198,184 | 388,883 | 45,848 |
| Oregon | 598,015 | 1,368,162 | 124.107 |
| Utah | 132,655 | 523,121 | 38,131 |
| Nebraska | 1,113,247 | 227,453 | 204 864 |
| Kansas | 1,033,133 | 629,671 | 430,907 |
| Dakota | 206,783 | 85,244 | 41,670 |

In addition, there were in Arkansas, Missouri, Texas and New Mexico, 8,032,009 head of cattle; 9,248,519 sheep; and 1,633,-262 head of horses. At least twenty-five per cent. of these would reach the northern ranges in the fall of the year 1884 (to say nothing of the corn-fed cattle of western Iowa, that would seek an Omaha market), if proper opportunities were offered for handling stock at this point.* Not only most of this immense number of cattle, sheep and horses, but an enormous number of hogs also, might be better marketed here, than farther east. In or near Omaha, then, it was clear to the minds of these men, that stock yards, on a large scale, were demanded; and they proceeded to act upon (for they had the courage of) their convictions,

"The best practicable place on the tract was chosen for the creation of pens, and work was commenced on the eighth day of April, 1884, under the immediate direction of William A. Paxton, the president of the

*See the *Chicago Times* of March 18, 1884.

company, who must be considered the real founder of South Omaha—a man extensively known as having a big purse but a bigger heart." A large force of men and teams were employed, and soon a remarkable transformation was wrought on the "Drexel Tract," a portion of which constituted the company's purchase Many obstacles had to be overcome

"The first point of attack by the workmen under the eye of Mr. Paxton, was the low swamp or marshy slough that extended from the present west end of the stock yards to what is now the George H Hammond Company's packing house

"The work was continued uninterruptedly, and with such success, not only in grading and filling, but in making pens (the pens then covered about ten acres, and five thousand cattle could have been handled daily), and arranging other conveniences, that by the first day of August the yards, under the superintendency of John F. Boyd, were sufficiently completed to have received live stock had any arrived on that day But none reached the place until the thirteenth, at noon, when a train of twenty-five cars, by the Union Pacific Railroad, came in, loaded with 531 cattle. The consignor was F. Walcott, of Medicine Bow. * * *

"The hay furnished the cattle was 3,750 pounds, and the next day (August 14, 1884), the stock was reshipped, in twenty-five other cars, on the Rock Island Railroad, bound for Chicago—six of the cars having twenty-two head each, and nineteen taking each twenty-one head Thus it was, that the Union Stock Yards of South Omaha entered upon its successful career, and "The Union Stock Yards Company of Omaha (Limited)" booked its first consignment of cattle.

"The first hogs received at the stock yards was on August 27, 1884, by way of the Union Pacific Railroad. The consignors were Black & Nash, of Kearney, Neb, the hogs being consigned to themselves at Chicago, and were shipped in cars No 5,097 (fifty-six hogs) and No 16,525 (fifty-two hogs) They were reshipped by way of the Chicago and Milwaukee Railroad, the same day, and were fed in the yards four bushels of corn, for which four dollars was charged

' Now, let us listen to some of the 'prophetic voices' concerning the new stock yards This is what C F Goodman, president of the Omaha Board of Trade, said, at the close of 1883 'The recent forming of the Union Stock Yards Company, of Omaha, composed of large and enterprising capitalists, for the purpose of doing a general stock yards business, near [but outside] the southern limits of this city, and to establish slaughter and packing houses, are destined to exceed our most sanguine expectations, and while this enterprise is yet in embryo, it is already beginning to make itself felt over the country tributary to this city '

"And this is the language of Thomas Gibson, secretary ' Our stock yards and packing interests, just now so largely increasing, will help immensely to swell our population and extend the limits of Omaha, and this board will use every means available to assist these new companies in their advancement, and in securing any desired public improvement which will facilitate business in opening the avenues of connection between their establishments and the business center of our city '"*

As a forecast of the future, a writer, soon after the stock yards had been made ready for occupation, had this to say

" While it is not necessary that the crack of the cowboy's whip should be sounded continually in the vicinity of the shambles, it is important that all great cattle grounds should have as convenient facilities for reaching the demand markets as is consistent with the proper raising and growth of cattle It was this reason, among others, that induced some of the leading and most enterprising capitalists of Omaha, many of whom are leading stockmen, to establish a stock yard there No city in the west offered better inducements, especially because of its extra fine railroad conveniences, nearness to the cattle grounds, and suitability in all other respects So honorable, business-like, feasible and fair did the original founders of this company enter upon their business, that they were soon joined by some of the most active and enterprising capitalists in the East, as well as in England and Scotland To-day it is one of the strongest and most important corporations of the kind in the world, and there is not the slightest doubt but the extent of its business will fully justify operations on the largest possible scale, and the heaviest investments. * *

The Union Stock Yards Company is certainly

*The Drovers Journal, December 31, 1892

one of the most creditable industries ever established in the Central West. * * * It has an authorized capital of one million dollars and 260 acres of land located exactly three and a half miles southwest of Omaha."*

Six days before the stock yards were declared ready for business, the directors (July 25, 1884,) purchased the residue of the stock of the Council Bluffs Company, so that the Union Stock Yards Company of Omaha, became sole owner of both.†

Enough has already been stated to clearly show that the year 1884 was the one in which was established, in what is now the city of South Omaha, the Union Stock Yards, by "The Union Stock Yards Company of Omaha (Limited)." It was the year in which the "Magic City" was really founded; and the day (April 8th) of that year (the date of breaking ground by the Union Stock Yards Company), is appropriately the day to celebrate as South Omaha's anniversary.‡

At the same time that the stock yards were being urged forward, there was another undertaking in the hands of the company. A building (not large, as the people of South Omaha would *now* look upon it) was erected for packing purposes, and leased to a responsible firm in Detroit for a term of three years. It was the beginning (as will hereafter be shown) of a great industry built up in the immediate vicinity of the yards.§

* *The Leading Industries of the West* (1884), pp. 27, 28.
† "The stock of this [the Council Bluffs] company, which was $400,000, par value, was bought by the stockholders of the Union Stock Yards Company, as a private investment, for $75,000, and was turned in to this [latter] company by them at a par value of $450,000, this amount to apply on their subscriptions to the capital stock of this company. (See resolution unanimously adopted at a directors' meeting, held July 25th, 1884 .]"—From the report of M. A Upton, secretary, for the year ending November 15, 1884. The secretary adds: "The purchasers of the stock of the Transfer Yards (at Council Bluffs) constituted the whole of stockholders of the Union Yards [of Omaha] and none others."
‡ "South Omaha dates its founding on that day [April 8, 1884] which, it is believed, beginning with the 8th of April, 1894, will be duly celebrated [at the end of] each successive ten years; at least, it should be."—*The Drovers Journal*, December 31, 1892.
§ The "Dressed Meat and Packing Concerns," of South Omaha, will form the subject of a subsequent chapter.

It has already been explained that numerous obstacles had to be removed before the "opening day" of the stock yards. Not the least of these was the obtaining of sufficient water. It was at first forced in by steam pumps, from wells sunk at the pens and from a pond adjacent; but, it may be premised, this plan afforded only a limited supply, and other means had to be resorted to. A small stream was found, over a mile away, in a northeast direction, which was fed by springs. Across this stream, on land owned by the syndicate before spoken of, a dam was thrown, and a small lake formed, of clear, cold water. From this, at a large expense, hereafter to be more particularly mentioned, the water was conveyed to the yards. But even this (so great was soon the demand) proved ineffectual in the end, and the American Water Works Company, of Omaha, finally came to the relief, and the cattle of the yards "drink Missouri River water the same as common folks."*

NOTE.—The credit of giving to South Omaha the popular name of the "Magic City" belongs to J. B. Erion, who, in an address read before the Board of Trade. used the words, which (so far as the writer of this history can find) was their first application to this place. It is true, the same name had been applied to Lincoln. also to Hastings, but, in neither case. with that fitness as when given to South Omaha; and, as to those places. it was soon discontinued.

"Such is South Omaha of to-day. Four years ago her site was a cornfield. Her future is an unknown quantity. Situated as she is. however, in the heart of the great corn belt, centrally located on the great overland route between ocean and ocean, in the 'happy medium' of latitude, where she does not freeze in winter nor scorch in summer, there is the indication that certain commercial greatness is in store for her. With her past so near the present, truly has she earned the title of the 'Magic City'."—M. A. Upton, in *Mag. of Western Hist.*, Vol IX (April, 1889), p. 681.

* J B. Erion, in *The Eagle*, April 25, 1891. See, also, an article by M. A. Upton, in *Mag. of Western Hist.*, Vol. IX (April, 1889), p. 681.

## CHAPTER II.

### PROGRESS AND PRESENT CONDITION OF THE UNION STOCK YARDS.

Although the business at the Union Stock Yards did not spring into enormous proportions at a single bound, yet the volume transacted from August 13, 1884, to the end of November was gratifying. The receipts were as follow cattle, 86,095, hogs, 1,402, sheep, 3,479, horses, 447 Total, 91,423 The car loads were as follow cattle, 4,245, hogs, 25, sheep, 34, horses, 20 Total 4,324 There was received during August, 516 car loads, September, 1,265; October, 1,907, November, 636 This stock was disposed of as follows Shipped over the Chicago, Rock Island & Pacific,1,419 car loads, Burlington & Missouri River Railroad, 1,228, Chicago, Milwaukee & St Paul, 757; Chicago & Northwestern, 516, Wabash, 84, Missouri Pacific, 22, Union Pacific Railway, 148, driven out, 150 car loads Average net earnings per car, $2 37¾

A recent writer, in recording pioneer events connected with the stock yards, says

"John F Boyd, now [May 9, 1891] sheriff of Douglas County, was the first superintendent of the yards, and performed the first active labor toward organizing the work, and building the yards He came here from the Council Bluffs yards, and continued to serve as superintendent until elected sheriff in 1888

"Arthur Shriver was among the first men here, having come in April, 1884, and was followed in June by Frank Boyd, D R Scott, Ed Cullen and 'Ike' Brayton Frank Boyd is now [May 9, 1891] superintendent I A Brayton, or 'Ike' as he is known by everybody, was the first yard master and assistant superintendent The yards could not be run successfully without him, to this day Billy Williams came in April, 1884, and Dan Williams, Billy's brother, arrived in July of the same year The latter is known as 'happy Dan,' on account of his faculty of always seeming contented under all circumstances * * *

"Ed Hulett was the first weighmaster, and was succeeded by Ed. Stearns, in the spring of 1885 Ed. held down the job for over four years, and then left it for the position of live stock reporter for *The Drovers Journal*, which position he fills with much ability

"James Paxton, a nephew of W A Paxton, was the first time-keeper He now [May 9, 1891] has charge of the Council Bluffs yards.

"Mr Hutchins was the first foreman of the yards, and was succeeded by William Stewart, who landed May 2, 1884 * * At that time not a post had been set or a board sawed, neither did Mr Stewart, as recently stated in the [*Omaha*] *Bee* [of May 3, 1891] drive the first stakes, but took up the work where Mr Hutchins left off, in the fall following "*

A little over a year after the purchase of their first tract of land, on which to locate their yards, the Union Stock Yards Company had deeded to it an additional tract, amounting to ninety-seven and eight-hundredths acres, by L M Anderson,† for the sum of $14,562, the deed for this having been executed February 25, 1885, so that then the company owned in all two hundred and fifty-three and fifty-six hundredths acres.

On the 28th of May, 1887, the stock yards company purchased for $14,183, from the South Omaha Land Company (the syndicate's successor, really), seventy-six acres and three-tenths of an acre, "excepting, however, all lands that have hitherto been conveyed to the Omaha & Southwestern Railway Company and the Omaha Belt Railway Company for right-of-way purposes, which right-of-way contains 8 64 acres, more or less leaving the amount of land conveyed

---

*J B Erion, in *The Eagle*, of May 9, 1891 The article in the *Bee* referred to by Mr Erion, was in these words "Seven years ago the start—William Stewart, the old-time and reliable carpenter at the stock yards arrived where South Omaha now is seven years ago yesterday, and drove the first stake and erected the first of the improvements for the Union Stock Yards Company Mr Stewart thinks the transformation from half-tilled farm lands to a city of ten thousand inhabitants, and the third packing center in the United States, within seven years, is past fiction and almost equals table "

† This was, in reality, a purchase from the syndicate already mentioned

by this instrument sixty-seven acres and sixty-six hundredths of an acre."

This conveyance was made upon the condition that the Union Stock Yards Company should cause to be opened through the tract an extension of L Street to the Union Pacific Railway right-of-way; also, a street sixty-six feet wide along the north line of the ground of the said Union Stock Yards Company from the north and south center line of section four west to the west line of section four.

The Stock Yards Company also purchased for one dollar, of the syndicate, June 3, 1887, seven acres and seven hundred and forty-six thousandths of an acre. This conveyance was made upon the condition that the grant should be used for track purposes only, and as a means of connection for different railroads with the Union Stock Yards.

On September 15, following, the company purchased of the syndicate, one acre and seven hundred and eighty-three thousandths of an acre for the consideration of $1,947.60.

These before-mentioned tracts constitute all the conveyances heretofore made by the syndicate and its successor to the Union Stock Yards Company. But other parties have conveyed to the last mentioned company, lands at different times, as follow: The Omaha and North Platte Railroad Company, November 23, 1887; L. A. Walker, July 11, 1889; Michael Cudahy, December 5, 1890; the Omaha Packing Company, January 31,1891; Balthas Jetter, June 30, 1892;* and Omaha Belt Line Railway Company, November 11, same year.

The Union Stock Yards Company have conveyed at various dates, to different parties, small tracts: March 20, 1888, to the Omaha and North Platte Railroad Company; June 30, 1888, to Anderson Fowler, and others; January 26, 1889, to the George H. Hammond Co.; January 7, 1891, to Michael Cudahy; January 31, 1891, to the Omaha Packing Company; July 30, 1892, to Michael Cudahy; November 11, 1892, to the Union Pacific Railroad Company; November 11, 1892, to the Omaha Belt Line Railroad Company.

* "The Union Stock Yards Company has purchased two and one-half acres of ground from B. Jetter. The property is the old Jetter homestead at the west end of the Q Street viaduct, and lying north of that street. The price paid is $30,000. For some time negotiations have been pending for this piece of property, and its purchase means that the Stock Yards Company intends to make further improvements, which will be of a substantial and extensive character."—From the *Omaha Bee* of July 5, 1892.

At the time of the opening of the yards, there had not been erected any Exchange building by the Union Stock Yards Company, for the accommodation of its patrons, so the old Fred. Drexel house—a frame structure of two stories in height, and in size about twenty-eight by forty feet—standing upon the ground first purchased by the company, was utilized for that purpose. The building stood just a little east of the southeast corner of the present Exchange; it had six rooms up-stairs and four on the first floor.

The first commission man to do business at the yards was Edward Howe. Howe & Co. was the style of the firm, which received three cars of stock and quit the business. Several other firms started up, but all, in a short time, got tired and left. W. F. Brown & Co. (W. F. Brown and George Brown), began business in January, 1885, in the Exchange—that is, in the old farm house, before described—and was the first commission firm "to stick." W. F. Brown, the senior member of this pioneer firm, was also one of the first men in the Chicago yards. The firm of Wagner, Savage & Sanders, took a bedroom in the farm house, and began to receive and sell stock, February 9, 1885; but the old bedroom has given place to room five, in the new Exchange. Green & Burke, also, did business in one of the best rooms in that same white frame house, and both are still, at the yards, although members of different firms.* The Stock Yards Company occupied the kitchen of the Drexel Exchange for their office, using the pantry, in lieu of a vault, for their valuables. In the cellar was a saloon. The Union Rendering Company had a bed-room for an office; and D. R. Scott, Frank Boyd and several others lived in the house. But the old farm-house, in 1888, took unto itself wheels, and rolled away—nigh to the Burlington & Missouri

* The commission men doing business at the stock yards (January 1893), are: Gasmann & Dudley, Perry Bros. & Co., Dorsey Bros. & Co., Garrow, Kelly & Co., Lawrence, Sweeney & Hare Live Stock Commission Co., H. Krebbs & Co., M. H. Hegarty & Co., Perrine, Green & Co , Paddock & Co., Crill, Denny & Co., Wood Bros., Clay, Robieson & Co., W. F. Brown & Co., Jackson, Acker & Co., Martin Bros., Parkhurst & Hopper, Hake & Reddington, Keenan & Smith, George Burke & Frazier, Byers Bros. & Co., Foley & Chittenden, Spelts, Hitchcock & Olney, Jackson, Higgins & Co., Gilchrist, Hanna & Acker, Smith, Cary & Co., George Adams & Burke, Brainard, Richardson & Carpenter, Allen Root & Co., Boyer Bros. & Co., Frazier & Goodwin, McCloud-Love Live Stock Commission Co., Gosney Live Stock Co., Coffman-Smiley & Co., Campbell Commission Co., Waggoner, Birney & Co , The Boyer-McCoy Co., Moore, Campbell & Co., Benton & Uederwood, Cudahy Packing Co., E. T. Durland. & Co., The G H. Hammond Co., Omaha Packing Co., Lee Rothchild, Smith-Carey Co., Tuefel & Mo-Vicker, Vansant & Carey.

## PROGRESS OF THE UNION STOCK YARDS. 603

River depot, on L Street—transformed into a residence more comely in its appearance, now the dwelling of I A Brayton

The first building erected on the stock yards' site was a boarding house, or "hotel" It stood a few feet east of the Drexel farm house. Here, before the yards were opened, graders and other workmen were boarded and lodged It was first known as the "Canfield House," afterwards as the "Union Stock Yards Hotel" After cattle began to come to the yards, not only those having charge of the pens, but "the knights of the prod-pole," who came in with stock, found accommodation there During the summer and fall of 1885, several commission firms took rooms in the "hotel," for offices, among them Wood Bros, Malloy & Son and Keenan & Hancock Subsequently, the old frame building—two stories high—was torn down, giving place to cattle-pens, and South Omaha's first hostelry—its first "hotel"—was a thing of the past *

The following, from the *South Omaha Globe,* of October 30, 1885, contains information of what was then a new enterprise for the Union Stock Yards Company

"The brick walls of the new Exchange building, at the Union Stock Yards, will soon be completed if the present rate of progress is continued They have gone up like magic during the past few weeks of splendid weather The contractors are under bonds to finish the building by a certain date—January 1st [1886], consequently a large force of men are engaged on the work Mills & Delaney have charge of the brick work, J. Douglas, the wood work, while the iron contracts have been placed with Chicago and St Louis firms The west end of the building will be but a few steps from the yards, while the east front will face the main line of the Union Pacific, about two hundred yards distant, and will be reached by a broad driveway, constructed by means of a heavy fill across the low grounds, and which constitutes the approaches to a high bridge across a small stream [Mud Creek] which intervenes between the building and the main road The building * * * will be four stories in height, surmounted by a tower eighty feet high The ground floor will contain the public office, and private parlors of the

*For nearly all these items concerning the first "Exchange building," credit is to be given J B Erion (See *The Eagle,* of April 25, 1891)

Union Stock Yards Company—large dining room and accessories (kitchen, laundry, refrigerator room, etc.), lunch room and bar room

"The banking department will be on the second floor, directly over the stock yards company's offices, and occupy exactly the same amount of space This floor, which is the main one, will also contain fifteen handsome office rooms for the use of commission men A wide corridor runs through the center of the building on each floor.

"The third floor will be divided into twenty-six sleeping rooms, stock room and parlor The fourth (or Mansard roof floor) will contain thirty sleeping rooms.

'The contracts in the different departments of mechanical work call for the best material and most skillful workmanship When completed it will be an imposing edifice, costing from forty to fifty thousand dollars The men doing business at the yards have, so far, been cooped up in a little frame building, and we almost fear some of them will get lost when first they begin to tread the spacious corridors, broad staircases and wide piazzas of the new stock exchange building"

The Exchange building, as it now stands, is a handsome structure of red brick, four stories high, with a basement That portion of the building facing south was finished in 1886, and is 145 feet long and 42 feet in width, with ornamental projections at the ends and in the center, which adds to the beauty of the front and increases the width to sixty feet Twelve foot corridors extend from end to end through the center of the building

The rapidly-increasing business of the yards soon outgrew the accommodations afforded by the structure as first planned and a wing facing east forty-four feet in width, extending northward one hundred feet, of the same style and height as the main building, was added later Along the south and east sides extends a porch, which forms the favorite resort of the habitues of the Exchange during warm weather

The first story of the Exchange is occupied by offices of the commission men, the hotel, the bar and barber shop The second story is occupied by commission men and the telegraph and railroad companies, for offices

The third floor of the main building is also used for offices, and the wing is used for sleeping apartments. The Exchange Hall occupies one-half of the fourth floor of the wing, the other half being used for storage purposes. All this story of the main building is used for sleeping rooms. The Exchange Hotel uses the basement as a kitchen dining room, and for other purposes.

The year 1885, thoroughly tested the full capacities of the improvements made at the stock yards, and forced the able management in charge to make additional improvements of still greater proportions to meet the demands of the surrounding country. The company was officered as already stated, while J. F. Boyd was made superintendent of yards. The directors were W. A. Paxton, J. A. McShane, Thomas Sturgis, P. E. Iler, J. F. Boyd, B. F. Smith, Joseph Frank and J. M. Woolworth.

Much opposition to the establishment of the stock yards at first was experienced from other cattle markets farther east, but the western cattle men kindly encouraged, in fact demanded the enlargement of the yards, promising to ship their stock to South Omaha as soon as the company could handle the shipments. It was but the natural course of events that South Omaha should become a very large stock market. Albany, N. Y., was forced to give up its hold on the stock business to Buffalo, at the foot of the lake, and Buffalo afterwards graciously surrendered her supremacy to Chicago.

Thus far it seemed apparent that every dollar invested by the Union Stock Yards Company had been warranted, even to the $60,000 Exchange building.

Receipts from, and shipments by the following roads during 1885, were of car loads of stock as follow:

| | Receipts. | Shipments. |
|---|---|---|
| Chicago, Milwaukee & St. Paul | 38 | 932 |
| Omaha & St. Louis | 25 | 85 |
| Missouri Pacific | 343 | 69 |
| Union Pacific | 6,547 | 295 |
| Chicago & Northwestern | 30 | 1,033 |
| Burlington & Missouri River | 692 | 1,680 |
| Chicago, Rock Island & Pacific | 45 | 1,101 |
| Chicago St Paul, Minneapolis&Omaha. | 145 | 108 |
| Fremont, Elkhorn & Missouri Valley. | 360 | ... |

Receipts at, and shipments from the stock yards during 1885, of live stock, were as follow:

| | Receipts. | Shipments. |
|---|---|---|
| Cattle | 114,163 | 83,233 |
| Hogs | 130,867 | 71,919 |
| Sheep | 18,985 | 8,404 |
| Horses and Mules | 1,959 | 1,415 |

In 1885, there were driven out of the yards or sold to Omaha packers:

| | Driven Out | Sold to Omaha Packers. |
|---|---|---|
| Cattle | 337 | 1,273 |
| Hogs | 1 | 819 |
| Sheep | 28 | 59 |
| Horses | 25 | .... |

"What are they doing in South Omaha?" asked the *Omaha Bee*, about the middle of May, 1886. "Does the business there amount to anything? Are they getting much live stock at the yards? Will it ever be a great cattle and hog market? and will it ever amount to anything as a slaughtering point? These and many other similar questions are daily asked by citizens of Omaha who do not realize that, just south of our city limits, a business is growing up that in the near future will surpass, in point of capital employed and business importance, the entire wholesale and manufacturing interests of Omaha in 1886." And the *Bee*, in this its draft upon the future, as will presently be seen, was entirely right—only the the half was not declared!

"The careless observer who may have visited the Chicago yards, and who estimates the importance of a business by the number of acres of land it occupies, and does not take into consideration the length of time it has been established, might take a casual survey of the yards and go away satisfied in his own mind that the South Omaha Stock Yards amount to very little."

But the paper quoted also says: "It was only a short time ago that a few enterprising men met in the open prairie, set their stakes and said: 'Here we will build stock yards which can be enlarged as the business develops; here we will build packing houses that shall have a capacity sufficient to handle all the live stock of the Northwest; here we will lay out town lots to be built upon and occupied by our employes and by others having interests here.' The yards were built; a packing house [Hammond's] was built; stores and private dwellings went up; but no sooner was it known that stock would be shipped to the yards, that it would be sold here for shipment and for slaughtering, than the most violent opposition was encountered from other markets. Chicago sent men here, not to establish commission houses, but to turn business away from here, to spy out sales made to speculators and then telegraph the price to Chi-

## PROGRESS OF THE UNION STOCK YARDS 605

cago, that the stock on arrival might be sold at a loss to the speculator, thereby making it unprofitable for him to operate on this market. In spite of all the opposition the market continued to thrive, the yards were enlarged, the capacity of the packing house was increased, western cattlemen gave every encouragement and promised to ship all their stock here as soon as the yards could handle it. * * *

"That something more than talk and cheap advertising," continues the *Bee*, "are necessary to make a market, was at once realized by the stock yards company; and it is to be doubted if any enterprise in the West has been pushed with greater vigor, or if any company has been more ready to take advantage of the opportunities presented than the Union Stock Yards Company, of South Omaha. They have worked quietly and without any display, if anything, they have been too quiet, and should have made more noise in the world

"To-day the company are moving into the new Stock Exchange building, a structure which would be a credit to any city or any market. It has just been completed at a cost of sixty thousand dollars, and is sixty by one hundred and forty feet on the ground, four stories in height. It will be occupied by the stock yards company and by the commission firms—the balance being used for banking and hotel purposes The old building, together with the hotel, will be removed to make 100m for the extension of the yards A force of men are engaged in making brick which will be used in building the new packing house to be occupied by Fowler Bros, of Chicago The plans and exact dimensions of this packing house have not been completed yet, though the ground is being graded down ready for it. This much, however, is known, that it will be fully as large as Hammond's, and will be used exclusively for slaughtering hogs * * *

"To give some idea of the growth of the business done at the yards, compare receipts of the present year with a year ago In April, 1885, the receipts were 955 cattle, 8,506 hogs, 375 sheep and 56 horses, in April, 1886, the receipts amounted to 8,217 cattle, 20,780 hogs, 822 sheep and 84 horses The bulk of all the receipts are handled by commission men, who are well represented by M Burke & Sons, George Burke, manager, [W F Brown & Co], Savage & Green,

Keenan & Hancock, represented by Draper Smith, Wood Bros, represented by Walter Wood and John Dadisman, and George Adams & Burke, represented by Andy Gillespie and Frank Chittenden"

The Union Stock Yards Bank, with an authorized capital of $500,000, and a subscribed capital of $200,000, opened for business November 24, 1886 Officers John A McShane, president; W A Paxton, vice president, E. B Branch, cashier Directors John A McShane, Herman Kountze, W A. Paxton, Peter E Iler, John A Creighton, Frederick H Davis, Samuel W Allerton, Chicago; Robert D Fowler, Chicago; M C. Keith, North Platte The establishing of this bank had become a necessity as well as convenience, for the transaction of the banking business rapidly accumulating at the stock yards The volume of business had daily swelled by increasing shipments of live stock to the yards, and these large transactions could not well be managed without a local bank It occupied the banking office in the Exchange building, and transacted a general banking business in all its departments It has since given place to the Union Stock Yards National Bank.

The receipts of live stock at the Union Stock Yards, and the shipments from them during the year of 1886, were—

|  | Receipts | Shipments |
|---|---|---|
| Cattle | 144,457 | 73,120 |
| Hogs | 390,187 | 187,369 |
| Sheep | 40,195 | 17,728 |
| Horses and Mules | 3,028 | 1,857 |

The receipts of car loads of stock at the yards from the different roads, in 1886, and the shipments over the same roads for the same period, were—

|  | Receipts | Shipments |
|---|---|---|
| Chicago Milwaukee & St Paul | 13 | 762 |
| Omaha & St Louis | 47 | 68 |
| Missouri Pacific | 1,519 | 69 |
| Union Pacific | 7,802 | 314 |
| Chicago & Northwestern | 43 | 1,741 |
| Burlington & Missouri River | 2,163 | 2,104 |
| Chicago, Rock Island & Pacific | 14 | 1,431 |
| Chicago, St Paul, Minneapolis & Omaha | 901 | 118 |
| Fremont, Elkhorn & Missouri Valley | 1,068 |  |

These tabular statements convey "in language too plain to be misunderstood," the volume of business at the Union Stock Yards, for the year 1886 And the following as clearly shows the increase for the first six months of 1886 over the same months of 1885

Receipts for six months ending June—

|  | 1885 | 1886 |
|---|---|---|
| Cattle | 15,113 | 43,605 |
| Hogs | 55,043 | 149,242 |
| Sheep | 4,561 | 12,546 |
| Horses | 598 | 1,339 |

Shipments for six months ending June—

|  | 1885 | 1886 |
|---|---|---|
| Cattle | 10,520 | 14,718 |
| Hogs | 24,485 | 82,355 |
| Sheep | 2,700 | 5,092 |
| Horses | 530 | 561 |

Consumed in Omaha during six months ending June—

|  | 1885 | 1886 |
|---|---|---|
| Cattle | 4,593 | 28,887 |
| Hogs | 30,555 | 66,887 |
| Sheep | 1,861 | 7,454 |

The ending of the year 1886 made it evident to all parties immediately concerned, as well as to the public at large, that the Union Stock Yards of South Omaha, were placed upon a firm and permanent basis, that its business was sure to increase from year to year for an indefinite period, and that it would always be a great live stock center. The statistics accessible to all, of its business ever since its first receipt of cattle, clearly and emphatically demonstrated (as in this chapter has already been shown) how complete was the success of the yards.

From (and including) the first day of 1887 to (and including) the last day of 1892, there has been no time when any resident of South Omaha—of Omaha—of Nebraska—of the entire West—could reasonably doubt the permanent character of the Union Stock Yards, of this city. It is only necessary then, hereafter, to mention in a general way the progress of these yards to the beginning of 1893, and their present condition.

The receipts of car loads of stock by the different railroads connected with the yards since the first, in 1884, to the close of 1892, were, by the—

|  | 1884 | 1885 | 1886 | 1887 | 1888 | 1889 | 1890 | 1891 | 1892 |
|---|---|---|---|---|---|---|---|---|---|
| Chicago, Milwaukee & St. Paul | 16 | 38 | 13 | 538 | 589 | 1,263 | 1,290 | 1,516 | 1,180 |
| Omaha & St. Louis | | 25 | 47 | 599 | 656 | 956 | 1,342 | 1,245 | 950 |
| Missouri Pacific | | 343 | 1,519 | 1,332 | 1,594 | 1,845 | 2,239 | 2,589 | 2,443 |
| Union Pacific | 4,322 | 6,547 | 7,802 | 10,842 | 13,080 | 12,412 | 14,391 | 11,466 | 15,016 |
| Chicago & Northwestern | 10 | 30 | 43 | 370 | 454 | 1,074 | 1,158 | 921 | 494 |
| Burlington & Missouri River | 1 | 692 | 2,163 | 7,788 | 10,806 | 12,153 | 17,056 | 11,423 | 17,616 |
| Chicago, Burlington & Quincy | | | | | | 1,206 | 2,026 | 2,466 | 1,261 |
| Chicago, Rock Island & Pacific (East) | 21 | 45 | 14 | 490 | 540 | 903 | 1,083 | 1,582 | 819 |
| Chicago, St. Paul, Minneapolis & Omaha | 17 | 115 | 901 | 2,214 | 2,084 | 3,071 | 3,708 | 4,265 | 4,938 |
| Fremont, Elkhorn & Missouri Valley | | 360 | 1,068 | 3,300 | 689 | 7,838 | 9,990 | 10,281 | 12,371 |
| Chicago, Rock Island & Pacific (West) | | | | | | | | | 1,556 |
| Total | 4,887 | 8,195 | 13,570 | 27,428 | 30,492 | 42,721 | 54,283 | 47,754 | 58,644 |

The shipments of car loads of stock by the different railroads connected with the yards, during the same period were, by the—

|  | 1884 | 1885 | 1886 | 1887 | 1888 | 1889 | 1890 | 1891 | 1892 |
|---|---|---|---|---|---|---|---|---|---|
| Chicago, Milwaukee & St. Paul | 755 | 932 | 762 | 1,737 | 2,468 | 1,426 | 2,457 | 2,082 | 5,417 |
| Omaha & St. Louis | 85 | 85 | 68 | 98 | 336 | 272 | 246 | 592 | 384 |
| Missouri Pacific | 9 | 69 | 69 | 130 | 99 | 262 | 363 | 267 | 247 |
| Union Pacific | 112 | 295 | 314 | 477 | 521 | 911 | 774 | 801 | 663 |
| Chicago & Northwestern | 516 | 1,033 | 1,741 | 2,341 | 2,604 | 3,206 | 3,825 | 3,234 | 2,264 |
| Burlington & Missouri River | 1,145 | 1,680 | 2,104 | 2,637 | 3,741 | 747 | 615 | 656 | 778 |
| Chicago, Burlington & Quincy | | | | | | 5,611 | 7,234 | 4,738 | 5,117 |
| Chicago, Rock Island & Pacific (East) | 1,480 | 1,104 | 1,431 | 2,661 | 4,249 | 1,031 | 781 | 1,263 | 1,276 |
| Chicago, St. Paul, Minneapolis & Omaha | 37 | 108 | 118 | 147 | 171 | 227 | 428 | 554 | 715 |
| Fremont, Elkhorn & Missouri Valley | | | | | 176 | 329 | 437 | 415 | 470 |
| Chicago, Rock Island & Pacific (West) | | | | | | | | | 56 |
| Total | 4,089 | 5,306 | 6,607 | 10,228 | 14,365 | 14,022 | 17,160 | 14,597 | 17,387 |

The receipts of stock at the yards from their opening in 1884, to the close of 1892, were—

| | Cattle | Hogs | Sheep | Horses and Mules |
|---|---|---|---|---|
| 1884 | 86,898 | 1,868 | 4 188 | 466 |
| 1885 | 114 168 | 130 867 | 18,985 | 1,959 |
| 1886 | 144,457 | 390,487 | 40 195 | 3,028 |
| 1887 | 235,723 | 1,011,706 | 76,014 | 3,202 |
| 1888 | 340,469 | 1,283,600 | 158 503 | 5,035 |
| 1889 | 467,340 | 1 206 605 | 159,053 | 7,595 |
| 1890 | 606,699 | 1,673,314 | 156,186 | 5,318 |
| 1891 | 593,044 | 1,462,428 | 170,849 | 8 592 |
| 1892 | 738.186 | 1.705 687 | 185,457 | 14,183 |

The receipts of stock driven in by local stock raisers, received via the "Sarpy Central," as it is locally known, during the past seven years are as follow

| | Cattle | Hogs | Sheep |
|---|---|---|---|
| 1886 | 1,778 | 5,130 | 485 |
| 1887 | 3,990 | 5 548 | 1,360 |
| 1888 | 3,201 | 8,977 | 1,456 |
| 1889 | 4,284 | 11,200 | 1,234 |
| 1890 | 4,385 | 14 344 | 1,311 |
| 1891 | 8,026 | 16,763 | 175 |
| 1892 | 8,871 | 15,884 | 1 092 |

The shipments of stock from the yards during the same period, were—

| | Cattle | Hogs | Sheep | Horses and Mules |
|---|---|---|---|---|
| 1884 | 81,935 | 500 | 1,278 | 417 |
| 1885 | 83 233 | 71 919 | 8,408 | 1,415 |
| 1886 | 78,120 | 187,869 | 17,728 | 1,857 |
| 1887 | 151,419 | 140,726 | 56,444 | 1,856 |
| 1888 | 206,064 | 333 228 | 118,208 | 3,799 |
| 1889 | 227,921 | 179 916 | 108 250 | 6 744 |
| 1890 | 283,880 | 275,638 | 94,464 | 4 935 |
| 1891 | 267,730 | 245,046 | 89,416 | 7 895 |
| 1892 | 280,703 | 380,647 | 83 338 | 12,048 |

From the opening of the yards in 1884, to the close of 1892, the largest recipts of stock in one day, were—

Cattle, October 19, 1891,   6,784
Hogs, August, 12, 1890   16 725
Sheep, September 24, 1891   8,782
Horses and mules, June 6, 1889   718
Cars, May 17, 1892   420

Largest receipts of stock in one week were—

Cattle week ending October 31. 1891   37,190
Hogs, week ending July 31, 1890   75,797
Sheep, week ending September 30, 1890   12,817
Horses and mules week ending September 14, 1892.   1,083
Cars, week ending October 31, 1890   1,947

Largest receipts of stock in one month, were—

Cattle, October, 1892   90 037
Hogs, August, 1890   256,322
Sheep, October 1888   31,829
Horses and mules, June, 1889   2,073
Cars, August, 1890   5,859

Largest receipts of stock in one year were—

Cattle, 1892   738,186
Hogs, 1892   1,705 687
Sheep, 1892   185,457
Horses and mules, 1892   14,183
Cars, 1892   58,644

The following facts are gleaned from the Eighth Annual Live Stock Report of the yards, made by J C Sharp, secretary of the Union Stock Yards Company, at the close of 1891

Twenty miles of railroad track traverse the yards and six locomotives are kept in almost constant service day and night. The switch tracks are the property of the Stock Yards Company They are connected with all the various railroads centering here, and all switching, both of live stock, dead freight and packing house products to and from the packing houses and yards are done by the employes of the company. The four leading dressed meat and packing concerns of the United States have houses here,[*] with capacities only limited by the amount of stock received, while shippers, speculators and buyers for eastern and western houses are always on the market in direct competition with the buyers for local slaughterers, shippers being thus assured of a sure and ready sale for their stock at the market value. The same is true of the hog market

In addition to the local packers, Boston, New York, New Haven, Indianapolis, Cleveland, Baltimore, St. Louis and other eastern cities as well as Denver, Salt Lake City, Helena and others on the west are liberal purchasers of live hogs here. South Omaha is at present second to no market west of Chicago, and in a few years at most will be second to none in the country As a distributive point for stockers and feeders, this market has no superior, its position in the heart of the best stock raising and feeding country under the sun, making it the natural trading point for stockmen. The number of feeding cattle shipped to the country from

[*] Of these, a particular account is given in a subsequent chapter

this point during the past year is more than double the number shipped last year, each succeeding year witnessing the development of this branch of trade and recording additional tributary territory. The horse market has been placed in charge of gentlemen who will conduct it on a "strictly commission" basis. They are thorough horse men, having an extensive business acquaintance both east and west, and their facilities for handling horses here are unexcelled.

The revenue of the stock yards company is derived entirely from yardage charges and the sale of feed for stock. When stock is sold, yardage charges are: for cattle and horses, 25 cents a head; hogs, 8 cents a head; sheep, 5 cents a head; calves, 10 cents a head. Feed charges are, for hay, $1.00 per hundred; corn, $1.00 per bushel; oats, $1.00 per bushel.

Looking at the yards on the first day of July, 1892, and extending our view in retrospection to the commencement of that year, and certainly in no previous six months in the history of the yards, could improvements have been so extensive, nor at any time were the prospects for the development of an immense live stock market at this point more promising. The Stock Yards Company were expending something over two hundred thousand dollars in the erection of new pens and better equipment of the older portions of the yards. Nine acres of the ground north and east of the Exchange building had been recently graded and covered with cattle pens, completely surrounding it. This brought the total area of the yards up to fifty acres, and the capacity to 10,000 cattle, 20,000 hogs, 5,000 sheep and 600 horses and mules. Of the new pens, twenty-eight were paved with vitrified brick. Forty-one new loading and unloading chutes were being constructed for the new division, and another new scale house, No. 6, was about completed. Two miles of track had been added to the yards equipage, and another locomotive bought and placed in service. Old division B had been completely remodeled—changed from cattle yards to hog pens. There had also been several changes in the Exchange building itself. The old dining-room had been cut up into several new office rooms, and the dining room and kitchen re-located in the basement. In fact a person who had not seen the yards for a year or so would hardly have been able to recognize them now. These extensive improvements and alterations were not made without good reason, as the record of receipts for those six months with the same period for the years 1890 and 1891, abundantly attested. It was to be noted that the supplies of all kinds of stock had steadily increased for the previous three years:

| 1890. | Cattle. | Hogs. | Sheep. |
|---|---|---|---|
| January | 43,985 | 99,509 | 10,987 |
| February | 41,427 | 66,194 | 15,009 |
| March | 55.980 | 75.351 | 18.211 |
| April | 52,778 | 92,581 | 11.969 |
| May | 63,054 | 127,698 | 10,956 |
| June | 48,991 | 153,599 | 5,135 |
| Total | 306,215 | 614,982 | 72,267 |

| 1891. | Cattle. | Hogs. | Sheep. |
|---|---|---|---|
| January | 50,972 | 162,105 | 11,364 |
| February | 47,057 | 130,681 | 12.421 |
| March | 49,923 | 145,223 | 16,351 |
| April | 35,945 | 106,842 | 18,682 |
| May | 31,576 | 120,991 | 8,456 |
| June | 34.066 | 142,105 | 5,095 |
| Total | 249,539 | 807,947 | 72,369 |

| 1892. | Cattle. | Hogs. | Sheep |
|---|---|---|---|
| January | 58,138 | 201,557 | 11,774 |
| February | 55.563 | 127,549 | 17.620 |
| March | 61.105 | 102,384 | 20,071 |
| April | 61.563 | 97,826 | 17,283 |
| May | 62,102 | 149,574 | 12.013 |
| June | 44,230 | 202.912 | 7,923 |
| Total | 342,761 | 881,652 | 86.684 |

On the whole, then, the first half of the year 1892 was a most prosperous season for the South Omaha stock market. Within the history of the Union Stock Yards no period (we may repeat) can be recalled when the improvements made had been so extensive, the receipts so large, and the prices paid so good, as has characterized those six months.

When it is recalled that more than $1,000,000 was being expended in improvements by the packers (whose extensive plants will be found described in a subsequent chapter) and the Stock Yards Company, the fact was apparent that a large and successful stock market and packing center was being reared in South Omaha. When, therefore, at the beginning of the year, the packers gave notice of their intention to expend several hundred thousand dollars in improving and enlarging their mammoth establishments, no one seemed surprised. Later, when the Union Stock Yards Company began improvements costing $200,000, to meet increased business, it was regarded as a natural consequence When new territory was opened up, and the stock shipped to South Omaha, it was no more than was expected When the differential rate on stock from Indian Territory points was reduced to $12 50 per car, it was received with the feeling that justice had been done, and that the railroads desired to get into the South Omaha column of progressiveness and enterprise, and every new improvement, each day's increase in receipts and slaughterings, and the whole general prosperity were calmly considered and attributed to the fact that it was but the natural acquiring of all that was necessary in the grand march for second place which South Omaha was (it was believed) so rapidly and gloriously accomplishing There had been no loud sounding of trumpets, no pyrotechnical display of accomplishments, but a calm, determined, enterprising effort on behalf of all to take advantage of the opportunity and place, within a short time, the Magic City where she properly and naturally belonged

The large improvements then making by the Union Stock Yards Company were made necessary by the increase in the receipts of stock and in the outlook for increased business in the future

The Union Stock Yards Company and the Union Stock Yards Railroad Company have the same officers, who are the same as previously given, but with W N Babcock, general manager The board of directors consists of W A Paxton, John A McShane, John A Creighton, A C Foster, Milton Rogers, E A Cudahy, B F Smith, of Omaha, M C Keith, of North Platte, and P A Valentine, of Chicago

Of the two hundred and fifty acres of grounds owned by the company, thirty-seven and one-half acres were covered by stock pens January 1, 1892, twelve acres being allotted to hogs, twenty and one-half acres to cattle and five acres to sheep. Fifteen additional acres have since been graded at an expense of $15,000 in removing 60,000 yards of earth, and have been covered with pens Of these, five acres are for hogs and ten acres for cattle Many of the new pens have been paved with vitrified brick, which will make the yards among the finest in the world Every pen in the yards has ample supply of good fresh, pure water The supply is received through two eight-inch mains, two miles long A standpipe eighty-five feet high and twenty feet in diameter, situated seventy-five feet above the level of the Exchange, insures ample pressure at all times Two additional scales for weighing stock have been added, making six in all A storm water sluice twelve by fourteen feet and four thousand feet long, has been constructed during the year at a cost of $40,000 This connects with the sewerage system A tunnel six by six and 1,700 feet long, costing $23,000, ten miles of sewers through every alley and connecting with every stock pen in the yards, at a cost of $25,000 and a sewer two miles long to the Missouri river, make the sewerage system absolutely faultless Fifty-five new loading and unloading chutes have been built, thirty-one of them single and eighteen double The new Union Stock Yards office building is 44 by 67 feet, costing $40,000

To the eighteen miles of railroad trackage, costing $250 000, more than two miles were added during 1892, at a cost of $20,000 The sixth locomotive engine was received during the year, thus furnishing motor power for almost any needs To the immense new brick barn of the horse market, 62 by 260 feet, costing $18,000, a new horse shed, 54 by 300 feet has been completed, with a capacity of two hundred head and costing $5,000 Between the exchange and the horse barn a fine race track, one-eighth of a mile, has been constructed and fenced, and an elegant pavilion, with a seating capacity of four hundred, has been constructed for the benefit of buyers and sellers of horses and for the pleasure of those who delight in seeing fine and fast horses Not the least successful and gratifying of the additions to the yards is the horse and mule department The receipts of horses and mules in 1891 were 8,592, while the receipts of 1892 were 14,183, an increase of 5,591, or 65 79 per cent Of the receipts 9,218, or 65 per cent, were sold at this market This, too, in less than a year, for the horse and mule department has been in operation only ten months, while nearly half that time was spent in preparation for the promised business The sheep pens burned last summer are being rebuilt and will cost $8.000

Another sewer, one thousand feet long, eight feet in diameter, is being constructed from the Exchange building to connect with the sewer at the south side of The G. H. Hammond Company packing houses. This sewer will be circular, built of brick, and will cost $20,000.

Fifty men are now (January 1, 1893,) at work on the new interlocking switch, which promises much benefit to the yards and the packing plant. The switch will be 1,300 feet long and will be located west of the Union Pacific Railway tracks, with the center about opposite the Union Pacific Depot, and will be under the control of the Union Pacific Railway Company. It will cost $65,000, and will enable the Burlington & Missouri River Railroad Company to run all of its trains via this point and over its union cut-off, and likewise the Missouri Pacific all trains over its fort cut-off. The tracks will be laid by the middle of this month.

South Omaha has gained a standing among the very first as a feeder market. During 1892 the sales of feeders increased from 91,500 to 131,231, or 46 per cent.

During the same year, 255,500 cars were handled by the Union Stock Yards Railroad Company, an average of 816 for every working day in the year, equal to forty-one trains of twenty cars to each train.

The feed-master's report shows that nearly $100,000 was expended during 1892 for feed. Eight thousand five hundred tons of hay, costing, on an average, $6.50, were required, entailing an outlay of $55,250; and 90,000 bushels of oats, averaging 35 cents a bushel, cost $31,500.

Eleven teams, with teamsters, averaging ten loads per day, are now (January 1, 1893), required to clean the yards. Three to four cars per day are used, averaging about 1,000 cars per year, to remove the gatherings, while 7,600 cart-loads are annually thrown in the dump.

The water system is among the best in the country, and the supply inexhaustible. Four meters are used, and all the water consumed is accurately accounted for. About 15,000,000 gallons are consumed per month or 250,000,000 gallons per year.

The present pay-roll contains the names of 351 persons, and the salaries amount to $155,000 per year.

The South Omaha Live Stock Exchange has now (January 1, 1893), a membership of 202. During the past year just one hundred new members were added to the roll. On May 22, 1892, the initiation fee was increased from twenty dollars to $500, and the transfer fee raised to $100. It is regularly chartered under the laws of Nebraska, and is a member of the national association. The regular election of officers occurs on the first Monday of January of each year. The present officers are: President, J. A. Hake; vice-president, M. R. Murphy; secretary, A. L. Lott; treasurer, H. C. Bostwick; directors, David L. Campbell, Jerome B. Blanchard, J. E. Byers, L. C. Redington, and Walter E. Wood.*

The secretary of the Union Stock Yards Company, J. C. Sharp, in the Ninth Annual Report of the yards made at the close of 1892, says:

"With less than a decade of years to its credit, the position occupied by the Union Stock Yards, of South Omaha as the third largest live stock market in the country, is an excellent example of the wonderful possibilities of the country and the age.

"In August, 1884, the yards were first opened for business. The start was in a comparatively small way, but the country naturally tributary to this point, was filling up with settlers and rapidly developing, and the projectors of the scheme, with characteristic foresight and energy, having made ample preparations in the way of securing grounds and the location of new packeries, now have the gratification of seeing the infant industry of 1884, the third packing center of the country, with possibilities second to none.

"Geographic, agricultural and climatic conditions have been all that could be desired for the building up and maintenance of a great live stock market, while the construction of the great net-work of railroads, of which Omaha is the center, and the constant changing of the face of the country from rolling prairie to fruitful farm and

*Adapted from the *Omaha Bee* of Sunday, January 1, 1893.

"To supply the market with live stock, the Union Stock Yards Company occupies 275 acres of ground, and has a capacity for 10,000 cattle, 20,000 hogs, 5,000 sheep, 500 horses and mules. Its Stock Yards Railway now has forty-five miles of tracks, six engines and other facilities for hauling stock. An interlocking switching plant, costing $65 000, is being constructed, which, it is claimed, will be the most complete in the United States. All the switches in the yard will be operated by one man, in a high tower, and electricity will be the power used. The tracks of the company connect with the Union Pacific, Burlington & Missouri River; Fremont, Elkhorn & Missouri Valley; Missouri Pacific; Chicago, Burlington & Quincy; Chicago & Northwestern; Chicago, St. Paul, Minneapolis & Omaha; Chicago, Milwaukee & St. Paul; Chicago, Rock Island & Pacific; Kansas City, St. Joseph & Council Bluffs; Wabash; and the Belt Line Railroad. The principal sources of supply for this market are the States of Nebraska, Kansas, Iowa, Colorado, Wyoming, Montana, and the two Dakotas. Arizona, New Mexico and Texas furnish considerable especially for stock and feeders."—*South Omaha Daily Tribune*, December 31, 1892.

ranch, only improved the situation, and made doubly sure the success of the enterprise. With a live stock market, situation is everything, and in this respect South Omaha certainly has no superior to-day. The vast, rich cattle and sheep ranges of Colorado, Wyoming, the two Dakotas, Montana, Utah, New Mexico and the Panhandle of Texas, furnish an almost limitless supply of beef and canning cattle for the slaughterers, while they also furnish thousands of young animals to be fattened and finished in innumerable feed lots on corn, the staple product of the great state of Nebraska, as well as of her sister states, of Kansas and Missouri, on the south, Iowa on the east, and South Dakota on the north.

"At present the yards cover an area of about fifty-five acres, while nearly as many acres more are already graded and ready for the construction of pens as soon as the necessities of the situation demand it. The present capacity of the yards is estimated at 600 cars of cattle, 13,000 head; 375 cars of hogs, 25,000 head; 50 double decks of sheep, 10,000 head, and 25 cars of horses, about 500 head. Over twenty miles of railroad tracks traverse the company's property, these switching tracks being owned and operated entirely by the Stock Yards Company. They connect with all the various lines of railways centering at this point, and six locomotives are required in switching the live stock and packing house product to and from the stock yards and packeries.

"Water from the city mains traverses the entire yards, and a complete system of sewerage and drainage makes these yards second to none in this respect. The yard company's employes yard, feed and water all stock on arrival as well as look after the weighing when sold. Every shipper is assured of the best of treatment for his stock, whether he accompanies his shipment or not. But one charge for yarding is made, this to cover the entire time the stock remains in the yards, however long, and in no case to be collected unless the stock sells here. Western shippers thus have an opportunity to stop off here and try the market on their way east without any additional expense for yarding. All through billed stock that stops off here is taken care of entirely by the company's employes, and the only charge made is for such feed as may be ordered. * * *

"The position of this market, situated as it is in the very heart and center of the greatest corn belt in the world, makes it of necessity a natural distributing point for stock cattle and feeders. The vast breeding grounds of the west and southwest furnish the feed lots of the states further east with thousands of cattle, which in turn find their way back here again ready for the butcher's block, the refrigerator car, or often to make a journey across the Atlantic 'on the hoof.' This branch of the business has increased rapidly from year to year, and the increase must, in the very nature of the case, continue.

"A new feature has been added to the business of the yards during the past year in the way of a horse market. * * * These sales [auction sales of horses] are attended by buyers from all over the country, although it has been practically demonstrated that Omaha alone demands enough good horses of all kinds to support a very respectable sale stable."

The expenditure, during 1892, of $200,000 in enlarging an improving the yards was only deemed necessary for the future growth and needs of the stock business at this point. But with this immense sum of money, judiciously handled, so rapid has the growth of business been, that the improvements have scarcely kept ahead of the needs. The Union Stock Yards Company has increased its capital from time to time until it has now resolved to make it six million dollars. The stock is considered an excellent investment, as it now sells at fifty-three cents above par, and the character of its officers is a guaranty to the holders, and the public generally, that all is well at the Union Stock Yards in South Omaha.

In a most reliable published work, just issued, is this statement.

"In the entire history of the live stock business * * * there has been nothing to compare with the building up of the market at South Omaha. The magnitude of Chicago, as a live stock center, is the result of over twenty-five years of effort. St. Louis and Kansas City are both comparatively old markets. But here, on a spot where eight years ago [this was written in July, 1892] the corn was growing luxuriantly, has sprung up the third largest market in the country. A glance at the conditions and circumstances will show that the building up of a trading center here, for live stock of all kinds, has been as much a necessity as a commercial enterprise.

"Corn is the cheapest and best ration yet discovered for fattening stock, and the genial clime and rich soil capable of producing this cereal are also particularly adapted to the raising of cattle, hogs and sheep. No country under the sun can compete, in this respect, with the territory surrounding South Omaha. There are Nebraska, Iowa, Kansas, Missouri and the Dakotas—all rich agricultural States, which find this a market for a good share of their live stock. In addition to furnishing beef cattle for the slaughterers, the ranges of Wyoming, Colorado, Utah, New Mexico and Texas, furnish unlimited numbers of feeders for the corn States. Numerous railroads, whose facilities are being constantly increased, bring the live stock from all points of the compass to this place, to be slaughtered and distributed to the world. The establishment of a market here was a convenience, even a necessity, for the surrounding naturally tributary country, and its situation in the very center of the greatest corn belt in the world, places its permanence beyond question."*

The Union Stock Yards Company, at its last annual meeting, decided to expend at least $200,000 in improvements during the coming year (1893). The interlocking switching system, now in course of construction, and the building of an eight-foot square tunnel, to connect with the main sewer, for the better drainage of the yards, will be pushed to completion. Sometime during the year about sixteen acres of the original hog and cattle pens, at the south side of the yards, will be torn down, and the area covered with new and improved hog houses and sheds for cattle, hogs and sheep. The new pens will be paved with brick, as, in fact, will be the entire yards at no distant day. Additional cattle pens are all the time being built. About fifty acres of ground is now graded, ready for pens, in addition to what is already occupied.

The Union Stock Yards Company shows what capital, enterprise and persevering endeavor can do when rightly and thoughtfully directed. Experiments, as every business man knows, made in the line of attempted progress, are to be entered upon with great caution, especially where large sums are necessary to carry them forward. It is, then, really a matter of wonder that so many of Omaha capitalists should have so quickly and unreservedly invested large amounts, in 1883 and in the next two years, in broad acres south of the city, which were then little else than corn-fields, following up their purchases by starting and urging forward with great energy and forethought, the Union Stock Yards, of South Omaha.

But our wonder is greatly increased when we reflect that, in less than nine years of development, their very purchases—these very yards—have brought to the "Magic City" the Union Stock Yards and all the industries connected therewith. Can the live stock industry in the Great West make, anywhere, a better (or even as good), a showing as this? We think not. The success of the "experiment" has, really, been unparalled. And what is also gratifying to everyone interested, is the fact that there is an undoubted permanency in all this—as lasting as the extensive ranges and grass-fields of the growing states now stretching away from the Missouri River to the Pacific Ocean.

A great live stock market carries with it not only millions of capital, but an overshadowing display of bewildering activity. Any one doubting the truth of this, has only to spend a few hours at the Union Stock Yards of South Omaha, to be thoroughly convinced that such is the fact. But South Omaha does not alone feel the impulse—it is carried into Omaha—into Nebraska—into the entire West.*

But to particularize: It is not alone that the stock yards proper disclose activities such as are an evidence of success. There are the many commission merchants, of honorable dealings, to aid in all that gives prominence and character to the extensive transactions carried on there; and there, also, and in the city near by, are the national banks, to help carry forward the great work. And last, but not least, we hear the busy hum of four large packing industries,† which add wonderfully to the lively scene, and to the greatness and durability of South Omaha.

*Union Stock Yards Directory, by Bert Anderson and A. F. Stryker, p. 4.

*See The Drovers Journal for December 31, 1892; art.; "Our Review."
†Fully described in a subsequent chapter.

# CHAPTER III.

### THE "SYNDICATE" AND SOUTH OMAHA LAND COMPANY

The pioneers of the territory included within what is now the incorporated limits of South Omaha, came not to form a city, but to secure themselves farms, and some of them came early, even at a date when Omaha was only known on paper And they continued to live, until a recent period, in Douglas Precinct — a division of Douglas County not yet wholly wiped out by the onward march of a "metropolitan city," or ot a "city of the second class, having over eight and less than twenty-five thousand inhabitants"

Those pioneer times just antedating the founding of South Omaha are well remembered by those who are now living But how many of them, ten years ago, for one moment imagined that, of some one of their farms, a single acre might be picked out, which, if cleared of all its buildings, would, on the first day of January 1893, be worth $100,000? But the future was not open to the score of farmers in this goodly portion of what was then Douglas Precinct, who, in the spring of 1883, sowed their grain and planted the corn on land worth, as they believed, fifty dollars an acre, although one or more gifted with a far-seeing eye, would not be anxious to sell at four times that figure

The men who first conceived the idea of, and who formed themselves into a "syndicate" to purchase the few farms and tracts lying to the southward of the City of Omaha, and to create, upon the tracts so bought, stock yards and packing houses, also a town — to these men, South Omaha owes largely whatever is to-day of the city  It is proper, therefore, that the names of these men, who, on the 30th of August, 1883, were deeply interested in the movement, should be made a matter of record  A H Swan, C A Righter, Colin J MacKenzie, M C Keith, August Richard, W A Paxton, Milton Rogers, J E Markel, Thos Swobe, John A McShane, Iler & Co, Caldwell, Hamilton & Co, Frank Murphy, Ben B Woods Geo E Barker, Samuel E Rogers, J M Woolworth, J H Dumont, Charles F Manderson, Benj F Smith, Samuel Allerton

What the syndicate accomplished is first to be considered

It is to be borne in mind that on the first day of December, 1883, was formed, in Omaha, "The Union Stock Yards Company (Limited)", and it has already been shown that, previous to that date, a large tract of land (including several farms) had been purchased by a syndicate, not only for stock yards and packing houses, but also for the laying out of a town contiguous thereto *

And here it may be explained that the tracts thus secured were from the following named gentlemen, to whom were paid the following sums

|  | Acres | Amount |
|---|---|---|
| John Kennelly | 220 | $41,552 00 |
| Fred Drexel | 365 | 47 808 57 |
| Geo Holmes | 148 15 | 25 483 50 |
| John Bagley | 147 | 38,220 00 |
| Patrick Bagley | 31 | 8,060 00 |
| S A Orchard | 120 50† | 20,166 66 |
| C L Clark | 160 | 40,000 00 |
| J W Lee | 300 | 75,000 00 |
| R Hendricks | 118‡ | 4 068 00 |
| J Thompson | 266§ | 12,620 00 |

The whole number of acres was 1,875 65, at a cost of $312.978 73, but 464 acres lay outside the present South Omaha, costing $30,076 67  This leaves the actual purchase inside what are now the city's limits, 1,411 65 acres, costing $282,902 06, equivalent, on an average, of a small fraction over $200 an acre

On the first day of January, 1884, all these lands, inside and outside the present limits of South Omaha, were conveyed in a trust-deed to the syndicate—that is, executed by Leverett M Anderson and wife

---

*Ante, p 597

"Scarcely eight years ago the site where twelve thousand people now live and prosper, where 100,000 car loads of traffic are annually handled, where business to the extent of more than $50,000,000 is done every year was common farming land "
— *South Omaha—The Magic City*, by Samuel P Brigham, Joseph J Breen and Z Cuddington, May 7, 1894

† Eighty acres of this tract lies west of, and outside the limits of South Omaha

‡ Wholly in Sarpy County and outside South Omaha

§ All in Sarpy County and beyond the city limits

(who had secured the title to them), to Alexander H. Swan, William A. Paxton, Thomas Swobe, Frank Murphy, Charles W. Hamilton, Peter E. Iler, and James M. Woolworth, trustees,—the whole lying in the counties of Douglas and Sarpy, Nebraska—to secure the payment of bonds to the amount of $1,400,000; but it was stipulated in the deed that there should be conveyed to the Union Stock Yards Company, of Omaha, (limited), the 156.48 acre tract which has already been described; and it was also stipulated that the trustees should lay out the remainder of the lands, or so much and such parts as they in their discretion, might think expedient, into a town, with streets, passage-ways, public grounds, lots, blocks, and reserves, and improve the same, or cause the same to be improved by roads, walks, railroads, water-works, gasworks, and other convenient and proper structures and works of whatsoever nature, the planting of trees and pleasure grounds, and otherwise, and they might establish and maintain, or cause to be established and maintained, lines of transportation of persons and property, and reserve and donate and convey to proper parties, lots and parcels of these lands for schools, churches and other public buildings.

Now all these lots, except such as were reserved, were to be disposed of under certain regulations mentioned in the deed, and the proceeds were to be held by the the trustees in lieu of the lands for the security of the bonds issued by them.

The trustees before mentioned, at once organized with A. H. Swan, as president; Frank Murphy, as treasurer; and Thomas Swobe, as secretary;—appointing for directors, A. H. Swan, Thomas Swobe, Peter E. Iler, W. A. Paxton, Frank Murphy, Charles W. Hamilton and J. M. Woolworth. The organization, it must be understood, was wholly and legally distinct from the Union Stock Yards Company. After the organization of the syndicate, M. A. Upton was appointed assistant secretary and manager, and L. M. Anderson, superintendent. The prospective plans of the syndicate and their expectations of what would be the result of their scheme, is thus set forth at that date by one who understood how strong were the convictions of all in its ultimate success.

"The adjacent lands to Omaha were carefully looked over, and certain properties situated on the line of the Union Pacific Railway, and adjoining the City of Omaha, were selected, being only seven minutes from the Union Pacific Depot; and an arrangement was entered into with that railway to continue the present [1884] dummy train, which runs to and from Council Bluffs, on the east side of the Missouri River, every hour, to the lands that were thus chosen.       *       *       *

"It is hard to form or convey an accurate mental picture of a country one has never seen. The imagination is an uncertain quality, and it plays fantastic tricks with merely written descriptions. Nevertheless, I will essay the difficult task of describing this portion of the Nebraska prairie, with the object of delineating the country and its natural adaptation for the purposes required, viz.: *A suburban town to Omaha, and the stock yards, packing houses, etc.*, for the development of a vast trade, yet in its infancy.

"It must be borne in mind that the stock yards and packing houses (lands for which have been reserved and set apart) are to be so far removed from this vast purchase for a suburban town, that they will offer no ground of objection to sale for residential purposes. The yards and packing houses, etc., will be out of the sight of the residential portions of the main estate, and be sufficiently far removed to render them no objection. The estate will be laid out into a well arranged and carefully studied town for workingmen nearest to the yards. The more easterly portions will be subdivided into lots suitable for more wealthy residents. By reference to the map it will be seen that this suburban town will not only be reached by the Union Pacific main line, but by a belt or circular line of railway, now fully established, connecting all the six eastern roads at this one point, and thus giving every facility, at very low rates, for merchants, clerks, employes of the various railroads, to reach their homes in a few minutes from their various occupations and employments; and, also, by a cable line. The undertaking has had the entire support of the Union Pacific Railway and its local management, as well as the Burlington & Missouri River Railroad in Nebraska.

"So that the main features of the lands chosen may be rightly comprehended by one who is a stranger to such lands, a common error should be corrected, and that is to suppose a prairie to be a dead level It is not so, but on the contrary, the American plain is ever ascending to the higher altitudes until it merges into the lower slopes of the Rocky Mountains The tract of land referred to comprises low hills through nicely graded little slopes or valleys, nearly all gently sloping to the present main line of the Union Pacific Railway, with rising ground on each hand In fact, the contours of the land are pretty hills or dells, and when the landscape is clothed with a due proportion of wood, as this property is, the scene is exceedingly pleasing, and, certainly, most picturesque Where not under cultivation there is a rich mould clothed with a luxurious growth of grass, like an English meadow The entire tract is underlaid by a bed of gravel, which forms a vast storehouse for water, with a never-failing stream running through the entire estate, from the north to the south

"This is a fair description of the purchase in its outline feature This tract of land being secured, it was offered to certain gentlemen upon the most advantageous terms, viz That the owner would convey the same to any responsible parties as trustees, who would agree to lay it out into a suburban town and promote a system of stock yards, and organize companies to erect packing houses for dressing beef, cattle, sheep and hogs for packing or shipment by refrigerator cars to the Eastern cities and Europe, and the utilization of all the products by aid of fertilizing works, canning establishments, glue and bone factories, etc , and other such important manufactories, and in such case he agreed to accept bonds running over a long series of years, with the very low rate of five per cent interest, receiving such bonds as in full payment and consideration for his lands

"After a careful examination of the title to the property, and in accordance with the agreement, a certain trust was formed and deed executed to the following gentlemen: William A Paxton, A H Swan, Charles W Hamilton, Frank Murphy, Peter Iler, Thomas Swobe and J. M Woolworth One of the most important features in this trust deed is, that under no circumstances, of any nature or kind, can this trust be wound up, and the entire lands sold without the consent of a majority in interest of the holders of the bonds, and thus virtually vesting the sole control in the bondholders It also provides that all property sold from time to time shall be applied to the liquidation of the bonds and interest due thereon Printed copies of this trust deed may be obtained The trust deed is entirely in accordance with the laws of the State of Nebraska, and the terms of trust have been settled and agreed to by a gentleman of the highest standing and professional reputation—the Hon J M Woolworth, who is an attorney and counsellor of years' standing in Nebraska, and who, it may be asserted, is of United States repute

"The next question that to any inquiring mind will arise is,—' How is this property to be sub-divided and dealt with, and what are the probable returns for the investment ?" The great question of drainage arises first The draining is by means of the slopes or valleys all running into the main drainage formed by the creek that follows the line of the Union Pacific Railway (as will be seen on the map), which empties into the Papillion River, and thence passes on into the Missouri, rendering the natural drainage perfect in every respect, and in the place of running into the City of Omaha, passes directly away from it Nearly all American cities are laid out in right angles, and to preserve these streets in a direct line of the compass, a vast expense is often incurred in grading, cutting down high lots and filling in low lands The intention is to abandon this plan, and to deal with this property in laying it out in natural grades, using what nature has so freely given, and to sub-divide by means of the gentle sloping valleys so as to have an easy ascent or descent to and from the hills, which offer the most picturesque sites for the residential portion of the town In Omaha, during the year 1883, $150,000 was expended in merely grading the streets, and with paving and sewerage over half a million dollars

"The stock yards and packing houses are [to be] located in a valley at the southern extremity of the purchase, entirely out of view, and to comprise in such re-sale to that company about 156 48 acres Two hundred feet on each side of the Union Pacific Railway, about two miles in length, are to be reserved for warehouses, stores, elevators, shops, and such premises as may require switches, and are directly dependent on railway facilities. The balance of the lands is to be sub-divided into lots and sold for cash or on long credit, with a reasonable rate of interest, payments for which being received either by bonds, cash or monthly.

"The taxes of Omaha are comparatively high, by reason of the vast expense of grading. It is intended to inaugurate a proper system of self-government, independent of Omaha, confining the taxation within the limits of the South Omaha corporation; nevertheless the growth of South Omaha will be the prosperity of Omaha, and so vice versa.

"The probable returns must next be considered, and they are so carefully studied that they are decidedly underrated rather than overdrawn:

The entire property, less the 200 feet herein referred to, will be divided into about 3,070 lots of about 60x150 feet each, which may be fairly estimated at $250 to $2,000 per lot, and will average $1,125 per lot ........ $3,453,750
The 200 feet reservation, divided into lots of 50x200 feet, will produce about 350 lots for the purposes before mentioned, as also for stores and retail business. These may be estimated at from $300 to $1,500 per lot, making an average of $900 per lot ............................ 315,000

Total ...... .................... $3,768,750

"This does not take into consideration the great advance by reason of improvements, buildings, etc., in the value of the property remaining from time to time unsold, but is based upon actual value, with a due consideration, to a limited extent, of the assured improvements.

"The population of Omaha, together with Council Bluffs, which is on the east side of the Missouri, and if properly called would be 'East Omaha,' and is now connected with Omaha by local trains of the Union Pacific Railway, is over 75,000, and with the addition of the proposed important business, within five years from the present date at least double, or 150,000, may be relied upon. However, this would only be a fair calculation in proportion to the growth of the city within the last three years, even without the impetus now contemplated. The bonds therefore as an investment,—being secured by this property, speak for themselves. It may be asked, what about the interest on the capital invested, which is always increasing. Bear in mind that the great increase in the value of the lots as each resident builds his house, effects an advance in fact that can scarcely be estimated. Following a judicious plan, which has proved highly successful in the sale of railway lands, the trustees will reserve each alternate lot, and thereby gain the benefit of the adjoining improvements."*

It will provoke a smile to consider, at this date (1893), the declaration made in the foregoing extract, " that the stock yards and packing houses * * * are to be so far removed from this vast purchase for a suburban town, that they will offer no ground of objection to sale for residential purposes;" and again, that " the yards and packing houses, etc., will be out of sight of the residential portions of the main estate, and be sufficiently far removed to render them no objection." And the following (the italicising is ours) is even more facetious: "The estate will be laid out into a well-arranged and carefully studied town *for working-men*, nearest to the yards. The more easterly portions will be sub-divided into lots suitable *for more wealthy residents.*"

The map mentioned in the extract just given is the first attempt ever made to deliniate South Omaha on paper. It is a map of Omaha, with South Omaha added on the south; but the latter is wholly fanciful, as it was drawn before the " town " of South Omaha was first surveyed (which survey is mentioned in the next paragraph). In some respects it conforms to the first recorded plat. East and west streets, lying east of the Union Pacific Railroad, are designated (as now) by letters, beginning with A and going south until I Street is reached. But north and south streets are not indicated either by names or numbers, except that what is now Twenty-Fourth Street is given as " Bellevue Avenue." A cable line enters South Omaha, where, from the north, the motor line now enters it, turning off of " Bellevue Avenue " at E Street, and running thence in a southwest course until the Union Pacific Railroad track is reached.

During the first half of the year 1884, the syndicate caused to be surveyed and platted three hundred and eighty-nine acres of their

---
*Omaha; Its Past, Present and Future. By C. R. Schaller. Printed in the "Seventh Annual Report of the Board of Trade of Omaha, for the Year ending December, 1883." Published in the first half of the year 1884.

land, one hundred and forty-four acres lying in section 33, of township 15, north, in range 13, east, and twenty-five acres in section 34, of the same township, also, one hundred and sixty-five acres lying in section 4, and fifty-five acres in section 3, of township 14, north in the same range. The plat was completed and certified to by George Smith, county surveyor, July 18, 1884. The tract thus laid out was named South Omaha. It included considerably over one-fourth of the syndicate lands and was laid out into one hundred blocks, containing 1070 lots, each 60x150 feet in size, with streets 80 feet and alleys 20 feet in width. Trees were planted on each side of every street, twelve feet from the line of the lot, and near the north end of the town two entire blocks were reserved for park purposes. The tract as surveyed and platted was bounded on the north by a part of the present south line of the City of Omaha, on the east by (the present) Twenty-third Street, on the west by the Union Pacific Railroad right-of-way, and on the south by an east and west line running about one hundred and twenty feet south of (the present) O Street.

Says a writer soon after "A tract of land has been selected a short distance south of Omaha, and in addition to having completely appointed stock yards, this company (Union Stock Yards Company of Omaha) intend to build a little annex, or suburban city around their operating premises. It will be a location of pleasant, comfortable and cheap homes, especially for those connected with the stock yards, where there will be every desirable social, religious and educational advantage."*

Even before lots were put on sale, we have this published Omaha statement, entitled,—"A word to Omaha Workmen." "Thousands of suburban lots have been sold [in Omaha] for a small cash payment, the balance to be paid in installments of ten or fifteen dollars per month. There are a very large number of workingmen, and people of limited means generally, who have thus made a start toward acquiring homes and hundreds who are on the lookout for just such opportunities. Every cent is being saved by these people, and applied to lots which they have purchased and upon which they are building small but comfortable houses. They are punctual in their payments, and a most desirable class of purchasers. Applications are coming every day from just such people for lots in South Omaha. This includes thousands of workingmen in this community, and the realization of permanent work in the stock yards, packing houses, etc., and of homes to be had on easy terms near then work, will make them substantial citizens. It encourages them to take a deeper interest in the welfare of the city and stop abuses through the ballot-box. Many of the Omaha workingmen already have comfortable homes entirely paid for, and now are looking out for, and acquiring additional property upon which they are erecting small houses to rent.

'The almost universal movement on the part of Omaha workingmen shows that they are a frugal and industrious class, who are the backbone of the city, and ever ready to maintain law and order. This may open the question whether rents will maintain their upward tendency. There is no doubt on this point, for Omaha will next year, 1885, and for years to come, continue to grow rapidly. It follows, therefore, that all who now secure homes or put money in real estate will reap a handsome profit."

After the syndicate had made the plat of a part of their lands before mentioned and duly recorded the same, a system of extensive improvements began.* Water works, at an expense of $30,872.07 were erected, clear cold water having been furnished the Union Stock Yards as early as August 1, 1884, by the syndicate, from a point in the northeast portion of their lands, which was not included in what had before been laid off as a town.

"Not among the least of the natural advantages of South Omaha, as a residence place," said a resident of the town, writing on the twenty-fifth of September, 1885, "is the splendid water from the South Omaha water works. In the northeastern part of

---
*The Leading Industries of the West (1884), p 27. But it will be observed the writer confounds the Union Stock Yards Company with the syndicate. "A little annex" is good, certainly.

*¹ The syndicate on New Years day 1884 deeded their entire possessions (except what had been determined upon for the Stock Yards Company) to trustees in trust to secure the payment of $1,400,000 in bonds. These trustees then organized for business—they would have a town surveyed and platted * * * and then they would put on sale their lots and by every inducement legally and fairly held out encourage emigration to South Omaha. They succeeded * * * Emigration thus far had been promoted not only by inducements held out for work at the stock yards and by the two packing firms, but had been stimulated by the liberal policy of the syndicate in selling lots at a moderate price and on long time at a fair rate of interest, besides many improvements were entered upon by the town proprietors which it was clearly seen by all newcomers would redound to their benefit."—*The Drovers Journal*, Dec 31, 1892 [the syndicate tract, adjoining] the town site, which is covered with a dense growth of timber, is a deep gorge through which runs a stream of pure sparkling water, fed by a number of living springs. Across this stream has been erected a dam and on its banks are situated the crib, pump and boiler house. The supply of water, furnished as it is by never failing springs, is inexhaustable, and has the advantage of being free from Missouri river mud, to say nothing of other filth. Since the first plant was made, additions have been built to the pump house, an additional boiler put in, and many other minor improvements made. There are two pumps with a joint capacity of 1,500 gallons per minute. The water is pumped, but as a matter of precaution a stand-pipe has been erected at an elevation of two hundred feet from the works, with a capacity for nearly one million gallons. This is kept full, for use in case of accident to the pumps or pipes. With this elevation a stream can be thrown fifty feet high at the stock yards, a mile distant, with stand-pipe pressure alone.

"The reservoir is in a most romantic spot, surrounded by a vast body of timber, which is to be underbrushed and otherwise improved for park purposes. At no distant day it will furnish a shady resort for the increasing population of South Omaha, and for tired [Omaha] city people as well." *

In laying out South Omaha—that is, in making the first survey and plat—the streets running north and south were wisely made to correspond in number to, and to connect with the streets of Omaha, beginning on the east line of the town plat with Twenty-third Street. The east and west streets were designated by the letters of the alphabet, the most northerly being marked A, the next south B, and so on, until the south line of the plat was reached.†

The lots were, soon after the platting, put upon the market. From the first sales‡ there has been, on the average, a steady increase in values. In some instances, however, there have been fancy prices obtained after purchase from the syndicate; in other instances, lots have been sold much below what the situation would seem to have demanded. Thus far, the highest values and prices have been reached on N Street, where, in one case, a corner lot, 60x150, sold, April 12, 1884, for $300, is now worth, without improvements, $30,000; another lot, sold in the spring of 1885, for $300, was afterwards cut up by the purchaser into six business lots, 25x60 feet each, the last of which the owner subsequently sold for $7,000.

In 1885, I S. Hascall had the sale of all lots north of G Street, and Bedford & Souer, all lots south of G Street. An advertisement of Hascall's reads as follows:

"Bargains in Lots.—Long Time.—Easy Terms.—I will sell any or all lots north of G Street, South Omaha, on the following terms: One-fourth cash, balance in one, two and three years, at seven per cent. No other suburb of Omaha can offer superior inducements in the way of land, conveniences, nearness to center of the city, and beauty of location. Inquire of I. S. Hascall, or at the *Globe* office."*

The *South Omaha Globe*, of October 30, 1885, says, in speaking of the "grand scheme" of establishing stock yards and laying out a town near them:

"As to the finances back of all this enter-enterprise, we will simply give the names of some of those interested. Their number includes some of the most wealthy and influential men of this country and Europe, among whom may be mentioned: Colen J. MacKenzie, of the British Linen Bank, of Edinburgh, Scotland, and president of the Swan Land and Cattle Company; Hon. A. II. Swan and Thomas Sturgis, of Cheyenne, Wyoming; Samuel W. Allerton, Joseph Frank, Nelson Morris and Isaac Waixel, of Chicago; C. A. Righter, of William Clark & Co., and Auguste Richard, ex-president of the Ogallala Land and Cattle Company, New York; while among the resident members [of Omaha] are Hon. W. A. Paxton, Caldwell, Hamilton & Co., Hon. John A. A. McShane, Hon. J. M. Woolworth, Hon. C. F. Manderson, Frank Murphy and B. B. Wood, president and cashier of the Merchants National Bank; Milton Rogers, Her

---

* J. B. Erion, in the *South Omaha Globe*, October 30, 1885. But the article, as stated in the text, was written over a month previous.

†It is to be borne in mind that the surveying, platting and naming of the tract already described (and, it may be premised, of all subsequent additions thereto, whether made by the successor of the syndicate or other parties, and lying within the present limits of the City of South Omaha), had nothing to do with, nor had any relation to the establishing of the village (afterwards the city) of South Omaha, or defining its limits. All these surveys, plattings, and the giving of them names, have been private matters; but the organization of the village and defining its limits was wholly a public affair, and will be treated of in a subsequent chapter.

‡The first lots sold were Nos. 5 and 6, in block 12, on the twelfth day of April, 1884, to George W. Masson, for the sum of $1,400. (See records of the South Omaha Land Co.)

*From the *South Omaha Globe*, October 30, 1885.

& Co., Markel and Swobe, George E. Barker, Samuel E. Rogers and J H Dumont. There are also, Anthony & Denhart, of Washington, Ill., B F Smith, of Boston, and M C Keith, of North Platte, Nebraska.

"The syndicate is managed by a board of trustees who are Hon A H Swan, president, C. W Hamilton, vice-president, Thomas Swobe, secretary, Frank Murphy, treasurer, Hon. W A Paxton, Hon J M Woolworth, Peter E Iler * * *

"We have thus given our readers a hurried and somewhat disconnected outline of the main features of a grand scheme, which, it is acknowledged by all, will materially add to the already wonderful progress of Omaha in its efforts to become one of the most important commercial centers in this country It means that the cattle of a thousand hills, which have heretofore been shipped through to Chicago at great risk and expense, will find a ready market nearer home South Omaha, with her network of railroads and central location, of all points on the Missouri, is best adapted to command this business, while the beautiful town site, withal, so near the center of the business portion of the city [Omaha], will furnish pleasant, healthy and profitable homes for thousands of people * * *

And thus, the *Omaha Daily Bee*, in May, 1886 "The town of South Omaha is building up rapidly, and hundreds of men are finding there pleasant and agreeable homes, while town lots are increasing in value at a rate which promises to rival the boom in Omaha city lots It is not surprising that those who are posted on the affairs of the stock yards are enthusiastic over the outlook and future prosperity of the business enterprises established there"

The trustees of the syndicate—Alexander H. Swan, William A Paxton, Peter E Iler, James M Woolworth, Morrill C Keith, Samuel W. Allerton, and Robert D Fowler —in consideration of $750,000, conveyed, by their deed, to John H Bosler, on the last day of January, 1887, all the lands belonging to the syndicate Nineteen days thereafter, Bosler and wife, by a special warranty deed, conveyed these lands to a number of persons who had associated themselves, a short time previous, as "The South Omaha Land Company" This company "stepped into the shoes" of the syndicate, for all purposes for which the latter had been formed It was in their articles of association stipulated that their principal place of business should be Omaha, and that the capital stock of the company should be $1,000,000, to be divided into shares of $100 each The bonds issued by the syndicate, amounting to $500,000, were canceled The board of directors was to consist of nine members, five of whom should be residents of Omaha The officers of the company, for 1887, were William A Paxton, president; John H Bosler, vice-president Peter E Iler, secretary and John A Creighton, treasurer The officers at this time (1893) are the same, except that Herman Kountze is president

The directors for the first year, which terminated December 7, 1887, were Alexander H. Swan, Robert D Fowler, John H Bosler, William A Paxton, John A McShane, Peter E Iler, John A. Creighton, Benjamin F Smith, and James M Woolworth It was determined that the officers and directors should be elected thereafter annually, the election to be held on Tuesday after the first Monday of December of each year, but this was subsequently changed to the Tuesday after the second Monday of that month

The laying out and platting of the tract already described, has been followed by four other separate surveys and plattings by the land company, all lying within the present limits of the City of South Omaha *

The land lying inside the City of South Omaha belonging to the South Omaha Land Company, which has not, at this date (January, 1893), been surveyed into lots and platted, or sold to the Union Stock Yards Company, comprises 108 acres, lying east of Twenty-third Street and north of G Street, (part of which is usually known as ' Spring Lake Park," or "Syndicate Park ")†

Many have heretofore supposed that *all* the land—all the farms—lying within what are now the limits of South Omaha, were purchased by the syndicate Such, however, was not the fact, only about 1411 acres, as before mentioned, were bought by that com-

---

* These subsequent surveys are not to be considered original surveys of South Omaha only the *first* was the original The four subsequent surveys of the company are not, as usually mapped 'additions to South Omaha " The lots marked on maps outside of the western limits of the city as belonging to the company, are a myth, no lots having been laid out

†"The South Omaha Land Company still retains the ownership of much land They have expended $ 000 [about $30,000] in improving Spring Lake Park, a tract of land consisting of 63 acres"—*South Omaha Daily Tribune*, December 31, 1892.

pany. Some persons who did not sell have since had cause to congratulate themselves. One of these recently disposed of forty acres for $80,000. Upon tracts disposed of at various times have been laid out many additions lying within the corporate limits of the city, made by parties upon lands not included in the syndicate purchase, some extending across the city's southern boundary into Sarpy County, and others across its western boundary into Douglas Precinct. There are, also, some entire additions in this precinct and in Sarpy County.*

At the present time (January, 1893) nearly all the company's lots, on the east side of the Union Pacific Railroad tracks, have been disposed of, and a portion of those in what is generally known as "the half circle" (third survey), in all, not less than fifteen hundred. West of the Burlington & Missouri River Railroad ("Lincoln Line"), very few lots have been sold. About sixteen hundred lots, in all, are yet in the market.

On the whole, the policy which has from the start been pursued by the syndicate and its successor, the South Omaha Land Company, while it has tended to the aggrandizement of those particularly interested (and why should it not?), has been a liberal one. It has not exhibited the spirit of "grinding the poor," so common in corporations of the kind.

---

*"Besides the marketing of their [the syndicate] lots, a large number of "additions" have been surveyed and platted by outside parties, who have not been slow, by the purchase of lands near by, to "turn an honest penny"—some of their surveys extending even outside of what are now the limits of South Omaha."—*The Drovers Journal*, December 31, 1892.

NOTE.—It was supposed when the syndicate made their first survey of lots, streets and alleys, that the town would spring up some distance to the northward of the stock yards, particularly because it was expected that packing houses would soon be erected; hence, the original plat extended no further southward than between the present O and P Streets, this being the southern boundary, while A Street was nearly the northern boundary. Now the streets running east and west were given the names of the letters of the alphabet, while the north and south streets, beginning at Twenty-third (which was run out as a continuation of Twenty-third Street in Omaha) were designated by consecutive numbers, going west. But the land lying west of Twenty-seventh and south of L streets, having been previously sold to the Union Stock Yards Company, was not, of course, laid out into lots. As the city grew, the houses, contrary to expectation, continued to crowd closer to the yards and to the packing houses (hereafter to be described); and N Street became the central part of the city. The second survey and platting by the syndicate was then made of their land lying east of the Union Pacific Railroad tracks and south of their first (or original) survey. The blocks conformed with the first survey, on the north and south streets—that is, on such as were designated by numbers; but not so on the east and west streets—the letters of the alphabet being abandoned and other names substituted—the blocks being much longer in the second survey than in the first. What has added to the confusion is the fact that numerous small additions have been platted west of the railroad tracks, and their east and west streets, although conforming to the second survey and platting by the syndicate, were given new names. It has been suggested that the trouble will soon be remedied, by the city authorities abolishing all the names as at present used for the east and west streets south of Q Street, and substituting therefor the letters of the alphabet, commencing with R. in regular order so far as they will go, and after that giving other names, but in every case extending them throughout their *entire length*.

# CHAPTER IV.

### DRESSED MEAT AND PACKING CONCERNS

Packing houses in Omaha were established several years before it was determined to induce packers from abroad to locate near the Union Stock Yards in South Omaha.

"The leading packers were James E Boyd, David Cook and J Phipps Roe Mr Boyd began business in this line in 1872 For the season of 1872-3 he bought and packed 4,515 hogs, at an average cost of $3 40 per hundred, 1873-4, 13 546 head, average cost, $3 65, 1874-5, 11,418 head, average cost, $5 75, 1875-6, 15,042 head, average cost, $6 42, 1876-7,33,561 head, average cost, $5 45; 1877, to January 1, 1878, 12,000 head, average cost, $3 65

"David Cook commenced packing in 1871, in a small way In 1873, O H Ballou bought an interest in the business, and the following season Cook & Ballou killed three thousand hogs, and the next season about the same number. The firm dissolved in the spring of 1877 Mr Cook carrying on the business alone, and up to the middle of December he had killed two thousand head of hogs, when a fire destroyed part of his buildings, causing him severe loss and temporary suspension of business With characteristic energy, however, he was soon rebuilding a packing house and smoke house, with brick, the former twenty by eighty feet and the latter thirty by forty feet

"J Phipps Roe invested $7,000 in the packing business, in buildings and grounds He began with the season of 1874-5, and packed 1,700 head that season In the winter of 1877-8, he packed 2,500 head, and in May and June, 1877, 2,000 more Up to the first of January, 1878, he had packed during the season 2,200 head, the average net weight of which was 260 pounds

"In 1877, James E Boyd's packing house was on South Chestnut and Second Streets, a good half a mile south of the "Bridge Yards," his office was at 495 Thirteenth Street J Phipps Roe's office was at 193 Farnam Street, David Cook's at the Union Pacific Railway track

"In addition to the gentlemen we have named, many of the leading butchers of the city packed more or less each season Sheely Bros, R A Harris, A Aust, William Aust & Knuth, F Hickenstine, and several others, packed from 1,000 to 2,500 head each In 1878-9, Mr Boyd packed 60,000 hogs On the 18th of January, 1880, his plant was destroyed by fire, but he rebuilt on a larger scale, at a cost of $50,000 He continued in the business nearly seven years longer His chief competitors were Harris & Fisher, and Joseph F Sheely & Company Harris & Fisher's packing house was near the "Upper Yards," but on the north side of the track Joseph F Sheely & Company's was east of Harris & Fisher's, and near the same yards The firm last named staid as long as they could do business successfully

"The packing house of Harris & Fisher was completed in the latter part of 1878 The entire cost of their building was $10,-000 They employed from twenty to fifty men, according to their necessity for help, at an average of from $1 50 to $3 00 per day The capacity of their packing house was four hundred cattle, with three hundred to four hundred hogs, per day They packed some mess pork, but made more of a specialty in dry, smoked and salt meats, and beef-curing and canning.

"The packing house of D Cook was purchased, January 15, 1880, by Joseph F Sheely & Co The firm killed about 15,000 hogs annually, also about 1,200 head of cattle and 5,000 sheep, and employed fifteen hands The establishment was subsequently [December 3, 1886,] burned down, and the firm went out of the packing business

"But the packing industry in Omaha, was, finally, nearly all given up, there having been established such a competition near by (outside the city limits), that it was futile to continue the business inside its boundary lines."*

It has already been shown who it was that first conceived the idea of establishing at or near Omaha not only stock yards, but packing houses, on a scale commensurate with the needs of the territory lying to the westward and southwestward of the Missouri River and extending to the Pacific and the Gulf.

A close observer, even before a single packing house had been built in South Omaha, wrote thus of the prospects:

"As regards the cattle interests, Omaha is reached from all of the cattle ranges of Nebraska, Wyoming, Colorado, Idaho, Montana, Utah and Oregon by the Union Pacific Railway, the Burlington & Missouri, and through the latter with the Atchison, Topeka & Santa Fe, and is the point above all others in the United States that offers facilities for stock yards, beef packing houses, etc. The English capitalists who control investments of $15,000,000 in cattle, some time since combined and agreed to start a competing market at Omaha, and to ship beef dressed to eastern and European markets. The project is not a new one, but has been under consideration by the far-seeing ones for some length of time. The treatment they have received in Chicago justified such a step, and when they considered it, the saving of 500 miles haul of beef on the hoof, between Omaha and Chicago, was of itself sufficient to determine to take the step. There was no point farther west than Omaha possessing the necessary facilities needed, and the choice naturally fell upon this city.

"The stock yards project has enlisted and secured $1,000,000 of English stock and American capital, and the beef packing, canning and other projects have been promised $2,000,000 of English capital, while these together with the bone manufactory, tannery, soap factory, glue factory, and several other concerns already assured, will at once add at least *ten* thousand to the present population of Omaha, all of whom will desire, naturally, to reside in that beautiful portion of the city thrown open in South Omaha, reached as it is, by the main line of the Union Pacific, seven minutes from the Union Depot in the city, and also by the Belt Railway, now partly *built*, and soon to be finished, which encircles the city. It has at once the advantages of metropolitan convenience, without the burden of metropolitan taxes.

"The following from the *Chicago Tribune* [of December 12, 1883,] speaks for itself as to how this new enterprise was received:

"'If the newly developed project of certain Chicago and Omaha capitalists proves as great a success as anticipated, there is a boom of prosperity in store for the busy little city across the bridge. The rapid strides Omaha has made during the last few years has attracted the attention of many wealthy men who believe she is to take high rank among the inland cities of the great northwestern territory.

"'Samuel Allerton, one of the heavy stockholders in the new company, says he and his two partners, who own yards in Council Bluffs, will join all their interests with the syndicate, which contemplates building new yards at Omaha. He says the cash capital of the new company is $1,000,000, and that it has secured a large tract of land in South Omaha, upon which buildings will have been erected by June 1st. Mr. Allerton says: 'I consider Nebraska and Dakota the greatest country in the West. Their cattle and hog-raising interests are unsurpassed. If Chicago can pack pork and beef for Europe cheaper than New York, then Omaha can do the same thing. I don't mean to say Omaha can hurt Chicago, as Chicago is on a solid rock foundation, but I do think Omaha is destined to become one of the best business points in the West, and in a few years will walk away from Kansas City.'"*

It was not alone the idea, then, of forming stock yards south of the city and contiguous thereto, which induced the organization, in 1883, of the Union Stock Yards Company of Omaha. They would not only create there a live stock market, but make it also a dressed meat and pork-packing center. Therefore it was that, while the yards were being urged forward, subsequently, to such a state as would justify the reception in them of live stock, a building was commenced, intended

---

*The Drovers Journal*, December 31, 1892.

"Packing in the city [Omaha] had been for a number of years carried on, but hogs only were slaughtered to any extent. During the previous few years Omaha had built up what was, at the commencement of 1879, thought to be a large business in pork-packing."—*Id.*

*Omaha: Its Past, Present and Future, (1884), in the Seventh Annual Report of the Omaha Board of Trade.

for packing purposes. This, as before stated, was in 1884

| | |
|---|---|
| The original contract for the packing house was | $60,000 00 |
| Add for changes in plans as per agreement July 7, 1884 | 4,095 00 |
| Extra for stand-pipes not included in original contract | 348 00 |
| Lumber furnished by the contractor for stock yards | 208 00 |
| Total | $64,651 00 |
| Deduct account changes in contract $4,370 00 | |
| Deduct for one tank furnished by the Union Stock Yards Company 350 00 | |
| Deduct for earthwork done by same company 725 46 | —5 445 46 |
| | $59 205 54 |
| Add to this the earth-work and tank as above, which had been charged to the construction account of the yards | 1 075 46 |
| | $60,281 00 |
| Deduct from this amount for lumber charged to packing house which went to build stock yards | 208 00 |
| Makes actual cost of packing house | $60,073 00 |

The building thus erected was a three-story frame, irregular in shape, running 350 feet along the railroad tracks, and 170 feet back. Connected with it was about six acres of ground. It was soon seen that consumers near by were appropriating to themselves a considerable amount of the live stock received at the Union Stock Yards. This hurried up the Union Stock Yards Company to look around for some heavy packing firm to locate near the yards. Success soon crowned their effort. Their packing house was leased for three years to G H Hammond & Co, a firm first organized in Michigan, in 1869, extensively engaged in the packing business. The company was duly incorporated, with a large capital, in the State just named

"While it is true that, in their articles of incorporation, the Union Stock Yards Company set forth that, among other things, the feeding and caring for live stock was to be carried on by them, and also that they were to slaughter, dress and pack cattle, hogs and sheep, nevertheless, it was the intention of the company, from the start, to induce others, if possible, to establish packing houses near the yards, by liberal gratuities extended them. Fortunate it was that so well-known and successful a firm as George H Hammond & Co was the first to accept an offer of the stock yards company, which was, to lease to them for a nominal amount, a packing house already erected, at a cost of nearly $65,000, near the yards, for a term of three years. And it may here be said that the entire plant was afterwards generously donated to the firm This, truly, was a policy, which, from the beginning, could but have the effect to induce packers of large means to locate in South Omaha. And the same liberality has, it may be said, been steadily pursued to this day, and to an extent which really seems surprising"*

An early writer says

"The great packing house at South Omaha was opened for business Saturday, May 23 [19], 1885, with great expectations of prosperous business, and, although the managers are men of generous business ideas, not one of them had a proper conception of the magnitude of the enterprise In nearly every department of the business supplies and capacity have fallen short of what the business demands." * * * But what is here referred to was the date of the first slaughtering of cattle

Hogs were killed as early as January 25th An agent† was sent into the country and purchased three car loads "to open the house" After the opening, cars commenced to come in slowly, but throughout the year Kansas City had to be mainly relied upon The reason was, Boyd's packing house was running in Omaha and there were stock yards at the bridge, where there was no "yardage," which operated against the Hammond enterprise, as "raidage" had to be paid in South Omaha Finally Boyd was obliged to come to the yards here to purchase hogs, also Stewart & Co, of Council Bluffs, and then Sheely Bros for their packing house in Omaha ‡ So much did Joseph F Sheely & Co and Harris & Fisher rely upon the Union Stock Yards toward the close of 1886 that these firms were put down as South Omaha packers

The packing house of Hammond & Co

---
* *The Drovers Journal*, December 31, 1892,
†W F Brown
‡ ' But the facilities early in the year [1885] for purchasing cattle and hogs at the Union Yards were limited, though they soon improved, stimulating also the business of packing inside the city of Omaha—carrried on, as already shown by James E Boyd Joseph F Sheely & Co, and by Harris & Fisher The first named, the heaviest packer killed 143 890 hogs during the year, aggregating in value $1 531,393 71 and the last mentioned killed 15,000 hogs, 12 000 sheep and 9,354 cattle, aggregating in value $4 00,000 "—*The Drovers Journal*, Dec 31, 1892

had, even in 1885, a daily capacity of 500 cattle and 1,000 hogs. Their products were shipped in their own refrigerator cars to eastern markets. This company—the pioneer packer in South Omaha—has from the start been shippers of dressed beef and hog products. In 1889, the firm sold their entire plant (including packing houses belonging to them not in South Omaha) to a company of eastern and European capitalists. The latter own the greater part of the stock. The firm was incorporated and the name changed to "The G. H. Hammond Company." The officers of the American board of this company are Andrew Comstock, president, Providence, R. I.; J. P. Lyman, general manager, Chicago; J. D. Standish, secretary and treasurer, Detroit; A. H. Noyes, superintendent South Omaha branch. It has its principal offices in Hammond, Indiana, where it has extensive slaughter houses.

The plant in South Omaha is located near the Union Stock Yards, west of the Union Pacific Railroad tracks. Both loading and unloading tracks connect all the railroads directly with the buildings.*

The number of hands employed by the company in South Omaha were, in—

1885 ............................................. 105
1886 ............................................. 170
1887 ............................................. 210
1888 ............................................. 220
1889 ............................................. 325
1890 ............................................. 330
1891 ............................................. 320
1892 ............................................. 585

The record of slaughtering by this firm is as follows:

|      | Cattle. | Hogs. | Sheep. |
|------|---------|---------|--------|
| 1885 | 24,106  | 13,576  |        |
| 1886 | 56,437  | 122,191 |        |
| 1887 | 62,563  | 138,319 |        |
| 1888 | 62,511  | 144,734 | 6,614  |
| 1889 | 66,759  | 155,074 | 10,959 |
| 1890 | 72,734  | 145,678 | 10,869 |
| 1891 | 64,387  | 123,738 | 9,379  |
| 1892 | 52,167  | 123,371 | 9,814  |

*A committee, consisting of Samuel P. Brigham, Joseph J. Breen and Z. Cuddington, in *South Omaha—The Magic City*, published the 7th of May, 1892, the following, concerning the company:

"The G. H. Hammond Company has torn down the frame beef house and has commenced the work of rebuilding. Two large brick buildings are being erected this year. The new beef house will be 144 by 172 feet and six stories high. The new hog house will be 178 by 231 feet and six stories high. The floor area of the two new buildings will be ten and one-half acres. Two arctic or ice machines of seventy-five tons per day will be used to chill these houses. The beef house will be completed and ready for occupancy July 1, and the hog house September 1, 1892. When completed the capacity of the plant will be 1,000 cattle, 2,500 hogs and 600 sheep per day. This is treble the present capacity of the house for cattle and more than quadruple that for hogs and sheep. The pay-roll will be more than trebled, as the additional capacity will necessitate the employment of from seven hundred to eight hundred hands.

"'The above is substantially as given by me to the committee and is correct. A. H. NOYES, Manager'."

The company's plant during a part of the summer of 1892 was entirely shut down owing to raising the old buildings and building new ones.*

The company has a capital stock, in all, of $6,500,000. During the year 1892, the South Omaha plant was (as, in May, it had been predicted) more than doubled in its capacity, two mammoth brick buildings, a beef house 144x172 feet, and a hog house 178x231 feet, were erected, with a floor area of ten and a half acres, increasing the entire floor area to about sixteen acres.

The new houses are supplied with every modern invention or improvement and are considered the perfection of packing house buildings. Two ice machines of seventy-five tons each, a lard refinery of 250 tierces per day, a tankage grinder with a cyclone grinder, costing $2,500, three dynamos of a total of 420 amperes, stationary engines increasing the horse power to 805, and six seventy-horse power tubular and two 225-horse power, Sterling boilers, costing $5,000, and two artesian wells of a capacity of 120 gallons per minute, were of the 1892 improvement. A perfect fire system, with a company, carts, hose and fire plugs and the American District Telegraph electrical fire alarm, insures practical safety. The retail market accommodates many citizens, as well as employes. The present capacity is hogs, 5,000; cattle, 1,200; sheep, 1,000; and calves 500 per day; and in its present shape 600 hogs, 200 cattle and 100 sheep can be slaughtered in an hour. In 1892 the hogs weighed 28,943,782, or 251 pounds each, costing $1,208,398.62 or $9.80 each, or $3.86 per 100 pounds; the cattle weighed 58,717,-550 or 1,126 pounds each, costing $1,868,-692.27, averaging $35.82 each or $3.18 per 100 pounds.

The G. H. Hammond Company now (January, 1893) has 1,000 refrigerator cars. The 585 employes drew $258,386.72, averaging $580.72 for 1892, and the distributive sales were $4,301,650.87 as compared with $4,219,-356.06 in 1891. The product of 1892 consisted in pounds of 2,228,198 short rib sides, 2,355,476 short clear sides, 829,353 other dry salt meats, 733,387 sweet pickle shoul-

*"On the 6th of April, 1892, a large force of workmen began the work of tearing down the old wooden part of the Hammond plant. This was the original building—the first constructed in South Omaha for packing purposes—and the object of its demolition was to give way to a modern constructed brick structure, with the latest improved machinery."—*The South Omaha Daily Stockman*.

ders, 3,806,478 sweet pickle hams, 1,616,618 other sweet pickle meats, 8,442,831 tallow, 1,069,853 bones, and 855,450 tierces of prime steamed lard and 3,112,460 tierces of other lard

From the beginning the business of this company at South Omaha has had a steady but marked annual increase. This prosperous condition augurs well for its future.

After the erection of a building and its lease to George H Hammond & Co for packing purposes, by the Union Stock Yards Company, the latter did not stop their good work in that direction. Their next enterprise was the building of another packing house, with a capacity of 4,000 hogs per day for Fowler Brothers, of Chicago, who were given a bonus of $185,000 to locate a plant here, work upon which began by grading the site in the spring of 1886

"Since work has actually begun on the new packing house [of Fowler & Brothers]," says a writer on the twenty-first of May, 1886, "everybody is trying to see who can secure the most real estate. The same lot, in one or two instances, has been bought by different parties on the same day, one purchasing of one agent and the other of another, neither having any knowledge that he had a rival until headquarters were reached, when 'first come, first served,' rule settled the matter. There is nothing succeeds like success, and the success of the live stock business at South Omaha has assured the future of the place. Men of means are scrambling over each other in their efforts to secure a slice in the thriving town where so much money has been and is being invested. The completion of the Exchange building has marked a new era in the progress and importance of the stock business, and that event being supplemented by the still greater one [of the commencement] of the building of the Fowler Brothers & Co's mammoth packing house and the prospect of others to follow, has put new life into every branch of the business represented here. Our lumber men are doing a big business, and the rapid increase of population is giving our provision stores a genuine boom and imparting an air of activity not seen in most other towns."*

*J B Erion, in the *South Omaha Globe-Journal*
"In the spring of 1884 a large tract of land was purchased south of Omaha's city limits and called South Omaha. Work was commenced on the yards April 8, 1884, and they were opened August 25 [13th] of the same year. In the year following the yards company built and leased to Hammond & Company a large

The successors in business of Fowler Bros. were, finally, "The Omaha Packing Company," which is the present organization. They commenced in South Omaha, as the "Anglo-American Packing Company," November 9, 1886, the present firm began February 1, 1888. The whole number of hogs slaughtered during that year was 285,188. A warehouse, 113x160 feet, was built in the meantime.

When Fowler Brothers began packing, on account of the little importance the packers at other points attached to South Omaha, the competition at this point was quite limited, and this company was able to buy stock at low rates, and consequently did a large business which was profitable. Since that time competition is sharper, prices are higher, proportionately. In early days, the firm frequently purchased all the hogs offered in the market.

"And here, it may be said, that this year to 1888, was the turning point, so to speak, in packing interests in Omaha and South Omaha, in the former those interests went down, never to be restored, in the latter they took a tremendous bound upward and onward. And so they continue to move to the present moment."*

It is unnecessary, in this connection, to follow, year by year, the magnitude and increase of the business of the Omaha Packing Company. Material, in July, 1892, was on the ground and work was being actively pushed in the enlargement of the plant †

"The company's South Omaha works are located near the stock yards, and have an packing house, and when that was fairly under way another packing house was built which was taken by Fowler Brothers, of Chicago, who were given a bonus of $135,000 to locate here. The opening of these two houses was the first sign of the city now known as South Omaha. Land was given different individuals and corporations as a bonus to build Houses sprung as if by magic and people found their way to the busy little city as fast as they cast their lot "—*South Omaha Daily Tribune*, December 31, 1892

But Fowler & Brothers can claim to be the *next after* Hammond only because of their contract to locate here and the beginning of work on their packing house. In the matter of *opening* their plant, they were the third in South Omaha by one day

*The Drovers Journal*, December 31, 1892

† On the seventh of May 1892, a committee of South Omaha citizens published the following

"An additional story will be put on the present cold storage house, making a hanging room of 160x32 feet, and a new chill room 128x30 feet of a capacity of 1,000 hogs per day in summer A new brick building for cold storage purposes, 65x285 feet and three stories high, will be erected south of the present buildings and facing the south railroad track. These improvements, when completed, will increase the capacity of the plant more than twenty per cent, and will give a capacity of 3,500 hogs in summer and 4,500 in winter, 125 cattle, 250 sheep and 50 calves per day

"'The above is the statement made by me to the committee and is correct

"'T W TALIAFERRO, Manager'"

area of several acres; also excellent railway facilities, and sheds and pens to accommodate 200 head of cattle and 5,000 hogs. Their houses are fully equipped with the latest improvements. On the premises are nine boilers of seventy-five horse-power each, and two of one hundred horse-power each; there are, also, three steam engines, each of one hundred and twenty-five horse-power. The electric plant furnishes nine hundred electric lights, and the cold storage is complete in every detail. The company owns a number of refrigerator and tank cars, and deal in fresh pork and beef, lard, oils, dry salt meats, mess pork, special meats, green hams, shoulders, smoked meats, and glue stock. Their business from the beginning has constantly increased. During the year 1892, their transactions reached $4,000,000; the amount paid by them, as shown by their pay-roll, was $156,000. The daily average of men employed was 325."*

The following additional particulars are given in the *Omaha Bee* on the 1st of January, 1893:

"During the year [1892] a new cold storage building, 67x130, and three stories high was erected south of the main building and facing on the south railroad tracks. An additional story 32x160 feet was built on the cold-storage department and a new chill room, 30x128, with a capacity of 1,000 hogs per day was erected. A retail meat market was erected on Thirty-third Street, primarily to supply the demands of employes, but with the additional view of supplying the local wants. * * * The improvements and enlargements made in 1892 increase the capacity of the house from 20 to 30 per cent. This house makes a specialty of hogs, and is the only packing house in the city given almost exclusively to that special industry. A few cattle, sheep and calves are slaughtered only to supply demands of regular customers.

"Twenty-seven electric alarm boxes, connected with the American District Telegraph office, together with a well drilled fire department, are of the protections against fire.

"Five artesian wells of a daily capacity of 125,000 gallons each, furnish part of the water supply. About 70,000,000 gallons of water are consumed annually.

"A Bundy automatic timekeeper has just been added as one of the latest improvements. Each employe is given a key, and on going to work, quitting or laying off, registers the hour and minute, by inserting the key in the machine.

"The plant is now thoroughly equipped, and is complete in every particular. * *

"The slaughterings were 348,046 hogs, 4,349 cattle and 207 sheep in 1891, and 304,620 hogs, 4,450 cattle and 87 sheep in 1892. The hogs weighed 77,125,876, or 255 pounds each, costing $3,768,550.90 or $11.84 each, or $4.89 per 100 pounds. The present daily capacity is 5,000 hogs, 125 cattle, 250 sheep and 100 calves. * * * The company has two car lines, 252 refrigerator cars and 25 tank line cars; $1,000,000 insurance is carried. The material consumed consisted of 450 carloads of coal, 301 carloads of salt, 30,000 tons of ice per year, 5,000 barrels and 100,000 boxes annually, and ten carloads of paper. The 1892 product consisted in pounds of 23,000,000 short rib sides, 8,500,000 shoulders, 9,000,000 hams, 14,500,000 lard, 1,812,000 fertilizer and 190,000 grease."

"This company's principal offices and headquarters are in Chicago, and they have also large packing houses in Hutchinson, Kansas. The officers are P. L. Underwood, president; Anderson Fowler, vice-president; Robert Stobo, secretary; James Viles, Jr., treasurer—all of Chicago. T. W. Taliaferro is the South Omaha manager."* The present company was, upon its organization, duly incorporated under the laws of Illinois, with a paid-up capital of $500,000, and its trade from all its plants extends not only throughout the entire United States and Canada, but also to Mexico, the West Indies, Central and South America and Europe.

"It must not be supposed that the locating in South Omaha of the packing firms of George H. Hammond & Co., and Fowler Brothers, discouraged others from coming in. In the fall of 1886 [commencing business in packing November 8], the third packing establishment was started here by Thomas J. Lipton," with a daily capacity of one thousand hogs. And here we may introduce an extract from the only South Omaha paper then published:

"It is, indeed, gratifying to those who have braved the inconveniences of a new town, and are yet wading the mud and enduring many unpleasant things to secure

*The Drovers Journal, December 31, 1892.  *The Drovers Journal, December 31, 1892.

something for the future, as South Omaha people have done, and are doing, to contemplate the sure foundation upon which they have builded Surely the stock yards pioneers have a brilliant future before them, to compensate for the hardships they have endured and the risks they have run Mr. B. F Smith, a heavy stockholder in the South Omaha Stock Yards Company, who lives in the East, was at the Paxton last night [December 12, 1886] says the *Herald* 'Mr Smith is very hopeful of the growth and prosperity of Omaha, and especially of the meat industry He said that Hammond was killing 1,000 hogs a day, Fowler Bros 3,500, Lipton 1,000—a total of 5,500, and the houses are not running to near their full capacity Fowler and Lipton have been running only four weeks Said Mr Smith ' We have plenty of water and the best facilities for drainage at the South Omaha Yards All offal is utilized, and there is not likely to be any such stench as at the Chicago yards with their dead river there Our improved methods will do away with that The Stock Yards Company has 276 acres left and the syndicate 1,400 acres The new Exchange building is crowded with offices, and more new buildings must be put up right away to accommodate the increased business Omaha is bound to be a great market Here is the place where the cattle are—the feed is There is a grand country here and it is only in its infancy yet. Take Omaha as a pivot and strike a circle of three hundred miles out and you've got the richest spot on the face of the earth The people of Omaha are in the center of this wealth and are getting rich fast The biggest boom Omaha ever saw will be during the coming year ' "

" ' The Missouri Pacific [Railroad] helps us greatly, because it is possible to get the cattle here from Kansas City Mr. Hammond's buyer goes on the Kansas City market each day and sends the cattle on here for dressing Rates on the railroads are so low that Omaha is at a great advantage over Kansas City Omaha beef is called the finest in Boston, because it goes there whithout being bruised, as beef is when shipped as far as Chicago before being slaughtered The Missouri Pacific is of great advantage to the stock yards

" ' There will be many other beef packing houses here soon Negotiations are pending to have some of the most prominent dressed beef films of Chicago come to Omaha The names I'll not give, as the negotiations are not yet completed, but Omaha will be the equal of Chicago if these films come here

" ' Armour, Swift and Fowler are among them, I suppose [queried the *Herald*] '

" ' You may have your own surmises about that The films you name are not asleep in matters of this kind Omaha is to be larger than Cincinnati, and perhaps as big as Chicago itself, in time, and in a few years, too [as a packing center] South Omaha then will be part of the city The best residence parts will be west and north Hammond now kills two hundred to three hundred cattle a day The development of the meat business at South Omaha is certain ' "*

Early in July 1887, the Lipton property was transferred to the Armour-Cudahy Packing Company, to whom the Union Stock Yards Company gave a bonus of $150,000, for locating a plant in South Omaha They immediately began the erection of a large packing house The slaughtering of hogs commenced by them on the 10th of November, 1887, cattle killing, in the month following The number of hogs slaughtered in November was 41,933, in December, 16,198 Their building was completed in 1888, when the value of the plant was estimated at $800,000

On the 15th of December, 1890, the Armour-Cudahy Packing Company was dissolved, Philip D Armour retiring from the South Omaha house, and Michael Cudahy and Edward A Cudahy obtaining ownership of the plant — doing business as " The Cudahy Packing Company,"† which is incorporated; Michael Cudahy is president, and Edward A Cudahy vice president and general manager The buildings are located directly west of the Union Stock Yards

A committee of citizens of South Omaha made on the 7th of May, 1892, the following report concerning the company

" The Cudahy Packing Company has begun work on the enlargement of its immense plant The enterprise of this company, the confidence of its managers in the South Omaha markets and the marvelous increase

---

* From the *South Omaha Daily Stockman* December 13, 1886

† " T J Lipton opened a packing house in 1887 with a capacity of one thousand hogs, which was sold in the same year to the Armour-Cudahy Packing Company, now the Cudahy Packing Company The stock yards people gave Armour-Cudahy a bonus of $150,000 "—*South Omaha Daily Tribune*, December 31, 1892

of the business of that house, have been the pride of South Omaha, the wonder of packing interests, and the admiration of Nebraska.

"The improvements commenced will cost not less than $200,000, and are the most important ever made in South Omaha since laying foundations for the packing plants, and will consist of six large buildings, covering three and one-half acres of ground.

"A beef house, 90x225 feet and five stories high, is being erected immediately west of the present beef house, extending to Thirty-third Street. A warehouse, 278x165 feet and two stories high, is being erected west of Thirty-third Street and just north of the pepsin works. This will be used as a hide cellar and for the storage of canned goods and cooperage.

"A tin shop, 125x150 feet, and two stories high, is being built west of Thirty-third Street and north of the new tin shop, which will just double the capacity, and allow 75,000 [50,000] packages to be turned out daily.

"A new butterine factory, 60x100 feet and three stories high, west of the present butterine factory, to be supplied with the most improved machinery, will give a capacity of [over] 150,000 pounds a week.

"Repair shops, 75x150 feet, for repairing the company's railroad cars, will be located immediately east of the old hog house and fertilizer department. To allow this, the loading chutes of the Stock Yards Company have been removed, and the switches and tracks running up to the east end of the building, are being removed north of the new buildings and the old repair shops.

"The fertilizer department will be increased by a building 50x100 feet. The canning department will be increased by the use of the present tin shop quarters, and will then have a capacity of 150,000 to 200,000 pounds a day.

"The old butterine factory will be added to the oleo department.

"Eight new 100-horse power boilers will be added to the power-producing equipments, an additional 150 ton arctic or ice machine will be put in the new engine rooms, and a complete and well-equipped machine shop will make this one of the largest and most perfect packing plants in the West. * * *

"With every legitimate branch of packing house business in operation, from cattle and hog slaughtering, and curing, to sausage making, canning, making butterine, beef extract and pepsin, the Cudahy Packing Company has the most complete packing house in the West, and doing a business of $15,000,000 a year, is one of the largest.

"'I have read the above article, and it is substantially correct.

"'E. A. CUDAHY.'"*

The value of their manufactured products for the year ending July 1, 1892, was about $12,000,000. In their report given the writer in the month last mentioned, they say:

"We own and operate 300 refrigerator cars, for the shipment of dressed beef, 10 tank cars for shipment of liquids. There has been added to the plant during the current year the following buildings [being those already mentioned by the citizens' committee of South Omaha; also a] machinery shop, car repair shop and blacksmith shop, besides numerous additions to old buildings; total cost of such improvements being about $250,000.

"Branch houses have been established in the following places:

"Jacksonville, Florida; Los Angeles, California; Brooklyn, New York; Nashua, New Hampshire; Lincoln, Nebraska; Seattle, Washington; New Orleans, Louisiana; three in the City of New York; Minneapolis, Minnesota; St. Louis, Missouri; three in Chicago; [and now, 1893, one in Sioux City.]

"Our packing house is fitted out competely with electric fire-alarms, connecting directly with the Omaha Fire Department, the South Omaha Fire Department, and the private department of the company, the latter of which consists of ten men and a professional chief, who have spacious quarters on the floor above the office, where a restaurant is run, with a capacity for serving 150 at a single time.

"Within the last twelve months we have added a manufactory for the production of pepsin, in all its various forms, beef extract, pancreatin and oleomargarine, the latter of which we produce about 20,000 pounds per day. [The capacity of the beef extract department is about 125,000 pounds per annum; that of the pepsin department, 15,000 pounds].

---

* See report of Samuel P. Brigham, Joseph J. Breen and Z. Cuddington, advertising committee, in *South Omaha—The Magic City.*

## DRESSED MEAT AND PACKING CONCERNS.    629

" In our tin shop we consume about $350,-000 worth of tin in the manufacture of boxes into which is packed lard and cans for the packing of preserved meats

" In our office we employ at present ninety-five men Our market extends throughout the whole United States, Canada, England, and the Continent. [The office staff is divided into departments, twenty-five in number· Provision, south and east, west and jobbing, fresh meat, foreign, butterine, chemical and pharmaceutical, traffic; shipping; paymaster, store-keeping, electrical; telegraphic; credit, auditor's, cashiers, book-keeping, billing, consignment, mailing Each of these departments has a manager].

' We carry, consigned on sale, about $1,000 000 worth of product, in the hands of about one hundred or more consignees, for convenience in exporting, from $300,-000 to $500,000 worth of canned meats are stored in New York "

There was published, on the last day of 1892, in a South Omaha paper, the following

" This company, which is the second in size in the world, * * * has been incorporated under the laws of Illinois, and its trade now extends, not only throughout the entire United States and Canada, but into Great Britain and other European countries, Mexico, the West Indies, and Central and South America * * *

" They ship a large number of car-loads of meats and provisions daily Their plant, as might be expected, is, in all respects, first class "*

A still later published statement giving particulars of the Cudahy Packing Company's plant in South Omaha, is that to be found in the *Omaha Bee* of January 1, 1893 " The Cudahy Packing Company has a capital of $3,500,000 and it increased its distributive sales from $15,182,001 87 in 1891 to $19,070,540 00 in 1892 The improvements [were in accordance with the report of the citizens' committee already given, with the addition of a] beef extract and pepsin laboratory 80x125 feet, chill room to the old hog house, with a capacity of 1,500 hogs per day, an additional story to the canning department, and a game and poultry department, with a capacity of 3,000 chickens, 1,000 turkeys and 500 ducks and geese per day * * * Five new artesian wells, of sixty gallons per minute, have been drilled An efficient fire brigade and American District Telegraph system guard against fire * * * A $12,000 booth will be erected and stocked at the Chicago Exposition * * * The hogs bought in 1892 weighed 153,784,248 pounds, averaged 248 pounds, cost $6 743,441 27, or $10 87 each, or $4 38 per 100 pounds The cattle weighed 164,988,252 pounds, averaged 1,053 pounds, and cost $4,479,431 04, or $28 65 each, or $2 71 per 100 pounds. The sheep weighed 1,664,-618 or 92 pounds each, and cost $76 906 74, or $4 25 each, equal to $4 62 per 100 pounds

" The present daily capacity of the house is 6 000 hogs, 1,200 cattle and 1,000 sheep. * * * The consumption during 1892 consisted of 3,300 car loads of coal, 700 of salt, 1,621 of ice, 100 of wood, 50,000 boxes of tin plate, 12,300,000 tin packages, 210,000 barrels, tierces and kegs, 1,230,000 boxes and 1,800 barrels of vinegar, 13,371 car loads of product were shipped in 1892 Under the 80 per cent clause the company carries $2,750,000 insurance and pays annually $55,000 in premiums The year's exportations amounted to $3,250,000 The telegraphic tolls are $65,000 yearly and the letters received and sent are 1,200 daily, besides 15,000 circulars weekly, costing $12,-000 a year The company is represented by twenty-eight branch house managers, with a force of 187 brokerage agencies, twenty-eight traveling salaried representatives and fourteen European general agencies * * * The product for 1892 consisted of * * * [besides what has already been given] beef extract, 236,300 pounds, and pepsin, 31,683 pounds "

But the latest account is the one from the *Commercial Enquirer*, of March, 1893 It says

"Wonder at the immensity of the plant required is one's first sensation upon viewing the great packing establishments of the West, wonder at the marvelous economy and the diversity of processes and products by which it is possible, is the second. Nothing is wasted. The meat, the hide and the fat, once summed up the value of an ox. He has many other virtues long hidden, now active. What he and his friend the hog, are capable of one may see by following them on their progress through the works of the Cudahy Packing Company At the end

---
* *The Drovers Journal* December 31, 1892

they will have assumed a dozen, perhaps twenty, novel, ingenious, economical or obscure shapes; and the waste product could be carried in one's hat.

"That an establishment with an annual product worth $20,000,000 is a large one, is a matter of course; but the impression conveyed by dollars alone, is vague. What one sees tells much more.

"When one has walked exactly a quarter of a mile in a straight line, past a row of buildings continuous and unbroken, occupied by a single firm, his idea of the extent and importance of the meat business very suddenly enlarges. When his experience has been further enlarged by a tramp of several miles contemplating beef and pork in various forms at every step, without going from beneath a roof, he conceives a profound respect for the great American hog. After he has spent two solid days, with no time wasted, in viewing the various departments of the Cudahy Packing Company, he revises all previous notions of a "big" concern, dismisses all old standards with a touch of contempt, and finds himself disposed to wondering admiration for the marvelous organizing talent, the remarkable executive ability that built up and directs so vast and complex a business.

"Many a 'down-east' farmer would think himself fortunate with a farm equal in area to the Cudahy Packing Company's floor-space. Twenty-three and a half acres are covered by buildings; there are over seventy-five acres of floor-room; and fifteen acres of cold-storage rooms. About 500,000 cattle are killed annually; 2,000,000 hogs are converted into pork, etc.; and many thousands of sheep, calves, poultry, etc., are disposed of. Besides this immense establishment, the Cudahy Packing Company have another large plant at Sioux City, Iowa, recently purchased from Ed. Hankinson & Company. Six hundred men are employed, the annual product is worth $8,000,000, and the plant has facilities for killing 3,500 hogs daily. This packing house is simply an adjunct controlled and managed from South Omaha. Besides the more usual animal food-products in every variety, [over] 200,000 pounds of . . . beef extract—a comparatively new and very valuable food preparation—and 4,000,000 pounds of butterine are annually produced. The mere catalogue of what we may call by-products is formidable; not long ago hog-stomachs were useless except for the rendering tank and fertilizers; now they supply [more than] 30,000 pounds of pepsin annually—a business of several hundred thousands of dollars. Then there is pancreatine, ox gall and glycerole compounds; knife-handle bones; comb and button stock from horns; glue; bone phosphates; blood phosphates; other fertilizers; blood albumen; sausage casings, and several other manufactured by-products; not to mention a factory for making the tin cans used in the canning department, where 50,000 boxes of tin plates are consumed every year; and an ice-making plant producing over 200 tons of ice every day."

The business statistics of the company for the year ending December 31, 1892, were as follow:

| | |
|---|---|
| Total distributive sales | $19,070,540 |
| Total pay-roll | 1,200,000 |
| Number of employes | 2,400 |
| Total ground covered by buildings | acres, 23½ |
| Total floor area in buildings | acres, 75 |
| Total cold storage area in buildings | acres, 15 |
| Hogs killed | 620,501 |
| Cattle killed | 156,684 |
| Sheep killed | 18,094 |
| Made pork (all kinds) | barrels, 21,426 |
| Made beef (all kinds) | barrels, 31,421 |
| Made lard (all kinds) | pounds, 28,936,679 |
| Made dry salt meats | pounds, 51,583,668 |
| Made sweet pickled meats | pounds, 38,192,051 |
| Made smoked meats | pounds, 28,587,039 |
| Made canned meats | pounds, 10,713,120 |
| Made butterine | pounds, 2,583,467 |
| Made fertilizers | pounds, 11,250,000 |
| Made sausage | pounds, 3,232,295 |

The company have a retail meat market for the convenience of their employes and outsiders, and, in this line, they do a flourishing business.

It was early in the summer of 1887 that negotiations were concluded between the Union Stock Yards Company and G. F. Swift, pork packers and shippers of dressed beef, mutton and pork, of Chicago, for still another packing house in South Omaha. Mr. Swift was given a bonus of eleven acres of land and about $135,000. The house was built and the slaughtering of cattle commenced April 1, 1888, but that of hogs not until in December following. The value of the buildings was $300,000. The plant was then run, and still is, under the name of Swift & Company.

A published description of Swift & Company's South Omaha plant for the year 1888, is this: "G. F. Swift, president; A. C. Foster, general manager The buildings are located west of the Union Pacific Railroad tracks and south of the " Y," and has front and rear railroad switch tracks, with facilities for loading fifty cars of dressed meats per day The buildings are brick and cover an area of two and one-half acres, and have a floor area of about six acres, the chill-room covers about two acres, the machinery consists of four boilers, of one thousand horse-power, and two Corliss engines of two hundred and twenty-five horse-power, and two dynamos, with arc and electric circuits, with twenty arc and six hundred incandescent lights The slaughter, tank, and fertilizer houses are each three stories high, the oil house four, and the bone house five Four elevators are in use. New ice houses, with a capacity of 7,500 tons, were erected at South Omaha during the year, and the ice houses at Cut Off Lake were enlarged to hold 150,000 tons The capacity of the ice boxes is 6,000 tons The monthly pay-roll is from $12,000 to 15,000 About 6,500 tons of salt and 12,000 tons of coal are used per year Ten to twelve cars of dressed meats a week are shipped to G F. Swift & Son's market in Omaha * * *

"From April 1, to December 31, 1888, the slaughterings were Cattle, 62,370, sheep, 23,963, hogs, 8,260, calves, 1 803; total, 96,396 Hog slaughtering was not commenced until December 4th The business of this well-managed packing house has increased from $104 990 in December, 1887, to $415,640 in December, 1888. The value of the product shipped from April 1, to December 31, 1888, was $3,790,151 "

The capacity of the plant at the close of 1888, was 800 cattle, 1.000 hogs, and 800 sheep per day

"During 1890, a cold storage building was erected, the structure is brick, 128x214 feet, and six stories A brick tank-house and hog-killing brick building, 80x153 feet, three stories was erected A frame ice house, 144x160 feet, of 14,000 tons capacity, was erected immediately south of the main building Besides these local improvements the company bought 145 acres of land, near Ashland, for ice fields, and has erected an ice house, 192x420 feet, of 60,000 tons capacity Eleven new boilers of one hundred horse-power each, was added to the four old ones, making the motor power 1,800 horse-power, and one new 125 horse-power engine was added to the three old ones, increasing the horse-power to eight hundred An arctic, or ice machine, of one hundred tons per day, was added, giving a product equal to two hundred tons of ice daily A dynamo, with a capacity of one thousand incandescent electric lights gave the plant sixteen hundred incandescent and thirty-five arc lights ot two thousand candle power These improvements nearly doubled the capacity of the plant."

In May, 1892, the improvements of the company were published by a South Omaha committee *

" Work has already been commenced by Swift & Company on improvements that will increase the capacity of that establishment fully twenty-five per cent One large building, 64x193 feet and six stories high, has been built along the unloading tracks running between the old and the new houses This building extends from the new pork house north 193 feet and is divided into three departments The first department, or southern end, will be constructed for cold storage on the first and second stories the third story for the lard department, the fourth story for sausage, the fifth story for cooperage, and the sixth for general storage The second department will be the smoked meat department, and then will come six smoke houses 14x14 feet

"'I have read the above article and it is substantially correct

"'A C Foster, Manager'

[Superintendent]"

A late publication—one made on the last day of the year 1892—says

"It was in the summer of 1887 that another packing house was established in South Omaha—thanks to the munificent action of the Union Stock Yards Company, Swift & Company located here, and then the " Magic City " could boast of four large plants, and of that number it is still assured

" The principal offices and headquarters of Swift & Company are located at the Union Stock Yards, Chicago, and they have likewise an extensive plant at Kansas City. Their general business is packing, and the shipping of dressed beef mutton and pork The South Omaha Works are under the management of Mr. A C Foster. The

*Samuel P Brigham Joseph J Breen, Z Cuddington, in *South Omaha—The Magic City*

company own hundreds of refrigerator cars, and they have fresh meat depots in all the principal cities of the United States. The various departments of their South Omaha works are fully equipped with all the latest improved, appliances, apparatus and machinery known to the trade, operated by steam power." * * *

A still later account given to the public is this:

"During 1892 extensive improvements were made by this company. * * * North of the old fertilizer department, a building 80x176 feet has been erected, and is used for engine and boiler rooms and additional fertilizer department. This building is connected with the old fertilizer building on the south and the new hog killing building on the north. Eight new boilers of 1,000 horse power and one engine of 225 horse power are the additional machinery equipments of this power plant. South of the old beef house a beef killing addition has been erected. This building is 144x236 feet and three stories high, and is used for cooling beef, hogs and sheep.

"The slaughterings during 1892 were, hogs, 276,766; cattle, 233,583 and sheep, 76,143, as compared with 197,009 hogs; 151,468 cattle, and 55,406 sheep."†

The latest published account gives these (among other) particulars:

"During the last year the capacity [of the plant] has been increased materially. Among other improvements two immense beef and hog slaughtering houses have been erected and equipped with the latest improved devices for turning out packing house products.

"Swift & Company, not alone are prepared and do supply home trade, but ship their products to all parts of the civilized world. * * *

"It was in the month of March [May, 1887], a blustering day [a warm day], when Swift & Co. began to lay the foundation for their future great plant in South Omaha. Manager [Superintendent,] A. C. Foster had charge of the work then and has to-day. Work was pushed as rapidly as possible, and within a year the house was ready for operation. Since then it has been almost a continual addition of new buildings."‡

*The Drovers Journal, Dec. 31, 1892.
†The Omaha Bee, Jan. 1, 1893.
‡The Omaha World-Herald, January 6, 1893.

When it is considered that South Omaha eight years ago had no packing interests and that now it has four packing houses that compare favorably with the largest in the world; when it is seen that each year thousands of cattle, hogs and sheep are slaughtered here, the whole number on the average of more than 6,000 head each day; when it is learned that more than two millions of dollars were paid out in this city in 1892 for labor performed in these four establishments; when it is known that more than $28,000,000 were paid out by the South Omaha packers each year to drovers and farmers for live stock to be slaughtered here—can it be considered a gross exaggeration to say that the growth of South Omaha as a packing center is without a parallel in the West? We think not.*

"One or two commission firms handled all the stock received [at the stock yards in South Omaha at their opening,] and one packer had no difficulty in taking care of the entire receipts [for some time after.] The record since then has been one of enlargement and improvement in every essential particular. Even in this age of commercial miracles, men are compelled to wonder at the rapidity and substantial nature of the growth of the live stock industry at this point. The law of supply and demand has brought the producer and consumer of meat closer together each year—the distributing point gradually moving westward with the growth and development of the country. In this way, Chicago displaced New York as a live stock market and distributing center, and this position she has been enabled to hold for a quarter of a century on account of unequaled resources and facilties."†

The four packing establishments of South Omaha do a business third in magnitude of the chief packing centers in the United States; which business, if the increase is carried on two or three years longer, as it has been for a brief period just passed, will be second in the country; that is, it will only be excelled by Chicago. In 1886, the year in which the business of packing in South Omaha may be said to have been fairly under way, the wages paid by all the packers (as nearly as it could be esti-

*Adapted from The Drovers Journal of December 31, 1892.
†Union Stock Yards Directory. By Bert Anderson and A. F. Stryker.

mated,) was $216,000, the amount paid to farmers and stockmen for live stock something over $5,700,000, in 1892, the employes, (4,246 in number,) received $2,345,400, and the amount paid for hogs, cattle and sheep slaughtered, $28,450,000 The number of hogs cattle and sheep packed during the year last mentioned, was hogs, 1,320,386, cattle, 453,113, sheep, 103,406

The total weight of this live stock was over 800,000,000 pounds, and in round numbers the packers paid for it about $30,000,000

The total number of hogs, cattle and sheep packed in the eight years in which packing houses have been established in South Omaha is, for

| | |
|---|---|
| 1885 | 109 683 |
| 1886 | 312 999 |
| 1887 | 903 460 |
| 1888 | 1 039 366 |
| 1889 | 1,323,764 |
| 1890 | 1 792 772 |
| 1891 | 1 768,466 |
| 1892 | 1 876,905 |

The aggregated distributed sales of packing house products for 1892 in South Omaha were $45,160,885

It is safe to say that there are not now in South Omaha—in Omaha—in Nebraska—in the entire West—any croakers or timid spirits who say or believe that the Union Stock Yards of the Magic City will "soon become a waste place, or its packing houses a solitude"* Says Secretary Sharp, of the Union Stock Yards, in his report for 1892

"In addition to the constant improvements being made by the stock yards company, all the time, one of the most encouraging features of the market here is the enormous outlays made by all the different slaughterers in enlarging their plants, and thus preparing for increased receipts and increased business Over a million and a quarter of dollars have been expended by Hammond, Cudahy, Swift, and the Omaha Packing Company, during the past twelve months in increasing their killing and storing capacity for cattle, hogs and sheep The capacity has beeen increased over thirty per cent The management of these houses are not known as "rain-bow chasers," and the substantial nature of the improvements made, gives the market an assurance of permanency, which could come from no other source.

*The Drovers Journal, December 31, 1892

"But in addition to the buyers for the local killers, eastern and western slaughterers and exporters have buyers here at all times, for cattle, hogs and sheep, so that complete local control of the market is absolutely out of the question, and the shipper is always sure of a ready sale at full market value. This is especially true as to hogs, for hardly a day passes on which eastern houses do not take from 200 to 2,000 or 4,000 hogs There never has been a time, however, when local houses have been compelled to turn away stock of any kind for lack of accommodations"

Government meat inspection at South Omaha was inaugurated by the secretary of agriculture, July 1, 1891, Swift & Company being the first packers to receive the inspection—the other packers soon following. The inspection consists in an examination while in the yards, of all cattle, sheep and hogs, by the inspectors in charge of the various abattoirs, all animals presenting evidence of disease, being rejected After the animals reach the killing floors they are again subjected to a critical post-mortem examination, and all carcasses found diseased are removed to the fertilizing tanks in the presence of the veterinary inspector in charge The carcasses of those animals found perfectly healthy, receive the government certificate

September 12th, 1891, the microscopic inspection of pork intended for export, was granted to the Cudahy Packing Company, and the Omaha Packing Company. The other packers afterwards applied for inspection, owing to the great demand for inspected pork, and have received it The microscopic force examine samples taken from the slaughtered hogs, for trichinæ spiralis (an animal parasite), which so often infests the flesh of hogs The microscopic work consists in taking three small pieces of meat from different parts of the hog, tagging the animal, and sending the samples with corresponding tag numbers to the microscopical rooms Those animals found diseased are removed from the abattoir in the presence of the veterinary inspector in charge of the cooling rooms, and the healthy carcasses receive the government stamp, and are then ready for export

"The work [meat inspection]," says a recent writer, "requires the utmost care and painstaking, and upon the thoroughness with which it is accomplished depends the reputation of South Omaha meat in the markets of the world. Before each operator is a pile of small, round wooden boxes. Each of these contains two pieces of meat, one cut from the neck and one from the diaphragm of a hog. The box is opened and with a tiny pair of scissors the operator clips small oblong slips from each of the specimens and arranges them upon the glass of the microscope. The lens is properly adjusted and the hunt for trichænial germs is begun. The examination is continued until it is certain that no lurking bacilli remain undiscovered; and then, if the result is favorable, it is so reported, and the animal from which the specimens were clipped is eligible for shipment to the European markets. Each specimen is accompanied by a slip of paper bearing a printed number that corresponds to a number attached to the hog from which the specimens were taken, and if any bacilli are discovered, the animal is condemned and cannot be exported.

"Considering the fact that the meat inspection bill was only passed a little over a year ago, and that its expense was only provided for by a limited appropriation of $200,000, the meat inspection department has attained a marvelous degree of proficiency. This is especially the case in South Omaha."

The microscopic inspection of pork is performed largely by ladies. A description in detail of the work might be interesting, but suffice it to say that, generally, they are seated at tables, in groups of four or six, each with a mounted and highly polished microscope before her, through which she squints with one eye at two tiny strips of pork from as many different portions of the deceased hog's anatomy, tightly compressed between two pieces of heavy plate glass, held in place by a metal frame. He who looks at an infected specimen, will see, instead of a reptile as large as a boa constrictor, as he expected, a vicious little animal (against which France and Germany turned their diplomatic batteries), which looks like the hair spring of a watch, coiled up in a transparent paper sack. The trichinæ are always coiled and encysted, and appear dormant, unless released by the compression between the plates of glass, when they continually lengthen and contract the coils, similar to a watch spring in motion. The proper adjustment and use of the microscope is the first lesson the microscopist has to learn, and the duties of the chief microscopists, when giving their first lesson, are very much those of the old-fashioned country schoolmaster.[*]

---

[*] Adapted from the *Omaha Bee*.

# CHAPTER V.

### PIONEERS AND PIONEER TIMES.

The pioneers of South Omaha—"ye ancient pioneers"—are those who were dwellers here a few months after the farms within the city's present limits were sold to the syndicate, or who had previously been residents within what are now its established boundary lines. We may mention of the class first named, the following heads of families, each home having, as nearly as can be remembered (including hired help), the number given. J Bagley, Sr., 4, J. Bagley, Jr., 5, Q O Reily, 9, Ed Cassady, 6, Philip Cassady, 4, B Jetter, 7, Thomas Ryan, 7, J J O'Rourke, 5 Patrick Hoctor, 4, Chas Williams, 6, Ferdinand Wendt, 6, Michael Dee, 5, Jacob Jetter, 6, Mr Shipright, 6, Wm Schmeling, 5, John Schwenck, 5, Christian Sautter, 5, Mr Thomas, 5, Fred Drexel, 10 total, 110 But there are others, also, to whom belong the title of pioneers Those who came here after the Union Stock Yards Company began work upon their stock yards, but before the village of South Omaha was organized, which event took place, it may be premised, in October, 1886 "The pioneers of the territory included within what is now its incorporated limits, came not to form a city, but to secure themselves farms, and some of them came early, even when Omaha was only known on paper And they continued to live, until a recent period, in 'Douglas Precinct'—a division of Douglas County not yet wholly wiped out by the onward march of a 'metropolitan city,' or of a 'city of the first class, having over eight and less than twenty-five thousand inhabitants'"*

West of the Union Pacific tracks, in 1875, and for ten years previous, was a county road, commencing in Omaha near the north end of the present Sixteenth Street viaduct, running thence westerly near to what is now the "government corral," thence to what was then, and is now known as Quealey's Soap Factory, from there it took a southwesterly course, reaching the present northern limits of South Omaha at the north end of South Omaha Boulevard near blocks 203 and 204 of the syndicate survey, thence to the northwest corner of block 237, thence south on what is now Thirty-sixth Street, to the Sarpy County line There was also a traveled road leading south from the "poor farm" in Omaha which reached the northern boundary of South Omaha, as afterward defined, at the northwest corner of block 3, of Thomas and Sears' addition to South Omaha, running thence on the present Forty-tourth Street, south, leaving it at about the crossing of Spring Street, in Hascall's subdivision, running thence in a southwesterly course to Papillion These were the only two roads west of the Union Pacific tracks at the time the syndicate began their purchases Nearly all country travel, coming in from the southwest of Omaha, came in on these two roads

In the present Thomas and Sears' addition there lived Mr Thomas, at the time of the syndicate purchases, at a point north of the Fremont, Elkhorn & Missouri Valley Railroad track, on the country road last traced in the preceding paragraph He is still a resident there

John Bagley, Sr., resided at what is now F Street, blocks 256 and 257 being a part of what was his orchard, the house he lived in being now known as the "Savage House," west of the Union Pacific tracks Mr Bagley is now a resident of Papillion While living here on his farm, he had a private road, leading from the county road, to his house

John Bagley, Jr, had his home at what is now Thirty-sixth and F Streets, on block 266, now known as the "Johnston homestead" Mr Bagley now lives at Springfield, Nebraska

Mrs Cornelius Smith lived in a small frame house on the present Spring Street and Thirty-ninth on what is now known as "Smith's Reserve"

Philip Cassady dwelt in a large frame

---
*The Drovers Journal, December 31, 1892

farm-house (still in good repair) east of what is now Forty-fourth Street, and just north of the present Fowler Street. None of his farm was purchased by the syndicate.

Edward Cassady, son of Philip, lived about a block west of what is now Thirty-sixth Street, and just south of the present "Burlington Square" addition, east of the Omaha & North Platte Railroad track. His dwelling was (and the house still remains) a small frame farm-house.

Just over the western boundary line of South Omaha (now Forty-fourth Street) two blocks south of Q Street, was the farm-house of Mrs. Ann Corrigan, which was built several years prior to the beginning of South Omaha, and still stands. The Corrigan farm is now platted into several additions, some in and some outside the city, all south of Q Street.

The farm-house of George Holmes stood about a block south and a little east of the west end of the present L Street viaduct, on the property now covered by the stockyards. It was a log house and was torn to pieces by a cyclone about the time his farm was sold to the syndicate.

Then came the "Fred Drexel house," on the syndicate tract, afterwards purchased by the Union Stock Yards Company, which house is described in a previous chapter.

The house of Balthas Jetter was situated north of what is now Q Street, immediately west of Twenty-seventh Street. It is still there—a large frame building—a farm house, and is still in good repair.

Thomas Ryan's farm house was located about one block southwest of the present G. F. Swift & Co.'s packing house plant, and one block east of Twenty-seventh street. The building is a large frame, and is still (January, 1893), occupied by Mr. Ryan.

A house at St. Mary's (Catholic) Cemetery, south of Q and east of Thirty-sixth Streets, has been built about twelve years, and was first occupied by Francis Toner, and subsequently by one having charge of the cemetery.

Michael Dee's house still stands; it is about one block west of Thirtieth Street, and about a block northwest of Jetter's brewery. This farm house was built about 1879. Dee sold his farm to Jetter, and moved to Omaha.

The farm house of Mrs. Mary O'Rourke stood (and still stands) two blocks west of Thirtieth Street, and three blocks north of the Sarpy County line. It is now owned and occupied by her son, John J. O'Rourke.

Michael Melia lived in a frame farm house, two blocks west of what is now Thirty-sixth street, and two blocks north of the Sarpy County line. The building is still habitable.

Not later than 1880, a Polish Catholic priest, Rev. Father Strupenski, built a small frame cottage, just west of the present Thirty-sixth Street, and about eighty rods north of the Sarpy County line. It still stands.

The farm house of George, Frank, and Mary Sautter was built before 1880, in what is now known as "Albright's Annex," a half block west of the County Road, and about the same distance south of the Union Pacific Railway tracks. The building is still standing, and is occupied.

The building now occupied by Patrick Hoctor, which was erected after the burning down of the original farm house, in 1883, is situated just north of the Sarpy County line, and immediately west of Twenty-seventh Street. The first house was built by Dennis Dee, in about the year 1857, and the building and farm was purchased by Mr. Hoctor in 1875. It is a frame farm house, in good repair. Mr. Hoctor came from Minnesota where he settled, in 1855.[*]

The appearance of things upon the east side of the track of the Union Pacific Railroad, was much like that on the west side. First, there was the "Old Bellevue Road," which came in from the north, following what is now Twenty-fourth Street to F Street, running thence in a southwesterly direction to what is now Twenty-eighth Street, between J and K Streets; thence following along the east side of the Union Pacific Railroad track to what are now the southern limits of the city. The first farm house to be seen, in going south, after entering the present limits of South Omaha, was

---

[*] "These pioneer times just antedating the founding of South Omaha are well remembered by those who are now living, of the Bagleys, the Cassadys, the Corrigans, the Holmes, the Thomases, the Melias, the Sautters, the Drexels, the Jetters, the Ryans, the Dees, the O'Rourkes, the Hoctors, the Kennellys, * * * and others. But how many of them, ten years ago, for a moment imagined that, of some one of their farms, a single acre might be picked out, which, if cleared of all of its buildings, would, on the 1st day of January, 893, be worth $100,000? But the future was not open to the score of farmers in this goodly portion of Douglas Precinct, who, in the spring of 1883, sowed their grain and planted the corn on land worth, as they believed, fifty dollars an acre, although one or more, gifted with a far-seeing eye, would not be anxious to sell at four times that figure."—*The Drovers Journal*, December 31, 1892.

that of John Kennelly, situated in the present Twenty-fifth Street, near the intersection of G Street The house is still standing, and is occupied It is a story-and-a-half frame. A log house, built by Frederick Drexel, stood on what is now the southeast corner of Twenty-sixth and M streets, and was torn down about 1882 It was occupied as a dwelling house Then the Drexel School house was next seen, standing in what is now block 76, east of Twenty-seventh street, and south of M street It was a frame one-story, about thirty by sixty feet It is still used as a school building, it having been removed to the fourth ward of the city

The next building reached going south was what was called the "Widow Brown House" It was situated just south of the present Q Street and west of Twenty-fourth Street, in what is commonly known as "Brown Park" It was a two-story frame building occupied as a farm house It was burned down in 1892 The next building was the "Bohme" farm house, located on what is now block A, in Morrison's addition to South Omaha, between Wyman and Milroy Streets, just east of Twentieth Street It was a large two-story frame and is still standing There was also what was known as "the Half-Way House," standing on what is now block C, in Potter and Cobb's second addition, east of the old Bellevue Road and north of Armour Street It was a one-story frame, occupied as a dwelling and saloon It got its name from the circumstance of its being situated half way between Omaha and Bellevue It still stands, and is occupied as of old The next was Christian Sautter's farm house—a large two-story frame (now known as the "Sautter Homestead") in what is the present "Albright's Choice" east of Bellevue Avenue and west of Nineteenth Street

The reason why the eastern portion of what is now South Omaha was not built upon was that, owing to the fact that it was a wooded district the land was divided up into small parcels and used by the farmers for their supplies of wood

After South Omaha was founded—after work actually commenced on the Union Stock Yards—the first person to settle here was Martin Spoettle, who located on lot 14, block 78, southeast corner of Twenty-fifth and M Streets, where he built a one-story frame house, in which he subsequently started a saloon Mr Spoettle is still a resident of South Omaha Others soon followed him to the new city—that was to be

In the first number of the first paper printed in South Omaha, the following is found

"Wonderful growth of South Omaha A brief eighteen months of time metamorphoses a large tract of cultivated land into a busy mart of trade Sketch of the progress of the enterprise from its inception to the present Personnel of the land syndicate, stock yards company, water works, etc

"A year and a half ago [in the spring of 1884], what is now a beautifully laid out town site, ornamented with trees and parks and enlivened with the hum of industry, employing millions of money, was simply a series of grain fields grown too valuble for farming purposes on account of their proximity to the great and growing city of Omaha A number of prominent resident capitalists, forecasting the future value of this large tract of land, both as a residence and business place, formed a syndicate and purchased 1,400 acres, lying one-half mile south of the southern limits of the city About one-third of the tract was at once platted and laid out in town lots 60 by 150 feet in size, with streets eighty feet and alleys twenty feet in width Trees were planted on either side of each street, twelve feet from the lot line, thus giving ample room for sidewalks between the trees and lots Near the north end of the town plat, two entire blocks were reserved for park purposes This has been fenced and planted in evergreens, shade trees and shrubbery In the near future a fountain of pure water will be playing in the center of the park, supplied from the splendid water works, of which further mention will be made in this article In the meantime, the same men who to-day [fall of 1885] form the land syndicate, organized the Union Stock Yards Company, the operations of which, in this brief space of time, has commanded the attention of live stock markets and stock men all over the West"*

In May and June, 1891, J B Furon, published, in *The Eagle*, some of his recollections of "ye olden times" in the "Magic City." He says

"In 1885, there were no dummy trains on

* From the *South Omaha Globe*, October 30, 1885

the Union Pacific, no street-car lines, [in South Omaha] and no paved streets nearer to the [stock] yards than Thirteenth and Hickory Streets, Omaha. Thirteenth Street was then the route between the yards and the city, and the hill was as steep as ever, no grading having been done between Hickory and Vinton [Streets]. The reader can easily imagine, though not realize, the difficulty of doing business in South Omaha, which was itself a mud hole the greater part of the time, the streets not graded, no sidewalks, and all supplies to be brought down from the city [of Omaha].

"W. G. Sloane, present mayor of the city,* was the pioneer store-keeper of the packing town. He came to this place June 22, 1884, and built a small frame business house in the midst of a wilderness of cornstalks and jimpson weeds, on the spot where now [May, 1891], stands the drug store of A. W. Saxe. His stock of goods consisted of drugs and medicines, groceries and provisions, butchers' jackets and overalls, and other things too numerous to mention. The writer has seen the narrow space between the counters so blockaded with barrels of potatoes, sacks of beans, sides of bacon and cow-boys, as to make it extremely difficult, if not utterly impossible for a modest man or woman to get farther than a molasses barrel. All the same, Mr. Sloane can testify that, even under such difficulties, as high as four hundred dollars in cash has been 'fired' at him as the proceeds of a single day's business. Mr. Sloane—he was plain 'Mr.,' then—was also the first postmaster, having been appointed in October, 1884, and served for over three years, with Mrs. Sloane as deputy postmaster, and Al. Carpenter as chief clerk. The records show that the first day's business of the new postoffice amounted to twenty-three cents, and involved the handling of at least a dozen letters.

"Frank Pivonka, the now wealthy Bohemian, is entitled to the distinction of selling the first goods in South Omaha, and they were wet goods. Frank opened up a beer hall on the same block where his saloon now [May, 1891], stands, and sold pale lager to the thirsty adventurers without even asking for a license. His hall was not a palace. It consisted of a shed-roof shanty, a plank fastened to posts driven into the ground for a bar, and his first stock of liquors was two

*Written May 23, 1891.

kegs of beer with a wet blanket thrown over them. The beverage was hardly as cool and palatable as it is now served over the bars of some of the sixty-odd saloons of this city, but it was beer, and seemed to have more fight in it to the gallon than a whole keg has now-a-days. But, Mr. Pivonka did not have a monopoly of the beer trade very long. In a short time there were five saloons on the ground, and only one provision store. Then, J. C. Carroll, seeing that the fluids and solids were out of proportion, started another grocery store in a patch of jimpson weeds, cornstalks and dog fennel, at the corner of Twenty-sixth and N Streets. John was, at that time, a single man, and his sister, now Mrs. T. Geary, was unmarried. Miss Carroll was the district school ma'am, and trained the susceptible minds of a small squad of pupils in the little old frame school house near the railroad. When her term expired she went behind the counter in her brother's store, or, more properly, her own, as she had an interest there.

"During the summer of 1885, the population increased rapidly. Chicago transferred a large number of her commission men to this city, placing them in charge of branch houses here. Already they saw the inevitable coming, but accepted it with anything but good grace. Most of them cursed the new town, called it anything but pet names, and swore long and loud that it would never be anything more than a feeding station, and not much of that. The opening of the Hammond house, though a small affair, brought in a few hundred butchers, who assisted materially in making the place lively, especially at night. Most of them were young men, without family ties here, living in boarding houses, or, rather, eating there and living in the saloons. There was no police, no local authority, no organization, no legal restraints, except that of county and state. The reader can imagine that the 'boys' made it very lively at times. It was an unusually quiet, lonesome evening when there was not, at least, a half-dozen fist-fights, and a shooting-scrape or two, and yet nearly all the heroes of that day still live to tell the tale.

"On December 20, 1885, ground was broken for the first brick building, on N Street. Clark & Laufenberg, of St. Paul, brick masons, having faith in the town, laid the walls of the building with their own hands, working all through the winter, sometimes when the mercury was knocking at the back door of the thermometer

"The following mention of it, in the *South Omaha Globe*, of Christmas day, 1885, will give an idea of the importance attached to such a wonderful improvement at that date The item was headed,' A New Brick Block for South Omaha,' and read thus 'Ground is broken, and laborers are now at work on N Street, between the postoffice and Carroll's grocery store Clark & Laufenberg, a St Paul firm, are the proprietors, and, being masons, propose to do the brick work themselves The building is to be 40x50 feet, two stories high, the upper story to be finished off for families or furnished rooms, the whole for rent Mr G Voth, a rising young architect, formerly of Cleveland, Ohio, but late of Salt Lake, where he took the prize on drawing plans for the grand Masonic Hall, drew the plans, and will assist in the work The firm say they base their judgment of the enterprise on their faith in South Omaha, and are not in the least afraid of the result'

"The 'brick block' was a small, low building, very plain, and, later, an eyesore to the street The grading of N Street left it below grade, which added to its squatty appearance Two years ago [that is, in 1889], it was torn down and replaced with the Pioneer Block, a fine brick, finished in modern style, and is a perfect hive of industry John Ritchhart had the original building rented before it was finished, and leaving the Stock Exchange Hotel, of which he was the landlord, moved into the 'brick block,' and opened it as a hotel and saloon Mr Ritchhart seems to be wedded to the spot, for he continued to occupy the old building until it was torn down, and the new building was built under his supervision He still occupies it, but instead of selling whisky and beer, and making plenty of money, he now [1891] publishes the *South Omaha Daily Tribune*
\* \* \* \* \* \* \*

"George W Masson, now a wealthy business man, came here from Michigan in a very early day, with a large stock of ambition and a very small amount of cash With the latter, he purchased lots 5 and 6 in block 12, on Twenty-fourth Street, the same being the first sold by the syndicate Mr Masson afterward purchased block 47 entire, and built thereon four tenement houses in one of which Doctor Miller has lived ever since it was a house The Masson block on the hill on Twenty-eighth Street, is known to everybody The two lots on Twenty-fourth Street were purchased in April, 1884

"Doctor Glasgow was the pioneer physician of South Omaha He came to the new town from Auburn, in June, 1886, and is still here The first practice of the new doctor was principally sewing up scalp wounds and probing for stray bullets, with occasionally an obstetric case Dr Overton came soon after, followed by Dr Einhout, and the latter by Kirkpatrick Overton was soon shelved, while the others mentioned are still [May, 1891], the leading physicians Dr Glasgow has always stood at the head of the profession here in spite of all comers, and although he has virtually quit practicing, being now postmaster, he is still obliged to respond to more calls than he cares to have

"There are now [1891] fourteen physicians in the city doing regular business At one time when there were only four or five doctors in the town, and rivalry was quite sharp, with not enough practice to go around, the doctors themselves carried guns for each other, and threatened to make work for the coroner, and at the same time cut off competition among members of the profession However, the guns, knives and hatchets have all been long since buried, and the brethren now dwell together in unity. \* \* \*

"All the old settlers will remember the little frame shanty near the Exchange crossing [wherein was] a bar which was always, night and day, lined in front with a row of thirsty customers, but that was nothing, as there were several more in town of the same kind The remarkable part of it was, that, in addition to the bar, there were two real estate offices and a lunch counter in the same room which was narrow, short and low The lunch counter man had six stools and many a time while six were eating, a dozen hung around awaiting their turn to pay twenty cents for liver and bacon The real estate men did a business, which, at the present time would make the entire Real Estate Exchange of Omaha happy

"The building stood alone, almost directly

opposite the crossing, and, as the mud was generally knee deep in that vicinity, the continual procession of humanity which passed that way, walked in at the front door of the saloon and out at the back, *to avoid the mud.*   *   *   *

"The mud was something fearful in those days. It must have rained every day and some at night. Teams and wagons at times went out of sight on N Street, and the writer has seen a dozen rails or broken plank stuck up in dangerous holes on every street to mark a bottomless mire. One day a green-looking granger with hayseed in his shaggy beard, got off the train and started for the city hotel, which was only a few yards from the depot. Somehow he did not take the saloon route, and consequently, he stuck in the mud, and there he stood, pulling first at one foot and then the other. Seeing the writer wading along with gum boots on, he accosted him with, 'Say stranger is this a good town?' Receiving an affirmative answer, he continued, 'Well, I haven't seen much of it yet, having just got off the train and got this far, but by —— I'm stuck on it,' and he again made an unsuccessful effort to extricate his brogans.

"At that time what is now a nicely graded site for cattle pens, bounded on the west by the Exchange building, north by the L Street viaduct, east by the Union Pacific tracks and south by Exchange Avenue, was a lake, from the bosom of which, in winter, the supply of ice was cut for the use of the then small packing house. It was called Lake Pivonka, because Frank Pivonka cut ice there.

"In warm weather the lake was generally full of bathers in the evening time, the proprieties being less observed then than now. On the evening of October 10th, 1886, Daniel Kilroy, an employe of Fowler and Company, who had just arrived from Chicago, went in bathing and was drowned.
*   *   *   *   *   *

"The old district school house, a little dilapidated frame building without a lock for the door or shutters for the windows, was the only school house in the place, when on June 5, 1886, a tragedy occurred there. For a long time the school house grounds had been a rendezvous for tramps, although the police repeatedly run in the gang. In summer the motly crowd lounged, slept and insulted passers-by, beneath the shade of large cottonwood trees with which the grounds were ornamented and in winter they entered the building, built a fire in the stove and made themselves at home.

"On the evening named, the usual hard crowd were there, when a stock shipper in the employ of Lobman and Rothschild, undertook to assist a man named Williams, whom the gang were attempting to hold up and rob. The shipper, who was none other than "Sheeney" Martin, was promptly shot and a few minutes later came limping up to the Exchange, with a bullet through the thigh. The ball entered in front near the groin and was taken out at the point of the hip, having passed clear through the thickest part of the thigh and yet Martin still lives to tell the story. The tramps were not disturbed to any great extent.

"Fire bugs too, got in their work occasionally. Many will remember the Wishart-Jones tragedy in which a building was burned and Jones was shot though not fatally. Also the burning of the "Sans Souci." The place was fitted up like a palace and opened with an elaborate banquet; but it was not allowed to stand very long. Good people get desperate sometimes and do things which they would condemn in others under ordinary circumstances."

From the *Globe-Journal*, the successor to the *Globe*, we make the following extracts:

March 19, 1886.—"South Omaha! Beautiful residence lots! for sale. Also business lots. Look on the large map of Omaha and observe that the two-and-one-half mile belt from the Omaha postoffice runs south of section 33, and through the north end of South Omaha. Take a string and pencil, then get one of J. M. Wolfe & Co.'s maps of Omaha and South Omaha combined, put your finger on the string at Thirteenth and Farnam, Omaha's business center, and your pencil on the string at where Bellevue [Twenty-fourth] Street enters South Omaha from the north, then draw a circle and note where South Omaha is, and also that many 'Additions,' 'Places' and 'Hills' are far outside this magic circle. Then stop and think a moment what will make outside property increase in value. The growth of Omaha is all that will enhance the value of real estate other than at South Omaha. At the latter point we have three important factors to build up and make valuable the property. (1) The growth of Omaha, which has and always will follow the transportation lines, (2) all the great railways center there, thus making it the best manufacturing point of any in or near the city [of Omaha], (3) the immense stock yards interests

"Dressed beef business and pork-packing industry will make a town of themselves Two new packing houses [are] going up this year [1886] A gigantic beef-canning establishment [is] to be put into operation by that prince of meat producers, Nels Morris, of Chicago You fool away your day of grace when you do not get an interest in South Omaha before a higher appraisement is made [by the syndicate] The best locations are being taken Make your selections now Lots that sold for three hundred dollars in 1884 cannot now be bought for one thousand dollars The viaducts over the railway track will make safe and splendid thoroughfares between this [Omaha] city and South Omaha A street car line will run to the stock yards this year [No street cars entered South Omaha for many months after that was written ] The minute it does, lots will double in value, as this will afford cheap and quick transportation either by dummy, cable or horse cars * * * [Signed] M A Upton, manager"

April 23, 1886 —"South Omaha — her present status and future prospects Two years ago, the land which now comprises the town plat of South Omaha, was a wilderness of cornstalks Not a 'lick' had been struck at the stock yards, and farm houses were the only buildings in sight For a year past the fame of the little city [village], which has sprung up as if by magic, and the immense packing canning and live stock business, which has been so successfully planted here has acquainted the public with the fact of the wonderful transformation
* * * * * * *

"As an example of the natural growth of the business at the [stock] yards, we will mention the erection of the Exchange building, the contract for which was let last fall, and which is now nearly ready for occupancy. When work began on the foundation, we heard the remark, time and again that the stock yards company were foolish for putting up so large and costly a building, that it was more for show than service, and that it would never be half filled Now that it is about completed, its magnificent proportions and four stories are found to be entirely too small, and the company are contemplating adding a wing In a few days the company will break ground for another mammoth packing house, and ere the summer wanes still another will be added Twice they have been obliged to enlarge the [stock] yards for the accommodation of the increasing receipts of stock

"Besides the live stock business, the new town has three general stores, one drug store, and postoffice, four meat markets, three blacksmith shops, five hotels, eight saloons, two lumber yards two coal yards, one feed and flour store, and boarding-houses without number"

April 30, 1886 —"South Omaha is to have a resident deputy sheriff from and after May 1, [1886] Mr Walker, a former [Omaha] city policeman, is the man who will run the cowboys in when they get obstreperous"

May 7, 1886 —"Mr. [Thomas] and Mrs [Anna M Carroll] Geary will continue in the grocery business, or, rather, Mr Geary will run the store while his wife attends to household duties"

In a newspaper published early in May, 1886, under the heading of "South Omaha," a description of what the settlement was at that date and what her "grand future," "without the shadow of doubt," was to be, are clearly set forth

"Any one would suppose that the above name [South Omaha] would indicate the southern part of the city of Omaha This, however, is not the case South Omaha is the name of a thriving town [reference here being to the territory then platted by the syndicate] whose northern boundary is one-half mile south of the city limits of Omaha, and runs from there one and a quarter miles south to the Union Stock Yards

"Two years ago the 1,400 acres which the South Omaha Company [the syndicate] own were cornfields and pastures Since that time over one million dollars have been expended in stock yards, railway tracks, packing houses, water works, and a fifty thousand dollar Exchange building, so that now [May 1886] there is quite a village built up and the town has its own post office, railway stations and newspaper

"New buildings are going up every day, and it is only a question of a few years when South Omaha will be to Omaha what Brooklyn is to New York At the north end of the town site, [between Twenty-fourth Street on the east and the Union Pacific Railroad right-of-way on the west] one mile north of the stock yards, and only two and one-half miles from the business center of the city of Omaha, are four hundred as finely located residence lots as ever gladdened the eye of the lover of the beauties of nature [and, strange as it may seem, many are still (1892) unoccupied]. These beautiful lots are on an elevation far above their surroundings, the altitude being 250 feet above the Missouri River. Omaha has some handsome suburbs, but this one hundred acres in South Omaha is without doubt the most lovely spot and will make the finest suburban homes around the city. Beautiful shade trees are planted on each side of the streets, twelve feet from the lot line. Near the center of the north end [of the platted town] is a pretty little park of six acres, in which are evergreens, shrubs and ornamental trees, surrounded at present by a wire fence [which, in July, 1892, is still there]. It is the intention of the company [that is, the syndicate] to put an attractive fence around this park and place in the center of the same a fountain to be fed by their water works—which, by the way, is a fine system, costing over thirty thousand dollars, furnishing pure spring water, clear as crystal [but now (1892) supplanted by the mains from the Omaha works, supplying an abundance of Missouri River water of a consistency decidedly clouded]. So much for that part of South Omaha, where the finest residences will be located, and where lots ten years from now [May, 1886] will sell for thousands that now sell for hundreds.

"At the south end [of the syndicate's first survey], as before stated, there has quite a town sprung up and is growing rapidly. One brick block has just been completed and another one is under way. Near here are located the stock yards, which are fast becoming headquarters for stockmen and their herds. Here is also the large dressed beef house operated by Geo. H. Hammond & Co., who own four hundred refrigerator cars and have meat houses in all the principal eastern cities of this country and in Europe. This house cost $156,000. The brick Exchange building, erected by the Stock Yards Company, is a model of beauty and grandeur. This will be used for stock yards, bank, telegraph and commission men's offices, with a restaurant and bar in the basement. The third and fourth floors will be used as a hotel.

"Beyond a shadow of doubt, South Omaha has a grand future. Backed [as it is] by a syndicate who represent forty millions of dollars, located on the edge of the most prosperous city [that is, one of the most prosperous cities] on the continent, having the support and presence of all the great railways, having already established a large and rapidly increasing live stock market, having a location unsurpassed in beauty and utility —what other outcome can there be for this young giant but that which is most favorable?

"Manufactories and packing houses will rapidly be erected. To show that Chicago packers are seeing that this is the point for their future business, we quote from the [Omaha] Bee, of April 19 [1886]:

"'Another step towards assuring Omaha's future has been taken by the South Omaha syndicate. A contract has been closed with Fowler & Bros., of Chicago, who rank among the largest pork packers in the world, by which that firm will operate a great packing house at the stock yards, just as soon as the building for that purpose can be erected. When we say that the capacity of this concern is to be three times that of Boyd's packing house [in Omaha], and that it will be operated the year around—winter and summer—the magnitude of the enterprise can be best appreciated.'"*

We copy from the files of the *South Omaha Daily Stockman*, of September 24, 1886, the following pen sketch of South Omaha at that date:

"For the benefit of our readers at a distance who have never visited South Omaha, but have heard a great deal about it and didn't believe it, we will briefly mention the principal business firms and houses of the stock yards town. To begin at a convenient point, we will start on the north side of N Street at its confluence with the Bellevue road, and name the business places on both sides of the street as we go east. First, then, is J. Nielson's blacksmith shop, next Captain Rigby's shoe shop, next Sliter and Gould's wholesale and retail lumber yards and office, which is also headquarters for B. J. Coy, the contractor and builder. Next the city pharmacy, by E. Wert, late of Au-

*From the *American Real Estate Criterion*, May, 1886.

burn, who has opened up a large and very fine drug store Crossing the street diagonally we come to T Geary's dry goods and grocery house, E. K Well's boarding house, with fourteen boarders, the brick Stock Exchange hotel, by J F Ritchhart, with thirty-eight regular boarders and a large transient patronage Next, on the same side of the street, comes the postoffice, drug and provision store of Sloane and Saxe, and the retail meat market of McGuire and Curtis, the large two-story frame dry goods house of M J Degraff, formerly of Oakland, Iowa, farther on and on the same side of the street, Mrs W. O Thayer's boarding house, with eighteen boarders On the other side of the street is the two-story and basement brick hardware store of Holmes and Smith, with their tin shop next door The public telephone station, recently established, is also in this store, and Dr E L Einhout has his office and consultation rooms on the second floor The fruit and confectionery store of F Block and the new livery stable of J Hogate, late of Oakland, Iowa, finishes up the business of N Street Beginning at the north end of business on Twenty-sixth Street, we will mention the South Omaha Hotel, a large two-story frame building, with a bar attachment and twenty boarders Mr Belolevek is the proprietor The next business place south of the hotel is the justice office of D O'Connell Attorney Grice also offices with the justice, and the two carry on an extensive real estate business under the firm name of 'O'Connell and Grice' Then comes 'Doug's Place' a saloon and 'free and easy' Nearly opposite is the Wisconsin House, by Bruno Strathman, one of the largest and nicest hotels in the place This house also has a bar and entertains twenty-two regular boarders Across the street, opposite, is the justice office and news stand of G Reuther, next to which is Ed Kaufmann's barber shop. Frank Pivonka's saloon comes next, one of the oldest and best known bars in the town Mr Pivonka is a prominent property owner and proprietor of several business houses Crossing N Street and continuing south is the Walker House, a large and nicely furnished two-story frame hotel, managed by the wife of Deputy Sheriff Walker The house at present has fourteen regular boarders and a good transient business Next is the large, new merchandise store just completed and occupied to-day by the owner, J Levy

" Adjoining is the Iowa saloon, and next to that McGuire and Driscoll's saloon Mr McGuire is also associated with Frank Slater in the wholesale butcher business under the firm name of McGuire and Slater Further on is Pat Rowley's saloon and boarding house, and at the further end of the row is Mrs Rigby's boarding house, with ten boarders Across the street is J Boyles' saloon, which ends the business on that street On Twenty-seventh, facing the railroad, is the saloon and lunch counter of Geary and Co, the Central Hotel, with thirty-six boarders, and the new City Hotel, a large, airy structure, nicely furnished, and owned and managed by Daniel Rafferty Dr Overton has rooms at the Stock Exchange Hotel and Dr Glasgow resides in a new and splendid home he has lately finished He practices from Sloane and Saxe's drug store The resident population is in the neighborhood of fifteen hundred and there is enough floating population to swell the number to at least two thousand. While this is a good showing for so young a place, the real business and wealth of South Omaha has not been mentioned, and it is not the intention to more than touch upon it in this article The live stock trade and its adjuncts are the real foundation of South Omaha's business When we remember that nearly one million dollars has been invested in the yards and packing houses, and other necessary improvements for carrying on the business, the reader may form some idea of the extent of the business Oberne. Hosick & Company have a large accommodation slaughtering house, rendering establishment and soap works, all under the same roof The Union Rendering Company have extensive works near them, and farther up is the Hammond house, too well known to need mention The Fowler Brothers packing house, a five-story brick of giant proportions, is nearly ready for business, as is also the Lipton packing house near it, which is also built of brick. The two latter houses are located at the western extremity of the yards and are surrounded by boarding houses for the men, the two employing 450 hands in their construction S H Pague, of Kansas City, Mr. Bright, of Omaha, and E E. Palsley, of South Omaha, each have boarding houses near the buildings, for the convenience of the hands. The Stock Yards Hotel, formerly known as the 'Canfield House,' run by Daniel Walker, boards and lodges a large number of the yard men, while the grand Exchange Hotel, in the Exchange building, takes care of stock men and visitors to the yards. Now, if the reader will remember that the *Daily Stockman* is also a South Omaha production, we will excuse him."

NOTE.—Some of the "First Things" in the settlement, after it received the name of "South Omaha," but before it became an organized village. are these:

Charles Akofer came to South Omaha August 28, 1886. He was the first permanent butcher.

The first male child born was Henry Wordeman, at the corner of Twenty-fifth and M Streets, in July, 1885.

The first boarding house. May, 1884. was kept by a man named Jones—"Bill Jones," they called him. He had seventy-five boarders in a small frame building on the east side of Twenty-fifth Street, between N and M Streets.

John Howe, called "Jack," for short, had the first blacksmith shop. It was on Twenty-fifth Street. between N and O.

The first female child born was Catherine Rowley, daughter of Patrick and Annie Rowley. She was born on Railroad Avenue, between N and O Streets, on the third of August, 1886.

The first two lots sold after the list price was set and the town blocked out. were purchased by William Kerr and Martin Spoettle, on June 4. 1884; although George Masson bought lots 5 and 6, in block 12, in April, before any lots had been placed upon the market.

The first marriage was that of John F. Ritchhart and Mrs. Anna Williams on the 22d of August, 1885, by the Rev. Dr. Patterson, rector of St. Marks' Episcopal Church. Omaha.

The first death occurred the 4th of July, 1884. Thomas Kerr. infant son of William and Onie Kerr, died on that day.

The first Catholic service in South Omaha was the celebration of mass the first Sunday of November, 1885, in the Ryan School House, on Twenty-seventh Street. between N and M Streets, by the Rev. John Jeanette, pastor of St. Patrick's Church, Omaha.

L. J. Carpenter came to South Omaha in 1885 and bought out Jesse Hogate, who started the first livery stable in the village. In September, 1891, he erected the building he now occupies, near the corner of Twenty-fourth and N Streets.

# CHAPTER VI.

### South Omaha as a Municipality

The surveying of South Omaha and the recording of the plat, on the 18th of July, 1884, were not immediately followed by village organization, as it was then, to a great extent, without inhabitants to enjoy or be protected by a municipal government To lay out a town site was one thing, to secure a population for it of sufficient numbers to justify the county commissioners in incorporating it—to actually induce that body to form it (with perhaps other territory) into a municipality—was quite another matter

For more than two years, the people (few, at first, of course) who had emigrated to South Omaha, were governed by such officers and regulations as were provided by law for ordinary country precincts However, as will now be seen, there seemed to be a necessity for at least the removing to the settlement of a justice of the peace to have his office there for the accommodation and security of residents who had determined to make South Omaha their permanent home, but as yet they lived, not in an organized village or in any city, but simply in one of those precincts which had before been established in Douglas County As late as May 7, 1886, we find the following in the *South Omaha Globe-Journal*

"Douglas Precinct Without a Constable. —Douglas Precinct has a good, live justice of the peace but no constable. The attention of the county board [County Commissioners of Douglas County] was called to this fact last week, by Justice O'Connell, and through his recommendation H F Jasper was appointed to that office but declined to serve He would have made a good officer, but there are other good men for the place who would accept and the matter should not be dropped In this connection we will say that Squire O'Connell may be found at South Omaha every forenoon, where complaints may be entered His office at present is at his residence, on Twentieth Street and Bellevue Road [just south of Omaha], but he intends opening a permanent office at South Omaha as soon as he can secure a building" * * *

But more than a justice of the peace and an officer to execute his will were demanded So largely had the population of that part of Douglas precinct then designated as "South Omaha" increased by the middle of the summer of 1886, and there was so much lawlessness, that many residents were desirous that a village should be incorporated—a village government established as a public necessity to preserve peace and order, so, on the 8th of July, a petition was drawn up in these words and signed by a large number of residents

"South Omaha, July 8, 1886
*To the Honorable County Commissioners of the County of Douglas, State of Nebraska*

"We, the undersigned citizens of South Omaha, Douglas County, beg to offer you a petition praying that you incorporate the portion of South Omaha hereafter mentioned and marked with the red line on the map, hoping that you will grant our prayer, knowing as you do, how we are exposed without any protection against tramps and murderers—having no jail, no church, one school house (and that falling to decay) one saloon for every twenty inhabitants, one gambling house, two houses of ill-fame, one justice of the peace, one deputy sheriff (he is paid by three corporations), one postoffice, no constable proper here We earnestly pray that you grant us incorporation of the following lines, under the name of the village of South Omaha (proposed lands to be incorporated in the village of South Omaha are illustrated with red lines), viz The west half of the west half of section 3, township 14, range 13 east, all of section 4, in township and range just mentioned, the north half of the north half of section 9, in the same township and range, all that part of the south half of section 33, in township 15, in the same range, lying south of the north line of the South Omaha

645

Syndicate's lands; and all that part of the west half of the southwest quarter of section 34, in the last named township and range, lying south of the north line of the lands of South Omaha Syndicate." Hoping to receive a favorable reply we remain yours truly—[Signed by]:

"George Clarke, W. G. Sloane, W. O. Thayer, J. D. Jones, G. W. Klingaman, W. A. Dixon, F. J. Persons, E. H. Howland, I. A. Brayton, N. Purinton, S. K. Krigbaum, F. J. Sliter, Larue Williams, C. A. Rapp, Gust Ekbam. E. C. Davis, L. R. Davis, Charles Lee, A. N. Shriver, W. Richardson, Thomas Richardson, A. Howell, Henry Laufenburg, A. A. Gary, Joseph Odwarker, L. Dey, J. D. Meagher, Fred Wasem, E. D. Wiers, Dudley Sullivan, J. L. Davis, John N. Burke, Ed. Lee, F. Jonnscheit, John A. Nelson, C. Williams, Ed. Kaufmann, Bruno Strathmann, Fred. Kessner, John Hedderman, Daniel O'Connell, Sr., Louis Grundmeier, Thomas Kenny, John Reiper, Oliof Haga."

Added to the foregoing were the following names:

"Moritz Kuptery, Theodore Gehrtre, Paul Dodenhoff, Charles Kohm, Frank Waack, C. Lueed, F. Pivonka, C. Stiliry, Thomas Kozat, V. Pivonka, A. L. Black, W. F. Martin, James Ward, Pat. Lynch, William Long, Thomas Cullen, Albert Bloom, John Day, Edward Corrigan, D. H. Reynolds, J. Cook, B. F. Walker, B. McCaffrey, J. C. Carroll, H. V. Rice, D. Mahoney, L. B. Gorham, C. A. Withrow, F. E. Pearl, Bill Binit, P. F. Hayes, H. Sullivan, Philip Korn, George Ball, Frank Gillean, F. Stuart, Frank Iona, J. D. Robinson, J. S. Haskins, W. Schmeling, James Ball, P. Baer, George Jones, Ch. Simmert, D. Eden, Martin W. Kierkendall, Thomas Adams, C. E. Wood, E. E. Palsley, Pat. Scanlan, Frank Martzahn, L. P. C. Larsen, W. G. Larsen, James McVeigh, J. E. Vance, R. Pearl, F. Joneshite, P. Wetzel, J. Peters, C. E. Jones, J. Kiesbina, Jim Heckelman, Daniel Malone, Herman Trenkle, Gideon Hood, Fred. Ribo, Patrick Sullivan, O. F. Johnson."

Additional names signed to the petition were these:

"S. C. Malin, Joe Wardyan, John Borda, Christian Haga, H. B. Mengel, Moses Livingstone, Peter Petersen, Thomas Kaysen, J. Jacobson, T. B. Whittlesey, T. Long, D. Loescher, D. R, Swett, C. W. Glynn, T. Crawley, M. Hagen, Charles Segebart, William McKay, J. A. Doe, Union Rendering Company, B. Lovell, David P. Barber, W. J. Slate, William Horton, J. P. S. Wallwork, William Saunders, Michael Woulf, Thomas O'Connor, Daniel DeLancey, Thomas Haley, D. F. Donoghue, Thomas Kozak, W. A. Bennett, E. A. Stearns, Dan. Williams, William Stewart, E. P. Savage, George E. Heis, Henry Rigby, E. T. Gadd, C. F. Fahs, Anton Beloiavek, Amos Elgner, Frederick Sahlberg, John O'Connell, Thomas Geary, P. Climtsetus, Patrick Keenan, C. Lewis, J. R. Anderson, John Jacobs, L. T. Fimicim, W. H. Gould, Steve Kaiser, Henry Fingado, Ed. T. Levis, T. B. Bohn, W. Daly."

The foregoing petition was duly presented to the county commissioners, but soon thereafter two remonstrances, one dated July 10, the other August 14, were handed in to the board, the former signed by Frank Murphy, Ben B. Wood, Milton Rogers, T. B. Hatcher, M. A. Upton, John A. McShane and Joseph Barker; the latter, by C. W. Hamilton as vice-president, and Frank Murphy as treasurer for the board of trustees—that is, for the syndicate. The first remonstrance claimed that a large number of the signers to the petition were, as they had been informed, non-residents; that a majority of property owners did not desire their village incorporated; and that the corporate limits proposed would be unjust and would "work great and irreparable injury to citizens and owners of property;" the other remonstrance objected to incorporation because the signers had been informed that it was intended to limit the boundary lines to those of the syndicate, east of the Union Pacific Railroad track; and they asked that no action should be taken by the board for thirty or sixty days. Thereupon the whole matter was postponed for two months.

When sixty days had expired there was apparently an amicable agreement with all parties that South Omaha should be incorporated; and its limits had been fixed upon. Besides the citizens generally, the Union Stock Yards Company had acquiesced in the arrangement; although the syndicate still stood aloof. On the 16th of October there was presented to the board of commissioners the following:

"Petition for the Incorporation of South Omaha.

" *To the Honorable, the County Commissioners, Douglas County, Nebraska*

"Gentlemen We, the undersigned, hereby petition your honorable body for the incorporation of the village of South Omaha, Nebraska, as shown on the above plat within the red lines [marked on a map of Omaha and of considerable of Douglas precinct] *

' Union Stock Yards Company, S B Fenno, C H Moody, D H Reynolds, C M Carson, F W Biddle, C H Bradrick, J H Wallwork, L B Gorham, F. S Dewey, F W Gasmann, D Smith, Joseph H Nash, L Rothschild, D R Scott, E A Stearns, Daniel O'Connell, J R Grice, G W Klingaman, C. C. Bosworth, J W Lowe, John E McCann, Richard A Haga, W G Sloane, Sloane & Saxe, W S Anderson, D L Holmes, F M Smith, E K Wells, John Lacey, Thomas Hennessy John Hartnett R T Maxwell, Dr E. L. Einhout, E M Overton, J. Nigh, W L Sears, E D Weus, J H Jacobs, Charles Clapp, Thomas P McDowell, J. W Ridings, John Nelson, Iohn Hogan, J. D Jones, L Carpenter, M J DeGraff & Co, Larue Williams, Axel Kallstrom, Andro Janson, Thomas Hoctor, H Sullivan, J M Glasgow, J H Johnson, M F Anderson, E C Dries Lee Dries, Martin Lynn, John York, George Zenor, William Saunders "

The following names also were added "Moses C Livingstone, William McCraith, F McLaughlin, E F Crowley W Kane, John Sistor, Patrick Sweeney, Charles Jones, Dudley Sullivan, John N Burke, Patrick Rice, Daniel P O Connell, Charles Segebart, James Edney, John Hemming, F J Sliter, Geo E Heis, R R Keller, V Pivonka, J Patek, Edward Goodman, T Geary, Charles Lear, P Mooney, J W Smith, John Carey, J Cook, L C Gibson, P M Livsy, John A Doe, S K Kirgbaum, Fr Pivonka C M Hunt, Ziba Crawford, A J Stoll, M Barnhart, John Hedeman, Patrick Lynch, John Clay, George Gibbons, J D Robinson Charles W Glynn, John H Wallwork, G Reuther, M Meyer, M Reichenberg, Charles H Rich, William Moore, S L Caldwell, E C Deckson, D Kratzer A Winegard, J M Eversole, Isaac Myers, W E Haines, James S Brown, C H Urquhart, Jacob Levy, R B Sarles, C W Sumner, A C Shepard, David Hoban, P. McMahon, Jim O'Gorman,

* This red line indicated the north boundary for South Omaha which had been agreed upon and, as will be presently seen, it was the result of a careful survey previously made

John Kenney, Joe Moly, John Lee, O E. Shannon, Willmore Davis, F Williamson "

The record of the transactions of the county commissioners upon this petition is in these words

" Omaha, Saturday, October 16, 1886 — The board met this day, pursuant to adjournment, present, F W. Corliss, Geo E Timme and R O'Keefe This day came up the incorporation of South Omaha, and the following was offered and adopted

" ' WHEREAS, a petition having [has] been presented to this board, signed by the majority of the taxable inhabitants of South Omaha, praying for the incorporation of the Village of South Omaha and

" 'WHEREAS, said petition having [has] been duly considered by this board of county commissioners, and

" 'WHEREAS, it appears to this board that said incorporation is a public necessity, to preserve peace and order, and

" ' WHEREAS, under the law [there is full power] authorizing county commissioners to declare villages incorporated, therefore, be it

" ' *Resolved*, that the Village of South Omaha be, and is hereby declared incorporated, as petitioned for, being more fully described as follows, to-wit

" Commencing at the southwest quarter section corner of section eight (8), township fourteen (14), range thirteen (13), and running thence north two and one-half (2½) miles to the center of section thirty two (32) township fifteen (15), range thirteen (13); thence east thirty-one chains, more or less, to the center line of Howe Street, in Melrose Hill, thence south one hundred and sixty-four feet (164), to the center line of Morse Street, in said Melrose Hill, thence east in the center of said Morse Street to the southwest corner of lot nine (9) in section thirty-three (33), township fifteen (15), range thirteen (13), thence north eighty-six degrees (86°) east thirty chains and forty-seven links, more or less, to a point sixty-five links (65) south of the center of section thirty three (33), township fifteen (15), range thirteen (13), thence north eighty-one degrees (81°) east ten chains and seventy-two links (10 72), thence south eighty degrees and forty-five minutes (80° 45′) east thirty-one chains and thirty-seven links (31 37), thence south eighty-five degrees and thirty minutes (85° 30′) east ten chains and thirty-three links to a hickory stump; thence south forty degrees (40°) east fifty-eight chains and seventy-one links (58.71) to the northeast corner of lot four (4) in section three (3), township fourteen (14), range thirteen (13); thence west ten chains and seventy-six links (10.76); thence south forty-five degrees (45°) east fourteen chains and fifteen links (14.15); thence east ten chains and seventy-six links (10.76); thence south forty-five degrees (45°) east one chain and thirty-nine links (1.39); thence north thirty-two degrees (32°) east nineteen chains and twenty-five links(19.25); thence north forty-five degrees (45°) west one chain and fifty links (1.50) to the section line between sections three (3) and thirty-four (34); thence east to the center of the Missouri River; thence in the center of said river to the south line of section eleven (11), township fourteen (14), range thirteen (13); thence west to the place of beginning.''"*

"And be it further *Resolved*, that the following named persons be and are hereby appointed trustees of the Village of South Omaha, Douglas county, Nebraska, who shall hold their office and perform the duties required of them by law, and until the election and qualification of their successors: C. M. Hunt. E. P. Savage, W. G. Sloane, I. A. Brayton and F. J. Sliter."

It will be borne in mind that the area of the village as established by the County Commissioners was much larger than the town as surveyed and platted by the syndicate, but it did not reach Omaha, at its nearest point, by about half a mile. That the two municipalities now join is because Omaha extended its area south after the limits of South Omaha had been established by the County Commissioners. Douglas precinct therefore bounded South Omaha, when it was incorporated as a village, on the north and west.

The purchasers of all the land by patents from the general government on which South Omaha is now located, were: George M. Ballew, Samuel Moffat, Patrick Bagley, John E. Allen, James W. Lee, Levi Van Camp, John Kennelly, George Holmes, John Bagley, Patrick Corrigan, George Scott, William Holmes, Louis A. Walker, Peter Cassady, Micael Bagley, Frederick Drexel,Terence Cassady, Samuel A. Orchard, Ellen Cassady, Andrew R. Orchard, Philip Cassidy, Thomas Garry, Thomas Ryan, Timothy Sullivan, James Walker, Robert Furgerson, Erastus J. Burr, Clement Lambert, Wm. Riggs, Joab McKenzie, Albert C. Strickland, Morris Dee, Samuel M. Breckenridge. All the patents were issued between November 10, 1859, and September 14, 1861.*

The trustees of the village organized on the eighteenth of October, by the appointment of E. P. Savage, chairman; Daniel O'Connell, village clerk; John R. Grice, village attorney; M. J. De Graff, treasurer; and Patrick Lynch, marshal. A writer, two and a half months after the organization, says: "South Omaha has now between 1,200 and 1,500 inhabitants. For several months past has the subject of incorporation been uppermost in the minds of all her people. The the town was getting too large to be without municipal government. Mr. W. G. Sloane, the present postmaster; Daniel O'Connell, a lawyer and justice of the peace, and Mr. Frank Pivonka, owner of the first brick building erected in the place, took the matter in hand and proceeded with the good work in the interest of law and order. Of the busines houses, twenty-one were saloons, and disgraceful scenes were constantly taking place. * * * A license of five hundred dollars was imposed upon them."†

"As the town grew at a rapid rate," says a recent publication, "and the population was made up principally of homeless men, who cared but little for appearances, it may be surmised that those who were looking forward to future homes, began early to agitate the question of municipal organization. Strange as it may appear now, there was strong opposition to such a measure and it was not confined to the loose element, but found more influential advocates among the moneyed men,who talked expenses and cared more for the present nickel than for the future good of the city. But the inevitable came, and on Saturday, October 16, 1886, the county commissioners of Douglas County, in compliance with a petition signed by the

---

* From the center of section 32 the boundary eastward to the river, as described, was indicated on a map by the red line before mentioned, which map accompanied the petition.

*For the above statement of the patentees of the land on which South Omaha is now located, the writer of this history is indebted to The Midland Guarantee and Trust Company, of Omaha.

†The *Industries of Omaha* (January 1, 1887), p. 47.

best citizens of the town, incorporated South Omaha as a village

"The following account of the action is copied from the *Daily Stockman,* of October 18, 1886 'At a meeting of the county commissioners of Douglas County, held at their rooms in the 'Temple on the Hill,' Saturday afternoon, a petition from the citizens of South Omaha was presented, praying that honorable body to incorporate the village of South Omaha Favorable action was taken, and the following trustees were appointed to act in an official capacity until their successors shall have been elected and qualified C M. Hunt, Frank J Shter, E P Savage, I A Brayton and W G Sloane The appointed officers will hold a meeting this evening and effect an organization The boundary lines of the village were defined in the *Stockman* of a previous date We want to congratulate the citizens and business men of the new village on the consummation of this important scheme. It means for South Omaha, protection to both public business and private enterprise, the regulation of license and the control of unlawfully disposed persons, the care of streets and precaution against fire, in short, the legalized supervision of the business interests of the community, whether individual or collective The incorporation of the town will mark a new era in the prosperity of the phenomenal Gate City suburb, whose wonderful progress has been heralded by the newspapers of the entire world It is only a question of time, and a short time at that, when South Omaha will be the center of the live stock business of the country, as she is now the geographical center of the United States The little village of probably three thousand souls, incorporated only last Saturday, will be a city of ten thousand or fifteen thousand in a few brief months' [but in all this, ' the wish is father of the thought,' evidently, besides, the 'little village' could not have had a population anywhere near '3,000 souls,' judging from the number forming 'a majority' of the taxable inhabitants' who signed the last petition for incorporation.]

"A few days later [October 18] the trustees met and elected Col E P Savage chairman John Grice was elected city attorney, and to him was assigned the task of drafting the first ordinances for the new village, but in point of fact Colonel Savage was the real author of those important documents

"Saloons * * * which had up to this time run wide open without even so much as saying, 'by your leave,' were forced by law to pay license or shut up shop Nearly all chose the former * * *

'Saloon licenses were placed at five hundred dollars, and they still remain at the same figure The number of drinking places grew in proportion to the increase in population, and the revenue derived therefrom laid the foundation for the splendid schools of which this city is now justly proud

"For a time the officers had a hard time enforcing the ordinances, in fact some of the peace officers were too much in sympathy with the lawless classes to take effective steps against them There seemed to be a general disposition on the part of nearly all to wink at perversion of morals if not at actual crime Another thing, everybody seemed to be too eager to secure the almighty dollar to care much what their neighbors did "*

Just here we may say, parenthetically, that, on the very day of the organization of the village (October 18, 1886), was born John Ritchhart, son of J F and Annie Ritchhart. That boy was the first child born within South Omaha's corporate limits

The name "South Omaha" was given by the syndicate to the settlement before the time of the surveying and platting of the town † When the latter was "laid out," it, also, took the same name as before mentioned So, too, when the postoffice was afterwards established, it was called the "South Omaha" office; and the name, of course, was continued to the city when the village no longer existed ‡

Late in 1886, W G Albright, who had a large sale, in the previous August, of lots in his "Albright's Annex," completed the purchase of the Christian Sautter farm, consisting of 280 acres, which adjoins and lies east

---

*The *Eagle*, May 30, 1891

†Ante, p 617 This is proved by the published (but fanciful) "map of the City of Omaha, published with *Omaha, Its Past, Present and Future,* compiled by C R Schaller Issued by special authority of the Board of Trade—N B Falconer, president, Thomas Gibson, secretary 1884 *Herald* Litho, Omaha, Neb" An examination of this map shows not only that it was gotten up before the survey and platting of the town, but that the settlement had already received the name of South Omaha

‡The name "New Edinburg" had been suggested and considered by the syndicate before the adoption of 'South Omaha," and rejected

of the "Annex," and a half mile south of the stock yards—extending from the Burlington & Missouri River Railroad on the east, to beyond the Union Pacific Railroad on the west. This farm he laid out into lots.

"The population [of the village of South Omaha] is increasing every day," says an early account, "and by next spring [1887] it will surely double. Already is she gifted with water works, the water being supplied from a number of wells and from a lake which lies between the Stock Exchange and the railroad tracks. This lake has also an outlet which is used to carry off the refuse from the packing houses. * * * The education of the youth of South Omaha is not being neglected. A large school house will be built next spring [1887]. Mr. L. S. Caldwell, the principal of the public schools, is a gentleman, thorough in all his methods of instruction, and will look after the good of the community to the interest of each and every member. Already has a daily newspaper been established. It is a spicy, five-column folio, sailing under the name of *South Omaha Stockman*, owned and edited by Messrs. J. B. Erion and C. H. Rich. They issued the first number on the 12th of June, [1886], as a four-column folio, and continued it in that form until the first of last December [this was written January 1, 1887], when they moved to their new quarters on the east side of the [Union Pacific Railroad] track. They have a circulation of from fifteen hundred to eighteen hundred copies, which is increasing day by day. They publish the market reports, and the paper is held in high estimation by the stock men." * * *

"South Omaha [January 1, 1887] is a curious community, and well worth a day's time of the sight-seer. It is a combination of the city and the western country town. East of the railroad tracks, upon a rough, ungraded hillside, are bunched the frame and brick houses composing the general trading-point of the village. The dwellings scatter in all directions and vary in point of architecture from a plain, unpainted house of one room, to the two-story structure upon which the designer must have passed sleepless nights in originating fancy work. There are no sidewalks, and the man with the broadest sole makes the best progress after a rainstorm. Across the tracks [west], in direct comparison with the rural-looking stores, is the magnificent Stock Exchange, a four-story brick of a decided metropolitan appearance; while further west are the mammoth packing houses of Fowler Brothers and Lipton & Company, surrounded by the sheds and yards of the Union Stock Yards Company. * * *

"Here there is a wonderful absence of social distinction. The elegantly attired business man, with head covered with a shiny tile, hobnobs with the farmer, who has come to town with his wagon load of truck, wearing his blue jeans and sou'wester, which has weathered many a storm; the cowboy with his long boots, flannel shirt and wide-brimmed hat, is to be seen chatting familiarly with the daintily-dressed city chap, whose stylish pants are rolled up out of the way of dirt, which clings to his pointed shoes. Everything gives way to the one idea of building up South Omaha. Merchant and farmer, capitalist and laborer, Christian and skeptic, prince and pauper, are all equal, when on bended knee before the shrine of the almighty dollar."*

Another writer, early in 1887, says: "The really wonderful activity in South Omaha real estate, where property has advanced in value from one hundred to one thousand per cent. during the past few months, has caused a great many grave head-shakings and predictions of a reaction. Fortunately, however, this rise is based upon sound business principles and rests upon the established law of supply and demand. There is a demand for South Omaha property, and the supply for the purpose for which it is sought being rapidly exhausted, the value of real estate in this new Porkopolis must of necessity be based upon the changed condition of affairs, and not in the light of past values.

"South Omaha is now an incorporated city [village] of its own, not merely a suburb of Omaha. It was founded by the Union Stock Yards Company as a place for slaughtering, packing and auxiliary industries, and being so favorably located from a geographical standpoint, as well as a railway center, its future can only be measured by the experience of other cities, in which packing is an important industry. Cincinnati has lost its prestige because it lies in too thickly a populated section, where cattle

* *The Industries of Omaha*, pp. 46, 47, 49.

ranges can not exist and the supply is limited. Chicago took the lead on account of its unexcelled railroad facilities, its supply of cattle and hogs coming from every section of the west. Its packing establishments will continue to remain and to grow in importance, notwithstanding the founding of other packing centres. The Chicago Stock Yards and packing houses now support a population of over one hundred thousand and cover a vast area. Kansas City next comes to the front, and although it has not near as good a country to draw from for its supply, its packing industry has assumed vast proportions. South Omaha is destined to be a more important packing point from the fact of its being located in the midst of a rich cattle and hog growing country and at the very gate to the immense stock country of the northwest—Nebraska, Dakota, Colorado, Idaho, Montana, all being tributary to it.

"The world is using more meat every year, provisions never being a drug upon the market, and while prices may fluctuate, the demand keeps fully abreast of the supply. The population of Europe has doubled during the past eighty years, notwithstanding its terrific wars and an emigration unparalleled in the annals of history. At the same ratio of increase there is really a grave question as to whether a sufficient food supply can be secured for Europe in this country a few decades hence, when the rapid increase of our own population is taken into consideration. The demand certainly can never fall off. Thus the founding of South Omaha as a stock yards and packing point became an urgent necessity. It was not a speculation, and its success was assured from the start. The houses now operating there have found their business profitable, others are coming this year and every foot of the land contained in the present corporation limits of South Omaha will soon be occupied by vast establishments, employing armies of men, necessarily followed by residences, stores, schools, churches and other buildings found in a thriving, industrious city."*

The village of South Omaha was divided into three wards February 14, 1887. All that part lying west of the Union Pacific

Railroad track was designated as "ward three," east of the track and south of N Street, "ward two;" east of the track and north of N Street, "ward one." But the village government was of short duration, because of the rapid increase of the population. By the first of March it was certain there were within the village limits more than one thousand residents. It was entitled, then, by law, to be formed into a city of the second class (of the lower degree) "having more than one thousand and less than twenty-five thousand inhabitants." Steps were taken, therefore, to organize a city government. So it was that, by ordinance No 11, the *village* of South Omaha was divided into wards for the purpose of a *city* government. The three wards established were identical with those previously formed by the village. This was done on the seventh of March, 1887.

The next meeting of the village board of trustees was held March 14, 1887. The proceedings were as follow: "South Omaha, Nebraska, March 14, 1887. An adjourned meeting of the village board of trustees [was] held at the office of the village clerk, at 7 o'clock, P M. Meeting opened in regular order, E. P. Savage in the chair. E. P. Savage, C. M. Hunt, I. A. Braxton, present; W. G. Sloane and F. J. Sliter, absent. Minutes of previous meeting read and approved. Moved and carried that the chairman be instructed to issue a proclamation for holding an election on the 5th day of April, A D, 1887, in the several wards of the village of South Omaha, for the election of a mayor, a treasurer, one police judge, a city clerk, city engineer, and two councilmen for each ward, the polls to be open between the hours of 9 o'clock A M and 7 o'clock P M, at the following places: First ward, at the office of John R. Grice, attorney, second ward [at] Carpenter & Blackwell's office; third ward [at] the Exchange building, stock yards [Signed] Daniel O'Connell, clerk, E. P. Savage, chairman."

At the election E. P. Savage was chosen mayor, C M. Hunt, treasurer, E. K. Wells, clerk, F. M. Smith and Bruno Strathman, councilmen, first ward; Daniel Rafferty and Alfred A Gary, second ward, and David Loescher and John N Burke, third ward. G. Reuther was elected police judge and Hugo Theinhart, city engineer. On the 7th of April, 1887, these gentlemen took the

---
*Omaha Bee, January 9, 1887. But the "vast establishments" and "armies of men" were drafts upon the imagination which have not yet, in all respects, been fully realized.

oath of office. The village records end with: "Here the old board retired with a few remarks from Mr. Hunt." The village government lasted a little less than six months. Mr. Hunt pronounced its valedictory.

On that day the city council met at the office of Ritchhart & Persons. Present: Mayor Savage, and Councilmen Smith, Strathman, Rafferty, Gary, Loescher and Burke—when an adjournment was taken to April 12, following.

At the meeting of the council on the 12th of April, Frederick M. Smith was chosen president; David Loescher, acting president; J. R. Grice, city attorney; and Patrick Rice, city marshal. George Dixon was appointed night watch. The marshal was instructed to act as street commissioner. The bond of the city treasurer was increased from five thousand dollars to ten thousand dollars. A proposition from Mr. Ritchhart was received, wherein he proposed to furnish room, lights and fuel for council meetings at one dollar per night. The proposition was promptly accepted. The meeting then adjourned. It will be seen that the wheels of the city government were now fairly in motion.

"In April, 1887," says a recent publication, "there being the requisite population, the village of South Omaha was organized into a city of the second class. * * * The moment this movement was talked of it created a breeze, and everybody prepared for a battle of ballots, the contest being between the law-abiding citizens, on the one side, and those who cared more for money and a license to do as they pleased than for for law and order, on the other. The nominating convention, itself, was a picnic which occurs only once in a man's lifetime, and indeed but few men are blest with the privilege of witnessing such an exhibition.

"The meeting was held in the old frame school house, near the Union Pacific tracks, and the house was jammed full of embryo politicians, half-drunken bummers, tipsy candidates and rocky heelers, sandwiched in with honest citizens, respectable members of society, business men and capitalists. Colonel Savage was elected chairman, and Edward Stearns, secretary. Nominations for city officers were made, beginning with candidate for mayor, of which there were several, and it was agreed that all nominations should be decided by ballot. There were many present who had not the slightest idea of what the object of a primary or nominating meeting was, although they were there under instructions, from their candidates, to carry the meeting if it had to be done by force. Many of them thought, or, at least, acted as if the nomination of a candidate meant an election, not seeming to know that they could have another whack at an objectionable candidate at the polls. Consequently, when balloting began, and it commenced to dawn upon the mob that the law-and-order people would succeed in placing their men on the ticket, a scene of wild confusion took place. The multitude surged back and forth, seats began cracking all over the house, like old dry timber, fist-fights occurred in various parts of the room, knives and pistols were drawn, and several heads were broken by policemen's clubs. Brave men became panic-stricken, and in several instances climbed out of the windows at the imminent risk of breaking their necks, and for aught the writer knows, some of them are still running. In the midst of the confusion lights were extinguished, and the convention was virtually broken up. For once in his life Colonel Savage, the chairman, could not command attention, although he mounted a desk and exercised his lung power to its utmost capacity. However, the ticket was afterward completed, and nearly all of it elected.

"A bitter contest took place at the polls, and some blood was shed, though it came mostly from broken noses. * * *

"It was not without some murmuring that opposing factions accepted the situation, and for a time at least, the most arduous duty of the city officials was to preserve order. But the extraordinary growth of the city, both in population and in commercial importance, soon over-shadowed everything else, and gave the city fathers so much to do to provide for necessary improvements, that the lawlessly inclined had things pretty much as they wanted them. Gradually, however, the reins were tightened, and at least a show of police authority was made, Patrick Rice was made chief, and Pat had a rough time of it. At times it was a difficult matter to say whether he was chief of police, acting under orders of the city council, or whether the saloons and their customers had been clothed with authority to run the chief and his men.

"These were small matters—too small to cut much of a figure, except with those who naturally would find fault if they lived in Heaven."*

At a meeting of the council, on the 18th of April, another night watch was appointed, and on the 25th, James Lasher was authorized to act as policeman. An ordinance (No 15) was introduced at a meeting held on the 29th, establishing and regulating a police department. It was read the first time—put upon its final passage and carried. On the 9th of May, the committee on boundary lines introduced the written opinion of John M Thurston, on the subject of the encroachment of the City of Omaha on the territory of South Omaha. The "encroachment," here referred to, was the passage of an ordinance, on the ninth day of the previous month, by Omaha, extending its jurisdiction over all of South Omaha north of F Street. However, as Omaha took no action under the ordinance—not attempting to exercise any municipal jurisdiction over the territory mentioned, the City of South Omaha continued to make good the autonomy and integrity of its original boundaries, in all respects, as though her more powerful neighbor had laid no claim to the northern half of her possessions.

"In the following June," are the words of a recent writer who has already been frequently quoted, "the city council passed a resolution agreeing to submit a proposition of the Omaha Motor Railway Company and also of the South Omaha Street Railway Company to a vote of the people. At the same time the Union Pacific Railway Company asked the council to donate to them thirty feet of the west side of Twenty-seventh Street, nearly opposite the foot of N Street, for depot purposes.

"In July 1887, Armour closed a deal with Lipton whereby he became the possessor of the Lipton plant and the 'King of Packers' became a South Omaha operator. If any doubts remained in the minds of the weak-kneed, this move of Armour dispelled them. Even the most skeptical from that date forward felt that it was only a question of time when South Omaha would be second if not first in the list of packing centres. From that day the Armour plant began to grow and is still growing.

"On Monday, July 25, 1887, a special

*The Eagle, July 4 1891

election was held to vote upon the street railway proposition mentioned above. The election resulted in defeating the home company and in granting the Omaha company a franchise. This was the first step towards our present splendid facilities for travel between the two cities. * * *

"On the same day of the election, [July 25, 1887], the City of St Joseph offered P D Armour $100,000 in cold cash and twenty acres of ground, as an inducement to him to establish a packing house there, but Mr Armour declined with thanks, preferring to make South Omaha his principal place of business on the Missouri River. That was another example of Mr Armour's good business judgment, and another indication of the future of this city. The sequel is all that could have been desired, both on the part of Mr Armour and of the city.

"On August 4th, 1887, the following item appeared in the *Stockman*

"'An even half dozen new commission firms have been added to the number doing business in South Omaha, within the past few days. Hill & Smiley, Regan & Lowry, Brainard & Richardson, Horne & Sharp, Alexander & Fitch, Gosney & Chumbley.

"'These firms do not count in numbers alone, but are all good, strong, substantial firms of established reputation. In fact there is not a snide live stock commission firm at the yards, whether old or late accessions. They are nearly all men who have been in business for years, in New York, Chicago, and other eastern markets, who have been driven to Omaha by the stern hand of fate, which has from time to time decreed that the live stock markets shall go farther west, nearer the source of supply. They are composed of the most enterprising of the large army of eastern operators, who have both the means and experience necessary to a successful business.'

"It was about this date that Fowler Brothers, packers, served an injunction on the Stock Yards Company to restrain them from issuing a block of shares of their stock to Armour. The matter was afterward amicably adjusted.

"An ordinance providing for the grading of N Street from the railroad to Twentieth Street, was passed in August, 1887, and on the 12th of that month the School Board met, opened the bids, and let the contract for erecting the High School building.

Mackey & McDonald put in a bid of $8,400, which being the lowest, entitled them to the contract.   *   *   *

"In the same month of August, the K. S. Newcomb Lumber Company located its yards in this city, and the new Union Pacific passenger depot was located at the foot of N Street. Many other important improvements were inaugurated at this time, and a number of accessions to the ranks of the business men of the city were made, most of whom are [in 1891], still here, and doing well." *

At the meeting of the council, October 17th, a motion was made and carried, that the mayor notify the Governor of Nebraska that the City of South Omaha has a population of over five thousand. This was a proceeding looking to the incorporation of South Omaha as a city of the second class of the highest degree.

By a proclamation of the Governor of the State, issued December 13, 1887, South Omaha became a city of the second class (of the highest degree), "having more than five thousand and less than twenty-five thousand inhabitants." This change took place a little more than eight months after its organization as a city of the lesser degree—that is, having over *one* thousand, but less than twenty-five thousand inhabitants.†

The election for city officers was held on Tuesday, April 3, 1888, and resulted in the choice of W. G. Sloane for mayor, Thomas Hocter for city clerk, Thomas Geary for treasurer. On the 12th of April, J. McMillan was elected president of the council; Eli H. Doud was appointed city attorney, and E. B. Towle city engineer. Edwin Driggs was authorized to number the houses of the city at the cost of the owners. On the 16th C. J. Collins was appointed inspector of plumbing; and on the 23rd, David Hoban was made street commissioner.

On the 28th of August, the city engineer was instructed to advertise for bids to build the Q Street and L Street viaducts, the issuing of thirty-five thousand dollars in bonds for the former, and forty-three thousand for the latter of these viaducts having the day previous been voted for by the citizens of South Omaha, each proposition receiving a majority of over eight hundred votes. A proposition also carried at the same election to issue sixty-two thousand dollars in bonds for sewerage purposes; another for twelve thousand dollars to pave street and alley intersections; and still another for thirty-five thousand dollars to fund outstanding indebtedness. J. J. Breen was appointed and confirmed building inspector on the 22nd of October following.

Let us now glance at the material progress of the village—the city—of South Omaha. Here is the showing for the ending of the year 1888: It had a population of not less than eight thousand, and the number of firms and individuals doing business was 243. Nothing, in Nebraska, during the four years preceding, equaled that increase, considering the fact that it started from almost nothing.

It was submitted to the city council on the 18th of April, 1889, by a special committee appointed for that purpose, that the total indebtedness of the municipality was $271,912.14; total assets, $816,982.32. The expenditures for the previous year were $190,390.37.

On the 1st of May a committee reported to the city council that the new fire alarm system had been completed and was working satisfactorily. An issue of seventy thousand dollars funding bonds was voted by the South Omaha electors on the 21st. It was soon after shown that the assessed valuation of the city was $2,167,000.

When, in the spring of 1889, it became evident that South Omaha had a sufficient population for the city to be organized under the statute [that is, under one particular statute] as a city of the first class "having more than eight thousand and less than twenty-five thousand inhabitants," a proposition to that effect was submitted to a vote of the people. This was on May 21, 1889, and the question was carried in the affirmative. Thereupon the Governor of Nebraska issued his proclamation in these words:

"WHEREAS, a certificate has been filed in the executive office, by the mayor of the City of South Omaha, in the State of Nebraska, in which it is certified that the said

---
* J. B. Erion, in *The Eagle*, July 4 and 11, 1891.

† "On October 16, 1886, only a little over six years ago, so many of the people of 'Douglas Precinct' as felt the necessity of having a form of local government established, which should immediately protect them in their homes and at their work, caused to be organized the village of South Omaha, with boundary lines exactly identical with those of the present city. The trustees of the village organized by the election of E. P. Savage as chairman, who thus became the first chief executive officer of South Omaha. But the very next year (1887), the village began to put on "metropolitan airs." It became a city of the second class, of the lesser degree, and Mr. Savage was elected first mayor; then it soon became a city of the second class of a 'higher degree.'"—*The Drovers Journal*, December 31, 1892.

City of South Omaha contains a population of more than eight thousand inhabitants, the said certificate having been given by the mayor acting under authority of law and in accordance with the facts

"Now, therefore, I, John M Thayer, governor of the State of Nebraska, do hereby issue my proclamation and declare said City of South Omaha a city of the first class and subject to all the provisions of an act to provide for the organization, government and powers of cities of the first class, having more than eight thousand and less than twenty-five thousand inhabitants

"In testimony whereof, I have hereunto set my hand, and caused to be affixed the great seal of the State

"Done at Lincoln this eighth day of June, A D 1889

"*By the Governor*,       JOHN M THAYER
"[L S]       G. L LAWS, *Secretary of State*"*

On Tuesday, April 1, 1890, an election for city officers resulted in the choice of W G Sloane, mayor, T E McGuire, clerk, Thomas Hoctor, treasurer, P J King, police judge

But just here it is proper to state that the Supreme Court of Nebraska, in the case of the "State ex rel School Board of South Omaha *vs* County Board of Douglas County," in a decision handed down February 15, 1893, nullifies the proclamation of Governor Thayer in these words "South Omaha, as shown by the census of 1890, is a city of the second class, having more than eight thousand and less than twenty-five thousand inhabitants, and not a city of the first class"

That Omaha and the "Magic City" would be benefited in various ways were South Omaha to be included in the municipality first named, and become a part thereof, was a proposition that early had advocates in both cities It was now (April, 1890) agitated with vigor Steps were taken to bring the matter, according to law, before the citizens of Omaha and South Omaha for them to vote upon the proposition There was no great interest manifested in the city first mentioned, but in South Omaha the excitement was intense The election was held May 8, 1890

*On October 18 [16] 1886, South Omaha was incorporated as a village and on December 19 1887, by the governor's proclamation it was made a city of the second class, the requirements being that it should have a population of over five thousand In March 1890, [June 1889,] the city was granted a charter as a city of the first class, having a population over eight thousand and less than twenty five thousand —*South Omaha Daily Tribune*, December 31, 1892

Omaha went *for* annexation, but in South Omaha the result was as follows

| Wards | For | Against |
|---|---|---|
| First | 235 | 309 |
| Second | 178 | 302 |
| Third | 191 | 198 |
| Fourth | 123 | 16 |
|  | 727 | 825 |

Majority *against* annexation    .    98

So the annexation project was defeated, and South Omaha is still a city, duly incorporated under the statute, but there was left them a source of disquietude It was threatened that Omaha had a good claim to all of the territory north of F Street, and that, if annexation failed, the metropolitan city would soon assert its rights in the courts The attempt was made, but with what success we shall now see

The City of Omaha commenced suit in the Supreme Court of Nebraska against the City of South Omaha, September 1, 1890, in effect to recover from the latter all the territory lying north of F Street as extended east and west to its east and west limits — the city first named claiming (as before mentioned) this extensive area as rightfully belonging to that municipality, and that jurisdiction over it was wrongfully exercised by South Omaha   But the court decreed the territory to the last mentioned city, which leaves its boundaries exactly as established by the county commissioners, October 16, 1886, when the board fixed the limits of the village of South Omaha *

On Tuesday, April 5, 1892, the successful candidates for the following city offices were C P Miller, mayor, Thomas Hoctor, treasurer, Henry Ditzen, clerk, James M Fowler, police judge

Mayor Miller was found in an unconscious condition in the weeds in the vicinity of Eighth and Dodge Streets, Omaha, on Tuesday evening, October 4, 1892, at about 5 30 o'clock   There was a hole in his forehead, showing where a 45-caliber bullet had entered, and his left eye was entirely out of its socket hanging down on his cheek by only a few shreds of flesh   The patrol wagon was called and he was taken to the Methodist hospital   Dr Somers probed for the bullet, but was unable to find it   Mr Miller died at 4 30 o'clock in the afternoon of the next day

The coroner's jury returned the following

*Nebraska Reports*, Vol 31, pp 378-385

verdict on the afternoon of October 14: "After a searching examination we find that ex-Mayor Miller, of South Omaha, came to his death from a gun-shot wound in his left temple, and after having exhausted all means in our power we, the jury, do say that we are unable to determine by whom the fatal shot was fired.

"Gustav Anderson, W. A. Sharp, J. T. Withrow, John P. Durler, C. J. Mentor."

The funeral of Mayor Miller occurred on the afternoon of Sunday, October 9. A large part of the population of South Omaha attended to pay a last tribute to his memory, the streets being crowded with thousands of people. Many houses were draped. The funeral was in charge of the Knights of Pythias, of which order Mayor Miller had been a member. The First Presbyterian Church, where the services were held, was filled to its utmost capacity and many were unable to obtain admission, while hundreds realized the uselessness of attempting to gain entrance and remained upon the streets. The remains were buried in Laurel Hill Cemetery, whither they were followed by a long cortege, composed of citizens and members of various secret orders.

The successor of Mayor Miller, as chief executive of South Omaha, was J. S. Walters, who, by virtue of his office as president of the council, became acting mayor, in which capacity he is now (January, 1893) officiating.

The councilmen of South Omaha who have been, or are now, in office, with the years of their incumbency, are:

1887—First ward, F. M. Smith,. Bruno Strathman (the latter having resigned, J. M. Glasgow was appointed in his place); second ward, Daniel Rafferty, Alfred A. Gary; third ward, David Loescher, John N. Burke (during the year this ward was divided and a fourth ward formed); fourth ward, T. B. Whittlesey and Charles Bogart were appointed by the mayor.

1888—First ward, D. F. Bayless (who resigned, and F. H. Boyd was appointed to fill the vacancy), Fred. M. Smith; second ward, John McMillan; third ward, J. J. O'Rourke; fourth ward, S. B. Fenno for the long term, and B. Jetter for the short term. Mr. Fenno resigned and E. P. Savage was appointed to fill his place.

1889—First ward, E. B. Towle; in the second ward a contest between D. Rafferty and Christian A. Melcher was decided in favor of the latter; third ward, J N. Burke; fourth ward, Ed. Johnston.

1890—Patrick Rowley, James J. Dougherty, Edward T. Conley, and John J. O'Rourke were elected councilmen at large.

1891—First ward, William M. Wood; second ward, A. B. Haley; third ward, F. Bowley; fourth ward, J. S. Walters.

1892—James H. Bulla, Ora Edwin Bruce, John F. Schultz and Walstein B. Wyman were elected from the city at large.

The following persons have filled the position of police judge in South Omaha: G. Reuther, P. J. King, and J. M. Fowler now (January, 1893) in office.

Residents of South Omaha who have held county and state offices are: Peter J. Corrigan and C. C. Stanley, county commissioners; J. J. Breen, John McMillan and A. L. Sutton, assemblymen.

NOTE I.— The City of South Omaha has an efficient fire department. An ordinance creating this department was passed on the 5th of August, 1889, by the council and approved the same day by Mayor Sloane. Fred. M. Smith organized the department, and has served as chief continuously since that time.

The police department is well organized, and its work effective. The number of police is ten. The names of those who have held the office of chief are: Patrick Rice, A. C. McCracken, J. P. Maloney, Thomas Brennan, W. H. Beckett.

NOTE II.— The city has, as before mentioned two viaducts: one on L Street, with a length of 1474 feet, costing $41,717.25; the other on Q Street, with a length of 816 feet, costing $45 300. Bonds have been issued on the L Street viaduct for $42,000, and on the Q Street viaduct for $35,000. The structures are of great utility, crossing, as they do, above the Union Pacific and other railroad tracks, closely uniting the east and west parts of the city.

# CHAPTER VII.

### Minor Industries and Public and Private Institutions

The first newspaper printed in South Omaha was the *South Omaha Globe*, J B Erion, editor and proprietor. It commenced its existence October 30, 1885 Some of the editor's "locals," in that issue are worthy of preservation

"The Carroll grocery house is one of the new institutions of South Omaha They have a large, convenient building, recently finished, and neat and clean as a new pin It is well filled with a new, fresh stock of groceries and provisions "

"The U P Company has had a large force of hands at work for months past, directly opposite this office [the *Globe*], at the Summit, grading yards and laying switches The result is extensive yards two hundred feet wide and half a mile long Next season a union depot will be built at this point by the B & M and U P [It was built (a small frame building) but was removed in 1890] '

' South Omaha needs a physician. One would naturally think, with the thousand of M D 's turned out by the medical colleges every year, some young fledgling or other would stick out his shingle in every village and hamlet in the country, but it seems that no saw-bones has struck South Omaha as yet The town is supplied with a good drug store, but no doctor "

" H Rigby & Co have opened a boot and shoe shop at South Omaha Mr Rigby is an Ames, Iowa, man and is a thorough workman "

"South Omaha now has a coal dealer, which will be quite a convenience Heretofore the town was obliged to order its supply of coal from the city [Omaha] "

" It has been positively asserted by those who know, that the street cars will run to the Stock Yards next season If the present company does not extend its line, the syndicate will build a line of its own and operate it "

" It may seem rather odd to some people that the *Globe* office has been established at the Summit, a mile and a quarter [north] from the stock yards, and about two miles from the [Omaha] city post office, but we have reasons for so doing The wonderful growth of Omaha warrants us in the prediction that we will be in the heart of a business community in a short time. At present, however, we must admit it is a little lonesome ['This ' heart of a business community ' has not as yet materialized, as on the first day of January, 1893, all the lots in the immediate vicinity are still vacant, and ' the *Globe* office ' has been moved away ]"

On the first day of January, 1886, the *South Omaha Globe* was combined with the *Omaha Live Stock Journal* and the paper named the *South Omaha Globe-Journal*, J B Erion continuing as editor and proprietor

A daily paper — the first in South Omaha — was issued by J B Erion, June 12, 1886, and called the *South Omaha Stockman*, taking the place of the *South Omaha Globe-Journal* It was first printed in the parlor of the " Union Stock Yards Hotel" formerly the " Canfield House "

Not long after the advent of the *Stockman*, C H Rich bought an interest in the paper, and it was, thereafter, until March 25, 1889, published by Erion and Rich On the day last named, the concern passed into the hands of "The Stockman Publishing Company," who have since been proprietors It is, as its name implies, largely a live-stock paper It is also issued as a weekly and a semi-weekly.

The *Hoof and Horn* was first issued December 20, 1887, by John A MacMurphy as editor and manager On November 3, 1888, MacMurphy retired, his successor being L F. Hilton On the 17th of December following, the name was changed to the *Daily Drovers Journal* On March 21, 1890, Mr Hilton associated with himself in the publication of the paper, Denna Allbery It so continued until January 15, 1891, when Hilton turned the paper over to Perry Selden who held a mortgage on the property Selden, on the 30th of April following, came into possession of the paper under a mortgage sale, Mr Allbery being continued on the paper as agent. It was run by Selden until June 4th when "The Drovers Journal Company" was organized and purchased the plant, continuing Mr. Allbery as editor to the present time (January, 1893). The *Journal* is also issued as a weekly and a semi-weekly. The paper is principally a live-stock publication.

The first number of the *South Omaha Tribune* was issued November 21, 1890, by J. F. Ritchhart, editor and proprietor. The *Tribune* passed into the possession of "The Tribune Printing Company" March 1, 1892. This company is organized under state laws, and the paper is still (January, 1893), run by the same company. The *Tribune* is democratic in politics.

Several newspapers of South Omaha have "gone the way of all the earth":

(1) The *Times* was first issued February 24, 1887. The successive editors were Geo. Southmayd, James H. Van Dusen, M. M. Parrish, E. O. Mayfield and Samuel P. Brigham. The *Times* was republican until the last editor changed it to independent. Its final issue was October 26, 1890.

(2) The *Boomer* made its bow to the public for the first time, February 15, 1889; but gave up its "individual being" April 15, 1890. It was independent in its political sentiments and was edited by A. E. Brigham.

(3) The *News* (independent democrat) was born June 19, 1890. W. A. Root edited the paper, which expired on the twenty-ninth of the following November.

(4) The *Enterprise* was first issued July 21, 1891, but "departed this life" November 27th, thereafter. It was edited by A. E. Brigham and A. H. Powers. In politics it was independent.

(5) The *Bulletin* made its first appearance January 18, 1892, and succumbed June 27th, following. It was a commercial sheet and was conducted by Samuel P. Brigham.*

Although not the latest attempt at the newspaper enterprise which has "failure" written across its face, yet we have reserved the *Eagle* for the last. Its first number was issued April 13, 1891. It was a weekly publication, in pamphlet form — established by Erion & Hart and edited by J. B. Erion.

* To Mr. Brigham, the author is indebted for the facts concerning these several papers that are no longer in existence.

After a brief existence the *Eagle* was consolidated with the *Omaha Republican*.

From a consideration of the press of South Omaha, a transition to its schools is a natural one, the newspaper powerfully assisting in the promotion of education.

When the first movement was made looking to the founding of a town south of the city of Omaha, there was only a common school district in that part of Douglas precinct, known as District No. 3, which was united with District No. 4, in the same precinct.* The school organization extended over territory bounded on the east by the Missouri river; by Sarpy County on the south; by section 8, in township 14, of range 13, on the west; and by Omaha on the north.

The first organization was in 1858 with John Bagley, Philip Cassady and Patrick Corrigan as directors. The district was divided in 1864. The first school house was built in 1867, and was removed to what is now known as the fourth ward in 1888. The directors of the new district were L. A. Walker, Fred. Drexel and Thomas Ryan.

Little interest can attach to the school, from the first one taught, down to the time when a great change was impending, for the reason that its history for more than twenty-five years (1858-1885) was the usual one of that appertaining to a Nebraska common school as carried on in a country district.

When South Omaha began to put on the appearance of a village, Miss Anna M. Carroll (now Mrs. Thomas Geary), was the teacher in the "Stock Yard's School District"—that is, in District No. 3, of Douglas precinct. She commenced teaching on the twenty-first of September, 1885, being first employed for three months at $40 a month; the succeeding three months she was paid $50 a month.

From the *South Omaha Globe* of November 6, 1885, the following is taken:

"Judging from the increase in the school attendance for the present time as compared with that of last year, the board of education [district directors] will soon have to furnish other and better accommodations for the little ones. At present there are more than fifty pupils crowded together in a small room, with not a sufficient number

* District No. 3, originally extended north to Vinton street, east to the river, south to the Sarpy county line, and west to the present Thirty-sixth street. When the village was established it took in a portion of the east side of District No. 4, extending one-half mile west of Thirty-sixth street. That strip, although in South Omaha, still belongs to District No. 4.

of seats for half the number of scholars. Day after day the pupils and their teacher are cheered on in their labors by the consoling thought that there are better days coming."

"[November 20, 1885.]--The public school building at South Omaha is a small, one-story frame, the worse for age and rough usage, poorly and sparely seated, and entirely too small to accommodate the number of pupils in attendance, much less the number enrolled. We understand the teacher, Miss Carroll, who, by the way, has given excellent satisfaction, has repeatedly asked the directors to at least put in some additional seats and desks, but so far in vain. It seems to us that good economy, if nothing else, should prompt those in authority to make the needed repairs at the South Omaha school. It is throwing money away to pay a teacher $40.00 per month, furnish fuel, etc., and then destroy the efficacy of the whole thing by neglecting to furnish desk and seating capacity for the pupils. A teacher in a common school, obliged to teach all grades in one room, has a hard row to hoe, even when supplied with all necessary conveniences. Give the teacher a chance."

From the *Globe-Journal:* "[April 9, 1886],—The people of South Omaha took a lively interest in the annual school election which took place last Monday. If there is any one thing of which the average American citizen is justly proud, it is our public school system, and there is no one thing for which the people are as willing to spend their money as for the education of their children. The rapidly increasing population of South Omaha demanded something better than a little, old, dilapidated, one-room frame pen, cold as a barn, in which to teach 'the young idea how to shoot', hence the interest above mentioned. For some time past Col. E. P. Savage has been talked of as a proper person for the position of director, especially at this time when a live business man is needed to manage the affairs of the district; and as an evidence of the unanimity of the people, we will just state that out of seventy-two votes cast, the Colonel received seventy. No. 3 in which South Omaha is located, is a large district extending to the river on the east and contains but one good school house [the small brick, now in Omaha, on Boulevard] and that with only one room. With the present board the voters of the district can rest assured that the wants of the *whole* district will be regarded. Before another election day rolls around, No. 3 will have two new school houses, one at South Omaha and one in the east end of the district."

HIGH SCHOOL BUILDING.

So rapid was the increase in the population of South Omaha in the next twelve months, that three teachers were necessary for the public schools. At the end of the school year 1886-'87, S. L. Caldwell was chosen principal and Miss Grace Glasgow (now Mrs. Manly Raley) assistant. Another frame building was erected adjoining the old one. The following school year (1887-'88) beginning September 1st, a course of study was adopted. There were three rooms and eight grades were represented in the schools which were taught in the two school buildings and the Methodist church. This was the beginning of the graded school. H. E. Grimm was elected to succeed Mr. Caldwell, but he only served one month when he resigned. A. A. Munroe was then (October 17, 1887) elected superintendent to finish the school year, at a salary of $1,000. He was re-elected in June, 1888, for one year at a salary of $1,200; also in June, 1889, again chosen for one year, at the same salary; and in June, 1890, re-elected for three years at a salary of $1,500. During the school year of 1887-'88, E. P. Savage, Walter J. Slate and J. B. Erion constituted the school board and foreseeing the rapid growth of population they purchased three lots on the corner of Twenty-fifth and L Streets for $5,500 and built thereon a high school building at a cost of $10,323. On the first day of January, 1888, the high school building being finished, Superintendent Munroe moved in.

At the end of the school year of 1891-'92, there were thirty-two teachers employed including the superintendent.

The following table shows the growth of the schools:

| Year Ending July | Children of school age | Enrolled during year | Av. daily attendance | Number Teachers employ'd |
|---|---|---|---|---|
| 1885 | 204 | 107 | 35 | 1 |
| 1886 | 321 | 188 | 132 | 2 |
| 1887 | 784 | 348 | 153 | 2 |
| 1888 | 1,091 | 631 | 235 | 4-10 |
| 1889 | 1,468 | 1,172 | 590 | 15 |
| 1890 | 2,048 | 1,248 | 740 | 23 |
| 1891 | 2,255 | 1,586 | 788 | 25 |
| 1892 | 2,931 | 1,751 | 909 | 32 |
| 1892-3* | | | | 88 |

The records show a total enrollment in the public schools since September 1, 1892, of 1,765 pupils. The average daily attendance during November, 1892, was 1,260.

In 1887, Savage, Slate and Erion constituted the board under the district laws. In April, 1888, a board of six were elected as follows: F. J. Persons, C. T. VanAkin, W. J. Slate, David Hoban, and J. D. Robinson. The following year, 1889, the board consisted of Persons, J. C. Carroll, Van Akin, Slate, Hoban and Robinson. In April 1890, the new board consisted of Persons, Swift, Funston, Slate, Robinson, VanAkin.

The board for 1891 was: C. T. VanAkin, president; J. D. Robinson, vice-president; Robert Funston, secretary; W. J. Slate, J. D. Jones and James Bulla. For 1892: W. B. Cheek, president; J. D. Jones, vice-president; Robert Funston, secretary; Jas. H. Bulla, F. E. Pearl, Ivor Thomas.

In 1888, at the urgent request of Supt. Munroe the free text book system was adopted with many misgivings on the part of the board. The scheme proved to be a long stride in advance and has since been embodied in the state law and adopted in all districts.

From one school house, one teacher and a handful of scholars, in September, 1885, to eight school houses (some of them fine brick structures), thirty-eight teachers and 1,765 pupils, eight years thereafter, is the progress made in the South Omaha schools.

There are a number of other institutions in South Omaha, some public, others private, demanding attention because of their importance. There may now be mentioned the Postoffice, the South Omaha Board of Trade, the Street Railways, the Express Companies, the Telephone Exchange, the American District Telegraph Company, the Banks, and the South Omaha Electric Light, Heat and Power Company.

The first postmaster in South Omaha was W. G. Sloane, whose commission was dated October 3, 1884. Before the establishing of the postoffice, the few citizens of the settlement were obliged to have their papers and letters sent them to Omaha.

Mr. Sloane was finally compelled on account of ill health to resign his office.

The successor of Mr. Sloane was Peter Cockrell, in whose favor the former resigned. He received his appointment November 3, 1887, and took charge of the office on the 16th of the same month. Mr. Cockrell was re-appointed as a postmaster of the second-class, January 16, 1888, assuming his duties as such on the fourteenth of the ensuing month. During his term of office the business continued to increase rapidly. The free delivery system, after a good deal of effort, was established by him, on the first day of July, 1889. Mr. Cockrell went out of office in the fall of 1890, a change in the administration having made his resignation desirable.

Dr. J. M. Glasgow was Mr. Cockrell's successor and he still (January, 1893,) holds the office. He was appointed August 13th, receiving his commission September 1st, and assuming the duties of office October 4th, 1890.

The South Omaha Board of Trade was organized in the winter of 1887-8. The first officers were David Anderson, president; John Doe, vice-president; J. B. Erion, secretary; and J. C. Farral, treasurer. By its united and timely efforts, this organization has accomplished much toward aiding the building up of South Omaha.

The Omaha Street Railway Company's track enters the City of South Omaha from the north at the beginning of Twenty-fourth street, and continues south along that street to and across N street. Their cars are pro-

---
*The number of pupils enrolled during the year 1892-3 up to March 1st was 1765. The average daily attendance for the month of February, 1893, was 1228.

pelled by electricity, and they have an eight minute service This track was opened to the public in December, 1890

The Metropolitan Street Railway Company lately opened a short road from Q street to the lower part of Albright's addition The cars are propelled by horse power Recently the track has been extended

There are in South Omaha four Express Companies, the Adams, the Pacific, the American and the United States The Adams Express Company was opened January 22, 1890; the American, September 17th of the same year, the Pacific about six years ago, while the United States has been in operation about two years

The South Omaha Telephone Exchange was established October 31, 1888, with about twenty-five telephones and now numbers ninety Besides these there are several private telephones not connected with the central office On account of the large amount of business done with Omaha parties, about twenty-five firms have telephones connected direct with the Omaha exchange South Omaha is connected with all towns having a telephone exchange in this territory.

The American District Telegraph Company opened in South Omaha in September, 1886, with twenty-two night watch and fire alarm boxes There was a night man in charge the first eight months H P Ryner was appointed manager September, 1887. The system has steadily grown until it has reached nearly three hundred (July, 1892) Their business is to protect stock yards and packing house interests, from which they recieve two signals each minute all night. They have charge of thirty watchmen Their central office is connected with electric wires running throughout the packing houses and stock yards They handle all fire alarms in South Omaha

Nothing more unquestionably evinces the solid foundation of South Omaha than the banks of the city—affording, as they do, every facility for commercial and monetary transactions and giving an insight of the thrift and prosperity of its citizens The national banking institutions are the Packers National Bank. the South Omaha National Bank and the Union Stock Yards National Bank

The business of these banks is in a highly prosperous condition The Savings Banks of South Omaha are the Packers Savings Bank and the South Omaha Savings Bank According to the statements of these two banks, $108,422 69 are on deposit The undivided profits and surplus is $15,981 06

The annual business of the three National Banks represents the handling of $561,000,-000. These banks are, of course, independent of those in Omaha, and, as a result, do not figure in the clearing house reports of that city

The South Omaha Electric Light, Heat and Power Company was organized in June, 1888, consisting of a number of persons, mostly residents of the city A board of directors of nine members was elected, from whom were chosen John Boyd, president, C M Hunt, vice-president, John Doe, secretary, J L. Miles, treasurer, and J T. Smith, general manager The capital stock was fixed at $25,000

The religious organizations and secret societies of South Omaha are not the least among the important and influential institutions of the Magic City. And these, too, now demand attention.

The St Agnes Parish Church was organized in 1888, by the Rev D W Moriarty, the first resident priest in South Omaha During the two preceding years, services were held in a frame building (now known as St Bridget's), but, in November, 1889, a large brick structure was completed and services have since been held therein. There is a parochial school connected with the church

The First Methodist Church was organized in 1886, Rev T B Hilton being the first pastor A church building and parsonage were erected the same year, but the former soon becoming too small for the increasing attendance, a larger structure in 1886 took its place This was nearly all burned down January 18, 1893

The South Omaha Presbyterian Mission was organized May 29, 1887, by the Rev. Geo W Dodge. A new church building was organized in August, 1891, and dedicated in February, 1892 The Fourth Ward Mission was organized October 20, 1889, the Missouri Avenue Mission, in May, 1890

The organization of the Baptist Church by Rev. F W Foster. took place September 11, 1887, and was recognized as a regular organization on the twenty-eighth of October, 1888. A church edifice now completed was commenced early in the spring of 1892.

The German Evangelical Lutheran Zion Congregation started over six years ago, under the direction of the Rev. E. J. Frese, of Omaha. Later, Rev. John Iler took charge. In the fall of 1891, Rev. N. Adam was called to this field.

In 1889, the Episcopal Church Society was organized in South Omaha—Rev. R. L. Knox, priest in charge. The congregation have a church building on Twenty-third Street.

Besides the Roman Catholic parochial school already mentioned, there is one under direction of the Lutheran Church. This was organized by H. S. Rullmann.

The other religous organizations in South Omaha are: The First Christian Church on 23rd and K Streets; the Albright M. E. Church, 17th and D Streets; the German M. E. Church, on North 28th Street; the First Presbyterian Church, on 25th and J Streets.

The secret societies of South Omaha are numerous and in general prosperous.

The Bee Hive Lodge, No. 184, of Free and Accepted Masons was created January 22, 1889, and chartered June 30, thereafter. The first officers were: Jas. Gilbert, master; W. M. Wood, secretary; G. H. Brewer, S.W; C. C. Stanley, S. D.; A. V. Miller, J. W.; F. M. Smith, J. D.; D. S. Holmes, T.; J. Emerick, T.

The organization of Lodge No. 148, I. O. O. F., took place with Grand Master Adam Ferguson in the chair, the following being the charter members: J. H. Johnson, W. S. Anderson, J. B. Erion, L. Carpenter, Peter Cockrell, D. Loesher, James Carlin, James Sattizan, C. C. Van Kuran, A. H. Miller, Geo. Clark.

Enterprise Lodge, No, 79, K. of P., was organized June 22, 1887. The first officers were: C. C., Adam Kellner; V. C., William Baumann; P. C., A. J. Baldwin; M. of E., Harry Miller; M. of F., J. H. Johnson; K. of R. & S., J. F. Ritchhart; P., Frank Lake; M. of A., John D. Robinson; O. G., A. D. Slater; I. G., A. J. Stoll; trustees, J. H. Johnson, A. J. Baldwin, Frank Lake.

The Uniform Rank of this lodge was organized February 12, 1891, with the following as first officers: Captain, A. L. Lott; first lieutenant, W. B. Cheek; second lieutenant, T. B. Hatcher; right guide, J. D. Robinson; left guide, Geo. Hatcher.

The Robert R. Livingston Post, No. 282, G. A. R., was organized February 18, 1889, with the following charter members: Jacob W. Cress, S. W. Dennis, E. K. Wells, W. A. Root, J. O. Eastman, Chas. R. Burgess, J. M. Lambert, Amos Thurlaw. Chas. Howe, N. Gooden, J. S. Oviatt, John E. Hart.

The Women's Relief Corps of the Robert R. Livingston Post, No. 143, was instituted October 5, 1891, with members as follows: Mrs. May M. Cress, Coe E. Cress, Emma A. Bayless, Mary A. McDaugal, Maria S. Raworth, Elizabeth Candon, Flavilla Etter, Edith Smith, Mary Hill, Ethel Eddy, Jennie Tylee.

The E. K. Wells Camp, No. 72, Sons of Veterans, was organized August 2, 1889, with: Captain, John P. Harris; first lieutenant, F. E. Hart; second lieutenant, Harry Dennis.

The Ancient Order of United Workmen (Lodge 66) was organized May 23, 1888, with the following elected officers: Past master workman, Jacob Jaskalek; master workman, James A. Kelly; foreman, C. W. Miller; overseer, J. L. Anderson; recorder, W. H. Slabaugh; financier, Dan Sullivan; receiver, S. G. Wright; guide, Chas. Lear; inside watchman, Frank Walweber; outside watchman, P. E. Sullivan. Nebraska Lodge 227 was organized on the 22d of January and instituted by Jacob Jaskalek, of South Omaha. This lodge had a charter list of thirty members and the following were elected as its officers: Past master workman, P. E. Sullivan; master workman, A. M. Gallagher; foreman, John J. Sexton; overseer, James Carmody; recorder, James Gallagher; financier, Joseph Duffy; receiver, Richard Swift; guide, Patrick Buntz; inside watchman, P. McMahon; outside watchman, J. J. O'Brien.

Division No. 3, A. O. H., was organized June 24, 1888, with the following officers: James P. Maloney, president; Thomas Hoctor, vice-president; Patrick Rowley, treasurer; Henry McKendry, financial secretary; Thomas Dowling, recording secretary; Martin Hannigan, sergeant-at-arms; board of trustees, Lawrence Connors, Frank Boyle and Jno. McNetty.

Rad Hvezda Svobody, (Star of Liberty), C. 145, C. S. P. S. Lodge, was organized January 15, 1888, with charter members as follows: Mark Boukal, Alois Novak, John

Dudicha, Anton Pivonka, Joseph Sinkule, Anton Sekyra, Joseph Capek, Frank Vlcek, John Svejda, Anton Dragoun, Vaclav Riha, Vaclav Pivonka, Joseph Kadavy, A W Oswald, John Hudec Frank Rypka, Joseph Markytan

Besides the above named there are three Courts of Foresters, viz Magic City, No 168, Prokop Volky, No 200, and Teutonia, No 195, Magic City Lodge No 100 of Good Templars, Crusader Encampment No 37 of Odd Fellows, South Omaha Lodge No 55, of Tieu Bund, Olivova Ratolest, J C D, No 35, South Omaha Assembly K of L, Lilian Temple No 1 Pythian Sisters, South Omaha Camp No 1,075 Modern Woodmen of America, South Omaha Union W C T U, Bohemian Turner Sokol, South Omaha Carmens Union, South Omaha Plattdeutscher Verein, United Bohemian Lodges, Vlastmil Bohemian Singing Association, Young People's Social Club

NOTE I — Less than eight years ago M A Upton, assistant secretary and manager of the South Omaha Land Syndicate, wrote the following letter, which clearly shows he had that faith in the future of South Omaha that time has fully justified Mr Upton had, it may be safe to assume, never dreamed of the magnitude of the packing houses then in the prospective, when he wrote the lines — "the slaughtering of beef commences tomorrow," indeed the imagination cannot even now scarcely take in the immensity of the great interests involved in the four establishments of South Omaha As to any paper not paying expenses the first year — that was a safe prediction, which, probably (as Mr Erion may have a full realization of), subsequent facts fully attested

But the Magic City has now (1893) three daily papers, as before mentioned, all in flourishing condition

" OFFICE OF SOUTH OMAHA LAND SYNDICATE }
(LAND DEPARTMENT),
OMAHA, NEB May 18, 1885 }
" *J B Erion Esq , Lewis Iowa*

'DEAR SIR Replying to yours of 14th inst, we think the prospects for South Omaha and the stock yards very flattering However, as regards the publishing a paper there, don't think any more than expenses could be made the first year, but have no doubt but that in connection with job work it would eventually work into a splendid business There is every reason for us to be justified in thinking that a very large live stock market will be built up here and that the killing and shipping of dressed beef, in refrigerator cars, will be carried on very extensively, likewise pork packing canning of meats and vegetables etc

I enclose you map and descriptive circular of South Omaha The slaughtering of beef commences tomorrow

' Yours truly,
"M A UPTON
Asst Sec'y "

NOTE II — In September 1890 a special teacher of drawing was employed to supervise the teaching of drawing in the schools In September, 1891 music was added to the course of study and a specialist elected to take charge of it Music and drawing are now taught through the whole course, from the primary up Pupils who finish the eighth grade, thus completing the common school course of study, are offered three years' instruction in each of three courses the Latin, the German and the English, fitting them to enter the freshman class of the Nebraska State University The first class of five was graduated from the high school in June, 1892 Mr W J Taylor, a graduate of the Nebraska State University is the principal, Miss Helen Seeley Miss Hettie Moore and Miss Hattie M Wood are assistants

# CHAPTER VIII.

### Social Life.*

It is not easy for any one living in South Omaha, or enjoying the hospitality of its people at this time, to imagine the chaotic state of its social life in the early days, or how hard its pioneers worked to get a little pleasure. The residents of to-day, with their beautiful homes and grounds, their receptions, church socials, balls, club entertainments, secret society events, kettle drums, lawn parties, carriages and short service of electric motors—surely do not enter into the spirit of their entertainments with the pleasure we did, they having lost those enjoyment-givers, the necessity of and inconvenience in getting, only known to the early settler.

Three things were needed in the social life of those days: More wives, mothers and daughters, there being but five in the town proper up to July, 1884. During the latter part of that year and all of 1885, South Omaha, with its army of workingmen of all ages and degrees of skill, nearly all strangers to one another, with their abundance of wage-money, the most meagre home accommodations, little to eat and plenty to drink—is it any wonder these were needed or that its history reads like a romance.

Perhaps some workingman had taken his dinner with a boarding-house matron who had carried the meat for the meal from a packing-house in an adjacent city upon her back, if no switch engine were available, and was back in time to place a smoking repast before her guest, upon pine boards laid upon other pine boards, in the center of a room into which the guest entered from any side, and, while dining, threw the cobs of the much enjoyed roasting ears into the entry ways.

Some of the earliest social events I will pass lightly over.

Gradually, toward the fall and winter of 1884, South Omaha's social life began to change. Those who took part in the early festivities were gone to greener fields; so that the many social gatherings which took place upon a temporary platform erected under the willows of "Lake Pivonka," near the first Exchange building, where some of our best citizens tripped "the light fantastic toe," and drank lemonade from the same glass with the dining-room girls, were of not nearly so dangerous or hilarious a nature.

How glad the hearts of Mrs. W. G. Sloane and Mrs. Isaac Brayton, those pioneer mothers, must have been made when they saw their labors crowned by the organization of a Union Sunday school, by Rev. Charles Savidge, of Omaha, that first Sunday of September, 1884. Wm. Stewart was elected temporary superintendent. This Sunday school continued two years with Mrs. Sloane and Mrs. Brayton attending as superintendents. Never did the Rev. Charles Savidge have a more appreciative audience, not even on that memorable Decoration Day in 1888, when he was cheered to the echo by five hundred voices, for rendering Sheridan's Ride, and he and the Rev. Mrs. Andrews, of Omaha, drew tears of sorrow, by their eloquence for the patriotic dead.

A refining influence was abroad; so, when a Fourth of July celebration was talked of, all joined hands; and it must be said that the social life of South Omaha began in 1885 with that celebration. It was held at Kavan's garden, on Twenty-fourth Street, between J and K Streets, now known as "Turner Park." Wagons made hourly trips to and from Omaha to accommodate the celebrators. Hundreds came, and more than one of our wealthy taxpayers dates his development from a common laborer, to a land-owner and influential citizen, to that day, by combining business with pleasure, in negotiating for cheap lots, which have since advanced many fold.

About this time, those pious old settlers, Mr. and Mrs. Peter Hedderman and Thomas Ryan, deploring the state of affairs, within their vision, made a Sunday trip afoot, as was their wont, to Omaha and interested that noble pioneer priest John Jeannette, in behalf of the young men of his creed who

---

*Written for this History by Mrs. John C. Carroll, one of South Omaha's pioneers.

were fast going to ruin. By their combined efforts the first mass celebrated in South Omaha, was said, Sunday, the 8th of November, 1885, in the Ryan school house (where Miss Anna Carroll taught the children of the district), which stood near the tracks, on Twenty-seventh Street, between N and M Streets, in the same building in which the Union Sunday School was organized some time before.

Both church services were held here till the 31st of October, 1886, when St Bridget's Catholic Church was opened by the same priest—Rev John Jeannette.

South Omaha, where cattle and hogs constituted the stock in trade, was beginning to be known, and every train brought new comers. It welcomed to its fold such pioneer wives, mothers and daughters as Mrs Annie Maxwell, Mrs. John Doe, Mrs Cary M Hunt and daughters (Lu and Coe), Mrs J M Glasgow and daughters (Grace and Anna), Miss Helen Leavitt, and a little later her sister, Mrs. Frank Hayward, and daughter Maud, Mrs. Frank Boyd, Mrs Daniel Rafferty, Mrs Patrick Rowley, Mrs J B. Erion and daughter Alice, and Miss Jessie Savage.

Thenceforth the social life of South Omaha was much changed. Until the winter of 1886 no event called out, as Mr Erion would say, "our best people," unless an especially chartered train to Omaha and return would convey a select few to some opera or banquet.

Some of our feelings can be imagined when cards bearing the information that the stock commission men would give a banquet to celebrate the opening of the new brick Exchange building, came to us. It was to be upon Washington's birthday, with George Canfield, the veteran hotel keeper, as caterer. What were we to wear and how to get it? were the questions, we who had lived in our valises, with five miles—it might as well have been fifty—between us and the modiste and the milliner, with no way for many of us to get there unless on the 6 15 a. m workingman's train, and if not fortunate enough to finish in time to catch the returning 8 15 train, to remain at the other end till the evening workingman's train. The way to get there was inconvenient and the necessity of going great, but any one who had been upon that train, would rather dispense with entertainments, new clothes and of necessity food than go again. Ladies, can't you smell those cars yet?

We went to the banquet and enjoyed ourselves nearly as well as at that noted electric light banquet December 20th, after the Exchange building had been enlarged, in 1888.

By the year 1887 so many society people had come among us, that the necessity of clubs, musicales and literary doings had become apparent, and the young people, equal to the emergency, formed the La Veta Club and the Young People's Literary Society.

Nothing has been upon the boards since in South Omaha that gave half the pleasure, as did that little drama "Above the Clouds," given by home talent—the out-come of the La Veta club—to open Hunt's Opera House, on N Street, between Twenty-sixth and Twenty-seventh Streets, in the year 1888. How we waited longingly for the first night, spent hours in furbishing up long laid-by garments, fans and bonnets, and when at last the night arrived, lifted our skirts high above the mud that went in at the tops of our rubber boots, and went to see J H Van Duzen and L C Gibson grow eloquent in their love-making, Dr C E C Smith portray the funny character to perfection, and Maud Hayward, the leading lady, be recalled a half dozen times. What a success it was, no wonder it had to be repeated three nights after.

In October of that same year, when the Reed House, now the Great Western Hotel, on Twenty-fifth Street, between L and M Streets, was opened under the auspices of the Odd Fellows, what a time we had! To this day, one lady has part of the 2x16 plank, she sat upon between dances, in the meshes of the lace upon her dress! What matter that the plastering was green, and the floor half swept, we danced with more gusto and felt for our partners than if the clouds of lime had not prevented us seeing them. James Smith, the barber, sang and played the band, and Lyman Carpenter, J B Erion, Col Savage, H Heyman and William Anderson did the honors.

In the moonlight nights of November, 1889, there appeared an oasis to the vision of the church folks. The Rev D W. Moriarty of St Bridget's and the ladies of his congregation gave a church fair, the first of the kind held in South Omaha, and the first entertainment given in Rowley's Hall on Twenty-sixth Street between N and O Streets. Everybody went, and for thirteen nights everybody enjoyed themselves.

# CHAPTER IX.

## SOME OF SOUTH OMAHA'S ENTERPRISING MEN.

Thomas Geary (real estate agent) began business in South Omaha at an early day as grocer, being among the first to foresee the rapid growth of the city. Being the choice of the people for city treasurer, he disposed of his grocery and devoted his attention to the office. When his term expired he resumed business on his own account as a real estate, loan and insurance agent. Mr. Geary is a native of New York, settled in Nebraska about ten years ago, having previously been located in Colorado.

J. H. Eggers and Peter J. Bock, a firm doing business as Eggers & Bock, are contractors, builders and manufacturers of brick. They began operations here in 1886 and rapidly came to the front as the leading firm in their line. Many of the substantial brick structures which now adorn the city were erected by them. Among these are the South Omaha National Bank, the addition to the Stockyards Exchange, the Joslyn, Hardy and Brandeis Blocks, and the *Stockman* building. They erected on their own account the Eggers Block, a three-story brick structure near the corner of Twenty-fourth and N Streets. This firm also own and operate brick yards covering nearly three acres. They manufacture about two and three-quarters millions of brick annually. In this enterprise alone they employ thirty men. The members of the firm are both natives of Germany and bricklayers by trade, and capable and successful business men. Mr. Bock came to America in 1882 and joined Mr. Eggers in 1886. Mr. Eggers is a practical architect and a graduate of a school of architects in Germany.

The firm of Smith & Carter Bros. is formed of D. W. Smith, N. E. Carter, and A. E. Carter, owners of a planing mill in the Magic City. Mr. Smith is a native of Michigan; settled in Nebraska eight years ago; he is a carpenter and mill man of long experience, and a member of the A. O. U. W. Mr. N. E. Carter is a native of Ohio, who has lived for many years in Iowa, Kansas and Nebraska; settled here about four and a half years ago; he was for a time a contractor and builder; he is a turner by trade. A. E. Carter, a native of Iowa, is a practical turner, was engineer at the mill and has recently become a partner.

In July, 1890, S. V. Decker, architect, began business in this city. He is a carpenter and builder by trade. Mr. Decker is a native of New Jersey.

The proprietors of the General Transfer Line and Boarding Stable, are W. S. Glynn and D. L. Holmes, doing business as Glynn & Holmes. This partnership was formed September 1, 1892. Mr. Glynn, a native of Michigan, came to South Omaha April 1, 1887. Mr. Holmes is a native of New York, but subsequently did business in Iowa in the hardware line, and came to the Magic City in July, 1886. The firm has erected a fine building, 34x150 feet, well adapted for the business intended.

The South Omaha Roller Mill, now the property of Axel L. Berquist, is located close to the county line in Albright's Addition, and is connected with the railroad tracks running through that part of the city. It was built in 1887 and has a capacity of seventy-five barrels of flour per day. It has also machinery for feed and corn meal. The total cost of the mill was $11,000. Mr. Berquist is a native of Sweden and came to America in 1869, reaching South Omaha in 1887.

W. H. Slabaugh, physician and surgeon of South Omaha, was born in Elkhart, Ind.; he was educated in Mount Union, Ohio. He studied medicine at the Bellevue Medical Hospital College, New York, taking a three years' course and graduating in 1883. He practised for one year in the Charity Hospital, New York, and afterwards for three years in Ohio. In 1877 the doctor settled here. He is a K. P. and a member of the A. O. U. W. and the Modern Woodmen.

One of the brick firms of the city is that of Kritenbrink Bros., established six years

## SOME ENTERPRISING MEN.

ago The capacity of their works is 24,000 bricks daily; they employ from twenty to twenty-five men

One of the dealers in clothing and men's furnishing goods, in South Omaha, is H Heyman, who came to the city in 1887, and began business in a small way, gradually increasing until the spring of 1892, when he removed to 2405 and 2407 N Street, occupying a new building which had been arranged for him

The house of The Babcock Paint, Glass and Wall Paper Company, A W Babcock, manager, 413 Twenty-fourth Street, was established August 3d, 1888, as a branch of the Carter Manufacturing Company of Omaha In 1889 Mr Babcock became proprietor, and on January 25th T. J Beard succeeded to the business, with A W Babcock as manager They occupy store-room and basement 24 by 75 feet They carry a ten thousand dollar stock A force of from ten to twenty men is employed The manager was born in Waukesha, Wisconsin, in April, 1852 In 1880 he accepted a position with the Omaha White Lead Company as superintendent, and remained there until the South Omaha house was established

O'Neil's Real Estate Loan and Insurance Agency was lately established by T. J O'Neil, who is a native of Ireland, and came to this country at the age of seventeen In the year 1881 he came to Omaha and was employed as a clerk until he came to South Omaha in March, 1888, and opened a wholesale flour and feed business, which he conducted for two years At the end of that time he became a partner in the firm of Monahan & O'Neil, dealers in real estate In August, 1892, Mr O'Neil retired from the partnership and now conducts a prosperous business alone on Twenty-fourth Street

In the coal, flour, grain and hay business are Sage Brothers (W N and W R Sage) W. R Sage came to South Omaha in February, 1886, and established the business as dealer in feed, which he conducted until September, 1887, when his brother (W N ) became his partner Afterwards they added coal to their business The brothers are natives of Illinois.

Burnett Brothers are dealers in clothing and men's furnishing goods and occupy Nos. 407 409 and 411 north Twenty-fourth Street —a new building, into which they put, August 13, 1892, a thirty thousand dollar stock These brothers are natives of Indiana The proprietors are O P, and L. D Burnett, who had been in Omaha for thirteen years, the greater part of the time with A Pollock, clothier

Frank Pivonka has contributed largely to the building of the Magic City A native of Bohemia, he came to America in 1865, and gradually worked west till he reached Omaha in 1874, remaining three years In April, 1884 he came to South Omaha and soon after built a small building, which was replaced by a two-story brick building in 1886 In the last year he built a block of five stores of brick, three stories with basement, costing $15,000, the corner-stone being laid July 23, 1892, with appropriate ceremonies

A C Raymer, late of Omaha, is the successor in business of Holmes & Smith, who started a small hardware business in June, 1886, at 2516 N Street In 1890 this firm erected the large three-story brick building now occupied by the business at 2408 N Street, at a cost of $14,000, which was occupied by a $10,000 stock in December of that year. In February, 1892, D H. Huston succeeded Holmes & Smith, and in September, 1892, Mr Raymer succeeded him, and now carries a $20,000 stock

J M Waugh & Son opened a real estate and insurance office in South Omaha in the spring of 1886 Their fire insurance agency was the first to be located in this place D B Waugh, the junior partner, had the management of the business In July, 1889, John M Westerfield became a member of the firm, which has since that time been Waugh & Westerfield,—J M Waugh returning D B Waugh is a native of Canton, Illinois In 1882 he came to Omaha and took a position in a commission house, remaining there till his removal to this place in 1886 John M Westerfield was born in Knoxville, Illinois He came to Omaha in 1883 and took a position as bookkeeper, and later engaged in the commission business In 1887 he was engaged in the live stock commission business in South Omaha, which he quit to enter the present firm in 1889

Among the earliest settlers in Albright's addition was John S Mullen, whose residence dates from the spring of 1887, when there were just four families in that suburb Born in New York, raised in Iowa, Mr

Mullen served through the war as a volunteer in the Union army, graduated as a physician from Ann Arbor University, practiced medicine, with which he became dissatisfied in a year and abandoned it for railroad employment. In 1887 he built the first store in Albright, a two-story frame, which was afterwards burned and succeeded by the large frame building, he now occupies as a grocery store, in the summer of 1891.

Since the early part of 1888, Ed. Johnston & Co., real estate agents and abstracters, have been sole agents at South Omaha for the South Omaha Land Company and have handled no lots in this city outside the company's plats, although doing a business in real estate lying outside the city. From 1869 till the time he took charge of the company's business here Mr. Johnston was a citizen of Omaha.

Vaclav Pivonka, proprietor of the Bohemian National Hall (Naroni Sin), is a native of Bohemia. He settled in South Omaha in 1885 and has built two buildings in the city—one 36x70 feet and the other 24x60, both brick and two stories in height, situated on Twenty-fourth Street. Mr. Pivonka was in the Austro-Prussian war of 1866 and was wounded at the battle of Koeniggratz.

The firm of Persons & Berry is engaged in real estate, loan and rental business. The partnership was formed in June, 1888, and has prospered. Frank J. Persons, the senior partner, is a native of New York. He reached South Omaha July 22, 1885, after several progressive steps westward—having been a resident of various localities in Illinois and Iowa. His first employment in this city was about the stock yards, and later he was a partner in the firm of Ritchhart & Persons, real estate dealers. William B. Berry, of the above named firm, began life as a sailor on board the good ship Washington, in a great storm off Cape Horn, December 23, 1866. His father was the ship's captain and his mother a passenger, who frequently accompanied her husband on his voyages. Since that time Mr. Berry has traveled over the world a great deal. He settled in this city in August, 1888.

The firm of J. B. Watkins & Company, dealers in lumber, consists of J. B. Watkins and George A. Hoagland, and has been established in South Omaha since January 1, 1888, during which time Mr. Watkins has had charge of the business, which has been second to none in this line in this city. J. B. Watkins is a native of Illinois, was raised and educated in Iowa and has been in the lumber business since 1879, having spent considerable time in the camps and mills of Wisconsin.

Thomas Hoctor is a native of Minnesota. On May 5, 1875, he came to Douglas County with his father's family and settled on a portion of what was known as the Dennis Dee farm, now a part of South Omaha. In 1888 he was elected city clerk of South Omaha and held that office two years. In 1890, he was elected city treasurer, for a term of two years and re-elected in 1892.

P. L. Monahan is in the real estate, loan and insurance business, in which he started in this city, in March 1891. The firm of Monahan & O'Neil, which was then established, existed till recently, Mr. Monahan continuing the business at the old stand. P. L. Monahan was born in Detroit, Michigan, and grew up in Iowa. Previous to coming to this city, he spent four years in Omaha as a clerk, first with the Commercial National Bank and later with the Bates-Smith Investment Company.

Nathan T. Gordon, a soldier in the Union army during the rebellion and the first settler on Missouri Avenue, east of Twentieth Street, is a native of New York. He settled where he now resides in October, 1887.

Alexander A. Munro for the past six years superintendent of the public schools of South Omaha, is a native of Prince Edward Island. In 1872 he graduated from the Normal School, at Charlottetown. He has resided in Nebraska since May, 1874. He entered the Nebraska State University at Lincoln in 1879, and graduated from there five years later. Mr. Munro's life work has been teaching and to him the present excellence of the South Omaha schools is largely due.

W. S. King is a native of Platte County, Nebraska, and is the son of a pioneer couple. From 1878 to 1887, he was in the employ of the Union Pacific Railroad, chiefly as an engineer in the Rocky Mountains. Since the latter date he has been engineer for the South Omaha Stock Yards Company, and for four years past city engineer for South Omaha, having in charge a great amount of work on construction of stock yards, grading, paving and viaducts

Among the early settlers of South Omaha is J C Carroll, who was born at Ardee, County Louth, Ireland, and came to Milwaukee with his father at an early age He spent his youth in Wisconsin and Iowa, and in 1880 visited Ireland for a year Later he spent some years in the Rocky Mountains where he bought buffalo robes and furs In August, 1885, he reached South Omaha and started the second store in the town on N and Twenty-sixth Streets, where the Packers National Bank now stands A few months later he opened the first general merchandize store in the young city At the end of three years, he went out of commercial business and invested largely in real estate to which he now devotes his time Mr Carroll was married August 17, 1886, to Mrs Josephine Egan, widow of Michael J Egan, and daughter of John Godola, who came to Omaha in 1857, and was a pioneer merchant in that city

John Flynn & Company, are clothiers and mens outfitters The company is Arnold Cohn, of Chicago This house has been in business here since September, 1889, and now occupies 2404 and 2406, on N Street, and employs three clerks and eight tailors Mr. Flynn was formerly a clerk in the house of M Hellman & Company, and has built up the present trade from a small 14x18 house, which he first occupied

G H Brewer settled in the great packing center January 15, 1888, and went into business with D Sullivan under the firm name of Brewer & Sullivan, furniture dealers and undertakers In 1891 the partnership was dissolved, Mr Brewer continuing in the undertaking business. In June, 1892, the firm of Brewer, Sloane & Co, was formed by G H Brewer, W G Sloane, and Eli H Dowd

Jacob Jaskalek is a native of Cleveland, Ohio He came to Omaha in 1880, and worked at the cigar trade till he opened a small factory and retail store in South Omaha, December 15, 1887, where he made cigars alone From that beginning he has built up a business that now gives employment to thirteen persons and turns out four hundred and seventy-five thousand cigars annually, being the second largest factory in the state of Nebraska. The cigars are sold mainly in Omaha and South Omaha

J H Bulla, weighmaster at the stockyards, is a member of the board of education, a place to which he was elected in April, 1891, receiving the largest vote of any of the four candidates running In April, 1892, he was elected councilman-at-large receiving the largest vote out of a total of twelve candidates in the field Mr Bulla was born at Albany, Gentry County, Missouri, and has lived in South Omaha since October, 1887

The Oberne Rendering Works, owned by George and George N Oberne, have been in successful operation at South Omaha from the date of beginning business at the stock yards by the pioneer packers These works have a capacity of twenty-five cattle and one hundred hogs per day The principal business of this establishment is rendering rough tallow and slaughtering on commission W H Looker, who has been connected with the firm four years, is manager He is a native of Pennsylvania, and has been in Nebraska since 1879

W G Sloane was born in Franklin county, Vermont When about twenty years of age, he spent a year seeing the sights in Colorado and New Mexico He then returned to Vermont and engaged in the drug business for over three years, and then came to Omaha, where he was connected with prominent drug houses as a traveling salesman On June 23, 1884, he came to South Omaha and, with D W Saxe, started the first drug store in this city on N Street, between Twenty-fifth and Twenty sixth Streets, where they also carried a stock of groceries In October of the same year he was appointed postmaster of South Omaha which office he held for about three and a half years He also served as one of the village trustees and was twice elected mayor of the city, an account of which is given elsewhere in this history In 1888 he was a candidate for presidential elector-at-large on the state democratic ticket In 1887 Mr Sloane retired from the firm of Sloane & Saxe and has since been interested in the real estate business with E H Dowd, and lately in the furniture business is a member of the firm of Brewer, Sloane & Co

William N Babcock is a native of Canandaigua New York He entered the railway service in June, 1863, as joint operator for the Chicago and Alton and Wabash railroads at Springfield Junction, Illinois. From 1866 to October 1872 he was station agent at different points on Illinois railroads. At the latter date he became agent of the United States Express company, at Crawfordsville, Indiana, where he remained four years. From August 1876 to January 1881 he was connected with the Colorado Central Railroad, successively as superintendent of construction, general freight and passenger agent and general agent. January 1, 1881, he took the position of general agent of the Chicago & Northwestern railway at Denver, and in August, 1883, became general western agent of the same road at Omaha. July 1, 1889, he took the position of general manager of the Union Stock Yards and Railroad Company, at South Omaha, which position he still holds. In 1892 he was elected state senator from Douglas County on the democratic ticket. He is vice-president of the Omaha Board of Trade and also holds other responsible offices.

Dr. E. L. Ernhout is a native of Pennsylvania and a graduate of the Bellevue Medical College of New York City. For seven years after graduating he practiced in Wilcox, in his native state. The doctor is a Modern Woodman and a liberal-hearted, genial gentleman.

J. C. Brennan came to Omaha sixteen years ago. He lives in Clontarf precinct which he named in honor of the suburb of the city of Dublin, Ireland, of that name. While a journeyman plasterer he organized the Plasterers' Union in Omaha. In 1890 he was elected on the democratic ticket to the lower house of the Nebraska legislature. On account of his services in the house he was nominated for state senator in 1892. His opponent was declared elected, but on account of alleged irregularities in the election Mr. Brennan and other candidates have entered contests which have not now (January 1893) been decided.

Peter Cockrell was born August 16, 1832, in Delaware county, Ohio, and is of Virginia stock. From 1852 to 1860 he was engaged in shipping cattle and sheep raising. September 11, 1862, he was mustered into the United States service as captain of Company H, 121st Ohio Volunteer Infantry, and served till January, 1864. Soon after the war he moved to Paris, Edgar County, Illinois, and engaged in the stock business, remaining there till 1886, when he removed his family to South Omaha. Since that time he has been engaged in the real estate business, handling his own property to a great extent.

George W. Masson was born at Dayton, Ohio, December 8th, 1848. At the age of 21 he engaged in the retail meat business. Five years later he went into the business of pork packing at Plainwell, Michigan, where he remained fifteen years. In August, 1885, he came to Omaha and became a wholesale and retail dealer in meats. He has made his home in South Omaha since January, 1887, and carried on a real estate business. For four years past he has held the position of official inspector of provisions.

Carey M. Hunt is a native of Delaware County, Ohio. In 1863 he settled near Chillicothe, Missouri, and conducted a grocery store, dealt in live stock, and also carried on a packing business for ten or twelve years. Later on for four years he was engaged in mining in Colorado. For seven years previous to coming to South Omaha Mr. Hunt was general agent for the Singer Sewing Machine Company, at Lincoln, Nebraska, where he also handled real estate. He came to South Omaha in 1886, and since that time has been engaged in the real estate business and closely connected with many enterprises that have developed the city. Mr. Hunt is a scion of an old Pennsylvania family.

George Parks is one of the prominent contractors of this state. He has erected some of the largest buildings in South Omaha, and among his late contracts are large establishments in St. Joseph, Missouri, and Sioux City, Iowa.

E. F. Hooker—known far and wide as the "Colonel"—is a veteran of the early western stage lines. His first experience in transportation was in 1843, with a six-horse freight wagon, between Columbus and Cincinnati, Ohio. Two years later, he became conected with Neil, Moore & Company, afterwards merged into the Ohio Stage Company. This company ran all the stages from Wheeling, Pittsburg and Buffalo west, with the cross lines. Later as the Western Stage Company it controlled all the routes in Indiana and Southern Illinois. In 1852 the Western Stage Company's stock and vehicles were removed to Iowa. Colonel Hooker

## SOME ENTERPRISING MEN

removed to Iowa permanently in 1856, making Des Moines headquarters, and having charge of all western lines. The route from Omaha extended to Columbus, then to Fort Kearney and to Denver. The first contract for carrying the mail from Fort Kearney to Denver was made in Colonel Hooker's name, the daily mail being three or four sacks. From 1869 to 1873 Colonel Hooker had charge of the California and Oregon Stage Line between Chico, California, and Portland, Oregon. For twenty years past he has been connected with the freight department of the Rock Island Railroad and is still actively employed at South Omaha.

NOTE.—Besides those who are already mentioned in this chapter as among South Omaha's enterprising and active men, there are the following David Anderson, real estate, W Berry, physician, C J Collins, waterworks, T A Berwick, physician, J F Cornish, jeweler, J M Glasgow physician and surgeon, John F Ritchhart, journalist, J H Van Dusen, lawyer, J J Gorman, paints, T F Elliott, lawyer T H Ensor, physician, L C Gibson real estate, A C Raymer, hardware, Thomas Kelly, physician, Mabery Bros hardware, Milo Kirkpatrick, physician, D H Mahoney, railroad agent, E J Seykora, drugs, C H Sobotker, cigars, C C Stanley, real estate Morris Yost, jeweler, Walker & Vincent, grocers Howard Meyers drugs, A Cohen, tailor, J H Kopietz, coal, A Stein, steam dye works, Chas Singer, dry goods, S M Press, clothing, E Truehait, dry goods

Also, Theo Volz, tailor, M Wollstein, liquors, E Sullivan, furniture, H E Hogle, boots and shoes, Charles Block liquors, L J Carpenter, livery · Templeton Bros, dry goods Z Cuddington, coal, Dickman Bros, grocers, J S Stott, newsdealer, F J Etter grocer, Rudolph Hartz, bottling works, C A Melcher drugs, Fred M Smith, fire department, D Morrill, flour A H Morrow repair works, J M Schenck, restaurant, P S Casey, meats Ben S Adams, lawyer, J H Adams restaurant Thomas Alison meats, Samuel P Brigham, journalist, J F Burt, plumbing F Bowen, feed store, D F Bayless, lawyer, Buck & Son, produce, George Dare, plumbing

In addition to the foregoing are these Cook Bros, electricians D Davidson grocer, E Diamond, clothing John Yates, packing house, Max Gusowski clothing, Howland & Bradford lumber, Paul Henni, meats, Z P Hedges real estate, James Kelley, physician, Isaac Reichenberg, furniture, Gust Raff, meats, J W Sipe real estate A Spigle grocer, Henry Ditson city clerk, B Jetter brewer, L T Sunderland & Co, coal P H Toner harness shop, Herman Tombrink, grocer, Wright & Schmitz, meats, J B Erion, journalist Chas Hinz grocer, W B Cheek railroad agent R B Montgomery lawyer, Egan & Israel, blacksmiths Pringle Bros, bakers Spiri Bro. bakery, E C Lane, lawyer, R A Maxwell, real estate D L McGuckin, hotel, A Madson, photographer, Eli H Doud, lawyer, Thomas B Whittlesey packing house, Joseph Rasner, meats, A N Hagan, capitalist, J H Hale, packer, John J Ryan, bookkeeper, Daniel Rafferty, capitalist

# CHAPTER X.

### South Omaha of To-Day.

The total number of all firms and individuals doing business in South Omaha January 1, 1889, was 243. There were 76 that commenced business during the year and 33 retired, a net gain of 43; so that, at the end of 1889, there were 286 in all, including the banks, packing houses and commission firms. This total, at the end of 1890, had increased to 314; at the close of 1891 to 327; and on the last day of 1892 to more than 350. The population of the city cannot be less than 12,000, and were a census now (January, 1893,) to be taken, it would probably show a considerably larger number.

As a railway center, South Omaha, considering its size, has no superior in the West, and few equals. Its railroads bring with them, as a matter of course, every facility for shipping by express, and nearly all the leading express companies of the country have offices here. Street railways (electric motors) carry passengers to various parts of the city, but particularly to and from Omaha. And in telegraph and telephone service there is nothing lacking.

While it is true that South Omaha has for its four corner-stones in its substantial foundation the Union Stock Yards, the packing interests, its banks and its real estate interests—there are others, as already shown, of great substantiality. Nothing more clearly indicates the prosperity of a city than the number of its building permits for a given period. If this number is large in a place of moderate size it is a certain proof of rapid progress. The whole number in South Omaha during the year 1892 was 377, showing an expenditure of $497,238.*

Prominent among the institutions making South Omaha a desirable location for home enjoyment are, as before shown, its schools and religious organizations. The former have a high standard of excellence; the latter evince, by the numbers and liberality of those who are identified with them, clearly and unmistakably the great good accomplished by them. The city has reason to be proud of both.

The center of the city of South Omaha is now about four miles south of the business center of Omaha.

A comparison of the industrial statistics of the two Omahas shows well for South Omaha. The total value of factory output in the city of Omaha for the year 1892 was $34,104,200, while the total value at South Omaha for the same period was $45,503,258. The amount of capital employed in manufacturing industries in Omaha at the close of 1892 was $11,508,400, while in South Omaha the same item foots up to $10,397,300. The total wages paid during the year 1892 in Omaha was $3,569,905, and at South Omaha $2,219,565.

The number of persons employed January 1, 1893, in Omaha was 5,641, and the number employed in South Omaha on the same date was 3,618. These figures do not present a fair showing for South Omaha as to number employed, as the force of men at the packing houses is always at a minimum in midwinter, besides the light receipts of hogs has compelled the packing houses to run a limited supply.

Separating the industries from each other in South Omaha, and we have this showing for the Magic City for 1892:

| | Number of Firms. | Number of People Employed During the Year. | Number Employed January 1, 1893. | Wages Paid During the Year 1892. | Capital Employed Including the Value of Plant. | Value of Output at the Factory. |
|---|---|---|---|---|---|---|
| Breweries | 1 | 33 | 32 | $27,000 | $300,000 | 160,000 |
| Brick Yards | 2 | 37 | ...... | 12,000 | 19,500 | 25,400 |
| Cigar Factories | 1 | 14 | 14 | 6,760 | 3,000 | 18,000 |
| Flour Mills | 1 | 5 | 5 | 2,840 | 25,000 | 60,000 |
| Laundries | 2 | 24 | 26 | 8,244 | 18,800 | 20,000 |
| Printers | 3 | 52 | 50 | 31,121 | 31,000 | 65,000 |
| Pack'g Houses | 4 | 4,099 | 3,491 | 2,131,640 | 10,000,000 | 45,153,858 |

The city's rapid growth continues unabated. Thrift and energy constitute a proud monument of its greatness, and insure its future prosperity.

---

*See *The Drovers Journal*, of December 31, 1892.

# INDEX

[This Index refers to both the History of Omaha and of South Omaha]

## A

Abbe, J G , 64 71
Abbott, L D , 361
Abbott, L I , 227
Abbott, L L , 178 183
Abbott, S C , 470
Aberly Harry, 453
Abraham, H J , 467
Abraham L , 337
Ackerman A S , 469
Ackermann Bros & Heintze, 502
Adair, J M , 323
Adam N , 662
Adams, Ben S , 227, 671
Adams, Charles Francis, 301
Adams, Emma 382
Adams, George and Burke, 605
Adams, Isaac, 227, 264
Adams J H , 671
Adams, Thomas, 646
Adams, William L , 414, 438
Adams William R , 438
Adamsky, Eliza S , 382
Adamsky S , 381
Adler & Heller, 484
Agee, J W , 278
Ahmanson, John, 81, 364
Aiken, H C , 502
Aiken, Mrs H C , 205
Aiken, J C , 358
Akin, F M , 86
Akofer, Charles, 644
Albright W G , 649
Alexander, E L , 365
Alexander & Fitch, 653
Alexander W H , 126, 442, 444, 445
Algotelmen, Claes, 170.
Allman, Mrs , 257
Alison, Thomas, 671
Allan, Blanche, 263
Allan, James T , 106, 109, 110, 163, 252, 436
Allan, Jean M , 257, 258
Allan Jessie, 260 263
Allan Mary P , 259
Allbery, Denna, 658
Allee, H D , 404
Allen, Mr , 86
Allen B F , 422
Allen Bros , 478
Allen, C W , 158
Allen, E A , 80, 96, 162, 278. 400, 480
Allen, Edgar 505
Allen, E T , 212, 365
Allen I E , 386
Allen, J , 308
Allen, J B , 95, 147, 386
Allen, J R , 222
Allen, J W , 334
Allen, James S , 71

Allen, John E , 154
Allen, P H , 257
Allen, W C B , 172, 279, 594
Allen, W F , 281, 432
Allis, Samuel, 34, 35
Allison, Benjamin S , 458
Allison, C C , 358, 361
Allison, Daniel W , 155
Allison Thomas H , 78 671
Allison, William L , 380
Aloe, A S , 481
Aloe, A S & Co , 480
Aloe & Penfold Co , 480
Althaus, A C , 78, 239
Althaus, Anton, 154
Althouse, W H , 335
Altman D , 465
Alven, J O , 326
Alvord, Benjamin, 317
Alvord Gen , 162
Ambler, Henry, 414
Ambrose, Geo W , 77, 81, 94, 102, 221, 237 239, 276 370, 519
Ambrose, J C , 95, 224, 225
Ames, Edward P , 121
Ames, Elizabeth H , 121
Ames, Fred L , 166, 218, 303
Ames George C , 419
Ames George W , 278, 419
Ames William, 121
Anderson, Bennett C , 358
Anderson, C A , 94
Anderson, David, 430, 660
Anderson, Gustave, 94, 656
Anderson, H C , 83, 385 386
Anderson, Lafayette, 381
Anderson, Leavitt M , 78, 596, 597 601, 613
Anderson, Mrs Leavitt M , 613
Anderson, Lew 211
Anderson, O B , 500
Anderson, William, 96
Anderson W S , 662
Andreen, G , 494
Andreesen, E M , 428, 473
Andries Philip, 82
Andrus, Guy S , 186
Angel, D P , 95
Angel, F B , 157
Angel W W 95
Annin, Mrs W E , 115
Arbuckle, G A , 356
Archibald, R B , 405
Armstrong & Co , 124
Armstrong Ella Rebecca, 124
Armstrong, Ewing Latham, 124 308, 476
Armstrong, George Robert, 67, 75, 78, 79 86, 94, 105, 123, 124, 143, 155, 156, 217, 224, 228, 249, 250 264 378, 380, 383, 384 385, 386, 387, 419, 476

Armstrong, Mrs George R , 124
Armstrong Robert, 124, 308
Armstrong Rose, 124
Arnd, Frederick, 473
Arndt, August, 177
Arnold, Anselum, 53, 149
Arnstein, S , 464
Artemus. Sahler & Co , 423
Arthur, President, 378
Arthur, William 76
Ashley. William H , 36
Askwith, Anna E , 381
Askwith, Nellie, 381
Askwith, W S , 381
Aston, William 156
Astor, Mrs John Jacob, 205
Atkinson, Henry M , 155
Atkisson, R V 333
Atwood, Florence M , 120
Aubrey, F X , 200
Auchmoedy, S S 96
Aultman & Taylor Co , 476
Aumock, Charles M , 106
Aust, August 96 621
Aust, William and Keith 621
Ayer, F C , 474
Ayres, Geo B , 355, 356, 357, 360
Axtater, H L , 500

## B

Babcock, A W , 667
Babcock Charles E , 96, 317
Babcock L F , 354, 387
Babcock, W N 317, 609, 669
Back, Peter M 96, 97 478
Bacon, Frederick, 358
Bacon, John M , 160
Baer, Lewis, 504
Baer, P , 646
Bagley, J 635 638
Bagley, J Jr , 635
Bailey, Francis E , 96, 281, 436
Bailey, J D , 451
Baker, Alexander H , 81, 223, 224, 277
Baker, Ben S , 227, 242, 249, 431
Baker, Joseph Jr , 95, 98, 124
Baker Ottway G , 137, 225, 233, 234, 235
Baker, W I , 96
Balbach, Charles, 496
Balbach, Leopold, 496
Balch. Edward E , 426
Balcombe, Selma, 449
Balcombe, St A D , 119, 142, 168, 173, 215, 216 257 281
Baldridge, Howard H , 227
Baldwin, A J , 662
Baldwin, Arthur E , 227
Baldwin C A , 96, 225, 227, 238, 239, 264, 351

## INDEX.

Baldwin, Frank, 239.
Baldwin, H. R., 465.
Baldwin, Leona, 239.
Baldwin, W. W., 404.
Ball, B. R., 211, 381.
Ball, George, 646.
Ball, James H., 646.
Ball, Kate M., 451.
Balliet, C. H., 227.
Ballou Bros., 279.
Bamford, John, 96.
Bamford, T. E., 158.
Bancker, William D. jr., 471.
Bangs, D., 383.
Bangs, Stephen D., 242.
Bank, S., 470.
Banks, Charles, 96, 172.
Banks, W. A., 511.
Barkalow, B. B., 308.
Barkalow Bros., 447, 471.
Barkalow, D. V., 471.
Barkalow Family, 106.
Barkalow, S. D., 471.
Barker, E C., 74.
Barker, George E., 98, 106, 124, 270, 429, 430, 434, 498, 613.
Barker, Joseph, 98, 106, 124, 204, 215, 281, 303, 646.
Barlow, 275.
Barlow, J. H., 157.
Barlow, Mrs. Joseph, 106.
Barlow, Milton, 424.
Barnard, Frank, 431.
Barnard, J. C., 227.
Barnard, R. C., 95.
Barnes, J. J., 374.
Barnes, Rev., 331.
Barnes, T. B., 186, 228.
Barnes, Viola M., 186.
Barnsdall, J. W., 365.
Barrett, Jackson, 68.
Barrett, J. H., 280, 505.
Barritt, W. M., 358, 362.
Barrows, B. H., 81.
Barrows, Carrie G., 113.
Barrows, Millard & Co., 113, 117, 424.
Barrows, Miss S. J., 205.
Barriger, David S., 420.
Barringer, Reuben, 76, 116.
Bartels, C., 481.
Bartels, Louis F., 383.
Bartholomew William O., 78, 227, 246, 249.
Bartlett, Edmund M., 81, 227.
Bartlett, E. W., 502.
Bartlett, J. A., 158.
Bartlett, J. C., 404.
Bartlett, J. J., 280.
Bartlett, J. P., 94, 96.
Bartlett, W. R., 81, 169.
Barton, Guy C., 204, 282, 412, 413, 415, 419, 433, 454, 496, 510.
Barton, Thomas M., 366.
Bates & Co., 479.
Bates, C. R., 479.
Bates, J. E., 479.
Battin, Isaac, 498.
Baugher, H. L., 320.
Baughman, R. C., 483.

Baum Iron Co., 473.
Bauman, William, 662.
Baumer, John, 78, 278, 366, 375, 470.
Baumer, Theodore, 96, 313.
Baumer, William, 80, 154.
Baumley, Charles, 490.
Baumley, Edward, 490.
Bay, John P., 488.
Bayless, D. F., 656, 671.
Bayless, Emma A, 662.
Bayless, Lizzie, 200.
Bayliss, Samuel S., 100, 104, 122, 141, 142.
Bayne, John J., 155.
Bayne, Oliver P., 155.
Baxter, Irving T., 227, 317.
Beall, Roger T., 155, 156.
Beals, S. D., 78, 311, 315, 522.
Bean, Samuel, 466.
Beans, D. T., 404.
Beans, W. K., 324.
Beans, Mrs. W. L., 186.
Beard, T. J., 471, 667.
Beard, T. J. & Bro., 471.
Bebbington, George, 485, 486.
Bechel, W. F., 96, 97, 164, 380, 382, 448.
Bechel, William S., 96.
Beck, W. B., 71.
Becker, C. G., 825.
Becker, F. W., 380.
Beckett, William D., 227.
Beckett, W. H., 656.
Beckman, Joseph, 510.
Bedford, Jeff W., 96, 281, 431, 488, 495.
Bedford, Thomas W., 155.
Bedwell, C. E., 480.
Beebe, C. A., 500.
Beebe, E., 500.
Beebe, Runyan, 500.
Beebe, W., 500.
Beechler, A. L., 382.
Beechler, Lizzie, 239.
Beekman, W. H., 227.
Begley, James, 380.
Behm, Fred., 96.
Behm, Charles, 106.
Behm, Jeremiah, 78, 172.
Behm, John F, 106, 375.
Beile, Austin, 265.
Beindorff, Charles F., 106, 442.
Belden, David D., 79, 80, 94.
Belden, George P., 155, 156.
Bell, Alexander Graham, 202.
Bell, James A., 151.
Bell, John T., 259, 260, 280, 439.
Bell, John W, 405, 481.
Bell, Joseph, 334.
Bell, Maria, 205.
Bell, W. B. T., 158.
Bell & McCandlish, 279.
Bell, William H., 160.
Bellecourt, Joseph, 13.
Belolevek, Mr., 643.
Bemis, George P., 94, 97, 101, 102, 103, 253, 279, 281, 524.
Bemis Omaha Bag Co., 503.
Bend, W. R., 400.

Bender, Victor E., 171.
Benedict, A. J., 71.
Beneke, Gustave, 78, 94, 375, 378.
Benham, Alex., 489.
Bennett, Gideon, 149.
Bennett, George, 54, 78.
Bennett, H. P., 54, 79.
Bennett, Lewis M., 81, 163, 253, 368, 427.
Bennett, S. F., 469.
Bennett, Sophia M., 381.
Bennett, W. R., 469.
Bennett, W. R. Co., 469.
Bennison Bros., 464.
Bennison, David, 429.
Benson, E. A., 203, 281, 414, 430.
Benson, H. H., 227, 352, 380.
Benson, Mrs. J., 466.
Benson, Mrs. M. T., 202.
Benson, N. I., 227, 337.
Benson, Roanna E., 382.
Benton, Thomas H., 284, 422.
Benton, Thomas H. jr., 284, 308, 422.
Benzinger, Frederick, 172.
Berg, P. J., 326.
Bergen, George P., 332.
Bergen, W. W., 322.
Berger, Jacob R., 155.
Berger, Reuben C., 154.
Bergman Jewelry Co., 470.
Berka, Louis, 94, 97.
Berlin, Max, 338.
Berlin, Richard S., 78, 82, 278, 279.
Berquist, Axtel L., 666.
Berry, W., 668, 671.
Berthold, H., 375.
Bertrand, George E., 82, 227.
Berwick, T. A., 671.
Beselin, H., 510.
Besen, P., 375.
Beslot, Michael, 13.
Betts, George C., 317, 329.
Bevins, Andrew, 227.
Biart, C. M. G., 358, 361.
Bickford, Maggie, 202.
Bierbower, Ellis L., 272, 429.
Bierbower, Mrs. Ellis L., 111.
Bierce, L. V., 238.
Billings, A. S., 366, 367.
Billman, Rev., 329.
Billow & Doup, 500.
Billow, N. K., 500.
Bilz Bros., 503.
Bimmerman, Ernest, 154.
Binit, Bill, 646.
Bird, Charles, 211, 309.
Bird, R. A., 309, 380, 412.
Birkett, Charles P., 78, 91, 95, 106, 224, 227, 238.
Birkett, J. H., 279.
Birkhauser, P. W., 97, 216, 552.
Bishop, A. S., 384, 385.
Bissell, Col., 164.
Black, A. L., 646.
Black, C. E., 479.
Black, Samuel W., 72, 123, 143, 150, 151.
Black, Witt, 151.

Blackburn T W , 96
Blacker Allen, 154
Blackman & Garton 171
Blackman Mis L C , 206
Blackmore, Thomas, 81, 96
Blau, John H , 196
Blair, Joseph H , 189, 227, 245
Blake Bruce & Co , 480
Blake. C F , 480
Blake F H . 488
Blanchard George F , 81, 317
Blanchard, Jerome B , 610
Blayney, F S 332
Blenkhorn Thomas, 476
Bliss & Isaacs, 472.
Bliss, J 381
Bliss, M H 339, 352, 472
Block Charles, 671
Block, F 643
Bloom, Albert. 646
Bloom Simeon 96, 227, 381
Blose. R H . 481
Blotcky Bros 465
Blotcky & Cohen. 465
Blotcky Jos , 465
Blotcky M I . 465
Blotcky, Sol , 465
Blum A 508
Blum, E A . 488
Blumer F L , 96, 352
Bock, Mary Allan, 257
Bock, Peter. 666
Boegle Alwilda, 119
Boehl, W , 493.
Boehne, Adolph, 96 313
Boekhoff John, 484
Bogart Charles, 656
Boggs Geo H 96 281
Bohn, Robert H 366
Boien P S. 508
Bollard Fred B 458
Bolln, Henry, 78, 81, 94, 97, 157, 258, 432
Boltz Mis L L . 204
Boluss H G , 171
Bond, H F , 335, 336, 366
Bond Dr , 366
Bonewitz, John E , 97
Bonner George C , 96, 381
Bonney Mi , 207
Boone. A C , 416
Booth Packing Co , 479
Borden A F , 388
Borglum J G 453
Borglum Mrs J G , 453
Borglum. J M , 364
Borie. 162
Bostwick H C , 489, 610
Boucher, J J 227
Boudinot C T . 505
Bourke, John G , 118
Bourve, James F , 136
Bovey, G C , 83, 86, 95, 105, 123
Bovey & Armstrong, 74, 118, 123, 145, 345
Boweman John S , 151
Bowen, Aurelius, 126, 155, 201, 354
Bowen, F , 671
Bowen John S , 80, 81, 201

Bowen Leavitt L , 64, 69, 71, 79, 222, 383
Bowen, Thomas M , 154
Bowen, William R , 154, 156, 383
Bowie, R E , 151
Bowley, F , 656
Bowman, G G , 227
Bowman Ralph, 106
Boyd, Eleanora 111
Boyd, Frank, 601, 602, 656
Boyd, Mrs Frank 665
Boyd, James E , 72. 74, 78, 79, 94 96, 105, 110 111, 138, 162, 164, 188, 190, 191, 194, 196, 204, 217, 220, 226, 241, 267, 268, 269, 277, 279, 303 304, 305, 306, 377, 403, 427, 527, 621
Boyd, Mrs James E , 111
Boyd, James E & Bro , 77
Boyd, James E jr , 111, 384
Boyd, John F , 137, 138, 599, 601, 604, 661
Boyd. John M , 74, 78, 96, 184
Boyd, Joseph, 188, 192, 403
Boyd, Margaret, 111
Boyd, Mis , 277
Boyd, Thomas, 304, 305
Boyer, Louis J , 154
Boyer, P & Co , 474
Boyle Gen , 142
Boyle, Father, 348
Boysen, P J , 485, 621
Brackan, John H , 352
Brackenridge, H M 27, 30, 31, 37, 127
Bradbury, Mr , 31
Bradbury Frank A , 380
Braden, Harvey, 135
Bradford, A A , 54, 71
Bradford, Henry, 354
Bradford, Louis, 246, 487, 488
Bradley Edgar S , 227
Bradley, James, 222, 297
Bradley, L H , 227, 249
Bradley, L P , 159
Bradley, Mary, 318
Bradshaw, 239
Brady, John S 478
Brainard, D , 35
Brainard & Richardson, 653
Bramsan, 338
Branch & Co , 482
Branch, E B , 605
Brandenburg, G & Co , 482
Brandeis, J L & Sons, 465
Brando, E E . 483
Brandt, Edward O , 404
Brash, G H , 362
Brash Lewis 268
Braston, James W , 338
Brayton Isaac A . 601, 603, 646, 648 649 651
Brayton Mrs Isaac. 664
Breck, Charles H , 227, 246, 249
Breck. Daniel, 246
Breckenridge, C F , 245
Breckenridge, John C , 62
Breckenridge. Ralph W . 227, 245, 419

Breckinridge. Mary J , 365
Breen, John Paul, 105, 227, 247 249
Breen, Joseph J , 82, 654, 656
Bremer, Mr and Mrs , 346
Brennan, James C 82, 670
Brennan, Thomas. 656
Brenton, E J , 333
Brewer, G H , 662. 669
Brewer, William M , 94, 276
Brewster, C E , 212
Brewster, E P , 80
Brewster, S C , 80 81
Brewster, Mrs Sardis C , 309 342
Bridge, George, 84
Bridges, Lyman, 435
Bridges, W O , 356, 358, 361
Briggs, Ansel. 383
Briggs, Clinton, 79, 94, 106, 169, 221, 224, 225, 228, 238, 249, 364 403, 529
Briggs, John S , 168, 169, 173
Briggs, Mrs John S , 451
Brigham, A E 658
Brigham, Nat M , 158
Brigham, Samuel P , 658
Brinkmeyer Henry, 325
Bristol, C L , 94 381, 400
Bristol, L L . 96
Britt, L F , 322
Broatch, William J , 81, 94 96, 184, 212, 217, 219, 279, 304, 380, 382, 431, 473, 495, 530, 594
Broderick, John P , 227
Brogan, F A , 227, 246
Brome, H C , 227
Bronson Mrs , 252
Brooke John R . 160, 382
Bross, William 134
Brown, C B , 413
Brown, C E . 502
Brown Charles H . 80 81 94 95, 116, 136, 165, 215, 221, 223 224, 227, 228, 234, 257, 277, 278, 352, 372, 458
Brown, Clara, 116
Brown, C T , 421
Brown, Ewing 356, 357, 361
Brown, Frank D , 278 402
Brown, Mrs F J , 187
Brown, F W 469
Brown George 602
Brown George F , 227
Brown, George L , 81
Brown, G M , 211, 324
Brown, Harrison J , 106, 168
Brown I , 467
Brown J H , 79, 80
Brown James J , 74, 95, 98 106, 112, 116 218 277, 278, 306 352. 413, 414, 433
Brown James N , 162, 402, 431
Brown J Morris 382
Brown. Jeanie Dean, 116
Brown, Jennie, 311
Brown, Lewis, 96 116
Brown Martha 113
Brown M H 96
Brown, Miss 35

# INDEX.

Brown, Nat, 255.
Brown, Nellie, 308.
Brown, Percy T., 392.
Brown, R. A., 112.
Brown, Randall K., 106, 116.
Brown, O. P., 667.
Brown, R. H., 94.
Brown, Richard, 149.
Brown, Samuel, 454.
Brown, S. R., 106.
Brown, William B., 105.
Brown, William Young, 86, 308, 423.
Brown, Willie, 308.
Brown, W. F., 602.
Brown, W. F. & Co., 605.
Brown, W. M., 358.
Brown, W. P., 381.
Browning, King & Co., 463, 464.
Browning, O., 343.
Brownlee, E. C., 428.
Bruce, E. E., 279, 480.
Bruce, Ora Edwin, 656.
Bruechert, F. H. W., 334, 335.
Brugger, C., 325.
Bruner, Andrew J., 106.
Bruner, Charles E., 96, 384, 388.
Bruner, James B., 78.
Bruner, John J., 106.
Bruner, Uriah, 106.
Bruning, A., 75.
Bruning, Henry, 95.
Brunner, Thomas C., 81, 215, 281, 387, 388.
Bruns, H., 325.
Bryant, Dewitt C., 357, 358, 362.
Bryant, F. B., 387.
Bryant, James S., 227.
Bryson, Elmer E., 506.
Buchanan, James, 62, 236.
Buchanan, William H., 156.
Buck & Son, 671.
Buck, Truman, 94.
Buck, Willis, 365.
Buckingham, E. H., 79, 402.
Buckingham, J. R., 308.
Buckley, S. F., 202.
Bulla, James H., 656, 660, 669.
Buman, A. M., 314.
Bunn, F., 106.
Burbank, B. G., 227.
Burbank, J. H., 446.
Burdish, Richard, 96, 97.
Burgess, Charles R., 662.
Burgess, Lucy E., 318.
Burgess, W. J., 304.
Burgner, John Q., 227.
Burke, George, 605.
Burke, John N., 646, 651, 656.
Burke, M. & Sons, 605.
Burket, H. K., 277, 431, 490.
Burkhard, Mrs., 348.
Burkley, Celia E., 346, 548.
Burkley, Frank J., 122, 170, 350, 502.
Burkley, Harry, 122.
Burkley, Miss, 311.
Burkley, Vincent, 80, 95, 96, 106, 122, 311, 313, 395, 445, 460, 503.
Burkley, Mrs. Vincent, 346.
Burley, Alfred, 412.

Burlington, Mrs. W. E., 205.
Burmester, Charles E., 380, 382, 495.
Burnett, L. D., 667.
Burnett, O. P., 667.
Burnham, E. C. M., 331.
Burnham, Leavitt, 96, 227, 243, 253, 258, 369.
Burnham, Nathan J., 79, 367.
Burns, George W., 154.
Burns, Samuel, 322, 366.
Burns, Mrs. Samuel, 451.
Burr, Mrs. Horace, 318, 472.
Burr, Sherwood, 81, 82.
Burrell, H. L., 358, 362.
Burrett, J. H., 505.
Burroughs, Amelia, 365, 533.
Bursler, Julius, 485.
Burstall, Theodora, 263.
Burt, Charles W., 78, 313.
Burt, Francis, 50, 51, 52, 72, 222.
Burt, J. F., 671.
Burt, J. S., 308, 309.
Bush, F. S., 483.
Bush, Henrietta M., 117.
Bushman, William M., 445, 477.
Butler, David, 72, 224, 312, 412.
Butler, Jacob, 155.
Butler, John H., 95, 373, 375.
Butler, S. Wright, 327.
Butterfield, Fanny, 449.
Butts, P. W., 481.
Byers, J. E., 610.
Byers, J. L., 218.
Byers, William N., 52, 54, 74, 79, 83, 85, 91, 95, 105, 119, 308, 384.
Byrne, Father, 347.

## C

Cabanne, John, 34, 199.
Cady & Gray, 486.
Cady, H. F., 280, 486.
Cahn, Aaron, 80, 106, 119, 143, 253, 373, 375, 383, 460.
Cahn, Albert, 320, 465.
Cahn, Martin, 320.
Calder, George O., 212, 227.
Calderwood, Robert, 96.
Caldwell, E. W. 387.
Caldwell, Hamilton & Co., 117, 613.
Caldwell, L. S., 650, 659.
Caldwell, Samuel, 117, 403.
Caldwell, Smith S., 94, 106, 117, 257, 303, 368, 424.
Caldwell, Mrs. Smith S., 117.
Caldwell, Victor, 117.
Calhoun, John C., 33.
Calhoun, Simon H., 446.
Callahan, Mr., 98.
Callahan, Kate, 201.
Callahan, James B., 95.
Calvert, T. E., 404.
Campbell, Clara, 320.
Campbell, C. M., 365.
Campbell, David L., 610.
Campbell, H. C., 151.
Campbell, John C., 69, 71, 96, 106, 354, 444.

Campbell, O. C., 96, 268.
Campbell, William, 200.
Canan, C. J., 504.
Candon, Elizabeth, 662.
Canfield, George, 81, 251, 277, 419.
Canfield, L. G., 365.
Cannon, Father, 346.
Capek, Thomas, 82, 227.
Capron, Edwin R., 154.
Carlin, James, 662.
Carlin, William P., 159.
Carpenter, Al., 638.
Carpenter, Dan W., 108, 141, 168.
Carpenter, L. J., 644, 662, 671.
Carpenter, Lieutenant, 273.
Carpenter, Lucinda, 119.
Carpenter Paper Co., 471.
Carr, D. D., 385, 386.
Carr, James, 227.
Carr, John L., 227.
Carr, J. W., 264.
Carrier, Richard, 314, 426.
Carroll, Anna M., 658.
Carroll, Dennis, 105.
Carroll, Father, 348.
Carroll, J. C., 638, 646, 660, 669.
Carroll, W. J., 227, 402.
Carson, A. L., 476.
Carson, J. C., 106.
Carson, W. F., 511.
Carstons, H. G., 332.
Cartan, D. L., 227.
Cartan, William J., 505.
Carter, A. E., 666.
Carter, David, 388.
Carter, James, 355, 356, 360, 361.
Carter, Levi, 497.
Carter, Michael, 255.
Carter, N. E., 666.
Carter, O. M., 220, 281, 291, 304, 433.
Carter & Son, 494.
Carver, Jonathan, 42, 43.
Cary, John W., 301.
Case, B. B., 95.
Casey, J., 255.
Casey, P. S., 671.
Cassady, Ed., 635, 636.
Cassady, Philip, 635, 636, 658.
Cassidy, J. P., 384, 385.
Cassidy, P., 222.
Cathers, John T., 227, 281.
Catlin, C. F., 39, 46, 48, 351.
Catlin, Mrs. C. F., 449.
Catlin, L., 338.
Caulfield, John S., 122, 380, 470.
Cavanaugh, J. A., 227.
Chabono, Toussaint, 23.
Chadwick, Aaron M., 78, 249, 480, 505.
Chaffee, Clarence L., 96, 97, 487.
Chamberlain, Anderson & O'Connell, 467.
Chambers, A. B., 200.
Chambers, John M., 199.
Chambers, S. A., 71.
Champlin, C. M., 421.
Chandler, E. B., 94, 106, 110, 249, 412.

INDEX 677

Chapin, W F  80
Chaplin, Edward M , 78
Chaplin, Francis B , 155
Chapman, Bud B , 72 83, 167
Chapman, H Z , 206, 207
Chapman, James G , 99, 101, 106, 237, 238, 426
Chapman Samuel M , 81
Chappel, A , 95, 353, 354
Charles, J S , 366
Charlton, Alex G , 211, 428, 429, 510
Charlton Paul, 227
Chase, Champion S  94, 162, 163, 217, 225, 227, 228, 264, 268, 270, 281, 317, 380, 412
Chase Clement, 171, 451 470
Chase & Eddy, 470
Chase, E W , 358, 361
Chase, Salmon P , 233
Cheek, W B  662 671
Cheney, Charles D , 96
Cheney & Olsen 480
Chestnut, Thomas M , 308
Child, Abel L , 201
Child, E P , 80 157, 279
Childs, Charles, 106, 141
Chittenden, Frank 605
Chivington, J M  322 323, 383
Choate 275
Choka William 348
Christie, Sarah M , 382
Christie William H , 357, 358, 361 380
Christofferson, George, 82  227
Christopherson John, 81
Chubbuck H E  419
Church, F S , 449
Churchill A S , 227, 249
Churchill Pump Co , 474
Claiborne, Wm C C , 18, 19, 20
Clair, John, 374
Clari, W J , 227
Clancy, William, 52, 54, 59, 71 79 101
Clapp Charles E  227, 247
Clapp, Dorland L , 225
Clark Albert S , 95
Clark, A W , 212, 331
Clark, C F , 358
Clark, C H  227 473
Clark, Cora B  318
Clark, Elias Hicks, 155, 384
Clark & French  279
Clark, G W  183, 662
Clark Mrs G W , 178, 186, 206
Clark Hugh G , 81, 96, 278 279, 431, 490
Clark, James T , 410
Clark John T  270 417, 419
Clark Joseph 106
Clark & Laufenberg, 638, 639
Clark, Lewis, 99
Clark M B  119
Clark, Merrill H , 80, 93, 167, 354, 371
Clark Oyster Company, 479
Clark, Robert W  410
Clark S H H , 162, 251, 376, 402, 409, 412  417

Clark, Walter G , 490
Clark, W E , 506
Clarke, Albert S  95
Clarke, George K , 23, 54
Clarke George Rogers  23
Clarke, Henry T , 96, 160, 383, 403 419 473
Clarke, John M  106, 147
Clarke, William, 23, 24, 27, 28, 29 30, 41
Clarke, William T , 151, 154, 225
Clarkson & Hunt 245
Clarkson Joseph R , 94, 137, 184, 186, 226, 227 241 245
Clarkson, Robert H , 205, 258, 317, 340, 341, 342, 533
Clarkson, Mrs Robert H , 205, 449
Clarkson T S , 164 380, 441
Claussen, J E , 358
Clautman, Captain, 200
Clayes, George, 66, 67, 68 72, 79, 147
Cleburne William 318 384
Clements, D O  381
Clements Nellie 381
Clendenning, T C  323
Cleveland Bessie 320
Cleveland, Grover, 242, 442
Cleveland, H W S , 438
Cleveland, Pres and Mrs , 164
Clifford, Patrick, 106
Clifton, Thomas, 383
Clinton, Samuel 90
Cloppet, John Y , 149, 154, 303, 386 403
Clowry, Mrs Cole, 311
Clowry, Robert C , 277, 416
Clowry, Mrs Robert C , 231
Coady, Michael 380
Coates, Frank J , 470
Cobb, Amasa, 81 382
Cobb, Howell, 92
Cobb, Judge, 190  195
Cobb Silas, 227
Coburn, William, 78  96, 380, 381, 429
Cochran, B F  227, 591
Cochran, Col , 122
Cochran H E  227
Cochran S B  420
Cockrell, Peter, 660, 662, 670
Coe, Charles A  277  280, 468
Coe Charles A Co , 467, 468
Coffman, P Frank, 106, 412
Coffman, V H  354, 356, 359, 419 489, 534
Cohen, A  671
Cohen, Rabbi, 338
Cohn H  464
Colby, Col , 378
Cole, Ella, 311
Cole H C , 389
Cole, Henry J , 488
Cole W W  280 506
Coleman James, 155
Colfax, Schuyler, 125, 134
Collett, A M , 496
Collier, David L , 90, 106
Collier, Hattie, 203

Collins, Charles, 144  171
Collins, C J , 654, 671
Collins C K , 451
Collins, Ella S , 382
Collins, George W , 81
Collins, G H , 387 482
Collins Gun Co , 473
Collins, Isaac F , 106 322, 342
Collins, John, 23
Collins, J F , 383
Collins J S , 387, 473
Collins, M  490
Collins & Morrison 482
Collins & Petty, 473
Collins Robert A  154
Collins, W A , 74
Colpetzer, Frank C , 81, 487
Colpetzer, Mrs Frank C , 450, 451
Colter, John, 23
Colville, R W , 356
Combs, T L , 186
Comp, C E , 203
Comp, Mrs C E , 203
Comstock A H , 171 502
Cone, A P , 158
Congdon Isaac 227 245
Congdon J H , 267
Conger, O T , 331
Conkling J R , 79 95 354
Conkling Roscoe, 245
Conley, Edward T , 656
Connell R W  365
Connell, William J  72 79 94, 102, 146, 227, 228 238 240 264, 270, 281, 414
Conner, A H  81
Conners, Charlie L , 388
Connolly, Michael 106
Connolly Patrick, 106
Connor, C B , 485
Connor, General, 124
Connor Joseph A , 279
Conoyer, Charles M , 80 96, 105, 313, 315, 317
Conrad, George A  327
Converse J M  200
Conway, Father, 348
Conway, Madame 350
Conway Timothy, 96 97
Cook Bros , 671
Cook, David, 621
Cook, E F , 106 144, 386
Cook, George W & Son 468
Cook Howard  358
Cook, J D , 269 646
Cook, William E  171
Cooke, M H , 461
Cooker, P G , 71
Cooley Mrs A H , 311
Cooley, Julius Smith, 227
Cooper  68
Cooper, F D , 96
Cooper, George W , 227.
Cooper, Peter, 106, 322
Cooper, Stearns F , 155
Cooter, Virginia, 123
Coots, John F , 77, 210, 217, 499
Copeland, Kate, 172, 320
Copeland, M B , 498

678

INDEX.

Copeland, L. B., 227.
Copeland, W. E., 96, 336.
Copeland, W. W., 126, 200, 444.
Copp, C. M., 377.
Corby, J. O., 96.
Corkhill, George B., 247.
Corliss, F. W., 78, 207.
Cormody, Michael, 106.
Cornish, Edward, 227.
Cornish, J. F., 671.
Cornish, J. N., 281, 429, 434.
Corri, Henry, 303.
Corrigan, Ann, 636.
Corrigan, Edward, 646.
Corrigan, John C., 76, 77, 239, 264, 268, 275, 285, 370.
Corrigan, Patrick, 658.
Corrigan, Peter J., 78, 656.
Corson, W. A., 227.
Cortelyou, J. G., 432.
Cortez, 37.
Coryell, H. B., 96, 317.
Cost, A. S., 474.
Cotner, Samuel, 430.
Cotter, Thomas, 172.
Cotton, F. L., 489.
Cotton, J. W., 318, 489.
Coulter, F. E., 358, 362.
Counsman, Jacob M., 96.
Court, Frederick, 106.
Courtney, S., 374.
Coutant, Charles K., 81, 96, 315, 441.
Coutant & Squires, 488.
Covell, George W., 227, 245.
Cowell, Robert, 462.
Cowgill, J. B., 493.
Cowgill, J. E., 211.
Cowherd, William M., 227.
Cowin, John C., 162, 163, 164, 196, 207, 224, 225, 227, 243, 360, 380, 414.
Cowles, 54.
Cox, Charles W., 68.
Coy, B. J., 642.
Crager, George H., 157, 387, 388, 390.
Craig, James Y., 124, 352.
Craig, R. A., 169.
Craine, Josiah, 354.
Cralle, C. K., 227.
Cramblet, T. E., 335.
Cramer, Francis I., 154.
Cramer, Joseph E., 441.
Crane Co., 474.
Crane, Frank, 323.
Crane, H. A., 211, 324, 327.
Crane, H. C., 327.
Crane, Herbert, 227.
Crane, Isaiah H., 149.
Crane, Thomas, 227.
Crary, Mrs. B. D., 454.
Crary, Martha, 172.
Crary, Nathan, 320.
Crary, William H., 281.
Crawford, Andrew, 358.
Crawford, Anna, 381.
Crawford, Frank, 311.
Crawford, G. M., 172, 278.
Crawford, L. M., 304, 305.

Creighton, Augustus, 113.
Creighton, Charles, 113.
Creighton, Edward, 106, 112, 113, 157, 254, 350, 373, 403, 415.
Creighton, Mrs. Edward, 346, 350.
Creighton, Frank, 106.
Creighton, Harry, 106.
Creighton, James, 81, 91, 95, 96, 106, 112, 215, 267, 313, 397, 495.
Creighton, John A., 112, 204, 286, 350, 425, 495, 597, 605, 609.
Creighton, John D., 106, 172, 204, 265, 277, 278, 320, 362.
Creighton, Joseph, 106.
Creighton, Luther, 113.
Creighton, Morgan, 112.
Cremer, John, 511.
Cremer, W. H., 218.
Crenshaw, N., 382.
Cress, Coe E., 662.
Cress, Jacob W., 662.
Cress, May M., 662.
Critchfield, A. J., 78, 80.
Croft, John T., 156.
Crofoot, Lodowick F., 227.
Cromelien, John F., 227.
Cromwell, A. F., 66.
Cronk, G. P., 488.
Crook, George, 162, 163, 273, 274, 275.
Crooks, Ramsey, 33.
Cropsey, Lew E., 81.
Crosby, George E., 162, 466.
Crosby, George H., 404.
Crosby, O. E., 162, 257.
Crosby, S. M., 227.
Cross, Frank, 473.
Cross Gun Co., 473.
Crounse, Lorenzo, 224, 446.
Crow, Joseph, 227.
Crow, William H., 227.
Crowell, Edward, 227, 378.
Crowell, George W., 106, 386.
Crowell, Henry C., 106.
Crowell, William B., 106.
Crowley, Stacia, 172, 314, 320, 345.
Crozatte, Pierre, 23.
Cruickshank, A. & Co., 463.
Crueger, H., 325.
Crumb, H. C., 445.
Crummer, Benjamin F., 357, 358, 362.
Cryer, J. H., 115.
Cudahy, E. A., 609, 628.
Cudahy, Michael, 602.
Cuddington, Z., 671.
Cullen, Ed., 601.
Cullen, Thomas, 606.
Cultin, John B., 382.
Cuming, Thomas B., 50, 51, 52, 54, 57, 68, 69, 73, 77, 95, 98, 99, 131, 140, 143, 221, 222, 253, 308, 328, 345, 351, 374, 537.
Cuming, Mrs. Thomas, 114, 147.
Cumings, M., 96.
Cunningham, Dennis, 96.
Cunningham, E. E., 81.
Cunningham, Michael, 146.

Cunningham, Sylvester, 458.
Curl, William, 156.
Curran, Sterritt M., 68, 79, 80, 106, 154.
Currier, Frank C., 259, 366.
Curry, Henry C., 314.
Curtis, Captain, 252.
Curtis, Edward, 227.
Curtis, Father, 346, 348.
Curtis, H. Z., 95, 108, 371.
Curtis, John, 314, 387.
Curtis & Keysor, 248.
Curtis, O. H., 466.
Curtis, Samuel R., 104, 107, 108, 151, 168, 232.
Curtis, S. S., 413.
Curtis, W. S., 248, 260.
Cuscaden, Gertrude, 358.
Cushing, J. T., 268.
Cushing, Richard C., 82, 94, 164, 165, 184, 217, 233, 284, 286, 427, 455, 459.
Cutler, Martin B., 156.
Cutler, Robert R. B., 154.
Cutts, G. E., 503.

D

Dadisman, John, 605.
Dailey, Eleanor S., 356, 358.
Dailey, Howland, 333.
Dailey, Mrs. Howland, 333.
Dailey, John E., 95.
Dailey, Thomas H., 96, 268.
Dailey, William, 96.
Dake, O. C., 311, 317, 329.
Daken, T. D., 158.
Dakin, Charles R., 317.
Dale, John, 178, 211, 324.
Daley, John, 135.
Dallow, E., 79, 94, 106.
Dandy, Geo. B., 164.
Daniels, Edward, 227.
Daniels, J. W., 331.
Darrow & Logan, 465.
Darst, L. M., 485.
Darst, William, 485.
Daughty, George, 385.
Davenport, Ethel, 318.
David, John, 13.
Davidson, C., 277.
Davidson, Fleming, 52, 54, 79, 423.
Davidson, James, 71, 380.
Davies, Emma J., 365.
Davies, Mrs. H. B., 365.
Davis, Alexander, 79, 105, 141, 222.
Davis, Annie, 308.
Davis, Charles D., 155.
Davis, E. C., 646.
Davis, Edwin P., 96, 97, 280, 387, 493.
Davis, Eliza P., 118.
Davis, Elizabeth, 113, 308, 311.
Davis, Frederick H., 106, 311, 420, 421, 605.
Davis, H. E., 96, 310.
Davis, Herbert J., 226, 227, 240, 248, 264, 379, 413, 414.

Davis, H T, 322
Davis, James 239
Davis, Mrs James, 239
Davis, Jeft C, 159
Davis, John P, 75, 105, 227, 465
Davis, John R, 487
Davis, Justin, 308
Davis, Katie, 308
Davis, L R, 646
Davis & Morris, 241
Davis & Nicholas, 251
Davis Oscar F, 80, 91, 95, 105, 116, 117, 260
Davis, R T Milling Co, 479
Davis, Thomas, 52, 54 73, 74, 78, 79, 83, 85, 88, 95 100, 105, 140, 147, 312, 313, 492
Davis, William M, 358
Dawes A C 162
Dawes James W, 72, 225, 236
Dawson, C W, 323
Dawson Mrs C 187
Daxacher Father, 346
Dav, Curtis L, 227
Day, F P, 476
Day, George A, 227, 433, 434
Day, H L 227
Day, H R, 211
Day, John, 646
Deane. A L 474
Deane A L & Co, 474
Deane. H H, 474
Deane & Horton, 474
Deaming, Moses H., 155
DeBienville, M, 9
DeBord, W A, 227
DeCasky M, 474
Decatur. Stephen, 129, 131, 132, 133 134 143
Decker J H, 79
Decker O G, 381
Decker S V, 54 65, 66, 67, 68, 70 71, 666
Dee, Dennis, 105
Dee, Jeremiah, 345
Dee, Maurice, 105
Dee, Michael 105, 635, 636
Deering, William & Co, 476
DeForest D C, 422
DeFrance W, H 227
Degraff, M J, 643
DeJerry 95
DeLamatyr, C W, 227
DeLamatyr. G W, 322, 323
Dellecker O K, 510
Dellone, Andrew, 78, 224, 255
Dellone, Frank, 106, 218, 375
Dellone, Frederick. 96, 106, 147
Demaree, 149
Demarest, P A, 322
Demarest, W H. 106
Demerest, W R 74
Demorest, William H, 383
Dempster A R, 280
Den E H, 354
Denise, Jacob C, 79, 202, 203, 211, 339, 352, 356, 358 359 360, 362
Dennis Harvey 662
Dennis, J B, 431 446, 447

Dennis, S W, 662
Denton, W A, 80
DePuy, Henry, 80
DeRoin, Francis, 34
DeSmet, Father, 37
Detweiler, J S, 329, 330
Detwiler, J O, 227
Deuel, Blanche L, 163, 172, 314
Deuel, Charles, 234
Deuel, Harry P, 106, 118, 200, 314, 384
Devalon, H P, 475
Devitt, Mary, 263
DeVol, P C, 473
Devries J S, 79
Deweese, J W 404
Dewey, C H, 270, 466, 540
Dewey, Rosa 186
Dewey & Sons, 218
Dewey & Stone, 77, 466
Dewey, Trimble & Co, 466
Dey, L, 646
Dey Peter A, 391 393, 394
Deyo, Abraham 155, 157
Dick, R A L, 227
Dickens, Roger, 186
Dickey, J J, 417, 418, 419
Dickey, Samuel, 179
Dickey, William I yle & Co, 475
Dickinson. E, 402
Dickinson, Hiram M, 78, 80, 249
Didam, John, 184
Dietz, C N, 487
Dillingham, E D, 145
Dillon, John F, 196, 229, 239, 292, 297
Dillon, John T, 227, 239, 433
Dillon, Father, 346
Dillon, Sidney, 166, 398, 401, 402, 448
Dimnick, F M, 332
Dimmock, W S 417
Dinan Patrick. 106
Dinsmore, C M, 364 365
Dinsmore, J B, 81
Dinsmore, Orpha C 205
Disbrow, M A & Co, 498
Ditzen, Henry 655
Dix General, 393
Dixon. George. 652
Dixon, W A, 646
Dixon, Wiley, 106
Doane, George W, 79 80 81 95, 106, 137, 138, 184 224. 226, 227, 233, 234, 236, 239, 242, 264, 268, 283, 284, 285, 301, 302, 317, 378, 413, 541
Doane, Guy R, 438
Doane William G, 227
Dodd, Richard, 410
Dodge, George M, 297 391, 403
Dodge, George W, 661
Dodge Henry. 87
Dodge, Hugh L, 81
Dodge, Orrin G, 96, 268
Dodge, Sylvanus, 78, 206, 222
Doe, John, 489, 660 661
Doe Mrs John 665
Doherty, Emma 318
Doherty, Robt, 317 318, 450 543

Dohle, Henry, 468
Dolan, Bernard, 227
Doll, Leopold, 439
Dominis, John O, 162
Donelan, E A, 68, 69, 71, 80, 354
Donnell, J W, 474
Donnelly, James 96
Donnelly, James, jr, 96, 157, 375, 390, 419
Donnelly, J W, 331
Donnelly, John H, 597
Donovan, D. 227
Donovan, Edward, 154, 155
Doolittle, Ida, 320
Doran, 283
Dori, Philip 376
Dorrington, G E, 409
Dort, A C 313
Doud, Eli H 654 669
Dougherty, James J, 656
Douglas, Gay & Hoar, 255
Douglas House, 251
Douglas, J, 603
Doup, L G, 500
Dowdel, Peter, 374
Downey, C A, 78
Downs, Anna, 121
Downs, Carlotta 121
Downs, C H, 83, 91, 95, 104, 121, 147, 403, 496
Downs, Hiram P, 154
Downs, Thomas 255
Doyle, A J, 54, 95
Drake, Amelia E, 381
Drake, Flemon, 96, 313, 315, 417, 418
Drake, Mrs Flemon 311, 318
Drake, Luther J, 427, 483
Draper, Geo E, 433, 434
Dreschlinger Joseph, 380
Drexel, Anthony J. 458
Drexel & Foll, 498
Drexel, Fred, 78, 80, 106, 204, 413, 498, 635, 637, 658
Drexel, H P 498
Drexel & Hart, 255
Drexel, John 498
Drexel, John C, 79 468
Drexel & Maul, 490
Drexel & Rosenzweig. 468
Drezmal, Alexander, 410
Driggs, Edwin, 654
Driskall, S, 222
Drishaus, Herman, 465
Droste, August, 501
Drulyard, George 23
Drummond & Co, 493
Drummond, William R, 211, 280
Dryer, Henry C, 325
Dubois. Mary S, 450
Dudley Edgar S, 156
Dudley, Edwin G, 81 94
Dudley, Erwin 81, 94
Duff John, 400
Duffie, E R 227, 245, 249, 379
Dufrene, A R, 428
Duke, E T, 474
Duke, O C, 311, 317, 329

## INDEX.

Dumont, J. H., 281, 283, 286, 290, 291, 419, 480, 613.
Dunbar, John, 34, 35.
Duncan, George W., 419.
Duncan, James, 334.
Duncan, Robert D., 95, 97.
Duncker, H., 467.
Dundy, E. S., 177, 178, 184, 235, 272, 273, 275, 276, 301, 302, 317, 382, 442.
Dundy, E. S., jr., 249, 382.
Dunham, Martin, 80, 81, 96, 106, 156, 157, 386.
Dunmire, J. W., 473.
Dunn, E., 259.
Dunn, I. J., 227.
Dutcher, Rodney, 368.
Dunwarden, Elbert H., 380.
Durant, Thomas C., 92, 392, 393, 398.
Durham, Harry, 356.
Durkee, W. P., 299, 404.
Durlee, John, 656.
Durnall, Henry, 219.
Durnall Family, 106.
Durr, E., 484.
Duryea, Joseph J., 184, 186, 326, 449.
Dyball, R. W., jr., 331.
Dyson, Joseph, 79.
Dwyer, John, 96.
Dwyer, William N., 96.

### E

Earhart, Dr., 364.
Easter, John C., 329.
Eastman, J. O., 662.
Eaton, C. M., 474.
Eaton, E. L., 106, 142.
Eaton, Harry, 453.
Eddy, Edward, 496.
Eddy, Ethel, 662.
Eddy, George B., 171, 470.
Eden, D., 646.
Edgar, John T., 96, 257, 313, 473, 474.
Edgerton, G. H., 280.
Edholm, N. G., 389.
Edmiston, A. W., 357, 358.
Edmunds, L. B., 158.
Edwards, A. G., 96, 97.
Edwards, Billy, 171.
Edwards, C. D., 477.
Edwards, Isaac, 251.
Edwards, Thomas L., 155.
Edwards, Ogden, 392.
Egan, Father, 346.
Egan, Michael J., 669.
Egbert, Augustus A., 215, 384, 411.
Egbert, A. E., 97.
Eggers, J. H., 666.
Eichelberger, T. O., 476.
Eicke, Henry, 76, 78, 278.
Ekbaln, Gust., 646.
Elder, S. M., 82, 189, 190.
Elk, Big, 127.
Elk, John, 275.
Elgutter, Charles S., 96, 227, 317.

Eller, J. W., 78, 81, 227, 249.
Elliott, Charles, 308.
Elliott, Clarence D., 227.
Elliott, Mrs. M. A., 203.
Ellis, Jennie, 248.
Elmer, W. D., 227.
Elsasser, Peter, 96, 97.
Elson, Charles, 183.
Emerick, J., 662.
Emery, Charles J., 320.
Emery, E. L., 80, 142, 144, 145.
Emonds, Father W., 345.
Engel, August, 331.
Engelmann, Richard, 278, 482.
English, E. A., 477.
English, Father, 347.
English, J. P., 227.
English, P. A., 477.
Ensign, J. E., 325.
Epeneter, John, 494.
Erb, G. S., 255.
Erion, Alice, 665.
Erion, J. B., 600, 637, 650, 657, 660, 662.
Erion, Mrs. J. B., 665.
Erlich & Langstadter, 484.
Erling, E. E., 183.
Ernout, E. L., 639, 643, 670.
Ernst, C. J., 404.
Estabrook, Augusta, 231, 277, 311.
Estabrook, Experience, 79, 105, 150, 151, 152, 157, 207, 221, 222, 223, 224, 228, 231, 332, 245.
Estabrook, Mrs. E., 231.
Estabrook, Henry D., 172, 189, 196, 223, 227, 245, 247, 319, 544.
Estabrook & Irvine, 247.
Estel, J. C., 490.
Estelle, Lee, S., 79, 137, 226, 227, 241, 315, 380.
Evans, Charles, 118, 260.
Evans, Edward D., 118.
Evans, Mrs. E. J., 203.
Evans, James A., 392.
Evans, John, 95, 118, 279, 312, 383, 386, 387, 482.
Evans, John B., 118.
Evans, John B. & Co., 279.
Evans, J. H., 280, 430, 490.
Evans, J. T., 78.
Evans, J. W., 227.
Evans, Mary, 118.
Evans, Perla, 118.
Evans, Thomas L., 282.
Etter, Flavilla, 662.
Ewing, Alexander, 124.
Ewing, Julia A., 124.
Ewing, T. H., 338.

### F.

Fairbanks, Morse & Co., 474.
Fairfield, E. B., 258.
Fairlie, John F., 501.
Faist, Louie, 375.
Falconer, N. B., 259, 260, 279, 463.
Faris, S. J., 251.
Farnsworth, E. T., 227.

Farnum, Henry, 391.
Farral J. C., 660.
Farrell, D. jr., 280, 506.
Farrell, D. & Co., 280, 505.
Farrell, Gregory, 380.
Fassett, William, 374.
Faust, Emil, 388.
Faust, J. J., 325.
Fawcett, Jacob, 227, 249.
Fay, J. H., 335.
Feckenscher, F. C., 499.
Fee, Edward, 157.
Feeman, M. J., 511.
Feil, N. P., 170.
Fellbach, J. H. & Co., 482.
Felix, Sophia, 275.
Felker, W. S., 82, 227.
Felton, S. K., 96.
Fenno, S. B., 82, 656.
Ferguson, Adam, 662.
Ferguson, Arthur N., 79, 96, 102, 106, 127, 223, 226, 227, 241, 268, 547.
Ferguson, Ben. S., 115.
Ferguson, Fenner, 72, 115, 222, 223, 230, 241, 308, 546.
Feris, J. O., 329.
Ferris, James, 308.
Ferry, G. E., 499.
Ferry, James, 105, 142, 352.
Festner, F. C., 170, 501, 502.
Festner, Julius T., 501.
Field, Allen W., 81.
Field, Amos, 480.
Field, General, 307.
Field, Joseph N., 307, 425.
Fields, Joseph, 23.
Filley, James F., 95.
Fillmore, Hall & Haren, 124.
Fillmore, Millard, 124.
Finney, John, 54, 60, 79.
Fischer, Charles, 375.
Fish, John T., 301.
Fisher, Charles, 374.
Fisher, H. D., 273, 322.
Fitch, F. W., 227.
Fitch, William, 488.
Fitzpatrick, Frank A., 315, 317.
Flack, William S., 151.
Flagg, E. S., 306.
Flagler, T. T., 267, 270.
Flanagan & Heafey, 489.
Flanagan, P., 381.
Flannagan, J. H., 382.
Fleming, Wm., 339, 429.
Florence, Hattie, 200.
Florkee, William G., 106, 251.
Floyd, Charles, 23, 28.
Floyd, J. G., 404.
Flynn, John & Co., 669.
Fogelstrom, E. A., 204.
Folsom, Benjamin R., 54, 132.
Fontenelle, 199.
Fontenelle, Henry, 127, 133.
Fontenelle, Logan, 127, 128, 129, 132, 140, 200.
Fontenelle, Lucien, 127.
Fontenelle, Susan, 132, 133.
Foote, D. A., 365.
Foote, Lelia, 203.

INDEX 681

Forbes Family, 106
Forbes, F S 327
Forbes George W, 73, 78, 322
Forby, Lee 186
Forby Mrs S L, 186
Ford Charles E 429
Ford James H, 151
Ford, Patrick 82 95, 96 431
Fordyce, William B, 410
Forsythe James 252, 481
Forsythe, Mrs James 311
Foster, A C, 459 609, 630
Foster, Frank W, 332 661
Foster & Gray 488
Foster, Judge 178
Foster, William M 486
Foushee Rev, 338
Fowler, B A, 170 421
Fowler & Beindorf, 216
Fowler Bros & Co, 625
Fowler C A, 227
Fowler, C H, 279 421
Fowler, Edward G 323
Fowler James M, 655, 656
Fowler L D 432
Fowler Robert D 605
Fox Joseph 81
France, James S 333 374 380
381 382
France Mrs James, 333
Francis, J, 405
Francis John H 151
Frank E D, 249, 250
Frank Jacob 360
Frank, Joseph, 604
Franklin, L 338
Fraser, A A 227
Frazer, G M 186
Frazier Robert 23
Frederick C H 380
Frederick, C H & Co, 465
Freeland, Loomis & Co 464
Fremont Gen, 37 55
French, Egbert E, 383 387, 388
390
French, E R, 227
French, John M 334
French, W M, 201, 202
Frenzer, Joseph P 106, 470
Frenzer Peter 120
Frese E J, 662
Frick, A F 106, 484
Frick & Herbertz 484
Fritscher Charles L, 510
Frost & Harris, 492
Frost, Harry, 492
Frost George 171, 313
Fuller, J A, 480
Fuller, J A Drug Co, 480
Fulton, Henry, 387
Funston Robert, 660
Furay John B, 81 96 97, 163,
215, 381 382
Furnas Robert W, 71, 72, 80,
155, 384

**G**

Gage, W D 308
Gaines George W 338
Galbraith, William J, 357, 362,
402
Gallagher Benjamin, 478
Gallagher, C V 96, 259, 267,
375, 441
Gallien, Manuel, 13
Galligan, John J, 95, 369, 373
374, 375
Gambell, C L, 95
Gamble, Samuel, 308
Gamewell & Co, 373
Gannett, Earle W, 494
Gannett J W, 257, 417, 448 548
Gannon & Brogan, 247
Gannon, M V, 170, 227, 246, 247,
249
Gantt, Daniel, 80 94 106, 221
Gapen, Clark, 90, 357 358
Gardner C H, 158, 184 329
Gardner W A 82
Garfield, Mrs Pres, 239
Garland, Gen, 196
Garlichs & Johnson, 434
Garlichs Robert L, 429
Garneau James W, 428
Garneau, Joseph, 279, 505
Garneau, Joseph jr, 277, 505
Garner, L A 447
Garrett, A C, 329
Garrison G L, 472
Garrity F 381
Garton, A E 227
Gary Alfred A, 646, 651, 656
Gaslin William 228
Gass, Patrick, 23 24, 27, 28 29
Gatch & Lauman 472
Gate City Hat Co, 465
Gates, Amos, 71
Gates, George C 157
Gates, H E. 425
Gatewood, James M, 129, 383
Gayer, Alfred D, 79
Gaylord M C, 98, 99, 105
Gaylord, Ralph E, 81, 96, 227,
311, 319, 342
Gaylord, Reuben, 105, 147, 309
322, 326 342
Gaylord, Sarah, 308, 311
Gawey, John, 350
Gawey, Patrick, 82
Gawey, Thomas 350
Geary, T, 643 654
Gealy, Mrs T, 638, 658
Gedney, C P 280, 506
Gehrtie, Theodore, 646
Geisscke H, 381
Gemeck, William, 325
Genius, A, 332
Gentleman, William, 478
Geralde, H H, 168
Gere C H 51
Getty, Samuel 200
Giacomini, George, 255
Gibbs, I L, 79
Gibbs, W S, 79, 96, 317, 356,
358, 360, 361 430
Gibbon, W A L, 96, 259, 419
430, 465, 549
Gibson, A A, 96 374, 496, 549
Gibson George, 23, 172
Gibson, James S, 81, 96, 106,
280
Gibson, J I, 304
Gibson, L B, 78, 249
Gibson, L C 671
Gibson, R W, 96, 317
Gibson, Thomas, 119 279, 495
Gibson, William 208
Gideon, J L, 382, 470
Gifford, Harold, 357, 358, 361,
362
Gifford, Miles P, 364
Gilbert, George I, 91, 94, 102,
106, 184, 227, 228 234, 235 264,
310, 368, 435
Gilbert, Mrs G I, 450, 451
Gilbert, James, 95 97, 662
Gilbert, Wolcott, & Co, 235
Gilleau Frank, 648
Giller, W M 227
Gillett, S B 358
Gillette, Lee P 154
Gillespie, Andy, 605
Gillespie, John A 72 154, 202,
203, 212, 432
Gilman, S F, 479
Gilmore Annie, 308
Gilmore, A R, 94 106, 118, 143,
303
Gilmore, George F, 227
Gilmore Harry, 409
Gilmore Robert, 358
Gilmore & Ruhl, 465
Gilmore, Willie, 308.
Giltner, N M, 308
Ginn, A P, 357
Gise, Cassius 172 320
Gise, Jonas, 76, 78 95 267 312,
403
Gish Jacob, 78, 490
Giteau, 247
Gladstone, Addie H, 314, 320
Gladstone, A H 478 479
Glandt, Peter, 430
Glasgow, J M 639, 656, 660,
671
Glasgow, Mrs J M, 665
Glass, Herman 92, 93
Glauber, Father, 347
Glover, E V, 387
Glynn, W S, 666
Goble, M H, 418
Goddard S O 404
Goddard W O 432
Godfrey, T F, 251, 409
Godola John 669
Godwin Parke, 79 227
Goldstein M, 338
Good, W H, 308
Goodall, W B, 480
Gooden J S 662
Goodman, C F, 81, 96, 212 279,
380, 480, 481, 594 599
Goodman Drug Co 480
Goodman, Ida M, 314
Goodman, Mary, 212
Goodman O P 480
Goodrich Chas S 95, 96, 141,
157, 168, 251, 254
Goodrich, D H, 413, 415

Goodrich, Silas, 23, 141.
Goodrich, St. John, 78, 95, 251, 386, 387.
Goos, Peter, 429.
Goodwill, Carrie E., 308.
Goodwill, Miss J. A., 308.
Goodwill, Taylor G., 52, 54, 73, 74, 78, 79, 83, 84, 85, 95, 147, 384.
Gordon, Albert M., 314.
Gordon, Mrs. Albert M., 343.
Gordon, John, 319.
Gordon, Nathan T., 668.
Gorham, L. B., 646.
Gorman, J. J., 671.
Gosney & Chumbley, 653.
Goss, Charles A., 227.
Goss, John Q., 155, 388.
Goss, J. W., 431.
Goss, Peter, 429.
Gossert, Wi lis, 380.
Gossman, John G., 329, 333.
Golheimer, B., 503.
Gougar, Helen, 180.
Gould, Jay, 106, 300, 301, 409.
Gould, George S., 124.
Gould, H. R., 433.
Gowdy, M. M. 496.
Goyer, Alfred D., 52, 54.
Graddy, L. B., 355, 356.
Graham, D. T., 362.
Graham, E. B., 334.
Graham, Martin, 200.
Grant, Charles, 85, 94.
Grant, Fred and wife, 162, 163.
Grant, James B., 596.
Grant, John, 148, 510.
Grant & Sons, 506.
Grant, U. S., 125, 162, 163, 238, 242, 342.
Grattan, George W., 95.
Gratton, Mrs. M. E., 186, 187.
Graves, George A., 68, 386.
Gray, Fred W., 81, 96, 215, 304.
Gray Henry, 94, 95, 106, 155, 371, 403.
Gray, William, 106.
Grebe, Henry, 80, 95, 106, 120, 250, 384.
Grebe, Mrs., 134.
Grebe, Louis, 120.
Grebe, Theodore, 120.
Greeley, Horace, 134.
Green, Alex. D., 227.
Green & Burke, 602.
Green, Charles J., 79, 381.
Green, Dora, 381.
Green, J. H., 95, 312, 384.
Green, John, 74, 545.
Green, M. A., 338.
Greene, C. J., 79, 227, 244, 245, 381.
Greene, W. E., 183.
Greenabaum, Father, 346.
Gregory, D. D., 227, 249.
Gregory, Frank L., 280.
Gregory, Hadley, 279.
Grensel, E. S., 227.
Grice, John I., 648, 649, 651, 652.
Gridley & Co., 488.

Gridley, F., 86, 423.
Gridley, M. Isidore, 239.
Griffin, Joel T., 68, 75, 80, 81, 106, 110, 277, 383, 384, 412, 441.
Griffith, J. E., 227.
Griffith, J. G., 330.
Griffith, J. W., 402.
Griffith, Washington, 253.
Griffey, T. L., 149.
Grigor, T. S. & Co., 478.
Grimm, H. E., 659.
Grimes, Joseph S., 308.
Groff, George B., 384, 497.
Groff, Lewis A., 226, 241, 242, 413.
Grooms, George, 378.
Gross, M. D., 314.
Gross, J. W., 431.
Grossman, J. H., 227.
Grossman, Paul, 356, 358, 362, 550.
Grotte & Co., 486.
Grotte, R. R., 485.
Groves, J., 94, 97.
Gue, G. W., 322.
Gugler, O. E., 496.
Guild, D. S., 405.
Guiou, Charles H., 486, 487.
Gunderson, G. M., 498.
Gunther Alexander, 465.
Gurley, W. F., 170, 227, 246.
Gushart, W., 374.
Guthrie, Roger C., 95.
Guy, George H., 78, 106.
Gwyer, Gwynnie, 449.
Gwyer, William A., 79, 81, 95, 96, 106, 251.
Gyger, William, 466.

## H

Haarman Bros., 505.
Haarman, F., 505.
Habock, Jacob H., 151, 155.
Haga, Oliof, 646.
Hagan, A. N., 671.
Hagood, J. McF., 68.
Hahn, W. J., 380.
Hail, W. B., 54, 69, 71.
Hake, J. A., 610.
Hale, J. H., 671.
Hale, L. F., 227.
Haley, A. B., 656.
Hall, Augustus, 222, 223, 242, 383.
Hall, Charles W., 155.
Hall, Hugh, 23.
Hall, H. J., 280.
Hall, John, 333.
Hall, Joseph B., 169.
Hall, M. A., 227.
Hall, McCulloch & English, 223.
Hall, Mrs. P. C., 317.
Hall, R. S., 96, 223, 227, 242, 243, 428.
Hall, Silas, 292, 386.
Hall, Thomas F., 81, 96, 313, 431.
Hall, William D., 158.
Halle, A., 97.
Halleck, I. P., 222.
Haller, C. W., 227, 264.

Haller, F. L., 475.
Halligan, C. P., 227.
Halligan, J. J., 227.
Hallock, H. P., 474.
Hamilton, Charles W., 96, 105, 113, 117, 253, 313, 328, 383, 424, 425, 615, 646.
Hamilton, C. Will, 114, 424.
Hamilton, Ed. O., 317.
Hamilton, Frank, 114.
Hamilton, Frederick, 114.
Hamilton House, 253.
Hamilton, H. P., 358.
Hamilton, Isaac M., 494.
Hamilton, James W., 227, 234.
Hamilton, May, 114.
Hamilton, Millard Caldwell, 114.
Hamilton, Miss, 310.
Hamilton & McEwan, 473.
Hamilton, Stella, 114.
Hamilton, William, 50, 130, 308.
Humilton, W. J., 96.
Hance, Morgan A., 154.
Hanchett, W. H., 363, 365, 552.
Hancock, John, 308.
Hancock, Rev., 338.
Hanlon, Frank P., 375, 496.
Hanna, H. G., 155.
Hanscom, Andrew J., 52, 60, 66, 67, 79, 95, 97, 98, 99, 100, 101, 105, 109, 123, 136, 142, 143, 149, 222, 328, 394, 412, 437.
Hanscom, Mrs. Andrew J., 109.
Hanscom, Duane, 109.
Hanscom, Georgia, 109, 311.
Hanscom, Virginia, 109.
Harard, W. L., 338.
Harden, J. J., 473.
Hardenbergh, J. R., 333.
Hardenbergh, Mrs. J. R., 333.
Hardin, Edwin R., 222.
Hardy, H. & Co., 460.
Harfield, E. H., 337.
Hargreaves, Geo., 405.
Harlan, N. V., 82, 275.
Harmon, A. J., 106.
Harmon, Luther A., 178.
Harmon, Paul, 106, 323.
Harpster, David, 96, 106.
Harrigan, C. P., 79, 357, 358.
Harrigan, J. D., 227.
Harris, Benjamin, 380.
Harris, Charles L., 421.
Harris, E. N., 331.
Harris & Fisher, 621.
Harris & Foster, 486.
Harris, J. P., 662.
Harris, J. R., 431.
Harris, J. W., 331, 431.
Harris, L. D., 492.
Harris, M. H., 501.
Harris, R. A., 621.
Harris, Taft & Woodman, 501.
Harrison, C. F., 414.
Harrison, C. H., 227.
Harrison, George B., 404.
Harrison President, 115, 165, 225, 241, 242.
Harrison, Mrs., 165.
Harrison, Mrs. Russell, 111, 165.

# INDEX

Harrison William H  503
Harsh Levi, 79
Halsha W J  184, 186, 273, 319, 322 323
Hait, C L, 365
Hart, David, 322
Hart F E  662
Hart, John E  662
Hart, Ed, 504
Hartman, Chris  94, 106, 184, 208, 277 281 368, 497
Hartman & Gibson, 279
Hatty, H C  510
Harvey, Charles A, 158 472
Harvey W E  80 95, 310
Hattenback Godfrey 385
Havens, C B  487
Havens, W H  495
Haverly, D M, 381
Haverly, Nettie  382
Hawes, P O, 94 227 239
Hawes, Wilbur F, 95
Hawkins, James L, 225
Hawksworth, D  405
Hawley J B  227
Hax, Louis  466
Hay, Charlotte J  344
Haybrook, L G, 494
Hayden Bros  469
Hayden, Edward  469
Hayden, Prof, 147
Hayden, S B, 497
Hayden William, 469
Hayes Abbie  310
Hayes, C W, 365
Hayes, Father  346
Hayes Mrs  163
Hayes, P F  646
Hayes President, 163
Haymaker, Edward, 501
Haymount Henry  151
Hainer W C, 500
Haynes, D W, 304
Haynes Mrs J B  125
Hays, Frank H, 333
Hayward, Mrs Frank  665
Hazen R W, 151
Heafy & Heafy  490
Healey, William E  227
Heath, John, 447
Hebburn Major, 129
Hecht Abram  385
Heckelman Jim, 646
Heckerman G W  511, 667
Heddelman John  646
Heft, Frank R, 499
Heilman, J C, 78
Heimrod George, 72, 432
Heimrod Louis  181 215
Heissenbuttel, Otto D, 340
Helm, Thompson & Co  504
Heller, Frank  227
Heller J J, 504
Hellings W P  331
Hellman, M & Co  119, 504
Hellman, Meyer  106, 119, 141, 375 384 460
Helsey, L  94 227
Henderson Mrs A, 281
Henderson John A, 334

Henderson, John H, 183
Henderson, John S, 79, 381
Henderson, William R, 332
Hendrickson  433
Henn, Bernhardt, 104, 441
Henn, Charles, 381
Hennessey, Bishop, 341
Hennig H A, 337
Henry, Ann H  110
Henry, A M, 257, 264
Henty, Dr, 110
Henry, Mr, 30
Hepburn, G W, 385, 386
Hepner, George  353
Her, John S, 136, 662
Herdman, R E L  227
Herman Samuel H, 96, 317
Hernandez, 238
Hernandez Mrs, 239
Herndon House, 251
Herney, G W  211
Hertzman, J F, 413
Herzog, George, 106
Hess, C D  305
Hewett, O B, 80, 155
Heyd, C, 453
Heyman, H  667
Heyn, S  472
Hibbard, Frank B  278
Hickman, Charles F, 169
Hickman, Henry, 158
Hicks George N, 279, 281
Hickstein, Frederick, 97, 621
Higby, Mary E, 238
Higgins, Woolsey D, 137, 233
Hill George W, 78
Hill, Lewis W, 165, 281
Hill, Mary  662
Hill & Smiley, 653
Hill & Young, 467
Hiller, Henry, 484
Hillman, Father, 348
Hills F W, 211 402 433
Hilmes, J H, 325
Hilton, F B, 661
Hilton L F, 657
Himebaugh, Pierce C, 340, 419, 420 432 552
Hinds Marion A, 156
Hine C D, 259
Hines, William F, 78 149
Hitchcock, Gilbert M, 162, 164, 169 170 234 242, 334
Hitchcock, P W, 72, 89, 90 106, 169, 228, 234 310, 371, 384
Hitchcock, Mrs W, 119
Hitt H C  227
Hoagland, George A, 485, 486, 554, 668
Hoagland George T, 485, 486
Hoban, David, 654, 660
Hobrecker, John Jr, 475
Hochstetler, F B, 473
Hoctor, Patrick, 635 636
Hoctor, Thomas  654, 655, 660
Hodgetts, A, 211 323
Hodgins Eli  158
Hodgins, R F  280
Hoefter James  350
Hoel Alfred A  78

Hoel, A R, 95
Hoel Frank J, 478
Hoffman, Oscar, 357, 361
Hogate, J, 643
Hogeboom, R  222
Holbrook, L L, 80, 100
Holcomb, W H  299
Holden, S E, 227
Holdrege, George W, 164, 299, 404, 405, 453, 459
Holland, John S, 227
Holliday, A S  354 446
Hollins William G  95, 154
Hollinshead J W  80
Hollo, Charles, 388
Holloway, C T  71, 79
Holmes, D L, 666
Holmes, D S, 662
Holmes, George, 636
Holmes, H P, 365
Holmes L D, 227, 249
Holmes, O C, 512
Holovtschiner E  358
Holsman H B  227
Holt, M L  180, 328
Holtorf, J C, 380
Homan George W, 95, 96, 106 322
Honey Louise, 257
Honin, Daniel B, 171
Hood, Gideon, 646
Hooker E F, 670
Hooper John Y, 154
Hooper E F, 670
Hootum, J S, 385
Hope, Henry C, 410
Hope & Labouchere  18
Hopewell, M R, 226 263
Hopkins, A P, 212, 281, 318, 375 422, 428
Hopkins, Mrs A P  212
Hopkins, George C, 137, 224 225
Hopkins J H, 308
Horbach, John A, 83, 96, 100 106, 118, 119 200, 211, 267, 281, 413 448 458, 483, 496
Horbach, Mrs John A  118
Horbach Molhe F, 118
Horbach, Paul W, 118
Hornberger Henry, 96
Horne Bishop  221
Horne & Sharpe  653
Horton, Charles B  417
Horton, Richard S, 227
Hospe A, 281
Hospe, A jr, 471
Hotel Barker  255
Hotel Brunswick  255
Hotel Casey, 255
Hotel Dellone  255
Hotel Esmond  255
Hotel Falls  251
Hotel Metropolitan  255
Hotel Windsor, 255
Houder J W, 227
House, George C, 391
House H L  331
House J F, 79, 95, 215, 267, 391 392 438

**683**

House, T. M., 323.
Housel, C. C., 279, 304, 387, 462.
Houston, Mrs. Samuel, 118.
Howard, C. O., 510.
Howard, John, 171.
Howard, Kate, 200.
Howard, O. O., 164.
Howard, Robert A., 68, 136, 155.
Howard, Robert H., 151.
Howard, Thomas, 23.
Howe, Charles H., 79, 662.
Howe, Church, 82, 382.
Howe, Edward, 602.
Howe, John D., 81, 94, 196, 224, 227, 258, 268, 284, 285, 286, 414, 644.
Howe, O., 410.
Howland, E. H., 646.
Howland, T. S., 404.
Howell, A., 646.
Howell, Charles L., 380.
Howell, Edward E., 96, 97.
Howell, Maria, 343.
Howell, S. J., 414.
Howell, W. D., 343.
Hoyt, E. F., 364.
Hoyt, Helen, 318.
Hubbard, John M., 338.
Hubbard, N. M., 227.
Hubbard, P. A., 338.
Huberman, A. B., 339, 388.
Hubert, Sieur, 10.
Hughes, M. A., 357.
Hughes, William B., 160.
Hughes, W. H. S., 96, 106, 278, 315, 424, 427.
Hughitt, Marvin, 410.
Hugus, John W., 426.
Hugus, Peter, 78, 93, 106.
Hugus, Wilbur B., 155.
Hulett, Ed., 601.
Hull, T. L., 381.
Hull, Mrs. E. A., 381.
Hullinger & Railey, 480.
Hulse, E. M., 500.
Hultman, J. A., 335.
Hume, Mrs., 450.
Hummel, T. F., 280.
Humphrey, Charles F., 161.
Humphrey, George E., 81, 382.
Humphrey, W. A., 365.
Hungate, J. H., 82, 278, 489.
Hunt, Asa, 95, 386.
Hunt, C. M., 648, 649, 651, 670.
Hunt, Mrs. Cary M., 665.
Hunt, Charles L., 374, 471.
Hunt, George I., 227, 245.
Hunt & Manning, 74.
Hunt, Wilson P., 31.
Hunter, E. Irene, 481.
Hunter, General, 233.
Hunter, Hom. Phar., 481.
Hunter, J. P., 481.
Huntington, Arthur S., 320, 482.
Huntington, Charles S., 449, 450, 482.
Huntington, David, 453.
Huntington, L. C., 95, 482.
Huntoon, S. A., 447.
Hurd, T. A., 246.

Hurford, Etta, 172, 320.
Hurford, O. P., 106, 403.
Hurlbut, E. M., 365.
Hurlburt, S. A., 380.
Huse, Jesse B., 82, 509.
Hussey & Day Co., 473.
Hussey, F. B., 473.
Hussey, N. B., 473.
Huston, D. H., 667.
Hutchins, 601.
Hutchinson, A. E., 402.
Hyde, 451.
Hyde, H. W., 357, 358.
Hyde, J. R., 78, 106, 249.
Hyde, M. D., 227.

I

Icken & Wohlers, 482.
Ijams, William H., 78, 250, 382, 400.
Iler & Co., 485, 613.
Iler, J. D., 507.
Iler, Peter E., 597, 604, 605, 615.
Iler, Mrs. P. E., 451.
Ingalls, Helen, 311, 318.
Ingalls, O. P., 94, 95, 105, 373, 384, 468.
Ingraham, R. E., 170.
Ingram, J. W., 335.
Ingram, R. H., 335.
Iona, Frank, 646.
Irish, W. N., 328.
Irvine, Frank J., 226, 227, 247, 248, 316.
Irving, 92.
Irwin, H. B., 227.
Irwin, Mrs., 239.
Irwin, Selden, 238.
Irwin, Thomas, 429.
Isaacs, Bertha, 311, 314, 320.
Isaacs, N. P., 95, 106, 322.
Ish, Jas. K., 95, 122, 268, 384, 555.
Ittner, Martin, 281, 511.
Ives, W. C., 227.
Ivory, William W., 154.
Izard, James, 147.
Izard, J. S., 74.
Izard, Mark W., 57, 58, 61, 62, 64, 72, 90, 308.

J

Jackson, Abijah S., 154.
Jackson, Alfred H., 167.
Jackson, E. C., 382.
Jackson, Mrs. E., 187.
Jackson, Francis, 365.
Jackson, James, 104.
Jackson, Jerembe, 156.
Jackson, Stephen K., 81, 381.
Jackson, W. H., 387.
Jackson, Zaremba, 155.
Jacobs, Esther, 314, 320.
Jacobs, John G., 79, 490.
Jacobs, W. K., 382.
Jacobson, C. A., 170.
Jacobson, Halfdan, 96, 97, 172.
Jago, A. H., 358.
James, Edwin, 197, 198, 199.

James, Henry L., 106.
James, Henry M., 315.
James, William B., 155.
James, William C., 149.
James, W. H., 72.
Jameson, E. H. E., 273, 331.
Jamieson, David, 280.
Jaquith, A. B., 420.
Jardine, J. B., 212.
Jardine, Mrs. J. B., 203, 212.
Jaskalek, Jacob, 669.
Jaynes, C. L., 96, 317.
Jaynes, H. S., 410.
Jeffcoat, Helen B., 382.
Jeffcoat, John, 380.
Jefferson, Thomas, 16, 18, 21, 22, 23.
Jeffrey, George, 227.
Jeffries, T., 101.
Jenkins, Gertrude, 202.
Jenkins, John, 431.
Jenkins, Robert G., 95, 96.
Jennette, Father, 347, 348, 644.
Jennings, Edward, 256.
Jennings House, 255.
Jennison, H. E., 417.
Jensen, J. A., 332.
Jensen, H. P., 356, 357, 358, 362.
Jenter, H., 500.
Jesson, H. C., 364.
Jetter, Balthas, 602, 635, 636, 656.
Jetter, Jacob, 635.
Jewett, George, 172, 320.
Jewett, J. J. L. C., 450.
Johnson, A., 362.
Johnson, A. P., 366.
Johnson, Anthony, 183, 204.
Johnson, Benjamin, 308.
Johnson Bros., 488.
Johnson, Charles W., 410.
Johnson, David M., 149.
Johnson, D. L., 227.
Johnson, Edward A., 94.
Johnson, Enos, 308.
Johnson, Eric, 82.
Johnson, F. C., 433, 434.
Johnson, Frank B., 168, 429, 430.
Johnson, Mrs. Frank B., 111.
Johnson, Hadley D., 101, 105, 140, 168, 222, 277, 384, 385.
Johnson, Harrison, 78, 79, 95, 105, 144, 146, 206, 222, 347.
Johnson, Isaac, 433.
Johnson, James, 308.
Johnson, James M., 156.
Johnson, J. E., 167.
Johnson, J. H., 662.
Johnson, John, 204.
Johnson, O. F., 646.
Johnson, P. C., 323.
Johnson, President, 124, 235, 238.
Johnson, Samuel R., 270, 413, 427, 428, 594.
Johnson, W. H., 380.
Johnston & Co., 668.
Johnston, Col., 150.
Johnston, Ed., 656.
Johnston, John W., 227.
Jonas, A. F., 357, 358, 361.

INDEX. 685

Jonas, M Helfritz 357 358
Jones, Alfred D 52, 54, 73, 79, 80 83, 84 95 97, 98, 99, 101, 104, 105 107, 222, 239, 268, 309, 310, 383, 384, 385, 386, 387, 388, 389, 390, 441
Jones Allen 137
Jones, C D 308
Jones, C E 646
Jones, George, 646
Jones John C, 357 358
Jones John D, 96, 100, 312, 646, 660
Jones J G, 358
Jones Lizzie 308 311
Jones, L O, 465
Jones Salina 320
Jones Samuel B, 380
Jones William, 95, 101, 120
Jordan Robert C, 94, 95, 106, 317, 284 445
Jordensen C F, 494
Joslyn George A, 171, 502
Joslyn Mrs G A 205
Josselyn S T 352
Joy Clarence S, 458
Judson H M 95 106, 253

K

Kaempfer Charles F, 227,
Kuhn I 508
Kahn, M, 508
Kalakaua King 162
Kaley, J L, 227
Kalish, R 504
Kapena John M 162
Karbach, Charles J, 81 96, 106 120 218 432 493
Karbach Peter J, 106, 375, 493
Kasper Frank S 96, 505
Katon 137
Katz, Samuel 503
Kaufman, Charles 96, 268
Kaufman E N 227 643, 646
Kavanaugh Father, 346
Keeler Henry, 380
Keenan & Hancock 603, 605
Keenan Nicholas, 146
Keith Alma E 205
Keith, M C, 605 609, 613
Keith M W 88, 93, 136, 252
Keith N W, 106
Keith, William 95
Kellar, Charles B, 227, 383
Kellar, James A 337
Keller, Charles D, 227, 383
Keller, G D, 500
Kelley, E A 356
Kelley Edward, 310
Kelley, Father, 346
Kelley J A A, 358
Kelley, J E, 95, 264
Kelley, John M 78
Kelley, John P 96 345
Kelley, Stiger & Co 464, 467
Kelley, Thomas, 358
Kelley, Timothy, 93, 105, 146
Kelley, William A 96
Kelley, W R, 227 244, 402

Kellner, Adam, 662
Kellogg, J D, 386
Kellogg, William, 136, 223
Kellogg, William Pitt, 136, 144, 223, 233, 234
Kellom John H, 83, 91, 93, 94, 95, 106, 110 258, 259, 308, 309, 310, 311, 319 320 321, 423, 441
Kellom, Mrs J H, 311, 312, 321
Kelsey, William, 156
Kemper Bishop, 328
Kemper, W G 357
Kempton 54
Kennard F B, 483
Kennard, Frank, 311
Kennard, Levi J, 96, 106, 268, 483
Kennard, Marsh, 106, 508
Kennard, Thomas P, 72, 257
Kenneally, John 105, 637
Kennedy Alfred C, 212
Kennedy B E B, 79 80 94 95, 106, 121 217, 221, 227, 228, 235, 236 264 311, 312 395 397, 555
Kennedy, Charlotte, 121
Kennedy, E L 227
Kennedy, George F, 79 151, 154
Kennedy Howard 96, 142, 227, 309, 310, 313
Kennedy, Missouri, 116
Kennedy, Theodocia 119
Kennedy W J, 95, 106, 119, 141, 371, 374 423
Kenney, Thomas, 69, 646
Kennon L W V, 157
Kensley, H, 381
Kent, C D, 451
Kent C H 450, 451
Kent Josiah 95
Kent L H 227
Kent, W H 79
Keogh P S, 79
Kermott W J, 331
Kerr, David R, 333
Kerr, Hugh, 380
Kerr, William, 644
Kessner Fred 646
Kettler, C H, 381
Keysor, William W 226, 227, 248 264
Kibbe M G 496
Kierkendall M W, 646
Kierstead, William I, 208, 215, 270 466
Kiesbina J 646
Kilpatrick Koch Co, 462, 503, 505
Kilpatrick, Thomas, 212, 438, 462
Kilroy, Daniel, 640
Kilsay, Daniel, 640
Kimball, Daniel E, 381
Kimball, J F 222
Kimball, Richard P, 79, 95, 96, 105
Kimball, Thomas L 114 164, 284, 285, 299, 417, 433, 454, 556
Kimball, Mrs T L, 205
Kimball, W E 380
Kinder, Otto 170

King, A D, 432
King, A L 95, 496
King, Charles B, 106
King, Charles H, 155
King F S, 503
King, George 485
King, Harry, 239
King, Jacob 106
King, John H 157, 159, 163
King, O J 442
King Paper Co, 471
King, P J, 655, 656
King, Rufus, 15
King & Smead, 503
King Wingate, 71
King Wm R, 137, 144
King W S 668
Kingman & Co 476
Kinney, Kate, 200
Kinney R H 202
Kinsler Drug Co, 480
Kinsler, J C, 480
Kinsler, J T, 382 480
Kinsler M J, 480
Kipp, William 95
Kirby, Louisa 381
Kirkendall F P, 281
Kirkpatrick, 59, 62
Kirkpatrick Dr, 639
Kirkpatrick, S M, 71 80
Kirschbaun L 477, 482
Kirschbaun & Sons, 482
Kirscht L 484
Kitchen, Charles W 218, 254
Kitchen, James B, 218, 254 281
Kitchen, Richard 218 254
Kleffner, Frank 95, 106 373
Klima, Father, 348
Kline, William 194 151
Klingaman, G W, 646
Klopp A T 502
Klopp, Bartlett & Co, 502
Klopp C H, 502
Knapp, F S 158 499
Knight, Benjamin 78, 79
Knight, Frederick 172, 320, 449 452
Knight, Julia, 320
Knight, William, 95
Knode R S, 358
Knowles, H S, 365
Knox, David 82
Knox Robert S, 106, 662
Koch, Allen 462
Koenig, W H, 126 331
Koenig, Mrs C W, 106
Koenig, Henry, 154
Kohl Charles, 381
Kohm Charles, 646
Kohnstamm L J 358
Koon & Bramhall, 222
Kooser H B, 409
Kopp, Dierbus & Co, 506
Kopp, Jacob, 506
Kopp, Michael, 506
Korn, Philip, 646
Korty, L H, 331 402, 417, 418, 419
Koster, Bernard, 106
Kosters F H, 375

INDEX.

Kosters, Henry A., 105, 141, 471.
Kountze, Augustus, 100, 105, 113, 126, 254, 279, 283, 312, 329, 394, 395, 397, 398, 403, 412, 424.
Kountze, Mrs. Augustus, 114, 158.
Kountze Bros., 113, 144, 300, 423, 427.
Kountze, Charles, 424.
Kountze, Herman, 105, 113, 114, 257, 267, 281, 317, 327, 352, 384, 403, 424, 454, 594, 605.
Kountze, Mrs. Herman, 311.
Kountze, Katie P., 200.
Kountze, Luther, 424.
Kountze & Ruth, 92, 93.
Kozak, Thomas, 646.
Kozarink, Father, 348.
Kozat, Thomas, 646.
Koze, Frank, 211.
Kratz, L. G., 430.
Krause, Frederick, 500.
Krigbaum, S. K., 846.
Kroeger, Emily, 120.
Kroitzsch, L., 375.
Kroner, L., 489.
Krug, Edward, 507.
Krug, Frederick, 106, 218, 281, 432, 506, 507, 558.
Krug, John A., 482.
Krug & Selzer, 507.
Krug, William, 278, 279, 507.
Krumme, Henry F. C., 155, 156.
Kuhl, Henry, 156.
Kuhn & Co., 481.
Kuhn, J. F., 388.
Kuhn, L. M., 308.
Kuhn, Norman A., 281, 430, 481.
Kuhns, H. W., 106, 201, 329, 330, 344, 372, 384.
Kuhns, J. H., 81.
Kuhns, Luther M., 126, 330, 544.
Kuhns, Paul W., 126, 344.
Kumme, F. C., 156.
Kumpf, Frederick, 106.
Kumptery, Moritz, 646.
Kunda, H. 375.
Kyner, James H., 81.
Kynett, Dr., 179.

L

Labagh, George F., 268.
La Barge, Capt., 199.
Labinche, Frances, 23.
Laboo, Dominie, 155.
Lacey, Jesse H., 96, 115, 116, 200, 461.
Lacey & McCormick, 116, 461.
Lafferty, John A., 385.
Lake, Carrie J., 234.
Lake, Frank, 662.
Lake, Fred, 234.
Lake, George B., 79, 80, 94, 106, 116, 136, 137, 221, 224, 225, 227, 228, 234, 235, 264, 311, 312, 313, 370, 394, 395, 433, 438.
Lake, George E., 234, 320.
Lake, Mrs. Judge, 310.
Lake, Mary, 234.

Lake, O. F., 79.
Lally, H. T., 474.
Lambert, J. M., 662.
Lambertson, G. M., 196, 249, 274, 275.
Lamar, A. W., 331.
Lamaster, Joseph E., 446.
Lamont, Daniel S., 164.
Lander, Dana S., 227.
Landergren, Victor, 380.
Landeryou, Prof., 449.
Lane, C. J., 402.
Lane, E. C., 227.
Lane, George B., 315.
Langdon, Charles A. B., 156.
Langdon, Martin, 227.
Langstadter, Henry, 484.
Lankton, Freda M., 365.
Lapsley, D. L., 227.
Larimer, A. V.
Larimer, William jr., 68, 79.
Larocque, 275.
Larrabee, Gov., 179.
Larsen, L. P. C., 646.
Larsen, W. G., 646.
Larsh, Napoleon B., 154.
La Salle, 9.
Lasher, James, 653.
Latey, Family, 106.
Latham, Mr., 53, 54.
Lathrop, Mary, 180.
Latta, Samuel G., 155.
Latta, William S., 155.
Lauer, 240.
Laufenburg, Henry, 646.
Laussat, Peter Clement, 18, 19.
Lavender, W. R., 358, 361.
Lawler, Edward, 155.
Lawler, William, 305.
Lawless, Michael, 374.
Lawrence, Father, 346.
Lawrence, F. B., 496.
Lawrie, Harry, 211.
Laws, G. L., 445, 655.
Lawson, John N., 377.
Leach, J. W., 342.
Leach, William, 106, 322, 331, 366, 385, 386.
Leard, Asa, 333.
Learned, M. L., 227.
Learning, Silas T., 155.
Leary, C. A., 81.
Leavenworth, Col., 55.
Leavitt, Herbert T., 78.
Leddy, J. J., 494.
Ledwick, James, 227.
Ledyard, John, 22.
Lee, Bishop, 328.
Lee, Charles C., 170, 227, 646.
Lee-Clarke-Andreesen Co., 473.
Lee, Edward, 646.
Lee, E. W., 158.
Lee, Fried & Co., 473.
Lee, H. J., 474.
Lee, John A., 254.
Lee, Lewis, 496.
Lee, Michael, 96, 170, 369.
Lee, R., 481.
Leeder, Edward, 96.
Leeveen, Rabbi, 338.

Le Flesche, Joseph, 129.
Legge, George, 227.
Lehman, A., 500.
Lehmann, Henry, 471.
Lehmer, Emma, 311.
Lehmer, Laura, 311.
Lehmer, Nelia, 163, 314, 320.
Lehmer, William, 106.
Leisenring, P. S., 95, 212, 356, 358, 360, 361.
Leisge, Henry, 387.
Lemist, H. F., 487.
Lemmon, John S., 156.
Lemon, Thomas B., 105, 322, 343.
Lemon, T. W., 212.
Lemp, W. J., 485.
Leo, Mother, 350.
LePage, John Baptiste, 23.
Leslie & Leslie, 481.
Leslie, M., 482.
Levinston Bros., 465.
Levy, J., 643.
Lewis, E. V., 474.
Lewis, H. P., 259, 260.
Lewis, Meriwether, 23, 24, 26, 27, 28, 29, 30, 41.
Lewis, Samuel A., 98, 156.
Lichtenbergen, J. A., 475.
Linahan, Jerry, 106, 349.
Linahan, Michael, 106.
Lincoln, President, 144, 222, 233, 234, 235, 236, 238, 292, 293, 295, 343.
Lincoln, Mrs. President, 144, 233.
Lindell, Carl, 154.
Lindley, David, 441.
Lindley, William L., 381.
Lindquist, G. A., 204, 504.
Lindquist, J. L., 326.
Lindsay, M. S., 227.
Lindsay, S. W., 211.
Lindsey, Z. T., 211, 468.
Lininger, George W., 82, 96, 281, 304, 438, 451, 453, 475.
Lininger, Mrs. G. W., 451, 475.
Lininger, Metcalf & Co., 475.
Link, Harvey, 80, 355.
Lipe, W. A., 329.
Lipton, Thomas J., 626.
Lisa, Manuel, 30, 31, 37, 47, 198.
Litchfield, Col., 162.
Little, May, 200.
Little & Williams, 478.
Little, William A., 80, 106, 136, 221, 224.
Littlefield, Mr., 311.
Littlefield, Mrs., 311.
Livesey, Henry, 96, 106, 345, 511.
Livesey, Leonard, 172.
Livesey, Robert, 311.
Livingston, Robert R., 19, 154, 360.
Lobeck, C. O., 281.
Lobeck & Linn, 473.
Locke, S. E., 270, 497.
Lockfield, Henry, 254.
Lockwood, William F., 223.
Loescher, David, 651, 652, 656, 662.

INDEX 687

Logan, Emma 308
Logan John A , 381
Logan John, 94, 95, 105, 141
Lomax, E L 402
Long, Eben K 95, 96
Long Stephen H , 33, 48, 197
Long, William, 646
Looker, W H 669
Loomis, F L , 476
Lord J P , 357, 358, 362
Lorenzen W F 317
Lorimer, W M , 334
Loring. David R 333
Loring, Mrs David R , 333
Lott, A L , 610 662
Lounsbury John W , 389
Loveland, Carrie, 311
Loveland Edwin, 81, 95, 96, 106, 310 322
Lovett, James L 115, 594
Lowe, D , 89
Lowe, Enos 98 99, 101 104, 105 106, 107, 114, 154, 232 354, 397 398, 497, 558
Lowe, Frederick B , 279
Lowe, Jesse, 73 74, 78, 83, 85, 94, 98, 99 100 105, 114, 140, 147, 157, 222, 230 277, 310, 351, 352 560
Lowe, Samuel A , 80, 151
Lowe, W W , 107, 115, 147, 155, 281, 303, 305, 313, 496, 559
Lowenstein, E , 477
Lower, John J , 156.
Lowes, Henrietta M , 343
Lowrie, Mathew B , 319
Lowry, Lewis, 155
Lowry, T J . 96, 97
Lubbee, Theodore, 154
Lucas, D R . 335
Lucas Henry J 258 259
Lucas J H 200
Ludington Horace, 163, 382
Ludington, Mrs H , 203
Ludlow, O C , 94
Lueed C 646
Luhens Henry 96
Lund, John G 480
Lunt A J 227
Luyties, Herman jr , 481
Lyford & Co 145
Lyman C W , 420
Lyman. K T , 318
Lynch Pat 646
Lyon, E L , 430 431
Lyons, Perry A , 380
Lytle, John W , 561

### Mc

MacDonagh F M 171
MacKenzie, Colin J 613
MacMurphy, John A , 131, 657
McAllaster, B A , 402
McArdle, James H , 73, 78, 206, 400
McArdle, John F , 278
McArdle Patrick, 81
McAusland, Andrew 311
McAusland, Kate, 311

McAusland Family, 106
McBreath, William C , 156
McBride, John C , 106, 142
McBrien & Carter, 494
McCabe, James, 227
McCaffrey, B , 646
McCague Anna N , 343
McCague Bros 428
McCague, Brower E , 344
McCague George S 344
McCague, Mrs H M 203, 204
McCague, John L , 208, 220, 286, 290, 291 343 428, 429
McCague, Josie M , 343
McCague, Lydia S , 344
McCague, Margaret M , 314, 343
McCague, Thomas, 323, 334, 343
McCague, Thomas H , jr , 343, 428, 429
McCague William L 204, 212, 320, 343, 414, 428, 429
McCahan, Hannah C 358
McCandlish Cora 263
McCandlish, Isabella S 343
McCandlish, Robert C , 343
McCandlish, William, 333, 342, 343
McCandlish, Mrs William, 343
McCandlish, W N 155, 178, 343, 495
McCarthy, Joseph, 334, 347
McCartney, James F , 94, 172
McCheane, Helen, 203
McCheane, Jeremiah, 93, 106.
McClanahan, A A , 227
McClannahan, W L , 357
McClatchan & Andrews 500
McClelland, Robert, 33, 211
McClelland, William, 141, 151, 152 154, 353, 384
McCloud, Imri L , 227
McClure, E A , 168
McClure, E J , 405
McClure J A , 202
McComhie, John, 151, 154, 252
McConnell, A B , 481
McConnell, Frederick R , 96, 258, 314, 321
McConnell, Mrs Frederick, 311
McConnell, J H , 402 495
McConnell, Robert, 96
McCook, Gen , 163
McCord-Brady Co , 478
McCord, James, 478
McCord, William H , 478
McCord, William D , 154
McCormick, Albert, 116
McCormick, Finley 116
McCormick, John, 80 86, 95, 100, 106, 115, 147, 386, 394, 412, 420, 423, 426, 461, 480
McCormick John & Co , 116
McCormick, Josiah S , 95, 106, 116, 155 239 371
McCormick & Lund 480
McCoy, F L , 227, 264
McCoy, George A , 106
McCracken, A C , 656
McCrary, Judge, 275
McCreary, John, 106

McCulloch, J H , 78, 208, 227, 242, 249, 429
McCulloch, Mrs J H 343
McCune Joseph M , 94
McDaugal, Mary A , 662
McDermott, Father, 347
McDermott, Luke, 106
McDonald, Alexander, 483
McDonald, Charles, 66, 68
McDonald, Francis A , 154, 155
McDonald, H S , 493
McDonald, John, 374
McDonald, Robert, 358
McDonnell, Joseph, 358
McDonough, Patrick, 77, 106
McDougal, Mr , 56
McDowell, J V , 431
McDuffie, Robert A , 227
McElwee William, 353, 354
McFadden, A A , 430
McFaley, Gen , 162
McGavock, A , 81, 96
McGee, Miss L C , 318
McGill, T C 200
McGilton, E G , 227
McGovern Bros , 350
McGovern, John 487, 488
McGuckin, D L . 96, 671
McGuire & Co , 485
McGuire & Curtis, 643
McGuire, T E , 655
McHugh, William D , 170, 227
McIntosh, James H , 227, 243
McKaig, R N , 323
McKee, Mrs , 165
McKellgon, M J , 96
McKenna, L F , 356, 357, 358, 361
McKenney, A F , 154
McKenzie, Mrs Alex , 105
McKenzie Colin J , 613
McKeon, Gen , 124
McKinney Mary 381
McKinnon, M , 405
McKoon, M G , 96
McLain, J J , 211
McLain, W C , 211 381
McLaughlin, A T , 256
McLearie, John, 96, 97, 493
McLennan, William, 81 149 •
McMahon, Father, 346
McMahon, M , 381
McMaten, Andrew C , 154
McMenamy, J T 256
McMenamy M A 419
McMillan, John, 82, 654, 656
McMurty Edward 239
McNair Mrs C W, 187
McNamara, M A , 96
McNamara William 254
McNeal Hugh, 23
McNealy Russell 149
McNeeley Erastus G , 79, 151, 156
McNeil Abram, 151
McPherson, John P , 105, 201
McPherson Miss 340
McShane Edward C , 96, 304
McShane F J 96
McShane James 489

McShane, John A., 72, 81, 82, 164, 169, 278, 283, 304, 350, 375, 419, 495, 563, 597, 604, 605, 609, 613, 646.
McShane, Mary Lee, 350.
McVann, Edward, 157.
McVeigh, James. 646.
McWhorter, S. A., 279.
McWilliams, H. L., 227.

## M

Macfarland, J. M., 227.
Mack, Susie, 115.
Mack, William, 375.
Mackay, T J., 329.
Macke, August, 325.
Mackey & McDonald, 654.
Mackey, V. M., 311.
Macleod, Samuel, 183.
Macomber, J. H., 227, 249.
Macrae, Donald, 361.
Madsen, B. F., 95.
Madsen, N., 332.
Madson, A., 671.
Madson, James, 18, 19.
Maginn, L. F., 381.
Magney, George A, 227.
Maguire, Charles, 95.
Mahoney, D., 646.
Mahoney, Jeremiah, 95, 105, 106.
Mahoney, J. J., 137, 349, 350, 208, 209.
Mahoney, Minnehan & Smythe, 244.
Mahoney, Mrs., 210.
Mahoney, P. H. & Co., 488.
Mahoney, T. J., 79, 139, 227, 244, 350.
Maile, J. L., 327.
Majors, Thomas J., 154, 446.
Majors, William E., 154.
Malcomb, A. B., 80, 354.
Mallet, Paul, 11, 13.
Mallet, Peter, 11, 13.
Mallette, Samuel G., 183.
Mallory & Son, 603.
Malloy, Thomas, 493.
Malone, Daniel, 646.
Maloney, J. P., 656.
Manchester, John R., 78, 402.
Manchester, Mrs. John R., 311.
Manden, Dr., 364.
Manderson, Charles F., 72, 79, 94, 159, 162, 163, 164, 228, 230, 242, 245, 246, 259, 264, 304, 380, 427, 442, 446.
Manderson & Congdon, 245.
Manderville, Sieur, 10.
Mangrum, E. C., 382.
Manix, M. J., 485.
Mann, John H., 155.
Mann, Newton, 336.
Mannien, Joseph, 105.
Manning, J. H., 495.
Manning, Joseph P., 106, 384.
Manning, Mrs. J. P., 308.
Mansfelde, A. S. v., 360.
Manypenny, Col., 129, 143.
Marbois, Francis Barbe, 19, 20.

Marder, Luse & Co., 474.
Mardis, William, 306.
Maret, Hugues, 19.
Margry, M., 10.
Marhover John, 485.
Marlus, Caius, 39.
Markel, J. E., 95, 255, 273, 375, 613.
Markel & Swobe, 255.
Markham, George S., 387.
Marple, C. H., 227.
Marquette, D., 323.
Marquette, Father, 38, 42.
Marquette, Joseph, 8, 9.
Marquette, T. M., 71, 404.
Marsh, Allen, 120.
Marsh, Charles, 120.
Marsh, Frank, 120.
Marsh, R. L., 324.
Marsh, William, 120, 505.
Marsh, W. W., 96, 119, 120, 267, 412, 413, 415, 429, 562.
Marshall, John W., 155, 280.
Marshall & Lobeck, 279.
Marshall, M. M., 494.
Marshall, William, 81.
Marshland, T., 405.
Marston, Mrs., 187.
Marston, S. M., 105.
Martin, A., 335.
Martin, C. D., 308.
Martin, Euclid, 279, 317, 476.
Martin, J. J., 385.
Martin & Morrisey, 494.
Martin, Paul, 333.
Martin, T., 74, 96, 106.
Martin, W. F., 646.
Martin, W. R., 362.
Martzahn, Frank, 646.
Masilka, Anton, 504.
Mason, Mrs., 202.
Mason, O. P., 80, 196, 222, 224.
Mason, Robert, 155.
Masson, George W., 639, 644, 670.
Matheas, Alfred, 156.
Mathews, A., 78.
Mathews, J. F., 358.
Mathewson, C. P., 81.
Mathewson, H. P., 359, 360.
Mathieson, John, 82.
Mattice, Sarah, 205.
Maul, M. O., 79, 490.
Maul, W. G., 428, 460.
Maurer, Ed., 375.
Maxfield, J. B., 163, 323.
Maxwell, Annie, 665.
Maxwell, H. E, 227, 234.
Maxwell, Judge, 195, 234.
Maxwell, R. A., 671.
May, George, 80.
May, Mary E., 238.
May, P. J., 325.
May, W. H., 375.
May, William L., 94, 428.
Mayewski, Andrew, 380.
Mayfield, E. O., 658.
Maynard, J. W., 343.
Mayne, C. E., 215, 413, 414, 431.
Mead, C. W., 417, 496, 497.

Mead & Jamieson, 279.
Mead, W. D., 220.
Meadimber, E. D., 493.
Meagher, J. D., 646.
Mealio, Stephen N., 95, 373, 374.
Meaney, Michael C., 95.
Medlock, George, 106.
Meelens, W. G., 382.
Megeath, Bettie T., 123.
Megeath, George W., 123, 402, 487.
Megeath, James G., 78, 80, 95, 96, 105, 122, 123, 141, 384, 437, 508.
Megeath, Jeff, 311.
Megeath, Joseph P., 123, 470.
Megeath, Richards & Co., 122.
Megeath, Samuel A., 106, 122, 508.
Megeath, Samuel A., 123.
Megeath, S. A. & Co., 122, 461.
Megeath, S. J., 123.
Megeath Stationery Co., 470.
Megeath, T. A., 78, 225.
Megguire, W. H., 425.
Meigs, Bishop, 352.
Meikeljohn, George D., 82, 189.
Meikle, James B., 227.
Melcher, Christian A., 656.
Melcher, F. W., 352.
Meldrum, Thomas, 374.
Melquist, Benjamin, 498.
Mendelssohn, Louis, 304, 451.
Mentor, C. J., 656.
Mercer, D. H., 227, 563.
Mercer, D. S., 279.
Mercer Hotel, 255.
Mercer, Samuel D., 79, 80, 95, 96, 105, 122, 123, 141, 356, 359, 360, 384, 413, 414, 437, 508, 564.
Merchants Hotel, 255.
Meredith, John R., 95, 106, 144, 224, 225, 233, 264, 412.
Merriam, Henry, 172, 389.
Merriam, L. A., 356, 358.
Merriam, Nathan, 419, 420, 430, 432.
Merrill, George C., 95.
Merrill, H. W., 80.
Merrill, Lewis, 153, 157.
Merrill, Moses, 34, 35.
Merrill, S. P., 34.
Merriman, T. H., 496.
Merritt, Rev., 322.
Merrow, D. R. V., 227.
Mertzheimer, Mrs. Frederick, 239.
Metcalf, J. M., 475.
Metcalf, Thomas, 475.
Metz, Charles, 280.
Metz, Frederick, 81, 82, 482.
Metzger, J. P., 259.
Meyer, Adolph, 451, 470.
Meyer, Henry, 325.
Meyer, Julius, 306.
Meyer, Max, 164, 279, 281, 304, 337, 375, 469, 470, 484.
Meyer, Max & Bros., 218, 469.
Meyer, Max & Co., 484.
Meyer, Moritz, 470, 484.

## INDEX. 689

Meyer & Raapke, 478
Meyers, E E 76
Meyers, Henry B , 106, 432
Michaels, W H 352
Michaelson, C O , 494
Michan, M 23
Michener, E C , 421
Miles, Andrew, 430
Miles, Colonel 152 153
Miles, J L , 430, 661
Millard Alfred 96 113, 170, 204, 311, 428, 438
Millard, Caldwell & Co , 113, 117
Millard, Ezra 80, 94, 106, 112, 117, 162, 218, 255, 257, 267, 304, 333, 397, 398 403, 412, 425, 427, 428
Millard, Frederick, 320
Millard, H H, 324
Millard Hotel 255
Millard, Jessie H , 113
Millard Joseph H 94 106, 113, 164, 201, 217, 253, 255, 282, 403, 413, 414, 426, 433
Millard W B , 414, 426, 433
Millard, Willard D , 113
Miller, A H , 662
Miller, A V 662
Miller, Colonel, 49
Miller, C P 655, 656
Miller David N , 78 378
Miller, D C , 157
Miller, D D , 467
Miller, D R , 334
Miller, F H 498
Miller, Miss F J 118
Miller George L . 79 80, 84, 87, 95, 98, 108, 109, 110, 116, 125, 126 141, 149 164, 168, 169, 173, 184 204, 251 252, 257, 318, 319, 353, 354, 384, 386, 397, 438 447, 471 565 639
Miller, George L & Co , 140
Miller & Gunderson, 498
Miller, Harvey 662
Miller, J A , 83, 95
Miller, J B , 506
Miller, J S , 158
Miller, Judge, 221
Miller, Lorin 94 95, 100, 105, 311, 312, 384 395
Miller Mrs , 109
Miller & Richardson, 169, 204
Milligan John A , 327
Mills & Delaney, 603
Mills, George H , 394
Mills George M , 74, 95, 105, 106
Mills, Hannah 116
Mills S F 158
Millspaugh, Frank R , 329, 338
Milnes, G S 358
Milroy, W F , 353, 357, 358, 361
Miner, Isaac W , 96, 106, 304 305
Minick, J S 66
Mink, O W 448
Misner, Mrs E A , 187
Mitchell, —— , 99

Mitchel, General, 124
Mitchell Burrell 338
Mitchell, James C , 54, 57, 60
Moffatt David H , 106, 447
Moffatt Samuel, 73, 78,86, 106, 328, 422
Mold, J B , 345
Monahan, P L , 668
Monell, Annie 234
Monell & Co , 423
Monell, Gilbert C , 74, 86, 95, 106, 119, 168, 201, 212, 252 310, 317, 353, 354 395, 402, 423
Monell Mrs Gilbert C 119
Monell, John J 119, 310, 353, 390, 423
Monier H A , 387
Monroe, James 19
Montague R V , 419
Montgomery, C S , 227, 241, 301, 433
Montgomery Eugene, 227
Monzingo, Emma C , 317
Moody, H C 469
Moore Alfred F , 380
Moore F A , 205
Moore, Hettie, 663
Moore James W , 80
Moore, Richard C 95 354, 356, 377, 358 359, 360, 361
Moore, Mrs R C , 450
Moore, Stephen W , 154
Moore, William A , 338
Moore, William E , 79, 149, 167, 252
Moores, Frank E , 250, 382
More, A B 105
Morearty Edward F , 96, 227
Morgan, A S M , 85, 95
Morgan B T C 95
Moriarty, D W , 661
Morin, Louis 13
Morrell H B , 488
Morrell, John 96
Morris, 241
Morris, A D , 380
Morris, James 96
Morris L M , 227
Morris, Nels, 641
Morris William R , 227, 228, 449, 450
Morris, Mrs W R , 117
Morrissey, F R , 82
Morrissey, John, 94
Morrison John 483
Morrison, Morris 96, 317, 430
Morrow, John A , 403
Morrow Henry M , 227
Morse, A D 468
Morse-Coe Shoe Co , 467
Morse Dry Goods Co , 463
Morse, H H , 327
Morse, John W 292
Morse, S P , 464
Morse, W V , 281, 413, 451, 464, 467, 468
Morse, Mrs W V 311
Morse, W V & Co , 467
Morsman E M , 428, 447, 448
Morsman, W W , 227, 249

Morton, Carl, 280
Morton, C W 474
Morton, Cyrus, 414
Morton, James F , 227, 474
Morton, James & Son, 473
Morton, Mrs J , 234
Morton, J Sterling, 66, 67, 68, 72, 111, 222, 223, 224, 426
Morton, Thomas, 141
Morton, W D 426
Moseley, T F 202, 203
Moseley, Mrs T F , 203
Mosier, Caroline M , 141
Mount, David T , 95, 141, 157, 251, 277, 278, 431, 488
Mount & Griffin, 488
Mount, W J 78
Moyer, A , 498
Mueller, F M , 318
Mueller Music Co , 470
Mueller & Schmoller, 470
Muffitt, E E , 481
Muhlenbrock, Henry, 325
Mulford, Henry B , 158, 280
Mulford, H B & Co , 499
Mulhall, Mamie, 381
Mulhall, W , 96
Mullen, John J , 157
Mullen, John S , 667
Mullen & McClain 482
Mullen, P O , 81
Mullins, C L , 362
Mulvihill, Jeremiah 349
Mulvihill, John, 81, 105, 349
Mulvihill, Martin 254
Mumaugh, Mrs Frances, 451, 453, 454
Mundie Mary M , 119
Mungen, Thomas, 380
Munn, F E , 227
Munro, Alex A , 659 668
Munro, George F , 96 97
Munroe, J A , 402
Munroe, Mr , 198
Murdock, A H , 227
Murdock, L H , 227
Murphy, E J , 445
Murphy, Fannie, 113
Murphy, Frank, 65, 66, 67, 78, 94, 101 106 114 115 282, 412, 413, 415, 427, 498, 597, 613, 615, 618, 646
Murphy, James F , 280, 500
Murphy, John P , 154, 155
Murphy, M , 79
Murphy M J , 500
Murphy, M R , 610
Murphy, P F , 94, 96
Murphy, Wasey & Co , 500
Murray, C , 477
Murray H M , 158
Murray, Miss M F , 203, 451
Murray, Thomas, 105, 218, 255
Murray, William P , 324
Myers, A J , 162
Myers E E , 206, 208
Myers, John C 79, 81
Myers, Mrs S R , 490
Myers, William, 162

44

690                                     INDEX.

## N

Nance, Albinus, 72, 81, 163, 177, 240, 377.
Nash, E. W., 413, 414, 433, 496, 510.
Nash, F. M., 291.
Nash, Samuel, 320.
Nash, William, 320.
Nasler, James M., 156.
Nason, A. W., 366.
Nason, W. N., 279.
Nattinger. G. M., 279, 432.
Nave, McCord & Co., 144.
Neal, C. E., 137.
Neal, Edward D., 137, 138.
Neal, J. E., 387.
Neale, Mary A., 238.
Neble, Sophus, F., 170.
Nebraska Seed Co., 482.
Needham, Charles P., 78, 429.
Neff. Isaac H., 136.
Neighly, William, 225.
Neil, Louis, 132, 133.
Neilson, Paul. 93.
Nelson, Captain, 197.
Nelson, Daniel H., 68.
Nelson, John A., 646.
Nelson, O. R., 172.
Nelson, William T., 227.
Neve, Edward, 366.
Neve, William, 82.
Neville, James, 77, 225, 226, 227, 228, 242, 249, 264.
Neville, Joseph, 79, 358, 361, 363.
Neville, William, 81.
Nevin, J. E., 227.
Nevins, Charles F., 613.
New, Ike. 485.
Newcomb, Henry, 155.
Newell, C. G., 496.
Newell, John, 96.
Newman, C. B., 335.
Newman, Henry A., 446.
Newman, John P., 23, 341, 342.
Nicholls, 74.
Nichols, P. J., 402.
Nicholson, A. P., 594.
Nicholson, S. W., 211.
Nielson, J., 642.
Nightingale, A. F., 313, 315, 319.
Nile, William, 106.
Nims, Francis, 235.
Norberg. L. P., 331.
Norris, Chauncy H., 155, 446.
Norris & Wilcox, 468.
North, Frank. 383.
Northwall, T. G., 476.
Norval, Judge, 195.
Nosler, James N., 154.
Noyes, A. H., 624.
Nuckolls, 54.
Nutter, John P., 325.
Nye, Fred, 168.
Nye & Johnson, 168.
Nye, Mrs., 310.
Nye, Ray, 502.

## O

Ober, Frank W., 340.
Oberfelder, I. & Co., 465.
Oberne, George, 669.
Oberne, George N., 669.
Oberne, George & Co., 483.
Oberne, Hosick & Co., 643.
O'Brien, Bessie C., 264.
O'Brien, Edward, 137.
O'Brien, Father, 347.
O'Brien, George M., 82, 224, 225, 228, 230, 264, 412, 566.
O'Brien, George M. jr., 227, 231.
O'Brien, Joanna, 348.
O'Brien, Maggie. 263.
O'Brien, Moses P., 227, 231.
O'Brien, Thomas F., 431.
O'Callaghan, Father, 348.
O'Connell, Daniel, 227, 643, 646, 648.
O'Connell & Grice, 643.
O'Connor, Edward. 96.
O'Connor, James, 258, 340, 341, 347, 350.
O'Connor, J. J., 227, 458.
O'Connor, Michael, 341.
O'Connor, Thomas. 77, 78, 83, 91, 95, 105, 106, 142. 352.
O'Connor, Mrs. Thomas, 345.
Odwarker. Joseph. 646.
Oehrle, E., 493.
O'Fallon, William. 36.
Officer, Thomas. 308.
Offutt. Chas. 227, 249.
Ogden, Charles, 196, 227, 244. 275, 449.
Ogden, E. A., 200.
Ogden, Mrs., 205.
Ogden, William R., 391.
O'Gorman, James M., 309, 340, 341, 346, 347, 348.
O'Hanlon, Philip, 80.
O'Hollaren, F. C., 227.
O'Keefe, Daniel, 378.
O'Keefe, Richard, 77, 78, 96, 207.
Olive. 240.
Olmsted, R. H., 227.
Olsen, Theodore, 95, 96, 97.
Omaha Basket Manufactory, 499.
Omaha Carpet Co., 457.
Omaha Casket Co., 500.
Omaha Furniture Co., 467.
Omaha Gas Co., 497.
Omaha Mattress Co., 500.
Omaha Oil and Paint Co., 483.
Omaha Paper Box Factory. 499.
Omaha Real Estate and Trust Co., 279.
Omaha Rubber Co., 466.
Omaha Tent and Awning Co., 466.
Omaha Upholstering Co., 500.
O'Malley, Peter, 78, 96.
O'Neil, J. K., 451, 454.
O'Neil, T. J., 667.
Orchard, A. R., 106.
Orchard & Bean. 466.
Orchard, Samuel A., 106, 444, 464, 466, 467, 567, 613, 648.

Orcutt, Clinton. 430.
Ord, E. O. C., 162, 351, 436.
Ord, Josie, 172.
Ordway, John, 23.
O'Reily, Q., 635.
Orendorf & Martin, 218.
O'Rourke, J. J., 635, 656.
O'Rourke, Mrs. Mary, 636.
Orr, Mrs. Thomas M., 205, 451.
Osterholm. M., 183.
Osterhoudt, B. H., 493.
Osthoff, Henry. 96, 471.
O'Sullivan, P. F., 171.
Outhwaite, Milton C., 225.
Ousley, W. B., 338.
Overton, Dr., 639.
Oviatt, J. S., 662.
Owen, T. S., 358.

## P

Pabin, John, 494.
Paddock, A. S., 106, 151, 162, 164, 218, 252, 397, 403, 413.
Paddock, Ben. S., 115.
Paddock, Joseph W., 52, 65, 66, 67, 78, 79, 80, 96, 105, 115, 125, 155, 251, 252, 259, 412, 419.
Page, E. C., 227.
Page, Henry, 151.
Page, W. A., 280, 510, 512.
Page, W. A., Soap Co., 280, 509.
Pague, S. H., 643.
Paine, H. A., 162.
Palmer. E. S., 326.
Palmer, Henry E., 382.
Palmer, James N., 159, 162.
Palsley. E. E., 643, 646.
Pandow, August, 501.
Papez, Joseph, 504.
Parish, J. W., 227.
Park, George J., 308.
Park, Mrs. Graham, 187.
Parke, Wm. S., 328.
Parker, A. A., 96, 356, 357, 358.
Parker, Celestial, 311.
Parker, Churchill, 278, 419.
Parker, Diederick, 450.
Parker, F. A., 227.
Parker, I. W., 381.
Parker, J., 55, 78.
Parker, James M., 225.
Parker, John A., jr., 143.
Parker, O. F., 308.
Parker, Samuel, 34, 35, 36.
Parker, W. F., 454.
Parks, H. B., 338.
Parks, George, 670.
Parks, Mr., 137.
Parlin, Orendorff & Martin, 476.
Parmalee, Daniel S., 80, 81.
Parmalee, E. A., 380.
Parmalee, Edward E., 96.
Parmalee, F. S., 473.
Parrish, M. M., 658.
Parrotte, C. S., 430.
Parrotte, J. H., 430.
Parrotte, Scripps & Co., 465.
Parsell. G. E., 365.
Parsons. J. H., 275.

INDEX 691

Parsons, W H , 365
Paterson, George, 488
Patrick, A S , 106, 277
Patrick, Edwin, 105, 155, 157, 277
Patrick, Eliza, 124
Patrick, J A , 433
Patrick John, 106, 257
Patrick, J N H , 80, 106, 154, 415, 454
Patrick, M T , 106, 147, 156, 275, 276, 277, 278
Patrick, Robert W  227
Pattee, J M , 145, 257, 303
Patterson, R C , 411
Pattison, John W , 149, 167
Paul C H , 366
Paul George J , 157
Paul, J N , 505
Paul, Samuel 156
Paull, J L W , 325
Paulson, J T , 82, 278, 414
Paxton & Gallagher, 478
Paxton Hotel, 239, 254
Paxton, James 601
Paxton William A , 81, 82, 106, 114 218 264. 268, 277, 281, 403, 417 427, 478, 494, 594. 507, 567, 594, 597, 598, 599 601, 604, 605, 609, 613, 614, 615, 618
Paxton, William A , jr , 114, 220
Payne, G H , 432
Payne, John F  34
Peabody, James H , 354, 355, 356, 357
Peabody, John D , 79, 358, 359, 342, 569
Peabody William L , 78, 249
Peall, F E , 646 660
Pearl, R , 646
Pearman, John W , 155
Pearson, William Osgood, 329
Peart, W L , 227
Peattie, Robert B , 170
Pease Bros , 465
Peasley, J C , 404
Peavey, C T , 421
Peavey F H , 420
Peck Edward P , 106, 311, 353, 420, 421
Peck, Emery, 155
Peck, George P  332
Peck, James P , 95, 106, 277, 353, 354 359
Peebles, G H , 360 361
Pegram B R , 422
Pelton, George S , 327
Penfold H J , 362, 481
Pennell Lizzie, 450
Penniman, Alford B , 327
Pennock Henry W , 227
Perine, P L , 126, 281
Perine Mrs P L , 203
Perkins, Alonzo 71, 72
Perkins C E , 404, 455
Perkins, Melissa 311
Perkins M G 171
Perley, Lyman O , 227
Perley, Maude H , 247

Perrigo, A H & Co , 477
Perry, Ed , 483
Perry, General, 162
Persons, Frank J , 646, 668
Persons & Berry, 668
Peters, John, 447, 646
Peters M C , 280, 503
Peterson, Christian, 83
Peterson, Mrs Christian, 93
Peterson, Emma, 308
Peterson James 308
Peterson, Mary 308
Peterson, Nancy, 308
Peterson, P G  73, 78, 105
Peterson, R , 508
Peterson, Sarah, 308
Peterson & Son, 255
Petty, John, 106
Peycke Bros , 481
Peycke, Ernest, 481
Peycke, Edmund, 481, 506
Peycke, Julius 481
Pfeiffer, William 493
Pflimmer, Miss, 211
Phelps Stephen, 319
Philleo F A , 183
Phillipi, J O , 409
Phillips, James N , 444
Philpot J E  380
Phipps William H  410
Piatti L J , 227
Pichon Louis Andre 19
Pickard, James W , 80
Pickard, Oscar J , 278, 499
Pickard, W L , 106
Pickering H J , 380, 474
Pickering, J L , 506
Pier, William H  496
Pierce Charles W , 382
Pierce, John H  172
Pierce, President, 130, 222, 236
Pierce Roswell G , 98 100, 132, 223, 224
Pierson A T C , 384
Pierson, John, 282
Pilcher, Doctor 36
Pilcher, J D , 227
Pinney C H  79, 137, 354, 359
Piper, J B , 315
Pine, A B , 405
Pirtle, C H  82
Pivonka, Frank, 638, 643, 646, 648, 667
Pivonka, Vaclav, 646, 668
Pizarro 37
Place, George H , 227
Platt Oyster Co , 479
Plumb, H I  352
Plumbeck, George 81
Plumber, J , 55
Plumer, William L , 308.
Plummer J B , 106
Points, John J , 78, 96, 317
Pollard, R D  404
Pollock A , 667
Pollock, A L  171
Pollock, J F , 488
Pollock, W A , 80, 134
Pomeroy, Charles E , 417
Pomy, Gustav, 508

Pond, Charles L , 382
Poole, Edward L , 410
Poor, C S , 490
Poor, Henry B , 391
Pope, J S & Co , 208
Pope, O G  227
Poppleton, Andrew J , 51, 52, 54, 66, 67, 68, 70, 72 79, 80, 94, 97, 98, 105, 117, 123, 131, 136, 140, 143, 217, 221, 222, 224, 227, 228 232, 234, 239, 240, 243, 251, 254 257, 258, 260, 264, 266, 269, 273, 275, 276, 279, 285, 286, 292, 293, 301, 304, 305, 315, 339, 395, 400, 448 570
Poppleton, Mrs Andrew J , 205, 241, 449
Poppleton, Miss E J , 259
Poppleton, Will S , 126, 227, 317, 428
Poppleton, Mrs Will S , 236
Porter Bros  481
Porter, Charles F , 155, 156
Porter & Deuel, 118, 200
Porter, Don H , 255
Porter, H A , 389
Porter, H B , 386
Porter, J P , 366
Porter, John R , 79, 80, 94, 95, 106, 156, 200, 383, 386, 446
Porter, M , 149
Post George W  446
Potter, Arthur S , 286, 455, 457, 459, 572
Potter, Mrs A S , 206
Potter, Charles S , 447, 448
Potter, Jerome, 381
Potter, Philip, 433
Potter, W A , 474
Potter, Waldo M , 168
Potts John, 23, 154
Powell, A C , 433
Powell, Archie, 311
Powell, Charles, 97, 105, 155, 225
Powell, Clinton N , 96, 227, 268, 317
Powell, George E , 387
Powell, G J , 327
Power, John 511
Powers A H , 658
Powers, Father, 346
Powers, James A , 227
Powers, John H  188 189
Powers, H E , 227
Poynter W A , 82
Poynton G W , 227
Pratt, August 96 138
Pratt E D  jr , 227
Presnell, J F , 357, 358
Preston Alfred 429
Preston Walter G , 479
Preston, William 479
Prichard George A , 227
Prince, John S , 306
Prince Solomon 96 97, 374, 375
Prior Nathaniel, 23
Pritchett George E , 81, 94, 227, 228 242 249 268, 382
Pritchett, Mrs George E , 311

# INDEX.

Provost, Charles E., 154.
Prugh, Walter B., 183.
Puett, A. W., 66, 71.
Pundt, Henry, 106, 279, 281, 375, 477.
Pundt & Koening, 477.
Pundt, Meyer & Raapke, 477.
Purchase, M. W. E., 78, 400.
Purinton. N., 646.
Purple, Hascal C., 54, 149.
Purvis, Robert, 482.
Putnam, Jaynes, 453.

## Q

Quealey, P. J., 280, 509.
Quealey, P. J. Soap Co., 280.
Quincy, Josiah, 21.
Quinlan, Joseph, 79.
Quinland, Patrick, 105.
Quinn, Father, 348.
Quinn, John, 378.

## R

Rafferty, Daniel, 643, 651, 656, 671.
Rafferty, Mrs. Daniel, 665.
Raley, Mrs. Manley, 659.
Ralph, J. B., 95, 355, 356, 357.
Ramacciotti, H. L., 97.
Ramge, Frank J., 218, 504.
Ramsay, Alfred, 314.
Ramsey, O. N., 495.
Ramsey, Mrs. O. N., 258.
Ramsey, Secretary, 163.
Ramsyer, J. S., 333.
Ramsyer, Mrs. J. S., 333.
Randall, Alonzo, 254.
Randall, G. R., 313.
Randall, W., 404.
Rankin, B. P., 253.
Ransom, F. T., 227.
Rapp, C. A., 646.
Rariden, H. C. & Co., 423.
Rasner, Joseph, 671.
Rathbun, George R, 318, 381.
Rau, Maria, 119.
Rawitzer, A. H., 280, 466.
Rawitzer, Sophia, 381.
Raworth, Maria S., 662.
Ray, P. Henry, 160.
Raymer, A. C., 667.
Raymond, Alfred, 358.
Raymond & Campbell, 283.
Raymond, C. S., 470.
Rayner, W. H., 474.
Read, A. C., 227.
Read, Guy R. C., 227.
Reagan, C. G., 419.
Reagan, J. C., 419.
Reagan, John, 380.
Reardon, J. P., 405.
Reavis, Daniel, 155.
Rebut, M. A., 356, 358.
Reck, John, 383, 384.
Rector, Allen, 434, 473.
Rector & Wilhelmy, 218, 473.
Rector, W. S., 278, 429.
Redfield, Josiah B., 78.

Redick & Briggs, 224.
Redick, Charles R., 172, 238.
Redick & Chapman, 238.
Redick, Chatham, 238.
Redick, Clarke, 238, 320.
Redick, Elmer, 238.
Redick, George M., 238.
Redick, John I., 80, 85, 98, 99, 102, 106, 117, 137, 168, 221, 224, 228, 237, 238, 264, 303, 317, 403.
Redick, John I., jr., 238.
Redick, W. A., 227, 228.
Redick, William R., 320.
Redington, L. C., 610.
Redman, Joseph, 96, 106, 268, 313.
Reed, Abraham L., 111, 261.
Reed, Byron, 70, 78, 92, 94, 96, 98, 105, 111, 147, 253, 261, 262, 265, 266, 351, 384, 386, 398, 416, 458.
Reed, Mrs. Byron, 311.
Reed, Chauncy, 255.
Reed, Peter, 151, 155.
Reed, S. B., 158, 392.
Rees Printing Co., 280.
Rees, Samuel, 96, 280, 379, 501.
Reeves, Cameron, 78, 106.
Reeves, George W., 154.
Reeves, J. C., 142, 151, 222.
Reeves, Mills S., 69, 71.
Reeves, W. C., 357.
Reeves, William Nebraska, 142.
Regan & Lowry, 653.
Reichenbach, H. A., 332.
Reid, F. S., 202.
Reiper, John, 646.
Reis, Charles, 380.
Remington, Arthur, 172.
Renner, F., 446.
Rensselaer, Cortland, 308.
Reuther, G., 643, 651, 656.
Reynolds, D. H., 646.
Rheem, L. M., 280, 379, 418, 419.
Rhoades, Addie M., 381.
Rhoades, A. K., 381.
Rhoades, Juliette, 382.
Rhoades, Mattie, 381.
Rhoads Mrs. M., 187.
Rhodes, George H., 381.
Ricara, 12.
Ribble & George, 482.
Ribble, Henry H., 155.
Ribo, Fred, 646.
Ribyl, John P., 505.
Rice, H. V., 646.
Rice, N. L., 308.
Rice, Patrick, 652.
Rich, C. H., 650, 657.
Rich, Joseph, 156.
Richard, August, 613.
Richards, Anna, 203.
Richards, Burr H., 122.
Richards, David, 105, 227.
Richards, D. F., 95.
Richards, D. J., 203.
Richards, J. H., 510.
Richards, John, 95.
Richards, L. C., 95.
Richards, L, D, 188, 189.

Richards, T. W. T., 264, 494.
Richardson, Cornelia, 235.
Richardson Drug Co., 479, 480.
Richardson, George, 479.
Richardson, J. C., 480.
Richardson, J. R., 339.
Richardson, Lyman, 73, 77, 78, 83, 84, 98, 100, 105, 108, 110, 116, 117, 155, 168, 221, 251, 253, 258, 259, 346, 439, 574.
Richardson, Mrs. Lyman, 117.
Richardson, Minnie, 117.
Richardson, Mrs. M. J., 187, 216.
Richardson, N. C., 106.
Richardson, O. D., 52, 54, 69, 78, 88, 95, 98, 105, 117, 222, 235, 423, 574.
Richardson, Ralph, 117.
Richardson, R. W., 226.
Richardson, Thomas, 646.
Richardson, W., 646.
Richardson, William A., 69, 70, 72.
Richelieu, Edward, 496.
Richmond, R. M., 227.
Richthart, J. F., 639, 643, 644, 658, 662.
Ricketts, M. O., 358.
Ricketts, Reverend, 338.
Rickley, John, 68.
Ricks, John, 385.
Riepen, Fritz, 96, 268.
Rigby, H., 642.
Rigby, H. & Co., 657.
Righter, C. A., 613.
Riis, C., 358.
Riley, A. K., 227.
Riley, Allen F., 156.
Riley, Andrew, 484.
Riley, A. W., 357, 358, 362.
Riley, Bernard, 484.
Riley, Bros., 484.
Riley, E. F., 484.
Riley, James E., 81, 419.
Riley, John, 105.
Riley, Thomas, 95, 136, 142, 208.
Riordan, Father, 347.
Rippey, I. N., 311, 354.
Risdon, M. R., 380, 381.
Risk, James, 462.
Ritchhart, John F., 644, 658.
Ritchie, A. S., 227.
Ritchie, Frank E., 421, 501.
Ritchie, John 80, 95, 322.
Ritchie, Thomas W., 156.
Rittenhouse & Embree, 487.
Roche, M. D., 78, 79.
Robb, D. B., 71.
Robb, Fleming W., 446.
Robbins, Silas, 227, 451.
Roberson, Frank R., 340.
Roberts, C. J., 499.
Roberts, George W., 94.
Roberts, George H., 224, 225, 228.
Roberts, John B., 149.
Roberts, W. R., 433, 434.
Robertson, Bernard N., 227.
Robertson, Beverly H., 150, 151.
Robertson, E. B., 123.

## INDEX  693

Robertson E L & Bro , 484
Robertson John B  308
Robertson Theodore H , 54, 83, 105 143 167
Robidoux, Joseph 34
Robinson E R , 355
Robinson Franklin, 239
Robinson, John M , 154
Robinson J D , 646, 660, 662
Robinson, J T  280
Robinson, J W  324
Robinson Lewis A , 410
Robinson M W  385
Robinson W S , 362
Robitaille Philip 13
Roddis, Edward, 96
Rodefer J W , 429
Rodgers, P M  71
Rodgers W O , 358
Rodis Jessie, 320
Roe, Edward J , 465
Roe, Fayette W  161
Roe J Phipps 183, 323, 621
Roe Mary 187
Roebling Michael 105
Roebling, Moritz, 106
Roeder Agustus, 79, 106, 354 384
Roeder, Julius 311
Roeder, Maggie, 451
Rogers, Alice L , 122
Rogers E A , 80
Rogers, E H  80, 201
Rogers, G S , 115
Rogers Herbert M , 122
Rogers H W , 420
Rogers, John N , 292, 294, 297.
Rogers, J W , 227
Rogers Milton, 121, 144, 270, 385, 475 609, 613, 646
Rogers Milton & Sons 122 475
Rogers Samuel E , 52. 54, 66, 78, 79, 86 101, 102, 105, 114, 115 140, 222 281 303, 306, 383, 423 427, 613
Rogers, Thomas J , 122, 281, 311, 475
Rogers Warren M  122, 475
Rogers, Will S  122
Rogers William, 105
Rogers, William R , 114
Rogers, W T , 381
Roggen Edward P , 164, 181
Rohrbough G A , 318
Rohrbough L J  318
Rohrbough, M G , 318
Ruhwer, Henry 95
Rollins R H , 400
Rood, E S  227
Rocker, W V , 170
Root Aaron 117, 251
Root, Allen 105, 222.
Root, Mrs Allen, 308
Root, W A  658 662
Roper William R , 154
Rose J M  472
Rose, S C  96
Rose William, 326
Rosenau, William, 338
Rosenberg A , 314

Rosenberry A  498
Rosenstein, Joseph, 388  389
Rosenstock & Co , 484
Rosenthal, B , 167
Rosewater Andrew 79, 95, 97, 258, 259, 283, 430
Rosewater, Chas , 357, 358, 362
Rosewater, Edward, 81, 164 169 170 179, 180 182, 184 268 281, 417, 575
Rosewater & Webster, 180
Rosicky John 170
Roskee W F , 509
Ross Christina, 449
Ross & Cruickshank, 463
Ross, F  474
Ross, George H  405
Ross. James M , 172, 208  259
Ross W L  357, 358
Rothery, Albert, 453, 454
Rotholz Joseph 375
Roundebush J W , 228
Roundibaugh, Alfred, 155
Rounds S P  168
Rounds & Taylor, 168
Rowley Annie 644
Rowley, Catherine 644
Rowley, Edwin S , 220, 428
Rowley, Patrick  644, 656
Rowley Mrs Patrick 665
Royal, W B , 497
Royce, J B , 37
Roye, T B , 37
Rudd, Ella M , 203.
Rudowsky Julius, 95, 106
Rudowsky M  74
Ruf, F L , 106
Ruggles General 162
Rugh Emma R , 317
Rullman, H S , 662
Rumsey, Philo 255, 256
Runyan, W , 500
Rupert Prince, 44
Rush, John 78  94, 141, 208, 349, 430
Rush Mrs John, 352
Rush, S R , 228
Rusk Jerry, 165
Russell W H , 220, 340, 432
Russell, Mrs , 176
Russell. Patrick 380
Rust, Geo W , 106
Rust, Mary P  310
Rustin, Charles B , 413, 496
Rustin Claire 172, 260 320
Rustin Gilbert 95
Ruth, John B , 483
Ruth, William, 93, 106, 114, 384, 412
Rutherford, G A , 228
Ryan, Bishop 341
Ryan, James, 308
Ryan, Jerry 206
Ryan, John J , 671
Ryan, Mary, 308
Ryan, Thomas 635, 636, 658
Ryan & Walsh 208 210
Ryan William M , 81
Ryland E M , 200
Ryner, H P , 661

## S

Sabin George W , 390
Sackett, Fred J  78
Sackett, H B , 423
Sackett J E , 305
Safford Jacob 59, 71
Safford W , 79
Saft, Reverend, 337
Sage, W N , 667
Sage, W R , 667
Sahler, John H  88, 94, 106
Sailing, J , 222
Salisbury, Alonzo F , 66, 79, 106, 328 351
Salsbury, J C , 405
Salter Charles 374
Sample, Samuel E  430
Sanders, A H , 96, 375, 433
Sanders A P , 368
Sanford Major 40, 48
Sapp William F , 80, 95, 155
Sarpy, John A , 131
Sarpy, Peter A  33, 34 37, 51, 127, 128, 129 130, 131, 132 143, 223, 383
Sattizan James, 662
Saunders, Alvin, 72 96, 111 153, 163, 165 267 280, 284, 302, 312, 313 386 387, 395, 397 399, 400, 401 403, 577
Saunders, Charles L , 111, 320, 505
Saunders W A , 228
Sautter, Christian 645, 649
Sautter, Frank, 636
Sautter, George. 636
Sautter, Mary, 636
Savage, E P , 648 649, 651, 656, 659
Savage & Green, 605
Savage James W , 71 137, 158, 221, 225, 228 229 240 241, 242, 259 260 264 268, 298 269, 359, 380, 382 589, 660
Savage Jessie 665
Savage, Morris & Davis, 241
Savidge Charles W , 323, 324, 325 336
Savidge, Mrs Charles W , 337
Saville, J J , 96
Sawhill, John B , 380
Sawyer, Lyman M , 154
Sawyer, W G , 476
Sayre, Alfred, 384
Saxe, A W , 638
Saxe D W , 480, 669
Saxenberger F  364
Scanlan, Father, 345
Scanlan, John 380
Scannel R , 204 341
Schaible, John G , 334
Schall & Hering, 498
Schaller, C R , 596, 616, 649
Schaller, Miss 320
Schlank & Prince, 255
Schaff A H  157
Schaul Albert 215
Scherblich A C , 280
Schell J V  423

# INDEX.

Scherbe, Enos, 225.
Schlank, Charles, 374, 375.
Schlick, E., 481.
Schmeling, William, 635, 646.
Schmidt, Charles, 154.
Schmidt, F., 375.
Schnake, Frederick F., 170, 171.
Schneider, Edward F., 168.
Schneider, Frederick A., 106, 253.
Schnur, George H., 330.
Schock, Thresa, 186.
Schoelply, J. W., 468.
Schomp & Corson, 243.
Schomp, John, 228, 243, 244.
Schroeder & Co., 482.
Schroeder, H., 332.
Schroeder, Louis, 507.
Schultz, John F., 656.
Schulze, William, 471.
Schuyler, Lieutenant, 449.
Schwenck, John, 635.
Schwenk, P., 505.
Schwerin, W. F., 335.
Scism, W. L., 171, 389.
Scofield, Shurmer & Teagle, 483.
Scott, Alexander H., 154, 381.
Scott, Alzina, 311.
Scott, C. R., 226, 228, 281.
Scott, D. R., 601, 602.
Scott, Edward Harlan, 228.
Scott, E. H., 228.
Scott, Judge, 249.
Scott, Walter A., 410.
Scott, Willard, 326, 227.
Scott, William, 73.
Scribner, A. W., 402.
Seagrave, A. A., 78.
Seaman, W. T., 476.
Search, Joseph W., 356.
Searight, William, 151.
Searle, B. L., 158.
Sears, Delia M., 241, 257.
Seaton, John S., 154.
Seavey, Webber S., 95, 184, 368, 370.
Sebring, William S., 171.
Sedgwick, C. H., 78, 249.
Seeley, Helen, 663.
Seeley, Jona, 79, 85, 95, 106, 221, 252, 328.
Seeley, Silas E., 95.
Seeley, Walter M., 82.
Segelke, William, 508.
Selden, J. C., 472.
Selden, O. B., 105, 157, 308, 492.
Selden, Perry, 657.
Selzer, Rudolph, 506.
Sessions, M. H., 81.
Seward, H. L., 95.
Sexauer, William, 106.
Sexton, Thomas L., 319.
Seybolt George L., 80.
Seymour, Ellen J., 158.
Seymour, Emerson D., 79, 106, 136, 158.
Seymour, E. S., 387.
Seymour, Miss F., 310.
Seymour, James H., 79, 80, 106, 154, 353.

Seymour, Silas, 392.
Shade, Robert, 453.
Shaffel, Roman, 265, 348.
Shahler John H., 74.
Shain, R C., 423.
Shane, Daniel L., 77, 208, 210.
Shank, J. W., 211.
Shannon, Bernard, 96, 268, 378.
Shannon, George, 23.
Sharp, C. A., 434.
Sharp, J. C., 489, 598, 610, 633.
Sharp, Joseph L., 52, 54, 79.
Sharp, J. S., 117
Sharp, Neal J., 154.
Sharp, W. A., 656.
Sharpe, Henry, 320.
Shaw, E A., 108.
Shaw, T L., 136.
Shea, John C., 82, 137.
Shears, Samuel, 255.
Sheean, J. B., 228.
Sheed, H. H., 81, 82.
Sheeks, Benjamin, 137, 224, 225, 249.
Sheely, John M., 106.
Sheely, Joseph F., 95, 106, 218, 373, 374, 375.
Sheiks, Ben., 137.
Shelby, P. P., 81, 96.
Sheldon, L, 71.
Sheldon, W, S., 340.
Shelley, Daniel, 172.
Shelley, D. C., 502.
Shelley, B. T., 353, 354.
Shelton, D. O., 497.
Shelton, Nathan, 257, 270, 411.
Shennehan, Mr., 88.
Shepard, J., 447.
Sheridan, General, 161, 162.
Sheridan, Michael, 160.
Sherrill, A. F., 273, 326, 327.
Sherman, Charles R., 141, 481.
Sherman, Charles W., 168.
Sherman & McConnell, 480.
Sherman, W. T., 94, 163.
Sherwood, E. H., 78, 489.
Sherwood, W. H., 183.
Shields, George W., 78, 228, 244, 249, 262, 320.
Shields, John, 23.
Shields, Reverend, 332.
Shields, Robert, 383.
Shimonski, Mr., 310, 311.
Shimonski, Mrs., 310, 311.
Shinn, Edward, 186.
Shinn, Moses F., 105, 142, 277, 308, 350.
Shinn, Q. A., 183.
Shinn, Q. H., 337, 380.
Shinn, Q. R., 186.
Shipman, Mr., 275.
Shipman, H. A., 600.
Shipwright, Mr., 635.
Shirlaw, Walter, 449.
Shiverick, Arthur, 467.
Shiverick, Chas. & Co., 467.
Shoaf, John, 106.
Shoaf, Randal, 106.
Shoemaker, W. S., 228.
Sholes, D. V., 96.

Sholes, Lyman, 410.
Shriver, Arthur N., 601, 646.
Shriver, William G., 96, 279, 280.
Shroeder, Alfred, 419.
Shroeder, Louis, 96.
Shropshire, J. S., 388, 390.
Shugert, E. L., 475.
Shukert, C. E., 504.
Shull, Daniel W., 351, 375.
Shull, Jacob S., 98, 106.
Shull, Mrs. Jacob, 98.
Shull, William, 351, 375.
Shultz, Cal. D., 171, 172.
Shultz, George, 154.
Shultze, Mrs. E. J., 451.
Sickles, T. E., 257, 282, 398.
Sievers, William, 434.
Silkworth, M. S., 451.
Silloway, Benton, 255.
Silsby, H. A., 373.
Simeral, Edward W., 79, 228, 246, 249, 264, 268, 370.
Simeral, William, 228.
Simmert, Charles, 646.
Simmonds, Edward, 157.
Simons, Henry, 388.
Simpson, Andrew J., 95, 106, 277, 281, 312, 371, 373, 386, 419, 492.
Simpson, Charles, 95, 373.
Simpson, F. W., 493.
Simpson, John, 161.
Sinclair, William, 159.
Singleton, 54.
Sinsley, John, 105.
Sisson, W. H. H., 364.
Skinner, Charles, 387.
Slabaugh, W. H., 357, 666.
Slabaugh, W. W., 228.
Slate, Walter J., 659, 660.
Slater, A. B., 506.
Slater, A. D., 505, 662.
Slaughter, B. D., 81, 82.
Slaughter, W. B., 322.
Slaughter, Mrs., 186.
Slightman, James, 225.
Sliter, Frank J., 646, 648, 649, 651.
Sliter & Gould, 642.
Sloan, Johnson & Co., 478.
Sloane, W. G., 638, 646, 648, 649, 651, 654, 655, 656, 660, 669.
Sloane, Mrs. W. G., 664.
Sloane & Saxe, 643.
Sloman E. E., 358.
Small, Samuel, 179.
Smead, J. P., 283, 503.
Smiley, John A., 593, 594.
Smiley, Miss, 310, 311.
Smilie, G. H., 453.
Smith, Allen B., 404.
Smith, Mrs. A. B., 343.
Smith, Arthur, 405, 463.
Smith, Benjamin F., 281, 304, 413, 597, 604, 609, 613, 627.
Smith, Charles, B., 105, 253, 308.
Smith, Cornelia C., 121.
Smith, Mrs. Cornelius, 635.
Smith, David W., 154, 666.

INDEX. 695

Smith Draper 605
Smith Dudley 477, 505
Smith Edith 662
Smith, Ed P 228 361, 402
Smith E V 92, 96 106
Smith, Mrs E V 277
Smith Father, 348
Smith Francis, 95, 136, 403
Smith Frank 106, 397
Smith, Frank S, 336
Smith, Fred 154
Smith Fred L, 465
Smith, F M, 651, 652, 656, 662
Smith General 198
Smith, George 138
Smith, George, 617
Smith, George R 79 95 98, 100, 441
Smith, George S 228
Smith H A, 222
Smith H K 444 463, 594
Smith & Hopkins 462
Smith Hopkins & Housel, 462
Smith Howard B, 78, 228, 249, 368
Smith, H S 172
Smith, H W 327
Smith, James Jr 68
Smith, J E Jr 389
Smith, John E 389
Smith, J Ed 157
Smith Joel S, 80
Smith, Jessie, 186
Smith J S & Co, 483
Smith, J T, 661
Smith M E, 463
Smith, M E & Co, 463, 503
Smith, M J, 183
Smith & Parmalee, 423
Smith, Richard, 209, 511
Smith, W A 415 429, 505
Smith Watson B 177, 178, 187, 228 243, 249 250, 339
Smith, Mrs Watson B, 187, 206
Smith, W C, 280, 494
Smith, W D, 463
Smith, W Franklin 336
Smith W M, 322
Smyth C J 82, 96, 157, 228 317 379
Smyth, Edwin F, 228, 230
Snowden Tenie 454
Snowden, William P, 95, 105, 251, 322
Snowden, Mrs William P, 105
Snyder, Adam, 78 82, 96
Snyder, H W, 508
Snyder, Webster, 436
Snyder, William 492
Somers A B 95 97, 357, 358
Sommer Bros, 478
Sommer C A, 453
Sorenson, Alfred, 62
Sorenson, Mrs Alfred, 105
Soudenberg Charles, 97
Southard, J B, 94
Southmayd George 658
Spalding S K 96, 281, 317, 356, 358 362, 381

Spaulding H W, 334
Spaun, J S 242
Spaun & Pritchett, 242
Specht, Christian, 82, 96, 97, 494
Spencer, B, 365
Spencer, W A, 170
Sperry, Charles C, 96
Spitko A, 171
Spoettle, Martin 637, 644
Spoor Alice L 122
Spoor Frank 96
Spoor, Herbert, 122
Spoor, Jennie S, 122
Spoor N D, 122
Spoor, N T, 258
Spoor Thomas J 122
Spoor, Warren M, 122
Spoor, Will S, 122
Sprague C G 363 365
Spratlin Lee W 434
Squires C E 304 380, 381, 510
Squires, Mrs C E 311
Sreeves, Alice A, 382
St Clair L E 228
St John, Governor 179, 180
St Julien G, 489
St Julien L 489
Stafford J H, 402
Staley, Thomas J, 96, 315
Stanley, C C, 656, 662
Stanley, Henry M 164
Stansbury Captain, 55
Stanton, Edwin M, 233, 387
Starks, Theodore, 476
Starr C A 211 340
Stearns, Edward 601 651
Steckles Benjamin, 95, 136, 365 361, 371 372
Steel, I R, 96
Steel, John. 96, 97, 281, 477
Steele Dudley M, 477
Steele Dudley M & Co, 477
Steele, James, 155
Steele, Johnson & Co, 477
Steele, R W, 79
Steen, John, 94
Steen, O, 381
Stein J H, 504
Steinberger, J, 79
Stelling, George F, 329, 336
Stenberg, E M, 78, 94, 431
Stephens, Lucien, 465
Stephens & Smith 465
Stephens & Wilcox 105, 200, 461
Stephens, William J, 96 461
Stephenson, James, 96, 268, 269, 277 279 377 489, 579
Stephenson, Thomas 332
Stephenson & Williams, 489
Sterling Charles G, 319, 333
Stein David, 337
Sternsdorf George J, 82
Sterry, C N 247
Stevens, Douglas H, 156
Stevens, Richard & Sons, 499
Stevenson, Renfrew 487
Stewart, A A & Co, 472
Stewart, Alexander S, 155

Stewart, George D, 332
Stewart, John M, 154
Stewart, John T, 282
Stewart J S 71, 79
Stewart, J W, 323
Stewart, L L E, 512
Stewart, R E, 203
Stewart Robert, 33
Stewart, William, 601
Stickles, Benjamin, 106
Stillery C, 646
Stillman, E, 365
Stimmel Phil 482
Stoddard, H P, 228
Stokes, James, 354
Stokes, Joseph R, 94
Stoll, A J, 662
Stone, E L, 413, 466
Stone, R M 79 357
Storey, N F, 482
Story P C 482
Storz, G 507
Stout, W H B 154, 156
Stowe, W A, 226
Strang, A L, 218
Strasburger, Levy M, 464
Strawn Win S, 228, 249
Street, Joseph H D, 104
Street & Redfield, 104
Streeter Rienzi 80
Strietz, Ferdinand 320
Strickland Silas A, 67, 68, 71, 72, 79 80, 124 125, 143, 154, 222, 224, 225, 228, 230, 239, 249, 380
Strickler, V O, 228
Stryker, A F, 632
Strong, Mary 358
Stuart, F, 646
Stuart William, 381
Stubbendorf, Frederick, 507
Stuck, R J, 78 249
Stuht Ernest 284, 285, 302
Stull, Homer 96
Sturdevant, F M, 228
Sturges, Hiram A, 228
Sturgis, Thomas 604
Sudborough Grace, 317
Sudborough, T K, 260
Sues, G W 228
Sullivan, Daniel 96, 106
Sullivan Dudley 646 669
Sullivan, H 646
Sullivan, Maurice, 368
Sullivan, Patrick 646
Sullivan, P C, 79
Sullivan Tim 105
Summers, J E, Jr, 357, 358, 361
Sumner, Milton S, 156
Sunder, Fred 467
Sunderland J A, 488
Sunderland, L T 488
Sussenbach, Henry 81
Sutherland, R, 402
Sutphen, D C, 92, 93 95, 96, 126, 386
Sutphen, Mrs D C, 186
Sutphen & Son, 477
Sutter, Mamie 203
Sutton Aaron L, 78, 656

Sutton, Thomas L., 95, 106.
Swaim, W. E., 267.
Swan, Alexander H., 596, 597, 598, 613, 615.
Swanson, Olin, 326.
Swanson & Vallen, 490.
Swartzlander, Albert, 224, 228, 257, 264.
Swartzlander, Fred, 358.
Sweet, E. N., 171.
Sweet, J., 446.
Sweesy, Charles C., 117, 320.
Sweesy, Frank, 117.
Sweesy & Root, 117, 251.
Sweesy, William F., 106, 117, 251, 255.
Sweesy William K., 117.
Swetman, J. M., 279, 355, 356.
Swezey, Field W., 228.
Swift & Company, 630, 631, 632, 633.
Swift, G. F., 630.
Swift John, 349.
Swift, Patrick, 94, 105, 349.
Swift, Thomas, 105.
Switzler & McIntosh, 243.
Switzler, Warren, 82, 228, 243, 281.
Swobe, J. A., 331.
Swobe, Thomas, 78, 96, 164, 255, 278, 279, 281, 382, 597, 613, 615.
Swobe, Mrs. Thomas, 311.
Sykes, Martin L., 410.
Sylvester, George, 106.

**T**

Taffe, John, 80, 155, 157, 264.
Taft, Robert K., 96, 501.
Taggart & Co., 490.
Taggart, Harry, 374, 375.
Taggart, J. M., 69, 71.
Tagger & Walker, 503.
Talbot, Bishop, 317.
Talbot, David, 488.
Talbot, John, 155, 156.
Talbott, John F., 228.
Taliaferro, T. W., 625, 626.
Tallon, Thomas, 504.
Taney, Judge, 276.
Tanner & Downs, 104.
Tator, Cyrus, 136, 234, 235.
Tatum, David, 200.
Tatum, Fannie, 200.
Taylor Bros., 172.
Taylor, Cadet, 168, 281, 431.
Taylor, C. H., 153.
Taylor, Charles T., 411, 489.
Taylor, D. E., 200.
Taylor, E. B., 81, 168, 394.
Taylor, F. H., 432.
Taylor, Frederick W., 171.
Taylor, Mrs. George, 135, 136.
Taylor, J. C., 299, 404.
Taylor, John F., 106.
Taylor, J. M., 183.
Taylor, J. W., 228, 322.
Taylor, V. C., 385.
Taylor, W. E., 203.
Taylor, William H., 80, 495.

Taylor, W. J., 663.
Taylor, Zachary, 94.
Teasdale, Thomas W., 410.
Teeter, Joseph, 380.
Teetzel, W. Y., 511.
Tehon, Joseph, 375.
Templeton, W. G., 432, 433, 434.
Ten Eyck, William B., 158, 228.
Test, J. D., 385.
Tex, Jacob, 106.
Thain, A. R., 327.
Thayer vs. Boyd, 243.
Thayer, Emma H., 452.
Thayer, John M., 72, 97, 98, 99, 105, 142, 151, 152, 154, 162, 164, 167, 169, 189, 191, 194, 195, 196, 226, 228, 233, 235, 241, 253, 312, 342, 368, 384, 386, 387, 655.
Thayer, W. O., 646.
Thayer, Mrs. W. O., 643.
The Cozzens Hotel, 251.
The Douglas House, 251.
The Farnam House, 251.
The Grand Central Hotel, 253.
The Metropolitan Hotel, 251.
The Pacific House, 251.
The Union Depot Hotel, 251.
The Union Hotel, 251.
The Wyoming House, 251.
Thembart, Hugo, 651.
Theurer, Jacob, 380.
Thieman, Charles A., 96.
Thomas, A., 183.
Thomas, B. F., 228.
Thomas, C. B., 169.
Thomas, Charles L., 381.
Thomas, Dexter L., 228, 430.
Thomas, E. E., 228.
Thomas, E. G., 228, 249.
Thomas, F. S., 361.
Thomas, Iver, 660.
Thomas, Mr., 635.
Thompson, Belden & Co., 464.
Thompson, Charles A., 154.
Thompson, Charles, 154.
Thompson, C. W., 280, 504.
Thompson, Doctor, 132.
Thompson, F. W., 366.
Thompson, George W., 380.
Thompson, Henry A., 281.
Thompson, H., 228.
Thompson, James, 430.
Thompson, J. D. N., 149, 154.
Thompson, J. Hurd, 466.
Thompson, John B., 23, 54.
Thompson, M., 89.
Thompson, Mr., 132.
Thompson, Mrs. S. A., 202.
Thompson, William, 458.
Thrall, George, 96, 254.
Thrall, W. R., 66, 67, 68, 72, 79, 353, 354.
Thrane, C. C., 96.
Thurlow, Amos, 662.
Thurston, John M., 94, 96, 225, 228, 239, 242, 244, 258, 280, 285, 301, 305, 342, 367, 402, 580.
Thurston & Hall, 246.
Tibbles, T. H., 273, 275, 323.
Tibbs, George M., 280, 463.

Tibke, Martin, 433.
Tiffany, F. B., 228.
Tilden, George, 354, 357, 359.
Tilden, Ida C., 203, 204.
Tillson, George W., 95.
Tilly, James F., 97.
Timme, George W., 78, 207.
Tindall, D. K., 324.
Tipton, J. G., 228.
Tipton, Thomas W., 154, 446.
Tobbitts, Madame, 350.
Tobitt, Edith, 263.
Todd, Charles L., 479.
Todd, Governor, 125.
Toland, Hartford, 431.
Tooley, T. J., 228.
Tootle & Jackson, 460.
Tootle & Maul, 240, 462.
Tootle, Milton, 104, 460.
Torrey, Isabella, 310, 311.
Torrey, T. J., 95.
Tousley, J. W., 106, 277, 322.
Touzalin, A. E., 427, 455.
Towle, George C., 281, 488, 495.
Towne, S. R., 316, 357, 358.
Townsend, George W., 228.
Townsend, Robert, 78, 249, 264.
Townsend, W. D., 473.
Trace, Mrs. E. L., 187.
Train, George Francis, 101, 102, 103, 166, 201, 253, 255, 395, 581.
Trauerman, Moses R., 228.
Travis, W. E., 382.
Treitschke, Julius, 278, 375.
Tremont House, 251.
Trenkle, Herman, 646.
Trevett, T. M., 493.
Trimble, A. W., 222.
Trimble, John, 466.
Trorlicht, J. H., 467.
Trostler, B., 510.
Trostler, I. S., 280.
Troup, A. C., 81, 228.
Troxel & Williams, 462.
Truitt, Charles M., 161.
Truman Bros., 490.
Trussell, E. A., 475.
Tucker, F. A., 415.
Tukey, A. P., 340.
Tule, Anna, 381.
Tulleys, L. W., 220, 431.
Tunnicliff, N. H., 228.
Turk, John C., 66.
Turkington, George E., 228.
Turkle, A. J., 328.
Turner vs. Althaus, 239.
Turner, Charles, 106, 121, 218, 383, 428.
Turner, Mrs. Charles, 121.
Turner, Charles F., 228.
Turner, Mrs. Charles R., 311.
Turner, Curtis, 121.
Turner, Mary, 121.
Turner, William R., 78.
Turtle, William, 81.
Tutt, F. E., 200.
Tuttle, Charles F., 228.
Tuttle, Leroy, 308, 422.
Tuttle, Merrill S., 154, 156.
Tuttle, Thomas F., 96, 97.

## INDEX

Tuttle. W H , 386
Tutwiler, Joseph N , 156
Tyler, B B , 334
Tyler, Jennie 662
Tzschuck, Bruno, 82, 130, 131, 171
Tzschuck, George B , 170, 501

### U

Uhlig, Robert 475
Umsted, W W , 417
Underwood, P L , 626
Underwood. W A 270 271, 283.
Union, Jennie Smith. 187
Upton, M A , 597 600, 641, 646, 663
Upton, M A & Co , 279

### V

Valentine, E K 163 380
Valentine, Mrs E K , 311.
Valentine P A , 609
Valentine, S I & Co , 482
Van, C C , 385
Van Akin, C T 660
Van Antwerp, William H , 317, 329
Van Buren, President, 107
Van Camp, Charles L 78, 96
Van Camp, Helen A 171
Van Court, Mrs E D , 205
Van Dervoort, Paul 380, 381
Van Dusen, J H , 228, 658
Van Dusen M S , 506
Van Etten, D . 228
Van Gieson, H C , 357, 358, 361, 381
Van Gilder, W C 228
Van Horn, J . 66, 71
Van Horn. M M , 211
Van Kuran, A S 402
Van Kuran, Mrs A S , 311
Van Kuran, C C , 662
Van Namee. D A . 251
Van Ness, Sherman, 358, 361
Van Nostrand, James W , 78, 94, 312. 313, 371
Van Nostrand, Mrs James W , 205 311 450
Van Oman George, 255
Van Orman 378 '
Van Rensselaer, Cortland, 308
Vance, J E , 646
Vance, J H . 357
Vaughan, W R , 170
Venable, Joseph, 354
Venable, W D , 338
Venner, C H , 272
Victor, General, 18
Vierling, A J , 280 494, 512
Vierling, Lewis, 494
Vierling, Robert , 494
Vifquain, Victor, 190, 382
Vilas, General 164
Viles, James 11 , 626
Vincent, Doctor, 143
Vincent, General, 162
Vinsonhaler, D M , 228

Visscher H H , 74, 83, 95, 105, 310, 373, 384
Vodica, Frank, 389, 504
Vogele & Dinning, 506
Vogel Bros . 499
Vogel, J W , 499
Vogel, L D 499
Voght, Henry, 154
VonRaven, H H , 259
VonWindheim, August, 374
VonWindheim Philip, 106, 375
Voss, Henry, 215
Voth, G , 639

### W

Waack, Frank. 646
Wade, Joseph S , 155
Waggener, Baily P , 301
Wagner, C H , 510
Wagner, Savage & Saunders, 602
Waixel, Isaac 618
Wakefield, John A , 279, 304, 487
Wakeley, Arthur C , 172, 223, 228, 264 320
Wakeley, Bird, 320
Wakeley, Eleazer, 77, 79 94, 184, 186, 222, 223, 225 226, 228, 236, 237, 252, 263, 264, 268, 281, 313, 378 413, 582
Wakeley, Lucius, 172
Walcott, F , 599
Walker, Ada T , 205.
Walker, B F 646
Walker Charles H , 81
Walker, E H , 278
Walker, E P , 503
Walker, G T , 495
Walker, L A .602, 658
Walker, S T , 170
Walker, Will I , 228
Walker, W M , 255
Walker W W , 403
Wall, Miss F D 318
Wallace, George C , 172
Wallace, J Laurie 453, 454
Wallace, Lewis S . 458
Wallace, Miss M E , 318
Wallace, Robert, 172
Wallace, Sallie, 118
Wallace, William, 258, 259, 263, 266 304, 382, 426, 496
Walsh, Edward 378
Walter, Daniel 325
Walter, Horace, 156
Walter, Peter, 154
Walters, Frank, 306
Walters, J S 625
Waltmeyer, T S 483
Wanamaker John, 165
Wappich, W F , 228
Ward James 646
Wardell Thomas, 147
Ware J A 317, 426
Ware, J A & Co , 426
Ware J D 228
Ware, Mary J , 114
Ware S M , 211 333
Warner, George E . 504

Warner, Harry T , 483
Warren, C C , 419
Warren, Frank, 419
Wasem Fred 646
Wasey E , 500
Washburn. F 402
Wasserman, Andrew, 106
Wasserman Frank, 429
Waters, A R , 343
Waters, Della M 343
Waters, Maggie E , 343
Waters, Margaret B . 343
Waters, Thomas B W , 343
Waters, Walter W , 343
Watkins, J B 668
Watson, Ben, 338
Watson, George W , 328, 329
Watson James M , 426
Watson, John C 82, 189
Wattles G W , 429
Watts, Charles. 178
Waugh D B , 667
Waugh J M & Son, 667
Wearne Bros . 494
Weatherwax Thomas J , 154
Weaver, F L , 228
Weaver, General, 307
Webster, Fannie, 187
Webster, George 332
Webster John L , 79, 81, 94, 179 180 196, 228, 239, 240, 249, 264, 273, 275, 276, 379, 584
Webster John R 228
Weeks, I S P 405
Welch Frank, 80
Well, E K 643 651, 662
Weller C F , 480
Wells Bros 251
Wells William L , 388
Wells, N W 413
Welsh, Thomas 68, 94
Welshans, Joseph L , 211, 333
Welshans, Mrs Joseph L , 333
Welshans Joseph L & Co , 473
Wendt Ferdinand 635
Wentz, C C 203
Wentz Mrs C C , 203
Werner William, 23
Wert, E , 642
Wertz G W , 366
Wessells, Frank W , 228, 264, 427
West. C H 489
West Joel W 228
West John 329
West, Joseph B., 381, 510
Westerdahl C J 95
Westerfield John M 667
Western Button Co 505
Westwood H C 322
Westwood Hay & Whitney, 87
Wettling L F , 479
Wetzel P , 646
Whaley E E 430 431
Wharton J C 228 249
Wheaton Frank 124. 159
Wheeler, Daniel H , 81, 96, 278, 431
Wheeler, James L, 386
Wheeler, J H , 95

## INDEX.

Wherry, William M., 162.
Whidden, A. J., 487.
White, B. T., 228.
White, John F., 228.
White. W. C.. 211.
Whitehorn, Edward, 225.
Whitehouse, Joseph, 23.
Whitlock, George C., 95, 154, 316.
Whitman, Doctor, 35.
Whitmarsh, Angelina, 381.
Whitmore, E. E., 484.
Whitmore, H. P., 472.
Whitmore, R. F., 358.
Whitmore. William C., 81, 82.
Whitney, David, 106.
Whitney, Henry, 500.
Whitney, Mr., 55, 87.
Whitney, W. N., 468.
Whitted, James M., 383.
Whitted, Robert B.. 52, 54, 79, 98, 99.
Whitten. William I., 154.
Whittlesey. T. B.. 656, 671.
Wiedemann, Conrad, 507.
Wiers, E. D., 646.
Wigman. John E., 314.
Wilber, William, 320.
Wilbur, John E.. 427.
Wilbur, Mathew C., 78, 80, 384.
Wilbur, R. E., 162.
Wilbur, R. H.. 94, 381.
Wilbur, R. J.. 212.
Wilbur, W. H.. 380.
Wilcox, J. D., 197.
Wilcox, Jeremiah C., 106, 156, 168, 170.
Wilcox. L. L., 81.
Wilcox, R. S., 380.
Wilcox, Seymour G., 228.
Wilcox, S. K., 331.
Wilcox. S. M.. 388.
Wilcox, William P., 105, 200, 356, 358, 461.
Wilde, Oscar, 450.
Wilder, William F., 68, 106.
Wiles, Isaac, 155.
Wiley, S. L., 270, 419, 585.
Wiley, S. L. & Co., 268, 270.
Wilgocke, A. J., 95.
Wilhelmy, J. F., 473.
Wilhite. William T., 156.
Wilkie, J. J., 499.
Wilkins, Charles. 275.
Wilkins. General. 96.
Wilkins, H. L., 490.
Wilkinson, George P., 154, 358, 361, 362, 363.
Wilkinson, James, 18, 19.
Wilkinson, John L., 499.
Wilkinson, Thomas, 78.
Willard, Alexander, 23.
Willard, Frances E., 180, 181.
Willard, W. B., 365.
Willever, E. E., 263.
Williams. Charles, 635, 646.
Williams, C. H., 404.
Williams & Cross, 482.
Williams, Dan, 601.
Williams. Fred A.. 156.

Williams, George O., 95, 96.
Williams, General, 163.
Williams, G. W., 365.
Williams, G. R., 278.
Williams, Jesse, 104.
Williams, John A., 338.
Williams, John T., 228.
Williams, John, 184, 186, 329, 338.
Williams, J. L., 435.
Williams, Larue, 646.
Williams, L. B., 211, 259, 339, 413, 428, 469.
Williams, Mrs. Anna, 644.
Williams. Mrs. Oscar, 122.
Williams, Phillip P., 155.
Williams, Virgil, 453.
Williams, William, 601.
Williams, William N., 228.
Williamson, Charles E., 340, 431, 465.
Williamson, John, 334.
Willis, J. G., 381.
Willmasser, May, 451.
Wills. Doctor, 121.
Wilson, C. H., 158.
Wilson, Crockett, 95.
Wilson & Drake, 494.
Wilson. Fannie E., 314.
Wilson, Jennie, 201, 202.
Wilson, J. H., 338.
Wilson, J. M., 333.
Wilson, John, 215, 259, 260.
Wilson, Lewis, 254.
Wilson, O., 81.
Wilson, Posey, 426.
Wilson, Robert W., 495.
Wilson, Samuel, 354.
Wilson, Silas, 183, 187.
Wilson. Thomas, 410.
Wilson, T. T., 511.
Wiltse, Chauncy, 95, 264.
Winchester, Ben, 492.
Windheim, August. 374.
Windheim, Peter, 106, 141, 277, 375, 384.
Windheim, Mrs. Philip, 482.
Windsor, Henry J., 281.
Windsor, Richard, 23.
Windsor, Mrs. S. H., 318.
Wing, James H., 156.
Wing, W. S., 402.
Winship, James M., 106.
Win hip, J. L., 350.
Winspear, James H., 81, 95, 97.
Winter, Edwin H., 410.
Winter, Phil. E., 228.
Wirth, Fritz, 380, 381.
Wiser, Peter, 23.
Withnell, Alwilda, 119.
Withnell, Blanch C., 119.
Withnell Bros. & McCafferty, 254.
Withnell, Charles H., 119.
Withnell, Cora B, 119.
Withnell, Eliza A., 118.
Withnell, Elizabeth C., 118.
Withnell, Frank R., 119.
Withnell, John, 105, 118, 119, 160, 218, 511.

Withnell, Richard N., 105, 118, 119, 160, 218, 281, 511.
Withrow, C. A., 656.
Withrow, J. T., 656.
Withrow, J. T. & Co., 489.
Wittig, Ed., 375.
Wittum, George F., 228.
Wolcott, E. C., 228.
Wolcott, Oscar, 386.
Wolf, Thomas, 171.
Wolfel & Baker, 345.
Wollstein, M. & Co., 484.
Womersley, E. E., 356, 357, 358, 363.
Wood, A. M., 382.
Wood, A. P., 281, 352.
Wood, Benjamin, 277, 426, 427.
Wood. Ben. B.. 646.
Wood Bros., 603, 605.
Wood, C. E., 646.
Wood, C. T., 356.
Wood, E. C., 228.
Wood, Elmer H., 402.
Wood, F. W., 453.
Wood, G. W., 54, 95.
Wood, Hattie, 663.
Wood, H. N., 434.
Wood, John A., 484.
Wood, John S., 380, 381.
Wood, O. S., 352, 364, 365, 586.
Wood, Rubin, 106.
Wood, S., 380.
Wood, Walter E., 605, 610.
Wood, William M., 656, 662.
Woodard, James I., 441.
Woodbridge, S. F., 314.
Woodburn, J. M., 356.
Woodman, Clark, 215, 421, 428, 501.
Woodman, Mrs. Clark, 450, 451.
Woodman, Edwin E., 410.
Woods, Ben. B., 613, 646.
Woodworth, Charles D., 96, 151, 315.
Woodworth, C. D. & Co., 482.
Woodworth, L., 482.
Woolworth, Charles C., 106, 447.
Woolworth, James M., 76, 79, 85, 90, 94, 98, 102, 106, 117, 144, 146, 164, 206, 218, 221, 224, 228, 231, 253, 258, 266, 286, 292, 301, 312, 317, 422, 447, 453, 587, 597, 604, 613, 615.
Woolworth, Miss, 164.
Wordeman, Henry, 644.
Worden, C. C., 161.
Worley, H. A., 364.
Worley, W. M., 324.
Wortenberger, Joseph, 170.
Worthington, Bishop, 184, 186, 318.
Worthington, Richard, 23.
Woten, George W., 322.
Wren, Thaddeus, 146.
Wright, A. S., 364, 365.
Wright, C., 496.
Wright, Clark, 322.
Wright, George F., 282.
Wright, L. R., 228.
Wright, William H. S., 410.

Wright, W L 472
Wright, W S , 473
Wurtz, 311
Wyckoff, Helen L , 317
Wyman A U , 105 110, 151,
 220, 291 422, 433, 434
Wyman, Carrie, 320, 449
Wyman, Henry F , 428
Wyman, Walstein B , 656
Wyman, W T , 433
Wyman, W W , 91, 95, 105, 110,
 167, 168, 441

Wyman, W U , 83, 86, 91

**Y**

Yates, C E , 405
Yates, Henry W , 106, 144, 257,
 286, 317, 329 427, 455, 459, 497
Yeiser, John O , 228
Yerga, John M , 106
Yoemans, George, 405
Yost, Casper E 80, 110, 168, 413,
 417, 441

Young, Brigham 71, 73
Young, Erastus, 402
Young, J Morris 156, 467
Young, Miss J M , 318
Young, J R K2
Youngerman George H , 511

**Z**

Zahner, Louis, 329
Zedikei James F , 81
Zimmerman, Andrew, 388